THE BUILDINGS OF SCOTLAND

FOUNDING EDITORS:
NIKOLAUS PEVSNER AND COLIN McWILLIAM

# STIRLING AND CENTRAL SCOTLAND

JOHN GIFFORD
FRANK ARNEIL WALKER

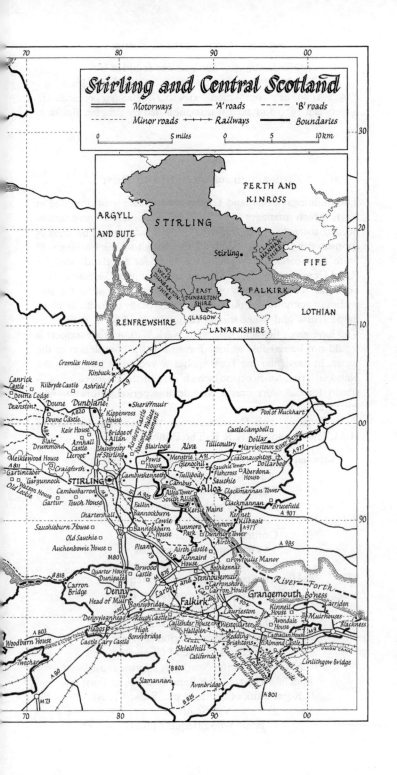

# Stirling and Central Scotland

Motorways    'A' roads    'B' roads

Minor roads    Railways    Boundaries

0    5 miles    0    5    10 km

PERTH AND KINROSS

ARGYLL AND BUTE

STIRLING

Stirling

CLACKMANNANSHIRE

FIFE

WEST DUNBARTONSHIRE

EAST DUNBARTONSHIRE

FALKIRK

RENFREWSHIRE

GLASGOW

LOTHIAN

LANARKSHIRE

Cromlix House

Kinbuck

Lanrick Castle

Kilbryde Castle

Ashfield

Doune Lodge

Deanston

Doune

Dunblane

Sheriffmuir

Pool of Muckhart

Doune Castle

Kippenross House

A9

Keir House

Bridge of Allan

Airthrey Castle

National Wallace Monument

Castle Campbell

Blair Drummond

Arnhall Castle

University of Stirling

Blairlogie

Dollar

Meiklewood House

Lecropt

Powis House

Menstrie

A91

Alva

Tillicoultry

Harviestoun

River Devon

A977

Craigforth

Glenochil

Coalsnaughton

A811

Gartincaber

Cambuskenneth

Tullibody

Fishcross

Sauchie Tower

Dollarbeg

Old Leckie

Watson House

STIRLING

Cambus

Sauchie

Aberdona House

Gargunnock

A9

Cambusbarron

A905

Alloa Tower

South Alloa

Alloa

Clackmannan Tower

Gartur

Touch House

A91

Clackmannan

Brucefield

Chartershall

Fallin

Kersie Mains

Kennet

A907

Sauchieburn House

Bannockburn

Cowie

Kilbagie

Dunmore Park

Dunmore Tower

A977

Old Sauchie

Bannockburn House

Dunmore

A985

Auchenbowie House

Plean

Airth Castle

Airth

M80

Kinnaird House

Powfoulis Manor

Quarter House

Torwood Castle

M876

Bothkennar

River Forth

Carron Bridge

Dunipace

Larbert and Stenhousemuir

Carronshore

Bo'ness

Carriden

Head of Muir

Bonnybridge

Carron House

Grangemouth

Denny

Falkirk

A904

Kinneil House

Muirhouses

B818

Dennyloanhead

Rough Castle

Callendar House

Laurieston

Avondale House

Blackness

M9

Haggs

High Bonnybridge

Hallglen

Westquarter

Redding

Lathallan House

A803

Castle Cary Castle

Shieldhill

Brightons

Almond Castle

Union Canal

Woodburn House

California

Redding Muirhead

Kinneil Priory

Linlithgow Bridge

Twechar

A80

B803

Rumford

Maddiston

A801

M73

Slamannan

B825

Avonbridge

A801

PEVSNER ARCHITECTURAL GUIDES

*The Buildings of Scotland* was founded by
Sir Nikolaus Pevsner (1902–83) and Colin McWilliam
(1928–1989) as a companion series to *The Buildings of England*.
Between 1979 and 2001 it was published by Penguin Books.

THE BUILDINGS OF SCOTLAND TRUST

The Buildings of Scotland Trust is a charitable trust, founded in
1991, which manages and finances the research programme
needed to sustain *The Buildings of Scotland* series. The trust is
sponsored by Historic Scotland (on behalf of the Secretary of
State for Scotland), the National Trust for Scotland, and the
Royal Commission on the Ancient and Historical Monuments of
Scotland. The Buildings of Scotland Trust is grateful for and
wishes to acknowledge the support of the many individuals, charitable trusts and foundations, companies and local authorities
who have given financial help to its work. Without that support it
would not be possible to look forward to the completion of the
series. In particular the Trust wishes to record its thanks to the
National Trust for Scotland, which carried the financial responsibility for this work over a considerable period before the new
trust was set up.

The Trustees wish to acknowledge the generous support of
H.M. The Queen and H.R.H. The Prince of Wales.

Special thanks are due to the following major donors
Aberbrothock Charitable Trust
Binks Trust, Dulverton Trust
Esmée Fairbairn Charitable Trust
Marc Fitch Fund
Gordon Fraser Charitable Trust
Gargunnock Estate Trust
A.S. and Miss M.I. Henderson Trust
Historic Scotland, Imlay Foundation Inc.
Sir Peter Leslie, Leverhulme Trust
MacRobert Trusts
Colin McWilliam Memorial Fund
Nancie Massey Charitable Trust
Merchants House of Glasgow
National Trust for Scotland, Pilgrim Trust
Radcliffe Trust, Joseph Rank Benevolent Trust
Royal Bank of Scotland plc, Russell Trust
VisitScotland
James Wood Bequest Fund

# Stirling
# and
# Central Scotland

BY

JOHN GIFFORD

AND

FRANK ARNEIL WALKER

WITH CONTRIBUTIONS FROM

RICHARD FAWCETT

THE BUILDINGS OF SCOTLAND

YALE UNIVERSITY PRESS

NEW HAVEN AND LONDON

IN ASSOCIATION WITH
THE BUILDINGS OF SCOTLAND TRUST

YALE UNIVERSITY PRESS
NEW HAVEN AND LONDON
302 Temple Street, New Haven CT 06511
47 Bedford Square, London WC1B 3DP
www.pevsner.co.uk
www.yalebooks.co.uk
www.yalebooks.com

Published by Yale University Press 2002
Reprinted with corrections, 2006
2 4 6 8 10 9 7 5 3

ISBN 0 300 09594 5

Copyright © John Gifford and Frank Arneil Walker,
Richard Fawcett, David J. Breeze, Ian Fisher,
Judith Lawson, J.N. Graham Ritchie, 2002

Printed in China
through World Print
Set in Monotype Plantin

FOR
CHARLES AND DAVID

# CONTENTS

# LIST OF TEXT FIGURES AND MAPS

# ARRANGEMENT OF THE GAZETTEER

*Stirling and Central Scotland* covers the former Central Region (1975–96), i.e. the present local government areas of Clackmannanshire, Falkirk and Stirling, and also the present East Dunbartonshire and West Dunbartonshire. The map on pp. ii–iii shows the boundaries of the area covered.

All the entries for towns, villages and major rural buildings in the gazetteer are amalgamated into a single alphabetical run but the local government area of each is indicated by one or two letters (e.g. C for Clackmannanshire or WD for West Dunbartonshire).

## MAP REFERENCES

The numbers printed in italic type in the margin against the place names in the gazetteer indicate the position of the place in question on the area map, which is divided into sections by the 10-kilometre reference lines of the National Grid. The reference given here omits the two initial letters (formerly numbers), which in a full grid reference refer to the 100-kilometre squares into which the county is divided. The first two numbers indicate the western boundary, and the last two the southern boundary, of the 10-kilometre square in which the place is situated. For example, Callander, reference 6000, will be found in the 10-kilometre square bounded by grid lines 60 (on the *west*) and 70, and 00 (on the *south*) and 10; Blair Drummond, reference 7090, in the square bounded by grid lines 70 (on the *west*) and 80, and 90 (on the *south*) and 00.

# ACCESS TO BUILDINGS

Many of the buildings described in this book are public places, and in some obvious cases their interiors (at least the public sections of them) can be seen without formality. But it must be emphasized that the mention of buildings or lands does not imply any rights of public access to them, or the existence of any arrangements for visiting them.

Some churches are open within regular hours, and it is usually possible to see the interiors of others by arrangement with the minister or church officer. Particulars of admission to Ancient Monuments and other buildings in the care of Scottish Ministers (free to the Friends of Historic Scotland) are available from Historic Scotland, Longmore House, Salisbury Place, Edinburgh EH9 1SH or its website, www.historic-scotland.gov.uk. Details of access to properties of the National Trust for Scotland are available from the Trust's head office at 5 Charlotte Square, Edinburgh EH2 4DU or via its website, www.nts.org.uk. Admission is free to members, on whose subscriptions and donations the Trust's work depends.

Scotland's Gardens Scheme, 22 Rutland Square, Edinburgh EH1 2BB, provides a list of gardens open to visitors, also available on the National Gardens Scheme website, www.ngs.org.uk. Scotland's Churches Scheme, Dunedin, Holehouse Road, Eaglesham, Glasgow G76 0JF, publishes an annual directory of churches open to visitors while *Hudson's Historic Houses, Castles and Gardens Open to the Public* includes many private houses.

Local Tourist Offices can advise the visitor on what properties in each area are open to the public and will usually give helpful directions as to how to get to them.

# ACKNOWLEDGEMENTS FOR
# THE PLATES

# FOREWORD

*The first volume of Sir Nikolaus Pevsner's* The Buildings of England *was published in 1951, the last in 1974, when several of the earlier volumes had already been republished in revised editions. Not long before his completion of the English series Pevsner set out to launch equivalent series for Ireland, Scotland and Wales, entrusting the editorship of the Scottish series to Colin McWilliam, who himself wrote* Lothian, *the first volume, published in 1978, and was co-author of the next volume,* Edinburgh. *Colin's death in 1989 deprived the series of his polite but not always uncritical oversight but he had already established a standard for the series which its authors have attempted to observe.*

*The authors have divided responsibility for the gazetteer on geographical lines, John Gifford having written Clackmannanshire, East Dunbartonshire and Falkirk (including revisions of a few entries first published in* Lothian*), and Frank Arneil Walker Stirling (both burgh and landward) and West Dunbartonshire but with the accounts of Dunblane Cathedral, the Church of the Holy Rude, Stirling, Stirling Castle and Argyll's Lodging, Stirling, contributed by Richard Fawcett. The entries for prehistoric monuments are by J. N. Graham Ritchie and for Roman remains by David Breeze. The opening chapters of the Introduction are also specialist contributions, the chapter on geology and building materials being by Judith Lawson, that on prehistory by J. N. Graham Ritchie, that on the Romans in Central Scotland by David Breeze, that on Early Christian work by Ian Fisher, and that on medieval churches by Richard Fawcett. The rest of the Introduction has been divided between the authors, although each saw and commented on the other's drafts. John Gifford wrote the chapters on post-Reformation churches, mausolea, monuments and statues, roads, railways, canals and harbours, rural manses, farmhouses and steadings, and industrial buildings. The chapters on castles and tower houses, country houses, and burgh and village buildings are by Frank Arneil Walker.*

*At the beginning of* The Buildings of Scotland *series Colin McWilliam stated its objectives as being 'to present all the buildings that merit attention on architectural grounds, to do it for the whole country, and to do it with all possible speed'. To those objectives must be added the aim that the volumes be thoroughly researched and their authors sceptical of information unsupported by documentation. Starting points for research have been provided by David MacGibbon and Thomas Ross's two works,* The Castellated and Domestic Architecture of Scotland *(5 vols., 1887–92) and* The Ecclesiastical Architecture of Scotland *(3 vols., 1896–7), and by the Royal Commission on the Ancient and Historical Monuments of Scotland's Inventories of* Clackmannanshire *(1933) and* Stirlingshire *(1963), but only the last covers buildings dating from after 1707 and it adopted 1840 as a cut-off date. For buildings of the* C18, C19 *and early to mid* C20, *much information is provided by Historic Scotland's List of Buildings of Special Architectural or Historic Interest and the list has proved a useful pointer to information on the buildings it includes. For the series as a whole, John Gifford extracted some years ago all Scottish references from* C19 *and* C20 *architectural and building periodicals (*The Builder, The Building News, The Architect, *etc.). The arrangement of these notes by individual buildings grouped within parishes was undertaken for this volume by John Gifford, Margaret Stewart, Alexandra Jones and Siobhan Marples. They also greatly supplemented these notes with information collected from such sources as the various* Statistical Accounts of Scotland, C19 *gazetteers (*The Ordnance Gazetteer of Scotland, *ed. Francis H. Groome, 5 vols., 1882–5, being the fullest), a mass of local histories and guidebooks (those produced by Historic Scotland to the monuments in its care of particular value) and more specialized works (e.g. James Ronald's* The Story of the Argyle Lodging *or John Dunbar's* The Stirling Heads *and* Scottish Royal Palaces). *Work was also carried out on manuscript sources, especially those held by the National Archives of Scotland, Falkirk History Research Centre, Glasgow City (formerly Strathclyde Regional) Archives, Stirling (formerly Central Region) Archives, and the Archive of Historical Architecture at the University of Strathclyde. Much work, especially on local newspapers, was done in the public libraries at Alloa, Clydebank, Dumbarton, Falkirk, Kirkintilloch and Stirling, as well as in the National Library of Scotland, the Edinburgh Central Public Library (especially the Scottish and Fine Art Departments), the Andersonian Library of the University of Strathclyde and, the most frequented of all, the National Monuments Record of Scotland. The staffs of all these institutions have been consistently helpful, forbearing and long-suffering. The research notes for published volumes in the series are deposited in the National Monuments Record of Scotland.*

*Information on individual buildings has been given by local authority building control and planning departments and by many architects. Thanks are especially due to Iona Beauly, David Cowling, Jocelyn Cunliffe, Philip Flockhart, Bob Heath, David Page, Brian Park, John Sanders, Richard Shorter and James Simpson. Architectural historians and enthusiasts have shared information and ideas. Particular mention must be made of Malcolm Allan, Gordon Barclay, Lyndsey Bowditch, Constance Brodie, Alistair Campbell of Airds, the Rev. Morris Coull, Patricia Douglas, John Dunbar, Gordon Ewart, Richard Fawcett, James Fife, Simon Green, John Harrison, Willy McEwan, Iain MacIvor, Charles McKean, Aonghus MacKechnie, Debbie Mays, Simon Montgomery, Duncan Peet, Joe Rock, John and Ann Ross, Geoffrey Stell, Margaret Stewart, David Walker, Diane Watters and John Weston. Many priests, ministers, church officers and the owners of country houses and other private buildings put themselves to considerable trouble to let the authors see over the buildings in their care and, not infrequently, provided welcome hospitality and valuable information.*

*The book's Editor, Charles O'Brien, read the whole text and comments on parts of it were provided by Bridget Cherry and John Dunbar. Their contributions have added immeasurably to the book's scholarship and verbal felicity. Elisabeth Ingles and Amanda Howard prepared the typescript for the printer. At Penguin Books, with whom this volume was originally undertaken, valuable assistance was provided by Andrew Henty and Georgina Widdrington, who designed the text. The Index of Artists was prepared by John Gifford and the Index of Places by Judith Wardman. Many of the photographs were taken specially for this volume by the photographers of the Royal Commission on the Ancient and Historical Monuments of Scotland but a search for existing suitable photographs was also carried out by Graham Ritchie in Edinburgh. Commissioning and co-ordination of the illustrations was undertaken by Fleur Richards and Emily Rawlinson with Ruth Wimberley at the National Monuments Record providing valuable assistance in fulfilling last-minute requests for prints. Reg and Marjorie Piggott drew up the maps of the general area, its geology and the line of the Antonine Wall along with maps of Stirling and Falkirk. All other town maps, and the plans of buildings, are by Alan Fagan. Source material for many of the maps was helpfully provided by Nick Haynes at Historic Scotland.*

*In* Stirling and Central Scotland, *as in the preceding volumes of* The Buildings of Scotland, *certain general policies have been adopted. The format remains that established by Sir Nikolaus Pevsner in* The Buildings of England, *but with some Scottish quirks. Almost all churches and public buildings are included as a matter of course, as are buildings, especially in towns and villages, which, whatever their architectural quality, are too conspicuous to be entirely ignored. With some minor buildings, such as late Georgian farmhouses, those which are in or immediately next to a village have been mentioned but isolated examples left out. The more important rural buildings such as castles and country houses have individual entries in the gazetteer. An entry in brackets shows that the building has not, for whatever reason, been personally visited. There are bound to be mistakes and omissions in this volume. The authors will be grateful to anyone who takes the trouble to tell them of these.*

*The research and travelling costs for this series are necessarily high and for many years were underwritten by the National Trust for Scotland. The task has now been taken over by The Buildings of Scotland Trust, which is raising from public and private sources the funds necessary to see the series through to completion. The authors thank the Trust for this assistance.*

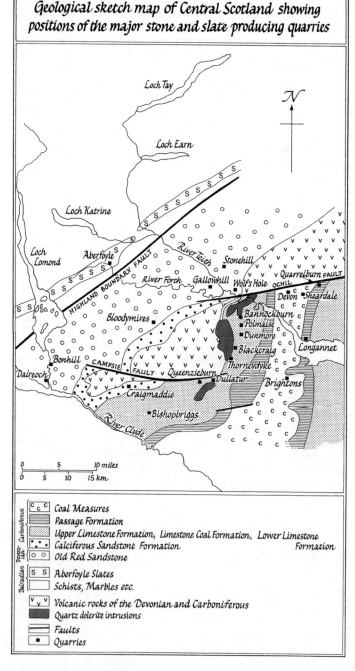

# Geological sketch map of Central Scotland showing positions of the major stone and slate producing quarries

Loch Tay

Loch Earn

Loch Katrine

Loch Lomond

Aberfoyle

River Teith

Stonehill

Gallowhill

Wolf's Hole

Quarrelburn FAULT

River Forth

HIGHLAND BOUNDARY FAULT

OCHIL

Devon

Sheardale

Bloodymires

Bannockburn

Polmaise

Dunmore

Blackcraig

Longannet

Bonhill

CAMPSIE FAULT

Queenzieburn

Thorneydyke

Dullatur

Brightons

Dalreoch

Craigmaddie

Bishopbriggs

River Clyde

𝒩

| 0 | 5 | 10 miles |
| 0 | 5 | 10 | 15 km |

| | |
|---|---|
| C C C | Coal Measures |
| | Passage Formation |
| | Upper Limestone Formation, Limestone Coal Formation, Lower Limestone Formation |
| •.•.• | Calciferous Sandstone Formation |
| o o o | Old Red Sandstone |
| S S | Aberfoyle Slates |
| | Schists, Marbles etc. |
| v v v | Volcanic rocks of the Devonian and Carboniferous |
| | Quartz dolerite intrusions |
| | Faults |
| ■ | Quarries |

Carboniferous — Devonian — Dalradian

FIGURE I. Map of the area covered by this volume, with simplified geology and positions of quarries.

# INTRODUCTION

## GEOLOGY

### BY JUDITH LAWSON

Stirling and Central Scotland includes spectacular, dramatic and varied scenery. N of the Highland Boundary Fault (or Highland Line), which crosses the area from Callander to Loch Lomond, is the high ground of the Caledonian Mountain Range, deeply dissected by valleys, often occupied by ribbon lakes. To the S is a broad area of lower, rolling country covered by pastures and woods. Further S again rise the rocky hills of the Ochils, Campsie Fells and Kilpatrick Hills. Yet further S lies a rolling area, once a low density rural economy, then an important coal mining and industrial area and now dominated by C20 housing.

*Geology and Scenery*

N of the Highland Boundary Fault are peaks rising to over 3,000ft (912m.). The highest mountains, Ben Lomond, Ben More, Stobinian and Stuc a'Chroin, with rocky, sharp-edged tops and ridges and scree-covered slopes, tower over the deep, broad valleys. The prevailing W winds bring high rainfall and much snow on the hills in winter, when conditions can be extreme. Even in summer patches of snow may be found. Originally mixed oak woodland would have covered the lower slopes, with pine forests higher up. A relict pine forest can still be seen in Glen Falloch N of Loch Lomond. The highest ground was clothed with peat and heather. Man has greatly modified the original vegetation by cutting or coppicing the oak woods for charcoal, clearing the land for grazing and, in the last century, planting vast areas with conifers. Different farming methods have also left their mark with the clearance of the crofting communities and small farms, for example at Sallochy, based on cattle, for the open tracts favoured by sheep farmers. Since the depopulation of the Highlands in the C19 there has been some movement of people back to these areas but this is still a relatively underpopulated part of the British Isles, with few towns and villages.

Many of the valleys were originally pre-glacial river courses which more recently were modified into the typical U-shaped cross-section by the action of ice. The valleys may be smooth or covered with hummocks of glacial debris left as the ice melted. The valley floor near Tyndrum is an excellent example of such terrain. Deep lochs may occupy the valley bottoms, which were often overdeepened by the scouring action of the ice. Loch Lomond, the largest freshwater lake in Britain, with its surface only a few metres above sea level, plunges in its northern reaches to 200m. below sea level. The valleys have always been vital arteries for the transport of people, animals and goods, and roads, railways and villages have been confined to the valley floors. Villages such as Tyndrum, Crianlarich or Lochearnhead exist primarily as service areas on the main routes through the hills.

In the s Highlands the ground is lower and more wooded. Birch and oak woodland, perhaps similar to that which once covered a much wider area, is well seen around Loch Katrine, the main reservoir for Glasgow and a spot much favoured by visitors from a wide area.

A marked change in the scenery occurs s of the Highland Boundary Fault. The lower ground, generally less than 300m., would once have been extensively wooded but has long been used for mainly pastoral farming. Rising above the low ground are the rocky hills of the Kilpatricks, Campsies and Ochils. Often rising to over 500m., the ground is used as rough grazing or has been planted with conifers. The sheep that grazed the Ochils were vital to the development of the woollen industry of the hillfoot villages to the s.

The framework of the Highlands is formed of metamorphic rocks of Precambrian age, approximately 800–600 million years old, belonging to the Dalradian Supergroup. Of sedimentary and igneous origin, these rocks have been altered by heat and pressure from shales, sandstones and limestones to become SLATE, SCHISTS, QUARTZITES and MARBLES. Basic lavas and intrusions have become 'green beds' – GREEN SCHISTS and EPIDIORITES. The original sediments were deposited in the sea at the edges of a large ocean, called Iapetus, which separated an older continental area in the NW of Scotland from that in England and Wales. Major earth movements caused the ocean to shrink in size as the two continents moved together until they finally collided and the rocks were folded, faulted, metamorphosed and finally intruded by massive GRANITES. By the end of this Caledonian mountain-building episode, about 400 million years ago, the Highlands probably looked something like the Himalayas today. An immense amount of erosion has occurred since then, so that only the lowest part of that mountain chain still exists. The rocks that now outcrop are resistant to erosion and the Highlands are today an area of generally high ground. One of the final events was the formation of the major fault that brings two very different geological areas together – the Highland Boundary Fault.

To the s of the fault, in Devonian (Old Red Sandstone) times, approximately 400–350 million years ago, products of the erosion of the high ground were deposited by rivers as sands and gravels. These sediments were consolidated into SANDSTONES and CONGLOMERATES. Near the top of the Old Red Sandstone there are also AEOLIAN SANDSTONES formed in large sand dunes, and occasional CORNSTONES, which represent fossil soils. The rocks, deposited on a barren land surface with little vegetation, are often strongly coloured red and brown. These relatively soft rocks outcrop extensively as generally flat-lying beds in Strathmore, between Callander and Loch Lomond. Near the Highland Boundary Fault they have been tilted up by later movements along the fault and form the ridges of the Menteith Hills, Conic Hill, near Balmaha, and some of the islands in Loch Lomond. There was also some localized volcanic activity at this time, with outpourings of mainly ANDESITIC LAVAS in what are now the Ochils. The IGNEOUS ROCKS are much more resistant to erosion and so stand up as prominent hills rising to over 600m.

Later, during the Carboniferous Period, 350–270 million years ago, the Highlands had been greatly reduced by erosion. To the south, extensive lowlands were covered by dense tropical forests through which large rivers flowed. Although the trees were very different from those of today the general appearance was probably similar to that now found in the Amazon Basin. As the mountains were now much lower and erosion less rapid there are few conglomerates in the Carboniferous. The commonest sediments are shale, originally mud deposited in lakes and on river banks, and the somewhat coarser sandstone. In Scotland limestones are rare. The sea level fluctuated constantly, sometimes flooding the land, at which time the forests were killed off and buried under new sediment. Gradually, over millions of years, the vegetation was converted, first to PEAT and then to COAL. Most coal seams are relatively thin, up to 1.5m., but usually very much less, and may be separated by considerable thicknesses of shales and sandstones. It was the presence of the coal seams that led to the great coal-mining industry of the Central Coalfield of Scotland. Numerous villages were built to house the miners. Commercially, the most valuable resource, in terms of value not volume, was the refractory FIRECLAY often found underlying the coal seams, which was the original soil on which the trees grew.

There was also volcanic activity during Carboniferous times. BASALT LAVAS form the Kilpatrick Hills and the Campsie Fells. The nearly horizontal lavas form a typical 'trap' scenery, with the resistant centre of the lava flows forming cliffs and the softer material between forming ledges. This is particularly well seen in the SW of the Campsie Fells, overlooking Strathblane, and in the Gargunnock Hills, especially after a light fall of snow. Intrusions of dolerite in the form of volcanic plugs, once the cores of the volcanoes, can be seen at, for example, Duncryne, S of Gartocharn, and at Dumgoyne at the W end of the Campsie Fells. Dykes and sills are also common. Stirling Castle and the Wallace Monument are built on the crags of a quartz dolerite sill. At the end of the Carboniferous Period further, fairly minor, earth movements caused the large Ochil Fault to form. This brings the resistant Old Red Sandstone lavas of the Ochils against the younger, much softer Carboniferous sediments to the S, forming the steep fault-line scarp so dominant over the coalfield. Some mineralization occurred near the fault. Silver ores were profitably mined near Alva for some years in the early part of the C18 and there were other mines also producing lead and cobalt from Bridge of Allan to Dollar. Another large fault formed at the S edge of the Campsie Fells. Numerous small faults affected the coalfield, disturbing the coal seams and causing many problems to the miners. Large open folds were formed in Stirling and Central Scotland; the main coalfields are found in the downfolds or synclines.

For most of the time since the Carboniferous Period Scotland has been a land surface, part of a large continent which did not break up to form the Atlantic Ocean until much later. Major rivers drained this continent flowing to the E and S. These cut deep into the mountains and must, in time, have removed enormous thicknesses of rock. In the last 100,000 years huge glaciers filled the valleys and all but covered the highest peaks. The river valleys were modified into U-shapes and the ice often scoured them well below sea level. Higher up, corries mark the position of later, smaller glaciers and there are sharp arêtes and peaks. Screes formed on the hillsides as a result of frost shattering. As the ice melted MORAINE was dumped on the lower ground, whether as irregular mounds, as can be seen near Tyndrum, or as ridges of terminal moraine marking the positions of the snouts of glaciers as the ice front advanced and retreated many times. The last major advance, the Loch Lomond Readvance, about 11,000 years ago, reached a little way S of the Highland Boundary Fault where ridges of terminal moraines can be seen around the S end of Loch Lomond and to the W of Stirling. Much of the lower ground is covered with the elongated, rounded, small hills of boulder clay called DRUMLINS. Other glacial features include the CRAG (a volcanic plug) and TAIL (softer rock protected from erosion by the crag), well seen at Duncryne.

After the ice melted, the rise in the volume of water, combined with the depression of the land that had occurred under the great weight of the ice, allowed the sea level to rise. The sea flooded into Loch Lomond, which for a time became a sea loch, and the estuary of the Forth extended much further W than at present. W of Stirling is an extensive tract of low, flat land (the carse), beneath which are shelly marine clays. The land rose as the weight of ice dispersed and raised beaches can be seen on the shores of Loch Lomond and the carseland across which the River Forth now meanders in a series of classic loops.

The geological position of Stirling, between two areas of high, volcanic hills, at a point where the river could be bridged, and with the easily defensible dolerite sill for the site of a castle, led to its becoming the most important town of the region, defending and monitoring one of the main routes into the Highlands.

### Building Materials

Timber buildings are not common in this area, just as in most of Scotland. BRICKMAKING has a relatively recent history, and is often a by-product of the coal-mining industry, using the shales associated with the coal. Many bings were recycled in 'composition' bricks, which were widely used in industrial buildings. Boulder clay is not generally suitable for brickmaking as it contains too many fragments, which would cause the bricks to shatter on firing. Occasionally, small areas of brick clay are found in the superficial deposits associated with the reworking of the boulder clay by rivers or the sea. A brickworks existed at Shires Mill, Bogside, for some time producing both tiles and bricks.

For most of the time STONE was used for small houses and farm buildings as well as for castles and mansions, with the available timber being confined to roofs. Rubble walls, random or laid to courses, would have been usual for most buildings with ashlar confined to larger buildings where money and labour were available. In much of the area a common source of stone for the building of dykes, byres and small dwellings would have been boulders and pebbles from river beds, glacial debris or weathered rock surfaces. Such loose material was easily won and, having survived transport by water or ice, was often very durable. The usually rounded shape was not very convenient for building neat walls, hence the irregular nature of many of the rubble walls. Castle Campbell shows an interesting mix of building materials. The lowest part of the tower has very angular andesite lava blocks, while above is squared sandstone rubble laid in courses. Other walls are of random rubble while the C16 part, the most recent, is of ashlar. A great variety of stone can be found in buildings using this material. Igneous and metamorphic rocks from the Highlands may be found anywhere in the area and sediments may occur as well. Some of the oldest buildings in Stirling used rounded core stones left on the surface after the weathering of the dolerite on which the town is built. There were also numerous small quarries producing stone on a small scale for local use. In most cases there is now little to be seen on the surface. 'Millstone Wood' s of Ballikinrain Castle is a reminder of the presence of a small quarry in a coarse sandstone once used for such stones. The volcanic plug of Catythirsty, on the Stockiemuir Road, has several small quarries, probably used for dykes and road metal. Many estates had their own quarries supplying stone for their own needs. Where a particularly good stratum was found much larger quarries were developed which sent their stone further afield. Some of these were very large and were worked for a long period of time.

In the Highlands by far the most important rock used was SLATE. Slate was originally a fine-grained sediment later altered by high pressure at a relatively low temperature so that the flakes of the clay minerals were realigned perpendicular to the direction of pressure, along a slaty cleavage. The rock breaks easily into thin sheets along this cleavage allowing the production of thin, relatively light, impermeable slates ideal for roofing material. North of Aberfoyle, at the Duke's Pass, were several large quarries which produced millions of slates, mainly for the Central Belt of Scotland. The slates were variously coloured blue, green, grey and purple and could also be striped or mottled green and purple, called tartan. They contain little pyrite in contrast to those from many other areas of Scotland. The slates were carried to the railhead at Aberfoyle by a mineral railway. These quarries closed in the middle of the last century. Some impure LIMESTONES are found near Loch Tay but have mainly been used for lime-making, not building.

Other metamorphic rocks are of limited use as they tend to break too easily along their more irregular cleavage and so do not make good building stone.

s of the Highland Boundary Fault SANDSTONES have long been the preferred building stone. Sandstones occur at numerous horizons in both the Old Red Sandstone and the Carboniferous and large quarries have been developed at some levels where there is good stone in large volume (figs. 1, 2). Many of the sandstones are of excellent quality. In the Old Red Sandstone the sandstones are often brown, red, pink or cream, while in most of the Carboniferous they are buff or cream becoming pink or red near the top of the succession. Sometimes they may be streaky or irregularly blotched.

In the Lower Old Red Sandstone there were quarries in the grey or dull brown sandstones of the Sherriffmuir Formation which overlies the Ochil lavas. At Gallowhill quarry the working faces can still be seen but at Stonehill near Dunblane and Wolf's Hole near Stirling little is now visible as the quarries have been filled and landscaped. A brown sandstone, used in the lower part of Dunblane Cathedral, came from Dunblane itself. Higher in the succession, in the Upper Old Red Sandstone, good-quality, more uniform sandstones occur which were widely used throughout Strathmore. Extensive quarrying took place SW of Kippen and at Culcreuch where the very bright red Gargunnock Sandstone outcrops and several quarries can still be seen. At Bloodymires Quarry about 7m. of face is still visible. There are many C18 and C19 cottages built of this in Gargunnock, and it was used in lintels and quoins over a wide area. Culcreuch Castle was built of this sandstone. There are many small quarries throughout the area. For example some of the C18 and C19 buildings and the Buchanan Monument (1788) in Killearn were built of a cream sandstone quarried just above the village. Small quarries at much the same horizon were opened for the construction of the Loch Katrine aqueduct. Further W a pink stone was quarried at Bonhill and at Dalreoch in the Leven valley. The coarser sediments of the Old Red Sandstone are not so often used, as the pebbles may drop out, although some conglomerates have been used in Callander.

The Carboniferous rocks contain many sandstones suitable for buildings and various quarries have been opened since medieval times for use locally. Once the railways developed many quarries had their own sidings and stone was exported to other parts of Scotland or even overseas. Many of the divisions of the Carboniferous were named in the C19 and are not particularly descriptive of Scottish rocks. The Upper Limestone Formation, for example, contains very little limestone. In the W, in the lowest part of the succession, the Calcareous Sandstone Formation, there were quarries on Craigmaddie Muir although this sandstone was not of particularly good quality. Further E rock of similar age was quarried near Stirling. Much stone was required for the various stages of the building of Stirling Castle and a quarry in the Raploch area in Stirling was almost certainly used in medieval times. A small quarry was opened in Abbeycraig Park, Causewayhead, in a rather coarse, pebbly sandstone, for the building of the National Wallace Monument between 1861 and 1869. A little higher in the succession was Ballengeich quarry, near Stirling although its exact site is not known. It was used in the castle, the parish church and the old bridge over the Forth. Catcraig quarry, Bannockburn, was also used for the castle and in Stirling town.

In the Upper Limestone Formation thick sandstones occur over a wide area. The famous Bishopbriggs quarries, although mainly used outwith the area, particularly in Glasgow, produced a stone of uniform cream colour. Crowhill quarry was opened in the early C18 and others including Kenmuir and the Coltpark area were developed in the C19 when Glasgow was rapidly expanding. More than 1,000 men worked here at one time. Most of the quarries were worked out by the end of the C19. The sandstone dipped gently to the E and Huntershill quarry extended underground as a mine in that direction. Miners cut horizontally into the top of the stone and quarriers cut down to extract it. The resulting galleries were some 15m. high. A fatal roof collapse in 1908 brought about the mine's abandonment and quarrying came to an end in this area. Sandstone can still be seen in the railway cutting S of Bishopbriggs but otherwise little remains of this once flourishing industry. Other quarries were worked at much the same horizon at Queenzieburn and at Dullatur, in N Lanarkshire, which supplied stone for Kirkintilloch Town Hall and the Woodilee Hospital, Lenzie. Further E similar stone, the 'Plean White Freestone', was quarried at Blackcraig. This was a cream, medium-grained, slightly mica-ceous stone used in Plean, Stirling Public Library and Falkirk Post Office. A little above this was the 'Cowie Rock'. Thorneydyke quarry supplied stone for many buildings in Stirling including the North Parish Church and the Albert Hall. It closed finally in 1903. Dunmore had a long history and it too has been extensively used in Scotland and, together with Polmaise next door, can be seen all over the Central Belt. Polmaise stone was used in Holy Trinity church in Stirling, Cambusbarron Church and Denny Parish Council Offices. New Dunmore quarry was opened in 1985 to sup-ply dimension stone for restoration work, and some new buildings. In the Passage Formation above were the Longannet quarries, in Fife, which provided stone for Stirling Castle, possibly for the Chapel Royal, and for the Christie Memorial Clock, Stirling. Further E were quarries at Sheardale, near Dollar, used in the older part of Dollar Academy, and Quarrelburn, used in Dollar Parish Church.

In the higher Carboniferous, in the Coal Measure Formation, the sandstones are often pink or red in colour. Schawpark stone was a dark colour and the reddish stone from Devon quarry was also used. The warm, reddish colour of the buildings of Alloa and Alva comes from this local sandstone.

Most estates had their own quarries. There were, for example, four small quarries on the Hill of Dunmore (Dunmore Park), others at Torwood (Torwood Castle), Carbrook and Harviestoun (Harviestoun Castle, now demolished).

In the S, in the Falkirk area, bedrock is often covered by thick drift materials and there were fewer quarries. A quarry at Brightons, near Falkirk, supplied stone for local use. Thinly bedded sandstones,

FIGURE 2. Sandstones used as building stone in Stirling and
Central Scotland

| | | |
|---|---|---|
| **Permian** | | |
| New Red Sandstone | Closeburn | Clydesdale Bank, Stirling |
| | Locharbriggs | St Mary's Church, Stirling |
| | Gatelawbridge | Nos. 21–25 Baker Street, Stirling |
| **Carboniferous** | | |
| Coal Measures Formation | Bothwell Park | |
| | Devon | } Alloa |
| | Schawpark | |
| Passage Formation | Longannet | Stirling Castle |
| Upper Limestone Formation | Blackpasture | Stirling Municipal Buildings |
| | New Dunmore | |
| | Dunmore | Stirling Post Office |
| | Auchenheath | Bridge Clock Tower, Stirling |
| | Polmaise | Cambusbarron Church |
| | Thorneydyke | North Parish Church, Stirling |
| | Blackcraig | Stirling Public Library |
| | Dullatur | Kirkintilloch Town Hall |
| | Bishopbriggs | |
| | Blaxter | Stirling Municipal Buildings |
| Calciferous Sandstone Formation | Craigmaddie | local |
| **Devonian** | | |
| Old Red Sandstone | | |
| Gargunnock Sandstone | Gargunnock | Gargunnock Village |
| | Culcreuch | Culcreuch Castle |
| Dunblane Formation | Dunblane | Dunblane Cathedral |
| Sherriffmuir Formation | Stonehill | } Dunblane, |
| | Gallowhill | Bridge of Allan, Stirling |
| | Wolf's Hole | |

FLAGSTONES, were usually imported from Caithness or Arbroath.
Some were however quarried N of Kilsyth in the Garrel flagstone.

Although sandstones were the main building stones in most of
the area there were also quarries in the lavas and intrusions.
DOLERITE and QUARTZ DOLERITE were exploited for kerbstones
and setts at Cambusbarron. Generally, igneous rocks may be
either difficult to fashion to shape or closely jointed so that it is
difficult to extract large blocks. There is a grain, or 'reed', along
which it is relatively easy to split it and perpendicular to this is the
'hem'. In expert hands, small setts and kerbstones could be
quickly and easily made. They can still be seen in use in many roads
throughout the Central Belt. Otherwise they were mainly confined
to walls or small farm buildings. One building where dark, basic
rock, possibly from Craigend quarry, can be seen is in the old stable
block now used as a visitor centre at Mugdock Country Park.

Many of the Scottish sandstone quarries were becoming worked out by the end of the C19. Between 1890 and 1914 red sandstones of Permian and Triassic age were commonly imported from the S of Scotland and some have been reopened to supply stone for both new building and renovation work. This New Red Sandstone, formed in sand dunes on land, is even-grained and often shows large-scale cross-bedding. It is hundreds of metres thick and is easily quarried. There were relatively few, but very large quarries in Ayrshire and Dumfriesshire. By 1898 some 1,500 men were employed. Quarries included Locharbriggs (St Mary's R.C. Church, Stirling), Gatelawbridge (Lawsons in Baker Street, Stirling) and Closeburn (Clydesdale Bank, Stirling).

Carboniferous sandstone was also imported from quarries in the Central Belt, for example Auchenheath, near Lesmahagow, and from the N of England, particularly Northumberland. These were cream sandstones similar to many of the Scottish ones. Blackpasture stone was used in Stirling's Municipal Buildings. Blaxter stone was also used here and in the new Railway Station and the War Memorial in Stirling.

# PREHISTORIC AND EARLY HISTORIC STIRLING AND CENTRAL SCOTLAND

## BY J.N. GRAHAM RITCHIE

The navigable Firths of Forth and Clyde provided ready points of entry to the first folk who made their way into Stirling and Central Scotland about 10,000 years ago. Periods of glaciation were past and a woodland landscape rich in game greeted the newcomers. From the E the River Forth offered a natural highway into the area and would have formed a wide sea-firth stretching far inland along the course of the present river. From the W the Firth of Clyde offered access to the Vale of Leven and Loch Lomond, with routes into Central Scotland provided by the river systems that flow into the Clyde and Loch Lomond such as the Blane Water, the Endrick Water and the Kelvin. The way of life of these early folk, known as MESOLITHIC, was one that relied on the use of the natural resources of the countryside, hunting and gathering at different seasons of the year. Often their campsites are discovered as a result of finding carefully formed tiny flint implements, or the debris of their manufacture. In Stirling and Central Scotland such flint scatters are rare, but this may be more a reflection of a lack of field inspection than a genuine absence. Finds of whalebone and worked antler in the inner basins of the Forth show the activities of Mesolithic peoples, and in at least two examples the bones of a whale appear to be associated with antler axes with wooden handles, which suggests that an adventitious stranding of a whale has been the occasion for feasting. The bones would also have been useful in the preparation of tools and as elements of the temporary structures that such a peripatetic way of life required. Culinary habits of another sort are indicated by the mounds of discarded limpet shells between Mumrills and Inveravon.

A knowledge of agriculture and stock-rearing was introduced to Stirling and Central Scotland around 4000 B.C., the beginning of the NEOLITHIC PERIOD, but again the surviving evidence is slight and concentrated in the sw part of the area. The major architectural monuments of the period, known as CHAMBERED CAIRNS, were designed as communal burial places. Many have been badly ruined over time, and mention is made here only of the better preserved. The scale of the monuments varies considerably, but at Auchenlaich, Callander, Scotland's longest cairn has been identified, a man-made mound some 320m. in length. Its scale and that of other long cairns such as Stockie Muir (Croftamie) and Craigmaddie provide an indication of the human resources that might be mustered for a communal building project.

Comparable monuments in the E, possibly of timber and turf construction, have not survived centuries of ploughing. In 2001, excavation at Claish Farm, near Callander, revealed the plan of a Neolithic timber building measuring about 25m. by 9m., closely comparable in plan to one at Balbridie (Aberdeenshire), and dating to about 4000 B.C.

The practice of decorating rock surfaces with small pecked hollows known as CUPMARKS, sometimes additionally ornamented with surrounding rings (CUP-AND-RING MARKINGS), may also have begun at this time. Although individual sites are not listed, examples from Greenland, West Dunbartonshire, may be seen in the Hunterian Museum, University of Glasgow. Boulders from Bowling are in Glasgow Art Gallery and Museum, Kelvingrove. STANDING STONES and STONE CIRCLES were erected in the Neolithic period; many are known to have been moved from their original positions, but there is an interesting linear setting at Drumgoyach and a fine stone circle near Killin.

Most later Neolithic and BRONZE AGE monuments are burial sites, either CAIRNS of stone or BARROWS (earthen mounds) covering or containing individual burials in slab-built graves or cists (from the Scots word for a chest). Many barrows and cairns have been destroyed, but discovery and recording of such finds across the area suggests a growing intensity of settlement by the second millennium B.C. The cairns at Kippenross House and Fairy Knowe, Bridge of Allan, are surviving examples of a type of monument that would have been commonplace in the landscape until the Age of Improvement and industrial and urban development. Many stray bronze objects have been discovered. There are also a few Late Bronze Age swords and spearheads, as well as a beaten bronze vessel from Flanders Moss.

In the IRON AGE, the major monuments are those built for 3 defence; e.g. that at Dunmore (Kilmahog) or as stout homesteads; indeed some hilltop fortifications were already in use in the later Bronze Age (categorization of periods of prehistory in Scotland is sometimes only a useful shorthand terminology). In a number of cases the stone wall of a FORT was additionally strengthened by the use of timber beams to assist in the consolidation of the struc-

ture. If a timber-laced wall were set alight either deliberately in the
course of attack, or perhaps ceremonially after capture, or indeed
accidentally, the heat fused the stones together to form a vitrified
mass. Examples of such vitrified forts include Dumyat (Blairlogie)
and Sheep Hill (Dumbarton). Smaller stone-walled defended
homesteads are also found, known as 'duns'. Several BROCHS, a
class more commonly found in the far N and W of Scotland, have
been identified, including that at Tappoch, Tor Wood (Plean),
but many of these are not well preserved. Excavation of the broch
at Leckie, near Gargunnock, suggested that its occupation fell
between the later 80s A.D. and not much after 140 A.D.; the range
of artefacts recovered included iron spearheads, sword-blades,
sheep shears and a spade, as well as querns, stone loomweights,
beads and imported Roman goods. These objects suggest that the
broch was a stoutly constructed working farm. At Fairy Knowe,
Buchlyvie, radiocarbon dates provide a similar date for a broch,
which had been preceded by a timber round house, a type of structure that was probably far more common than surviving stone-built
structures. Most of the pottery found was of Roman origin, and
sherds of Roman glass were also discovered, along with brooches
and a fine enamelled ring of Iron Age type. A pair of compasses
was among an unusually wide range of iron artefacts (this metal
does not survive well in Scottish conditions). The range of com-
paratively well dated material found at these sites raises intriguing
questions about the relationship between the native populations
and the Roman occupations. CRANNOGS, structures within lochs
using the surrounding water as a form of defence, were also probably common both on the Clyde and in Loch Lomond and Loch
Tay. The skills of the native population in metallurgy may be shown
by the beaten bronze cauldron found in 1768 in Kincardine Moss.

In the W and central parts of the region the tribal grouping was
that of the Dumnonii, and in the E the Venicones and Votadini,
the latter to the S of the Forth. A confederation of tribes, comparable to that of the Caledonii in the N, was known as the Maeatae,
a name that may survive in Dumyat and Myot Hill today. The
political importance of central Scotland in the early first millennium
A.D. is clear as the tribal units of the Iron Age were transformed
into the kingships of the Early Medieval period, later to form the
kingdom of Scotland. This is most readily identifiable in the W of
the region where the Dumnonii became the Britons of Strathclyde
with a capital at Dumbarton. In the central part it is more complex,
as this area became known as Manau Gododdin, a name that is
cognate with the Votadini. This is of more than passing interest, if
susceptible to many interpretations, as the first element remains to
this day in the place-names Clackmannan and Slamannan, and a
stone with the traditional name 'Clach Manau' survives outside
the tolbooth of Clackmannan.

# THE ROMANS IN STIRLING AND CENTRAL SCOTLAND

## BY DAVID J. BREEZE

In A.D. 68 Nero, the last of the family of Julius Caesar to reign as emperor, committed suicide. The ensuing civil war ('The Year of the Four Emperors') ended with the success of Titus Flavius Vespasianus, commander of the army of Judaea. The new emperor, better known to history as Vespasian, had served in Britain during the Roman invasion of 43, and he decided on a new forward policy, presumably with the intention of completing the conquest of the island. The Brigantes of N England were subdued in the early 70s and completion of the conquest of Wales followed.

In 79 (or, less probably, 80) the Roman army, under Gnaeus Julius Agricola, the governor of Britain, advanced as far N as the River Tay. The following season, Tacitus recorded, a line of BASES was constructed across the Forth–Clyde isthmus and 'if the valour of the army and the glory of Rome had allowed it, a halting place would have been found within the island'. Little is definitely known of these Agricolan bases but they probably included Camelon at Falkirk, Mollins by Moodiesburn, Lanarkshire, and Barochan Hill near Bishopton in Renfrew. The line of timber towers beside the Roman road running N to the Tay may also date to these years.

The Forth–Clyde isthmus was not to be the final frontier in Britain. In 83 and 84 Agricola advanced beyond the Forth and achieved victory over the Caledonians at the battle of Mons Graupius, probably somewhere in NE Scotland. Following this victory Roman control over E central Scotland was consolidated through the construction of two lines of FORTS, one running up Strathmore and the other along the edge of the Highlands. Each of the Highland Line forts was strategically placed at the mouth of a glen. They include Drumquhassle near Drymen, Malling by the Lake of Menteith and Bochastle at Callander.

It is still a matter of debate as to whether the purpose of the forts was to guard against unauthorized entry to the province or act as springboards for an advance up the glens into the Highlands. The placing of a legion at Inchtuthil at the entrance to Strath Tay, the route followed by the modern A9, might be thought to support the latter view. There was, however, to be no advance into the Highlands, nor were those forts to have a long life. Defeats on the continent only two years after Mons Graupius led to the withdrawal of troops from Britain and the abandonment of most forts N of the Cheviot Hills, even before Inchtuthil was completed.

During the reigns of two emperors, Trajan (98–117) and Hadrian (117–138), the Roman army consolidated the Tyne–Solway line as the northern frontier of the province of Britain. On this line Hadrian ordered the construction of the Wall which still bears his name.

The Emperor Hadrian died in July 138, and in the following year preparations were put in hand for a second major advance into Scotland. The reasons for this change in policy are unclear. It has been variously suggested that there was trouble in s Scotland serious enough to require military intervention, that Hadrian's Wall was out of touch with the Caledonians, the main enemy in the N, or that the new emperor, Antoninus Pius, required a military triumph to help secure his position. Certainly Cornelius Fronto recorded the emperor controlling the activities in Britain from his palace as the helmsman controls a ship. Victory was celebrated in 142.

The northern advance resulted in the reoccupation of the land between Hadrian's Wall and the River Tay and the construction of the ANTONINE WALL (fig. 3) from Bo'ness on the Firth of Forth to Old Kilpatrick on the River Clyde. Hadrian's Wall was abandoned. The new wall was of turf, 15 Roman feet (4.3m.) wide, placed on a stone base. It stood perhaps 10 feet (3m.) high and may have been surmounted by a timber breastwork. In front lay a wide and deep ditch, the material from which was tipped out on to the N side to form a low, wide mound.

The first plan appears to have been for six forts along the Wall eight miles apart, with fortlets at mile intervals between. Before construction was completed the number of forts was increased through the addition of at least eleven forts so that the average spacing was reduced to a little over two miles for much of the length of the Wall. These forts were connected by a road, possibly planned from the beginning. In certain locations southern expansions of the rampart have been recorded. Each consists of a platform about 5m. square. These 'expansions' appear in pairs and the best explanation of their function relates them to signalling. In one area three small enclosures have been noted but their purpose is unknown.

The placing of the forts on the Wall, and their close relationship with the rampart, blurred the distinction between the two essential functions. The purpose of the linear barrier together with the fortlets was the bureaucratic function of frontier control, whereas the task of the units in the forts was to defend the province from attack and, if necessary, interfere in affairs to the N.

The Antonine Wall was built by soldiers from the three legions of the province, II Augusta from Caerleon, VI Victrix from York and XX Valeria Victrix from Chester. These soldiers left records of their work in the form of elaborately carved 'distance slabs'. The forts, however, were mostly manned by soldiers of the second-line units of the *auxilia*. Unusually, some legionaries are attested at some forts and it is possible that the occupation of the Antonine Wall overstretched the resources of the army in Britain.

The forts on the Wall followed the basic arrangements for such military installations. The principal buildings included the headquarters, commander's house and granaries, often, though not always, of stone, or at least based on stone foundations. The barrack-blocks and other buildings were of timber. Each fort usually had its own bath-house. However, the internal plans of forts could vary considerably as could the defensive arrangements, from one to four ditches being provided. In size the forts ranged from tiny Duntocher

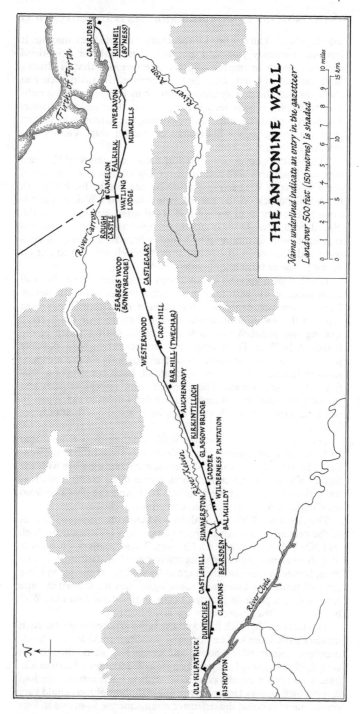

FIGURE 3. Map of the Antonine Wall

at o.2ha to Mumrills at 2.6ha. Some, such as Rough Castle, were patently too small to hold a complete regiment and part of the *cohors VI Nerviorum* attested here must have been outposted.

Many forts had an annexe attached to one side. The purpose of this was probably military, protection of the bath-house, workshops etc. Inscriptions furnish some evidence for the existence of officers' families and other civilians though excavation has largely failed to provide physical evidence of civil settlements. Field systems are, however, known outside several forts.

Today the most visible feature of the Antonine Wall is the ditch that survives particularly well from Falkirk to Bonnybridge, where 4 the rampart is also visible, and over Croy and Bar Hills. The best forts are at Rough Castle and Bar Hill (Twechar). The only visible fortlet is at Kinneil (Bo'ness), whereas all 'expansions' can be seen on either side of Rough Castle fort and on the w brow of Croy Hill (North Lanarkshire). The Military Way is preserved at Seabegs Wood (Bonnybridge) and Rough Castle. The rampart base may be seen in New Kilpatrick Cemetery, Bearsden, and a bath-house 5 and latrine at Bearsden.

The Antonine Wall was probably abandoned over a period of years in the early 160s, but coins and an inscription may indicate continued military interest in the area.

The campaigns of the Emperors Septimius Severus and Caracalla in Scotland do not appear to have affected the Antonine Wall, although there was military activity at Cramond on the Forth and a new base was constructed at Carpow on the Tay. But the campaigning which had begun in 208 ended with the death of Severus at York on 4 February 211.

Treaties are known to have existed between Rome and the Caledonians in the second century and are again mentioned in the fourth century: it is possible that they existed throughout these years. The Ravenna Cosmography records '*diversa loca*' in southern Scotland and these have been interpreted as official tribal meeting places sanctioned by Rome, but this is uncertain. The Barbarian Conspiracy of 367 when the Picts and Scots and the otherwise unknown Attacotti attacked the empire caused considerable disruption. Although the Romans retrieved the situation, it would appear that they had lost any remaining control over central Scotland.

# THE EARLY CHRISTIAN PERIOD IN STIRLING AND CENTRAL SCOTLAND

## BY IAN FISHER

In the period from the C7 to the C9, the area covered in this volume lay between the territories of the Scots of Argyll, the Picts of E Scotland and the Northumbrians in Lothian. One might expect the region to be influenced by the rich sculptural traditions of these neighbours, but much of the area followed the practice of the British kingdom of Strathclyde, which appears to have produced no sculpture before the late C9 or C10. The British name *Eccles*, indicating an early church, was originally applied to three places including Falkirk and St Ninian's, but the S part of the area was more notable for battles between the neighbouring peoples than for religious activity.

Evidence of Irish/Scottish missionary work is more widespread, including place-names in Kil- (*Cill*, 'church' or 'burial-ground') and *Annat* ('abandoned church'). Dedications to Irish saints include Columba (Drymen, and possibly Inchmahome), Blaan or Blane (Dunblane), Findoca (Inchcailloch) and Ronan (Kilmaronock). Surviving CARVED STONES are concentrated in the Strathfillan–Glen Dochart corridor and the adjoining highland glens which enjoyed ready communication with Argyll. Most of these are simple linear CROSSES of types found throughout the West Highlands, and single examples or small groups are preserved at Strathfillan Priory (Crianlarich), at Suie in Glen Dochart, at the W end of Loch Earn and the S end of Loch Lubnaig. The largest group, at Balquhidder, includes a slab with a wedge-armed 'sunken' cross with recessed centre. The relics of St Fillan, a bronze bell and a crozier encased in an elaborate late medieval shrine, are now among the principal treasures of the National Museum of Scotland. For centuries they were guarded by hereditary keepers, the bell (the 'Bernane') at Suie and the crozier (the 'Quigrich') at Killin, and another lost relic, the arm of the saint, may be represented on a slab at Strathfillan.

By the C10 the kingdoms of the Picts and Scots had been united, and there are records in E Scotland of a number of communities of clerics or *Céle Dé* ('clients of God'), perhaps based on older monasteries. In the C12 one such community was recorded as serving the new cathedral of Dunblane, and two CROSS-SLABS there suggest that it may have had an earlier origin. The larger slab shows on one face a plain ringed cross, and on the other a medley of motifs including confronted animals, a free-standing ringed cross, an ill-proportioned horse and rider, coarse geometrical ornament and a figure with a staff or crozier. The second slab may have been trimmed for re-use as a grave-slab, but one edge preserves original interlace, fret and animal ORNAMENT. The connections of both stones are with E Scotland, and the same is true of the tall slab that surmounts a low summit at Hawkhill (Fife), enjoying fine views to the Forth and the Ochils. Although much worn, this preserves on each face the outline of a plain cross with semicircular armpits, resembling in shape the more ornate crosses at St Andrews.

Also of the C10 is a small group of carved stones from the N bank of the Clyde. Two of these, at Dumbarton Castle, are incomplete grave-slabs with plain crosses set against interlaced backgrounds, as on examples at Govan and Inchinnan. The other stones, one from Old Kilpatrick and another from the grounds of the nearby Mountblow House, are both fragments of free-standing crosses, the most widely distributed monuments in Strathclyde at this period. Both have neat panels of interlace, and the Mountblow cross-shaft, which is almost complete, also shows a beast and a rider. Belonging to the following century there are a complete hog-back monument and a fragment of another of the same type, both at

Logie (Blairlogie). These have imitation tiled roofs, and the ridges are less curved than those of earlier examples such as at Govan. A small wheel-cross with wedge-shaped arms and a gabled base at St Ninian's is probably also of the CII and may have stood at one end of a coped grave-cover.

# MEDIEVAL CHURCHES

### BY RICHARD FAWCETT

Stirling and Central Scotland does not have large numbers of medieval churches, though the range of types is more fully representative than might be anticipated from such a short list. At the more ambitious end of the scale are the virtually complete (partly thanks to modern restorations) cathedral of Dunblane and the great collegiate burgh church of Stirling, while the royal abbey of Cambuskenneth survives as little more than a ruined fragment with a complete tower. In the middle rank are the priory of Inchmahome, a tiny portion of the nunnery at Manuel (the latter being an example of a particularly rare type) and the enigmatic remains of Strathfillan Priory (Crianlarich). Churches of parochial scale are represented mainly by structures of the simplest form, though greater complexity is seen at Airth, and indications that churches of even the most basic plan type might nevertheless have high-quality architectural detailing are seen at Inchcailloch. Perhaps the most significant absence from this range of types is a house of one of the mendicant orders, the only slight compensation for this being the excavations on the site of the church of the Dominican Friars in Stirling, which have revealed parts of the S and E walls of the church there.

Several of the churches had a longer history of religious activity than their present buildings might suggest. Dunblane is traditionally associated with the late C6 or C7 mission of St Blane, and surviving CROSS-SLABS certainly point to religious life by the C8 or C9. The island sites of Inchmahome and Inchcailloch are also said to have been home to earlier communities, the latter being associated with St Kentigerna (perhaps † c. 733), while Strathfillan may have been the site of St Fillan's activities in the C8. But we enter into more certain territory in saying that many of the buildings we now see had their origins in the revival of the Church that began at the turn of the CII and CI2, and that took on particular momentum in the reign of David I (1124–53). The first bishop of the revived diocese of Dunblane, which was sometimes referred to as Strathearn, appears on record by 1155, and the lower storeys of the cathedral tower are probably of a little before that date. Two of the religious houses were founded by the royal family as part of their policy of introducing European monasticism in all its varied manifestations. Cambuskenneth had a relationship with the favourite royal residence of Stirling Castle similar to that of Holyrood Abbey (Edinburgh) with Edinburgh Castle or Kelso Abbey (Scottish

6, 7, 8, 9, 10, 11

Borders) with Roxburgh Castle. It was probably established soon
after 1140 for the order of canons of Arrouaise, which was soon
subsumed within the mainstream of the Augustinian order. Manuel
was founded at a date before 1164 for Cistercian nuns by David's
grandson and successor on the throne, Malcolm IV. The efforts of
the royal house for the diocesan system and the religious orders were
paralleled in the encouragement of the establishment of parishes
across the kingdom. That at Stirling was probably established by
David I himself, as was perhaps also that at Airth, while Kinneil
was evidently a creation of the king's chamberlain, and Tillicoultry
appears to have been a royal creation of no later than the reign of
William I.

Inchmahome Priory represents a later type of foundation than
those so far discussed, having been established in 1238 by the earls
of Menteith as their family mausoleum. This foundation took
place at a time when the pressure on the great families to set up a
major abbey, both as an act of high patronage and as a statement
of their own prestige, was being replaced by a preference for
smaller foundations. The choice of the highly adaptable Augustinian
order, however, could be because the canons continued to be viewed
as particularly well suited to absorbing or replacing older foundations. But in this case there is at least a possibility that there were
less pure motives behind the foundation, the priory possibly being
a recipient of funds the earls had improperly diverted from the
diocese of Dunblane during a period of episcopal instability, and
which they preferred to devote to a project that was more to their
taste. The adaptability of the Augustinians was probably also a
factor behind Robert I's fostering of a small priory at Strathfillan
in about 1317, a house that never flourished, and where the physical
remains are, to say the least, unilluminating.

The planning of these churches demonstrates well the gamut of
forms that might be expected among such a range of types.
Having possibly been initially housed in temporary buildings,
Cambuskenneth Abbey's church was eventually set out in the earlier
C13 to a plan that had been introduced into Scotland by the
Cistercian order. It has a short rectangular presbytery for the high
altar, a pair of transepts with two-bay chapel-aisles on the E side of
each, and an extended nave which housed both the canons' choir
and a space that could be used by layfolk, though in the Cistercian
prototypes the W part of the nave had been given over to the lay
brethren. The lack of correspondence between the wall-shafts on
the S side of the nave and the arcade piers and wall-shafts of the
single nave aisle, on the N side, suggests the aisle at Cambuskenneth
was a later addition to an initially aisleless nave, being set on the
side away from the cloister, where there was no need to relocate
other buildings. The original plan would thus have been essentially
like that of the Cistercian abbey of Culross (Fife). Evidence for
the similar addition of a single aisle is to be seen elsewhere at a
number of other monastic churches, as at the Cistercian abbeys of
Deer (Aberdeenshire) and Balmerino (Fife) and the Tironensian
abbey of Lindores (Fife). Similarities between Lindores and
Cambuskenneth are also evident in the way that both had free-

standing bell-towers to the N of the W front of the nave. At Cambuskenneth, where the restored tower is the best-preserved part, it had been placed far enough away to allow the aisle to be added without difficulty, though at Lindores the tower was much closer, meaning that the new aisle could not extend the full length of the nave.

Dunblane Cathedral and Inchmahome Priory were both probably set out in the 1230s on variants of a plan type that came to be greatly favoured for churches of middling scale, with an extended aisleless E limb for the presbytery and chancel, a nave of similar length but with one or more flanking aisles, and a single engaged bell-tower. Dunblane had two nave aisles, with the retained C12 tower projecting rather unexpectedly part-way down the S aisle; it also had a two-storeyed sacristy, treasury and chapter-house block running along much of the N side of the chancel. But in the basic combination of rectangular unaisled chancel and aisled nave, it was related to the cathedrals at Brechin (Angus) and Dunkeld (Perth and Kinross), with other versions of the idea being employed at the cathedrals of Aberdeen, Dornoch (Highland) and Fortrose (Highland). Inchmahome had only a single aisle, on the side away from the cloister, with a squat tower rising over its W bay; it also had a sacristy off the N side of the choir.

Inchmahome Priory's church was not large, though it was certainly more ambitious than that of the Cistercian nuns of Manuel. Nuns seldom attracted the lavish benefactions of the monks, canons or even friars, and the church at Manuel was evidently never more than an unaugmented rectangle, though C18 views suggest it was a building of simple elegance, with carefully proportioned and grouped lancets along its flanks and gables. From the later C12, a rectangular plan came to be common for many types of churches of smaller scale, and this appears to have been the plan at Blackness, Inchcailloch and Tullibody. Kinneil Parish Church, (Bo'ness), was more ambitious in having separate compartments for chancel and nave. The survival of the superb carving of the (presumably) C12 crucifixion from there, (now displayed in Kinneil House, Bo'ness) which was perhaps once placed over the chancel arch, is an early reminder that even relatively simple churches might once have had splendid fixtures and furnishings. At the old parish church of Airth the plan was further enriched by having a N aisle, the arcade piers and responds of which were decorated with fine carved capitals, one being of waterleaf form. Waterleaf capitals are also to be found at Inchcailloch Church among the fragments of what appears to have been a handsomely detailed late C12 doorway.

We know nothing of the original parish church at Stirling. What we have there is a vast building of the C15 and earlier C16 which provides us with one of the clearest expressions anywhere in Scotland of the importance of their parish church to the burgesses of the great trading burghs, and of the central role it played in their civic life. Stirling's church was rebuilt in two stages, with a large aisled nave and an axial W tower built first; this was followed by a shorter but even more impressively conceived aisled choir once the burgh had agreed to assume the full financial responsibility for rebuilding. Although the church was never entirely finished, the cosmopolitan outlook of its builders is evident in the apsidal E termination of the choir and the telescoped form of the W tower. The former was a feature probably reintroduced into Scotland from the continent in the 1450s at St Salvator's College in St Andrews (Fife), and that was to be taken up at other burgh churches at Linlithgow (West Lothian) and Aberdeen around the same time as at Stirling. The form of the tower is likely to have been a borrowing from the Netherlands, and it is seen in even more sophisticated form at the burgh church at Dundee. Other signs of the soaring ambitions of the builders of Stirling's church are the apparent intention to build a three-storeyed chancel, though only two storeys were ever built, and what appears to have been an abortive plan for a second tower at the crossing. Parallels for a three-storeyed elevation in a burgh church are to be found in the nave at Linlithgow, though the only likely Scottish prototype for having two towers ranged along the principal axis is at the C12 abbey church at Kelso.

The burgh churches benefited from the growing late medieval tendency of layfolk to prefer the spiritual ministrations of their local church over those of some great religious institution. Another manifestation of this was the endowment by wealthier individuals or by trade and religious guilds of CHANTRY ALTARS, at which prayers might be offered for the welfare of the living and the salvation of the dead, at a time when the fear of damnation was of greater concern than is now possible for most of us to imagine. Many of these altars were simply set at aisle ends or against arcade piers but, for those who could afford it, the preferred choice was often to build CHAPELS, usually referred to as aisles, that projected from the flank of the building. One of these, built for the Forestar family, survives virtually intact off the E end of the N nave aisle at Stirling, and at least two others are known to have existed there.

Chantry chapels were not confined to the greatest churches, however, and one built for the Bruce of Stenhouse and Airth family survives in roofless state at Airth Church. It is characteristic of many such chapels in being of rectangular plan, in being entered from the church through a wide arch, and in having windows in only the W and gable walls, the E wall being left blank to permit an elaborately carved and painted altar retable to be placed there. But imposing chapels might also be formed within the main spaces of churches, where they would once have been enclosed by traceried timber SCREENS, and a clue to their former existence can often be the insertion of enlarged WINDOWS. At Dunblane in the C16, for example, Bishop William Chisholm displayed an aspect of the late medieval wish to identify more closely with the sufferings of Christ in adding a dedication to the Holy Blood to an altar already dedicated to St Blaise at the W end of the N aisle. The only pointer to what must have been an extensive remodelling of the chapel, presumably in order to provide an imposing burial place for the bishop, was the insertion of two large windows; these would almost certainly have taken large areas of stained glass in which Christ's Passion was graphically depicted.

Burial within a church was a much sought-after goal for those who could afford the high costs, and the area covered by this book has several fine MEMORIALS and EFFIGIES, including a number of unique interest. Cambuskenneth has some notable C13 coped GRAVESTONES of polygonal section, one having a foliate-headed cross with sprigs of stiff-leaf foliage along its shaft. A more orthodox foliate-headed cross is to be seen on a ledger slab at Inchmahome. But the best C13 memorials are effigies at Dunblane and Inchmahome. Dunblane has two episcopal effigies in mass vestments, one re-set in a recess in the N wall of the chancel that is thought to commemorate the rebuilder of the cathedral, Bishop Clement, and the other in a recess in the chapel at the E end of the S nave aisle. Dunblane also has a fine double effigy thought to represent one of the earls of Strathearn and his countess. Rather more remarkable is a double effigy, now in the chapter-house at Inchmahome, which is assumed to represent Walter Stewart, earl of Menteith († c. 1295), who is shown in a fond embrace with his countess. This embrace may have been for dynastic purposes, though it has always struck a sympathetic chord with the romantically inclined.

Armoured figures were always the most common form of high-relief male effigy, and a further C13 member of the Stewart family is commemorated in this way at Inchmahome, while there is a fragment of yet another knightly effigy, in this case probably of the C15, at Cambuskenneth. A somewhat more gauche depiction of a knight is that of Sir John Drummond (probably † early C15); his incised slab, which may be of West Highland production, is in the Inchmahome chapter-house. Another striking C15 effigy is within a tomb recess below the S gable wall at Airth, in which a lady is shown with her hands raised in prayer above a drawn-back shroud. Unfortunately we know very little about the design of the tombs in which most of these effigies were once set. It is intriguing to speculate that some fragments of enriched canopy work surviving at Cambuskenneth may have been from the tomb of King James III, who was buried there after his murder at Sauchieburn in 1488, but there can be no certainty on this.

The areas in which these effigies were located would probably always have been lavishly furnished but, from the increased number of references to liturgical fixtures and furnishings in accounts of the activities of the great patrons, we know that a growing emphasis was being placed on creating a beautiful setting for all aspects of worship in the later Middle Ages. This was especially the case in the vicinity of the growing numbers of altars and in the areas used by the clergy; pitifully few such furnishings survived the 'cleansing' operations of the Reformation, however, and it is therefore particularly fortunate that a number of the choir stalls of Dunblane Cathedral have survived. Six of them still have their canopies, while in the adjacent cathedral museum part of the arch over the processional entrance between the returned stalls at the W end of the choir is to be seen. These provide tantalizing reminders of the magnificent furnishings that were once such an important feature of our greater churches, and that might even overshadow the architecture in their rich detailing and elaborate polychromy.

## POST-REFORMATION CHURCHES

The Scottish Reformation of 1560 broke the Church's link to the papacy, abolished episcopacy (re-established briefly in 1610–38 and again in 1660–89), suppressed the religious orders and established a Presbyterian system of church government. English supplanted Latin as the language of worship in which reading of the Scriptures, prayer and preaching became the dominant features. Celebration of the sacrament of the Lord's Supper or Eucharist, despite the intention of the early Reformers, became infrequent, taking place generally twice a year. The 'idolatrous' furnishings of churches, such as stone altars, rood screens or beams, statues and stained glass, were destroyed. However, the buildings themselves continued to be used for worship.

The post-Reformation stress on the proclamation of the Word of God by reading of the Scriptures, prayer and preaching meant that audibility of the minister to his congregation assumed prime importance. The largest of the existing medieval churches, their size often the result of a monastic or collegiate function, were subdivided to serve two or more congregations (e.g. the Church of the Holy Rude at Stirling in 1656) or abandoned partly (e.g. Dunblane Cathedral) or wholly (e.g. Cambuskenneth Abbey). However, parish churches continued in use but adapted to the new forms of worship, the minister standing in a pulpit, if one existed, either at one end of the nave or, more frequently, at the centre of one side. Chancels and side chapels lost their function of housing altars and were often taken over by local lairds, who placed their own pews or galleries in them, sometimes with a burial vault below. At Alloa the chancel of Old St Mungo's Church was taken over by the Earl of Mar, whose family burial place below was constructed in 1582. The pew of the Bruces of Airth was placed in the Lady Chapel of the now former Airth Parish Church. Airth was a parish that contained estates of three prominent families and the church was
12 soon enlarged by the addition of two more transeptal 'aisles', those of the Elphinstones of Dunmore in 1593 and of the Bruces of Powfoulis in 1614, each containing a laird's pew.

Replacement of medieval churches by buildings better suited to reformed worship took place in only a few parishes and burghs in the late C16 and C17. A new parish church (later itself replaced) was built at Dumbarton c. 1565. It seems to have been T-shaped, with a transeptal N 'aisle', a very early example of what was to become a standard post-Reformation plan. Alva Parish Church, rebuilt in 1631, may have been cruciform, as certainly was Kirkintilloch Parish
13 Church (now Auld Kirk Museum) of 1644. Other C17 churches, e.g. Balquhidder Old Church of 1631, the (now demolished) Bo'ness Parish Church of 1634, the former Fintry Parish Church of 1642 or the former Kippen Parish Church of 1691, were simple rectangles. Despite the classical detail of the Chapel Royal built at Stirling Castle in 1594, these parish churches had doors and windows that were either unadorned rectangles (e.g. the 'aisles' and

remodelled body of the former Airth Parish Church) or of Gothic
survival character, as at the former Kirkintilloch Parish Church 13
and Logie Old Church. Most seem to have had birdcage bellcotes
such as survive at Logie Old Church and the former Kippen Parish
Church. Exceptional are the towers added to the former Airth 12
Parish Church in 1647 and to Old St Mungo's Church at Alloa 14
c. 1681–3, the first originally pyramid-roofed, the roof of the second
consisting of an ogee dome atop a truncated pyramid, this tower
further dignified by its roundheaded windows with consoled keystones.

Rebuilding of parish churches continued in the c18. These new
edifices may be characterized as decent but economical, the local
heritors (landowners) responsible for the erection and repair of
churches, manses and schools seldom willing to pay more than
required of them by law. Almost all these churches were straightforward oblongs, like Drymen Parish Church of 1771, the Old
Parish Church of 1774 at Aberfoyle, or on a T-plan, like *John Adam*'s
Buchanan Parish Church (Milton of Buchanan) of 1761–4, the
windows rectangular (with stone mullions used as late as 1766 at
the former Carriden Parish Church), or roundheaded, the keystones
projecting at Killearn Old Church of 1734. Gables were sometimes
crowstepped (e.g. at Gargunnock Parish Church of 1774) and occasionally crossed by forestairs giving access to galleries inside (e.g.
at Gargunnock and Baldernock Parish Churches). Birdcage bellcotes were standard. The position of the pulpit, often placed in the
centre of the s side, was commonly marked by tall flanking windows
and a minister's door, as at Baldernock Parish Church of 1795 which 16
further marks the pulpit's position by a bellcote-topped pediment
at the centre of the s side. Some churches were grander. Consciously
urbane, and not unreasonably so since it formed the centrepiece of
the main square of a planned new town, was the pedimented front
of the Callander Parish Church (demolished) designed by *John
Baxter Jun.* in 1771. Unusual in plan is the now badly altered Killin
and Ardeonaig Parish Church of 1744, its body an octagon from
which projected three 'aisles'. Two notable towers were erected in
the c18. At St Ninian's Church, Stirling, the medieval tower was 15
rebuilt in 1734 by *Robert Henderson* and *Charles Bachop*, its design
derived from that used fifty years before at Old St Mungo's Church 14
in Alloa but with urns on the corners of the cornice and a domed
roof surmounted by a cupola. At Falkirk Old and St Modan's 17
Church four years later *William Adam* designed a new crossing
tower, its belfry stage octagonal.

Churches other than parish churches were erected as the result
of two c18 secessions from the established Church of Scotland,
one in 1733 leading to the formation of the SECESSION CHURCH
(soon split into Burgher and Antiburgher factions, later coming
together as the United Associate (subsequently United Secession)
Church), the other leading to the founding of the RELIEF CHURCH
in 1752. Most of the buildings erected for these secessionist denominations reflected the poverty of their congregations. The earliest
of their surviving buildings in the area is the Holm Secession
Church, near Balfron, of 1739–40, a humble meeting house but

with symmetrically placed door and window openings and a cavetto eaves cornice. Little grander is the starkly detailed former Relief Church of *c.* 1795 at Old Kilpatrick. More assertive are the Buchlyvie Antiburgher Church (later Buchlyvie North Church) of 1751–2, with Gibbsian projecting keystones to the roundheaded openings, and the Burgher Church of 1797 at Bannockburn, its pilastered entrance surmounted by a Venetian window. Unusually large were the Relief Churches at Dumbarton (since demolished) of 1793–4 and at Falkirk (now The People's Church) of 1799. Also at Falkirk is a former Antiburgher Church (the 'Tattie Kirk') of 1806, a tall octagon squeezed into a tight site set back from the street.

The EARLY NINETEENTH CENTURY saw a marked increase in new churches, partly the result of previous failure to carry out repairs but also the result of growing prosperity. Some new rural churches, such as Muiravonside Parish Church of 1811, were no more ambitious architecturally than the generality of their predecessors but a few showed development from the standard C18 type. At Baldernock Parish Church of 1795 the position of the pulpit at the centre of the S wall was marked externally by a pediment. This external emphasis on the position of the pulpit was followed in 1805 at Logie Parish Church, near Blairlogie, by *William Stirling I* who provided it with a tower, pedimented at eaves level, projecting from the centre of the S side. This tower contained the vestry behind the pulpit and was finished with an octagonal belfry and spire. Another version of the formula, but on a vast scale and in Perp dress, occurs at *James Gillespie Graham*'s St Mungo's Parish Church in Alloa of 1816–19. A few churches were classical. Kilmaronock Parish Church of 1813 has pedimented gables and round-arched windows. The pedimented main gable of *John Brash*'s Dumbarton (now Riverside) Parish Church of 1810–11 contains a pilastered doorpiece and is surmounted by an Ionic pilastered and urn-finialled steeple, its belfry and spire octagonal. At Stirling the Burgher Church (later Erskine Marykirk) designed by *Allan Johnstone* in 1824 appears like a heavily detailed piend-roofed two-storey villa, its centrepiece pilastered and pedimented. Alva United Secession (now Parish) Church of 1842 is a curiosity, the front gable dressed up in the Georgian castellated manner. Unarchaeological Romanesque was employed at the chapels of ease (churches to relieve overcrowded parish churches) built at Camelon St John in Falkirk and Haggs in 1839–40. But the dominant style was Gothic. Two of the first early C19 Gothic churches, New Kilpatrick Parish Church, Bearsden, of 1807–8 and Falkirk Old and St Modan's Parish Church of 1810–11, both designed by *James Gillespie Graham*, were little more than crowstep-gabled rubble-built broad boxes. Then in 1812–13 Old Kilpatrick Bowling Church and *Gillespie Graham*'s Clackmannan Parish Church established a norm for churches built in the area during the next twenty-five years. Clackmannan Parish Church is a broad buttressed oblong, the gables crowstepped, the side walls battlemented, with a battlemented tower at one end and identically detailed Gothic windows. The outcome is expressive of the respectable religion of the established Church. The formula was repeated by Gillespie

Graham at Kilmadock Parish Church, Doune, in 1822–4 and, with minor variations (e.g. the omission of crowsteps or battlements), by other architects working in the area: notably by *William Stirling I* at the parish churches of Airth (1817–20), Kippen (1823–7), Lecropt (1824–6) and Dunipace (1832–4); by *David Hamilton* at Larbert Old Parish Church (1818–20), the dramatically sited former Campsie Parish Church at Lennoxtown (1827–8) and Cadder Parish Church at Bishopbriggs (1829–30); by *John Baird I* at Bonhill Parish Church (1834–6) and, with a steeple, by *John Henderson* at Bannockburn Allan Church (1837–8). The formula but with innocently lighthearted detail was used enjoyably by the wright-architect *Thomas Aitken* at Denny Old Parish Church in 1812–14. Also enjoyable are the towers of the almost identical Fintry Parish Church of 1823 and the former Killearn Parish Church of 1825–6. A more scholarly variant occurs at Kincardine-in-Menteith Parish Church, Blair Drummond, of 1814–16 where *Richard Crichton* provided a nave and aisles in place of the standard unaisled box.

The dominant position of the Church of Scotland, established by law and the spiritual home of the great majority of the population, was rudely challenged in 1843 when a third of its ministers walked out of the General Assembly and convened in a rented hall to found the FREE CHURCH OF SCOTLAND in direct opposition to the liberal theology and social conservatism of the established Church. The Free Church was not intended to be a sect but a replacement of the Church of Scotland. One initial aim, largely achieved within a few years, was to provide a Free church, manse and school in every parish in Scotland. These early Free churches, some to standard designs provided by *Cousin & Gale*, were mostly cheap, rubble-walled boxes with a bellcote at one end. A surviving example is Clackmannan Free Church (by *John Burnet*, 1845), its very modest architectural adornment (roundheaded windows and bellcote) reserved for the front gable, while the former Dunblane Free Church of 1843 has only tall roundheaded windows. Tullibody Free Church of 1844 is larger and Gothic but of the plainest sort. Some early Free churches showed greater ambition, e.g. the T-plan Millburn Free Church at Renton of 1843–5, with a steeple at the front gable, and Polmont Free (now Brightons Parish) Church at Brightons of 1846–7, both carpenter's Gothic with an enjoyable display of pinnacles. Alva Free Church of 1848 has a shaped gable and Tudor detail.

In 1847 the United Secession and Relief Churches, descendants of the c18 seceders, joined to form the UNITED PRESBYTERIAN CHURCH. So, from the mid-1840s, Scottish Presbyterianism was divided into three not hugely unequal denominations, the Church of Scotland, the Free Church of Scotland and the United Presbyterian Church of Scotland. Rivalry between these competitors was shown by the size and cost of the churches they erected in the 1850s and 1860s. Although *Kennedy & Dalglish*'s Callander Free (now Parish) Church of 1861 was Italianate, the general style was Gothic, now of an archaeological type. In 1851–6 *J., W. H. & J. M. Hay* of Liverpool designed new churches for the Free Church congregations of Dunblane (now St Blane's Church),

Stirling South (now Stirling Baptist Church), Bridge of Allan
(now Chalmers Church) and Alloa West (now disused), all Dec or
Geometric in style and, except at Dunblane, with gable fronts and
boldly detailed prominent steeples. Similar but in a more austere
E.E. manner was *John Honeyman*'s Dumbarton Free (now High
Parish) church of 1863–4. Also gable-fronted and steepled Gothic,
but of French inspiration, were the large United Presbyterian
churches designed by *Peddie & Kinnear* at Alloa (now Alloa West
Church) and Stirling (now Allan Park South Church) in the 1860s.
Less demonstrative but not without presence were two established
parish churches rebuilt at this time, the sturdy buttressed and bell-
coted lancet Gothic Balquhidder Parish Church (by *David Bryce*,
1853–5) and the scholarly Gothic Aberfoyle Parish Church (by
*John Honeyman*, begun in 1869). A Church of Scotland church
built in 1874–5 for an area of rapidly expanding population was
Grahamston (now Grahamston United) Church at Falkirk where
*T. B. McFadzen* produced a large nave-and-aisles edifice, the tall
steeple at one corner of the front gable and the early French
Gothic style apparently derived from Peddie & Kinnear's work
for the United Presbyterian Church.

By the 1870s the Presbyterian churches were being challenged
by the ROMAN CATHOLICS, their numbers swelled by Irish
immigrants to the industrial towns and villages of the area, and,
more significantly in terms of the numbers of church buildings of
pretension, by the EPISCOPALIANS. Both bodies had been freed
in the 1790s from legal prohibitions on public worship but, until
the 1840s, they made do with a handful of chapels, usually small
and cheap like the Episcopal chapel built at Stirling in 1797, which
seated only two hundred and cost about £600, or the unambitious
Gothic Roman Catholic Church of the Most Holy Trinity, also at
Stirling, of 1836–8. But in 1846 the Roman Catholics put up St
Machan's Church at Lennoxtown, an impressively large example
of unarchaeological 'Saxon' architecture. Two years before, at St
Mary's (Episcopal) Church, Dunblane, *John Henderson* had used
the same elements of a nave, lower chancel, s porch and w bellcote
as appear at St Machan's but in a simple lancet style. Henderson's
adoption of Tractarian principles for this church was followed
generally by succeeding Episcopal churches. At St Saviour's, Bridge
of Allan, of 1856–7 *Henderson* again produced a bellcoted nave
and chancel, the chancel containing a stone sedilia in accordance
with the teachings of *The Ecclesiologist*. After Henderson's death in
1862 *R. Rowand Anderson*, a former assistant of George Gilbert
Scott, became the favoured architect of the Episcopalians. His first
church, Christ Church, Falkirk, built in 1863–4, continued the
simple Gothic nave and chancel formula but with the bellcote placed
on the E, not the w, gable of the nave. At St John the Evangelist,
Alloa, of 1867–9 the nave has a N aisle, and a sw steeple proclaims
the building's importance. Steeples were also intended by Anderson
for St Augustine, Dumbarton, of 1871–3 and Holy Trinity, Stirling,
of 1875–8 but not executed. Both these churches have fully aisled
naves and long chancels, their interiors imbued with an unfussy
spirituality. Also expressive of Episcopalian well-heeled self-

confidence is the prominently steepled and tall St Cyprian, Lenzie, of 1872–3 by *Alexander Ross*, its Tractarianism influenced by Slater & Carpenter. By contrast, St Madoc, Doune, by *James Brooks*, 1876–8, and St James the Great, Dollar, by *Thomas Frame & Son*, 1879–82, and, in Arts and Crafts Gothic, St Angus, Lochearnhead, by *G. T. Ewing*, 1888, and St Mary, Aberfoyle, by *James Miller*, 1893–4, revert to the ideal of the small English rural church which underlay Henderson's work of the 1840s and 1850s.

Between 1891 and 1905 the Roman Catholics built a number of large and tall churches, all late Gothic in style, with walls of red sandstone and prominent front gables. Of these, three (the Church of the Holy Family and St Ninian, Kirkintilloch, of 1891–3, the Church of Our Holy Redeemer, Clydebank, of 1901–3 and St Mary, Stirling, of 1904–5) were designed by *Pugin & Pugin* and another (St Patrick, Dumbarton, of 1901–3) by *Dunn & Hansom*. Each is to a standard basilican plan with a broad nave and aisles, the widely spaced arcades allowing open views to the high altar standing in a shallow chancel flanked by chapels containing altars of Our Lady and the Sacred Heart at the ends of the aisles. At the (liturgical) w end were a vestibule under a choir and organ gallery, a baptistery and mortuary chapel. The style was late Gothic with inventive tracery and strongly vertical emphasis.

Some large PRESBYTERIAN CHURCHES were built in the later years of the C19 and the first of the C20. The Hamilton Memorial Free Church, Clydebank, of 1884–6 was Neo-Norman but most were Gothic, often derived from Scottish late medieval work, e.g. *David Barclay*'s Renton Trinity Parish Church of 1891–2 or *John* 22 *McLeod*'s Bridgend United Presbyterian Church (now The West Kirk) at Dumbarton of 1886–8, a ten-light wheel window in the front gable. Sometimes they seem eager to proclaim sectarian superiority, as at Stirling where *J. J. Stevenson*'s free Gothic St Columba's (originally North United Free Church) dominates the suburb of King's Park. The angle-buttressed steeple of Killearn Parish Church (by *John Bryce*, 1881–2) lords it over both its nearby predecessor and its Free Church rival, while at Grangemouth the towers of the nearly adjoining Grange United Free Church (by *John B. Wilson*, 1902–3) and Zetland Parish Church (by *Wilson & Tait*, 1910–11) battle for supremacy. At Bo'ness three churches parade along the steep side of the hill above the old town, *R. Thornton Shiell*'s massively steepled Bo'ness Old Kirk of 1885–8, *J. McKissack & W. G. Rowan*'s Craigmailen United Free Church of 1883–5, its tall tower topped by a crown spire, and *J. N. Scott & A. Lorne Campbell*'s Bo'ness St Andrew's Parish (originally United Free) Church of 1904–6, its tower with welcome Art Nouveau detail and a green copper flèche.

Attempts were made to reorder or rebuild Presbyterian churches according to 'ecclesiological' principles after the foundation in 1886 of the Aberdeen (later, Scottish) Ecclesiological Society which advocated expression of the unity of Word and sacrament by placing a communion table as the focal point of a church, preferably in a chancel whose entrance was flanked by the pulpit and font. As a result, some Georgian churches were reordered (e.g. Killin

and Ardeonaig Parish Church in 1890). Others had short chancels added, the work sometimes accompanied by the removal of galleries as at Logie Parish Church, Blairlogie, in 1900–1, Kincardine-in-Menteith Parish Church, Blair Drummond, in 1907 and Larbert Old Church in 1909–11. Exceptionally far-reaching and expensive was *Sydney Mitchell & Wilson*'s reconstruction of Alloa West United
28 Free (now Alloa West) Church in 1902–4, with the addition of transepts and a chancel to provide a marble-clad sanctuary under the crossing where the spired oak pulpit (placed centrally contrary to true 'ecclesiological' principles) serves as a reredos to the marble communion table. Also expensive but without the ostentation of Mitchell & Wilson's work was the McLaren Memorial (now Stenhouse and Carron Parish) Church at Larbert of 1897–1900, designed by *John J. Burnet* developing a formula he had previously used for the Dundas United Presbyterian (now Dundas) Church at Grangemouth in 1894. Each church has a nave and one aisle, a massive tower at one end, a prominent porch and an attached hall block at r. angles to the church, the detail a confident stylistic mixture of Romanesque, Gothic and Arts and Crafts. The interior of the McLaren Memorial Church was in full accordance with 'ecclesiological' principles, the chancel entrance marked by a rood beam and flanked by the pulpit and font, the chancel itself containing choir stalls and a centrally placed communion table, the organ sited in a chamber at the E end of the aisle. One of the leading exponents of 'ecclesiological' ideals, *Peter Macgregor Chalmers*, designed three new churches in the area between 1904 and 1914. One, St Serf's Parish Church at Tullibody, is small and simple, consisting of a nave with one aisle and an apse. St Modan's Church at Falkirk is larger, with a fully aisled nave. Also sizeable is the cruci-
27 form Carriden Parish Church, with a W tower, a fully aisled nave, a baptistery in one transept, and the communion table in the chancel. Chalmers' churches are in a stripped Romanesque or Early Christian manner evocative of the supposed purity of the Scottish Church before the Romanizing reforms of the C12.

In the INTER-WAR years the 'ecclesiological' movement triumphed across denominational divides. One major church, St David's United Free (now St David's Memorial Park) Church at Kirkintilloch, to a design of *c.* 1921 by Chalmers executed by *J. Jeffrey Waddell* in 1924–6, comprised an aisled nave with semi-octagonal chancel and SW steeple, the Gothic style quite without fussiness. Simple Gothic but on a humbler scale was employed by *John Bruce* for St John Vianney (R.C.) Church at Alva in 1925–6 and for Sauchie and Fishcross United Free Church at Sauchie in 1931–2. But stripped Romanesque was the favoured architectural language, used by the Church of Scotland at *Wilson & Tait*'s St Helen's (now Baptist) Church of 1932 at High Bonnybridge, by the Episcopalians at *Dick Peddie & Walker Todd*'s uncompleted St Catharine's, Bo'ness, of 1921 and *J. Maxton Craig*'s St Mary's, Grangemouth, of 1937–8, and by the Roman Catholics at *Reginald Fairlie*'s Church of the Holy Family, Dunblane, of 1935 and *Archibald Macpherson*'s Church of the Sacred Heart, Grangemouth, of 1925–7, where a semicircular portico provides a hint of ultramontanism, and his

brightly coloured and idiosyncratic Church of Our Lady and St
Ninian, Bannockburn, of 1927. At Cowie in 1935 *Reginald Fairlie*
produced a plan as much prefiguring the late C20 as looking back
to the Renaissance, an octagon with only a small projecting chancel
to house the high altar, the walls built of uncompromising red brick.

The first POST-1945 church built in the area, Duntocher Trinity
Parish Church, of 1951–2 to *William Reid*'s design of 1949, is
brick-built and traditional but with a shallow-pitched roof and
parabolic arches in the gables. However, most of the significant new
churches of the later C20 were built for the Roman Catholics. In
the 1950s *Gillespie, Kidd & Coia* designed several, all brick-built
and traditional in plan, those at Bishopbriggs (St Matthew of 1950),
Clydebank (St Euan of 1950–1) and, the brick covered with white
render, at Balloch (St Kessog of 1957–8) decidedly economical,
the prominently sited St Michael's, Dumbarton, of 1952–4 larger
and much more powerful, with diamond-shaped clearstorey
windows and a sculptural brick and glass bell-tower. At St Mary's,
Duntocher, of 1952–4 and St Stephen's, Clydebank, of 1957–8
*Thomas S. Cordiner* produced brick-built modern-traditional
churches, the structure's portal frames exposed inside St Stephen's.
Also modern traditional and with a low bell-tower is *Allan &
Friskin*'s St Mungo's, Alloa, of 1959–61. Much more dramatic is
the chevron-patterned screen front of St Francis Xavier, Falkirk,
by *R. Fairlie & Partners*, 1958–61, bearing a huge relief of the patron
saint calling on passers-by to enter. From the 1960s, and given
impetus by the liturgical reforms associated with the Second Vatican
Council, Roman Catholic (and Protestant) churches have sought
to express worship as a communal participation of the gathered
people of God as close as possible to the altar or communion table.
One (now demolished) attempt to achieve this was *Gillespie, Kidd
& Coia*'s wedge-shaped St Mary's (R.C.), Bo'ness, of 1962 but
most churches have been built as broad rectangles. Patterned brick
walls and horizontal glazing mark out *Gillespie, Kidd & Coia*'s St
Mary of the Angels (R.C.), Camelon, at Falkirk of 1960 and the
same firm's St Margaret's (R.C.), Clydebank, of 1970–2, the second
having the liturgical axis running diagonally across the square
interior. A continuing distinction between nave and sanctuary but
without physical separation can be given by the use of monopitch
roofs, forming a V-shape at *King, Main & Ellison*'s Radnor Park
Parish Church, Clydebank, of 1969–70 or, more usually, intersecting
to provide a clearstorey as at *Peter Whiston*'s St Bernadette's (R.C.),
Tullibody, of 1961–3, *Garner, Preston & Strebel*'s St Peter's
(R.C.), Dumbarton, of 1970–1, *Nicholson & Jacobsen*'s St Patrick's
(R.C.), Old Kilpatrick, of 1979–80, or *Watson, Salmond & Gray*'s
St Andrew's (R.C.), Bearsden, of 1987. That these recent churches
need not be devoid of a sense of the sacred is demonstrated by
the lofty dark interior of St Peter's (R.C.), Dumbarton, and,
triumphantly, in the glass-sided numinously light chapel designed
in 1997 by *James F. Stephen* for Scotus College at Bearsden.

GALLERIES were erected from soon after the Reformation in
burgh churches, often by trade incorporations to seat their members.
By the late C16 the Church of the Holy Rude, Stirling, contained

lofts and in the early c17 these included the King's Loft surmounted by the royal coat of arms. At Falkirk Parish Church lofts
were put up in 1643 and at Dunblane Cathedral in 1653 and 1664.
Rural parish churches might contain lairds' lofts, sometimes occupying the medieval chancel, as at Old St Mungo's Church, Alloa,
or placed in a transeptal 'aisle' which also contained a family burial
vault, as at the former Airth Parish Church. Galleries became
increasingly common in the c18 but disappointingly few of them
have survived, many having fallen victim to high-minded c20
restorations or rearrangements. There is an c18 laird's loft, its front
and sides panelled, at Killin and Ardeonaig Parish Church and
galleries remain in Baldernock Parish Church and the former
Kirkintilloch Parish Church. Many more survive from the early c19,
their fronts panelled, sometimes with Gothic blind arcading as
at Airth Parish Church of 1817–21, the supporting columns of
wood or cast iron. Exceptionally grand is the Keir Loft of 1826 in
Lecropt Parish Church, its panelled front supporting bundle-
shafted columns from which spring Gothic arches, the ceiling over
the laird's seats formed as plaster vaults. Many Victorian Presbyterian
churches contain galleries, often of dark-stained wood and with
Gothic detail, but 'ecclesiological' disapproval ensured their omission from c20 churches.

PULPITS were often the most important items in post-
Reformation Protestant churches. The entablature of the Corinthian
pilastered back of a pulpit of 1655 survives in Carriden Parish
Church, the pilasters and inlaid oak panels of a c17 pulpit imported
from the Netherlands are incorporated in the present pulpit at
Bo'ness Old Kirk, and the pilastered and panelled body of a c17
pulpit is still used in the Church of the Holy Rude, Stirling. Of
c18 pulpits, that of Baldernock Parish Church of 1795 has an
Ionic pilastered back. More elaborate is the pulpit of 1782 in the
former Kirkintilloch Parish Church, its back again pilastered but
also decorated with Gothic panels and surmounted by a plaster
shell. Of a little later is the ambitious pedimented pulpit of 1810 at
Slamannan Parish Church. The carved and gilded eagle that served
as the finial of the pulpit in the demolished Falkirk Burgher Church
is preserved in Erskine Parish Church, Falkirk. Most Victorian
pulpits were designed either in a heavy Georgian survival manner
or with routine Gothic detail. The alabaster and marble pulpit of
1878 at Holy Trinity (Episcopal) Church, Stirling, is unusually
expensive. So too are the wooden pulpits of 1895 in Callander
Parish Church and Dunblane Cathedral, the first displaying reliefs
of Our Lord and saints, the other with carved figures. Reliefs (of
the *Agnus Dei* and an angel) together with two consecration crosses
appear also on the pulpit of 1899 at Stenhouse and Carron Parish
Church, Larbert. Almost Georgian Gothick in feeling but wonderfully elaborate is the crocketed finialled spire of the pulpit canopy
provided by *Sydney Mitchell & Wilson* in their reconstruction of
28 Alloa West Church in 1902–4.

Episcopalians and Roman Catholics had no doubts about the
permissibility of ORGANS to accompany worship and two of the
earliest organs in the area, instruments by *Forster & Andrews* and

*Conacher*, were erected in Episcopal churches at Bridge of Allan and Stirling in the 1870s. The use of instrumental music in Presbyterian worship was first permitted in the Church of Scotland by its General Assembly of 1866, a decision soon followed by the United Presbyterian and Free Churches, and organs appeared in churches of these denominations in the area from the 1880s, sometimes, as at Charing Cross and West Church, Grangemouth, in 1884 and Craigmailen United Free Church, Bo'ness, *c.* 1900, combined with the pulpit to provide a dominating focal point. An apse to house the organ was added to Old Kilpatrick Bowling Church in 1897–8. At St Columba's Church, Stirling, of 1899–1902 the chancel was designed to be occupied by the organ, which takes on the appearance of a reredos. In the same position is the organ at Holy Trinity Church, Bridge of Allan, but placed above *Charles Rennie Mackintosh*'s modern Gothic oak screen which hides the organist and console. A more conventionally elaborate organ case, decorated with carved birds and fruit, was provided by *Robert S. Lorimer* at St John the Evangelist (Episcopal) Church, Alloa, in 1913. Many pipe organs were replaced by electronic instruments in the late C20. A welcome counterblast has been given by the erection of a new pipe organ by *Flentrop Orgelbouw* at Dunblane Cathedral in 1990.

Mackintosh's organ screen at Holy Trinity, Bridge of Allan, was part of an ensemble of CHANCEL FURNISHINGS of 1904 which also comprised choir stalls, a communion table and pulpit (integral with the screen but at one end of it). Another such ensemble (reredos, choir stalls and organ case, with an earlier communion table in the central position) was provided by *Lorimer* at Dunblane Cathedral in 1912–14, its intricate Gothic carved detail hinting at Art Nouveau. Less showy and with Celtic detail are the chancel furnishings of 1925–6 by *J. Jeffrey Waddell* at Dollar Parish Church.

COMMUNION TABLES in Presbyterian churches from the Reformation until the later C19 were generally utilitarian, either a long fixed table filling the middle of the church or, more commonly, trestle tables erected only on the infrequent communion Sundays. For Episcopalians and Roman Catholics a fixed altar was an essential, often with a reredos rising behind. An example of what a prosperous Tractarian-minded Episcopal congregation could aspire to is provided by the altar and reredos of 1869 at St John the Evangelist, Alloa, the stone altar slab supported on Gothic capitalled marble columns, the reredos (by *Farmer & Brindley*) with angel-filled niches flanking the central mosaic (by *Antonio Salviati*) of the Last Supper. Even more accomplished is the reredos of 1878 by *C. E. Kempe* in Holy Trinity (Episcopal) Church, Stirling, with a carved and painted depiction of the Nativity of Our Lord. At St Augustine (Episcopal), Dumbarton, in 1893 *R. Rowand Anderson* designed a stone altar and reredos (executed by *Rhind*) with reliefs of Our Lord in Glory and the *Agnus Dei* and small statues of the Evangelists. The Episcopal Church's move towards a more advanced Catholic position, perhaps to distinguish itself from the increasingly 'ecclesiologically'-minded Presbyterian

Churches, at the end of the C19 and the beginning of the C20 was accompanied by a move away from the depictions of purely scriptural scenes on altars and reredoses and towards the inclusion of saints, especially Scottish ones. St James the Less (Episcopal) Church at Bishopbriggs now contains the altar and reredos made for St Andrew-by-the-Green (Episcopal) Church in Glasgow in 1907–8, the altar stone itself a fragment of the medieval high altar of Iona Abbey, the panels of the altar front containing gesso figures of SS. Andrew, Mungo, Columba and Margaret of Scotland. The reredos above is more soberly restricted to showing Our Lord and the Apostles. However, at St Angus (Episcopal) Church, Lochearnhead, the reredos of 1909 displays (except when its doors are closed in Passiontide) four Scottish saints.

The Roman Catholics in the late C19 and earlier C20 tried, if money permitted, to have a sumptuous reredos above the high altar, its tabernacle containing the reserved sacrament, the focus of public worship, with flanking chapels, usually dedicated to the Virgin Mary and the Sacred Heart of Jesus, serving for private devotion. Such a high altar reredos was executed with a lavish use of marble and alabaster by *Boulton & Son* at the Church of the Holy Family and St Ninian, Kirkintilloch, in the 1890s, in painted stone and gilded wood at the Church of Our Holy Redeemer, Clydebank, in 1923, and in white marble at St Patrick's, Dumbarton, in 1936.

From the late C19 'ecclesiologically'-minded Presbyterians championed the installation of centrally placed communion tables. At its second meeting in 1886 the Aberdeen Ecclesiological Society agreed unanimously 'that the Holy Table should occupy a permanent place of prominence and honour'. In 1893 *R. Rowand Anderson* designed a heavy Gothic table for the choir of Dunblane Cathedral and wooden communion tables, usually of late Gothic style and often carved with vines and oak leaves, were introduced to most Presbyterian churches during the next forty years. In Alloa West Church the communion table of 1902–4 is of marble. The oak communion table designed by *John J. Burnet* in 1921 for Stenhouse and Carron Parish Church, Larbert, has niches containing statues of angels and saints as well as one of Our Lord.

FONTS were standard in Roman Catholic and Episcopalian churches. Most are of stone and routine Gothic in character. The Presbyterians until the late C19 contented themselves with baptismal basins, sometimes fixed on a bracket to the pulpit. The Presbyterian adoption of freestanding fonts was another success of the 'ecclesiological' movement. Few are of much aesthetic interest but the font of 1901 at Logie Parish Church, Blairlogie, is of Caen stone with alabaster pillars, and at Balfron Parish Church the font introduced *c.* 1909 is of onyx and carved with angels. Quite exceptional is the font of silvered bronze made by *Albert H. Hodge* in 1909 for Stenhouse and Carron Parish Church, Larbert, panels on its stem filled with reliefs of naked dancing children.

STATUES have been generally frowned upon by Presbyterians as idolatrous although Kippen Parish Church contains a bronze 'Charity' by *Alfred Gilbert*. The Roman Catholics have had no such inhibitions but have too often favoured the kitsch productions of Continental factories. One exception is *Eric Gill*'s contribution in 1920 to the varied statuary in St Patrick's, Dumbarton, a powerful representation of St Michael, others the powerfully modelled Stations of the Cross by *Vincent Butler, c.* 1978, in St Anthony's, Rumford, the figures of Our Lord of 1961 by *Scott Sutherland* on the crucifix behind the high altar in St Mungo's, Alloa, and of 1997 on the N wall of St Kessog's, Balloch, by *Andrew Ramsay*, who also provided the Stations of the Cross in the church's garden. Most dramatic is the translucent resin figure of Our Lord by *Kate* 31 *Robinson*, 1997, which hangs over the altar in the chapel of Scotus College, Bearsden.

STAINED GLASS appeared in churches of all denominations from the 1860s, the earliest examples in the area being two windows of 1868 at Stirling, one in the Church of the Holy Rude, the other in Holy Trinity (Episcopal) Church. Both are by the Edinburgh firm of *James Ballantine & Son* which (from 1892 as *A. Ballantine & Gardiner* and from 1905 as *A. Ballantine & Son*) produced many windows during the next fifty years, usually competent but never exciting. Presbyterians until the early C20 generally restricted the subject matter to scriptural scenes or depictions of Our Lord as the Good Shepherd. Episcopalians, although far from eschewing such matter, were readier, certainly by the 1890s, to admit figures of non-scriptural saints, as at St Columba's, Clydebank, where the N transept window of 1896 depicts SS. Patrick, Columba and Mungo, or at St Augustine's, Dumbarton, whose S (liturgical W) window of 1903 shows Scottish saints and the Fathers of the Western Church, an iconographical counterblast to Presbyterian claims for descent from a supposedly pure Celtic Church standing apart from the rest of Christendom. Probably as the result of most windows having been given as memorials and the donors' wishes having been taken into account, iconographical coherence is rare, even in incomplete form. However, St Cyprian's (Episcopal) Church, Lenzie, does have windows of 1873 showing the Nativity, Crucifixion, Resurrection and Ascension of Our Lord round two sides of the sanctuary, and the N (liturgical E) windows in the transepts of Alloa West Church of 1904 depict scenes from the life of Our Lord from the Annunciation to the Finding in the Temple and the Road to Calvary (i.e. four of the five Joyful Mysteries and four of the five Sorrowful Mysteries of the Rosary). A late C20 co-ordinated scheme of glass was provided by *Douglas Hamilton* in St Stephen's (R.C.), Clydebank. The stained glass panels of the Stations of the Cross by *Shona McInnes* hung along the sides of the chapel of Scotus College, Bearsden, in 1997 form the only complete scheme unified both by subject matter and artist.

Episcopalians in the late C19 and early C20 often patronized English artists as well as the ubiquitous Ballantine firm. *John Hardman & Co.* produced the sanctuary windows at St Cyprian's, Lenzie, in 1873, *Burlison & Grylls* glass for St Columba's, Clydebank, and Holy Trinity, Stirling, in 1896, *Shrigley & Hunt* and *Morris & Co.* windows at St Augustine's, Dumbarton, in the early C20, and *C. E. Kempe* work at St John the Evangelist's, Alloa, in 1890 and

1902. Kempe was also employed by Presbyterian congregations for the E window of Dunblane Cathedral in 1901 and the transept windows at Alloa West Church in 1904. Other English firms employed by Presbyterians were *Cottier & Co.* at the Church of the Holy Rude, Stirling, in 1880, *James Powell & Sons* for the w window of Logie Parish Church, Blairlogie, in 1903, *Clayton & Bell* for the w window of Dunblane Cathedral in 1906, and *Louis Davis* for the cathedral's superbly coloured Art Nouveau-ish glass of 1915–17. The magnificent four windows by *Morris & Co.*, 1882, depicting the Evangelists, now in St James the Less (Episcopal) Church, Bishopbriggs, were originally commissioned for Woodlands Road United Presbyterian Church, Glasgow. But Presbyterian and some Episcopalian churches in the area were strong patrons of Glasgow firms of glass-stainers. *W. & J. J. Kier* provided glass for Dumbarton (now Riverside) Parish Church in 1876 and they and *Adam & Small* produced windows at the Church of the Holy Rude, Stirling, in the 1870s. The Kiers and *J. & W. Guthrie* worked at Strathblane Parish Church in the 1870s and 1890s. *William Meikle & Sons* produced two brightly coloured realistic windows for Bo'ness Old Kirk in 1902–8. Accomplished windows of 1908–24 from *Oscar Paterson*'s studio can be found in St Andrew's Parish Church, Bo'ness, and Renton Trinity Parish Church. Most distinctively Glaswegian is the lushly coloured painterly stained glass made by *Stephen Adam* and his pupil *Alfred A. Webster*, represented by windows at St Columba's (Episcopal) Church, Clydebank, St Augustine's (Episcopal) Church, Dumbarton, Gartmore Parish Church, St Serf's Parish Church, Tullibody, and a remarkable 23, 24 collection of glass at New Kilpatrick Parish Church, Bearsden. The richest Glaswegian windows of the early C20 now in the area are those of 1909 depicting scenes from the life of Our Lord made by *Stephen Adam Jun.* and now in St James the Less (Episcopal) Church, Bishopbriggs.

Almost all the C20 STAINED GLASS in the area has come from Scottish studios. Usually strongly coloured, most effectively in *Herbert Hendrie*'s windows at Kippen Parish Church, it has seldom departed far from realism, often expressionist or stylized. One of the most prolific artists was *Douglas Strachan* who provided St John the Evangelist's (Episcopal) Church at Alloa with its E window in 1913, the clearly drawn figures set against pale glass. The next 25 year he made the E window of Stenhouse and Carron Parish Church, Larbert, a splendid combination of jewel-like colour and swirling movement. Examples of his later and sometimes disappointing expressionist manner can be found at New Kilpatrick Parish Church, Bearsden, and the Church of the Holy Rude, Stirling. More even in quality is the work of *Margaret Chilton*, best seen in the strongly coloured depiction of the Annunciation at St John the Evangelist's (Episcopal) Church, Alloa, and in the aisle lights at Holy Trinity (Episcopal) Church, Stirling, of 1947–55. *Gordon Webster*'s windows (e.g. at St David's Park Church, Kirkintilloch, the South Parish Church at Bearsden, Dunblane Cathedral and Clackmannan Parish Church) are examples of squared-up modernism, always of reliable quality but never quite providing a tingle of the spine. The most colourful and least disciplined C20 artist was *William Wilson* who filled windows at Dundas Parish Church, Grangemouth, St Mungo's Parish Church, Alloa, and Bo'ness Old Kirk between 1938 and 1954. The most recent work, *Willie Rodger*'s glass at St Mary's Parish Church, Kirkintilloch, and the near-abstract stained glass Stations of the Cross by *Shona McInnes* in the chapel of Scotus College, Bearsden, is arguably the best.

## MAUSOLEA, MONUMENTS AND STATUES

In 1581 the General Assembly of the Church of Scotland forbade burial within churches. Some noble and lairdly families circumvented the spirit of this edict by taking over the chancel or existing transeptal chapels or 'aisles' or building new 'aisles' as burial places and sites for their pews or galleries (*see* Introduction: Post-Reformation Churches), as at the Elphinstone Aisle of the former Airth Parish Church which still contains late C16 and early C17 graveslabs decorated with coats of arms. Others built detached BURIAL ENCLOSURES or MAUSOLEA in the graveyard. The earliest of these in Stirling and Central Scotland is the mausoleum built for the Stirlings of Law in Old Kilpatrick Bowling Churchyard in 1658, with ball finials on its corners. Also of the late C17 are two enclosures in Kincardine-in-Menteith graveyard, Blair Drummond, that of the Muschets of 1689 decorated with the relief of a coat of arms under a skeleton, that of the Drummonds of 1699 with rusticated quoins. More ambitious is the Lennox Mausoleum of 34 1715 in the former Campsie Parish Churchyard at Clachan of Campsie, a square pavilion, probably originally covered by a domed roof even before its early C19 heightening to two storeys, the entrance through a basket-arched door. Suaver and a pioneering work of Neo-classicism is the Johnstone Mausoleum in the Old Parish Churchyard at Alva designed by *Robert Adam* in 1789, a Greek cross on plan, the pediment over the entrance carried on columns whose fluted shafts are Greek Doric, their rosetted capitals Roman Doric. More stodgily classical, despite its ogee-arched entrance, is the Graham Mausoleum (by *William Stirling I*, *c.* 1817) at Port of Menteith. At Larbert Old Churchyard William Dawson's mausoleum of *c.* 1875 is a Doric temple but staid in comparison with the Doric rotunda provided by *Archibald Elliot* in 1815–16 for the Forbes Mausoleum at Callendar House, Falkirk. 35 Other C19 mausolea are Gothic. *James Gillespie Graham* designed a couple, both buttressed and crowstepped rectangles, their windows hoodmoulded, the Zetland Mausoleum at Falkirk Old and St Modan's Church in 1810–11 and the Mar Mausoleum in Old St Mungo's Churchyard, Alloa, in 1819. Also crowstepgabled but with paired windows and a porch on one side is the mausoleum of 1864 (Kilbryde Chapel) built for the Campbells of Aberuchill near Kilbryde Castle. Less earthbound is the Edmonstone Mausoleum of 1802 in Strathblane Parish Churchyard, its absurdly tall and pointed entrance pushing up towards a coat of arms under the apex of the extravagantly steep pitched roof. *William Atkinson*'s Breadalbane Mausoleum of 1829–30 at Finlarig Castle, a buttressed nave and chancel, is now derelict.

CHURCH MONUMENTS, generally tablets of marble, stone, bronze or brass commemorating the modestly prosperous as well as lairds and nobles, are common. One of the earliest and largest is the late C16 or early C17 monument to members of the Strathallan family in Dunblane Cathedral, a roundheaded recess set in a corniced aedicule with superimposed fluted Doric attached columns. The monument of *c.* 1700 to George Abercromby inside the now roofless former Tullibody Parish Church is a Corinthian-columned aedicule adorned with reminders of death and a coat of arms. Two very smart monuments, erected in 1709 in the Mar Aisle of Old St Mungo's Church, Alloa, and now in the Mar Mausoleum, are convex white marble ovals, their Baroque frames carved with cherubs' heads and surmounted by coroneted coats of arms. The more expensive late Georgian monuments were generally white marble classical aedicules, that of 1791 to Janet Roger in the Church of the Holy Rude, Stirling, surmounted by a lady weeping over an urn, the same church's monuments to David Doig, the Rector of Stirling High School, †1800 and of 1819 to the Rev. James Somerville also surmounted by urns, Doig's with the accompaniment of books and a pen. The monument by *Alexander Ritchie*, 1838, to the Rev. John B. Patterson at Falkirk Old and St Modan's Church is carved with the relief of a mourning lady and cherub beside an urn-topped sarcophagus whose side bears a portrait bust of the dead minister. Less elaborate (a mourning lady and an urn) but in a Gothic frame is *Peter Turnerelli*'s monument of 1819 to John and Patrick Stirling in Dunblane Cathedral. Gothic surrounds were also provided for the Home and Drummond monuments of *c.* 1800–20 at Kincardine-in-Menteith Parish Church, Blair Drummond. Unusually opulent is the Baroque aedicule, of dove-coloured marble and alabaster with red and yellow marble columns, designed by *R. Rowand Anderson* in 1910 to commemorate William Stirling of Keir in Dunblane Cathedral. Monuments bearing relief busts are not uncommon from the later C19. Sober examples commemorating ministers are those to the Rev. Lewis Irving (by *William Brodie*, 1879) in St Andrew's West Church, Falkirk, and to the Rev. William Begg (by *J. & G. Mossman*, 1889) in Falkirk Old and St Modan's Church. Justifiably sentimental is *Percy Portsmouth*'s relief bust of 1950 at Tullibody to Alistair Ramsay Tullis who died aged only eighteen months. Unusual for their quantity and being fully rounded sculptures are the C19 busts of the Stirlings of Keir in Lecropt Church. Portraiture of a more generalized type is found at the silver tablet of 1902 to Edward John Younger, killed in the South African War, at St John the Evangelist's (Episcopal) Church, Alloa, one corner bearing an exquisitely executed depiction by *Phoebe Traquair* of an angel taking the hand of a fallen soldier. A more joyful war memorial tablet is the First World War Memorial bronze (designed by *D. Forrester Wilson* and executed by *James Gray*) erected at Cairns Church, Milngavie, in 1921, its relief showing a kilted soldier embraced by a dancing angel. By far the grandest of church monuments, in a class and, indeed, aisle of its own, is that in St John the Evangelist's (Episcopal) Church, Alloa, to Walter Coningsby, Earl of Kellie, designed by *R. Rowand Anderson* and executed by *John Rhind* in 1873. It is a conscious revival of the medieval sarcophagus and effigy class of monument, carried out in marble, the head of the figure of the dead earl lying on a cushion carried by angels, the feet on a recumbent lion. One of the most emotive monuments is the sandstone pillar by *Richard Kindersley* incised with elegantly lettered inscriptions which was erected at Dunblane Cathedral in 2000 to commemorate the schoolchildren and teacher murdered in 1996.

Until the use of cremation became widespread in the C20 the vast majority of burials took place in CHURCHYARDS and, from the 1850s, CEMETERIES. Churchyards, by the early C18, were usually enclosed by stone walls, the entrances sometimes dignified by corniced ashlar GATEPIERS. Exceptional for their height are the rusticated gatepiers, probably of the later C17, at Old St Mungo's Church in Alloa, one bearing the relief of a skull and crossbones, the other of an hourglass. It was usual for elders to stand at the gate of a churchyard on a Sunday to take a collection for relief of the poor of the parish. Not surprisingly, some sort of shelter for these collectors was often provided. Most were humble and have been removed. Some were larger and used also as session houses for meetings of the kirk session (e.g. at Gargunnock Parish Churchyard) or as watchhouses where men kept a look-out for 'resurrectionists' come to rob graves of newly interred corpses to be taken to medical schools for dissection (e.g. the house of 1828 at Baldernock Parish Churchyard and the early C19 house at Logie Old Kirkyard, Blairlogie). The watchhouse of 1832 in Callander Churchyard is octagonal and at Cadder Parish Church, Bishopbriggs, the watch house of 1828, sited not at the entrance but in the middle of the burial ground, is unusually decorative with roundheaded dummy windows and a hoodmoulded entrance.

CEMETERIES, divorced from churches, were formed from the mid C19, the earliest in the area, at Dumbarton, laid out by *Stewart Murray* in 1854, its landscaping and planting of high quality, followed in 1857 by Clackmannan Cemetery and the Valley Cemetery at Stirling. Many have an entrance lodge, sometimes with bargeboarded gables, but the lodge of 1903–4 at New Kilpatrick Cemetery, Bearsden, is larger and Scots Jacobean in style.

The marking, indeed the ownership, of a churchyard grave was the prerogative of the moderately prosperous, often until the later C19 granted only on payment of money towards relief of the poor. C16 and C17 grave markers in Stirling and Central Scotland were usually GRAVESLABS. A number of these early slabs survive but most are badly weathered. Some, like the coped slabs in the Old Kirkyard of the Church of the Holy Rude, Stirling, probably of the C17, continue medieval tradition but with pie-crust borders. Two of the best preserved and most elaborate, but not *in situ* and perhaps formerly in a laird's 'aisle', are those of *c.* 1606 to the Kincaids of that Ilk in the blocked entrance to the Lennox Mausoleum in the former Campsie Parish Churchyard, Clachan of Campsie, both with marginal inscriptions and coats of arms. One of the earliest slabs (dated 1579) is in the Old Kirkyard of the Church of the Holy Rude, Stirling, and bears in relief the tools of a mason (pick, mallet and chisel). In the graveyard at Fir Park, Tillicoultry, the graveslab of Robert Meiklejohn, skinner and burgess of Edinburgh, †1651 displays a shield incised with a glove. Other trade emblems appear on slabs in the Old Kirkyard of the Church of the Holy Rude, Stirling, one of 1699 having a shield bearing a merchant's mark, the shield of another (of 1700) carved with a weaver's shuttle.

A few C17 and C18 TABLE STONES survive (e.g. the one to Robert Kirk †1692 in the Old Parish Churchyard at Aberfoyle) but HEADSTONES are the most usual grave markers. The earliest surviving in the area is probably the stone of 1621 to Agnes Sharp in the Old Parish Churchyard at Bo'ness, its top with scrolled sides. Some C18 stones are aedicular (e.g. in Old St Mungo's Churchyard at Alloa, Bo'ness Old Churchyard, Clackmannan Parish Churchyard or the graveyard at Fir Park, Tillicoultry), the classical language often imperfectly understood. Common motifs recur – reminders of death (skulls, crossbones, hourglasses), the soul (an angel's head), coats of arms and trade emblems. Sometimes the carvings are crowded, with unconsciously comical effect as at the stone of 1687 in Tillicoultry Parish Churchyard where a skeleton wears an hourglass as a hat. Several are ambitious. In the Old Parish Churchyard, Bo'ness, a stone, again of 1687, is carved on one side with angels who hold a crown above a figure climbing out of its coffin and, on the other, with a joyful angel who flourishes a trumpet while trampling on a skull and crossbones. In the same churchyard one C18 stone depicts an angel waking a corpse and another is carved with caryatids with baskets of fruit on their heads. A stone of 1761 in Muiravonside Parish Churchyard bears figures who stand on coffins and blow looped trumpets. At Polmont Old Parish Churchyard are stones of 1754 and 1786 depicting Adam and Eve in the Garden of Eden. A few include portraits of the dead. The top of one C18 stone in the Old Parish Churchyard, Bo'ness, is carved with the head of a wigged man. Touchingly inept is the depiction in Kincardine-in-Menteith Churchyard, Blair Drummond, of George Bachop and Jennet Ferguson †1750 and their ten children. Some, perhaps many, of the designs were derived from engravings. A stone of 1637 to John Service in the Old Kirkyard of the Church of the Holy Rude, Stirling, bears a panel depicting a woman with an hourglass under her foot and pointing to a sundial while an angel leads her to death and eternity (symbolized by a snake with its tail in its mouth), the subject taken directly from an engraving in Francis Quarles' *Emblems Moral and Divine* of 1635. The dyester's press carved on a stone of 1708 in the Old Parish Churchyard at Alva seems to have been copied from an engraving, even including the accompanying identification ('A PRESS').

Most headstones of the C17 and C18 seem to have been the work of local masons and a particular churchyard often contains a collection of stones of marked stylistic and iconographical similarity. In the Old Kirkyard of the Church of the Holy Rude, Stirling, the tops of fifteen headstones erected between 1696 and 1736 have mirrored s-scrolls. All the late C17 and many of the C18 stones in the graveyard of the former Tullibody Parish Church have incised decoration instead of the more usual relief carving. The C18 stones in Muiravonside Parish Churchyard are unusually thick and display a number of motifs (naked boys and grapes as well as the commoner coats of arms, emblems of death and angels' heads) variously combined. In the C19 headstones became much more routine and carved decoration increasingly uncommon, partly perhaps the result of the establishment of specialist firms of monumental masons in middling and larger towns. However, *Alexander 'Greek' Thomson* designed a Neo-Greek stone for the Rev. James Thomson †1864 in Balfron Parish Churchyard. Table stones also became more common but the area contains disappointingly few of note. Improved transport in the C19 brought materials, especially granite, from outwith the area. In the C20 polished slate became another popular material for headstones. Few C20 stones are worth mention but Dalnottar Cemetery, Clydebank, contains Art Deco headstones of *c.* 1935 by *J. Gilfillan* to members of the Kirk family as well as the tall and austere stone to the artist Leslie Hunter †1931 by *Gray & Co.* One welcome recent example of elegant simplicity is the sandstone headstone to David Russell †1999 in St Thomas's Cemetery, Stirling.

Some GRAVEYARD MONUMENTS go far beyond their primary function of marking a burial site. One of the earliest and weirdest is the monument to Sir John Graham of Dundaff in Falkirk Old and St Modan's Churchyard, composed of a stack of slabs, the lowest medieval and carved with a robed effigy, perhaps of a woman, the one above probably erected in the late C16 and apparently bearing an inscription to Sir John taken from Blind Harry's *Schir William Wallace*, the two top slabs successive replacements (of *c.* 1723 and 1772) for the inscription slab. The surrounding cast iron cage was erected in 1860. More conventional are large wall monuments. In the S wall of the Old Kirkyard of the Church of the Holy Rude, Stirling, is the monument of 1689, originally erected for John McCulloch but later taken over by the Sconce family, an aedicule with coupled columns and a shaped pediment, adorned with carved reliefs of a cherub, angels, strapwork and emblems of death. Smaller but accomplished is the Moodie monument of 1702 in Clackmannan Parish Churchyard, with reliefs of dancing angels flanking the aedicule whose corkscrew columns support a segmental pediment topped by fruit. A rustic version of a Corinthian-columned aedicule appears in the graveyard of the former Tullibody Parish Church, the tympanum of its curvaceous pediment carved with an angel trumpeter and a skull and crossbones. It is of 1715 and commemorates George Haig. Two early C18 aedicular monuments in the Old Parish Churchyard at Bo'ness have barley-sugar columns and segmental pediments. So too does the large and more elaborate Baroque monument of *c.* 1725 to Patrick Murehead in Falkirk Old and St Modan's Churchyard, its pediment a support for reclining angels. A recess at the base of the aedicule used to contain effigies, a surprising archaism for the date. Large churchyard monuments of the mid and later C18 are few but one which impresses by both size and swagger is the sarcophagus monument of 1751 to Sir Robert and Dr Duncan Munro, again in Falkirk Old and St Modan's Churchyard, carved with drapery, grotesque heads, angels' heads, heraldry and trophies.

C19 AND C20 CHURCHYARD AND CEMETERY MONUMENTS are many but mostly standardized. Statues of angels are distressingly common. Obelisks and lopped trees abound, the obelisk commemorating William Denny †1854 in Dumbarton Cemetery exceptionally tall. Urn-topped columns, the tall Doric column to Joseph Stainton †1825 in Larbert Old Churchyard one of the better examples, recur. So too do Celtic crosses, popular from the later C19 but often routine in execution. Two which stand out are the tall grey granite cross erected in 1877 in Falkirk Old and St Modan's Churchyard by the third Marquess of Bute to commemorate the men of Bute killed at the Battle of Falkirk in 1278 and the richly decorated cross to Alexander Brown in New Kilpatrick Parish Churchyard, Bearsden, which was made by *Donaldson & Burns*, c. 1930. Gothic spires were erected to some inhabitants of Dumbarton Cemetery in the later C19, the tallest and most elaborate example to Janet Rankin †1867 executed by *Charles B. Grassby*. A variety of sarcophagi is represented by the monuments to members of the Dawson family in Larbert Old Churchyard – Baroque for William Dawson †1867, Gothic for Thomas Dawson †1873 and Celtic for Anne Dawson †1888. Some monuments inspire curiosity. Why was the relief of a lady clasping a book to her bosom thought appropriate to commemorate George Walker in 1859 at Tillicoultry Parish Churchyard or the polished granite statue of a horse chosen for William Alexander †1936 in Cadder Cemetery, Bishopbriggs? Others are self-explanatory to those with some knowledge, like the large monument of 1891 in the Old Aisle Cemetery, Kirkintilloch, to Beatrice Clugston, the founder of Broomhill Hospital, its bronze relief by *Pittendrigh MacGillivray* showing a nurse tending a patient under a portrait bust of Miss Clugston accompanied by cherubs. In Valley Cemetery, Stirling, is a group of monuments, not marking graves but celebrating the heroes and heroines of the Scottish Reformation, all erected by the 'seedsman and evangelist' William Drummond. At the entrance to the

38 cemetery is the Star Pyramid of 1863 by *William Barclay*, each hammer-dressed face carved with pious texts and with marble Bibles at the bottom. Statues of Presbyterian divines by *A. Handyside Ritchie*, 1858–9, are scattered through the cemetery which also con-

39 tains the monument erected by Drummond in honour of Margaret Wilson, reputedly drowned in the Solway in 1685 for refusing to abjure the Covenant, here depicted in marble together with 'her like-minded sister Agnes' and an angel.

The principal monuments to national or local heroes were erected outside graveyards. At Renton, the novelist Tobias Smollett is

36 commemorated by an urn-finialled Tuscan column of 1774. An

37 obelisk, over 31m. high, was designed in 1788 by *James Craig* to

honour the memory of George Buchanan at Killearn and another obelisk was put up in 1836 at Dunglass Castle overlooking the Clyde to the memory of Henry Bell, the pioneer of steamship construction. The memory of the C18 Secession leader, the Rev. Ebenezer Erskine, is celebrated by a Tempietto designed by *Peddie* 40 *& Kinnear* in 1859 and erected outside the former Erskine Marykirk Church at Stirling. Others were commemorated by clock towers, e.g. Dr William Spence at Dollar in 1912 and Lady Muir at Deanston *c.* 1930, both with touches of martial detail. At Gartmore the writer, nationalist and eccentric R. B. Cunninghame Graham is commemorated by a whinstone wall bearing a relief portrait bust by *Alexander Proudfoot*, 1937. At Alexandria, the former Dunbartonshire M.P. Alexander Smollett was honoured in 1870 by the erection of a fountain designed by *Adamson & McLeod* in the form of three superimposed Baronially parapeted church fonts of diminishing size topped by a cast iron heron. More lighthearted and commemorating no one in particular is the tall Fountain of Nineveh erected 41 at Bridge of Allan in 1853, its Doric column supporting a bowl adorned with dolphins.

STATUES stand as commemorations of the famous, their likenesses serving as inspiration to future generations and as works of art to adorn public spaces. The not very proficient stone statue of the Duke of Wellington by *Robert Forrest*, *c.* 1830, was put up at Falkirk in 1854. In 1876–7 *Andrew Currie*'s statue of Robert the Bruce was erected on The Esplanade outside Stirling Castle and another, much larger, equestrian statue of Bruce by *C. d'O. Pilkington Jackson* was placed outside the Bannockburn Heritage Centre, Stirling, in 1964. At Dumbarton, a bronze statue of the shipbuilder Peter Denny by *W. Hamo Thornycroft*, 1898, was erected outside the former Municipal Buildings in 1902 and an outsize bronze of Sir William Mackinnon (by *Charles McBride*, 1899) placed in the garden of Helenslee in the 1920s when Keil School which he had endowed moved there. Behind Dumbarton Road in Stirling stand the figures of the Prime Minister and local M.P. Sir Henry Campbell Bannerman by *Paul R. Montford*, 1911–13, the poet Robert Burns, by *Albert H. Hodge*, 1914, and, more disappointingly, *Benno Schotz*'s statue of Rob Roy.

WAR MEMORIALS, especially those put up after the First World War, are commonplace. Some are symbolic, like *G. H. Paulin*'s bronze figures of a lady holding a lamp at Milngavie (*c.* 1920), of 'Victory' at Denny (1922) and 'Youth' at Dollar Academy (1922), *Alexander Proudfoot*'s 'Sacrifice' and 'Victory' at Bearsden (1924) or *C. d'O. Pilkington Jackson*'s kneeling angel holding a sword at Tillicoultry (1948). Others are more direct representations of the fallen. On The Esplanade at Stirling and at Crianlarich are figures of kilted Scots soldiers, by *W. Hubert Paton*, 1905–7 and by *Beveridge* of Perth, *c.* 1922. More ambitious are statuary groups. In Stirling Road, Alloa, and Newmarket Street, Falkirk, each of the South African War Memorials by *W. Birnie Rhind*, 1904, and *W. Grant Stevenson*, 1905–6, depicts a soldier guarding the body of a fallen comrade. The First World War Memorial at Bedford Place, Alloa, sculpted by *Pilkington Jackson* in 1924, shows a group of soldiers

crawling into attack with, above, a standing female figure symbolizing 'The Thought of Alloa'. Other memorials take the form of
cross-finialled shafts, the shaft at Kilmaronock, designed by *D. Y.
Cameron* in 1921, standing on a cairn, the memorials provided by
*Robert S. Lorimer* in 1921 at Clackmannan and Strathblane more
reminiscent of market crosses, the memorial at Sauchie, designed
in 1922 by *William Kerr*, with angels holding a crown in front of
the cross. The shaft of *Alexander N. Paterson*'s War Memorial at
Kippen is an unusual Ionic column. The two most powerful
memorials in the area, both designed by *John J. Burnet*, are of
1920 in Levengrove Park, Dumbarton, and of 1922–3 in Zetland
Park at Grangemouth. Both are ashlar cenotaphs, the one at
Dumbarton serving as a backdrop for the bronze figure of an angel,
43  the one at Grangemouth surmounted by a bronze of the British
Lion killing the eagle of German militarism. Weirdly old-fashioned
is the castellated and pinnacled War Memorial Gateway to the
former Campsie Parish Church at Lennoxtown erected in 1923.
By contrast, the memorial gateway to Peel Park, Kirkintilloch,
designed by *John Shanks* in 1925, is classical, its New Zealand
marble masonry giving it a chilly precision.

   Two monuments in the area defy categorization. The MacGregor
Monument at Lanrick Castle, erected as a clan memorial *c.* 1800,
rises from an exceptionally tall ashlar-faced base which simulates a
truncated tree trunk whose branches have been lopped off. This
supports a classical rotunda, the Roman Doric columns absurdly
attenuated, topped by a single (originally urn-finialled) column.
The National Wallace Monument designed by *John T. Rochead* in
1861 and completed eight years later is the definitive expression of
nationalism as experienced by Victorian Scotland. Perched on top
of the Abbey Crag, overlooking the site of Wallace's defeat of the
English army at the Battle of Stirling Bridge in 1297, the huge
battered Baronial tower, over 60m. high, rises into a crown spire,
both outline and detail making this a prickly assertion of Scottish
self-esteem, the nationalism further emphasized inside by the
combination of stained glass and statuary filling the vaulted
chambers (the Hall of Honour, the Hall of Heroes and the Royal
Chamber).

## CASTLES AND TOWER-HOUSES

Two sites above all others in the landscape of Stirling and Central
Scotland assert their pre-eminence as defensive strongholds:
Stirling and Dumbarton. Both are topographical anomalies, ancient
volcanic rocks erupting unexpectedly on the marches of that swathe
of low fertile land that stretches across the country from Forth to
Clyde. Both command important routes. Overlooking the lowest
bridging point of the Forth, Stirling stands at Scotland's crossroads guarding communications not only N–S between Highlands
and Lowlands but W–E between land and sea. The dominance of

Dumbarton is scarcely less significant: while to the w the Clyde broadens and divides into the long lochs that lead to the Western Isles, the road N follows the coiling course of the Leven to Loch Lomond and on into Argyll and Perthshire. Seen from carse or estuary, each rock is visually stunning and provocative. Such a geography must surely have a history. Yet hard evidence for the early strategic conscription and fortification of either location is surprisingly lacking. Stirling may well have been the primitive citadel from which the Maeatae, Votadini and Gododdin repulsed the Roman invaders; it could conceivably have been King Arthur's Camelot; and it was probably besieged by Kenneth MacAlpin in his campaign to unify Scotland in the C9. The Britons, too, may have resisted Agricola from their fortress of Dumbarton; at the recommendation of St Mungo, Merlin may have spent time at the court of Rhydderych Hael on the 'two-headed rock'; and there the Scottish kings were certainly denied suzerainty until the beginning of the C11. By the end of the first millennium a number of written sources, varying in their reliability, support the inference that to hold these two fortified rocks was to command Central Scotland. But of archaeological corroboration there is little. While it seems likely that some form of stone castle existed at Stirling at least from the C12 and at Dumbarton from the C13, no physical remains can be identified prior to the later medieval period. At Stirling, the earliest masonry appears to be in the lower walling of the North Gate; at Dumbarton, the oldest structure is the Portcullis 50 Arch which guards the narrow s approach to the summit: both are believed to date from the C14.

Elsewhere there is little that antedates these vestiges. At Castle Craig in Tillicoultry the foundations of a motte-and-bailey castle have been excavated. Similar circular fortresses protected by ditching and timber palisades probably existed across the region from the C12 or before, but the evidence is scant. At Castle Rankine near Denny, a simple stone peel, now gone, is thought to have been erected as early as the C13. Stretches of ruinous walling at Dunglass Castle and some fragmentary remains of the Earl of Lennox's island redoubt of Inchmurrin on Loch Lomond survive from the C14, as does the shell of Craigmaddie Castle. Not until the last years of the C14 (*see* below), however, is there an example of those stone-built castles which had replaced the motte-and-bailey model in some other parts of the country. These CASTLES OF ENCLOSURE were much stronger defensive structures, their domestic lodgings, grand hall and often separate kitchen block all accommodated around a courtyard ringed with high walls. The invading English monarch Edward I had planned to raise strongholds at Tullibody and Polmaise in 1304–5 but next to nothing was built. Indeed, during the unstable period of the Wars of Independence, which dragged on through most of the C14, serious building construction seems to have been at a standstill. By the 1380s, however, Robert Stewart, Duke of Albany and Regent of Scotland, had begun to erect the great castle of Doune on an 49 elevated eminently defensible site wedged in the confluence of the rivers Teith and Ardoch. Building on earthworks surviving from some ancient settlement raised on the dun that gives the castle and adjacent burgh their name, Albany created a walled fortress of impressive dimension. Its quadrilateral plan is marked out by masonry curtains with parapet walks and corbelled turrets at the corners and mid-points. But, unlike the great castles of a century and more before, the bulk of its accommodation is gathered on the N side in a frontal mass of high, strongly fortified keep-gatehouse and battlemented Great Hall. At the NW corner a link is made to a structurally distinct kitchen block. All apartments at ground-level are vaulted, as is the Duke's Hall located on first-floor level in the gatehouse tower. Planning is sophisticated with a careful arrangement of activities and circulation routes. Doune is a formidable stone structure, exceptional and without contemporary parallel between Forth and Clyde.

Two lesser structures, one in the E more or less intact, the other in the W minimal and problematical in extent, provide evidence of the more modest architectural qualities characteristic of revived castellar building in the late 1300s. Well sited on King's Seat Hill, Clackmannan Tower rose three storeys high, of coursed and squared sandstone on a splayed base. Its original single tower (heightened and extended in the C15) provides an example of the simple plan and scale of the tower-house building type that would soon proliferate across central Scotland. Mugdock Castle, on the other hand, presents a different, apparently more ambitious, configuration. Begun in the late C14 by the Graham family who had acquired the estate from the Lennox earls in the previous century, it, too, has a surviving tower. This, however, does not stand alone but is linked by a long length of wall to a second, more ruinous, tower, an arrangement suggesting that the *enceinte* may have continued to form a castle of enclosure. If this was indeed the case, Mugdock seems to have remained an all but solitary example of this grander type.

While it is safe to assume that by the beginning of the C15 masonry curtains, probably more akin to those at Mugdock than those at Doune, gave defensive definition to the hilltop fortresses at Stirling and Dumbarton, only one other castle can properly be said to have developed a plan of walled and towered containment in some sense comparable to that hypothesized for Mugdock. Constructed in the second quarter of the C15 by Sir George Crichton, Earl of Caithness and Admiral of Scotland, the dark whin
51 rubble curtain walls of Blackness Castle wrap themselves around a small promontory on the S shore of the Forth estuary. The layout, doubtless conceived by its nautical patron in the spirit of *l'architecture parlante*, is shipshape, launched into the firth with stem and stern towers N and S (the prow structure appropriately triangular in plan) and a central 'mainmast' tower. This last, oblong in plan, rises five storeys to a wallhead where some C15 corbelling survives below replacement rounds. And it is Blackness's towers rather than its enclosure plan, unique or not, that best exemplify the starkly straightforward nature of C15 castle architecture.

TOWER-HOUSES, combining defence and accommodation in a single structure, were built across the region, though by far the majority can be found E of Stirling on the low-lying ground S of the Forth estuary and N of the river along the Hillfoots of Clackmannanshire. Plans are oblong, though a few structures have integral jambs. In most cases the walls rise at least four storeys to a corbelled battlement often with rounds at the corners. Some have corner caphouses with crowstepped gables. The location of stairs varies, with turnpikes frequent. Carnock Tower near Plean, sometimes known as Bruce's Castle, is probably the oldest and may date from the early C15, though it is now little more than a tall fragment of standing masonry. Plean Tower, of the mid C15, survived to the wallhead until an archaeologically indifferent restoration began at the start of the C20. Comparable in date, Sauchie Tower is constructed in squared coursed sandstone similar 53 to the rough ashlar masonry of Clackmannan Tower where the earlier tower was raised and a higher SE jamb added. Callendar House at Falkirk has absorbed an oblong tower which was certainly in existence by 1458. The small, late C15 tower at Airth is now no more than an indistinguishable corner of a successively enlarged house finally fronted by a castellated Gothic façade. Another, much larger tower, five storeys high and probably constructed some time between 1470 and 1490, forms most of the W wing of Kinneil 57 House, Bo'ness, its first-floor hall, already remarkably prestigious by virtue of size, adapted as the Great Dining Room of the castle's later transformation into a Restoration showhouse. Although the tower is now without floors and partitions, plasterwork decoration and several stone chimneypieces from the late C17 reconstruction can still be seen. Castle Cary Castle, c. 1480, betrays an intention to build to an L-plan, though this was never realized, whereas at the now ruinous Almond Castle a NE jamb was constructed to house the kitchen. In West Dunbartonshire, Kilmaronock Castle and Duntreath Castle provide the only examples of C15 towers; the former a high but blasted, ivy-cloaked shell, the latter assimilated by C19 conversion. Of all the castles built in Stirling and Central Scotland, Castle Campbell, dramatically poised above a deep 52 wooded cleft in the Ochil Hills, is perhaps the most picturesquely sited. Built by Colin Campbell, first Earl of Argyll, the original tower, c. 1475, vaulted not only over the ground floor but over the first floor also, has remained the erect core of later aggrandizement. Much less striking in its setting now that local authority housing has swamped its once magnificent grounds, Alloa Tower, 54 completed by the 1490s (from which date its oak roof has survived), is none the less grander in scale. Like Castle Campbell it rises four storeys (the lower stages perhaps C14) but from a much larger plan base, a measure of the wealth and prestige of the Erskine Earls of Mar who built it.

Also in the 1490s, major reconstruction began at STIRLING CASTLE. Over the next century or so, thanks to the patronage of the Stewart kings, the Rock evolved into a royal fortress and residence thoroughly European in its cultural pretension. Essentially forming a castle of enclosure, the buildings within the peripheral 44 fortifications differed markedly in scale and stylistic character from the humbler tower-house architecture of the local lairds. To the late

C15 belong much of the extensive perimeter wall masonry and the
47 stout forework with its French-inspired gatehouse, which originally boasted four three-storeyed towers with corbelled parapets
and conically roofed caphouses. But it was around the inner close
or court that the most radical changes were to occur as a new more
regularized right-angled relationship of buildings was devised, perhaps
by James IV himself, to transform the castle from medieval
stronghold to Renaissance palace.

One of the first elements to be realized in this distinctly classical
conception was the King's Old Building laid out on an elongated
L-plan above the craggy W face of the Rock. Its linear arrangement
of principal rooms, raised on a series of barrel-vaulted basement
chambers, was reached from the courtyard by a turnpike stair.
This still medieval means of access was not expressed as a stone
cylinder but housed in a square projection topped by an octagonal
caphouse – a sequence of superimposed forms copied at Castle
Campbell and more sculpturally echoed in the contemporary
staircase projection at Duntreath Castle.

Across the Close from the King's Old Building, James IV built
48 the Great Hall, a vast single-space chamber lit at the S end by tall,
symmetrically placed, oriels and throughout at high level by pairs
of large, segmentally-arched, clearstorey windows. Its castellated
battlements, like the crowstepped skews of the gables, are clearly a
consequence of deliberate stylistic choice; decorative sophistication rather than defensive consideration is paramount. But if the
forms of Franco-Scots castellar architecture linger superficially, there
are other more potent influences at work here. Unprecedented in
Scotland, the Great Hall almost certainly owes its conception to
the example set by Eltham Palace and other similar royal halls in
England.

Over a generation later when James V commissioned the build-
45 ing of a new royal palace on the S side of the inner close, fresh
Franco-Italian models brought the Renaissance into the heart of
Scotland. The palace plan has strong classical affinities: more or
less identical royal suites are grouped symmetrically around three
sides of an inner courtyard with a linking gallery on the fourth, W,
side, where connection with the King's Old Building may have
been intended. But it is in the elevations to N, E and S that the new
international culture so enthusiastically espoused by the Scottish
monarchy is most apparent. Here again crowstepped gables and
battlemented parapets persist but there is otherwise an unexpectedly
precocious commitment to the sculptural and allegorical possibilities of Mannerist art. Many elements of the design, which from
the late 1530s seems to have been the responsibility of *Sir James
Hamilton* of Finnart, can be ascribed to European precedent: the
articulation of the façades in which windows alternate with niches
housing statues, increasingly common across the continent; the
adoption of multi-cusped arches over recesses framing statues
placed on balusters, decidedly French; the disposition and decorum of the statues themselves, based on Germanic interpretations
of classical themes.

In 1594 James VI completed the enclosure of the inner close on

the N side by building the Chapel Royal, the most classically calm 46
and assured of the four buildings fronting the courtyard envisaged
by James IV; a symmetrical façade with paired round-arched
windows of Florentine provenance and a central arched entrance
doorway framed by coupled columns carrying an entablature. In
place of a crenellated parapet there is a simple moulded eaves
course and only modest crowstepping survives to resonate with
the rest of the gabled skyline surrounding the close.

The C16 aggrandizement of Stirling must be seen in national
terms. Such prestigious commissions and contracts were only to be
found at the royal palaces of Falkland, Holyrood and Linlithgow
where the Stewart kings had built with comparable style. Across
the countryside of central Scotland there were few echoes of these
achievements, for while the monarchy may not have been alone in
its awareness of the latest European trends in art and architecture,
only the Crown could be expected to build at such a scale, only the
exchequer could sustain the necessary expenditure and perhaps
only the Court find the skills to turn familiarity with fashion into
physical fact. At the start of the century the second Earl of Argyll
had erected a two-storey-and-attic SE range beside his Castle
Campbell tower-house, placing the principal rooms on the upper
floor over a vaulted basement in much the same manner as had
been done a few years previously at the King's Old Building in
Stirling. But no other patron found the funds or the daring to
follow any of the innovations made by later buildings on the Rock.
Outside the royal battlements the fundamental exigencies of security still remained relevant for most builders, the introduction of
Renaissance forms confined here and there to matters of ornament
and detail. At Blackness between 1536 and 1544, the involvement
of the king's principal master of works *Sir James Hamilton* of Finnart
was largely focused on the strengthening of the curtain walls and 51
the provision of a new, more defensible entrance to the castle. At
Kinneil House, on the other hand, a new 'palice' range, the NE 57
wing, was added to the C15 tower, 1553–c.1555. More palace than
castle, its large windows suggest a reduced need for security, its
interior decoration of wall painting simulating tapestries a more 58
cultured lifestyle. And, indeed, in the second half of the century
the popularity of the traditional tower-house model did begin to
weaken. Even then the emergence of an unfortified domestic
architecture was tentative and unresolved.

EARLY C16 TOWER-HOUSES in the region are unremarkable
and in many cases fragmentary. Dunmore Tower is a ruin. Still
less remains at Rednock Castle. At Touch House, the SE tower, 60
which may even be late C15, has become a romantic appendage to
the Georgian mansion, while a second tower, C16, is hidden in the
fabric of the N range built a century later. Culcreuch Castle near
Fintry survives as a hotel but gentrified by later interference and
all but overwhelmed by additions made in the C18 and C19.
Further S, close to the suburban fringes of Glasgow, Bardowie,
too, is substantially intact and much less architecturally impaired
by the remodelling of its upper structure in 1566; alterations which,
by removing the original battlements and adding a new top-floor

gallery under an arch-braced roof structure, seem to indicate an early willingness to dispense with the trappings of fortification. Several surviving tower-houses appear to confirm the tendency towards domesticity and comfort over defence. The Blair at Blairlogie, a mini-tower of 1543 to which an equally small E wing was added in 1582, is decidedly domesticated, while the hall-house built alongside Plean Tower on the other side of the Forth some time in the middle years of the century is further proof that the defensible castle was no longer *de rigueur*. Torwood Castle, which was probably built in 1566, is also a hall-house. It is an L-plan structure with gunloops to the vaulted chambers of the lowest storey, a hall at first-floor level and a turnpike stair in the re-entrant angle. But the windows to the upper storeys are perhaps just a little more generous than hitherto and, filling the jamb, a second turn-pike rises from ground to first floor; both signs of an increasing concern for domestic amenity. Greater privacy and comfort were, indeed, a significant consequence of L-plan and Z-plan arrange-ments which offered flexibility in the internal layout of accommo-dation and circulation hitherto limited by the geometry of the older rectangular plan. Stairs could be much more conveniently located, frequently in the re-entrant angle, and the more private apartments of the laird's household accommodated 'deeper' in the jamb or towers of the plan.

This trend becomes more marked in LATE C16 TOWER-HOUSES. At Dunglass, Sir Humphrey Colquhoun of Luss built a dwelling house inside the protective walls of the earlier castle. In 1581, at Airth Castle, a two-storey, L-plan wing was added against the E side of the old tower to make the house more agreeably habitable; it maintained a pseudo-defensive wallhead but with only 'little battlements' and broken by dormers. At Old Sauchie, defensive concerns are still much in evidence in the array of pistol-holes, peep-holes and gunloops, but generously sized windows point to increased domestic considerations. Edinample Castle, for all its conformity to the classic Z-plan formula with drum towers at the NW and SE corners, is no fortress. Built by the Campbells of Breadalbane *c.* 1584 in a wooded hillside setting of picturesque Scottishness, it is correctly, if uncolourfully, described by MacGibbon and Ross as 'a fine old mansion'. Duchray Castle, a less complete Z with a single round tower at the SE corner and only a corbelled turret on the NW, seems no less residential, though the later transformation of its original windows to pointed-arched openings certainly con-tributes much to this impression. The ruinous walls of the late C16 tower-house of Gartartan Castle betray little more than their Z-plan configuration, but at Cardross House, an L-plan tower of similar date has proved amenable to absorption into the residential expansion of the C18. At Gargunnock, too, both a late C16, four-storey, L-plan tower-house and the three-storey wing which in the following century completed the Z-plan have been swallowed up by the later C18 mansion-house. Still to be seen a kilometre W of Gargunnock is the T-plan arrangement at Old Leckie, also late C16. Here, while the short stem of the T has a castellar appearance with turnpike stair turrets tucked into the re-entrants on each side of a high crowstepped gable, the main accommodation block behind is wholly domestic in character, barely distinguishable from the c18 wing which extends it to the E, except perhaps in the size of its windows. Much restored and marooned in a housing scheme, Menstrie Castle, raised by Sir William Alexander, first Earl of Stirling, c. 1600, is broadly similar; 'a large wealthy manor house, rather than a castle that could have withstood a determined enemy'*. Further improvements at Castle Campbell, made around the turn of the century, also introduced more salubrious residential accommodation. This new E range, essentially a self-contained dwelling rising through three storeys and attic, is well appointed with good staircases, generous garderobes and a small but pleasant loggia of elliptically-arched bays opening on to the castle yard.

Confidence in a peaceful future was growing but tradition was by no means abandoned. Though both structures are in ruin, neither Arnhall Castle nor the island fortalice of Inchtalla in the Lake of Menteith appears to depart much from a tower-house model which, by the time of their erection at the start of the c17, was already almost four hundred years old. Defence still seems to have held the upper hand at Finlarig Castle and the islanded Loch Dochart Castle, both built in the first years of the c17 by Sir Duncan Campbell, seventh of Glenorchy. No doubt caution and parsimony played their part in such conservatism. The former was certainly not misplaced, as the civil and religious disturbances of the mid c17 would show. Castle Campbell, for example, suffered badly. In 1654 it was burned by Royalist troops in the course of the Earl of Glencairn's action against the Cromwellian occupation and remained derelict until repairs were begun in the c19. But the Restoration brought some renewed calm and with it a return to a style of lordly living at once more comfortable and more cultured. In many castles, windows and doors were enlarged, additional openings inserted, more fireplaces introduced, better stairs provided and new wings built. Through this transition the tower-house became the forerunner of the country house.

If the walled castle of enclosure had any equivalent progeny it was to be found a century later in the spate of BARRACKS building which followed the Jacobite revolts of the first half of the c18. Remotely sited close to the E shore of Loch Lomond, Inversnaid Garrison, of which little remains, was one of several erected across the country to a more or less standard pattern with three-storey tenement-like blocks built to accommodate soldiers around a parade ground. At Dumbarton Castle, where during the c17 the fortifications had fallen into ruin, a prolonged programme of reconstruction took place. Particularly intense in the 1730s, by the late 1790s work on a series of masonry batteries strengthening the defences around the Rock had been completed. Stirling Castle, since 1603 surplus to royal residential requirements, was also reinforced. Events linked to the Jacobite cause, from the rising of James Graham of Claverhouse in 1689 to the unsuccessful siege laid by the Young Pretender's retreating army in 1746, completed its transformation

---

* Adam Swan, *Clackmannan and the Ochils* (1987), 64.

from palace to barracks. In the last decade of the C18 the Main
Guard House and Fort Major's House were built – and well built
– but, as the military demands of the garrison had grown, the
character of the castle had changed. Several of the great Renaissance
buildings of the C16 were radically altered and damaged. Not until
the C20 would this trend be reversed and the castle regain its regal
dignity.

## COUNTRY HOUSES

Throughout the C17 the transition from tower-house to country
house was prolonged and ambivalent. While several of the older
fortified structures were cautiously adapted to meet the demands
of a new, more relaxed, more civilizing lifestyle, a number of
smaller dwellings were being built with no more than the most
perfunctory acknowledgement of defensive criteria. These MANOR
HOUSES, built by the lesser lairds, were frequently constructed to
three or more storeys on an L-plan and, though otherwise lacking
in the defensive attributes of martial design, to that extent at least
might still be regarded as coming under the influence of the castellar
tradition. By the middle years of the century, Carriden House,
Cawder House, Kersie Mains near Alloa (now a farmhouse) and,
possibly, Newton of Doune all seem to have followed this pattern,
though later changes make it difficult to be definitive about their
original form. Newton of Doune is L-plan with a small cone-roofed
turret clasped in the re-entrant and a staircase in the w jamb given
a rounded crowstepped gable. Auchenbowie House, from *c.* 1666,
is a grander version of this arrangement. It began as an L-plan
structure, its harled walls rising through three storeys to an attic
floor which is still dormered in the s wing. In the re-entrant is a
four-storey, octagonal entrance tower which originally housed the
staircase. Erect and assured, Auchenbowie remains a country house
of wholly Scottish provenance, no longer castellar but still traditional in form and detail.

Two larger POST-RESTORATION houses set a different, more
classical pattern. Bannockburn House, built by the Rollo family from
*c.* 1675, is still recognizably Scots. Its three-storeyed harled walls,
crowstepped gables, and pedimented dormers breaking through
the eaves recall Auchenbowie which is, indeed, little more than a
kilometre distant to the s. But, instead of the long-established
L-plan, the layout is now almost wholly symmetrical. w and e wings,
containing balanced apartments and staircases, are linked by a
five-bay central block entered axially through a pedimented doorway. Internally, however, the symmetry is disrupted by a 1:4 subdivision of this connecting core. The overall H-plan arrangement
may be derived from precedent set by some of the great Elizabethan
mansions built in England a century or so earlier. In any event,
both in its external appearance and in the magnificent plasterwork
of the interior, Bannockburn merits its designation by the RCAHMS

Inventory on *Stirlingshire* (1963) as 'the most remarkable' country house to be built in Stirling and Central Scotland during the C17. Its only rival is Kinneil House, Bo'ness, where between 1675 and 1686, the old C15 tower became the core of a wide-fronted symmetrical composition, its façade regularized and given a classical entrance, a conception that may well have been influenced by the work of John Mylne Jun., at Panmure House, 1666, or Sir William Bruce at Balcaskie House, 1668. Unlike these precedents where the centrepiece was lower, Kinneil's five-storey height, topped off by a balustraded wallhead, is flanked N and S by slightly lower advancing end pavilions with pyramidal roofs, the former itself a remodelling of mid-C16 fabric. Inside, in the new SW pavilion, a staircase was designed as a prelude to a state apartment. Although the intention to create an open U-plan forecourt to the E of this splendidly balanced façade by reflecting the C16 palace range already built on the N was never achieved, the transformation from the contingent forms of medieval building to the self-conscious axiality of classical architecture was significant. Evidently what the third Duke of Hamilton wanted was not so much a castle as a country house, but a country house with a state apartment, that prestigious suite of rooms provided by every self-respecting nobleman who could afford to entertain the possibility of a royal visit. And this aristocratic preference soon became a widespread fashion. In the late C17, for example, Callendar House, Falkirk, was extended to a U, the inner angles containing stair towers and, at the same time, a state apartment was formed to fill the first floor of the S range and approached by the new state stair in the SE corner of the addition.

During the last quarter of the C17 one architect was largely responsible for introducing the CLASSICAL MANSION-HOUSE to Scotland. This was Sir William Bruce whose houses at Kinross, Craigiehall and Hopetoun, all of which shared an austere classicism raised on a compact oblong plan, set a model that would prove influential well into the C18. The attributes of the new style – the adoption of symmetrically composed elevations, the provision of the state apartment at first-floor level, the formal emphasis on this *piano nobile*, and the introduction of the pediment whether as a major element in the design of the façade or merely as a decorative stress to windows and doors – were soon in vogue across Scotland, for Bruce's authority was widespread and ramified, his impact on country house design related not only to the direct appeal of his built work but, as John Dunbar has pointed out, to 'the indirect ascendancy that he was able to establish over the work of other designers' through his extensive range of contacts among the nobility. His advice was sought by many patrons; so much so, indeed, that where he was not engaged as architect his influence was often no less evident. This indirect link could have occurred at Strathleven House in West Dunbartonshire, though *James Smith*, who had succeeded Bruce as the Crown's Master of Works in 1683, is the more likely designer. Begun perhaps as early as the 1690s, the buildings commissioned by William Cochrane for his Vale of Leven estate were not complete until the late 1720s. A pedimented three-storey block sits between lower advancing pavilions, roofs are steep, piended and bellcast, chimneystacks rise from cross-walls. The flanking wings do not return to form a U-plan forecourt but stretch out to magnify the façade in a plane parallel to that of the main block.

Other attempts were made to interpret the compositional discipline of classical order adumbrated by Bruce and Smith. Two of these were located in the small county of Clackmannanshire. Begun by the Abercromby family *c.* 1710, Tullibody House was rigorously symmetrical, a six-bay, three-storey block flanked by lower wings advancing on each side of a wide forecourt. Piended roofs were steeply pitched above a bellcast eaves. Piercing the ridge of the central block, chimneystacks rose from the two structural cross-walls that divided the plan. Tullibody was demolished in the 1960s but a comparable composition survives at Brucefield, 1724. The three-storey centrepiece is similar though not so large, the piended roofs again steep and bellcast, the chimneystacks identically placed. But, whereas at Tullibody the principal entrance remained at ground level (with the state apartment on the floor above), here a staircase, or perhaps an earth banking, originally rose to a once pedimented doorway opening directly to the *piano nobile* at the centre of the E front. Here, too, flanking wings were built, though later and never in balance. None the less, both Brucefield and Tullibody are clearly conceived in accord with the same architectural model and, though no designer can be securely ascribed to either house, both bear the serious high-hatted countenance of a classicism that might derive at some distance from Bruce, who had died in 1710, but which again seems more likely to be the achievement of *James Smith*. Similarities in layout and detail link both residences to Blair Drummond House, another piended, three-storey mansion with lower flanking wings, built 1715–17 to a design by *Alexander McGill*. Like Tullibody, McGill's Blair Drummond had a state apartment plan. Like Tullibody, too, it has gone, demolished in 1870.

A third architectural enterprise undertaken in Clackmannanshire in the early years of the C18 merits mention. In 1703–15, as part of improvements to his estate (*see* Parkland below), the *Earl of Mar* (whose name has also been associated with the design of Tullibody) began to make extensive changes to the old Alloa Tower, remodelling the interior and adding a new SE block. These alterations, on which Mar took advice from a number of architect-contractors including *James Smith* and *Alexander McGill*, were completed later in the same century; they included a regularization of the façade fenestration and, internally, the creation of a two-storey entrance hall and state stair leading to the new house behind. More architecturally sophisticated proposals later prepared by the Earl himself, exiled as a result of his ill-fated support for the Jacobite cause at Sheriffmuir in 1715, remained on paper. Had Mar's fantasies been realized, their French Baroque elegance would have been unique in Scotland. Much of what was in fact built has been lost, destroyed after a fire in 1800.

In the early 1740s *William Adam* prepared a design for Gartmore House, later published in *Vitruvius Scoticus*. The concept is clearly Palladian; set back behind low flanking pavilions to which it is linked by r.-angled screen walls is a tall, three-bay, piend-roofed house, pedimented at the centre, with a Gibbsian Venetian doorway defining the entrance. The plan retains the traditional state apartment. But it is unclear whether this design was ever built. Even if some or all of Adam's ideas were realized, they have long since been submerged in later transformations. By the middle of the century there were only two country houses of more than provincial architectural quality: Touch House, which lay not far from Stirling a little to the w of Cambusbarron, and Wrightpark, more remotely sited on the Kippen Muir.

Until the late 1740s, Touch followed a traditional L-plan arrangement resulting from the building of a N range in the C17 which had linked two earlier towers. Its C18 aggrandizement entailed the creation of a large three-storeyed mansion, introduced into the SW re-entrant angle of the older composite structure, which presented a handsome seven-bay façade to the S. Placed axially at the rear of the plan, tangential to the older building, is an elegant elliptical staircase which returns to an upper landing leading to the Drawing Room located at the three-bay centre of the S façade between Dining Room and Principal Bedroom. Though it has no portico and lacks any development of flanking outbuildings, Touch comes close to Palladian refinement. So, too, does Wrightpark, 1750–1. On a ground-floor storey of channelled ashlar, giant Ionic pilasters articulate a sober five-bay front. Carried on a façade-wide entablature, a pediment holed by an oculus rises from the central three bays. Urns punctuate the skyline in front of a piended roof. Like Touch, Wrightpark is a country house without pretension to royal entertainment. The principal rooms on the first floor, no longer reserved for regal splendour, are now the lived-in apartments of a family. By the middle of the C18 the state apartment had become a thing of the past. With William Adam dead and the Jacobite rising of 1745–6 defeated, the lairds and nobility of North Britain aspired to a new, more comfortable, more convenient and more private lifestyle, shorn of any dependent deference to the Court.

Cochno House, built *c.* 1757 in the hills above Clydebank, is, like Touch, seven bays wide with a pedimented centre. But the similarity ends there; Cochno is without architectural ornament, plain, not to say dull, the proportions of its harled walls ill served by later additions. Catter House, on the other hand, which shares with Wrightpark a five-bay front but none of its grand *gravitas*, is delightful in scale and detail. Pleasantly sited overlooking the coiling course of the Endrick Water s of Drymen, it is pert and pretty with a small eaves-pediment peak repeated over the front entrance, from the landing platt of which stairs curve down to the l. and r. Less infused with charm but respectably staid is the s front of Gargunnock House, 1794. It is fashionably contrived in seven bays, with a pediment centred between eaves balustrades, essentially a façade concealing C16 and C17 building absorbed in more up-to-date accommodation. At Keir House, the three central bays of the eleven-bay mansion built towards the end of the C18 were pedimented, though later interventions make it all but impossible to envisage this wide and perhaps rather unimaginative Georgian façade.

A much simpler expression of the new addiction to symmetrical order appears in Stirling district in the design of a handful of SMALL HOUSES OF THE EARLY EIGHTEENTH CENTURY. These generally conform to a three-bay, two-storey, gable-ended model with a central entrance door and staircase behind. Ballewan near Strathblane, Blawlowan at Bridge of Allan and Lochend on the SE shore of the Lake of Menteith adopt this formula, though all are in some way unbalanced by subsequent additions. Old Auchentroig, near Buchlyvie built as early as 1702 (it may have incorporated some earlier fabric), remains uncompromised by any later encroachment; the symmetry of its low-scale SE front is, engagingly, not quite perfect. Its nail-studded door is framed by roll-and-hollow architrave mouldings, a decorative gesture recurring at the centre of the five-bay façade of Old Ballikinrain where the early C18 house is flanked by lower wings forming a symmetrical U-plan court. Examples of the familiar three-bay formula can be seen at Glengyle at the NW end of Loch Katrine and at Old Glassingal House near Kinbuck, the latter modestly enhanced by a Roman Doric doorpiece. Birdston at Milton of Campsie and Huntershill House, Bishopbriggs, which has an ill-proportioned Gibbsian doorway, are five bays wide; both have scrolled skewputts at the gables but are otherwise plain. At Mains of Glinn, on the moor S of Kippen, the entrance door defers more intelligently to Gibbs's example. Kinnell House, Killin, is similar in scale but has a chimneyed gable at the centre. This proto-pediment also appears at the Roman Camp Hotel in Callander where a built-in datestone avers a doubtful C17 provenance. While some built wider, others raised the eaves to three storeys. N of Thornhill, Braendam House, built 1742–4 but remodelled c. 1790, is hip-roofed with three tripartite windows at first floor and thermal windows flanking a Roman Doric porch. Auchlyne in Glen Dochart, c. 1760, also three-bay and three-storeyed, is more austere but has a central pediment with armorial carving. Powis House, 1746–7, lacks a pediment but, three-bayed on the façade and sides, is classically compact, its small-windowed cubic solidity emphasized by ashlar quoins.

SMALLER HOUSES OF THE LATER EIGHTEENTH CENTURY proliferate. Simple five-bay, two-storeyed houses, most skew-gabled with a pedimented façade and a central doorway leading directly to a stair at the rear of the plan, were common. Kippenross at Dunblane, c. 1770, is a classic example. Lacking a pediment, Boquhan Old House, 1784, is even more archetypal. Quarter House, N of Dunipace, is piend-roofed with a chimneyed pediment. Also piend-roofed is Craigmaddie House, N of Baldernock, c. 1790, a mansion commissioned not by a landed patron but by Glasgow's Lord Provost; panelled pilasters define an unusual four-bayed front with a chimneyed gable rising over the two central bays. Candie House, near Loan, is also four-bayed. Woodbank House, a decaying shell on the edge of Balloch, c. 1774, and Milton House, built for the manager of the mill established on the Milton Burn E of Dumbarton, c. 1792, are more orthodox, both pedimented, both with flying stairs; the former distinguished by buckle quoins and a Gibbsian door, the latter by tall windows and a humbler pilastered doorpiece. Still smaller, still symmetrical dwellings might be lairds' houses or farmhouses or both. Among such are Leddriegreen near Strathblane, Gartinstarry w of Buchlyvie, Arnprior and, at Milton of Campsie, Woodburn House. Flanking the unremarkable three-bay house at Leddriegreen, which was built some time between 1760 and 1770, are pedimented pavilion wings with Venetian windows, a small-scale parochial echo of distant Palladian norms. But precedent seems to play no part in the tripartite composition adopted some years later at Old Kippenross. Here, raised on the barrel-vaulted cellars of some earlier structure, are three side-by-side units, similar in plan but with the centre a storey higher in section than its single-storey neighbours. Each harled block is roofed with a slated pyramid, the elevated centre given a gable to the N – adding to the aberrant delight of this unique little building just a hint of Gothick whimsy.

The standard Georgian mansion, only occasionally pedimented though never dignified by a full-height temple-front portico, retained its popularity well into the NINETEENTH CENTURY. Columned porches became more common: Roman Doric at Doune Lodge, c. 1805, and Garden House, 1830, where *William Stirling I*'s five-bay 64 mansion masked its mid-C18 predecessor; Greek Doric at Plean House, c. 1802, Carbeth Guthrie, c. 1810, and Rednock House, c. 1821; Ionic at Killermont House, Bearsden, c. 1805, and Westerton House, Bridge of Allan, 1803. At Glenarbuck House, Old Kilpatrick, the Roman Doric porch is small but sits between pedimented tripartite windows. Perhaps the most finely judged façade of all the classical houses built in these first decades of the C19 is Gartur, w of Cambusbarron, where, though there is neither portico nor porch, a columned entrance screen, semicircular fanlight and iron-work balcony enhance the centre of an austere front otherwise no more than subtly inflected on the flanks.

Meanwhile, more assured signs of a shift in stylistic preference had followed the tentative Gothic intimations of Old Kippenross. In 1790 the building of Airthrey Castle began. It is among the last 61 of *Robert Adam*'s Castle Style houses but the only one in Stirling and Central Scotland. There are, of course, no pointed arches at Airthrey, no tracery, no finials, no Gothick fripperies. The house is seriously solid and symmetrical, its plan uniquely D-shaped with rectangular, apsidal and octagonal rooms balanced around a circulation core, its elevations reverberating with tripartite relationships. But, if these strategies may still be considered classical, the building's bulging mass, battlemented and towered, is medieval in its evocation. And it is this still-axial castellar medievalism that begins to make an impact on the design of the country house. Halfway between Falkirk and Linlithgow, Vellore, c. 1800, a small-scale version of the pavilioned Palladian layout, has its central block and linked wings mantled lightly in Gothick. But while Vellore is playful, the CASTELLATED GOTHIC style can be said to emerge in earnest in the domestic work of *David Hamilton*, an admirer if not indeed an employee of the Adam practice. Hamilton's designs for Airth Castle, 1807, and Kincaid House, c. 1812, the former a three-storey 62 dwelling forming a diagonal link between the ends of the old L-plan buildings of the c15 and c16, have a serious cast. Battlements, arched openings, hooded windows and octagonal turrets and chimneys arrange themselves in disciplined order; a rather grave Gothic gripped in symmetry. But this is only half the story, for in the w the revived interest in things medieval took a different course.

In West Dunbartonshire it was not Adam but the English architect *Robert Lugar* who challenged Georgian classicism. His designs for Balloch Castle, 1808–9, Tullichewan Castle, 1808–9 (demolished 1954), and later for the remodelling of Boturich Castle, 1834, all of which are (or, in Tullichewan's case, were) in sight of the s end of Loch Lomond, are conceived in a looser, more picturesque spirit than those of Adam or Hamilton. Lugar's is a Castellated Gothic romantically attuned to dreams of a monastic medievalism, as much ecclesiastical in its allusion as it remains military in its quasi-fortified forms. Elements of plan and section group freely below ragged skylines that rise and fall around battlemented towers. At Balloch and Tullichewan, for the first time in Scotland, Gothic affords that more general release from the constraints of classical composition which, begun in fanciful nostalgia, would prove to be the *sine qua non* of country house design in a c19 of ramifying social demands and growing stylistic pluralism. Room shapes and room relationships could now be designed for convenience rather than formal rigour.

The new Gothic gained converts, the possibilities of asymmetrical planning as seductive as the imagined associations of wallhead battlements and pointed arches. At Ross Priory, 1810–16, *James Gillespie Graham* seems tempted but does not fully succumb. Wrapping the new around the old, he still clings to the classical idea of the symmetrical tripartite façade with its central flying stair rising to the *piano nobile*. Yet, no doubt in acknowledgement of the building's mythical religious history, the detail is all ecclesiastical Gothic: tall crocketed finials, a buttressed porch, cusped pointed-arched window sashes, fan-vaulted plasterwork. A few years later at Mugdock, *Alexander Ramsay*, wholly in thrall to the asymmetric precedents set by Lugar, built Craigend Castle, 1816–17. Now reduced to a shell, its empty blasted towers and broken tracery are no less romantic in overgrown decay. Near Killearn, Carbeth House, *c.* 1840, a less robustly castellated make-over of an earlier dwelling, remains unimpaired by later Victorian additions. Three decades later, Dalmoak House near Renton, 1866–9, is still battlemented Gothic and still symmetrical.

In the E, a few houses catch the medievalizing infection. More villa than mansion house, Powfoulis Manor, *c.* 1820, is symmetrical Gothic and, with its spired buttresses, traceried parapets and hooded windows, so much akin to Ross Priory as to suggest the hand of Gillespie Graham. N of Airth, Dunmore Park, designed by *William Wilkins* for the fifth Earl of Dunmore, 1820–5, is rather less rigidly composed, its towered and battlemented architecture, sadly blighted by assault and neglect, best described as Tudor. Similar symptoms appeared elsewhere as, in the search for secular rather than ecclesiastical precedent, the Gothic Revival deferred to Elizabethan and Jacobean models. *Thomas Hamilton*'s Lathallan House, E of

Polmont, 1826, is Tudor too, as is the S front of nearby Avondale House. Watson House near Gargunnock, 1829–35, though it does possess a tall Perp Gothic staircase window, is already fevered with Jacobean. Not far away, Meiklewood, *c.* 1832, is both; quintessen- 65 tially JACOBETHAN REVIVAL. No longer dependent solely on castellar or ecclesiastical sources, the country house became more domesticated, its massing asymmetrical and flexible, its planning increasingly adapted to need, its architectural ornament more freely derived and freely applied. It began to seem as if the Elizabethan period, seen as an age of prosperity and, moreover, one in rapid cultural transition, might have a special relevance for the C19 and the prodigy house of the late C16, *mutatis mutandis*, prove a more appropriate model than medieval castle or church.

One building stands out from these trends. Lennox Castle, built 68 at Campsie Glen for the wealthy J. L. Kincaid Lennox, 1837–41, more than merits its castellar designation. Designed by *David Hamilton*, it is monumental in scale with high square towers rising to machicolated battlements. But it is not Gothic. Behind a massive *porte cochère* the N front soars to four tall storeys on a raised base- ment, its tiered ranks of round-arched windows set between twin turrets, 'almost evocative', as Diane Watters has observed, 'of a Romanesque cathedral front'*. Ecclesiastical perhaps, but une- quivocally fort-like in form and aspiration, Lennox Castle is unique. Hamilton's debt is to Adam and the Castle Style, though there is none of the cylindrical movement seen at Airthrey and elsewhere. Symmetries survive even if not all-embracing. The round arch is favoured, its ubiquitous presence emphasized, as Adam never did, in strongly moulded repetition. Perhaps because of its sheer size, perhaps because, despite its medieval affinities, it eschews Gothic liberation, this is a building without residential parallel or progeny – unless there is something in these planar walls and regularized rows of windows precociously redolent of Alexander 'Greek' Thomson. If there is, it makes no impact on country house design in Stirling and Central Scotland. Rather it was in the accommo- dation of the Jacobethan Revival to the Scottish context that progress was to be made.

No architect in Britain was a more prolific designer of country houses than *William Burn*. If any was more stylistically versatile, none was more skilled in tailoring the formal attributes of Tudor Gothic and Jacobean to the complex planning demands of his privileged clients. Nor was any architect more adept in the creative elaboration of the asymmetric plan not only to assimilate the grow- ing appendage of ancillary accommodation required to service the complex day-to-day running of the C19 country estate but also to achieve that conventional separation of family, guests and servants deemed so necessary to the proper conduct of Victorian social inter- course. From his office in Edinburgh, Burn established a far-flung practice. Yet he was responsible for no more than a handful of domestic commissions in Stirling and Central Scotland. The earliest of these, Gart House (or The Gart) near Callander, 1833–5, survives,

* Diane M. Watters, 'Domestic Works', in *David Hamilton, Architect*, ed. Aonghus MacKechnie (1993), 19.

though its original cottagey character is now invisible under a Baronial re-working of 1903–4. Paradoxically, it was Burn's own engagement with the detail and syntax of the Scots Baronial style as a kind of national alternative to the more English Jacobethan that would prove immensely influential. In 1836 at Stenhouse, Larbert, he carried out a remodelling of the early c17 L-plan tower-house (now demolished). It was not the first time he had attempted to adapt the indigenous architectural tradition to the present but at Stenhouse, able to study the original at close quarters, he was particularly successful. Burn's younger partner *David Bryce* continued to elaborate and exploit this new style. At The Parsonage, Dunmore Park, 1845–6, Bryce is still in restrained Elizabethan mode, but at Leny House, Kilmahog, 1845–6, Stronvar, Balquhidder, 1850, and, most spectacularly, at Ballikinrain Castle between Balfron and Fintry, 1864–70, he asserts his mastery of the BARONIAL REVIVAL. Ballikinrain, a huge estate project which entailed the building of arched gatehouse, lodges, bridges, a large stables court and walled garden as well as the great house itself, engrosses all the formal attributes of the mature style: crowstepped gables, bartizans with conical roofs, gabled eaves dormers, corbelled turnpikes, stepping stringcourses, cable mouldings, and so on. All this was fused with the canted bays and mullioned and transomed windows of Tudor England. But, for Bryce, the important prodigy house precedents were not those of the South but those of Scotland, especially those to be found in that last flowering of the tower-house tradition that had erupted between the Dee and the Don in late c16 Aberdeenshire; at Ballikinrain, for example, the great drum tower is a reincarnation of Castle Fraser.

While the desire to recover and re-interpret the Baronial tradition was stimulated initially by an apolitical romantic nationalism, the successful development of the style was driven by a detailed, if not yet archaeologically founded, knowledge of the historical evidence. Between 1845 and 1852 R.W. Billings compiled his four-volume *Baronial and Ecclesiastical Antiquities of Scotland*. Burn was a leading subscriber but many of the most prominent architects in Victorian Scotland also sponsored the publication. Once in print, the volumes lay on their desks, their detailed engravings frequently consulted as commissions for houses cast in a recognizably Scottish mould multiplied. From the middle of the century, Baronial was everywhere in demand.

A fire at Buchanan Castle in 1850 gave *William Burn* the opportunity to realize his largest and last commission in Stirling District. Little more than the high entrance tower with its bartizans and pedimented eaves dormers survives; enough to reveal Baronial intention without Brycean invention. In 1852, the accommodation at Dunglass Castle, which had been repaired and reinhabited in the 1830s, was further improved; the enlargement, though small, was Baronial. Six years later *Charles Wilson* and *David Thomson* began the restoration of the abandoned ruins of Duntreath Castle, adding a new wing and gatehouse in a manner sympathetic to the original medieval buildings. With no need to concern itself with any of the niceties of historical conservation, *James Smith*'s Overtoun

House, built near Dumbarton, 1859–62, is immense, confident and 69
rudely ebullient with all the creative benefits of Billings. Blair
Drummond House, 1868–72, by *James C. Walker*, is large, too, with
a four-storey E entrance tower reminiscent of Burn. Callendar
House at Falkirk, where improvements in internal planning had
been made in 1841–3 with the introduction of a central stair hall
permitting access to the principal rooms to be gained from a landing rather than through each other, was given its final form by
*Brown & Wardrop*, 1869–77. It is widely and impressively sym- 66
metrical and rightly described as 'Frenchified', yet the cylindrical
stair towers with high candle-snuffer roofs at the ends of this
expansive façade, seem Scottish too. Perhaps this very ambivalence
of categorization is not surprising, serving as it does to recall the
Franco-Scots origins of the Baronial tradition.

Among many other Baronial Revival interventions and transformations are the W wing of Argaty House near Doune carried
out in the early 1860s, *William Spence*'s towered additions to
Cameron House on Loch Lomond in 1866–7, a comprehensive
remodelling of the C17 Kilbryde Castle by *Andrew Heiton Jun.* in
1877, the rebuilding of Cromlix House by *Brown & Wardrop* in 1874
and, at Mugdock Castle in the late 1870s, the 'Old Scotch' house
created by *James Sellars*. When it came to a new build, extremes
were possible; the style that could conjure up picturesque fairytale
delight at Broom Hall, a mini-castle with a tall, thin, Rapunzel-
turreted tower built below the Ochils in 1874 for a mill-owner in
Menstrie, could also wallow in the gargantuan vulgarity of Dalnair
House, Croftamie, 1884. This range of scale and interpretation,
coupled with the flexible uncodified nature of the style, ensured
that the popularity of Baronial did not wane. Edinbarnet House,
for example, was completed by *John J. Burnet* (admittedly for the
second time) as late as 1889–91, while *Ebenezer Simpson*'s contemporary Dollarbeg, *c.* 1890, indulges itself to the full, piling
Pelion on Ossa in an outrageous display of Baronial bluster.

Dollarbeg is the last C19 Baronial Revival mansion to be built in
Stirling and Central Scotland. It marks the almost absurd summit
of confidence in the style and, indeed, the beginning of the end for
the country house idea. The thesis that architecture might be
invested with some national characteristics continued to appeal,
but with changing social conditions and a corresponding shift in
patronage away from the large, rambling estate residence to the
suburban villa this tended to express itself in a softer, more vernacular Scottishness. A few older houses were still recast in Baronial
dress. Simpson himself reshaped Auchentroig House, Buchlyvie in
this manner, 1901–3, while the facelift that *David Barclay* gave to
Gartmore House, 1901–2, grafted Baronial elements on to a frontispiece tower otherwise Franco-Italianate in character. But now, as
the influence of the ARTS and CRAFTS MOVEMENT spread N of
the border, the cottage began to seem a more fitting model for design
than the castle. Simple slated roofs, white, harled or roughcast walls,
perhaps a crowstepped gable or turnpike stair, were often enough
to identify as Scottish those few country houses still being built.
*H. E. Clifford*'s turn-of-the-century Arntamie, W of Port of Menteith,

has cone-roofed rounds and a low pyramid-roofed entrance tower. Bridgend of Teith, Doune, by *Robert S. Lorimer*, 1902–3, has overtones of Voysey. At Kilmaronock House, 1901, the bellcast leaded dome over the round entrance tower is certainly Scots, though the two-storey glazing grid to the hall has a rough-and-ready Lutyens look. Bargeboarded gables and half-timbering make *John A. Campbell*'s 1903 enlargement of Duncryne House near Gartocharn more decidedly English. Perhaps more villa than country house, Boghall near Baldernock, built in random masonry, 1907, remains Scottish with crowstep gables, corbelled corners, and catslide-roofed dormers. So, too, in a more relaxed way, are the revisions made at Invertrossachs House, near Kilmahog, in 1911.

70      BETWEEN THE WARS only one country house commands serious critical attention. This is Gribloch near Kippen, 1937–9, designed by *Basil Spence* (in consultation with the American architect *Perry Duncan*) for a steel magnate able to indulge himself in what had by now become an anomalous lifestyle. The white walls of the vernacular are here more polemical. In place of gabled slopes, parapets simulate the flat-roofed asceticism of the International Style. But much is pretence, the aesthetic effect more that of an effete late-onset Georgian taste than hard-edged European Modernism. Near Blanefield, the contemporary Levern Towers is no more attuned to the spirit of the age; the best that can be said for its latter-day Baronialism is that it is at least vigorous in form.

Only a handful of private houses were built in the country in the first two decades AFTER 1945. Those that were erected were conservative in mood. Boquhan House, 1959–63, aspires to an anachronistic classicism but cannot accept its strict disciplines. In a radical transformation of Mill of Argaty, near Doune, 1958–60, *William H. Kininmonth* perpetuates something of the pleasant but pusillanimous Modernism of Spence's Gribloch. On the other hand, at much the same time, *Jack Holmes* is more adventurous; Deil's Craig Dam, Strathblane, is a small house but boldly planar in its waterside setting. A decade later, *Morris & Steedman*'s Principal's House on the University of Stirling's campus, recasts the traditional L-plan in sleek and stylish terms. Less ambitious but no less of an achievement, Little Carbeth, built near Killearn, 1977–8, by the *Boys, Jarvis Partnership*, marks a return to the rural vernacular; simple, elegantly modern and altogether convincing.

The earliest country house INTERIORS are those of the C17 at Kinneil House and Bannockburn House. Wall paintings of the 1620s in a room of the N range at Kinneil attempt to simulate panelling and plasterwork. Half a century later at Bannockburn there is some splendid plasterwork, its design and execution evidently related to contemporary work at Holyrood Palace. Above the rose and bracket cornice of what was the Drawing Room is a magnificent ceiling, oval at the centre, richly modelled with flowers, fruit and foliage in high relief. In the Library is a second splendid plaster ceiling in similar style.

At Strathleven House, which at the turn of the C18 set a new standard of pedimented dignity for the country house, some of the original long-neglected classical interiors (though not those of the state apartment) are now restored. These include the Hall's hanging stone staircase, its timber balustrade carved with roses and foliage, and the wall panelling in the Pine Room and Oak Room. The ornamental character of the oak panelling, which is articulated by Corinthian pilasters and carved in the frieze with fruit, flowers and angels below a rose and bracket cornice, bears a marked likeness to that installed at Sir William Bruce's Kinross House.

From the rest of the C18 there is, however, surprisingly little of note. At Touch House, 1747, an elegant elliptical staircase of cantilevered treads rises at the centre of the plan. The walls of both the Dining Room and Drawing Room are panelled full height in pine, the frieze of the former carved with acorns and oak leaves. Both rooms have plaster ceilings with tendril-light Rococo motifs by *Thomas Clayton*. There is, too, some mid-C18 timber panelling in the Dining Room at Gargunnock House and a plaster ceiling with scroll motifs on a rose and bracket cornice.

The decorative impact of the early C19 Gothic Revival is much more in evidence. Several houses have entrance halls with plaster vaulting. At Airth Castle, 1807–9, the vault is groined; at Balloch Castle, 1808–9, ribs rise from cluster shaft columns; there are fanned squinches at Ross Priory, 1810–16; while at Powfoulis Manor, *c.* 1820, the plaster vault springs from corbelstones carved in medieval manner with expressive faces. At both Balloch and nearby Ross Priory there are Gothic fireplaces and pointed-arched panelling on some of the doors. Friezes, cornices and ceilings at Balloch are ornamented with tracery and vine motifs, the latter reappearing at Boturich Castle in the 1830s. In the same decade Gothic becomes Tudor in the panelled plaster ceilings at Meiklewood House, but plaster vaulting is still in vogue with fan and pendant forms appearing over the upper landing of the main staircase. Behind Romanesque towers and rows of round-arched windows, the abandoned apartments of Lennox Castle, 1837–41, have a number of vaulted and compartmented Tudor ceilings; more ribs, bosses, fans and pendants.

The interiors created in the C19 remodelling of Callendar House, Falkirk, say much about changing stylistic preferences. Two major phases of reconstruction and refurbishment were carried out; the first, 1825–8, by *David Hamilton*, the second, 1841–3, by *Patrick Wilson*. The earlier decorative treatment is the more orthodoxly classical: foliage, urns and anthemia ornament the plasterwork in the Morning Room, there are swagged friezes and corniced doorpieces in the Drawing Room, and, in what was probably the late C17 entrance hall, an egg-and-dart cornice. In the Library, 67 Hamilton set pilastered bookcases along the walls below a coffered barrel-vaulted ceiling of oak. *Wilson*'s timber panelling on the walls and ceiling of the main stair hall is, however, Jacobean in character with strapwork enrichment.

Among several later decorative schemes that remain relatively unscathed is the Drawing Room at Dalmoak House, Renton, 1866–9, which has a splendid gorge cornice of acanthus leaves and a white marble chimneypiece lavishly carved with floral ornament. From the 1880s, the well stair introduced by *R. Rowand*

*Anderson* at Kippenross House and the imperial staircase and hall at Balfunning House merit mention for their spatial impact. The character of many rooms, especially those of Baronial Revival houses, is indiscriminately classical, often Mannerist, confidently robust if not exactly elegant in form. By far the most memorable late Victorian interior is that at Airthrey Castle where *David Thomson* destroyed much of Robert Adam's work but left an astonishing eclectic legacy that seems almost as much museum as it is refurbishment. The oak-panelled walls lining Thomson's irregularly shaped but spacious Hall, Flemish in style and surmounted by a leather frieze of umbrous richness, are an immediate delight. Elsewhere in the house, a fascinating assortment of decorative art of varied provenance – Italian, German, Flemish, Arabic – can be discovered and enjoyed. The C20 has nothing to compare with
71 this. The Hall of *Basil Spence*'s Gribloch House, with its lacily balustraded curving stair rising against the light, preserves a genuine period feel, though the comfortable 'good taste' of the late 1930s, however respectably elegant, seems no more than bland compensation for the vigorous interior design of the Victorian country house.

When first built, many houses enjoyed both the natural beauties of their rural location and the more calculated pleasures of landscaped PARKLAND and WOODLAND. But few proprietors have been able to sustain or maintain such privilege into the C20. The policies at Alloa Tower laid out from *c.* 1700 by the *Earl of Mar*, much influenced by recent French design, entailed a series of far-flung *pas d'oie* axial alignments related to local landmarks such as Clackmannan Tower, Dunmore Tower, Sauchie Tower and Stirling Castle. These magnificent gardens, alleys, meadows and woods have vanished. Several estates planted in later, more picturesque style, and now in whole or in part in the hands of local authorities, have, however, been given a new lease of life: country parks open to the public surround Balloch Castle, Craigend Castle, Overtoun House, the ruinous Plean House and the little that remains of Muiravonside House. Airthrey Castle estate is now the green campus of the University of Stirling. Much of the parkland at Callendar House survives, though encroached upon by tower blocks. Since the mid C20 an industrial estate has surrounded Strathleven House. Well-trimmed lawns and wooded walks, once the prerogative of a private household, now enhance the amenity of those mansions converted to hotel use, as at Airth Castle and Cameron House. More than twenty WALLED GARDENS are still in existence, though most are overgrown and in disrepair. There are no surviving greenhouses of note but hollow walls constructed to conceal heating pipes can still be seen at Rednock House and at Dunmore Park, where two brick-walled gardens sit side by side, one of the mid C18, the other probably 1822. The first of these is wonderfully
72 enhanced by the amazing Pineapple, an outrageously domed pavilion from which the ordered landscape at Dunmore could be viewed. At Ballikinrain the garden walls are now integrated into the construction of a new housing enclave, while at Cameron House they conceal sports and leisure activities. But at Craigend Castle

and Ross Priory, the original gardens have been restored and brought back into production. At Ross Priory a new Moongate has been formed and a pentagonal summerhouse built. Older summerhouses survive at Cardross House and Finnich Malise, the latter rotating to catch the sun.

DOOCOTS, though not specially numerous, are remarkably varied in form. There are C18 examples, square in plan, at Kippen, Bannockburn House, Strathleven House and Blairhoyle, the last still with a pyramid roof. Lectern doocots at Drumquhassle, near Gartness, and Westquarter, also C18, have crowstepped gables and ball finials on the parapeted walls. At Cawder House the plan is circular, at Dougalston, Milngavie, hexagonal, at Gargunnock octagonal; all these from the early C19. 73

Many of the STABLE BLOCKS that originally housed the animals, carts and implements necessary to support life on the estate of local laird or *parvenu* landowner still stand. While some are ruinous, others have fared better; better, indeed, than the estate mansion, their size and scale rendering them more amenable to some continued use long after the demolition of the country house they once served. Almost all date from the fifty years between 1780 and 1830, though the roofless offices at Strathleven House carry the date 1727. Two plan types predominate: a square or nearly square yard enclosed by ranges of offices on all four sides or an open U-plan court. The composition is classical with a frontal range given some form of architectural emphasis on the axis of entry. *William Stirling I*'s stable block at Doune Lodge, 1807–9, is the outstand- 74 ing example: at the centre, above a pedimented entrance archway, is a tall octagonal clock tower and spire; on the flanks, hip-roofed pavilions. Perhaps only slightly later in date, the still surviving stable block of Tillicoultry House, with its three-bay frontispiece and strangely phallic cupola, is scarcely less distinguished. Entry arches can be semicircular, segmental, elliptical or four-centred. At Plean House, where the stables are otherwise almost totally degraded, a segmental arch set between coupled Roman Doric pilasters still makes an impressive portal. Above the pend entries to stable yards the symmetry of the façade may be stressed by some form of gable, pedimented as at Touch House, crowstepped as at Muiravonside House and Balfunning House, and frequently, as is the case at Dalmoak House, penetrated by pigeon entries. A pyramid roof may be enough to stress the centre but some form of tower, sometimes incorporating a belfry or perhaps a doocot, often adds a more vertical accent. At the ruinous stables of Inverardoch House near Doune, an octagonal belfry tower surmounts a barrel-vaulted entrance on each side of which are convex walls indented with niches.

This façade formula remains at first largely unaffected by changes in stylistic preference. The late C18 stables at Cardross House, and those at Tullichewan Castle, 1808–9, Craigend Castle, 1812, Lanrick Castle, *c.* 1820, and Dunmore Park, *c.* 1825, all conform despite their differing interpretations of Gothic. Craigend and Dunmore are both battlemented but Tullichewan's central tower is a thin kiosk of open lancet arches with a crenellated tiara.

Asymmetry begins to appear with the Baronial Revival. *Bryce*'s
bartizaned clock tower at Ballikinrain, more municipal than rural,
does not rise above but beside the arched portal to the yard. At
the home farm of Keir House, the tall clock tower sits not at the
centre but on the corner of the cattle court.

A few buildings remain in agricultural use. Some have been
converted to housing, among them Blairhoyle, Rednock, Dalmoak
and Blair Drummond. At Craigend the court of offices has been
adapted to form the focus of a leisure centre while the stables at
Sauchieburn House now function as a riding school. The successor
to the stables block, the MOTOR HOUSE or garage, appears in
1907 at Meiklewood House as a half-timbered gabled structure,
and at Gribloch, where staff flats are provided above the cars, in
the white-walled livery of Thirties Modernism.

LODGES generally echo, or rather preview, the style of the
country house at the foot of whose driveway they stand sentinel.
The S Lodge at Keir House with its pilastered drum and nearby
estate gates soberly dignified by Greek Doric columns, 1820, is the
best of the classical examples, of which there are few. Much more
in evidence are Baronial crowstepped gables and drum towers. The
W Lodge at Ballikinrain Castle, built in the 1860s, is outstanding,
the gabled dwelling linked to the battlemented walls and gateway
that guard the driveway. Less intimidating are a number of smaller,
later lodges built in a softer Scots idiom: harled vernacular at
Balfunning House, *c.* 1905, perhaps by *Robert S. Lorimer*, perhaps
*William Leiper*; the same at Touch House, with a slated bell roof,
almost certainly a consequence of *Lorimer*'s involvement in the
late 1920s; and the Mid Lodge which served Auchentorlie House
at Bowling, 1925, constructed in random rubble with a red-tiled
bell roof, by the Dumbarton County Architect, *Joseph Weekes*.

# ROADS, RAILWAYS, CANALS AND HARBOURS

In Stirling and Central Scotland before the late C18 roads were
few and the rivers often more convenient thoroughfares for travel
and the transport of goods. However, roads did exist. The Roman
military way behind and parallel to the Antonine Wall and the
Roman road leading N through Dunblane into Perthshire and Angus
survived despite neglect and there were established tracks or drove
roads along which cattle from the Highlands were herded into S
Scotland and England. There is clear evidence that, by the time of
the Wars of Independence of the late C13 and early C14, there existed
roads, probably gravelled, capable of carrying wheeled traffic, which
extended from the Borders at least as far N as Stirling. In 1304 wages
for the army of Edward I were conveyed from York to Stirling in
two carts, each pulled by five horses, the journey taking only five
days. In the same year twenty-one carts carried a large siege engine
from Linlithgow to Stirling. It seems probable that the 'carte road'
from Edinburgh to Stirling and Doune that existed by the begin-

ning of the C18 was medieval. The existence of a BRIDGE over the River Forth at Stirling in 1297 is well attested by the battle to which it gave its name and accounts of that battle suggest that it was narrow and constructed of wood, possibly with stone abutments. Probably the area's earliest surviving stone bridge, though widened and reconstructed, is the bridge over the Allan Water at Dunblane erected by Bishop Finlay Dermoch in 1409, a single semicircular arch, the abutments founded on rock above the usual water level of the river. The original width of the roadway between the parapets was *c*. 3.05m., amply broad enough for a single cart but probably too narrow for two-way traffic. Much larger and broader, its carriageway 4.57m. wide, is the Old Bridge over the River 75 Forth at Stirling which was rebuilt in the C15. It is four-span, the moulded segmental arches springing from abutments and piers rising from massive oval bases that also support triangular cutwaters, the centre cutwater on each side surmounted by a rectangular buttress that provides a pedestrian refuge at parapet level. These refuges originally rose higher as crowstep-gabled towers, an architectural flourish probably provided as a display of burghal pride rather than for utility. At each end stood a gateway at which tolls could be collected but also emphasizing the importance of the bridge as the approach to the royal burgh from the N.

Two bridges of the early C16, the Old Bridge at Bannockburn of 1516 and the Bridge of Teith at Doune of 1535, were built by Robert Spittal, tailor to the Crown, which may have prompted his improvements to the road system, the Bannockburn bridge providing a crossing for wheeled traffic over the Forth on the road between Linlithgow and Stirling, the Bridge of Teith access for wheeled traffic from Stirling to Doune Castle, at that time a royal stronghold commanding the route from central Scotland to the W Highlands. Both are relatively narrow (carriageways of *c*. 2.9m. and 3.05m.), the Old Bridge at Bannockburn a single segmental arch, the Bridge of Teith two-span, the abutments founded on rock at or just below the summer water level of the river, the central pier of the Bridge of Teith founded on rock at a lower level, construction probably having been carried out with the aid of a coffer dam to divert the river round the site. The land route to Stirling on the N side of the Forth was eased in the C16 by the Old Bridge near Tullibody, a combination of causeways and arches carrying a road across the River Devon and its flood plain.

In 1617 an act of the Scottish Parliament placed an obligation to maintain roads in each parish on its inhabitants under the supervision of the local Justices of the Peace and also stipulated that roads to markets and sea ports be 20 feet (6m.) broad. The legislation was further strengthened by acts of 1669 and 1676, which gave responsibility for oversight to Commissioners of Supply (local landowners charged with valuation of lands for taxation purposes) as well as the Justices of the Peace. However, these acts produced only a fairly rudimentary and indifferently maintained road system, dependent on the work of peasant farmers whose labour and carts could be provided only at certain seasons of the year. In the mid C18 these locally constructed and maintained roads were supplemented

in Stirling and Central Scotland by new MILITARY ROADS constructed by soldiers under the direction of *Major William Caulfield*
and intended, by their linking of the Highlands to central Scotland,
both to make easier military control over potentially disaffected or
Jacobite areas and to bring trade and civilization to the Highlands.
A military road from Stirling to Crieff was constructed in 1741–2,
another from Dumbarton along the w side of Loch Lomond to
Inveraray in 1744–50, the road from Stirling via Crianlarich and
Tyndrum to Fort William in 1748–53 and, after Caulfield's retire-
ment, a new road from Stirling via Kippen and Drymen to
Dumbarton in 1770–80. Bridges along both the local and military
roads became more common in the C17 and C18, generally built
with abutments and piers standing on solid rock foundations, their
stonework usually of rubble instead of the dressed masonry of their
C15 and C16 predecessors. Often they have narrow carriageways and
limited architectural ambition. One of the simplest is the Bridge of
Ardoch erected at Doune in 1735, a narrow humpbacked single span.
Several were of two or three spans, the arches generally segmental,
usually with triangular cutwaters and plain parapets (e.g. Luggie
Bridge at Kirkintilloch of 1672, Cobleland Bridge at Gartmore of
1752, Cardross Bridge at Dykehead of 1774 or Gartchonzie Bridge,
Invertrossachs, of 1777). Kinbuck Bridge of 1752 has exceptionally
heavy cutwaters. The Low Bridge of Gonachan built in 1750–1 at
Fintry is adorned with hoodmoulds over the arches and one keystone is decorated with a palmette under a panel surmounted by
a stone carved with a human head. The military bridge over the
Endrick Water at Drymen of 1765 (reconstructed in 1928–9) is of
five arches. So too is Drip Old Bridge at Craigforth, built by public
subscription in 1773, the design decidedly architectural with symmetrical side elevations, the arches increasing in size towards the centre
where the cutwaters are carried up to form small semi-hexagonal
pedestrian refuges.

A major improvement to the road system took place in the late
C18 and early C19 when acts of Parliament were passed for the
making of TURNPIKE ROADS, often replacements for existing
roads, by bodies of trustees who recouped the costs of construc-
tion and maintenance by levying tolls. By the 1790s Stirling and
Central Scotland contained turnpike roads from Edinburgh to
Falkirk and thence to Glasgow and Stirling, from Glasgow to
Stirling, from Glasgow via Bearsden to Kilmaronock, from Glasgow
to Kippen, from Glasgow to Balfron and a new turnpike road to
replace the military road from Stirling to Dumbarton. In the early
C19 the network was extended by new roads from Stirling into
Clackmannanshire and from Dumbarton to Helensburgh. Some
TOLLHOUSES survive, e.g. an early C19 one with a canted bay
window at Port of Menteith, one of the earlier C19 in Glasgow
Road, Kirkintilloch, its dummy windows designed to display the
charges, or the Tudor Gothic tollhouse by *Peter Frederick Robinson*,
1831, at Blair Drummond. Construction of new roads was accompanied by new bridges, many replaced in C20 attempts to further
upgrade the road network. One major survivor is the New Bridge
built at Stirling in 1831–2 to a design prepared five years before by

*Robert Stevenson*, its five segmental arches clad with rough-faced whinstone. Also of rough-faced masonry but of startling appearance is the 'New Road' Bridge at Bannockburn designed by *Thomas Telford* in 1819, its roundheaded arch over the river surmounted by a large circular opening under the carriageway. Later in the C19 and in the C20 many existing bridges were widened or rebuilt and some new ones constructed. Generally these are unexciting but the Erskine Bridge over the Clyde at Old Kilpatrick, by *Freeman,* 77 *Fox & Partners*, 1967–71, is monumental yet slender, the Artizan Bridge of 1972–4 at Dumbarton, by *Babtie, Shaw & Morton* in association with *Garner, Preston & Strebel*, an elegant crossing of the River Leven, and the design of the Bonhill Bridge of 1987 at Alexandria, by *Strathclyde Regional Council*, pays homage to its two predecessors, a suspension bridge of 1836 and a bowstring lattice girder bridge of 1898.

Before the construction of turnpike roads and the C19 development of a railway system most goods and many travellers in the area, as elsewhere in Scotland, were transported by boat. The River Forth bisects the E end of the area and the River Clyde defines its SW boundary. HARBOURS were built along these rivers from the Middle Ages. The royal burgh of Dumbarton, founded in 1222, was sited at the confluence of the River Leven with the Clyde, the mouth of the Leven providing a sheltered anchorage. Along the Forth, Blackness is on record as a landing place by 1304 and became the port of the royal burgh of Linlithgow in 1389. Bo'ness, just to the W, was described as a port by 1565. Further up the River Forth, Alloa, that river's W natural harbour easily accessible to larger vessels, certainly served as a port by 1502 and probably had done so for many years before. Small boats could reach Stirling, which may be identifiable as the *Giudi* mentioned by Bede in the C8, and the existence of a harbour or quays there seems implicit in documents of the mid C12. Most of these early harbours or ports probably consisted of little more than naturally sheltered anchorages, perhaps with wooden or stone-built quays along the shore. However, Dumbarton had a shipyard by 1505, a pier seems to have been built at Blackness in the early C17 and Airth possessed a shipyard by 1723. Construction of a harbour, including a tidal basin and a sluice to wash out silt, at Bo'ness was carried out in 1707–33, probably some years after similar work had been carried out at Alloa. These harbours were largely rebuilt in the later C19 but by then were far outstripped in importance by two harbours, Grangemouth and Bowling, which had been begun in the late C18 at the E and W ends of the Forth & Clyde Canal. Each developed in the C19 into a complex of docks impressive for sheer size.

Two major CANALS were cut through the S part of the area in the late C18 and early C19. The Forth & Clyde Canal, designed by *John Smeaton*, was constructed in 1768–75 from Grangemouth to Stockingfield in Glasgow, and extended W to Bowling on the Clyde by *Robert Whitworth* in 1786–90. The 62.4km. of terrain which it passes through is rolling rather than dramatic and the canal, originally equipped with thirty-nine locks, performs no feat of constructional drama. The 50.7km.-long Union Canal, designed

by *Hugh Baird*, was constructed in 1818–22 as a link between Edinburgh and the Forth & Clyde Canal which it joins at Camelon in Falkirk. Like the Forth & Clyde Canal, its progress through the area is mostly unobtrusive and its final stretch to Camelon is
76 through a 640m.-long tunnel but its entry by the Avon Aqueduct near Muiravonside is assertive, carried on twenty segmental arches supported on tapering piers of hammer-dressed masonry. The bridges which cross it are plain except for one near Hallglen, the keystones of its arch carved with laughing and weeping human heads. Other canals were projected but not executed. One, suggested in 1835, would have connected Stirling to the Forth & Clyde Canal. Another, first proposed in 1815 when *Robert Stevenson* surveyed the route and again considered in 1889–90 and 1946–7, would have been cut from Stirling to Loch Lomond. Both the Forth & Clyde and the Union canals were closed to traffic in the C20 and the ladder of locks that connected them removed but the waterways were then restored, with much use of cement at locks and bridges, and reopened in 2001 when a wheel of gondola containers was erected to carry boats from one canal to the other.

RAILWAYS developed to serve the area in the C19. The earliest, the Monkland & Kirkintilloch Railway, designed by *Thomas Grainger* and opened in 1826, was constructed to carry coal from the mining district near Airdrie (Lanarkshire) to the Forth & Clyde Canal at Kirkintilloch whence it could be shipped to Edinburgh. This railway's wagons were at first drawn by horses, which were replaced by locomotives in 1831. The Slamannan Railway, opened in 1840, was also intended to transport coal, in this case from Airdriehill (on the Monkland–Ballochney Railway in Lanarkshire) to Causewayend on the Union Canal. Soon after, main railway lines through the area were constructed. The Edinburgh & Glasgow Railway, linking Scotland's two principal cities and running through Polmont, Falkirk, Kirkintilloch and Bishopbriggs, was opened in 1842. Six years later the Caledonian Railway opened a line from Glasgow N to Greenhill near Falkirk where it joined the Scottish Central Railway's line to Stirling, Dunblane and Perth, constructed in 1845–8 under the supervision of *Joseph Locke* and *John Edward Errington*. In the SW of the area the Caledonian & Dunbartonshire Railway from Bowling to Dumbarton and then N to Balloch was opened in 1850 and a line from Dumbarton to Helensburgh in 1858. In the E of the area, a line was opened in 1850 from Dunfermline and Oakley (Fife) to Alloa and extended W to Stirling in 1852. The Forth & Clyde Junction Railway from Stirling W via Buchlyvie to join the Caledonian & Dunbartonshire Railway opened in 1856. Construction of minor and branch lines accompanied or quickly followed that of the main routes. In 1847–8 the Edinburgh & Glasgow Railway opened branches to Shieldhill and Lennoxtown, while the Slamannan & Borrowstounness Railway cutting diagonally across S Stirlingshire was constructed in 1851, the same year in which a branch line was opened from Alloa to Tillicoultry. Branch lines from the Caledonian Railway to Denny and from Dunblane to Callander were completed in 1858, a branch line from the Alloa–Stirling line to Alva and another from Glasgow to Bearsden and

Milngavie in 1863, the Callander & Oban Railway begun in 1865, and the line to Lennoxtown extended W as the Blane Valley Railway to Blanefield in 1866. The Alloa–Tillicoultry branch was extended to Dollar in 1869 and two years later E from Dollar to Kinross to join the North British Railway's line from Edinburgh to Perth, and the line from Callander was extended N to Killin in 1870. Further railway construction continued through the last three decades of the C19. The Kelvin Valley Railway from Glasgow to Lenzie and Kilsyth opened in 1878, the line to Killearn was extended to Aberfoyle in 1882, a line from Alloa to Larbert with a viaduct over the River Forth was constructed in 1885, a line from Killin E along Loch Tay in 1886, a line from Alloa to Kincardine-on-Forth (Fife) in 1893, and the Lanarkshire & Dunbartonshire Railway from Glasgow to Clydebank, then on to join the line to Dumbarton in 1896.

Many of these railways faced financial difficulties from an early stage and, by the later C20, rapidly increasing competition from the roads. Sadly, if not surprisingly, most of the smaller lines were closed after *c.* 1960 and the opening of the Bo'ness & Kinneil Railway is testimony to the determination of railway enthusiasts rather than the likely prelude to a new expansion of the network.

RAILWAY VIADUCTS survive although not all are still in use. One of the earliest and most impressive is the twenty-three-span Avon Viaduct near Linlithgow Bridge, designed by *Grainger & Miller* in 1838 for the Edinburgh & Glasgow Railway, its stonework of stugged and channelled ashlar. Similar but of only eight spans is the same firm's contemporary Castlecary Viaduct near Haggs. Aggressively rough stonework characterizes *Locke & Errington*'s viaducts of 1845–8 for the Scottish Central Railway, the viaduct at Larbert of sixteen segmental arches, the Dunblane viaduct of four. Rock-faced masonry was used for the two viaducts (of three and twelve spans) of 1869–70 in Glen Ogle near Lochearnhead, their arches again segmental. A third viaduct in Glen Ogle is of 1901–5, constructed of concrete and curved, its nine arches semicircular. The laminated timber arches of 1847–8 of the Dalreoch Viaduct over the Leven at Dumbarton were replaced in steel *c.* 1870. At Bowling Basin in 1896 *Crouch & Hogg* designed a viaduct of segmental arches and lattice girders, including a swing bridge, for the Lanarkshire & Dunbartonshire Railway.

RAILWAY STATIONS, often designed by the railway companies' own engineers, were architectural expressions of the companies' corporate identity. The station put up *c.* 1842 at Polmont by the Edinburgh & Glasgow Railway is piend-roofed Georgian survival, the Scottish Central Railway's Dunblane Station of *c.* 1848 brick-built with crowstepped gables, the Milngavie Junction Railway's terminus at Milngavie a broad-eaved *cottage orné*. In contrast to these villa-like buildings, the Lanarkshire & Dunbartonshire Railway's red brick and sandstone station at Clydebank, designed by *John J. Burnet* in 1896, is a public edifice, albeit on a small scale. It is V-plan, the hinge provided by the pyramid-roofed hexagonal booking hall, its entrances canopied, the corbelled and panelled parapet decorated with carved foliage and breaking into round bartizans at the corners. Much larger but without the same punch is *James Miller*'s Stirling Railway Station of 1913–16, its exterior low and sprawling despite its battlement and crowstepped gables. This is only a front, however, for a masterful manipulation of light and space inside, with glazed roofs over the sinuously curved internal structures around the semicircular concourse.

MOTORWAYS have been the late C20's major contribution to the communications infrastructure of Stirling and Central Scotland. The M8 from Edinburgh to Glasgow and the M9 from Edinburgh to Stirling were both opened in 1970 and the M80 and M9 extension running N from Haggs past Stirling to just S of Dunblane in 1974. They have contributed little to the architectural excitement of the area but much to its development as Silicon Glen, the home of new industry and dormitory suburbs.

## BURGH AND VILLAGE BUILDINGS

Burghs, formally constituted towns with trading rights, divided into two types. The first, ROYAL BURGHS, holding property and privileges directly from the Crown, to which they paid taxes and duties, were founded from the C12 as part of David I's introduction of feudal administration and control. These communities enjoyed a monopoly of foreign trade within their extensive surrounding areas and were colonized first by merchants, many from outside Scotland. The merchant guild of each burgh would continue to dominate civil government until 1833, though representatives of craft incorporations had been admitted to town councils by the C16. Typically, a royal burgh was laid out as a single street wide enough to enfold the local market (Broad Street in Stirling is well named) with a chain of narrow but long plots of land (riggs or tofts) at r. angles to it, each containing the house and garden of a burgess. Important royal burghs were founded at Stirling, *c.* 1125, and Dumbarton, 1222, both castellar strongholds of the Crown.

BURGHS OF BARONY or REGALITY* were founded by lairds, nobles, abbeys and cathedrals. In the relatively fertile region of Stirling and Central Scotland there were many such burghs: Kirkintilloch, *c.* 1212 (refounded 1526), Dunblane, *c.* 1300, Port of Menteith, 1467 (refounded 1680), Alloa, 1497, Clackmannan, 1511, Airth, 1597, Falkirk, 1600, Doune, 1611, Tillicoultry, 1634, Bo'ness, 1668, Old Kilpatrick and Buchlyvie, both 1672, Gargunnock, 1677, Killin, 1694, and Dollar, 1702. The inhabitants of these burghs were allowed to take part in domestic trade and fairs were held each year. Most remained rural and agricultural in character, housing a handful of craftsmen. A few became centres of specialized manufacture, e.g. Doune for pistols and leather-working, while others, such as the ports at Alloa and Bo'ness, were by the late C17 able to challenge the royal burghs' monopolies.

---

* The distinction was one of nomenclature. In the case of a burgh of barony its feudal superior held his lands from the Crown as a barony, in the case of a burgh of regality the feudal superior held his lands as a regality.

From the early years of the C18, improvements in land and animal husbandry began to change the face of the countryside. A combination of reformed estate management and speculative enterprise led to the establishment of many PLANNED VILLAGES; among them, Thornhill, Alva, Strathyre and Gartmore, the last a good example of the simple orthogonal layout often adopted by improving landowners. The plan of Callander, laid down in the 1730s, was ambitious enough to introduce a central square but Laurieston, founded in 1756, was no more than a ribbon development along the road from Falkirk to Linlithgow. Some villages served a specific industrial need. Grangemouth, laid out on a grid-iron plan in the 1770s, was designed as a port at the E end of the new Forth & Clyde Canal. Communities in Deanston, Balfron, Fintry, Lennoxtown, Renton and Duntocher worked in the local textile mills that developed rapidly in the late C18 and early C19. Stenhousemuir housed workers at the Carron Ironworks, Chartershall nailmakers, and Kennet's single terraced row of c. 1800 miners. Picturesque estate villages were built at Dunmore and Muirhouses, their relaxed scale adopted on a larger scale at Westquarter, a miners' garden suburb of 1936.

Thirteen PARLIAMENTARY BURGHS were created by the 1832 Reform Act, all existing burghs of barony or regality and including Falkirk, to add to the royal burghs already represented in Parliament. The 1833 Act provided for the election of town councils in each of the burghs and allowed for the adoption of a 'police system'. This made councils responsible for the employment of police constables, the provision of fire engines, and the administration of lighting, paving, cleansing, drainage and sewerage, with further responsibilities added by the 1850s. By an act of 1850, 'populous places', defined as having more than 1,200 inhabitants, could also adopt a 'police system', those that did becoming POLICE BURGHS, including Callander (1866), Bridge of Allan (1870), Grangemouth (1872), Milngavie (1875), Denny and Dunipace (1876), Alva (1882) and Clydebank (1886). The adoption of burgh status came late to the Glasgow dormitories of Bearsden (1958) and Bishopbriggs (1964).

Effective local government in villages and rural areas began only in 1667 under the newly appointed Commissioners of Supply (usually the major landowners). Their civic responsibilities were taken over by elected COUNTY COUNCILS in 1889. Elected parochial School Boards supervised education from 1872 to 1918 when they were succeeded by county education authorities who in turn passed this responsibility on to the county councils in 1929. In 1975 burgh and county councils were superseded by a two-tier system of district and regional councils, themselves replaced in 1996 by unitary authorities (in Stirling and Central Scotland, the present Stirling, Falkirk, Clackmannanshire, East Dunbartonshire and West Dunbartonshire).

*Public Buildings*

In many burghs founded before the C19 MARKET CROSSES provided a focus for trade and public affairs. The majority took the form of a finialled shaft standing on a stepped base; many were probably of wood but some were constructed in stone. An early stone example, probably of *c.* 1600, is the Old Market Cross at Airth, its shaft much weathered, its head carved in a crudely cubic manner. The shaft and base of the Cross at Stirling were replaced in 1891 but the original C16 finial carved with a unicorn supporting the royal arms survives. At the burghs of barony of Doune, Alloa, Clackmannan and Airth, the crosses, all probably of the C17, display the arms of their feudal superiors.

78

TOLBOOTHS or TOWN HOUSES, designed to accommodate the meetings of town councils and courts, to deal with the receipt of taxes and tolls and to provide prison cells, were built near the market crosses in all royal burghs and larger burghs of barony. Prominent towers and steeples could express civic pride, notably at Clackmannan, whose bell-roofed tower of 1680 survives, and at Stirling's Town House, by *Sir William Bruce*, of 1703–5, where an early dourly regular classical building is raised to municipal distinction by its high square corner tower. In Falkirk's town house of 1812–14, *David Hamilton* housed council chamber and prison within the splendid, six-stage, Neo-classical steeple (the Town Steeple), still a significant landmark in the burgh's townscape. MUNICIPAL and BURGH BUILDINGS, housing a multitude of civic and administrative functions, appear from the later C19. Many continue to announce their presence with towers. They range from Alloa's small palazzo design by *Thomas Frame & Son*, 1872–4 with Roman Renaissance aspirations, to the robust Baronial bulk of *A. & W. Black*'s Burgh Buildings, Falkirk, of 1876–9, with its Frenchy truncated spire. Baronial and Jacobean mix together at Dumbarton (1899–1903) while at Clydebank, *James Miller*'s tempietto-topped corner tower not only cleverly separates one elevational composition from another but makes maximum impact in the long straight-street perspective. Stirling's Municipal Buildings, by *J. Gaff Gillespie*, 1914–18, are even more imposing but confidently eclectic with a strong Scottish cast. The C20 is less rewarding for such buildings, from ponderous Baronial at Denny's Town House, of 1930, to stripped Neo-Georgian at Grangemouth and half-hearted, albeit well-scaled, Modernism at Milngavie Town Hall of 1961–2. More pretentious but less civic, Falkirk's Municipal Buildings by *Baron Bercott & Associates*, 1962, are distinguishable from a contemporary commercial office block only by the mirrored glass front of the Town Hall. Only with the adoption of responsibility for education in 1929, together with an increasing role in the provision of rural and village housing, did the county councils begin to construct COUNTY COUNCIL OFFICES. The very small county of Clackmannanshire put up a correspondingly small-scale but well-detailed Neo-Jacobean building, by *William Kerr* and *John Gray*, in 1926. At Stirling, in 1932, the County Council took over a large villa, Viewforth, to which *James Miller* added a stripped Neo-Georgian wing in 1934–7. In 1968, *A. J. Smith* designed a vast five-storey office block (now Stirling Council Offices) in the grounds. Also of five storeys and very like commercial developments of the time are the offices (now West Dunbartonshire Council Offices)

79

82

87

86

built at Dumbarton by *Lane, Bremner & Garnett* for Dumbarton
County Council in 1962–5. DISTRICT COUNCIL OFFICES, constructed after 1975, range only from the bleak to the dull.

Purpose-built SHERIFF COURT HOUSES and PRISONS were
provided in the major burghs from the early C19. Stirling's former
Court House and Jail was constructed to a design by *Richard
Crichton* in 1806–11, adding a block behind the Town House for
double-height court room and cells, its symmetrical ashlar façade
one of austere Neo-classical elegance. At Dumbarton, *James
Gillespie Graham* and *Robert Scott* designed a pedimented mansion- 84
like court house in 1822–6, with separate prison (now demolished).
As prisons began to acquire a reformatory function besides that of
incarceration, more sanitary and humane conditions prevailed and
in 1839 a General Board of Directors of Prisons in Scotland was
established to ensure better standards of criminal detention. The
new prisons at Dunblane, by *William Stirling II*, 1842–4, and at
Stirling (now the Old Jail), by *Thomas Brown Jun.*, 1845–7, were 81
scarcely less grim than their predecessors, however, the latter a
castellated fort, sombre, authoritarian and forbidding. In 1860 the
Sheriff Court Houses (Scotland) Act provided proper funding for
new courts. The best of those in Stirling and Central Scotland were
designed by *Brown & Wardrop*. At Alloa, 1862–5, and Stirling,
1874–6, (adapting a design of 1860), their combination of Baronial 85
gables and turrets, steep roofs with French dormers and a scatter-
ing of Flemish strapwork exemplifies the increasingly eclectic nature
of Victorian civic architecture. At Falkirk they are decidedly more
Scottish. A late C20 contrast is provided by *Robert Matthew,
Johnson-Marshall & Partners*' Postmodern Falkirk Sheriff Court
built at Camelon in 1990.

Surviving POLICE STATIONS are mostly C20. Those at Larbert,
by *A. & W. Black*, 1900–1, Denny, by *Ebenezer Simpson*, 1908,
and Bishopbriggs, by *James Lochead*, 1914–15, are small-scale
Jacobean; *A. & W. Black*'s station at Falkirk is much larger and in
a blowsy Italianate idiom. Alexandria, *c.* 1930, and Kirkintilloch,
1934, both by *Joseph Weekes*, have a Scottish character, their low
rural look and roughcast vernacular almost welcoming. But the
late C20 has produced either long runs of repetitive office-block
wallpaper, as at the regional headquarters at Dumbarton and
Stirling, or aggressive blocks, such as that at Bo'ness. At Alloa,
1990 by *Central Regional Council*, attempts are made to camouflage
size in would-be cottagey detail.

A national Government postal service was established in 1808
and sizeable POST OFFICES erected in the larger towns. At Alloa,
the Post Office of 1882 by *Thomas Frame & Son* is Renaissance in
style. Larger post office buildings at Falkirk, *c.* 1893, and Stirling,
1894–5, were by *H.M. Office of Works*. They exhibit no house
style: one a Tudor Gothic concoction with a turreted corner, the
other a smart ashlar-faced palazzo.

Late Georgian urban social life – dancing, card-playing and
conversation – seems to have centred on ASSEMBLY ROOMS
attached to inns and hotels. At Stirling, however, the Athenaeum, 83
designed by *William Stirling I*, was built in 1816–17 as 'a genteel

building of three stories. . .containing two elegant shops with suitable apartments above for an assembly room, library and reading
room with a steeple in the centre'.* This tall steeple, topped by a
1 round belfry and spire, still dominates the view up King Street.
From the mid C19 almost every town and many villages began to
acquire PUBLIC HALLS or INSTITUTES, their accommodation
generally including one or more halls, reading rooms and spaces
for sober recreation. These could be impressive affirmations of
local pride and sometimes of the philanthropy of local citizens.
Presiding over the E approach to the town, the Public Hall at
Alexandria, by *Hugh H. Maclure*, 1862–3, survive in tarnished
grandeur, their high Doric portico a deceptive mask to a later descent
through cinema to bingo hall. Also in Alexandria is a pair of buildings gifted by William Ewing Gilmour for the moral good and self-
improvement of young workers in the local dyeworks and print-
91 works. One, the Ewing Gilmour Institute (now Library), 1881–4,
was designed with an elegant Grecian façade by *Robert Thomson* as
92 a men's institute; the other was a women's institute (now Masonic
Temple), by *John A. Campbell*, 1888–91, imaginatively fusing Scots
Renaissance, Baronial and Arts and Crafts forms. One of the
grandest halls is Stirling's Albert Hall of 1881–3, by *William Simpson*,
built by a joint stock company in a strongly modelled free Italianate
manner. Grangemouth Town Hall, by *A. & W. Black*, 1884–5, is
free classical. In 1888 the local textile magnate, John Thomson
Paton, gifted to Alloa what now seems its incongruously inflated
Town Hall, the front block containing a library, designed by the
English architect *Alfred Waterhouse* in François I style. *George
Washington Browne*'s Bo'ness Town Hall of 1902–4, more like a
church than a civic building, has two lightly domed towers set
between hall and library. In smaller burghs halls were more modest.
Tillicoultry's Popular Institute, 1858–60, was Baronial; its idio-
syncratic tall tower, launched between bartizans by *John Melvin &
Son* some twenty years later, still stands. Clackmannan's utilitarian
Town Hall has a front block, its Jacobean tinged with Art Nouveau
and an ogee-domed cupola centred on the roof, added by *Ebenezer
Simpson* in 1903. The Muir Hall at Doune, 1921–2, is mechanical
Baronial but the red sandstone buttresses, parapets and curvilinear
gables of Dunblane's Victoria Hall, 1926, have a more crafted
look. Late C20 Brutalism appears at Bearsden Public Hall, by
*A. McInnes Gardner & Partners*, 1975.
   In smaller communities VILLAGE HALLS are often the only
buildings to rise above the vernacular, literally so at Buchlyvie Village
Hall, by *Wilson & Stewart*, 1884–5, where a small ogee-domed
tower pops up on the edge of the village. Stylistic pretension varies
following the precedents set by the towns. Lenzie Town Hall,
1892, and the Muirhead Memorial Hall, Dennyloanhead, 1893,
are Jacobean, the Dobbie Hall in Larbert, by *A. & W. Black*, 1900–1,
heavy Baroque. The most attractive examples are those content to
apply an Arts and Crafts gloss to vernacular scale. In the leafy,
almost suburban context of Strathblane, the tiled roofs and half-
timbered gables of the Village Club by the English architects *Davis*

* Extract from Stirling Guildry Records in RCAHMS, *Stirlingshire* i (1963), 303.

*& Emanuel*, 1911, seem almost at home. The Clackmannanshire
halls and institutes at Coalsnaughton, 1907, extended in 1925,
Sauchie, 1925, Alva, 1928, and Fishcross, 1930, all wholly or
partly by *William Kerr* and *John Gray* of *John Melvin & Son*, share
a similar anglicized vocabulary of hipped roofs, harled walls and
multi-paned square bay windows spiced up with some Cape Dutch
gabling. From the second half of the C20 there is nothing of
note save, finally, the Village Hall at Gartocharn, by *Maclachlan &
Monaghan*, 1999–2000, a trim, pyramid-roofed building set neatly
into a gently sloping site.

Halls of a more specialized nature were provided in some towns
and villages. Amongst others of the late C19, DRILL HALLS for
the Argyll and Sutherland Highlanders were erected at Stirling in
1892, with crowstepped gable between conical-roofed drum towers,
and Falkirk (now Falkirk School of Gymnastics) in 1898–9.
Freemasonry has flourished in Stirling and Central Scotland and
there are many purpose-built MASONIC HALLS. The Masonic
Hall, Falkirk, by *Thomas M. Copland*, 1906, provides a swaggering
Baroque centrepiece for one side of Lint Riggs, *Matthew Steele*'s
Masonic Hall at Bo'ness, 1909, is characteristically idiosyncratic
and, in Dumbarton, the severely elegant Masonic Temple by *Garner,
Preston & Strebel*, 1973–4, gives a touch of civic dignity to the town
centre development. In the village of Thornhill the crossroads
tower of Blairhoyle Masonic Hall by *S. Henbest Capper*, 1893, is a
delight, its wide-eaved, red-tiled roof a piquant contrast to the hard-
edged slated streetscape. A reminder of the organized strength
and well-heeled backing of political parties is given by *William
Kerr*'s Liberal Club of 1904 in Alloa, the smooth Jacobean dress 94
exuding a hint of smugness. Evidence of another form of social
concern is provided in St John Street in the Old Town of Stirling
by *Eric S. Bell*'s couthy Scots Boys' Club of 1929.

LIBRARIES and MUSEUMS were the products of philanthropy
and civic largesse. The earliest, Leighton Library in Dunblane,
was built in 1685–7 to house more than 1,200 books collected by
the cleric and scholar Robert Leighton, Archbishop of Glasgow,
from 1670. But until the late C19 this simple harled and crowstep-
gabled structure remained a lonely shrine to scholarship. Then, in
1871–4, *John Lessels* designed Stirling's Smith Art Gallery and
Museum (endowed by the painter and collector Thomas Stewart
Smith), a sober temple to culture, its classical reserve ennobled by
a tetrastyle Doric portico. Perhaps inspired by this example, the
Clackmannanshire Natural History and Archaeological Society
built the Alloa Museum and Library, designed somewhat in the 88
Ægypto-Greek manner of Alexander 'Greek' Thomson by *John
Melvin & Son*, 1874. Twelve years later a Museum Hall (combining art gallery, museum and hall) was put up at nearby Bridge of
Allan, its architect, *Ebenezer Simpson*, confining Grecian allusion
to an interior hidden behind a street façade of *Rundbogenstil* arcading. Although burghs had from 1854 been empowered to levy
rates to provide public libraries, it was only from the 1880s, when
the steel magnate Andrew Carnegie provided generous funding,
that building got under way. The Grangemouth Public Library,
by *A. & W. Black*, 1888–9, incorporates Ionic, Corinthian and

Composite pilasters in a two-storey five-bay front. The former Larbert Public Library, 1902–4, is modestly classical. The libraries
90 at Dumbarton, by *William Reid*, 1908–10, and Clydebank, by *A. McInnes Gardner*, 1912–13, draw on Renaissance sources, the latter
89 with a fine front of giant columns. At Falkirk Library, by *McArthy & Watson*, 1900–2, the mood is Gothic. Part Renaissance, part Tudor, *Harry Ramsay Taylor*'s Stirling Public Library takes full advantage of Carnegie funding, its high walls of mullioned and transomed glazing dramatizing the hillside at Corn Exchange Road. Later libraries are more reserved, even mundane. *Falkirk District*
89 *Council*'s 1992 extension to Falkirk Public Library is sympathetic while the William Patrick Memorial Library at Kirkintilloch, by *Strathkelvin District Council*, 1994, has some Postmodern civic presence.

In the late C20 a number of museums have been formed out of existing buildings but HERITAGE AND VISITOR CENTRES have been the most prominent developments. On the edge of Stirling, national pride is hallowed in the white-walled Modernism of Bannockburn Heritage Centre, by *Wheeler & Sproson*, 1966–7,
102 while at Balloch *Page & Park*'s Lomond Shores Visitor Centre, 1998–2002, acts as a gateway to the Highlands and, perhaps, vehicle for the post-industrial regeneration of the Vale of Leven.

SCHOOLS are ubiquitous. The Education Act of 1696, which gave legal backing to the Protestant Reformers' aim of providing a school in every parish, obliged the heritors to pay a schoolmaster and provide him with schoolroom, house and garden. Most were simple structures although by the mid C19 they might display a modest dignity, as at Larbert Parish School, 1826, reconstructed in 1862. From the early C19 some mine owners and industrialists built schools to give part-time education to the children they employed. These might be more ambitious in their architectural detail, as at Alloa Colliery School, Sauchie, 1819; Dalmonach School, Bonhill, built *c.* 1830 for children working in the print-works, and Paton's School, Alloa, of 1864–5 where *John Melvin* provided shaped gables and an idiosyncratic battlemented tower. Following the Disruption of 1843 the Free Church of Scotland put up its own schools while the Episcopalians, Roman Catholics and a few charitable trusts also contributed to the educational infrastructure. St Mary's Episcopal School, Dunblane, *c.* 1850, is unequivocally if modestly Gothic, as are the Victorian parish schools at Jamestown, 1859–61, and Aberfoyle, 1870, the latter by *John Honeyman*. In the burghs schools showed greater stylistic pretension. Stirling Grammar School (now the Portcullis Hotel) by *Gideon Gray*, 1788, is austere, its erect pedimented front recalling the stiff-backed discipline no doubt endured by its pupils. The s front of Falkirk Grammar School, by *John Tait*, 1845–6, is artic- ulated by architraved and corniced windows. At Stirling a decade later *J.*, *W. H. & J. M. Hay* designed two Gothic Revival academies, the Old High School and Snowdon School, the first arranged around a collegiate quadrangle entered through a vaulted pend under a bell-tower. In Dumbarton, *Melvin & Leiper*'s Burgh Academy of 1865–6 (now Burgh Hall) is no less medieval in

provenance, two tall French Gothic storeys accented with a high
pinnacled belfry at the centre. Dollar Academy is exceptional in
size, function and architectural quality. Endowed as a 'school for
the poor of the parish', it developed into one of national repute.
The wide Neo-Classical façade designed by *W.H. Playfair* in 98
1818–21 is erudite and elevating, a pedimented Doric portico at
the centre, columned pavilions on the flanks. Located mid-plan,
between boys' and girls' classrooms, was a shallow-domed library
(reconstructed in the 1960s after a fire) whose fluted Ionic columns
gave a special grace to the interior.

The Education Act of 1872 established School Boards and laid
down standards for school buildings. The new schools were plain
gabled blocks, usually symmetrical in layout and, until the last
years of the C19, almost always single-storey. A few had modest
architectural ambition. Gothic detailing is widespread in the
earlier buildings, e.g. Dunblane (now Braeport Community Centre),
Polmont and Coalsnaughton, all of the 1870s, a more secular
Jacobean developing at Alloa Burgh School, 1875–6, Slamannan,
1876, Twechar, 1886, Falkirk High School, 1898, and, with a
steeple, Bishopbriggs High School (now Public Library), 1895–6.
Milngavie High School, 1874–5, Larbert High School (now demolished), 1891, and Lennoxtown Primary School, 1894–6, were all
more classical or, at any rate, Renaissance-derived in design.
Extensions to existing buildings freely borrowed from the song-
book of architectural styles into the C20. Only a few distinguish
themselves: *James MacLaren*'s towered extensions of 1887–90 to
the Old High School in Stirling are a notable exception in size and
quality, their imaginative eclecticism embracing a variety of sources.
Recollections of Scots Renaissance and Scots Baronial were incorporated into the high roughcast walls of *John A. Campbell*'s Queen
Victoria School, built at Dunblane for the children of servicemen,
1906–10. Grange School, Alloa, of 1907–8 (now St John's Primary 99
School) escapes from historicist norms. There, around an orthodox
School Board plan centred on a galleried hall, *Kerr & McCulloch*
gave external expression to those aberrant Art Nouveau forms
already evident in the contemporary school work of Charles Rennie
Mackintosh in Glasgow and J.H. Langlands and W.G. Lamond
in Dundee. Between the World Wars the scene is less inspiring,
typified by red brick county council designs only occasionally rising
above the ordinary, as at St Mary's Primary School, Stirling, by
*A.N. Malcolm*, 1938–9, where glazed corridors and round-ended
classroom wings give a grudging *envoi* to Thirties style. The school
building boom up to the 1970s produced designs of dully repetitive character, generally single-storey glazed box primary schools
in the first decades, followed by secondary schools of grid-glazed
infill frame construction, many of them several storeys high. From
this later phase McLaren High School, Callander, by *Perth & Kinross
County Council*, 1963–5, stands out mostly for its slated roofs and
roughcast walls which manage, just, to retain some sense of vernacular context. Douglas Academy, Milngavie, by *Boissevain & Osmond*,
1964, is long, low and respectable but Bannockburn High School 101
by *Central Regional Council*, 1977–9, is exceptional, a stunning

step-section solution on a boomerang plan. After 1980 the boxy mould is occasionally broken with some success, whether in the experiments with polygonal planning topped by glazed cupolas made at Torrance Primary School or Drymen Primary School's cleverly conceived ridge-lit barn, by *Central Regional Council*, 1990. Stimulating and attractive educational environments have also been made in the family of schools (Bo'ness Academy, Braes High School at Reddingmuirhead, Graeme High School at Falkirk, and Carrongrange School and an extension to Larbert High School at Larbert) designed by *The Parr Partnership* for Falkirk Council in the 1990s.

FURTHER AND HIGHER EDUCATION BUILDINGS are few but present a spectrum of quality. St Andrew's College, Bearsden by *Gillespie, Kidd & Coia*, 1968, endeavours to avoid banality with multi-pitched roofs and a chequerboard of white cubic boxes spilling down the hillside site and there is an undeniable spit-and-polish sophistication about the panelled walls of Stirling Centre for Further Education, by *Reiach & Hall*, 1997–8. But the outstanding achieve-
100 ment is *Robert Matthew, Johnson-Marshall & Partners'* University of Stirling, 1966–72, where the consequence of placing scrupulously disciplined architecture in an estate landscape of exceptional beauty is as memorable in its more ramified way as the lawn-aproned prospect of Dollar Academy.

ALMSHOUSES are not common. Robert Spittal, the King's tailor, founded Spittal's Hospital (since demolished) in Stirling to accommodate a number of poor men in 1530. Also in Stirling, Cowane's Hospital, endowed by the merchant John Cowane to house 'decayed
80 gild breither', was built to a design by *John Mylne Jun.* in 1637–48, the centrepiece of its front an ogee-roofed tower with a statue of the founder in an aediculed niche. In the C18 these almshouses were turned over to other uses, the endowment income being used to support the indigent in their own homes. Money raised by kirk sessions and from heritors supported the poor and insane from the C16. A Poor Law of 1845 regularized the system, still on a parochial basis, and soon after some POORHOUSES were built; at Falkirk in 1850, Stirling (now part of Orchard House Hospital) in 1856, and Dumbarton in 1865. ASYLUMS for the mentally ill appeared about the same time. The Royal Scottish National Institution (now Hospital) for the mentally defective at Larbert, housed in buildings designed by *F. T. Pilkington* in his characteristic rogue Ruskinian Gothic, was opened in 1862. Italianate touches mix with the generally free Jacobean of *Salmon, Son & Ritchie*'s Barony Parochial Asylum (later Woodilee Hospital) at Lenzie, built in 1871–5 to house pauper lunatics from the Barony parish of Glasgow.

HOSPITALS for the physically sick were built in the later C19 when typhus and cholera were still not uncommon. In 1868 a small hospital was opened at Alloa. Six years later in Stirling the former Commercial Bank (now Forth Valley Health Board) was converted to form the Stirling Royal Infirmary. At the same time an epidemic hospital was built at Dumbarton and in 1875 Broomhill Hospital for incurables was founded at Kirkintilloch. More followed. Some were isolation hospitals with ward pavilions for patients suffering different infectious diseases; the earliest is Falkirk Infectious Diseases Hospital, thrifty Jacobean by *A. & W. Black*, 1881. Others were cottage hospitals, like the minimally Gothic Dumbarton Cottage Hospital, 1888–9. A new general hospital, the Clackmannan County Hospital, designed by *R. A. Bryden*, was built at Alloa in 1898–9. Such general provision in the larger centres of population came between the wars at Stirling Royal Infirmary, 1925–8, Falkirk Royal Infirmary, 1926–32 and Canniesburn Hospital, Bearsden, 1935. Vale of Leven Hospital, Alexandria, by *J. L. Gleave*, 1952–5, was originally built to a standardized module thought to be readily responsive to probable growth but it too has developed in piecemeal fashion. At Clydebank the Health Care International Hospital, by *The Architects Collaborative*, 1991–4, is the latest attempt to come to terms with the exponential explosion of need, a vast brick-clad fortress of private medicine. Villa-like CONVALESCENT HOMES were also built in the late C19 but none can match *James Thomson*'s Schaw Convalescent Home at Bearsden, 1891. Towered, gabled and bay-windowed, it sits on a hilltop like some latter-day Tudor prodigy house.

Several burghs built PUBLIC BATHS in the later C19. Most were utilitarian and many demolished in the C20 as domestic bath-rooms became general. Exceptional as a survivor is the free Scots Renaissance Public Baths and Gymnasium (now the Speirs Centre) at Alloa, designed by *John Burnet, Son & Campbell*, 1895–8. 93 SPORTS AND LEISURE CENTRES, largely a late C20 phenomenon driven by fashionable enthusiasms for health, have appeared since the 1970s. Of that decade, the Allan Leisure Centre, Bridge of Allan, Rainbow Slides Leisure Centre, Stirling, and the Antonine Sports Centre, Duntocher, are crudely utilitarian. At Alva Academy's Swimming Pool and Leisure Centre, by *Central Regional Council*, 1980, a sloping wall of glass lights the pool and collects solar energy, but its raking concrete beams are over-aggressive. Later efforts do better. Clydebank's Playdome Leisure Centre, by the *Ellis Williams* 103 *Partnership*, 1991–4, has something of the brash fun-fair feel of the circus. At Callander, by contrast, the McLaren Leisure Centre, by *Gaia Architects*, 1997–8, is pleasantly understated, concerned with green rather than formal issues.

### Commercial Buildings

In most villages and small burghs in the C18 and early C19 INNS were the largest buildings other than churches and manses. Perhaps the oldest surviving is the Lion and Unicorn Hotel at Thornhill whose high open fireplace with salt-box recess alongside provides some corroboration for its claim to date from 1635. The pantiled former West Pier Tavern, Bo'ness, the Black Bull at Kippen, the old village inn in Torbrex, and Stirling burgh's oldest alehouse, the crowstep-gabled Settle Inn in St Mary's Wynd, all date from the first three decades of the C18. Inns from the latter half of the C18 are to be found at Ardeonaig, Doune, Gargunnock, Inverarnan, Killearn, Killin and Kippen. Most are two-storey three-bay units, with little to distinguish them from contemporary 'improved' farmhouses, a pattern which continued into the C19. Domestic plainness may only be relieved by a pilastered doorpiece, architraved windows or a wallhead cornice, e.g. inns at Clachan of Campsie (now Altessan Gallery), Balfron, Milngavie, Tillicoultry and Buchlyvie.

Larger Georgian HOTELS were built in some burghs and occasionally in villages. At Falkirk the former Royal Hotel was constructed *c.* 1760, its ground floor of channelled ashlar with a Corinthian-columned doorpiece. Stirling's Golden Lion Hotel of 1786 is dignified by a broad pediment. The rubble-built Dreadnought Hotel, Callander, *c.* 1805, is big but originally severely plain. Smarter is *William Stirling I*'s former Red Lion Inn of 1828 in Falkirk, ashlar-fronted, the first-floor windows dressed up with lugged architraves and pediments, those at the second floor corniced. In Alloa, the nearly contemporary Royal Oak Hotel, with angle pilasters and a pilastered doorpiece, is set in a late Georgian extension to the town. Also in Alloa, the pedimented, villa-like Tontine Hotel (now Ochil House) of 1806. Later, from the mid C19, rail travel gave a new impetus to hotel building. Some were placed in town centre buildings above street-level shops. In Stirling the former Douglas Hotel, 1879–82, rose above the entrance to Crawford's Arcade while in Falkirk a large hotel by *Alexander Gauld*, 1904–6, occupied much of the w side of Lint Riggs. Station hotels appeared at Alloa, 1880, and Larbert, *c.* 1900, the former Georgian survival but with a Gothic entrance, the latter half-timbered, with a slated copper spire. New hotels were constructed and older inns enlarged to serve tourists visiting the picturesque hills and lochs of N Stirlingshire and Perthshire, especially in the resort towns of Bridge of Allan and Callander where classical and Baronial vied for popularity. By far the largest such hotel was the dramatically sited and towered Dunblane Hydropathic (now Hotel Dunblane) by *Peddie & Kinnear*, 1875–8. In the C20 conversion of existing buildings to hotel use has become common, usually country houses but also the Old High School in Stirling. This last has helped reinvigorate the Old Town, though the new bedroom wings closing an intelligently contrived courtyard plan are less than adequate to their skyline exposure on the castle rock.

BANKS, emphatic interruptions to the mid-C19 tenemental streetscape, almost always affect architectural assurance. From the early C19 to the early C20 each branch bank was run by an agent, usually a lawyer, provided with offices and family home in a building whose only significant accommodation for banking was the banking hall. The Commercial Bank, founded in 1810, established itself with considerable classical dignity on Spittal Street, Stirling (now Forth Valley Health Board), 1825–7, and on Falkirk's
95 High Street, 1829–31, the former certainly, the latter probably, designed by *James Gillespie Graham*. Both are Greek temples, the Stirling bank with a Doric portico, the Falkirk branch with giant Ionic columns *in antis*. Other banks of the 1830s were more restrained. *William Burn*'s Bank of Scotland of 1833 on King Street, Stirling, was designed as a large and elegant classical residence. Even more residential in character is the Union Bank (now Bank

of Scotland) of 1832 on Mar Street, Alloa, a large villa with a pedimented Doric portico. Also in Alloa but more austerely classical is
the former Commercial Bank of *c*. 1840 on Bank Street. In the
same street is the richly detailed palazzo put up for the Clydesdale
Bank in 1852, the banking and office accommodation marked off
by a cornice from the agent's house above. By the mid C19 the
Renaissance palazzo had become the standard model. Stirling's
King Street has several: the former Clydesdale Bank, *c*. 1840, with
a Roman Doric colonnaded ground floor, the contemporary double-
porticoed Bank of Scotland, 1863, notably *Peddie & Kinnear*'s
former Royal Bank of Scotland of 1863, with its impressive Greek
Doric granite entrance. True to its name, the National Bank adopted
national, i.e. Scots Baronial, dress for their banks of which survives
an example in Upper Newmarket Street, Falkirk, of 1862–3 by
*MacGibbon & Ross*. In the 1890s and early 1900s *George Washington
Browne* provided the British Linen Bank with inventive compositions,
using Gothic, Tudor and Jacobean motifs at Alloa, Dumbarton, 96
Falkirk and Grangemouth. In the w, *Peddie & Kinnear*'s palazzo
for the Royal Bank, 1891, rises above the two-storey townscape
of Alexandria. More rumbustious is *J. M. Dick Peddie*'s English
Baroque Royal Bank of Scotland of 1908–11 in Alloa. The
Clydesdale Bank became positively opulent at the head of King
Street, Stirling, in 1899–1900 but their banks in the smaller towns
and villages were much less assertive: large villas in Larbert, *c*. 1865,
and Denny, 1866; blandly Italianate edifices at Tillicoultry and
Dollar, both *c*. 1870.

Most C20 banks, eschewing the need to accommodate agents
on the premises, lack the scale and *gravitas* of their predecessors.
In High Street, Dumbarton, the Savings Bank, by *Eric Sutherland*,
and the former Clydesdale Bank, by *John Baird & James Thomson*,
contemporary in date, 1938–9, though distinct in material and
composition, share a fascination with flat Art Deco classicism. Of
the glossy high-tech image of late C20 banking there is no architectural reflection. Instead, in a conversion of 1994–5, the Bank of
Scotland's flagship offices in Stirling have been located in Craigs
House, Upper Craigs, an early C19 mansion replete with the re-
assuring conservatism of Georgian classicism.

THEATRES are rare in Stirling and Central Scotland. The circular
auditorium of the Hippodrome, Bo'ness, by *Matthew Steele*, 1911–12,
survives but unused. The only active centres of live stage entertainment are at Dumbarton in the bleak, blue-black brick box of
the Denny Civic Theatre, by *Reiach & Hall*, 1968–9, and at the
University of Stirling's more welcoming MacRobert Arts Centre,
by *Robert Matthew, Johnson-Marshall & Partners*, 1969–72. *Richard
Murphy*'s introduction of an auditorium into the converted former
Court House adjacent to the Town House, Stirling, in 2001–2,
promises an architecturally exciting urban venue for music and
drama. CINEMAS were built from the early C20 and by the 1930s
almost every small town had its picture house and the larger centres
of population several. Only a handful remain, mostly consigned to
neglect or bingo. The oldest is the Empire Electric, Grangemouth,
1913, its auditorium shed fronted by a pavilioned vestibule block

in Scots Renaissance dress. Others surviving include the Rialto, Dumbarton, 1914, Falkirk's Bank Street Picture House, 1920, and ABC Cinema, 1935, and the Black Bull Cinema, Kirkintilloch, 1921. The Carlton Allanpark Cinema, Stirling, 1936–8, and the Gaumont, Alloa, 1938, are little more than large utilitarian blocks. So, too, behind its electrographic mask, is the late C20 multiplex at Clydebank.

By the mid C19 the central streets of towns in Stirling and Central Scotland were generally lined with three- or four-storey tenements, their ground floors occupied by SHOPS. Shopfronts were relatively discreet although with large windows and often marked off by a cornice from the housing above. One smart early C19 survivor is at Nos. 19–23 Bank Street, Alloa. From the 1860s, redevelopment produced buildings with higher ground-floor shops influencing the design of upper floors which might still be for residential accommodation but could be intended for commercial or office use. In 1862–3 the Drummond Tract Depot (now Bank of Scotland) was built on the corner of King Street and Murray Place, Stirling. Designed by *J., W. H. & J. M. Hay*, it is a palazzo, a porch at the splayed corner, the ground-floor windows originally surmounted by the carved heads of Protestant divines honoured by the books and pamphlets for sale within. A more commercial and less high-minded function is evident in the glazed cast iron front of Nos. 36–38 King Street, Stirling. King Street also contains the entrance to Crawford's Arcade, by *John McLean*, 1879–82. In Alloa *Thomas Frame & Son* designed a tall commercial block, Nos. 39–45 Mill Street, whose sandstone front displays a wealth of Ægypto-Greek detail in the manner of Alexander 'Greek' Thomson. Also in Mill Street, Alloa, is *George Kerr*'s Flemish gable front at No. 38, 1903, a style earlier adopted in more lighthearted vein at No. 65 High Street, Falkirk, 1886. No. 42 and Nos. 52–56 Port Street, Stirling, are turn-of-the-century five-floor emporia designed with characteristically weird idiosyncrasy by *John Allan*. Staider was the redevelopment of Lint Riggs, Falkirk, in 1903–6, the free Jacobean design for the commercial façades (except that of the Masonic Hall, q.v.) prepared under the direction of the Burgh Surveyor, *David Ronald*. At Grangemouth, a new commercial centre was built *c.* 1900–14, with free Renaissance buildings by *Wilson & Tait* along Station Road and an Edwardian Queen Anne block by *John P. Goodsir* in Union Road.

The Co-operative movement was strong in Stirling and Central Scotland and Co-operative Stores appear in many towns and size-able villages, sometimes disproportionately large for the settlement, e.g. at Reddingmuirhead, *c.* 1900, and Bonnybridge, 1928. The store on the corner of Alexander Street and Chalmers Street, Clydebank, by *Robert Stewart*, 1914, has a four-storeyed galleried interior under a glazed cupola. Between the wars Art Deco was enthusiastically adopted for stores in Primrose Street, Alloa, and Kirk Wynd, Falkirk, where the same style forms the dominant note of the town's 1930s commercial redevelopments, e.g. at Callendar Riggs and No. 10 West Bridge Street. Other notable examples are found in the faience façades of the former Burton's store on Port

Street, Stirling, 1928, the former Woolworth's of 1938–9 in Wallace Street, Clydebank, and most appealingly in the black, green and orange chevron ornament of Nos. 55–63 High Street, Dumbarton, by *W. J. B. Wright*. At *William Kerr* and *John Gray*'s gas showrooms, Bank Street, Alloa, Art Deco is combined with stripped Georgian 97 to convincing effect.

Since the late 1960s major REDEVELOPMENTS have sought to maintain, augment or re-create a genuinely urban context for shopping in several towns. In schemes at Duke Street and Stirling Street in Denny, by *Wilson & Wilson*, 1966–72, La Porte Precinct at Grangemouth, by *Wheeler & Sproson*, 1967, and Douglas Street in Milngavie, by *Jack Holmes & Partners*, *c*. 1970, existing street lines have been respected but wholly rebuilt. Mitchell Way, Alexandria, 1976, stitches two older streets together but the patch is untidy. Dumbarton's Town Square, by *Garner, Preston & Strebel*, 1966–9, is tidy enough in plan but otherwise bleak, Brutalist and commercially moribund. Falkirk's Callendar Square Shopping Centre, by *Clark, Tribble, Harris & Li*, 1992, has better scale and is at least integrated with existing streets. In Stirling, too, the malls of the Thistle Centre, by *Walter Underwood & Partners* (Phase 1), 1973–6, and *Comprehensive Design* (Phase 2), 1995–7, link well to the older shopping streets of Port Street and Murray Place, while the whole complex, augmented by car parking and bus station, acts as a robust bulwark along the E marches of the town centre. Other recent attempts to integrate supermarkets into the urban fabric have generally failed, compromised by sheer size and perverse efforts to domesticate this size with the pusillanimous camouflage of tiled roofs and facing brick.

### Domestic Buildings

Before the C18 aristocrats' TOWN HOUSES were erected close to the centres of power. In Stirling, the seat of the court, two such prestigious buildings survive not far from the castle. The empty shell of Mar's Wark, a once splendid mansion built by the Regent 104 of Scotland, 1570–2, sits alone, a little aloof at the head of Broad Street, its twin-towered façade an impressive, now ruinous, backdrop to the events in the market-place below. On Castle Wynd, a gateway breaches a tall screen wall to open into the courtyard of Argyll's Lodging, a detached residence begun in the late C16 and 105 completed by the Earl of Argyll in 1674. Built around three sides of its forecourt with conically capped staircase towers in the corners, it is three storeys high, generously ornamented with strapwork above windows and dormers, the most important town house of its period. In High Street, Dumbarton, once the w's castellar equivalent of Stirling, is the Earl of Glencairn's Greit House of 1623, a 106 three-storey building with pedimented eaves dormers. While far from the equal of aristocratic houses like Mar's Wark or Argyll's Lodging, it closely parallels the architecture of some lesser, but still relatively well appointed, residences.

For, unlike the nobility, the burghers and gentry of Stirling lived not in palatial detachment but shoulder-to-shoulder on the streets of the town itself. Humbler in style, many of these LAIRDS' AND MERCHANTS' TOWN HOUSES, built tall and thin on their narrow-fronted tofts, possessed that solid dignity so characteristic of much Scottish townscape. A good deal of this remains, though much is restored. The scale is four-storeyed, the narrow façades gabled, or dormered along the eaves, the materials ashlar or rendered rubble. One of the earliest of these tall town houses is Bruce of Auchenbowie's Lodging, begun c. 1520, where, recalling the tower-house, the basement is vaulted and a turnpike stair pushes forward on to the pavement of St John Street. Darnley's House, Bow Street (also known as Erskine of Gogar's House), c. 1600, has a vaulted street-level storey and pedimented dormerheads. Other examples include Provost Stevenson's Lodging, Town Clerk Norrie's Lodging, and the Graham of Panholes Lodging, all 107 on Broad Street, all dating from the C17. The Darrow Lodging, Spittal Street, has a restored frontal turnpike. John Cowane's House, erected on St Mary's Wynd in 1603, remains only in ruins.

There is one other survivor from the C17 the stylistic nature of which is particularly significant. The dwelling which the master 109 mason *Tobias Bachop* built for his family at 25 Kirkgate, Alloa, in 1695, is a rare example but one which in its design seems to stand conveniently halfway between the grander compositional provenance of the country houses of Sir William Bruce, James Smith, and others (on several of which Bachop had worked) and the humbler but still dignified hand-me-down classicism which from the early years of the C18 began to characterize Scottish burghs and villages. Bachop's house is a symmetrical two-storeyed dwelling with crowstepped gables. All the windows of its five-bay ashlar street front have lugged architraves, those at ground floor (and the door-way centred between them) enhanced with pulvinated friezes and 78 cornices. View Villa, Airth, dated 1722, is also crowstep-gabled with a five-bay front and central street door under a pulvinated frieze and cornice. But it is rubble-built, pantile-roofed, and less carefully controlled in the size and disposition of its windows.

The desire to assert social distinction remained a potent factor shaping the appearance of most villages and towns in the C18 and C19 and the detached dwelling continued to be an important element in the street scene. In its architectural aspiration, the piend-roofed, two-storey classical house, with its Roman Doric or Ionic doorpiece or portico, declared itself a superior residence, one which, by virtue of what was originally often a peripheral location, might be considered as much suburban villa as town house (*see* below). In Stirling, the oddly four-bay façade of the townhouse at No. 80 Port Street, c. 1775, has urns raised on pedestals above a fine eaves cornice and pediment; a sober intimation of Georgian residences soon to be built nearby on Melville Terrace and Allan Park (*see* below). Tower House in Clackmannan, c. 1840, Brockville House in Falkirk, c. 1840, and Marshill House in Alloa, c. 1835, follow the standard model. On the w edge of Dollar is Devongrove, 1821 by *W. H. Playfair*. In the Old Town of Stirling, Dalgleish Court, c. 1810, which is approached up a flying stair, and Sauchie House, 1830, framed with coupled pilaster quoins, are each located axially at the end of a short alley opening N off Baker Street. Further N, beyond the limit of the Baker Street tofts, the more modest mansions of Irvine Place appeared. Similar houses appeared in, or close to, a few villages, though there was little to differentiate these from many of the smaller mansions or farmhouses built in the country-side at the time. The degree of architectural ornament, never more than modest, might vary but the compositional formula remained the same. Typical is Spittalton House, Buchlyvie, 1738, a detached one-family residence, two storeys high, skew-gabled and three bays wide. Among later C18 village examples of this two-storey, three-bay model are Orchardlands and Clachan House in Balfron, and Hillside House, Kippen.

Few families could afford to live in the upstairs-and-downstairs style of the minor lairds, merchants and professional classes and it seems likely that FLATTED DWELLINGS in the towns would have been common from the C17 onwards. Indeed some of Stirling's lesser town houses (*see* above) may originally have been flatted. Such examples might well have had a frontal turnpike but this would have been a semi-public staircase off which each floor of the property would have been given over to one or more tenanted flats. But of all this there is now no physical evidence. In the smaller towns and some villages flatted dwellings, although perhaps exceptional, also existed. A few examples survive. In Shore Road, Airth, is a crowstep-gabled, rubble-built house from the early C18 with a five-bay front, the upper floor of which is reached by a forestair. Forestairs also survive in a small group of much-restored housing on Kirk Wynd in the village of St Ninian's, now a suburb of Stirling, and at No. 101 Corbiehall, Bo'ness.

The customary form of housing in the smaller towns to the end of the C18 was identical to that of the rural settlements (*see* p. 92–3). Built of mud or drystone rubble-walls with thatched roofs, these were increasingly replaced by three-bay, single-storey cottages or two-storey, often flatted, dwellings, plain but almost always symmet-rical; in Doune their presence is so constant and consistent along Main Street and Balkerach Street that they define the very town-scape of the place, tight narrow corridors of two-storey housing of the late C18 or early C19 accented by columned or pilastered door-ways, later shopfronts, or the occasional Victorian intrusion. It is hardly surprising that such repetitive order should characterize the housing in PLANNED VILLAGES since there the control of layout and architectural uniformity could be readily exercised over a depen-dent community whose working population was tied to the local estate, mill or mine. The repetition of simple symmetrical dwellings set in contiguous relationship became the architectural hallmark of the new village. The colliery hamlet of Kennet is exactly this, a long, pantiled row of twenty single-storey three-bay, miners' cottages, constructed *c.* 1800 as improved housing for the workers in the local pit. At Deanston the mill workers were accommodated in flatted two-storey ranges. Begun in 1785, the village retained a visual order which, almost a century later, was impressive enough to lead Groome to grant it 'an appearance greatly superior to that of most seats of manufacture'. Cottages, some with two-storey centrepieces, form a U-plan arrangement in the small riverside estate community of Dunmore, established *c.* 1840. Dwellings on the Carriden estate in the mid-C19 hamlet of Muirhouses are similar but more picturesque in style.

In the early C19 ordered sequences of similar houses coalesced into TERRACES. Gable-to-gable Georgian houses ranged together, their repetitive façades punctuated by paired pilastered doorways, survive at Stirling, e.g. Viewfield Place, Queen Street, Princes Street and Forth Place, all built before 1850. In the later C19, the urban terrace took two quite distinct forms, each related to a different housing market. In the larger towns, ranges of two- or three-storey TOWN HOUSE TERRACES filled a social gap between the select isolation of the detached mansion or villa and the less private, generally more proletarian, accommodation of the tenement flat (*see* below). It was usual for this type of terrace to be treated as a parade of more or less identical architectural elements, perhaps with reflected elevations and doorways, but there are no examples of the palace-fronted terraces found in Georgian Edinburgh or Glasgow. Humbler terrace rows of one-and-a-half storeys, based on the aggregation of the cottage–villa type, appear in the late C19 Knoxland suburb of Dumbarton. The six three-storey houses of Craighuchty Terrace, Aberfoyle, by *James Miller*, 1895, are animated by Arts and Crafts colours, textures and forms drawn from an enthusiasm for Shavian Tudor. Also influenced by the Arts and Crafts Movement but in a more intimate, more Scots way, are the quaintly grouped houses at 1–11 George Street, Doune, 1894, by *T. MacLaren*.

Where town house terraces housed the professional and *petit bourgeois* classes, FLATTED TERRACES accommodated workers employed in local industries. These terraces might flatter to deceive, seeming to be ranges of individual two-storey houses. In fact their street doorway led only to the ground-floor flat or flats, or perhaps, in addition, to a close access leading to the stair to the flat (or flats) on the upper level. From the early 1880s many such red sandstone rows appeared in the Vale of Leven, housing the workers serving the booming printing, dyeing and bleaching industries. The best of these two-storey terraces are in Alexandria: Main Street, Middleton Street and Smollett Street. In Bonhill, Dillichip Terrace, 1885, survives; in Balloch, Charles Terrace, also from the 1880s. Probably contemporary, Edmond Terrace in the village of Croftamie may be a rural offshoot of this Vale of Leven type. Although these workers' flats are almost invariably plainly detailed, exceptions occur, e.g. the crowstepped gables and shouldered-arched doorways that enliven the façades of the terraces in West Bridge Street, Falkirk, 1898.

Like the flatted terraces, TENEMENTS line the street in repetitive ranges, providing self-contained dwellings grouped around a common stair not merely on two but on three, four and even five floors. Examples of this quintessentially urban type survive from the C18 onwards in the major towns of Stirling, Falkirk and Bo'ness. By the mid C19, the main streets of most larger burghs in Stirling and Central Scotland were tenemented to a greater or lesser extent, invariably combined with shops (*see* Commercial Buildings, above) and providing accommodation of a more generous size, increasingly appropriate to middle-class inhabitants. These buildings still contribute to the street scene above shop fascia level, many evincing an increasing architectural awareness to complement commercial display. In Stirling's Port Street, King Street and Murray Place are short stretches of three-storey tenements c. 1840–50 with ashlar façades, some with architraved windows and consoled cornices. On Falkirk's High Street, Wilson's Buildings at Nos. 105–111, 1848, has consoled cornices spread over large tripartite windows and there are cornices and pediments over the windows of Nos. 147–149, by *William Stirling III*, 1862. In Dumbarton, Nos. 127–135 High Street, 1854, is notable for pilastered Venetian windows at the centre of a wide five-bay range. In Alloa, at Nos. 39–45 Mill Street, 1874–5, the stringcourse stepping over the first-floor windows and coupled dwarf pilasters on the storey above are derived from the terrace and tenement work of Alexander 'Greek' Thomson in Glasgow. The formal devices and ornament of classical architecture remained the *sine qua non* of most tenement building until the end of the century, e.g. Nos. 2–14 Townhead, Kirkintilloch, 1896–1900, but by then stylistic changes were already varying the street-wall scene. Both Italianate sources and Jacobean variations were popular but it was the Scots Baronial style that responded best to the challenge of the gushet or street junction site. Conically roofed corners appear at Baronial Buildings on Coalgate, Alloa, 1887, and in Bo'ness at North Street's meeting with Scotland's Close, 1884. Four storeys above the entrance to a pub at the junction of College Way and Station Road in Dumbarton, *J. M. Crawford*'s 1898 Baronial tenement soars to a crowstepped gablet with an offset bartizan. Away from the principal town streets, most tenements were plainer as at Bruce Street and Wallace Street, Stirling (1890s), but bayed examples from the turn-of-the-century years are plentiful in Dumbarton and Clydebank. Here and there oddities appear: the aberrant rough-faced Mona Place, 1897, on Newhouse, Stirling; touches of Glasgow Style Art Nouveau at No. 32 Spittal Street, Stirling, 1903, and Nos. 60–62 West High Street, Kirkintilloch, 1905.

The building of SUBURBAN VILLAS AND MANSIONS began in the late C18 as variants of the Georgian town house or country house model. Elegant examples from the first decades of the C19 can be found in Allan Park, Pitt Terrace and Melville Terrace, Stirling, where a whole suburb of such houses sprang up between 1810 and 1835. Each villa, whether a single three-bayed dwelling or a four-bayed semi-detached unit, is an elegant variation on the prevailing Georgian theme. On Alloa's Bedford Place several villas dating from c. 1815 to c. 1855 are especially fine in composition and detail. By the 1850s and 60s, however, as villa-land expanded rapidly, most notably in Stirling's King's Park suburb, in Lenzie and in the Upper Town of Bridge of Allan, stylistic approaches began to change. Renaissance details were introduced, with Italianate towers a recurring element, but there were allusions, too, to other styles.

This ramifying historicism was especially strongly developed in some of the much larger MANSIONS built in the second half of the

C19, where greater emphasis was placed upon privacy not afforded by the smaller villas. Usually erected for the wealthy owners of local industries and placed within easy reach of their works, these buildings provided accommodation and a setting comparable to that of a country house, within their own grounds and often hidden from the street. In Dumbarton's leafy Kirktonhill are houses for the local shipbuilding elite. Both Helenslee, by *John T. Rochead*, 1855–6, and Methlan Park, by *John McLeod*, 1880–1, have tall Italianate towers but on the edge of the same suburb, *Rochead*'s Levenford House, 1852–3, rose from the hillside like a latter-day Scots castle. Nearby, Garmoyle by *John Burnet, Son & Campbell*, 1890–2, adduces Scots Renaissance and Baronial forms to its snecked sandstone bulk. Baronial sources were also plundered for Springwood House, *c.* 1870, and Brentham Park House, 1871, both in Stirling, and for Glenhead House, Lenzie, built *c.* 1875. The Jacobean style was employed in the remodelling of Carronvale House, Larbert, for George Sheriff by *John J. Burnet* in 1897 but used to best effect in a most remarkable sequence of industrialists' mansions in Alloa. First, elevated on terraced banks, is the multi-gabled red rubble mansion of the Younger family, Arnsbrae House by *Alfred Waterhouse*, 1885–6. Then come three houses built for the Paton family, owners of the prosperous local textile firm. Greenfield House, by *Sydney Mitchell & Wilson*, 1891–4 is an impressive gabled and bay-windowed pile, with a high tower carrying a glazed caphouse with leaded ogee roof, and interiors that maintain the Mannerist Jacobean idiom.

113 By the same architects, Inglewood House, 1895, is distinguished by its bulky parapeted tower with turret and bartizan. Its interior is again Jacobean and magnificent: decorative plaster friezes and compartmented pendant ceilings, timber arcading and panelling,
115 inglenook fireplaces and fine stained glass. Gean House by *William Kerr* of *John Melvin & Son*, 1912, is an Arts and Crafts adaptation of the English Tudor manor house to modern living but in its planning the house is strikingly similar to that of Inglewood built a generation earlier. However, with mullioned and transomed windows, red tiles, tall chimneys and dormers, the influence of Sir Edwin Lutyens does not seem far removed.

These styles, augmented by the occasional flirtation with Gothic or Baroque motifs, were also developed in the SMALLER VILLAS, although the simple compositional formula of an accented doorpiece set symmetrically between canted bays, however much enriched by ornament, remained the recurrent model for most suburban living. Orthodox Renaissance detail generally prevailed and only rarely were classical forms elaborated with the kind of idiosyncratic Thomsonesque invention seen in such smaller villas as Warwick Croft, Lenzie, *c.* 1880, and Melbourne House, Clydebank, 1877–80. By the last decade of the C19, stylistic options had begun to proliferate. The Jacobean style, so prevalent in the larger mansions (*see* above), is evident as early as *c.* 1860 in the design of No. 3 Arnothill, Falkirk, and enhances the still Scottish references in *James M.*
112 *MacLaren*'s Avondhu at No. 168 Bo'ness Road, Grangemouth, 1878. English Tudor, increasingly viewed through Arts and Crafts eyes, developed more intimate domestic interpretations suited to

the scale of most suburban villa building. Woodcroft, Larbert, by *Thomas L. Watson*, *c.* 1890, is replete with the necessary half-timbering, bargeboards and red tiles, while *John Allan*'s brick-red Batterflatts in Stirling, 1893–5, interprets the same language of form and material with almost industrial vigour. *William Leiper*'s Endrick Lodge, off Polmaise Road, Stirling, 1899–1900, is better than most. More typical in scale and in their informal collages of red tiling, render and timber are Fisherwood, Balloch, *c.* 1900, Tidings Hill in Cadzow Crescent, Bo'ness, by *A. Hunter Crawford*, 1908, and *James E. Ronald*'s 23–25 Randolph Road, Stirling, *c.* 1910.

There is little evidence of that break from tradition seen elsewhere in the contemporary domestic work of Charles Rennie Mackintosh. Some touches of Art Nouveau at Grangewells, Muirhouses, by *Matthew Steele*, 1911, and Glasgow Style interiors exist in *George Walton*'s Ault Wharrie, Dunblane, *c.* 1900, and in Hatherley, Arnothill, Falkirk, by *Thomas M. Copland*, *c.* 1904–5. Curiously, at Auchenibert, Killearn, *Mackintosh* himself could only compromise; Cotswold style, comfortable but uncontroversial. On the other hand, the white-harled, skew-gabled walls of *William Kerr*'s Struan House, Claremont, Alloa, 1905, hint at formal austerities to come. In the 1920s and 30s, however, private housing notably failed to come to terms with the abstemious programme of international Modernism. *William Kerr* and *John Gray*'s The Pines in Dollar, 1938, is white and severe but clings to a Scots vernacular idiom already exploited a generation earlier by Mackintosh. Only in Bearsden where *John R. H. McDonald* designed White Lodge on Kilmardinny Crescent, *c.* 1930, and a curving line of small villas on Carse View Drive, 1933–6, did flat roofs, flat white walls and corner windows make an appearance. In the later c20 there is much uninspired speculative housing. Only a few privately commissioned houses merit notice. The Ostlers, Dollar, by *Andrew Whalley* and *Fiona Galbraith*, is a geometrically tight, energy-efficient dwelling planned around a roof-lit court, while at *Robert Halliday*'s Howard Lodge, Bridge of Allan, nostalgia for Mackintosh lingers on.

Since the end of the First World War, LOCAL AUTHORITY HOUS-ING has contributed prodigiously to the streetscape of almost every town and village. There is an Art Deco flavour to the 1930s flats built by *Matthew Steele* in Bo'ness, the work of *J. G. Callander* and 117 *Wilson & Tait* on the E side of Callendar Riggs, Falkirk, and in *Arthur Bracewell*'s mill workers' houses on Moss Road, Tillicoultry. Later flat-roofed houses at Braehead, Alva, by *John Fraser & Son*, 118 1938, Margaret Avenue, Haggs, by *Wilson & Wilson*, 1939, and Winston Crescent, Lennoxtown, by *T. O. W. Gratton*, 1940–1, are more uncompromisingly modern.

Throughout the 1920s and 30s, in what was then the county of Dunbartonshire, the cottages and flats built by the County Architect, *Joseph Weekes*, gave new expression to the Scottish vernacular tradition. Whyte's Corner, Milton, 1933, and Hawcraigs, Old Kilpatrick, *c.* 1935, near Dumbarton are particularly inventive and intimate. At the Veterans' Houses in Callander, Lorimer-like 116 Scotstyle prevailed while building in the Raploch suburb of Stirling also began in strong Scottish form with *Eric S. Bell*'s 1936 housing

at Nos. 66–74 Drip Road. A similar allegiance naturally governed the rehabilitation of Stirling's Old Town initiated by the Thistle Property Trust in 1928. Designs re-animating the old townscape in a marriage of restoration and sympathetic new-build were prepared by *Frank C. Mears* before the Second World War, though reconstruction and infill began only in the 1950s. The Scottish burgh vernacular subsequently re-created by Mears' firm working in collaboration with Stirling's Burgh Architect in the 1950s, 60s and 70s also appeared elsewhere with modest success. As in Stirling so in, for example, Airth, Balfron, Cambus, Clackmannan and Menstrie efforts were made to continue the revival of the vernacular tradition. This modest architecture of harled walls, doorways with roll-moulded stone surrounds, crowstepped gables and the occasional ogee-domed turret worked well in village streets but it could not respond to the urban housing problem. By the 1970s, vast bleak swathes of low- and medium-rise housing, harshly economic in form and material, were being built in the spreading suburbs of Stirling, Falkirk and larger neighbouring towns on both sides of the River Forth and in the w in Clydebank, Dumbarton and the Vale of Leven. Tower blocks erupted on the 60s skyline, their impact most evident in
120 Falkirk and Clydebank. Yet within a generation this boom in local-authority house building was all but over. Attitudes to urban housing changed as tenement rehabilitation and infill, much of it in the hands of housing associations, gathered pace. Respectable late C20 examples of flatted housing, all of it careful to respect existing street lines, include Parkgate Court, Mar Place, by *Campbell & Arnott*, 1990, and Bridge Terrace, Shillinghill, by *Simister Monaghan*, 1995, both in Alloa, and the fittingly red brick O'Neil Terrace in Alexandria
119 by *Chris Stewart*, of *Vernon Monaghan Architects*. Mitchell Court, Bridge Street, Dollar, by *Keir & Fraser* is a convincing Postmodern interpretation of traditional forms.

## RURAL MANSES, FARMHOUSES AND STEADINGS

Until the late C18 the rural economy of Stirling and Central Scotland, as elsewhere in the country, was based largely on peasant agriculture. Tenants grouped in 'fermtouns' or 'townships' worked the arable land, which was usually enclosed by a dyke to protect crops from cattle or sheep, turned out in the spring to graze on the land beyond or taken to hill pasture further away. There was little security of tenure and rents were paid in kind.

The most substantial dwelling houses, besides lairds' houses, were the ministers' MANSES. The parish minister was a farmer as well as a spiritual leader, dependent on the produce of his glebe (the land allocated him) as well as on the tiend (or tithe) paid him for his livelihood. Ministers might work the land themselves or rent it to others and, after 1866, glebe land could be feued, the resultant feu duty used for support of the incumbent.

The minister's house or manse in the C17 and early C18 was a dwelling of modest comfort suited to the social standing of the minister. The housing of successive ministers of Campsie parish may have been not untypical. There, the first post-Reformation manse appears to have been the house formerly occupied by the parish priest, a vicar appointed by the canons of Glasgow Cathedral, which held the rectory and major part of the tiends. That house, probably humble, was replaced in 1627 by a new one described as of two storeys but small and thatched with straw. An act of Parliament in 1663 obliged the heritors (landowners) of each parish to provide a 'competent' manse costing between £27 15s. 6d. and £83 6s. 8d. sterling, the cost proportionate to the wealth of the parish, and in 1727 a new manse was built at Campsie. By the late C18, when agricultural improvement had raised the income and expectations of some farmers, larger manses, their character not dissimilar from that of contemporary middle-class suburban villas, were being built, a process aided both by the rising social status of ministers and a decision of the Court of Session in 1760 that the upper limit on the cost of a manse laid down in 1663 did not apply to the rebuilding of an existing manse. In 1798 Campsie Parish Manse was rebuilt at a cost of £447 16s. 0d. and the previous manse converted to offices at a further cost of £68 10s. 0d. Rebuilding of manses in the late C18 and early C19 was general. A comparison between the size, comfort and architectural pretension of these new manses and those of their predecessors is provided at Fintry where the manse of 1732 (now Dunmore Cottage) stands near its successor (the New Manse) of 1836, the first low and rubble-built with crow-stepped gables, the second taller, its windows architraved, the door set in a pilastered surround. The early C19 Fintry Manse is a simply detailed example of a standard type, a three-bay-fronted house of two storeys with an attic originally lit by windows in the gables, perhaps supplemented by skylights, and invariably covered with a slated roof. Very similar are Logie Manse (now Logie House), Bridge of Allan, of 1803, Lecropt Manse of 1812 and Muckhart Manse, Pool of Muckhart, of c. 1832, all designed by *William Stirling I*, the off-centre doorpiece of the first a pedimented aedicule, the second's Roman Doric pilastered doorpiece containing a round-headed fanlight, the doorpiece of the third with a block pediment. Slightly more pretentious is the former Bothkennar Parish Manse, by *David Hamilton*, 1815–16, its eaves cornice surmounted by a blocking course which rises to a parapet over the centre bay, the ground-floor windows three-light and elliptically arched, the entrance pilastered and corniced. Later in the C19 manses were enlarged, almost all being given dormer windows and many one or two bay windows. Rear wings were often added or rebuilt, generally to provide a new kitchen with bedrooms and a bathroom above.

Each C18 or early C19 manse was accompanied by offices (a barn, byre and stable, cellar and brewhouse) of unassuming character, e.g. the (now ruinous) early C19 U-plan court at Kilmaronock Manse, although these were sometimes partially removed in the late C19 when ministers had ceased to farm their glebes. Often, at the same time, one of the offices was converted or rebuilt as a gig house to shelter the two-wheeled horse-drawn trap which was, by then, the usual mode of ministerial transport.

FARMHOUSES, until the late C18 agricultural improvements that replaced 'townships' or 'fermtouns' by individual tenanted farms, were primitive, described by John Francis Erskine in his *General View of the Agriculture of the County of Clackmannan* (1795) as 'miserable hovels'. In the area of Stirling and Central Scotland these were single-storey buildings, the walls, *c.* 2.13m. high, constructed of stone, either without mortar or with clay mortar. The roofs were supported by inelegant structures of which the most important components were pairs of curved crucks, their feet built into the lower part of the walls, their tops often joined by collar and tie beams and sometimes supporting a saddle of small uprights under the ridge-pole. A number of purlins, usually of branches or saplings, were laid on the crucks and in turn covered by smaller pieces of wood to form a mat under the roof covering, which was of ferns, turf or heather. These farmhouses usually contained two rooms, each *c.* 3.66m.–4.27m. square, sometimes with a small closet between them. One of the rooms was the kitchen, also used for sleeping, the other (the 'spence') the bedroom of the head of the family and used also to receive visitors. The windows, one to each room, were generally closed by partly glazed shutters. Under the same roof and separated from the kitchen by a partition of clay-plastered willow was the byre and stable. One survivor of these farmhouses is Moirlanich Longhouse near Killin, its thatched roof now covered with corrugated iron, the spence containing a hanging lum (flue) constructed of wood and clay. Others, also with corrugated iron roofs covering their thatch, remain at Lochearnhead.

Improved agriculture became general in the area in the late C18 and early C19. Tenants practised a regular rotation of crops and increased the fertility of the land by the application of lime. This was accompanied by the erection of new farmhouses and steadings, the cost of their construction usually paid by the landlord, the tenant providing carriage for the materials. Many of the farms in Stirling and Central Scotland were small and their farmhouses and steadings correspondingly modest but all the new houses were built of lime-mortared stone, with roofs constructed on an A-frame of usually imported timber and covered with slates, pantiles or, sometimes, straw thatch. They were often of a single storey and attic, *c.* 12m. by 6m. externally, with side walls *c.* 2.74m. high, and contained two rooms and a closet on the ground floor and two attic rooms above. The steading at Lochend, near Carron Bridge, is typical of a small farm of the earlier C19. The farmhouse and offices form a rubble-walled U-plan court, the single-storey and attic farmhouse in the middle of the long centre range, the office buildings slightly lower, their projecting wings ending in piend-roofed gables. A circular horsemill was attached to the outer side of the barn, which occupied one wing, the stable and byre filling the opposite wing. At Muirmill, also near Carron Bridge, the early C19 barn's threshing mill was powered by a water wheel. On larger farms the houses were of two storeys, e.g. at Gartinstarry, near Buchlyvie, of 1789, the probably late C18 Gartur, near Dykehead, or the early C19

Kipperoch, near Renton, and Tullochan, near Gartocharn, all plain, with three-bay fronts, standing in the main range of the steading. At Burnshot, near Blackness, the farmhouse and pantile-roofed steading of the earlier C19 are adjacent but do not make up a formal courtyard. Some two-storey farmhouses enjoyed modest architectural pretension, much like contemporary manses. At Arnprior Farm, Arnprior, the late C18 house displays a pilastered doorpiece and wallhead cornice surmounted by a blocking course. The centre bay of the early C19 house at King O' Muirs, near Glenochil, is bowed and contains a three-light first-floor window. The mid- or late C18 house at Birdston Farm, near Milton of Campsie, is of five bays, with a first-floor lintel course under the moulded wallhead cornice, scrolled and rosetted skewputts, and false keystones to the window surrounds. The two-storey house of the early C19 Buchanan Home Farm in the grounds of Buchanan Castle is joined by single-storey links to pavilions. This modest sophistication must have resulted from the farm's proximity to a ducal residence. A stronger assertion of being part of a plutocratic complex is the steeple on the early C19 Home Farm at Harviestoun, an exceptional gesture in this area of generally modest farms and farm buildings.

COTTAGES to house smallholders or farm labourers were, until the late C18 and early C19, squalid, the low walls built of drystone, occasionally with clay mortar, the cruck-framed roofs covered with turf and straw or ferns, the fire sited in the middle of the floor, the smoke escaping through a hole in the roof. New cottages commensurate with the new farmhouses and steading began to be built by the late C18. They remained humble but the masonry of their walls was mortared, windows were glazed and chimneys provided at the gables. The roofs were of A-frame construction and covered with pantiles or thatch. A recognizable surviving late C18 cottage range is the present Post Office at Arnprior, the walls rising from a base of boulders but scrolled skewputts providing a minor architectural flourish. This building's thatch was replaced by slates early in the C20. By the mid C19 rural cottages were modest single-storey versions of the smaller farmhouses and generally plain. Unusually picturesque are the cottages in Cadder Road, Bishopbriggs, built for workers on the Cawder House estate, their harled walls enlivened with red sandstone dressings, some of the windows corniced and gables dressed up with scrolled skewputts.

# INDUSTRIAL BUILDINGS

The towns and villages of much of Stirling and Central Scotland were founded or developed in the late C18 and C19 to house factory workers and miners. By the mid C19 the s part of the region was one of the most heavily industrialized in Scotland. Economic changes in the C20 destroyed most of the industry, depriving the associated settlements of obvious reasons for existence.

In 1750 Stirling and Central Scotland was a predominantly rural area, the burghs small and home to merchants and craftsmen (masons, wrights, smiths, glaziers, tailors, glovers, cobblers, etc.) who, for the most part, worked either on site in the case of the building trades or in what can be termed, not inaccurately, cottage industries. A few towns were noted for specialities, notably Doune for its late medieval leather-working and pistol manufacture, but purpose-built workshops, except for smithies and bakeries, were few and all were small.

From the Middle Ages until the end of the C18 the most significant rural buildings after churches and castles or lairds' houses were the monasteries', lairds' or burghs' GRAIN MILLS to which peasants were thirled, i.e. bound to bring their produce for milling. An act of 1799 allowed commutation of this feudal servitude and improved farms of the early C19 were almost always equipped with their own threshing mills; many of the earlier grain mills were converted to other purposes or demolished. One of the few that has survived is the rubble-built and crowstep-gabled Inverallan Mill of 1710 at Bridge of Allan, its eight-spoke undershot wheel powered by a lade from the Allan Water. An underground lade from the Burn of Mar powered the wheel of the C18 Buchanan Mill at Milton of Buchanan. An alternative to water power was wind and the rubble-built round tower of a windmill of c. 1700 (later converted to a doocot) stands on a hill to the s of Sauchie.

Lime, long used in mortar and harling of stone buildings but usually burnt on site in temporary and inefficient horizontal or clamp kilns, acquired much greater importance in the later C18 when its use to improve the fertility of land came to be generally accepted. As a result permanent LIME KILNS were erected. These were vertical stone-built draw kilns, often circular, in which the lime was burnt over coal-fired furnace pots. Many stood alone but at Cambusbarron the late C18 Murrayshall and Craigend Limeworks were composed of ranges containing respectively three and four kilns, built against a bank, enabling the coal and limestone to be packed in from the top, the quicklime produced discharging through draw-holes. Here the limeworks became an industrial operation, being linked by a tramway to the Forth & Clyde Junction Railway which was opened in 1856.

DISTILLERIES in the area existed from the C18, e.g. the Tambowie Distillery at Milngavie, the Glenochil Distillery founded in 1746, the Rosebank Distillery at Falkirk and the Carsebridge Distillery at Alloa, both begun in the 1790s, the Littlemill Distillery at Bowling founded c. 1800 and the Cambus Distillery established in 1806. However, these were small, the whisky being made in pot stills, and the industry suffered under punitive excise duties imposed in the late C18. In 1828 the duties were reduced sharply and the invention in 1829–30 of the Stein and Coffey stills enabled continuous distillation. As a result existing distilleries were redeveloped and new ones founded, e.g. the Bankier Distillery at Denny in 1828, the Bo'ness Distillery in 1830 and the Burnfoot (later Glengoyne) Distillery at Killearn in 1833. Although the Kilbagie Distillery boasted a Boulton & Watt steam engine in the 1790s, water was the main power source for the machinery of most of these until the mid C19 when steam engines became more general. Most distilleries, if they continued in business, were largely rebuilt in the later C19, like the Rosebank Distillery at Falkirk whose surviving brick and stone buildings date from 1864 or the Littlemill Distillery at Bowling, its pyramidal-roofed kilns part of a reconstruction of 1875. Further rebuilding of the few distilleries in the area that continued production took place in the C20, the resultant buildings, e.g. of 1937 at the Cambus Distillery, utilitarian but at the Hiram Walker distillery in Dumbarton, developed from 1937, on a massive scale.

BREWING was a craft industry organized on domestic lines, sometimes carried out at inns, until the early C19 when it came to be concentrated in larger breweries founded or developed in towns, e.g. at Falkirk and Stirling. Alloa was a brewing centre, its Meadow Brewery founded in 1762 but much enlarged seventy years later; the Candleriggs Brewery opened in 1787, the Mills Brewery c. 1804, the Alloa Brewery in 1810 and the Shore Brewery in 1816. In the early and mid C19 a typical brewery comprised a courtyard of two- or three-storey buildings including maltings, stores, a granary, cooperage, stables and, perhaps, an office, the machinery powered by water, horses or, increasingly, steam engines. Steam power became general in the later C19 when the industry became more concentrated in a relatively small number of breweries. Their architecture made little attempt at display, e.g. the plain buildings of 1910 at the Thistle Brewery in Alloa. Redevelopment of breweries in the later C20, e.g. the reconstruction of the Alloa Brewery in 1958–68 (demolished 2001), impressed by size alone.

TANNERIES such as had existed in most medieval towns continued without much alteration in their nature until the late C19 when large centralized tanneries were built. The largest of these in Scotland was the tannery of c. 1880 at Tullibody (demolished 2001), its four-storey main block's two top floors where the hides were laid to dry after tanning having louvred walls, a round brick chimney disclosing the use of a steam engine to power machinery.

LINEN MANUFACTURE was practised in Scotland by the C17 but for long the workers were handloom weavers working in or outside their own cottages and, until the C18, producing coarse cloth which was left unbleached. However, the C18 saw a rise in both the quantity (from c. 3,200,000m. to c. 21,760,000m. of officially stamped linen) and quality of Scottish linen. Lint mills containing water-powered machinery for scutching flax (i.e. beating it to separate the fibres from the woody parts) copied from Dutch examples were built in Scotland from the 1730s and increased rapidly after Robert McPherson's improved 'perpendicular' construction for water power was introduced in the 1760s, although even in 1800 machine-scutched flax amounted to only about a quarter of the total used in the linen industry. The next stage in the processing of flax, heckling (combing the fibres to draw them out before spinning), remained unmechanized until the C19. A large factory for the spinning of linen thread was put up at Renton c. 1763, its seven thread mills powered by water from the River

Leven. Factory spinning of linen cloth did not become common until after the invention of wet spinning (allowing mechanical moistening of the brittle flax) in 1825. The cottage industry of hand-loom weaving was replaced by factory-housed power looms later in the C19.

COTTON was woven in Scotland by the mid C18 when it was combined with linen to produce fustian. A significant development of cotton manufacture took place after 1775, aided by the invention of Richard Crompton's mule which combined features of Hargreaves's spinning jenny and Arkwright's water frame to increase immensely the amount of yarn that could be spun. Much of the production was the work of handloom weavers but these could be and often were employed in factories rather than working at home. One late C18 cotton-spinning mill was at Dunipace on the River Carron, others at Deanston (of 1785) on the River Teith, at Bannockburn beside the eponymous burn, and at Milton (of c. 1790) on the Milton Burn. Three, Ballikinrain Mill of 1792, the five-storey Ballindalloch Mill of 1790 at Balfron, and the four-storey mill of 1792–4 at Fintry, were on the River Endrick, all employing large workforces, that of Ballindalloch Mill reportedly amounting to 390 men, women and children in the 1790s. All these were water-powered. So too were the four mills taken over or built by William Dunn at Duntocher between 1808 and 1831. However, by 1835 Dunn had introduced steam power to three of these. Most of the mill buildings seem to have been architecturally austere and barracks-like, although Milton Mill had Palladian Gothick windows in its battlemented towers. Some were short-lived. The mills at Deanston and Ballikinrain were destroyed by fire in 1796 and 1806 and not rebuilt. Of the others, several burnt down and the rest closed in the later C19.

WOOLLEN MANUFACTURE, formerly conducted by handloom weavers, expanded and became industrialized in the late C18 and early C19, the mechanization applied first to the spinning of the wool and then to the weaving of the cloth. Early woollen mills could be sizeable, one at Old Kilpatrick employing c. 320 workers by the 1790s. Again, they were water-powered. Many were built along the foot of the Ochil Hills to take advantage of their precipitous burns, the earliest perhaps a mill put up at Alva in 1798. The Clock
122 Mill of 1824 at Tillicoultry is given modest pretension by its ball-finialled S gable, which contains a clock face. Much larger but austere are the tall and narrow Royal George Mill of c. 1822 at Bannockburn, whose wooden floors span from wall to wall unsup-
123 ported by columns, and the Deanston Spinning Mill of 1830–1, its severity barely relieved by the roundheaded windows of its ashlar ground floor. From the mid C19 the mills became broader, the floors usually supported by cast iron columns as well as at the outer walls, although the external dress was still severe late Georgian as at the mid-C19 Strude Mill at Alva, whose twenty-six-bay frontage is relieved only by a slightly advanced and pedimented centrepiece topped by a bellcote. Steam power became common from the 1850s for both spinning and weaving, hand looms being replaced by power looms, usually housed in sawtooth-roofed sheds. The

largest of the late C19 mills in Stirling and Central Scotland are
the Hayford Mills at Cambusbarron, by *Wylie & Davie* (later
*James Davie & Sons*), *c.* 1860–80, the buildings Italianate in red
brick with white trimmings and consciously polite in their architecture. Other mills developed in piecemeal fashion. The sizeable
Kilncraigs Factory at Alloa began *c.* 1830 with a rectangular mill
building of *c.* 17m. by 7m. and of at least two storeys above a basement, with an adjoining wheel-house containing a wheel powered
by water from the Brathie Burn. Two further buildings, a wareroom
or store, and the West Mill, apparently steam-powered, were put
up *c.* 1850, the Burnside or East Mill in 1859 and the North Mill
in 1868. In 1878 the original mill was rebuilt and provided with an
engine house for its steam engine, which replaced the earlier water
wheel. All these buildings of the mid and later C19 were deep, their
floors supported on cast iron columns, but fire-proof construction
was used only at the stair towers. It was only in the C20 and at the
firm's offices that the Kilncraigs Factory's architectural ambitions
rose much above the utilitarian. In 1903–4 *William Kerr* of *John
Melvin & Son* provided a tall English Baroque office block and, in
1936, together with *John Gray*, extended it with an example of 127
white harled modernity belied only by its piended roofs, just visible
above the tall parapet.

  PAPER MILLS in the C18 and early C19 were by-products of the
textile industry, the raw material for manufacture being rags of
bleached linen and, later, of cotton, largely replaced in the later
C19 by esparto grass and then wood pulp. A mill was founded at
Sauchie *c.* 1787, two mills at Dunipace in 1789 and 1806, three
mills at Airthrey in 1803, 1825 and 1832, and mills at Bearsden in
1793, Falkirk in *c.* 1799, Stirling in 1806 and Keir in *c.* 1825, all
powered by water which was also important in the manufacturing
process. From the mid C19 steam became the motive power for
the machinery which, as in other industries, became more sophisticated and powerful. One of the few surviving mills is the late C19
Kilbagie Mill, utilitarian except for its water tower.

  BLEACHING (for linen and cotton) and dyeing were intimately
associated with the textile industries. A bleachfield, its design copied
from Dutch examples, was constructed at Renton in 1728 and three
more, at Dalmuir (Clydebank), Glorat and Keir, between 1746 and
1760. By the 1790s bleachfields were common in the area, the
heaviest concentration being in the Vale of Leven, their buildings,
now long demolished, having louvred roofs. Bleaching required
the cloth to be steeped in a hot alkaline solution and then, after it
was washed and dried, the application to it of acid. For most of
the C18 the alkali was provided by wood, weed or kelp but chlorine
was introduced in 1788 and its use became common after Charles
Tennant patented his invention of a dry bleaching powder formed
from chlorine and lime and manufactured in the huge St Rollox
Works in Glasgow. An alternative alkali, sal ammoniac, was also
used and made in Stirling and Central Scotland (e.g. at the Dalmuir
Shore Soda Works at Clydebank) from the late C18. From the mid
C18 the acid commonly used in the bleaching process was vitriol
(sulphuric acid) and chemical works for its production were put

up. DYEING of textiles, often with printed patterns, was frequently associated with bleaching by the later C18. Two of the earliest print-works were established at Kirkintilloch and Cordale, near Renton, by the 1770s. From the early C19 the most frequently used dyes were Prussian blue and Turkey red. Prussian blue (made from iron cyanides) was manufactured at Lennoxtown and Millburn and Turkey red (a madder-based dye) in a string of works (e.g. Dalquharn, Croftinglea, Levenbank, Milton and Dillichip) in the Vale of Leven, which enjoyed pure water from Loch Lomond and clean air. Fixing of the colours in dyeing was achieved by the use of alum (or copperas) or ferrous sulphate. An alum works at Lennoxtown, its buildings' roofs covered with tarred paper, was founded in 1806 and the Bo'ness Copperas Works c. 1808. At the end of the C19 these dyes were replaced by synthetic dyes, many imported from Germany. German dyes were unavailable during the First World War and anthraquinone dyestuffs were developed as an alternative, leading to the establishment in 1919 of the Scottish Dyers (now Avecia) Factory at Grangemouth.

COAL is found under almost all of Clackmannanshire and SE Stirlingshire. It was mined from the Middle Ages but the problem and expense of draining mines long limited development of the industry. For his mines near Alloa John, sixth and eleventh Earl of Mar, developed a drainage system by which buckets hung from a wheel hauled up the water, the wheel's motive power provided by water from the Brathie Burn, itself fed from the reservoir behind the Gartmorn Dam which he had constructed at the beginning of the C18. Steam pumping engines, although introduced from the 1720s, were rare before the late C18. In the C19 when the canal and railway systems made transport easy, mining developed as a major industry in the area. One memento of its former importance is
125 provided by the late C19 beam engine house of the former Devon Colliery near Fishcross, but in the late C20 the industry was all but killed by government action or inaction in the face of cheaper foreign imports and alternative sources of energy. GASWORKS abounded in the C19 and much of the C20, the fuel being produced from the redistillation of coal tar. One was founded at Alloa as early as 1828 and another at Kirkintilloch c. 1835. The Herbertshire Paper Mill at Dunipace was lit by gas by 1839 and the Deanston Mill by 1844. Gasworks were erected in the village of Slamannan in 1855 and by the later C19 all towns, many villages and some country houses had their own gasworks. One of the few surviving mementoes of an industry once almost ubiquitous is the gasholder of 1906 at Grahamston (Falkirk). OIL REFINING in the area began in 1924 at Grangemouth and developed in the later C20 into a
128 huge refining and petrochemical complex, its small-scale office buildings polite irrelevancies beside the unashamed functionalism of the industrial structures.

SALT PANNING, one early industry literally fuelled by coal, took place along the River Forth, notably at Bo'ness and at Kennetpans near Clackmannan, from the C15 until destroyed by English imports after the removal of the salt duty in 1825. In salt panning salt water was placed in iron pans heated by coal, the process usually carried out in stone-built pan houses, their steeply pitched roofs covered with turf or heather and, later, with pantiles. Another industry dependent on coal was GLASS MANUFACTURE in which high temperatures were required to fuse sand and soda. Glass works were opened at Alloa in 1750 and Dumbarton in 1777, the glass being made in tall truncated cone structures, originally fuelled by pot furnaces. One early C19 cone survives at Alloa.

IRON MANUFACTURE was the major coal-powered industry in Stirling and Central Scotland. Until the mid C18 this had been concentrated in Argyll where wood for charcoal-heated smelting furnaces was readily available, but one charcoal-fired furnace at Achray near Aberfoyle enjoyed a brief existence in the 1720s. However, in 1759 a trio of entrepreneurs founded the Carron Ironworks sited conveniently near ironstone and coal deposits and linked by a canal to the River Carron and thence to the River Forth. The Carron Works, modelled on the coke-fired ironworks

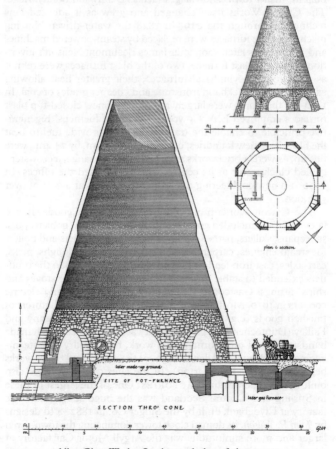

Alloa Glass Works. Section and plan of glass cone.

at Coalbrookdale (Shropshire), combined production of pig iron with the extraction from it of wrought iron and the casting and forging of metal goods, the most notable in the Works' early years being the 'Carronade', a gun used principally by privateers. As first built in 1759–66 the Carron Works contained four coke-heated blast furnaces, the blasts of cold air provided by water-driven blowing machines designed by *John Smeaton*. Although the Carron Works remained of exceptional size, employing 2,000 men by *c*. 1776, rival ironworks appeared before the end of the C18, the Devon Ironworks near Fishcross being founded in 1792 and a foundry at Alloa and a smithing and iron factory at Old Kilpatrick by the 1790s. In 1819 former employees of the Carron Works founded the Falkirk Ironworks as a foundry and factory for the manufacture of steam engines. By the 1830s there was an iron foundry at Dumbarton and the Kinneil Works at Bo'ness was founded in 1845. In the mid and later C19 thirteen further ironworks were founded at Falkirk, most standing beside the Forth & Clyde Canal, and other ironworks were built in smaller towns and villages such as Denny and Bonnybridge. The Carron Works itself changed and grew as it adopted new technology through the C19. In 1828 the water-driven blowing machines at the furnaces were replaced by steam-powered machines and, seven years later, soon after James Beaumont Neilson's invention of the hot blast furnace, two of the blast furnaces were rebuilt as open-topped cylindrical furnaces, their greater heat allowing exploitation of blackband ironstone and cheaper grades of coal. In 1874–83 the works were largely rebuilt. Four new closed-top blast furnaces employed E. A. Cowper's version of Siemens' regenerative principle to enable the trapped gases to provide fuel to heat the blast. Two new foundries, one a massive 46.9m. by 24.4m., were put up, as were a brickworks and the long front range, a crowstepgabled clock tower at its centre, which contained the offices. In 1900–1 a new engineering department was built at a cost of over £30,000.

The Carron Works produced a huge variety of goods. In the later C18 these included guns, hand grenades, kettles, goblets, pots, saucepans, skillets, parts for millwheels, pipes, cylinders and boilers for steam engines, carpenters' tools, spades, hoes, ploughs, picks, cart-axles, cast iron fenders and pedestal stoves. By 1880 the products extended to stable fittings, kitchen ranges, register stoves and ships' fittings. Gas cookers were introduced in 1902 and electric cookers in 1910. Most other ironworks were also manufacturers of finished goods (e.g. the early C19 spade factories at Denny and Faifley (Duntocher), the Lion Foundry at Kirkintilloch which made bandstands and other ornamental work, the foundry and steam-engine factory built at Alloa in 1832, or the engine and boiler works begun in 1847 at Dumbarton). In the later C19 there were also built large single-product FACTORIES. One of the largest of these in Stirling and Central Scotland was the huge sewing-machine factory at Clydebank built by the Singer Co. in 1882–4 to designs by *John B. Wilson*, its domed clock tower dominating the town. Even larger and more sumptuous was the Argyll Motor Car factory at Alexandria designed by *Halley & Neil* in 1905, the factory sheds and workshops single-storey and utilitarian, the 165m.-long two-storey office range a sumptuous red sandstone essay in Beaux-Arts-influenced free Baroque, the pedimented centrepiece supporting a domed tempietto.

SHIPBUILDING took place in the area by 1494, when rowing barges were built for James IV at Dumbarton, and in 1505 construction of the ship *Columba* was begun at the same town. On a smaller scale, ships were being built at Airth by 1723, the shipyard equipped with a wind-powered sawmill. In the 1830s there were yards on the Clyde at Dumbarton and Bowling but huge expansion of the Clydeside industry took place in the mid and later C19. A. MacMillan & Son Ltd. established a shipbuilding yard in 1834 at Dumbarton where, ten years later, William Denny & Bros. founded another from which they moved to a new yard in 1867, the same year in which the MacMillan yard was extended. The first iron steamer built at Dumbarton was launched in 1844, the first screw-propeller steamer the next year and the first steel steamer in 1879. Clydebank developed rapidly from a village into a shipbuilding conurbation after 1871 when James & George Thomson moved their business there from Govan (Glasgow), constructing a six-berth shipbuilding yard with a fitting-out basin at its w end. A second shipbuilding yard was made *c.* 1900 and a test tank opened in 1903. In 1906 the company erected a hammer-head crane, capable of lifting 152.4 tonnes, for installing boilers and engines in the ships. In the Thomsons' yard (owned from 1899 by John Brown & Co.) were built the great liners of the Cunard shipping company, the *Servia*, launched in 1881, the *Carmania* in 1906, the *Lusitania* in 1907, the *Queen Mary* in 1934 and the *Queen Elizabeth* in 1938, as well as H.M.S. *Hood* in 1918 and the royal yacht *Britannia* in 1953. A second shipbuilding firm, William Beardmore & Co., opened another yard at Clydebank in 1905, largely but not exclusively for the construction of warships. Two of its six berths were *c.* 305m. long and one of these was equipped with an overhead gantry, 228.7m. long, 35.7m. wide and 40.5m. high.

Almost all of Stirling and Central Scotland's C19 industries have gone. Cotton, linen and alkali manufacture were virtually abandoned by 1900. Woollen manufacture, although just alive, has never recovered from the punitive import duties imposed by the United States of America in 1890. The manufacture of iron collapsed in the face of the switch to steel produced outside the area from the early C20. The Argyll Motor Works at Alexandria closed as a car factory in 1914, the Singer sewing machine factory at Clydebank in 1980, and the last working shipyard on the Clyde, except for the production of a few oil rigs, in 1973. Coal mining is now all but extinct.

New industries came in the late C20, especially ones related to INFORMATION TECHNOLOGY, housed, for the most part, in discreetly sited sheds and low office blocks packaged in a variety of Modern and Postmodern styles. The buildings of the Castle Business Park at Stirling, developed in the 1990s to designs by the *Hurd, Rolland Partnership*, have attempted to be of their time but with references to traditional Scottish architecture. Architectural quality is shown at some of the University of Stirling's Innovation Park buildings, the most elegant being *Davis, Duncan, Harrold*'s steel-framed E.R.D.C. Building of 1999–2000, the gently bent long elevations covered with grids of glass, glass brick and tiling. *Cobban & Lironi*'s Wallaceview Business Park near Blairlogie is a dark-glass-walled symbol of the new technology's promise of a future far removed from that of the heavy industry of the area's past.

# STIRLING AND
# CENTRAL SCOTLAND

## ABER WD *4080*

A hamlet of scattered dwellings 1.3km. N of Gartocharn. A few cottages cluster casually around ABER MILL which retains a lintel stone dated 1806.

## ABERDONA HOUSE C *9090*
### 2.7km. ESE of Coalsnaughton

Rubble-built L-plan laird's house which has developed in three stages. The first is represented by the early C18 two-storey NE range, quite plain except for three-light windows in the S bay. These may be early C19 insertions made when the shorter S range was built. This is again of two storeys and has three-light windows in the E bay. At its W bay, a hoodmoulded Tudor door, presumably given its present form in the mid C19 when the notched heel of the L was filled with a three-storey battlemented tower, its windows hoodmoulded.

## ABERFOYLE S *5000*

A clachan of 'miserable little bourocks' until Sir Walter Scott brought the hamlet to the attentions of C19 travellers in search of the picturesque. Since then its location E of Loch Ard and S of Lochs Achray and Venachar has made it the gateway to the Trossachs. It remains a tourist stop, rather more car park than village.

OLD PARISH CHURCH, Kirkton, 0.5km. SSW. Rebuilt 1744, repaired 1839, a roofless rubble shell, the walls standing to eaves height. Session house at E gable. Four lintelled windows with sandstone margins in the S wall. False wallhead belfry contrived on the E gable over the relieving arch. – Within, several headstones and, high on the N wall, a sarcophagus TABLET inscribed under a shallow pediment block with wreath carving in memory of Jane Dent †1846. – Two cast iron MORT-SAFES, early C19, sit outside the W doorway. – In the GRAVEYARD are lying SLABS and TABLE-TOMBS, C17 and C18, including one commemorating Robert Kirk †1692, pastor at Aberfoyle, LINGUAE HIBERNIAE LUMEN (as the tomb records) and author of a strange essay on the subject of fairies. Several mantled HEADSTONES with fluted pilasters and edges, early C19. Celtic CROSS covered in vines within a

cable-moulded edge and raised on a convex base; to Robert Blair
†1903, and his family.

PARISH CHURCH, 0.75km. WNW. Gothic Revival at its scholarly
best by *John Honeyman*. Begun in 1869–70 as a simple oblong
built in greenish whin rubble with ochre sandstone dressings, and
in 1883–4 elaborated into a cruciform plan with gabled transepts
N and S, with an octagonal vestry added in the NE re-entrant
and the entrance porch moved to the W end of the S wall. In the
W gable and transepts, a cusped circle over three lancets. All
doors and windows have moulded arches and shafted jambs.
The four-bay nave is roofed with arch-braced trusses carrying
purlins, diagonal bracing and counter-diagonal boarding. A
moulded pointed chancel arch rises from clustered shafts with
floral capitals. In the sanctuary, *Minton* tile chequer-board floor
pattern in red, rust, cream, black and green. Cusped-arch N doorway to vestry and, on the S wall, a stone PISCINA. – PULPIT of
Caen stone and Italian alabaster, a rounded square in plan with
three Gothic aedicules inset, each carved with vines, wheat and
passion flowers. – Recessed in the N wall beside the transept is
the ORGAN, by *Bryceson Bros.* of London, 1887; timber tracery
and painted pipes. – Original paraffin LAMPS, now electrified,
wall-mounted N and S. – MEMORIALS. N side sanctuary, a pink
granite TABLET in cusp-arched sandstone surround, to Richard
Hampson †1866, in whose memory the church was begun. N
transept, brass memorial PANELS to his wife, Mary †1886, and
brother, Robert †1888, patrons. – S wall, mounted on veined
white marble, another brass PLATE with knot-pattern edging to
the Rev. W. Moncrieff Taylor, 1919, under whose ministry the
church took its present form. – STAINED GLASS. W gable:
orthodox Victorian personifications of Faith, Charity and Hope
by *Alfred O. Hemming & Co.*, 1884. – A single S lancet pictures
Loch Ard and Ben Lomond. – S transept: in memory of Isabella
Dalziel †1897, a conventional Mary with the Infant Jesus
flanked by a knight in vigil and an elderly couple, both representations bathed in olive-brown colour, *c*. 1900. – N transept: a
crowned Christ between St Francis and the Virgin; by *Gordon
Webster*, 1974. – E wall, below a cherub amid pink angel wings,
Moses with a Commandments tablet and a scarlet-cloaked
Good Shepherd; in memory of Mary and Robert Hampson,
*c*. 1890.

   The BELL presented to the Old Parish Church (*see* above) by
the Duke of Montrose in 1725 hangs in a small saddleback-
roofed structure close to the E gable. – Downhill is the village
WAR MEMORIAL, 1921, a swollen octagonal-plan sandstone
shaft carrying a cross with inscribed pink granite panels on the
plinth and steps.

ST MARY (Episcopal), Main Street. Arts and Crafts Gothic by
*James Miller*, 1893–4, charmingly perched on a leafy hillside.
Walls are roughcast with red sandstone for window and door
dressings, and for the weathered stringcourse capping a high
rubble base. The saddleback-roofed belfry wall rises high above
the ridge from the chancel-arch wall below. Timber-framed S

porch. Plastered interior. Four-bay roof arch-braced under simple kingpost trusses; spars stripe the ceiling soffits and upper walls. – FURNISHINGS mostly contemporary. At the W end, the egg-shaped FONT in red sandstone. – To l. of chancel arch, a circular stone PULPIT, 1899, pierced by cusped pointed-arched openings. – Stained oak LECTERN, cruciform in plan, with cusped tracery and finials. – Massive stone ALTAR block carved with simple ringed cross motif and commemorative inscription. – Pipe ORGAN, installed 1900 but replaced by *Willis & Sons*, 1957. – Behind this, the church's treasure, an impressive, ruggedly assembled oak REREDOS of unknown provenance bearing the date 1683. At its centre, the head, shoulders and (mutilated) hands of Christ, around which are disposed dragon scrolls, leaves, diamond patterns and tracery daggers in a composition more appealing for its naïveté than any stylistic conviction. – STAINED GLASS depicting scenes from Christ's life in the four lancets above the altar, C20; in one N lancet, a cloaked scholar and the words MEDICINA, RELIGIO, ARS recalling the interests of the church's organist, Anne Smith, 1966; in another N lancet, St Anne, by *Gordon Webster* (?).

ABERFOYLE BRIDGE. C18. Rubble structure with narrow parapeted carriageway widening on N bank. Two segmental arches span the River Forth. Central faceted cutwater.

BRAEVAL MILL, 1.5km. SE. Mid C19. Single-storey-and-attic gabled rubble; now a restaurant. The wheel has gone. Across the road, BRAEVAL FARM, late C18, standard two-storey, three-bay, with a later single-storey wing extended E.

DAVID MARSHALL LODGE, Queen Elizabeth Forest Park, 0.5km. N. 1958–60, by *James Shearer & Annand* of Dunfermline. Hilltop leisure centre with viewing loggias of twin-tubed concrete columns. Built in Lake District masonry and inexplicably flat-roofed apart from a small pyramidally roofed tower. Stained timber N additions by *Ian G. Lindsay & Partners*, 1978. Delightful landscape setting.

SCHOOL, 0.6km. WNW. By *John Honeyman*. Dated 1870 on the schoolhouse gable; enlarged 1890. L-plan classrooms in unexpectedly good Gothic Revival with S and W buttressed porches. Detached SE block, 1906; also by *Honeyman*.

DESCRIPTION. MAIN STREET is straight and short, alive with holiday buzz but with no continuity of enclosure and little architectural quality. The N side is the better. Built in whin rubble and red sandstone, the shops and flats of the BANK OF SCOTLAND BUILDINGS, *c*. 1900, have octagonal corners with slated peaks, mullioned and transomed windows, gabled porch canopies and a solidly Scottish sense of Arts and Crafts worth. More English is CRAIGHUCHTY TERRACE by *James Miller*, 1895: red sandstone but with a tile-hung first floor and roof just as red; six three-storeyed houses in a row with bay windows, coupled doorways, and half-timbered gables at the ends. Nothing else measures up to this standard, except perhaps the same architect's St Mary's Church (*see* above).

# AIRTH

Village close to the River Forth. It began as a burgh of barony under the superiority of the Bruces of Airth in 1597, the first houses being built on high ground *c.* 0.3km NNW of Airth Castle and the former Airth Parish Church. Apparently in 1697 (the date on the new Market Cross) a 'new town' was begun further N on low ground closer to the shore. In 1724 Alexander Graham of Duchray noted of this that '. . .there's building a tolbooth and fleshmarket. There's several good houses already built, and others building.' He also mentioned the existence of a harbour, shipbuilding yard and sawmill but Airth failed to develop as an industrial centre and now serves as a dormitory for nearby towns.

## CHURCHES

12 Former AIRTH PARISH CHURCH, in a graveyard immediately E of Airth Castle. Roofless and ivy-clad remains of a medieval church which was remodelled and overlaid by outshots shortly before and after the Reformation.

A church at Airth was in existence by *c.* 1130 when it was granted by David I to the Abbey of Holyrood. Its nave almost certainly occupied the site of the w half of the present building's main block and was *c.* 13.4m. by 7.6m. A three-bay N aisle was added to the nave at the end of the C12. Of this aisle's arcade there survive the keeled E and W responds and the round E pier, all visible inside the present building. They have bases of an early waterholding type, the lower roll of flat and semi-elliptical profile. The capital of the pier has a square abacus above concave sides which are carved with crude foliage. The E respond's waterleaf capital (its exposed s face badly weathered, its N face preserved within later walling) has been much more accomplished and was presumably the work of a different mason. The present semicircular arch carried by the E respond and pier is C17, probably constructed in 1614 when the Bruce Aisle was built behind it.

Also surviving from the pre-Reformation church is the ashlar-walled transeptal Lady Chapel (the AIRTH AISLE) added on the s by Alexander Bruce of Airth *c.* 1480. The s gable's skew-putts are carved with the Bruce coat of arms; weathered finial at the apex. Below the gable's cope are several carved flowers. Large pointed s window with a chamfered surround. Its present form dates from the C17 when the original window was contracted. The hoodmould is C15, the pendant label stops carved with foliage. On the window's C17 E jamb, an incised sundial. In the Aisle's W wall, a small mullioned window of two rectangular lights, probably a C17 insertion. On the E wall, a canopied image niche, its bracket carved with the Bruce coat of arms. Inside the Aisle, at the s end of the E wall, an aumbry. Under the s window, an elliptical-arched recess. It now contains the sandstone EFFIGY of a recumbent woman, her head resting on a pillow, her hands joined in prayer. The lower half of her body is covered with a sheet or blanket on which, at the figure's feet, lie a pair of curled-up dogs. The effigy may be C14. It was moved to its present position from the E end of the church in the C20.

Immediately W of the Airth Aisle is the rubble-walled ELPHINSTONE AISLE added to the medieval nave in 1593. Cavetto-moulded eaves course. Rectangular door with rounded margins at the W side. In the crowstepped gable, a large rectangular window, again with rounded margins; it has been narrowed by the insertion of a chamfered jamb on the E side. Above the window, a badly weathered heraldic panel which was recorded in 1896 as displaying the quartered arms of Elphinstone and Livingstone. It is flanked by the initials A$^M$E (for Alexander, Master of Elphinstone) and IL/ME (for his wife, Janet Livingstone, Mistress of Elphinstone) and surmounts the date 1593. The Aisle opens into the nave of the church through a roundheaded arch of two orders, the inner chamfered. On the floor of the Aisle, seven GRAVESLABS of various dates between 1593 and 1638. They bear rather small coats of arms and inscriptions, all except one carved in relief.

A third addition to the pre-Reformation nave was made in 1614 with the construction of the transeptal BRUCE AISLE on the site of the E bay of the medieval N aisle. This was probably removed at this time except for the responds and one pier (*see* above), the two W bays of the arcade being replaced by a wall. Crowstepped N gable containing a rectangular door, the lintel inscribed 'I$^S$B M$^D$R.THE LORD IS MY TRVST', the initials those of Sir James Bruce of Powfoulis and Dame Margaret Rollox, his wife. Above the door, a moulded frame which contains a panel bearing the Bruce coat of arms under the initials of Sir James Bruce. His initials and those of his wife reappear on the W skewputt; on the E skewputt, the date 1614. On two stones at the W end of the gable have been scratched crude human figures and initials, probably by a vandalistic visitor at an indeterminate date.

Except for the Airth, Elphinstone and Bruce Aisles, the church was completely recast in 1647. The nave's W gable was rebuilt in rubble. Low down at its S end, a small window. Rectangular centre door and, higher up to its S, a second door formerly reached by a stone forestair, which gave access to a gallery. Above the main door and sharing a surround is a tall rectangular window. At the same time the pre-Reformation choir was removed and the nave extended E by *c.* 12.2m. In the new E gable, a rectangular door (originally a window) with a round-arched gallery window above. On the N side of this E extension, a three-bay arcade, the semicircular arches carried on corniced square piers. The arcade opened into an aisle, *c.* 3.35m. broad, which extended E of the Bruce Aisle. In the stonework of the arcade are postholes for the beams of galleries in the aisle and the E end of the nave. The aisle's N wall has been demolished. In the E gable, a roundheaded window.

Against the S wall of the 1640s extension of the nave, a stone forestair to an E gallery which was supported by a scarcement on the inner face of the gable. W of the forestair are two rectangular windows (now blocked) unaligned with the arcade openings opposite. Built into the external surround of the W of these windows, a panel carved with the date 1630 and the initials PH and KM; it is probably not *in situ*. Between the two windows, on the external face, a segmental-arched tomb recess, the initials PH and IC crudely incised on its keystone. W of the windows is a tower, its four intaken stages marked off by cavetto-moulded stringcourses. At the lowest stage, a S door, its margin hollow-chamfered; above the lintel, the inscription 'IVLY THE 15 1647'. At the second stage, near the N end of the E side, a door (probably for the minister) which was presumably reached originally by wooden steps. At this stage's SE corner, a weathered sundial. At the top stage, a round-arched belfry opening in each face. Moulded eaves course. There used to be a pyramidal slated roof with a small dormer window in each face. At the tower's N side, doors into the church at the two lowest stages; the upper door probably opened on to a high pulpit. Also on this face, corbels which apparently carried a wall-plate but above them is the raggle of a double-pitched roof (i.e. at r. angles to the main roof over the nave). Inside the tower, at the bottom stage, stone benches along the E and W sides.

AIRTH PARISH CHURCH, Main Street. By *William Stirling I*, 1817–20. Georgian Perp, faced with ashlar, droved horizontally at the main walling but vertically at the buttresses. On the buttresses, crocketed pinnacles. Hoodmoulds with corbel label stops over the mullioned and transomed windows whose heads are filled with cusped loop tracery. At the SE gable, a sturdily buttressed low semi-octagonal vestry; like the body of the church it is finished with a parapet pierced with Gothic arcading. Square NW tower, the wallhead now bereft of its parapet and the corners of their pinnacles. At the first stage, Tudor arched doors under rectangular hoodmoulds, the spandrels decorated with quatrefoil panels. Sill courses mark off the second and third stages, the second having hoodmoulded two-light windows, again with cusped loop tracery. At the third stage, tall hoodmoulded paired belfry openings under an arcaded frieze.

Inside, a D-plan gallery of 1817–20, with a Gothic panelled front. – The gallery SEATING was made in 1823–4 by *James Burn*. – The area's PEWS and the PULPIT date from *A. & W. Black*'s alterations of 1890. – Also of 1890 is the five-light SE STAINED GLASS window ('Oh come let us walk in the light of the Lord') by *Stephen Adam*, in characteristic Glasgow style with lots of flowers and the figure of a musician. – COMMUNION TABLE of 1904.

CHURCHYARD WALL built by *Robert Walker*, 1821, with low corniced gatepiers. – Just SE of the church, the Georgian survival MONUMENT (an obelisk on a corniced pedestal) erected by John Duncan in memory of his mother, Ann Bowie, 1863.

## PUBLIC BUILDINGS

AIRTH PRIMARY SCHOOL, Paul Drive. By *James Strang*, 1906. Tall single-storey, with broad eaves and half-timbering in the gables.

COMMUNITY HALL, Main Street. By *G. C. A. Architects Ltd.*, 1995. Harled rectangle, with a gablet-roof.

MARKET CROSS, High Street. Erected in the late C17. Stepped octagonal base supporting an octagonal shaft, its square capital 78 of quasi-Doric design. Above the capital, an acorn-finialled topknot, its corners carved with Ionic columns supporting a segmental pediment over each face. The SE and SW faces bear sundials. The SE pediment is carved with the date 1697, presumably for the cross's erection, the SW with crossed branches. On the NW face, the coat of arms of Elphinstone, and, in the pediment, the initials CE for Charles Elphinstone of Airth. The initials of his parents, Richard Elphinstone of Calderhall and Janet Bruce of Airth, are on the NE pediment and their coat of arms (Elphinstone quartered with Bruce) on the face below.

OLD MARKET CROSS, Airth Castle Park. Crudely squared shaft bearing an almost cubical head, its SE face apparently formerly used as a sundial. It is probably of *c.* 1600.

## DESCRIPTION

MAIN STREET's S end begins with the drive leading uphill to Airth Castle (*see* below) and the former Airth Parish Church (*see* Churches, above). The next incident on the l. is the Community Hall (*see* Public Buildings, above). This stands on the corner of High Street which curves away to the NW as an informal crescent while Main Street forms an answering rough crescent to the NE. In this stretch of Main Street, 1930s housing (by *Tatlock & Thomson*) on the r. On the l., two-storey terraced housing (FORRESTER PLACE) of *c.* 1962. It is of early C18 vernacular inspiration with moulded doorpieces and pantiled roofs, their eaves broken by catslide dormerheads. Reset in the front wall of No. 6 Forrester Place, a stone recording the Burgher Church which stood on the site ('THIS HOUSE WAS ERECTED AT The expence of The Burgher Meeting at Airth A.D. 1809'). More housing of the same type on the r. side of HIGH STREET (Nos. 2–38). At its N end, the ELPHINSTONE INN of *c.* 1800, with a central chimneyed gablet and a cornice over the off-centre door. Here the street broadens into a rough triangle in which stands the Market Cross (*see* Public Buildings, above). N of this is the crowstep-gabled, rubble-built and pantile-roofed VIEW VILLA, 78 its date provided by an oval panel inscribed 'SP/JH/1722' above the entrance. Five evenly spaced windows at the first floor. At the ground floor, a central door in a bolection-moulded surround under a pulvinated frieze and cornice. Originally there were windows only at the end bays, broader than those above and placed just out of alignment with them. Two further windows were inserted *c.* 1960. Small attic windows in the gables. High Street slides N past View Villa. On the r., another crowstep-gabled, rubble-built and pantiled house of the early C18, its windows randomly disposed. The datestone of 1893 presumably refers to a restoration. High Street now rejoins Main Street.

On the N corner of MAIN STREET and Shore Road, the harled CROWN HOTEL, its present two-storey appearance mid-C19 with a heavy pilastered doorpiece, but the bolection-moulded windows of the W front suggest an early C18 origin and that the upper floor may be an addition. Opposite, on Main Street's W side, more housing of the 1960s (Nos. 1–8 KIRKWAY), the front wall boasting a stone carved with the relief of a ship. NW wing stepping up THE PATH. On this lane's N side, sited high above Main Street, is the rubble-walled ROSEBANK built in the later C19. Steeply pitched roofs (now covered with concrete tiles) and Gothic windows; in the inner angle, a conical-roofed round porch. N of The Path, on Main Street's W side, a routine Celtic cross WAR MEMORIAL by *W. Roberts & Son*, 1923, followed by Airth Parish Church (*see* Churches, above). Set well back from Main Street's W side at the N end of the village, the PARISH MANSE by *William Stirling I*, 1813–14. Piend-roofed main block of two storeys and three bays, with giant pilasters at the corners. Pilastered doorpiece at the slightly advanced centre; cornices over the ground-floor windows. Single-storey lateral wings, their windows set in overarches, the front walls carried up to screen the roofs.

SHORE ROAD runs NE from Main Street towards the River Forth. On its r. side, Nos. 6–10, rubble-built early C19 houses of one and two storeys, with pantiled roofs (No. 6 now with concrete tiles). Taller two-storey crowstep-gabled house at Nos. 14–16, again rubble-built and pantiled but of the early C18, the central door of its symmetrical five-bay first floor reached by a forestair; cavetto eaves cornice. Another cavetto cornice at the lower No. 18, also rubble-built and pantiled but probably early C19. On the l., more 1960s housing (CRAWFORD SQUARE). At the N end of Shore Road, in a garden on the r., a piend-roofed villa (ROTHESAY VILLA) of *c.* 1840. On the l., the rubble-built pantile-roofed BAREND COTTAGE, probably of the C18, one of its gables crowstepped. This stands on the corner of NETHERBY ROAD in which is NETHERBY, an early C19 house, the two-storey main block's front of three bays; fluted frieze and cornice over the door.

PAUL DRIVE runs SE from Shore Road. At its NW corner, the early C18 two-storey No. 44. Rubble-built and pantile-roofed, with crowstepped gables. Five-bay front but the broad centre window of the first floor has been converted from a door (its lower part built up) and there is no opening below it. Ground-floor entrance at the l. bay with a bolection-moulded surround and pulvinated frieze and cornice, the ends topped by upright lugs. To the SE, more housing of the 1960s followed by Nos. 2–14 MILLER PLACE, a small development by *Carronvale Homes*, 1989, a determined but ignorant evocation of Scottish vernacular. In Paul Drive's SE stretch returning to Main Street, Airth Primary School (*see* Public Buildings, above).

House of two contrasting faces, to the S a rubble-walled (formerly harled) laird's house of the late C15 and C16, to the N an ashlar-clad late Georgian toy fort. This part of the lands of the Airth was 62 acquired by Alexander Bruce of Stenhouse in the mid C15 and a house built here by 1485 when Alexander Bruce's grandson, Robert Bruce of Airth, signed a charter '*Apud maneriem de Erth*' ('at the manor of Airth'). However, that house seems to have been destroyed or wrecked by James III's army after the Battle of Sauchieburn in 1488. The same year the Lord High Treasurer of Scotland granted a precept for £100 to Robert Bruce 'to the byggin of his place that wes byrnt' and the earliest part of the present house, the SW tower, probably dates from this time. In the early or mid C16 the house was extended by a sizeable E addition. Then in 1581 Alexander Bruce added a NE wing, making the building L-plan. In 1717 the estate was sold to James Graham, Judge-Admiral of Scotland, and in 1807–9 his grandson, Thomas Graham Stirling, employed *David Hamilton* to infill the inner angle of the L with a new block. The house was converted to an hotel in the later C20.

The late C15 tower at the W end of the S range is a rubble-built rectangle of three storeys and an attic. One of the first-floor windows in the W gable is set in a plain rectangular recess. Is this original or a later remodelling? The other windows of the exposed S and W walls (one converted to a door in the late C20) are large with roll-and-hollow moulding; they probably date from the alterations of 1581. Ashlar battlement on the same plane as the walling but marked off by a moulded stringcourse under the semicircular spouts which drain the wall walk. Rising inside the battlement is the crowstep-gabled attic, its appearance probably dating from a C16 remodelling.

The rest of the S range is of the early or mid C16, again rubble-built and of three storeys but the wallhead slightly below that of the C15 tower. S front with fairly regularly spaced windows, again with roll-and-hollow mouldings, but the two lower floors have clearly been altered, perhaps first in the 1680s (an heraldic panel, now preserved inside, suggests work was done then) and again in 1807–9. At the ground floor, one jamb of a built-up C16 window to the l. of the present W window and the jamb of another blocked C16 window at the E end. The first-floor windows were deepened in 1807–9, the second from the W being an insertion of that date. Jamb of a blocked C16 window to the l. of the next opening. Over the four second-floor windows, gablet dormer-heads standing above the moulded eaves course.

The wing of 1581, which contained a ground-floor kitchen and stores with lodging rooms above, is tenuously attached to the S range's NE corner. At the S end of the wing's W side was the new principal entrance. In the SE inner angle and rising above the main ranges is a square stair tower, its S battlement flush with the walling below, its E battlement projected on continuous corbelling. More continuous corbelling under the tall round turret at the tower's SE corner and under the shorter turret squeezed into the inner angle of the tower's SW corner and the gable of the S range. At both the stair tower and the NE wing, windows with roll-and-hollow mouldings. Along the wing's E front, a moulded wallhead cornice stretched between little battlements. Rising through the wallhead are the two second-floor windows' dormerheads, the ends of their pediments carried on attached columns rising from pendant corbels. The tympanum of the S pediment is carved with low-relief foliage, that of the N with latticework in which are set mullets (the armorial motif of the Bruces) and, in the top compartment, a fleur-de-lys. The pediments' finials are missing.

62    *Hamilton*'s Georgian castellated addition of 1807–9 is a triangle which fills the courtyard bounded by the C15 and C16 ranges, completely covering their N and W fronts and with its ground floor (above a sunk basement) at the first-floor level of the earlier work. The NW front is faced with grey ashlar droved to a corduroy texture. Rigorously symmetrical elevation with three-storey round towers at the outer corners and a broad centre bay carried up as a battlemented rectangular tower. At its corners, massive piers, their fronts panelled with pointed arches surmounted by fluting, which are topped by battlemented octagonal turrets. Between the piers, a porch with pointed openings to front and back, the front arch springing from clustered shafts, the back arch containing the entrance into the house and flanked by Gothic side lights. Quatrefoils pierce the porch's parapet. Above the porch, a giant pointed overarch containing the central first- and second-floor windows, the first floor's hoodmoulded, the round-headed second-floor window standing on an Adamish sill course. The outer bays of the front are of two storeys and a basement, the hoodmoulded ground- and first-floor windows linked by sill courses. Corbelled battlement at the wallhead. At the three-storey and basement corner towers the windows are narrower and only those of the ground floor have a sill course. Square windows to the second floor. Moulded and arcaded corbelling under the battlement.

Inside, the principal rooms were created or remodelled in 1807–9. *Hamilton*'s front door opens into an entrance hall covered by a plaster groin vault; at the SE end, a Gothick niche flanked by two doors, the r. opening into a cupboard, the l. into the Saloon squeezed into the SE corner of the earlier courtyard. This is a two-storey segment, top-lit from a cupola of the same shape. Round the room's upper level, a balcony, its plastered soffit ornamented with oval rosettes and husks. Console-corniced doors open from the Saloon into the main public rooms. On the N is the Dining Room. Expensive but simple plasterwork. Marble chimneypiece with paired fluted Doric columns and rosette decoration. S of the Saloon, in the early or mid-C16 S range, are the Drawing Room and Morning Room, probably originally a hall and chamber. They retain their C16 dimensions but their

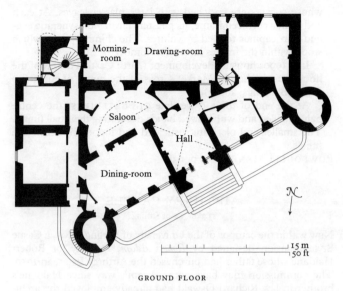

GROUND FLOOR

Airth Castle. Ground-floor plan.

appearance otherwise is of 1807–9 when *Hamilton* provided their interconnecting double door. Again the plasterwork is fairly simple but expensive with large sunburst ceiling roses. In each room, a marble chimneypiece, its paired fluted Doric columns of skinny proportions; rosettes at the ends of the fluted frieze. The room (now Cocktail Bar) at the SW corner of the house was the first-floor hall of the late C15 tower. On its N wall has been placed a large stone PANEL carved with an heraldic achievement displaying the quartered arms of Elphinstone and Bruce (for Richard Elphinstone of Calderhall and his wife, Janet Bruce, the heiress of Airth, who married *c.* 1680). It was moved here in the later C20 from the stables but probably was originally placed over the former main entrance to the house at the S end of the W side of the NE wing of 1581.

STABLES 0.46m. W of the house. U-plan arrangement of three mid-C18 rubble-built two-storey blocks, now linked by late C20 additions. The E and W blocks contained stabling. Each has a pedimented S gable, a round window in the tympanum. The N block was the coach house. Piended roof with bellcast eaves. At its S front, segmental-arched ground-floor openings; five windows above. The N elevation, now ensconced in a late C20 courtyard, is grander. At the centre, a twin-flight forestair, its landing sheltering the basket-arched ground-floor door. The principal entrance, at the first floor, has a lugged surround and pulvinated frieze surmounted by a pediment. This door gave access to a single room (formerly 'the Long Room above the Coach Houses') of *c.* 12.9m. by 5.2m. which occupies the whole of the upper floor. Egg-and-dart cornice under the ceiling's cove

whose corners are enriched with large plaster leaves. At each
end wall, a corniced frame, its pilasters having idiosyncratic egg-
and-dart capitals topped by volutes. The chimneypieces which
stood within the frames have been removed.

In a 1990s housing development (Airth Castle Park) N of the
house stands the old Market Cross of the burgh of Airth (*see*
Public Buildings, above).

At the end of the E drive, late C18 GATEPIERS, the centre
pair panelled and with carved bands decorating their ball finials.
The smaller end piers are rusticated and topped by acorn-like
finials.

POWFOULIS MANOR. *See* p. 638.

AIRTHREY CASTLE                     s
                        3.3km. NE of Stirling

61  Now within the campus of the University of Stirling (q.v.), a Castle
Style mansion designed by *Robert Adam*, 1790–1, for Robert
Haldane whose father had purchased the Airthrey Estate in 1759.
The commission may have come Adam's way since Haldane's
brother-in-law Richard Oswald had already employed the architect at Auchencruive in Ayrshire. But this had been over thirty
years earlier and it seems likely that the reputation which Adam
had acquired nationally over that period would have been a more
compelling reason. Things did not, however, run smoothly. A first
design, less compact and more classical than the built project, was
rejected. Haldane, however, professed himself 'charmed' with a
second, Castle Style, proposal. But, following negotiations with
the builder, *Thomas Russell*, who had worked under Adam's supervision at Seton House in East Lothian, Haldane decided to dismiss
Adam, redirecting the money saved on fees to pay for droved rather
than rubble masonry.

Exactly a century later the house was radically altered. Robert
Graham, who had acquired the estate in 1889, engaged *David
Thomson* to provide additional accommodation, a commission
which entailed the demolition of Adam's N façade, the building of
a new wing in its place and the almost complete reconfiguration of
the internal plan. In 1939 the house became a maternity hospital.
A low, two-storey nurses' home, wholly inappropriate in architectural idiom, was built extending E from the services court which
Thomson had created. Since 1969 the Castle has belonged to the
University of Stirling which has effected considerable refurbishment. It is now the University's Division of Academic Innovation
and Continuing Education.

The plan is unusual: an ingenious D-shaped arrangement of rooms
on three storeys around a central staircase hall. At the centre of
the curving S front, which enjoys the views, a shallow bow rises
into an attic storey between two small square towers. From the
*piano nobile*, where a narrow terrace fronts three tall round-arched
openings lighting the drawing room, a wide stair falls to the lawn.
Oval openings are cut into the low walls of terrace and staircase.

On each side of the towered frontispiece, the D bends back in
five-bay arcs, the three-bay centres of which, lugged with tiny
bartizans, advance slightly. Round-arched openings again dignify
the principal rooms. On the flanks the composition is closed by
book-end blocks facing w and E, each three bays wide, a single
window framed between square towers that repeat those at the
centre of the D, though without the attic. Binding all this movement together are moulded stringcourses at ground-floor sill
height and first-floor level and a parapet corbelled on mock
machicolation, with mock cruciform gunloops in the towers
and crenellation over the three bowed parts of the façade.

The original N entrance elevation – parapeted with broad
wings and a castellated cylinder at the centre, 'as fine as any of
Adam's castle façades'* – disappeared in the dull, barely Baronial
additions made by Thomson in 1891. These present a blocky
asymmetrical façade built in a droved ashlar sandstone more
ochre in colour than the late C18 work. Two storeys and attic
rise over a basement, with a four-storey square tower advancing
r. of centre. All wallheads have corbelled castellated parapets
considerably cruder in detail than those built to Adam's design.
To the E, the frontal block returns with octagonal turrets topped
by dumpy stone obelisks at the NE and SE corners. In the w, a
three-quarter drum, fenestrated in two tiers of four two-light
mullioned and transomed windows separated by pilaster strips,
returns against the greyer stonework of the earlier building. A
semicircular bow, castellated above the ground-floor storey,
projects from the centre of Adam's w front.

The principal entrance, a hooded round-arched doorway, with
monogram and date, 1891, carved in the tympanum, is located
at the base of the tower. Placed off-centre in Thomson's façade,
the entrance nevertheless aligns exactly with the axis of Adam's
plan. The INTERIOR, however, retains little of its original
arrangement, the nice ingenuities of Adam's geometry all but
lost. The lower vestibule is square in plan with a mosaic margin
of floral scrollwork in pink, grey, white and blue. Above is a
simple rib-gridded plaster ceiling. Four stone steps rise to the inner
vestibule where the ceiling is similar and the mosaic border
repeated. Inset in the s wall in a panelled oak dado, an Italian
tabernacle, Renaissance in style but probably of later date. It is
carved in frontal perspective to show a coffered arched recess in
which two angel figures stand below a dove, symbol of the Holy
Spirit. Above it, a large freely shaped plaster cast of three angel
heads in high relief; perhaps C17. A door r. opens to the HALL,
a remarkably generous inner space, largely unfurnished but
lavishly panelled, which envelops the central staircase from
Adam's original Drawing Room in the s to the bulging arc of
Thomson's NW bow. The late C19 oak panelling is executed in
a highly detailed C16 Flemish idiom. The design is organized
in three horizontal layers, each marked by a carved frieze and
cornice, the first at sill height, the second coincident with the

* David King, *The Complete Works of Robert and James Adam* (1991), 173.

chimneypiece mantel (*see* below), the third at door lintel height. Thin vertical elements, shaped with miniature terms, heads, figural motifs, consoles, and projecting cornice mouldings, articulate these bands at regular intervals. Of the three layers the middle is the most intensely decorative; each section of coupled panels is covered in low relief carving, inventively tortile and varied, a different medallion head at the centre of each panel, another in the frieze above. Above the topmost cornice of the oak panelling a deep leather frieze, full of floral and fruit motifs, scrolling and classical figures, glows with dark colour. Oak ceiling panelled and boarded. In the NW bow, panels radiate from a central octagon. Two wide high-level openings on the E wall, one to the inner vestibule, the other to the staircase, have Cantonese enamel plaques set in the reveals.

Dominating the Hall on the W wall is an ostentatiously magnificent oak chimneypiece vigorously sculpted in C17 style. A deep simply moulded mantel divides the design. Below, the fireplace is flanked by Solomonic Corinthian columns, carved with plant forms and *putti* between helical twists. Each advances between Corinthian half-columns with part-fluted shafts. Above the fire but below the central projecting bow of the mantel, an almost fully three-dimensional relief of three *putti* linking arms bursts forward. Islamic (?) ceramic tiles on the sides of the fire opening. Cast iron fire-back depicts the Virgin and Child with St John. Hearth of brown glazed tiles. Carved in high relief above the mantel is a high bow-fronted central panel showing a battle scene from the life of Sir William Wallace. This is surmounted at ceiling level by a deep somewhat crudely moulded oak cornice supported by obliquely set Corinthian columns, their shafts part-fluted, part-carved with cloaked classical figures. On each side of the central panel, corniced at a lower level, are two more martial scenes flanked by aberrant Ionic columns.

Panelled oak doors open from the Hall to the Adam rooms on the W and S. These have lost their original designations and are now numbered. Almost nothing of late C18 date survives. In Room 19, where the five-light bow window is a late C19 addition, there is a narrow Arabic door with bronze bossing which may be of C19 Egyptian provenance. In Room 18, which is apsidal at both ends, there is a similar door and an Italian walnut door of *c.* 1550, its six panels carved with horsemen. Also in this room, a huge white marble chimneypiece carved with a fine classical cornice and plump *putti* celebrating Bacchus in a drunken dance through trailing vines. At the centre of the plan in Room 17, a plain black marble fireplace with floral Victorian tile ingoes in ultramarine, turquoise and dark green. On the adjacent door, two C17 Flemish oak panels illustrating the Annunciation and Nativity. Rooms 22 and 24 together constitute the doubly apsidal reflection of Room 18. In the former, part of a ribbed and bossed plaster ceiling patterned in triangular and vesica shapes can be seen. In the latter, a stone chimneypiece in Italian Renaissance style: floral pilasters and a deep frieze with shield, urns, and male and female figures swept up into plant arabesques; inner oak surround inlaid with majolica panels depicting the toilet of Venus, Apollo slaying the Python, and a landscape scene with girl; intensely turquoise tiles in the fireplace.

A broad well stair of three flights balustraded with timber strapwork leads to the upper floor. Acting as a balustrade to the passage on the N side (originally open but now glazed) is an oak altar front, possibly c18 German. Gently undulating in plan, its carvings depict Christ breaking bread at Emmaus, the Samaritan woman at the well, and a third scene that may represent the feast held to celebrate the Prodigal Son's return. Above this, in a moulded plaster frame, an Arabic window case with shutters. Opposite, over the s upper landing, a c15 Italian grey marble roundel of the Virgin and Child surrounded by angels. Above this is an attic gallery with a timber balcony carved with wheatsheaves and vines and fronted by a large panel showing the children of Israel collecting manna and Moses bringing water out of the rock. The staircase well is lit from a gabled saddle-back roof-light. Decorative plaster console brackets. On the upper landing wall, an Arabic timber door of staggeringly daedal detail. A few Adam-type fireplaces, now heavily painted, survive in first-floor rooms.

EAST LODGE by *William Stirling I*, 1809; a two-storey battlemented octagon with hooded windows and a circular stair turret, also battlemented. Formerly the gate-house to the castle, it survives uninhabited.

HERMITAGE, in Hermitage Wood. Late c18. Clifftop folly overlooking Airthrey Loch and the University of Stirling campus. Created as a woodland retreat by Robert Haldane but now a ruinous rubble pile.

STANDING STONE, 0.3km. SSE. An impressive monolith of grey dolerite, 2.7m. high.

# ALEXANDRIA                WD *3070*

A red sandstone town no more than two-storey in scale with a fractured but still perceptible urban order. Following the successful introduction of bleaching along the Leven banks in the c18, industrialized calico printing and Turkey-red dyeing in the c19 brought the Orr-Ewing family the prosperity with which to transform 'an ill-planned, straggling and rather mean-looking place where every bit lairdie planted down his ain bit biggin anywhere he liked' into a gridded town of flatted terrace rows. But the blight of c20 recession is all too evident. Redevelopment has largely scorned the red Levenside legacy.

## CHURCHES

ALEXANDRIA METHODIST CHURCH, Albert Street. Dull Gothic by *Malcolm Stark*, 1877–8. In the s gable, a pointed-arched doorway moulded above the springing line.

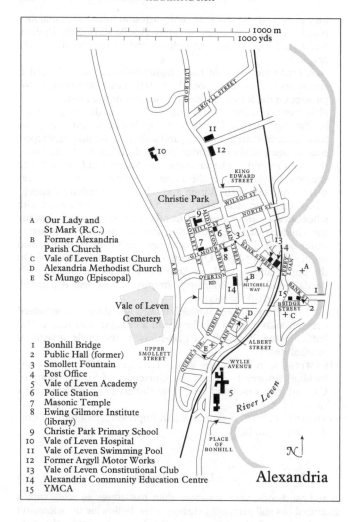

A   Our Lady and
    St Mark (R.C.)
B   Former Alexandria
    Parish Church
C   Vale of Leven Baptist Church
D   Alexandria Methodist Church
E   St Mungo (Episcopal)

1   Bonhill Bridge
2   Public Hall (former)
3   Smollett Fountain
4   Post Office
5   Vale of Leven Academy
6   Police Station
7   Masonic Temple
8   Ewing Gilmore Institute
    (library)
9   Christie Park Primary School
10  Vale of Leven Hospital
11  Vale of Leven Swimming Pool
12  Former Argyll Motor Works
13  Vale of Leven Constitutional Club
14  Alexandria Community Education Centre
15  YMCA

Former ALEXANDRIA PARISH CHURCH. 1840. Best described,
paradoxically, as round-arched Gothic. Gable front with hunched
steeple set forward slightly at the centre. Buttress quoins clasp
the skews and tower, each carrying a short octagonal shaft and
dumpy obelisk. On the tower, clock faces are positioned between
these shafts but there is no belfry stage. Instead, louvred lucarnes
project from the base of a spire that emerges abruptly and uncomfortably. Yet despite this architectural solecism, the steeple works
well in the townscape, a familiar marker at the s end of Main
Street. Interior recast in 1906 when kingpost trusses were exposed.
U-plan gallery supported on cast iron columns with bell capitals.
In 1997, the church became a children's play centre.
   Victorian tombs fill the GRAVEYARD which surrounds the

church. On the N wall, set in a low-walled plot, a large HEAD-
STONE, erected *c.* 1865, more Baroque altarpiece than Presbyterian gravemarker, records the deaths of William Barlas †1894,
his wife Veir Forrest †1863 and their two-year-old son Archibald
†1849. – Interrupting the E wall is the gabled T-plan SMOLLETT
MAUSOLEUM, richly Romanesque in detail, but without inscription.

ALEXANDRIA PARISH CHURCH. *See* Balloch.

OUR LADY AND ST MARK (R.C.), Ferry Loan. By *Donald J.
Cameron* of *S. B. Lithgow & Cameron*, 1926. A long roughcast
hall church with little pretension to religious distinction. Seven
bays of tall round-arched windows. At the piended S (liturgical
E) end, a single similar opening, hooded and flanked by coupled
pilasters. Venetian windows l. and r. light the Sacred Heart and
Lady Chapels. Unencumbered interior with shallow segmental
ceiling. Plain furnishings installed in 1959.

ST MUNGO (Episcopal), Main Street. By *J. M. Crawford*, 1893–4.
Tentative in extent and unambitious in style; built in square-
snecked red sandstone with ashlar dressings but without decorative elaboration. At first only the six-bay nave and the low
parapeted porch to the SE gable were built. Pointed arches down
each side of the nave below coupled clearstorey lancets were
simply filled in. SW aisle added, 1902–3. The intended chancel,
betrayed by a pointed arch in the NW gable of the church, has
never been completed. Simple interior with Lady Chapel to l.
Stained red pine roof of arch-braced trusses on stone corbels. –
Stone ALTAR and carved PULPIT from St Augustine's Church,
Dumbarton. – Brass eagle LECTERN. – STAINED GLASS in the
triple lancet SE window: Christ in glory flanked by SS Agnes
and Dorcas, by *Clayton & Bell*, London, 1897. – In 1908–9, the
detached rough cast Hall, modestly Arts and Crafts in character
rather than ecclesiastical, was built to the design of *James Chalmers*.

VALE OF LEVEN BAPTIST CHURCH, Bridge Street. 1847; alterations and additions, 1897. Piend-roofed preaching box for
the Relief Church. Three-bay N front of painted droved ashlar
with a small central pediment on the eaves cornice. Pilastered
doorpiece with entablature.

## PUBLIC BUILDINGS

ALEXANDRIA COMMUNITY EDUCATION CENTRE, Main Street.
1972–3. Fascia-banded flat-roofed Modernism. Single-storey
street-front offices faced in fawn brick. Rising behind, an eight-
bay HALL with clearstorey glazing to W, S and E.

Former ARGYLL MOTOR WORKS, Main Street. By *Halley &    126
Neil*, 1905–6. The most architecturally spectacular industrial
enterprise to be built in the Vale of Leven. The massed ranks of
factory sheds and north-light workshops, which prior to the
First World War were producing sixty 14–16 h.p. cars each week,
have all been razed, but the offices survive. And what offices!
An immensely wide W façade in red sandstone ashlar stretches
out on either side of a dominant central dome flanked by lower

pyramid-roofed towers. This is Beaux Arts Baroque, conception and execution more fitted for the shores of the Bosphorus or some Vatican piazza than the Leven valley. But here it is, in Dunbartonshire, preserved and adapted to new commercial use as Loch Lomond Outlets by *Page & Park*, 1996–8.

Like some grand Seicento Roman church the central mass of the composition advances in five broad bays under a continuous entablature, characteristically Edwardian with its deeply shadowed cornice punctuated by mutule blocks. Giant pilasters of pink Peterhead granite flank the outer bays below the towers; three-quarter columns in the same material define the centre. Above a Gibbsian round-arched entrance is a balconied Mannerist aedicule. Overall, an open pediment, deeply carved with allegorical figures gathered around the bonnet of an Argyll motor car. A stepped parapet behind carries plinths l. and r. on which hefty ball finials sit on scrolled supports. These repeat at the corners of the outer towers which rise as solid cubic blocks framed by coupled Tuscan half-columns on all four faces. Above the capitals, robustly consoled cornices carry the sprocketed eaves of red-tiled pyramid roofs. The central clock tower rises higher, chamfered at the corners, with coupled Composite columns standing free under entablature blocks. Behind a balustraded parapet the distinctively egg-shaped dome emerges, clad in copper sheet. Perched at the apex is a louvred tempietto with balustraded bow balconies at its base. Flanking this whole grandiloquent pile, nine bays of offices (two storeys to Main Street, three to the rear) extend the façade N and S, picking up the line of the main cornice under a balustraded skyline. Pilaster strips mark each structural bay; superimposed two-light windows repeated in segmental-arched recesses with a double-height canted bay in the last. Gone are the ventilator-topped pyramid roofs which originally accented these outermost bays. A wall of five further open bays continues N, terminating in a two-storey HOUSE with portico entrance and balustraded loggia over. Along Main Street iron railings with repetitive scrolled ornament have survived, as have three sets of channelled ashlar GATEPIERS with cornices and ball finials. L-plan LODGE.

The main Hall under the dome, in which a generous T-plan staircase rises in a galleried well, is lavishly finished in polychromatic marbles, with black and white marble chequer-board floor at entrance level and marble terrazzo on the upper floor. Stair treads are in white Sicilian marble, the balusters in Derbyshire alabaster, the handrail of Pavonazzo marble. Ceramic tile dado panelled and bordered in green, cream and white with Art Nouveau motifs. Four substantial piers with Composite columns on the corners, all in scagliola white marble clouded with greys and pale mauve, support the beams carrying the superstructure. Over the stairwell square, a shallow plaster dome ceiling. Shopping aisles now run N and S from the Hall behind the W façade. Retail space opens E at ground- and first-floor levels and at lower-ground-floor level opening to the car park at the rear. Original fireproof construction retained to ground-floor

ceiling: white glazed brick vaults arching between closely spaced
riveted steel flanges. White glazed brick also survives on the
inner face of the w façade and on the exterior face of the e wall
where it traces the profile of the demolished factory sheds.

BONHILL BRIDGE. First, a chain suspension bridge, designed by
the Glasgow engineer *Charles Atherton*, was built to replace the
ferry over the Leven; the so-called Bawbee Brig of 1836, where
tolls were collected until 1895. Then, in 1898, came a second
bridge formed of two bowstring lattice girders carried on red
sandstone abutments; engineers, *Crouch & Hogg*. Finally these
two structural principles were combined in the present bow suspension bridge, designed by *Strathclyde Regional Council* in
1987.

CHRISTIE PARK, Main Street. Opened 1902. Tall, ochre sandstone GATEPIERS with cornices and ball finials. High, vertically
ribbed ironwork GATES carried on iron piers. Baronial L-plan
LODGE by *James Miller*, 1902. – In the park is the town's WAR
MEMORIAL, *c*. 1920, a massive stone pylon-form inlaid with
slate panels bearing many names; Celtic cross carved on the
sides. – Squat cast iron FOUNTAIN with Grecian ornament,
half-circle bowls and lion's-head spouts; it carries a golden
female figure crowned with a laurel wreath.

CHRISTIE PARK PRIMARY SCHOOL, Middleton Street. Built
as the North Public School, 1884. High two-storeyed symmetry
in the town's ubiquitous red sandstone. Below the heavily consoled eaves, at the centre of the e façade, three round-arched
lights over a windowed mezzanine and pupils' entrances l. and r.
The plan is deep; N and S banks of classrooms around a balconied
hall. Additions made w and N by *Boston, Menzies & Morton*,
1894 and in 1902, when the school became known as the Vale
of Leven Academy Public School.

EWING GILMOUR INSTITUTE, Gilmour Street. Now a library.  91
By *Robert Thomson*, 1881–4; extended at rear, 1927. Endowed
by William Ewing Gilmour to foster the education and moral
well-being of the boys of the Vale. A pink sandstone building of
exceptional Classical refinement evidently and providently
under the assimilated tutelage of Alexander 'Greek' Thomson,
to whom the eponymous and altogether mysterious Robert was,
it seems, no kin. Pediments and pilasters reverberate across the
pink sandstone ashlar of the asymmetrical Ewing Street façade.
To the l., an unorthodox two-storey gable. To the r., equally
high but fronting a single inner space, is a three-bay temple front,
inventively *in antis*. An inscription in the tympanum records
the donor's gift. Between the two pedimented gables is a lower
pilastrade with a pedimented, square-columned Ionic porch
pushed l. A subtle layering of detail permeates the façade, for
the line of the entablature over this central zone extends l. over
the porch and on into the sill of a four-light pilastrade under the
e pediment while to the r. it is picked up in the stringcourse and
transom that pass across the temple front and return down the
w elevation. Delicate carving complements the success of the
composition. Above the string/transom line crossing the temple

to the r., for example, the two tall stone mullion-columns become fluted.

The interior matches the sophistication of the façade. In the VESTIBULE, oak doors, framed by partly fluted pilaster architraves, have pedimented entablatures with dentilled cornicing. Wainscoting of Riga oak. Dentilled plaster ceiling cornice with modillions. On the floor, marble mosaic in a bold Greek fret border. To the l. are offices and a small flat at first-floor level. The principal central space, originally known as the CONVERSATION HALL, has an oak-panelled dado and doors similar but not identical to those in the Vestibule; above their dentilled cornice is a scrolled pediment broken to receive an inverted shell motif. Coved panelled plaster ceiling with three round rooflights. The modillion cornice, repeated in the roof-light drums, has an unorthodox frieze of alternating triglyphs and anthemion sprays. The high-ceilinged Reading Room, now rather perversely serving as a children's library, possesses a simple volumetric elegance. The tall windows, three N, four W, fill the space with light, each individually framed by narrow pilaster strips and dentilled cornices. Beamed plaster ceiling panels with dentilled modillion cornices and central ventilation roses. Riga oak floor.

MEETING ROOM, at first-floor level in the C20 extension, has oak-panelled walls and coupled windows with leaded glass inner casements. Long round-ended council table and heavily Classical chairman's chair.

92 MASONIC TEMPLE, Gilmour Street. Built 1888–91 as an institute to benefit 'those humble women who live by toil', this astonishing building was the gift of William Ewing Gilmour. A few years after he had provided for the young men of the Leven valley (see Ewing Gilmour Institute, above), he ensured that the young women of the Vale, many labouring in noxious dyeing shops and printworks, would have similar opportunities for self-improvement. Nor did this second exercise in built philanthropy fail to match the first in architectural quality – though it was decidedly different in style. Indeed, the two buildings, located at opposite ends of the same street, are without peer in Alexandria.

*John A. Campbell* of *John Burnet, Son & Campbell* was engaged as architect. The result is an imaginative fusion of Scots Renaissance, Baronial and Arts and Crafts forms, at once rugged and refined, intimidating and intimate. The material is polychromatic sandstone laid in rough-faced snecked courses with red ashlar carvings and dressings. L-plan arrangement disposed in three linked parts at the corner of Gilmour Street and Smollett Street, along which lies a high gabled HALL. Punching through a balustraded eaves, three tall mullioned and transomed dormers with broken segmental pediments in equilateral gables, carrying balls on the skews and a thistle at the apex. Below, under relieving arches and segmental hoodmouldings, are three lintelled windows with convex jambs. From the lower part of the s gable on Gilmour Street a canted bay pushes forward, solid but for a small light in each splay. Broad buttresses, linked by an open balustrade, surge back to flank a first-floor window elaborately framed and pedimented. In the tympanum is the date, 1888. At the gable apex, a thick chimneystack with an inset niche. A second element in the composition develops E. Lower in ridge and eaves, it too has three eaves dormers linked by a balustrade and crowned with broken pediments full of scroll and strapwork carving. Third comes the TOWER, no higher than the Hall but vigorous in form and detail. A corbelled stair turret rises in the SW re-entrant, rounds adhere on the SW and SE corners, a chimney slab erupts at the NE. High on the S face is an ornamental panel carved to represent the Tree of Knowledge (?). Only the wide spacing of the balusters on the corbelled parapet (no different from the spacing adopted elsewhere but here exposed on the skyline) seems ill-judged. From the Tower a balustraded wall, concealing the caretaker's dwelling, leads E to a buttressed, segmentally arched gateway with a single high ogee-domed pier.

The principal entrance, asymmetrically placed at the base of the Tower, is dramatized by a flamboyantly Baroque door over which a carved inscription asserts the building's latter-day function as a Masonic Temple. Through this portal is a small VESTIBULE and, beyond, an inner HALL. The floor is panelled in rust-red tiles set in a black-line grid. Walls are first red ashlar, then panelled in stained timber to door cornice height. Above this high dado is an oil-painted frieze: pastoral scenes inhabited by maidenly figures; by *Harrington Mann*. To the r. are the kitchens occupying an area originally equipped for bathing, retaining its segmental plaster ceiling vault and ceramic wall tiling with decorative dado of shell motif inserts. To the l. the Hall extends W, also tiled. Five windowed bays with decorative glazing grids provide a view out under overhanging eaves to the garden. The lean-to, arch-braced trusses of the roof are exposed over this light-filled space, more loggia than corridor. Along the S wall, where the painted frieze runs on, are three pedimented stone doorways. Each is cut with a Scots aphorism. WARK . BEARS. WITNESS / WHA . DOES . WEEL. GUDE . COUNSEL / IS . ABUNE . A' . PRICE. WANT . O'WIT . IS. WAUR / NOR . WANT . O'GEAR. There is a good deal more of this cosy wisdom in stone and timber throughout the building, but the homespun tone remains the same. The two rooms S of the loggia-corridor (originally a classroom and library) have been refurnished, but some wall panelling survives. In the E ROOM, a fireplace, thinly edged with marble, with a lugged architrave frame beneath a Mannerist overmantel of Tuscan columns under an open-and-broken pediment. Stone corbelling from the tower stair turret intrudes into the SE corner of the room. A framed perspective view of the architect's design, drawn by *McGibbon*, 1888, hangs on the wall.

The Hall is entered at the W end of the loggia. The dark, lofty interior is stunning. High arch-braced trusses soar into the darkness, shallow-arched purlins crossing the five bays to support spars and boarding. Tall eaves dormers break into the roof timbering in complicated joinery, and false hammerbeams terminate in carved lions' heads, each with a brass ring in its mouth. Trusses fall to a continuous convex corbel cornice carved with biblical injunctions. Between the trusses are narrow, barely negotiable balustraded galleries. In the s gable is an inglenook, deep and wide. Above the fireplace, curving back to the splayed sides of the recess is an overmantel mural which 'treats of the duties and industries of women', by *Harrington Mann* (restored by the artist in 1936 and in 1988 by others). Heavy stone corbels emerge l. and r. of the fireplace to carry a timber-beamed balcony across the s wall. This gable gallery, balustraded like those on the lateral walls but set at a slightly higher level, is reached by a mural stair hidden in the e wall. On the n gable is an immense C16-style chimneypiece in red sandstone ashlar which rises from the mantel line in a wide masonry plane tapering upwards to a moulded cornice high in the shadows. All seems carried over the wide void of the fireplace opening by a flat voussoir arch and inner segmental arch. Centred above the fireplace, an armorial cartouche.

POLICE STATION, Hill Street. Built *c.* 1930; refurbished 1967 and 1997. Rural vernacular (almost) in cream roughcast with grey ashlar dressings; all pleasant enough if a little incongruous in the midst of red sandstone terraces. The word LEVENAX (i.e. Lennox), inscribed in a circle above the gabled entrance, asserts street cred. Linked physically and stylistically, round the chamfered corner in Middleton Street are some piend-roofed flats with segmentally arched recesses shading the doorways.

POST OFFICE, Bank Street. Dated 1904. A single storey of square snecked red sandstone with a balustraded parapet. Central pediment with inner segmental pediment over a tripartite window. Tuscan column mullions.

Former PUBLIC HALL, Bridge Street. Competition-winning design by *Hugh H. Maclure* of Glasgow, 1862–3, cleverly composed to take advantage of the gushet site at the junction of Bridge Street and Bank Street. Confronting the Bonhill Bridge over the Leven (*see* above), the tetrastyle Doric portico, balustraded above the entablature and pedimented behind, makes a formidable propylaeum at the e approach to the town. Detached Classical portals stand l. and r. ahead of the temple front. The plan contains a principal hall, lesser halls and offices. Converted to a cinema by 1911; outer bays added *c.* 1930; since 1973 the building has survived in accelerating shabbiness as a bingo hall.

SMOLLETT FOUNTAIN, Main Street. 1870; refurbished 1996. An unequivocally Victorian compilation of mercat cross confectionery won in competition by *Adamson & McLeod*. It was raised to honour the philanthropy of the local laird and MP Alexander Smollett by his 'feuars, tenants and other admirers in the county'. Pools, pillars and panelled parapets accumulate in a diminishing pile of ringed cylinders. On the top, a cast iron heron. Built in Bannockburn freestone with shafts of red and grey Aberdeen granite.

VALE OF LEVEN ACADEMY, Place of Bonhill. A vast educational ghetto. The original glazed classroom blocks, framed with brick infill, by *A. Buchanan Campbell*, 1962–3. Later blocks constructed in prefabricated CLASP system by *Lane, Bremner & Garnett* in association with *Dumbarton County Council*.

VALE OF LEVEN CEMETERY, Overton Road. 'Garden Cemetery' laid out by *James Wilson* of Greenock, 1880–1; enlarged 1898. A large and well-tended graveyard on the W slopes of the Vale denied stillness by the incessant hiss of traffic on the nearby A82. Many fine trees including two tall Chilean pines. Pierced iron GATEPIERS with urn finials, GATES and spear-headed RAILINGS manufactured by the *Saracen Foundry*, Glasgow. Ironwork FOOTBRIDGE. – Grey granite wall MONUMENT, its pediment block carried on the flanks by Tuscan columns; to John Izatt †1906 and family. – A similar, smaller, but more classically correct MONUMENT with Ionic half-columns on the sides; to Andrew Izatt †1977 and his wife †1912. – To John Cullen Brown †1908 and family, a Celtic CROSS, the shaft carved with panels of interlacing, florets and nailhead. – High tapering HEADSTONE with funeral urn, to Thomas Kinloch, builder, †1890; sculpted by *W. Kinloch*. Set on an open-arched base within which sits a tiny sarcophagus commemorating Kinloch's infant son who died aged one month in 1888.

VALE OF LEVEN CONSTITUTIONAL CLUB, Bank Street. By *Boston, Menzies & Morton*, 1900. Red ashlar with a bellcast roof and a witch's hat over a corbelled corner bow. Segmental-arched entrance with roll-moulded jambs. A cornice string-course hints at Art Nouveau.

VALE OF LEVEN HOSPITAL, Luss Road. By *J. L. Gleave* of *John Keppie, Henderson & J. L. Gleave*, 1952–5. Two-storey ward units and other departments standardized in elevation by regularly spaced concrete mullions infilled with glazing or red cedar boarding. Service buildings in roughcast brick. The five-storey maternity block by *Ivor Dorward*, 1968, maintains repetitive rhythm in glazing.

VALE OF LEVEN SWIMMING POOL, Luss Road. By *Blair & McWiggan*, 1972–3. Brown facing brick walls freely arranged in a well-scaled relationship with the inner order of the rectangular pool, the roof of which rises higher to obtain clearstorey light. Mansard-slope fascia of profiled metal sheeting conceals roof structure. Some poolside glazing E between brick fins.

YMCA, 105–111 Bridge Street. *c.* 1900. Six-bay red sandstone façade with a central half-timbered gable corbelled on twinned fluted consoles. Five windowed gables project W from hall. Abandoned.

## DESCRIPTION

MAIN STREET is the bent spine of the town. Unlike the eponymous ramrod route through Renton to the S, it twice alters direction, though only just. The longest and straightest stretch runs past the Smollett Fountain (*see* Public Buildings, above). Two early three-bay properties with shouldered frontal chimneys, flats over shops, *c.* 1840, form the oblique junction with Bank

Street. Beyond North Street, McKENZIE'S BAR is similar, barely better, but seven bays long with the date 1852 in the frontal stack. Then, at Nos.13–33, a flatted terrace in red ashlar, c. 1880, the consistent two-storeyed building block of Alexandria's late Victorian townscape. These terraces continue N as far as the old Argyll Works (*see* Public Buildings, above) interrupted only, in form but not material, by BELLEVILLE, c. 1885, a semi-detached villa with Jacobean gables and leaded ogee caps to its canted bays. WILSON STREET and KING EDWARD STREET, accented with a slated pyramid on the corner, maintain the 1880s terrace theme, the latter in marginally better condition. Opposite the Fountain on the W side of Main Street, more red shops and flats at FINDLAY'S CORNER, 1880. An older, lower, two-storey row, badly mauled, but a part preserving its eaves cornice, runs N; probably 1840–50. Over the gate in the Bowling Green wall, the date 1867. Otherwise, nothing to catch the eye before Christie Park. Opposite the Argyll Works, early C19 gableted Gothic GATEPIERS and a Gothic LODGE with crenellated gable and porch still mark the entrance to the driveway that led to Tullichewan Castle (*see* p. 786), demolished in 1954.

Red ashlar shops and flats, 1895, fill Main Street's chamfered gushet with Bank Street. Parapet peaked with pediments and chimneys; original shopfronts with roll-moulded openings. S along Main Street, the ROYAL BANK OF SCOTLAND by *Peddie & Kinnear*, 1891, a high dignified palazzo, almost too suave for its indifferent location. Pedimented attic dormers linked by a balustraded parapet, a segmental shell pediment centred at first floor and a good classical porch with fluted Ionic columns. Across the street, Nos. 118–144, another red terrace of shops and flats, 1887. Then, the same commercial-residential mix in parallel stretches of 1970s roughcast redevelopment. Steps drop down to the shops in MITCHELL WAY, 1976, part of the same attempt at renewal.

The spire of St Andrew's Parish Church (*see* Churches, above) fills the view S marking a slight swing in the direction of Main Street. Opposite the church is the Community Education Centre (*see* Public Buildings, above). From here continuity of enclosure is broken and the street less urban. No. 274 (LEA PARK), c. 1840, a three-bay cottage villa of sophisticated plainness. Its contemporary neighbour at No. 280 (SOUTHEND COTTAGE), is a little grander with a pilastered doorpiece and a good eaves cornice but marred by an added mansard. Then comes a second swing W. Now the street equivocates between urban and suburban. On the E, the red flatted terraces return; Nos. 297–301 (PLANE TREE BANK), Nos. 305–325 (DALMARY PLACE), 1884, Nos. 329–333 (MULBERRY BANK), 1887, and the unnamed Nos. 335–337 which have oddly low close entries. But across the street, past the curved corner of ROWAN TREE BANK, c. 1880, and the painted street-front austerity of ROWANTREEBANK HOUSE, c. 1840, is a series of late Victorian villas incongruously contemporary with the workers' rows they confront. ARDENLEE is muted Gothic; NIAGARA carries its gables on console brackets;

four-in-a-block SOUTHFIELD PLACE has double-height bows; ST ANN'S, stilted round-arched windows under fretted barge-boards.

On the W side of town, gridded streets lie parallel or perpendicular to the three stretches of Main Street. Red sandstone dominates. In MIDDLETON STREET, flatted terraces with close entries to rear stairs, then detached cottage villas, 1880s. More flats from the same time in SMOLLETT STREET; Nos. 1–23 with a particularly attractive back-lane range of outside stair projections giving access to the upper flats across bridging platts. Uphill on UPPER SMOLLETT STREET, some grander late C19 villas. GLEN LEVEN has some quatrefoil carving and two-storey bows with trefoil-headed windows. ALEXANDRIA HOUSE, red sandstone with grey dressings, stands tall and erect, its tripartite windows pilastered at ground floor and round-arched above. HILLSIDE has good gatepiers. Above a bend on Overton Road is the old manse, KIRKLAND, dated 1915; domesticated Baronial with an octagonal entrance tower carved with a burning bush tablet and the Church of Scotland motto NEC TAMEN CONSUMEBATUR. All these are in red sandstone. So, too, though rough-faced, are the four-in-a-block 1920s houses in QUEEN'S DRIVE and WYLIE AVENUE; by *Joseph Weekes*, housing architect for Dumbarton County Council from 1919.

Between Main Street and the river there is none of this built coherence, the original arrow-head clarity of BANK STREET and BRIDGE STREET converging on Bonhill Bridge (*see* Public Buildings, above) lost in a vortex of looping roads, footbridges and underpasses. Some individual buildings of modest quality stand isolated. Only O'NEIL TERRACE, *c.* 1998, a long wall of crisply detailed two-storey red brick housing rising to a balconied third floor at the ends, gives a sense of what redevelopment might have been. Designed by *Chris Stewart* of *Vernon Monaghan Architects* with glass butterfly-canopied porches and forecourts.

FORT, Carman. 2km. SW, on the summit of a rounded hill to the S of Overton Muir. The fort comprises an outer enclosure measuring 180m. by 140m. overall with an inner stone-walled fortification 55m. by 40m. internally. At least a dozen hut-circles are visible in the interior of the larger enclosure.

TULLICHEWAN CASTLE. *See* p. 786

# ALLOA
C *8090*

The largest town and, since 1822, the administrative centre of Clackmannanshire, Alloa was erected a burgh of regality under the feudal superiority of the Lords Erskine (later, Earls of Mar) in 1497.

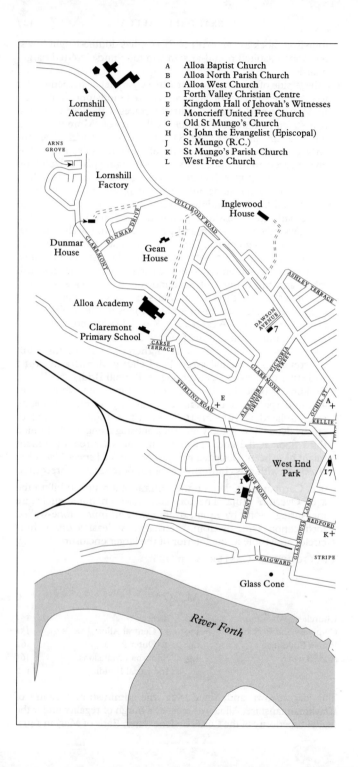

A   Alloa Baptist Church
B   Alloa North Parish Church
C   Alloa West Church
D   Forth Valley Christian Centre
E   Kingdom Hall of Jehovah's Witnesses
F   Moncrieff United Free Church
G   Old St Mungo's Church
H   St John the Evangelist (Episcopal)
J   St Mungo (R.C.)
K   St Mungo's Parish Church
L   West Free Church

Lornshill
Academy

ARNS
GROVE

Lornshill
Factory

Dunmar
House

Gean
House

Inglewood
House

TULLIBODY ROAD

CLAREMONT

DUNMAR DRIVE

ASHLEY TERRACE

Alloa Academy

Claremont
Primary School

CARSE
TERRACE

DAWSON
AVENUE

7

STIRLING ROAD

ALEXANDRA
DRIVE

CLAREMONT

VICTORIA
STREET

E

OCHIL ST.

A

KELLIE

West End
Park

GRANGE ROAD

1

2

17

GLASSHOUSE
LOAN

BEDFORD

K

CRAIGWARD

STRIPE

Glass Cone

River Forth

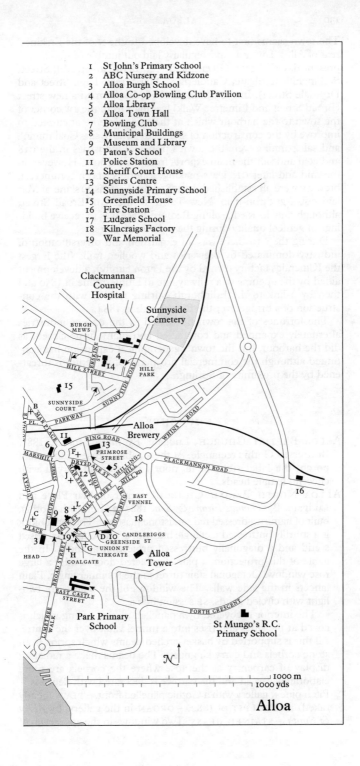

1   St John's Primary School
2   ABC Nursery and Kidzone
3   Alloa Burgh School
4   Alloa Co-op Bowling Club Pavilion
5   Alloa Library
6   Alloa Town Hall
7   Bowling Club
8   Municipal Buildings
9   Museum and Library
10  Paton's School
11  Police Station
12  Sheriff Court House
13  Speirs Centre
14  Sunnyside Primary School
15  Greenfield House
16  Fire Station
17  Ludgate School
18  Kilncraigs Factory
19  War Memorial

Clackmannan County Hospital

Sunnyside Cemetery

BURGH MEWS

ERSKINE

HILL STREET

HILL PARK

SUNNYSIDE ROAD

15

SUNNYSIDE COURT

LUDGATE

B

MR PLACE

PL.

PARKWAY

11

RING ROAD

6

13

PRIMROSE STREET

F

MARSHILL

J

12

DRYSDALE ST

SHILLING

5

MAR STREET

MILL STREET

BANK ST

MILL RD

EAST VENNEL

Alloa Brewery

WHINS ROAD

CLACKMANNAN ROAD

16

C

9

8

L

18

PLACE

3

HEAD

19

10

D

G

H

CANDLERIGGS ST

GREENSIDE ST

UNION ST

KIRKGATE

COALGATE

Alloa Tower

EAST CASTLE STREET

LIMETREE WALK

Park Primary School

FORTH CRESCENT

St Mungo's R.C. Primary School

BROAD STREET

CHURCH STREET

AULDSBY

N

|_____| 1000 m
|_____| 1000 yds

Alloa

The town seems first to have developed to the N of the Erskines' seat of Alloa Tower as an irregularly laid out jumble of streets (the present day Kirkgate, Greenside Street, Bank Street, Mill Street, Shillinghill, Coalgate, Candleriggs, Mar Street, High Street and Drysdale Street). In 1705 John, Earl of Mar, formed a new street (Broad Street and Limetree Walk) leading s from the sw corner of the town to the harbour which at the same time he attempted to improve by the construction of sluices to remove silt. Coal mining and salt panning were the town's principal industries in the c18 and coal and salt the main exports from the harbour. However, in the mid and later c18 glass-making, a pottery and a commercial brewery were all established. In 1785 John Francis Erskine of Mar laid out a gridiron-plan 'New Town' to the w of Broad Street, although only its N edge along Bedford Place was to receive buildings of genteel quality during the next thirty years.

During the c19 there was an expansion and diversification of industry dominated by breweries and woollen mills (the largest the Kilncraigs factory owned by the Paton family), a development aided by the opening of a railway line to Dunfermline in 1850 and then by a link to the Edinburgh–Stirling railway with the construction of a bridge over the River Forth in 1884.

The fortunes of the town fluctuated in the c20 as industries alternately expanded and contracted and many firms closed, as did the harbour, but the town's geographical expansion has continued although the commercial prosperity of its centre is threatened by the proximity of Stirling.

## CHURCHES

ALLOA BAPTIST CHURCH, Ludgate. By *James Mitchell*, 1881. Buttressed Gothic rectangle. At the E gable, a rose window and porch, the label stops of its door's hoodmould carved with cheerful female heads.

ALLOA NORTH PARISH CHURCH, corner of Mar Place and Ludgate. By *Thomas Frame & Son*, 1881–2. Lumpish Gothic, built of hammer-dressed red sandstone masonry. The main block is a sturdily buttressed rectangle but with a semi-octagonal apsed s end and a diagonally buttressed projection at the N. In the gable of this projection, a pair of gableted doors under a large rose window. Octagonal stair turret in the NE inner angle. Plain lancets in the side walls. The windows of the s apse are two-light with circled heads. SE session house.

The interior is covered by a panelled plaster ceiling which is coved at the sides and rises into a tunnel vault over the centre. All this is supported by basket-arched beams which spring from stone corbels and carry kingposts. The beams make a radiating display of carpentry at the apse where the corbels are more elaborately carved and the cornice is decorated with fleurons. – Pitch pine N gallery with a Gothic panelled front. – PEWS (gently raked) and PULPIT of 1882. – ORGAN in the gallery, by *Abbot & Smith*. – STAINED GLASS. Two windows in the apse, each of two lights. The sw (St Andrew, St Michael the Archangel) is of 1921, darkly coloured, much of the detail now lost. – The brighter and more clearly drawn se (Our Lord and St Andrew) is by *Herbert Hendrie*, 1937. It was formerly in the West Free (later Chalmers) Church and was brought here in 1970. Extra panels to fill the opening were added in the same manner by *John Blyth*, 1982.

ALLOA WEST CHURCH, Bedford Place. Originally Alloa West United Presbyterian Church, it is by *Peddie & Kinnear*, 1863–4, but enlarged and altered by *Sydney Mitchell & Wilson*, 1902–4, the later masonry of squared and stugged rubble like that of the 1860s but a little yellower in colour.

The 1860s church, comprising a three-bay nave and aisles, sw steeple and se porch, is early French Gothic. At the front (s) gable of the nave, small vestibule windows; above, a pair of large two-light gallery windows, plate-traceried cinquefoils in their heads, the hoodmoulds' label stops carved with tight knots of foliage and human heads. Vesica in the apex of the gable. Under the gallery windows, a stringcourse which steps down at the ends of the gable. From there it is carried across the sw tower to form a hoodmould over the s door which has squat nook-shafts with foliaged capitals and a moulded pointed arch. Projecting from the stringcourse at the e corner of the nave gable, the sculpture of a grotesque beast. It is balanced by the figure of an angel flying out from the gable's w corner at the junction of its roof with the tower. Over the se porch, an iron-crested French pavilion roof.

The tower but not the spire of Peddie & Kinnear's sw steeple survives. Originally this was of four stages. In the w face of the second stage, a two-light window with broad mullions and a plate-traceried quatrefoil in the head; the hoodmould's label stops are carved with the heads of a king and queen. Under the small paired lights of the s face's third stage, a long sill, its ends carved with balls of foliage. At the original top stage, a round opening. This stage is finished with a bandcourse studded with blind quatrefoils. *Sydney Mitchell & Wilson* heightened the tower by the addition of a very tall belfry, its faces filled with three-light openings of late Gothic type, its slender columns having stiffleaf capitals. More stiffleaf capitals on the piers at the corners. Above, arcaded corbelling under a high battlement. Inside the battlement, a dumpy fish-scale-slated spire topped by a weathercock.

Over each bay of the 1860s aisles is a roof at r. angles to that of the nave, producing triple-gabled side elevations. In each of these gables, two tiers of windows, the upper with plate-traceried cinquefoils in their heads and foliaged label stops to the hood-moulds.

The church was extended N in 1902–4 by the addition of transepts and a chancel, the N inner angles filled with triangular organ chambers; slate-spired ventilator-flèche over the cross-ing. The new work is of the same height as the old but the detail is evocative of Scots late Gothic. In the transept gables, two tiers of windows, the lower rectangular with cusping in the heads.

Pointed three-light windows, their heads containing bar-traceried cinquefoils. These are flanked by blind arcading springing from foliage-capitalled attached columns. More blind arcading across the upper storey of the organ chambers. In the chancel's gable, a four-light window with cusped loop tracery; it is flanked by blind arches. At the corners of the gable, angle buttresses supporting Tudorish octagonal turrets, their sides panelled. Partly covering the gable, a low vestry, also of 1902–4.

On the E side of the church, a Gothic HALL by *Thomas Frame & Son*, 1891, spired zinc ventilators rising from the red-tiled roof ridge.

Inside the church, *Peddie & Kinnear*'s nave arcades are carried on tall and slender columns with foliage capitals. Galleries in the aisles and at the S end. Ribbed ceilings. *Sydney Mitchell & Wilson*'s additions created a sanctuary under the new crossing, a choir loft in the N chancel, the loft's semi-octagonal front projecting into the sanctuary, organ pipes in the NE and NW organ chambers, and galleries in the transepts. The sanctuary is semi-
28   octagonal, with pointed arches opening into the other limbs of the building. Broad arch into the nave, its soffit decorated with carved and painted fruit and foliage, the responds' small capitals carved with foliage. The arches into the other parts spring from foliage-capitalled marble-shafted columns standing on high bases whose tops are carved with birds and fruits. Over the sanctuary, a ribbed wooden vault with carved bosses. Over the N chancel, a pointed tunnel vault, again ribbed. Under the transept galleries, oak screens. Below the organ pipes the splayed NE and NW sanctuary walls are clad with bands of marble (now covered over); marble floor.

The PULPIT of 1902–4 occupies the centre of the sanctuary. It is of oak with an elaborate crocketed-finialled spired canopy. – In front of the pulpit, a marble COMMUNION TABLE of the same date, its frieze carved with birds and foliage. – ORGAN CASES again of 1902–4 in a late Gothic manner. – ORGAN by *Lewis & Co. Ltd.*, 1904. – STAINED GLASS. In the nave windows, Glasgow-style abstract glass, probably of 1904. – Accomplished N window (the Road to Calvary) by *C. E. Kempe*, 1904. – Also of 1904 and by *Kempe* are the transept windows (the E depicting Our Lord among the Doctors in the Temple and the Presentation of Our Lord in the Temple, the W the Annunciation, the Nativity of Our Lord, and the Adoration of the Magi).

Inside the hall, a braced roof, its boarded ceiling surprisingly smart, the ventilation outlets contained in decorative panels.

FORTH VALLEY CHRISTIAN CENTRE, Greenside Street. Built as Greenside Mission Church in 1873. Tall single-storey hall-church. At its E end, a Frenchy tower, the truncated pyramidal roof covered with fish-scale slating and topped by iron cresting. At the W end, two-storey housing of the same height as the church proper. The general manner is thrifty Jacobean.

KINGDOM HALL OF JEHOVAH'S WITNESSES, Stirling Road. By *Forth Computer Graphics*, 1993. Polite but unexciting, with harled walls and a slated roof.

MONCRIEFF UNITED FREE CHURCH, Drysdale Street. Originally Alloa Townhead United Presbyterian Church. Late Georgian Gothic survival, by *John Melvin*, 1850–1. Big box, the breadth of its front (s) gable disguised by a firescreen front divided into a 'nave' and 'aisles' by stepped buttresses with big foliaged finials. At the outer corner, diagonal buttresses, also with foliaged finials. The verticality of all these buttresses is emphasized by vertical broaching. In each of the front's outer bays (the 'aisle ends'), an immmensely tall pointed and hood-moulded window, its surround again vertically broached. At the centrepiece ('nave gable'), a broad Tudor-arched door with bell-capitalled nook-shafts, flanked by cusped-arched dummy windows. Above the door, a rectangular hoodmould with pendant label stops; in the spandrels, quatrefoil panels. This lower part of the centrepiece, its stonework of polished ashlar in contrast to the horizontally broached ashlar of the rest of the walling, is finished with a broad bandcourse divided into panels containing blank shields. Above, a four-light mullioned and transomed window, again with vertical broaching, under a hoodmould. Harled side walls pierced by two tiers of windows.

Inside, an arched and ribbed plaster ceiling. – U-plan GALLERY, its cast iron columns with capitals of stylized foliage. At the centre of the front, a cartouche containing a clock. – Boxy PEWS, raked within and under the gallery. – The roomy plat-form PULPIT incorporating the organ console was introduced in 1884. – Semi-octagonal N apse, the angular arch at its entrance springing from bundle-shafted columns. – Filling the apse is the ORGAN, by *Lewis & Co. Ltd.*, 1884.

OLD ST MUNGO'S CHURCH, Kirkgate. Most of the former 14 parish church of Alloa was demolished in 1817 and little more than the W gable of the nave and the W tower now survive. The present form of both largely dates from the repair and recon-struction of the church carried out *c.* 1681–3.* At the rubble-built gable, each side of the tower, a tall rectangular gallery window with a cavetto moulded surround, probably of the 1680s but perhaps enlarged in 1717 when a second W gallery was erected. Small rectangular window at the S end of the gable to light the area under the gallery. At the inner (E) face of the gable, at ground-floor level, a crude recess marking the position of a door from the tower. Built-up door of the 1680s from the tower to the former gallery. Above this door, a hollowed-out niche, probably made in the earlier C19, its consoled keystone perhaps re-used from the N door of the tower. In this niche, a statue, probably of *c.* 1683, of a man in C17 dress holding a book. The statue formerly stood in a niche in the S wall of the church and has been regarded since at least 1791 as representing St Mungo, an identification made explicit by the C19 inscription

---

* This followed a report on the costs of the proposed work prepared in 1680 by *John Buchanan, Tobias Bachop* and *Patrick Main*, masons, *James Houston* and *James Allan*, wrights, *William Johnston*, smith, and *William Bow*, slater, but there is no firm evidence that the work carried out more than a year later was executed by these craftsmen or to their design.

on the lintel of the present niche. At the apex of the gable, a small
rectangular window into the tower. At the S end of the gable, a
stub of the S wall of the nave. This is ashlar-built and probably
of the 1680s; at its E end, one jamb of a pointed window. At the
N end of the gable, a fragment of the W wall of the church's N
aisle including part of a window jamb. Projecting from this stub
are the semicircular respond and springing of the W arch of the
aisle's three-bay arcade into the nave. The aisle is likely to have
been built c. 1500, its construction perhaps connected to
Alexander, Lord Erskine's endowment of a chaplainry at the
altar of St Kentigern in Alloa Church in 1502.

The W tower seems to be all of c. 1681–3. Its rubble-walled
lower three stages rise unbroken by stringcourses to a moulded
cornice under the ashlar-faced belfry. At the first stage, a round-
arched door in each of the N and S sides, the N a dummy, the S
with a consoled keystone and roll-and-hollow surround. At the
second stage, a cavetto-splayed rectangular W window. At the
third stage, in each of the exposed faces, a cavetto-splayed round-
arched window with a consoled keystone. Tiers of narrow rectangular stair windows at the SW corner. The belfry stage is dignified with rusticated quoins as well as ashlar masonry. At each
face, a round-arched and console-keystoned opening. The
imposts of these openings are continued across the walling as a
moulded stringcourse. The belfry is finished with a frieze and
cornice under the bellcast eaves of the slated roof. This is very
similar to the roof of the Tolbooth tower at Clackmannan
(q.v.), a truncated pyramid topped by an ogee dome rising into
a spirelet topped by a weathercock.

The medieval chancel of the church became the 'Mar Aisle'
after the Reformation. Following the demolition of the nave in
1817, it was rebuilt in 1819 as the MAUSOLEUM of the Earls of
Mar (later, Mar and Kellie); *James Gillespie Graham* was the
architect. Heavily buttressed and crowstep-gabled three-bay
ashlar box. Hoodmoulded pointed windows, those of the N and
S sides nook-shafted; W window of two cusped lights under a
quatrefoil. Broad pointed E entrance with large foliaged label
stops to the hoodmould. The interior's plaster vaulting and
lavish Victorian decoration have been stripped out. Of the
MONUMENTS the best are on the W wall. Low down at its S
end, a weathered C16 stone tablet is carved at its top l. corner
with a cross on a triangular base. This marks the beginning of
its inscription recording the construction of the burial vault
under the medieval chancel: 'I.E [John Erskine, Earl of
Mar]:RESTIT./YE.XXVII DAY.OF.OCTOBAR/1572:ÆD:ORDAIT/
YIS TO.BE.DONE'. The narrative is continued on a second
tablet at the N end of the wall which states: 'AT/QVHAIS.
C/OMAND.HIS./LADY:A:M [Annabella Murray]:/DYD:1582:' –
Above are two white marble monuments, identical except for
their inscriptions, which were erected in 1709 by John, sixth and
eleventh Earl of Mar, one commemorating his first wife, Lady
Margaret Hay, and a son who died in infancy, the other his
father and three brothers who died in childhood. They are oval,

with convex inscription panels set in baroque frames, each carved with cherubs' heads and surmounted by a coroneted coat of arms.

GRAVEYARD. In the N wall along Kirkgate, a built-up basket-arched DOORWAY, perhaps of the early C18. – To its E, a pair of rusticated ashlar GATEPIERS (the opening between now blocked), probably of the later C17. The top stone of one is carved with the relief of a skull and crossbones, the other with a winged hourglass. – At the entrance to the older part of the grave-yard from a large Victorian E extension, rusticated GATEPIERS with belted ball finials (one fallen); they look early C18.

HEADSTONES. At the W end of the graveyard, a fair number of stones of the mid and later C18, carved with angels' heads (souls) and emblems of death; most are now largely buried. An exceptionally large one, commemorating George Forester (?), bears the relief of an anchor (the emblem of a sailor). – About halfway between the W wall of the graveyard and the W end of the church, a headstone of 1761, its E face divided into two panels, one displaying a skull, crossbones and hourglass, the other a crowned hammer (for a smith) or shoemaker's knife. – SE of this, two C18 stones with fluted Doric pilasters at the sides and, on top, scrolls which form the outlines of swan-neck pedi-ments, both bearing reminders of death and one with a crowned hammer and an unidentified implement. – To their S, a stone of 1729 to IA and IN, decorated with emblems of mortality, together with the comb, razor and bleeding bowl of a barber. – S of this, the large MONUMENT to Robert Johnston †1739, a Roman Doric columned aedicule, the swan-neck pediment broken by an angel's head. Triglyphs and rosettes on the frieze; emblems of death at the base. Inscription:

Before this monument of stones
Lie honest Robert Johnstons bones
He lived devoutly died in Peace
Prompt by religion and Grace
Endowd a Preacher for this Place
With consent of his Wife to lie
Here by him when she falls to die
At her Expence This Tomb was raisd
For him whose Worth she prized & praisd

– On the S side of the monument, a headstone of 1724 with two angels' heads at the top. – S of this, a headstone of 1723 bearing a skull, crossbones and hourglass, and a plough. – Beside it, another farmer's stone of 1725, with a skull and crossbones in relief and an incised plough. – N of the Johnston monument, two headstones of 1751, one with a skull and crossbones and a plough, the other with emblems of death accompanied by a broom, shovel and loaf of bread (?). – To the SE, against the S wall, a stone, probably of the C18, with reliefs of a skull, cross-bones and hourglass on the l. of its face and, on the r., nautical emblems including an anchor. – NE of this, a small ineptly exe-cuted C18 aedicular headstone, the front carved with a skull wearing an hourglass as a hat. – To the E, near the S wall, a headstone of 1741 to JC and MB, with a weaver's shuttle and loom, together with the usual skull, crossbones and hourglass. – Beside it, a small curly-topped stone dated 1673, one face incised with a weaver's shuttle and stretcher, the other with the inscription:

REMEMBER MAN AS THOV GOSE.BY.THAT THOV.WITH.ME IN.
DUST.MOST.LY SERVE.THOV.THE.LORD.IN FEAR.THERFOR.AND.
THOV SHAL.LIVE.FOR.EVRMORE

– E of this, a large stone of 1750 bearing a plough. – To the N, another big stone but of 1705, again with a plough and symbols of death. – To its E, a stone of 1718 with the standard grisly emblems and a crowned hammer. – N of this, a stone of 1799, again with reminders of mortality and with a broom, shovel and loaf.

ST JOHN THE EVANGELIST (Episcopal), Broad Street. Simple Geometric, the character more rural than urban, by *R. Rowand Anderson*. The nave, chancel and SW steeple were built in 1867–9, the double-pitch roofed N aisle, its slightly taller E bay containing a choir vestry and organ chamber, added in 1872. Low sacristy of 1900 at the E end of the aisle. Walls of hammer-dressed grey stone. Hoodmoulds over the windows, their boldly projecting label stops clearly intended to be carved. The steeple consists of an angle-buttressed tower and a broach spire, its masonry enlivened by bands of red stone.

INTERIOR. In 1992 *Machin Associates* put up a simplified Gothic screen to make a vestibule from the W bay of the nave and converted the W end of the aisle into meeting rooms. Otherwise the Victorian and early C20 interior survives. Arcade to the aisle, its pointed arches springing from alternately round and quatrefoil-plan pillars with simply moulded capitals. At the E end of the aisle, a pointed arch to the choir vestry and organ chamber. The arch from the nave into the slightly narrower two-bay chancel springs from short corbelled-out wall-shafts with stiffleaf capitals. Over the nave and aisle, wooden pointed tunnel vaults divided into panels by transverse ribs, their painted decoration rather more elaborate in the aisle. The panels of the nave ceiling are decorated with roundels displaying alternately the IHS monogram and the Star of David together with floral motifs. On the panels of the aisle ceiling, coats of arms of male ancestors of the Earls of Mar and Kellie. The wooden chancel ceiling, another pointed tunnel vault, dates from alterations of 1913 by *Robert S. Lorimer*. It is encrusted with carved and gilded ribs and bosses, the carving richer in the E bay (the sanctuary). Over the step at the entrance to the sanctuary, a broad rib bearing gilt reliefs of angels holding shields blazoned with emblems of the Passion. On the ridge rib of the sanctuary, shields displaying a chalice, the *Agnus Dei* and an eagle (the emblem of St John the Evangelist).

On the nave and aisle floors, encaustic TILES of 1869 by *William Goodwin*. The chancel floor was laid with white-veined red marble and porphyry by *Allan & Son*, 1902–3.

Stone ALTAR of 1869, the slab supported on stiffleaf-capitalled marble columns. – Above it, the contemporary REREDOS (height-

ened by the insertion of a marble slip in 1913). Its marble framework and carving are by *Farmer & Brindley*. In Gothic niches at
the ends, figures of angels, one holding a crown of thorns, the
other a cross. The centre of the reredos is filled with a mosaic
by *Antonio Salviati* depicting the Last Supper. Over the central
figure of Our Lord, a stone canopy rising from the framework.

Round the chancel, a panelled oak DADO of 1913 in *Lorimer*'s
characteristic late Gothic manner, the frieze carved with birds and
fruit. – Oak CHOIR STALLS designed by *Lorimer* and executed
by *Nathaniel Grieve*, 1901–2, with linenfold panelling and carved
vines. On the back of the Rector's stall (the W on the S side), a
memorial TABLET of 1902 recording the erection of the stalls; in
one corner of the tablet, an enamel plaque depicting the Pelican
in Piety by *Phoebe Traquair*. – Tall ORGAN CASE (the organ
itself removed) by *Lorimer*, 1913, the elaborate carved decoration again incorporating birds and fruit.

The wrought iron CHANCEL SCREEN was designed by *Lorimer*
and executed by *Singer & Sons* of Frome, 1902–3. Floral decoration on the screen and its surmounting cross; also small shields
bearing emblems of the Passion. – Flanking the chancel arch,
the FONT and PULPIT of 1869, both routine Gothic.

Oak SCREEN (by *Lorimer*, 1913) cutting off the vestry and
organ chamber from the aisle. At the top, a sculptured depiction
of the Crucifixion, the four ends of the cross bearing emblems
of the Evangelists. On the front of the screen, a WAR MEMORIAL
PANEL by *Lorimer*, 1920.

In the N aisle, a huge marble MONUMENT to Walter
Coningsby, Earl of Kellie, designed by *R. Rowand Anderson* and
executed by *John Rhind* in 1873. Gothic sarcophagus on which
lies the life-size effigy of the heavily moustachioed Earl dressed
in peer's robes, his head resting on a pillow held by kneeling
angels, his feet on a recumbent lion. – At the W end of the N wall
of the choir, a silver TABLET of 1902 to Edward John Younger
†1901 in the South African War, one corner bearing an enamel
by *Phoebe Traquair* showing an angel taking a fallen soldier by
the hand. – On the S wall of the nave, a metal TABLET to the
Rev. Alexander Penrose Forbes Erskine †1925, with the low
relief of a Gothic arch framing a chalice and host.

STAINED GLASS. E window of the chancel (the Crucifixion,
flanked by scenes from the lives of Our Lady and Our Lord) by
*Douglas Strachan*, 1913. Clearly drawn narrative panels set against
a background of variegated pale glass. – In the side windows of
the chancel, glass (the Arrest of Our Lord in the N wall, Resurrection appearances in the S) by *C. A. Gibbs*, 1869. – The three S
windows of the nave (Our Lord's descent into Hell; the Resurrection; Pentecost) are all by *C. E. Kempe*, 1890. – In the N wall of
the aisle, the E window's centre light, a strongly coloured depiction of the Annunciation set against a background of obscured
plain glass, is by *Margaret Chilton*, 1939. The side lights (heraldic
crests) were added in 1955. – Next to it, an accomplished
narrative window (St Oswald, King of Northumbria, raising the
Cross at Hevenfelth) by *Kempe*, 1902. – To its W, a window of

*c.* 1900 (Hope, Faith and Charity), much weaker in design and colouring. – In the aisle's w bay, a window of the later C19 (scenes in the life of Our Lady), strongly coloured but the detail badly eroded. – The two-light w window of the aisle (St Andrew and St Thomas) is also of the later C19 and has lost most of its detail. – Colourful w window of the nave (the Last Judgment in the centre light, the expulsion from Eden, the building of the Ark, the denial of St Peter and the conversion of St Paul in the side lights) of 1869 to a design by *R. Rowand Anderson*; it was restored by *Christian Shaw*, 1996.

ST MUNGO (R.C.), Mar Street. Modern-traditional in dark brown brick, by *Allan & Friskin*, 1959–61. Broad nave flanked by flat-roofed narrow aisles; w projection (containing vestibule and gallery) from the centre of the nave. Low square bell-tower at the nave's NW corner. Tall rectangular windows.

Spacious interior, the passage-aisles marked off from the nave by octagonal pillars. – Tall wooden BALDACCHINO over the altar. – On the E wall, a CRUCIFIX, its bronze figure by *Scott Sutherland*, 1961. – In the Lady Chapel at the NE, a three-light STAINED GLASS WINDOW (Our Lady) by *Sadie McLellan*, 1960. Strongly coloured expressionist.

N of the church, the PRESBYTERY, also of 1961 and by *Allan & Friskin*. Brown brick again, the manner a sort of updated English Arts and Crafts.

19 ST MUNGO'S PARISH CHURCH, Bedford Place. By *James Gillespie Graham*, 1816–19. Late Georgian Perp, built of broached greyish ashlar, the windows all hoodmoulded. The body is a huge battlemented rectangle, corners clasped by diagonally buttressed low towers containing entrances. Each of the gables has a firescreen front suggestive of a nave and aisles, the slightly advanced centrepiece finished with crocketed pinnacles at the corners and a stone cross on the apex. The gables are partly covered by single-storey additions by *Leslie Grahame Thomson*, 1966–7, in the Lorimerian manner of fifty years before. The w addition, containing a session house complex, is blocky, its buff-coloured polished ashlar a not very happy contrast to Gillespie Graham's masonry. The E addition is a chancel-like porch, a tall carved relief of the Church of Scotland's Burning Bush emblem on its E face. The long street (N) elevation is of five bays between the corner towers, the centre slightly advanced under a gable, again with crocketed pinnacles and a cross finial; in the gable, a dummy roundel containing cusped loop tracery.

The church's dominant feature from a distance, but half-hidden from the street, is the steeple which projects from the centre of its s side. The corners of the tower are clasped by octagonal buttresses terminating in crocketed pinnacles. At the tower's bottom stage, a Tudor Gothic s door under a rectangular hoodmould, the label stops carved with bearded heads; quatrefoil panels in the spandrels. Plainer doors in the E and w faces. At the second stage, in each exposed face, a two-light window. At the third stage, paired belfry openings with slender nookshafts. In each face of the top stage, a round clockface contained in a foliaged border which rises at the top to support a foliaged finial. At the wallhead, sturdy moulded corbels supporting an arcaded parapet within which rises the spire, tied by flying buttresses to the corner buttresses of the tower. The spire itself is a delicate octagonal needle, its corners lavishly crocketed and the cardinal faces bearing lucarnes; foliaged finial supporting a weathervane.

The INTERIOR is a huge single space. Its rather bare character dates largely from 1936–7 when *Leslie Grahame Thomson* removed the galleries and introduced the present panelled wooden ceiling. At the W end, a chancel formed by Thomson in 1966–7 from a former vestibule and the choir loft above. The vaulted plaster ceiling over the chancel is of 1819. In the chancel, PULPIT, LECTERN and FONT of 1936–7, designed by *Thomson*, the chancel's wrought-iron RAILING executed by *Charles Henshaw*, with panels showing a bear, ship, crossed croziers and mitres, and a salmon with a ring (the emblem of St Mungo). – The COMMUNION TABLE looks a little earlier. – In the nave, oak PEWS of 1936–7 in a plain sub-Lorimer manner.

STAINED GLASS. In the S wall, one light of the W window (the Good Shepherd) was filled in 1895 by *William Meikle & Sons*. – In the N wall, one light of the W window (St Mungo and St Andrew) is by *John Blyth*, 1991. – In the window to its E, all three lights (Our Lord in Glory, with St Michael the Archangel and St Andrew) were filled in 1951–2 by *William Wilson* in characteristically expressionist fashion. – To its E, another three-light window (*Te Deum*), darkly coloured and muddily drawn, by *A. L. Moore & Co.*, 1901. – E of that, a lushly coloured narrative window (the Agony in the Garden) of 1908.

WEST FREE CHURCH, Bank Street. Disused. A characteristic work by *J., W. H. & J. M. Hay* of Liverpool, 1854–6. Geometric Gothic rectangle, with stepped buttresses along the sides. Projecting from the front gable, a powerful steeple. Muscular diagonal buttresses appear to push up the tower before dying into it below a stringcourse above the second stage. In the front face of the first stage, a pointed entrance decorated with ballflower ornament, its nook-shafted capitals carved with naturalistic oak leaves and acorns; the hoodmould's label stops are sculpted as the heads of a bearded king and a woman. At the second stage, a three-light window. Intake at the low belfry, a gableted opening at each of its faces; plain pinnacles above its cut-out corners. Tall lucarnes on four faces of the octagonal stone spire.

## CEMETERY AND PARK

SUNNYSIDE CEMETERY, Sunnyside Road. Opened in 1878. At the entrance, concave dwarf walls topped by railings; at their ends and centre, banded and corniced red sandstone piers, their curvy pediments carved with anthemion decoration. – Plain LODGE with a broad-eaved piended roof. – MONUMENTS. In the NW part, a fair number of Celtic crosses and some broken columns and urn-topped memorials, as well as late C19 and C20 headstones. The best of the crosses is against the w boundary, near the N end. It commemorates David Paton Thomson †1917. Large and elaborately carved, by *Robert Gray* of Glasgow.

WEST END PARK, Grange Road. Opened in 1878. At the entrance, corniced GATEPIERS with Ægypto-Greek ornament.

## PUBLIC BUILDINGS

ABC NURSERY AND KIDZONE, Grant Street. Originally St John's (Episcopal) School. By *John Melvin & Son*, 1902. Single-storey, the walls of glazed red brick and render; cupola on the roof. It is beset by later additions.

ALLOA ACADEMY, Claremont. Originally by the Clackmannan County Architect, *W. H. Henry*, 1958–9, in the lightweight Festival of Britain manner. Much of this is still visible but a new N front and extensions were added by *Central Regional Council* (Director of Architectural Services: *G. M. Crossan*) in 1986–90. This is of patterned brick and red tiles, a wild mixture of neo-vernacular (e.g. the tiers of huge catslide-roofed dormer windows) and neo-Victorian (the piend-roofed towers); low octagonal entrance pavilion and a clock tower.

ALLOA BURGH SCHOOL, Bedford Place. Now in other use. Free Jacobean, by *John Melvin*, 1875–6. Crowstep-gabled L-plan front of one storey (a basement exposed in the steeply falling ground behind). In the inner angle, a round tower with huge crosslet 'arrowslits' in its walling; fish-scale-slated conical roof.

ALLOA CO-OP BOWLING CLUB PAVILION, Sunnyside Road and Hill Park. Free early Georgian, by *George A. Kerr*, 1924–7. Harled, with a pantiled roof. Balconied verandah across the recessed centre of the E front; segmental-shaped dormer windows.

ALLOA LIBRARY, Drysdale Street. Originally a supermarket and offices, it is by *Wagner & Associates*, 1974. Flat-roofed two-storey block, the walls of dark brown brick.

ALLOA TOWN HALL, Marshill. By *Alfred Waterhouse*, 1887–8. Thriftily detailed François I but on a huge scale, built of squared and stugged buff-coloured masonry. T-plan, the three-storey and attic front (s) block designed to house a public library and art school as well as the vestibule to the hall which occupies the two-storey N wing. Immensely tall mullioned and transomed windows at the two lower floors of the front block. Its E and W gables are shaped, with obelisk finials on the corners. Another shaped and obelisk-finialled gable at the broad centrepiece containing the huge round-arched principal entrance. The centrepiece's upper floors are dignified with superimposed pilasters, the lowest order supported on semicircular corbels, their fronts carved with sunbursts; stumpy Ionic pilasters fronting the mullions of the second-floor windows.

The hall wing is plain except for polished ashlar roundheaded overarches containing the tall mullioned and transomed gallery windows. Across the N end, a block containing three floors within

the same height as the hall, the detailing more Jacobean. On the
N side of this block, a very tall and slim octagonal chimney, the
top projected on arcaded corbelling.

Inside the front block, a square entrance-cum-stair hall, the
walls covered with olive and pale green tiles decorated with
flowers and stars, the toplit central well pierced by openings to
the landings. On either side, rooms with thinly detailed Jacobean
plaster ceilings. Behind, the large but unexciting public hall, a
gallery round three sides, a stage at the end where there formerly
stood a grandiose organ.

BOWLING CLUB, Dawson Avenue. Free Queen Anne, by *William
Kerr* and *John Gray* of *John Melvin & Son*, 1925. Harled, with
pantiled bellcast-eaved roofs. Verandah (now glazed) across the
recessed centre of the U-plan front. At the ends of the front,
octagonal towers with ogee-profiled copper domes. In the centre
of the roof, a narrow cupola with a tall ogee-domed spire.

CLACKMANNAN COUNTY HOSPITAL, Ashley Terrace. By *R. A.
Bryden*, 1898–9. Long villa-like spread consisting of a two-storey
administrative block and single-storey wings containing the wards;
some half-timbering in the gables but the idiom is generally plain
Jacobean Renaissance. E addition by *Keppie, Henderson & J. L.
Gleave*, 1954, in the Festival of Britain manner.

CLAREMONT PRIMARY SCHOOL, Carse Terrace. Designed and
built by *Crudens Ltd.*, 1968. Of one and two storeys, built into
the hillside. Flat-roofed and sensible, with long windows piercing the dry-dashed walls.

FIRE STATION, Clackmannan Road. By *A. J. Smith*, 1962–4.
Flat-roofed, with brown brick walling and a hosepipe tower.

LORNSHILL ACADEMY, Tullibody Road. Large complex. The
main part is by *Baron Bercott & Associates*, 1967–70. Two and
three storeys, the exposed concrete frame with segmental arches
over the windows and projecting fins.

LUDGATE SCHOOL, corner of Ludgate and Glasshouse Loan.
Now in other use. The single-storey main block was built *c.* 1837.
Irregular H-plan, the roofs piended; some flat-roofed C20 additions. Single-storey NE block by *Kerr & McCulloch*, 1910.
Edwardian Baroque, the masonry of the front channelled. At
the E gable, a consoled pediment with a dummy oculus in the
tympanum; above, a three-light window with Corinthian
columned mullions.

MUNICIPAL BUILDINGS, Bank Street. Two blocks, now unified
internally. The NE, formerly the POST OFFICE, is by *Thomas
Frame & Son*, 1882. Three-storey Renaissance front of polished
ashlar. The ground floor (rather altered) is plain except for the
keystone of the off-centre round-arched entrance carved with
the head of Queen Victoria. The windows of the upper floor are
linked by sill courses, that of the second floor moulded as a
cornice. Architraves and cornices to the first-floor windows, the
tripartite windows in the second and fourth bays with pediments
over their centre lights. The second-floor windows rise through
the eaves, those of the end bays surmounted by triangular pediments, the intermediate windows by segmental pediments. The

centre window is tripartite, the cornice topped by scrolls above
the side lights, an urn-finialled consoled pediment above the
centre light.

The sw block, built as the Municipal Buildings, is by *Thomas
Frame & Son*, 1872–4. It is of the same height as the NE block
but contains only two tall storeys. Tight Baroque, the end bays
advanced and balustraded, and with Composite pilasters at the
corners of their upper floor; over the three-bay centrepiece, a
panelled parapet. The stonework is polished ashlar, channelled
at the ground floor where a round-arched pend entrance occupies
the l. bay; at the r. bay, a Composite columned portico topped
by a huge cartouche, its bottom swagged, carved with the burgh
coat of arms. Over the first-floor windows, consoled open pediments, alternately triangular and segmental; panelled aprons
under the three windows of the centrepiece. Inside this block, at
the principal stair, green tiles decorated with Art Nouveau flowers
and abstract patterned Art Nouveau stained glass; these date
from the interior's reinstatement in 1906 after a fire. On the first
floor of the former Post Office, the DISTRICT COURT, fitted
up *c.* 1925 with a Holyrood-revival plaster ceiling and oak
panelling.

In front of the Municipal Buildings, the early C17 BURGH
CROSS, its octagonal stepped pedestal a C19 replacement. The
shaft is square at the base and then broached to an octagon which,
at the top, is corbelled out to the square on reversed broaching;
capital of a very simplified Doric order. On top of the capital, a
corniced square stone with scrolls at the bottom looking like
upside-down volutes. The front and back of the stone are each
carved with a cross of chains, a rectangular panel at the intersection of the arms. On top, a badly worn stone carved with the
head of a gryphon* but one side is left in block. Has this been
brought from somewhere else?

88 MUSEUM AND LIBRARY, Church Street. Now a club. Built for
the Natural History and Archaeological Society in 1874, by *John
Melvin & Son* in the manner of 'Greek' Thomson. Two-storey
rectangle of purplish stugged ashlar with dressings of buff-
coloured polished ashlar. Five-bay elevation to Church Street,
the centre (containing the entrance) slightly advanced. Heavy
entasis at the corniced window surrounds, their friezes incised
with Ægypto-Greek decoration. Over the door, a pedimental
entablature with an anthemion finial. More anthemion finials
on the wallhead pediment of the centrepiece, its frieze supported
on squat neo-Egyptian columns. Balustrades over the outer bays.
The S front is shorter, again with a pedimented centrepiece, the
only opening a door like that of the W elevation. Above the
door, a long stone panel. On this front, a couple of lotus-flower
chimney pots are still in place.

PARK PRIMARY SCHOOL, East Castle Street. By *William Kerr*
and *John Gray* of *John Melvin & Son*, 1935. Long single-storey

---

*The heraldic achievement of the Earls of Mar (feudal superiors of the burgh of
Alloa) had gryphon supporters and the coat of arms used by the burgh from 1892 to
1902 displayed a gryphon.

U-plan, the short W front faintly neo-Georgian with a centre block and lower pavilions behind which are long E wings, utilitarian with tall metal-framed windows.

PATON'S SCHOOL, Greenside Street. Now a mill shop. The main block, built in 1864–5 as a school for children working at the nearby Kilncraigs Factory, is by *John Melvin*. Tall two storeys. Three bays, the outer two under shaped gables. Projecting from the centre, a tower, its four stages marked off by stringcourses, the lowest jumping up to form a hoodmould over the entrance. At the tower's second stage, a three-light window which would be Venetian were it not for the narrowness of its centre light. Above, a clock stage, the round faces (the N replaced in the later C20) placed in moulded lozenges. Pedestals at the corners of the idiosyncratic battlement.

At the ends of the main block, tall single-storey wings added by *John Melvin & Son* in 1900; they contained dining and recreation rooms for workers at the Kilncraigs Factory. Both have shaped gables and swags over Gibbsian doorpieces but the W wing is broader and has a three-light window as its principal feature.

POLICE STATION, Ring Road and Mar Place. By *Central Regional Council* (Director of Architectural Services: *G. M. Crossan*), 1990. Overblown and heavy-handed cottage style, the walls of buff-coloured brick with dark brown dressings, the roofs tiled; glazed porch at the heel of the L-shape.

Former POST OFFICE, Bank Street. *See* Municipal Buildings, above.

Former POST OFFICE, Bedford Place. *See* Streets: Central Alloa, below.

ST JOHN'S PRIMARY SCHOOL, Grange Road. Originally Grange 99 School. By *Kerr & McCulloch*, 1907–8. Accomplished squared-up Art Nouveau; two storeys of stugged red sandstone masonry. Single-storey W addition of *c.* 1940.

ST MUNGO'S R.C. PRIMARY SCHOOL, Forth Crescent. By *Central Regional Council* (Director of Architectural Services: *G. M. Crossan*), 1982–3. Single-storey, of brown brick, with prominent monopitch roofs.

SHERIFF COURT HOUSE, Mar Street and Drysdale Street. 85 Large crowstep-gabled Scoto–Flemish edifice of two tall storeys and a NE tower, by *Brown & Wardrop*, 1862–5. The main front is to Mar Street. Symmetrical seven bays with crowstepped gablets over the second, fourth and sixth bays. Mullioned and transomed windows of two or three basket-arched lights; pendant label stops at the hoodmoulds. Broad basket-arched centre door set between stepped buttresses. On their sloping tops, large moulded corbels supporting the ends of a stone balcony, the corner piers of its arcaded parapet topped by lions holding shields which display the crosses of St Andrew and St George. The central wallhead gablet, carved with the Royal Arms, is larger than the others. On its apex, a stone lion holding a metal flagpole weathervane; at the bottom corners of the gablet, Tudor finials standing on piers with gryphons projecting from their bases. At the apex of each of the other gablets, a Tudor finial. The s gable is plain except for carved stone panels, one bearing monograms, the other a crest. On the similar N gable, a panel carved with the date 'AD 1863' under a crowned monogram of 'VICTORIA'.

The tower's NE corner is canted at the base and corbelled out to a rectangle above. In the second stage of the N face, a hood-moulded mullioned and transomed window. At each face of the third stage, a basket-arched single light, again hoodmoulded. High parapet rising at the centre of each face into a crowstepped and Tudor-finialled gablet set between diagonal buttresses from which project gryphons; in each gablet, a round clock face. Inside the parapet, a fish-scale-slated Frenchy roof topped by tall iron cresting; on the E and W sides, bargeboarded belfry dormers.

Plain E wing to Drysdale Street, the NE corner canted at the ground floor and corbelled out to a rectangle above. The building was extended E by *William Kerr* of *John Melvin & Son*, 1910, with the addition of a lower two-storey two-bay block. Crowstep-gabled squared-up Jacobean, with mullioned and transomed windows and a large W chimney. A further two bays in the same manner were added by the same firm in 1937–8.

Inside the main block, first-floor COURT ROOM of the 1860s. Hammerbeam roof; large ornamental brass fittings for gasoliers.

93 SPEIRS CENTRE, Primrose Street. Built as public baths and gymnasium in 1895–8; *John Burnet, Son & Campbell* were the architects. Free Franco–Scots Renaissance, the masonry of stugged red sandstone. Tall front block of two storeys with an attic lit from skylights and small windows in the gables; bracketed broad eaves. Principal (W) elevation of five bays. The plain S bay contains a ground-floor window. At the next bay, a gabled two-storey porch, a polished granite surround to the tall entrance whose lintel bears two sandstone reliefs displaying *putti*, a bird and a ship. At the ends of the porch's upper storey, attached Roman Doric columns standing on corbels; flanking the strapwork-topped two-light window, figures of a healthy youth and maiden. On the outer corners of the porch's gable, obelisk finials; on the top, a small Dutch-gabled and columned aedicule containing a shield. N of the porch, the ground floor projects from the walling above as a long three-bay rectangle lit by two-light mullioned windows and decorated with beautifully carved François I detail. This projection is surmounted by a balustrade, the bays marked off by niched pedestals, presumably intended for sculpture. At the first floor the three bays N of the porch are separated by slender attached baluster columns supporting consoles under the main cornice; at each corner of the front the cornice is supported on a console rising from a corbel carved with a grotesque head.

At the S gable of the front block, a rectangular ground-floor projection with a curvilinear lean-to roof. At the top of the projection's front, a segmental open pedimented aedicule containing the gryphon rampant coat of arms of the burgh of Alloa.* Across

* This coat of arms was used by the burgh of Alloa from 1892 to 1902.

the inner angles of the projection and the main gable are round-headed arches with console-keystones, flanked by tall slender columns. These support balconies with angle rounds at their ends.

Behind the main block, a narrow corridor block of two storeys in the height of the main block's ground floor. At its s end, set back from the main block's gable, an elliptical-arched recess whose back wall contains a three-light window, its Roman Doric column-mullions standing on consoles. Behind this block, the irregular H-plan swimming-pool block. Its sw jamb is provided by a squat square tower with round turrets and a broad-eaved roof. The rest is long and low. At the e end, a tall octagonal chimney of red bricks banded with white.

SUNNYSIDE PRIMARY SCHOOL, Erskine Street. By *John B. Wilson*, 1892. Free Jacobean two-storey block, built of hammer-dressed red sandstone with polished dressings; cupolas on the roof. – To the NE, CLASSROOM AND GYMNASIUM BLOCK, by *Clackmannanshire Council*, 1998, looking rather like a Georgian barracks but some of the upper-floor windows suggestive of a prison.

## ALLOA TOWER

off Devon Road

8090

Exceptionally large tower-house, a symbol of the feudal superiority of the Erskines, later Earls of Mar, over the barony and burgh of Alloa whose c20 housing and factory buildings now besiege it.

54

The barony of Alloa was granted by David II to Sir Robert Erskine of that Ilk in 1368 but the first mention of a tower-house here was not made until 1497 when Alexander, third Lord Erskine, signed a charter '*Apud maneriem sive castrum de Alway*' ('at the manor or castle of Alloa'). The house was probably built a few years before,\* possibly incorporating earlier work (*see* below), and stood among lower ancillary buildings. The tower house itself was enlarged in the c17 by the addition of a sw wing.‡ In 1689 the estate of Alloa was inherited by the fourteen-year-old *John Erskine, sixth and eleventh Earl of Mar*.§ During the earl's minority his mother demolished at least one of the ancillary buildings (the 'old tower') and from *c.* 1700 the earl himself set about a plethora of estate improvements including the layout of great formal plantations, the development of mining and the construction of a new harbour at Alloa. The great new landscape garden he created was crossed by avenues radiating from Alloa Tower and focused on natural and historical features, among them Sauchie Tower, Clackmannan

---

\*There is no mention of it in a Crown charter of the lands and barony of Alloa granted to Alexander Erskine, son and heir of Thomas, second Lord Erskine, in 1489.

‡For ease of description I have taken the house as being entered from the N (instead of the NW)

§From the c15 the Erskines claimed to be the rightful heirs of the ancient earldom of Mar, a claim apparently admitted in 1565 when John, sixth Lord Erskine, was created Earl of Mar. In the late c19 the House of Lords decided that after 1565 the Erskines held both the ancient earldom of Mar and a second earldom (also of Mar) created in 1565.

Tower, Dunmore Tower and Stirling Castle. Alloa Tower itself underwent remodelling and extension, including the addition of a SE block in the inner angle of the tower and the C17 SW wing. Work was begun by 1703 and continued until broken off in 1715 by Mar's leadership of the Jacobite rising and his subsequent exile and attainder. Mar acted as his own architect but with advice from *Alexander Edward* and from *James Smith* and *Alexander McGill* who were contractors for at least some of the work. The additions were completed later in the C18, almost certainly not to any of Mar's designs, but were demolished, along with the C17 wing, after a fire in 1800. The medieval tower-house survived the fire and was later repaired (in the earlier C19 and again in 1867) as an antique curios-ity rather than a dwelling, a new mansion house (Alloa House) being built some way to the NE in 1834–8.* In 1989–96 the tower was again repaired and fitted up for opening to the public by the Alloa Tower Preservation Trust; the architect was *Bob Heath* in association with *Martin Hadlington*. It is now administered by the National Trust for Scotland.

The general external appearance of Alloa Tower today is of a late C15 house, a severe four-storey and attic rectangle, *c.* 19m. by 12m., the walls rising unbroken by offsets or stringcourses to flush battlements, with rounds projected on continuous corbelling at the four corners and the centre of the N front. Conical-roofed caphouse inside the SW round. Extending from the SE round, a rectangular N projection carried on machicolation and contain-ing a garderobe. The masonry is all of buff-coloured sandstone, the two lower storeys of rubble, the floors above of rough ashlar. Presumably the change indicates two stages of construction but was there only a temporary interruption followed by a switch to a grander material or was the tower originally a two-storey building, perhaps of the late C14, and then raised to the present height in the late C15? Some of the upper part of the N front has been refaced, perhaps in the C18. Below the battlements, regu-larly spaced round openings draining the parapet walk. The battlements of the rounds are conventionally crenellated, as is the centre of the S battlement, but at the N front, both gables and the ends of the S front the merlons are crowstepped and the crenelles V-shaped. The battlements of the N rounds are pierced by large square gunloops. In each of the three central merlons of the S battlement, a rectangular gunloop with splays to the inside as well as the outside. A couple of smaller and much more crudely formed gunholes in the battlement of the SE round. Another roughly formed gunhole under the E first-floor window of the N front. Two more gunholes near the top of the W gable. At the S end of this gable, a tier of slit windows lighting the stair inside. Below them and to their S, at first-floor level, a pair of shorter but slightly broader rectangular openings, now built up. More slit windows (lighting a stack of garderobes) near the S end of the E gable.

---

*This was designed by *George Angus*. It was reconstructed and extended by *John Melvin* in 1866–72 and demolished *c.* 1954.

Most of the remainder of the external detail dates from *Mar*'s remodelling in *c.* 1703–15. The upper floors of the entrance (N) front are all of a regularly fenestrated five bays, the windows having chamfered margins. The ground floor is of seven bays and less regular. E of the entrance, three dummy windows, the centre one smaller than the other two. W of the entrance, a window and two dummies, the window (in the bay next to the entrance) slightly smaller than the dummies. The central entrance has been in this position since the early C18 and perhaps since the C15 but there is evidence of a wall chamber (now blocked at each end) which could have been an entrance lobby behind the second of the dummy windows to its E. The present entrance's door surround with banded Ionic pilasters supporting an entablature is clearly a mid-C19 replacement, although the bases of the pilasters may be earlier, but the design is almost identical to that of a door shown as existing here in a drawing produced by the exiled Earl of Mar in 1727. Not shown in that drawing are the gryphon supporters and crest and motto from the armorial achievement of the Earls of Mar which are carved on the ends and centre of the frieze. In the door's round-arched fanlight, early C18 ironwork decorated with a rinceau ornament and flowers; it was repaired by *P. Johnson & Co.*, 1996. Less decorative are the 1990s grilles of the ground- and first-floor windows which seem out of keeping with both the windows' early C18 surrounds and their Neo-Late Georgian astragals.

At the E gable, two roof raggles of a single-storey building show the former existence of a C19 caretaker's cottage. Below the raggles, at the S end of the gable, a built-up door opening, probably for a cupboard quarried out of the gable wall of the tower. In the centre of the gable, a tier of early C18 windows, again with chamfered margins; the one at second-floor level has been partly built up in brick, perhaps in the late C18.

The W gable is now of four bays. In the three N bays, regularly spaced early C18 windows (several of them dummies), all with chamfered margins. At the centre of these three N bays, the ground-floor window was formerly a door (probably converted to a window in the C19) opening on to steps down to a terrace which used to stretch along the W side of the tower and its SW wing. In the S bay of the gable, smaller C18 windows, again with chamfered margins and one a dummy, interspersed with the C15 slit windows.

At the S elevation, roof raggles of the C17 and C18 extensions which formerly overlaid its lower storeys. Three ground-floor door openings, the W C17 and rectangular, the others (segmental-headed and roundheaded) early C18. All are now blocked and contain C19 horizontal-shaped windows with concrete margins. At the E end of the ground floor, a blocked window of reasonable size and set quite high; it may have been inserted in the C17. At the first floor, the C17 door opening into the SW wing was converted to a window in the C19; chamfered surround of the 1990s. W of this, two roundheaded early C18 door openings into Mar's SE addition, the W now blocked, the E containing a 1990s

double-leaf partly glazed door and fanlight of late Georgian
character. Also of the 1990s the balcony, whose sinuous thin railings are unabashedly late C20. E of this door, a built-up early
C18 window which gave borrowed light from *Mar*'s Great Saloon
to a garderobe in the tower house. At the second-floor level, at
the W end, two windows, both C19, their surrounds renewed in
the 1990s. The lower, r. window occupies the position of a C17
door from the tower-house into the SW wing; the l. window lights
the stair in the tower-house's SW corner. E of these, an early C18
window. At the third floor, three regularly spaced early C18
windows, their chamfered margins much renewed in the 1990s.
    The attic rising within the battlement is best seen from the
wall-walk. In each gable, a decent-sized early C18 window. Above
the W window, a smaller blocked window also with chamfered
jambs and perhaps contemporary. S of the E window, one jamb
of an earlier window and, to its N (clearly visible from inside), a
built-up doorway. On top of each gable of the attic, a ball finial,
the E of the early C18, the W of the 1990s. The floors of the
rounds are set quite high above the wall-walk. Immediately N of
the SE round, a garderobe covered with a roof and equipped
with a lamp recess.
    INTERIOR. The lower storeys of the present interior are better
understood as the surviving fragment of a grandiose early C18
show house than as belonging to a C15 tower-house. The ground
and first floors may originally have been covered by a single stone
vault (i.e. the first floor was an entresol). If so, *Mar*'s work of
c. 1703–15 removed the vault and the entresol to produce a two-
storey Saloon or Entrance Hall, occupying the W three-fifths of
the tower, which opened at the E into a circular Stair Hall. At
the lower level of the Entrance Hall, doors formerly opened
into the C17 SW wing and into Mar's SE block whose ground
floor was occupied by a Waiting Hall. The principal function of
the Great Stair in the Stair Hall was to serve as a formal approach
to a two-storey Great Saloon which occupied the upper part of
the SE block.
    The Entrance Hall is now divided horizontally by a floor,
possibly introduced in the later C18, at the likely level of the
medieval first (or, perhaps, entresol) floor. The ground-floor
room (the lower part of Mar's Entrance Hall) is plain. In the S
wall, a stone chimneypiece, perhaps C18, flanked by roundheaded
openings whose fanlit doors are of the 1990s. In the early C18
doors in these positions opened into mural lobbies leading to
the SW wing and the SE Waiting Hall. These lobbies were converted to a toilet and kitchen in the 1990s. In the toilet's W wall,
an opening into a rectangular wall chamber, probably of C15
origin. Over it, a segmental-arched vault whose W end has been
cut away so as not to run into the early C18 window. The toilet's
W wall is straight but its E is splayed; perhaps this was the ingo of
a medieval window. The same combination of one splayed and
one straight ingo occurs at the N window of the Entrance Hall.
The only break at the ground floor between the Entrance Hall and
Stair Hall is provided by inward projections from the N and S

walls, which formed a visually more decided division in the early C18 when they could be seen to form the lower parts of a giant arch between the Entrance and Stair Halls.

Under the E half of the Stair Hall, a cellar, perhaps medieval, its access formed in the 1990s. Off the Stair Hall's S side, another early C18 lobby (now another toilet), again with a splayed wall on one side and a straight wall on the other. Its segmental-arched ceiling is probably of the early C18 when this lobby formed a second access from the tower to the Waiting Hall. The Great Stair itself climbs as a broad semicircle filling the W half of the round Stair Hall. Shallow stone steps. The very plain balustrade is probably a replacement of the late C18 or early C19 when the top of the stair was altered and a landing inserted across the W side of the Stair Hall. Before then, the stair had ended at a balcony-landing in front of a lobby at the entrance to the SE block's Great Saloon. There is now no visible sign of the early C18 spur stair which led off the lower part of the Great Stair, rising in the thickness of the house's N wall up to the embrasure of the Stair Hall's first-floor N window. Instead there are a couple of steps constructed in the 1990s which lead off the Great Stair to a medieval L-plan wall chamber which had been blocked off in the early C18. The chamber's W limb is tunnel-vaulted. At the heel of the L, a well shaft of good-quality ashlar. Light was provided by a small window (now blocked) at the end of the NE jamb. At the second-floor level of the Stair Hall, an E balcony reached by steps constructed against the E side of the embrasure of the first-floor N window. This is probably of 1867, with balustrades in a late Georgian manner. Over the Stair Hall, a domed plaster ceiling, presumably early C18 and intended to have painted or stucco enrichment. On the E side of the Stair Hall's first-floor lobby to the missing SE block, a medieval garderobe.

In the early C18, before the erection of the present floor, the upper part of the Entrance Hall had a balcony across its W end. Access to the balcony from the Stair Hall was provided by tunnel-vaulted wall passages, possibly extending medieval chambers, the S (beginning at the lobby to the SE block) now divided into cupboards, the N (from the Stair Hall's N window embrasure, formerly reached by the spur stair) punctuated by the embrasures of the N windows, each formerly with its own balcony to the Entrance Hall. This passage's curved W end which opened on to the W balcony has been blocked off. In this upper part of the Entrance Hall, a heavy cornice with a foliaged frieze, in appearance more likely to be late C17 than early C18. Off-centre W window, its opening enlarged in the C18. On one of its splayed ingoes, a fragment of C19 painted decoration. To its S, a Neo-Jacobean fireplace of 1867. At the SW corner, a wall lobby which formerly gave access to the SW wing. In this lobby's W side, the entrance to a spiral stair constructed by *John Melvin* in 1867 in the position of a medieval stair giving access to the floors above and ending in the caphouse opening on to the wall-walk.

The second floor, entered by a straight flight of 1867 down from the spiral stair, was occupied in the C15 by a Hall or Great

Alloa Tower. Part of proposed C18 first floor plan.

Chamber covered by a stone groin vault (now plastered). *Mar*'s early C18 remodelling cut off the Great Chamber's E end in an awkwardly contrived manner to make it part of his Stair Hall whose ceiling hides the vaulting above; the surviving part became the Charter Room. Again the windows were enlarged, several now having one straight and one splayed ingo. On the walls, diaper-patterned stencilling.

On the third floor, another large room. Lime concrete floor. All the windows except the E ones of the N and S walls have arched embrasures and are medieval although their openings have been enlarged in the early C18. Stone seats on both sides of the embrasures of the central N and S windows and the W window; wall cupboard at the central N window. The embrasure of the E window has a seat under a cupboard along its N side. In its S side, a low roundheaded and chamfered entrance into a garderobe, its stone latrine seat and lamp recess surviving. The attic floor above is missing but the stubs of the sawn-off corbels which supported its joists are visible. The oak roof is late C15, each pair of rafters joined with two collars, all lightly repaired in the 1990s.

A little E of Alloa Tower is TOWER SQUARE, the former stable courtyard of Alloa House. It is by *John Melvin*, 1867–9. Not quite symmetrical, built of stugged grey ashlar. The general

character is Georgian survival but over the segmental-arched N
entrance is a low piend-roofed tower with a window of three
round-arched lights under a circular clock face; block corbels
under the dwarf parapet. Inside the courtyard, segmental-arched
cartshed openings and simple porticoes with wooden columns
and pyramidal roofs. The buildings were converted to housing by
*Bob Heath*, 1992. – Just to the E, a pair of pinnacled GATEPIERS of
the 1990s, simplified miniature versions of the early C18 piers in
Limetree Walk (*see* Streets: Central Alloa), by *Martin Hadlington*.
WALLED GARDEN, *c.* 0.27km. NE on the NE side of Devon Road.
Probably begun in the 1830s but remodelled *c.* 1870. The N, W
and E walls are of rubble, faced internally with grey brick. The S
wall is all of brick. At its centre, gatepiers of channelled ashlar
with shallow pyramidal tops.


## STREETS

### 1. Central Alloa

#### BANK STREET

At the NE end, at the junction with Coalgate, the early C19
segment-cornered No. 1. Two storeys, the front of painted
ashlar, channelled at the ground floor, droved above. Also early
C19 in origin but more vernacular is the adjoining block at Nos.
3–7. Shops at the ground floor, first floor of broached ashlar.
The slightly jettied second floor was added in 1992–4. Then the
two-storey but much taller CLYDESDALE BANK of 1852.
Renaissance, the fronts of polished ashlar. Six-bay elevation to
Bank Street, the ground-floor windows set in tall rectangular
overarches. Cornice above the ground floor marking off the
agent's flat on the upper floor from the banking hall and offices
below. The entrance to the agent's flat was moved from the
third bay to the l. bay as part of *John Baird & James Thomson*'s
alterations of 1905. At the first floor, corniced and aproned
windows. Mutuled wallhead cornice under a parapet on which
stands an off-centre chimneystack with scrolled sides and a
panelled front. Quadrant W corner where a new entrance to the
bank was made in 1905, the door framed by granite-shafted Ionic
columns and an open pediment. The original bank entrance was
at the SW front whose ground floor has channelled masonry and
segmental-arched windows flanking the central porch (its doors
blocked in 1905); over the porch, a Tudorish pierced parapet.
First-floor detail repeating that of the NW elevation but the wallhead chimney stack is centred.

Opposite the Clydesdale Bank, on the NW side of Bank
Street, the former West Free Church (*see* Churches, above). To
its SW, across Burgh Mews, the former CROWN HOTEL of
1866–7. Tall two storeys and attic, the polished ashlar of the
three-bay front badly eroded. At the recessed centre, a broad
door under a segmental fanlight; round-arched windows at the
upper floors, the first floor's with projecting keystones and

imposts, the attic window contained in a Jacobean finialled stepped gablet. This centrepiece is flanked by big two-storey rectangular bay windows. Behind their iron cresting the attic windows rise through the wallhead into scroll-sided semicircular dormerheads. Beside this but set back, the Municipal Buildings (*see* Public Buildings, above).

On Bank Street's SE side, opposite the Municipal Buildings, Nos. 19–23. Small-scale but quite smart early C19 commercial classicism, the concrete-tiled roof an unfortunate alteration. Ground-floor shopfront with Doric half-columns and a cornice over the centre door. Balustered aprons under the first-floor windows. Also of two storeys but lower, the adjoining double house (Nos. 25–27) of *c.* 1840, with pilastered and corniced door-pieces. Lintel course linking the ground-floor windows; elliptical-arched windows above. Bowed corner to Union Street whose short elevation is surmounted by a scroll-buttressed wallhead chimney.

On Bank Street's NW side, looking down Union Street, is the former COMMERCIAL BANK OF SCOTLAND (Nos. 18–22) of *c.* 1840. Austere front of polished ashlar, channelled at the ground floor. Lugged architraves and cornices to the first-floor windows; blocky consoles under the wallhead cornice. SW of this, a mid-C19 vernacular two-storey terrace (Nos. 24–38), the end house sporting an oriel window added *c.* 1895.

97    Bank Street's SE side ends with a large building (originally the municipal GAS SHOWROOMS) by *William Kerr* and *John Gray* of *John Melvin & Son*, 1935–6. It is of reinforced concrete construction, the shape an acutely angled L to keep the street pattern of Bank Street and Stripehead. The architecture mixes stripped neo-Georgian and Art Deco. Symmetrical two-storey front to Bank Street faced with polished ashlar. Broad recessed centre containing a shopfront under a balcony. Concave SW corner from which projects a single-storey canted bay window. The rendered S elevation to Stripehead acquires a third storey in the fall of the ground. The top floor's horizontal windows with widely spaced green-tiled mullions are Art Deco but the E end's vertical first-floor windows, one fronted by a balcony, are reminiscent of Lorimerian early C18 revival. E front to Coalgate, again rendered, with projecting bows at the corners and, between them, a long first-floor balcony (but with no door on to it) providing a strong horizontal.

### BEDFORD PLACE

At the E end, on the S side the former POST OFFICE, by *H.M. Office of Works*, 1924. Single-storey front of polished ashlar, the minimally advanced end bays (each originally containing a door, the E now converted to a window) marked off by broad strips of rustication. Basement in the fall of the ground to the rear. Opposite, a segmental-shaped enclosure houses the WAR MEMORIAL by *Robert S. Lorimer*, 1924. In the front wall, a wrought-iron gate decorated with stylized foliage. In the centre of the enclosure, a tall bow-ended pedestal of diagonally broached

ashlar supports a bronze SCULPTURE (now painted) by *C. d'O.
Pilkington Jackson*, depicting a group of soldiers crawling into
attack, the front one cutting wire. Above, the standing figure of
a crowned woman ('The Thought of Alloa') holding a shield
emblazoned with the arms of the burgh of Alloa in one hand
and blessing with the other. Set into the back wall of the enclosure, a bronze tablet inscribed with the names of the dead.

On the S side, closing the vista down Church Street, the
former Alloa Burgh School (*see* Public Buildings, above) followed
by the nondescript flat-roofed TELEPHONE EXCHANGE, by
*H.M. Office of Works*, *c.* 1960; rear addition by the *Ministry of
Public Building and Works*, 1971. Then, a former CHURCH HALL
(now housing) by *William Kerr* and *John Gray* of *John Melvin &
Son*, 1926. Neo-Georgian except for the spired ventilator of
Victorian School Board type on the centre of the piended roof.

On the N side, a short early C19 two-storey terrace, the house
fronts all of painted broached ashlar. It begins with a four-bay
double house (Nos. 1–3), quite smart, with rusticated quoins,
a bandcourse between the ground and first floors, and paired
segmental-arched entrances. Two-bay No. 5, plain except for a
roundheaded door in the r. bay; the l. bay's rectangular pend
entrance has been partly built up and now contains a door. This
was formerly a wing of the ROYAL OAK HOTEL (No. 7) whose
main block has simplified giant pilasters at the corners and a
Roman Doric pilastered doorpiece. Late C19 bay window. Set
back behind a small front garden, No. 9, built as the Burgher
Manse *c.* 1815. Plain two-storey main block flanked by single-
storey wings, all of buff-coloured droved ashlar. Beside it, the
Burgher Church's Victorian replacement, Alloa West Church,
confronting St Mungo's Parish Church across the street (for
these *see* Churches, above).

To the W of St Mungo's Parish Church, the S side continues
with two-storey villas. The first (No. 12) faces S away from the
street. Piend-roofed main block, its front's bay windows added
in the later C19. They flank the Roman Doric columned doorpiece. Single-storey E wing, its front window overarched, balanced
by a screen wall on the W. No. 14 was built for the mining engineer Robert Bald in 1815. Piend-roofed main block and single-
storey wings, the E overlaid by a N addition. At the street (N)
front, an Ionic portico below a three-light window. The principal
elevation is the S, its ground-floor masonry channelled. Roman
Doric bowed porch flanked by overarched three-light windows.
The windows of the wings are set in overarches. (Inside, a domed
circular stairhall, the wall decorated with a mural showing
Edinburgh from the Firth of Forth, with steamboats in the foreground.) The front of No. 16 is also to the S. In the slightly
advanced end bays, overarched ground-floor windows; at the
centre, a skinny pilastered and corniced doorpiece.

On the N side, W of Alloa West Church, a prosperous pair of
early Victorian two-storey villas. No. 11 is of *c.* 1840. Three-bay
front of polished ashlar. Architraves at the windows, those of the
ground floor surmounted by consoled cornices. Central portico,

the piers' capitals carved with short acanthus leaves; mutuled cornice. Oriel windows were added to the w gable *c.* 1900. The front of the Italianate No. 13 of *c.* 1855 is also of polished ashlar and of three bays but the scale is larger and the manner more opulent. Again a central portico but its piers' Roman Doric capitals are decorated with rosettes and the cornice is dentillated and surmounted by antefixae. Flanking the portico, pilastered round-arched windows set in rectangular surrounds, the spandrels carved with foliage. Shouldered arches to the first-floor windows, the corners of their surrounds bearing rosettes. More antefixae above the mutuled wallhead cornice.

### BROAD STREET AND LIMETREE WALK

Broad Street was originally John Street, named after John, Earl of Mar, who laid it out in 1705. At the top, on the E side, St John the Evangelist's Episcopal Church (*see* Churches, above) followed by a plain late C19 tenement and some housing of 1930 by *William Kerr* and *John Gray* of *John Melvin & Son*. On the w side, planting to screen the Castle Street Industrial Estate. At the s end of Broad Street begins the narrow avenue first planted with lime trees in 1714 which continues down Limetree Walk as a formal approach to the harbour. On the w side of Limetree Walk, more C20 industrial buildings; on its E, a park. At the entrance to East Castle Street, a development along the former principal approach to Alloa Tower, two tall quatrefoil-plan cornined pillars, each topped by four stone balls which support immense pinnacles, all built of polished pinky ashlar. These are early C18, perhaps contemporary with the planting of the lime avenue.* They are linked by curvaceous dwarf walls (the s surviving but bereft of its railing) to GATEPIERS which probably date from *John Melvin*'s alterations of 1866–72 to the grounds of Alloa Tower. V-jointed rusticated masonry. On each face, a tall roundheaded panel. Belted ball finials.

### CANDLERIGGS

For the development occupying the sw side, *see* Mill Street. On the NE side, after the corner building with Mill Street, Nos. 2–6, a three-storey block of the later C19. The Victorian shopfront survives. Cornined first-floor windows, the outer two each two-light. Small-scale early C19 vernacular at the two-storey Nos. 8–22, the front of painted broached ashlar. No. 24 on the corner of East Vennel is probably mid-C19. Piended roof at the sw gable, crowsteps on the NE gable.

### COALGATE

For the building on the NW corner, *see* Bank Street above. The E side starts with the early C19 two-storey Nos. 1–3; scrolled

---

*And certainly of before 1739 when one of the 'Pyramids in the Grand Alley' is recorded as having been broken by a gale.

skewputts and a pilastered and corniced doorpiece. There follows a large block (BARONIAL BUILDINGS) by *Thomas Frame & Son*, 1887. In keeping with the name it is Scottish Baronial, with crowstepped gables and jettied upper floors, but the fat conical-roofed corner tower is quite pacific. Then Coalgate jinks SW, its S side occupied by a car park. On the N side, a small garden, followed by the mid-C19 No. 20, a former brewery; in the ball-finialled front gable, a window of three stepped lights. Beyond and returning along Union Street is a rubble-walled L-plan building (No. 22 Coalgate and Nos. 3–9 Union Street). It seems to have been built in the mid C19 as a four-storey S range and a two-storey NW wing. All this was recast as a billiards hall and reading room for brewery employees by *William Kerr* of *John Melvin & Son* in 1903, the S range having its original windows built up and the interior remodelled as a two-storey building. New windows with lugged cement architraves were provided, as was a pair of oriels with half-timbered and bargeboarded gables. The windows of the NW wing were also given lugged architraves. Red-tiled cresting of 1903 on the ridge of the slated roofs. Late C19 tower in the inner angle, its piended pantiled roof added in 1903.

## DRYSDALE STREET

On the SE side, between Mill Street and High Street, late C20 blocks, Nos. 1–15, neo-traditional by *Baxter, Clark & Paul*, 1998. On the NW side, after Maple Court (*see* Shillinghill) and Alloa Library (*see* Public Buildings, above), the pitched-roofed TSB (No. 30) by *John Deans*, 1980, brick-faced like the library but the colour is a lighter brown and the bricks are laid vertically above and below the first-floor windows. Then a big block built for the Alloa Co-operative Society in 1895; it is by *Thomas Frame & Son*. Free but bare Jacobean, near-symmetrical with a large centre gablet. It is followed by two-storey vernacular buildings of the earlier C19. On the SW corner with High Street, the former TOWNHEAD INSTITUTE by *William Kerr* and *John Gray* of *John Melvin & Son*, 1914–15. Long two-storey block, dry-dashed with painted stone dressings and a tiled roof, the manner cottagey neo-Georgian. Consoled balcony over the main entrance. To its W, the Sheriff Court House (*see* Public Buildings, above).

After the block on Drysdale Street's NW corner with Primrose Street (q.v.), No. 68, a two-storey vernacular building of the earlier C19. No. 70 (originally Clackmannan County Council Offices) is by *William Kerr* and *John Gray* of *John Melvin & Son*, 1926. Accomplished neo-Jacobean. Symmetrical two-storey front with mullioned and transomed windows. Simplified pilasters and a cornice framing the entrance; rosetted frieze at the wall-head. MONCRIEFF HOUSE, built as the Antiburgher Manse *c.* 1840, is set behind a small front garden. Two-storey piend-roofed villa, with a pilastered and corniced doorpiece. Beside it, Moncrieff United Free Church (*see* Churches, above).

The N side is devoted to car parking. On the s, the Forth Valley
    Christian Centre and the former Paton's School (*see* Churches
    and Public Buildings, above).

On the E side, after Nos. 1–7 on the s corner with Mill Street
    (q.v.), the mid-C19 Nos. 9–15, with one window of two lights
    and one of three at the broached ashlar upper floor. The free
    English Baroque ROYAL BANK OF SCOTLAND (No. 19) is by
    *J. M. Dick Peddie*, 1909–11. Two-storey polished ashlar front.
    The very tall ground floor was remodelled by *Gordon Biggar* of
    *John Melvin & Son*, 1971, but is still articulated by the lower
    parts of the giant fluted Corinthian pilasters which mark off the
    ends of the building and the broad open-pedimented centre-
    piece. In this centrepiece, a tripartite first-floor window, its centre
    light with a projecting keystone under a segmental pediment. In
    the tympanum of the main pediment, a high relief sculpture of
    the Bank's heraldic achievement but the shield bearing only its
    initials. Moulded architraves to the windows of the outer bays
    where the wallhead is topped by balustrades. After some late
    C20 shops, the late Georgian two-storey No. 37, a rope-moulded
    scrolled skewputt at its s gable. More skewputts of the same sort
    at the contemporary Nos. 39–43. At Nos. 45–47, by *William
    Kerr* and *John Gray* of *John Melvin & Son*, 1923, a pair of
    canted oriel windows. Then No. 49 on the corner with Drysdale
    Street, by *Alex Strang & Associates*, 1968, with a metal-clad
    oversailing upper floor and a bowed corner.

    w side. For the building on the s corner, *see* Mill Street. Then
    drab stugged ashlar frontages of the later C19, the long three-
    storey block at Nos. 18–32 dated 1873, followed by late C20
    shops. More welcome is the late C19 three-storey three-bay
    block at Nos. 52–58. Original shopfronts with a dentillated
    frieze. Corniced first-floor windows. The second-floor windows
    of the outer bays are topped by bargeboarded gablets, the smaller
    centre window by a piended dormerhead. Next, a four-bay
    block of two tall storeys, its ground floor occupied by a late C20
    shopfront. The upper floor is of 1874, the stonework of pinkish
    stugged ashlar pierced by round-arched and keystoned windows,
    their architraves lugged at the bottom. Wallhead cornice sur-
    mounted by a balustrade broken by urn-topped pedestals and,
    in the centre, a panel carved with the Co-operative Society's
    emblem of clasped hands and the inscription 'CO-OPERATION/
    1862/INDUSTRY'. Above this there was erected in 1912 (the
    Society's golden jubilee) a curvaceously pedimented aedicule
    framing a clockface.

On the s side, the wall of the graveyard surrounding Old St
    Mungo's Church (*see* Churches, above). w of the graveyard,

two-storey housing by *Clackmannan District Council*, 1984.
Pitched-roofed and sensible, the walls of reddish-coloured concrete blockwork. The two-storey house (No. 25) on the N side
was built and presumably designed for himself by *Tobias Bachop*, 109
a master mason who had previously worked on Sir William
Bruce's Kinross House (Perth and Kinross). It serves to advertise
the owner's skills as both craftsman and up-to-date architect.
Five-bay polished ashlar front with rusticated quoins and a
moulded eaves cornice, the openings grouped 1/3/1. At the centre
three bays of the ground floor, two windows serving as sidelights
for the door. At the upper floor the centre bay is occupied by
a V-shaped swag-topped sundial projected on a large corbel
sculpted as a grotesque head. Below the sundial, a panel, its surround carved with fruit; on the face of the panel, the date 1695
and the initials TB and ML (for Tobias Bachop and his wife,
Margaret Lapsley). All the openings of this front elevation have
lugged architraves with pulvinated friezes; cornices over the
ground-floor windows and door. Crowstepped gables, their skewputts carved with acanthus leaf decoration. The sides and rear
are harled, as is the plain NE wing.

LIMETREE WALK *see* BROAD STREET

MAR STREET

The SW side begins with the former British Linen Bank on the
corner of Mill Street (q.v.). Then, Nos. 5–11, an early C19
block of two storeys and attic, its shopfront late Victorian. At
the first floor, broached ashlar masonry pierced by three broadly
spaced windows, the centre one tripartite, its centre light a
dummy. Two late C19 bargeboarded dormers at the attic. The
scale rises at No. 15, originally the LIBERAL CLUB, by *William
Kerr* of *John Melvin & Son*, 1904. Symmetrical Jacobean two- 94
storey and attic three-bay front of polished buff sandstone ashlar.
At the outer bays of the ground floor, low four-light windows
with broad centre mullions; blank shields in the corners of the
lintels which are surmounted by egg-and-dart cornices. Round-
arched and keystoned central entrance framed by Roman Doric
columns *in antis* supporting an entablature; in the centre of the
triglyphed frieze, a strapwork panel containing the date '1904'.
The first floor's status is emphasized by a tall three-light window
flanked by oriels, all mullioned and transomed. The dentillated
main cornice breaks forward over the oriels where it is surmounted by parapets. Behind these parapets, mullioned attic
windows placed between Artisan Mannerist Ionic pilasters,
their shafts tapering towards the bottom and decorated with
carved foliage. The pilasters support obelisk-finialled curvilinear
gablets. Inside, the windows of the first-floor room contain
stained glass (depictions of domestic, urban and commercial
life) by *Oscar Paterson*. NW of the old Liberal Club, No. 17,
formerly the offices of the Alloa Co-operative Society, by *William
Kerr* and *John Gray* of *John Melvin & Son*, 1932. Authoritarian
neo-Georgian faced with polished red sandstone ashlar.

After the corner building with Mill Street (q.v.), the NE side starts at Nos. 2–14 with late Georgian two-storey vernacular housing above shops. The height is maintained at Nos. 16–18 but this building is of 1952 by *Arthur Bracewell*, with an Art Deco inflexion. Then a symmetrical two-storey and attic block (No. 20) by *Simister, Monaghan*, 1991, the influence of Charles Rennie Mackintosh apparent at the ground- and first-floor windows; heavy lead-clad dormers.

On the SW side, behind a front garden, No. 19, a piend-roofed villa of *c.* 1830. Giant pilaster strips at the ends of its polished ashlar front, the centre slightly advanced under a pediment. Fanlit entrance in an Ionic columned and corniced surround. Corniced ground-floor windows with panelled aprons; sill course linking the first-floor windows. Low parapet above the wallhead cornice. Next door and also set back, the villa-like BANK OF SCOTLAND (originally Glasgow Union Bank) of 1832. Again a polished ashlar front of two storeys and three bays with the centre advanced and pedimented, but the scale is slightly larger. Channelled masonry at the ground floor, its segmental-headed and aproned windows in segmental-headed overarches. Doric portico. At the ends of the first floor, pilaster strips with incised ornament. This floor's windows have aprons and lugged architraves. Blocking course above the main cornice. To the N, St Mungo's (R.C.) Church and presbytery (*see* Churches, above).

On the SE side, opposite St Mungo's, the two-storeyed near-symmetrical Nos. 56–58 of the later C19, the windows all of two segmental-headed lights, the paired doors elliptically arched. Next door and of about the same date, Nos. 60–62 of three tall storeys. Three-bay broached ashlar front. Shouldered-arched ground-floor openings under hoodmoulds which rise into 'gablets'. At the central door and adjacent window, foliage-capitalled columns. Elliptically arched first-floor windows. Over the second-floor windows, crowstepped gablets. This side of the street ends with the bulk of the Sheriff Court House (*see* Public Buildings, above). Opposite, No. 27, a mid-Victorian villa, Georgian survival with a corniced doorpiece.

## MARSHILL

At the E end, on the N, MAR PLACE HOUSE, a two-storey early C19 villa, its front of painted broached ashlar. Three-bay main block, the Ionic-columned doorpiece flanked by bay windows of the later C19. Single-storey lateral wing at each end. On the S side of the street, OCHIL HOUSE, built as the Tontine Inn in 1806. Villa-like, of two storeys and three bays, the façade's ashlar badly weathered. Slightly advanced centrepiece with a chimneyed pediment. Attached to the W gable, a broached ashlar GATEWAY, its cornice and blocking course stepped up at the centre. Above the chamfered elliptical arch, a panel dated 1882 stating that this was the access to a drill hall but the gateway itself looks like work of *c.* 1840. On the site of the drill hall now stands EARL OF MAR COURT, housing by *Bracewell, Stirling*, 1993–4.

To the W of the roundabout which cuts off the main stretch of Marshill from its E end, the S side is a large vacant site. The N begins with the huge Alloa Town Hall (*see* Public Buildings, above). Beyond, the former LODGE of Marshill House, originally Jacobean of *c.* 1840 but a two-storey bay window was added to the S gable and Frenchy dormers to the attic in the late C19. MARSHILL HOUSE itself is a villa of *c.* 1835. Roman Doric portico at the slightly advanced centre where the wallhead's blocking course is studded with rosettes. The next villa (No. 6) is probably of *c.* 1840. Main block of two storeys and three bays, with an Ionic portico and consoled cornices over the ground-floor windows. Slightly recessed additions at the E, probably of the mid C19.

## MILL STREET

The NW side begins with a pair of two-storey buildings (Nos. 3–13) of *c.* 1800 containing housing over shops, the upper floors of painted broached ashlar. This late Georgian low-scale vernacular continues at Nos. 15–19 but with the addition of two large gableted dormers of *c.* 1900, their windows framed by paired Roman Doric wooden pilasters; at Nos. 19–25 the upper floors' masonry is harled. The two-bay No. 27, of the same height but with a more steeply pitched roof, narrower windows and a crowstepped S gable, is probably C18. On the corner of Mar Street, the former BRITISH LINEN BANK (No. 31) of 1906 is by *Peddie & Washington Browne* in their best François I manner. Tall two storeys and an attic, the street elevations of polished red sandstone ashlar. The principal but narrower near-symmetrical front is to Mill Street. At the ground floor, four-light mullioned and transomed main window, a fluted frieze under its rather small cornice. To the l. of this, a small window set in an aedicule, the tympanum of its flaming finialled pediment carved with a stylized shell. To the r. of the main window, the principal entrance, again in a pedimented aedicule, the panelled pilasters decorated with foliaged lozenges, the frieze with linked ovals. On the ends and apex of the shell-decorated pediment, obelisks standing on balls; leafy scrolls on the sides. The mullioned and transomed two-light first-floor windows are framed by Ionic attached columns supported by corbels carved with swagged cartouches. Above the columns, the wallhead entablature. Above the ends of the entablature, balustrades. Over the centre, the balustrading is broken by a shaped gable containing another pair of two-light windows but smaller than those of the first floor. Again they are framed by Ionic columns which here support a cornice under the gable's ogee-arched and pinnacled top; in this top, the coat of arms of the burgh of Alloa. The more simply detailed four-bay Mar Street frontage again just avoids symmetry. Over the centre, a pair of ogee-topped shaped gables flanking a wallhead chimney.

Mill Street's SE side between Coalgate and Candleriggs is filled by a development by *Hendry & Legge*, 1993–6. Three and four storeys to Mill Street containing housing above tall ground-floor shops, faced with a mixture of dry-dash and rough-textured dark red blockwork. Tall staircase windows but otherwise neo-vernacular with bargeboarded wallhead gablets. The development continues down Candleriggs, the scale dropping from three to two storeys and finally to a single storey at the entrance to a supermarket, by *Percy Johnson-Marshall & Partners* in association with *Hendry & Legge*, 1994–6, which stretches back to the SW behind a car park fronting Greenside Street. On the super-market's S gable, a RELIEF of scenes from Alloa life in the past, by *W. Aikman*, 1995.

On the NW corner of Mar Street, a mid-C19 three-storey block (Nos. 33–37) containing flats above shops, the original cornice over the shopfronts now lost. The upper floors are of painted broached ashlar, the windows architraved, those of the second floor with aprons. Anta pilasters frame the splayed corner. The next building (Nos. 39–45), extending to the corner with High Street, is a tall 'Greek' Thomsonesque commercial block by *Thomas Frame & Son*, 1874–5, with a wealth of Ægypto–Greek detail. On the opposite corner with High Street, a perfunctorily neo-vernacular late C20 block (Nos. 47–53 Mill Street and Nos. 1–7 High Street). After it, Mill Street continues with a couple of early C19 buildings (Nos. 55–57 and Nos. 59–61), unpretentious except for the pilastered shopfronts of Nos. 59–61; the single first-floor window of Nos. 55–57 looks as if it has been lowered. The scale soars at the late C19 Nos. 65–71. Plain Italianate front of polished ashlar, with consoled cornices over the first-floor windows and a broad pedimented gablet at the centre of the wallhead. Two-storeyed Nos. 73–77 of *c.* 1835, the first-floor windows architraved, the ground-floor shopfronts added in the later C19. Then, the corner building with Drysdale Street (q.v.).

The SE side of Mill Street beyond Candleriggs continues with No. 26. Free Jacobean Renaissance of the later C19. Consoled cornices over the mullioned two-light first-floor windows. Segmental-arched lights at the second-floor windows which rise into gablets pushing above the eaves cornice. Over the quadrant corner, a witch's hat spire. Then a couple of early or mid-C19 buildings (Nos. 28–36) followed by the large-scale Flemish gable front of No. 38, by *George A. Kerr*, 1903. Late C20 shops occupy the ground floor of the otherwise late Victorian Nos. 42–46. At the first floor, broad panelled pilasters between the windows. No. 50, by the Construction Department of *F. W. Woolworth & Co. Ltd.*, 1961, is jazz-modern but not enjoyable. Packaging of a more elegant sort is provided next door by the gently Art Deco cinema front of cream-coloured tiling divided into panels by lines of blue tiles. This is the former GAUMONT CINEMA (now a bingo hall) by *W. E. Trent*, 1938. Then a grimly plain late C19 block (Nos. 66–72) followed by a two-storey show-room (SCOTTISH POWER), by *A. M. & W. McMichael*, 1961, and early C19 vernacular (Nos. 78–82). At the end of Mill Street, the obtusely angled mid-C19 JUNCTION PLACE, the first-floor windows architraved.

PRIMROSE STREET

On the E side, at the S end, the two-storey Nos. 1–3 of *c.* 1840, with a gentle bow on the corner to Drysdale Street. Then the bulk of the CO-OPERATIVE DEPARTMENT STORE, a tall three-storey Art Deco building by the *Scottish Co-operative Wholesale Society's Architectural Department*, 1933–5; low N extension by *E. Pollard & Co.*, 1957. The rest of this side is occupied by the Speirs Centre (*see* Public Buildings, above).

On the W side, on the S corner with Drysdale Street, No. 2, a 1920s version of the small-town vernacular of a century earlier. The three-storey No. 6 is Victorian, with crowstep-gabled dormerheads. Also Victorian but more aggressive is No. 8, presenting a crowstepped gable to the street. The two-storey block of 1878 at Nos. 10–14 has been altered but the front's first-floor foliage-capitalled cast iron columns and piers survive. Mid-C19 Georgian survival at Nos. 20–22 followed by the contemporary PRIMROSE COTTAGE set behind a front garden. The building line is re-established by Nos. 30–36 of *c.* 1860, its ground-floor openings segmental-arched, the first-floor windows roundheaded. Of about the same date, Nos. 38–44, a modillion cornice with consoled ends over the shop-fronts. Consoled pediments over the first-floor windows of the outer bays; wallhead chimney. At the N end of the street, the STATION HOTEL, by *James Mitchell*, 1880. Georgian survival except for the Victorian Gothic main entrance and an oriel window on the splayed NE corner.

SHILLINGHILL

The SE side begins with squared-up Art Deco of 1938 at Nos. 1–2. The two-storey scale continues at No. 3 but this is of *c.* 1800, with a mutuled eaves cornice; the pilastered doorpiece looks a mid-C19 addition. Then two-storey buildings of the earlier C19, Nos. 7–8 with a round-arched window at the centre of the first floor, No. 9 with a pilastered and corniced doorpiece. At the end, BRIDGE TERRACE, flatted housing by *Simister, Monaghan*, 1995. The pitched-roofed frontage is broken into 'house' units by the use of different materials but the street line is kept and the neo-Mackintosh touches restrained.

On the SW side and extending along Drysdale Street, MAPLE COURT by the Clackmannan County Architect, *W. H. Henry*, in association with *City Wall Properties (Scotland) Ltd.*, 1967–9, a large development of flats above shops. At the front the shops are set back behind a loggia but their flat-roofed rears project behind as a terrace off which are the flats' entrances. At the end of this side of Shillinghill, a large single-storey supermarket by *Ian Burke Associates*, 1982–3.

## 2. Outer Alloa

### ALEXANDRA DRIVE

On the SE side, No. 5, a piend-roofed two-storey villa of *c.* 1830.
Polished ashlar front, a beltcourse under the first floor. Architraved windows; Roman Doric pilastered doorpiece. A bay
window was added to the SW gable in the early C20.

### ARNS GROVE

At the S end, GEAN LODGE by *William Kerr* of *John Melvin &
Son*, built in 1912–13 as the S lodge to Gean House (*see* Suburban
Mansions, below). Long and low English picturesque cottage.
Harled walls with half-timbering in the gables; big red tiled roof.

### CLACKMANNAN ROAD

The N side begins at the W with small Victorian villas. At the centre
bays of Nos. 1–3, paired tree-trunk porches; slightly advanced
and gabled end bays, each with a hoodmoulded ground-floor
window and a roundheaded window above. Another double
house at Nos. 10–11, the paired doors sheltered by a decorative
cast iron portico. Another cast iron portico at Nos. 13–15 but
here the windows have semi-octagonal heads and the attic
gablets carved bargeboards. Opposite, on the S side of the road,
at the entrance to a former drive to the demolished Alloa House,
a single-storey LODGE of *c.* 1835. Three-bay W front of painted
ashlar, the centre slightly advanced; boldly projecting cornice
under the eaves of the piended roof. To its E, a rubbly GATEPIER
topped by three superimposed pyramids above 'flight holes'. It
is of *c.* 1950 and marks the entrance to the Hawkhill housing
development begun in 1946. Quite far out, on the N, the Fire
Station (*see* Public Buildings, above) and, on the S, SAFEWAY,
by *Dalziel Design Partnership*, 1997, a large tidily packaged commercial shed with a Postmodern entrance.

### CLAREMONT

At the SE end, on the NE side, two originally identical houses, the
badly altered No. 23 (CLAREMONT LODGE HOTEL) and Nos.
27–29 KELLIE PLACE, entered from Kellie Place but with
their fronts to Claremont. They are by *John Melvin*, *c.* 1865. Each
is of two storeys, built of painted ashlar, with free Jacobean detail
and enjoying a two-storey bow window and French pavilion-
roofed tower. Beyond the roundabout at the junction with Stirling
Road, on Claremont's SW side, Nos. 15–17, a tall symmetrical
Jacobean double house of the mid C19. Also mid-C19 is No. 19,
a large *cottage orné* with carved bargeboards and hoodmoulded
windows; the roof's slates have been replaced by pantiles. The
villa of *c.* 1900 at No. 21 (CLAREMONT GROVE) is cold-blooded
neo-Georgian to the N but with bay windows overlooking the
garden; English Arts and Crafts wing added by *William Kerr* and

*John Gray* of *John Melvin & Son*, 1913. On the NE side, on the
SE corner of Victoria Street, No. 30 Claremont, an unremarkable
small late Victorian villa given a weird post-Mackintosh bowed
portico in 1924. Diagonally across the street, on the NW corner
of Alexandra Drive, is STRUAN HOUSE (No. 33 Claremont),
by *William Kerr* of *John Melvin & Son*, 1905. Harled walls with red
sandstone dressings; red tiled roof. Arts and Crafts with mullioned
windows, the inspiration as much English as Scots despite the large
thistle carved on the datestone beside the entrance. Further on,
No. 37 (CRAIG-NA-ARD) of 1902 and also by *John Melvin & Son*
but dour despite half-timbering in the gables. Next door, No. 39
(CLAREMONT HOUSE) built as Alloa Parish Manse in 1901–2;
yet again the architects were *John Melvin & Son*. Peaceable
Scots Renaissance with carving over the door and a rainwater
outlet sculpted as a fish. In the garden, a large monkey-puzzle
tree.

For Dunmar House, *see* Suburban Mansions, below.

### GRANGE ROAD

At the E end, on the N side, Nos. 1–2, a double house of *c.* 1840.
Piend-roofed two-storey and attic main block, its five-bay front
of polished ashlar. At each end bay, a door in a heavy pilastered
and corniced surround; the dormer windows are later additions.
Lateral wings, each originally of one storey (the E now of two),
with canted bay windows at their gables. No. 3 is a villa of *c.* 1835.
Broached ashlar front with a pilastered and corniced doorpiece.
Another symmetrical double house at Nos. 4–5 but Jacobean of
*c.* 1845, with stugged ashlar masonry and horizontal glazing in
the windows. Then THE OLD RECTORY, a piend-roofed villa
of *c.* 1840. Front of polished ashlar with a first-floor beltcourse.
Architraved and corniced windows at the ground floor; aprons
under the first-floor windows, all with horizontal panes. Roman
Doric columned doorpiece. GARVALLY is Georgian survival of
*c.* 1850. Giant pilasters at the corners of the painted ashlar front;
canted bay windows at the ground floor. After the West End Park
(*see* Cemetery and Park, above), smaller villas of the mid and
later C19. Near their end, opposite St John's Primary School (*see*
Public Buildings, above), No. 67 of *c.* 1865. Single-storey, with
hoodmoulded two-light windows flanking the entrance which is
sheltered by a gablet topped by a cast iron weathervane.

### GRANT STREET

On the E side, at the top, No. 40, an early C19 piend-roofed villa.
Polished ashlar front with a Roman Doric columned doorpiece.
On the W side, the ABC Nursery and Kidzone (*see* Public
Buildings, above).

### MAR PLACE

At the S end, on the corner of Ring Road, the Police Station (*see*
Public Buildings, above). N of the railway bridge, on the W side,

a mid-C19 house with hoodmoulded openings at the ground floor. On the E side, PARKGATE COURT, a block of flats by *Campbell & Arnott*, 1990. Roughly U-plan, of three storeys, the lower two faced with buff brick, the top floor of grey brick and marked off by a stringcourse. Sparing decoration provided by square panels of blue and black tiles; on the S elevation, a painted sundial. Broad-eaved shallow-pitched roofs. The effect is conventional but not without style.

### OCHIL STREET

On the E side, Nos. 2–4, a two-storey double house of *c.* 1870, now rather altered. Generally Italianate but with idiosyncratic detail. Carved zigzag decoration on the lintel of the outer windows of the first floor whose two-light centre windows each have two stilted roundheaded arches springing from a foliage-capitalled column-mullion.

### STIRLING ROAD

At the E end, a small public garden containing the SOUTH AFRICAN WAR MEMORIAL by *Robert S. Lorimer*, 1904. Tall stone pedestal, its bowed front carved with a garlanded roundel bearing reliefs of the coats of arms of the county of Clackmannan\* and the burgh of Alloa. On top of the pedestal, a stone sculpture by *W. Birnie Rhind* of a kilted officer and a fallen soldier, both heavily moustachioed.

Further W, on the N side, COWDEN PARK, a sizeable harled mid-C19 Jacobethan villa, by *John Melvin*. The principal front to the S is a just asymmetrical U-plan with bay windows at the advanced ends, the r. canted, the l. rectangular and with a three-light window above. In the centre of this front, a shield in a strapwork surround. To the S, the Kingdom Hall of Jehovah's Witnesses (*see* Churches, above). To the SW, an L-plan LODGE to the demolished Norwood. It is by *John Melvin, c.* 1875. Baronial, with a fish-scale-slated witch's hat roof over the round tower in the inner angle.

For Arnsbrae House, *see* Suburban Mansions, below.

### SUNNYSIDE COURT

On the NW corner with Parkway, GREENFIELD LODGE, *c.* 1900. Single-storey and attic, English picturesque. Harled walls with half-timbering in the gables; red tiled roof.

### TULLIBODY ROAD

At the SE end, set well back on the NE side, Greenfield House (*see* Suburban Mansions, below). On the SW, Nos. 3–7, a terrace of three mid-C19 cottages, with broad eaves and gableted canopies bracketed out over two of the entrances. Further out, on the

---

\* As used between 1890 and 1927.

NE, Nos. 36–38, a double cottage of the later C19, again with broad eaves and bracketed gablet canopies but the detail is heavier and there are consoled cornices over the doors. More bracketed gablet canopies over the doors of the single-storey late C19 Nos. 46 and 48, No. 48 enjoying a canted bay corner window under a squashed spire roof. Then, single-storey and attic and two-storey small houses of the late C19, several with bargeboards at their gables and dormer windows. More relaxed is the early C20 double house at Nos. 96–98. Single-storey and attic, in an accomplished English Arts and Crafts manner. Big red tiled roofs swept down to form porches at the cut-out corners of the front. At the front's centre, an M-roofed double gablet; small catslide-roofed dormers. Half-timbering at the attic storeys jettied out at the end gables. Further out, on the NE side, the mansion house and ancillary buildings of Inglewood House and, still further out on the SW, the lodge at the entrance to the drive of Gean House (for these, *see* Suburban Mansions, below). At Tullibody Road's exit from Alloa, the Lornshill Factory (*see* Industrial Buildings, below) and Lornshill Academy (*see* Public Buildings, above).

## SUBURBAN MANSIONS

ARNSBRAE HOUSE, Stirling Road. Designed by *Alfred Waterhouse* for the brewer James Younger, and built in 1885-6; N extension in the same manner by *Paul Waterhouse*, 1919. Flatly detailed multi-gabled Jacobean, the walls of pinkish-purple hammer-dressed masonry. Arched entrance on the E side. Asymmetrical s front overlooking the garden and to the River Forth, a two bay loggia at its W end. Broad eaved LODGE with half-timbered gables, presumably also by Waterhouse, 1885-6.

DUNMAR HOUSE, Dunmar Drive and Claremont. Built *c.* 1900. Walls of red brick set off by creamy harling and half-timbering; red tiled roof. It is a mansion in size but the soul is *petit bourgeois*.

GEAN HOUSE, Tullibody Road. English Arts and Crafts manor house built in 1912 as a wedding present to Alexander Forrester Paton from his parents, the owners of Inglewood House (q.v.). The architect was *William Kerr* of *John Melvin & Son*. Walls of hammer-dressed purplish stone with buff-coloured polished ashlar dressings, the roofs covered with red Rosemary tiles.

Irregular Z-plan. Two-storey SE wing containing the kitchen and offices. At r. angles to this, a two-storey and attic block and, at r. angles to that, the NW wing, also of two storeys and an attic. At the W end of this Z, a single-storey billiard room projecting to the s.

Entrance from the E. Here the centre block and SE wing form two sides of an informal courtyard, entered through urn-finialled corniced gatepiers on the E side and open to the garden on the N. The centre block's E front is asymmetrical, gabled and gableted, with stone mullioned windows. Below the tall five-light stair window, a lean-to single-storey corridor running from the kitchen wing to the advanced broad gable at the N end of the centre block's front; abutting the gable, a huge chimney for vertical emphasis. In the gable, the round-arched front door framed in a Roman Doric-columned Jacobean classical aedicule; above the cornice, a shield in a strapwork surround and, at the ends, lions holding more shields.

The N gable of the centre block provides the advanced end bay of the house's N elevation; projecting from it, a sloping-roofed two-storey canted bay window. Adjoining, the NW wing whose gabled and chimneyed l. bay has a round-arched recess to its ground floor. The three bays to the r. make a near-symmetrical composition, with parapeted two-storey bay windows flanking a four-light window at each floor of the centre. The symmetry is just disturbed by the glazing of the l. bay window (lighting a double-height living hall) which rises through two storeys broken only by mullions and transoms, while the r. bay window is divided by a band of masonry to mark the division between the ground- and first-floor rooms inside. Piend-roofed dormer windows over the two r. bays but not the l.

Set back at the W end of the house, a verandah along the N side of the single-storey SW (billiard room) wing, whose S gable is the backdrop for a broad canted bay window. The S front of the main NW wing just avoids symmetry. Mullioned and transomed ground-floor windows, the r. projecting as a bow. Low mullioned windows of horizontal proportions at the first floor. Again there are two dormers instead of the expected three on the roof. At the E end, the boldly projecting L formed by the E range and the SE wing. At the wing, mullioned ground-floor windows, the r. a canted bay; horizontal first-floor windows, also mullioned, each rising through the eaves into a pair of piended dormer-heads. Further E, a low service wing, a cupola on the roof.

INTERIOR. The front door opens into a panelled vestibule, its ceiling a groined plaster vault. Beyond, a panelled stair hall, the Jacobean stair rising on the S side. On the N side of the stair hall, a door into the panelled business room at the house's NE corner. In its SE corner, an inglenook, with a small window overlooking the front door. On the W side of the stair hall, the entrance to the double-height beam-ceilinged living hall, the bay window at the N end giving a spectacular view to the Ochils. The lower half of the walls is covered with panelling. Ionic pilasters support the beam ends of a silhouette-balustered gallery across the S end of the room. More Ionic pilasters frame the flat-arched and niche-topped opening to a broad inglenook at the E wall. Along the sides of the inglenook are bench seats; small two-light window to the N. Stone chimneypiece in the manner of *c.* 1700.

S of the hall is the dining room lit from a large S-facing bow window. Panelled walls. Holyrood-revival moulded plaster ceiling, its big centre roundel heavily enriched with fruit.

W of the hall is a drawing room of late C17/early C18 character. Another Holyrood-revival moulded plaster ceiling, with a large central octagon. At the room's W end, an exceptionally broad inglenook, its flat-arched entrance framed by a lugged architraved wooden surround. Inside the inglenook, a small window on the N side of the panelled overmantel, balanced by a glass-fronted cupboard on the S. In the SW wing of the house, the billiard room. One and a half storeys in height, the elliptically arched plaster ceiling sparingly enriched with roses, thistles, etc., in a neo-Elizabethan manner. Panelling rising half the height of the walls. On the W side, a panelled inglenook, its floor raised by one step as a dais.

NE of the house and of the same date, a LODGE (also by *William Kerr*) at the entrance to the drive from Tullibody Road. Huge pyramidal red tiled roof; Roman Doric columned verandah. For the former S lodge, *see* Outer Alloa: Streets: Arns Grove, above.

GREENFIELD HOUSE, Mar Place. Villa-mansion designed by *Sydney Mitchell & Wilson* and built in 1891–4 for David Paton Thomson, a partner in the Patons' textile firm. The style is Scots Jacobean. Walls of squared Corncockle rubble, the roofs covered with green Elterwater slates. L-plan, the W block a triple pile, the S range one room thick.

Asymmetrical entrance (W) front. At the N end, a one-bay recessed section bearing a panel inscribed 'WHA/THOLIS/WINS'. Then, on the principal building line of the two-storey and attic front, a first-floor canted oriel window carried on continuous corbelling. Roughly in the centre of the front, a two-storey rectangular bay window. Between its four-light ground- and first-floor openings are panels suggestive of a dummy window but carved with shields bearing the dates 1892 and 1894 and the initials of Thomson and his wife. Behind the bay window's scalloped parapet, one of a trio of attic gablets which enliven the wallhead. In the next bay of the front, large stair windows. Then the tower which proclaims the house's importance. At its base, a slightly projecting porch with attached Ionic columns at the corners. Splay-sided entrance, the soffit of its segmental arch carved with a rosetted guilloche ornament. The porch supports a canted oriel window, its cornice topped by a stone shell. Overall battlement but its rounded merlons are pacific. Inside the battlement, a glass-walled caphouse with an ogee-profiled lead roof ('a curious erection' thought *The Builder*, which condemned it as robbing the tower of its dignity\*). On the r. of the porch, a single-storey section.

The three-storey three-bay S elevation is symmetrical. At each of the outer bays, a two-storey canted bay window under a scalloped and ball-finialled parapet. At the top floor, a three-light window rising into a gablet. At the ground and first floors of the centre bay, mullioned and transomed two-light windows; second-floor window of three squat lights. The symmetry is fractionally disturbed by the chimneystacks. The l. has octagonal chimneys, the r. spiral-fluted chimneys flanking a rectangular one. At the E gable of this range, a projection (housing inglenooks)

\* *The Builder*, lxi, 481.

which bears a panel inscribed 'SEN. VORD.IS./ THRALL.AND./
THOCHT.IS.FRE./ KEEP.VELL.THY./ TONGVE. I.COVNSILL.
THE.'

Simply treated E elevation, with mullioned and transomed
windows and a shell niche in one of the gablets. At the N end,
service blocks of one and two storeys, one surmounted by an
ogee-roofed cupola.

Attached by a glazed link to the E end of the house is the
EXTENSION by *Clackmannan District Council*, 1987, providing
further accommodation for its present use as council offices.
Brick-built, single-storey and attic, with triangular dormer
windows. The style is a sort of rustic vernacular.

INTERIOR. The front door at the house's W side opens into a
plain Jacobean vestibule. In the inner doors, stained glass of
'aesthetic' character displaying the Thomson crest and the greeting 'SALVE'. The vestibule opens on to a broad corridor articulated by Artisan Mannerist Ionic pilasters supporting the ends of
transverse ribs. On the N side of the corridor, at its W end, is the
stair, its character again Jacobean. On the S side of the corridor,
two inter-connecting rooms (library and drawing room), both
with routine Jacobean ceilings, the drawing room's the more
elaborate of the two. In the library at the W, an oak dado and, at
the W wall, low bookcases flanking an Artisan Mannerist wooden
chimneypiece. At the canopied overmantel, a recess containing
a mirror; on the frieze of the overmantel, the inscription 'EAST
OR WEST HAME'S BEST'. Above the dado the room's walls are
covered with varnished dark gold Tynecastle Tapestry embossed
with depictions of cherubs among foliage. In the drawing room,
a panelled dado with Ionic pilasters supporting consoled projections from its cornice. Elliptical arches over the double doors
from the library, at the window embrasures and to the inglenook in the E wall. The inglenook contains a veined marble
Gothic fireplace in an Ionic pilastered surround; open pedimented
and mirrored overmantel flanked by shell-headed niches. In each
of the inglenook's N and S sides, a small window with leaded
round panes, bottle glass at the borders.

In the SE corner of the house's N block, the dining room.
High panelled dado of simple Artisan Mannerist character and
a panelled wooden ceiling. At the N wall, a low sideboard recess,
its top coved. At the S end of the E wall, an elliptical arch into a
fully panelled recess ending in a rectangular bay window; this
space was probably intended to contain a small table for informal family meals.

On the first floor, at the NW corner of the house, the double-
height billiard room. Swagged frieze under the main cornice;
above, a simply compartmented segmental-arched plaster ceiling. At the N end of the room, a screen of fluted Doric pilasters
marking off a recess containing a dais. Over the recess, a panelled
oak ceiling. In the N wall of the recess, a fireplace, with arched
niches at its projecting semi-octagonal overmantel. On the E
and W sides of the recess, elliptical arches, the E to a wall recess,
the W to the window embrasure. At the NW corner of the dais

recess, another arch which opens into a small room, again with a panelled oak ceiling.

Across the main corridor from the billiard room, a bedroom with a high white-painted dado and built-in cupboards, their doors with full-height mirrors; in one cupboard, a small safe. A pair of glass-fronted bookcases or china cabinets flank the fireplace, a round mirror in its overmantel.

INGLEWOOD HOUSE, Tullibody Road. Villa-mansion designed by *Sydney Mitchell & Wilson* for A.P. Forrester Paton of the Paton textiles family who bought *c.* 8 hectares of land here in 1895. The house is placed on a terrace about three-quarters of the way up the gently sloping hillside, with densely planted specimen trees behind and, in front, a formal garden divided by a ha-ha from parkland intended for occupation by Highland cattle.

The style of the architecture is free Jacobean. Masonry of squared and hammer-dressed purplish stone with lightly broached buff-coloured dressings; red Rosemary tiles covering the main roofs. The house is composed of three principal parts. At the E end, a low service wing containing the laundry, scullery, etc. Intermediate section comprising a N tower which contains the servants' hall and billiard room, and a low kitchen block on its S. At the W, the main block containing the principal rooms.

Asymmetrical entrance (N) front. At the service wing, a relatively narrow saddleback-roofed tower abutting a broad gable. Then the massive four-storey battlemented tower. At the E end of its front, a full-height semi-octagonal turret, its three front faces almost fully glazed at each floor to form canted bay windows, the windows of the first and second floors linked by mullions which rise in front of the intervening stone panels. Over each light of the second-floor window, a swan-necked pediment. The other N windows of the tower are all mullioned, those of the first floor also transomed and, like the other principal windows, with lozenged glazing in their upper lights. At the SE corner of the tower, a semi-octagonal bartizan. At the SW corner, a semi-octagonal buttress-like projection topped by an ogee-roofed caphouse. Large stone spouts project from the tower's battlement.

The tower's first-floor sill course is continued across the main block, which has a second stringcourse under the attic. This block's N front is L-plan with the E jamb projecting slightly forward of the tower. In the jamb's triangular-gabled front, an asymmetrical arrangement of a tall stair window under an oculus on the l. and a tier of small two-light windows on the r. Jutting out of the inner angle of the L, a porch fronted by Roman Doric coupled columns which support an entablature under a tall shaped parapet. W of the porch, a full-height mullioned and transomed window. Next, a rectangular bay window and, at the attic, a shaped gable. At the slightly recessed W end of the front, another shaped gable but steeper and with a prominent chimney. W of this, a plain addition of the later C20, partly covering the W end of the house.

The S front overlooking the garden begins at the W end with a conservatory projecting from the end of the main block. E of the conservatory, the main block's three W bays form a symmetrical composition. At the outer bays, shaped gables and two-storey canted bay windows topped by pierced parapets. At the centre bay, a broad depressed-arched ground-floor recess; above, a loggia fronted by paired elliptical arches and a balcony, its front a repeat of the bay windows' parapets. The symmetry of this section is disturbed by the very slightly recessed E bay of the main block, which has a triangular gable and a two-storey rectangular bay window. Set well back at the E end of the main block, the single-storey semi-octagonal fronted kitchen in front of the tower. E of the kitchen, the service wing.

INTERIOR. The vestibule behind the front door opens into the Hall. The general framework of this room is a two-storey rectangle. High oak dado with sparing Jacobean detail. Above the dado, superimposed pilasters, the lower orderless but decorated with carved fruit dropping from shields, the upper Ionic with fluted shafts. Plaster frieze modelled with foliage and cherubs who support shields bearing emblems (crowns, anchors, etc.). On the E and W sides the frieze is broken by foliaged brackets supporting the beams which divide the ceiling into compartments, each containing geometrically panelled neo-Jacobean plasterwork enriched with pendants. But this general framework is broken on every side, each displaying an individual identity. Along the upper floor level of the E and S sides, set behind the pilasters of the framework, are wooden arcades whose round-headed arches are carried on Artisan Mannerist Roman Doric columns; the arcades provide borrowed light to the first-floor corridors behind. Under the S arcade and across the full width of the room, a very broad depressed arch with projecting keystone and voussoirs which opens into a ground-floor corridor-recess; floral enrichment on the panelled soffit of the arch. Another depressed arch of similar character occupies a little more than the N half of the E side; behind this is the principal stair. At the W end of the N side, an opening above the door from the vestibule was designed to be filled with the front pipes of an organ (now removed). W of this, a full-height rectangular recess, its huge mullioned and transomed N window containing STAINED GLASS, a depiction in pale greens and yellows of an idealized streetscape inscribed 'GO EAST GO WEST HOMES BEST'. Like the other stained glass in the house it is by *Oscar Paterson*. In the centre of the W side of the Hall, a segmental-arched inglenook, the arch soffit divided into panels enriched with egg-and-dart moulding and with rosettes at their intersections. Along the N and S sides of the inglenook are bench seats. Artisan Mannerist stone chimneypiece with bulging jambs like simplified consoles; Doric frieze, its metopes carved with cartouches.

The principal Stair occupying the NE corner of the main block continues the Artisan Mannerist character of the Hall. Silhouette balusters; carved strapwork on the newel posts, the first topped by a lamp. Plaster ceiling of the same type as in the Hall. On the half landing, another STAINED GLASS window ('Morn'). It depicts a cock crowing as the sun rises behind a church steeple.

At the first floor the corridors behind the E and S sides of the hall are covered with simply panelled plaster tunnel vaults. E of the Stair and occupying the first floor of the tower is the Billiard Room. High dado along the walls. Compartmented ceiling decorated with foliaged panels. Bay window recess at the NE corner. At the SE corner, an inglenook but now without its chimneypiece and seats. At the SW corner, a door on to a flat roof from which to enjoy the view.

The NW corner of the ground floor of the main block was originally occupied by the Business Room (opening off the Hall) and, reached from the corridor-recess at the S end of the Hall, the Family Bedroom and Dressing Room. The principal public rooms are all entered from the corridor-recess and ranged along the S front of the main block. The largest, at the W end, is the Drawing Room (now Forrester Room), its ceiling enriched with Jacobean *pâtisserie* ornament. The room is asymmetrical, with recesses along the E side and at the S bay window, both with beamed flat arches into the body of the room. Depressed arch framed by fluted Ionic pilasters to the inglenook at the W end of the N wall. Basket-arched chimneypiece of black-veined white marble in an oak border. The walls of the inglenook are covered with painted panelling. On the W side, a small window filled with abstract STAINED GLASS. Another Ionic pilastered arch opens into a recess at the N end of the room's W side; off this recess is the Conservatory. E of the Drawing Room, a lobby off the corridor-recess leads to a door into the garden. E of this, the Morning Room or Library. On its E and S sides, depressed arches to a shallow recess and the bay window. At the N and W walls, roundheaded blind arcading above a base formed by glass-fronted bookcases whose Artisan Mannerist Ionic columns support an egg-and-dart cornice. This bookcase cornice breaks forward at the centre of the W wall to form a mantelpiece over the fireplace. Compartmented ceiling, some of the panels enriched with foliage. The SE room of the main block is the Dining Room (now Inglenook Room). Low dado of walnut, this wood used also to frame the bay window and at the keystoned depressed arch and panelling of the inglenook in the centre of the E wall. The inglenook's chimneypiece is of dark red marble under a swagged frieze and egg-and-dart cornice; at the overmantel, shellheaded niches flanking the frame for a painting. In the canted SE corner of the inglenook, another STAINED GLASS window. It depicts a stylized tree, its significance explained by the inscription 'Friendship Is the Sheltering Tree'.

The 1890s entrance to the drive from Tullibody Road (a little SE of the present entrance) was through urn-topped and V-jointed ashlar GATEPIERS. The fronts of the lower stones are faceted, those of the upper fluted. SE of the gatepiers, a contemporary LODGE, built of the same masonry as the house and also roofed with Rosemary tiles but the manner is broad-eaved English picturesque. At the front gable, a wide and shallowly projecting canted bay window under a jettied and half-timbered attic. At the NW end, a semi-octagonal-ended projection whose windows are framed by thin Roman Doric columns on corbelled bases. Catslide dormer at the SE end. A little to the SE and now separated by late C20 housing, the 1890s GARAGE. Again it displays the same masonry and Rosemary tiles as the main house but is more decidedly Scots Jacobean. In the inner angle of the main block and SE wing, a round tower, the tiles of the domed roof shaped as fish-scales. The upper windows are set in curvaceously pedimented aedicules. At the rear (NE) elevation, the main block's upper floor is jettied, its twin gables harled and half-timbered.

## INDUSTRIAL BUILDINGS

GLASS CONE, Craigward. Early C19 cone, originally containing a pot furnace for the manufacture of glass. Octagonal stone base with round-arched openings in the sloping sides. Above, a tall truncated cone built of red brick.

KILNCRAIGS FACTORY, Auld Brig Road. Woollen mill developed from the early C19 for the firm of John Paton, Son & Co. (later Patons & Baldwin). It is a large complex of buildings, their main fronts facing a roughly triangular courtyard. On the courtyard's E side, the EAST or BURNSIDE MILL of 1860. Rubble-built thirteen-bay frontage, originally of three storeys except for the S bay, which rose for a further two floors as a pedimented tower topped by a bellcote. Later in the C19 the twelve N bays were raised to the same height as the tower and given piended sawtooth roofs. On the N side of the courtyard, the NORTH MILL of 1868. Again rubble-built and of thirteen bays but four storeys in height and with a double-M piended roof. In the inner angle of these two buildings, a square tower contemporary with and originally of the same height as the North Mill; round-arched windows at the lower stages, an oculus at the top stage. It was heightened in brick by *John A. G. McLean*, 1906; the pyramidal roof is the same shape as its predecessor. At the E end of the S side of the courtyard, the WEST MILL, the rubble-walled lower three storeys again late C19, the brick-built top three floors added by *John Melvin & Son* in 1902. To its E, projecting behind the courtyard, the bow-ended OLD MILL AND ENGINE HOUSE, by *John Melvin*, 1878, but heightened in brick in 1913. W of the West Mill, THE WAREROOM, its three lower floors mid-C19, the two top floors of *c.* 1880; it is rubble-walled and quite plain. The height is maintained by the OFFICE BLOCK at the W end of the courtyard's S side. This is by *William Kerr* of *John Melvin & Son*, 1903–4. Short N elevation, a long W elevation stretching down the lane to the S. Enjoyably pompous English Baroque, the stonework of buff-coloured polished ashlar. At the N front, an aedicule with giant Ionic columns topped by lions holding shields. The first- and second-floor windows of the W front are framed by aedicules, again Ionic but with pilasters rather than columns. Inside, the principal rooms are finished in a mixture of Baroque and Art Nouveau. In 1936 *William Kerr* and *John Gray* of *John Melvin & Son* extended this SW block to

127

the S with a six-storey building, its ground floor of stugged red sandstone with two-light windows a survivor of the previous building (of 1924) on the site. The five floors above are of steel-framed construction, the brick walling harled and painted white. Horizontal metal-framed windows, those of the fourth floor lower than those below, the top floor's windows lower again. The walling is carried up as a flush parapet to hide the piended roofs which belie the building's determined modernity. Round the edge of the complex, C20 single-storey brick-built weaving sheds. In the wall of these facing Auld Brig Road, a reset stone bearing the date 1770, the initials IG and CL, and the emblems of a smith (a crowned hammer, anvil and horseshoe).

LORNSHILL FACTORY, Tullibody Road. Built in 1956. Curtain-walled two-storey office block. Behind, sawtooth-roofed weaving sheds.

THISTLE BREWERY, Mill Road. Complex bounded on the SE by a late C20 brick wall bearing large panels with reliefs of thistles. The principal buildings are of the later C19 but reconstructed and partly rebuilt in 1910 after a fire. At the SE, a three-storey piend-roofed malt store of the later C19. Five bays by three, built of red brick with white brick dressings. To its N, a tall brewhouse, again piend-roofed and built of red and white brick, with a louvred ventilator and a tower, now with a flat roof but formerly piend-roofed. At the SW corner of the complex, facing East Vennel, a two-storey and attic office block, dated 1896. Façade of ashlar, hammer-dressed at the ground floor and polished above. At the ground floor, round-arched doors (one enlarged as a garage entrance) and large round windows. Carved decoration at the corners of the first-floor windows.

<h1 style="text-align:center">ALMOND CASTLE</h1>

0.4km. N of Muiravonside

F 9070

Substantial ruin of a C15 tower house built for the Crawfords of Haining and encased on two sides by now fragmentary additions of the late C16 or early C17.

The C15 tower is L-plan, the main block aligned SE–NW, the jamb protruding to the NE, of four storeys and an attic, built of grey sandstone rubble, many of the stones roughly squared, with ashlar in-and-out flush quoins. The walling rises unrelieved by stringcourses to the parapet, now mostly fallen but probably originally crenellated; a bartizan at the centre of the main block's SE gable is recorded in C19 views. Some utilitarian drainage spouts survive under the parapet, e.g. on the NW side. Narrow ground-floor windows in the gables of the main block and the NW and NE walls of the jamb, the jamb's NW window now built up, its NE converted to a door in the late C16. At the NE end of the main block's SE gable, a roundheaded ground-floor door with double-splayed jambs. The house's main entrance is at the first floor immediately above the ground-floor door. The stone-work of the rectangular opening has been shaved and a lintel

with a splayed arris inserted, probably in the late C16. Another
door, with roll-moulded jambs, used to exist immediately to the
l. of this entrance. It was probably an early C17 insertion, replacing a window, but the stonework is now missing. At the first floor
and those above, windows of generous size with chamfered
margins, probably all enlarged in the C16.

INTERIOR. On the ground floor, a tunnel-vaulted cellar in
the main block and another in the jamb. The only access from
these to the first floor is by a hatch in the vault at the SE end of
the main block's cellar. Above the ground floor the thickness of
the walls is reduced from c. 2.17m. to c. 1.92m. Ashlar tunnel
vault over the attic but the storeys below have had wooden floors,
their wall-beams carried on rounded stone corbels. The first-
floor room of the main block was originally the hall. At its NW
end, a large but plain C15 fireplace. Also C15 are the roundheaded
rear-arches of the NW windows in the SW and NE walls but their
daylights have been enlarged, probably in the C16; a locker in
the NW ingo of the NE window. The SW wall's centre window is
a C16 insertion, with a segmental rear-arch. Part of the stonework
of the hall's SE gable has been cut away in the C16 or C17, the
original thickness shown by a stub between the two doors. The
small windows at this end were probably inserted at the same
time. At the SE end of the NE wall, a pointed arch with splayed
arrises gives access to a tight turnpike stair contained in the wall
thickness of the SE corner of the main block. To its l., two
doors, both with splayed jambs and lintels. The r. door is C15,
the l. a C16 insertion made when the NW wall of the jamb was
thinned from the original c. 2.17m. to a mere c. 0.46m.

Inside the jamb is the C15 kitchen. Originally the whole length
of its NE end was occupied by a fireplace with a splayed segmental
arch. Small window in its back and, to the l. of this window, a
sink with a drain to the outside. Probably in the late C16 or early
C17, after the construction of a new kitchen in the additions to
the tower, a small fireplace (blocking the sink) was inserted in
the NW end of the original fireplace and a door (later blocked)
made in the SE end. In the SE wall, a narrow C15 window, its
daylight blocked by a wall of the C16 SE addition to the tower.

On the second floor of the main block, an upper hall. As at
the floor below, part of its SE gable has been thinned; originally
it must have contained a short passage from the stair. Comfortably sized windows, perhaps all enlarged in the C16. Fireplace
towards the NW end of the NE side. At each end of the gable, a
wall cupboard; another at the NW end of the SW side. In the S
corner, remains of a piscina, its surround's stepped and chamfered
jambs rising into a pointed arch. Immediately l. of the doorway
to the stair, the entrance to the room in the jamb. A straight lintel
has been inserted into this opening's pointed arch, probably in
the C16. As at the original kitchen below, the NW wall has been
thinned and now contains a small C16 window. The SE window
is of the C15 but blocked. Off-centre fireplace in the SE wall.

The C15 turnpike stair originally rose to the top of the tower
but was cut off at second-floor level in the late C16 when a new

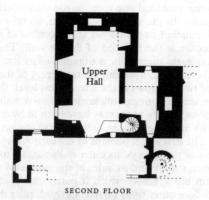

SECOND FLOOR

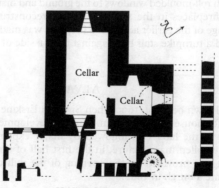

FIRST FLOOR

GROUND FLOOR

15 m
50 ft

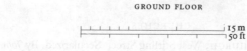

Almond Castle. Plans.

stair was provided in the SE addition. The third floor of the C15 tower again provided one room in the main block and another in the jamb. In the main block's room, an off-centre NW fireplace. Unaltered C15 windows at the centres of the SW and SE walls; locker at the NW end of the NE wall. The room in the jamb has again undergone a thinning of its NW wall. No fireplace. At the attic, a window in the centre of the SE gable and traces of two windows at the NW. At this level, the room in the jamb retains the original thickness of its NW wall. No evidence of windows but the room may have been lit by dormers.

The NE and SE additions, now very ruinous, were built in two stages. The first stage, perhaps of the early C16, was L-plan and probably of two storeys, its outer walls parallel to and c. 2.74m. away from the NE and SE sides of the jamb and the SE gable of the main block across which it partly extended. Parts of the ground-floor outer walls survive. On both sides they are pierced by narrow unsplayed slits, probably crude windows to light cellars behind. Above the tower's C15 ground-floor door, a raggle to support the springing of a stone vault over the SW cellar of the extension. The second stage, possibly of 1586 (the date on an heraldic stone from Almond Castle which was removed to the farmhouse at Gilmeadowland) but more likely to be early C17, extended the SE range of the earlier addition to the SW beyond the S corner of the tower and raised the height of the earlier addition to its own of three storeys and an attic, the roof raggle cutting across the third floor S windows of the tower. The new walling is of smaller blocks of rubble than the earlier work and with an admixture of reddish stone. C19 drawings show this second addition's SE front to have been a symmetrical U-plan, with oval windows at the top floor of the jambs. Part of the S jamb survives, with roll-moulded windows to the ground and first floors; evidence of fireplaces in the SW wall. In the reconstruction of the SE range of the earlier addition a fireplace was made in the SW side and a turnpike stair built against the NE side of its cross-wall.

8090                           ALVA                           C

Small town begun c. 1690 when Sir John Erskine of Alva granted feus for houses at The Green. Further development to the N took place in the later C18 followed by major expansion, associated with woollen manufacture, in the first half of the C19. A further boost was provided by the opening of the railway in 1863. Alva became a burgh in 1882.

### CHURCHES

ALVA FREE CHURCH, West Stirling Street. Secularized. By *John Melvin*, 1848. The rubble-built front has survived the building's conversion to housing. Broad shaped gable, with hoodmoulded round-arched narrow windows and a Tudor Gothic door; on top, a curvy-headed birdcage bellcote.

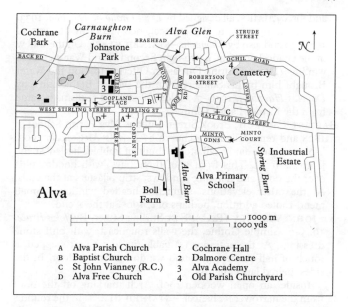

A   Alva Parish Church          1   Cochrane Hall
B   Baptist Church              2   Dalmore Centre
C   St John Vianney (R.C.)      3   Alva Academy
D   Alva Free Church            4   Old Parish Churchyard

ALVA PARISH CHURCH, Stirling Street. Sneck-harled rubble-walled box, built as a United Secession church in 1842. Georgian castellated detail of a type more often associated with secular buildings. The centre of the front (N) gable is slightly advanced to suggest a nave flanked by aisles. At the corners of the centre-piece and the outer corners, conical-finialled round turrets. Over the 'aisle' ends, sloping battlements; the 'nave' gable is stepped and surmounted by a gableted bellcote. Unmoulded round-arched windows at the side walls and the 'aisle' ends. At the 'nave' gable, a roundheaded ashlar overarch containing a quatrefoil panel above a window which would be Venetian were not all the lights round-arched. This is half-hidden by a big step-gabled porch added by *Thomas Frame & Son* in 1888. In the front of the porch, a dummy oculus above the entrance's Doric columned and battlemented surround, apparently re-used work of 1842.

To the W, a low plain HALL by *George Plenderleith*, 1883–4. Fleur-de-lis finialled N gable, its ground-floor openings round-headed; small oculus above.

Inside the church, a panelled plaster ceiling of Tudorish character, with small pendants and a central rose of Prince of Wales feathers. Deep N gallery erected in 1861–2 and enlarged by *Thomas Frame & Son*, 1888. At the S end, a rectangular chancel added in 1989; it houses the ORGAN by *Forster & Andrews*, 1893, brought to this church in 1948 when it was rebuilt by *William Hill & Sons and Norman & Beard*.★ – In front of the chancel, an oak COMMUNION TABLE, the Agnus Dei carved on a front panel,

★ It was formerly in Millport West Church, Cumbrae, Ayrshire.

and three CHAIRS, all designed by *Leslie Grahame Thomson*, 1933.
– E of the opening to the chancel, neo-Jacobean PULPIT of
1948–50 and also by *Thomson*. – STAINED GLASS. On the wall W
of the chancel opening, a two-light Second World War memorial
window (David Pouring Out as an Offering to God the Water
Brought him by his Soldiers from the Well at Bethlehem), by
*Douglas Hamilton*, 1956–7. Colourful stylized realism. It came
from the former Parish Church.

BAPTIST CHURCH, Brook Street. Built as Alva Parish School in
1828 and remodelled as a church by *Kerr & McCulloch*, 1907.
L-plan, of one fairly tall storey, built of rubble, harled at the
jamb's S front. This front is of three bays, with hoodmoulds
over the door and flanking windows; strip pilasters at the ends.
At the other elevations, segmental-headed windows. Small
piend-roofed addition, perhaps of *c.* 1905, at the N end.

ST JOHN VIANNEY (R.C.), East Stirling Street. By *John Bruce*,
1925–6. Simple Gothic, the walls roughcast, with buff stone
dressings. At the entrance (s) gable, its lower part stepped, a
touch of half-timbering; round window over the door. In the
sides, paired lancet lights.

Inside, an open wooden roof. Arch marking off the nave
from the narrower N chancel. – STAINED GLASS. In the round S
window, glass ('Sing to the Mountains') by *Veronica J. Lynch*,
1996. – In the E wall, a sketchy two-light window (St Columba
and St Ninian) of 1997 and also by *Lynch*.

CEMETERIES

CEMETERY, Lovers Loan. Laid out in 1873; corniced and ball-
finialled GATEPIERS at the S entrance.

OLD PARISH CHURCHYARD, Ochil Road. The site of the former
Parish Church (a C17 building which had been reconstructed in
1815, and enlarged in 1854 and 1877; destroyed by fire in 1984)
is laid out as a low grassed mound of rough Greek cross shape.
Built into the dwarf retaining walls are some stones from the
church. On the E side is one carved with the date 1631 above a
shield bearing the Bruce coat of arms flanked by the initials A B
(for Alexander Bruce of Alva). Another bears the initials J J (for
James Johnstone of Alva) and the date 1854. At the E end of the
S side, a stone inscribed 'REMEMBER./TO.KEEP/HOLY.THE.
SABBOTH.DAY.1637'.

E of the site of the church is the JOHNSTONE MAUSOLEUM
by *Robert Adam*, 1789–90. It is a droved ashlar parapeted Greek
cross, the pedimented arms projecting only minimally. In each
of the N and S faces, a roundheaded niche. The W face contains
the entrance, its roundheaded door, the keystone carved with a
bearded human head, set in a rectangular overarch. The pediment above is here carried on Doric columns which have Greek
fluted shafts and rosetted Roman Doric capitals; a triglyph at
each end of the frieze. On the S and E sides where the ground falls
away abruptly, the walls of the undercroft are exposed. In the later
C19 the undercroft was extended E, the new walling of rock-

faced ashlar, the extension's piended roof butting into the upper part of Adam's E face which was originally a repeat of the N and s sides but whose niche has been opened up as a window into the extension. Also of the later C19 is the plain stone cross on the E pediment. Inside the original mausoleum, a groin vault over each arm, a flat ceiling over the centre. On the walls, roundels bearing relief busts, and three monuments.

Immediately W of the mausoleum, a GRAVESLAB, its piended platform top carved with weathered reminders of mortality; it is probably early C18. – Plenty of C18 HEADSTONES, their decoration either carved in relief or incised. Beside the graveslab, a headstone with the initials WM and the date 1773; reliefs of a skull, crossbones and hourglass. – Behind, a stone of 1727 incised with a skull and crossbones. – NW of the Johnstone Mausoleum, a stone with the initials IA and MG, an angel's head (the soul) in the swan-neck pediment. The main front panel displays motifs which include dividers and a set-square. On the back, the date 1785. – Behind, a stone with the initials IH and MV, the curvaceous pediment supported by Ionic columns. On the front, a bipartite panel, the l. half with the relief of a gardener's tools, the r. with emblems of death. – Just to its N, a large headstone dated 1727 and with the initials TB and MC. It is incised with a blacksmith's tongs and a skull and crossbones.

Most of the graveyard's C18 HEADSTONES are to the s and w of the site of the church. To the s, a stone of 1729 with the initials AS and MD. Front with two roundheaded panels carved with reliefs, the l. of a skull above crossbones. – To its N, a small pilastered and curly pedimented stone, dated 1719 (?), an angel's head in the tympanum. – SW of this, a well preserved curvy-topped stone, the front divided into three segmental-arched panels, the r. bearing reliefs of a skull, crossbones and hourglass, the centre the date 1729 and a weaver's shuttle and loom. – Further W, several stones of the earlier C18 incised with crude reminders of death. One, of 1736 or 1756, also displays a crossed gun and fishing rod, so presumably commemorates a gamekeeper. Another (of 1748) has a weaver's shuttle. – N of these and just NW of the church, a stone of 1719, the front tripartite with roundheaded outer panels, the l. carved with reliefs of an hourglass, skull and crossbones, the r. with a shuttle and loom. – Further N, W of the centre of the church, a small stone of 1685 (?) with the initials IM and MB. It is a pilastered aedicule, with scrolls on the sides of the open pediment. – Behind, a large stone of 1760 carved in relief with emblems of death and a merchant's mark (like a figure 4). – To its NW, a stone dated 1708, again with emblems of death and also the depiction of a dyester's press, helpfully but unnecessarily labelled 'A PRESS', the depiction together with the label perhaps copied from an engraving. – Just NE of this, a headstone whose W face has the date 1751 and an incised skull, crossbones and shuttle. – Immediately NE again, a stone, perhaps of c. 1700, its W face carved with the relief of a trumpeting angel, its E with a cartouche whose top is held in the mouth of a grotesque head. – To its NE, a stone of 1725 with

an incised skull and crossbones. – Immediately in front of the
churchyard's w gate, a plain stone with the initials 'HR.IB.MD'
and the unusually early date of 1673.


## PUBLIC BUILDINGS

ALVA ACADEMY, Queen Street. At the NW, an assemblage of flat-
roofed boxes, red brick the chief walling material, by *Clackmannan
County Council* (architect in charge: *A. J. McLaren*), 1967. E of
Queen Street, two-storey U-plan building by *Central Regional
Council*, 1981, the E and S ranges of brown brick banded with
red; shallow-pitched slated roofs carried down between the
windows of the upper floor in a mansard effect. The N range,
partly dry-dashed, has a slated mansard roof. At the SW of the
school, the SWIMMING POOL AND LEISURE CENTRE by *Central
Regional Council*, 1980. Heavy slate-hung top hamper oversailing
a low ground floor; at the S end the upper storey forms a monopitch roof (largely glazed), its line continued to the ground by
sloping concrete buttresses.

ALVA PRIMARY SCHOOL, Brook Street. By *Central Regional
Council*, 1976. Flimsy-looking, with dark brown brick and panels
of curtain walling.

COCHRANE HALL, West Stirling Street. By *William Kerr* and *John
Gray* of *John Melvin & Son*, 1928–9. Symmetrical Lutyensesque
Queen Anne. Tall single-storey main block and corner pavilions,
the walls rendered, the roofs covered with red tiles. Cupola over
the centre. Cape Dutch gabled S porch flanked by flat-roofed
Roman Doric columned verandahs. Inside, the hall is covered
by a plaster segmental tunnel vault.

DALMORE CENTRE, West Stirling Street. Originally Alva Infant
School. Best School Board Gothic, by *John Melvin & Son*,
1885–6, in hammer-dressed pinkish sandstone. H-plan, with a
gabled and bellcoted centrepiece.


## DESCRIPTION

Set back from the A91 on a hillside at the E end of the town, ALVA
HOUSE by *Montgomery, Forgan*, 1998–9, a Postmodern classical
bad joke. The main road becomes EAST STIRLING STREET,
an unpromising introduction, with an industrial estate on its S
and late C20 housing on the N. But after *c.* 0.35km., LOVERS
LOAN leads N to the Cemetery and, on the hill above, the Old
Parish Churchyard, now dominated by the Johnstone Mausoleum
(*see* Cemeteries, above). In OCHIL ROAD W of the churchyard,
a mixture of C19 and C20 villas, the larger on the S side where
they have uninterrupted views over the town below. One house
of the later C19 on the N (No. 43) has hoodmoulded windows
and carved bargeboards. ROBERTSON STREET, going uphill
to the N, contains cottages of the mid and later C19, Nos. 14–16
with a corbelled and rosetted eaves cornice. At the top, the
Strude Mill (*see* Industrial Buildings, below). From near the
top of Robertson Street, BRAEHEAD curves SW down to rejoin

Ochil Road past blocks of two-storey houses by *John Fraser &* 118
*Son*, 1938. Flat-roofed, with prominent chimneys with unmoulded
copes, decidedly modern despite the neo-Georgian architraves
at the doors. Off the W end of Ochil Road, on the N side beside
the E bank of the Alva Burn, the former Braehead Mill (*see*
Industrial Buildings, below). To its SW, on the N side of Ochil
Road's final stretch to the Alva Burn, a short terrace (THE
ISLAND) of little-altered mid-C19 cottages.

East Stirling Street develops some architectural interest on the
W corner of Lovers Loan with ST SERF'S, a mid-C19 *cottage
orné*, with broad eaves, hoodmoulds and a canted bay window.
The N side continues with C19 and C20 villas. On the S side of
East Stirling Street, Ochilvale Mill (*see* Industrial Buildings,
below) followed by MINTO GARDENS, decent local authority
housing of 1919. Opposite, on the N side of East Stirling Street,
St John Vianney Church (*see* Churches, above) attached to a
broad-eaved villa of the later C19, its porch enjoying a Jacobean
shaped gable. Then, on the street's S side, plain terraced housing of the later C19 (Nos. 93–99 dated 1867); on the N, small
C19 and C20 villas and cottages, followed by the mid-C19 Nos.
56–62. Two-storey, No. 56 with a segmental-arched pend
entrance, Nos. 58–62 with heavy corniced doorpieces, pilastered
at Nos. 58 and 62. On the W side of Croftshaw Road, a jolly
little BUS SHELTER AND PUBLIC CONVENIENCE of 1934.
Pantiled piended roof; porch with half timbering in its gable
from which projects a clock by *James Ritchie & Son* of Edinburgh.
Adjoining, a sizeable two-storey late C19 commercial building
on the corner of Brook Street. Semi-octagonal tops to the first-
floor windows. Large moulded skewputts and a low battlement
at the wallhead, a big chimney corbelled out at the centre of the
S front.

BROOK STREET runs N–S. On its W side, N of East Stirling Street,
the Baptist Church (*see* Churches, above). S of East Stirling Street,
on the E side, a former woollen mill (*see* Industrial Buildings,
below) and, a little to the S, Alva Primary School (*see* Public
Buildings, above). Beyond, THE MEADOW, a two-storey harled
house of *c.* 1845. S front of four bays with, from the l., a corniced
ground-floor window, a pilastered and corniced doorpiece, a
two-storey canted bay window, and a shallow rectangular bay
window, also of two storeys. NW wing of the later C19, the upper
windows with bargeboarded dormerheads. At the S end of Brook
Street, on the W, BOLL FARM. Jacobean single-storey and attic
farmhouse of *c.* 1860. The steading behind may be of about the
same date.

STIRLING STREET continues the line of East Stirling Street. On
the NW corner with Brook Street, the JOHNSTONE ARMS
HOTEL is mid-C19 Georgian survival. On Brook Street's SW
corner, the ALVA GLEN HOTEL, the main block dating from
1807 but reconstructed in the later C19 with energetic Ruskinian
detail. The street then establishes a plain two-storey norm of
housing over shops, mostly of the mid and later C19 but with
some C20 redevelopment. Hoodmoulds over the ground-floor

openings of the mid-C19 CROWN HOTEL on the s. On the N, gableted dormerheads with obelisk finials at Nos. 84–86, dated 1874. Opposite, on the E corner of Cobden Street, Nos 85–93, the former Alva Co-operative Society premises of 1873. A wall-head dormer containing a clock instead of a window was added for the Society's jubilee in 1895; scroll-sided with an urn-finialled segmental pediment, the tympanum carved with a relief of the Society's clasped hands emblem. Pilastered and corniced door-piece at No. 108 on the N, a mid-C19 two-storey house. A little w, on the s side, Alva Parish Church (see Churches, above). Beside it, the former UNITED SECESSION MANSE (No. 121) of c. 1845; Georgian survival, with a heavy pilastered and corniced doorpiece. Opposite, on the N, a former CINEMA of 1921. w of this, on the corner of Queen Street, the single-storey Nos. 128–130 Stirling Street, the former STIRLING DISTRICT AND COUNTY SAVINGS BANK by A. M. McMichael, 1932. Ashlar-fronted and piend-roofed, a shaped gablet over the canted corner containing the entrance.

QUEEN STREET runs N and s of Stirling Street. To the N, on the w side, No. 46, a mid-C19 house, Georgian survival but the (painted) ashlar is stugged and the window surrounds moulded in a Victorian manner. At the N end, on both sides of the street, Alva Academy (see Public Buildings, above). In Queen Street's s part, on the E, No. 63, by John Melvin & Son, 1878. Two tall storeys of stugged purplish ashlar with polished buff dressings. Three-bay front, the heads of the openings all stilted. At the ground floor, segmental-headed and nook-shafted door flanked by bipartite windows, their lights again segmental-headed. A band of stiffleaf ornament is carried across the front, forming capitals at the nook-shafts of the door and the columned mul-lions of the windows and, at the ends, shaft-rings enclosing the downpipes. First-floor windows of two rectangular lights with bell-capitalled nook-shafts.

WEST STIRLING STREET is the main road's exit from the town. In its E stretch, two-storey buildings, mostly of the mid C19. On the N side, the building line is broken by the front garden of the BANK OF SCOTLAND (former Union Bank) of 1863, a piend-roofed Georgian survival villa, the pilastered and corniced door-piece flanked by shallow rectangular bay windows. On the s side, the former Alva Free Church (see Churches, above). Beside it, its former MANSE of c. 1850, a piend-roofed rubble-walled villa, the front windows corniced, rather meanly at the upper floor; heavy door surround which forms a balcony under the window above. Further w, on West Stirling Street's NW corner with Copland Place, a two-storey block (Nos. 176–180) of 1877, with corbels under the eaves. Gablet over the canted corner; chimney (now truncated) corbelled out from the s front. Of about the same date and also with a corbelled-out chimney the adjoin-ing Nos. 182–186, followed by the Dalmore Centre (see Public Buildings, above) and the former Glentana Mills (see Industrial Buildings, below). Behind and to the w, the COCHRANE and JOHNSTONE PARKS, the E part (Johnstone Park) laid out in 1856, the W (Cochrane Park) in 1922, the Cochrane Hall (*see* Public Buildings, above) standing at its SE corner. In BACK ROAD to the NE of Johnstone Park, No. 106, a late C19 overgrown barge-boarded *cottage orné* with a tower, its French pavilion roof covered with bands of fish-scale slating.

## INDUSTRIAL BUILDINGS

BRAEHEAD MILL, off Ochil Road. Now Masonic Hall. Woollen mill of the later C19. Three-storey triple pile with double-pitched roofs, the walls of stugged ashlar. Forestairs to the first-floor entrances at the ends of the five-bay S front.

GLENTANA MILLS, West Stirling Street. Now Mill Trail Visitor Centre. Main range of *c.* 1945, flat-roofed single-storey, built of brick. At its W end, the former power loom shed of 1873, a double pile of one storey over a basement. Red brick with dressings of glazed white bricks which are used as corbels under the lintels of the rectangular overarches framing the ground-floor window; more corbels under the eaves of the slated roof, its W end piended. Round-arched windows in the W gable. Inside, cast iron columns supporting the valley of the M-roof.

OCHILVALE MILL, East Stirling Street. Late C19 woollen mill. Rubble-built NE range. The two-storey W range is the main block. Long (thirty-bay) double pile with piended roofs, red brick with dressings of glazed white bricks; corbels of white bricks under the eaves. At the N end, a single-storey seven-bay wing, perhaps a slightly later addition, again a double pile with piended roofs. Red and white brick except for the N front to the street which is of rubble. This front's windows and round-arched door are late C20.

STRUDE MILL, Robertson Street. Now housing. Mid-C19 woollen mill, of large blocks of pink sandstone rubble with buff-coloured dressings. Tall (six storeys) and relatively narrow piend-roofed block of twenty-six bays by three. The centre four bays of the front are slightly advanced under a rather steep pediment, the surround for a clock in its tympanum, topped by a round-arched bellcote. Simple rectangular window openings except for a pair of round-arched windows flanking the front entrance. Elliptical-arched entrances front and rear. NW wing demolished.

WOOLLEN MILL, Brook Street. Now housing. Mid-C19. Rubble-built, the roof jerkin-headed at the N gable. Two storeys, the W front of eight bays. Attached to the S end, a two-bay house, also of two storeys but taller and with a corniced doorpiece; probably contemporary with the mill.

## ARDCHULLARIE MORE S 5010
### 4.2km. SSE of Strathyre

Dated 1910; by *Stewart & Paterson*. A skew-gabled, L-plan shooting lodge well sited above Loch Lubnaig. White roughcast with Scots Renaissance detail and dressings in sandstone.

# ARDEONAIG                                        S

Hamlet on the s side of Loch Tay.

ARDEONAIG HOTEL. Roughcast inn; C18 core (?). Four gabled
dormers have antler-like bargeboards. Pillared and gabled porch
with decorative wrought iron under canopy.

MAINS CASTLE. A few stones near the lochside.


# ARNHALL CASTLE *see* KEIR HOUSE


# ARNPRIOR                                        S

T-junction hamlet.

ARNPRIOR FARM. Late C18, three-bay farmhouse formula
inflated to mansion-house pretension. Stiff-backed, two-storey
N façade with eaves cornice and blocking course. Steps span a
sunk area to reach the pilastered doorpiece. Three storeys at
rear with rusticated ashlar basement. A square central hall at
the entrance level with pilastered corners from which spring
four arches with panelled soffits. Cantilevered stone stair with
rounded end to s.

ARNPRIOR PRIMARY SCHOOL. Dated 1875. Tripartite window
to gabled classroom with integral schoolmaster's house. Both in
tooled red sandstone. Reconstructed and extended E, *c.* 1960.

POST OFFICE. C18. Roughcast cottage row built on rubble-
bouldered base. Rolled skewputts.

ARNGIBBON, 1.4km. SW. Dated 1863. Baronial villa with a battlemented NE entrance tower and moulded crowstep gables. Over
the door an armorial panel and the motto IT'S GOOD TO BE
LOUN.

GARDEN HOUSE. *See* p. 513.


# ARNTAMIE                                        S
### 1.8km. W of Port of Menteith

By *H. E. Clifford, c.*1895. A well-set hillside house with splendid views
s to the Lake of Menteith. White roughcast walls with painted
dressings. Rounds at the SW and SE corners capped by slated cone
roofs and a pyramid-roofed square tower over the entrance at the
centre of the s front. This principal façade, thus contrived to be
symmetrical in mass though not in detail, suggests the incorporation of earlier domestic structures. LODGE at drive entry dated
1902.


# ASHFIELD                                        S
### 2.5km. N of Dunblane

An industrial hamlet on the Allan Water. Founded in the 1880s as
a model village to serve a new bleachworks. It survived as a working community until 1975, but is now wholly residential.

At the N entry to the village, three, three-in-a-row, three-bay
dwellings form a single-storey U-plan group. All are rubble-built
with segmental lintels to doors and windows. So, too, is THE
SQUARE, a symmetrical two-storey row with four delightfully
curving forestairs giving access to upper flats. THE STEADING
forms an L-plan, each entrance given an ashlar surround with a
steep pediment. At the S end are THE COTTAGES, a softer and
more rural single-storey row with pointed-arched entrances
under gablets.

## ASHFIELD HOUSE

3.2km. SW of Gartocharn

WD  *4080*

Built *c.* 1844. A small but neat three-bay classical house, piend-
roofed with single-storey pavilion wings. Pilastered and pedimented doorpiece. WALLED GARDEN.

## AUCHENBOWIE HOUSE

3.2km. S of Bannockburn

S  *7080*

An austerely upright Scottish house, three-storeys-and-attic high,
built to an L-plan, *c.* 1666, then altered to assimilate enlargement
on the W, 1768. Restored 1967.

The walls, which rise off a tabled plinth, are harled cream, with
margins, dormers and gable crowstepping of dressed sandstone.
An octagonal four-storey tower, pyramidal-roofed, is engaged in
the SE re-entrant of the C17 L-plan; at its base, the original
entrance, framed by a bolection-moulded surround. Above the
door is an inset panel, reputedly found during re-harling, 1952,
when its then illegible inscription was confusingly recut with
the date 1506. To the l., the two-bay S wing is dormered above
the eaves; to the r., the E wing, also two bays wide, has no
dormers, the windows to the second floor having been raised in
height when the attic was eliminated in the C18. These later
changes were more radical on the W side of the house where a
narrow strip of accommodation, matching the height and character of the C17 work, was added. Contrived to respond to a
new approach from this direction, a re-located entrance was
placed a short distance S of the existing N gable. Like its predecessor, it is housed at the foot of an octagonal four-storey tower,
here battlemented but again capped by a slated pyramidal roof.
This tower links S to a one-room, crowstep-gabled wing which
returns to abut the S gable of the old house. On the pediment of
the single attic eaves dormer on this return is the date 1768.

The provision of the W entrance resulted in the removal of
the turnpike from the old re-entrant tower and the creation of a
new geometric stair at the heart of the original L-plan. Along
the S side of the curving stair well a generous HALL dog-legs N to
the new entrance tower. N of the stair, in the NW angle of the C17
house, is a barrel-vaulted cellar and beyond it some two-storey

service accommodation added in the C19. The interiors remain substantially those created in the C18; most notable is the second-floor LIBRARY in the E wing, a tall room timber-panelled to cornice height below a coved ceiling.

An obelisk SUNDIAL, truncated above its polyhedron head, sits on a moulded base a short distance across the lawn from the old entrance tower. On opposite sides of the shaft base are two sets of marriage initials and the dates 1702 and 1919; both inscriptions are thought to be of C20 date. Marooned further E, sculptural events in a landscape of terraced lawns and topiary, are two tall round GATEPIERS with large ball finials.

## AUCHENGILLAN

*5080*                                                              WD

Hamlet on the A809.

LOW AUCHENGILLAN. Dated 1750 and 1846. A long three-bay farmhouse. Harled two-storey core and lower wings. Central NE doorpiece with block pediment.

TOWNHEAD OF AUCHENGILLAN. A cluster of cottages; the oldest early C19. The ALLANDER CHALET, by *Drew Samuel*, 1970, is a chunky block containing hall and dormitory accommodation, which serves the Outdoor Centre. White harl below, the upper floor of log construction with a split monopitch roof. Inset balconies in the gables; SW wall glazed to hall.

## AUCHLYNE

*5020*                                                               S

Chapel and house in Glen Dochart.

CHAPEL (Caibeal na Fairge). Date unknown. Roofless oblong preserving N door and two small S windows.

AUCHLYNE. Built *c.* 1765. Austere three-storey, three-bay house; centre S bay projects under a pediment carrying armorial insignia. Turnpike at N rear. Bow projections N, W and E. Rubble-built WALLED GARDEN, C18, with octagonal shed.

DOCHART BRIDGE. 1.5 km SW. Early C19. Rubble structure of three wide segmental-arch spans on cutwater piers with stepped copings. Concrete strengthening to all bases

## AUCHMAR

*4090*                                                               S

1km. NNW of Milton of Buchanan

By *Stewart & Paterson*, 1932. Built for the Duke of Montrose when Buchanan Castle (q.v.) was abandoned. Cream roughcast walls under a busy roofscape of bellcast piends, gables and chimneystacks. Roman Doric NW porch in sandstone. Well windowed to the SW for the view of Loch Lomond and to the SE where the garden terraces steeply to Burn of Mar.

## AUCHMORE HOUSE *see* KILLIN

### AVONBRIDGE

F 9070

Village of late C19 and C20 housing.

AVONBRIDGE CONGREGATIONAL CHURCH, Main Road. Dated 1860. Broad rubble-built box, with roundheaded windows in the sides. At the front (w) gable, a roundheaded door flanked by cusped and pointed windows; Venetian window over the door. Bellcote with a steep pyramidal roof.

AVONBRIDGE PARISH CHURCH, Falkirk Road. Originally Avonbridge United Presbyterian Church. Cheap Gothic rectangle, by *A. & W. Black*, 1889–90. Large wheel window and a bellcote at the front (w) gable.

BRIDGE, Falkirk Road. Single segmental arch over the Avon, built in 1886 and widened to the E in C20 utilitarian fashion. On the w side, a stone carved with a coat of arms, the initials IA, and the dates 1640 (for the bridge's predecessor) and 1886.

### AVONDALE HOUSE

F 9070

1.8km. NE of Polmont

Enjoyable double-pile mansion house, the front block light-hearted Tudor Gothic of the early C19, the rear block C18.

The main elevation is the early C19 rendered s front, a long two-storey battlemented spread. The centrepiece is a crowstepped gable grasped by pinnacled diagonal buttresses. Pointed door under a tall pointed window, both hoodmoulded. Each side, a long one-bay recessed link to broad ends. At the w end, pinnacles standing on the corners of the battlement; the E end is framed by pinnacled octagonal buttresses, their fronts decorated with dummy gunloops. Pointed lights in the rectangular window openings. Battlemented bows at the gables.

The rear block, its front covered by the early C19 block, is stodgy piend-roofed early Georgian but with diagonally set chimneys of the early C19. Off-centre bow-ended back wing. A pointed dummy window in the w gable.

To the w, an early C19 castellated courtyard STEADING. Towers at the corners and over the E and w entrances, the E of these containing flightholes for a doocot. Pointed ground-floor openings in the external walls; circular openings under the wall-head battlement. At the entrance to the w drive, early C19 urn-topped classical GATEPIERS.

On a hill to the s of the house, an early C19 FOLLY. It is a battlemented square, with a round tower at each corner.

Just the church and inn of a rural parish.

BALDERNOCK PARISH CHURCH. Built and perhaps designed
by *John McMurrich*, wright in Paisley, 1795. Generally straightforward oblong kirk, built of squared rubble, with forestairs to
the gables' gallery doors. All the openings are rectangular except
the two tall roundheaded s windows with projecting keystones.
They flank a slightly advanced and pedimented centrepiece
containing the (built-up) minister's door. Above the pediment,
a pedestal of two stages, the upper with concave sides, supporting a spireleted birdcage bellcote. Below the pediment, a panel
inscribed: 'DEO OPTIMO MAXIMO! P[ATRI].F[ILIO].S[PIRI-
TUI].Q[UE].S[ANCTO]/MDCCXCV' ['To God the good and
great! To the Father, the Son and the Holy Spirit. 1795']. On
the N side of the church, a vestry addition.

Inside, simple Victorian PEWS. The ceiling rose also looks
C19. – Semi-octagonal GALLERY of 1795, panelled front with
fluted frieze and mutuled cornice; supported on wooden Doric
columns. – Also beneath the bow-fronted PULPIT, its back with
Ionic pilasters supporting a mutuled cornice.

At the SE entrance to the churchyard, an octagonal WATCH-
HOUSE designed by *Robert Baird*, wright in Milngavie, 1828
(the date on the door lintel).

BOGHALL, 0.7km. SSE. Scots Arts and Crafts villa designed in
1907 by *T. A. Millar* of *Gardner & Millar* for his own occupation.
The house is composed of three blocks, all built of crazy-paved
masonry, the roofs slated. Crowstep-gabled s block of two storeys
and an attic. Symmetrical three-bay s front, the re-used door
lintel inscribed '1796 J. H.' said to have come from the house's
predecessor which stood further E. Canted NW corner corbelled
to the square at the first floor. Catslide-roofed dormers. At r.
angles to this, the double-pile central block, its pitch-roofed w
half set back from the s block's w gable. w elevation of six bays
at the first floor, the windows grouped 3/3, but the ground floor
is asymmetrical with one rectangular bay window and one
mullioned four-light window. The E half, projecting E of the s
block, is flat-roofed and battlemented. Main entrance to the
house in the s gable, rounded at the ground floor but jettied out
to the square above. In the E elevation, a large mullioned and
transomed stair window. The house's third component is a low
service block at the N end.

Contemporary LODGE in the same manner, with crowstepped
gables and a conical-roofed round tower containing the entrance.

THE KIRKHOUSE, immediately w of the churchyard. Originally
an inn. Early C19, single-storey and attic, built of white painted
rubble. Roman Doric columned and pedimented doorpiece.
Piend-roofed offices at the back.

# BALFRON
3.5km. NE of Killearn

Village, transformed in 1790 by the construction of the five-storey Ballindalloch Cotton Mill on the N bank of the Endrich Water. By the beginning of the C19, 400 workers were employed, a population of cotton spinners and hand-loom weavers housed in gable-to-gable cottages lining the village's main street from the ancient Clachan down to the Mill. By mid century the industry was in recession and in 1898 the Mill was finally demolished. Most of the old houses have also gone, replaced by C20 local authority redevelopment.

PARISH CHURCH, Clachan. By *John Herbertson*, 1832. A red sandstone rubble structure which, though 'commodious enough', was constructed with the expressed intention 'that every possible expense ... should be avoided'*. By 1882 transepts and tower had been added by *Stewart & Wilson*. These transepts and the W end are gabled; E end hipped. The square tower, capped by a slated pyramid, fills the centre of the S front in the transept re-entrant. Three stages tall, the belfry stage, altered 1889, recessed slightly between gabled corner buttresses below a plain parapet with angled gargoyles. A door at the W end of the S front leads to the vestibule. The body of the church has a flat plaster ceiling with cornice, but behind the transept arches (pointed-arched openings on double stub-column corbels) are timber roofs with a single arch-braced truss. W gallery carried on two cast iron pillars cased as timber columns. Gallery front and E wall panelled with a cusp-arch motif. – Central half-octagon PULPIT canopied by a Gothic gable on thin timber columns. – Heavy onyx FONT carved with shield-bearing angels, *c.* 1909. – ORGAN, S transept, by *Rushworth & Dreaper*, Liverpool, 1951. – Various TABLETS. – Unremarkable STAINED GLASS to triple lancets in transepts: N, the Good Shepherd between a sower and harvester, to the Rev. Alexander Slessor †1904; S, Dorcas flanked l. by Faith and Hope and r. Charity, to his wife †1914.

In the GRAVEYARD, numerous lying SLABS from the C18 and at least one with a late C17 date; few are legible. – A number of early C19 red sandstone HEADSTONES are of interest. Mantled stone to Corporal Walter Buchanan 'who fell in the memorable battle of Waterloo on the 18 June, 1815'. – Aedicule formed by Roman Doric shafts carrying a winged cherub pediment below which two snakes coil symmetrically in heavy relief; to Catherine Maxwell †1827. – Another with a round sunburst pediment on fluted pilasters to Grissel McLew †1839. – Dumpy milestone-like tomb erected by the Balfron Abstinence Society in memory of their president, John McGilchrist †1842. – Later memorials include a plain neo-Greek HEADSTONE, carved by *J. & G. Mossman* to a design by *Alexander 'Greek' Thomson*, to Rev. James Thomson †1864, and the grave of Rev. Alexander Slessor †1904, a much patterned and bossed Celtic CROSS.

* *The New Statistical Account of Scotland*, viii (1845), 297.

Former HOLM SECESSION CHURCH, Edinbellie, 3km. E. Built
1739–40. More farm building than church, it seems, and so it
has served since the mid C19. Gabled oblong of pink and grey
sandstone rubble, its originally symmetrical arrangement of
doors and windows just discernible. Cavetto eaves course.

Former HOLM UNITED PRESBYTERIAN CHURCH, 3.5km. ESE.
Built 1860–1 for a congregation descended from the Anti-
Burgher Holm kirk (*see* above). Dated 1861. Gabled hall lit by
chamfered lancets. Two-storey manse, with ground-floor canted
bays l. and r. of central door, built across W gable of church.
The latter's bare interior preserves the original floor, two fireplaces, two pointed-arched W doors (one false) and, flanked by
stairs with scrolled balustrading, a half-round central PULPIT,
the detailing of which suggests the hand of *Alexander 'Greek'
Thomson*. Thomson, who was born in the village, produced an
unexecuted 'design for a small church and manse at Balfron'*
which, though more sophisticated and characteristic, shares the
same connection between manse stair and pulpit; this may be as
close as he came to its realization.

ST ANTHONY (R.C.), Dunmore Street. 1867–9. Small four-bay
chapel in tooled red sandstone. Skew-gable front with pointed-
arched door and circular window over, both hooded.

Former SOUTH CHURCH, Spinner's Street. 1881. Five buttressed
bays with cusped lancets. Thinly traceried, pointed-arched W
window over cusp-arched entrance doorway. Converted to
residential use, 1994.

BALFRON HIGH SCHOOL. On Cotton Street, the School Board
school, late C19; a symmetrical classroom block with central
gable and tripartite windows with quasi-pilaster mullions. Hip-
roofed, roughcast extensions, 1929. New buildings were erected
on Roman Road in 1959–62, but these were demolished following construction of an entirely new Balfron High School on the
opposite side of the road in 2000–01. Designed by *Boswell,
Mitchell & Johnston* for Stirling Council.

BRIDGE, crossing the Endrick Water below Holm U.P. Church.
By *Walter Paul*, engineer; dated 1865. Two segmental arches in
rough-faced red sandstone. Central rounded cutwater pier.

FIELD BRIDGE (a contraction of Endrickfield Bridge), 1.3km.
SSW. Late C18 (?). Two wide segmental arches in coursed and
tooled red sandstone spanning the Endrick Water. Hoodmoulding over voussoirs. Central cutwater pier splayed on
top.

WAR MEMORIAL AND MCCANDLISH FOUNTAIN, Clachan.
High, circular cairn on triple-stepped base; erected *c.* 1920.
Dressed sandstone surround to painted panels recording the
dead. – Nearby, a public FOUNTAIN, pink granite bowl on grey
granite pedestal, still preserves the hooks for its drinking cups; a
memorial to the local doctor William McCandlish †1892.

---

*Andrew MacMillan, 'Frontiers of the West – Glasgow and Chicago', in *'Greek'
Thomson*, ed. Gavin Stamp and Sam McKinstry (1994), 211.

DESCRIPTION

CLACHAN is the oldest part of the village, a hilltop chicane where several narrow roads knot together immediately W of the Parish Church (*see* above). Between road and kirkyard is a small public space: room for the Clachan Oak, McCandlish Fountain and War Memorial (*see* above). ORCHARDLANDS, an unpretentious late C18 dwelling with a tall stair window at the centre of its three-bay front, closes the S side. Across the road, CLACHAN HOUSE, symmetrical and gabled like its neighbour, is smarter: angle pilasters, a good eaves cornice and a central half-octagon bay with an architraved door above the cornice of which is a scrolled panel bearing the dates 1766.1922. A white wall undulates W over a round-arched entry to the garden.

From the Clachan the road dips SW through a wooded bend before opening S into BUCHANAN STREET. The impact of Campsie Fells is immediate, filling the downhill view S and framed by well-scaled local authority housing which, in the 1950s and 60s, superseded the village's coherent early C19 townscape. Designed by *Stirling County Council*, this comprehensive transformation tries to maintain a certain Scottish quality and, though it lacks the austere aesthetic of its predecessors, it succeeds. Variegated roughcast, moulded stone dressings, swept dormers, the occasional crowstepped gable: DUNKELD COURT, 1965, is typical. Shops, Library, Post Office and Police Station all find accommodation. Some traces of the past survive (HELENSLEA, 1904, has some good Gothic railings) but it is only at the lower S end of the street that the original weavers' dwellings remain. LAVEROCK HOUSE has gabled eaves dormers to the upper floor as has No. 11; both are roughcast. Nos. 15–19 is a full two storeys; it was once the Ballindalloch Hotel but has lost its iron-crested porch. These, and a few others, are built hard to the pavement, unlike their C20 neighbours uphill. Further S on the bend of Printers Row is ENDRICK COTTAGE, birthplace of Alexander 'Greek' Thomson.

In DUNMORE STREET, past the ugly corner of the MCLINTOCK HALL, *c.* 1930, inset with curious fasces tablets, some older cottages survive. No. 46, however, is bungalow-like; two battlemented canted bays flanking a hefty doorpiece of Roman Doric half-columns and pediment. MANSEFIELD, the former U.P. (later Old South) manse, 1856–8, by *Alexander 'Greek' Thomson*, is much more sophisticated, though with its five-light timber-framed bay at first floor and ill-at-ease blocky porch, a somewhat provincial variant of the architect's Italianate villa theme. Up Banker's Brae is THE PIRN INN, in part an early C19 three-bay rubble house, combined with the former British Linen Bank, *c.* 1860, three-bay too but taller with a fine eaves cornice.

BALLINDALLOCH, 1.2km. W. A charming one-and-a-half storey, crowstep-gabled, three-bay house reconstituted from fragments of its predecessor by naval architect *Alexander Stephen*, 1978–9. Two centuries earlier Old Ballindalloch had been built by mill owner Robert Dunmore. In 1868–9 this first dwelling was replaced by a two-storey-and-attic, mildly Scots mansion designed by *David Thomson*, of which elements have been creatively conscripted to architectural service in the present more modest house. Of three gabled dormers on the S front only one is in its original position (part of the old services wing). Bold roll-moulded details reincorporated at window and door jambs.

A delightful garden to the S is romantically enhanced by the retention of ruinous bay-windowed walling from the C19 mansion. C17 obelisk SUNDIAL.

BALLINDALLOCH LODGE, 0.7km. SW, immediately N of Field Bridge. By *Launcelot H. Ross*. Dated 1924 over pedimented door. Crowstep gables and pedimented eaves dormers: suburban sub-Baronial in cream roughcast with red sandstone dressings.

MOTTE, Woodend, 1km. SE of Clachan. Readily defensible natural mound, *c.* 3m. high, flattened on top to form an oval platform 40m. by 34m.

BALLIKINRAIN CASTLE. *See* p. 193.

## BALFUNNING HOUSE     s
1.1km. w of Balfron

By *James Thomson* of *John Baird & James Thomson*, 1883–7. Castellated Baronial in rough-faced snecked red sandstone. A battlemented ashlar parapet carried on two corbel courses surmounts the S and W façades and the round SW tower. Roll-moulded windows, crowstepped gables W and E and, at the centre of the S front, a battlemented block porch with stop-chamfered corners. Inside is a splendidly spacious and symmetrically arranged STAIR-HALL. A central stair flight returns l. and r. to a deep U-plan gallery at first floor. Above, over a consoled cornice, is a plaster barrel vault, panelled and roof-lit and overlooked from a balustraded balcony at attic level which is reached by a stair at the S end of the first-floor gallery. Panelled hall doors have a cornice both castellated and dentillated. In the DRAWING ROOM and ANTE-ROOM, ground floor W, a delicate acanthus leaf cornice, central rose and a plaster panelled ceiling patterned with segmental curves. In the DINING ROOM, ground floor E, the plaster ceiling is divided by beams and the cornice carried on consoles. Arch-braced trusses and timber-lined ceiling in the BILLIARD ROOM which is incorporated into the lower service wing N.

Between the house and the A811 are the STABLES, a small U-plan block in matching style. Symmetrical S front with a central crowstep gable and segmental-arched pend leading to a cobbled court. Marriage stone lintel bears the inscription AB.1723.HC. At the roadway, the Lorimeresque LODGE, *c.* 1905, harled with red sandstone dressings; a captivating essay in geometrical whimsy. The plan is square, the roof pyramidal, each elevation has a single gabled eaves dormer and the exposed roadside corner a conically capped round tower.

# BALLIKINRAIN CASTLE          S *5080*

2.1km. SE of Balfron

In its original form the biggest and possibly the best of all the Baronial Revival country houses by *David Bryce*. Built 1864–70 for Archibald Orr Ewing whose vast dyeing and printing interests in the Vale of Leven had enabled him to purchase the lands of Old Ballikinrain (*see* below) in 1862. For exactly half a century the estate remained in the family's hands but in 1913, already stripped of furnishings and abandoned, the house was gutted by fire. Bought by Sir Charles Cayzer, it was later restored in somewhat reduced form by *C. H. Greig*. In 1967 it was purchased by the Church of Scotland and has since served as an approved school for boys.

Ballikinrain Castle. Watercolour perspective by David Bryce, 1865.

Bryce's methods are at once apparent in the WEST LODGE, a twin-gabled composition of subtly infracted symmetry enunciated through a vocabulary of Baronial elements which include crowsteps, corbelled corners and a small but forceful stair tower with fish-scale-slated, conical roof. Linked s is a battlemented wall with segmental-arched GATEWAY, not quite symmetrical. Syntax and semantic intent are determinedly Scottish, a stylistic programme even more declamatory over a kilometre up the drive when the castle itself is revealed. Dominating the three-storeyed N front is a cylindrical Castle Fraser-derived entrance tower embedded just off centre of the house's oblong plan. A buttressed *porte cochère* with shouldered-arched openings W and E projects from it into the forecourt. High mullioned and transomed windows light the principal apartments at first-floor level on the N, W and S façades. Eaves dormers with steep, heavily scrolled pediments punctuate the skyline on the N and W. Bartizans mark the corners. But it is along the S elevation that the distinctive character of Baronial composition becomes most apparent: a succession of vertical groupings, each stack of superimposed windows more or less symmetrical whether axially tied under a crowstep gable or tiered through the three-dimensional modelling of a canted bay or cylindrical stair tower and all packed together in wholly asymmetrical aggregation. Stretching W is a complex mesh of service courts and offices entered from the N through a battlemented pointed-arched portal defined by a gargantuan cable moulding knotted below impost level. Linked W is the STABLES block, town-hall Baronial, reaching three storeys, boldly accented by a tall clock tower spiked with bartizan cones.

Big as it is, Ballikinrain was reduced by Greig's rebuilding. The great N tower is now two storeys lower than it was as Bryce built it, though its balustraded parapet and copper, ogee-domed tourelle have been re-used. The W end of the building has been curtailed and a vast conservatory at the SW corner has gone. The house has also lost its lavish Jacobean-Baronial interiors, though these have been in part replaced by panelling, door-casings and a staircase brought from Ralston House, Paisley, which *J. J. Stevenson* had refurbished in 1864.

Long drives approach the house through the wooded estate from the W and E. Each crosses the valley of a stream flowing N to the Endrick Water. The WEST BRIDGE is a single pointed-arched span set between cutwater piers which rise into half-octagon inshots from the parapets. The EAST BRIDGE is similar in design but longer and much higher. Five spectacularly tall pointed arches span a deep gorge, their cutwater piers, too, transformed above into recesses off the parapets. Both structures are built in a mixture of ashlar and rough-faced sandstone. Near the road, the high shaped boundary walls of the WALLED GARDEN have recently been integrated into a late C20 housing development.

OLD BALLIKINRAIN, 0.8km. N. C18, with part perhaps C17. Five-bay, two-storey gabled house. SE front in droved ashlar with rusticated quoins, dressed margins and a central door with lugged, double-roll-and-hollow architraves, pulvinated frieze and cornice. Single-storey ranges project l. and r. to form an open U-plan court. A short NW projection from the centre of the house connects with a second two-storey block, late 1780s, parallel to the first. The centre of its NW façade is pedimented on Ionic pilasters but is unsatisfactorily filled by two bays of bipartite windows. SW and NE gables are shaped as half-octagon bays.

The OFFICES lie N; single-storey outbuildings gabled with scroll skewputts.

# BALLOCH    WD

A village of cafés, car parks and a castle at the outflow of the River Leven from Loch Lomond. Since 1850, when it became the terminus of the North British and Forth & Clyde Railway, it has been committed to tourism. Small craft throng the moorings N and S of Balloch Bridge. Cruises leave for the Loch.

CHURCHES

ALEXANDRIA PARISH CHURCH, Lomond Road. By *T. J. Beveridge*. Built 1963–4 as part of the National Church Extension programme. Church, hall and campanile tower in white dry-dash render, all with shallow-pitched roofs. Ladder-pattern glazing in the E gable and on the N and S sides of the chancel. Carved MEMORIAL STONE at the base of the tower records the date of building. Rough-faced grey granite WAR MEMORIAL, a Celtic cross on a cairn-like base, badly re-sited close to the S wall.

ST KESSOG (R.C.), Balloch Road. By *Gillespie, Kidd & Coia*, 1957–8. White-rendered and respectably plain, but little more. Only the figure of the archer saint, hanging below a canopied bell on the S gable, gives the religious game away. The bell originally hung in the United Turkey Red Printworks, Alexandria. Central S porch with segmental roof and stone flanks. The interior, eleven bays long lit by tall slot windows, is enriched by a timber-lined segmental-vaulted ceiling. Red quarry tile floor with travertine insets. Sanctuary refurbished, 1997. Original black altar-rail marble re-used as sanctuary steps. Trapezoidal block ALTAR, tapering FONT and LECTERN clad in flecked fawn marble; each incorporates a white marble frieze of vines, grapes and birds taken from the original altar. Raised on the N wall is the sculpted figure of Christ, by *Andrew Ramsay*, 1997. Also by Ramsay, STATIONS OF THE CROSS; small painted clay images mounted on railway sleepers in a garden behind the church.

PUBLIC BUILDINGS

BALLOCH BRIDGE, Balloch Road. Opened 1887; a replacement for the suspension bridge of 1841. By engineers *Hanna, Donald & Wilson* of Paisley. Five-span steel girder crossing of the Leven. Three central spans are lattice girders, the outer two plated girders; each rests on cylindrical sandstone piers which become octagonal above the carriageway level. Two remaining lamp standards.

BALLOCH LIBRARY, Carrochan Road. 1974. Simple planar relationships of glass, buff facing brick and black fascias. A single monopitch roof-light.

DUNCAN MILLS MEMORIAL SLIPWAY, beside Balloch Pier. By architects *Wren Rutherford*, 1999–2000. White and shipshape at the water's edge. Rectangular in plan, the building is aligned in parallel with the jetties and pier beyond. N and S glazed gables are of different height so that the raking ridge results in curving slated slopes. This almost hull-like inversion finds nautical echo in the balcony prow jutting N out towards the Loch. Inside, a mezzanine gallery runs longitudinally.

LOMOND BRIDGE, Lomond Road. By engineers *Blyth & Blyth*, 1933–4. Three spans on segmental-arched plated steel girders with lattice cross-bracing. Red sandstone abutments, deep piers with segmental-arched openings and advanced prow-like cutwaters. Cast iron lamp standards.

LOMOND SHORES, at Drumkinnon Bay. 1998–2002. An architecture of national ambition and achievement by *Page & Park*;
literally and metaphorically a *tour de force*. Instinct with strategic
intention, this remarkable development has been created as a
gateway to the lacustrine beauties of Loch Lomond National
Park. While the Loch itself more than justifies such investment,
economic spin-offs are envisaged as much for regional regeneration back down the Vale of Leven as for Scotland's wider tourist
industry to the N. But whatever fortune the future unfolds,
perhaps no other building in Scotland has more memorably
marked the millennial moment.

The design conception is expansive, effectively reshaping the
S end of the Loch. W of Balloch Pier an area of 100 acres,
including a brownfield site raked by sand and gravel workings,
has been wonderfully transformed by landscape architects *Ian
White Associates*. In place of some ill-defined stretches of loch-
edge water, a new lagoon has been formed. A thick curtain of
trees wraps itself around the water from Drumkinnon Wood on
the W through lavish new woodland planted back from the shore
on the S. This broad bank of greenery, coupled with a series of
landscaped mounds, helps to screen the large areas of car- and
coach-parking necessarily provided for the 1,200 or so tourists
stopping *en route* to the Highlands and Islands. At the water's
edge, looking out across the lagoon to the Loch and mountains
beyond, are the three buildings which, sequentially, shape the
visitor's experience.

At the end of a long timber screen wall, the ORIENTATION
BUILDING, by *Bennetts Associates*, nestles against the dense
edge of Drumkinnon Wood. It is low, horizontal and rigorously
rectilineal, a Miesian box of glass walls enclosing goalpost
frames of black steel. Marred only at the S corner by an out-
of-scale excrescence from prismatic simplicity, the otherwise
uncompromised geometry works well against the natural background of trees. A balcony cantilevers NE over the lagoon shore
giving views E to the tall Visitor Centre (*see* below) and across
the water to the new Slipway (*see* above) and the *Maid of the Loch*
steamer tied up at Balloch Pier. Lured by all of these attractions,
but tempted in particular by the massive impact and intriguingly
allusive mystery of the first, the visitor now follows a curving
promenade held out on concrete brackets over the rock-strewn
shore. An esplanade wall of RETAIL ACCOMMODATION (by
*Percy Johnson-Marshall & Partners* but not yet under construction in spring 2001) marches with this walkway.

Halfway along, the gentle concave curve of the shoreline
reverses to become the convex edge of a widening forecourt
102  approach to *Page & Park*'s VISITOR CENTRE, a stunning building of rare architectural presence, bold enough to confront
nature with austerity of form and material. This in itself is
Scottish; but there is more that is eloquently expressive of a
national tradition revitalized to address the cultural exigencies
of the present. This is an immense broch built to a height of 26m.

– an architecture drawn from indigenous Iron Age precedent – enfolded by a towering cylinder of black whin rubble. Emerging unwrapped from this embrace is a second, inner drum, its implicit vulnerability toughened by white-harled solidity. This, too, has its provenance as, for example, in the gatehouse gables and turret that rise tentatively behind the great masonry of Dunstaffnage Castle (Argyll and Bute). Between the two drums, a slow stair-case ramp fills the circumferential gap. As the stair descends, so too does the dark immuring hug of whinstone, falling from its parapeted summit under a helical helter-skelter of glazing and stepping roof. So this is broch and castle too, but more than these – a tower to tourism, a cultural power-station perhaps. For there is no pastiche here, and there is no sentimental nostalgia either; the building bursts with contemporary architectural energy. It knows both its place in geography and its moment in history.

On the w side, a two-storey rectangular void, lugged with balconies under a long lintel at the upper level, opens through the black rubble. Curved forms bend back into the depth between outer and inner drums, with a hint of Le Corbusier. To the l., entrance doors open into the ring of space trapped between the drums. A short ramp leads to a landing from which the visitor turns r. into a lofty Public Hall filling half the circular plan of the building and rising through four floors. From the n, light floods into this inner space through a 16m.-high wall of glass engulfing the interior with the prospect of loch, hills and sky. At the centre of the Hall is an astonishing structure, an inverted six-pronged concrete talon emerging tree-like from a sculptural bole rooted into the floor. From its base, column branches splay symmetrically n and s to support accommodation above, and a high-level triangulated network of tubular steel braces for the great curtain of glass on the n. A retail shop is located on the w side of the Hall with a café opposite on the e. Symmetrically arranged fire stairs and toilets fill the remainder of these flank-ing segments of the plan. On the s side, placed rather uncom-fortably close to the base of the concrete tree, a leaning wall of Douglas fir divides the Hall from a large 'black box' ante space entered symmetrically from w and e. Beyond, located in the outer ring space, stairs rise to the Film Theatre above. This upper volume, entered centrally at pit level below a 17m.-high screen, is dramatically tiered to the n to accommodate an audience of 350.

From the rear of the Theatre visitors may proceed to the covered Viewing Gallery located over the Public Hall. From here, 18m. above water level, and from the open roof terrace at a higher level still, the views n are panoramic. Thrilled by legend and landscape, the visitor then leaves the Gallery at its w end to descend from the heights by the glazed stepped ramp. This falls in a slow circumferential route around the building, held between the inner and outer drums, finally arriving close to the café at the ne corner of the Public Hall.

## DESCRIPTION

BALLOCH ROAD busies itself with the passing tourists, so much
so that the early dignity of the BALLOCH HOTEL, from *c.* 1820,
has been compromised by agglutinative addition. A rough row
of red sandstone flats survives at CHARLES TERRACE, Dalvait
Road; a legacy from the Vale's industrial days. On DRYMEN
ROAD, leafy suburbia; ROSELEA, 1888, distinguished by decorative bargeboards, WARWICK HOUSE and THE COTTAGE,
both *c.* 1930, by a mansard roof swept over dormers and canted
bays. At the S end of Old Luss Road, behind quadrant walls
with Gothic gatepiers, is TULLICHEWAN EAST LODGE, early
C19, by *Robert Lugar* (*see* Tullichewan Castle). Now a private
dwelling, its ironwork verandah, curved below the eaves of a
bow-ended wing, retains real Regency charm.

W along the bank of the Leven, dreaming among riparian trees,
two Arts and Crafts houses. TULLICHEWAN HOTEL, *c.* 1900, by
Balloch Bridge (*see* Public Buildings, above), is awash with half-
timbered tile-hung gables. But the contemporary FISHERWOOD
HOUSE, down-river beside the Lomond Bridge (*see* Public Buildings, above), is even more picturesquely English, a charm-laden
pot-pourri of gables, canted bays and curve-topped buttresses
rendered in red tiles, red brick, red sandstone and roughcast. A
low ogee tower emerges at the SE. Carved below the shell tympanum of the W door pediment are the words FAR . FROM .
COURT . FAR . FROM . CARE. On the S wall, a sundial. These
two houses, evidently by the same architect (still unknown), are
precious surprises, recalling an Edwardian residential lifestyle
more representative of the Home Counties than the edge of the
Highland Line.

Off the Stirling Road on the N edge of the village is NETHER
HALDANE, an undistinguished late C19 house in red sandstone,
tired, a little dreary, but unexpectedly distinguished by a small
Studio wing added on the W gable by *Christopher Platt*, 1999–
2000. Here the quality of the new embarrasses the old. Tiny,
cunningly devised galleries overlook a Dining Room whose
glazed walls slide open to the garden on the SW corner.

WOODBANK HOUSE, off Old Luss Road at the N end of the
village. A well-bred mansion house burnt out by fire, 1996, and
sullied by neglect. An earlier house on the site, known as
Stuckrodger, seems to have been built in the late C17 but the
surviving shell is a century or so later. Facing E is a five-bay
Classical front of two storeys set over a basement, stuccoed, with
raised ashlar margins and buckle quoins; this is the Woodbank
built by the Glasgow merchant Charles Scott of Dalquhurn,
*c.* 1774–5. A pediment, bracketed at the ends and middle on
small consoles, surmounts the three central bays. Blind oculus
in the tympanum. Urns at the eaves and apex. Central first-floor
window with a lugged surround and fluted keystone. Below this,
a pedimented doorway in a Gibbsian frame to which rises a broad
stair with wrought iron handrails. The house is roofless, partially
blocked up and dangerous. A S-facing wing, added *c.* 1885,

extends W. This, too, is a symmetrical five-bay façade of two
principal storeys, but, with a bay-windowed pedimented centre
rising to three storeys between flanking dormers, scarcely deferential enough. – Timber GAZEBO, octagonal in plan, with a
finialled pagoda roof of terracotta tiles, broken by gablets at
alternate eaves.

## BALLOCH CASTLE
1km. N

A picturesque effusion of mock medievalism of 1808–9 overlooking the S end of Loch Lomond. As the centrepiece of a landscaped
estate which became a country park in 1981, the castle is accessible to the public. Commissioned by John Buchanan of Ardoch
from London architect *Robert Lugar* who published his design as
'Balloch Abbey'. With Tullichewan and Boturich (qq.v.), both also
realized by Lugar in Dunbartonshire, Balloch proved influential in
establishing a new Castellated Gothic fashion whose romantic and
seemingly arbitrary asymmetries broke free from the still-Classical
order of the Adam Castle style. As if to validate familial and architectural lineage, stone was quarried from the ruinous C13 Balloch
Castle, stronghold of the Earls of Lennox until they moved to the
insular safety of Inchmurrin Castle (q.v.) towards the end of the
C14. The site of this earlier fortress, still barely perceptible in the
landscape, lies closer to the loch shore some 400m. SSW.

Lugar's mansion is constructed in diagonally droved grey ashlar,
now weathered and badly patched in places. The entrance façade,
which looks E, swings in a gentle concave curve of battlemented
wall diminishing in height to the N where the offices are absorbed
into the composition. The higher part of this wall defers to
symmetry, the castellated three-bay front of the two-storey house
being raised and stepped at the centre between bartizans.
Windows are lintelled with lugged hoodmouldings. A hefty
basket-arched porch, buttressed by square piers broached to
domed octagonal shafts above its battlements, advances axially.
An octagonal tower marking the SE corner is reflected by a
round tower to the r. Both are battlemented; both have pointed-
arched openings and blind gun loops. A lower battlemented wall
continues r. to another round tower, machicolated, castellated
and capped by an ogee-domed open-arched bellcote. Beyond
this the wall height drops again, accented at the NE corner by a
domed bartizan reminiscent of an C18 sentinel turret. The S
elevation is surprisingly planar: first, a three-bay section with a
tripartite window of three round arches at ground floor, then, at
the SW corner, a square tower of three storeys with superimposed
hooded windows. The W façade, which enjoys splendid views
down across a terraced lawn to the loch, is more varied in plan,
elevation and skyline. At the centre is an engaged octagonal
tower, machicolated and castellated, with two sets of tripled
lancets at second-floor level. Behind this, embedded in the plan,
a higher round tower rises to dominate the whole medieval conceit. The chamfered planes of a second tower further articulate

the W front before the wall drops to enclose the offices. Another domed bartizan perches on the NW corner.

An INTERPRETATION CENTRE, designed by *Page & Park* in 1986, occupies the principal public rooms. Original plaster-work includes cornices and friezes variously ornamented with vine motifs, Gothic tracery, paterae and fleurons. Three bays of ribbed plaster vaulting arch over the ENTRANCE HALL from clus-tered shafts. Gothic panelling to some doors. Marble fireplaces with Gothic ornament.

NORTH LODGE, *c.* 0.5km. E, also by *Lugar* (?), is Gothic too, with a four-centred arched entrance and hooded lintelled windows. A carved owl sits in a circular recess in the E gable. – On Drymen Road, the contemporary SOUTH LODGE in similar style. Octagonal ashlar GATEPIERS with blind arrow slits set between quadrant walls. – A WALLED GARDEN, square in plan with a depressed-arched gate in the E wall, lies 0.5km. S of the castle.

BOTURICH CASTLE. *See* p. 276.

CAMERON HOUSE. *See* p. 305.

4090                    BALMAHA                          S

A hamlet of white cottages on a boat-spattered bay on the E shore of Loch Lomond opposite Inchcailloch (q.v.). No evidence now of the so-called 'Liquor Works' where, from the early C19 until 1920, the pyroligneous acid needed for Turkey Red dyeing in the Vale of Leven was manufactured.

CASHEL FARM, 3.8km. NW. Early C19 (?). Three-bay, two-storey, gabled house with short, single-storey, piended wings.

MONTROSE HOUSE. Built 1891. Commissioned by the Duchess of Montrose as a holiday home for Glasgow children. A stolid villa in rough-faced red sandstone with gabled eaves dormers pushing through a steeply pitched roof.

OLD MANSE, above the narrow Pass of Balmaha which climbs abruptly N of the village. L-plan, white-harled house, 1910, with conically roofed, bowed wings flanking front door. Lower wing, also two-storey, has dormers. Part may date from the C17, for the manse originally served the church on Inchcailloch Island.

CASHEL, Strathcashell Point, 3.5km. NW. Despite its promontory location the site is unfortified. The drystone wall structure, a ruinous irregular oval some 28m. at its widest and standing little more than 1m. at its highest, may be 'a religious establish-ment of Dark Ages date'*. Rubble remains of an oblong cham-ber in the NE arc.

5020                  BALQUHIDDER                        S

Picturesque kirktoun hamlet at the E end of Loch Voil.

BALQUHIDDER CHURCH. 1853–5. The design appears to be by *J., J. H. and W. M. Hay*, with some involvement by *David Bryce*

* RCAHMS, *Stirlingshire*, i (1963), 168.

who had just completed Stronvar House (*see* below) for David
Carnegie. Carnegie's links with Sweden, where his wealth had
accumulated from brewing and sugar refining, led to the same
design being used at St Bridget, Gothenburg. A skew-gabled
Gothic oblong of five buttressed bays rising from a battered base
to a steep slated roof. Cusped lancets. The W gable rises to a tall
apex bellcote. S porch. Constructed in roughly coursed bull-faced
masonry. Arch-braced trusses on corbelstones carry purlins, spars
and diagonal boarding. E gallery, panelled with ogee arch and
trefoil motifs, beamed and borne on two timber columns and
reached by a straight-flight N stair. A timber partition, 1989,
screens the 'Friendship Room' under the gallery. – Pitch pine
hexagonal PULPIT on boldly moulded pedestal base; each face
has a cusped ogee arch with quatrefoils in the spandrels. – Resting
on an octagonal stone base of 1917 is a rough stone FONT, holed
for a lid. Of uncertain age but unquestionably ancient, it was
found in the walls of the C17 church (*see* below) during its dis-
mantling in the mid C19. – Placed against the N wall since 1917,
the ST ANGUS STONE, a tapered slab, C8 or C9, on which the
saint is carved holding the cup of salvation. – A cracked BELL
bears the date 1684 and the initials IM, probably for *John
Meikle*, ironfounder in Edinburgh.

OLD CHURCH. Roofless yew-shaded ruin; a romantic backdrop
for the grave of Rob Roy MacGregor (*see* below). Dated 1631
on the lintel of the blocked S door. Reconstructed 1774 when the
walls were raised and the ogee arches of the two S windows
were formed, but abandoned in 1855 for the new church (*see*
above). The E wall with its apex birdcage bellcote still stands
above the MacGregor grave and the vestigial foundations of a
pre-Reformation church, the so-called 'eaglais beag', but, apart
from the windowed stretch of the S wall, the remaining masonry
is much reduced.

The C17 church and its C19 replacement are surrounded by
the hillside GRAVEYARD which contains many interesting graves.
Latter-day pilgrims converge on the MACGREGOR TOMBS
which lie in front of the E gable of the Old Church: buried in a
low-railed plot are the outlaw Rob Roy †1734, his wife (Helen)
Mary, and his sons Coll †1735 and Robert †1754. – But there
are many TABLE-TOMBS and lying SLABS of earlier date. – A
pointed-arched HEADSTONE, early C19, commemorates John
MacLaurin †1788, and carries a long inscription dealing with
the origins of the McLaren family whose name is associated
with Balquhidder since the C13. – Set into the inside face of the
blocked S door of the Old Church is a granite TABLET to the
parvenu laird, David Carnegie †1890. – Tucked high in the NW
corner a HEADSTONE to Christina Macnaughton †1947, who is
shown in carved relief kneeling with two owls and a rose, and
named in exquisitely incised lettering.

CALAIR BRIDGE. C18. Humped crossing of Calair Burn; a single
segmental arch.

MACGREGOR MURRAY MAUSOLEUM, Auchtoo, 1.5km. E. 1830.
Three-bay buttressed Gothic with pointed-arched N entrance

and blind lancets W and E. N and S gables crowstepped, the latter with pointed-arched entrance to basement. Stone-slabbed roof.

OLD KIRKTON BRIDGE. Late C18 (?). Rubble-built segmental arch span.

SCHOOL. Mid C19. Perhaps by *David Bryce*. Similar in style and masonry to his adjacent church. Eaves-dormered schoolhouse and Gothic classroom with triple lancet in the gable.

STRONVAR BRIDGE. C18. Three segmental rubble arches across the River Balvag. Cutwater piers and flood arches to the N.

WAR MEMORIAL. Tall Celtic cross by *George Washington Browne*, c.1920.

STRONVAR HOUSE, 0.9km. SW of Balquhidder Church. Built for David Carnegie by *David Bryce*; dated 1850. Good architectonic Baronial in warm ochre sandstone somewhat dulled by moss. A conic stair turret, r. of the crowstepped E entrance gable, corbels from first floor. To the S, more crowstep gables. On the N, a second cone-topped turret, this time full height, and the familiar canted bay splay-back to yet another crowstep gable. At the centre of the plan, a top-lit stairwell. STRONVAR FARM, 100m. W, is a symmetrical court of offices, built in harled rubble with dressed margins, *c.* 1828, to serve Glenbuckie House, Stronvar's predecessor.

CRAIGRUIE. *See* p. 351.

BANNOCKBURN                    S

A place of ancient origin and national renown on the S edge of Stirling. Robert I's victory over a vastly superior English invading force in 1314 welded the country into a nation and 'secured Scotland's independence – for a time'*. It left the scene of the battle sacred but bleak. No more than a village existed at the end of the C18 but this grew rapidly to become a centre of tartan and carpet weaving: a single mill building and several ruinous relics of this textile industry are scattered along the course of the Bannock Burn. The heart of the town has been brutally assaulted by redevelopment in the second half of the C20.

### CHURCHES

ALLAN CHURCH, Main Street and New Road. Originally Bannockburn Chapel-of-Ease. By *John Henderson*, 1837–8. Wide-gabled, four-bay church in a thin late-Gothic idiom. The slender E steeple, dominating the gushet site, works wonders in an otherwise blasted townscape. At its base is the ogee-hooded, four-centred arch entrance leading to a vestibule with a quadripartite plaster vault. The interior is galleried on three sides, the galleries supported by timber columns which, below balcony height, coalesce with similar columns of larger diameter rising to the plastered ceiling. Undistinguished furnishings. – On the

---

* William Croft Dickinson, *Scotland from the earliest times to 1603* (1961), 169.

w wall are two white marble MEMORIAL TABLETS: l., 1923, rectangular with a small cornice over a four-centred arch, to Rev. James Allan †1920; r., also rectangular but with a block pediment, to Rev. Thomas Smith †1883. – The HALL adjoins w, 1881. Vestry and kitchen added by *James Stevenson*, 1933.

Former BURGHER CHAPEL. Built 1797–8. Now abandoned and marooned behind the s side of Main Street. Two-bay gabled kirk with round-arched lateral windows and a Venetian window with intersecting tracery above the pilastered doorpiece in the entrance gable.

LADYWELL CHURCH, Morrison Drive. 1958–59. Dull roughcast walls barely enlivened by a steeply pitched roof. Sheltered by oversailing eaves, a bell sits in an ironwork cage in the apex of the SE entrance gable.

MURRAYFIELD UNITED FREE CHURCH, Main Street. Originally Bannockburn Free Church. By *James Harley*, 1849–50. Four-bay in coursed rubble with tall round-arched windows. Square s entrance tower, added 1853 (clock, 1854), rises in three stages to a castellated parapet with block obelisk finials. – STAINED GLASS in the two-light chancel window by *Gordon Webster*, 1951. – Roughcast HALLS N, 1900 and 1929.

OUR LADY AND ST NINIAN (R.C.), Quakerfield. 1927. By *Archibald Macpherson*. A strange affair concocted in biscuit-coloured brick in an idiosyncratic, almost Hansel and Gretel Romanesque which Historic Scotland generously describes as 'Modified Early Christian'. Bright orange tiling, a copper-green belfry spire, and swollen eaves packed with red tile fragments like some chocolate-chip confection add to the puzzle. It is difficult to decide whether the steeply pitched w gable with its tiered combination of pillared porch, round-arched recess and sub-Gothic pointed-arched window in the apex is whimsical (*The Brick Builder* of 1928 called it 'playful fancy') or simply inept. Segmental-arched arcaded interior in grey brick. High arch to square-ended NE sanctuary. Open timber roof; the principals carried on corbelled pilasters over the nave piers. Presbytery to NW linked by open arched screen.

PUBLIC BUILDINGS

BANNOCKBURN HERITAGE CENTRE. *See* Stirling. Outer Stirling: Public Buildings.

BANNOCKBURN HIGH SCHOOL, Bannockburn Road. By *Central* 101
*Regional Council*, 1977–9. Boomerang plan, splayed asymmetrically from the main stair and glazed to the N in a stunning section stepping s from one to four storeys in cleverly layered accommodation. Orange fascias and brickwork match the boldness of the idea, each bay of the four-storeyed s elevation striped by brick buttressing. Powerful, uncompromising stuff.

BANNOCKBURN HOSPITAL, 1km. SE of Allan Church. Begun in red facing brick as Bannockburn Fever Hospital by *McLuckie & Walker*, 1892–4. The Convalescent Home, added by *Ebenezer Simpson*, 1905–6, is appropriately domestic in scale; a bay-fronted villa with a canopied entrance and some good red brick detailing. Red sandstone tablet medallion of Queen Victoria, carved by *Albert H. Hodge*. Two hip-ended single-storey wards by *A. N. Malcolm*, County Architect, 1936. Roughcast Psychiatric Assessment Unit enlivened by octagonal room with slated rooflight peak.

LIBRARY, Quakerfield. By *Stirling County Council*, 1974–5. A low white building, square in plan, trimly edged on all four sides by series of brick boxes with lean-to glazing.

'NEW ROAD' BRIDGE. By *Thomas Telford*, 1819. A masonry structure of spectacularly unusual design carrying the A9 over the Bannock Burn. Under the carriageway a semicircular barrel vault is inverted to create a circular void, the lower arc of which is formed in three broad ribs which are in turn borne below by a second semicircular barrel vault over the stream. Rough-faced coursed stonework with diminishing abutments curving gently outwards from the bridge openings. Altogether 'singular and striking'*.

OLD BRIDGE. Segmental-arched span of 10.3m. crossing the Bannock Burn. Erected 1516 at the expense of Robert Spittal, a local tailor, but repaired 1631 and 1710 and widened to 7.45m. (double its original width) in 1781. The older E side is of coursed ashlar with a broad chamfer on the voussoirs; the W half also in ashlar, but sharper. Rubble parapets. An inscribed panel, late C18, records the donor and date.

ST MARY'S PRIMARY SCHOOL, Park Drive. 1935–6, by *A. N. Malcolm*, the Stirling County Architect. Parallel to the pavement, a twelve-bay, hip-roofed assembly block with tall metal windows. Entrances l. and r., behind which are single-storey classroom wings.

DESCRIPTION

MAIN STREET barely lives up to its name. It begins well enough, the gushet junction with NEW ROAD marked in declamatory style by the spire of the Allan Church (*see* above). But the scale of the street wall is domestic, the quality indifferent. No. 33, the former schoolhouse of the James Wilson Academy, *c.* 1850, is the exception: an educated Classical façade in ashlar, three bays wide, pilastered, with a pedimented centre and architraved windows. The TARTAN ARMS (No. 45) and No. 47 are good gable-to-gable vernacular: the former has a Gibbsian keystone; both have rolled skewputts. Set back by Coal Wynd is another OLD SCHOOLHOUSE, 1833, a two-storey piended dwelling, five tall window bays wide and relentlessly plain. On the r., equally plain, the CHRISTADELPHIAN HALL (once a carpet factory) and Nos. 42–50 mark the beginning of a respectable run of restored houses stepping down the steep curve of THE BRAE. Most are flatted but materials vary. Nos. 1–5, early C19, are ashlar, three side-by-side doors at the centre of a symmetrical

---

*Robert Southey, *Journal of a Tour in Scotland in 1819*, ed. C. H. Herford (1929), 21.

front. No. 7 is roughcast. Nos. 9–15, probably C18 in origin, are droved ashlar with skewputts, lugged architraves to the doors and a small forestair on the slope at No. 15. No. 19, similar in date and detail, but with stepped skews, is the last house before Spittal's Old Bridge (*see* above). Beyond, past the few ruinous reminders of what was once the industrial heart of the village, THE PATH climbs NW out of the Bannock valley. Two late Georgian villas, ROSEMOUNT and BRAEMORE, survive on the hillside; both have pilastered doorpieces. Along the Burn, 200m. E of Spittal's Bridge, is the ROYAL GEORGE MILL: nine bays long and four-storeys-and-attic high, it was constructed in stone and timber as a hand-loom weaving factory, *c.* 1822, but is now abandoned. The E gable, its three lower storeys hidden by the A9 carriageway, has been remodelled at third-floor level with pilaster strips, a porthole window and an Ionic columned doorpiece, on the heavy block entablature of which are inscribed Greek key motifs and the words MASONIC HALL.

There is little else to remark. On New Road, VIEW VALE, *c.* 1880, is vast, a pompous jumble of French-roofed tower, pedimented dormers and a peaked canted bay; only the calm elegance of the Ionic-columned porch suggests that all this may be the aggrandized conceit of an earlier dwelling. Uphill, at QUAKERFIELD, the village centre has lost all sense of containment. Isolated by 'improvement' at Bannockburn Cross, the EMPIRE BAR, late C19, with its curvilinear gable front, and the string-banded terrace of DOWNIE PLACE, *c.* 1890, retain some dignity. Engulfed by housing on BELLFIELD ROAD, the former Manse, a three-bay early C19 dwelling with a piended roof and a pilastered doorpiece, brings some late Georgian order into mediocrity.

## BANNOCKBURN HOUSE

1.5km. S of Bannockburn

S *8080*

A tall symmetrical house built in the last quarter of the C17. It was probably commissioned *c.* 1675 by Hugh Paterson shortly after he had bought the estate from Andrew, 3rd Lord Rollo. The H-shaped plan is unusual, perhaps influenced by English precedent: a main E–W block with wings running N–S, all three storeys high on a basement. But the walls are decidedly Scots in character and detail, harled with chamfered dressed margins to plain lintelled windows. The original conception is still clear, though encumbered by offices built to the W in the late C18 or early C19 and by late C19 additions which conceal the S projection of the W wing. This latter intervention, by architects *Waller & Son, c.* 1884, also included significant interior alteration (*see* below).

The principal N façade, recessed between flanking wings, is five bays wide with windows regularly disposed at all three levels. Ground- and first-floor openings have moulded cornices. In the topmost storey the windows become eaves dormers with carved strapwork pediments. An ogival eaves cornice returns above the blank walls of the wings to moulded skewputts at the foot of crowstepped gables. Above the central window at first-floor level is an uncarved mural panel. Below this, the main entrance was 'protuberantly beporched'* as part of the 1880s changes. The s front repeats the same arrangement of openings, the central doorway here now leading to the garden. The gabled wings, however, project only a short distance.

At the same time as the Victorian porch was added to the N front, the interior of the house was radically altered by the removal of the ceiling over the ground-floor Hall. This opened up two-thirds of the central block through two storeys, creating a gallery and exposing the magnificent plaster ceiling of the first-floor Drawing Room. This ceiling has a large oval motif at the centre surrounded by geometric panels. The plaster is in high relief and is richly ornamented with fruit, flowers and foliage. There is a rose and bracket cornice and a frieze repeating motifs from the ceiling. The coincidence of style and date with work at Holyrood Palace in Edinburgh suggests that the same craftsmen may have been involved.

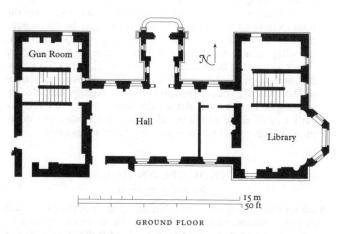

GROUND FLOOR

Bannockburn House. Ground-floor plan.

Dog-leg staircases, symmetrically placed in each wing, are reached along the N side of the ground-floor plan. There are rooms N and S of the stairs, those to the S being larger. The Library, which occupies the s end of the E wing, has a canted bay window added on the E elevation, c. 1884. The Gun Room, a smaller apartment on the N side of the W stair, has C18 panelling and a moulded plaster cornice. On the first floor the arrangement of rooms is similar. In the room over the Library is a second splendid plaster ceiling. Though rather more restrained than that over the Hall, it, too, features fruit and flowers in a border surrounding a central quatrefoil motif with corner panels

* Charles McKean, *Stirling and the Trossachs* (1985), 63.

outlined by a rod and ribbon border. In the s wall of this room, a stone fireplace with bolection moulding. The larger room in the w wing has an C18 fireplace and panelling. Its low relief plaster cornice is C17.

In a field, 220m. NE, is a ruinous square DOOCOT built in rubble with V-jointed quoins. Evidently of the penthouse type, it preserves a stringcourse at eaves height and below this, on the s and E walls, small circular entries for pigeons. The s doorway has a rusticated surround with mock voussoirs on the lintel and the date 1698 split by the letters S H P for Sir Hugh Paterson, second of Bannockburn. Above this, a smaller initialled stone dated 1768, perhaps the record of some reconstruction. All interior walls are gridded for nesting boxes.

# BARDOWIE                                          ED 5070

Small village built along the A807. At the w end, ROBINSFIELD, incorporating a farmhouse, probably of the early C19, but remodelled and much enlarged c. 1900 for the painter Robert Macaulay Stevenson. Rubble-built and now Arts and Crafts of a determinedly Scottish character with crowstepped gables and mullioned windows, some rising into gableted dormerheads. Round tower containing the entrance on the w side, a corbelled turret in one inner angle. Square tower at the NE corner.

## BARDOWIE CASTLE
### 0.6km. NW

Situated beside a loch in a dip of the hills, a C16 tower-house attached to a later laird's house, the result unaffectedly happy.

The lands of Baldernock including Bardowie were granted by Duncan, Earl of Lennox, to John Hamilton, a younger son of David Hamilton of Cadzow, c. 1390, but the first mention of a tower at Bardowie does not occur until 1532 and this had probably been built a few years before,* either by John Hamilton of Bardowie or his son, Alan. That tower is a rubble-walled crow-step-gabled rectangle, c. 9.75m. by 8.23m., but the corners are chamfered up to the level of a splayed stringcourse which is carried across the long N and S sides under the top floor. Near the w end of the s front, a ground-floor entrance, the semi-elliptically arched opening checked for an outer and inner door. Sticking out from the first floor to the l. of the door are a couple of corbels and there is the trace of a third to their r. Presumably they supported a wooden overhead defence above the entrance but there is now no obvious access to it. Reasonable-sized first-floor s windows, both enlarged, probably in the later C17. Slit window at the second floor. Three windows at the top floor, converted from crenelles as part of a remodelling, probably of 1566 (the date on an heraldic panel at this level on the N side),

* No mention of a tower is made in a charter of the lands issued in 1526.

when the gables were heightened and the tower given a new roof
that covered the parapet walks.

In the E gable, a ground-floor window, clearly inserted or
enlarged, probably in the later C17. Inserted first-floor window
near the N corner of this gable. It replaced a C16 window whose
outline is visible to its l. To the l. of this blocked window, the
outlet for a slop drain. At the second floor of the gable, near its
N corner, a C16 window. The N side of the tower is partly covered
by a C19 addition. At the top floor, three regularly spaced
windows, probably of 1566, formed in earlier crenelles. Beneath
the centre of these, a corniced panel carved with fluted pilasters
topped by stumpy pinnacles. Inside this frame are two shields,
the upper bearing the arms of Hamilton of Bardowie and flanked
by the initials I H (for John Hamilton), the lower the arms of
Colquhoun and flanked by the initials IC (presumably, the 'I' not-
withstanding, for John Hamilton's first wife, Marion Colquhoun).
At the top of the panel is the date 1566.

The house was extended W, probably in the later C17. The
addition, again rubble-built, was of two storeys, perhaps with
an attic, L-plan with a NW jamb. The only C17 detail now visible
externally is a blocked ground-floor window at the S front, to
the l. of the present mid-C18 main entrance. The extension seems
to have undergone alteration in 1713 when a door (now built
up) was inserted in the W gable, its lintel carved with that date
and the intricate monogram of the initials of John Hamilton of
Bardowie and his wife, Margaret Buchanan. Further remodelling
of the extension was carried out in the mid C18 but the extension
was again altered in the earlier C19 when the first-floor windows
were deepened and a second floor added, its wallhead surmounted
by a corbelled battlement. Later in the C19 further additions
were built against the N side of the house.

The S entrance to the C16 tower opens on to a short passage
through the 2.44m. thickness of the wall. Off the E side of the
passage, a straight stair contained in the wall, the C16 access to
the first floor but with its lower steps now removed and its top
blocked. The ground floor of the tower is occupied by a tunnel-
vaulted cellar, its E window enlarged or inserted probably in the
C17.

The first-floor hall of the tower, now entered from the C19 N
wing and with (blocked) doorways from the C17 extension, is
also covered by a tunnel vault but it is taller than the one below
and spans from N to S instead of E to W. The roll-and-hollow-
moulded E fireplace is C17, inserted in the built-up embrasure
of a C16 window. Beside it, a locker occupying the place of the
C16 sink whose outlet is visible outside. In the W jamb of the
enlarged window at the E end of the S wall, another C17 locker;
it marks the site of the former doorway of the C16 stair from the
ground floor. In the E jamb of the embrasure of the S wall's W
window, the entrance to a stair to the second floor, contained
within the thickness of the S wall and rising in a straight flight up
to a landing lit by a slit window. Off the landing is the base of a
turnpike stair mostly contained in the thickness of the tower's

SE corner but its NW segment nudging into the corner of the second- and third-floor rooms. A few steps up the turnpike is the entrance to the unvaulted second-floor room. C16 windows at the N end of the E gable and (blocked) at the S end of the W. In the W gable, a blocked fireplace, its jambs and lintel enriched with a bead moulding. N of the fireplace is the door to a stair in the thickness of the gable. This gives access to a narrow room on the tower's N side which was probably formed in the 1560s by roofing over the original parapet walk; the rafters are extensions of the principal trusses of the roof over the main third-floor room. Another room of the same type and presumably formed at the same time lies on the S side of the tower, entered from the SE turnpike stair. The turnpike rises above this level to give access to the principal third-floor or attic room. Low side walls support the arch-braced collar-beam roof. The timbers are now exposed but nail holes indicate that boards were once attached to them, so the room was formerly finished with a tunnel-vaulted wooden ceiling. One window to the E and two in the W gable but no fireplace. Presumably this was a gallery.

## BARNHILL HOUSE *see* MILTON [WD]

## BEARSDEN                                   ED *5070*

Large and leafy suburb of Glasgow. It began as a small village (known as New Kilpatrick) near New Kilpatrick Parish Church and in 1854 consisted of a dozen cottages 'set down with an admirable irregularity, with their patches of garden – a most agreeable rural picture'. Development began after 1863 when the railway to Glasgow was opened and by 1914 a sizeable assembly of villas had been built. A large amount of further construction, generally of smaller houses, took place during the mid and later C20. Bearsden was made a burgh in 1958 but the town centre has remained tiny in relation to the size of the population.

### CHURCHES

ALL SAINTS (Episcopal), corner of Drymen Road and Glenburn Road. By *Speirs & Co.*, 1897. English village picturesque, the walls harled and half-timbered above a red brick base; barge-boarded Rosemary tiled roof surmounted by a wooden bellcote. Inside, wooden pillars marking off the nave from the aisles; Gothic rood beam at the entrance to the S chancel. Open roof. – Gothic oak REREDOS of 1901. – STAINED GLASS S window (Our Lord in Glory worshipped by Angels) by *Norman M.*

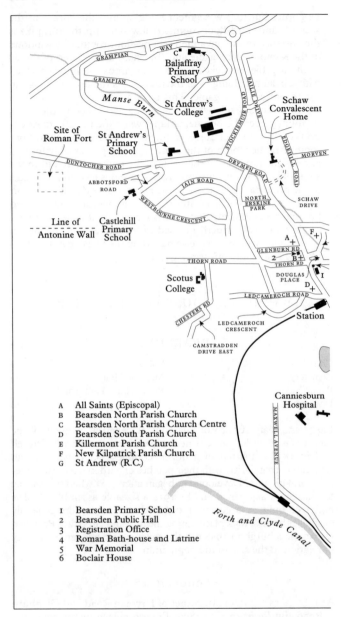

A    All Saints (Episcopal)
B    Bearsden North Parish Church
C    Bearsden North Parish Church Centre
D    Bearsden South Parish Church
E    Killermont Parish Church
F    New Kilpatrick Parish Church
G    St Andrew (R.C.)

1    Bearsden Primary School
2    Bearsden Public Hall
3    Registration Office
4    Roman Bath-house and Latrine
5    War Memorial
6    Boclair House

*Macdougall*, 1903. Colourful but not very good. – ORGAN by
*Sauer*, 1914, originally in Ballater United Free Church; rebuilt
here, 1995–6.
BEARSDEN NORTH PARISH CHURCH, corner of Drymen Road
and Thorn Road. Originally Bearsden Free Church. By *Henry*

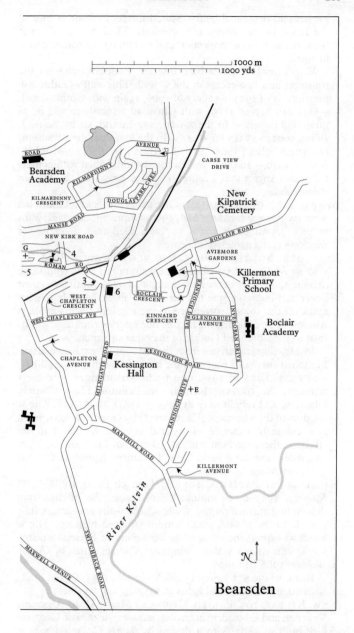

*Higgins*, 1888–9. Very simple Gothic but not without power, the red sandstone masonry of the prominent s and E elevations hammer-dressed; red Rosemary tiled roofs. Nave with E porch and w transepts, the s taller than the N. Steeple in the inner angle of the nave and s transept. Square and unadorned lower part beneath an octagonal belfry. Spired turrets in front of four of the faces; in the others, tall openings. Tiled octagonal spire. Semi-octagonal stair projection at the church's NE corner added in 1906.

Wagon-roofed rather bare interior. Pointed arches to the transepts and to a recess in the w wall. This wall's Gothic oak panelling is of 1923. E gallery of 1906, again with Gothic detail. – Oak PULPIT of 1889, with Christian symbols carved in its quatrefoil panels. – In the N transept, the ORGAN by *James J. Binns*, 1902. – STAINED GLASS. In the w wall of the s transept, two small lights ('Fides' and 'Patientia') by *William Meikle & Sons*, c. 1930. – In the w wall, a rose window filled with colourful glass (Angels and a laurel-wreathed cross) by the *Stephen Adam Studio*, c. 1920.

BEARSDEN NORTH PARISH CHURCH CENTRE, Grampian Way. By *Fleming Buildings Ltd.*, 1999. Unpretentious, with walls of pale brown brick and a concrete tiled roof. Rectangular windows and a gableted 'bellcote'.

BEARSDEN SOUTH PARISH CHURCH, Drymen Road. By *William McCrea*, 1955. Blocky, the walls of red brick with stone dressings, the sides of the nave articulated by flat buttresses, their lower part hidden inside the flat-roofed aisles. More buttresses mark off the stone centrepiece of the E gable. In this gable, a window of three lights, the middle one's curvaceous head a contrast to the simplified Gothic of the other openings.

Inside, elliptical arches from the nave into the passage-aisles. Flattened curve of a roof over the nave and w chancel. E gallery. – FURNISHINGS of 1955, in a traditional manner. – In the s transept, the ORGAN, formerly in Eglinton Elgin Church, Glasgow, and rebuilt here in 1955. – STAINED GLASS. The w window of the s transept (King David) by *Gordon Webster*, 1968, is a colourful example of stylized realism. Similar but less effective, the three-light window (the Risen Lord and St Mary Magdalene, with Old and New Testament figures in the side lights) by *Margaret Chilton*, 1955.

KILLERMONT PARISH CHURCH, Rannoch Drive. By *W. N. W. Ramsay*, 1955–6. Economical broad box, the pitched roof descending further on the s side whose walls are almost fully glazed. In the N side, small windows placed high up. The w windows express the shape of the ceiling inside. Skeletal N belfry. – STAINED GLASS in the w windows. Abstract panels by *Gordon Webster*, 1966 and 1969.

HALL to the N, by *Alan G. McNaughtan*, 1935. Of red brick, with three round-arched lights in the stepped w gable.

NEW KILPATRICK PARISH CHURCH, Manse Road. Ungainly Victorian and Edwardian accretions almost hide the late Georgian kirk built in 1807–8 to a design by *James Gillespie Graham*. Broad crowstep-gabled and rubble-walled rectangle. Tall pointed windows, their intersecting tracery probably original.

The first addition came in 1873 when *Hugh H. Maclure* designed a low extension at the E end, its parapet rising into a crowstepped gablet at the slightly advanced centre of the E front;

pointed windows. In 1877 an organ chamber was built against the centre of the church's s side. Three years later Maclure added a broad crowstep-gabled N jamb with a battlemented two-storey porch at its E end. He resumed work in 1885–6 when he added an outshot, very like that of his earlier E addition but its parapet given shallow crenelles, to the W end of the original church. At the same time he erected a tower in the inner angle of the original church and the N jamb. The tower has pointed windows and belfry openings. Corbelled battlement, its crenelles again shallow, with gryphons leaning out from under the corners; at the NW corner the battlement rises to suggest a caphouse. On the tower's W side, a two-storey vestry and session house, again battlemented. On the N side of the tower, a diagonally buttressed and crow-step-gabled porch, the soffit of its pointed door bearing foliaged bosses.

The last of the Victorian and Edwardian additions came in 1908–10 when *Henry Higgins* replaced the s organ chamber of 1877 with a chancel. In its gable, a stepped arrangement of four tall lancets; above, a hoodmoulded vesica panel carved with the dates 1649 (that of the parish's foundation) and 1807, 1885 and 1909 (for the major phases of the present church's building history). Flanking the chancel, narrow organ chambers, each with a pair of (empty) image niches in its side. Higgins also extended the N jamb by two slightly narrower bays, with simple lancet lights in the side windows and an economically traceried five-light gallery window in the N gable. Across this gable, a simply detailed Gothic porch added in 1972.

The INTERIOR was almost entirely recast by Higgins in 1908–10. Six-bay nave occupying the centre of the original church and the N extensions of 1885–6 and 1908–10. The four s bays have arcades, the columns all with granite shafts and foliaged capitals; at the ends of the arcades, the capitals are supported on corbels carved as human heads. The three s bays of each arcade open into transepts formed from the ends of the church of 1807–8 and extending into the E and W outshots added in 1873 and 1885–6. Over the nave, a shallow-pitched roof, its braces pierced by trefoils. U-plan gallery over the N end and filling the transepts, its oak front panelled in a simple Gothic manner. Pointed stone arch into the chancel whose arched boarded ceiling is panelled; gilded bosses carved with foliage at the intersections of the ribs.

On each side of the chancel, an organ case (the ORGAN itself is of 1877, reconstructed by *Norman & Beard Ltd.*, 1910, and rebuilt by *Rushworth & Dreaper*, 1974). – In the centre of the chancel, an oak COMMUNION TABLE of 1935, carved in a mixed Gothic and Celtic manner but with a naturalistic frieze of wheat and vines. – Simple Gothic CHOIR STALLS, again of oak, with poppyheads; they are presumably of 1910. – On the W side of the chancel arch, the PULPIT of 1910, designed by *Higgins*. Octagonal oak body, again of simple Gothic character, standing on a central Caen stone shaft surrounded by alabaster-shafted columns. – Brass LECTERN of Butterfieldian type, installed here in 1910 but it looks late C19. – On the W wall of the vestibule in the tower, an elaborate Gothic stone WAR MEMORIAL of c. 1920.

STAINED GLASS. Remarkable collection of windows, several of exceptionally high quality. In the chancel's S gable, four lights (the Nativity of Our Lord and Our Lord crowned with Thorns in the side lights; in the centre, the Maries at the Tomb) by *Stephen Adam*, 1910. Lushly coloured in the best Glasgow style. – In the S wall of the W transept, two windows by *Alfred A.*
23 *Webster*. One (Micah) of c. 1914, with figures in richly coloured clothing standing out against clear glass. The other (Prayer and
24 Praise) of 1914 depicts two darkly robed angels. – In the W wall of this transept, a disappointing S window ('Fides' and 'Caritas') by *James Ballantine II*, c. 1907. Beside it, a narrative window (the Good Samaritan) by *McCulloch & Gow*, 1885. – The third window of this wall ('Put on the Whole Armour of God', the depiction of a knight being dressed by a decidedly feminine angel) is by the *Stephen Adam Studio*, c. 1920.

In the W wall of the nave, N of the transept, a narrative window (Scenes from the Life of St John the Baptist and of Our Lord) of 1879. – Next, a colourful early C20 window (Our Lord holding a Chalice) by the *Stephen Adam Studio*. – This wall's N window ('Crossing the Bar') is painterly, by *C. E. Stewart*, c. 1940. – In the N gable of the nave, two realistic windows (an angel summoning a young man from the plough; an old woman symbolizing 'Light at Evening Time') of c. 1910, by *Alfred A. Webster*. – In the E wall of the nave, the three-light N window (the Risen Lord flanked by the Virtuous Woman in two guises) is by *Stephen Adam*, 1896, presumably resited here in 1910. – Single light (a soldier representing 'Victory') of c. 1920. – In the E wall of the E transept, a two-light window ('Virtue' and 'Valour' and small figures of Old and New Testament heroes and heroines) by *J. & W. Guthrie & Andrew Wells Ltd.*, 1934. – Three-light window (the Good Shepherd), unhappily realist by *W. H. Margetson*, c. 1910. – Two-light window (Our Lord blessing Children) by *Gordon Webster*, 1947. – In this transept's E wall, a painterly pictorial window (the Woman called Blessed) by *Alfred A. Webster*, 1912. – Also narrative but of far lower quality is the next window (Our Lord walking on the Water) by the *Stephen Adam Studio*, c. 1912.

In a short passage between the church and the tower's porch, an accomplished single light ('The First Fruits', with a colourful angel), a memorial to the glass-stainer Stephen Adam †1910, executed by his pupil, *Alfred A. Webster*.

The upper windows are best seen from the gallery. In the N gable, a five-light window (the Ascension), rather bittily drawn, by *J. T. & C. E. Stewart*, c. 1930. – In the surviving stubs of the N wall of the N jamb of 1880, two colourful lights (St Andrew and St Patrick) by *Gordon Webster*, 1965. – In the W wall of the W transept, three windows by *Eilidh M. Keith*, in a folk art manner bordering on kitsch. The N (Education and Music) is of 2000, the central three-light window (the Virtuous Woman) of 1994, and the window to its S (the New Jerusalem Coming down from Heaven) of 1997. – In the S wall of this transept, a three-light window (the Risen Lord appearing to the Apostles) by *Gordon Webster*, 1965, with characteristic small-scale drawing and strong colour. – The corresponding window in the E transept (the Risen Lord appearing to St Mary Magdalene) is of 1963 and also by *Webster*. – The three E windows of the E transept are all by *Douglas Strachan*, erected *c.* 1949 as a Second World War memorial. The centre window depicts Our Lord in Glory accompanied by saints and soldiers including St Michael the Archangel, St Patrick and Sir William Wallace. In the window to its l., Our Lord carrying the Cross, and the Crucifixion. In the r. window, the Risen Lord and the Disciples on the Road to Emmaus. All are typical of Strachan's expressionist late work but relatively restrained and the better for it.

Attached to the N porch by a long covered but open-sided walkway is the NEW HALL, by *Geoffrey Jarvis*, 1972. Two storeys, the exposed concrete frame infilled with panels of light brown brick. Pair of fin-like triangular towers with steep monopitch roofs.

GRAVEYARD. S of the church, the BURIAL ENCLOSURE of the Colquhouns of Garscadden, probably of the earlier C18. It is built of roughly dressed ashlar with polished dressings. Rusticated quoins and a moulded cornice; Gibbsian surround to the entrance. Only the bases of the crowning urns (?) survive. – Around it, C17 and C18 HEADSTONES. The best of these, immediately to its W, is C18 and marks the burial place of William Paterson. On the E face, an inscription panel bordered with egg-and-dart. The ends of this face are fluted and rosetted. On top of the face, a carved crown flanked by a weathered implement and hammer. – On the wall to its S, a MONUMENT dated 1663. Panelled piers at the ends; at the centre, a badly weathered inscription panel in a basket-arched and pedimented aedicule. – Further W, a free-standing very correct Corinthian aedicule erected in 1863 to commemorate the Rev. Alexander McNaughtan. It is by *James McClure & Son*. – At the NW corner of the graveyard, prosperous early C20 monuments. By far the most accomplished is the Celtic CROSS to Alexander Brown †1928, decorated with a wealth of Celtic motifs and signed by *Donaldson & Burns* of Edinburgh. – In the graveyard's NE corner, a triple-gabled MONUMENT with a bronze relief bust, to Robert Thomson †1901. – Immediately E of the church, the Victorian Gothic MAUSOLEUM of the Campbells of Garscube.

ST ANDREW (R.C.), off Douglas Place. By *Archie Crawford*, of *Watson, Salmond & Gray*, 1987. Tall block, the walls of brown brick. Tiled roofs, the ridges of the two pitches placed at differing heights and linked by a clearstorey-like but unglazed fascia. Inside, a sloping ceiling over the W sanctuary; stepped ceiling above the rest. – STAINED GLASS. Modernistic depictions of saints, by *Peter Connolly*, 1993–4.

## CEMETERY

NEW KILPATRICK CEMETERY, Boclair Road. Opened in 1903. At the SW corner, corniced and ball-finialled GATEPIERS, their

Art Nouveau flavour shared by the wrought iron gates. Harled
L-plan LODGE in a domestic Scots Jacobean manner, the entrance
placed in an ogee-domed bowed projection in the inner angle.

Plenty of monuments of a generally expensive but routine
character, including a goodly number of Celtic crosses and
alabaster angels. Near the s end of the e side, the MONUMENT
to Charles Gourlay †1926, with a bronze relief portrait bust in a
laurel-wreath frame. – To its w, the large HEADSTONE of
Alexander Melville †1937, carved with a panel depicting the
Sower. – N of this, on top of a hillock by the e boundary, a
TABLE STONE to Sir Archibald Campbell of Succoth †1941.
Craggy supports, one carved with an heraldic achievement. On
the slab, a Celtic cross in relief. Beside the monument, a length
of the stone base of the ANTONINE WALL of c. AD142 (see Introduction, p. 13). To the sw, on the s slope of a hill in the middle
of the cemetery, a second length, wider than normal but reduced
in width as it steps down the slope. The two lengths lie almost
at r. angles to each other, for here the Wall is striding from one
high point to another as it strikes w to Old Kilpatrick in order to
control fording points over the Clyde. Both stretches of the base
are crossed by culverts provided to aid drainage through the Wall.

In the middle of the cemetery is a hill. At the centre of its w
slope, a large stone CROSS to James Fyfe Morrison †1916,
lavishly decorated with motifs (beasts, interlacing, discs) and a
human figure derived from Pictish symbol stones. – To its N, on
top of the hill, another elaborately carved CROSS (to Douglas
Campbell Douglas of Mains †1927), its inspiration taken from
medieval West Highland sources and bearing the relief of a knight.
– N of this, a large granite HEADSTONE of 1941 commemorating Eliza Templeton Hammond Couper. It bears a bronze relief
of a pair of trumpeting boy angels. – Further N, the MONUMENT
to Robina Hutton or McLundie †1926. On the front, a coloured
mosaic roundel depicting a bird and inscribed 'FREEDOM AND
LIGHT'. On the back, a mosaic panel portraying a woman's
head.

## PUBLIC BUILDINGS

BALJAFFRAY PRIMARY SCHOOL, Grampian Way. By *Dumbarton
County Council*, 1972. Sensible collection of flat-roofed boxes of
one and two storeys, the walls of brown brick with wooden
fascias.

BEARSDEN ACADEMY, Morven Road. By the Dumbarton County
Architect, *James Miller*, 1955–8. Harled walls, with a sparing
use of stone and brick; tiled piended roofs. Not unpleasant but
undistinguished.

BEARSDEN PRIMARY SCHOOL, corner of Drymen Road and
Roman Road. Originally Bearsden Academy. By *James M. Monro
& Son*, 1909–11. Free Wrenaissance, the thrift emphasized
rather than relieved by occasional pieces of carved stonework.

BEARSDEN PUBLIC HALL, corner of Drymen Road and Glenburn
Road. By *A. McInnes Gardner & Partners*, 1975. Ill-mannered

lump of concrete blockwork topped by large triangular-headed windows rising into the canted underside of the deep fascia under the oversailing roof.

BOCLAIR ACADEMY, Inveroran Drive. By *Thomson, McCrea & Sanders*, in association with the Dumbarton County Architect, *Robert Sutherland*, 1974. Large and sensible group of flat-roofed blocks. The main building is of five and six storeys, the horizontal bands of aggregate cladding and glass interrupted by verticals of dark brown brickwork.

BOCLAIR HOUSE, corner of Milngavie Road and Boclair Road. Originally the Buchanan Retreat, built and endowed in 1890 by the Misses Buchanan of Bellefield as a home for twenty 'decayed Glasgow merchants'.

Curious mixture giving the impression that either something more ambitious was intended and scaled down or that an economical design was embellished without being rethought. The two-storey main part is straightforward Jacobean. Gableted dormerheads over the first-floor windows. Two-storey porch, with a stepped and pinnacled gable. Stretched incongruously across the front is a Gothic loggia, the columns' capitals carved with foliage. At the rear of the building and made inconsequential by its position is a tower, its battlement carried on arcaded corbelling.

CANNIESBURN HOSPITAL, Switchback Road. By *James Miller & Son*, 1935–8. The buildings are mostly flat-roofed and harled, of two storeys. Modern Movement but no fear of frightening the horses. – GERIATRIC UNIT by *Frank Burnet, Bell & Partners*, 1967. – PLASTIC SURGERY UNIT by *John Peters*, Assistant Architect to the Western Regional Hospitals Board, 1968.

CASTLEHILL PRIMARY SCHOOL, Westbourne Crescent and Abbotsford Road. By *Robert Rogerson & Philip Spence*, 1963–7. Curtain-walled and flat-roofed. A monopitch-roofed brick tower was added later and further extensions built to the E, with dry-dashed walls and shallow pitched roofs.

KESSINGTON HALL, corner of Kessington Road and Milngavie Road. Built as a tramway power station in 1924, the interior converted to a public hall in 1966. Not very decorative mixture of Wrenaissance and Jacobean, faced in hammer-dressed red sandstone with polished dressings. Pepperpot turrets at the corners. At the front (N) gable and the W elevation the openings are placed in rectangular overarches with corbelled sills. In the front gable, an elliptical-arched door surround surmounted by a cornice and flanked by corniced ground-floor windows. Segmental headed windows in the W side.

KILLERMONT PRIMARY SCHOOL, Aviemore Gardens and Kinnaird Crescent. By *Strathclyde Regional Council*, 1997. Single-storey, with red brick walls and large expanses of shallow-pitched tile roofs.

RAILWAY STATION, Drymen Road. Built in 1863. Piend-roofed two-storey block, Georgian survival of a sort. Awning with fretted pelmet over the platform. Lean-to addition on the S side and W extension.

REGISTRATION OFFICE, Roman Road. Originally Bearsden
Parish Council Chambers. By *Duncan McNaughtan*, 1906–7. Like
a standard villa, the ground floor walling of stugged masonry,
the upper floor half-timbered; bargeboarded gables. Balustraded
bowed porch, a consoled open pediment over the entrance.

ST ANDREW'S COLLEGE, Stockiemuir Road. Formerly Notre
Dame College of Education. By *Gillespie, Kidd & Coia*, 1968.
The administrative and teaching buildings are brick-walled with
copper fascias and multi-pitched copper roofs. – Boldly sited on
the ridge of a hill to the N, HALLS OF RESIDENCE. Cubist lines
of intersecting dry-dashed boxes.

ST ANDREW'S PRIMARY SCHOOL, Duntocher Road. By
*Dumbarton County Council*, 1967–9. Curtain-walled with pitched
roofs. It was extended later in the C20, with a flat-roofed link to a
SW block whose roof's opposing pitches are separated by a
lower flat-roofed centre.

SCHAW CONVALESCENT HOME, Schaw Drive. Now the
Lynedoch Private Nursing Home. Designed by *James Thomson*
of *John Baird & James Thomson* and built and endowed in 1891
with £40,000 given by Miss Schaw in memory of her father, it
was presented to Glasgow Royal Infirmary in 1895. Sited on a
hill for maximum effect, it is a 53.6m.-long three-storey range,
its inspiration taken from the prodigy houses of late C16 England.
French-roofed end pavilions, their corner turrets crowned by
crocketed ogee-profiled domes; two-storey canted bay windows
and aedicule-topped gablets at the front. Three-bay links, the
second-floor windows rising into pedimented and pinnacled
dormerheads. The centrepiece is an extravagantly tall battlemented
tower, the height emphasized by the domed octagonal turrets
clasping its corners. At the tower's two lower stages, hoodmoulded pointed openings. Above, a two-storey battlemented
oriel window, the panels marking the division of its floors decorated with shields.

SCOTUS COLLEGE, Chesters Road. The core of the college is a
prosperous late C19 bay-windowed and broad-eaved villa of
unassertive but squared-up Italianate character.
    CHAPEL immediately to the S, by *James F. Stephen*, 1997.
Externally very simple, a rectangle covered by a double-pitch
slated roof, its broad eaves covered in metal cladding, their
undersides boarded. Gables of polished ashlar, the N containing
the broad entrance under a large semicircular window divided
by a ladder-like central mullion (i.e. a variant on a Diocletian
window), the top of the S gable covered in metal cladding with
a broad semicircular arch at the centre expressing the ceiling
shape inside. The sidewalls, except for the ashlar-clad N bay
containing the vestibule, are fully glazed.

31        The interior is a magnificently calm setting for the drama of
the liturgy. Over the N vestibule, a glass-fronted deep gallery, its
stair rising in the building's NW corner, double doors under the
centre, ashlar walling under the E end. The ceiling over the
broad centre of the chapel is a tunnel vault. At the sides, narrow
'aisles' marked off only by flat-ceilinged inward projection of

the soffits of the eaves. At the s bay they rest on short ashlar cross-walls which screen fire exit doors. Floor of pale marble. – Free-standing and unadorned LECTERN (towards the N end) and ALTAR (towards the s), both of polished sandstone cut from the same block. – Flanking the altar are mild steel CANDLE-STICKS, in turn flanked by a PASCHAL CANDLESTICK and PROCESSIONAL CROSS, the cross's arms and central boss studded with spheres of coloured glass. All these are by *John Creed*, their inspiration taken from the Lindisfarne Gospels but their tactile sinuosity in no way derivative. – Behind the altar, a high-backed cherrywood CELEBRANT'S CHAIR, by *J. McNally*. – Hanging over the altar is a SCULPTURE of Our Lord, his arms outstretched but with no cross, by *Kate Robinson*. Translucent resin highlighted with gold leaf, cast from the body of a model and then partly reworked. – TABERNACLE set into the W cross-wall s of the altar. On its front, a simple Celtic cross design, also by *Creed*. – Hung along the glazed sides of the chapel are STAINED-GLASS PANELS (the Stations of the Cross) by *Shona McInnes*. Except for the cross which appears in each panel and a sparing use of symbols they are abstract, relying on colour to denote mood and meaning.

Undistinguished other buildings to the N, s and w of the house and chapel, built for the Royal College of Science and Technology which then occupied the site. They are by *Thomas S. Cordiner & Partners*, 1955.

## DESCRIPTION

DRYMEN ROAD, bringing the A809 in from the s, makes a leafy approach bordered by villas (for which *see* Villas, below). Small commercial interlude at the Railway Station (*see* Public Buildings, above) where, on the road's E side, is a development (MELVILLE PLACE, Nos. 68–76 Drymen Road) of 1881, a two-storey block of flats over shops. Georgian survival but the windows are two-light with chamfered margins. A little further N, Bearsden South Parish Church (*see* Churches, above) heralds the town centre. Just beyond, on the E, Bearsden Primary School (*see* Public Buildings, above). Immediately to its N, on the corner with Roman Road, the WAR MEMORIAL by *Alexander Proudfoot*, 1924. Large bronze of a young man ('Sacrifice'), naked except for carefully positioned drapery round his loins, falling into the arms of an angel ('Victory'). Bronze laurel-wreath frieze round the tall ashlar pedestal. On the back of the pedestal, a bronze panel bearing the relief of a laurel wreath, torch and a sunburst arrangement of flags. Diagonally opposite the War Memorial, on the corner of Thorn Road, Bearsden North Parish Church, followed by Bearsden Public Hall and All Saints Episcopal Church (*see* Churches and Public Buildings, above). The town's commercial centre is provided on the E side of Drymen Road by a U-plan block (Nos. 1–11 Roman Road, Nos. 102–116 Drymen Road and Nos. 2–22 New Kirk Road) of 1906. Two storeys and an attic, containing flats above shops. Squared-up free Jacobean.

Ogee-domed octagonal corner turrets and canted oriel windows
under steep gablets. Pediments, variously open, broken and swan-
neck, over the entrances to the flats' stairs. ROMAN ROAD lies
on top of the Military Way associated with the Antonine Wall,
constructed from Bo'ness to Old Kilpatrick after AD138 (*see*
Introduction, p. 13). On its N side, in front of flats and town-
houses (ROMAN COURT) by *Cordiner, Cunningham & Partners*,
1974, the remains of a Roman bath-house (*see* below).

NEW KIRK ROAD is L-shaped. Running S from the heel is
DOUGLAS PLACE, its start marked by NEW KILPATRICK
PARISH CHURCH OLD HALLS, by *Alan G. McNaughtan*,
1934–5. Harled with ashlar dressings; blocky porch at the S end.
Behind the halls, St Andrew's R.C. Church (*see* Churches, above).
The N stretch of New Kirk Road runs past the side of the grave-
yard of New Kilpatrick Parish Church (*see* Churches, above).
On the E side of the road, the office houses of New Kilpatrick
Parish Manse. They were built in 1812 by *John Crawford*, mason
in Milngavie. Rubble-walled and piend-roofed single-storey
U-shape; pointed windows in the W side.

VILLAS

BAILIE DRIVE. No. 32 is the epitome of 1930s builders' *moderne*.
Essentially a piend-roofed villa but the harling is jazzed up with
horizontal bands of red brick. Curved metal-framed windows at
the bowed and parapeted corners.

BOCLAIR CRESCENT. No. 26 (BLAVEN), designed for himself
by *Arthur Nicholson*, 1925. White harled walls and a pantiled
roof. Cape Dutch gable to the front and a single-storey bow
window.

BOCLAIR ROAD. No. 5, a late C19 broad-eaved villa, is unremarkable except for its battlemented round tower and elaborate
ironwork on top of the wooden porch. Harled double house of
the early C20 at Nos. 6–8. Half-timbering and canted single-
storey bay windows at the twin gables of the advanced centrepiece. In each inner angle of this centrepiece and the main block,
a porch whose outer corner is supported by a Roman Doric
column. No. 17, again early C20, in an Anglo-American cottage
manner. Ground floor of red brick, the upper floor harled. Roof
covered with red Rosemary tiles. Symmetrical three-bay front,
the inner pitches of the gables over the outer bays cut into by the
bracketed projecting eaves above the centre. Mullioned windows
of four and five lights; horseshoe-arched entrance. Large chimneys
with bulgy tops. Another early C20 house at No. 19 (ROMAN-
HURST) is a large English cottage in the manner approved by
*Country Life*. Walls of red brick, partly tile-hung. Tiled gambrel
roofs and an oriel window.

CAMSTRADDEN DRIVE EAST. No. 7 (RAHEEN) is by *Alexander
Cullen, Lochead & Brown*, 1914. Arts and Crafts Jacobean
domestic, in hammer-dressed ashlar. Shaped gable over the
entrance. PINEHURST of *c.* 1912, English cottage picturesque,
the walls harled and tile-hung, the roofs, some of gambrel form,

covered with Rosemary tiles. Small-paned windows; half-timbered porch.

CARSE VIEW DRIVE. A collection of houses (Nos. 1–2 and 5–10) stand in a curving line up a steep hill. Designed and built as a speculation by *John R. H. McDonald*, of *John McDonald (Contractors) Ltd.*, 1933–6 (*see* below). Originally all were flat-roofed, smooth rendered with metal-framed windows. Rounded corners and corner windows are much on display and at No. 9, a small triangular first-floor window perches on top of the entrance canopy. Most of the houses have been altered and their commanding views over to the Kilpatrick Hills interfered with.

CHAPELTON AVENUE. No. 1 is late C19. Plain but for a weird entrance whose pedimented aedicular surround is skied on corbels projecting from halfway up the door.

CHESTERS ROAD. STAC POLLY, a determinedly Scottish late C19 crowstep-gabled red sandstone villa. Tower topped by a corbelled parapet which rises to tall merlons at the corners but is topped by balusters along the sides. Large monkey-puzzle tree in the garden.

DOUGLAS PARK CRESCENT. No. 15 of *c.* 1935 is presumably by *John R. H. McDonald*. Flat-roofed and rendered, with touches of brickwork. Double pile, the front block of one storey, the rear of two. Corner windows.

DRYMEN ROAD. No. 40 (GREY GABLES) of *c.* 1900. Main walling of hammer-dressed stone, with half-timbering in the gables. Polished ashlar at the bay windows. The w of these is rectangular, its corniced parapet broken by a deep and narrow crenelle. A second bay window, projecting at the SW, is semi-octagonal and finished with a cornice. No. 88A (ARDOCH) is a large late C19 villa which mixes touches of half-timbering with Italianate round-arched windows and, at the attic, pedimented aedicules of 'Greek' Thomson character. No. 98, again late C19 but smaller. Extravagantly broad-eaved. Two-storey canted bay window in the gabled r. end of the front. At the other two bays, a corniced door and a two-light window, also with a cornice.

KILMARDINNY CRESCENT. WHITE LODGE of *c.* 1930 was designed for his own occupation by *John R. H. McDonald*, a partner in the building firm of *John McDonald (Contractors) Ltd.* and author of *Modern Housing* (1931). In accordance with the arguments put forward in that book the house is flat-roofed and designed to get the maximum amount of sunlight into the metal-windowed rooms. Symmetrical two-storey entrance front, the higher centre recessed, with a tall stair window at the upper floor. Corner windows at the blocky ends. The elevation to the garden steps forward from the almost fully glazed single-storey sun verandah at the SE via a two-storey bow and a rectangular two-storey block at the NE. Inside, the hall opens into the dining room to the l. and living room to the r. All three were intended to be used *en suite* for parties. At the living room's E end, French windows into the sun verandah. E of the hall, the D-plan library with a large bow window.

LEDCAMEROCH CRESCENT. No. 25. Late C19, built of bull-nosed red sandstone. Plain but with a battlemented tower.

LEDCAMEROCH ROAD. Nos. 23–25. Late C19 double house, the piended roof with bracketed eaves. At the centre of the six-bay main block, a pair of full-height bows, their upper windows with stilted roundheaded arches and Ionic column-mullions. The other first-floor windows are roundheaded and hoodmoulded. At each end, a single-storey porch containing a pedimented entrance. No. 27 (THE HIGH SCHOOL OF GLASGOW JUNIOR SCHOOL) is a large and lumpily detailed bay-windowed late C19 villa. Bargeboarded gables; shouldered arches to the first-floor windows. Tower over the entrance. The house is now beset by C20 additions.

MANSE ROAD. No. 45, a broad-eaved villa of c. 1900, the walls harled and with sandstone dressings. At the N front, a two-storey bow window and a single-storey bay window. Art Nouveau-ish tapered chimney.

MAXWELL AVENUE. Nos. 25–107 and Nos. 46–64 comprise single-storey and attic and two-storey terraced housing by *John A. W. Grant* built in 1913 as the beginning of the intended Glasgow Garden Suburb. English picturesque manner, with harled walls (half-timbered at Nos. 25–79), slate roofs and chimneys of glazed red brick (many now harled). Bracketed broad eaves and small-paned upper sashes in the windows. Advanced gables for emphasis.

MILNGAVIE ROAD. LOWER KILMARDINNY HOUSE is a two-storey three-bay house of the earlier C19. Heavy pilastered and corniced doorpiece at the rough ashlar front.

NORTH ERSKINE PARK. Nos. 29–31, a large double villa of c. 1890. Ground floor of stugged masonry, the first floor and attic harled and half-timbered. At the gabled ends of the front, jettied attics above a pair of two-storey canted bay windows, their upper storey intaken. Broad side-lit entrances under elliptical fanlights. In the upper panes of the windows, Glasgow-style stained glass.

ROMAN ROAD. No. 4 is a late C19 cottage. Consoled cornices over the two-light ground-floor windows. Carved bargeboards at the attic's dormer windows and the consoled gablet over the entrance. No. 6 is harled Scots Jacobean of 1902, with round corner towers and shaped dormerheads to the first-floor windows. Advanced gable containing the entrance which is surmounted by an Artisan Mannerist aedicule with barley-sugar columns. Above, a panel displaying a coat of arms and cherubs' heads. Well finished interior in prosperous but unflashy manner; some Glasgow-style stained glass. No. 10 is again harled Scots Jacobean, of c. 1900. It is L-plan, the NW jamb pierced by a pend arch. Dome carved detail, e.g. at the N stair projection, the lintel of one window carved with a cat's head and the semi-circular pediment of the window above bearing fleurs-de-lis and a rose.

THORN ROAD. No. 31 (GLENCOE) is best English Jacobean Arts and Crafts of c. 1895, built of stugged masonry with polished ashlar dressings. Bay windows of one and two storeys. Beside the door, a large panel inscribed 'PROPRIA DOMUS/OMNIUM OPTIMA' ('One's own house is the best house').

WEST CHAPELTON CRESCENT. No. 7 (BARONE) is of *c.* 1905. Small two-storey villa, built of stugged red sandstone. At the E front, an advanced and gabled centre. Low round SE tower with a convex profiled dome. Large double house of *c.* 1900 at Nos. 10–12. Harled, with half-timbering. Ball-finialled canted bay windows at the M-roofed centrepiece. Prominent tapered chimneys. No. 14, again of *c.* 1900, is free Jacobean, squared-up but with broad eaves. Mullioned and transomed windows, some of them bows. Small slated conical spire on top of the two-storey porch.

## MANSION HOUSES

KILLERMONT HOUSE, off Killermont Avenue. Restrained classical mansion house (now a golf club) of *c.* 1805. S-facing piend-roofed ashlar-built main block of nine bays by four. Two storeys over a tall basement which is largely hidden by the ramping of the ground in front. At the principal elevation the end and centre three bays are slightly advanced. Sill courses under the windows, the ground-floor windows taller and corniced, those of the end bays pedimented. At the pedimented centrepiece, an Ionic columned portico in front of the entrance and flanking windows. Plain rear additions of the later C19 and C20.

KILMARDINNY HOUSE, No. 50 Kilmardinny Avenue. Sizeable house which developed under successive C19 proprietors. The first of these, the Glasgow merchant John Leitch, added a new N front to an existing two-storey building at the beginning of the C19. This is of broached ashlar. Five broad bays tied together by a moulded bandcourse under the first floor. Advanced and parapeted ends, their ground-floor windows with balustered aprons and consoled cornices; aprons under the first-floor windows. Across the ground floor of the three-bay centrepiece, its parapet broken by balusters, is a balustraded Ionic columned stone screen (now painted). This is probably an addition by William Brown who acquired the house in 1833. Of the three openings behind the screen the central one is pilastered and round-arched and the other two corniced. Probably in the arrangement of the 1830s they served as windows flanking a door but the central opening is now a window and the r. the main entrance, a transposition likely to have been made *c.* 1860 by *James Smith* for a later owner, the Glasgow M.P. Robert Dalglish.

The W elevation is also a mixture. It is of four bays, the third advanced. At the two N bays, early C19 ground-floor windows with consoled cornices and balustered aprons. One of these bays' upper windows is aproned, the other made into a fire escape door in the C20. At the S bay, a consoled cornice over the ground-floor window but neither it nor the window above is aproned. The third bay was remodelled *c.* 1860 with corniced and aproned two-light windows; a pierced parapet surmounts the cornice of the ground-floor window.

The interior was largely recast in opulent style by *James Smith*, *c.* 1860. The small vestibule at the W end of the portico opens into a hall which occupies the house's centre. At its N end, a section with a foliaged ceiling rose, perhaps of the early rather than the later C19. The S side of this section has marble-shafted Corinthian pilasters of *c.* 1860 at its opening into the main part of the hall. Here the centre of the ceiling is cut out to form a balconied oval opening allowing top lighting from a cupola. Heavily classical plasterwork of the later C19. Over the doors from the hall to the ground floor NE and NW rooms, restrained Neo-Classical reliefs, perhaps of the early C19. At the S end of the hall, more marble-shafted Corinthian pilasters marking the entry to the Imperial staircase, its iron balusters shaped as rinceaux. At the half-landing a blind arcade, its roundheaded arches springing from marble-shafted pilasters. Pâtisserie classical Victorian ceiling over the stair. The W side of the ground floor is occupied by a double drawing room, its N half with an egg-and-dart cornice and foliaged ceiling rose probably early C19, the S half's coffered ceiling, enriched with acanthus leaves and naturalistic foliage, of *c.* 1860.

ANTONINE WALL, Boclair Road. *See* New Kilpatrick Cemetery, above.

ROMAN BATH-HOUSE AND LATRINE
Roman Road

5 Discovered during excavations for Roman Court flats in the 1970s, these buildings lay in the annexe attached to the C2 fort at Bearsden. The bath-house consists of a range of rooms along a main spine. It was entered from the W where there was a timber changing-room. In the second room the bather, that is the ordinary soldier, was offered a choice of bathing. To his left lay the hot dry room with its own furnace; straight ahead were the three rooms of the steam range (Turkish, really Roman, bath). To the side of the hottest room (the *caldarium*) lay the hot bath. Whichever form of bathing was chosen, the bather would return to the cold room to use the plunge bath. Several architectural features may be noted: the raised floors; the stones projecting from the walls of the hot dry room and the *caldarium* to support the wall jacketing, which survives in part in the *caldarium*. The doors in the steam range lie at opposite corners of each room. To the SE of the bath-house was a latrine flushed by water led by drains from the bath-house. The sewerage passed through the annexe rampart and accumulated in the fort ditch. Analysis of the sewage demonstrated that the soldiers had a mainly vegetarian diet, eating cereals, fruit and nuts, though bone fragments demonstrate that meat was on the menu too.

NE of the bath-house some evidence is visible of an earlier bath-house, abandoned when the plan of the fort was amended during construction.

# BISHOPBRIGGS

Three small villages (Bishopbriggs, Auchinairn to the s, and Cadder to the N) in the early C19 when mining and brickworks provided employment. Development of industry and massive expansion of housing to link the settlements came from the earlier C20 and the complex was made a burgh in 1964. It is now predominantly an area of C20 housing and supermarkets, just managing to safeguard its independence from Glasgow.

## CHURCHES

BISHOPBRIGGS FREE CHURCH, Auchinairn Road. Built in 1910. Small and cheap. Three lancet lights in the stepped s gable.

CADDER PARISH CHURCH, Cadder Road. Georgian Gothic, by *David Hamilton*, 1829–30. Tall and broad box, built of buff-coloured rubble from Possil Quarry. Y-traceried and hood-moulded windows. At the w end, lower parapeted projections containing stairs to the gallery. Rising between them is the square tower, its corners clasped by pinnacled octagonal buttresses. At the bottom of the tower, a hoodmoulded pointed door. Rather squat hoodmoulded windows at the two stages above. The top stage is the belfry with tall two-light openings, their hood-moulds' label stops carved with human heads.

The rectangular E chancel and flanking vestry and organ chamber were added by *Stewart & Paterson*, 1908–9. They are built of stugged masonry. Plain Gothic three-light window in the chancel's gable.

INTERIOR. Originally there were galleries at the w end and along the N and s sides. In 1914 *Stewart & Paterson* removed the side galleries and reconstructed the w gallery, providing a curvaceous oak front, the top and bottom bands carved with vines and foliage, the main panels with linenfold and coats of arms of the leading heritors (landowners) of the parish in the early C20 (Stirling of Keir and Cawder, Christie of Bedlay and Sprot of Garnkirk). Under the w gallery, a vestibule screen of 1980, its leaded lights and doors re-used from an earlier screen, probably of 1830, which was set further back. Plaster ceiling of 1829–30, flat over the missing side galleries and tunnel-vaulted with queen-post trusses over the central area. On the tie-beams are coats of arms of the heritors of 1830 which formerly decorated the gallery fronts. At the E end, a stone depressed arch, the responds' bundled shafts finished with foliaged capitals. This is of 1908–9 by *Stewart & Paterson* and opens into their chancel whose walls are lined with simple panelling.

In the nave, plain PEWS of 1908–9. – On the N side of the chancel arch, a late Gothic octagonal oak PULPIT, by *Stewart & Paterson*, 1910, the main faces with linenfold panelling, the corners bearing empty image niches. It was lowered slightly in 1914 and again in 1980. – On the s side of the chancel, ORGAN by *Norman & Beard*, 1914, imported from a church in Dumbarton in 1957. – STAINED GLASS. In the chancel, a three-light E window (Our Lord blessing Little Children) by *James Ballantine & Son*, 1890–1, originally in the E wall of the church. Moved here, and the tracery lights added, in 1909. – Flanking the chancel arch, two lights (Enoch and Jonah) by *A. Ballantine & Gardiner*, 1896. – At the E ends of the sides, a pair of windows, Faith, Hope and Charity (the Virgin and Child) on the S, 'Prayer and Praise' on the N, by *Alfred A. Webster*, 1914, in best Glasgow Art Nouveau-ish manner. – To their W, another pair, 'Sacrifice' (Abraham and Isaac, a soldier and, above, the Resurrection and Ascension of Our Lord) on the S, 'Supreme Sacrifice' (the Crucifixion, and Our Lord calling the Apostles) on the N, by the *Stephen Adam Studio*, 1921. – At the W end of the S wall, under the gallery, a competent but mundane depiction of Our Lord teaching ('In my Father's house are many mansions') by *J. & W. Guthrie & Andrew Wells Ltd.*, 1908. – Opposite, in the N wall, a modernistic window (Sower and Reaper) by *Sadie McLellan*, *c.* 1965.

GRAVEYARD. S of the E end of the church, a WATCHHOUSE of 1828. This is a single-storey broached ashlar oblong. In the W gable, a hoodmoulded rectangular entrance flanked by small roundheaded dummy windows. More roundheaded dummies in the side walls and E gable. Hefty octagonal chimneystacks on the gables. Inside, a fireplace on E wall. – S of the W end of the church, a curly pedimented C18 HEADSTONE marking the burial-place of John Paterson, its E face carved with inept Ionic pilasters and an angel's head (the soul). – S of this, a chunky OBELISK to – Thoms †1847 (?). – Immediately N of the church's W end, an early C19 MORT SAFE with elaborate spear-headed cast iron railings and urns on the corners.

KENMURE PARISH CHURCH, Viewfield Road. Originally Bishopbriggs Kenmure United Free Church. Gothic, by *Alexander Petrie*, 1905–6. N gable front of hammer-dressed masonry. Buttressed and advanced 'nave' centrepiece topped by a gableted bellcote. Above the door, a squat four-light window. Buttresses along the harled sides. Cupola-ventilators on the broad-eaved roof.

ST DOMINIC (R.C.), Kirriemuir Road. By *S. G. A. (Buildings) Ltd.*, 1977. Group of church, presbytery and hall, the walls of brown brick and render, the pitched roofs covered with concrete tiles.

ST JAMES THE LESS (Episcopal), Hilton Road. By *Weddell & Thomson*, 1980. Polygonal church with rectangular NE chapel and W hall, all with dry-dashed walls and pitched and slated roofs, those of the church and hall rising to triangular gablets; spirelet over the church.

Inside the church, white painted brick walls and a boarded ceiling. – Brass eagle LECTERN of *c.* 1920, originally in St James the Less Episcopal Church, Springburn, Glasgow (now demolished), the previous home of this congregation. – STAINED GLASS. In the SE sanctuary, four windows (the Four Evangelists) of knockout quality by *Morris & Co.*, 1882, from designs of 1872–4 by *Edward Burne-Jones* and formerly in Woodlands Road

United Presbyterian (now St Jude's Free Presbyterian) Church in Glasgow. – In the NW wall, three lushly coloured painterly lights (Our Lord crowned with Thorns; Our Lord in the Wilderness; the Agony in the Garden) by *Stephen Adam Jun.*, 1909, originally in the former Trinity Congregational Church, Glasgow. – From the same source, also by *Adam*, 1909, are the three lights in the SW wall (Our Lord blessing Children; the Sermon on the Mount; the Calling of St Andrew and St Peter).

Inside St Andrew's Chapel, an ALTAR AND REREDOS designed and painted by *Alexander M. McLellan*, the woodwork executed by *R. W. Reid*, 1907–8; they originally stood in St Andrew-by-the-Green Episcopal Church, Glasgow. The stone in the centre of the altar is a fragment of the medieval High Altar of Iona Abbey. Altar front divided into four round-arched panels, each containing the painted gesso figure of a saint (SS. Andrew, Mungo, Columba and Margaret of Scotland). Altar shelf decorated with painted gesso arcading containing figures of the twelve Apostles and, flanking the tabernacle, a pair of angels. The pediment of the reredos bears a depiction of Our Lord and saints, probably the Feeding of the Five Thousand. The altar is flanked by panelling, also of 1908, with fluted Ionic pilasters. On the panels, painted gesso figures of Old Testament prophets, each accompanied by a text. On the frieze above, New Testament scenes related to the prophetic texts. – STAINED GLASS. Two windows, both formerly in Woodlands Road United Presbyterian Church. One (St Columba) is strongly coloured realism at its best, *c.* 1920. The other (St Margaret of Scotland), very competent but without the same panache, is by *Douglas Hamilton*, *c.* 1935.

ST MATTHEW (R.C.), Kirkintilloch Road. By *Gillespie, Kidd & Coia*, 1950. Long brown brick rectangle with narrow rectangular windows. On the narrow W porch a pair of PANELS carved by *Benno Schotz* with scenes from the life of St Matthew.

SPRINGFIELD CAMBRIDGE CHURCH, Springfield Road and The Leys. Complex of various dates. The church itself, at the NE, is by *James Houston & Son*, 1971–2. Dry-dashed above a brick base. Monopitch roof and clearstorey windows in the high W end wall. It is joined by a hall extension of 1948–50 by *J. Ruthven* to a hall of *c.* 1910. This is a very broad simply detailed Gothic box, a four-light window in the S gable.

CADDER CEMETERY
Crosshill Road

Opened in 1887. At the SW corner, a two-storey LODGE by *Wharrie, Colledge & Brand*, 1886–7, plain despite its bargeboards and verandah. – Just N of the lodge, the craggy granite MONUMENT to Inspector James Allan of the Lanark Constabulary †1893; on it, a bronze relief portrait bust of a helmeted policeman. – On the cemetery's W side, the MONUMENT to William Alexander †1936, the pedestal surmounted by the polished granite statue of a horse.

PUBLIC BUILDINGS

AUCHINAIRN COMMUNITY EDUCATION CENTRE, Auchinairn
Road. Originally Auchinairn School. W block by *David Thomson*,
1874–5. Tall single-storey, with elliptically arched three-light
windows and a gabled porch. E block added 1906–7 by *Stewart
& Paterson*. Again single-storey, of three bays, the broad ends
gabled, with Venetian windows; columned cupola on the roof.

BALMUILDY PRIMARY SCHOOL, Stirling Drive. By *D. Harvey
& A. Scott & Associates*, 1962. Flat-roofed blocks, the three-storey
main building faced with bands of brick and glass.

Former BISHOPBRIGGS HIGH SCHOOL. *See* Public Library,
below.

BISHOPBRIGGS HIGH SCHOOL, South Crosshill Road. By the
Lanarkshire Deputy County Architect *Alexander Farquhar*, 1966.
Flat-roofed four-storey box. Symmetrical front, its horizontal
bands of glass and concrete aggregate interrupted by glazed
verticals.

CADDER PARISH CHURCH NORTH HALL, Cadder Road.
Built as Cadder Parish School in 1856–7. Tall single-storey, the
broad eaves supported on moulded corbels. At the N end, the
rubble-walled former schoolhouse (No. 21 Cadder Road) built
by *John Henderson*, wright in Bishopbriggs, 1826. Simple two-
storey three-bay house, with small windows at the upper floor.

CADDER PARISH CHURCH SOUTH HALLS, Kirkintilloch Road.
Gothic, by *David Sturrock*, 1896, the appearance that of a mission
church.

POLICE STATION, Kirkintilloch Road. By *James Lochead* of
*Alexander Cullen, Lochead & Brown*, 1914–15. Squared-up but
asymmetrical Scots Jacobean block originally containing the
police station, fire station and associated housing. Canted SE
corner topped by a conical-roofed low round tower. The main
entrance is Artisan Mannerist. Corbelled out at the springing level
of its roundheaded arch are urn-topped Ionic pilasters which
flank the mantled and crested coat of arms of Lanarkshire; cornice above.

PUBLIC LIBRARY, Kirkintilloch Road. Originally Bishopbriggs
High School. By *David Sturrock*, 1895–6. Tall single-storey main
block in a School Board Jacobean Gothic manner. Bargeboarded
eaves and hoodmoulded mullioned windows. Central entrance,
the spandrels of its pointed arch carved with roses and thistles,
placed at the base of a square tower. At the tower's second stage,
three-light mullioned and transomed belfry openings. Above
these, corbels carved with naturalistic flora (roses and thistles at
the front) on which stand cluster-shafted columns, their capitals
again naturalistically foliaged, supporting steep gablets containing clock faces. Rising from within the gablets is a slated spire
topped by a weathervane.

ST HELEN'S PRIMARY SCHOOL, Wester Cleddens Road. By
*Lanarkshire County Council*, 1970. Single-storey, the walls of
ribbed metal cladding or fully glazed. Tall round metal chimney
and a skeletal water tower provide vertical emphases.

THOMAS MUIR HIGH SCHOOL, Wester Cleddens Road. By *Strathclyde Regional Council*, 1977. Collection of flat-roofed buildings, the carefully asymmetrical main block with alternating bands of render and glass above a base of dark brick. Other blocks are lower, their brick walls under wooden fascias.

TURNBULL HIGH SCHOOL, St Mary's Road. By *Lanarkshire County Council*, 1974. A variant on the formula used at Thomas Muir High School (q.v.).

WATER TOWER, Boclair Road. Erected c. 1960. Large round concrete water tower (now painted) supported on stilts and a central octagonal shaft.

WESTER CLEDDENS PRIMARY SCHOOL, Wester Cleddens Road. By *Wright & Kirkwood*, 1962. Lightweight-looking in the Festival of Britain manner.

WOODHILL PRIMARY SCHOOL, Kirriemuir Road. By *Lanarkshire County Council*, 1973. Low and flat-roofed, the walls faced with aggregate and glass.

## DESCRIPTION

SPRINGBURN ROAD carries the A803 across Colston Road, the boundary between Bishopbriggs and Glasgow. The street name quickly changes to KIRKINTILLOCH ROAD. At its S end, small cottage villas of *c.* 1900. Among them, on the E side, Nos. 4–6, a single-storey and attic double house with extravagantly barge-boarded gabled end bays. A little further up, a bay-windowed tenement block (Nos. 24–38), again of *c.* 1900, stranded in this suburban context. It is followed by late C20 commercial garages until the road crosses the railway line. Immediately N of the railway VIEWFIELD ROAD going off to the W leads to Kenmure Parish Church (*see* Churches, above). Cottage villas of *c.* 1900 then resume on the W side of Kirkintilloch Road. Set back from them at Nos 1–1a BRACKENBRAE ROAD of 1997 is a Post-modern version of a 1930s double house.

The arrival of the town centre is announced on the W by the Police Station (*see* Public Buildings, above) followed by an ashlar-fronted and bay-windowed two-storey tenement (Nos. 119–121) of *c.* 1910. Opposite, the CROW TAVERN, its two-storey main block mid-C19 Georgian survival but remodelled in 1902–3 by *Alexander McDonald* of *McDonald & Currie* who added a gabled porch and, at each end, an ogee-domed round tower of late C17 inspiration. Then SPRINGFIELD ROAD exits to the E through a skewed segmental arch, presumably of 1842, under the railway embankment. In this street, some late C19 villas leading to Springfield Cambridge Church (*see* Churches, above).

On the N corner of Springfield Road, No. 130 Kirkintilloch Road, a three-storey tenement of *c.* 1900, with a couple of two-storey bow windows sitting on top of the console-corniced shopfronts. Then the TRIANGLE SHOPPING CENTRE, a two-storey pitched-roofed brick-walled commercial development by *The ADF Partnership*, 1989–91, the shops set behind a loggia. Opposite, on the S corner of KENMURE AVENUE and Kirkintilloch Road, a WAR MEMORIAL of 1919 by *H. Findlay & Son*. Polished granite Celtic cross, the front embellished with ball ornament and a relief of foliage. On Kenmure Avenue's N corner, Nos. 129–173 Kirkintilloch Road, a long three-storey tenement of 1898, with two-storey canted bay windows above the shopfronts. Further N and set below the present road level, St Matthew's R.C. Church (*see* Churches, above) followed by the Public Library backing on to Bishopbriggs High School (for these, *see* Public Buildings, above) whose main face is to SOUTH CROSSHILL ROAD. On this street's N side, No. 5 is an L-plan villa of *c.* 1910, built of hammer-dressed masonry. Broad-eaved, with mullioned and transomed windows. Two-storey bay window projecting from the bargeboarded SE main block; piend-roofed single-storey NW wing.

On Kirkintilloch Road's W side, a little N of South Crosshill Road, Cadder Parish Church South Halls (*see* Public Buildings, above). On the S corner of BALMUILDY ROAD, WOODHALL, a substantial villa of *c.* 1900. Crowstepped gables and gablets. Semi-octagonal bay window clasping the NW corner; a conical-roofed low tower at the NE. Opposite, No. 4 Balmuildy Road, an early C20 red sandstone villa, with Art Nouveau detailing at the entrance. This is overlooked from the E by the water tower in Boclair Road (*see* Public Buildings, above). On the E side of Kirkintilloch Road, N of Balmuildy Road, Nos. 204–206, an early C20 double house in hammer-dressed red sandstone. Squared-up symmetrical Jacobean, the twin-gabled centre flanked by two-storey semi-octagonal bay windows. Also Jacobean of *c.* 1900 and built of hammer-dressed red sandstone is No. 219 Kirkintilloch Road (RATHEARN) but it is much more vertical and determinedly asymmetrical. Some way further out, HILTON ROAD leads off Kirkintilloch Road to the W. On its N side, St James the Less Episcopal Church (*see* Churches, above).

At the N end of Kirkintilloch Road, almost on the edge of the town, CADDER ROAD goes off to the NW. On its N corner, a broad-eaved single-storey lodge (No. 2 Cadder Road) of the earlier C19, a hoodmoulded mullioned and transomed two-light window in its S side. Further along Cadder Road, on the SW side, Cadder Parish Church North Hall (*see* Public Buildings, above) followed by cottages built by Archibald Stirling of Keir and Cadder in 1909 to house estate workers. Harled walls with red sandstone dressings. Cornices over some windows; scrolled skewputts at the advanced and gabled ends. On the NE side of Cadder Road, THE OLD BRIDGE HOUSE, a white painted single-storey double cottage, probably of the early C19 and originally thatched. It overlooks the Forth & Clyde Canal which is crossed by a bridge; its ashlar abutments of *c.* 1775 survive but the drawbridge has been replaced by a fixed C20 roadway. On the other side of the canal, CADDER MILL. In its present broad-eaved form it is of the mid C19, of one and two storeys. Near-symmetrical front of five bays, the single-storey three-bay centrepiece with a gableted porch. Taller single-storey S bay. The N bay is of two storeys and incorporates earlier work. At the back, two projecting wings, each with a hoodmoulded first-floor window of two roundheaded lights. Segmental-arched ground-floor windows at the N wing. To the N, Cadder Parish Church (*see* Churches, above).

HUNTERSHILL HOUSE, Crowhill Road and Huntershill Road. Harled two-storey laird's house of *c.* 1765. Five-bay front with rusticated quoins and scrolled skewputts. Skinnily proportioned centre door in a Gibbs surround; projecting keystones at the window architraves. Inside, a basket arch from the entrance hall to the stair. Late C20 additions to the W and N.

CAWDER HOUSE. *See* p. 321.

## BLACKNESS*

F *0070*

Small village beside the Firth of Forth into which sticks the promontory surmounted by Blackness Castle.

BLACKNESS MISSION CHURCH. Originally St Ninian's (Episcopal) Church. By *James Thomson*, 1914–15. Dry-dashed, with triangular-topped windows and dominated by a large slated splay-foot spire. It was intended to be cruciform but only the crossing was built.

CHAPEL. On a small hill S of Blackness Castle, low remains of a rubble-built medieval chapel dedicated to St Ninian. The single-cell nave and chancel may be C13, the S transept probably a late medieval addition. The building was destroyed in 1650 when Cromwellian troops used the hill as a gun emplacement to bombard Blackness Castle.

HARBOUR. Small drystone-built and concrete-topped pier, by *W. M. Scott*, 1905.

### DESCRIPTION

C19 and C20 buildings. At the centre, a cast iron baluster PUMP with leafy base, dome and finial, 'the gift of Alexander McLeod Esq. of Nova Scotia to the inhabitants of his native village 1875'. Next to it a roughly contemporary DRINKING FOUNTAIN with similar top and lion's-head spout. N of these, GUILDRY is a redevelopment of *c.* 1960 by *West Lothian County Council*, a single harl and rubble block, intelligently concentrated at a point of vantage in relation to both land and water. To its N, the Harbour; to the S, Blackness Mission Church (for these, *see* above).

### BLACKNESS CASTLE

Blackness Castle on its headland sticks out into the Firth of Forth 51 like a ship. The two end towers are traditionally called the stem (N) and stern (S), with the curtain walls between them forming a deep rock-bottomed hold on which stands the 'mainmast' tower.

* Account based on that by Colin McWilliam, *The Buildings of Scotland: Lothian* (1978).

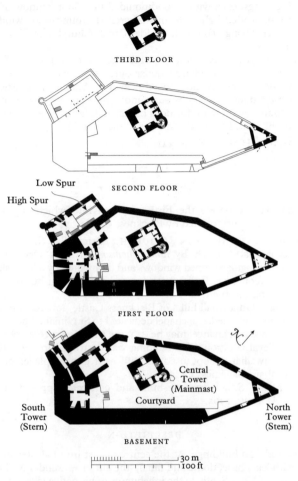

THIRD FLOOR

SECOND FLOOR

Low Spur

High Spur

FIRST FLOOR

Central
Tower
(Mainmast)

Courtyard

South
Tower
(Stern)

North
Tower
(Stem)

BASEMENT

30 m
100 ft

Blackness Castle. Plans.

The barony of Blackness was in the ownership of Sir George
Crichton, Earl of Caithness and Admiral of Scotland, by the 1440s
and he seems to have been responsible for building the castle,
which is first recorded in 1449. That work involved the construction of a curtain wall round the boat-shaped promontory, with a
small triangular tower (the 'stem tower') at its N end and a larger
tower (the 'stern tower') at the S. Roughly in the middle, a free-
standing tower (the 'mainmast tower').

As part of his assertion of royal power James II annexed
Blackness to the Crown in 1453 and the castle was thereafter held
by a royal captain or constable and keeper. From this time until the
Treaty of Union of 1707 the castle was used as a state prison, princi-
pally for political prisoners, the most notable being Cardinal David
Beaton, Archbishop of St Andrews, who was held there in 1543.

Probably by chance Cardinal Beaton's imprisonment came at the end of a major reconstruction of Blackness Castle begun by *Sir James Hamilton* of Finnart in 1536 and completed four years after his execution in 1540. The work included a massive strengthening of the defences at the landward (s) end and E side of the castle, the thickness of the curtain walls being increased from *c.* 1.5m. to *c.* 5.5m. and massive splayed gunloops (their throats up to 0.4m. in diameter and their external openings up to *c.* 1.5m.) being inserted. The C15 principal entrance on the E side, blocked by the thickening of the curtain, was replaced by an entrance near the s end of the W side, approached through a rectangular outshot (the Spur) containing a dog-leg passage commanded by gunloops. The first floor of the s tower was converted to a gun emplacement and the tower heightened to provide a new hall above. At the same time a stair tower was added at one corner of the central tower.

The castle, held by supporters of Mary, Queen of Scots, during the period of civil war after 1567, was blockaded and captured by trickery in 1573. During the civil wars of the next century Blackness was besieged by Cromwellian troops in 1650 and, after being badly damaged by bombardment from the hill to the s, surrendered and was then abandoned. After repairs, including alteration and thickening of the W curtain, in 1667 the castle was again garrisoned and brought back into use as a prison. The Spur was heightened as a gun emplacement in 1693. After the Treaty of Union of 1707 the castle ceased to be used as a prison until the late C18, when it housed French prisoners of war, but the garrison function continued and an area to the s and E was reclaimed and laid out as a parade ground. In 1870 the C15 castle was converted to the central ammunition depot for Scotland and new barracks buildings were put up to the W and s of the parade ground.

Blackness Castle's present role as an Ancient Monument began in 1912 when it was taken over by *H.M. Office of Works*. Major repairs and a remedievalizing of parts that had been altered were undertaken in 1926–35.

The approach from the s is across the flat parade ground formed in the C18 or C19. On the s side, a Georgian survival BARRACKS block of 1870–4. On the W side, a contemporary OFFICERS' QUARTERS, its appearance more aggressive with crowstepped gables and low towers over the entrance, all built of hammer-dressed ashlar. Also of the 1870s, a store, with bracketed eaves, at the parade ground's SE corner; cottage to its N.

The medieval castle at the N end of the parade ground is built of dark brown whinstone rubble with paler sandstone dressings. An area of paler stone at the E end of the s side is evidence of substantial late C17 patching after the damage caused by the Cromwellian bombardment. Otherwise the external masonry of the CURTAIN WALLS is almost all C15. At the s and E faces 51 of the South Tower, above the two lower floors, clear evidence of the C15 battlement, its crenelles infilled when the tower was heightened in 1536–44. Above this ghost battlement in the s face, a large segmental-arched hall window of *c.* 1540. The tower's battlement is a replacement of *c.* 1930. Also of *c.* 1540 are the huge oval gunloops which pierce the base of the tower and the main E stretch of the curtain wall. Near the S end of this E stretch, the C15 principal entrance to the castle, the inner end of its ashlar-walled transe blocked *c.* 1540 when the curtain wall was thickened. The entrance was originally segmental-arched but has been opened up into the roundheaded relieving arch. The vaulted short transe has been reopened for its original 1.5m. length. N of the entrance, one jamb of a C15 slit window, again blocked internally by the C16 thickening. This stretch of the curtain is finished with a C16 parapet projected on simple moulded corbels and broken only by a couple of broad crenelles intended for cannon. At the centre, double-moulded corbels supporting a slight forward break of the parapet in which is placed the surround intended for an oblong panel. N of this main stretch, the angled 'prow' of the castle, its plain parapet flush with the main walling. Just S of the North Tower, a garderobe chute. A tier of three garderobe openings at the tower itself. The height of the tower was reduced in 1693 when its top was remodelled as a gun emplacement with a large crenelle in the E side of the parapet. Near its N end, the walling of the W curtain is broken by a roundheaded water gate, its sill just above high tide level.

At the S end of the W curtain's main stretch, a broad pointed gateway in a segmental-arched surround which was inserted in 1868 to give access to a PIER constructed by *Head, Wrightson & Co.* in 1868 and reconstructed by *Briggs Marine Ltd.*, 1996. The pier is of iron. Drawbridge at the landward end; at the far end, a concrete mole on which stands a Victorian crane made by *T. Smith* of Rodley. The angled S stretch of the curtain abuts the NW corner of the South Tower's jamb. This has dressed quoins, possibly indicating that the jamb is an addition of *c.* 1540.

Built against this angled S end of the W curtain is the SPUR, a roughly rectangular outshot added *c.* 1540 to protect the new entrance to the castle. Because of the slope of the rock it is placed at a lower level than the C15 curtain. Originally one storey in height, the S end of the Spur (the HIGH SPUR) was heightened in 1693 to two storeys, the walling of the upper level (again a gun platform) projected on simple moulded corbels and pierced by elliptical-arched gun embrasures; at the SW corner, a round ashlar turret boldly projected on continuous corbelling. At the S end of the High Spur's W side, an oval gunloop of *c.* 1540 at the lower level and, beside it, the contemporary round-arched entrance surmounted by a large frame intended for an heraldic panel. In the W side, N of the entrance, a pair of oval gunloops which were blocked in 1693 when this part of the wall was thickened to provide a gun platform, the crenelles of its battlement formed by simple indentations in the rubble walling. In the N wall of the Spur, a rectangular-mouthed gunloop. The entrance to the Spur contains a yett of 1693 and a short tunnel-vaulted transe through the C16 wall. At its end, a door opening into an inner transe, also tunnel-vaulted, through the 1693 thickening of the wall. Under the platform of the S end's upper storey, a tunnel-vaulted chamber. This chamber, together with the inner transe, is commanded by a pair of rectangular gun-loops of *c.* 1540, their throats opening from a chamber contained in the immensely thick S wall. N of the chamber, a narrow courtyard. On its E side, steps up to the High Spur from which access is gained to the curtain's wall-walk. N of the steps, a rectangular C16 doorway, its surround chamfered, into the CASTLE COURTYARD, its irregular surface provided by the natural rock.

The internal faces of the curtain walls are enlivened by a few features of various dates. A little N of the entrance from the Spur is the Victorian entrance to the pier. To its N, a garderobe. A joint inside the garderobe makes clear the extent of the late C17 thickening of this part of the curtain. N of this, a stone roof ridge and large moulded corbels to support the wall-plate of the lean-to roof of a now demolished building, presumably of the late C17. In the W side of the 'prow', the elliptically arched embrasure of the water gate. In the 'prow's' E side, just S of the North Tower, the remains of a C15 garderobe, a mutilated stone seat at its S end and a low recess, perhaps for a lamp, in its N side. In the thickened main stretch of the E curtain, the round throats of two mid-C16 gunloops. Above them, corbels for a wall-plate so presumably there was a lean-to structure over the guns.

The S end of the castle is filled by the SOUTH TOWER (the 'stern'), its obtusely angled NW jamb set at a lower level because of the fall in the site, the inner angle occupied by a late C17 stair tower, probably replacing an earlier stair tower in the same position. The main block's N front, apparently remodelled *c.* 1540, has a nearly symmetrical arrangement of windows above the large segmental-arched central entrance, its importance emphasized by a box machicolation on simply moulded corbels at the wallhead. Chamfered margins to the door and windows but are these of *c.* 1540 or of 1667? At the basement of the jamb, a door in the N gable opening into an unvaulted store. At the ground floor of the main block, a tunnel-vaulted passage-room. The round throat of the C16 loop at its S end, like the other openings at this level, was blocked in 1667 but reopened *c.* 1930. To the E, another passage-like room, with the throats of two gunloops in its E side. W of the central passage, a slightly larger room, again tunnel-vaulted. High up in its N wall, a late C17 low door into the stair tower. Rectangular gunloop throats in the S wall and another (blocked by the C17 stair of the High Spur) at the N end of the W wall.

Also in this W wall, the entrance into a low C16 passage which steps down through the thickness of the wall to give access to a slit-like wall chamber at the S end of the Spur, the gunloops of this chamber's N side commanding the entrance passage. At the ground floor of the jamb, a comfortable unvaulted room, its N gable's plain chimneypiece probably of the late C17. The upper floors of both the main block and the jamb are reached from the stone turnpike in the stair tower. At the first floor of the jamb, a room very like the one below. In its S wall, two doors into an irregularly shaped tunnel-vaulted room in the main block, its N fireplace apparently late C17. E of this room, a tunnel-vaulted chamber which is raised by a few steps to allow for the height of the centre room below. It may have been a gun chamber; if so, the gunloops would have been destroyed by the 1650 bombardment of the castle and not replaced in the subsequent patching. E of this, a similar room, probably a powder magazine. At the second floor of the jamb, another unvaulted room. Its fireplace is probably late C17 but contains a cast iron basket of c. 1835 stamped with the initials W<sup>IV</sup>R and signed by the *Shotts Iron Co.*

The second floor of the main block contains the mid-C16 hall and kitchen. The tunnel-vaulted kitchen opening off the hall's W end is small and irregularly wedge-shaped. Plain and not very large fireplace. In the W wall, a slop drain. In the E wall, a door and service hatch into the hall. At the upper level of this side, the segmental-arched opening (blocked in the late C17 and reopened c. 1930) of a minstrels' gallery. The hall is entered from the stair through a moulded round-arched door; is this mid-C16 or late C17? There is another door at the E end of the N wall opening into a wall lobby from which a mutilated opening gives access to the curtain's wall-walk. The hall is large (c. 11.1m. by 7.0m.) and rises through the height of two storeys but is not vaulted. An upper floor inserted in 1667 was removed c. 1930 but a couple of late C17 fireplaces, each accompanied by a contemporary window, remain skied in the gables. The mid-C16 fireplace in the centre of the N side was contracted in 1667 but much of its original moulded E jamb and a little of the W survive. The fireplace now contains a stone crudely incised with the figure of a man and the date 1449 in Arabic numerals. Large windows in the S and E walls; the S is equipped with stone seats but also served as a gun embrasure. Smaller windows to the N, the E one again with seats. At the third floor of the jamb, another unvaulted room with a plain late C17 fireplace. Near the head of the turnpike, a door to the now missing inserted upper floor of the hall. Straight flight of steps from the top of the turnpike to the tower's wall-walk.

The CENTRAL TOWER (the 'mainmast') is externally plain, a five-storey rectangle, c. 10.97m. by 9.75m. At the top, the C15 continuous corbelling under the angle rounds (replacements of c. 1930) survives, as does one course along the E and W walls, but the chequer-set corbels and the battlement are of c. 1930. Round stair tower at the NE corner added in 1667, its roof another replacement of c. 1930. Immediately S of the stair tower is the rectangular entrance. In the N side of its transe through the 2.8m.-thick walls the door to the turnpike stair; the C15 stair was almost certainly contained in the wall thickness of the corner (removed when the stair tower was added). Ahead, a rock-floored ground-floor room, perhaps originally vaulted. In each wall, a segmental-arched embrasure with a stepped sill, containing a narrow window (all except the N restored in the C20). Three roughly formed aumbries unchecked for doors. No fireplace so presumably the room was a store. The first floor (the floor itself now missing) is reached from the C17 turnpike but originally was entered from a door, presumably reached by a wooden forestair, in the N gable. This door was converted to a window in 1667. Opening off its W ingo, a decent-sized wall chamber. Quite large windows in round-arched embrasures in the other walls, the S and W each accompanied by a wall chamber. Another wall chamber, perhaps originally a garderobe, in the N wall. Plain fireplace, probably late C17, in the E wall. The second-floor room is similar. Simple roll-moulded E fireplace, possibly C15. In the N wall, a garderobe. W wall chamber. Large aumbry in the E ingo of the S window. The third-floor room rises through two storeys. The crowning tunnel vault seems to be a C20 restoration, correct but tidy; stone cornice along the E and W sides. Another simply moulded fireplace, probably C15, in the W wall. Garderobe in the N wall. Large aumbry in the W ingo of the N window. Immediately NE of the Central Tower, a WELL or catch-pit.

The three-storey NORTH TOWER (the 'stem') is triangular, two of the faces formed by the curtain walls. It was built in the mid C15 but altered in 1693 when the top was remodelled as a gun platform reached by stairs from the wall-walks. First-floor S entrance opening into a tunnel-vaulted roughly triangular room. Fireplace in the SW corner, aumbries in the W and S walls. In the wall thickness at the N end, a garderobe equipped with a lamp recess. By the entrance to the garderobe, a hatch into the pit prison which occupies the floor below. In the floor of the prison, a drain which is flushed by the tide. The second-floor room is entered from the W wall-walk. Again it is a rough triangle and tunnel-vaulted. Stepped sills to the windows. At the N end, a garderobe with a narrow window and lamp recess.

## FARMS AND OTHER DWELLINGS

BLACKNESS HOUSE, 0.3km. W. Two-storey piend-roofed house of *c.* 1840. Ashlar front of three broad bays, the centre slightly advanced and containing the entrance under a block-consoled cornice. The flanking ground-floor windows are set in shallow projections.

BURNSHOT, 0.5km. SW. Two-storey farmhouse of the earlier C19. Three-bay ashlar front, the cornice over its entrance carried on block consoles. Slightly earlier extensive rubble-walled and pantile-roofed STEADING to the S, some at least of its buildings dating from 1826 when *Thomas Brown* of Uphall designed alterations and additions.

MANNERSTON, 1.3km. S. C17 laird's house, built of rendered rubble, the main block and NW jamb both with crowstepped gables. In the inner angle, an outshot, probably an addition, its E gable topped by a stone cross which looks mid-C19. C19 SE wing. Pantile-roofed single-storey office range, perhaps early C19, at the N end of the jamb.

MERRYLEES COTTAGES, 1.8km. S. Early C19 terrace of rubble-built single-storey cottages, their wallheads dressed up with obelisks at the skew ends. Hoodmoulds over the door and windows of No. 3.

# BLAIR DRUMMOND

An estate on the r. bank of the River Teith S of Doune.

KINCARDINE-IN-MENTEITH PARISH CHURCH. By *Richard Crichton*, 1814–16. A three-bay nave with lean-to aisles and a square W tower rising to an open parapet of cusped arches and with corner finials. In 1907 *Harold O. Tarbolton* removed the N, W and S galleries and added a chancel, in which he repositioned the original four-light neo-Perp E window. The diagonally buttressed entrance tower rises in three stages intaken at the buttress setbacks. The lowest stage, constructed in ashlar cut with a Latin inscription honouring the patron George Home Drummond, broadens N and S to the line of the nave walls. The nave gables W and E have raking arcaded parapets falling to crocketed finials. In the upper stages of the tower and in each bay of the nave, hooded windows with Perp tracery under four-centre arches. Quatrefoils light each clearstorey bay.

From the vestibule, which has a shallow eight-part ribbed vault, doors lead l. and r. into the nave. The central four-centred arch which once opened to a stair to the gallery is blocked. The nave, too, is similarly vaulted, the ribs bossed at ridge intersections and at the apex of the wall ribs over the quatrefoil windows. Arcades of four-centred arches separate nave from aisles; the ingoes are heavily moulded and on the nave side of the piers thin shafts rise to varied floral capitals. Over the later chancel is a four-centred arched ceiling divided by transverse ribs. Green veined marble steps to stone-flagged chancel.

FURNISHINGS date from 1907 alterations: seven-panel REREDOS in a vine frieze frame raised over three central ogee arch panels; finely carved five-panel COMMUNION TABLE with ogee-framed shields and cinquefoil holes, buff marble under table area; stone FONT, r. of chancel arch, a deep octagon carried on short octagonal pedestal. Also stone, a splendid half-octagon PULPIT, to l.; ogee arches cusped with rosettes over chamfered recesses, oak and vine leaves in the spandrels, and a grape-laden cornice. Seating for the laird behind a low partition at the rear of the nave.

MEMORIAL TABLETS. In the chancel l., on a black marble backing, a white marble panel, 1769, with egg-and-dart edging swept up into a curved pediment; to Lady Blair Drummond and George Drummond her brother. – To the r., flanked by pilasters of speckled brown-yellow marble, a cream marble panel, also C18, with a long elegantly phrased dedication to James Drummond of Blair Drummond and Lady Jane Grey his wife. – To the r. of the chancel arch, a vertical ellipse of grey-green marble on which is set proud a white marble panel with cornice and draped urn; to John Ramsay of Ochtertyre †1814. – Two stone memorials, tall Gothic aedicules, are mounted on the W wall: one inset with a white marble panel bearing a long laudatory inscription to Henry Home of Kames †1782 and his wife Agatha Drummond †1795; the other with a smaller marble inset in memory of George Home Drummond †1819. – Above the laird's

seats, in a drapery frame of cream-brown marble shaped with a
segmental head carrying the Drummond arms, an elliptical metal
PANEL incised with a lengthy familial description. – STAINED
GLASS fills every window. – In the four-light chancel window,
strongly coloured scenes from Christ's Passion, 1872. – At the E
end of the nave: N, SS. Matthew and Mark, 1873; S, SS. Luke
and John, each with his gospel and stylus, 1873. – Christ and St
Paul fill a third similar window at the centre of the S wall, 1872.
– Opposite this, St Andrew and St Margaret of Scotland, somewhat sentimentalized in sweet colour, 1952. – At the W end of
the nave: N, the War Memorial window, c. 1920; S, in warm
browns and reds, a crowned Christ carrying a lamp and Christ
the Good Shepherd, 1908.

GRAVEYARD, across the A84 from the Parish Church. Site of
former church. Irregular walled cemetery with several BURIAL
ENCLOSURES. Two are rubble-built standing to the wallhead:
in one, 1686, the resting place of the Muschets, a single gable
carries a tall armorial panel in relief, a skeleton with open Bible
(?) over the family coat of arms, while in the other, which has
corner rustication and is dated 1699, the Drummond arms sit
over the W gateway. A third, an oblong plot formerly railed,
terminates in a step-gabled sandstone wall in which are three
sharp pointed-arched recesses with cusp and dagger tracery
over inscribed pink granite panels. This is the burial place of the
Home Drummonds, reconstructed 1894, incorporating carved
stones brought from Dunblane Cathedral after the restoration
there in 1893. Within the plot, defined by a stone border with
antefixae, the grave of Henry Home, Lord Kames †1782, and
his wife Agatha Drummond †1795. – Numerous TABLE-TOMBS
and HEADSTONES, C18 and C19. Among the latter: George
Bachop †1717 (?) and family, who are represented by male and
female figures and ten infant figurines, all in relief and set within
a primitive frame of fluted pilasters under a winged angel; a
scrolled stone with a similar winged angel pediment and egg-
and-dart border, to James Bachop, his family and John Bachop,
merchant in Glasgow †1780; and a large pilastered and pedimented headstone to Robert Downie †1805, and his wife,
Margaret Morison, 'A Most Charitable and / Much Respected
Pair'.

BLAIR DRUMMOND SCHOOL, 2.4km. S of Blair Drummond
House. Dated 1850; Tudor Gothic symmetry, perhaps by R. &R.
Dickson. To the NW, between two-storey, gable-fronted wings, a
five-bay arcuated loggia interrupted by a solid centre carrying
an open octagonal spirelet. Now in residential use.

KINCARDINE MANSE. By William Stirling I, 1821. Two-storey,
three-bay S front with porch. Unusual jerkin-head roof forms.

KINCARDINE SCHOOL. 1855-7. By R. &R. Dickson, nephews
and probably pupils of Richard Crichton, architect of Kincardine-
in-Menteith Parish Church (q.v.). Single-storey classroom with
a tall gablet belfry rising from crowstepped E gable, dated 1855.
Ogee-capped ridge ventilator with finial. L-plan schoolhouse,
dated 1857, abuts W gable. Pyramid-roofed tower in re-entrant.

MILL OF TORR. Rubble shell, roofless and overgrown: part may
be C18 or earlier but extended in mid C19, perhaps by *R. &R.
Dickson*.

OLD FARM, s side of the narrow road leading to Cuthil Brae.
Perhaps by *William Stirling I*, 1829. Four-bay piended house,
harled pink. Red sandstone farm buildings incorporate a corner
porch with a single Roman Doric column.

TOLL HOUSE (Loch-hills Cottage) at the junction of the A84
and A873. 1831. Asymmetrical Tudor Gothic by *Peter Frederick
Robinson*.

BARROW, 0.6km. w. 25m. in diameter and 3.3m. high, excavated
by Sir Kay and Lady Muir in 1927–8, with the discovery of two
cists and other burials.

MOTTE, 0.8km. wsw, standing to a maximum height of 12m.,
surrounded by a broad ditch except on s. Summit area 21m. by
17m. surmounted by an obelisk.

## BLAIR DRUMMOND HOUSE

The original mansion, by *Alexander McGill*, 1715–17, illustrated in
*Vitruvius Scoticus*, was a vast if somewhat dull Classical pile; a
piended seven-bay, three-storey core linked by round stair towers
in the re-entrants to lower wings advancing s. In 1868 *James C.
Walker* prepared plans to alter and enlarge the house. These came
to nothing but his alternative proposals for a new Blair Drummond
found favour and the house took shape in 1868–72 on higher
ground to the w, while McGill's mansion was demolished.

Built in square-snecked sandstone, the conception is Baronial
but distinctly Burn-derived both in plan, where Drawing Room,
Library and Dining Room are aligned along the s front with a
complex 'scientific mode of arrangement' as advocated in Robert
Kerr, *The Gentleman's House* (1864), of corridors and courts
extending the service quarters N, and in the elevations, particularly the square E entrance tower which recalls that at Buchanan
Castle (q.v.) or the unbuilt Fonthill. This tower is the highest
element, four storeys below a heavily corbelled parapet with a
two-storey NE bartizan and a full-height, round stair tower set
in the SE re-entrant. The wide, three-storey-and-basement s front
is almost symmetrical, divided into three sections by small cylindrical towers which project from the façade and contain stairs and
closets. At the centre, a grand canted bay, dated 1869, corbels out
from the Library. Over all, E, s and w, slated cones and pedimented
eaves dormers spike the skyline. On the w, a dividing stair
descends to the garden from a balustraded balcony opening from
the main E–W corridor of the *piano nobile*. Service ranges spread
N, roof ridges enlivened by fringed coolie-hat ventilators.

The house is now used as a residential home and adapted to
the needs of its new community. Interiors, 1921–4, reconstructed
following a fire 'without any loss of grandeur'* by *James B.
Dunn*, survive.

---

* Charles McKean, *Stirling and the Trossachs* (1985), 110

Those parts of the estate grounds not given over to the nearby Safari Park are wooded or under cultivation. Walled garden and greenhouses have gone. The s lawn is terraced, the retaining wall enclosing a gigantic decorated URN set on a square base on the axis of the house. – A much-altered STABLES BLOCK, 1871, by *Walker*, lies W; it, too, is now residential. Through W gatepiers carrying knobbled ball finials is a U-plan court. In the SE corner, a low clock tower, corbelled from circular to square under a bellcast pyramid roof with gableted belfry dormers and a tall weathervane. Adjacent are the L-plan OFFICES of *c.* 1835; low random rubble ranges with gambrel roofs. S of this, a T-plan COTTAGE, *c.* 1839–40, with an arched false bellcote carrying a ball finial and cockerel weathervane. – Nearby SW, an octagonal STORE, *c.* 1800, its cornice decorated with paterae, and a rustic FOUNTAINHEAD, C18, with an illegible inscribed panel above the water-mouth. – N of the house, an egg-type ICE HOUSE, early C19.

Octagonal EAST LODGE, *c.* 1800, built in droved ashlar with lintelled windows in arched recesses and a pedimented gablet; remodelled by *R. & R. Dickson*, 1836. – WEST LODGE, *c.* 1830, gabled Tudor Gothic with porch, by *Peter Frederick Robinson* (?). – Similar in character, the NORTH LODGE ('Chain Lodge'), at Bridge of Teith (*see* Doune), dated 1859, may be by *R. & R. Dickson*. – Squat rubble OBELISK raised by Henry Home, Lord Kames, FOR HIS NEIGHBOURS AS WELL AS FOR HIMSELF, some time between 1766 and 1782; perhaps based on an Adam sketch. WALLED GARDEN, *c.* 1800, with good wrought iron E gates.

## BLAIRHOYLE                                           S *6000*
### 3km. E of Port of Menteith

The original mansion house was demolished in the 1950s to be replaced by a substantial but unremarkable dwelling. Early C19 U-plan court of OFFICES, now converted to residential use. Some basket-arched cart entries survive and a central clock tower, projecting into the courtyard on a square base but rising through an octagonal shaft to a leaded ogee roof with weathervane. – In the estate grounds, a tall square DOOCOT, possibly late C18, rubble-built with a slated pyramid roof. Three pigeon entries in a rectangular recess with ledge on the S face.

## BLAIRLOGIE                                           S *8090*

A small, picture-postcard-pretty village of whitewashed harled cottages nestling under Dumyat Hill at the W end of the Hillfoots. 2

BLAIRLOGIE UNITED FREE CHURCH. Originally Blairlogie Relief Church. Simple roughcast hall with a small bellcote on the E gable apex. In the S wall, three tall twinned windows under six equilateral arches. Above the W door a red sandstone tablet records Secessionist origins: THIS HOWSE WAS / BUILT AT THE

EXPENCE / OF THE DISSENTING / CONGREGATION OF /
LOGIE IN THE YEARS / 1761 & 1762. At the rear, another
date, 1765. Rebuilt 1846 after fire.

BLAIRLOGIE UNITED FREE CHURCH, Menstrie. *See* Menstrie.

LOGIE OLD KIRK, on the w bank of Logie Burn, 0.3km. NW of
Logie Parish Church. Only the w gable and part of the s wall of
the church built by *Tobias Bachop*, 1684, remain. At the centre of
the s wall is a lintelled door and above this another round-arched
window with Y-mullion divide. To the r., a similar window, taller
and wider, with a transom. To the l., a small square window with
a sill stone dated 1598, a fragment found (1874) in the ruins of
the session-house once located at the E end of the church. W of
this is an opening at upper level which, originally reached by a
forestair, must have provided access to one of the three lofts
known to have been constructed in 1686. The rubble gable,
carrying a columned bellcote with stone pyramid, has plain skews
and a scrolled SW skewputt; there is a small, round-arched,
bipartite window and below this, off-centre, a lintelled doorway.
– Above the door, an exfoliating stone TABLET with a carved
shield and an inscription recording its transposition (1804) from
the manse of 1698. – Inset under shingled timber canopies l.
and r. are several memorial PANELS. Best is a white marble
cornamd slab to Elizabeth Claire Graham and Cynthia Violet
Graham †1914; angels kneeling l. and r. of a radiant cross. –
Close to the gable's SW corner, a tabular SUNDIAL, dated 1684.

The ruined church sits within a walled GRAVEYARD entered
under rubble arches at the SW and NW. Beside the SW entrance
is a WATCHHOUSE. – Many lying SLABS and HEADSTONES,
most aligned in close-packed parallel rows N–S. In 1963 the
RCAHMS Inventory recorded 'nearly a hundred stones bearing
dates earlier than 1707'. Several carry armorial carving, trades
symbols, mottoes and inscriptions besides the usual initials and
dates. – Tapering HOG-BACK STONE, 1.73m. long with evidence
of tilework ornament. – E of the church a number of railed and
walled plots. Rev. Robert Clason †1831, a chimneypiece freestone MEMORIAL with long inscription. – Thomas Buchanan
of Powis †1842, and family, three stone TABLETS set in a shallow-pitched rubble gable.

LOGIE PARISH CHURCH, 1km. w of the village. By *William
Stirling I*, 1805; enlarged and altered 1900–1 by *Ronald Walker*
of *McLuckie & Walker*. In its original form, 'a plain, unpretend-
ing structure'* built in brown and grey whinstone rubble with
dressings of pale grey freestone; a piend-roofed preaching box
with a spired belfry tower centred s housing a session-room below
and a vestry above. Two round-arched windows (rather than only
one) appear on each side of the projecting steeple. The steeple
itself, low but elegant, rises on a square plan to eaves height,
where it is pedimented, before stepping into an octagonal drum
with four louvred belfry openings and four blind arches. Above
this is an ashlar spire inset with blind elliptical lucarnes. The

* *The New Statistical Account of Scotland*, viii (1845), 232.

internal arrangement originally focused on the pulpit at the centre of the s wall with galleries on the w, n and e.

In 1872 three round-arched windows were opened in the n wall, but the alterations of 1900–1 were more radical. 'With the exception of the tower, which has not been interfered with, and the side walls, which have been transformed by the putting in of new windows, nothing of the old edifice remains'*. A short gabled chancel was built e, seating re-orientated and, extending the original ridge, an imposing w end added, accommodating vestibule, cloakroom, n staircase and gallery. Finely moulded eaves cornice. The new w gable incorporates a relief carving of the Burning Bush (emblem of the Church of Scotland), three round-arched windows in a round-arched frame and wide-lintelled entrance doors flanked by plump engaged columns on plinth-blocks. Bifurcating stone tracery inserted in the n and s windows. Purlin roof carried on five arch-braced trusses from stone corbels. – Oak panelling and FURNISHINGS in the chancel with carvings of biblical subjects; by the Stirling joiner *William McPherson*, 1901. – Caen stone FONT, 1901, with alabaster pillars. – ORGAN built by *Ingram, Hope-Jones & Co.*, 1901. – STAINED GLASS. Three memorial windows in the s wall by *A. Ballantine & Gardiner*, 1901: youths armed with righteousness and faith, the good seed sown and reaped by angels, and the resurrected Christ, 'Light of the World'. – Celtic cross flanked by decorative motifs in the three-light w window by *James Powell & Sons*, London, 1903. – A Nativity and Annunciation dominate the centre of the three-light Ewing memorial e window, 1905. – In the middle of the n wall, Christ the Good Shepherd, 1904, by *A. Ballantine & Gardiner*.

In 1902 a carved oak-framed LYCH-GATE was erected at the roadside w of the new w front.

An extensive GRAVEYARD spreads s and e. The usual obelisks, draped urns, crosses, etc., all C19 and C20. Pink granite HEADSTONE to William Landell †1891; a heavily pedimented stele with crude anthemion bookends. – Pullar family MONU-MENT, *c.* 1905; low relief bronze panel in pale pink granite wall with Art Nouveau cornice and inset motifs. – At the cemetery gates, NW of the church, an L-plan COTTAGE, late C19 (?), incongruously appealing in red engineering brick with a conical-roofed entrance drum in the re-entrant.

## DESCRIPTION

The plan of the village is a simple cross, twisted attractively. A burn, channelled between rubble walls, runs N–S beside the narrow road that leads from the A91 up to The Blair. Passing W–E is the ancient track from Bridge of Allan to Menstrie. Several cottage dwellings, late C18, lend a picturesque definition to each arm of the cross. At the head of the village, where there is just the suggestion of a square, MONTANA, harled and pantiled,

* R. Menzies Fergusson, *Logie*, i (1905), 257.

faces S, the central of its three swept dormers merged into a later canted bay corbelled over a keystoned doorway. Set into the wall are a datestone (1765) and SUNDIAL. A low cottage row runs E. More swept dormers in pantiled roofs, a forestair and, in a much restored wall, another tabular sundial. Opposite this is TELFORD HOUSE, early C19; tall, gabled and inordinately severe. To the W, IVY COTTAGE, harled and pantiled, and, entered under a gabled timber porch, CROFT HOUSE, with a white-harled, chimneyed monopitch wing at the rear as sculptural as it is architectural. At right angles, Nos.1–2 ROWANBANK, attractively plain cottages, the latter with a Gothic finial on its gable dormer. THE CROFT is roughcast and dormered but short on pantiles. Beyond it, BLAIRLOGIE COTTAGE, a two-storey white piended box with an octagonal pyramid-roofed pavilion, c. 1975, by *Duncan Stirling*, in the garden. Closer to the main road is KIRKLEA, another pantiled cottage facing S, wide-fronted, with a block porch and an inset tablet inscribed AW . MG . 1758. Nearby is Blairlogie U.F. Church (*see* above) and the adjoining MANSE, 1843, gabled ashlar with pilastered ground-floor windows. To the E sits STRUAN, a mid-C19 villa carrying a full-width dormer painted reverentially with lancet astragals. Roughly contemporary but less pretentious, OCHIL NEUK, a barge-boarded cottage with an elliptical fanlight.

W of the village, facing the W gable of Logie Old Kirk (*see* above), is WARDEN COTTAGE, a harled single-storey row, probably early C19, with later gabled dormers and a gabled porch with a triglyph entablature.

THE BLAIR (Blairlogie Castle). Small L-plan tower-house erected in 1543 by Alexander Spittal with E wing added in 1582 by Adam Spittal; the date carved in the S skewputt of the E gable. Turnpike stair in corbelled SE turret retains an original balustrade at the attic. Three dormers with carved gablets: AS for Spittal himself with a fleur-de-lis; EH for his wife Elizabeth Hay and a thistle; and a rose or man's head with the date 1543. An aumbry survives in what is now the drawing room. Square bay window inserted in crowstepped S gable, probably in the C19. N wing and staircase, probably C19. Small formal garden W.

GOGAR HOUSE, 1km. SE. Mid C18. Harled three-bay, two-storey dwelling. Corner sundial.

LOGIE VILLA, 0.8km. W, on the A91. By *William Stirling I*, 1817; a school and schoolhouse in a low cottage style with half-hipped gables.

WALLACEVIEW BUSINESS PARK, 1.5km. WSW. By *Cobban & Lironi*; built in two phases 1983–86. Long, low and sleek: bronze-tinted, glazed walls below white exposed aggregate fascias. Severely but suavely landscaped with grassy banks and low privet hedge.

FORT, 1km. NE, on the SW shoulder of Dumyat Hill, a position with commanding views over the Forth, protected by steep crags to the S and E. Two walls protect the summit area on W and N, enclosing an area 130m. by 48m., with entrance to W. A small, possibly later, stone-walled dun, 27m. by 16m. in the

interior. Dumyat means 'fortress of the Maeatae', the name by
which the local Iron Age tribe was known.

POWIS HOUSE. *See* p. 639.


# BLANEFIELD *see* STRATHBLANE


# BO'NESS*                                          F *9080*

Bo'ness is short for Borrowstounness, the name of the headland
jutting into the Forth and providing a natural harbour. From the
mid C16 the Hamiltons, Earls of Arran and later Marquesses and
Dukes of Hamilton, the dominant landowners of the area, mined
and leased the local coal measures and encouraged a salt-panning
industry here. A town at Bo'ness seems to have been begun in the
early C17 and the Hamiltons promoted development of its harbour
and trading links with the Low Countries and the Baltic. A church
was built at Bo'ness in 1634 and this supplanted Kinneil Parish
Church in 1669, the year after Bo'ness was created a burgh of
regality. Daniel Defoe reported in the 1720s that the town 'consists
only of one straggling street, which is extended along the shore close
to the water' but noted also that 'It has been, and still is, a town of
the greatest trade to Holland and France of any in Scotland,
except Leith...' For much of the C18 Bo'ness served as the E coast
port for Glasgow but the opening of the Forth & Clyde Canal
with its own port at Grangemouth in 1790 robbed it of this special
position. Mining, a pottery, a distillery, a salt factory, chemical
and engineering works, brickyards, sawmills and iron foundries all
flourished at Bo'ness in the C19 but industry has largely disappeared
since the mid C20 and it is now primarily a dormitory town.


## CHURCHES

BO'NESS AND CARRIDEN FREE CHURCH, Links Road. Now
  Bo'ness United Social Club. Built in 1844–5 and originally a
  straightforward rectangle with pointed windows in the side walls
  and rectangular openings in the gables. The walls were heightened in 1850. In 1877 the S transept and W tower were added.
  At the transept, a huge two-light Gothic window, the capitals of
  its columns carved with downward-pointing acanthus leaves.
  The tower is square and squat Italianate. Roundheaded window
  openings and, at each face, a huge roundel containing a trefoil
  panel. The building was recast as an institute by *William Scott*
  for the iron and coal master Henry M. Cadell in 1908.

*Account based on that by Colin McWilliam, *The Buildings of Scotland: Lothian*
(1978).

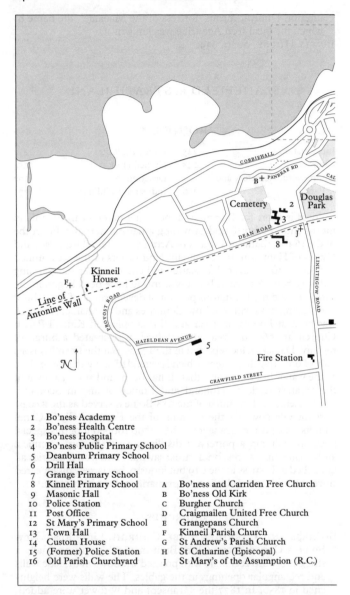

1   Bo'ness Academy
2   Bo'ness Health Centre
3   Bo'ness Hospital
4   Bo'ness Public Primary School
5   Deanburn Primary School
6   Drill Hall
7   Grange Primary School
8   Kinneil Primary School          A   Bo'ness and Carriden Free Church
9   Masonic Hall                    B   Bo'ness Old Kirk
10  Police Station                  C   Burgher Church
11  Post Office                     D   Craigmailen United Free Church
12  St Mary's Primary School        E   Grangepans Church
13  Town Hall                       F   Kinneil Parish Church
14  Custom House                    G   St Andrew's Parish Church
15  (Former) Police Station         H   St Catharine (Episcopal)
16  Old Parish Churchyard           J   St Mary's of the Assumption (R.C.)

BO'NESS OLD KIRK, Panbrae Road. Originally Bo'ness Parish
Church. Gothic with a Normandy inflection, by *R. Thornton
Shiells & Thomson*, 1885–8. Complicated composition because
of the need to provide stairs to the galleries, dominated by the N
(liturgical W) steeple. Behind the steeple, an aisled nave with
transeptal stair projections at its N end. S transepts with lower

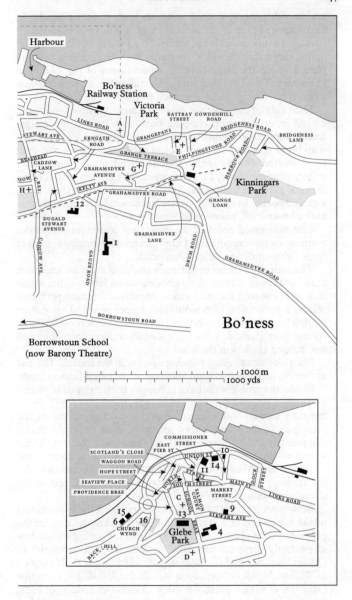

Harbour

Bo'ness
Railway Station

Victoria
Park

RATTRAY    COWDENHILL
STREET         ROAD

LINKS ROAD

A

ERNGATH
ROAD

STEWART AVE

GRANGEPANS

BRIDGENESS ROAD

BRIDGENESS
LANE

E

GRANGE TERRACE

PHILPINGSTONE ROAD

HARBOUR ROAD

BREAHEAD
CADZOW
LANE

GRAHAMSDYKE
AVENUE

G

CRES

KELTY AVE

H

GRAHAMSDYKE ROAD

7

Kinningars
Park

GRANGE
LOAN

CAZGOW AVE

DUGALD STEWART
AVENUE

12

I

GRAHAMSDYKE
LANE

GAUZE ROAD

DRUM ROAD

GRAHAMSDYKE ROAD

BORROWSTOUN ROAD

Bo'ness

Borrowstoun School
(now Barony Theatre)

1000 m
1000 yds

COMMISSIONER
STREET

EAST
PIER ST

SCOTLAND'S CLOSE

WAGGON ROAD

HOPE STREET

SEAVIEW PLACE

PROVIDENCE BRAE

UNION ST

10

11        14

NORTH STREET

SOUTH STREET

SALMON
COURT

SCHOOL BRAE

MAIN ST

DOCK STREET

LINKS ROAD

MARKET
STREET

STEWART AVE

9

C

13

15

6        16

CHURCH
WYND

BACK HILL

Glebe
Park

4

D

stair projections in their inner angles. Short s chancel a little lower
than the nave.

At the tower of the boldly projecting steeple, angle buttresses
surmounted by conical-spired turret pinnacles. In the N face of
the lowest stage, the entrance, its gable's tympanum carved with
the Burning Bush emblem of the Church of Scotland. In the E

and W sides, nook-shafted windows with trefoiled heads. In each exposed face of the second stage, a pair of hoodmoulded two-light windows with circled heads. At the third stage, tripled lights, very tall at the sides, shorter at the N front where they are placed above the large heraldic achievement of the Dukes of Hamilton. Two-light openings at the tall belfry stage; octagonal stone spire, a large lucarne at each face.

Each side of the nave's N gable, a transeptal stair projection, its tall inner part with clasping buttresses topped by foliage-finialled spired octagonal turret-pinnacles, their sides decorated with blind arcading. In the N face of each inner part, a two-light nook-shafted window with a trefoiled head; a taller but plainer gallery window above. Lower semi-octagonal ends with foliage-finialled gabled buttresses. At the N face of each of these ends, a gabled porch. In the other faces, lancet windows, nook-shafted at the lower level, plainer and squatter above.

The buttressed aisles of the nave have paired lancets under continuous hoodmoulding. Large clearstorey windows, each of three lights under a cinquefoiled head.

The stair projections in the inner angles of the nave and main S transepts have continuously hoodmoulded lancet lights which step up in line with the stairs inside. At each of the transepts themselves, a procession of hoodmoulded openings and, at gallery level, a large four-light window with cusped circlets in the head. At the short chancel, a five-light S window, large loop-traceried and cusped circlets in the head.

Plain Gothic SE vestry, contemporary with the church. The hall at the SW, also Gothic, is an addition of 1911 by *Matthew Steele*.

Inside, the rubble walls have unhappily been stripped of plaster and ribbon-pointed (the chancel in 1928, the rest in 1933). Four-bay nave arcades with alternate round and octagonal pillars, the principals of the wooden roof springing from corbelled shafts. Big pointed arches into the transepts and short chancel. At the N end of the nave, the Hamilton Loft, in the transepts, the Mariners' and Miners' Lofts, all of the 1880s. The spaces under the transept galleries were partitioned off from the rest of the church in *Kenneth Murdoch*'s alterations of 1998.

Bow-fronted PULPIT of 1886–8 incorporating the pilasters and inlaid oak panels of a Dutch pulpit imported in the C17 for the previous parish church. – STAINED GLASS. Five-light S window in perfectly clear colours (the Ascension, as a memorial to Queen Victoria) by *J. T. Stewart*, *J. S. Melville* and *R. Monaghan* of *William Meikle & Sons*, 1902–3. – In the W wall, the S window (saints) is of 1913. – Next, a window (Martha and Mary) of 1928, the detail badly eroded. – This wall's expressionist N window (St Michael and an airman, as a Royal Air Force memorial) is by *William Wilson*, 1948. – The E wall's S window (Our Lord healing blind Bartimaeus and washing the feet of St Peter) is again by *Wilson*, 1938. – Beside it a First World War memorial window (a knight, and an angel giving the wreath of victory to a fallen warrior), competent but unappealing, by *James Ballantine II*, 1919. – Next, a strongly coloured window (David and St Paul) by *William Meikle & Sons*, 1908. – In the E transept (now hidden from the church), five lights (Resurrection subjects) by *William Wilson*, 1954.

BURGHER CHURCH, Providence Brae. Disused. Rubble box built by *Nisbet*, mason in Edinburgh, 1796. Pointed windows in the side walls. In each gable a quasi-Venetian window, its centre light pointed. C19 W porch.

CRAIGMAILEN UNITED FREE CHURCH, Braehead. Originally Bo'ness United Presbyterian Church. By *J. McKissack & W. G. Rowan*, 1883–5. Simple E.E., built of blackened squared rubble. Vine carving over the N (liturgical W) door; above it, a four-light window, a cusped vesica in the head. Very tall NW tower with a crown spire composed of eight flying buttresses and an exceptionally tall central pinnacle.

Inside, the aisles are marked off from the nave by three-bay arcades, their cast iron columns hardly slender but still appearing too thin for the weight of the semicircular arches. Pointed arch into the shallow recess at the S end originally intended to house the pulpit. Galleries in the aisles and N end, their fronts of simple Gothic character. Boarded ceilings, all stencilled with stars. Original PEWS, like all the woodwork of pitch pine. The focus is a powerful combination of pulpit and organ contained in a railed enclosure. It builds up from the organ console (the ORGAN is by *Brindley & Foster*) to the pulpit which is integral with the organ case. This work is an alteration of *c.* 1900. – STAINED GLASS. Complete scheme of 1885, the side windows with roundels containing flowers and fruit. In the four-light N window, heads of the Evangelists set in a lavish floral display. In the two-light S window (largely hidden by the organ), figures of St Peter and St Paul.

GRANGEPANS CHURCH, Cowdenhill Road. Mission church of *c.* 1890. Rubble-built box, its breadth exaggerated at the E end by the lateral extension provided by the porch and by the seven-light Gothic window. Rectangular windows in the sides. Cupola-ventilators on the broad-eaved roof.

KINNEIL PARISH CHURCH, off Provost Road. Remains of an early or mid-C12 church on the W side of the gorge of the Gil Burn, abandoned for worship in 1669 and destroyed in 1745. It consisted of an oblong nave and small square-ended chancel, the footing of the side walls and E end exposed by excavation in 1951. These are of squared cubical stones as is the W gable which stands to its full height. The gable is windowless but contains three tiers of holes, some but not all penetrating through the wall as at the C12 churches of St Martin's, Haddington (East Lothian), St Helen's, Cockburnspath (Borders) and St Magnus', Egilsay (Orkney); possibly they were putlog holes. Corbelled out at the top of the gable, a double bellcote, the twin openings round-arched. There has been a transept on the S side of the chancel, probably an early C17 addition.

In the churchyard, to the S and W of the church, a number of weathered GRAVESLABS, probably all of the C17. Most are carved with shields, some of these bearing initials. The best preserved, aligned with the church's w gable, has a shield inscribed '1627/ GH K'; below, an incised depiction of an upside-down anchor.

St Andrew's Parish Church, Grange Terrace. Originally St Andrew's United Free Church. By *J. N. Scott & A. Lorne Campbell*, 1904–6, a cruciform church in pale hammer-dressed snecked rubble, its N (liturgical w) gable facing N over the Forth and nicely related, on its corner site, to a square tower which incorporates the main door. The tower has three stages: the first solid; the second with angle buttresses that send up Art Nouveau pedestals on to the clasping buttresses of the third; finally a green copper flèche. The smooth octagonal stair tower at one corner finishes with a concave, pointed roof whose eaves are pierced by eight delicate stalks with pedestals. Behind this front, a broad nave, N transepts and a short chancel. At the NE, contemporary hall dressed up with half-timbering and broad eaves.

Inside the church the plan is ingeniously simple: a four-bay nave with N gallery over the vestibule, chamfered arcade without capitals, and passage aisles merging into the transepts. Roof with concave principals and triple kingposts with tracery between. – Most of the FURNISHINGS are of 1904–6, in a restrained Art Nouveau manner, the original font now in the vestibule. – PULPIT of *c.* 1950. – STAINED GLASS. The chancel's s window (the Ascension) is by *James H. Leat* of *Oscar Paterson*'s studio, 1908. Good strong colours and hinting at Art Nouveau. – Similar N window (the Sermon on the Mount, flanked by figures of St Andrew and St Michael) by *Oscar Paterson*, 1920.

St Catharine (Episcopal), Cadzow Crescent. By *Dick Peddie & Walker Todd*, 1921. A fragment of a tiny church – sanctuary and chancel, crossing, N transept and s organ chamber, one bay of the nave, NW porch – stocky and solid in buttressed rubble (the w gable rendered) with clasping buttresses and slate-arched roundheaded windows, the transept's N window with nook-shafts. The N door has engaged shafts with unwrought block capitals and so does the rubble arch between the groin-vaulted crossing and the chancel. Plain segmental arch before the sanctuary. – ORGAN of the earlier C20. – STAINED GLASS. In the sanctuary six colourful lights (Isaac, David, Samuel, St John the Evangelist, St John the Baptist, and Timothy) of *c.* 1960. – In the N wall of the choir two lights, again colourful. One (St James) is by *Neil Hutchison*, 1982, the other (St Catherine) of 1939. – HALL on the N side added in 1924.

St Mary's of the Assumption (R.C.), Dean Road and Linlithgow Road. By *Fleming Buildings Ltd.*, 1990. Group containing church, hall and clergy house. Walls covered in dry-dash relieved by strips of brickwork; tiled roofs. The church is square with a pyramidal roof.

## CHURCHYARD, CEMETERY AND PARK

CEMETERY, Dean Road. Laid out on a steeply sloping site by *James Strang*, 1881. Dwarf boundary walls surmounted by spearhead railings.

GLEBE PARK, Braehead and Stewart Avenue. Laid out *c.* 1900. Contemporary cast iron BANDSTAND with slender Corinthianish columns and decoratively pierced brackets; open crown on the roof.

OLD PARISH CHURCHYARD, Corbiehall. Graveyard behind the site (now occupied by a former cinema) of the C17 Bo'ness Parish Church. On the w side of the entrance, the MONUMENT erected in 1796 by James Tod to the memory of his parents. Tall corniced pedestal topped by a swagged urn. Identical pedestal, now missing its urn, of 1828 on the E side of the entrance; it marks the burial place of William Shairp.

Along the churchyard's E wall, several MONUMENTS of the earlier C18 (some with later inscriptions). At the N end, a monument dated 1743 (renewed in 1874). Aedicular, the Doric pilasters' panelled fronts bearing emblems of death (arrow, scythe and spade), the swan-neck pediment broken by an angel's head (emblem of the soul); at the base, relief of a skull and bone. – Next, an C18 monument (now with an inscription to Andrew Milne †1817 and Mary Learmonth †1832). Again it is an aedicule but with barley-sugar columns and a segmental pediment broken by a cartouche topped by a grotesque head; angels' heads at the ends of the frieze. – Further s and badly overgrown with ivy another barley-sugar-columned and segmental pedimented aedicule (now with an inscription to John Burnett) dated 1722. Carved skull on one side of the pediment. – Similar monument, the columns with Corinthian capitals, just to its s.

Remarkable collection of C17 and C18 HEADSTONES (many now bearing C19 inscriptions). Near the NE corner, placed against the wall of a burial enclosure, a stone of *c.* 1800 to John and Frederick Duncan carved with a sailing ship. – To its w, a stone of 1728 to WH, WS and others, the w face incised with a mariner's quadrant. – The top of the stone to the s (inscription to Peter Steven and Isobel Maltman) is dated 1687. On the E face, a relief of two floating angels who hold a crown above a figure climbing out of a coffin. On the w side, a very jolly angel of the Resurrection flourishing a book and trumpet and trampling on a skull and hourglass. – Just SE of this, a stone dated 1738, the relief of a mariner's quadrant on the w face. – Immediately to its w, an C18 stone (now with a C19 inscription recording the burial place of Alexander Blair and Margaret Paris). On the w face, a large angel's head above an acanthus-bordered panel which is carved in high relief with a maltster's (?) implements and the initials JY and MJ. – w of this, another C18 stone (inscription noting the burial place of George Gunning). On the E face, caryatids with baskets of fruit on their heads. Above, an angel's head and a round panel bearing the initials WC/MM. – Immediately to the N, a small but richly carved scroll-topped stone displaying a high relief angel of the Resurrection. – N of this, a stone almost identical to the one before that. – Again to the N, an C18 stone (inscription noting the burial place of Thomas Smith and Janet Boag), the E face incised with a couple of weavers' shuttles. On the w, two round-arched panels each containing a human figure, one standing under a sun, the other under a moon. – To the N, a stone with initials including IB FC and IB MH. On the E side, the inscription flanked by begging angels; on the W, a sailing ship. – W of this, a large stone with the weathered high relief of an angel waking a corpse. – To its SW, large but charmless stone of 1838 (renewed in 1895) to Captain James Mackie, again with a sailing ship.

Near the S wall of the churchyard, a stone of 1742 (inscription noting the burial place of John Thomson and Janet Morton), an incised mariner's quadrant and anchor on the W face. – A little to its N, a stone of 1735 (inscription to Alexander Taylor and Janet Mair), the sides carved with torches and angels' heads. On the E face, an inscription cloth framed by Ionic pilasters; on the W, panelled pilasters and a shield bearing emblems of death. – W of this, an C18 stone (now noting the burial place of Richard Hamilton) again with an incised mariner's quadrant. – To its N, a stone to Thomas Grindlay †1741, also with a mariner's quadrant and anchor but in relief. – SW of this, the HEADSTONE, apparently C18, erected by James Arkley in memory of his relatives, the top carved with the head of a wigged man. – To its W, a large GRAVESLAB, perhaps of the C17. The top is carved with a very badly weathered angel's head over a cartouche, the bottom with a skull, crossbones and hourglass flanked by a mariner's quadrant and anchor. – N of this graveslab, a HEADSTONE bearing the initials IR IM and the date 1797. On its E side, fluted Doric columns and a pediment with skulls on the ends; on the W relief of angel of the Resurrection and an incised tailor's goose (?) and iron. – A little to the NE, an C18 stone (now with the date 1838 and noting the burial ground of John Boag and Margaret Meikle). Pair of cherubs' heads on top of the E face, a skull and winged hourglass on the W. – Immediately to the W, a stone of 1776 to Andrew Aikman, an angel's head at the top of each face.

Near the SW corner of the churchyard, several more C18 STONES. One (now inscribed to Alexander Glen, Janet Gardaner and Thomas Binnie) is dated 1792. Aedicular E face with fluted pilasters and a segmental pediment with angels' heads on its ends; angel of the Resurrection on the W face. – To the NW, a smaller C18 stone (now with an inscription to Helen Brown). Cheerful angel's head on the E face, reliefs of an anchor and mariner's quadrant on the W. – To its S, a stone of 1750 to RE, the W face displaying a butcher's cleaver, knife, sharpener and trestle (?). – To the SE, the stone to William Roy and Grizzel Henderson, the E side carved with fruit. – Just to its N, a stone to Agnes Shearp, the scroll-sided top bearing the date 1621. On the E face, the initials DS and IR and a crowned hammer, the emblem of the smiths. – Near the S end of the W wall, an C18 barley-sugar-columned MONUMENT almost hidden by ivy.

## PUBLIC BUILDINGS

BO'NESS ACADEMY, Gauze Road. By *The Parr Partnership*, 1998–2000. Large but unexciting, the walls faced in concrete blockwork and render, the shallow monopitch roofs covered with ribbed metal. Ventilators of C19 maltings inspiration.

BO'NESS HEALTH CENTRE, Dean Road. *Alison & Hutchison & Partners*, 1981. Brown brick walls and flat roofs.

BO'NESS HOSPITAL, Dean Road. By *John Nicol Jarvie*, 1999. Informally composed single-storey, with dry-dashed walls and pitched roofs, girdled by wheelchair ramps.

BO'NESS PUBLIC PRIMARY SCHOOL, Braehead and School Brae. Plain single-storey block by *John Paterson*, 1874–5, with prominent gables and bracketed eaves. It was thickened to the N by *Alexander Cullen*, 1900. NE addition by *Cullen*, 1902–3, in a Queen Anne manner. Simple late C20 NW addition. At the NW corner of the site, the INFANT SCHOOL of 1895.

BO'NESS RAILWAY STATION, off Dock Street. Collection of buildings acquired and rebuilt on this site by the Scottish Railway Preservation Society from 1981. At the E end, the main TICKET OFFICE AND REFRESHMENT ROOM of 1997-8, traditional in style, with a valenced canopy. – Opposite on the N side of the line, a RAILWAY SHED on the 1980s. Of red brick with white trimmings. At the ends, round-arched engine entrance under circular openings. – Then, on the S side, a wooden STATION BUILDING with red and white brick chimneystacks enlivening its S elevation. On the platform side, decorative bargeboards and a valenced awning. It was formerly at Wormit (Fife) where it was built in 1887. – Next, a TRAIN SHED by *John Miller*, 1840–2, originally of twelve bays and at Haymarket Station, Edinburgh. Its length was reduced to eight bays when rebuilt here in 1983–4. Roof supported on fluted cast iron columns from which spring elliptical arches, their spandrels with heavy rinceau decoration; upside down anthemions along the internal roof ridge. The S arcade has been filled with boarding. – Near the N side's W end, a broad-eaved pyramidal roofed SIGNAL BOX, probably of the late C19, which came from Garnqueen Junction (Glasgow). – At the W end of the station, a lattice-girder FOOTBRIDGE of the later C19, formerly at Murthly Railway Station (Perth and Kinross).

BORROWSTOUN SCHOOL, Borrowstoun Road. Now the Barony Theatre. By *John Paterson*, 1877. Tall single-storey. U-plan front, symmetrical except for the placing of one wallhead chimney. Jerkin-headed gables and porches; broad eaves.

CUSTOM HOUSE, Union Street. Now in other use. By *William Simpson*, c. 1881. Long but ponderously detailed two-storey block built of bullnosed rubble, the building's name spelt out in cast iron letters above the centre. Elliptically arched ground-floor openings, some emphasized by hoodmoulds; at the upper floor, basket-arched windows, some with piended dormerheads. At the E end, a first-floor window of two lights which are surmounted by panels carved with roses and thistles and flanked by canine 'gargoyles'; above, a Frenchy pavilion roof.

DEANBURN PRIMARY SCHOOL, Hazeldean Avenue. By *Marshall, Morison & Associates*, 1969. Single-storey, with brown brick walls and wooden fascias; monopitch rooflights provide vertical emphases.

D RILL HALL, Corbiehall. Now a garage and rather altered. Built
*c.* 1890. Long and low, symmetrical free Jacobean of a sort.
F IRE STATION, Crawfield Road. By *Central Regional Council*,
1981. Built of blockwork, with diagonally ribbed wooden fascias.
Sculptural concrete hose tower.
G RANGE PRIMARY SCHOOL, Grange Loan. By *H. &D. Barclay*,
1905–6. Long block on a towering site, with the two entrances
(for boys and girls) at the symmetrical w end. A mixture of
Art Nouveau and Queen Anne, boldly modelled in snecked
rubble.
K INNEIL PRIMARY SCHOOL, Dean Road. By *George L. Walls
& Duncan*, 1954. Lightweight-looking with shallow-pitched
copper roofs.
M ASONIC HALL, Stewart Avenue. By *Matthew Steele*, 1909, and
probably his best work. Piended roofs, the eaves supported by
stumpy tapered columns without any detail at all; the four centre
ones support a bell-profiled stone canopy over the door; above,
a boat-shaped dormer.
Former POLICE STATION, Corbiehall. Now offices. Built in
1891. Neo-Georgian U-plan front with consoled pediments over
the entrances.
P OLICE STATION, Union Street. Blocky, by *Central Regional
Council*, 1981.
P OST OFFICE, corner of East Pier Street and Union Street.
Eccentric but bureaucratic English Baroque, by *James Thomson*,
1911–12.
S T MARY'S PRIMARY SCHOOL, Gauze Road. By *Alison &
Hutchison & Partners*, 1954. A strong composition unimpaired
by a diversity of materials, in the Festival of Britain manner.
T OWN HALL, Stewart Avenue. By *George Washington Browne*,
1902–4. On a difficult site and with only £10,000 to spend,
Browne combined the two functions of Town Hall and Public
Library in one long block, symmetrical on its E–W axis but not
the side; in fact it looks like a secular church. Hall to the w with
a big lantern and an apsidal end, its upper windows of thermae
type; library to the E with single-storey bows to N and S, its
windows all domestic. The join is marked by a pair of little
domed clock towers related to those at Adam's Register House
(Edinburgh), and sections of the parapet are relieved with a
light Bramantesque balustrade. Vermiculated underbuilding
makes up for the steep slope on the N, and from here it presides
not too pompously over the town centre. From the S it is festive
but informal.

### KINNEIL HOUSE
off Provost Road

Large late medieval tower-house extended by the addition of a
pacific 'palice'* block in the mid C16, the medieval tower then
remodelled in the 1670s as a Restoration showhouse.

*The word 'palice' was used in C16 Scotland for a laird's or noble's house which
was not a tower.

The barony of Kinneil was granted by Robert I to Walter FitzGerald, ancestor of the Hamiltons (later Lords Hamilton, Earls of Arran, and Marquesses and Dukes of Hamilton) in the early C14. In 1473, on the eve of his marriage to the Princess Mary, sister of James III, James, first Lord Hamilton, was granted a royal licence '*construendi et edificandi castrum infra mare situatum nuncupat Craglyoune*' ('for the construction and building of a castle called Craglyoune sited above the sea') and the next year received a crown charter confirming his ownership of the lands of the barony of Kinneil and of the '*castrum de Kynneil nuncupatum Craglyoune*' ('the castle of Kinneil called Craglyoune'). Although it is improbable that the construction of a major tower house was completed within a year it seems likely that the W range of the present house was built in the 1470s and certainly before 1490 when another crown charter confirmed James, second Lord Hamilton (and later first Earl of Arran), in his ownership of the lands and barony of Kinneil '*unacum cum castro et fortalicio de Craiglioun*' ('together with the castle and fortalice of Craiglioun'). In 1532 Margaret Douglas, wife of James, second Earl of Arran, received a life rent of the '*turrim et fortalicium de Kinneil*' ('the tower and fortalice of Kinneil').

On the accession to the throne of his cousin, Mary, Queen of Scots, in 1542, the second Earl of Arran, who was then heir to the Crown, became Regent of Scotland and in 1549–50 the accounts of the Lord High Treasurer of Scotland record payments for wood (boards, deals and roof joists) supplied to Kinneil. Some significant reconstruction of the buildings there is indicated, probably a remodelling of the tower. This phase of work seems to have been completed by 1552 when the accounts note the supply of trees for the Earl's garden at Kinneil.

A second stage of building work attributable to the Regent Arran began in 1553 when the Lord High Treasurer's accounts record the provision of a horse for the 'stane carte in Kynneil' and payments of drink silver to *Thomas Bargany*, 'masoun wirkand in Kynnele', and to 'the masons in Kynnele... at the laying of the ground stanes of the palice of Kynnele'. This 'palice' consisted of a large NE wing added to the C15 tower and probably having the new garden on its N side. From the evidence of the heraldry incorporated in its internal decoration it was completed during the Regent Arran's lifetime and presumably before 1566 when he went into exile in France. Probably the work is all of 1553–c. 1555.

In 1570, during the civil war following the escape of Mary, Queen of Scots, from captivity in Lochleven Castle, the house at Kinneil was stated to have been blown up by the Earl of Morton. This seems to have entailed a wrecking of the C15 tower, the NE 'palice' range remaining apparently unharmed. It is likely that the tower was then abandoned but the NE range remained in use and was partly redecorated and probably extended by the second Marquess of Hamilton, grandson of the Regent Arran, in the early 1620s.

The second Duke of Hamilton was succeeded by his daughter, Anne, in 1651, her husband, the first Earl of Selkirk, being created Duke of Hamilton. In the 1670s this pair began a reconstruction of Kinneil House in which the C15 tower was remodelled as the formal centrepiece of an intended U-plan showhouse. Work continued until 1688 but the proposed SE range balancing the mid-C16 NE palace block was not built.

Kinneil House remained in the ownership of the Hamiltons until 1936 when it was acquired by the burgh of Bo'ness which granted to a housebreaker the right to demolish the building and remove such materials as he wished. Demolition began later that year but was halted after the discovery of C16 and C17 painted decoration in the palace block and this part of the house was then taken into state guardianship. Some internal restoration was carried out in 1936–41 and the corner turrets of the main block reroofed c. 1980.

The site of the house and the park to its E is a promontory bounded by the gorges of the Gil and Dean Burns on the W, N and E. The present house is placed at the promontory's NW corner and, before the planting of the woodland to its W and N, was a dominating presence above the low-lying coastal strip beside the Forth.

The approach is from the E where N and S garden walls enclose a broad forecourt bisected by a gravelled drive. At the entrance to the forecourt, ball-finialled PIERS, probably of the late C17; attached Roman Doric columns at their E faces.

57 Straight ahead is the W range. Its E front, as remodelled in 1675–86, owes its general conception to a series of houses built or remodelled in Scotland from the 1660s whose fronts have flat-roofed and balustraded centrepieces between projecting gables or towers. Where Kinneil differs from these is that the centre block (the remodelled C15 tower) is taller than the end towers or pavilions. The front of this centre block is of five storeys, the wallhead finished with a balustrade, the roof formerly topped by a cupola. Symmetrical three bays, the windows of the ground and fifth floors small, those of the first floor very tall to denote the *piano nobile*. The segmental-pedimented doorpiece has a pair of consoles accompanied by a lateral pair drawn in shadow-like relief, an unusual detail apparently taken from the churchyard gateway of 1662–3 at Rutherglen Old Parish Church (Glasgow). Projecting at each end of the front is a square four-storey pavilion, built of harled rubble, the top floor marked off by a moulded stringcourse. The pavilions' pyramidal roofs were removed in the 1930s and restored c. 1980. The windows are placed towards the inner corners, the unbroken walling beyond providing a tower-like strength. That the N pavilion is of mid-C16 origin, contemporary with the N range which it joins to the C15 tower, is indicated by built-up windows in the E, N and W walls. Its E front formerly displayed a large moulded frame containing the coats of arms and mottoes of the Regent Arran and his wife, Margaret Douglas, daughter of the third Earl of Morton. This pavilion was remodelled in 1675–86 when the balancing S pavilion was built. At the S pavilion, a large moulded frame for an heraldic panel. Tusking and blocked door openings in the pavilion's S wall show that the house was intended to have a SE

range to balance the palace block. The line of this range's intended N front is now marked by a wall which ends at a pier with an attached column; it used to have a ball finial.

At the back of each pavilion, in its inner angle with the main block, a rubble-built late C17 stair tower, its wallhead rising just above that of the pavilion. Over each stair tower, a crowstep-gabled monopitch roof abutting the main block.

The rear elevation of the main W block displays evidence of a complicated building history. It is rubble-built, of five storeys and a basement. At the basement and ground floor, large oval gunloops, possibly of the 1470s but their resemblance to those at the early C16 'Outer Entry' to Linlithgow Palace (West Lothian) suggests they are insertions of the 1540s. At the S end, a (blocked) comfortably sized window. Above, more blocked windows of various dates, several quite large. The tower's S gable is of ashlar and without openings; it seems to have been rebuilt in the 1670s. The lower part of the N gable is C15; the upper part may be C17.

The N side of the forecourt is occupied by the palace block of 1553–c. 1555, a substantial but pacific crowstep-gabled rubble-walled L-plan house with a NE jamb whose E side is flush with the gable of the main block. Both the main block and the jamb are of three storeys and an attic. Very large first-floor windows at the S and E elevations and the N gable of the jamb; like all the openings they have chamfered margins. The NW inner angle of the main block and jamb has been infilled, probably c. 1620. The addition (now roofless) is slightly lower than the original work but contains four storeys. At the W end of its N wall, moulded corbels carrying a very shallow garderobe projection.

INTERIOR. The late C15 tower originally included the principal accommodation although doubtless supplemented by ancillary buildings. The Regent Arran's construction of the N ('palice') range in the 1550s provided in it two virtually self-contained suites of rooms, that on the first floor for his own occupation, that on the second for his wife's, the planning apparently derived from the 'lodgings' of the King and Queen in contemporary Scottish royal palaces, each consisting of a hall, chamber and bedchamber. The late C17 remodelling integrated the tower and 'palice'. The new entrance at the centre of the tower led into a hall whose S end opened on to a state stair in the new SW pavilion. The stair rose to the first floor where the whole of the tower was occupied by the Great Dining Room, presumably a remodelling of the C15 hall. From this a room (the Small Dining Room) in the N pavilion gave access to the 'palice' range where the C16 first-floor hall became the Great Drawing Room, the chamber Duchess Anne's Bedchamber, and the bedchamber her dressing room; the floor above contained a drawing room, bedchamber and dressing room for her husband.

The main W block (the remodelled C15 tower), now without floors or partition walls, shows complicated signs of reconstruction and alteration. The outer walls are very thick at the ground-floor level, the W wall immensely so, almost certainly the result

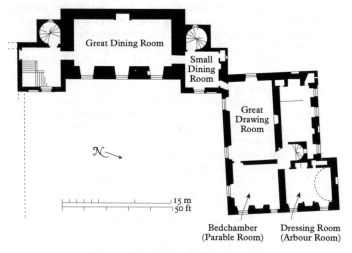

Bo'ness, Kinneil House. First-floor plan.

of its having been reinforced as an artillery fortification in the 1540s. In it are the (blocked) segmental-arched throats of three gunloops; the basement gunloops are no longer accessible from inside. Otherwise almost all of the few surviving features of this block and its N and S pavilions belong to the late C17 reconstruction. The state stair in the S pavilion was of stone with thickly bullnosed steps and corner landings. Only its lower part remains, bereft of its heavy balustrade. At the top of the stair, a plaster cornice and frieze whose amorini develop into foliage in which appear the heads of crocodiles. At the centre of the long W side of the first floor of the main block, a large bolection-moulded stone chimneypiece. Fireplaces in the end walls at the second and third floors of the main block, three of their bolection-moulded chimneypieces surviving. In the W wall of the fourth floor, a pair of fireplaces. At each floor of the S pavilion, a blocked S door to the intended but unbuilt SE range. At this pavilion's second and third floors, plain chimneypieces. Behind the pavilion, a comfortable turnpike stair, the unmoulded treads projecting beyond the risers and their inner ends partly hollowed out. Identical stair behind the N pavilion. At the ground floor of this pavilion there is clear evidence of blocked C16 windows, one at the W end of the N wall, the other at the N end of the W wall. In the NW corner of this room, a fragment of late C17 cornice. At the tall first-floor room (the late C17 Small Dining Room), a late C17 plaster frieze. Stone chimneypiece, its moulded surround crossed at the bottom by diagonal blocks. It looks early rather than late C17. In the N wall, immediately W of the fireplace, a blocked C16 window with a recess in its W side. Plain stone chimneypiece, probably late C17, in the room above. Except in the top room of this pavilion, the late C17 doors to the W tower and the N turnpike stair have moulded stone surrounds. Unornamented doorways

to the NE 'palice' range; they are squeezed rather awkwardly
into the NW corner.

The ground floor of the 'palice' range is largely intact although
with some C20 subdivision. Along the S side, a tunnel-vaulted
corridor off which open three tunnel-vaulted stores, the SW with
an aumbry in its N wall. N of the central store is a turnpike stair
and E of the stair another tunnel-vaulted room in the range's NE
jamb. The NW ground-floor room, also tunnel-vaulted but
probably an addition of *c.* 1620, has been a kitchen. Fireplace
and oven at the W end. At the E end of the N wall, an aumbry.
The addition of this kitchen and the rooms has been wrapped
round the originally external N and W sides of the stair.

The NW and SW rooms of the 'palice's' upper floors are roofless. The first-floor SE room (the C16 chamber, the late C17
Duchess Anne's Bedchamber, and now known as the PARABLE
ROOM) has a simple moulded chimneypiece, probably of the
1550s, at the E wall. It is placed between two windows, the
narrower S one built up and its embrasure converted to a
garderobe recess, perhaps in the late C17. Coffered oak ceiling,
probably of the 1550s, the design strongly geometrical; it has
been partly painted in red and black (simulating ebony). The
walls are covered with painted decoration of the 1550s (restored    58
by *John Houston*, 1936–8) executed in black for outlines, white,
grey and russet-red, with occasional touches of ochre. The scheme
seems intended to simulate tapestries or tapestry cartoons hung
within arched panels between a dado and frieze. At the dado,
massive piers from which spring elliptical arches, each containing a foliage-filled urn surmounted by a cherub's head. On the
dado band, arabesque decoration in which are placed a variety
of motifs, e.g. at the S wall medallion portraits placed in wreaths
supported by cupids who sprout fruiting acanthus-leaf tails, at
the W vases, children, ribbons, floral sprays and bunches of fruit,
and at the E a roundel containing a figure of Justice. The main
panels are set in three-centred arches springing from Corinthian
columns with clustered shafts; spandrels painted with simulated
ashlar, each containing a roundel framing a human head. On
the frieze which extends along the S, W and N walls are portrait
busts set within widely spaced wreaths linked by youths, their
torsos emerging from acanthus-leaf tails which curl round to end
in dolphins' heads. The principal panels contain scenes from the
parable of the Good Samaritan and three subsidiary panels figures
emblematic of Christian penitence, all probably derived from
woodcuts. On the E wall is shown the man falling among well-
armed and armour-clad thieves. Two trees are topped by laurel
wreaths enclosing shields, the N bearing the arms of the Regent
Arran collared with the insignia of the Order of St Michael which
he was granted in 1548, the S his arms impaling those of his wife,
Margaret Douglas. At the E end of the S wall, one of the subsidiary panels depicting St Jerome in the Wilderness, gazing on
a crucifix, his l. hand resting on a skull. This wall's main panel
shows the Priest and Levite passing by (the identifying inscriptions transposed), the Priest dressed in mitre and dalmatic, the

Levite wearing the square cap of a doctor of divinity; behind
them, a walled city (Jerusalem). On the w wall, the two main
panels, both badly defaced, show the Samaritan binding the
wounds of the victim and the Samaritan placing the victim on
his own horse while another horse looks on; behind, two more
views of Jerusalem. At the wall's N end, above a door, a subsidiary panel depicting the Penitent Magdalen. At the w end of
the N wall, the third subsidiary panel. This shows a woman
stabbing herself, probably a representation of Lucretia whose
suicide was seen as a symbol of penance. The two main panels
of this wall, again defaced, depict the arrival at the inn, the head
of the Samaritan still very clear, and the innkeeper being paid
by the Samaritan whose horse takes a benevolent interest in the
transaction.

The NE first-floor room (the mid-C16 bedchamber, late C17
dressing room and now known as the ARBOUR ROOM) is tunnel-
vaulted. Simply moulded stone chimneypiece, probably of the
1550s, at the E wall. At the w wall, an elliptical-arched buffet
recess; garderobe to its N. The walls and ceiling were decorated
in the mid C16, this scheme being painted over by a new one in
the 1620s. This second scheme was in turn covered over in the
late C17 when pine panelling and a new coat of plaster were
applied to the walls and ceiling. The plaster and panelling were
removed in 1936 followed by partial removal of the 1620s decoration to expose about half of the mid-C16 work. The result is
archaeologically interesting but aesthetically unsatisfactory.

The mid-C16 decorative scheme, its palette restricted to the
same colours as in the SE room, consisted of a dado painted with
foliage and finished with a foliaged dado band. Growing out of
the dado band are twinned branches covered with leaves and
flowers; set among these, but not necessarily supported by them,
are birds and animals (e.g. on the s wall, a greyhound coursing
a deer, a dove, a squirrel, a rabbit and a pheasant; on the w wall,
an owl, a unicorn, a rabbit and a dog). Scattered over the foliage
are scrolls bearing proverbial sayings and spiritual exhortations.
The branches curl round circular panels containing depictions
of scenes, on the s wall Samson and Delilah, on the w a badly
damaged Temptation of St Anthony, on the N Abraham and
Isaac, and David and Bathsheba. On the ceiling are two more
mid-C16 roundels. The s contains the arms of the Regent Arran
under a ducal coronet (for the French dukedom of Chatelherault
granted him in 1549) and circled by the collar of the Order of St
Michael (conferred on him in 1548). In the foliage below the
roundel, an antelope gorged with a coronet, the heraldic supporter
of the Hamiltons. The s roundel, half covered by the 1620s
decoration, bears the same coat of arms impaling another, presumably that of the Regent's wife, Margaret Douglas, again
under a ducal coronet and circled by a knotted cord; in the
roundel's border are displayed the cinquefoil emblem of the
Hamiltons and the mullet of the Douglases.

The early C17 decoration was much more architectural and
strongly coloured than the scheme it covered. It consisted of a

high dado painted to simulate oak panelling and finished with a frieze bearing the coats of arms of James, second Marquess of Hamilton, and his wife, Anne Cunningham, and surmounted by an acanthus-leaf cornice. At the upper part of the end walls above the 'panelling', a painted simulation of enriched plaster-work embellished with amorini. On the ceiling, the simulation of a compartmented plaster vault, the ribs imitating red marble. On the larger compartments are painted flying amorini who scatter fruit and flowers. At the centre of the ceiling, an oval panel bearing the heraldic achievement and initials of James, second Marquess of Hamilton, the arms circled by the Order of the Garter providing a date for the work of between 1621, when he was made a knight of that order, and his death in 1624. On the soffit of the E window, a panel decorated with the heraldic achievement and initials of his wife, Anne (Cunningham), Marchioness of Hamilton. Above the lintel of the window, a pair of cherubs placed among blossoms and holding cords from which hangs a plaque displaying the Marchioness's coroneted cypher. At the back of the buffet recess, a small C17 painted sketch of a naked spinster, probably contemporary with the decorative scheme but produced only for the artist's amusement.

On the second floor the NE room contains a stone roll-and-hollow moulded chimneypiece at the N end; garderobe in the W wall. In this room are kept fragments of plasterwork and painted wooden beams taken from elsewhere in the house.

SCULPTURED STONES from the house and from Kinneil Parish Church and its graveyard are preserved in the SW ground-floor room of the 'palice' block. Among them is the KINNEIL CROSS, a weathered slab carved in relief with a depiction of the Crucifixion (the figure of Our Lord surviving only in shadowy form except for his feet). As nothing very like it survives in Scotland or England there can be no certainty as to its date although the C12 seems likeliest. The hand of God above the head and the stiffly outstretched pose recall such late Anglo-Saxon roods as that at Romsey in Hampshire. The format of the cross, in particular the oblong ends and the disc behind, appears to be unique, at least in large-scale stone sculpture. It is not easy to know for what sort of setting the cross was designed. It was not free-standing because the back is rough, but the finished sides, those of the cross ends carved with crosses, mean that it was never let into a wall. The most likely answer is that it was supported on a corbel above the chancel arch.

Large HERALDIC STONE of the 1550s, formerly on the E front of the pavilion in the inner angle of the W and N ranges. It is divided into two panels by fluted attached columns, their capitals of Corinthian inspiration, supporting a would-be egg-and-dart cornice. In the l. panel, the coat of arms of the Regent Arran under a ducal coronet and circled with the order of St Michael from which is suspended a (now headless) antelope (the Hamilton supporter). In the r. panel, the arms of the Regent's wife, Margaret Douglas, again with a ducal coronet and circled by a knotted cord from which hangs a wild man or wodehouse,

the heraldic supporter of the Douglas earls of Morton. At the
bottom of the stone, panelled pilasters frame, on the l., the relief
of a saw and the Hamilton motto 'THROVGH', and, on the r.,
the relief of a fetterlock and the word 'SICHIR' for the Douglas
motto 'Lock Sicker'. A second ARMORIAL STONE is of the late
C17 and carved in high relief with the heraldic achievement of
Anne, Duchess of Hamilton. – Various GRAVESLABS from
Kinneil Parish Church. One bears the date 1632, the initials
DM and KV and a crown. Another has a marginal inscription
to John Hamilton †1607, son of the Chamberlain of Kinneil.
Stepped cross on the slab to William Graffard, perhaps of the
late C16 or early C17. Two more slabs bear incised crosses.
Another, probably late medieval, is carved with a circled cross,
roundels placed between the arms. Late medieval fragment of a
floriated CROSS.

Immediately SW of the house is WATT'S COTTAGE, a roofless and very plain single-storey workshop built *c.* 1769 for James
Watt who worked there on developing an improved model of a
steam engine to be used for pumping.

At the NE corner of the forecourt, an informal rubble-built
L-plan group. The pantile-roofed W range, formerly stables and
now a museum, looks of the mid C19. The slated E range contains a double house, probably of the early C18. Single-storey
pantile-roofed E addition, perhaps late Georgian.

## DESCRIPTION

It is the landward terrain that gives Bo'ness its extraordinary character. The old town, merging into Grangepans and Bridgeness to
the E, occupies a thin coastal strip. Villas and churches, Victorian
and Edwardian, look down on it from the airy heights immediately to the S. Town hall and board school stand halfway down,
and the slope is negotiated by steep pathways and hairpin roads,
workers' houses pushing uphill, villas gingerly downhill. The strong
personalities of two local architects, *Matthew Steele* and *James
Thomson*, supplemented by others of national repute, provide still
further interest. Post-1945 development has been concentrated,
though that is not exactly the word, in Grangepans and on the
plateau to the S; the centre has seen a modest late C20 recovery
after what threatened to be terminal decline.

DEAN ROAD carries the A993 in from the W along the edge of the
plateau above the coastal strip. The first incident is provided by
the Cemetery (*see* Churchyard, Cemetery and Park, above) on
the N. Beyond but set well back and below the level of the road,
Bo'ness Hospital and Bo'ness Health Centre. Opposite, on the S,
Kinneil Primary School (for all these, *see* Public Buildings, above)
followed by St Mary's of the Assumption (*see* Churches, above).
On the opposite corner of LINLITHGOW ROAD, SEAFORTH
(Nos. 109–111 Dean Road and Nos. 43–45 Linlithgow Road)
by *Matthew Steele*, 1909. Two-storey flatted block, the walls
pebble-dashed with hammer-dressed stone dressings. Canted
corner. Recessed entrances, those to the upper flats placed behind

balconies reached by external stairs. The free style hints at modernity despite the mullioned windows. Further E, No. 33 Dean Road, a broad-eaved single-storey and attic house of *c.* 1900. Roundheaded windows, a very large one in the front of its battlemented rectangular bay.

CADZOW AVENUE leads s to the MINGLE housing development of 1967 by *Alison & Hutchison & Partners*. Sensible but unexciting, boredom averted by the terraces' stepped frontages.

CADZOW CRESCENT leads downhill to the N. At its top, on the W corner, ROSEMOUNT by *James Dodds*, 1909–10; bayed and battlemented, i.e. quite Victorian in character. Further down, on the E side, four two-storey blocks of local authority housing (Nos. 25–47) by *Matthew Steele*, 1935. Traditional piended roofs but horizontal strips across the rendered frontages and cut-out corner windows strike a modernistic note. To the N, St Catharine's (Episcopal) Church (*see* Churches, above). On the corner of Cadzow Crescent and Cadzow Lane, TIDINGS HILL, an English Arts and Crafts villa of 1908 by *A. Hunter Crawford*. Relaxed composition in roughcast with red tile roofs and leaded windows; gable kept pointedly separate from the chimney stacks. At the foot of Cadzow Lane is BRAEHEAD. In it, to the E, is THE TOWER, a sizeable Victorian villa with an octagonal tower. Plain late C19 vernacular cottages to its E. No. 16, on the W corner of Cadzow Lane, was built as Bo'ness United Presbyterian Manse in 1859. Piend-roofed Georgian survival with a corniced doorpiece. Beside it, Craigmailen United Free Church (*see* Churches, above). On the N side of the street, Glebe Park (*see* Churchyard, Cemetery and Park, above). On the park's E side, in SCHOOL BRAE, Bo'ness Public Primary School (*see* Public Buildings, above).

N of this, in STEWART AVENUE, on the corner of Providence Brae, the former LIBERAL CLUB (No. 37 Stewart Avenue) by *J. McKissack & W. G. Rowan*, 1884. Scots Jacobean, with ball-finialled crowstepped gables, the W containing a large mullioned and transomed round-arched window. Balustraded balcony carried on heavy stone corbels. Steep pediments over a pair of first-floor windows at the s front. Immediately to the N, in PROVIDENCE BRAE, the former Burgher Church (*see* Churches, above). In Stewart Avenue E of Providence Brae, on the N, a block (Nos. 73–81) of local authority housing by *Matthew Steele*, 1935, again with horizontal cement strips enlivening the rendered walling and cut-out corner windows. To its E, OCHIL TOWER by *James Thomson*, 1903, a battlemented tower on the SW corner of the balustraded front. A little further E, the Masonic Hall (*see* Public Buildings, above). Some way further E, on the s side, more 1930s housing (Nos. 62–66), a pair of jerkin-head gables at the front. On the N, Nos. 131–135, a strange triple house by *Matthew Steele*, 1909; bays and gables all in rough snecked rubble – even the projecting eaves course – but the chimney stalks end in smooth tapered bells. In Stewart Avenue W of Providence Brae, the Town Hall (*see* Public Buildings, above) on the N side of Glebe Park. To its W, the WAR MEMORIAL by

*Galt & Barr*, 1924. Large fat obelisk with a flattened pyramidal top; a pulvinated frieze at the top of its pedestal. In PANBRAE ROAD to the w, Bo'ness Old Kirk (*see* Churches, above).

CORBIEHALL carrying the A904 along the coastal strip is reached by a path down from the church. Just w of the foot of the path, Nos. 191–199 Corbiehall, a long three-storey block of flats by *Matthew Steele*, 1935. The length is broken by five taller vertical sections containing the entrances and stairs, all with deep fluted friezes, the central three parapeted, the outer gabled. E of the foot of the path, on the s side of the road, the late C18 No. 101. Rubble-built with a pantiled roof and stone forestair. To the E plain blocks, Nos. 83–85 of 1908, Nos. 79–81 of 1935, and Nos. 75–77 of 1905. At their end, a U-plan development (Nos. 43–51) by *Matthew Steele*, 1932–3, of two- and three-storey flatted blocks. Doors at the bottom of tall chimney breasts decorated with fluting and rising to battered stacks. Further E again, on the site of the former Bo'ness Parish Church, the former BO'NESS PICTURE HOUSE by *Matthew Steele*, 1921. Tall shed-like auditorium set behind a modernistic two-storey foyer block, the centre of its shallowly convex front marked off by piers; pantiles on the sloped coping of the front wall. The yard beside the cinema gives access to the Old Parish Churchyard (*see* Churchyard, Cemetery and Park, above). On the yard's E side, a single-storey pyramid-roofed late Georgian session house refronted *c.* 1900. Opposite the cinema, the former Drill Hall and Police Station (*see* Public Buildings, above). The s side of the street ends with a two-storey terrace (Nos. 3–11) of *c.* 1905, with shallow canted oriel windows, and No. 1 by *James Thomson*, 1904, with a bowed quadrant corner to Church Wynd. On the E side of CHURCH WYND, a plain but unaltered harled cottage of the mid C19 (No. 19) and, to its s, a C19 extension of the churchyard.

SEAVIEW PLACE carries on the line of Corbiehall E of Church Wynd. Car park on the N side. On the s, Nos. 23–27 (the former CLYDESDALE HOTEL) of 1877 by *John Melvin & Son*, Georgian survival turning Baroque. The w wing was heightened by *James Thomson* in 1907. Then, Nos. 1–11, a long block of flats by *Matthew Steele*, 1937. Three-storey piend-roofed pavilions at the ends; two storeys for the rest. The projecting horizontal strips over the entrances and the banding of the concrete blockwork walling with green tinted blocks at the ground floor provide touches of Art Deco. Tightly bowed corner to Providence Brae.

The town centre is a triangle bounded by the V-shaped North Street on the N and the straight South Street on the s. At NORTH STREET's sw end the buildings on its SE side have been removed. On its NW side, filling the space between it and WAGGON ROAD, a big five-storey former warehouse (Nos. 1–13 North Street and No. 29 Waggon Road) of *c.* 1800. Rubble-built with rusticated quoins. Three-bay sw gable with tall hoist openings at the centre. Plain merlon-like chimneys top the wallhead at this gable and the long sides. Bowed stair tower to Waggon Road. Late C19 shopfronts to North Street. The building was converted to housing by *Falkirk District Council*, 1978–80. To its

NE and stepping forward is the late C19 Italianate No. 15 North Street. Another step forward at Nos. 19–21 by *D. Harvey, A. L. Scott & Partners*, 1979, a harled and pantiled essay in East Neuk vernacular revival. At the same time pantiles replaced slates on the roof of the mid-C19 ashlar-fronted Georgian survival two-storey block at Nos. 25–29. Also Georgian survival the near-contemporary Nos. 31–35 containing housing over shops. North Street now curves to the SE (*see* below) but its line to the NE is continued by Scotland's Close.

SCOTLAND'S CLOSE starts off, on its W side, with a building of two storeys and a basement. The front's cement render and pilastered doorpiece are of the mid C19 but may disguise an C18 origin. It is joined by a segmental arch to the S gable of a four-storey and attic warehouse. In this gable, a large segmental-arched entrance, its keystone carved with the initials IC and the date 1772. Projecting keystones (many renewed in the restoration by *Falkirk District Council*, 1978–80) at the first- and second-floor windows of the three-bay gables. Five-bay W elevation. Pyramid-roofed stair tower at the centre of the W side. The warehouse is joined by a low rubble and slate link of 1978–80 to a rubble-walled and pantile-roofed two-storey vernacular build-ing (the former WEST PIER TAVERN). Forestair to a first-floor door, its lintel inscribed with the date and initials '17 F.MG. MR 11'. The N gable was remodelled in the early C19 when it was given straight skews with scrolled skewputts, large windows joined by a sill course, and a pilastered doorpiece. Crowstepped S gable in which are remains of the demolished adjoining house. At the ground floor, a large fireplace, its lintel's W end supported by a rounded corbel; small aumbry, probably a salt box, imme-diately to its W. A moulded stone chimneypiece at the first floor. These suggest the house was C17. On the E side of Scotland's Close, the rubble wall of a two-storey building, probably of the early C18, its door and windows now blocked and the roof covered with corrugated iron. To its n, a rubble-walled lean-to, perhaps contemporary.

NORTH STREET to the NE of the junction with Scotland's Close starts with a Scottish Baronial block of 1884. Bowed corner jettied out to a low round tower bristling with cannon-spouts and finished with a tall slated conical roof. Crowstepped gablets; steep triangular and segmental pediments at the dormerheads. Opposite, on the E corner with HOPE STREET, a road formed in 1902, the ROYAL BANK OF SCOTLAND, authoritarian Neo-Georgian of the earlier C20. On the W corner of Hope Street, THE HIPPODROME, a theatre of 1911–12 by *Matthew Steele*. Harled circular auditorium with rectangular ticket-office projec-tions; the one at the street corner, with a low domed cupola, is an addition of 1936 by *John Taylor*.

Hope Street junction is the signal for North Street to turn to the N for a short stretch. On the W side, the rendered vernacular front of No. 45, C18 but altered. Stepping forward to its N, rubble walling of mostly roofless late C17 or early C18 buildings back-ing on to the building facing Scotland's Close (*see* above). In the gable of the N, remains of a broad segmental-arched entrance whose missing keystone bore the date 1717. On the E side of this stretch of North Street, Nos. 42–46, built as the ANCHOR TAVERN in 1891 to a design by *Arthur Colville*. Baronial, the bowed corner topped by a fish-scale-slated conical roof. This provides a hinge in the street which turns to run to the SE. On the NE side, No. 57 of 1879. Tall two storeys but plain except for a few Jacobean hints. E of this, buildings have been removed to make a small pedestrian precinct surrounded by planting and, to its N, bus stances; East Pier Street (its W buildings demolished) forms the E boundary. In the centre of the square, a tall late Victorian cast iron fluted LAMP STANDARD, with dolphins and shells at the base; it was made by *A. Ballantine & Sons, New Grange Foundry*, and erected here in 1985 when the clock (by *James Ritchie & Son*) was added.

At the N end of EAST PIER STREET, the Post Office and, in UNION STREET to its E, the Custom House (for these, *see* Public Buildings, above). The line of East Pier Street is carried N across the railway line to the harbour (*see* Public Buildings, above).

MARKET STREET was formed in 1902 as a S continuation of East Pier Street running from North Street to South Street. On its W corner with North Street, the CLYDESDALE BANK, by *John Baird & James Thomson* of Glasgow, 1904. Neo-Georgian in polished red sandstone ashlar. In the middle of the street, at its N end, the JUBILEE DRINKING FOUNTAIN gifted to the town in 1887. Granite pedestal (the fountain) topped by a tall lamp standard. On the N face of the pedestal, a bronze relief bust of Queen Victoria; on the S, the coat of arms of Bo'ness. At the E corner of North Street and Market Street, a couple of buildings set well back from North Street, the small square in front of them marking the old centre of the town. The first of these buildings (No. 1 Market Street) is a straightforward harled and piend-roofed two-storey block of the early C19. The adjoining No. 74 North Street is an imposing gable-fronted block of 1786. Three storeys and an attic, harled, with strip quoins. Front gable of three bays, the openings grouped 2/1, the upper windows linked by sill courses. Restored by *William A. Cadell, c.* 1980. E of this, North Street narrows again for its final stretch lined with a disappointing mixture of late C19 and C20 architecture. For the end block on the corner of Commissioner Street, *see* below.

SOUTH STREET is the second principal street of the town centre. Its N side begins at the W end with plain late C19 commercial architecture. Then, No. 9 of *c.* 1800, its three-bay front of roughish ashlar (refaced at the ground floor), the roof now pantiled. Pantiles also at No. 11 but used to more consciously picturesque effect. This is by *Matthew Steele*, 1907. Closely spaced windows at the upper storeys, those of the first floor pushed up through the eaves in a miniature turret. The ashlar-faced ground floor is almost entirely occupied by a horseshoe-arched shopfront which is to Steele's design but not executed until 1979 (by *William A. Cadell*) when it replaced a shop of more conventional design.

Pantiles again at No. 13 where a moulded panel provides the date 1750 together with the initials RB and EB. Three-storey harled front of a symmetrical five bays, the first-floor windows linked by sill and lintel courses. Moulded eaves cornice. (Inside, C18 panelling and stone chimneypieces survive at the first floor and chimneypieces at the second.) The corner block with Hope Street (Nos. 15–17 South Street) of 1884 is Baronial in hammer-dressed rubble, with a conical roof over the bowed corner. On the S side of South Street as far E as School Brae, low-scale buildings of the earlier and mid C20 (the single-storey block of shops at Nos. 24–32 by *John Taylor*, 1934); they lack presence.

E of Hope Street, the N side of South Street continues with Nos. 19–21, by *James Thomson*, 1903, Neo-Georgian of a sort, a balustrade over the bowed corner. ANDERSON BUILDING (Nos. 23–27) of 1902, also by *Thomson*, continues in similar manner but the pulvinated friezes over the first-floor windows and lugged architraves introduce late C17 Holyrood-revival touches. Next, Nos. 29–33 by *Peter L. Henderson*, 1901. Unexciting Scottish Baronial in hammer-dressed masonry except for an ashlar-faced conical-roofed round turret jettied out at the corner of Market Street. On the opposite corner, Nos 35–41 South Street by *James Thomson*, 1901–2, with some Jacobean detail. Much bolder and more idiosyncratic Artisan Mannerist detail at Nos. 43–45 and Georgian touches at Nos. 47–51, both blocks of *c.* 1900. Beyond this the N side of the street abandons architecture.

On the S, set back at the corner of School Brae, SALMON COURT by *Alison & Hutchison & Partners*, 1978, an unhappy exercise in Neo-Georgian. Then the Jacobean TURF TAVERN of 1900, a broken pediment over the canted NE corner. Small classical block of *c.* 1900 at No. 52. Much more ambitious the adjoining Renaissance palazzo (Nos. 54–60) by *James Thomson*, 1900, but the stugged ashlar is unappealing and the building is far too pompous for the site. The set-back DALRIADA HOUSE is a late Victorian former infants' school. Tall single-storey, the windows elliptically arched. Its central porch topped by a bellcote was removed in 1934 when *Miller & Black* converted the school to a Baptist church. The building line is re-established by the tripartite-windowed stepped gable of No. 62, by *James Thomson*, 1903. To its E, No. 66 of 1883. Jacobean, built of hammer-dressed rubble, an ogee dome over the canted corner. Then the large and urbane late C18 two-storey and attic block at No. 68. The ground floor is taken up by a shopfront. Five-bay first floor, the centre marked off by fluted Doric pilasters whose triglyphed individual entablatures are placed above the eaves level and support an open pedimented gablet containing a round-arched and keystoned attic window. Club skewputts at the ends. Tall but plain late Victorian former BO'NESS CO-OPERATIVE SOCIETY PREMISES enlivened only by a pair of panels in rope-moulded surrounds, one panel bearing the Society's coat of arms, the other the statement that it was

'INSTITUTED 1861'. A couple more plain late C19 buildings at the end of the street.

COMMISSIONER STREET runs N from the E end of North Street. At its S end, two blocks of local authority flats of 1934, both with canted corners. At the W block (Nos. 113–139 North Street), a tower and a semi-octagonal headed door; at the E (No. 2 Commissioner Street), narrow horizontal cement bands across the render. Opposite, on the S side of MAIN STREET, the English Baroque Nos. 2–6 of *c.* 1900. Beside it, YE OLDE CARRIERS QUARTERS by *James Thomson*, 1904–5, with a trio of barge-boarded gablets, the outer two containing half-timbering. Pub-Jacobean ground floor articulated by wall-shafts which rise from thistle-carved corbels; large foliaged stops at the ends of the cornice. It is followed by open space. On the N side of Main Street, a long two-storey flatted block (Nos. 1–3) by *Matthew Steele*, 1936–7 but recast in the late C20. Over the door of No. 1, a reset SUNDIAL bearing the date 1741 and the initials RS/MC. Beyond is TESCO by *Ian Burke Associates*, 1989, the windowless blockwork of the front wall hiding the large low shed behind; entrance in a pyramid-roofed pavilion. Very plain tenements of 1909, the W designed by *James Thomson*, on the corners of DOCK STREET whose entrance is announced by a lavishly decorated late Victorian LAMP STARDARD by *The Bo'ness Iron Co. Ltd*. At the N end of Dock Street, on the corner with Union Street, the former BO'NESS IRON CO. OFFICES by *Matthew Steele*, 1908. Two storeys, the main walling of hammer-dressed rubble but this constitutes little more than infill between the dressings which are of vertically droved ashlar with horizontal droving at the corners. Parade of recessed bay windows. Segmental pediment over the off-centre entrance, its position marked by a small battlement breaking the line of the bracketed broad eaves. Projecting from the NE corner, a canted bay window, a half-timbered gable appearing behind its battlement. At the NE corner of Dock Street, the entrance to Bo'ness Railway Station (*see* Public Buildings, above).

LINKS ROAD, the E continuation of Main Street, is mostly industrial or derelict. On the S side, near the end of the road, the New Grange Foundry (*see* Industrial Buildings, below). Opposite the foundry, the former Bo'ness and Carriden Free Church (*see* Churches, above).

GRANGEPANS to the E was largely rebuilt in 1958–69 to designs by *Alison & Hutchison & Partners*. Remarkably cogent layout of two-storey houses varied by three- and four-storey flats, all in grey brick and white roughcast, some with clearstorey windows. On the S side of the street, THE CROWN, a pub of 1909 by *James Thomson* and similar to his other one in Main Street (*see* above). Again a trio of bargeboarded gablets, all with half-timbering. At the ground floor, recessed bay windows under a cornice carried on wall-shafts springing from corbels, some carved with crowns, others with thistles. Further E, on the corner of Rattray Street, a couple of very plain blocks of flats over shops built for the Bo'ness Co-operative Society, one in the late C19, the

other by *John Taylor*, 1935–6. Further E, COWDENHILL ROAD
climbs uphill to the N. On its W side, the former Grangepans
Church (*see* Churches, above). On its E, two-storey housing by
*Matthew Steele*, 1932, the doors placed in coffin-shaped vertical
slits; rendered walls banded in brick. In BRIDGENESS ROAD,
the E continuation of Grangepans, on the S, Nos. 16–24
(CRAIGFOOT TERRACE), a two-storey and attic flatted block
of model housing built by the coal and iron master Henry M.
Cadell in 1890. Ground floor of hammer-dressed masonry, first
floor and attic gablets picturesquely harled and half-timbered.
At Nos. 38–40 Bridgeness Road, a pair of three-storey blocks
designed by *John Taylor* and built for Bo'ness Town Council in
1934. Piend-roofed Neo-Georgian except for the cement band-
courses across the harled walls. E of these, a mixture of late C19
and late C20 cottages along the main road with 1930s housing
to the S. On the corner of Harbour Road another three-storey
flatted block for Bo'ness Town Council, by *Matthew Steele*,
1932–3, a jazz-modern vertical panel rising above the door and
through the eaves. This block is placed between two roads
which rise uphill to the S. Harbour Road is the E one of these.
Near its foot, in BRIDGENESS LANE, is GRANGE HOUSE, its
present form largely of 1857. Low and rambling with plenty of
crowsteps and some Jacobean detail; NW wing of 1909. Further
up Harbour Road, off its W side in THE TOWER GARDENS is
BRIDGENESS TOWER, a harled circular windmill tower of
1750. In 1895 *Hippolyte J. Blanc* removed the sails and converted
the tower to an observatory, adding arcaded corbelling which
supports a brick battlement; also of 1895 the stair tower at the
SE. Pantile-roofed addition, perhaps late Georgian, at the SW.
The building was restored as a house by *William A. Cadell*, 1989.
On the E side of Harbour Road, in KINNINGARS PARK, an
exceptionally large rubble-built DOOCOT, formerly crowstepped,
probably of the early C18. Perhaps in the early C19 its lower part
was altered to house a winding engine for the adjacent mine-shaft.
Presumably at that time it was given a roundheaded opening in
each face. Later in the C19 the E opening was bricked up and
much of this gable rebuilt in brick. At the upper part survive
nesting boxes constructed of stone slabs resting on brick piers.

PHILPINGSTONE ROAD, the other route uphill from Bridgeness
Road, contains some mid and late C20 development at the
bottom but Edwardian model housing built by Henry M. Cadell
predominates. Best is the single-storey and attic red sandstone
ashlar terrace of CORONATION COTTAGES (Nos. 50–60) on
the l., by *G. Wightman*, 1902, with arcaded corbelling under the
eaves and gablets. On the r., the two-storey GLADSTONE
TERRACE of 1905 is more muscular with hammer-dressed
masonry. Elliptically arched openings, the doors pedimented.
Crowstepped chimney-topped gablets; club skews at the main
gables. At the top, in GRANGE LOAN, Grange Primary School
(*see* Public Buildings, above). To its E, CARNDENE, a substantial
late C19 villa. Generally Georgian survival but with a bay window
and heavy Jacobean Renaissance doorpiece at the N front.

GRANGE TERRACE, continuing the line of Grange Loan to the W, begins with small Edwardian villas. Among them, No. 62 with a conical-roofed squat round tower at one corner. Further w, St Andrew's Parish Church (*see* Churches, above). Some way to the w, among late Victorian villas, ST FILLANS (No. 32 Grange Terrace) of 1887. Bargeboarded gables and a bracketed canopy over the door; pierced red tile roof ridge. Y-junction at the w end of Grange Terrace. The NW fork is provided by Stewart Avenue (for which *see* above). In ERNGATH ROAD, the steeply rising sw fork, and in DUGALD STEWART AVENUE to the w, some cottages of *c.* 1900, surprisingly plain for their date. Set back on the E side of Erngath Road, No. 11, built as Bo'ness and Carriden Free Church Manse in 1857. Georgian survival with Jacobean hints. To its s, THE KNOWE designed by *A. Porteous* for George Cadell Stewart, 1879. In 1907 *Matthew Steele* filled one inner angle with a higher extension, its wild corner turret topped by a domed and columned cupola. s of that, in KELTY AVENUE, a cul-de-sac to the E, a double and a triple house (Nos. 4–8) by *Matthew Steele*, 1906. English Arts and Crafts with harled walls and red Rosemary tiled gambrel roofs. Battered chimneys and touches of half-timbering.

GRAHAMSDYKE ROAD continues the line of Dean Road (*see* above) E along the edge of the plateau at the s of the town. On the N, prosperous villas of the late C19 and early C20. At the w end, a single-storey and attic double house (Nos. 3–5) of *c.* 1890, the roof swept over the canted bay windows and carried between them as a canopy above the paired entrances; gableted tile-hung attic. Contemporary two-storey terrace at Nos. 7–13, the ground floor of red brick, the upper floor harled, with half-timbering in gables and gablets; some catslide dormerheads. Set well back, a late C19 villa (Nos. 15–17), again with half-timbered gables. HOLLYWOOD HOUSE (No. 25), also of *c.* 1890, has segmental-arched windows and large Rosemary tiled roofs. CAER-EDIN, occupying the site between GRAHAMSDYKE AVENUE and GRAHAMSDYKE LANE, was built in 1899–1900 for the timber importer Sir Robert Murray. Symmetrical Queen Anne with full-height canted bay windows and half-timbering in the gables. Open segmental pediment over the Ionic doorpiece whose banding is oddly echoed in the courses of the window margins, alternately square and rounded. In the front hall, lit by stained glass painted with the heraldry of the European timber-exporting towns, a free-standing central fireplace. In the rooms to each side, classical wooden chimneypieces in deep ingles. Further E, No. 71 Grahamsdyke Road is a bungalow designed for himself by *Matthew Steele*, 1924, but the round-arched entrance is now hidden by a shallow porch and the tall chimney stacks which buttressed the gables have been removed. The harled No. 73 is by *Andrew Mickel*, 1907. Jacobean Arts and Crafts but with Art Nouveau touches. s of the E end of Grahamsdyke Road, in DRUM ROAD and the streets to its E, a housing development by *Alison & Hutchison & Partners*, 1964. Weatherboard finish between roughcast spine walls.

### INDUSTRIAL BUILDINGS

NEW GRANGE FOUNDRY, Links Road. Beside the road, late
c19 two-storey harled blocks, now roofed with corrugated iron.
Segmental arched windows; small corbels under the wallheads.

HARBOUR, off Union Street. By *Thomas Meik & Son*, 1878–81.
Rubble-built West Pier and concrete L-plan East Pier. These
enclose the harbour. At the s end of the East Pier, a lock entrance
to the concrete-walled Wet Dock.

ROMAN FORTLET, 2.2km. SW at Kinneil on the Antonine Wall,
constructed after AD 142. The fortlet has been laid out following
excavation. 70m. by 60m., it contained two timber buildings
within a turf rampart, broken to N and S by timber gates: a well
lay in the NW corner.

## BONHILL                                           WD 4070

A linear village on the l. bank of the Leven lost in post-industrial
distress; a place with no sense of place. On the hillside E, vast dis-
orientating tracts of two-, three- and four-storey roughcast housing.

BONHILL PARISH CHURCH, Main Street. Gothic Revival of
1834–6 by *John Baird I*, the latest in a series of places of worship
to have existed here or hereabouts since at least the c13. Repairs
to what was in all probability a late medieval church are recorded
at the end of the c17, but in 1747 a new kirk was built. This in turn
fell into a dangerous condition and in 1799 the presbytery again
ordered rebuilding for which a plan was approved in 1802. By
1834 walls were found to be damp, some settling and cracking. On
Baird's recommendation, the heritors agreed to build another new
church, stipulating that materials from the old building be re-used.
   Groome describes the church as 'handsome Gothic' but the
design is no more than stiffly and symmetrically medieval; provincial parish Perp. A square tower, embedded for half its depth and
height, rises at the centre of the E gable. At its base is a hooded,
four-centred arched entrance door with roll-moulded surround.
Above this, also hooded, a two-light, four-centred arched window
with transom. A sill-level stringcourse steps up at the corners of
the tower where short angle buttresses are transformed into
elongated colonnette quoins that rise to corbel capitals below the
tower's four corner finials. The third stage of the tower, emerging above the gable skews, is marked by a lozenge-framed clock
on the E face; the fourth, at belfry level, by three-light louvred
openings below square hoodmouldings. Stabbing the skyline
above a castellated parapet carried on a cyma reversa stringcourse
are four octagonal finials spiked with obelisks. In the gable, l.
and r. of the tower below parapet skews, a hooded, four-centred
arched window with Y-tracery and transom. The droved ashlar
of the E front returns on the N and S walls, a narrow buttressed
bay defining the width of the stairs which originally gave access
to the church gallery. All other walls are roughcast with ashlar
dressings and a deep battered base.

The W gable has parapet skews with a blind quatrefoil in the apex. Organ chamber and two hooded lancets, 1882. Ill-judged vestry projection by *Boswell, Mitchell & Johnston*, 1957. Tall windows similar to those on the E gable light the four bays of the N wall. On the S side, however, the two central windows have been concealed by a piend-roofed extension constructed in tandem with alterations which radically reshaped the interior, 1987–9. These changes, by *Thomson, McCrea & Sanders*, removed the original horseshoe gallery to create a two-storey suite of halls and offices in the E, the much reduced area for worship recast with the sanctuary in the N and new galleries S and E. A new vestibule and staircase are housed in the S extension. Benefits have undoubtedly accrued to the work of the church in the community, but the architectural transformation is mundane and less than devout.

The much altered interior is unremarkable. An eight-part ribbed plaster vault survives over the E vestibule, a significant contrast with the flat panelled plaster ceiling in the rearranged church. Sanctuary raised by two steps. – Oak COMMUNION TABLE with fluted Ionic posts, 1915; the gift of the Dennistoun Brown family of Balloch Castle (q.v.). – Part-octagonal oak PULPIT, from Ashton Church, Gourock, pressed into the NW corner. – STAINED GLASS. Colourful abstract-design panels in the W lancets incorporate family arms and mottoes; installed 1883. On the l., to Alexander Smollett of Bonhill †1881; on the r., to James Dennistoun Brown of Balloch †1888. – Members of the McAlister family are remembered in the two windows which light the relocated sanctuary, by *James Wright* of Garelochhead and manufactured by the *St Enoch Glass Co.* of Glasgow. In one, Christ with Andrew and James (?); in the other, originally in the S window closest to the W gable, Dorcas with other women and children. The upper parts of these two windows contain glass installed in 1954: Rachael and Jacob on the l.; Philip and the Ethiopian eunuch to the r. Both by *Douglas Hamilton* of Glasgow. – Lighting the stone staircase rising on the N side of the original vestibule is a memorial to Rachel Sword Kippen of Westerton: a blue-robed Mary cradling the Christ child beneath pink- and purple-clad angels, by *R. F. Milligan*, 1939. – A companion window to William James Kippen mounted in the S staircase is now inaccessible. – In the new S staircase, a series of small windows by *Lesley Macfie*, 1992, adapting designs prepared by pupils of Vale of Leven Academy whose names are individually recorded.

The church sits in a walled GRAVEYARD. A few C18 graves can be found but several early recumbent stones have disappeared under the turf. One such, still to be seen near the S side of the church, remembers the miller of Balloch, Patrick McAlaster †1665. – Among many C19 gravemarkers is an engraved SLAB commemorating the Covenanter Robert Nairn †1685; erected 1826, restored 1892. – But the most interesting memorials are those ranged along the S boundary wall; defiled by decay and disregard these roofless mausolea, late C18–early C19, crumble with reproach. The TURNBULL OF BONHILL MAUSOLEUM,

a square enclosure with convex corners, is entered through a
segmental-arched opening with angel wings carved above the
arch. Walled in rough red sandstone with a strong eaves cornice
from which the acroteria have fallen. – Next, in red ashlar, the
ARTHUR OF LEVENBANK MAUSOLEUM, pedimented front
and back, with fluted pilasters flanking the entrance. Inside, the
death of Ann Crauford †1797 is recorded. – Then, an unnamed
enclosure with a pediment gable on the rear wall. – Several
more ruinous walled plots follow. A railed area, backed by a
hammered ashlar wall rising in a small gable above armorial
carving, is all that remains of the DENNISTOUN BROWN
MEMORIAL. – Finally, dated 1808, the BUCHANAN OF ARDOCH
MAUSOLEUM, a larger enclosure walled in red sandstone ashlar
with a battered pedimented portal framing a segmental-arched
opening. – In the NE corner of the kirkyard is the MARTIN OF
AUCHENDENNAN MAUSOLEUM, 1870, a gabled structure in
ochre sandstone. Under a ribbed roof slated in stone, a wide,
heavily moulded semicircular arch opens to an interior with
three white marble memorial tablets on the rear wall.

ST RONAN (R.C.), Ladyton. By *Bamber, Gray & Partners*, 1977.
Hall church in brick and dry-dash render. Glazed monopitch
peaks on flat roof.

BONHILL BRIDGE. *See* Alexandria.

BONHILL PRIMARY SCHOOL, Main Street. Erected 1874–5 to a
design by a *Mr Greenlees*. A single-storey four-gable front in square
snecked red sandstone. Segmental-headed windows symmetrically arranged. Additions, 1914, by *Boston, Menzies & Morton*.

Former DALMONACH SCHOOL, Main Street. Built *c.* 1835 as
the school for half-timer pupils from the adjacent Dalmonach
Print Works. Two-storey flatted dwelling with curved forestair.
Adjoining schoolroom/workshop with four pointed-arched bays
and pointed-arched door l.

ST RONAN'S PRIMARY SCHOOL, Ladyton. By the *Boys, Jarvis
Partnership*, 1974–5. Orange brick and monopitch roofs.

DESCRIPTION

MAIN STREET now belies its name; more rural road than urban.
Church and school are there but across the street the long run of
gable-to-gable dwellings that once stretched s from Dalmonach
Works for half a mile or more has gone. Now there are too many
gaps. Late Georgian cottage villas survive at Nos. 472 and 478,
*c.* 1830, and there is one red row, DILLICHIP TERRACE, 1885,
with straight-flight stairs at the rear rising to the upper flats.

BONNYBRIDGE          F *8080*

Large village which developed in the later C19 as housing for
workers at its paper mill, sawmill and iron foundries.

BONNYBRIDGE ST HELEN'S PARISH CHURCH, High Street.
Geometric, by *Alexander Watt*, 1877. Big box with a firescreen

front, its centre advanced between angle buttresses. Pinnacles on the corners; narrow gableted bellcote at the apex of the gable. To the E, a HALL extended in 1881.

The interior of the church is covered by a kingpost truss half-round roof, with quarter-round coving at the sides. S gallery, its cast iron columns with foliaged capitals. The walls were stripped of plaster and the COMMUNION TABLE (of 1927) replaced the pulpit as the N focus in 1956. – STAINED GLASS. In the N gable, two lights (the Maries at the Tomb; Samuel and Eli) of 1911. – In the E wall, the strongly coloured centre window (St Paul) is by *R. Douglas McLundie* of the *Abbey Studio*, 1950. – N window of this wall (St James) of *c.* 1992; an example of simplified realism. – The two narrative N windows of the W wall (Noah building an Altar after the Flood; Our Lord stilling the Sea) are by *Dickson & Walker*, 1894. – Also by *Dickson & Walker*, 1895, and in the same manner is the next window (the Virtuous Woman). – Another similar window (Joshua addressing the Israelites) of 1917 to the S. – ORGAN in the gallery, by *The John Compton Organ Co.*, 1956.

BONNYBRIDGE HOSPITAL, Falkirk Road. Built in 1988. Long and low, with brown brick walls and roofed with brown concrete tiles.

DESCRIPTION. At the W end of HIGH STREET, on its N side, Bonnybridge St Helen's Parish Church (*see* above). The next incident is provided by the ROYAL HOTEL on the corner of Wellpark Street. It is a three-storey harled building of *c.* 1900. Swan-neck pedimented doorpiece. Mullioned windows, corniced at the ground floor; the top-floor windows have gablets rising through the wallhead. Bowed SE corner. At the E end of High Street, on the S side, a tall two-storey block built for the CO-OPERATIVE SOCIETY in 1928; the architect was *William Mercer*. Front of polished red sandstone ashlar consisting of a 'centre-piece' and E range; the balancing W range was not built. Opposite, in a small public park on the corner with Main Street, the village's WAR MEMORIAL, a wrought iron arch topped by a clock and roses. It was designed by the Stirling County Architect, *A. J. Smith*, in 1949 and executed by *R. Smith & Co.*

ANTONINE WALL, Seabegs Wood. A length of rampart, ditch and upcast mound together with the best surviving length of the Military Way on the Wall constructed after AD138. At the W end of the wood, the Wall turns N, preparing to take in the site of the fortlet which lies in the next field.

BOQUHAN                    S

A few houses on the W side of the A875 halfway between Killearn and Balfron.

BOQUHAN OLD HOUSE. 1784. Two-storey-and-attic, harled house, five windows wide. Skew gables with scroll skewputts. – In the estate, 0.2km. W, an octagonal LARDER, C18, with pointed-

arched doorway and windows and a steeply pitched pyramid
roof. The interior dome is plastered and retains two hanging
hooks.

## BOQUHAN HOUSE
### 1.9km. E of Kippen

S *6090*

1959–63; constructed throughout in square-snecked Auchinlea
stone. The design has pretension but none of the symmetrical
composure of its pedimented late C18 predecessor. Wide N
front, gabled with a porch of fluted Doric columns not quite
Greek enough. Much balconied to the S. Panelling and flooring
in Australian walnut.

In the grounds, SW, a short wall of red sandstone rubble
incorporates a relief TABLET, late C18, bearing the arms of the
Campbells of Argyll. – Nearby, in a grotto-like setting, PRINCE'S
WELL, dated 1790, marked by a small swept obelisk on a plinth.
– A WALLED GARDEN, now only a lawn, lies NNW. – Beside it
is LADY'S WELL, a mock stone cylinder capped by a stone disc
on the edge of which is inscribed MARIE CAMPBELL IFC
POSUIT 1792. – Also, a two-storey octagonal FOLLY of coursed
red sandstone, roofless and empty but with cornices at first-
floor and eaves level.

Also N is the former STABLE BLOCK, early C19, a much
altered quadrangular grouping of old and new farm buildings.
The principal S range is all too evidently a recent reconstruction, *c.* 1985, except at the centre where its domed skyline is
largely original. – Adjacent is BOQUHAN FARMHOUSE, 1907–
14, a harled sub-Baronial villa more suburban than rural.

EAST LODGE, of the mid C19, with Jacobean gables and an
ogee-domed entrance tower in the re-entrant. At the EAST
GATES, four square piers topped by squat pyramid obelisks
sitting on stone balls.

## BOTHKENNAR

F *8080*

Isolated church and manse.

BOTHKENNAR PARISH CHURCH. Originally a straightforward
oblong kirk designed and built by *John Moir*, wright in Falkirk,
with advice from *John Adam* on the form of the roof, 1788–90,
but incorporating earlier work at the gables, probably of 1673
(the date incised high up at the S end of the W gable). Rubble
walls with strip quoins at the corners; piended roof with bellcast
eaves. Roundheaded windows. W tower built of a mixture of
droved ashlar and rubble. Three stepped base courses project
from its W face and return along half the S side. At the bottom
stage of the tower, a roundheaded S door. At the second stage,
round-arched windows in the S and W faces. The third and fourth
stages are both intaken. At the third, a rectangular window in
each face; at the fourth, round-arched belfry openings. Stone-
slabbed spire roof of pyramidal form but with concave sides.

In 1887–8 *Sydney Mitchell & Wilson* extended the church to the N and S in a curiously unsympathetic Neo-Georgian manner. Vestry on the N. On the S, a two-storey T-plan addition. The crossbar abuts the C18 church. In its gables' open pediments, Venetian windows to light the gallery inside. Circular windows in the S side. On the broad and shallow jamb's open-pedimented gable, a segmental-pedimented 'bellcote'. In the E side of the jamb, a re-used circular window, its blocking incised with the date 1789. Set into the W side of the jamb, a stone bearing the arms and initials of William Bruce of Newtoun and the date 1654. Projecting from the gable of the jamb, a semi-octagonal vestry. In the inner angles of the crossbar and jamb, single-storey porches, their entrances pedimented.

The interior is almost all of 1887–8, by *Sydney Mitchell & Wilson*. Coomb ceiling supported by rounded arches sitting on the tie-beam. Gallery along the S side, its front surmounted by Tudor arches springing from Ionic columns. – Neo-Jacobean PULPIT, its back pedimented. It stands, together with the communion table and font, in an enclosure formed by choir pews. – STAINED GLASS. In the N wall, flanking the pulpit, two windows (the Crucifixion; the Risen Christ), garishly modernistic of *c.* 1950. – In the E wall, a strongly coloured window (the Nativity of Our Lord), also modernistic, by *Felix McCullough*, 1968.

Immediately E of the church, a harled HALL of 1926, its front gable containing roundheaded windows.

GRAVEYARD. Just W of the church, a large headstone of 1818 to Alexander and Margaret Simpson carved with the relief of a ship. In the SW corner, another large stone bearing the relief of a ship. It commemorates James Sclanders and Ann Stewart and is dated 1794. The ends of the stone are sculpted with a face and a skull. Beside it, another stone of 1794 and also to James Sclanders and Ann Stewart. On the E face, at the top, a carved head and drapery; on the W face, an anchor.

Former MANSE to the NW, by *David Hamilton*, 1815–16. Two storeys and three bays, the rubble walls finished with a blocking course which becomes a parapet over the centre. Skinnily pilastered and corniced doorpiece flanked by elliptical-arched three-light ground-floor windows.

BOTURICH CASTLE         WD
                  2.5km. N of Balloch

A castellated mansion overlooking Loch Lomond. Like Balloch Castle (q.v.), by John Buchanan of Ardoch to a design by *Robert Lugar*. Here, however, the new house was raised on the walls of the old; cellars from the C15 castle can still be seen. But the precise extent of Lugar's original work and the role played in its erection by *Robert Scott* of the Glasgow architects *Scott, Stephen & Gale* are unclear. That it was 'entirely built in 1834 with the exception of some small additions' seems likely enough, though the SW entrance tower came later, probably the consequence of a fire, *c.* 1850. The principal accommodation is compacted within a more or less square plan. The walls, harled in dull cream render, have ashlar facings and battlements. In general they rise to three storeys except in the NE quarter of the plan where a five-storeyed 'tower-house', crowstep-gabled N and S, emerges. Centred on the W face of this higher block, and therefore rising from the core of the plan, is a cylindrical tower with bellcast eaves and a slated conical roof with a glazed apex. It seems possible that tower-house and tower are built on masonry remaining from the earlier castle. Well below battlement level, the N and S walls of the square extend E to enclose offices and service yard.

The approach is from the E. A straight drive passes between trees to open on to a gravel forecourt signposted by two stone urns. Smooth lawns spread S. Ahead is the Loch. To the r. is the Castle, entered through the octagonal tower added at the W end of the S front. The tower, machicolated and crenellated, rises above the main battlements. A small porch with a three-centred arched doorway projects centrally under a square oriel. To the r., lower rendered walls with a tall tripartite window at *piano nobile* level. A cone-capped bartizan marks the end of the main castle block. Then, much lower, a four-bay wing extends the S front further E. It, too, is rendered below a rubble top storey of gabled eaves dormers. A round tower with a slated bellcast roof articulates the junction with the crowstepped gable of the services wing. An eroded armorial panel dated 1380 (perhaps from some earlier structure), pointed-arched window and round-arched portal stress the romantic conceit. All but detached at the SE corner, slender and erect like a misplaced buttress, is a charming belfry shaft, the bell hanging in an open pointed arch.

The W façade, which is also rendered and battlemented, is surprisingly dull, its few asymmetrically arranged windows failing to take full advantage of the prospect to Loch Lomond. Nor is the N front of interest, though it first rises dramatically in the crowstepped gable of the five-storey 'tower-house' before falling to lower rubble walls screening the services court. Two segmental-arched cart entries open E below three piended eaves dormers.

A handsome stone staircase ascends through the entrance tower to the *piano nobile*. Cantilevered flights return to the upper floors in an open well while to the r. a corridor leads to dining room and drawing room. Both are generous spaces with fine plasterwork, the former having a vine motif cornice and frieze not dissimilar to that at Balloch Castle (q.v.).

# BOWLING                                          WD *4070*

A sleepy linear village on the N shore of the Clyde estuary between Glasgow and Dumbarton. In 1790 it became the W terminal of the Forth & Clyde Canal. Later, Clyde steamers arrived; several were berthed here in winter. Docking wharves were built and a small shipyard established. The railway came. But the stir of road, rail, river and canal traffic is long gone. Uphill, above wooded slopes, the A82 dual-carriageway bypass is relentlessly busy. In the village itself the road is quiet. Trains still stop, but the canal is dry, there are no steamers, riparian embankments crumble and the canal basin is feebly fashioned as a makeshift marina for a few tired craft.

BOWLING CHURCH, Dumbarton Road. Built in snecked sandstone, 1869. A low, five-bay, gabled nave of modest Gothic pretension. Buttressed bays with a hooded lancet in each. N porch tower, diagonally buttressed like the church gables, has a steeply pyramidal slated roof with bellcast eaves. Hooded pointed-arched entrance doorway. Intersecting tracery in E gable window. In 1911, *W. F. McGibbon* added transepts and a small sanctuary in sympathetic style. Adjacent gabled HALL, built as Bowling Free Church, 1893, has a squat parapeted tower on the w with a hooded, round-arched door.

BOWLING BASIN. From 1790 when the Forth & Clyde Canal was opened, the shoreline of Bowling Bay was repeatedly reshaped to accommodate the demands of river traffic. Bowling Harbour was created *c.* 1850, in part to protect the debouch of the canal. The long embankments that separated and sheltered this inner stretch of water from the estuary can still be seen. At the E end of the harbour are the canal's last lock-gates, *c.* 1820, controlling the water level through a narrow channel constructed of large blocks of droved ashlar stone now much repaired with blue engineering brick. A BASCULE BRIDGE with iron wheel and cog mechanism crosses the channel. The gates protect the LOWER BASIN, formed in 1790, later modified *c.* 1820, and now adapted as a quiet backwater for yachts and river launches. Constructed in channelled mass concrete, it is of irregular shape. The quayside is curved on the S side, where a second channel (the original lock connecting with the river) has been blocked, but is straight along the N. At the E end of this N quay is the roughcast CUSTOM HOUSE, *c.* 1800, a two-storey, three-bay house with steep pedimented gables. The house, which is of stark aspect, is raised on a high basement plinth necessitating a forestair, the parapeted ship's-bridge landing of which seems imbued with a rather hefty nautical allusion. The basin constricts at this point into a second channel, which passes under the disused tracks of the Lanarkshire & Dunbartonshire Railway crossing the canal obliquely on a VIADUCT of segmental concrete arches and lattice girders by engineers *Crouch & Hogg*, 1896. Part of this impressive structure includes a steel-trussed SWING BRIDGE with concrete abutments. The narrow channel of water is then crossed by a second timber BASCULE BRIDGE before opening out into the rectangular UPPER BASIN. Here an access driveway drops down from Dumbarton Road revealing the dramatic spatial interrelationship of railway and canal. To the E, an elevated track, parapeted along the N side of the basin, leads to a flatted Arts and Crafts villa, harled with red sandstone dressings, which served as LOCK-KEEPERS' HOUSES, 1896. At the end of the basin, lock gates now form a permanent barrier to the dried-up course of the canal beyond.

In 2001 a waterway link (*see* Introduction, p. 68) was reinstated between Glasgow and Edinburgh by connecting the Forth & Clyde Canal to the Union Canal over a total length of 110km.

BOWLING SCHOOL, Dumbarton Road. Built as the Village School and Public Hall, 1861. A five-bay, skew-gabled structure of roughly snecked ochre sandstone with tall lintelled windows. A crowstep-gabled N entrance porch, added 1906 (?).

LITTLEMILL DISTILLERY, Dumbarton Road. Abandoned one- and two-storey, whitewashed rubble maltings dating from the late C18 or early C19 but largely rebuilt 1875. Pyramidal slated roofs over kilns at SW and SE corners. A datestone, 1772, is incorporated in the rendered gable of the adjacent C20 office block. Comparably forlorn across the road is the former EXCISEMAN'S HOUSE, late C18 with some mid-C19 additions.

DESCRIPTION. The creation of the A82 boulevard in the 1920s, curtailing the access to Auchentorlie estate, led to the building of three new lodge houses just off the N carriageway. All are by *Joseph Weekes*. Best is MID LODGE, 1925, neatly constructed in polygonal rubble with a red-tiled bell roof. Auchentorlie House itself was later demolished leaving only a ruined LAUNDRY, early C19, picturesquely sited beside weir and waterfall. Down in the village, the older DUMBARTON ROAD is lined intermittently with tenements of varying material and date but consistently indifferent quality. Nos. 15–17, RED ROW, 1894, is unusual if scarcely attractive; a flat three-storey range of English bond common brickwork with stone sills, lintels and quoins. Nos. 89–95, AUCHENTORLIE TERRACE, *c.* 1885, is more pleasantly residential, though rigorously regular in its window spacing. A two-storey-and-basement range bridged to the road, its entrance doors have wide cornice tables bracketed and railed with decorative ironwork. Raised on a high plinth, the five-bay front of Nos. 76–78 has ashlar dignity; a central shouldered chimneystack stresses the symmetry, eaves cornice, stringcourse and pilastered doorways provide the ascetic Classical detail. But there is little else to remark. The church is meek, the school severe, the distillery dry and derelict (*see* above). Down by the canal, the canker of neglect eats away at stone and timber.

DUNGLASS CASTLE. *See* p. 449.

## BRIDGE OF ALLAN

A genteel town of suburban character lying between the Allan Water and the wooded slopes that mark the SW limit of the Ochils. Until the first years of the C19 no more than a hamlet existed, sustained from medieval times by the mealmill on the river's W bank and the copper mines in the hills to the E. But the discovery by Sir Robert Abercromby, Laird of Airthrey, that the mine waters had curative properties changed everything. The town became a spa, transformed 'from the sequestered retreat of rural life to the favoured resort of elegance and fashion'*. Development

---

* Charles Roger, *A Week at Bridge of Allan* (Edinburgh, 1851), 3.

was especially rapid following the purchase of the estate by Major
Henderson of Westerton in 1844 and the arrival of the railway from
Stirling four years later. Along Henderson Street villas were erected
for 'holiday letting'*. By mid century the Lower Town had been
laid out on a simple grid plan. Finally, over the next two decades,
a still more salubrious Upper Town took shape. Along the contours
E of the mineral wells, baths and hydropathic hotel which had
become the community's *raison d'être* a concatenated sequence of
fine mansion-houses stretched out among the trees. In 1870 the
town achieved burgh status.

## CHURCHES

CHALMERS CHURCH, Henderson Street. Built, as its name
implies, as the Free Church, 1854–6, by *J., W. H. & J. M. Hay*
of Liverpool. Impressively set back and raised above the town's
main street, it far outshone its modest predecessor (*see* below).
The axially placed steeple-front solution is typical of the Hays'
Gothic, the broaching of the spire and the S tower's diagonal
buttresses both generously splayed. Between the buttresses, a
broad flight of steps rises to the pointed-arched entrance. Above
the door, a Dec window, three louvred lancets at belfry level
and two-light lucarnes set into the spire base. Behind is a three-
bay buttressed nave with lower transepts gabled W and E.
Laminated arch-braced trusses articulate the interior, the low-
set corbelstones intensifying the impact of the roof. At the
crossing, raking valley rafters from the transepts reach collar
height. The S gallery, carried on timber pillars, narrows in the
tower over the vestibule. Pointed-arched N window all but hidden
by the organ-pipe SCREEN, probably of 1897, intricately carved
with grape-laden vines. – *Brindley & Foster* ORGAN, 1898. –
Central three-bay PULPIT panelled with ogee arches and quatrefoils; stairs l. and r. – STAINED GLASS in four-light transept
tracery – pale W window by *A. Ballantine & Son*, Christ healing
the sick, to William Haldane †1914. – E, four very vertical saints,
also lacking in colour (Bride, Christopher, Andrew and Cecilia)
dedicated to Rev. James Miller, 1927. – Best is the Burning
Bush in the high S gallery window, smouldering orange in the
afternoon sun. – HALLS added W, 1890.
Former FREE CHURCH, Union Street. Though now very evidently
a dwelling, octagonal stone finials at each side of the roughcast
W gable front suggest a grander provenance. This was the Free
Church from 1844 until 1853, after which until 1875 it functioned
as a school. The bellcote now sits over a garden gate in Melville
Place.
HOLY TRINITY CHURCH, Keir Street. Originally Bridge of
Allan Chapel-of-Ease. By *James Henderson*, Glasgow, 1858–9;
E.E. Gothic in coursed rubble, with gabled triple transepts W
and E of central aisle. Steep fishscale-slated ventilator over central
crossing. Added in 1876 by *Robert Baldie*, the gabled N front has

---

* J. Malcolm Allan, *Bridge of Allan in Old Photographs* (1989), 39.

a circular window over a splayed, pointed-arched entrance and l. a low, diagonally buttressed steeple, the ashlar spire broached from an octagonal belfry. Linked W is a four-bay gabled HALL with mullioned and transomed windows and Perp tracery in the gables; by *Honeyman & Keppie*, 1895.

Broad three-aisle, three-bay INTERIOR with a busy roof. Above the floral capitals of thick circular piers, arch-bracing spans the centre aisle between, and diagonally across, each bay. Over each outer aisle, three ridge-and-valley roofs, the valleys supported by beams carried from corbelstones to the central piers. The result: a stripey confusion of dark-stained arched ribs, purlins and spars. Filling the S wall, above the chancel area, is a timber, organ-pipe SCREEN of cusped pointed arches. – In front of the ORGAN, by *Lewis & Co.*, 1884 and 1904 (now replaced by an instrument by *Abbot & Smith*), a light oak SCREEN, 1904, its three-bay canopy attenuated above three flattened ogee arches in exquisitely fluted and fretted modern Gothic detail devised by *Charles Rennie Mackintosh* of *Honeyman, Keppie & Mackintosh*. By the same hand, CHOIR STALLS, COMMUNION TABLE and box PULPIT, all rhythmically ribbed with an erect, stem-like ornament drawn, it seems, appropriately enough, from some precious other-worldly nature. – STAINED GLASS. Four of the six triple lancets in the transept gables have memorial windows: NE bay, richly coloured and well drawn, Christ cleansing the temple and the Good Samaritan, to the Rev. James Muir †1900. – Next to this, the Peacemakers, depicted in rich reds, blues, etc., to the Rev. John Reid †1900. – In the vestibule, the same preacher is commemorated by a white marble TABLET with block pediment.

ST SAVIOUR'S CHURCH (Episcopal), Keir Street. 1856–7; by *John Henderson*. Tractarian early Dec nave-and-chancel formula in square-snecked rubble with steeply pitched roof and apex belfry. *Alexander Ross* enlarged the nave from three to four bays in 1871–2, replacing the original W door with a gabled N porch. Low, over-buttressed, hip-ended vestry, 1928. High dark-stained purlin roof carried by arch-braced trusses on moulded corbelstones. – Recessed in the N wall of the sanctuary, a PISCINA and three-seat SEDILIA, all with cusped arches. – At the W end, an octagonal stone FONT, 1877, by *William Pirret* of Glasgow; in each face quatrefoils carved with relief symbols. – Ashlar chancel arch. – BISHOP'S CHAIR, 1912, by *Isherwood* of Glasgow, with Dec Gothic carving. – ORGAN by *Forster & Andrews*, 1872, in pointed-arched recess S. – Polychromatic patterned *Minton* tiles, 1897. – STAINED GLASS in five-light Dec tracery above altar; a sentimental depiction of the Crucifixion, Mary and John, with flanking angels. – The four-light W window is more forceful though less colourful, 1922, by the *Stephen Adam Studio*; incongruously juxtaposed are a wounded knight and the Annunciation, imagery commemorating Anne Pullar †1919, and Lt.-Col. Harold Thompson †1917, in Palestine.

Single-storey RECTORY, 1857, with trefoil-headed windows. HALL behind, added 1896.

## PUBLIC BUILDINGS

ALLAN LEISURE CENTRE, Union Street. 1970–1, by *Stirling County Council*. A clearstorey-lit, sports hall box in dull orange brick. Single storey library and health centre link E, the latter extended to first floor in barely matching brickwork, 1999–2000.

BRIDGE OF ALLAN, Henderson Street. Reinforced concrete segmental-arched span of *c.* 44m. carrying the double carriageway of the A9 across the weir of the Allan Water. Designed by *F. A. MacDonald & Partners* in 1938 but not built until 1956–8. Grey Aberdeen granite facings. Squinch-like arch abutment at Blairforkie Drive.

BRIDGE OF ALLAN PRIMARY SCHOOL, Pullar Avenue. 1964–5; by *Stirling County Council*. Long, low classroom block banded by glazing, brick and render.

41 FOUNTAIN OF NINEVEH, Fountain Road. 1853. Colourfully painted column, over 12m. high, conceived as a *point-de-vue* landmark at the S end of the lower town developed by Major John Alexander Henderson, Laird of Westerton. Set on a stone base in a circular pond is a wide cast iron basin from which rises a fluted Doric shaft, half-Greek, half-Roman. On top of this, another bowl and four dolphins; and a stork, added 1895.

MUSEUM HALL, Henderson Street. An exercise in balanced round-arched rhythms by the Stirling architect *Ebenezer Simpson*, 1886–7. A heavy central balconied porch separates a pair of two-storey-and-basement blocks each with symmetrical arcaded windows and broad-eaved, hip-fronted roofs; 'a marriage between a Wesleyan Chapel and a romanesque Venetian palazzo'*. In the Hall, a figural Grecian frieze runs above arcaded galleries. Double-arched staircase window E with painted panels; tiger, lion and several species of bird. Disused.

PATERSON MEMORIAL, Henderson Street. 1898. Cast iron from the *Saracen Foundry* of *Walter Macfarlane & Co.*, Glasgow. Clock-topped column with fluting, foliage relief and claw-foot base on plinth. Disused fountain basin. Erected in memory of the town's Medical Officer, Dr Alexander Paterson.

WAR MEMORIAL, Pullar Park, Henderson Street. By *John Stewart*, 1923. Wreath-topped prismatic block on a stepped base of grey marble. Two short columns of polished pink granite mark the approach from Henderson Street.

## DESCRIPTION

The old village lies by the Allan Water, S of the A9. Not much survives. On STATION ROAD, the rehabilitated INVERALLAN MILL, 1710, an L-plan rubble building with crowstepped gables, retains its eight-spoke, undershot wheel; 1979 restoration by *Alex Strang & Partners*. INVERALLAN HOUSE (No. 5), late C18, skew-gabled with a pedimented Gibbsian door, has become the

---

* Charles McKean, *Stirling and the Trossachs* (1985), 75.

centrepiece of a small sympathetically designed residential development. Nearby, the three-bay BRIDGE INN, late C18, and Nos. 3–5 INVERALLAN ROAD, early C19, rubble cottages with a neat rural charm. All this is engulfed by later industry and housing, the best of which is the muted Scots of Nos. 6–28 INVERALLAN ROAD, 1922, by *Stewart & Paterson*, a series of four- and two-in-a-block rubble dwellings with varied gabled eaves dormers. At Nos. 5–9 HENDERSON STREET, three quasi-Scots villas, *c.* 1903, roughcast with lugged architraves round the doors.

Beyond the mill-lade and river HENDERSON STREET continues as the backbone of the town, an avenue of hotels, shops and mansions. Straight for more than a kilometre, it is leafy and, though scarcely grand, still seems to preserve the relaxed air of the C19 spa. A few buildings antedate the planned town of *c.* 1850, notably the gable-fronted WESTERTON ARMS (No. 34), 1842, and the more Classical QUEEN'S HOTEL, opened 1839. Both have grown to meet demand, the latter acquiring its third storey and a broad full-height bay window with convex returns. Still later tastes are served by the ALLAN WATER CAFÉ, the 1902 conversion of an earlier house to confident classicism with a vigorous entablature and cornice, Gibbsian keystones and Art Nouveau tiles at its central entrance. Nos. 17–37, *c.* 1968, three-storey shops and flats, articulated into five flat-faced, flat-roofed blocks, do little but preserve scale and street-line. At Union Street, the Paterson Memorial Clock (*see* Public Buildings, above) marks The Cross. Diagonally opposite stood the United Presbyterian Church, 1895, by *John Honeyman*, 'a pivot of the town'* until its demolition in 1948. In its place, a trivial garden, some public toilets and the fluted cast iron standard of a PROVOST'S LAMP, its lantern painted with views of the Bridge of Allan. Fortunately, Nos. 36–50 Henderson Street, PENZANCE BUILDINGS, 1868 and 1880, remain: ashlar façades with pilastered first-floor windows, neo-Greek incision and Mannerist aedicule dormers. Unfortunately, its Victorian shopfronts have gone, badly mauled by C20 change. The pedimented portal, Corinthian columns and obelisk finial of an ashlar ARCHWAY, 1868, leading to The Avenue, restore quality at street level. Then comes AVENUE HOUSE (No. 52), the first of many symmetrical mid-C19 villas bulging with twinned, double-height canted bays. Several have later shopfronts pushed out to the pavement. At Nos. 54–58, shops survive with slender cast iron columns, consoles, a modillioned cornice and urns; others, at Nos. 59–61 are framed by red sandstone pilasters and cornicing with Renaissance detail. There are, too, variations on the villa theme. Some have good pilastered doorpieces; others consoled cornices instead. No. 106 has a wrought iron balcony over the doorway. At THE OAKS (No. 108) the original, almost fragile, glazing bars remain. Nos. 113, 117 and 119 mass together with a Roman Doric porch at the centre. CONEYPARK (No. 121) is plain Jacobean. At Nos. 118–124, *c.* 1851, by *James Collie*, the bays are gabled with

* J. Malcolm Allan, *Bridge of Allan in Old Photographs* (1989), 42.

scrolled bargeboards. PROSPECT HOUSE (No. 122), where the notorious 'supposed' murderess Madeleine Smith stayed in 1857, enters from a flying stair. At RUBISLAW (No. 127) the bays are swept up into pagoda-like slated caps.

Not everything conforms to this domestic pattern. At the corner with Fountain Road, an open ogee-domed cupola rises above the low, red-brick-and-roughcast walls of the POST AND TELEGRAPH OFFICE of 1902–3. On the NE side of the street, the ROYAL HOTEL, 1842, a twin-bayed villa at first, has been much enlarged in modest neo-Jacobean style to the E and N, c. 1885–95. Chalmers Church (see Churches, above) intrudes its commanding symmetry and spire. Further E, recessed behind conifers and lawns, is the OLD MANOR HOTEL (No. 129); begun in 1766, an advancing E wing added early C19, it acquired a spacious pedimented porch with two Roman Doric columns in antis set into the re-entrant, 1849. Then comes HOWARD LODGE (No. 129), a harled, millennial hommage to Charles Rennie Mackintosh, by Robert Halliday, 2000-1, in which formal quotations, derived principally from The Hill House, Helensburgh (Argyll and Bute), are cleverly employed. This well-informed study, both respectful and creative, all but convinces. But perhaps the echoes are just too frequent and too loud; certainly the building's silver-grey simplicities are mildly compromised by a garden filled with heterogeneous objets d'art. Last in line and incongruously civic among the tree-smothered residences at the E end of town, the abandoned Museum Hall (see Public Buildings, above).

The Lower Town lies s of Henderson Street. Close to the bridge some small, late C19 tenements appear. ALLANVALE ROAD bends with the river. At No. 3, on the corner with New Street, a quaint chimneyed gushet is dated 1849. Nos. 27–29, 31–33, and 35 are earlier C19; three similar three-bay houses with varied doorways – cavetto splays, consoled cornice, pilasters. In UNION STREET, more of the same: Nos. 9 and 11, side-by-side three-bay, harled, with pilastered doorpieces. But here, at the edge of the mid-C19 holiday-town street grid, there is later development. Penzance Buildings (see above), dated 1880, crackles with Mannerist ornament, three stilted segmental arches grouped together above part-fluted pilasters to mark the entrances to Nos. 1, 3 and 5. Opposite is No. 6, built as a photographic studio and art gallery, 1888; black-and-white gabled Tudor over square-snecked red sandstone. KEIR STREET runs SE, parallel to Henderson Street. It begins with DRUMMOND COTTAGE, a late C19 conversion of the former Free Church (see above). And this proves symbolic, for the street is both ecclesiastical and residential. Holy Trinity Church and St Saviour's (see Churches, above) flank the axis of Fountain Road, while a string of villas, some of them modelled on the familiar twin-bayed formula, several with intricate bargeboarding, stretches SE to Pullar Park. Far s, on Pullar Avenue, is ORCHARD HOUSE, 1904–5: outside, a harled composition of gables, chimneys and bellcast tiled roofs in balanced asymmetry; inside, Glasgow Style detail.

From The Cross, WELL ROAD swings narrowly and steeply into the Upper Town. Its plain three-bay villas, all *c.* 1850, are among the earliest NE of Henderson Street. At Nos. 5–9, a flyover stair rises to a block porch set between double-height canted bays. Nos. 4–6 is similar but with an Ionic doorpiece; Nos. 10–12 more Jacobean with overlapping stone skews and gabled dormers standing on the eaves. Then, unexpectedly, there is space. Ahead is WELL HOUSE, 1861, by *William Mackison*, symmetrical gabled Gothic with a pointed-arched E porch. Once the focus of the C19 spa (the pumping machinery survives underground), it is now a quiet restaurant with a wide bow-fronted S extension by *George R. Davidson*, 1930. Close by, ALLAN WATER APARTMENTS, formerly a hydropathic hotel, built 1861–4 by *James Hamilton* and converted to flats a century later: a rambling L-plan hinged on a tall Italianate tower, good masonry details and some finely fretted timber and ironwork cresting. Hints of Alexander 'Greek' Thomson style, especially in the gatepiers. Beyond is MINE HOUSE, *c.* 1738, a two-storey row of house, bothy and workshop built for copper miners but enlarged and converted to a single dwelling, *c.* 1830; restored 1975.

Three streets, curving gently through the trees, parallel one another along the contours of this leafy hillside suburb. Uphill, on ABERCROMBY DRIVE, tall Italianate towers haul WOODLEE (No. 1) and ARDFARDACH (No. 3) out of green concealment. Most villas are mid-Victorian stone but UPLANDS (No. 15) follows a later Arts and Crafts fashion: red-tiled roofs, half-timbered walls, canted bays and bracketed oriels piled together by *William Leiper*, 1907, in complex, exciting bulk. Further E in CLAREMONT DRIVE, there is more tile-hung Englishness at DRUMPARK HOUSE (No. 7), 1904–5, a cream-harled, gabled sanatorium by *Charles G. Soutar* of Dundee, well endowed with verandahs and balconies. No. 9, despite its affected symmetry, is less grand: an overgrown, white roughcast cottage, hipped dormers pushing through a gable-flanked, mansard roof.

A more consistent pattern, dating from the 1850s and 60s, emerges on CHALTON ROAD, second of the Upper Town's three residential streets. Here the model is an upscaled, upmarket version of the earlier Henderson Street villa with its twinned double-height bays. LISMORE (Nos. 3–7) adds later wings l. and r. with bracketed oriels at first floor. Nos. 9–11 and 17–19 have decorative bargeboarded gables over their two-storey bays. Others are crowstepped. ROWANHURST (No. 15), dated 1863, has a single advancing gable with two-storey canted bay. At THORNTON LODGE (No. 21), cavetto corbelling sweeps the flanks of the bay into the gable above, a move repeated at Nos. 27–29, ASHCROFT (No. 31), ROKEBY (No. 33), ABBOTSLEIGH (No. 35), and CRAIGALLAN and EAST WOODSTOCK (Nos. 43–45). At DALNAIR (No. 47) the twinned-bay model submits to more Classical interpretation: a low-pitched piended roof, Ionic porch with coupled columns and balustraded parapet, and some fine ironwork. No. 2 has a tall, twin-gabled front with tripartite windows instead of bays and an elaborately consoled

entrance reached by a railed stairflight. Harled extensions, which
include a carefully grafted E wing with a conical-roofed NE
octagon, augment the plain, mid-Victorian Gothic of AUCHEN-
GARROCH (No. 16); dated 1906, perhaps by *William Leiper.*

KENILWORTH ROAD completes the three-street plan. At No. 14,
*c.* 1850, a wide-gabled N front, with wonderfully traceried
bargeboards and a full-width verandah canopy; a Swiss Cottage
in sandstone. Across the street, a three-storey Italianate tower
at KILORAN (Nos. 13–15). CONISTON (No. 18) by *Francis
Mackison, c.* 1853, is distinguished by semi-elliptically arched
openings and vesica windows in its bargeboarded gables.
Pedimented dormers at IONA LODGE (No. 17), dated 1848.
At INGLEWOOD (No. 23), muted Baronial: the twinned-bay
model under crowstepped gables. Tucked against the hillside
looking S, the crisp glazed geometry of THE ROWANS by *Archie
Ferguson,* 1968, intrudes without compromise. Quadrant walls,
with gatepier perches for confrontational eagles, mark the
entrance to CONEYHILL HOUSE (Nos. 26–28), 1863; a large
but unremarkable three-bay mansion with a pilastered doorpiece and bargeboarded gables. DEANVILLE (No. 27) reverts
to gabled, double-height bays, adding a central three-storey tower
and much good ironwork cresting. Nos. 33–37, dated 1861,
follow suit, though without the tower. LOGIE ASTON (No. 32)
has only a single gable over a double-height bay but gains interest from the crenellated bays, sundial, turret and semi-elliptically
arched porch added by *William Leiper,* 1905–6. The same single
gables surmount two-storey bays at WELLPARK (Nos. 41–43),
dated 1872, and EASTWELL (No. 47), perhaps by *William
Mackison*; the former Jacobean, the latter corbelled on cavetto
curves. At Beaconhurst School, where Kenilworth Road dips S
to join Henderson Street, a cluster of later teaching buildings
crowds together on the slope. But the original mansion house,
BEACONHURST GRANGE (No. 52), dated 1868, is still in service:
high-minded ashlar Baronial, cast in neo-Jacobean rather than
Brycean mould, caparisoned in gables, crowsteps and crenellations. Downhill, the fine detail of the dormers and bays of
MEADOW PARK HOTEL suggest a similar, if less Baronially
exuberant, hand.

BLAWLOWAN (formerly East Lodge), Pathfoot. Three-bay, two-
storey-and-attic, gabled house with a door lintel dated 1731 and
a lower, older E wing of C17 date in the E gable of which a half-
shuttered window, similar to those at The Palace, Culross
(Fife), was discovered.

LOGIE HOUSE, Logie Lane, off Sheriffmuir Road. Built 1803 by
*William Stirling I* as the manse for Logie Parish Church
(Blairlogie). Two-storey, three-bay house with a central chimney
gablet and an off-centre doorpiece with pilasters and pediment.
Early Victorian additions.

WESTERTON HOUSE, Gordon Crescent. Hidden uphill in a suburban backwater; a calm, Classical mansion house built for
the estate of Westertoun of Airthrey, 1803, perhaps by *William
Stirling I.* Three-storeyed NW wing, 'The Mayne Tower', added

*c.* 1871. Lower NE wing, 1912. The five-bay s façade, in pale pink ashlar, has no pediment but is fronted by an uncomfortably broad Ionic porch shading a Regency door screen and fanlight. Piended roof with two well-placed dormers. Two canted bays on w. The former Lodge, now known as MORVEN COTTAGE, sits downhill on Alexander Drive; piended T-plan with a projecting pedimented entrance, dated 1859.

CAIRN 800m. NNE. Known as the 'Fairy Knowe', excavation in 1868 revealed a central cist. The mound remains, 18m. in diameter and over 2m. high.

# BRIGHTONS

F *9070*

Village begun in the C19 to house workers at the nearby quarry.

BRIGHTONS PARISH CHURCH, Main Street. Originally Polmont Free Church. By *Brown & Carrick*, 1846–7. Spikily pinnacled unarchaeological Gothic. On the front (N) gable, a diagonally buttressed stone-spired bellcote.

Inside, N gallery of 1847; the E and W galleries were erected in 1893. – At the s end, a PULPIT and COMMUNION TABLE of 1936. – STAINED GLASS. Two s windows (celebrating the work of the Boys' and Girls' Brigades) by *Ruth Gollilaws*, 1993. Crude realism in very strong colours. – ORGAN from a Glasgow church, rebuilt here by *Andrew Watt & Son*, 1950.

SCOTTISH PRISON SERVICE COLLEGE, corner of Redding Road and Newlands Road. Built in 1970. Flat-roofed and boxy, the walls of dark brick and render.

WALLACESTONE PRIMARY SCHOOL, Braemar Gardens. Lightweight-looking, by the Stirling County Architect, *A. J. Smith*, 1961.

One enters the village from the E along REDDING ROAD. On its r. side, the Scottish Prison Service College (*see* above). On the diagonally opposite corner, ST CLAIR, a late C19 villa with bracketed broad eaves. This marks the start of the curving MAIN STREET, its late Victorian houses mostly single-storey, often with an attic. On the street's s side, Brightons Parish Church (*see* above).

# BRIG O' TURK

S *5000*

A hamlet between Loch Achray and Loch Venachar. Cottages scattered along the short wooded valley between the A821 and Glen Finglas Reservoir.

TROSSACHS CHURCH, 2.1km.w. By *G. P. Kennedy*, 1849. Three-bay rubble kirk picturesquely sited on a knoll overlooking Loch Achray but disappointingly chunky in detail. Gabled porch at the centre of the s wall. Bands of fish-scale slates stripe the roof diagonally. In 1894 the interior was re-orientated from W to E. Arch-braced trusses. Plain lancets with steeply sloped boarded sills. – Baroque memorial TABLET, N wall, in grey-green marble

to Major General David Limond; below a centurion standing in
a broken-scrolled pediment, a brass panel depicts a huntsman
and stag. – STAINED GLASS. The Good Samaritan story in the
three-lancet E gable window, by *A. Ballantine & Gardiner*, 1893,
in memory of Alexander Dunsmure of Glenbruach †1892. – A
small GRAVEYARD, retained by a low rubble wall, surrounds
the church.

GRAVEYARD, 0.4km. W. Small walled enclosure with lying slabs,
table-tombs and headstones, C18 and C19. HEADSTONE, dated
1782, to Katharine Stewart: fluted Ionic pilasters carry an
entablature with pulvinated frieze under a pediment formed by
scrolls set against an oval armorial disc.

BRIG O'MICHAEL. C18. Humped rubble arched span over Black
Water.

BRIG O'TURK, 0.5km. SW. Probably C18. A single segmental-
arched span in rubble.

GLEN FINGLAS DAM, 1.4km. NW. 1965. Curved concrete dam,
228.60m. long and 34.05m. high. Overflow spillway.

SCHOOL, 0.4km. NW. Dated 1875. Schoolhouse and classroom
block in grey-green rubble with sandstone dressings. Mullioned
and transomed window in SE gable.

ACHRAY FARM, 0.8km. SW. Harled single-storey-and-attic 'improved' farmhouse, C19, with a bothy block W and a double
range of rubble outhouses on boulder footings, late C18, to the
E. Some cruck timbers survive in the latter.

BLAIR HOUSE (formerly Glenbruach), 1.75km. W. Mid C19. A
rubble mansion with arch-braced bargeboarding and a Gothicized
timber porch.

TIGH MOR TROSSACHS. *See* p. 768.

BRUCEFIELD                    C
                     3km. E of Kennet

Georgian laird's house sited on a hilltop, its development into a
surprisingly unified grouping of main block and end pavilions of
considerable complexity.

The earliest part is the three-storey centre block built *c.* 1724 for
Alexander Bruce yr. of Kennet. Rubble walls, originally harled,
with strip quoins at the corners. A lintel course joins the second-
floor windows immediately below the cornice under the bellcast
eaves of the steeply pitched piended roof, its ridge crowned by a
pair of panelled chimneystacks. Tall first-floor windows denote
the *piano nobile*. The original main entrance was probably at
the E front. This is of four bays except at the first floor where a
door (now a window) is placed between the two centre windows;
it was formerly reached by an external stair and seems to have
been surmounted by a segmental pediment (the curved line
visible in the stonework). The N ground-floor window of this
front was converted to a French window in the restoration and
alterations to the house carried out in 1928–39 by *James Shearer*.
The gables seem, on the evidence of the surviving second-

floor openings (two now blocked) at the s, to have been of three bays.

w front of five bays, the central bay at the second floor occupied by an heraldic panel displaying the arms of Alexander Bruce impaling those of his wife, Mary Balfour. The panel was moved to the (now demolished) Kennet House c. 1760 and reinstated here in the 1930s. At the centre of the first floor was originally a door (now built up and its triangular pediment removed). The length of its sill suggests it may have opened on to the flat roof of a portico sheltering the ground-floor door below and that stairs may have descended from the top of the portico to the ground, cf. the garden front of Drumlanrig Castle (Dumfries and Galloway), or the present front entrance to Newhailes House (Lothian). The sill of the upper door is now covered by a portico, perhaps of the early c19, in front of the ground-floor entrance. Paired Tuscan columns and a steep pediment pierced by a large circular opening; urns at the ends and on the apex.

The house's two-storey s pavilion, directly abutting the main block's gable and projecting to the front and back, was probably added c. 1760. Like the main block it is built of rubble (formerly harled), has strip quoins at the corners and a lintel course carried round under the eaves cornice. Similar piended roof with bell-cast eaves, the ridge at r. angles to that of the main block. At each floor of the E and W gables, a window of the same size as those of the main block's *piano nobile*. The ground-floor windows of the s side have been widened, probably in the c19.

The N pavilion is a further addition, perhaps of the early c19. Its w front bears a general similarity to that of the s pavilion but is of three storeys and slightly broader, with two windows at each of the lower floors. The lintel course under the eaves is confined to the w gable. Irregularly composed rear elevations, with slit stair windows at the SE corner. N of this pavilion, a small single-storey service court, probably of the c19.

Originally the INTERIOR of the main block contained a ground-floor parlour and first-floor dining room, each occupying the three centre bays and probably with a passage behind on the E. The room in the SE corner of the ground floor was originally the kitchen and retains a segmental-arched large fireplace. In the house's SW corner, a scale-and-platt stone stair, presumably of c. 1724 but old-fashioned, with rounded edging forming a panel at each riser. The interior was recast by *Shearer*. The parlour (now entrance hall) and first-floor dining room (now drawing room) now occupy the full depth of the house and contain panelling of c18 inspiration made by *Maclean* of Clackmannan. More panelling (of 1939) in the library on the ground floor of the s pavilion, which was made by throwing together a kitchen of c. 1760 and another room. In the SE corner of the N pavilion, a stone spiral service stair. Some basket-arched chimneypieces at the upper floors which may be c18 but not necessarily *in situ*. In the bedroom N of the drawing room, an c18 chimneypiece with a lugged architrave.

On the sloping ground immediately s of the house, an C18 brick WALLED GARDEN, the centre of the N wall replaced by railings in the C19.

NW of the house, the C18 STABLES (BRUCEFIELD MAINS), a rubble-walled and pantile-roofed quadrangle, the SW part converted to housing and rendered. At each corner, a two-storey pyramid-roofed pavilion. In the centre of the s range, a low tower, its top containing a doocot; small cupola surmounting the pyramidal roof.

*4080*                    BUCHANAN CASTLE                    S
                          1km. W of Drymen

Held by Buchanans of that Ilk from the C13, the estate was bought by the 3rd Marquis of Montrose (later created first Duke) in 1682. In 1724 an earlier dwelling was demolished to be replaced by Buchanan Place. Subsequent alterations to the house and gardens were carried out for the second Duke by *John Adam* in 1751 and in 1789 additions were made by *James Playfair*. Some further enlargement of the Old House had been envisaged in 1837 when plans were prepared by *Charles Barry*, though it is doubtful if these were proceeded with. In 1850 this C18 residence, now known as Buchanan Old House, was destroyed by fire. Service wing fragments of the fabric survive, associated with the Clubhouse of Buchanan Castle Golf Club, while the outline of the main house, which faced SE, is marked out by stones set in the turf. Following the fire, a new mansion on a different site was commissioned from *William Burn*.

Of this Buchanan Castle, erected 1852–4, some 0.5km. ESE of its predecessor, only a fragmentary shell remains. But a tall tower, bartizaned and balustraded, and three storeys of rough-faced, coursed stonework enriched with stringcoursing, mock gargoyles and pedimented eaves dormers standing open on the skyline are enough to recall a lifestyle far removed from that of the suburban dwellings that now surround this uneasy ruin. The house was vast; a sprawling asymmetrical plan with two courtyards and six staircases carefully contrived to comply with the domestic protocol of Victorian country-house living, the whole conceit elaborated in a style which, no longer Jacobean and not yet Brycean, is perhaps best described as Early Baronial. Partially demolished with its roof stripped off, the house was abandoned exactly a century after its construction.

In the grounds is a circular rubble FOLLY with six square buttresses carried above the parapet. Small square openings above round-arched windows. Circular ICEHOUSE, early C19, with brick dome interior.

BUCHANAN HOME FARM. Early C19. Two-storey, three-bay farmhouse with links l. and r. to piend-ended pavilion wings.

EAST LODGE, on the A811. Early C19, by *W. H. Playfair*. Piend-roofed cottage. Round-arched windows and entrance. (For other estate lodges *see* Kilmaronock.)

## BUCHANAN SMITHY          S 4080

A one-line, one-sided hamlet. Along the N side of the B837 are two piend-roofed four-house rows, built by the 3rd Duke of Montrose, *c.* 1800. Roughcast or painted rubble. Nos. 1–4 are two-storeyed with a tree-trunk porch added to No. 1. Nos. 7–10 lower, each with two catslide dormers at first floor.

## BUCHLYVIE          S 5090

Ribbon village on the A811.

BUCHLYVIE NORTH CHURCH, Station Road. Built by the Antiburgher Seceders, 1751–2; now abandoned. Gabled meeting-house kirk in a walled churchyard. Walls, including cavetto eaves course on the N, reprehensibly covered in dry-dash render but ashlar margins preserved. On the N, five round-arched windows; on the S, five more, closely spaced between identical round-arched doors at W and E ends. Pronounced Gibbsian keystones and wedge-shaped impost blocks to all S openings except two windows where, over a projecting grotesque at the head of the arch, a palmette motif is preferred. Central S window formerly a door. In a carving placed above the W doorway, a declamatory finger points vertically into the spine of an open book in which is rudely incised 'The / Law / Came by / Moses / But / Grace & / Truth by / Jesus / Christ'. A finely lettered stone TABLET set into the S wall at low level commemorates one of the founders, James Risk †1772, and his son and grandson. – The GRAVEYARD is entered from the S through square gatepiers with obelisk finials. – Several TABLE-TOMBS, late C18 and early C19. – Close to the church's W gable stands a MONUMENT to Patrick Morrison †1781, a tall, plain, Classical block capped by a cornice and deep fluted frieze. – The former MANSE, also on Station Road and probably contemporary with the church, is a two-storey, five-bay dwelling with a 21-pane ogee stair window.

BUCHLYVIE PARISH CHURCH. 1835–6. Small, skew-gabled, cruciform church built predominantly of red sandstone, apparently in two stages. The S wall, facing the road, is coursed; the W gable is thinly harled, but the N wall of random whin rubble. An inscribed tablet built into the S wall below the eaves records that the church was 'Erected by Public Subscription . . .' Gabled transepts and E end, constructed in snecked sandstone, 1891. Pointed-arched windows: Y-tracery to nave, intersecting in transept gables; each with a transom. The W birdcage bellcote carries a stepped pyramid. Plastered interior with a flat ceiling, showing the ceiling ties on cusped brackets dropped to timber corbels. Broad, round arches open into short transepts and a timber-vaulted chancel. – Octagonal box PULPIT, stained and grained, with cinquefoil motifs on panelled faces. – Grey marble FONT; bowl and shaft octagonal on stepped, square base. – Brightly variegated STAINED GLASS in tripartite E window depicts Christ blessing the pure in heart; in memory of William McOnie †1905.

PRIMARY SCHOOL, Station Road. Gabled classrooms; built 1876, extended w, 1908. Roll-moulded cavetto corbelstones support overhang of bargeboarded gables l. and r. Cast iron railings on low wall to playground. Gatepiers with weathered copes and ball finials.

VILLAGE HALL. 1884–5, by Glasgow architects *William G. Wilson & J. B. Stewart*. A square tower, its topmost stage an octagonal ogee-domed belfry rising from ball finial corners, stands sentinel at the higher w end of the village. It fronts a gable-ended hall with new window grids in broad, round-arched openings, added after a fire in 1984.

### DESCRIPTION

MAIN STREET stretches downhill from the Village Hall tower at the w to the Parish Church at the E. White roughcast cottages abound. Close to the tower, BANK COTTAGE, probably early C19, could scarcely be simpler, or better. WEDNESDAY COTTAGE, dated 1871, is more expansive but still elegantly severe. Along the N side of the street, at Nos. 46–62, dull but earnest local authority housing predominates. There is more of this across the street at Nos. 37–43 but the s side is mostly older and lower: gable-to-gable, three-bay dwellings, early C19, of which the best are MARFIELD, RHUALLAN and WILLOW COTTAGE, all roughcast, and THE MILL COTTAGE, mid or late C18, stripped back to reveal red rubble walls and relieving arches. At the BUCHLYVIE POTTERY SHOP, *c.* 1910, above a delicately dentilled fascia, two canted bay eaves dormers are carried on Art Nouveau brackets. Canted bays re-appear on the N side, pushing out at first floor in the narrow three-bay front of the BUCHLYVIE INN, 1851. Further E, set apart physically and architecturally, SPITTALTON HOUSE, 1738, a three-bay, two-storey, skew-gabled residence; wide, white and the best in town. Nearby, off-street behind the church, ARIVAIN, four bays of decorative common brick domesticated by dormers; begun in 1914, it seems to have been subdivided by *David W. Glass* of Stirling in 1932 but was later restored to one residence in 1958.

GARTINSTARRY, 2.2km. w. Standard skew-gabled farmhouse, late C18. On the s skewputt, the date 1789. Linked l. and r., single-storey, parallel ranges, probably late C19, present portholed, bargeboarded gables to the road.

OLD AUCHENTROIG, 3km. w. 1702. A three-bay, thinly harled rubble laird's house surviving beside the walled garden of its successor, Auchentroig House (*see* below). Crowstep gables with cavetto skewputts. A slight asymmetry in the SE front adds to the charm. Original door studded with nail-heads. Roll and hollow surround with 17 MS IM BG 02 inscribed on the lintel and above this a heraldic tablet carrying the arms of the MacLachlan family.

*South-east Elevation*

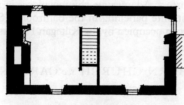

*First Floor Plan*

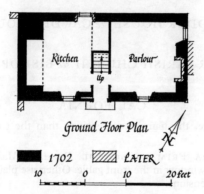

Buchlyvie, Old Auchentroig. Plans and reconstructed elevation.

ST PATRICK'S COLLEGE (Auchentroig House), 3km. w. A Scots
mansion in square-snecked red sandstone; drum towers, corbel
courses and bays but no crowsteps or slated cone roofs, its
beheaded Baronial appearance the result of the last of three
building programmes. First came a house of 1843 built to
supersede Old Auchentroig (q.v.). Then, 1901–3, a wholesale
remodelling and enlargement by the Stirling architect *Ebenezer
Simpson*. A three-storey tower from the earlier dwelling was
retained at the heart of the new NE front, which ranged three
crowstepped gables between cylindrical N and E towers with tall
conically capped roofs. The largest gable, projecting l. of entrance
porch, is splayed on twelve corbel courses over a corner bay

window. Beside it a stone tablet sentimentally inscribed: IF
THIS HOUSE/BE FINE OR NOT/THAT WAS NE ER MY/SERIOUS
THOUGHT/BUT IT WILL HAVE/GAINED ITS ENDS/SHOULD I
FILL IT/FULL OF FRIENDS. In the porch an 1850 datestone.
Principal apartments look SE across banked lawns. A gated
service court penetrates the plan on the NW. In 1923 the building
was gutted by fire. Rebuilding, completed *c.* 1930, transformed
the house: its serrated skyline cut down to a battlemented parapet,
a Gothicized porch, metal windows and entirely recast interior
decoration. Floor, wall panelling and beamed ceiling in the
spacious stair hall are in oak as are two fine elaborately carved
chimneypieces, one with marquetry inlays. Both hall fireplaces
have four-centred stone arches. Timber well stair with Mannerist
pilaster balusters. Adamesque chimneypieces in the bedrooms.
Splendid Vitrolite panelling in the bathrooms. Since 1965 the
house has been occupied by the Kiltegan Fathers.

BUCKIEBURN CHURCH *see* CARRON BRIDGE

CADDER CEMETERY *see* BISHOPBRIGGS

CADDER HOUSE *see* CAWDER HOUSE

CADDER PARISH CHURCH *see* BISHOPBRIGGS

*9070*                    CALIFORNIA                    F

Small village, the name more exciting than the C19 and C20
housing.

CALIFORNIA PRIMARY SCHOOL. By *A. N. Malcolm*, 1914.
Venetian window in the front gable. Otherwise plain with utilitarian extensions.

*6000*                    CALLANDER                    S

Though laid out as a planned village by the Duke of Perth in the
1730s, it took a generation before the town was firmly established
by the Commissioners for Forfeited Estates. By the end of the C18
the population exceeded 1,000. First cotton manufacture and
then, aided by the railway from Stirling, tourism stimulated further
development. Now no longer that 'place for summer rustication'
which Groome observed in Victorian times, the town continues
to attract visitors en route to the Trossachs and Highlands. The
original one-straight-street plan survives, grown altogether more
brash and commercial than its picturesque setting between the
Crags and the River Teith might suggest.

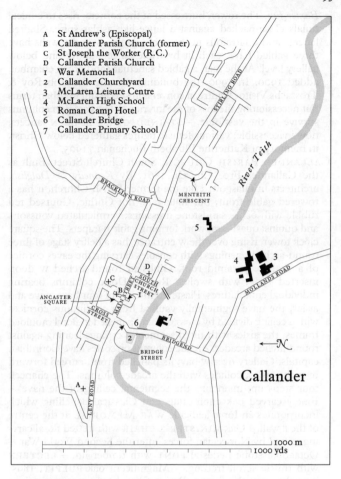

A   St Andrew's (Episcopal)
B   Callander Parish Church (former)
C   St Joseph the Worker (R.C.)
D   Callander Parish Church
1   War Memorial
2   Callander Churchyard
3   McLaren Leisure Centre
4   McLaren High School
5   Roman Camp Hotel
6   Callander Bridge
7   Callander Primary School

Callander

1000 m
1000 yds

CHURCHES

CALLANDER CHURCHYARD, Bridge Street. Walled graveyard on
    Tom na Cheasaig (the Mound of St Kessog) on the N bank of
    the Teith. Some lying SLABS may be C18 but most grave-
    markers are C19. The Robertson family tomb is a hefty stone
    SARCOPHAGUS framed by Gothic gables on colonnettes. –
    Built into the W wall, a hexagonal WATCHHOUSE, 1832; an
    inscription on the doorway lintel records that it was 'designed
    by *Duncan McNa* Joiner' and gives equally abbreviated clues to
    its three builders '*J.Par F.Bu & D.McGre*'.
Former CALLANDER PARISH CHURCH, Ancaster Square (N).
    By *Robert Baldie*, 1883. First Pointed, gable-front Gothic with a
    high steepled entrance at the centre. The church, facing S, and
    set back from Main Street behind a paved forecourt, occupies
    the same site as its pedimented predecessor of 1771–3 by *John*

*Baxter Jun.* The tower, buttressed at the corners, rises to conical finials close-packed against a lance-like ashlar spire. Shafted lancets and quatrefoils in the gable flanks. W and E walls have three gabled bays, each lit by triple lancets above and below gallery level. At the rear, a gabled sanctuary and organ chamber, added 1900. In 1990, the building became the Rob Roy & Trossachs Visitor Centre, a conversion successful in urban terms but necessitating the loss of the interior. A few cast iron columns survive in the vestibule. – STAINED GLASS in the N lancets, now inaccessible: various female figures gathered below Christ, in memory of Katherine Elizabeth Buchanan †1905.

CALLANDER PARISH CHURCH, South Church Street. Built as the Callander Free Church, 1861. By *Kennedy & Dalglish*, architects in Glasgow. Like the former Parish Church, it has a towered gable front, but Italianate, not Gothic. Coursed red rubble with ochre sandstone dressings; vermiculated voussoirs and quoins; quasi-strapwork forming gable parapets. The square clock tower, rising over the W entrance, has a belfry stage of three round-arched openings with consoles carrying the eaves cornice of a shallow pyramid roof. Gibbsian round-arched W door, inserted 1907, with swollen Roman Doric columns bearing individual entablatures. Plastered interior of four bays, nave and aisles, the nave segmentally vaulted from continuous cornices with a ceiling divided by cross ribs and panelled in floral moulded frames, the aisles with tilted segmental ceilings leaning against round-arched arcades. Arcade columns on socles have Corinthian capitals. Gallery over W bay; its panelled front, curved forward over the aisles, collides with the arcade columns. The chancel, four steps up, maintains the segmental ceiling of the nave. – Finely carved oak choir stalls and Classical panelling which incorporates an Ionic aedicule WAR MEMORIAL at the centre of the E wall. – Oak MINISTER'S CHAIR with fretted floral carving, gifted by Norwegian forces, after the Second World War. – Octagonal stone pedestal FONT with timber lid. – LECTERN with thistle scroll fretting. – Magnificent oak PULPIT, 1895, brought from the former Parish Church when congregations united: an elevated Gothic octagon with arcuated panels carved with the relief figures of Christ and the gospel saints. – ORGAN by *Abbot & Smith*, 1900. – STAINED GLASS in the three round-arched E windows: within variegated daedal margins, Christ offers the cup of salvation between Mary and St John of the Revelation.

ST ANDREW (Episcopal), Leny Road. 1857. Rural Dec Gothic by *J., W. H. & J. M. Hay* in red sandstone random rubble with ochre ashlar dressings. First, a simple nave with a bellcote on the W gable and a S porch; slated roofs falling in bellcast sweeps to sparred eaves. Added in 1872, a half-octagon sanctuary (E) and, in 1886, N and S transepts. Dark-stained, scissors-raftered roof with diagonal boarding; arch-bracing at crossing. Walls plastered above low dado, except W where rubble is exposed. Stone chancel arch. – Deep red *Minton* tiles in chancel and, more decoratively patterned, in the sanctuary. – ORGAN by *Abbot*

*& Smith* of Leeds, 1898. – Egg-cup FONT at w end; painted stone with trefoil and cross ornament. – STAINED GLASS. In the chancel, cusped lancets depict Christ with Mary, the Crucifixion, and the resurrected Christ, all figures canopied by Gothic niches, *c.* 1895. – s transept chapel, an Annunciation and a two-light window in warm browns, reds and yellows, showing Christ calling SS Andrew and Peter to discipleship, dedicated 1908. – w gable, two-light composition of baptismal themes; dedicated to the memory of the Rev. Thomas Wildman, 1882. – s wall, The Virtuous Woman by *Douglas Strachan*, 1947, commemorates Agnes Maude Thomson †1945. – HALL at rear added, 1891.

ST JOSEPH THE WORKER (R.C.), Ancaster Square, N of St Kessog. 1958. Roughcast hall with square concrete-framed windows.

## PUBLIC BUILDINGS

CALLANDER BRIDGE, Bridge Street. Built 1908 in square-snecked red sandstone as a replacement for an earlier crossing (1764) of the River Teith. Three wide four-centred arch spans on cutwaters. Heavy roll-moulding over voussoirs. Stepped parapet. Two cast iron light standards on the w side.

CALLANDER PRIMARY SCHOOL, Bridge Street. Former McLaren High School. By *Stewart & Paterson*, 1906–7 and 1924. Grand symmetrical w front with high piended roof. Lower storey projects with a concave centre recessed behind four Roman Doric columns, above which the first floor is pedimented. Segmental pediments on side elevations. Moulded architraves to all windows.

McLAREN HIGH SCHOOL, Mollands Road. By *Perth & Kinross County Council*, 1963–65. Swimming pool added 1967. Slated roofs, gable-ended, hipped and pyramidal, all but overcome the elongated bulk of two- and three-storey classroom wings.

McLAREN LEISURE CENTRE, Mollands Road. By *Gaia Architects*, 1997–8. Sports hall, bowling hall, squash courts and swimming pool collected in an L-plan arrangement under pitched roofs. Entrance in the re-entrant below raking eaves. Innovative breathing wall and ceiling systems reputedly the first major building of its kind in Britain. Heat usually lost to the outside is collected by air drawn through the insulation, the dynamic control of pressure differentials working as 'a counter-flow heat exchanger'. Green architecture at its most convincing; the forms at once traditional and responsive to the unconventional technology within.

ROMAN CAMP HOTEL, off Main Street. A picturesque grouping of pink-harled vernacular elements, genuine and contrived, and delightfully intimate. The main two-storey block, reputedly C17 but remodelled *c.* 1840, has the suggestion of a wallhead pediment. The low, bow-ended w wing may be of the mid C18. Following acquisition by the 2nd Viscount Esher, 1896, alterations and extensions were undertaken on the w and E by *Dunnage & Hartmann*, London, and *Stewart & Paterson*. These works continued over a period of two decades. Several conical roofs appeared, including one over the tiny, stone-domed Chapel added with the Library N of the W wing. Jacobean ceiling with plaster pendants in the LIBRARY, linenfold panelling to the STAIRCASE, and a splendid classical chimneypiece of white Sienna marble with coloured marble inlays in the DRAWING ROOM: all brought by Esher. Painted ceiling in the Dining Room by *James A. Gray*, using C16 and C17 Scots motifs. A carved overmantel depicting the Masque of Atalanta from the period of James VI.

Linked NE, a cottagey GUEST HOUSE with ashlar columns in the concave corners of its gabled E porch. Rubble-walled GARDEN with box parterres, herbaceous border and topiary. Italian STATUARY. Richly carved marble WELL-HEAD, brought from Windsor but said to be Italian Romanesque in provenance. SUNDIAL pillar at the centre of a yew-hedged square. – Entrance drive passes under a rustic rubble ARCH at THE CAMP HOUSE, a turreted, pink-harled lodge, mid C19, on Main Street.

WAR MEMORIAL, Ancaster Square (S). Erected *c.* 1920. Ashlar column with a Celtic capital on which an erect shield-bearing lion confronts the former Parish Church across the Square. Bronze plaques in a rubble-cube base are inscribed with the names of the town's dead; a bronze ring, enriched with Celtic ornament, has been added to the column base to record those who fell between 1939 and 1945.

### DESCRIPTION

Delineated in the C18, ANCASTER SQUARE is still the centre of town. It is, jejunely but precisely, a square of two halves, bisected by the W–E line of Main Street. Axially placed on the N, across a public space paved, seated, stepped and lively with people, is the former Parish Church (*see* Churches, above), now the tourist information centre. Nos. 1–7, a row of late C18 houses with a continuous eaves line and a pend at No. 5, flank the W side of the Square; at No. 1, a marriage lintel dated 1773. A little to the N is a rough-hewn MONUMENT in grey granite; a bouldered base carrying a table and obelisk in memory of the town clerk, William McMichael †1898. The E side is less uniform, though another pend appears. No. 10, dated 1878, has a projecting gabled porch with a round-arched doorway; first a school, it later became a Masonic Lodge. On the S, car parking presses on the War Memorial (*see* Public Buildings, above). Two-storey, three-bay houses, late C18, repeat on the W, Nos. 16–20, and on the S where No. 24 has a marriage lintel dated 1789, but the E wall is again poor. Nearby, MANSEFIELD, harled with margins, is vernacular C18 and perhaps earlier in part.

MAIN STREET numbers W–E, beginning at Station Road. It is straight and densely walled by a capricious variety of shops, cafés and hotels. The first event, in ochre sandstone, is the ROYAL HOTEL, an asymmetrical, three-storey palazzo with a balustraded parapet and a projecting first floor carried on heavy floral consoles; built 1883 as the Commercial Bank, probably designed by *David Rhind*. Nos. 7–19 are two-storey with a consistent eaves, *c.* 1800; No. 13, the black-and-white CROWN HOTEL, with a strong consoled doorpiece. More consoles at No. 27, with a chemist's mortar and pestle sign on the fascia. At Nos. 33–35, two shops with Art Nouveau glass under a three-storey corner, badly weathered but capped by a pyramid roof. Across Cross Street, the castellated, four-storey corner of the former ANCASTER ARMS HOTEL; rough red Baronial, dated 1893. Then, a two-storey wall as far as Ancaster Square. On the s side of the street, MILTON HOUSE (No. 4) is a late C18 domestic survivor, very plain, roughcast below a sparred eaves. At Nos. 12–14, a shopfront, probably Edwardian, with dentillated cornice and five mini-pediment motifs. Thereafter a two-storey scale predominates, but there are interruptions. Among them, the symmetrical KINNELL HOUSE (No. 24), 1861, breaking into an attic above tall tripartite windows; THE EAGLE, built as a hotel on the corner of Bridge Street, late C19, its gabled third storey, half-timbered and roughcast, jutting out over red brick and painted ashlar below; and the BANK OF SCOTLAND (No. 42), late C19, symmetry and tripartite windows again with three tall eaves dormers set into a mansard roof.

To the E of Ancaster Square, Main Street reverts gradually to its early residential character. On the N, shouldered-arched lintels and neat conically roofed attic dormers at Nos. 91–93, mid C19. Vulgar Baronial at THE CRAGS HOTEL, 1888; rough red rubble with heavily moulded dressings in ochre sandstone. GREENBANK GUEST HOUSE (No. 143), late C19, is calmer: three bays wide with more dormer cones, architraved windows and a consoled cornice over the central door. GARTLANDS (No. 151), 1884, has three gables to the street, each with fretted scrolls in the bargeboards. On the s, the two-storeyed range of the WAVERLEY HOTEL, *c.* 1880, is soundly urban, its rigorously repetitive windows, cornices, paterae, pilasters and doorway in debt to Alexander 'Greek' Thomson. Thereafter, domestic incidents catch the eye: lugged architraves and a pedimented entrance at BURNSIDE (No. 144); stop-chamfered pilasters and ingoes at Nos. 156–158; the bartizan corner of The Camp House (*see* Roman Camp Hotel: Public Buildings, above). Finally, MURDISTON (No. 192), a low two-storey, painted rubble house, dated 1790, with a later corbelled canted bay added to the r.

BRACKLINN ROAD climbs N leading to the Falls on the Keltie Water. A few villas enjoy the s-facing hillside. The gables of THE WHINNS, probably of *c.* 1880, have open timbering and fretted bargeboards. At ASHLEA, 1878, under a big hipped roof, the windows have pilastered mullions and jambs. But there is nothing here to compare with similar slopes at Bridge of Allan (q.v.). On the E, easily overlooked in the nondescript suburbia of STIRLING ROAD, are some gently curved VETERANS' 116 HOUSES by *Stewart & Paterson*, 1919–20: a short crescent of rough rubble cottages in Lorimer-like Scotstyle, all that was realized of a projected 'garden settlement' which included a hall, farm, greenhouses, workshops and more dwellings grouped in 'the true spirit of Scottish domesticity' (*The Builder*, 1925). s, by the river, is the Roman Camp Hotel (*see* Public Buildings, above).

At the w end of town LENY ROAD takes the tourists on towards the Trossachs. Many will have left from the DREADNOUGHT HOTEL; begun as a somewhat gaunt three-storey pile by Macnab of Macnab, *c.* 1805, it was later enlivened by corbelled octagonal corners and pyramid roofs, the result of extensive enlargements completed in 1891. Beyond lie WESTCOT, of the mid C19, with a flying stair, blocky ashlar porch and long Classically detailed dormer, St Andrew's Episcopal Church (*see* Churches, above), and the COPPICE HOTEL, mid C19, unremarkable but for its central Italianate tower.

Two routes go s from Main Street to cross the river. SOUTH CHURCH STREET leads to a metal footbridge; it is a short but pleasant avenue much enhanced by pavement trees. On the l. is Callander Parish Church (*see* Churches, above) and beside it, serving as the church hall, the former SCHOOL, dated 1849, a symmetrical block with a central gabled entrance, scalloped bargeboards and a pilastered doorway. Across the street, No. 8, the HIGHLAND HOUSE HOTEL, mid C19, a three-bay, two-storey dwelling of painted rubble, and the white roughcast wall of WATERSIDE HOUSE, late C18, three-bay too, but longer, lower and wonderfully simple. Set at right angles are WATERSIDE COTTAGE and AIRLIE, late C18, equally vernacular and charmingly distinguished by an unusual run of gabled, canted-bay eaves dormers, added *c.* 1835–40. And just before the bridge, a SUNDIAL, dated 1753, in the form of a short Ionic column, the volutes of its capital widespread under a cracked copper plate; incised on the column, a four-line rhyming verse.

BRIDGE STREET bends downhill to Callander Bridge (*see* Public Buildings, above). Nos. 4–6 make a short two-storey row; painted screed and random rubble. DUN WHINNY (No. 7) is similar but sits gable to road. Here, as rubble walls curve with the carriageway, there is an intimate sense of some earlier riverside hamlet. On the r., on a grassy knoll above the Teith, is Callander Churchyard (*see* Churches, above) and, across the bridge, what seems to be that very village. BRIDGEND is its single street. At the river are TEITHVIEW, C18, a simple streetside house, roughcast with no dressings, and, opposite, set well back from the road, the erect black-and-white symmetry of TEITHSIDE HOUSE, probably early C19, plain but decidedly more residence than house. Next to the latter is the Primary School (*see* Public Buildings, above) and then, adding pediment and pilastered door-piece to the familiar three-bay formula, ROBERTSON HOUSE, mid C19. The w side of the street has none of this detachment. Hard to the pavement is BRIDGEND HOUSE HOTEL, a two-storey wall (in part perhaps of C17 origin) speciously drenched in spindly C19 half-timbering. At IVY COTTAGE (No. 16), C19, an inset stone carved with the tools of building. In the gable front of No. 26, more carving; above the hoodmoulded door of a former Meeting Hall, the full incised text of John iii, 16 ('For God so loved the world. . .'). Other ornamental details include a rude Serlian entrance at GLENAIRLIE (No. 17), a heavily moulded lugged architrave to the doorway of ACHARN (No. 27), three tiny tile-topped gablets at No. 38, and some scalloped bargeboards at Nos. 48–54.

CALLANDRADE, 0.6km. SW. Asymmetrical gabled house, *c.* 1830–40, with gabled dormers and sparred eaves.

CAMBUSMORE. *See* p. 305.

GART HOUSE. *See* p. 516.

# CALLENDAR HOUSE *see* FALKIRK

# CAMBUS

C *8090*

Small village at the mouth of the River Devon, dominated by its distillery.

CAMBUS DISTILLERY, Station Road. Brown brick main block, by the *Distillers Company Ltd.'s Architect's Department*, 1937, at the SE of the complex. Behind and on the W side of the Devon, contemporary ranges, all built of dark brown brick. On the E side of Station Road, a two-storey office block of *c.* 1900, faced with red engineering brick. Piended roof, a curly-headed gablet at the centre of the wallhead.

W of the main complex, the CAMBUS IRON BRIDGE over the River Devon, built for the distillery in the early C19 and restored in 1997. It is a humped single span, *c.* 20.7m. long, of prefabricated lattice girder construction; curved parapets on the stone abutments. On the bridge's decking, iron guide rails for horse-drawn wagons.

DESCRIPTION: STATION ROAD is the approach from the N. On its W side, Cambus Distillery (*see* above). The village proper is L-plan consisting of FORTH STREET running S from the end of Station Road, with MAIN STREET projecting NE. In these streets, a huddled mixture of C19 cottages and C20 local authority housing which includes, at the hinge of the L, a development by the Clackmannan County Architect, *W. H. Henry*, *c.* 1960, dressed up to evoke Scots burgh vernacular of the C16 or C17. Late C20 private housing at the S end of Forth Street.

# CAMBUSBARRON

S *7090*

A hillside village which, despite its proximity to Stirling, has been saved from suburban absorption by the M9. Evidence of an industrial past survives in its weavers' cottages and textile mills.

BRUCE MEMORIAL CHURCH, Main Street. Originally Bruce Memorial United Free Church. Art Nouveau Gothic in rough-faced Polmaise stone; by *McLuckie & Walker*, 1909–10. Nipped in a gushet site, the square W tower has short finials and a small slated spire. Segmental-arched tripartite windows. Gabled transepts.

WAR MEMORIAL, in front of the church. Tall, pink granite cross on two-stage plinth, *c.* 1920.

DESCRIPTION. MAIN STREET is a short tight corridor of gable-to-gable cottages, late C18 and early C19, mixed with later higher housing. Between church (*see* above) and POST OFFICE, late C19, where two wide pediments over mullioned and transomed windows add some unexpected civic pretension, BIRKHALL ROAD branches downhill E. After more cottages, a few late C19 villas: LEDI VIEW with pilastered attic bay dormers; at BEECHVILLE, slate-hung gables and a first floor projected on huge concave overhangs.

HAYFORD MILLS, 0.5km. NNW. Founded 1833. A vast spread of piend-roofed, polychromatic brick buildings, one of the most complete surviving woollen mills in Scotland, constructed *c.* 1860–80 by *Wylie & Davie* of Stirling (*James Davie & Sons* from 1873). In the 1870s the company employed some 1,200 workers, yet in the last years of the C19 textile production ceased. Repeatedly adapted to new uses but now abandoned. Cast iron and wrought iron structure encased in walls of red brick with window surrounds, quoining and eaves banding in white. Single-storey and two-storey rubble WEAVING SHEDS, *c.* 1860–7: ashlar cornice at first-floor level with round-arched windows to floor above and dentillated eaves cornice. Elevation to Cutforth Road rebuilt 1870 in red and white brick. Five-storey MULE SPINNING MILL, *c.* 1865–71, twenty-five bays (NW and SE) by six. Adjacent ENGINE HOUSE has a complicated boarded and panelled ceiling with hooks and ventilators. Three-storey FINISHING DEPARTMENT, *c.* 1871–80, twelve bays by six. Windows lintelled at ground-floor, segmentally-arched at first-, and round-arched at second-floor level. Decorative key-pattern frieze picked out in white brick below eaves. Paired wall bays divided by pilaster strips in same material with alternate wall-head stacks, also polychromatic. Two rows of cast iron columns carry timber beams and kingpost trusses. Other buildings include the probable DYEHOUSE, *c.* 1865–70, in which cast iron columns carry twin timber beams tensioned by wrought iron; the WILLYING HOUSE, *c.* 1865–80 (the roof rebuilt after a fire in 1887) with a first floor of fireproof brick arches on cast iron beams and columns; and a tall circular CHIMNEYSTACK in banded brickwork. Though the earliest mill structures from the 1830s and 40s have gone, demolished 1914–15, the original rubble NW BOUNDARY WALL and ENTRANCE GATEPIERS survive, as does an oval COOLING POND, *c.* 1833–58.

LIMEWORKS. Late C18. At Murrayshall, a long line of kilns constructed in coursed stone and brick. Thirteen arched openings in line along the N face: eight 'draw arches' or vents, two to each of the two larger kilns, one to each of the four others; five tunnels giving access to 'draw holes'. A light rail track formerly ran along the top of the structure where brick charging holes, constructed as dished depressions, can still be seen. At Craigend, more ruinous remains built in random rubble.

HAYFORD HOUSE, beside Hayford Mills. 1850. Dull, asymmetrical, vaguely Jacobean villa. Coursed rubble front; otherwise harled. Finialled gables and dormers.

DUN, Castlehill Wood, 3km. SW. Oval, with entrance at W, 23m. by 15m. internally. Material from excavations in 1955 suggests C1 to C2 AD date.

GARTUR. *See* p. 522.

# CAMBUSKENNETH S 8090

Suburbanized village of little more than two parallel streets wrapped in a long loop of the Forth immediately E of Stirling. Along NORTH STREET and SOUTH STREET, a variety of three-bay, gabled cottages, early and mid C19; some are harled, some painted, some of pink square-snecked sandstone. Absorbed in Stirling Burgh from 1939.

CAMBUSKENNETH ABBEY, on the l. bank of the Forth, close to the NE edge of Stirling. Extensive but vestigial remains of an Augustinian foundation first known as the Abbey of St Mary of Stirling. Low lines of walling mark out the plan of the abbey church and a range on the flat carseland site. Evidence of the original C13 buildings is intermittent and in the main little more than footings. As early as 1378 the monastery was reported to be in poor condition with 'the choir greatly ruined'. Reconstruction was effected but at the Reformation, when the Erskine family took possession of the abbey, the structure was again 'ruined and cast down'*. By the end of the C18 the fabric had been further depleted by quarrying and all that remained were 'a few broken walls'‡ and the detached bell-tower, erected *c.* 1300 (*see* below). This was the state of the site in 1864 when the Burgh Architect of Stirling, *William Mackison*, undertook a programme of excavations leading to the stabilization of the surviving foundations. Though this has clarified the monastic layout, the introduction of C19 masonry to help define certain foundation strips has been criticized.

The ABBEY church is cruciform and conventionally orientated, almost 60m. overall W–E. Only the W door still stands; shafted splayed jambs carrying a pointed arch with deep moulded archivolt. On each side of the opening, the bases and bell capitals of five disengaged shafts remain, the decorative elaboration confined to some much-weathered dog-tooth ornament. The nave appears to have had a N aisle, though the footings of eight buttressed bays defining its N wall are largely C19 work and do not coincide with the spacing of responds in a short three-bay stretch of C13 wall which survives on the S side of the nave; an

---

* John Spottiswood, *The History of the Church of Scotland*, i (Bannatyne Club, 1850), 280.

‡ Francis Grose, *The Antiquities of Scotland*, ii (1791), 208.

anomaly which suggests that Mackison may have revealed some
later reconstruction on the N. At the W end of the nave, a cemetery, containing graves from the C18, has been created. At the
E end, some puzzling foundations may relate to a medieval
pulpitum. Traces of N and S transepts indicate that both had a
double chapel arrangement to the E, flanking the square-ended
chancel. Base-courses of buttresses and clustered shafts, C13,
give clues to the articulation of the transeptal walls, including
the likely arcading of the chapels. At the NW corner of the N
transept, evidence of a mural stair which presumably led to
triforium, clearstorey and roof. In the much less well defined S
transept, the N chapel retains stone seating for an altar, C13.
Nothing comparable exists in the chancel where a stone coffin
has been placed in a railed enclosure.

Beyond the S transept are the sacristy, slype passage and the
chapter-house; all, like the cloister itself, marked by low walls
and foundations 'reconstituted' in the C19. The base of a central
pillar, octagonal from square, makes it probable that the chapter-
house, square in plan, was roofed in four rib-vaulted compartments. Along the S side of the garth are the foundations of the
refectory. Some 53m. E of the chapter-house, footings betray a
long rectangular building, perhaps C15, aligned N–S and comprising three small cellars and one longer compartment in the N,
which may have been the Infirmary. Traces of another rectangular outbuilding lie 33m. S.

Situated 6m. N of the W end of the abbey is the BELL-
TOWER, c. 1300, 'an exceptional structure for Scotland'*. All the
more impressive for being the solitary intact piece of medieval
architecture rising out of this flat riparian landscape, at its
corbelled and crenellated parapet-walk the three-storeyed ashlar
tower reaches 19.5m. Square in plan, ribbed with buttressing at
the middle of each wall and at three corners, the NE corner stair
turret formed as an engaged octagon but terminating in a small,
spired heptagon with steep gablets on all sides. Weathered stringcourses continue the sill-lines at first- and second-floor levels.
At ground floor, three of the five lancet windows are blind. At
first floor, more lancets, except in the W wall where each bay is
centrally lit by a pointed-arched opening with two-light, foliated
tracery set between blind arcading. The top floor, the bell-
chamber, has two taller pointed-arched windows with Y-tracery
flanking the central buttress on each side. A moulded pointed-
arched doorway, advanced slightly under an isosceles triangle
gable containing a small cusped niche, enters the tower at the
centre of the S wall. A second E door is blocked. The ground
floor is vaulted with a tierceron vault which has a central circular
bell-hole. In the NE corner a short, shouldered-arched passage
leads diagonally to the stair. Access to the upper floors is by
dog-legged lobbies. Timber floors are supported on corbels and
there is evidence at both upper levels that intermediate framed
floors or platforms have existed. An account of C19 restoration

* RCAHMS, *Stirlingshire*, i (1963), 122.

work records that 'Stone sedilia have been put round the ground-floor apartment... A new wood belfry floor has been put in, and a flat roof constructed over the centre, leaving space round it and within the embrasure parapet wall, for an easy walk or pavement... Whatever materials were found not belonging to the original structure were removed... and the whole walls properly strengthened'*. Several stone fragments are preserved in the tower. – Broken coped GRAVE COVER, C13, with floral ornament, roundels, and a pair of shears. – Six FRAGMENTS of blue-black Tournai limestone; thought to come from the early C16 tomb of James III and his wife, Margaret of Denmark. – Eight more GRAVE COVERS, C13 or C14, all but one coped; varied carved ornament includes crosses, a long-bladed sword, chalice, open book, etc. – Lower part of a SLAB, late C14 or C15, showing the recumbent effigy of a crouching lion.

BRIDGE. Concrete footbridge across the Forth to Riverside, Stirling, by engineers *L. G. Mouchel & Partners*, 1934. Three-span structure (one elliptical arch and two half-arches) with low cutwaters at buttressed piers.

# CAMBUSMORE
3km. SE of Callander

S *6000*

Plain but attractively sited three-storey house, early C19, enlarged and enhanced by *Robert Baldie*, 1880. The red tiles, half-timbered attic dormers and W wing are his, as is the pyramid-roofed *porte cochère* tower placed at the centre of the S front. The allusions, vaguely medieval, seem more Germanic than Baronial.

The LODGE, early C19, a small piended cottage with lintelled windows in segmental-arched recesses flanking its central doorway, is oddly located on the opposite side of the A84 from the driveway entrance.

# CAMBUSWALLACE STABLES *see* DOUNE LODGE

# CAMERON HOUSE
1km. NW of Balloch

WD *3080*

An C18 mansion buried in later Baronial pretension, the resultant Victorian pile now the dominant core of a late C20 luxury hotel complex. In 1763 the estate was bought by the Smollett family who already held extensive lands in the Vale of Leven. With the purchase came the house; in April 1756 the *Edinburgh Evening Courant* had described Cameron House as 'new built, large and commodious'. Sixty years later it was no longer large enough and, as the Napoleonic Wars drew to a close, work began on

---

*W. Mackison, 'Notes on the Recent Excavations made at Cambuskenneth Abbey, and the subsequent Restoration of the Abbey Tower', *Papers read at the Royal Institute of British Architects* (1866–7).

alterations and additions 'all conform to the decision of James Gillespie architect', i.e. *James Gillespie Graham*, then also involved in the transformation of Ross Priory (q.v.), not far distant across the loch. Much of the fabric of this C18 and early C19 structure must be incorporated in the symmetrical five-bay, two-storey-and-basement house which now forms the principal E entrance to the hotel. Despite a rather heavy-handed proto-Baronial make-over, the Classical organization of this block is still clear. Nor is it irresponsible to suggest that both the tripartite Gothic porch and the battlemented tower that rises centrally behind the façade may bear the mark of Gillespie Graham. But later accretions and additions make it difficult to be sure. Following a fire in 1864, *William Spence* altered and vastly extended the accommodation to the W in a high Baronial wing, 1866–7, at the same time recasting the skyline of the older house with a crowstepped gable frontispiece and chunky pedimented dormer-heads to the first-floor windows. These same elements have been re-employed, much less convincingly, in the three- and four-storeyed bedroom block added to the SE, 1989–90. Yet, although the length of this wing is considerable and that of the contemporary Leisure Centre wing spreading NW no less, Spence's serrated skyline holds its own in an attractively landscaped lochside setting.

A low curved terrace wall, constructed in bull-faced rubble pierced here and there with gunloops, helps define the approach to the hotel entrance. In the forecourt is a circular fountain pool in which a *putto* holds a spouting fish. Axially located behind is the five-bay E entrance front. At its centre, built in warm ochre ashlar, is a three-storey crowstepped gable lugged with cone-roofed bartizans. Its upper floors have hooded lintelled windows but at ground-floor level, reached by a balustraded stair, a Gothic porch projects slightly under a stepped parapet with blind trac-ery and a central armorial panel bearing the Smollett motto 'VIRESCO'. A four-centred entrance archway is flanked by narrow lancets. The outer bays of the façade have been painted white with strings, dressings and dormerheads in ashlar. These last are in fact hefty hoodmouldings projected over the first-floor windows, carrying gablet pediments with carving in the tympa-num and small ball finials at the skews and apex. They recur on side elevations that repeat the treatment of the façade, with the exception of a single Palladian window at ground floor on the N. This N front is continued on a basement plinth by Spence's Victorian additions in good polished and tooled ashlar. First comes a three-storey gable lugged by bartizans and gently swollen with a two-storey four-light bow parapeted in open strapwork above first floor. Then a single bay with bipartites and another heavy dormerhead. Next, a four-storey tower with a parapeted square bay framing a tripartite window at ground floor. Finally, a five-storey square tower with bartizans at three corners and a battlemented round stair turret at the fourth. The tower returns W to be clutched disingenuously by blockwork walls rising from the 1990s Leisure Centre which extends NW under hipped roofs in a series of two-storey canted planes, most of which are fully glazed. In effecting this marriage of old and new, the bedroom wing to the SE is no more inspired. 'Keeping in keeping' with crowstepped gables, round stair towers and the repetition of the older house's idiosyncratic dormerheads seems an emollient compromise, certainly a strategy neither Gillespie Graham nor Spence would have adopted.

Rehabilitation as a luxury hotel in the early 1990s restored much of the house's original plasterwork and panelling. The architectural quality of the interior is not exceptional but there are several ribbed plaster ceilings in a variety of designs; the bossed square-and-octagon pattern in the Morning Room is the best. A timber chimneypiece in the Library has twinned barley-sugar columns under lions' heads. The Hall is lined to door height with a panelled dado incorporating an oak chimneypiece which has a shelved overmantel with three carved panel insets, one showing crossed pistols. In the main staircase well, four STAINED GLASS panels with portrait heads of Allan Bane, Helen MacGregor, wife of Rob Roy, Thomas Moore and the Duke of Wellington.

WALLED GARDEN to S, now given over to sports activities. – The L-plan MID LODGE, c. 1850, is modestly Tudor Gothic with a gabled porch in the re-entrant. – The NORTH LODGE, c. 1850, has mullioned and transomed windows and a canted bay gable topped by a thistle finial. – But it is the ebullient SOUTH LODGE, guarding the original (but now superseded) approach from the Old Luss Road, that is unequivocally Scots in allusion. Dated 1882, perhaps by *John Burnet*, it is an outrageous, beguilingly ugly compression of Baronial forms. Ironwork railings survive between large cylindrical GATEPIERS topped with ashlar cones.

# CARBETH GUTHRIE
## 2km. W of Strathblane

S *5070*

Built *c*. 1810. Tidy, two-storey-and-basement, three-bay mansion with a tall central SW window at first floor over semicircular Greek Doric porch. A low castellated wall decorated with urns protects the area. Architraved windows; those to the ground-floor apartments with cornices on consoles. In 1855 *John Baird I* extended the house NE (two NE windows have diagonally patterned ironwork balconies with Greek fretting) and in 1878 more accommodation was provided NW. Original mouldings and detail were maintained. Wide canted bays SE and NW may date from the 1920s, contemporary with the walled ROSE GARDEN to the SE. SUNDIAL with gnomon and world-wide directional plate. – Off the drive from the A809, the small STABLES block, 1817–18: flanking a central pavilion with pyramid roof, two windowed bays, each with a half-round loft window over a plain lintelled opening.

# CARBETH HOUSE                                    S
### 1.3km. N of Killearn

Foundations are said to survive from the late C15 'castle of the
birches' held by the Buchanans for four centuries. But, apart
from the find of a marriage stone bearing the family initials W B
and the date 1716, little is known of the house prior to its transformation into the 'castellated structure of 1840' noted by
Groome. In 1879 the W side of the house was added in a similar
but grander idiom; the tall square entrance tower with its asymmetrically placed corbelled turret appeared and the castellated,
pointed-arched porch. Inside, the tower rises to a nine-part
ribbed plaster vault lit by three pointed-arched windows flanking an octagonal cupola. Converted to flats in the 1980s. –
Octagonal GATEPIERS, also castellated, mark the W entrance to
the estate.

# CARDROSS HOUSE                                   S
### 0.8km. E of Dykehead

Built by the Erskine family who acquired the estate after the
Reformation. A long drive runs E across open parkland passing
the N forecourt *en route* to the stables beyond. The house, though
the irregular result of successive building phases, is unified by a
coating of old ochre roughcast, now redolent with an endearing,
almost Italianate decay. The N entrance façade, 1790, is wide,
symmetrical and Classical: elevated on a sunken basement,
two-storey, two-bay gabled wings flank a recessed centre from
which projects a lower entrance-hall block, added 1820. This is
flat-roofed with a full-width cornice and low parapet, a pilastered
doorway reached by steps and a sill-level stringcourse which
continues into the earlier wings l. and r. The original L-plan
house, late C16, is at the back, evident in the asymmetrical S
façade, where a skew-gabled tower-house, four-storeys-and-
attic high, advances at the W end of a long three-storey block.
Conically roofed bartizans at SW and SE gables. This S side was
remodelled in the C18. A classical doorpiece with Roman Doric
columns has been added to the three-storey wing. Two lintel-
stones over top-floor windows W of the SE bartizan record
Erskine marriage monograms with the differing dates of building: DE MH 1598 and JE AJ 1747. Abutting the tower-house W
is a two-storey wing of C18 date and, beyond that, further C19
service buildings.

In the garden, a log-built octagonal SUMMERHOUSE with
pantiled pyramid roof. – The STABLE BLOCK, 0.25km. NE, has
a two-storey S range with pointed-arched windows, piended end
pavilions and a raised centre now engulfed by ivy. Though
Gothic, it was probably built at the same time as the late C18 N
façade of the main house. – Small GRAVEYARD with a few plain
gravemarkers, the earliest from 1767. Neo-medieval CROSS,
1849, to George Keith Erskine.

# CARRIDEN*                                                 F *0080*

Little more than the present and former parish churches at the foot of Carriden Brae, with some late C20 housing to the W.

Former CARRIDEN PARISH CHURCH, Carriden Brae. Now roofless. Rubble-walled T-plan kirk of 1766. In the long S wall, a blocked door at each end and a third which is a little off-centre and gave the minister access to the pulpit. Rectangular door in the W side of the N 'aisle'. Two of the S windows and one window in the E side of the 'aisle' retain their C18 appearance with mullioned rectangular openings. The others have been Gothicized, probably in 1863 when a clock tower was added at the church's E end and a session house-cum-porch at the W. The tower, off-centre to the gable, has a lucarned stone spire. At the session house, a three-light plate-traceried W window. The interior formerly had galleries at the ends of the main block and in the 'aisle'; fireplace at the back of the 'aisle's' gallery.

On the outside of the gable of the 'aisle', a Gothic shelter erected in 1863 to protect the aedicular wall MONUMENT to William Maxwell of Carriden †1771 with its pretty Ionic order and pulvinated frieze. – In the NW inner angle of the church, a small late C19 cast iron DRINKING FOUNTAIN with dish and cup-hooks; it was made by *Walter Macfarlane & Co.*'s *Saracen Foundry*. – In the NW corner of the graveyard, the BURIAL PLOT of Admiral of the Fleet Sir James Hope †1881; an iron anchor chain is carried round the stone edging.

CARRIDEN PARISH CHURCH, Carriden Brae. Simple Romanesque in hammer-dressed snecked rubble, by *P. Macgregor Chalmers*, 1907–9. The plan is basically cruciform. Nave with attached W tower and lean-to aisles. The S transept is conventional except for a bow-fronted low tower at its SW corner. The N transept is formed by a broadening and heightening of the aisle, its roof double-pitched, the ridge running E–W instead of the usual N–S of a transept; apse on the E side. Apse-ended chancel, slightly lower than the nave. The W tower is tall, the upper stages marked off by chevroned stringcourses. Stone-slabbed steep pyramid roof, the eaves supported by chequer-set shallow corbels. At the base of the tower, the principal entrance with stylized foliage of Celtic inspiration carved on the semi-circular arch which springs from scallop-capitalled nook-shafts. Nook-shafted window over the door. At the stage above, a slit window in the W face. The two top stages, clear of the nave roof, have two-light belfry openings in each face. Small and studiedly simple windows to the aisles and clearstorey. Taller windows in the N side of the N transept. The windows of the two apses are taller again. Some consecration crosses show how determined were 'ecclesiologically' minded Edwardian Presbyterians to assert the continuity of the Church of Scotland with the pre-Reformation *Ecclesia Scoticana*.

---

* Account based on that by Colin McWilliam, *The Buildings of Scotland: Lothian* (1978).

27  Inside, the tower forms a tall narthex to the six-bay nave which is covered by a semicircular wooden ceiling. Roundheaded nave arcades. At the E end of each aisle, a half-arch into the transept. On the E side of the N transept, a chevroned arch into the apse containing the baptistery, its half-dome covered with MOSAIC depicting Our Lord and Little Children. Higher but plainer arch at the E end of the nave into the sanctuary. Eleven arcaded sedilia round its base. – FURNISHINGS. Oak PULPIT, LECTERN, PRECENTOR'S BOX and COMMUNION TABLE, all of 1909 in genteel Romanesque, as is the round arcaded stone font. – In the N transept, the Corinthian-capitalled wooden ENTABLA-TURE from the pulpit of the former Carriden Parish Church; it bears the date 1655. – ORGAN in the S transept, by *Blackett & Howden*, 1925, formerly in John Knox Church, Glasgow, and rebuilt here in 1943. – STAINED GLASS. In the apse, three windows (St George, Our Lord in Glory, St James), all good work of 1912. – In the baptistery, one light (Madonna and Child) of 1928. – Two lights (the Nativity and the Ascension of Our Lord) by the *St Enoch Glass Studios*, 1948, in the N transept. – In the N aisle, a rather pale light (St Margaret) by *A. Carrick Whalen*, 1983. – To its W, a window (St Cecilia) by *Roland Mitton*, 1999. – In the S aisle, four lights. Strongly coloured window (St Andrew) of 1974, also by *Whalen*. – The second window (Angels of the Resurrection) is of *c.* 1920. – The aisle's third window (St Francis) is by *G. T. S. Gould*, 1953.– The fourth window (St Leonard) is by *Mitton*, 1999. – In the tower, one light (Elijah) of *c.* 1935.

### CARRIDEN HOUSE
0.5km. E

Rubble-built agglomeration liberally sprinkled with dates from 1602 to 1890 which plausibly represent the many stages of the building's history, even though most were inscribed in the C19. The house was begun by John Hamilton of Lettrick who acquired the property in 1601 and (according to a date-stone now on the E front) put up an L-plan house the next year, its main block running N–S, the jamb projecting W from the N end. The estate was sold in 1678 to Alexander Myln, sometime Provost of Linlithgow, who in 1682 added a T-plan W addition, its principal range or crossbar extending from the jamb of the earlier house, its tail projecting to the N. Perhaps a little later the NW inner angle of this extension was partly filled by a further addition. After various changes of ownership in the C18 the estate was acquired in 1814 by Admiral Sir George Johnstone Hope who filled the remainder of this NW inner angle. In 1849 Hope's son, Captain (later Admiral Sir) James Johnstone Hope, added a castellated block in the inner angle formed by the original house and the extension of 1682 and also a porch in the SW inner angle of the original building. In 1863 Hope remodelled much of the exterior.

The original house was of five storeys (the lowest floor now a basement). Roll-moulded windows (many now blocked) survive;

some at the third floor are set above splayed gunloops. Round corner turrets, again with gunloops and projected on continuous corbelling, but these seem, except for the NE turret, to have been rebuilt in 1863 when they acquired their present slated conical roofs. Also of 1863 are the E front's oriel windows, one bowed and of two storeys, the other with canted sides. A third oriel window (but rectangular) was added to the main block's S gable at the same time. In the S inner angle of the original house, the large porch added in 1849, its battlement and four-centred arched entrance alterations of 1863.

The principal range of the extension of 1682 is of two storeys above a basement. The S front was probably always of six bays but refaced in 1863 when it was given a battlement whose continuous corbelling rises over the upper floor's windows; triangular merlons over the outer bays, a gablet above the two centre bays. At the W front of the additions in the late C17 NW inner angle, gablet dormerheads of 1863.

Inside the present basement of the E range, tunnel-vaulted rooms, the N probably the original kitchen. In the S room of this range's principal floor, a late C17 ceiling, deeply modelled in the manner of the contemporary plasterwork of the Palace of Holyroodhouse (Edinburgh). Central oval framed by a floriated band. At each corner of the ceiling, a triangular panel but with a concave inner side, the cable-moulded border enclosing floral scrolls. Swags and flowers on the coved cornice.

The rooms of the principal floor of the W range were remodelled c. 1815. In the drawing room, an elegant marble chimneypiece. Ceiling enriched with delicate plasterwork cords which form an oval enclosing a diamond containing the central rosette placed in an octofoil. Swagged frieze, perhaps work of 1890, the likely date for the introduction of panelling, and a china cabinet to the apsed E end of the room.

STABLES to the SE. The main (E) range, dated 1818, has piend-roofed end pavilions and a low centre tower containing a doocot.

# CARRON AND CARRONSHORE     F *8080*

Housing, some of the late C19 but mostly C20, built largely to house workers at the Carron Ironworks which had a dry dock at Carronshore with a railway link to the foundry.

CARRONSHORE CHURCH, Church Street. Built as a school, c. 1835, and reconstructed as a church by *A. & W. Black*, 1882–3. Rectangular windows, some hoodmoulded; gabled bellcote on the SE wing.

CARRON PRIMARY SCHOOL, Alloa Road. By *McLuckie & Walker*, 1898–9. Plain Jacobean but not without presence.

CARRON IRONWORKS, Stenhouse Road. Of the massive industrial complex of the Carron Company which was founded in 1759 and began operations in 1760 there survive utilitarian C19 and C20 workshops. The long E office range built of hammer-dressed masonry in 1876 as a grand front to the works has been demolished except for its central clock tower. Crowstepped two-storey gable containing a segmental-arched pend opening set in an elliptical overarch. At the first floor, a three-light window under a large panel bearing the coat of arms (three crossed cannons) of the Carron Company. Corbelled out at the top of the gable, a square clock turret with a tall pyramid roof and weathervane.

CARRON HOUSE. *See* below.

7080                    CARRON BRIDGE                    s

Crossroads on the B818.

BUCKIEBURN CHURCH, 0.17km. NNE. Erected *c.* 1750; reseated 1830. Thinly harled gabled oblong with session house and vestry adjunct on the E gable. Four lintelled windows S, two on N; all have timber shutters. Inside, MURALS painted by *William Crosbie*, 1946: Adam and Eve on the W gable; Christ at the centre of an allegorical composition on the E gable. Disused.

GRAVEYARD, Kirk o' Muir, 4.2km. W. Rubble-walled enclosure, gated but with stepping-stones in wall. Site of St Mary's Chapel, built in the mid C15, and extant until mid C17. Several well-weathered lying SLABS; two dated 1695 and 1705. Various small C18 stones. – HEADSTONE to John McKechnie †1857; inscribed framed disc shouldered with Ionic capitals cut in low relief.

CARRON BRIDGE. Rubble-built 1695, rebuilt 1715, and again repaired in 1907, all evidenced by dated stones, varied masonry and concrete buttressing. The narrow carriageway rises S over two unequal segmental arches, spanning 6.85m. and 14.48m., the larger S arch and vault reconstructed in engineering brick. W cutwater.

BENTEND, 0.6km. W. C19. Long, single-storey rubble farm with cone-roofed horsemill. Restored as dwelling.

LOCHEND, 2.4km. NE. Early or mid C19. Single-storey rubble steading around square court. Farmhouse centre S. Horsemill to E.

MUIRMILL, 1.5km. W. Single-storey farmhouse, probably C18, re-roofed, dormered and enlarged with N wing, late C19. Early C19 piend-roofed threshing mill range, built in rubble with tooled ashlar dressings, comprises central barn and cart bays with lofts over. Breast-shot water-wheel.

8080                    CARRON HOUSE                    F
                    0.4km. E of Carronshore

Late C18 merchant's house with aspirations to lairdly status. It is sited, not in the middle but on the edge of parkland, immediately beside the River Carron, allowing goods to be brought here by boat.

Four ranges round a quadrangle entered from the W. The house (partly derelict and partly rebuilt after a fire in the C19) apparently occupied the S and E ranges, the offices the N and W. The

now roofless two-storey S range overlooking the river possesses
the show front. Its main walling is of rough ashlar. Five bays,
the centre three minimally advanced under a pediment, its tympanum pierced by a round window with cross-wise keystones.
In front of the ground floor, a loggia of V-jointed polished ashlar,
the openings roundheaded. The loggia is gripped by the full-
height ends of the E and W ranges. The S half of the W range
(The Granary) is a store, covered by a triple-ridged piended roof.
At the outer corners of its S front, vermiculated pilaster strips.
Plain single-light windows at the slightly recessed centre. At the
W elevation of this block, a basket-arched entrance. The S end
of the E range, now partly demolished, was similar to that of the
W but dignified by a Venetian door under a window which was
of the same width and probably also Venetian. At each end of this
range's E front, overlooking the park, was a canted bay window.
The N of these is now incorporated in a very ordinary mid-C19
harled farmhouse occupying the N two thirds of the range. The
N range and N half of the W have brick walls to the courtyard
and pantiled roofs but no pretension to architectural display.

To the N, a brick-walled GARDEN, probably contemporary
with the building of the house. – c. 0.28km. S of the house, a
late C18 DOOCOT. It is a two-storey brick-walled octagon, the
upper floor marked off by an ashlar ratcourse and containing
oval windows (dummies except at the face containing the door).
The ground-floor entrance is a plain rectangular opening but
surmounted by an ogee-arched stone panel whose base line is
carried round the building as a stringcourse. The wallhead
parapet and roof are now missing.

## CASTLE CAMPBELL
### 1.2km. N of Dollar

C 9090

Spectacularly sited late medieval residence of the Campbells, 52
Earls of Argyll, high in the hills above Dollar. Abandoned after
being burned by Royalist forces during the Earl of Glencairn's
rising against the Cromwellian occupation in 1654, the castle was
repaired in the late C19. Further consolidation and a reroofing of
the NE tower have been carried out since 1948 when Dollar Glen
and Castle Campbell were acquired by the National Trust for
Scotland which placed the castle in state guardianship.

There was a house here before 1466 when a papal bull stated
that Walter Stewart, Lord of Lorne, who then held the lands in
feu ferme from the Bishop of Dunkeld, had destroyed 'a certain
manor with a tower of the place of Glowm situated in the territory
of Dolar'. In c. 1470 the lands were acquired by Colin Campbell,
first Earl of Argyll, after his marriage to Isabel or Elizabeth
Stewart, daughter and co-heiress of John, Lord of Lorne. It seems
clear that it was this Earl of Argyll who was responsible for the
construction of the NE tower, probably completed by 1490 when
he obtained an Act of Parliament to change 'the Name of the
castelle and place quhilk wes callit the gloume' to Castle Campbell.

The position is a decidedly odd one for a medieval laird's house or castle since it is formidably difficult to reach and without easily cultivable land nearby. What it does have, however, is a panoramic view over the broad valley of the Forth and the likeliest reason for the construction here of the earlier tower is that it was used as a regularly manned observation post from which to keep watch over the most important E–W land route across medieval Scotland. Whatever the original purpose of a tower here, the first Earl of Argyll's motive in beginning the construction of what must have been intended as a substantial group of buildings and renaming the complex after his family seems likely to have been self-advertisement. The C15 had seen his family establish itself as the dominant force in the West Highlands and he himself as a leading figure at the court and in politics, being granted the earldom in 1457, made Master of the King's Household in 1464 and Lord High Chancellor in 1483. The building of a princely new house of Castle Campbell was the opportunity to proclaim the extension of his possessions and power into the heartland of Scotland, the inconvenience of the site offset by the prominence of its position (now masked by trees). This was not a convenient residence but a status symbol.

The SITE is a roughly oval promontory bounded on the SW and SE by the gorges of the Burn of Sorrow and the Burn of Care (their names apparently products of late Georgian romanticism) which join at the promontory's S end to form the Dollar Burn. The relatively easy approach from the N has been cut across by a ditch (now filled in).

The castle buildings form a quadrangle spanning the summit of the promontory. At the quadrangle's NE corner is a tower house, the line of its N side continued W by a wall containing the gateway into the courtyard. On the S side of the quadrangle, a range containing a great hall overlooking the terraced garden which occupies the N end of the promontory. These buildings may well have been planned together, perhaps c. 1475, the tower built first, the S range following c. 1500, its executed design influenced by that of the contemporary King's Old Building at Stirling Castle. This S range is joined to the NE tower by a short E block, probably late C16 and perhaps designed as a jointure house. On the W side of the courtyard is a wall behind which there was probably a range of ancillary buildings.

The GATEWAY to the enclosure is placed near the W end of the N side. The rubble-built wall is a replacement, probably of the later C16. In it, two wide-splayed gunloops flank the shallow projection, perhaps formerly a low tower, containing the entrance. This is an unpretentious roundheaded arch with a simple roll-and-hollow moulding. It opens into a transe covered with an ashlar segmental tunnel vault. At the E wall of the transe, a bench and a recess; in its W wall, a built-up door into the adjoining single-storey guardroom, the survivor of the two buildings that flanked the transe. The rear (courtyard) elevation of the entrance tower is of ashlar.

At the E end of this side of the quadrangle, the NE TOWER. This is

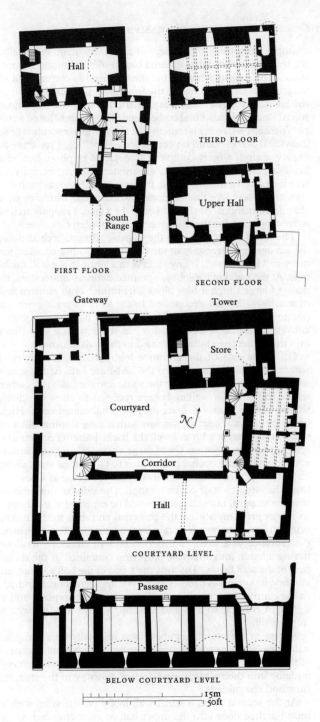

Hall

THIRD FLOOR

FIRST FLOOR

South
Range

Hall

Upper Hall

SECOND FLOOR

Gateway

Tower

Store

Courtyard

Corridor

Hall

COURTYARD LEVEL

Passage

BELOW COURTYARD LEVEL

15m
50ft

Castle Campbell. Plans.

a simple four-storey rectangle, *c.* 12.95m. by 9.1m. externally, the walls built of roughly squared blocks of buff-coloured sandstone. The masonry just below the wallhead is constructed of longer stones and the top of the tower was probably rebuilt in the late C16 when a vault was constructed over the third-floor room. Rounded individual corbels under the uncrenellated parapet (perhaps a C19 replacement); at the corners, rounds whose individual corbels stand on continuous corbelling. Projecting at the NW round, a fairly complete gargoyle (a gryphon, but now headless). Inside the parapet, a crowstep-gabled pitched roof which replaced a C19 flat roof in the later C20; there was probably something very like this originally. Rectangular windows with chamfered margins. At the bottom of the E face, a roughly arched narrow opening for the discharge from a garderobe chute.

The tower's entrance is in the W gable. Round-arched door, the sill lowered, probably in the C16, the surround checked for outer and inner doors. It gives access to a lobby in the wall thickness. At the E end of the lobby, a pointed doorway into a store, its walls of large rough ashlar blocks, its tunnel vault constructed of much smaller squared stones. In the store's S wall, a narrow pointed window. The late C16 doorway to its E was probably converted from a second window. In the E wall, a slop drain into the garderobe chute contained in the wall thickness.

Off the N side of the entrance lobby a straight stair rises within the wall thickness up to the first-floor hall. At the stair's top step, a pointed opening on the E side into the hall's NW corner whose rough ashlar walling is here recessed to allow the door, when open, to fit into it. Over the hall, a tall tunnel vault. High up in the W wall, a small window with a long sloping sill. S of this window and at a lower level, the hacked-about remains of a recess, perhaps a buffet. Quite large S window, its segmental-vaulted embrasure probably intended to have stone seats along its sides. E of this, another embrasure, now serving as a passage from the late C16 stair of the E range. The sides of this embrasure are straight, not splayed as would be expected at a window, so it was probably always the principal entrance to the room, originally reached by a forestair. In the E side of the embrasure, the entrance to a small tunnel-vaulted wall chamber, its floor having a hatch into a narrow pit prison contained in the thickness of the wall below. Towards the E end of the hall's N wall, an aumbry, its surround badly defaced but apparently ogee-arched. In the centre of the E gable, an elliptical-arched fireplace under a straight cornice; to its S and high up, a small window with a stepped sill.

Access to the two floors above was originally by a turnpike stair (now largely removed) mostly contained in the wall thickness of the tower's SW corner but the curved wall of its NE segment nudging into the rooms; round-arched doorway to the stair, its surround chamfered.

At the second floor, a small wall lobby off the stair, with a round-arched door into the upper hall or great chamber. Over this room, a wooden ceiling, its joists supported on rounded

corbels along the N and S walls. These are closely spaced at the
W end of the room but set very much further apart at the E end,
presumably to emphasize its importance. What is puzzling is
that the wider spacing begins above the window on the S side
and above the fireplace on the E (i.e. there are four corbels on
the S and only two on the E). In the W wall a window whose light
is not centred under the angular tunnel vault of its embrasure.
Another window, again off-centre in relation to its (semicircular)
vaulted embrasure, in the S wall. Both these windows have glazing
grooves in the jambs and their embrasures were probably intended
to have seats along their sides. Also in the S wall, what might
originally have been a wall closet, although its masonry is rough;
it now serves as a lobby from the late C16 range's stair. Towards
the end of the upper hall's N wall, at the point where the spacing
of the corbels becomes broader but not placed in a formal relationship to the corbelling, is the room's elliptical-arched fireplace,
a salt box in its E side. To the r. of the fireplace, the rectangular
doorway to a large dog-legged garderobe in the wall thickness of
the NE corner. It is well appointed, with windows to the N and
E. In the N wall, a basin with a drain through the wall; at the
garderobe's SE end, a stone latrine seat with a lamp recess beside
it. A second wall chamber, also dog-legged, is entered through a
round-arched broad door in the SE corner. This chamber's N
part is covered by a semicircular tunnel vault and lit by an E
window. In the SW part, a rectangular lamp recess in the E wall
and a cupboard in the W.

On the top floor, another single large room. Its original
entrance in the SW corner is roundheaded but set in a rectangular
over-arch. Over the room, a stone tunnel vault divided into
panels by a longitudinal ridge rib and transverse ribs, all heavily
moulded. On the two central panels, carved grotesque heads,
their open mouths intended to hold chains for lamps. The vault
is clearly not original and almost certainly dates from the construction of the present E range c. 1600. In the gables, large
windows, the E still with a stone seat along the N side of its
embrasure. Another window in the N wall but the top of its
embrasure was lowered when the vault was inserted over the
room. Slightly off-centre fireplace at the E gable, its straight lintel
supported on moulded capitals, the S one badly weathered. In
the wall thickness of the NE corner, a garderobe very like that of
the room below but without the refinement of a basin. At the W
end of the S wall, a vaulted mural closet which now serves as a
lobby from the E range's stair. Its window (at least in its present
form) is contemporary with the stair.

The rubble-walled SOUTH RANGE was probably built by the
second Earl of Argyll c. 1500 on the site of his father's intended
great hall. Now roofless and partly demolished, it provided a
princely lodging. It has been of two storeys and an attic above a
basement whose thick walling projects beyond that of the upper
floors on the S side. F-plan main block, the broad NW wing
incorporating a stair tower; smaller stair tower projecting near
the E end of the N side. The area between these projecting wings

was filled by a corridor below a gallery. The much altered and
largely ruinous courtyard (N) front is now featureless except for
the NW wing whose stair tower (occupying the S half of the
wing) survives to the wallhead. At its base, a simply moulded
entrance; above the lintel, a rectangular panel carved with three
weathered shields. The tower's top is broached to an octagon in
very similar fashion to the stair tower of *c.* 1500 at the King's Old
Building at Stirling Castle (q.v.); on the N face of the octagon,
the moulded frame for a missing armorial panel. W of the stair
tower, the entrance to a segmental tunnel-vaulted transe whose
floor slopes downwards through the range to the garden. The
range's garden (S) front is more intact than the N, the ends standing to the wallhead which has been surmounted by a parapet
carried on large individual moulded corbels; angle rounds at the
corners. At the basement, regularly spaced small windows, their
jambs and lintels splayed. The first-floor windows are all of decent
size, with chamfered margins; at each end, a tall window and, at
the centre, an exceptionally large one.

Inside the S range, the N corridor, a little below the courtyard
level, runs between the two stair towers. Opening off it, transes
through the wall of the main block which contain steps down to
storerooms, all covered with segmental tunnel vaults. At the E
end of the corridor, another store, its entrance sited awkwardly
under the NE stair. The main access to the principal floor was
from the NW stair. At the W end, a fairly narrow room, possibly
a kitchen. E of this, the hall which may have risen through the
height of two floors. Near the E end of its windowless N wall, a
big fireplace, the lower part of the jambs surviving; rectangular
aumbry to the E of the fireplace. The hall originally extended E
for a further bay but was contracted probably *c.* 1600 as part of
a remodelling in connection with the building of the E range.
This entailed the subdivision of the chamber E of the hall to
form two rooms, the E probably entered from the new E range.
Each room was provided with a garderobe hollowed out of the
thickness of the S wall. The gallery to the N was entered from a
door in each stair tower, the W door, opening on to steps, set at
a higher level than the E. At the E stair tower, above the level of
the gallery roof, a pair of windows whose rolled margins were
probably provided when the E range was built *c.* 1600.

The EAST RANGE was built *c.* 1600 as a largely self-contained
dwelling, perhaps a jointure house. It is of three storeys and
an attic, rubble-walled with crowstepped gables. At the rear (E)
elevation, an off-centre garderobe projection, a large wallhead
chimney, and dormer windows, their catslide roofs not necessarily
original. At the front, a tall saddleback-roofed and crowstep-
gabled NW stair tower in the inner angle of the main block of
the E range and the C15 NE tower. This stair tower, the main E
block and the NE stair tower of the S range form a U whose open
part is filled by a three-storey lean-to block (now roofless). The
front of this lean-to, like the NW stair tower, is of ashlar. At the
ground floor, a two-bay loggia whose elliptical arches spring
from a central pier and responds composed of clustered shafts

with elided capitals. Moulded stringcourses at the N stair tower are carried across the lean-to forming sill courses under the windows of the upper floors; another stringcourse steps down from the tower to form a cornice under the eaves of the lean-to. All the surviving windows of the lean-to and the stair tower have projecting rolled margins. Inside the lean-to, a first-floor gallery entered from the NE stair of the S range. In the E wall of this room, a pair of large cupboards. A second gallery above was entered by a door from the main block of the E range. The loggia provides a covered communication between the NE tower and the S range. At its N end, the entrance to the new stair, a broad turnpike, and, in the back wall, a door to the N of the two inter-communicating rooms which occupy the ground floor of the main block of the E range. These rooms are covered with heavily ribbed tunnel vaults similar to the one added to the top floor of the NE tower, apparently at the same time. Off each room, to the W, a former garderobe, the N entrance built up. The S room may have had a door into the E room of the S range. There have been two intercommunicating rooms on the first floor as well.

On the W side of the courtyard, a rubble WALL. There were probably buildings on the narrow piece of ground to its W but nothing of them is now visible.

S of the S range, terraced GARDENS, probably laid out c. 1500, fill-ing the S end of the promontory. At their SW, on a pillar of rock cut off from the promontory by a narrow gorge (now bridged over), a segmental stone ARCHWAY. It is more likely to be C19 than medieval and has been repaired in the C20.

# CASTLE CARY CASTLE     F 7070
## 1.7km. S of Haggs

Late C15 tower, later extended to form a comfortable laird's house.

The tower was built for Henry Livingstone of Myddilbynning, c. 1480. It was clearly intended to be L-plan but there is no evidence that the NW jamb was executed. Rectangular main block of four storeys and attic, the rubble walling incorporating a large number of dressed blocks, some bossed and others broached, probably re-used from the Roman fort of Castlecary (see Haggs). Continuous corbel course under the battlement which is studded with stone spouts. The parapet has been much renewed but the S face's central merlon carved with a weathered shield and a human head is probably original. At the tower's NW corner the battlement rises into a monopitch-roofed cap-house, its gables crowstepped like those of the attic storey inside the battlement. A little W of the centre of the tower's S front, a ground-floor gunloop, cross-shaped but with a circular upright; probably inserted in the later C16. One large off-centre window at the first floor of this front and another big window nearly at the centre of the second floor, both with roll-moulded margins and probably enlarged in the C16 or C17. A pair of smaller third-floor windows with chamfered margins, apparently original. At the ground floor of the w gable a blocked window and, to its n, a door (now a window) inserted to give access to a two-storey w addition, built perhaps in the c18 but since demolished. Above this door, a couple of small windows, probably insertions of the c16 or c17, lighting the stair in the tower's nw corner. At the n front of the tower tusking shows the original intention that there should be a broad nw jamb. Near the w end of this front, within the area which would have been covered by the jamb and aligned above each other, are three doors, that of the first floor blocked and the one above, at a level between the first and second floors, converted to a window lighting the stair behind. All three must have been intended to give access from the main block to the intended jamb. Small stair window at the third floor. It looks original, so either the jamb was intended to be lower than the main block and covered with an exceptionally shallow-pitched or flat roof, or the intention to build it was abandoned before completion of the main block. E of the position of the intended jamb, a slit window to the main block's ground floor. Above it, a larger but narrow first-floor window with a slit window (lighting a garderobe) to its l. Small square garderobe window at the second floor. At the third floor, a box machicolation which housed a garderobe chute.

A rubble-built two-storey and attic E extension was added, probably in the late c17. This is L-plan, its main block slightly narrower than the tower, the jamb projecting n from the w end. The E gable of the main block and that of the jamb are crow-stepped. In the jamb's w face a bolection-moulded doorway; above it but not necessarily *in situ*, a panel carved with the date 1679, possibly that of this addition. Higher up in this side and to the r. of the door, a small lozenge-shaped stair window. In the gable of the jamb, a couple of rectangular windows. Irregularly positioned ground- and first-floor windows in the s front of the main block. At the front, pairs of ground- and first-floor windows (one now a door) aligned with each other but asymmetrical in relation to the walling. Above them are the bottoms of two blocked attic windows which have formerly risen through the ogee-moulded eaves cornice into dormerheads.

Separated by a narrow close from this addition's E end is an informal range of single-storey outbuildings, the w gable of the lower w section crowstepped, the E end of the E section's roof piended. They were probably built *c.* 1800.

Inside the c15 tower, a tunnel-vaulted ground-floor store, the entrance lobby and foot of the turnpike stair nudging into its nw corner. In the E wall a sink, its outlet blocked by the E addition. s of the sink, a door made when the addition was built. This door now contains an iron yett, probably of the c15. First-floor hall. Fireplace at its E end with rather damaged late c16 bundle-shafted jambs, the lintel a replacement. The plastered wall above has been painted, probably in the earlier c17, in black, red and white, with an heraldic achievement, probably the Royal Arms. The originally beamed ceiling was supported on corbels, two near the E end of the room carved as human heads, the s of these now mutilated. An aumbry at each end of the s wall. There seems to have been a garderobe in the wall thickness of the NE corner but it has been altered to give access to the E addition. The second floor originally contained an upper hall or chamber, with an aumbry at the W end of the s wall and a garderobe in the wall thickness of the NE corner.

The ground floor of the E addition contains a kitchen, its large E fireplace with a segmental arch; brick oven, probably formed or altered in the C18, to its N. Two rooms on the first floor, the E with an early C18 basket-arched chimneypiece and panelling. More early C18 basket-arched chimneypieces and panelling in the attic.

## CATTER HOUSE
### 1.2km NNW of Croftamie

S 4080

Dated 1767 in central pediment. Splendidly sited Georgian: a five-bay, two-storey-and-basement laird's house, harled with painted dressings and rusticated quoins of local stone. Hip-ended pavilion roof with scrolled-shouldered chimneystacks on the gables. Roll skewputts. Centred on the NW front, a small pediment with a dated heraldic inset rises from the eaves cornice. The doorway below, framed by lugged architraves, is also pedimented. From a railed landing, curved stair-flights descend l. and r. Internal stone stair with oval cupola over. Dining Room panelled full height to consoled cornice. Plain dentilled cornice in Drawing Room; white marble fireplace with sand-coloured marble inserts.

Rectangular WALLED GARDEN, early C19. U-plan STABLES, also early C19, converted to residential use.

## CAUSEWAYHEAD see STIRLING

## CAWDER HOUSE
### 2.2km. NNW of Bishopbriggs

ED 6070

Substantial but externally unambitious mansion house of the Stirlings of Keir and Cawder, built in two principal stages, the first early C17, the second early C19.

The first stage, apparently completed in 1624 by Sir Archibald Stirling, provided a manor house. In 1813–15 Charles Stirling, a partner in the West Indies firm of Stirling, Gordon & Co. and younger brother of James Stirling of Keir, employed *David Hamilton* to alter and extend the house.

The C17 house was rubble-built, of three storeys and L- or possibly U-plan. Its main block and SW jamb survive as the centrepiece of the present building. The main block's s front is of a regular five bays. The C17 windows, their jambs and lintels rounded, survive at the ground and second floors. The first-floor windows were deepened and given new margins in the early C19. At the

same time were added the present wallhead cornice and blocking course and a Doric portico, the shafts of its unfluted columns
partly encased in vermiculated sleeves. The sw jamb survives
almost intact except that the early c19 cornice is returned along
its E side. Between the two first-floor windows of the gable, a
panel carved with the coat of arms of the Stirlings of Keir and
the date 1624. Moulded skews to the gable whose flat top is
surmounted by a chimney.

At the E end of the c17 house the early c19 alterations added
a minimally projecting SE jamb, possibly a replacement for a c17
jamb but it makes no attempt to balance the sw jamb and is
slightly broader and higher. In its front, an elliptical-arched
ground-floor window and, at the first floor, a stone mullioned
console-corniced three-light window, formerly with a balcony. E
of this jamb is a two-storey piend-roofed service block, its present
appearance early c19 but with a couple of blocked windows
(one cut across by a c19 window) at the S front, suggesting that
earlier work is incorporated. At the back of this wing, a slightly
taller NE jamb, again early c19. In its E gable, an elliptical-arched
ground-floor window and, at the first floor, a wooden-mullioned
three-light window with a lugged architrave and corniced sill.

At the w end of the c17 house and parallel to the sw jamb is
a second and slightly larger two-storey jamb added in 1813–15.
In its S gable, an elliptical-arched wooden-mullioned three-light
first-floor window surmounted by a consoled cornice. At this
jamb's w side, three tall and closely spaced first-floor windows,
all in architraved surrounds but sharing a common sill.

At the rear, an early c19 narrow addition parallel to the main
block; at its centre, a projection containing the early c19 stair.
Other additions are of the later c19 and quite plain.

INTERIOR. Opening off the portico is a low entrance hall, its
early c19 elliptical-arched and panelled plaster vault of Soanean
derivation. Elsewhere on the ground floor of the main block,
some rooms covered by c17 stone vaults. In one of these, a c2
PANEL from the Antonine Wall. It bears the relief of *Genii*
standing on eagles' heads and flanking a laurel wreath which
contains the inscription '*LEG/II/AVG/FEC*' ('the Second Legion
Augusta built this').

Behind the entrance hall, the early c19 main stair. It provides
a low-key approach to the principal rooms which occupy the first
floor of the c17 house and Hamilton's w addition. Their character
is almost entirely of 1813–15, with plasterwork of exceptional
quality, but they have lost most of their chimneypieces. Linking
them is a corridor contained in the early c19 addition behind the
main block, its main length covered by a plaster vault of the same
Soanean character as at the entrance hall. At the corridor's E end,
a groin-vaulted compartment, a convex grey marble chimneypiece fitted against its curved N wall. At the w end, a pair of
compartments with pendentive-domed ceilings. The whole first
floor of the w addition is filled by the drawing room, its deeply
modelled panelled ceiling Classical but with foliage enrichment
hinting at naturalism. The white marble chimneypiece survives.

Caryatids support an entablature carved with cornucopia and a Classical scene. In the C17 SW jamb to the E, a plain coomb ceiling. Is this C17 or early C19? Occupying the C17 main block are three rooms, now thrown into one, all with early C19 plaster ceilings of some elaboration, that of the centre room another Soanean elliptical-arched and panelled tunnel vault.

SE of the house are the STABLES. Front building of the early or mid C18 composed of a two-storey stable block (now roofless) flanked by slightly recessed single-storey carriage houses (the W now roofless, the E painted), all rubble-built and with rusticated quoins. At each end of the front of the stable block, a round-headed door with projecting keystone and imposts. Above, three small windows, the centre one later converted to a door and now back to a window. At each wing a large roundheaded Gibbsian-surrounded carriage entrance. Behind, plain buildings of the later C19 forming a courtyard.

E of the stables, standing on a low mound, an early C19 circular DOOCOT tower covered by a broad-eaved low conical roof. Rubble walling divided by a ratcourse and a moulded stringcourse into two storeys and an attic. In the S segment, the ground-floor entrance, its lugged architrave probably re-used as must be the curved lintel inscribed with the date 1723. Above, a louvred window with flight-holes at its base and a boldly projecting sill. Horizontal dummy windows at the attic, the three of the S segment pierced by flight-holes which stand on a landing ledge formed by a projection of the stringcourse supported on back-to-front corbels.

On the approach from the E the drive crosses an early C19 segmental-arched BRIDGE, its gently curved low parapets of broached ashlar ending in polished ashlar corniced pedestals. A utilitarian buttress has been added on the N side. At the entrance to the drive, a single-storey LODGE, also early C19, its roof's extravagantly broad eaves supported on carved brackets. Oblong main block, a small stone canopy over the front (S) window; hoodmoulded window in the E side. E porch, a pointed and hoodmoulded window in its E gable. Semi-octagonal W wing.

## CHARTERSHALL S 7090

A few cottage rows, formerly the homes and workshops of nail-makers, survive from the late C18. Of similar date, a single two-storey house at the N end of the bridge retains its roll skewputts and rusticated quoinstones.

BRIDGE. Built 1696, but substantially reconstructed in the mid C18. Rubble-built structure crossing the Bannock Burn in a single segmental-arched span of just over 8m. Inset panel on the W face records that THIS BRIDGE WAS RE / BUILT BY THE JUSTICES / OF THE PACE 1747. Voussoirs and intrados of the arch in dressed stone.

OLD SAUCHIE. *See* p. 628.

SAUCHIEBURN HOUSE. *See* p. 655.

## CLACHAN see FINTRY

CLACHAN OF CAMPSIE                    ED

Tiny village sited immediately S of the graveyard of the former
Campsie Parish Church.

Former CAMPSIE PARISH CHURCH. Only the W gable and a
stub of the N wall survive of the church, which was superseded
in 1828 when a new church was opened at Lennoxtown (q.v.).
The crowstepped gable, built of roughly squared large stones,
has an intake at the height of the lintel of the door. This lintel
serves as the sill of the window above. Both door and window
are rectangular and have chamfered margins. Inside, the window
is placed in an elliptically arched embrasure. All this looks C17.
So too may be the ashlar base of the now missing bellcote which
surmounted the gable. The E end of the surviving stub of the N
wall is plastered and presumably marks the position of a transeptal
N 'aisle'.

   At the entrance to the GRAVEYARD is a stone, probably C17,
bearing a skull and crossbones and the injunction 'MEMENTO
MORI'; it is flanked by a pair of stones carved with foliaged
scrolls. – On the E side of the graveyard, a square MAUSOLEUM
of two storeys, the walls harled, with strip quoins and a chunky
cornice under the parapet. The roof is a slated dome topped by
a lead cupola-like finial. At each corner, at the upper floor, a
diagonally projecting squared but unmoulded block of stone,
possibly intended to carry the plate of a sundial. In the W front,
a basket-arched door, its keystone incised with the date 1715.
Immediately above the entrance, a moulded frame contains an
heraldic achievement, the supporters now headless; the surmounting hoodmould looks C19. The upper floor is said* to
have been added by Miss Margaret Lennox in the early C19.
The lintel of its E door, reached by a forestair, bears the incised
inscription: 'REP.ᴿᴰ.1819.BY.M.L'. An inscribed stone inside
the top of the ground-floor entrance's arch states 'CLOSED 1884',
presumably the date when a pair of large early C17 GRAVE-
SLABS was erected in the arch. The l. slab bears the marginal inscription: 'HEIR.LYIS.ANE.HONORABIL.MAN.IAME[S]
KINKAID.OF.THAT.ILK.QVHA.DESISIT.YE.13.OF.FEBROVAR
.ANNO.1604.' In the centre, two shields, the upper flanked by
the initials IK for James Kincaid, the lower by the initials IF,
presumably those of his wife. The r. panel is similar. Almost
identical marginal inscription to another James Kincaid of that
Ilk †9 January 1606, and again there are two shields in the
centre. Both have impaled coats of arms (of Kincaid and Leslie,
and of Kincaid and Hamilton) which commemorate two successive lairds. The upper is surmounted by the initials IK (for
James Kincaid †1606) and flanked by the initials of his wife,
Christian Leslie. The lower is surmounted and flanked by the

34 (margin)

* By John Cameron, *The Parish of Campsie* (Kirkintilloch, 1892), 66.

initials I<sup>S</sup>K for their son, Sir James Kincaid. Below it, a less competently lettered inscription ('DESISIT/ 8 IA<sup>R</sup> D 1645/M.H.') records the death of Sir James Kincaid's wife, Dame Margaret Hamilton.

DESCRIPTION. The village has a sprinkling of C19 houses. At the N end, a square, its N side occupied by a harled former INN (now the ALTESSAN GALLERY) built in 1818 but remodelled in the mid C19 when it was given a new roof and a pilastered and corniced doorpiece. Long harled single-storey E wing, also of the earlier C19. Behind is the graveyard of the former Campsie Parish Church (*see* above). In front, a late C20 'bellcote' which houses the former church's BELL, inscribed 'FOR.THE PAROCH. OF.CAMPSIE. R.M.&.COMPY/FECIT.EDR.1729'.

# CLACKMANNAN

C 9090

Small town, founded in 1551 as a burgh of barony under the feudal superiority of the Bruces of Clackmannan whose residence, Clackmannan Tower, occupies a commanding position to the W. There was some industry (a distillery and a woollen mill) here in the C19 but the town now serves as a dormitory for Alloa.

## CHURCHES

CLACKMANNAN FREE CHURCH, Kirk Wynd. Now Masonic Hall. By *John Burnet*, 1845, looking more like a school than a church. Single-storey rectangle with bracketed broad eaves. At the front (W) gable, round-arched windows flanking the slightly advanced centrepiece, its door contained in a roundheaded over-arch. Surmounting the centrepiece, a roundheaded bellcote.

CLACKMANNAN PARISH CHURCH, Port Street and High Street. By *James Gillespie Graham*, 1813–15. Georgian Gothic, the flavour but not the detail Perp. It is built of buff-coloured stone, the main walling of rubble, the dressings of polished ashlar. Immensely broad crowstep-gabled box of four buttressed bays, with a W tower and E porch (the principal entry from the town). Battlemented N and S sides, their transomed windows, hoodmoulded like all the openings, each of three uncusped lights with small lancet lights serving as tracery in the head; the E window of the S wall has been partly blocked by a lean-to vestry added c. 1900. The cornice under the battlement is continued across the E gable as the base of a pediment, the tympanum enlivened by a sexfoil dummy opening. Below, a four-light window similar to those in the sides but its depth curtailed by the battlemented sturdy porch. Flanking this centrepiece, tall pointed dummy windows. W tower of four stages, each of the upper three intaken. At its corners, diagonal buttresses rising into gablets topped by foliage-finialled pinnacles.

Inside, a panelled wooden CEILING of c. 1960. – U-plan GALLERY, its panelled front of 1815, the supporting bundle-shafted columns replacements of 1882. – Round the walls, a

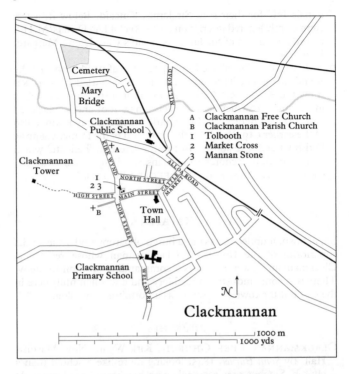

A  Clackmannan Free Church
B  Clackmannan Parish Church
1  Tolbooth
2  Market Cross
3  Mannan Stone

Clackmannan

1000 m
1000 yds

high panelled DADO of Kennet oak, the detail Lorimerian, by *Whytock & Reid, c.* 1935–8. – At the w end, contemporary PULPIT with an octagonal canopy. – Also of *c.* 1935 the CHANCEL FURNISHINGS. – C19 PEWS.

Impressive display of mid-C20 STAINED GLASS. In the s wall, the w window (St Serf; David; Jeremiah) is a display of colourful modern realism, by *Douglas Hamilton*, 1952. – The centre window of this wall (Our Lord; Abraham; Moses) is of 1964, by *Gordon Webster*, characteristic of his squared-up expressionist manner. – To its E, another example of colourful modern realism (the Good Shepherd; Our Lord healing the sick; the Good Samaritan) by *Herbert Hendrie*, 1938. – In the N wall, the w window (St Blasius; a carpenter; a seamstress) is again by *Douglas Hamilton*, 1953. – Centre window (the Risen Lord; giving drink to the thirsty; Our Lord and children), also modern-realist, by *Sadie McLellan*, 1966. – E window of this wall (St Margaret of Scotland; Our Lord and the Canaanite Woman; Dorcas) by *Herbert Hendrie*, 1940. – On the N wall, a stone MEMORIAL TABLET to Robert Bruce, Master of Burleigh, by *Robert S. Lorimer*, 1919, with carved heraldry.

The surrounding GRAVEYARD contains a collection of HEAD-STONES of the late C17 and early and mid C18, remarkable for both quality and quantity; the earliest (a little E of the church, commemorating Robert Duncan) dated 1684. All display carved reminders of mortality (skulls, crossbones, hourglasses, etc.) and some, although proportionately fewer than in most Scottish graveyards, angels' heads (symbols of the soul). Most bear emblems of the trades of the deceased, several having ploughs or weavers' shuttles. Among other trade emblems are the crowned last of a cobbler and the anchor of a sailor (both NW of the church), the sheaves and shovel of a maltster at the N end of the churchyard's W wall, and the scales of a merchant (E of the church). At the SE corner of the graveyard, a large stone, dated 1754, commemorating a farmer. In its shaped top, the inscription: 'YOU.LIVING.MEN.AS.YE.PAS.BY.AS YOW.AR.NOW ONC.WAS.I.AS.I.AM NOW SO WIL.YE REMEMBER.MAN YOW MOST DIE'. A few of the C18 headstones are aedicular, their masons' mastery of the classical orders not wholly accomplished. On the front of a stone immediately W of the church, the diagonally fluted columns are flanked by human figures. On the wall to the N of the church's tower, a MONUMENT erected in 1702 to the family of Robert Moodie, minister of Clackmannan. The inscription panel is framed by an aedicule whose attached corkscrew columns' foliaged capitals support a frieze carved with angels' heads at the ends and, at the centre, a datestone cartouche with a skull and crossbones either side. Above, a fruit-topped segmental pediment, a monogrammed cartouche in the tympanum. Each side of this aedicule, a relief of a dancing angel, one trumpeting the Resurrection.

## PUBLIC BUILDINGS

CLACKMANNAN PRIMARY SCHOOL, Wellmyre. By the Clackmannan County Architect, *A. J. McLaren*, 1971–2. Of one and three storeys, unexciting, with aggregate cladding and flat roofs.

CLACKMANNAN PUBLIC SCHOOL, Alloa Road. Disused. By *Thomas Frame & Son*, 1897. Tall two storeys, of hammer-dressed squared and coursed grey rubble. Symmetrical frontage, plain except for simplified Jacobean broad gablets and rather small cupola-ventilators of Wrenaissance inspiration. Plain rear addition of 1924–7, again by *Thomas Frame & Son*.

CLACKMANNAN TOWN HALL, Main Street. Front block (containing library and reading room) by *Ebenezer Simpson*, 1903. Symmetrical Jacobean in polished red sandstone ashlar. Mullioned and transomed windows, corniced at the ground floor; at the upper floor they are surmounted by gablets with ball-finialled ends. Above the door, a pedimented aedicule, the stumpy Doric pilasters framing the coat of arms of the burgh of Clackmannan. Ogee-domed cupola on the roof. Behind, the hall itself, by *Thomas Frame & Son*, 1887–8, built of brownish rubble. Stalk-and-ball finials on the gables, the S of which contains a round window. Along the E side of the hall, a low neo-vernacular addition by *Clackmannan District Council*, 1992–4.

TOLBOOTH, Main Street. Just a gable and the tower of the Tolbooth which was said to be 'a heap of ruins' by the 1790s and was probably demolished *c.* 1822 when the site of the Clackmannanshire sheriff court was transferred to Alloa.

Although a tolbooth was built here in 1592 the surviving W end is of *c.* 1680, built of buff-coloured rubble with grey polished ashlar dressings. Crowstepped gable with strip quoins. Rusticated quoins at the corners of the tower whose walls rise, unbroken by stringcourses, to a moulded cornice. Plain N door, its surround perhaps renewed, and small vertically proportioned rectangular windows. In each face of the belfry stage, a large round-arched opening; below, on the E and W sides, clock faces, probably of the C19. The roof is a broached ogee-domed slated spire very similar to that of Old St Mungo's Church at Alloa (q.v.); on top, a weathercock.

MARKET CROSS immediately to the NW. Chamfered stone shaft, tapered towards the bottom. Pedimental capital, its E and W faces broken by weathered coats of arms, the E face's still recognizable as those of the Bruces of Clackmannan, the superiors of the burgh. On top, a ball finial taken from the grounds of Clackmannan Tower and erected here in 1887 as a replacement for the original which had been removed forty years before. The shaft and finial may date from soon after the creation of the burgh in 1551 but are more likely to be C17. The plinth of octagonal concrete steps is of 1949.

MANNAN STONE (CLACH MANAU), N of the Tolbooth. Massive irregularly shaped whinstone block, *c.* 2.85m. high, topped by a capstone. It was moved here in 1833 but probably was erected originally near this site, perhaps in the third or second millennium BC.


DESCRIPTION

ALLOA ROAD is the entry from the NW, leading past the flush-pointed wall of the CEMETERY, opened in 1857, to the MARY BRIDGE, a plain nearly semicircular rubble arch of the late C19 but with a C20 footpath cantilevered out from its E side. On the hill to the S, blocks of flats (BACKWOOD COURT) by the Clackmannan County Architect, *W. H. Henry*, 1966, and, rising above them, Clackmannan Tower (*see* below). The road jinks to the SE. On the SW corner of Alloa Road and Kirk Wynd, the white-painted TOWER INN, its mid-C19 single-storey front block with bargeboarded and spike-finialled gablets and a pilastered doorpiece. To its S, in a small garden, the WAR MEMORIAL, by *Robert S. Lorimer*, 1921, of Market Cross type, the pillar-shaft bearing coats of arms; simplified capital decorated with rosettes and topped by a floriated cross. On the SE corner of Alloa Road and Kirk Wynd, the former Clackmannan Free Church (*see* Churches, above). Further E in Alloa Road, the former Clackmannan Public School (*see* Public Buildings, above). A little further E, MILL ROAD leads N. On its E side, CLACKMANNAN HOUSE of *c.* 1800. Two storeys above an exposed basement. Front of polished ashlar, rusticated at the ground floor whose windows are set in over-arches. At the slightly advanced centre, a Roman Doric columned surround to the fanlit door. To its S, MILL VILLA, a piend-roofed rendered house of the earlier C19, with rusticated quoins and segmental-arched windows, the ground-floor openings under Tudor hoodmoulds.

KIRK WYND leads uphill from the War Memorial. Prominent on its W side, No. 23 (originally the manse of the demolished United Presbyterian Church) of c. 1865, Georgian survival but with heavy surrounds to the ground-floor door and windows. On the E side, above the former Clackmannan Free Church (see Churches, above), the garden wall of MAYFIELD (the former Free Church Manse) of 1862, a plain piend-roofed box, rather altered in the late C20. At the top of Kirk Wynd, a housing development by the Clackmannan County Council Architect, W. H. Henry, 1957–8, mostly of two storeys, with dry-dashed walls and pantiled roofs, Scots burgh vernacular touches provided by rectangular gables corbelled out above rounded corners. On the S elevation, a reset panel carved with a garland enclosing the date 1702 and the initials TT and MC. Also a re-used door lintel bearing the dates 1668 and 1738 (either possible, the later perhaps more likely) above and below the initials WMCR; at the l. end of the lintel, a cleaver and axe, at the r., a knife, so presumably this came from the house of a butcher. The development was extended up HIGH STREET to the W in 1970, with concrete crowsteps on the gables. Incorporated in this extension, a pair of re-used roll-moulded skewputts, too large for their present position and of c. 1800 rather than the C16 or C17 date the architecture tries to evoke. Further up High Street's N side, two more roll-moulded late Georgian skewputts re-used on a late C20 house. On the S side of High Street, at the E end, single-storey pantile-roofed terraced cottages by W. H. Henry, 1963, followed by the churchyard wall of Clackmannan Parish Church (see Churches, above). At the W end of High Street, a path leading across a field to Clackmannan Tower (see below).

PORT STREET'S W side begins with a return of the 1963 development in High Street but here it is of two storeys and faces down Main Street. Two blocks, the gap between filled by a stolid LYCH GATE by W. H. Henry, 1966, at the entrance to a path to Clackmannan Parish Church (see Churches, above). S of the church, its garden entered from Port Street, THE MANSE by John Paterson, 1797, originally plain except for a bandcourse between the ground and first floors. The two-storey bay window on the S front was added by J. M. Wardrop in 1863. At the S end of Port Street, in WELLMYRE, Clackmannan Primary School (see Public Buildings, above).

MAIN STREET is Clackmannan's burghal and commercial centre. At its broad W end, standing on a small lawn, the remains of the Tolbooth, Market Cross and Mannan Stone (see Public Buildings, above). On the S side of the street, at its W corner with Port Street, No. 2 Main Street, a harled L-plan building of c. 1700, with a shaped N gable, was reconstructed by W. H. Henry, 1963, when a crowstep-gabled but chimneyless SW wing was added. Also by Henry and crowstepped is the block of 1970 at Nos. 4–6

Main Street. Then No. 8 (TOWER HOUSE) of *c.* 1840, crisply
white-harled with black-painted dressings. Two storeys and
three bays, a porch projecting at the E end of the front. Very tall
first-floor windows; piended roof, its rhones supported by
decorative cast iron brackets. Brackets of the same type under
the rhones of the contemporary Nos. 10–12, which stands
forward at No. 8's E end; the centre door has been converted to
a window. Again of *c.* 1840 but more vernacular, the next-door
building (Nos. 14–18). No. 20 of *c.* 1860, a pair of Jacobean
gablets over the first-floor windows, is followed by straightforward terraced housing of the mid and later C20.

The N side of Main Street begins with No. 1 of *c.* 1840, a two-
storey house with a badly weathered pilastered and corniced
doorpiece. Across the W gable, a bandcourse placed just too low
to be the base of a pediment. Another pilastered doorpiece at
No. 7, its l. bay's two-light windows suggesting a date of *c.* 1860.
Then Victorian vernacular leading to a tall two-storey commercial block (Nos. 25–31) of *c.* 1870. Free Jacobean, a gablet over
the console-corniced four-light window at the centre of the
upper floor. Built into the pend under the pantile-roofed low
tenement (Nos. 41–43) of the later C20 is a window lintel from
its predecessor, inscribed '16.TH.KP.[80]'. Pilastered doorpiece
on the mid-C19 No. 45, followed by neo-vernacular housing
(Nos. 47–59) by *Scott Bennett Associates*, 1991–2. Near the E end
of this side of Main Street is No. 61, a block of two tall storeys
built for the Clackmannan Co-operative Society in 1891 (its
date of 1863 is that of the Society's foundation); *James Johnston*
was the architect. Shaped and chimneyed central gablet of
Ruskinian Gothic inspiration. Two-light first-floor windows,
those of the outer bays under consoled pediments. At the E end
of Main Street's S side, Clackmannan Town Hall (*see* Public
Buildings, above).

CATTLEMARKET, the town centre's exit to the NE, begins with
single-storey C19 vernacular at Nos. 2–4 but then develops into
a mixture of C20 local authority housing and small late C19
villas. Off Cattlemarket's W side, running back behind Main
Street, is NORTH STREET. On its S side, behind No. 61 Main
Street, is a two-storey building put up for the Clackmannan
Co-operative Society in 1887. Plain industrial except for a
broad-eaved gablet over the hoist door at the centre of the first
floor. In this gablet, a panel bearing the Society's name and
clasped-hands emblem.

KENNET LODGE, E end of Alloa Road. Harled single-storey
bow-ended lodge of *c.* 1840 at the head of the drive to the
demolished Kennet House.

### CLACKMANNAN TOWER
0.5km. W

Medieval tower-house of the Bruces of Clackmannan, standing
on a hilltop to dominate the adjoining burgh and surrounding
countryside.

The house is ashlar-walled and L-plan, developed in two main phases. The first, probably of the C14, provided the lower floors of the main (N) block. The second, in the C15, remodelled and heightened that block and added the SE jamb. Some further alteration was carried out *c.* 1600. Part of the E front collapsed in 1955 and was rebuilt a few years later.

The main (N) block is rectangular, *c.* 10.97m. by 9.14m. externally. The three lower floors, the walling of the second floor taken in, belong to the first stage, constructed of squared and coursed buff sandstone with in-and-out quoins of grey stone. Splayed base except on the N side where it may have been removed when a later building (now demolished) was put up here. In the E gable, a tall slit window. Also in this wall, a large first-floor window with chamfered jambs and lintel; it may have been remodelled in the late C15. In the N side, a (blocked) window, glazing grooves in its rounded jambs. Is this C14 or C15? Another window, its surround chamfered, at the E end of this side. Plain first-floor window towards the S end of the W gable.

The C15 remodelling and extension heightened the original block to four storeys and an attic and added the SE jamb. The new work is again of ashlar. At the wallhead of the main block, a battlement (largely rebuilt in the C20) projected on individual moulded corbels, with timidly projecting rounds at the NE and SW corners. At the NW corner, a square caphouse, its outer sides upward projections of the main walling. Inside the battlement, the attic, with a crowstep-gabled roof. Very narrow stair windows at the N end of the W gable. The other windows are of reasonable size but plain.

The five-storey and attic jamb is, unusually, higher than the main block. Were both jamb and main block originally intended to be of the same height and the decision to keep the main block a storey lower taken as an afterthought, perhaps because of cost or because of worries about the strength of the lower parts of the walls? The jamb's windows have chamfered margins, the first floor E window larger than the others and perhaps altered in the C17. Boldly projecting parapet carried on moulded machicolation. Box machicolation towards the N end of the E side.*

The E entrance to the SE jamb was formed in the early C17. It is framed by fluted Doric pilasters, their bases panelled; from these springs a semicircular arch whose keystone is carved with a chalice (?). Not very comfortably skied above is a pediment, its tympanum carved with a tree; chunky but worn finials on the apex and ends of the pediment. Contemporary with this entrance is the low rubble-built outshot (now roofless) in the SW inner angle. Its S half was flat-roofed, its N covered with a lean-to roof, but both parts have been heightened in brick in the C20. In the W side of the outshot, a round-arched entrance.

Most of the interior of the jamb is now badly ruined. The principal entrance opens into the remains of a broad passage,

---

* Roughly the N half of this side of the jamb (including the box machicolation) was rebuilt *c.* 1960.

formed in the early C17 by erecting a partition wall to divide the jamb's ground-floor room into a passage and guardroom and by removing the C15 turnpike stair which had occupied the jamb's NW corner.* In the guardroom on the S, the springing of a tunnel-vaulted ceiling. C15 slit window in the E wall, a chamber in the thickness of the W. At the W end of the passage, a segmental-headed arch into the early C17 outshot which contained a scale-and-platt stone stair (the present stair a C20 replacement).

The C14 ground floor of the N block was reached from the first-floor hall by a straight stair in the thickness of the walling of the SW corner. A door from the jamb, its surround chamfered, was made in the C15. On this ground floor, a store. In the E wall, a slit window with a stepped sill. Stone corbels (restored in the C20) for the joists of a wooden ceiling which served as the floor to a tunnel-vaulted windowless entresol room above. The access to this entresol was through a hatch in the rough ashlar vault.

In the jamb, at the level of the entresol but entered from a half-landing of the SW scale-and-platt stair (originally from the now missing C15 turnpike), was a room with a S window, its embrasure having stone seats along both sides and a cupboard in the E. W of the window was a fireplace (blocked in the C17). In the room's N wall (originally the external S wall of the main block), a shallow recess covered by a flattened arch and incorporating the chamfered jamb of a built-up door into the main block; presumably it is a C15 feature. The room was divided in the early C17 but the partition wall has now fallen.

The outshot's scale-and-platt stair ends at the first floor where a door, its roll-and-hollow moulding preposterously exaggerated, gives access to a lobby formed from the space formerly occupied by the C15 stair in the thickness of the walling of the jamb's NW corner. In this lobby's diagonal SE wall, the entrance to the C15 kitchen in the jamb. This has been tunnel-vaulted. Across the S end, a large fireplace, a small window in its back. There have been comfortably sized windows in the E and W walls (the W blocked by the construction of the SW stair in the early C17). A garderobe used to open off the N side of the E window. At the NE corner of the kitchen, a door into the N block. This door was the C14 entrance to the house, originally reached by a forestair. It is segmental-headed with a sunk-chamfered and filleted margin; bolthole in the E jamb. A second entrance, from the lobby at the head of the SW stair, was made in the C17 when a curved passage was cut through the main block's S wall, by-passing the kitchen.

The first floor of the N block is occupied by the HALL, its floor still partly covered by stone paving. Rubble-built tunnel vault. The W fireplace is C15, its moulded jambs topped by bell capitals. At the W end of the S wall, a window which was blocked in the early C17 by the construction of the SW stair. In the W side of its embrasure, a door into a lobby at the head of the straight stair down to the ground-floor store. In the E wall of the hall, a

---

* Presumably the C15 entrance was on the W side of the jamb.

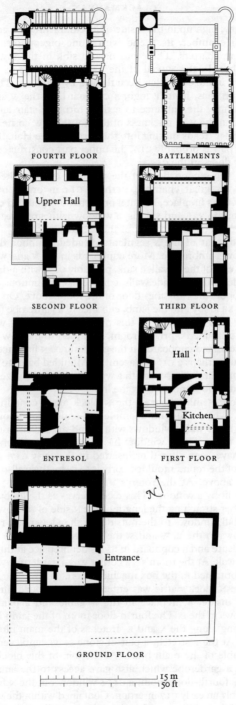

FOURTH FLOOR

BATTLEMENTS

Upper Hall

SECOND FLOOR

THIRD FLOOR

ENTRESOL

Hall

Kitchen

FIRST FLOOR

Entrance

GROUND FLOOR

15 m
50 ft

Clackmannan Tower. Plans.

window; high up in the N side of its embrasure, the entrance to a wall chamber, its E end with stone pigeonholes, possibly to store charters. There has been a sink in the E wall of the chamber. In the N wall of the hall, a buffet recess, probably formed in the C15. It has been flanked by windows. The W (now built up) has, in its E ingo, a cupboard. In the W side of the embrasure, the entrance to a tight turnpike stair largely contained in the wall thickness of the house's NW corner but with the upper treads butting into the corner of the Hall. The stair's lower part is probably C14, the upper part constructed with the upper floors in the C15.

On the second floor of the N block, an unvaulted Upper Hall or great chamber, perhaps C14 in origin but C15 in character. S fireplace, its lintel projected on moulded corbels. In each of the N, E and S walls, a window with stone seats or their remains. The embrasures of the N and E windows are round-arched, that of the S segmental-headed. Cupboard in the E window's embrasure. More cupboards in the N and W walls. At the W end of the N wall, a sink, probably C15, with a drain to the outside. Along the side walls, cornice-like continuous corbelling to support the (missing) floor of the room above. On the E side of the SE lobby into the jamb, entrance to a garderobe (replicated in the C20 rebuilding of this part of the jamb's E wall). The jamb contained a private room. Windows to the S, W and E, all with seats and cupboards in the embrasures. N fireplace, possibly C15 but perhaps a C16 replacement. Moulded bases to its jambs. The surround is carved with a wavy ribbon and stylized flowers. Moulded hoodmould over the lintel.

The C15 third floor of the N block again contains a single room. E fireplace with a simple roll-and-hollow moulding. In the W and S walls, windows with round-arched embrasures and stone seats. The E window has a rectangular embrasure and may have been altered or inserted in the early C17. Along the sides of the room, moulded corbels to carry the wall-plate of the room above. At the room's NE corner, a straight-sided wall recess lit by a window. This recess serves as the lobby to a wall chamber stretching the length of the N side of the tower and lit by small windows to the outside. In the SE jamb, a room with windows to the E, W and S, the last with stone seats along the embrasure and a cupboard in its E side; fireplace at the W end of the N wall. At the room's NE corner was a garderobe whose seat was contained in the box machicolation.

The N block's attic was entered by a W door from the wall walk. Inside, a fireplace in the W gable and a pair of small windows in the E. The fourth-floor room of the jamb is reached by going along the N and E stretches of the main block's wall-walk. At the E stretch, a pair of stone seats cantilevered out of the gable of the main block. At the join of this block and the jamb, a garderobe which also gave access to the jamb. In the jamb's fourth-floor room, a C15 S window but the N fireplace is probably an early C17 insertion. Contained within the wall thickness of the NW corner of the jamb is a turnpike stair entered not

from the room in the jamb but from the W wall-walk of the main
block. This stair gives access to the wall-walk round the top of
the jamb. Inside this walk is the jamb's attic entered by a door
in the S gable; small N window.

# CLYDEBANK          WD *4070*

Until the last quarter of the C19, those riparian lands later eponymously named Clydebank were wholly rural. A few farms; a
laird's house or two. If anything distinguished the scene it was the
skein of communications teased out E–W across the landscape.
The Clyde itself, of course, connected Central Scotland to the wider
world. The ancient land route W from Glasgow to Dumbarton
and the Highlands and Islands clung close to the river's edge,
where traces of the Antonine Wall, abandoned by the Romans in
185, may be found. Following a more or less parallel course, the
Forth & Clyde Canal, dug some 1,600 years later, cut a narrow
commercial conduit W to Bowling with a short straight Junction
Canal S to meet the Clyde opposite its confluence with the River
Cart. From 1858, a railway line linked Glasgow with Dumbarton,
Balloch and Helensburgh. Indeed, when James and George
Thomson bought the West Barns o' Clyde estate in 1871, moving
their shipbuilding business from Govan to the N bank, all the linking sinews of economic strength – river, road, canal and railway –
were already there. Two sets of berths beside a fitting-out basin
were formed, cranes were erected, boiler works and engineering
works built. Ten years later, the Singer Manufacturing Company
arrived from Bridgeton in Glasgow. Located between the
Helensburgh rail line and the canal, Singer's began producing
sewing machines in a second vast industrial complex at the heart
of the new community. Begun 1882–4, to designs by *John B. Wilson*,
these multi-storey red brick buildings eventually spread over 150
acres. For decades, until its demolition in 1980, the factory's domed
clock tower dominated the centre of town.

By the end of the C19 these two firms had to all intents and purposes created the new burgh of Clydebank, chartered in 1886. Rows
of tenements accommodating shipyard workers lined Dumbarton
Road. This was 'Tamson's Toon', though by 1899 the yards from
which the liners *Lusitania*, *Queen Mary*, *Queen Elizabeth* and *QE2*
would later slip into the Clyde had passed into the hands of John
Brown & Co. Close to 'The Cross' that marked the T-junction of
Kilbowie Road with the long E–W line of Dumbarton Road, the
town's new Municipal Buildings were opened in 1902. N and E of
Singer's plant, Kilbowie and Radnor Park developed with more
tenements and, on the higher slopes, detached dwellings. A similar
pattern evolved at Dalmuir to the W, where alongside the Lanarkshire
& Dunbartonshire Railway laid down in 1897, Beardmores began

to produce ships, airships and armaments. In the E near Yoker, the huge basin of Rothesay Dock was completed in 1907.

Stimulated by the boom of the First World War, Clydebank continued to grow. Civic and commercial life remained concentrated along Dumbarton Road and Kilbowie Road close to the yards and factories. By the 1930s, however, local authority housing schemes were spreading in Kilbowie, Park Hall, and Mountblow. Then came the Second World War and with it catastrophe. In March 1941 the town's shipyards and munitions factories were bombed with an unparalleled intensity. The blitz was the worst Scotland suffered; besides the damage to industry, over 4,000 houses were totally destroyed. After the war, a programme of reconstruction began. The residential areas of Radnor Park and Boquhanran were rebuilt. In Whitecrook and Linnvale, low-rise four-in-a-block 120 garden suburbs were laid out. High-rise flats appeared, first at Mountblow but later in Dalmuir, Drumry and elsewhere. But it was not until the 1980s that those few tenements that had survived the war and which, almost alone, contributed urban scale to the fractured street scene, were finally rehabilitated. By this time, however, the tide of prosperity was ebbing all along the Clyde. The shipyards were all but silent. Singer's had closed. Soon, with large areas of the burgh designated as Scotland's first Enterprise Zone in 1981, the town was awash with brownfield business parks sinking in a sea of housing estates. Almost nothing that is genuinely urban has survived. A new Town Centre turns its back on the streets. Roads, roundabouts and service yards inhibit pedestrian pleasure. Car parks proliferate. Eviscerated by renewal and redevelopment, Clydebank is a doubly tragic town.

## CHURCHES

ABBOTSFORD PARISH CHURCH, Abbotsford Road. Built 1978–9, as part of town centre redevelopment, with money given in compensation for the loss of the West Church and St James's Church. A high square box in white dry-dash render, its cubic solidity softened by rounded corners and glazed-gap splays providing side light to the sanctuary in the NE corner. A few small openings appear randomly. To the W, an entrance link to halls lit from a saw-tooth roof. Standing free at the SW corner of the church, a four-stage concrete-frame campanile – with no bells.

Worship is orientated on the diagonal of the square plan. Entrance below a concave-fronted choir gallery in the SW corner. Buttressed walls of rough and smooth brick. A high timber-gridded ceiling conceals roof-lighting catching W light behind parapet walls.

CLYDEBANK BAPTIST CHURCH, Alexander Street. Dated 1893. A plain street-front gable in red sandstone. Above the three-centred arched door, a single round-arched window. Roughcast, five-bay buttressed nave with small thermal windows to N.

CLYDEBANK FAIFLEY PARISH CHURCH. See Duntocher.

DALMUIR BARCLAY CHURCH, Dumbarton Road. An unconventional yet strangely unconvincing meeting hall by *Michael &*

*Sue Thornley*, 1994–5. The lofty cubic box of the church, over-lit by superimposed lintelled windows on three sides, sacrifices mystery but fails to find any compensating lustral clarity. The walls, built in bland buff blockwork, appear to be load-bearing but conceal a frame of laminated timber columns. The roof is pitched but the ceiling is a flat laminated timber grid. In the N gable, a small carved stone TABLET carries the text 'WILL YOU COME / AND FOLLOW ME / IF I BUT CALL / YOUR NAME'. Linked HALLS and offices in matching facing brick spread S down Durban Avenue.

HAMILTON MEMORIAL CHURCH, Glasgow Road. Originally Hamilton Memorial Free Church, 1884–6. Neo-Norman with a landmark spire seen in the long perspective of Glasgow Road. In the N gable, a large round-arched window with three round-arched lights and an eight-part circle. The steeple, which incorporates a memorial tablet in the tall first stage, rises without buttressing to obelisk-topped kiosk corners linked by round-arched balustrading at the base of the spire. Behind the vestibule zone, a four-bay unbuttressed nave. Abandoned.

KILBOWIE ST ANDREW'S PARISH CHURCH, Kilbowie Road. Originally St John's on the Hill Church. Red sandstone Gothic by *George A. Paterson*, 1902–4. A four-bay buttressed nave with transepts N and S. Dec tracery in the gable windows. Semi-octagonal roughcast chancel with two-light Dec windows in the splays and a quatrefoil in a small E gable. Marking the SW entrance at the junction with Melfort Avenue, a square belfry tower with battlemented parapet, added in 1933.

METHODIST CHURCH, Second Avenue. By *Roxby, Park & Baird*, 1978–80. A bold orange brick box poised on the hillside with glazed classrooms enjoying views S across railway and canal. To the N, below the church, the columns of the poured concrete frame create a shadowed streetside loggia perversely invalidated as much by the barrier of low brick walls and railings as by orientation.

MORISON MEMORIAL UNITED REFORM CHURCH, Glasgow Road. By *H. B. W. Steele & Balfour*, 1896–7. Dull Gothic in red Ballochmyle sandstone, the building a pale version of the design first proposed. Street gable lit by three lancets in a pointed arch. Triple lancets repeated down a four-bay buttressed nave raised on a semi-basement.

OUR HOLY REDEEMER (R.C.), Glasgow Road. 1901–3; the familiar *Pugin & Pugin* formula of high nave, aisles and chancel. Rough-faced red sandstone laid in thick and thin courses, the texture of the masonry a fitting foil for the severe E.E. style. A high NE gable faces the street, set back behind a low railed wall. There are two deeply recessed pointed doorways separated by two closely spaced buttresses rising halfway up the gable height. Emerging from their pincer grip, a thin lancet soars upwards at the centre of the façade. Above each door, two similar lights, equally narrow though not so tall, rise in parallel. Quatrefoils centred over each pair flank the head of the central lancet. In the triangular frame at the gable apex, a third quatrefoil. Angle

buttresses, slightly set back at the upper level, act as book-ends
breaking the skews in hefty chimneyhead-like finials. Low to the
r. is the BAPTISTERY, an apsidal semi-octagon advancing below
a roof of slated hips. To the l., under a conical roof, a higher
round-ended projection houses the winding stair from vestibule
to organ loft.

The nave is seven bays deep; the chancel, which drops in
height, only two. Lean-to aisle roofs continue over the Sacred
Heart and Lady Chapels, overlapping one bay of the chancel.
Behind the vestibule and gallery zone, the six buttressed bays of
the clearstorey are lit by tripartite lancets in large pointed-
arched openings. Triple lancets in rectangular frames light the
aisles. All eaves lines are strongly horizontal, uninterrupted by
finials. The SANCTUARY is generously lit: on the NW and SE
sides, a single three-light pointed window; in the SW gable a
high circle with quatrefoil tracery flanked below by two bipartite
pointed windows which repeat the quatrefoil theme. Sacristy
and presbytery abut the SW gable.

The INTERIOR is long but also wide. A succession of high
pointed arches carried on octagonal piers opens up the space,
while the pews continue uninterrupted through the line of the
arcading to walkways at the perimeter. Circulation aisles paved
in variegated marbles, 1948. Pale painted plastered walls. Dark
arch-braced trusses support the purlins of the panelled roof,
their wall members dropping to moulded corbels set in the spandrels of the arcade. Strutted lean-to trusses carry the aisle roofs
in similar manner. Along the NW aisle wall segmental arches define
confessionals. A high, pointed, chancel arch crosses the full width
of the nave. The arch is moulded and incorporates colonnette
shafts carried on angel corbels. Traceried screens, white-painted
stone with green marble colonnettes, lead l. and r. from the
chancel into side chapels. Above these screens the studded walls
are painted with a quatrefoil grid of stencilling in red, blue and
gold. More complex stencilled decoration covers the patterned
planes of the sanctuary ceiling. In the side chapels, painted ceiling ribs and painted panels.

FURNISHINGS. A magnificent ALTAR and REREDOS, installed
in 1923, fills the SW gable wall of the sanctuary. Raised high at
the centre in a cusped Gothic frame, a painted oak panel depicts
the crucified Christ, Mary and St John against a golden background. It is elevated between two elaborately carved canopied
niches, these in turn set at a slightly higher level than two similar
niches on the outer flanks. In the niches, SS Patrick, Joseph,
Andrew and Theresa of Lisieux. Linking the two outer saints in
a series of cusped openings are seven small painted panels
showing angels kneeling in prayer, swinging thuribles and, at
the centre, bearing rich embroidery. Two more angels fill niches
below SS Joseph and Andrew on either side of the tabernacle.
The stonework of this exuberant display is sumptuously, even
intricately, carved with Gothic detail; painted white, it dramatically intensifies the effect of the painted figures and panels. –
Painted stone ALTARS in the side chapels in similar Gothic

style. At the centre of the Sacred Heart altar l., a statue of Christ between oak panels with painted angels carrying shields bearing the instruments of the Passion. In the Lady Chapel r., Mary and Child. – Marble and alabaster ALTAR RAIL of traceried panels separated by banded colonnettes. – Gothic PULPIT, 1948, in white marble with ogee-arched tracery; carved figures of SS Columba and Mungo in Carrara marble and six mosaic panels with the words 'FACIAM / VOS FIERI / PISCATORES / HOMINUM'. – Set between the confessionals on the NW wall is a wooden SHRINE to the Madonna of Perpetual Succour brought from Rome. Painted decoration by local artist *James Brown*. – STATIONS OF THE CROSS by *Morgari* of Turin. – Pipe ORGAN in the NE gallery by *J. &A. Mirrlees* of Glasgow. Organ casing decoratively painted in grey, gold and red. – STAINED GLASS, from the late 1940s, largely by *John Hardman Studios*. In the sanctuary gable, a high four-quatrefoil window with a green cross and the instruments of Christ's Passion and a pair of two-light windows depicting the Resurrection and Annunciation respectively. In the bottom zone of the latter, scenes associated with the history of the Catholic faith locally. – In the NW and SE sanctuary windows, Christ raised up above sleeping disciples. – Appropriately, in the Sacred Heart Chapel, the words COR JESU appear in the decorative scheme. – In the Lady Chapel, the apparitions seen at Lourdes and Fatima are featured. – Scenes from the healing ministry of Jesus are portrayed in the six three-light windows over the confessionals. – Close to the Baptistery, a three-light window shows the three kings bringing gifts to the infant Jesus. – Baptismal scenes in the five Baptistery lancets. – In a three-light window at the stair to the organ gallery, the Assumption of Mary. – In the tall lancets of the NE gable, the prophets Isaiah, Jeremiah, Ezekiel and Daniel above the four gospel saints.

OUR LADY OF LORETO (R.C.), Dumbarton Road, Dalmuir. Built as Dalmuir Parish Church, 1902–3; by *George A. Paterson* of *Stewart & Paterson*. Adapted for Catholic worship, 1954. A six-bay gabled nave with double-gabled transepts built in square-snecked ochre sandstone. Five-light Perp-traceried windows in the principal gables, three-light in the transepts. At the centre of the NE entrance gable, an ogee-topped pointed doorway sits between thin finialled buttresses; square hoodmoulding raised above carved thistles and roses. Gallery stair housed to the r. of the vestibule is a WAR MEMORIAL CHAPEL with marble floor and ribbed ceiling. Church interior roofed by arch-braced trusses carried on corbels. Coupled pointed arches open to the transepts. Moulded chancel arch with half-octagonal shafts. Chancel dado with Perp detail at centre. – ORGAN by *Norman & Beard*, 1912, with pipes gathered in canted bays l. and r. of sanctuary. – STAINED GLASS in the SW gable: below a crimson-robed bearded God, Christ the Lamb surrounded by a host of figures including trumpeting angels. HALLS at rear in reconstituted stone, late 1940s.

RADNOR PARK PARISH CHURCH, Crown Avenue. By *King, Main & Ellison*. Built 1969–70 to replace a Gothic Revival church of 1894–5, by *Malcolm Stark & Rowntree*. Described as 'plain yet substantial', this original building had been damaged by fire in 1909, enlarged with transepts by *Duncan McNaughtan & Son* in 1910, blitzed in 1941, rebuilt by 1948, and finally destroyed by fire in 1968. Its successor is plain yet elegant. Fawn facing brick walls carry the slow flat slope of the nave roof up towards the E. Short steep monopitches tilt up on the E and W; the former rising to a hidden clearstorey over the trapezoidal sanctuary, the latter against the glazed gridded wall of the vestibule. Brick interior, clean and spacious under a wide pine-boarded ceiling. Octagonal PULPIT and COMMUNION TABLE, both suavely planar in oak and metal, designed by the architects. The church links W to the modestly Gothic ORR BROWN HALL, 1938.

ST COLUMBA (Episcopal), Glasgow Road. Disused. Cruciform E.E. Gothic in rough-faced square-snecked red sandstone by *M. McColl*, 1895–6. In the W gable, above a blocky porch, circular tracery fills a large pointed-arched window. Four-bay nave and transept gables lit by triple lancets. Five lancets fill the triangle of the E gable and an eroded bellcote sits at the apex. Side chapel and vestry gables flank the sanctuary, that to the N with a Star of David window. – STAINED GLASS in the W window: Iona by *Stephen Adam*, 1896. – In the N transept, SS Patrick, Columba and Mungo by *Burlison & Grylls*, 1896.

John Hutchinson Sharp Memorial HALL linked to S; by *H. D. Walton*, 1914. Eight roughcast buttressed bays, lancet-lit, fronted by a W gable in red Locharbriggs sandstone.

ST CUTHBERT'S PARISH CHURCH, Attlee Place, Linnvale. 1954. Red brick religion in a railed and grassed enclosure. A gabled hall with flat-roofed vestibule and offices. W entrance emphasized by a parapeted stone doorpiece carved with the Burning Bush and a perfunctory Gothic moulding.

ST EUNAN (R.C.), East Thomson Street. By *Gillespie, Kidd & Coia*, 1950–1. Long walls of buff-brown brick under a corrugated asbestos roof; bland and spiritless.

ST MARGARET (R.C.), Sinclair Street, Whitecrook. 1970–2. A wonderfully understated design by *Gillespie, Kidd & Coia* built to meet the new liturgical demands of the Second Vatican Council. There is no soaring roof, no campanile, only landscaped banks, walls of ochre brick, lead fascias and black planes of one-way glazing. Behind the glass, the widespread auditorium space for worship falls gently from the vestibule, scooped out below a still low space-frame roof. Entrance is without formality, casual almost, the subtlety and intimacy of the experience intensified by pews fanning around a liturgical axis that runs obliquely across the diagonal of a square plan. Dark at first, the church is lit along pine-boarded edges, light falling from above across the patterned and serrated planes of brickwork, the effect particularly dramatic over the sanctuary which is chamfered across the lowest corner. ALTAR, TABERNACLE, LECTERN and FONT in black slate with decorative lead treatment; by *Alfred Gruber* and *Jacqueline Stieger*. Mosaic PANEL honouring St Margaret by *Graven Images*, 1986.

However inspired the design decision to dig down, constructional inadequacies have led to repeated flooding. The original cut-and-fill landscape, open and indefensible, also proved vulnerable; not only the church but also the Presbytery and Halls, grouped around a hidden garden to the s, are now protected by obtruding railings.

ST STEPHEN (R.C.), Park Road, Dalmuir. By *Thomas S. Cordiner*, 1957–8. A tall cruciform church built in buff-brown brickwork with slated roofs. Above low aisles and side chapels, the lateral walls and gables rise to a high eaves, the ridge common to nave, transepts and chancel. Elongated pediment-arched windows fill each bay, with wider versions in the gables. Under a jutting ridge, the w entrance gable splays forward to a windowed wall set above concrete canopied doors. Linked N is a tall square campanile spired with a copper flèche. Concrete belfry grids on N, S and E faces; clock to the w.

Patterned terrazzo floor in the vestibule. To the r. a narrow stair rises to the rear gallery. To the l., located at the foot of the campanile, the baptistery. The church interior is light and lofty. On each side of the crossing, concrete portal frames, tapering downwards, mark out the structural bays: five in the nave, two in the chancel. Diagonal portals define the crossing itself. Woodblock floor. Marble steps (grey treads, white risers) to sanctuary. – Placed against a vertically boarded panel on the sanctuary gable wall is a large wooden RELIEF of the Martyrdom of St Stephen, carved by *J. McInally*. – ALTAR and splay-fronted PULPIT in white marble with grey and black edgings. – FONT, a tapering hexagonal prism in white marble veined green. – Carved wooden STATUES of Christ and Mary in the Sacred Heart and Lady Chapels by *McInally*. – Co-ordinated STAINED GLASS scheme by *Douglas Hamilton*. In the w gable, the crucified Christ on a purple cross with Mary and John below; at the base is a view of the original St Stephen's Church, bombed in 1941. – In the N transept, a gloriously blue St Andrew above SS Kentigern and Patrick with Glasgow Cathedral pictured at the base. – St Margaret mantled in purple dominates the s transept. – In the Baptistery chapel a colourful 'Ecce Agnus Dei'; Christ's immersion in the Jordan.

An undistinguished two-storey Presbytery links s to the HALLS, also by *Cordiner* and built in 1950 as a first replacement for the original church.

WESLEYAN REFORM UNITED CENTRAL CHURCH, Kilbowie Road. By *W. F. McGibbon*, 1886–7. Cheap gabled Gothic with a downmarket Arts and Crafts flavour. Stepping ridges and a low buttressed entrance tower in the sw re-entrant sit well on the hillside corner but the combination of Dorset pea render and white-pointed dull rust brickwork enervates charm.

## CEMETERIES

DALNOTTAR CEMETERY, Great Western Road. Four GATEPIERS, corniced, with high pyramidal prism copes. A few headstones

on the main driveway merit notice. Pink granite OBELISK with
bronze bearded head at the base of the shaft; to Alexander
Cameron †1922 and his wife Sarah Storms †1952, by *Hay &
Paterson*, Partick. – Perched on the tall battered base of the
Harvie MONUMENT, 1920s, a carved Ali Baba lamp lugged with
scrolls. – By *J. Gilfillan*, three Art Deco HEADSTONES to the
Kirk family, *c.* 1935. – High astringently plain HEADSTONE to
the artist Leslie Hunter (1879–1931), by *Gray & Co.*

KILBOWIE CEMETERY, Montrose Street. Opened 1897. Four
high GATEPIERS with corniced copes, the inner pair carrying
draped urns. Curving walks climb a grassy hill studded with the
customary gravemarkers. – To the l., the statue of a praying
angel sits on a pale grey granite base with corner columns; a
MONUMENT to William G. O'Beirne †1933. – Higher on the
hillside, another grey granite MONUMENT to David Winton
†1920 and his wife Christina Smith †1908: a draped urn flanked
by four flared vases on a high base cornered with pink granite
colonnettes. – To Mary Straiton †1914 and her husband William
Gaul †1917, a dark grey granite COLUMN from which capital
and urn have fallen. – Also in grey granite but lighter, an aedicule
MONUMENT with short Tuscan columns, cornice and block
pediment; erected by Andrew Moore to memorialize his wife,
Isabella Cameron †1911.

## PUBLIC BUILDINGS

CLYDE SHOPPING CENTRE. Built in two phases by *Hugh
Martin & Partners*, 1978–82. Almost half a kilometre of covered
shopping malls linking Alexander Street N across the Forth &
Clyde Canal to the supermarket and cinema sheds of a new
Town Centre. On the W, the urban integrity of Kilbowie Road
has been sacrificed. On the E, civic space defers to car parking,
(*see* Description, below).

CLYDEBANK COLLEGE, Kilbowie Road. Five-storey slab South
Building, 1960–5, by *Thomas S. Cordiner & Partners*; concrete
frame with brick infill. North Building added by *Cordiner,
Cunningham & Partners*, 1967–71.

CLYDEBANK CREMATORIUM, Dalnottar, off Mountblow Road.
1964. By *H. A. Rendel Govan* of *Sir Frank Mears & Partners*. A
clutter of lower roofs gathered around the pitched planes of the
chapel roof falling from a chimney tower in the E. Harled walls
with mock stone cladding. High glazing to W. Detached pentagonal Hall of Remembrance with two W walls glazed to the
Firth.

CLYDEBANK HEALTH CENTRE, West Thomson Street. 1972–3.
Bleak boxes of CLASP construction, clad in grey aggregate precast panels.

90 CLYDEBANK LIBRARY, Dumbarton Road. 1912–13. Competition-
winning design by *A. McInnes Gardner* of *Gardner, Millar &
Whyte*. Essentially a façade, but a good one. Seven Classical
bays in warm ochre Hunterston sandstone; a two-storeyed NE
front raised from the street on a basement of channelled ashlar.

Giant order three-quarter Composite columns carry a long entablature shadowed by an overhanging cornice studded with modillion blocks. Broad channelled pilasters act as quoins at the end of the façade. At the centre between coupled columns an arched entrance door is surmounted by the town's armorial bearings and the motto 'LABORE ET SCIENTIA'. A short length of ashlar façade faces Hall Street: the bold entablature maintained above superimposed tripartite windows set within a recessing stonework frame. Some remodelling of the interior, 1945–50; extensive modernization, 1967–9. In the foyer, a colourful STAINED GLASS collage celebrates the town's industrial past; by *Lesley Macfie*, 1991.

Former CLYDEBANK RIVERSIDE STATION, Cunard Street. By *John J. Burnet*, 1896–7. Single-storey and dormered attic, built in red brick and red sandstone for the Lanarkshire & Dunbartonshire Railway. V-plan arrangement dominated by a hexagonal booking hall on the corner fortified with corbelled parapet and topless bartizans. At the rear, a forestair rises to what was the stationmaster's house. All now in residential use.

HEALTH CARE INTERNATIONAL HOSPITAL, Beardmore Way. 1991–4. A fortress of private medicine designed by *The Architects Collaborative* of Cambridge, Massachusetts, with hospital planning consultants *Hamilton KSA* of Minneapolis. Everything seems overburdened with a blocky solidity; bulky and graceless in dull rust-coloured brick and precast concrete, the buildings pile up, almost ziggurat-like, to four, five, six and seven storeys. A long, roof-lit *porte cochère*, advancing diagonally from the cross-grid plan, leads to a Reception Hall serving the hospital and the inter-linked BEARDMORE CONFERENCE HOTEL, a four-storey slab with mock pediments. Comfortable 'business class' interiors.

MUNICIPAL BUILDINGS, Dumbarton Road. A design of some civic presence by *James Miller*, 1900–2, in creamy Bishopbriggs sandstone; classically organized and detailed with a creative lack of pedantry. The complex brief comprising Council Chamber, administrative offices, large and small Halls, Court Room and Police Station is resolved in two street façades hinged on a high corner tower. While the eaves lines along Dumbarton Road and 87 Hall Street maintain contextual tenement scale, the unbuttressed square tower rises more than twice this height to a prominent cornice shelf on which sits a domed tempietto. Four distyle pseudo-porticoes enrich the skyline silhouette. The bronze 'Angel', a conflation of Eros and Hermes transferred to Clydebank's tower in 1902 from the Glasgow International Exhibition of 1901, was blown from his perch on the small dome in 1968 to be relocated in the foyer off Dumbarton Road. Inserted at the base of the tower is the town's WAR MEMORIAL, 1931, by the sculptor *Donald Gilbert*; a gilt bronze figure of remembrance in archaic Greek style sheltering in her hands a lamp in the form of a galley.

The nine-bay NE front is symmetrical with an aedicular frontispiece and end bays projecting slightly under open segmental pediments. Guarded by cast iron lamp standard sentries, the central entrance is framed by channelled pilasters fronted by Ionic columns. The doorway's segmental pediment bustles with putti flanking the town arms and motto under the carved prow of a ship. Above, at first-floor level, a small balustrade links coupled Ionic columns under separate entablatures carrying an arched attic above eaves level. On the cornice of this decorative parapet a scrolled flagstaff base rises between urns while two female figures sit below on the consoled pediment of a central round-arched window. To l. and r. of the entrance are three bays of Gibbsian windows, round-arched at ground floor but taller and lintelled above. Set between banded pilasters in the end bays the windows to the *piano nobile* are taller still, arcuated under consoled open pediments. In the tympana, more naked allegorical figures celebrating the town's skills in engineering and shipbuilding. Gibbsian windows reappear at the base of the tower and again for five bays down Hall Street. Then comes a staircase element with pedimented street door, balustraded balcony and, raised above the eaves, an open pediment broken by an elaborate cartouche. A six-bay pilastrade fronting a first-floor lecture room continues the eaves line to meet the high gabled front of the large hall, i.e. the Town Hall. At street level a columned entrance loggia links two advancing staircase towers. Squat Venetian windows light lower landings. Above, the towers terminate in wide overhanging eaves (almost Wrightian in perspective) which return to meet the recessed plane of the gable. Filling the façade between the towers is a huge Diocletian window crossed by a dentilled entablature carried on four Ionic columns corbelled below the sill. At the gable apex a small obelisk breaks through a segmental pediment. Beyond this theatrical drama the street wall continues in lower, humbler vein across the Police Station. In 1935 the Town Hall was remodelled with a proscenium stage and a glazed ironwork canopy introduced along Hall Street.

In the rather cramped entrance hall to the Council Chamber, fawn scagliola columns and swollen pilasters on socles carry a beam supporting the first-floor gallery. Well stair rises below a large lintelled window divided into a nine-square grid of leaded glasswork and stained-glass armorial panels. Decorative plaster frieze with putti and swags at first-floor level. Columned screen to gallery similar to lower hall.

103 PLAYDOME LEISURE CENTRE, Abbotsford Road. By the *Ellis Williams Partnership*, 1991–4. Brash 'big-top' architecture pitched in a sea of downtown car parking. Dramatically slung on tension cables from seven tall steel masts, paired cellular rafter beams rise radially over the Pools Hall under stepping roof planes. At the central apex, a pyramid-like roof-light. Wave machine funnels add to the nautical allusion. Upper walls in blue and silver metal cladding on a ground-floor base of ochre brickwork. The same materials carried round 'big box' Bowling and Sports Halls to N.

ST MARGARET'S HOSPICE, East Barns Street. Begun 1970–2

by *Gillespie, Kidd & Coia* whose single-storey buildings in Dorset pea render are still detectable by square hole-in-the-wall windows, clearstorey strips and heavy splayed concrete eaves. In 1989 *Nicholson & Jacobsen* began to extend the accommodation by an additional top-heavy storey using aggressively coloured metal cladding panels in chocolate and tan. In 1997–8 the same architects added the adjacent two-storey CONVENT and single-storey SIR PATRICK HAMMILL EDUCATION CENTRE, preferring a light brown brick with darker banding.

WEST DUNBARTONSHIRE COUNCIL OFFICES, Rosebery Place. By *Baxter, Clark & Paul*, 1977–9. Four floors of cream-coloured, storey-height, precast concrete panels. The faceted units are identical, each with two window openings, the building bleakly repetitive. Staircase gaps and a splayed base of engineering bricks are the only relief.

## DESCRIPTION

On DUMBARTON ROAD the street-corner tower of the Municipal Buildings (*see* Public Buildings, above) sustains some sense of urban focus. It is not alone. Packed down the short length of HALL STREET is an unexpected enclave of civic architecture. On the E, Burgh Offices, Town Hall and Police Station (*see* Public Buildings, above). On the W, the wide, symmetrical gable front of the former CLYDEBANK BATHS, 1899–1902, and a now-rehabilitated tenement whose original role as the town's FIRE STATION, 1900–2, is betrayed by three round-arched pends. All of these are in ochre sandstone, consistently designed by *James Miller*. The red gable of Morison Memorial United Reform Church (*see* Churches, above) turns back into Dumbarton Road where Clydebank Library (*see* Public Buildings, above) completes the group. On both sides, the last of the tenement ranges of 'Tamson's Toon' stretch out along the S side of the road. To the W, Nos. 71–113, four-storeyed ashlar with canted bays from first floor. Then, Nos. 119–155, 1980s infill in grey blockwork with pink striping; canted bays continue but the scale drops and glazed stair slots interrupt the façade. Nos. 161–167 are original, rehabilitated 1988–9. E of the Municipal Buildings, a run of flat-fronted, three-storey shops and flats, *c.* 1890, reaches Bruce Street. Then Nos. 1–9 and 11–17 GLASGOW ROAD, two late C19 three-storey ranges, remodelled with rear porches as CENTENARY COURT, 1986–7. At WALLACE STREET, an abandoned Woolworth's corner, 1938–9; bricked up below but preserving the white faience fins and chevrons of Art Deco fashion above.

Across the road almost everything is new-build. Urban scale and continuity falter. KILBOWIE ROAD skews N from 'The Cross' junction. On the r., a flat wall of plain, late C19 shops and tenements, rehabilitated 1984–5, reaches the railway bridge; Nos. 16–42 in ochre sandstone, Nos. 44–48 in red. More red on the l.; Nos. 41–53, *c.* 1900, three-storeyed with canted bays from first floor. Thereafter eaves height and street lines are wilfully disregarded. Standing in a gratuitous ill-defined space, the grey granite STEVENSON MONUMENT, an octagonal Mercat Cross shaft topped by a sundial, cross and ball finial, raised in memory of the town's Medical Officer of Health, James Stevenson (1851–1909). Restoring scale but not dignity, West Dunbartonshire Council Offices (*see* Public Buildings, above) return four storeys of repetitive concrete into Rosebery Place. Beyond this, both sides of the road are engulfed in sudden suburban bleakness. On the E, the exposed backlands of Clyde Shopping Centre (*see* Public Buildings, above). On the W, Clydebank Business Park has replaced the Singer complex. The brown brick offices of ERSKINE HOUSE, 1983–4, are dully respectable; the tiled hipped roofs and brick soldier courses of *William Nimmo & Partners*' RADIO CLYDE BUILDING, 1983–4, attractive if incongruously rural; the mirror-glass walls and castellated beam verandahs of SCHERER LTD. by *Carl, Fisher, Sibbald & Partners*, 1984–5, more appropriately industrial. Clean and tidy as all this is, it is a cold heart for any town. Uphill, however, past Second Avenue, things begin to improve. Houses return to the street. Two church towers mark successive corners. Some shops and tenements have survived. But tawdriness prevails. And despite its size, Clydebank College (*see* Public Buildings, above), its forecourt depressed below pavement level, does nothing to restore urban credibility.

If, indeed, Clydebank retains any vestige of animated townscape, it is in ALEXANDER STREET. Running N parallel to Kilbowie Road, it, too, begins with shops and tenements. Three storeys of ochre ashlar on the r. with a chain of corniced windows at first-floor level; Nos. 2–32, dated 1895, rehabilitated 1984–5. Opposite, past the Baptist Church (*see* Churches, above), a second three-storey wall in polychromatic sandstone, *c.* 1897. The street then passes under the railway station bridge into the town's busiest public space. Buses and taxis contend with shoppers and commuters. Rounding the bend into Chalmers Street is the retail warehouse of CLYDEBANK CO-OPERATIVE SOCIETY by *John Stewart* of *Stewart & Paterson*, 1914–17; a high handsome wall of giant order pilasters with Ionic half columns and a skyline sculptured group dated 1916 over the corner entrance. Framed construction interior with a circular void passing through four storeys under a glazed cupola. Erect and architecturally assured, this sole survivor of Edwardian commerce is now a portal to lesser things. Alexander Street becomes SYLVANIA WAY SOUTH and plunges into the long milling mall of Clyde Shopping Centre (*see* Public Buildings, above). Castellated beams supporting a transparent canopy of acrylic pyramidal roof-lights cross the covered way between shops. Then comes a glazed elliptical barrel vault. Then, a space frame, as the internal street bridges the landscaped channel of the Forth & Clyde Canal. At FRANCONIA SQUARE the street side-steps into an open avenue, SYLVANIA WAY NORTH, planted with a few trees between covered walkways. At CARINTHIA SQUARE, steps lead up and out to Kilbowie Road. To the E is the TOWN

CENTRE, a place paradoxically more out-of-town than down-town: supermarkets, multiplex cinemas, fast-food restaurants and car parks. An open market-place on the s side of the canal, THREE QUEENS SQUARE, is only intermittently alive with trade. Relocated here, an octagonal, copper-domed BANDSTAND, manufactured in filigree-laced cast iron by the *Lion Foundry*, Kirkintilloch, 1907. Pitched further E, beyond Abbotsford Church (*see* Churches, above), the big, silver-and-blue-banded tent of the Playdome (*see* Public Buildings, above).

Around this ersatz centre the burgh seems little more than one vast and varied housing scheme. Of coherent streets or urban enclosure there are only fleeting reminders. The red sandstone, three-storey tenements in WHITECROOK STREET, *c.* 1900, have survived. Nos. 45–77, an extended range with canted bays at first and second floors and segmental hoods over the close entries; and opposite, Nos. 36–64, a long convex wall articulated only by strings, cornices and coupled windows. At the corner with GLASGOW ROAD, canted bays push through the eaves on each side of a leaded dome. There is more of this to the w. Dalmuir announces itself with a splendid onion dome marking the start of a four-storey range in red ashlar, Nos. 421–481 DUMBARTON ROAD. Carved on the façade below the dome, a naval Dread- 42 nought. Late C20 attempts to toughen the streetline proliferate; forms, heights and materials vary unconvincingly. But at STEWART STREET the red Edwardian tenements return. Then come DUNN STREET, PATTISON STREET, BURNS STREET and SCOTT STREET, all four-storeyed with canted bays, trun-cated canyons of rehabilitated urban living. At Nos. 709–727 and 733–781 DUMBARTON ROAD and in FRENCH STREET and CASTLE STREET the tenements are still red, three and four storeys high, but, strangely, flat-roofed. All have been revital-ized by alteration and addition in the 1980s. As a result, Dalmuir sustains a modest streetwise intensity. But not much else. A single Thomsonesque villa, MELBOURNE HOUSE on Regent Street, probably by *Robert Turnbull*, 1877–80, is the exception: a symmetrical dwelling with a façade-wide entabla-ture carried forward on square bays across an Egyptian-columned porch.

# COALSNAUGHTON                                                     C *9090*

Small village, the principal streets (MAIN STREET running N–S, and WARDLAW and RAMSAY STREETS running E–W) forming a T-plan. A few Victorian buildings but C20 housing is dominant.

COALSNAUGHTON UNITED PRESBYTERIAN CHURCH, Ramsay Street. Built in 1867. Broad box, the walling of large blocks of buff-coloured rubble. Round-arched windows in the sides. In the front (N) gable, a round-arched door under a heavy hood-mould. Oculus in the apex of the gable which is topped by a slate-spired ventilator.

COALSNAUGHTON PRIMARY SCHOOL, Blackfaulds Street.

Two blocks, the S of 1877–8, with quatrefoil dummy windows in the gables, the N, dated 1899, with bracketed eaves.

PUBLIC LIBRARY AND HALL, Main Street. Harled single-storey, built in two stages. The first, by *J. S. Leishman*, 1907, provided the library and a hall at the rear. Piend-roofed symmetrical front block (but one window is now a door) with a curvilinear gabled entrance at the centre of a bow-fronted E porch. Plain hall behind. The second stage, by *William Kerr* and *John Gray* of *John Melvin & Son*, 1925, added another hall to the S. Piend-roofed gable to the street containing a large window with wooden mullions and transoms.

ABERDONA HOUSE. *See* p. 103.

ABERDONA HOUSE. *See* p. 103.

*4070*                  COCHNO HOUSE                  s
                     1.5km. N of Duntocher

A harled Classical mansion house of *c.* 1757. Rudimentary in its architectural elaboration, it has been attributed to *John Adam*, but whether this is the son of William Adam or the more shadowy John Adam of Glasgow responsible for the design of Petershill House is unclear. Neither architect is credited with more than respectable competence and, indeed, Cochno's seven-bay, two-storey-and-basement composition is no more than that. Pediment over the three bays at the centre of the N entrance façade, with a circular oculus in the tympanum. Windows to first floor and basement are almost square, those to the ground floor vertical in proportion with a sill course crossing the façade. Only the Roman Doric porch, at the head of a perron stair, adds ornamental interest. A round arch set between elongated pilasters carrying an entablature, it seems likely that this rather overscaled element, raised high enough to shelter the original pedimented doorpiece, is C19, perhaps added in 1842 when a single-storey W wing was built. This Victorian enlargement created a lop-sided arrangement, but it was at least more respectful than the present two-storeyed wing which has resulted from the C20 addition of an upper storey. Side elevations are windowed but plain. To the S, the land falls away to make the elevation fully three storeys. A full-height canted bay projects at the centre with balustraded parapet and attic dormers behind.

The estate was bought by the University of Glasgow in 1954 but it was not until the 1990s that restoration began. Cochno House now serves as the teaching centre of a 355ha Farm and Research Centre.

0.1km. N, a large, late C18 STABLE COURT. Roughcast, two-storey buildings, only partly roofed, surround a U-plan cobbled court, open to the S. At the centre, a small pedimented gable on consoles with a round-arched window at first floor and a tiny opening set asymmetrically to the r. Round-arched doorways open on all three ranges. Pigeon entries grouped in the S gable of the W range. Derelict.

# COWIE

Bleak mining village.

CHURCH OF THE SACRED HEART (R.C.). By *Reginald Fairlie*, 1936–7. Despite its almost rural hilltop setting, this is hard-edged, redbrick religion. Pyramid-slated octagon with a leaded apex and round-ended W porch and apsidal E sanctuary projecting under lower conical roofs. Triple round-arched windows in four faces. Inside, eight mild steel lattice arches support purlins, spars and boarding. Sanctuary floor and altars in variegated marbles. Ill-at-ease N link to presbytery, also in red brick.

COWIE PARISH CHURCH. Originally Cowie United Free Church. By *McLuckie & Walker*, 1904–5. Gabled NW front in rough-faced, square-snecked sandstone: above, a triple lancet; below, a full-width, lean-to vestibule with gabled round-arched entrances l. and r. Unconvincing Gothic, uncomfortably exposed in peripheral isolation.

COWIE PRIMARY SCHOOL. Built by St Ninian's School Board, 1903–4, to a design of Stirling architect *Ronald Walker*. Extended 1911 by *McLuckie & Walker*. Earlier work in rough-faced, square-snecked stone; later in red brick. Both maintain the same forms: gabled classrooms with tripartite mullioned and transomed windows.

# CRAIGEND CASTLE *see* MUGDOCK

# CRAIGFORTH

A few houses by Drip Bridge 0.5km. S of the confluence of the Rivers Forth and Teith.

CRAIGFORTH HOUSE. The original house, still embedded in the present structure, was probably constructed in the last quarter of the C17. It was later enlarged and radically remodelled in the early C19, possibly by *William Stirling I, c.* 1830. This three-storey, seven-bay mansion house had a piended roof and, though otherwise elevationally plain, a columned, pedimented porch. In 1930 a fire swept through the property but a programme of conversion, begun in 1970, has restored the house as the headquarters of a large insurance company. Extensions made to the l. and r. of the original block have been seamlessly effected. A series of office buildings, clad in precast concrete panels, now surround the house; begun by *Bell Ingram*, 1972–80, and continued by *William Nimmo & Partners* in the 1980s.

DRIP OLD BRIDGE. Built in roughly coursed sandstone rubble by public subscription, 'perhaps before 1745'*, more likely *c.* 1773. Five segmental arches in symmetrically graduated spans cross the Forth (a distance of more than 60m.) carrying the old road from Stirling to Callander. The central span, 13.7m., springs from

* RCAHMS, *Stirlingshire*, ii (1963), 410.

cutwater piers which rise buttress-like to become half-hexagon refuges on each side of the narrow carriageway. Disused.

OLD INN COTTAGE. C18. Harled riverside dwelling; three bays, two storeys, with bow window added *c.* 1825. Later C19 house, similar but higher, sits at angle.

TOLLHOUSE. Built *c.* 1820. Single-storey cottage with a hipped half-octagon end, a skew-gabled porch set between gableted splays. Baluster SUNDIAL in the garden.

*4090*                    CRAIGIEVAIRN                    S
3.1km. NNE of Drymen

Three-storey laird's house, mid or late C18. T-plan with chimneyed skew-gables. The windows of the four-bayed SE front are vertically aligned, those to the first floor markedly taller. Off-centre entrance with moulded lugged architraves. In the gable-wall of the ground-floor NE apartment, a wide segmental-arched recess indicates the former kitchen fireplace.

CRAIGMADDIE CASTLE *see*
CRAIGMADDIE HOUSE

*5070*               CRAIGMADDIE HOUSE               ED
1.5km. N of Baldernock

Stolid but idiosyncratic Classical mansion house built for James Black, Lord Provost of Glasgow, *c.* 1790, and later enlarged in two successive stages.

The late Georgian house is a two-storey piend-roofed oblong faced with lightly broached buff-coloured ashlar. SW front of four bays with panelled pilasters at the outer corners. Windows all set in corniced architraves, those of the ground floor with small block-corbels under the ends of the sills; lugged windows at the first floor. The two centre bays are slightly advanced under a chimneyed pediment supported by three exceptionally broad panelled pilasters. This centrepiece was partially obscured *c.* 1910 by the addition of a porch fronted by a Tuscan columned portico. The portico's roof is pierced by round skylights, the openings decorated with bay leaf enrichment. At the back of the main block and projecting to the NW, an addition of 1842, the detail heavier than that of the original and the stone weathered to a grey colour. A second rear addition was built *c.* 1910, a first-floor Venetian window in each gable. Inside the house, some late Georgian detail but the predominant character is of *c.* 1910, with enriched plaster ceilings and woodwork in late C17 revival manner.

SE of the house, a GARDEN enclosed by rubble walls on its NW and NE sides, the NE wall screening piend-roofed office buildings and ending in a round DOOCOT tower. All this may be of 1842.

CRAIGMADDIE CASTLE stands on a wooded bank behind the mansion-house. This badly ruined tower was probably built for the Hamiltons of Baldernock soon after they acquired the lands *c.* 1390. It has been a rubble-walled rectangle, *c.* 8.58m. by 7.47m., and of at least three storeys. The walling survives up to the level of the first floor all round and higher at the W gable (much of its facing fallen), the E end of the N side and the S end of the E gable. In each gable, a ground-floor slit window. The first floor must have been reached by a forestair, apparently placed towards the W end of the N side where the base of the inner edge of a door jamb survives. There has been a first-floor window in the centre of the E gable.

Inside, the ground floor is covered by a tunnel vault, its E end pierced by a hatch which provided access from the floor above. At the first floor, in the S end of the E gable, a roundheaded recess, its middle grooved for a shelf. At the NE corner, remains of the bottom three treads of a turnpike stair to the floor or floors above. It has been partly contained in the wall thickness but also encroached on the room.

FORT. The ruined tower of Craigmaddie Castle is situated within an earlier fort with double ramparts.

## CRAIGRUIE

3.8km. W of Balquhidder

By *Peddie & Kinnear*, 1859. A fine house of steep bargeboarded gables spiked with timber finials. Symmetrical canted bays l. and r. of the entrance are corbelled to gables at first floor.

## CRIANLARICH

A T-junction village for road and rail at the intersection of Glen Falloch, Glen Dochart and Strath Fillan.

Former STRATHFILLAN FREE CHURCH, 5km. NW. Built in 1829 by the Scottish Society for Propagating Christian Knowledge but later used by the Free Church of Scotland. Simple four-bay whinstone Gothic. Both roughcast gables lit by a small circular window flanked below by lancets. Pointed doorway in SW gable sheltered by a gabled porch. Above, a saddleback-roofed bellcote clasps the apex.

STRATHFILLAN PARISH CHURCH. By *Thomas Ross*, 1901. Small two-bay church and vestry with a gabled porch canted across the SW re-entrant. Roughcast with inset buttresses, moulded sill course and Dec W gable window in red sandstone. Inside, a single kingpost truss arch-braced from corbelstones.

STRATHFILLAN PRIORY, Kirkton, 4.2km. NW. Probably C14. Rubble remains, rising to the sill height of a single window opening, suggest an aisleless nave-and-choir plan. A small GRAVE-YARD, sited on a knoll within a rubble enclosure, contains C18 and C19 tombs. Built into the N wall, a MURAL PANEL with guttae epaulettes flanking a flaming urn; to Captain Gregor Macgregor †1779. – Several lying SLABS may have come from the Priory. Among them is a broken stone incised with three simple Latin crosses.

VILLAGE HALL. By *Multiprofessional Architectural Practice*, 1991–2. Shallow-pitched roof of profiled metal from which a steeply gabled glazed porch projects. Roughcast walls with glazing in the W and E gables.

RAILWAY ENGINE SHED. Late C19. Brick-built gable-ended block, thirteen bays long with corbelled eaves between buttresses. Round-arched windows in alternate bays.

WAR MEMORIAL. *c.* 1922. Kilted soldier on a plinth of rough-faced sandstone into which is set a smooth stone panel with the names of the dead cut into it. Sculpted by *Beveridge* of Perth. A low wall with returns forms short stone benches l. and r. of the monument.

DESCRIPTION. Overhead the railway from Loch Lomond and the S swings NW en route to Oban and Fort William. Surviving between overgrown sidings, the island RAILWAY STATION, identifiable, but only just, as the standard brick and timber, West Highland Line design of *James Miller*, 1894, is unmanned but operative. E of the railway viaduct, a single-storey row of five railwaymen's COTTAGES. Across the road, a corrugated-iron-clad structure with porch, a N transept and an octagonal window in the W gable; a former CHURCH, *c.* 1910. Nearby is GLENBRUAR, early C20, attractively drenched in slated hips.

INVERARDRAN, 0.9km. ESE. Probably C18. Three-bay, two-storey, double-pile-plan house. Fretted curvilinear bargeboarding over first-floor windows and central porch, probably later.

LOCH DOCHART CASTLE. *See* p. 604.

*4080* CROFTAMIE S

A string of houses loosely tied round a deep wooded bend in the Catter Burn.

CROFTAMIE PRIMARY SCHOOL. Built 1907. Surprisingly sophisticated two-classroom block, its symmetry made all the grander by an elevated setting and axial approach. Roughcast with in-and-out sandstone dressings. Three half-timbered gables: at the centre a wide, segmentally-arched entrance with roll-moulded surrounds and pronounced keystones; l. and r., under similar lintels, tripartite mullioned and transomed windows. Pepperpot roof ventilator. Detached hip-roofed shelter symmetrically sited at rear. Adjacent gabled SCHOOLHOUSE in similar symmetrical vein.

DESCRIPTION. However picturesque the setting, there is no sense of built enclosure. N and S are small clusters of late C20 private housing. Between are some older properties, including the painted rubble ranges of CROFTAMIE FARM, early C19, surviving on the road edge and a strange domestic agglomeration of similar date, with glazed gabled porches and a conically roofed tower at

the rear. EDMOND TERRACE, late C19, a two-storey, tenement
row of three flatted dwellings of three bays built for sawmill
workers, and LANGWELL, a single-unit version of the same,
share moulded skewputts perversely turned to extend the eaves.

AUCHENECK HOUSE, 2.8km. SSE. Late C19. Red sandstone
Baronial, planar rather than bulbous. Two-storey house with
crowstepped gables and gablets abuts a square, four-storey
tower with toy-fort parapet and bartizans. Abandoned.

PIRNIEHALL, 0.7km. W. 1896. An 1886 datestone has been incorporated from an earlier building. Multi-gabled two-storey house
with a corner entrance drum ringed with roundels and capped
by a tall witch's-hat roof. The contemporary E LODGE, known
as 'Witch's Hat', has a steep piended roof sprocketed to a wide
overhanging eaves.

CAIRN, Stockie Muir. 5km. S. An impressive long cairn some 20m.
in length and 1.5m. high, with the portal stones and a few
stones of the chamber still surviving at the E end.

CATTER HOUSE. *See* p. 321.

DALNAIR HOUSE. *See* p. 356.

FINNICH MALISE. *See* p. 509.

## CROMLIX HOUSE          S 7000
### 1.4km. NW of Kinbuck

By *Brown & Wardrop*, 1874. Built as 'Cromlix Cottage' for Arthur
Hay Drummond, third son of the Earl of Kinnoull. All but the
chapel was destroyed by fire four years later, but rebuilt 1880.
Between 1900 and 1903 the estate was beautifully landscaped
and the house much enlarged to the E and N, incorporating the
residual apsidal chapel which somewhat incongruously projects
E beside a later battlemented entrance porch. The long E front,
rising three storeys to a multi-gabled eaves, terminates in a
Baronial S gable lugged with corbelled rounds above a two-storey
battlemented bow.

In the Morning Room, a white marble classical chimneypiece,
with deep entablature and inner margin of grey marble; Rococo
mirror over. Pilastered walls and two more white marble chimneypieces with swagged architraves and lugged frames in the Green
Room. An hotel since 1981.

The CHAPEL, though no more than a simple oblong with
semicircular E end, has an unexpectedly fine interior. Panelled
dado and plaster walls with stone dressings to the eight small
windows. Floor tiled in diagonal chequerboard pattern of red
and black. Military honours hang from a trussed-rafter roof
fanning around the apsidal sanctuary. – Above the altar, a white
marble PANEL with a Crucifixion scene carved below three
pointed arches. To the l., a stone PISCINA recess, and r. a taller
similar recess, both framed by cusped pointed arches. In the
sanctuary, decorative floor TILES with religious motifs and
texts; by *Campbell Tile Co.*, Stoke-on-Trent, 1883. – ORGAN by
*Rushworth & Dreaper Ltd.*, Liverpool; oak screen and pipes

housed at w end. – All eight windows have STAINED GLASS. On the N side, a Nativity scene, the figure of Sir Galahad commemorating Arthur Hay Drummond †1900, and the Annunciation, 1890. – On the s, Christ rising from the tomb, Sir Bors, and Christ in majesty above a priest at the altar. – Black Watch memorial windows flanking the altar feature SS. George and Andrew.

To the w, viewed from the 1880 wing across a fine lawn, a splendid URN sits on its wreathed plinth among the bushes. – To the s, down a grassed terrace beyond a beech hedge and buttressed retaining wall, is an obelisk SUNDIAL, c. 1630, its shaft and octagonal capital variously indented. Flanking this, two heavily moulded C16 fireplace jambs, late medieval fragments converted to GATEPIERS by the addition of splayed copes and ball finials.

## CULCREUCH CASTLE
1km. NNE of Fintry

Early C16 tower-house, now an hotel, with gabled caphouse, to which a four-storey gabled E wing and NE stair were added in the late C18 by the Glasgow merchant Peter Spiers whose industrial enterprise turned Fintry (q.v.) into a milltown. The conjunction of old and new is orderly but dull. The tower has chequered corbelling at the wallhead, gargoyles draining the parapet walk and rebuilt, less than convincing, battlements. The wing is of matching height, its moulded eaves course coincident with the line of gargoyles. On the s front three bays of windows are tiered regularly, those to the first and second floors taller than those below or above. The entrance door, taking up the bay closest to the tower, has roll-and-hollow-moulded architraves with two weathered panels above. The lower stone, presumably brought to the enlarged Culcreuch from some earlier construction, is carved with the initials IN and ML for John Napier and his wife Margaret Lennox and the date 1721. Windows, similar in size, detail and regularized placing to those of the wing, appear in the s and w walls of the C16 tower, indicating late C18 interference with the original openings. During the C19, further additions of varied length and height were made on the N, creating a U-plan: the E range, possibly by *John Honeyman*, 1879, is crowstepped with a projecting conically capped stair tower. Probably contemporary with this wing is the separate crowstepped range lying E, forming an L-plan court together with the earlier offices provided for the enlarged tower-house.

The castle's interior preserves some original features. The tower's two ground-floor chambers are barrel-vaulted. The Hall continues to occupy the whole of the first floor; though much altered, it retains an ogee-arched aumbry. Its yellow marble fireplace of curvaceous Frenchy design is of the mid C19. On the second floor the s bedroom still has its hand-painted Chinese wallpaper, reputedly brought to the castle in 1723. In the E wing the first-floor apartment, now the guests' dining room, has an ornate plaster ceiling, some richly decorative carving over the door and a white marble fireplace of elegant, strong simplicity; all probably of the mid C19.

Two LODGES mark entrances to the estate from the B822. The N, early C19, is the less traduced; nonetheless its naïve classicism, once rude, has been rendered crude by alteration. – The estate's PARKLAND is the landscape legacy of Peter Spiers. To the S lies a small loch partially enfolded by trees; W and E the woodland thickens, climbing N around the castle. On steep ground behind the house is a pinetum, planted by *A. G. Spiers*, 1842.

## DALMOAK HOUSE    WD *3070*
1.7km. S of Renton

An all but symmetrical castellated Gothic house in stugged sandstone ashlar. Built for the Ulster merchant James Aitken, 1866–9, on the W slopes of the Vale of Leven and since 1989 extensively restored by *John Szwed*. Opened as a nursing home, 1990.

The principal SE front, two high storeys on a battered plinth with mock gunloops, is five broad bays wide. A corbelled crenellated parapet masks the roof. The three central bays project slightly and are lugged by tall battlemented bartizans with round-arched niches. Lower octagonal bartizans cling to the outer corners of the façade. Windows are lintelled, paired and hooded, except at the outer ground-floor bays which have battlemented canted bays. A central porch, round-arched between battlemented octagonal buttresses, shelters approach stairs. Its shaped parapet is heavily carved and bears the patron's monogram JBA. In the spandrels, cable-moulded roundels with more monograms. Rising behind the façade, a tall square tower with a machicolated and crenellated parapet. At its W corner, a still higher octagonal stair turret, battlemented above a shield-on-saltire parapet. NE and SW elevations are identical; five bays deep, two recessing to three. Splayed chimneystacks add to the skyline accents. At the rear, the house's U-plan arrangement is revealed. In the central screen wall, an asymmetrically placed archway gives access to a small inner court.

Dalmoak's lavish interiors have also been restored by *Szwed*. A tripartite entrance screen with etched glass leads to the grand inner HALL. Between scagliola columns with Composite capitals an imperial stair returns to the first-floor gallery. Three tall, round-arched windows with thin colonnette shafts in the jambs and heads light the stair well on the NW. Ceilings are coffered with heavy cornices on paired brackets. Doors with strongly moulded architraves and raised cornices. In the Drawing Room, l. off the Hall, more sumptuous ceiling plasterwork; geometric layout with a deep gorge cornice of acanthus leaves. Scagliola columns. White marble chimneypiece voluptuously encrusted with floral ornament. Opening from the opposite side of the Hall, the Dining Room is more sombre; again, a panelled plaster ceiling, though more classically restrained with egg-and-dart moulding and a heavily dentilled cornice. STAINED GLASS fills the tall staircase windows. Three colourful mythological scenes depict the story of the red hand of Ulster. Various abstract patterns, thistle and acorn borders, armorial panels, monograms and the dates 1868 and 1869 appear.

The former STABLES, 1866–9, lie parallel a short distance NW. U-plan, opening to NE. Symmetrical SE front in square-snecked pink sandstone. Crowstepped gables l. and r. At the centre a smaller crowstepped gable with pigeon-holes. Contemporary single-storey MAINS LODGE, at the entrance to the s drive; more crenellated parapets. The GATEPIERS, too, at the s and N drive entries, have crenellated caps.

*4080*                    DALNAIR HOUSE                    s
                        0.5km. E of Croftamie

Brobdingnagian Baronial by *James Bell*, 1884. An immense mansion intent on bulk yet finely executed in honey-coloured Giffnock sandstone. The familiar forms are here: canted bays corbelled back to gables, mullioned and transomed windows, parapeted corner tower with mandatory engaged turret and battlemented bartizan. Ornament becomes sculpture: strapwork, thistles, a single parapet cannon, pipe-sized roll-mouldings framing windows and doors, and strange leonine creatures clinging to corbelled stringcourses. The house is now a nursing home with a long brick-and-roughcast bedroom wing of 1973, extending W and bay-windowed to enjoy views across the parkland to the s.

*7000*                      DEANSTON                      s

A textile village laid out along the s bank of the River Teith. The first mill was built 1785 but a fire destroyed much of the enterprise in 1796. By the second decade of the C19, serious steps towards industrialized manufacture were being taken under the direction of the mill manager, James Smith (1789–1850). The Teith was controlled by a massive gravity dam, sluices formed and a lade, one of the largest in Scotland, cut to a new spinning mill; four water wheels, each *c*. 11m. in diameter, harnessed the river's power; a weaving shed was constructed and workers' housing built. Not until 1949 did the wheels finally stop turning.

CLOCK TOWER, Teith Road. Village timekeeper with four clock faces; raised in memory of Lady Muir of Deanston †1929. Square-plan shaft constructed in rough red sandstone. Large loopholes formed in each face.

DEANSTON DAM. 1825–6. Diagonal dam faced in sandstone ashlar, built to serve the mill-lade or canal which, separated from the river by a promenade, runs parallel to the s side of the Teith.

DEANSTON DISTILLERY. By *Honeyman, Jack & Robertson*, 1949; altered and extended, 1966-7. Parapeted two-storey offices, warehouses etc. in dull terracotta brick. Glazed brick slot to staircase. The distillery has absorbed and adapted several structures originally part of Deanston Mill (*see* below).

o.5km. SE, on the B8032, is the GATE-LODGE, late C19, again Italianate by *John Burnet & Son*, rising to a low square tower with three-light mullioned and transomed windows under a wide-eaved pyramid roof. Linked r. by a falling crowstepped wall, four GATEPIERS, each topped by four orbs nestling against a squat eight-faced obelisk. Ironwork gate with honey-suckle scrolling and gilded shell-like leaves.

DEANSTON PRIMARY SCHOOL. 1897. Symmetrical gable-fronted classroom block in ochre sandstone. Segmental arches over doorways and mullioned and transomed windows. Central bellcote.

DEANSTON SPINNING MILL. Built 1830-1. Five-storey, attic 123 and basement L-plan structure, nine bays by seven. Tall round-arched ground-floor windows set in channelled ashlar; above, rubble walling with heavy ashlar parapet and cornice. Cast iron columns and beams with jack-arch construction. Single-storey WEAVING SHED, six bays by four, is contemporary. Its twenty-four compartments are vaulted from tall cast iron columns and were originally covered with soil to form a roof garden.

DESCRIPTION. The planned village (described by Garnett in 1800 as 'the new town of Doune', but in truth little more than a single street of workers' houses) lies NW of the mill. Teith Road runs parallel to lade and river. On the r., Nos. 1–7, designated First Division, form a gable-fronted row of flatted rubble cottages, early C19, the upper dwellings reached by stair-flights on leaning brick arches, the lower ones from the opposite, NE, side. Hard to the pavement on the l., Nos. 12–22, 24–34, 36–44 and 46–56; four straight stretches of plain, two-storey-and-attic terraces, early C19, built in dull red sandstone rubble. These, too, are flatted but have close entries. Much has been changed, but not the consistently mechanical cut of the street wall. At the entrance to the village are the later cottages, Nos. 1–7 and 8–11, *c.* 1875, still stone but less urban, almost Arts and Crafts in spirit with Gothic porches and complex, steep-slated gables and hips.

DEANSTON HOUSE. Mill manager's mansion in snecked sandstone, *c.* 1820; extended by *John Burnet & Son*, 1881–3. Since 1988 the house has been a nursing home. Burnet's additions are best, though the aggregated elements remain discrete rather than unified. They have a cultivated Italianate cast: five-storey SE entrance tower with a canted bay corbelled at third-floor level, and a porch with Roman Doric columns *in antis* projecting at its base; massive three-storey drum at the E corner capped by a shallow slated cone; and bow-ended SW conservatory symmetrically flanked by Roman Doric porches. Interiors, by the young *John J. Burnet*, are Classical: the entrance hall doorpieces, for example, are pedimented, dentilled and framed by half-pilasters, a motif drawn from the external treatment of second-floor eaves dormers.

Small burgh on the s bank of the River Carron. By the end of the c18 there was a village here which consisted of a single street (Broad Street) running e from the Parish Church. During the next forty years a parallel street to the n (Herbertshire Street) was laid out and woollen and paper mills established. Later in the c19 the village expanded to the w and an ironworks was founded. The village (together with Dunipace (q.v.) on the other side of the Carron) became a police burgh in 1876.

### CHURCHES

ANTIBURGHER CHURCH, Church Walk. Now Broompark Centre. A short and broad two-storey rubble box built for a short-lived Antiburgher ('Lifter') congregation *c.* 1787 and enlarged for a Burgher congregation in 1817. Some of the openings are round-headed, others rectangular. The n porch is an addition, probably part of *John Burnet*'s alterations of 1881. Shallow rectangular organ chamber at the s end, added in 1910 by *David Clark*.

DENNY BAPTIST CHURCH, Herbertshire Street. Late Gothic, by *J. & A. W. Money*, 1905. A broad and low buttressed rectangle. Gable front of hammer-dressed red sandstone containing a hoodmoulded and ogee-arched four-light window.

OLD PARISH CHURCH, corner of Glasgow Road and Duke Street. Lighthearted Gothick, built in 1812–14 to a design by *Thomas Aitken* who was also contractor for the wright work. Rubble-walled broad box with an e tower. In the w gable, a dummy oculus. The chancel at this end was added in 1927–8 by *J. Jeffrey Waddell & Young*. Across the e gable, an unmoulded stringcourse to suggest a pediment. The tower has a tall bottom stage; clock faces on the intaken and corniced second stage. Paired pointed belfry openings at the top stage which is finished with a battlement breaking out into pyramid-finialled bartizans at the corners. Inside the battlement, a slated octagonal spire. Projecting from the e front of the tower, a semi-octagonal stair turret of 1927–8.

Inside, the character is predominantly of 1927–8 when *J. Jeffrey Waddell & Young* removed the n and w galleries, provided a new e gallery and added the w chancel, its entrance a pointed stone arch, its flooring of green and white marble squares. Decoratively boarded ceiling over the nave, probably of 1838 when the church was 'beautified internally'.\* Panelled coomb wood ceiling over the chancel. – Simple but well-detailed late Gothic FURNISHINGS of 1927–8. – On the s side of the chancel,

\* According to the *New Statistical Account of Scotland* (1845).

ORGAN, *c.* 1900. – On the chancel's W wall, a REREDOS of 1960, with a sub-Lorimerian oak cornice above a hanging of Spanish *appliqué* cloth of *c.* 1600. – STAINED GLASS. Three-light W window (the Ascension) of 1928, an example of brightly coloured realism. – At the E stair to the gallery, three lights (the Nativity of Our Lord), modernistic by *Sadie McLellan*, *c.* 1970. – Also in the stair turret, a BELL bearing the date 1630 and the initials IM.

ST ALEXANDER (R.C.), Stirling Street. Built in 1890. Gothic of a generally unambitious kind but, in the front (S) gable, a weird gallery window of three lights, the taller centre opening with two tiers of nook-shafts. A SE jamb is provided by the parsonical Jacobean clergy house of 1871. The church's W aisle was extended N by four bays as part of *Joseph McKay*'s additions of 1932–3 which also provided the E aisle (curtailed because of the clergy house) and N sanctuary.

The interior is unbalanced by the aisles being of different lengths. They open into the nave through pointed arches springing from octagonal pillars. Broad pointed arch from the nave into the semi-octagonal N sanctuary whose walls are panelled with marble. – STAINED GLASS. In the sanctuary a strongly coloured round window (the Crucifixion) of *c.* 1900 flanked by contemporary pointed lights (St Patrick and St Alexander).

WESTPARK CHURCH, Duke Street. Originally Denny West United Free Church. By *James Strang*, 1898–1900. Broad Gothic box, the slated roof topped by a red tile ridge. Lancet windows in the buttressed sides whose masonry is of squared buff-coloured sandstone. The front (S) gable is of hammer-dressed red sandstone. In it, small vestibule windows with cusping in their pointed heads. Above, a pair of hoodmoulded cusped lights, their aprons panelled with blind arcading. Two-storey SW porch, its S entrance under a gablet. At the outer corner of the porch, an octagonal bell turret. Low SE porch now serving as a link to the extensive HALLS complex added by *Honeyman, Jack & Robertson*, 1979. Grey blockwork walls broken by tall vertical windows.

## CEMETERY
### Broad Street

Late Victorian cemetery laid out around and on top of several small hills; plenty of shrubs and trees including monkey-puzzles. On a hill at the E end, the WAR MEMORIAL by *G. H. Paulin*, 1922, a bronze figure of Victory.

## PUBLIC BUILDINGS

DENNY HIGH SCHOOL, Shanks Avenue. By *Alison & Hutchison & Partners*, 1957–9. Flat-roofed, with an exposed concrete frame and curtain walling. Low NE, NW and S additions by *Campbell & Arnott*, 1969.

NETHERMAINS PRIMARY SCHOOL, Bulloch Crescent. By the

Stirling County Architect, *A. J. Smith*, 1972. Sensible, with rendered walls and a flat roof.

PARISH COUNCIL OFFICES, No. 107 Stirling Street. Now in other use. By *Ebenezer Simpson*, 1910. Villa-like Jacobean, with lugged architraves to the windows (some corniced) and a heavy rusticated and corniced doorpiece. At the l. bay of the front, a gablet crowned by a ball finial; a crescent finial on the gable of the slightly advanced r. bay.

POLICE STATION, Broad Street. Plain Jacobean, by *Ebenezer Simpson*, 1908.

TOWN HOUSE, Glasgow Road. By *James Strang & Wilson*, 1930–1. Squared-up but asymmetrical Baronial, with crowstepped gables, an oriel window and a saddleback-roofed tower.

### DESCRIPTION

GLASGOW ROAD, the entry from the s, contains respectable but unexciting late Victorian and Edwardian villas. Among them, on the w side, the former DENNY IRON WORKS OFFICES, by *James Strang*, 1914. Single-storey Neo-Georgian, of red brick with dressings of polished buff sandstone. Balustraded E front of three broad bays, the entrance at the pedimented centre recessed behind Roman Doric columns *in antis*. In the outer bays, three-light windows with lugged architraves. A little further N, on the E side, the Town House (*see* Public Buildings, above). Opposite, No. 40 Glasgow Road, a conventional enough villa by *James Strang & Wilson*, 1933, but with Art Deco detailing on the rendered front. After the very plain late C19 short terrace at Nos. 30–38, the BINGO AND SOCIAL CLUB built as a cinema in 1938 by *Speirs Ltd.*, with a stepped front gable. At the N end of Glasgow Road, on the corner of Duke Street but set back on a small hill, the Old Parish Church (*see* Churches, above).

BROAD STREET leads E. At its start, plain C19 terraced buildings. Further E, the Police Station (*see* Public Buildings, above). In HERBERTSHIRE STREET, the next street N, Denny Baptist Church (*see* Churches, above).

DUKE STREET continues the line of Broad Street w past the Old Parish Church. On the street's N side and extending N along the w side of Stirling Street, a large development of flats over shops, by *Wilson & Wilson*, 1966–72. It is undecided whether to be Neo-Georgian or embrace the Modern Movement. More firmly anchored in a post-Festival of Britain manner is the two-storey octagon of brown brick and render, its copper roof rising into a spire, which projects at the sw corner. In CHURCH WALK, w of this development, the former Antiburgher Church (*see* Churches, above). On the w corner of Church Walk and Duke Street, the villa-like CLYDESDALE BANK, by *William Railton*, 1866, in a lighthearted Jacobethan manner. Further w, set well back behind a front garden, its centre occupied by a monkey-puzzle, is BROOMPARK (No. 30 Duke Street). It was built in the earlier C19 as a two-storey three-bay villa. At the centre of the droved ashlar front, an anta-pilastered doorpiece; at the outer bays, first-floor windows set in roundheaded overarches which rise through the wallhead cornice into gablets. The house was altered *c.* 1900 when mullioned and transomed bay windows were added at the outer bays, the gablets given consoled and jettied bargeboarded tops, and the centre window of the first floor enlarged. To the w, Westpark Parish Church (*see* Churches, above).

STIRLING STREET carries the line of Glasgow Road N. Its E side, facing the development on the corner of Duke Street (*see* above), is mostly occupied by two-storey buildings of the mid and later C19 and C20 containing housing above shops. Then the street turns to the w. On the corner, St Alexander's Church (*see* Churches, above). Further w, on the s side, the former Parish Council Offices at No. 107 (*see* Public Buildings, above). Then Stirling Street turns again to the N. On its E side, the ashlar-fronted No. 146 (BURNFOOT HOUSE) of *c.* 1840, the windows rather narrow, the doorpiece skinnily pilastered and corniced. At the end, on the w, the ROYAL OAK HOTEL, 'restored' in 1883 when it acquired its Jacobean character.

## DENNYLOANHEAD
F 8080

Village which developed from the early C19.

ANTIBURGHER CHURCH, Denny Road and Bonnybridge Road. Secularized. Built in 1815 on the site of a church of 1743 (the dates recorded on a weathered roundel at the centre of the E side); the architects were *Robert & Mark Shearer*. Broad harled box with tall pointed windows and, at the s end of the w side, two tiers of rectangular windows marking the former position of a gallery. Bellcote on the s gable; it looks a mid-C19 addition. Piend-roofed two-storey session house of 1840 at the s end. The N chancel was added by *J. Jeffrey Waddell* in 1932 when the interior was recast.

On the s, remains of a small graveyard. At its s side, classical MONUMENT to the Rev. James Stark †1850, a tall battered pedestal surmounted by an urn.

MUIRHEAD MEMORIAL HALL, Denny Road. By *Edmiston*, 1893. Jacobean, with mullioned and transomed windows and a sturdy gabled porch.

The VILLAGE is rather scattered, composed of houses of the mid and later C19, with C20 housing to the N. In DENNY ROAD, opposite the Antiburgher Church (*see* above), the piend-roofed former UNITED PRESBYTERIAN MANSE, by *Black*, 1851. Three-bay ashlar front, with cornices over the ground-floor windows and a pilastered doorpiece.

## DOLLAR
C 9090

Small town founded as a burgh of barony in 1702, the earliest development taking place around High Street. From the early C19 it grew as a one-company town, the company being Dollar Academy

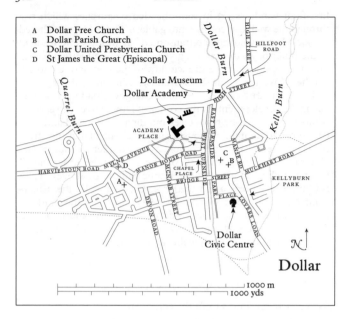

A   Dollar Free Church
B   Dollar Parish Church
C   Dollar United Presbyterian Church
D   St James the Great (Episcopal)

Dollar Museum
Dollar Academy

ACADEMY
PLACE

HARVIESTOUN ROAD   MYLNE AVENUE   MANOR HOUSE ROAD

CHAPEL
PLACE

BRIDGE

A

DEVON ROAD   BRIDGE STREET

WEST BURNSIDE   EAST BURNSIDE   HIGH STREET

C
B

MANSE ROAD   MUCKHART ROAD

KELLYBURN
PARK

PLACE   LOVERS LOAN

Dollar
Civic Centre

Quarrel Burn

Dollar Burn

HIGH STREET

HILLFOOT
ROAD

Kelly Burn

N

**Dollar**

1000 m
1000 yds

whose academic reputation attracted families and whose former
pupils, in surprising numbers, chose to retire here.


### CHURCHES

DOLLAR FREE CHURCH, Harviestoun Road. Secularized. Broad
   dumpy Gothic edifice by *Robert Hay*, 1858, enlarged in 1864.
   Nave flanked by double-pitch roofed aisles; barely projecting
   W transepts. Three-light Geometrical window in the main E
   gable.
DOLLAR PARISH CHURCH, Bridge Street. Unarchaeological
   Gothic of 1840–2, by *William Tite* of London, his design amended
   by *Robertson*, builder in Dollar. A tall building, originally T-plan
   consisting of a nave, N transepts and S tower. The main walling
   is of stugged ashlar above a base of broached ashlar. Broached
   ashlar also at the turrets, parapets and much of the upper part
   of the tower; window and door surrounds of polished ashlar. At
   the gables, uncrenellated parapets aligned with the roof pitches;
   battlemented octagonal turrets at the corners. In the side walls
   of the three-bay nave and the S walls of the transepts, two-light
   Y-traceried windows, hoodmoulded like all the openings. In the
   gable of each transept, a window of three stepped lancet lights.
   Small windows in the N walls of the transepts.
      At the tower, angle buttresses of broached ashlar. In the S
   front of the lower stage, a tall two-light window. Tall belfry above,
   its walling of broached ashlar, the two-light openings set in
   rectangular overarches with arcaded tops. The tower is finished

with a corbelled-out battlement. The tower's entrances are in the E and W sides, each under a cusped single light. The E entrance is still visible externally but the W was overlaid in 1964–5 by a battlemented porch (by *D. A. Flett*) which, although it tries hard to be in keeping, should not be here; a balancing porch on the E side was intended but not executed. Less obtrusive are the very short chancel and adjacent organ chamber added to the N end by *J. Jeffrey Waddell*, 1925. N of the chancel, a battlemented low vestry and session house.

Inside, the nave and transepts are covered by a plaster ceiling of plain late Georgian Perp character. Stone chancel arch of 1925–6. Over the chancel, a wooden wagon roof. – GALLERIES with free Jacobean detail were erected at the S end in 1862 and in the transepts in 1875. – In the nave, boxy PEWS, probably of 1843. – The Lorimerian late Gothic PULPIT on the W side of the chancel arch and the CHANCEL PANELLING, COMMUNION TABLE and STALLS (with Celtic interlaced decoration) are all of 1925–6, designed by *Waddell*. – On the E side of the chancel arch, a FONT of alabaster and marbles. It was erected here in 1926 but looks late Victorian. – ORGAN on the W side of the chancel, by *Rushworth & Dreaper*, 1926. – STAINED GLASS. In the E wall, a modern realist two-light window (St Columba and St Mungo) by the *St Enoch Glass Studios*, 1949. – In the W wall, another two-light window (Acts of Mercy), by *Douglas Hogg*, 1985, with strongly coloured small scenes, the realism very stylized. – N window of the chancel (the Baptism of Our Lord; the Sower; the Reaper) by *A. Ballantine & Son*, erected in the original N window in 1910 and re-erected here in 1926. – In the E wall of the chancel, a two-light window (Our Lord and Women) designed by *Jennifer Campbell* and *Adam Robson*, 1975, strong blues the dominant colours.

GRAVEYARD. At its NW corner, the roofless FORMER PARISH CHURCH, designed and built by *James Kirk* in 1774–5, the date of completion affirmed by a stone in the centre of the S side. It is rectangular, built of large roughly droved rubble blocks. Symmetrical S front of four bays with rectangular doors at the ends; at each of the centre bays, a roundheaded window, its inner half carried down as a low door (one presumably intended to be used by the minister). On the W gable, a birdcage BELLCOTE with keystoned roundheaded arches and a ball-finialled ogee roof. High up in this gable, a rectangular window. Windowless E gable. At the ends of the N wall, ruined forestairs to gallery doors. The interior used to have galleries at the ends and along the N wall. – SW of the former Parish Church, a rubble-walled and pantile-roofed SESSION HOUSE, with moulded skewputts; it is probably late C18.

HEADSTONES. S of the centre of the former Parish Church, a large stone, its curly top carved with the dates and initials '17TD HR37/17TD MT67'; below, two panels, the l. bearing a skull and crossbones, the r. with implements including a plough. – SE of this, a stone to Sophia Ballanden, dated 1719. The front again has two panels, the l. showing a skull, the r. a recumbent hourglass. – A little to the E, a stone whose W face bears well preserved reliefs of an hourglass, crossbones, harrow and plough. On the E face, the date 1759 and an angel's head (the soul) above the inscription:

CONFIDE.NOT.READER.IN.THY.YOUTH
OR.STRENGTH.BUT.MORE.THEN.BOTH
THE.PRESENT.MOMENT.PRIZE.
GRAVES.HERE.SURROUND.THEE.OF
EACH.BREADETH.&.LENGTH.AND.THOU.
MAY'ST.BE (PERHAPS) THE.NIXT.THAT.DIES.

– N of this, another well preserved stone, dated 1738. In its segmental pediment, the initials IH IL and an angel's head. Below, a shield flanked by attached columns of no recognized order. – E of this, a stone with an angel's head above the date 1763 and the initials WR and IS on the E face; on the W face, a weaver's shuttle and stretcher, and an hourglass and crossbones. – To its S, an C18 stone buried except for its curvy top which contains an angel's head carved in exceptionally high relief. – Further S, a small stone of 1712 to TC and ML, its E face carved with a crude but well preserved skull, hourglass, crossbones and heart. – Immediately E, a much larger stone of 1727, the W face bearing an hourglass and crossbones, the E two shouldered round-arched panels, with a skull on the space between. – Just to the SE, a stone of 1725 commemorating the Leslie children, with scales carved below the r. inscription panel of the W face; on the E face, two panels, one with an hourglass, the other with cross-bones. – To the E, another C18 stone displaying reminders of death.

DOLLAR UNITED PRESBYTERIAN CHURCH, East Burnside. Now a hall. By *Neil Macara* of Darlington, 1876–7. Buttressed Gothic rectangle, the side walls and E gable of rubble, the W front of stugged squared masonry. Lancet windows in the sides. At the front, a slightly advanced broad centre containing the double entrance, its paired arches sharing a fat centre column, the hoodmould's label stops carved with foliaged knots; above the entrance, a big rose window. On the N side of this centre-piece, a narrow 'aisle', its outer corner diagonally buttressed; cusped head to the pointed window, its label stops again foliaged knots. S of the centrepiece, a steeple. At the first stage of the diagonally buttressed square tower, windows like those in the front of the N 'aisle'. Narrow rectangular windows with cham-fered margins at the second stage. Above, broaching under the octagonal belfry stage, its tall pointed openings rising into gablets. Octagonal spire covered with purplish slates crossed by bands of green fish-scale slating.

ST JAMES THE GREAT (Episcopal), Harviestoun Road. By *Thomas Frame & Son*, 1879–82. Simple lancet Gothic, built of hammer-dressed and squared Dunmore stone. Sturdily buttressed nave, its proportions relatively tall and narrow, and a lower semi-octagonal-ended chancel, also buttressed. A steeple was intended but not built. In the nave's W gable, a window of three nook-shafted lights, the arch of the tall centre opening extravagantly stilted. The high-set windows of the chancel are all sexfoils contained in stumpily nook-shafted pointed overarches. On the s side of the chancel, a vestry added in 1934. sw porch by *Colin Campbell*, 1957, its front of stone, the sides of wood and glass, the roof shallow-pitched.

Inside, wooden pointed tunnel vaults over both nave and chancel, the nave roof stained, the chancel roof painted and with thicker and more closely spaced transverse ribs. The pointed chancel arch springs from attached shafts rising from corbels. Another arch (blocked) from the chancel into an organ chamber to the s. – At the w end, an octagonal FONT by *Jones & Willis*, 1884. It is of Caen stone, the faces bearing sacred emblems and the arms of the diocese of St Andrews, Dunkeld and Dunblane. – The SEATING is now provided by chairs. – Simple Gothic wooden PULPIT by *Nicholl* of Alloa, *c.* 1939. – Stumpily arcaded wooden ALTAR RAILS of 1886.

STAINED GLASS. The three sanctuary windows (the Nativity, Ascension and Baptism of Our Lord) are by *J. & W. Guthrie & Andrew Wells Ltd.*, 1915. Dark-coloured scenes set against pale quarries. – In the N wall of the nave, the colourful w window (St Andrew) was erected *c.* 1975 but it looks late C19 and presumably was imported from elsewhere. – In the s wall of the nave, the E window (St Philip) by *James Powell & Sons*, 1909, is paler and more sophisticated. – Beside it, a rather garishly realistic window (Our Lord and Little Children) by *Margaret Chilton*, 1949. – In the vestry, s window (St James) by *J. &. W. Guthrie & Andrew Wells Ltd.*, 1934, realistic and darkly coloured.

## PUBLIC BUILDINGS

DOLLAR ACADEMY, Academy Place, Manor House Road and Mylne Avenue. Greek Revival main building set in parkland, with later ancillary buildings in a variety of styles.

The Dollar Academy (originally Institution) was founded under the will of Captain John McNabb †1802 who had made a fortune as a London merchant and left £60,000 to endow 'a charity or school for the poor of the parish of Dollar wheir I was born'. After some years of dispute as to what should be established it was decided to build 'a great Academy and Seminary of Education' for the children of the parish and, in order 'to improve their manners and affect a new stimulus to exertion in prosecuting their studies', to admit to it also fee-paying boarders. The school was built in 1818–21. Since 1979 it has been solely a private institution.

At the centre of the complex is the PLAYFAIR BLOCK, the first 98 and by far the largest of the school buildings, by *W. H. Playfair*, 1818–21, extended by *John Burnet* in 1867–8 and reconstructed by *Watson, Salmond & Gray* after a fire, 1961–5. Originally rectangular, *c.* 56.7m. by 19.2m., of two storeys, built of broached Sheardale ashlar. Principal (sw) front of seventeen bays. The three bays at each end are slightly advanced behind attached unfluted Doric columns standing on a heavy base. Plain entablature and parapet which are continued across the three-bay links.

Slightly advanced centrepiece of five bays with a pedimented
hexastyle Doric portico (the columns again unfluted) surmounting a flight of shallow steps. The entrance's simplified Neo-
Georgian surround is an embellishment, perhaps of 1931 when
the panelled double-leaf bronze door was introduced.

The NW and SE elevations are identical except for the clock
added to the frieze of the SE. Each is of five bays, the ends
unbroken by openings. Three-bay centrepiece with attached
Doric columns, the broader centre bay containing an entrance
under a semicircular fanlight and a three-light first-floor window.

The rear (NE) elevation was originally a plain version of the
front, again with its centre and ends advanced but without
attached columns or portico. *Burnet*'s NE wing projects from
the centre, with Doric pilasters between its first-floor windows.
Following the fire in 1961 porches were added in the inner
angles and the wing extended in utilitarian fashion.

All the C19 interiors were destroyed by the fire, including
Playfair's centrally placed library which separated the boys' and
girls' classrooms either side. The ensuing reconstruction by
*Watson, Salmond & Gray*, 1961–5, provided three floors (the
top lit from the roof) within the shell. A new library was constructed on the site of the original and, like Playfair's, it is of two
storeys and Greek cross on plan, the central square covered by
a pendentived saucer dome. But Playfair's giant Ionic columns
marking off the limbs were not reproduced. Instead, the limbs
are now marked off by rectangular openings at the lower level
and walled off at the upper although the centre bay of each side
is framed by a giant roundheaded overarch, its pilasters' fluted
capitals bearing acanthus leaf decoration, within which is an
upper-floor window with a heavy architrave surmounted by the
school's coat of arms. The effect is more Neo-Baroque than
Greek Revival.

Attached to the NE corner of the Playfair Block is the GIBSON
BUILDING (music department and auditorium) by *The Law &
Dunbar-Nasmith Partnership*, 1991, lightweight-looking, with
broad-eaved ribbed metal roofs. – N of the Playfair Block but set
back from its building line, the SCIENCE AND DOMESTIC
BLOCK by *Rowand Anderson & Balfour Paul*, 1910, the harled
walls enlivened by pink sandstone dressings. Queen Anne, with
segmental-pedimented wooden dormers and an ogee-roofed
cupola. At the S front, an Ionic pilastered doorpiece topped by
a panelled pedestal which forms the base of a first-floor window
framed in a lugged architrave, its bottom corners scrolled, topped
by a segmental pediment. Utilitarian N extensions by *Hughes &
Waugh*, 1953, and *D. S. R. Waugh & Associates*, 1957–8, enlivened
by the addition of an extra floor in 1998. – NE of this, the
YOUNGER BUILDING (business, computing and mathematics
centre) by *Law & Dunbar-Nasmith*, 1995, with a broad-eaved
roof of ribbed metal.

SW of the Playfair Block and centred on its front, the WAR
MEMORIAL of 1922 by *G. H. Paulin*, a bronze of scantily clad
'Youth' offering itself as a sacrifice. The memorial stands on the

SE side of the present main drive which runs up to the school at a slightly oblique angle from Mylne Avenue to the SW. At the end of the drive, a GATEWAY erected in 1866 when this approach was formed. Cast iron gates, those of the carriage entrance set between block-pedimented piers. These are joined by convex dwarf walls (now deprived of their railings) to pedimented gateways containing the pedestrian entrances. To the SE, another GATEWAY at the top of McNabb Street. This is of *c.* 1820, the drive again obliquely angled on the front of the Playfair Block. Pyramid-topped gatepiers, those of the carriage entrance topped by lamps; the piers of the pedestrian gates are lower and linked by lintels. Another GATEWAY of similar design but of 1907 to the E at the head of Cairnpark Street. E of the Playfair Block and aligned diagonally on its SE end, the GATEWAY of *c.* 1910 from Academy Street. It is of similar design to the McNabb Street entrance but without the lintels joining the gatepiers of the pedestrian entrance and with all the piers of the same height.

The other school buildings are strung round the periphery of the parkland. Beside the Cairnpark Street entrance, the former DOLLAR BOARD SCHOOL, by *J. R. Baldie*, 1888. Tall single-storey block, built of stugged ashlar. At the W front, slightly advanced and pedimented ends containing five-light windows with Roman Doric pilaster-mullions; four-light window at the centre. – Behind the Playfair Block, the IONA BUILDING (home economics centre) by *Law & Dunbar-Nasmith*, 1995–6. Single-storey, with a few modish Postmodern touches. – To its NE, the PREPARATORY SCHOOL by *William Kerr* and *John Gray* of *John Melvin & Son*, 1936–7. Harled and pantile-roofed, with large metal-framed windows. Additions of 1997–8. – To its NW, beside the N boundary wall, an early C19 single-storey piend-roofed house, its walls built of large squared blocks of masonry. E front originally of three bays, the centre slightly advanced; hood-moulded doors and low windows. A fourth (N) bay appears an addition but cannot be much later. – Some way to the W, a harled and red-tiled GIRLS' PAVILION of 1953. – Beside it, the GAMES HALL of 1970. – A little further W, the ATHLETICS PAVILION, by *Hugh Dalrymple*, 1908. English picturesque, with a cupola on the red-tiled roof. It was extended in 1954. – Just outside the grounds, on the SW side of Mylne Road, the SWIMMING POOL AND DINING HALL COMPLEX, by *Honeyman, Jack & Robertson*, 1975–9.

DOLLAR CIVIC CENTRE, Park Place. By *Clackmannan District Council*, 1996. Octagonal, with blockwork walls. Ribbed metal roof topped by a large cupola, its sides glazed to provide clear-storey lighting.

DOLLAR MUSEUM, High Street. Built as a woollen mill, 1820, and converted to a hall in the late C19 when the top floor was removed and the windows of the ground and first floors were joined as tall vertical openings. These openings were partly built up in 1991 when the building was adapted to house a museum on the ground floor with flats above.

DESCRIPTION

MUCKHART ROAD is the approach from the E. At its start, on the
N, BURNBRAE LODGE, a stolid Georgian survival villa with a
heavy Roman Doric portico and very shallow rectangular bay
windows. Beside it, the discreetly sited THE OSTLERS, a single-
storey house by *Andrew Whalley* and *Fiona Galbraith*, 1990. Stone
walls and a shallow-pitched slated pavilion roof with a massive
array of skylights; fully glazed N wall overlooking the garden. A
sturdy rubble-built single-span BRIDGE, probably of the mid
C19, carries the road over the Kelly Burn. Then, on the S, THE
PINES, a white harled Lorimer-Scots style villa by *William Kerr*
and *John Gray* of *John Melvin & Son*, 1938. On the N, a double
villa (Nos. 7–9) of *c.* 1865. Two-storey canted bay windows
project from the slightly advanced gabled ends. Further on, on
the corner of Manse Road, another double villa (GLADSTONE
TERRACE, Nos. 1–3 Muckhart Road) of *c.* 1870. Sizeable but
dour despite its bargeboards and pyramidal-roofed low corner
tower. Large monkey-puzzle tree in the garden.
MANSE ROAD'S E side kicks off with a couple of mid-Victorian
villas, No. 2 with block-pedimented shallow rectangular bay
windows and a pilastered and pedimented doorpiece; at the upper
floor the outer windows rise into bargeboarded gabled dormerheads. At No. 4, carved bargeboards. On the W side, the graveyard of Dollar Parish Church (*see* Churches, above). N of the
graveyard, the former PARISH MANSE (now ST COLUMBA'S
HOUSE), the two-storey main block designed and built by
*Adam Turnbull* in 1794–5 but altered and extended to the rear
in the later C19.
BRIDGE STREET continues the line of Muckhart Road. On the N,
Dollar Parish Church (*see* Churches, above). On the S, between
Kellyburn Park and Lovers Loan, the broad-eaved No. 1
(SEBERHAM) of the earlier C19. Single-storey and attic main
block with bowed dormers; horizontal-paned glazing in the
windows. On the W side of LOVERS LOAN, a segmental-arched
GATEWAY with a roll-and-hollow moulding and a ball finial.
It looks C17. Round the corner in PARK PLACE, the Dollar
Civic Centre (*see* Public Buildings, above).
     W of Lovers Loan, on the S side of Bridge Street, Nos. 3–5 of
*c.* 1870, the ground floor occupied by a corniced shopfront;
the windows of the upper floor have segmental-arched lights.
There follows the villa-like CLYDESDALE BANK, piend-roofed
Italianate of *c.* 1870. On the N side of the street, Nos. 2–4, a
mid-Victorian double villa, the cornices over the ground-floor
openings and the mutuled main cornice Georgian survival but
the windows are two-light. Also mid-Victorian is No. 6 but the
walling is of reddish rubble and there are bargeboarded gabled
dormers. Next door, a harled cottage (No. 8), probably of the early
C19 but altered; a rope-moulded club skewputt at the E gable.
EAST and WEST BURNSIDE flank the Dollar Burn. At their
intersection with Bridge Street, a plain rubble BRIDGE of one
segmental arch across the burn; it was built in 1805. At the E

end of the bridge, a small square CLOCK TOWER built in 1912 as a monument to Dr William Spence. It is of hammer-dressed grey granite, a tall slit opening in each face; corbelled but uncrenellated parapet. In East Burnside, on the N corner with Bridge Street, No. 1 (BROOKSIDE), a mid-C19 bay-windowed villa (now harled), with bargeboards and horizontal-paned windows. Of similar date and *cottage orné* type is No. 2 to the N but its roughly squared masonry is left exposed. Then the former Dollar United Presbyterian Church (*see* Churches, above). To its N, the gable-ended No. 4 East Burnside is the former PARISH SCHOOL built *c*. 1780 and given an upper floor in 1800 by *James Dickson*, mason, and *Alexander Paterson*, wright. It is of sneck-harled rubble, with a pantiled roof; single-storey porch at the w end. In front, a cast iron PROVOST'S LAMP-POST of Victorian design presented to the burgh of Dollar in 1932. N of this, a second segmental-arched rubble BRIDGE over the Dollar Burn; it was built by *Beattie & Armstrong* in 1819. Then, No. 5 East Burnside, a single-storey and attic villa of *c*. 1860, its gableted dormers with carved bargeboards; one architraved and corniced window and one canted bay window flank the pilastered doorpiece. No. 6 is also of one storey and an attic but of *c*. 1835 with triangular bay windows and bowed dormers containing horizontal panes. Next, a double house (Nos. 7–8) dated 1870. Shallow rectangular bay windows and shouldered-arched doors with Jacobean hoodmoulds; over the first-floor windows, gableted dormerheads with fretted bargeboards. Another double villa at Nos. 9–10 but dourer and probably a little later; elliptical-headed first-floor windows and bargeboarded gables. More bargeboards on the plain late C19 No. 11. At the N end of East Burnside, three late C19 villas (Nos. 12–14), No. 13 with hood-moulded ground-floor windows and carved bargeboards. At the end of East Burnside, a third segmental-arched rubble BRIDGE over the Dollar Burn; it is probably early C19 like the other two.

HIGH STREET leads uphill to the E from East Burnside's N end. At its start, on the N side, the Dollar Museum (*see* Public Buildings, above). On the s side, No. 2 of *c*. 1840 with a corniced entrance. The adjoining single-storey No. 4 is late C20 behind a mid-C19 harled front whose vernacular character is continued at the rendered cottages of Nos. 6–8. Opposite these, on the N, Nos. 11–13 (MOUNT FORBES), a double house of 1909. Georgian survival rather than revival but with two-light windows. The long two-storey double house with rope-moulded skewputts at Nos. 15–17 is dated 1806 but the heavy console-corniced doorpiece on No. 17 looks a mid-C19 addition. Further up, High Street is mostly a mixture of mid-C19 vernacular and late C20 housing but the harled and pantile-roofed No. 32 on the s is dated 1799 on the lintel of a door (now window) in the gable. On the NW corner with Hillfoots Road, No. 37 High Street (THE TOWER), a tall two-storey villa with pacific Baronial detail, erected in 1867 by *Peter Sinclair*, an Edinburgh builder, who may have designed it; conical-roofed and weathervaned round tower containing the entrance. Returning downhill along

HILLFOOTS ROAD, on the NW side, vernacular housing of the late C18 and earlier C19; club skewputts on one early C19 cottage (No. 11). At the road's SW junction with High Street, a pair of harled and crowstep-gabled early C18 two-storey houses, the larger (No. 1) of three bays with a rustic Victorian porch, No. 3 with uncomfortably new-looking pantiles.

WEST BURNSIDE starts unpromisingly at the N end with small mid-C20 houses. They are followed by the early C19 No. 24 (BURNSIDE HOUSE), a villa of two storeys over a sunk basement, built of big blocks of rubble. Large chimneystacks at the ends of the piended roof. Over the door, a shallow block pediment supported on simplified consoles. To the S, beside the Dollar Burn, a small grey and red granite DRINKING FOUNTAIN topped by a cast iron column. It was erected c. 1890 and stands at the E end of the axis of ACADEMY PLACE whose W end is focused on the diagonally set SE end of Dollar Academy (see Public Buildings, above), this axial but not head-on view a gently picturesque touch. Each side of Academy Place consisted originally of three identical villas, the E two fronting the street, the W looking into the grounds of the Academy. They are linked by walls separating their front and back gardens and were designed by W. H. Playfair in 1819 to house masters at Dollar Academy. Each villa is of two storeys, with a mutuled cornice under the eaves of its piended roof. Three-bay fronts of broached grey ashlar; over the doors, consoled block pediments like that of Burnside House. The three N villas are now joined by rear additions. The W villa on the S side was altered and extended in the late C20.

s of Academy Place West Burnside continues with rubble garden walls flanking the entry to MANOR HOUSE ROAD. Here, on the N side, buildings belonging to Dollar Academy (see Public Buildings, above); on the S, the back gardens of houses in Chapel Place.

CHAPEL PLACE's N side starts at the E end with a plain piend-roofed early C19 house (No. 1), its front built of roughly droved ashlar. Next door is PARK HOUSE of 1822, also of two storeys and three bays but unsophisticated, the front faced with large blocks of rubble and the roof straight-gabled. Scrolled and rope-moulded skewputts; pilastered and corniced doorpiece. It is followed by a concrete-tile-roofed single-storey early C19 cottage (No. 5), originally of three bays but extended to the W and rear in the C20. Opposite, on the S side of the street, the STRATHALLAN HOTEL of c. 1860. A stylistic mixture, with pilasters at the ground floor, roundheaded Italianate first-floor windows and bracketed broad eaves. Further W, on the N side, Nos. 9–11, an early C19 harled two-storey double house which presents a two-bay piend-roofed gable to the street. In the gable, three-light windows, those of the ground floor set in corniced shallow rectangular bays. On the S, Nos. 16–18, a plain five-bay double house of the earlier C19.

s of Chapel Place, West Burnside continues with No. 21, a single-storey and attic house of c. 1840 with bowed dormers.

The bay-windowed additions at the ends are slightly later. Mid-
C19 piend-roofed Georgian survival at Nos. 18–19 and a contemporary cottage with bowed dormers at No. 17. There follows a
long garden wall leading to Bridge Street.

BRIDGE STREET's corner block (Nos. 12–14) with West Burnside
is of 1829. Two storeys, the E and S elevations faced with ashlar,
polished at the ground floor and broached above. Bowed quadrant corner set between open-pedimented gables, the main
gable to West Burnside having orderless pilaster strips, the S
gable being the slightly advanced E bay of the front to Bridge
Street. On the S corner of Bridge Street and West Burnside, the
harled CASTLE CAMPBELL HOTEL, probably of c. 1810 in
origin but its two-light and canted bay windows date from a
reconstruction of c. 1860. W of this, Bridge Street contains a
mixture of houses and shops with flats above, all of the early to
mid C19. Fluted panels on the friezes of the doorpieces of Nos. 15,
31 and 52; rosettes on that of No. 26.

MCNABB STREET runs N from Bridge Street. Villas on its E side.
SPEEDWELL is early C19, with a broached ashlar front, the
windows containing horizontal panes; scalloped valances under
the broad eaves of the piended roof. Beside it, the Georgian
survival No. 9 built for a joiner, James Baillie, in 1860, with two-
light windows, the ground-floor openings surmounted by heavily
consoled cornices. To its N, at Nos. 3–5, a two-storey double
house (ALBION VILLAS) of the later C19. Full-height canted
bay windows at the centre; tall cast iron balconies under the
first-floor windows of the outer bays. No. 1 is of the mid C19, a
two-storey bay window projecting at the advanced N end of
the front; Jacobean hoodmoulds over the other ground-floor
openings.

BRIDGE STREET W of McNabb Street is taken over by villas. On
the N, No. 70 of the earlier C19 with a pilastered doorpiece.
To its W, MITCHELL COURT by *Keir & Fraser*, 1995–7. Two-  119
storey and attic front block in an accomplished Postmodern
manner although its classical allusions refer more to the Neo-
Egyptian work of James Playfair than to the Greek Revival of his
nephew W. H. Playfair, the architect of Dollar Academy. On the
S side of the street, a Jacobean double villa (DEWAR HOUSE)
of the earlier C19. Another double villa of the same design (Nos.
1–3 Devon Road) facing W on the corner of DEVON ROAD. On
the N side of Bridge Street, facing down Devon Road, the early
C19 No. 86. Broached ashlar front, rosettes on the corniced
doorpiece.

W of Devon Road the main road turns to the NW and becomes
HARVIESTOUN ROAD. On its SW corner, the former Dollar
Free Church (*see* Churches, above). On the NE side, a terrace of
early C19 houses. The first (No. 2) is single-storey with an attic,
the dormers Victorian additions. The rough ashlar stonework of
its front nudges into the corner of the terrace's smarter continuation at Nos. 4–8 Harviestoun Road (CHARLOTTE PLACE) of
c. 1820, a symmetrical two-storey broached ashlar front of nine
bays at the ground floor but only six above. Then, No. 10, a

single-storey piend-roofed villa of *c.* 1840 with a pilastered and cornicted doorpiece. The battlemented bay windows, the l. canted, the r. a shallow rectangular projection, are additions, probably of 1867 (the date on the hoppers). No. 12, set well back behind a front garden, is early C19. Two-storey piend-roofed main block with a Roman Doric columned doorpiece; single-storey lateral wings. Beyond this, St James the Great (*see* Churches, above). W of the church, MYLNE AVENUE leads to the main entrance of Dollar Academy (*see* Public Buildings, above) but the Academy is set on a diagonal and just off-axis. Beyond Mylne Avenue, Harviestoun Road continues W with some prosperous Victorian villas on its N side. At No. 26, an early C19 ashlar-fronted single-storey villa, its centre slightly advanced and rising above the eaves to a cornice. In this centrepiece, a side-lit door under an overall elliptical fanlight. Projecting harled wings, probably mid-C19 additions. Set back from the W end of Harviestoun Road, on the S, DEVONGROVE, designed by *W. H. Playfair*, 1821, for the master of oriental languages at Dollar Academy. Piend-roofed main block of two storeys and three bays, the ground-floor windows set in overarches; pilastered doorpiece at the slightly advanced centre. Single-storey one-bay wings, their windows overarched, the walling carried up to screen the roofs.

CASTLE CAMPBELL. *See* p. 313.

*9090*                      DOLLARBEG                              C
                        1.9km. SE of Dollar

Crazed Baronial villa-mansion designed by *Ebenezer Simpson* for the tobacco merchant Henry Dobie, *c.* 1890. Panoply of crow-stepped gables and pedimented dormerheads (semicircular and steeply triangular). At the entrance (W) front, a balustraded square tower, a conical-roofed round turret at its NE corner; projecting from the tower, a *porte cochère*, its roundheaded arches carried on squat octagonal pillars, its corners surmounted by angle rounds. At this front block's N gable, a massively corbelled parapet between tall turrets. N range with canted bay windows, one full-height, its top corbelled to the square, the other balustraded. Conical-roofed tower bristling with cannon-spouts at the NE corner. Lower service wing at the E end of the house, a large rectangular oriel window in the N gable. Contemporary LODGE, also Baronial, at the entrance to the drive.

*7000*                          DOUNE                                 S

A small tightly introverted town. Famed in medieval times as a centre of pistol manufacture, purse-making and skinning, from the late C18 the town provided the labour for the cotton mill at nearby Deanston (q.v.).

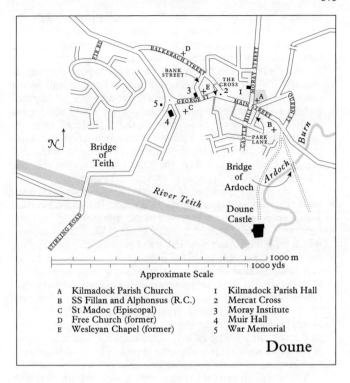

A  Kilmadock Parish Church
B  SS Fillan and Alphonsus (R.C.)
C  St Madoc (Episcopal)
D  Free Church (former)
E  Wesleyan Chapel (former)

I  Kilmadock Parish Hall
2  Mercat Cross
3  Moray Institute
4  Muir Hall
5  War Memorial

## Doune

## CHURCHES

Former FREE CHURCH (later West Church), Balkerach Street.
Built 1867. Dec Gothic still recognizable in three-light s gable
window but otherwise mauled by conversion to residential use
as West Kirk House, 1969. The church's arch-braced trusses,
pierced decoratively by trefoils, break through the timber-lined
ceiling of an attic billiard room.

KILMADOCK PARISH CHURCH, Main Street. By *James Gillespie
Graham*, 1822–4. Pretentiously scaled three-bay, buttressed nave
and three-stage, street-front tower, constructed in a disappointingly dull rust-coloured sandstone and far less appropriate in
the townscape than the 'plain affair' that preceded it, a simple
mid-C18 harled kirk. Evidently the Earl of Moray, whose carved
arms are set over the entrance door at the base of the s tower,
wanted nothing modest. Openings are generous in size, Late
Dec or Perp in style: hooded four-centred arches over wide
doorways and three- or four-light mullioned and transomed
windows. Backed by raking castellations on the s gable, the
square belfry tower rises to an ornamental parapet carried on
three corbel-courses and accented at the corners by scalped
rounds. A single tall pinnacle survives on the sw angle buttresses.

The church is entered under the s tower. Over the outer

vestibule is an eight-part ribbed and bossed plaster vault. An arched opening leads to an inner vestibule, symmetrically but irregularly configured across the full width of the church. At its centre, another ribbed and bossed plaster vault springs from floral corbel bosses in the corners. Floors are flagged, the original stones surviving in the inner vestibule. The rear wall of the church bends back convexly l. and r. creating space for entrance lobbies and stair flights rising to the gallery. These stairs, each of thirty cantilevered stone risers without landings, begin as straight flights against the S gable wall but then return in a semi-circular curve to upper landings defined above by an ovoid ceiling. Seen in perspective from the inner vestibule, each stair has a swinging sinuous elegance of exceptional beauty.

From lobbies and upper landings single doorways open under Perp arches to the church and gallery. The doors, panelled with pointed arches, are lintelled; in the arch-head a glazed fan-light with delicate cusped astragal tracery. Walls are plastered with a flush dado, part panelled, part boarded. The high ceiling, bordered by a simple moulded cornice, is flat. At its centre is a very large circular ventilator of thirty-four spokes, each narrow sector cusped at the circumference. The S gallery, carried on six cluster-shaft timber columns, has a boldly concave front panelled with coupled cusped arches flanking the gilded Moray family arms which bear the motto 'SALUS PER CHRISTUM REDEMPTOREM'. The gallery, which originally continued along the W and E walls returns abruptly at each side, its obliquely cut ends making awkward junction with adjacent window jambs.

The N wall (liturgical E) is unfortunately overburdened with ecclesiastical intervention and inheritance. To the l., added in 1936 to 'box in' a vestry, a low oak screened compartment panelled in blind Perp tracery pushes out from the NW corner. Concealing its ceiling, an open chevron and trefoil parapet returns untidily against the sill and jamb of the W window. To the r., the ORGAN by *Ingram & Co.*, Edinburgh with pipes framed in a massively and incongruously symmetrical timber screen from which canted bay clusters of pipes project on each side above the console. Gifted in 1908 by Margaret Morrison Muir in memory of her husband Sir John Muir of Deanston †1903, this vast assemblage was brought here from the West Church in the late 1960s. So, too, the raised PULPIT placed at the centre of the N wall; symmetrical, with a half octagon preaching projection and a high back panel with stepped frame and unusual depressed ogee arch moulding, its height encroaching over the lower part of the four-light N window.

On the W wall of the outer vestibule is a MURAL TABLET to the Rev. Patrick Murray †1837; on a black slate panel, a white marble sarcophagus bearing a long inscription and, above, the carved dove of the Holy Spirit.

In the GRAVEYARD, N and E, a variety of scattered stones, C19 and C20. That to Agnes Stewart †1813, her husband James Macruar and their children, has a rugged architectural dignity; a Classical aedicule of fluted pilasters bearing a pediment.

OLD KILMADOCK CHURCH. Fragmentary E gable survives.

SS FILLAN AND ALPHONSUS (R.C.), Main Street. By *John Laurie Fogo*, 1875. First Pointed Gothic. Five-bay buttressed nave in square-snecked sandstone. In the N gable front, a triple lancet window with column shafts and capitals; trefoils and canopied niche in the apex. Gabled NE porch. Plain plastered interior with arch-braced scissor trusses. Solid E end has a blind arcade of five pointed arches carried on stone shafts.

ST MADOC (Episcopal), George Street. By *James Brooks* of London, 1877–8. Constructed in warm ochre Polmaise sandstone rubble with dressed margins and mouldings. E.E. nave and chancel with N porch and transept (the intended N aisle and NW steeple were never built). Internally the walls are of roughly dressed stone. Barrel-vaulted nave ceiling lined with pitch pine and white pine boarding. Groined plaster ceiling over chancel. Chancel floor and nave passageways laid with *Minton* mosaic TILES. – ALTAR, PULPIT and low wall separating chancel from nave are all of red and grey stone. – Carved oak REREDOS with painted and gilded panels. – FONT carved from yellow freestone block. – ORGAN by *Bevington & Sons*, 1878; rebuilt 1951 and 1996. – STAINED GLASS: in the E window, the Worship of Heaven; in the round W gable window, the Descent of the Holy Spirit.

Former WESLEYAN CHAPEL, 13 George Street. Built 1844. Workaday Nonconformist Classicism. Gabled, two-storey, three-bay hall in rust-coloured rubble with ochre sandstone dressings. First-floor windows are round-arched with chamfered margins continuing down to frame lower lights. Now a house.

## PUBLIC BUILDINGS

BRIDGE OF ARDOCH. Rubble arch carrying a narrow hump-backed carriageway with splayed approaches. A mural TABLET in the parapet bears the inscription BUILT.UPON.THE. PUBLICK / EXPENSE.OF.THE.SHIRE / A.D.1735.

BRIDGE OF TEITH. Masonry structure of two wide semicircular arches; an inscribed armorial tablet set into the parapet records that it was commissioned by Robert Spittall in 1535. In 1866 it was widened and repaired by engineers *D. & T. Stevenson*. The changes are evident: on the W, rough-faced voussoirs and a faceted cutwater; on the E, plainer arches and a higher splayed cutwater.

KILMADOCK PARISH HALL, Moray Street. 1908. Three-light, mullioned and transomed window in street gable. Two metal ridge ventilators with small cusped openings under conical caps.

MERCAT CROSS, The Cross. 1620; re-erected on its present site in the early C18 and restored 1953. A tapered octagonal shaft on a six-stepped pyramidal base. At the head of the shaft, a carved block bearing the Moray and Campbell of Argyll arms and two sundials; above this, a much-weathered lion carrying a circular shield with the Moray crest.

MORAY INSTITUTE, George Street. Late C19. Three-bay hall in rust sandstone rubble with ochre dressings. Symmetrical gabled front; at the centre a lintelled doorway with round-arched fan-light flanked by round-arched windows. Deep eaves on stone brackets with four gabled dormers each side. Now in residential use.

MUIR HALL, at the w end of George Street. By *Eric S. Bell*, 1921–2. Crowstepped gables, bartizans, castellated parapets, eaves dormers and roughcast walls: Baronial, yet crudely mechanical in its symmetrical composition and dressed stone detail.

WAR MEMORIAL, on the A84 opposite George Street. Severe obelisk shaft on a square-cut, cubic plinth; *c.* 1920. Rubble wall and bench curve in a wide gentle arc behind.

### DESCRIPTION

Strongly Scottish townscape. Three narrow streets, in Y-plan relationship, converge at THE CROSS, a triangular breathing space at the heart of town. Directing the traffic, the C17 Mercat Cross (*see* Public Buildings, above). The scale is two-storey, rising to a gable-fronted three at the centre of the NW and NE sides; shops with flats above, of the mid to late C19. On the S side, JIMMUCK'S, early C19, has a good doorpiece with Roman Doric columns and entablature block set between pressed-in bay windows.

BALKERACH STREET runs NW, two-storey, gable-to-gable housing, much of it late C18, rubble or roughcast with plain or dressed margins; unremarkable but consistent.

MAIN STREET, going SE in a gentle curve, is similar but better: three- and five-bay dwellings, of the late C18 to mid C19, packed together in austere harled or painted walls; a very Scottish street, hard-edged and urban, its austerity subtly relieved by the varied detail of margins, quoins or doors (as, for example, in the almost Gibbsian doorpiece at the HIGHLAND HOTEL, *c.* 1770). There are, of course, interruptions. The BANK OF SCOTLAND, 1875, looms large, with high hooded windows and finials at the apex and skews of its street-front gable. Still grander, Kilmadock Parish Church (*see* Churches, above). At No. 52, across the street from the church, a three-storey slot, *c.* 1900, half-timbered at first and second floor with a crowstepped gable to Castle Hill; the ground-floor shop preserves some Edwardian stained glass. Next door, at No. 56, a tall flat-roofed frontage of three superimposed tripartite windows, by *John Allan*; a strange red brick intrusion dated 1900, with an inset tablet incised with what appear to be oversize masons' marks and the optimistic injunction 'LET / JUSTICE TRUTH HONOR / AND RESPECT / FOR OTHERS RIGHTS / BE WROUGHT / INTO EVERY PART / OF / OUR EMPIRE'. But vernacular townscape reasserts itself. Nos. 51–61 are low two-storey dwellings, *c.* 1800. Nos. 63–67, early C19; three single-storey, three-bay houses. BRAEHEAD HOUSE, of the mid C19, is again two-storey, but links to a further run of rubble cottages, Nos. 71–73, mid C19, curving downhill. Past Park Lane, No. 66, early C19, has a central front gable flanked by narrow conical-roofed bowed dormers; though rusticated quoins survive unscathed, the street wall has been badly refaced. Then come Nos. 68–76, early C19, more gable-to-gable, single-storey houses, roughcast or painted render. Marking the corner of Queen Street is MALTBARN HOUSE (No. 75), built in the late C18 but altered and enlarged *c.* 1835, perhaps by *William Stirling I*; its gable to Main Street enhanced by a corbelled oriel window.

GEORGE STREET falls W from The Cross, bridges the Dragon Burn, then rises again towards the War Memorial (*see* Public Buildings, above). Nos. 1–11, by *T. MacLaren*, 1894, step with the slope, quaint and quirky; a plainly harled yet kilted Arts and Crafts jig of crowsteps, corbels and conical-capped turret. More staid are Nos. 4–6, *c.* 1820, where five tall architraved windows line up at first floor. At No. 8, late C18, a chamfered corner.

## MANSIONS AND FARMHOUSES

ARGATY HOUSE, 1.9km. NNE. Two-storey-and-attic dwelling by *Stewart & Paterson*, 1920–3, linking vernacular house of *c.* 1840 with Brycean Baronial W wing of 1858–60, probably by the Stirling architect *William Simpson*. A curved screen wall, 1924, connects the house to the STABLES block, *c.* 1800, a symmetrical Gothick composition in random rubble with castellated parapets and skews, blind quatrefoils and small pointed-arched windows. Rear rebuilt 1840.

BRIDGEND OF TEITH. By *Robert S. Lorimer*, 1902–3. Two-storey Voyseyesque harled mansion with bay window and verandah.

HILLSIDE OF ROW, 3km. ESE. Built *c.* 1825. Three-bay two-storey farmhouse with symmetrical U-plan steading. Horsemill at rear.

INVERARDOCH, 1km. SSE. *David Bryce* built the estate mansion, reputedly in 'French' style, in 1859–61. Damaged by fire in 1879, it stood across the Ardoch Burn from Doune Castle until the 1950s. In the grounds are the ruined STABLES, *c.* 1800: convex walls, indented with niches, curving in to a central barrel-vaulted archway over which is the roofless shell of an octagonal belfry. A partially WALLED GARDEN retains two conically roofed corner towers. These, and the swept roof of a canted bay at the roadside LODGE, have fish-scale slating. All but overgrown by the riverside is a low, two-bay MORTUARY CHAPEL, 1876, built in a humble Gothic style by *John Campbell* of Inverardoch on the site of the ancient chapel of St Fillan. The rubble rump of this medieval structure, which 'by authentic records was in ruins in 1568', forms the E gable of Campbell's mausoleum.

INVERARDOCH MAINS, 1.5km. SE. Mid-C18, rubble-built out-building with three segmental-arched entries now built up. Circular DOOCOT tower, also of the mid C18. Crenellated parapet on corbel course; gargoyle spouts.

MILL OF ARGATY, 2km. E. 1958–60. By *William H. Kininmonth*. A two-storey roughcast house absorbing its C18 predecessor to the point of concealment. Pedimented to the S. Pergola link NW to octagonal summerhouse. Splendid forecourt paved in granite causeys laid in concentric circles. Nothing of the old mill survives.

NEWTON OF DOUNE. Harled and crowstepped three-storey house dating from the C16 and C17. L-plan with a corbelled stair in the re-entrant. Short two-storey W wing added to original dwelling. The courtyard wall has gone but part of an arched opening survives. Wrought iron GATES brought from Inverardoch (*see* above).

ROW, 2.7km. SSE. Three-bay house, perhaps late C18, aggrandized by *John Laurie Fogo*, 1862. A three-storey square tower, with a slated pyramid roof, anchors the resultant L-plan at its SE corner. Porch and dormerheads added to original E front, the latter carved with fleur-de-lis, thistle and crossed crooks.

WATSTON, 1.5km. SW. C18 and later. Harled three-bay, two-storey farmhouse. Octagonal horsemill.

DOUNE LODGE. *See* p. 382

7000                DOUNE CASTLE                S
On the SE edge of Doune, off Main Street

High-walled and dourly formidable, Doune Castle rides on a rolling swell of graded ground, banked and ridged, a defensive knuckle contrived at the end of the finger of land formed by the narrowed parallel flow of the Ardoch Water and River Teith, *c.* 0.45km. short of their confluence. Natural advantage is reinforced: the castle sits up, the landscape further shaped to the S where three ramparts separated by ditches cross the green finger between the rivers like a banded ring. There is no visible evidence of the C1 fort built here by the Romans. No doubt this fortified knoll is the ancient dun from which castle and town take their name.

Built over the last two decades of the C14 by Robert Stewart, Duke of Albany, 'the most powerful figure in the Scotland of his day'*, the castle rose from a site with advantages as much geographical as topographical. Like Stirling, Doune lay at the crossroads of Central Scotland, and it may be that Albany's ambitions led him to construct his own fortress less than 10km. from the royal stronghold. Though he commanded real financial power through his position as royal Chamberlain, and was even for a period Keeper of Stirling Castle, his construction of nearby Doune may have been political insurance. In the absence of the young King James I, held in protracted captivity in England, 1406–24, Albany ruled as Guardian until his death in 1420. His son, Duke Murdoch, proved less circumspect and considerably more venal. In 1425, after James's return to Scotland, Murdoch, his son and his father-in-law were beheaded at Stirling. Thereafter, royal governors were installed at Doune until, in the last years of the C16, it passed into the hands of the Earls of Moray who in the 1880s undertook a major restoration.

49  Approached from the N, the height and mass of masonry are impressive. The walls, rising from a sloping plinth, are of coursed sandstone rubble, generally brown in colour with quoinstones

* W. Douglas Simpson, *Doune Castle* (1966), 5.

and windows and door margins dressed in a lighter stone quarried at Ballengeich, near Stirling. To the l. is the Gatehouse Tower, accented by corbelled rounds on the NW, SW and SE corners but swollen on the NE angle by a full-height drum tower which returns against a broad rectangular projection on the E gable. This is the tallest part of the structure, four storeys high below a garret (five in the drum tower), the ragged skyline reaching almost 29m. at the gables. The upper works of the tower were repaired by the master mason, *Michael Ewing*, 1580–1. To the r., barely recessed from the N face of the gatehouse and scarcely half its height, the long front of the Great Hall extends W. At its mid-point, a half-round bastion rises to the parapet walk; at the W corner, a round turret at high level. Together, Gatehouse Tower and Hall constitute 'a powerful frontal mass behind which the curtain seems to trail'* for, apart from the Kitchen Tower which pushes W behind the W gable of the Hall and is itself a structure not much less in bulk and height than that of the Gatehouse, the castle is defined on the E, S and W only by CURTAIN WALLS over 2m. thick and 12m. high. These walls, parapeted, with ashlar circular turrets at the corners and mid-points on the E and S, have a continuous wallhead walk drained by weeper spouts regularly spaced below a projecting string-course. Interrupting the W parapet, above a blocked postern-gate, is a machicolated square turret built in ashlar and also partly restored. It is clear that the curtains were intended to enclose buildings ranged around the inner yard. Tusking stones are prominent on the SE corner of the Kitchen Tower close to a long forestair running down from first-floor level to the blocked W postern. Irregularly placed in the S wall are four pointed-arched windows, the larger possibly related to the castle's Chapel of St Fillan mentioned in 1570 but for which minimal foundation traces on the inner side of the S wall are scarcely convincing evidence. More traces indicate building which must have extended S from the Gatehouse along the E wall. At the centre of the courtyard is a circular stone WELL, reconstructed with old timbers and a modern windlass, 1884.

The GATEHOUSE TOWER was also the owner's residence, making it relatively easy for the duke to control the principal entrance to the castle. This arrangement, coupled with the perceived isolation of the tower from the remainder of the accommodation led the late W. Douglas Simpson to explain the planning of Doune as a response to 'bastard feudalism', a system under which late medieval magnates supposedly found it necessary to protect themselves against the potential treachery of their own mercenary soldiery no less than from attack by outside enemies. Today, however, most scholars would argue that this separation of accommodation was more apparent than real, seeing the arrangements at Doune – including those elements that were planned but not completed – as a step towards the fully integrated courtyard layouts found in later royal residences such as Linlithgow Palace.

* Stewart Cruden, *The Scottish Castle* (1981), 84.

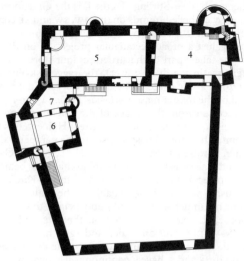

FIRST FLOOR

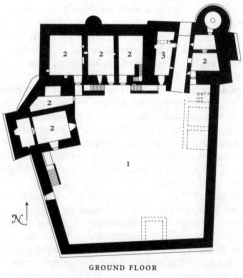

GROUND FLOOR

|⊢⊢⊢⊢⊢⊢⊢⊢⊢⊢⊢⊢⊢⊢⊢⊢⊢⊢⊢⊢|      30 m
                              100 ft

|   |            |   |            |
|---|------------|---|------------|
| 1 | Courtyard  | 5 | Great Hall |
| 2 | Cellar     | 6 | Kitchen    |
| 3 | Guard Room | 7 | Servery    |
| 4 | Duke's Hall |   |           |

Doune Castle. Plans.

While the original specification was clearly designed to provide Albany with an ample supply of well-organized accommodation, the needs of security were by no means neglected, although the presence of so many large windows in both gatehouse and curtain would have made the castle vulnerable to determined assault. The single shared entrance, passing under a flattish pointed arch, penetrates the tower obliquely below a barrel vault, the cobbled incline leading directly to the courtyard. Heavy outer doors (which are modern), a drawbar socket, a machicolation slot, a double-leaved iron yett (which is original) with its drawbar and beam, and checks in the masonry for an inner gate, all testify to the concern with security. On both sides of the passageway there are vaulted guardrooms and cellars, those on the l. giving access to a circular well-chamber in the round NE tower. Small ceiling hatches made it possible for water and provisions to be raised to the floor above. Access to the Duke's Hall on the first floor was gained by an external straight-flight stair rising from the courtyard W–E against the S wall of the Gatehouse. This approach, too, is protected; first by another iron gate, then by a high screen wall and finally by a round-arched door with a heavy drawbar.

The DUKE'S HALL is accessed through its W end. A lofty barrel-vaulted chamber at the E end of which is a double fireplace, framed by moulded elliptical arches and shafts. In the N wall, a single arched window recess from which the machicolation could be controlled. Opposite this, concealed in a thickening of the S wall, a mural chamber from which both activity in the Hall and around the entrance to the courtyard below can be observed. There is a spiral stair in the NW corner and beside it a doorway to the Great Hall, once thought to have been formed during *Andrew Kerr*'s renovations of 1883–6 but now generally accepted as an original opening, albeit heavily restored. The floor tiling, the music gallery at the W end, the oak panelling and screen, and the display of armorial bearings date from the 1880s. A second spiral stair is located at the NE. Here access is gained to a six-sided vaulted private apartment in the round tower and, by the turnpike, to an Upper Hall on the floor above, probably part of a separate suite for the Duchess. Approached from either stair, this second-floor hall, similar in plan and area to the one below, is reached along narrow vaulted passageways in the N wall, each opening into the deep arched recess of the single window that lights the chamber from this side. In the E wall, a wide fireplace, arched and moulded like those below. A recess in the S wall, coincident with the small mural chamber below, has been used as an oratory: there is an octagonal piscina, shallow sacrament house and credence niche, but the altar itself does not survive. To the l., a short passageway leads out to the parapet walk along the E curtain. Though high, the Upper Hall is not vaulted, its timber-beamed roof evidently supported on large carved corbels. The present ceiling, the timber construction of the rooms and roof above, and the repair of masonry at the NE stair, gables and wallhead, belong to the C19 restoration; together they make it

possible to climb to the N parapet walk and from this reach the
elevated E platform or beacon-stance and the still-open garret
over the NE drum.

The GREAT HALL, like the Gatehouse Tower, has its distinctly
separate entrance. It sits over three vaulted cellars each with its
arched door to the courtyard. An open unprotected parapeted
forestair climbs E–W to enter the irregularly shaped NW link which,
acting as both vestibule and servery, connects the N frontal range
with the Kitchen Tower. The Hall, similar in width to that of
the Duke's Hall but half as long again, was used for public and
ceremonial occasions and was probably warmed by some form of
central fire, now marked somewhat cosmetically by an octagonal
kerb. The Hall is high, 12m. or so to the apex of the restored
roof, erected in the 1880s, an open timber construction with hefty
cranked trusses resting on the original, grotesquely carved corbelstones. It is also well lit on the N, W and S by round-arched
windows which vary in size and level. The large two-light,
mullioned and transomed S window at the E end may not be
wholly original but certainly predates the late C19 restoration. A
service stair drops to the cellars from its E ingo; a privy opens W.
From the gable window recess, a mural stair rises to a gallery. In
the NW corner a second service stair descends to the wine cellar.
The footings of screens can still be seen at this end of the Hall
for it was here, through a door in the SW corner, that food and
drink arrived from the kitchens across the landing.

Two wide hatches spanned by elliptical arches, altogether aston-
ishingly modern and serviceable in appearance, break through
the N wall of the KITCHEN TOWER to the landing link. Wedged
between this servery wall and the top of the forestair entry is a
corbelled turnpike stair giving access to the so-called ROYAL
APARTMENTS, a group of chambers probably intended to
accommodate guests and members of the Duke's household.
The stair is clearly an insertion and may replace an earlier timber
staircase. The kitchen itself is a large vaulted space with a huge
fireplace taking up the full 5.5m. width of the W gable and 2.75m.
deep behind its low segmental arch. Within the fire recess there
is a slop drain; over the hatches, corbels for shelving; in the
vaults above windows and fireplace, openings giving ventilation; and in the SE corner, the remains of an oven. At the centre
of the S wall a door leads to a landing from which a spiral stair
rises within the wall to the parapet walk and a long open
forestair falls in a straight flight to the W postern.

DOUNE LODGE                    S
                        2km. NW of Doune

Formerly Cambuswallace or Doune Park. Built *c.* 1805. A wide
white mansion conspicuously poised on the lower slopes of the
Braes of Doune. The eaves cornice over the upper floor of the
seven-window S façade rises into a central pediment. Below,
reinforcing the stress provided by the pediment, a three-bay

Roman Doric portico carries a confident entablature and leaded blocking course. Behind this one-room-deep front, the stem of a symmetrical T-plan connects with a plain two-storey dwelling, C18, which lies parallel and was lineally enlarged E by *F. W. Deas*, *c.* 1913. Its vernacular simplicity is a delight; seductive enough, it seems, to persuade Deas to harl the main house (originally ashlar) too, a decision vindicated in the landscape but questionable at close quarters.

At the roadside is the LODGE, *c.* 1825, piend-roofed like the house on the hill and with a central Roman Doric porch, but still ashlar. Concave railed forecourt and ashlar GATEPIERS, dated 1897, with good cornices and torch-like coronet finials.

NE of the house is the WALLED GARDEN, early C19, with a SUNDIAL, formerly located at the front of the house, at its centre. A little to the N is the GARDEN HOUSE, *c.* 1825, with a semicircular verandah in ashlar.

STABLES, 0.5km. E. Quadrangular court by *William Stirling I*, 74 1807–9. Well described as a 'palace for horses'*: a wide two-storey ashlar front with hip-roofed end pavilions and a pedimented centre carrying a high belfry steeple. Below the pediment a round-arched entry leads to the quadrangular yard behind, the same arch form repeated in the windowed wings. The steeple is octagonal and rises through two tall stages (the lower with clocks dated 1809, the upper with round arches alternately louvred and blind) to a small leaded spire.

# DRYMEN S *4080*

First favoured in the C18 by its location on the E–W military road from Stirling to Dumbarton then stimulated by the tourist route N to Loch Lomond and the Trossachs. Now the A811 passes by on the E, giving the place space to dream. At its centre, a pleasant village green; soft, restful and unexpectedly English.

DRYMEN PARISH CHURCH. Dated 1771. By *George Taylor*, mason at Arnprior. Built in red sandstone but harled and painted white since 1962, it does not deserve its summary dismissal by the 1963 RCHAMS Inventory as 'of no particular interest'. The present building, begun as a simple oblong with two internal stairs which presumably rose to galleries in the W and E, has been successively altered. The church was reseated in 1810 and again in *c.* 1840–41 when a birdcage bellcote was added to the W gable. Changes made 1879–80, and again 1884–85, included reseating arrangements, the repositioning of the pulpit to the E wall where a new three-light window was created, the construction of the gabled W porch with its stair to the W gallery and probably (though the precise date of this enlargement is unclear) the addition of N and S transepts. In 1898 *James Thomson* inserted galleries in the transepts, with pyramid-roofed square stair towers set in the transept re-entrants to provide external access.

* Charles McKean, *Stirling and the Trossachs* (1985), 95.

The interior, painted in grey and pale blue, is pleasantly cool and intimate. The coomb ceiling is plastered. N and S galleries span the width of the transepts but the W gallery is carried on two slender cast iron columns, fluted with lily-like capitals. Plain panelling to the gallery fronts, E wall and vestibule. – Central octagonal PULPIT of pitch pine with lancet and quatrefoil motifs. – Pipe ORGAN, 1966, by *Rushworth & Dreaper*, Liverpool, in W gallery has asymmetrical pipe casing. – Two white marble sarcophagus TABLETS inset into vestibule panelling: one to David McFarlane MD †1884; the other to Rev. Alexander Lochore †1877. – In the three lancet lights behind the pulpit, STAINED GLASS depicting Christ between SS Peter and Paul; a memorial to the Macqueen family, 1884.

Former UNITED SECESSION CHAPEL, Stirling Road. Built 1819. Plain, two-bay gabled hall with round-arched windows. The E porch has steep gablets; above the door a bible-shaped TABLET taken from Duncryne, Gartocharn, with the inscription CHRIST / IS HEAD / OVER ALL / HIS BODY / THE / CHURCH and the date 1761. Used as the Parish Church Hall from 1953.

BUCHANAN ARMS HOTEL, Main Street. Two steeply pitched mid-C19 attic gables identify the original mid-C18 three-bay inn and farmhouse. In 1935 *J. W. Laird & Napier* created the hotel by building an L-plan S wing, its long eaves line jagged with gabled bedroom dormers. Conference rooms and a leisure centre were added in 1990.

DRYMEN BRIDGE, 1km. S. Built 1765 by *Major William Caulfield*. Widened and rebuilt 1929. Five segmental arches in red sandstone spanning the Endrick Water.

DRYMEN PRIMARY SCHOOL, Old Gartmore Road. By *Central Regional Council*, 1990. Long, high, pitched-roof oblong with shadowed gable-end glazing. The roof section determines all: ridge-lit to the high central assembly space which is overlooked by first-floor study pods at each end, it dips to widely sprocketed eaves over parallel classroom ranges. Two-tone brown brick walls and patterned tiling.

WAR MEMORIAL, at Balmaha Road junction. 1921. Silver granite cross, tall and tapered, sitting on a stepped base of rough whin.

DESCRIPTION

THE SQUARE, more trapezoidal in plan than its name implies, opens up a green space at the heart of the village. On the W, the WINNOCK HOTEL, a converted row of white two-storey houses, *c.* 1800, maintaining a common eaves and slated roof. Inside, a stone dated 1702 preserved from earlier buildings on the site. The CLACHAN INN, an L-plan cottage with a low piended corner to Main Street, may be an C18 survivor, though it has been much changed. On the E is THE POTTERY, two-storey red sandstone, mid C19, extended at the rear by *John Boys*, 1990, to form a hip-gabled tea-room with exposed pine trusses and glazed walls opening on to a brick-paved terrace. A neat bell-cast pyramid of Cumbrian slates sits nearby: this is the POTTERY

STUDIO, a glazed timber-framed workshop frugally designed and delightfully landscaped by *William A. Cadell*, 1993. Converted to a small restaurant in 1996; the studio's pyramidal roof is now fully glazed. Closing the S side of The Square, the LIBRARY is incorporated into a development of shops and flatted housing by *Central Regional Council*, 1977–9. Skew-gabled and dormered, this well-scaled but chunkily detailed group forms a pend-link with The Winnock, and continues across Balmaha Road as ALLANDER HOUSE, completed in the early 1980s.

BRAMBLEWOOD, set amid trees close to the Balmaha Road. 1982; timber-framed and clad, it sits neatly into sloping ground, its chalet-like SW gable glazed, canopied and balconied for sun and view.

MOTTE, Catter Law. A roughly oval motte shaped from a natural knoll overlooking the Endrick Water; standing up to 12m. high, measuring 30m. by 35m. across the top.

CRAIGIEVAIRN. *See* p. 350.

## DUCHRAY CASTLE
S *4090*
2.4km. SW of Milton

Late C16. A rubble-built block of three storeys with crowstepped W and E gables, a round stair tower with a conical roof at the SE corner and a NW turret corbelled at second-floor level; loosely, a Z-plan hall-house. Entrance to the barrel-vaulted ground floor in the SW re-entrant of the stair tower. Windows and doors gothicized, *c.* 1825, when the then ruinous castle was 'fitted up as a hunting lodge' (*Edinburgh Evening Courant*). A battlemented wall fronting the courtyard W is possibly also of C19 date.

## DUMBARTON
WD *4070*

Rock and river are the town's *raisons d'être*. Incongruously isolated and rugged in the low estuarial landscape, the great Rock is a happy accident of nature, a fortuitous fortress that has attracted settlement from the earliest times. Its location at the curving confluence of the River Leven with the Clyde intensifies this strategic potential. Here the upper reaches of the long seaward route into central Scotland could be guarded. Here, too, the ideal strategic base from which, N by the Vale of Leven and Loch Lomond or W by coast and sea-loch, the Scottish crown might exert its control over fractious and rebellious clans in the Highlands and Islands. But Dumbarton is no castletoun – at least, not in the sense of

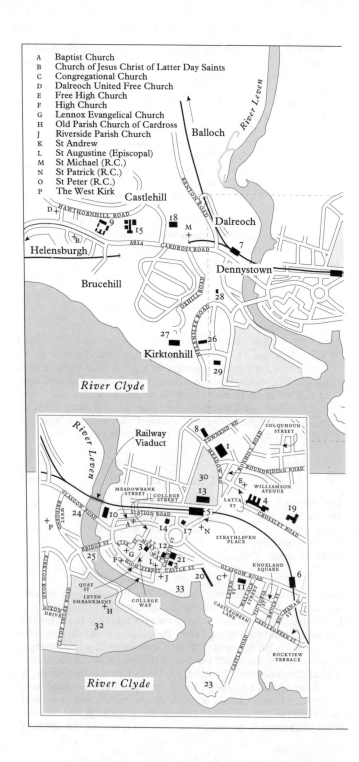

A   Baptist Church
B   Church of Jesus Christ of Latter Day Saints
C   Congregational Church
D   Dalreoch United Free Church
E   Free High Church
F   High Church
G   Lennox Evangelical Church
H   Old Parish Church of Cardross
J   Riverside Parish Church
K   St Andrew
L   St Augustine (Episcopal)
M   St Michael (R.C.)
N   St Patrick (R.C.)
O   St Peter (R.C.)
P   The West Kirk

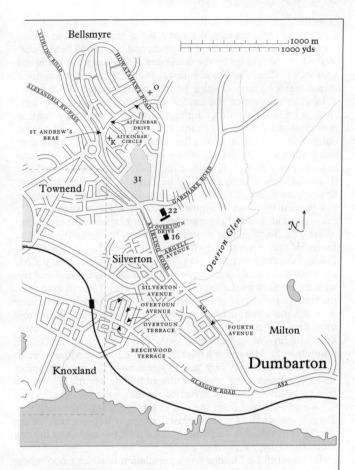

| | |
|---|---|
| 1 | Braehead Primary School and Meadowview Nursery |
| 2 | Burgh Hall |
| 3 | Denny Civic Theatre |
| 4 | Dumbarton Academy |
| 5 | Dumbarton Central Station |
| 6 | Dumbarton East Station |
| 7 | Dalreoch Station |
| 8 | Dumbarton Cottage Hospital |
| 9 | Dumbarton Joint Hospital |
| 10 | Health Centre |
| 11 | Knoxland Primary school |
| 12 | Masonic Temple |
| 13 | Meadow Sports Centre |
| 14 | (Former) Municipal Buildings |
| 15 | Our Lady and St Patrick's High School |
| 16 | Police Headquarters |
| 17 | Public Library |
| 18 | St Michael's Primary School |
| 19 | St Patrick's Primary School |
| 20 | Scottish Maritime Museum |
| 21 | Sheriff Court House |
| 22 | West Dunbartonshire Council Offices |
| 23 | Dumbarton Castle |
| 24 | Artizan Bridge |
| 25 | Dumbarton Bridge |
| 26 | Garmoyle |
| 27 | Helenslee |
| 28 | Levenford House |
| 29 | Methlan Park |
| 30 | Meadow Park |
| 31 | Dumbarton Cemetery |
| 32 | Levengrove Park |
| 33 | Distillery |

immediate proximity. The Rock provided little space for building.
Instead, the town developed about a kilometre N, folded in a wide
bend of the Leven. The site is low-lying and initially all but insular,
washed on three sides by the tidal river. From the E the landward
approach bridged the Knowle Burn, while for centuries the route
W necessitated a ferry crossing to the adjoining parish of Cardross.

In 1222 Alexander II founded the harbour town 'at my new
castle of Dumbarton', granting the small community trading
privileges and the right to charge tolls on Clyde traffic. As a royal
burgh linked to a royal castle, Dumbarton was conceived as a civilizing outpost of the realm, on the edge of the country's still law-
less western seaboard. A modest regional economy developed and
there was some overseas trade in herring and wine. Disputes over
shipping and fishing rights were frequent with Renfrew and Ayr
but particularly with Glasgow, a conflict which was not finally
resolved (and then to Dumbarton's detriment) until the beginning
of the C18. Shipbuilding prospered towards the end of the C15 as
James IV built a navy with which to subdue the Lords of the Isles.
Docks were constructed in 1505. Throughout this medieval period,
the town's physical extent was small; a single High Street curving
with the bend of the Leven from the C15 Parish Church at the S to
the ferry point not far to the NW. A number of vennels ran radially
from this main thoroughfare to the river; between them, the narrow
tofts were packed together. On the N side of High Street there was
little building while further N, beyond the site of the Collegiate
Church of St Mary, the Broad Meadow remained vulnerable to
inundation with every high tide. Some time in the third decade of
the C16, a 'water-gang' was constructed N of the church but in 1580
this protective dyke was breached, houses were lost, the area of
Townend separated from the rest of the burgh, and the road N to
Bonhill vanished. Despite repeated attempts to prevent flooding,
the 'Drowned Lands' were not drained until the middle of the C19
when the railway arrived.

It is doubtful if Dumbarton's population reached 1,000 before
the end of the C17. Its prosperity, never great, slowly increased.
The town's traders dealt in salmon, herring, coarse cloth, meal
and hides. The Leven quay was constructed in 1642 and a new
Tolbooth completed a few years later. The town mill was rebuilt,
1658. Two new streets now ran N from High Street: at its centre,
close to the Tolbooth and Meal Market, was Cross Vennel (later
College Street) and in the E, opposite the Parish Church, Kirk
Vennel (later Church Street). On High Street itself several substantial lairds' houses appeared, though only one of these, Glencairn
House, 1623, survives. In 1680 a petition to the Privy Council sought
permission to build a bridge over the Leven but it was not until
1765, after the third Duke of Argyll had been persuaded not to
route the Inveraray road through Bonhill to the N, that Dumbarton
Bridge was built. A new street was laid to the bridge and across
the river the suburb of West Bridgend (which remained adminis-
tratively outside the burgh until 1857) began to grow, its small but
rather well-to-do community served by the Relief Church of 1794.
By the end of the C18, with the population approaching 2,000,

industrial growth had begun. Shipbuilding continued, a foundry was established, there were tanning yards, sawmills, ropeworks, brickworks, a brewery, and, from 1777, the Dumbarton Glassworks Company, whose three tall kiln cones marked the town's skyline, until their demolition in 1850, like simplified replicas of the twin-peaked Rock. Close to the glassworks, which occupied a large riverside site north of the bridge, the Artizan settlement developed. Later, following the emergence in 1844 of William Denny & Brothers, a family firm which would dominate the town's productive shipbuilding industry well into the C20, more working-class districts were built: on the w bank, the two-storeyed flats of Dennystown, built in the 1850s, and in the e end, through the 1870s, 80s and 90s, the tenements, terraces and semi-detached villas of the so-called 'New Town' of Knoxland; both suburbs planned in a gridded network of streets. Meanwhile, on Kirktonhill a clutch of handsome villas and mansions formed the town's more salubrious West End. As the burgh expanded, the population rose rapidly; from just under 5,000 in 1851, it reached 15,000 in 1901. Fifty years later, however, the figure barely exceeded 16,000, a clear measure of economic recession.

Throughout the C20 the decline of heavy industry followed the national pattern, delayed at first by the impetus of two World Wars, but ultimately ineluctable. The shipyards and engine works closed, freeing the Leven banks but releasing, too, a large workforce. The introduction of whisky distilling in the 1930s did little to compensate for unemployment and nothing to enhance riverside or townscape. Through the 1920s and 30s, local authority housing schemes in Silverton Hill, Boghead and Brucehill improved the living conditions of many. In the aftermath of the Second World War similar developments spread over the slopes at Bellsmyre and Castlehill. In 1960 the results of a competition for the renewal of much of the central area were announced. For over a decade a massive programme of reconstruction rolled on. The A814, linking Glasgow to Helensburgh and beyond, was re-routed through the razed heart of town and on across the Leven. Old street lines disappeared N of High Street making way for new flatted housing, civic building and a shopping precinct. The riverside embankment was recast for parking and promenade. Fortunately, this radical surgery has only marginally scarred High Street which, close-packed with buildings of generally unremarkable quality but genuine urban vigour (not the least valuable contributors to which are a few Art Deco survivors), retains its historic bend concentric with the curving flow of the Leven.

## DUMBARTON CASTLE
### Castle Road

The craggy double-domed basalt of Dumbarton Rock, 'huge, mural, weather-worn', as Groome describes it, rises from coastal mud flats on the N side of the Clyde estuary. Its abrupt geological drama dominates an otherwise gentle riparian landscape. Eminently defensible, it seems to have remained beyond the fortified limits of

*Facies Arcis BRITANNODUNENSIS ab Oriente . The Prospect of ye Castle of DUMBRITTON from ye East.*
*This plate is most humbly Inscribed to the Right Honble the Lord Torryster &c.*

Dumbarton Castle. Engraving by John Slezer,
*Theatrum Scotiae*, 1693.

Roman Antonine occupation, though there may have been a
Roman naval station at the Rock. By the C5 it had emerged as the
power-base of the kingdom of Strathclyde, known as Alcluith,
Clyde Rock, or, as the Gaels of Dalriada called it, Dun Breatann,
the fortress of the Britons. Impregnable for centuries it finally fell
to the Norsemen, perhaps in 780, certainly in 870. Two years
later, Artgal, king of the Britons, was assassinated 'at the instigation of Constantine, king of Scots'. Not for at least a hundred
and fifty years, however, did Strathclyde become part of a united
Scotland. Thereafter, passing first into the hands of the Celtic
Earls of Lennox, in 1238 the castle on the Rock became a royal
stronghold. Despite capture by the English in the last years of the
C13 and later seizures by rebellious governors, the Rock remained
of strategic importance to the crown. Its position on the W coast
was crucial in the pacification of the islands in the late C15 and
throughout the C16. Geography also favoured Dumbarton with a
role in the events that followed upon Mary Stuart's accession to
the Scottish throne in 1542; links with France were strong and for
a time the fortress was held for the defeated queen after the battle of
Langside. In the religious conflict of the times the castle repeatedly
changed hands. During the first four decades of the C17 the
Accounts of the Masters of Works record payments made for the
many repairs to the fabric then carried out. The name of *Thomas
Fallisdaill*, a local bailie and, for a time, provost, is repeatedly mentioned as overseer of the works, while design direction and advice
appears to have come from *James Murray* of Kilbaberton, Principal
Master of all His Majesty's Works and Buildings in Scotland, master
mason *William Wallace* and master wright *Arthur Hamilton*. By the
time of the Restoration, however, the castle was in ruinous condition.
Repairs and reconstruction were again effected between 1675 and
the middle of the C18, in particular in 1735 under *Captain John
Romer*, General Wade's senior military engineer in Scotland. It is

essentially these defensive batteries and buildings that shape the architectural character of the Rock today. Abandoned as a military fort in 1865, the castle is now in the care of Historic Scotland.

The long straight approach to the castle down Victoria Street and Castle Road summons expectations. Finally, a slow swing W round the base of the Rock reveals a series of rising levels tiered in walled enclosures above the flat green lawn that spreads S to the river's edge. The scene is suddenly rural, the drama played before the wide prospect of the estuary. Centre stage is the Governor's House (*see* below) set low in the cleft that divides the Rock into two craggy summits, the architecture cushioned against black riven cliffs by bosky trees. The first wall, constructed in coursed polychromatic rubble with lintelled loopholes stepped under a raking coping stone, is penetrated by the C19 OUTER

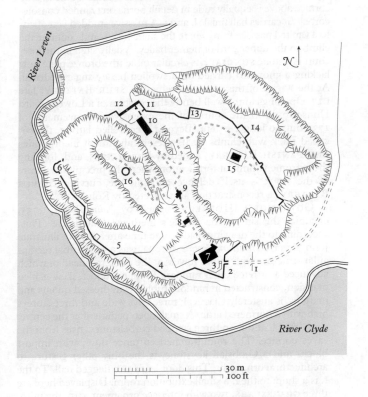

| | | | |
|---|---|---|---|
| 1 | Outer Gateway | 9 | Portcullis Arch |
| 2 | Inner Gate | 10 | French Prison |
| 3 | King George's Battery | 11 | Wallace Tower |
| 4 | Spur Battery | 12 | Duke of York's Battery |
| 5 | Spanish Battery | 13 | Duke of Argyll's Battery |
| 6 | Bower Battery | 14 | Prince of Wales Battery |
| 7 | Governor's House | 15 | Powder Magazine |
| 8 | Guard House | 16 | White Tower |

Dumbarton Castle. Plan.

GATEWAY. Square piers, boldly chamfered in the joints and capped above a hefty cornice by low domical swellings. Ahead, across a grassed inner court, is KING GEORGE'S BATTERY, designed in 1735 by *Romer*. This second wall advances sharply in an arrow-head plan almost but not quite coincident with the central axis of the house behind. At the apex of this projection, corbelled at the stringcourse which separates the whin rubble masonry of the wall from the coursed rubble of its parapet, is a cylindrical sentinel turret. Delightfully simple and sculptural, its domical stone roof topped off by a ball finial, it is identical to contemporary work at Edinburgh Castle and similar to earlier sentinel boxes at Stirling of 1708, and later examples at Fort George, *c.* 1750. An INNER GATE passes through the battery wall due w of the Outer Gateway. From here, steps rise to a portal arch stoutly articulated with a heavy keystone and impost blocks. The cornice above is equally rude in detail; borne on twinned console-corbels, it carries ball finials l. and r. A massive studded yett opens to a vaulted passage from where the stairs turn l. and continue the climb to the upper yard or nether bailey. Axially sited in the fore-court is a stone SUNDIAL, its circular table (the bronze plate now lacking a gnomon) carried on a swollen barley-sugar pedestal. At the w end of this second level is the SPUR BATTERY, late C17. Openings in the wall betray the position of a Lower Guard House, built in the course of the extensive improvements of 1735 but no longer extant. Beyond a corbelled latrine, the so-called Back Wall climbs w. Its present alignment incorporates the SPANISH BATTERY, added by Romer, 1735, and, forming the extreme w limit of fortification where the precipitous nature of the Rock is itself defence enough, the curving BOWER BATTERY, a reconstruction also effected by Romer.

GOVERNOR'S HOUSE, designed by *John Romer*, 1735, occupies the site of the Castle's medieval Gatehouse. This, according to the drawing made some time after 1678 to illustrate John Slezer's *Theatrum Scotiae* of 1693, was a substantial rectangular structure with round towers at the corners, ahead of which advanced a turreted outer rampart. Romer's robust, skew-gabled mansion, constructed in random rubble with dressed quoins and margins, is austerely Classical; three bays wide and three storeys high with a dormered attic. A small open pediment at the centre, supported l. and r. on three stepped corbelstones, rises from the eaves cornice. The round-arched entrance door, with impost blocks and a Gibbsian keystone, is the only other gesture to architectural ornament. This door leads to a flagged hall. To the r. is a shop; to the l. a small exhibition room. Displayed here are three GRAVESLABS, two with interlace ornament, C10, the third, C13 or C14, incised with the lines of a cross-shaft and clearly delineated scissors; a recumbent CROSS, C10; and a stone FRAGMENT from the Wallace Tower (*see* below) cut in 1704 with the words 'PERSECUTED FOR CHRIST & MISTAKEN / PRISON'D JOHN HARLAW, NOT FORSAKEN'. From this room a door exits w.

A terrace, supported by a rubble wall with blocked openings,

may be evidence of the medieval Hall and cellars which were
built in 1464 and recorded under repair as late as 1617 and 1633.
Of the C13 St Patrick's Chapel, rebuilt in 1456, there are no traces.
A straight flight of stairs rises from the terrace to the upper level.
To the r., a half-arch bridge, spanning from the retaining wall
which confines a narrow area immediately N of the Governor's
House, crosses to a door giving access at first-floor level to the
House's private accommodation. Immediately opposite this
entrance are two more steep staircases, side by side. That to the
l. leads to a small lawned garden. The other climbs higher, passing under the GUARD HOUSE, to which a return stair allows
entry from the N. The building may be C16; original windows to
the s are blocked but gunloops remain at high level. The accommodation provided is a single chamber at two levels, the lower
room lit s by two C18 lintelled windows.

Steps continue to ascend through a narrowing, rock-walled
defile to the PORTCULLIS ARCH, probably erected in the C14, 50
built to protect the more level ground which lies higher still
between the Rock's twin peaks and to afford more direct communication between these two summits. Tall pointed-arched opening, its weathered polychromatic sandstone masonry chamfered
on a double reveal at each face. In the vaulted passage, under
what is in effect a bridge, the portcullis slot can still be seen. More
stairs, shadowed by a leafy canopy of mature trees, climb on. On
a low wall, a fluted cast iron lantern standard, possibly C18,
similar to another surviving on one of the Outer Gateway piers.
On to the r., the path continues to rise following the contours
around the N side of the E summit, while the climb to the W crag
returns in a narrow, almost intimidating incline across the
Portcullis Arch bridge. Ahead, in the saddle, is a sunken WELL,
walled in below a segmental-arched vault in the 1730s. The
FRENCH PRISON, which dates from the third quarter of the
C18, is a five-bay, skew-gabled building in polychromatic rubble
with a round-arched w door positioned centrally below a circular
opening at first floor. Beyond this, on the N flank of the Rock
which overlooks the River Leven bending below, is a deep, walled,
basement area out of which rose the WALLACE TOWER. This
was constructed in 1617–18 to guard entry to the Castle, then
possible from the N. An earlier tower is known to have existed
here and in the late C16 batteries were constructed on the N
and E to reinforce the Castle's defences. These in turn were
strengthened, c. 1795, when the DUKE OF YORK'S BATTERY
encased the older walls. But of the four-storey gabled tower
shown by Slezer at the end of the C17 nothing but these lower
remains are to be seen.

From the vestigial walls of the Wallace Tower a defensive
curtain wraps itself around The Beak, the name given to the E
summit of the Rock. This N wall, as far as the platform of the
DUKE OF ARGYLL'S BATTERY, which was originally known
as the Belhouse Battery and conceived in the C16 as a flanking
defence opposite the contemporary One-Gun Battery just w of
the North Entry, was rebuilt some time before 1728 on the

instructions of General Wade. It continues E skewing S to the later PRINCE OF WALES BATTERY which, *c.* 1790, took the place of the C16 Round Battery. Beyond this is another sentinel turret by *Romer*, two-storeyed with a small forestair rising over an earlier turret to the tiny domed upper chamber. A further stretch of wall falls to an angled return above the cliffs on the SE face of the Rock. Close to the sentry cylinder, broken brickwork on the inner face of the wall reveals the location of an earlier gunpowder magazine. Nearby is the present POWDER MAGAZINE, 1748, set within a protective outer wall. Designed by *William Skinner*, Chief Engineer of North Britain, it is a detached skew-gabled rectangle with a barrel-vaulted interior.

On the more constricted space of the White Tower Crag, which is reached by a twisting path ascending from the Portcullis Arch bridge, little has been built. The medieval WHITE TOWER is no more than a small circular enclosure reduced to less than a metre in height. Groome's speculation that it may have been 'a windmill, a Roman fort (or) a Roman pharos' is unconvincing, but its original purpose remains unclear. Within its circumference is a square rubble plinth on which is a bronze direction indicator, 1932. Adjacent to the NW, at the summit, are a concrete triangulation point and a steel flagstaff.

## CHURCHES

BAPTIST CHURCH, Meadowbank Street. By *Archibald Craig*, 1897. Unprepossessing single-storey hall. In 1953 a circular opening over the main entrance was altered to create the tall central window with mullioned and transomed cross. Interior recast 1986–7. Boarded pine ceiling with partially exposed roof trusses. Adjacent halls, 1963.

CHURCH OF JESUS CHRIST OF LATTER DAY SAINTS, Cardross Road. 1963–4. T-plan, with hall and offices in the stem of the T. Steeply pitched roof over the church with a set-back in the gable to throw side light on the sanctuary. In the re-entrant, the canopied forecourt is pierced by a tall detached shaft, slender and elegant, more mast than spire.

COLLEGIATE CHURCH OF ST MARY. *See* p. 415.

CONGREGATIONAL CHURCH, Glasgow Road. 1878–82. A temple box, designed by a Mr *Dykes* (presumably *Thomas Dykes* of Glasgow); classical in aspiration with Thomsonesque touches. Completion was delayed by structural and financial collapse. Plain interior with beamed ceiling. Splendid iron railings scrolled and feathered.

DALREOCH UNITED FREE CHURCH, Hawthornhill Road, Dalreoch. By *Hamilton & McWiggan*, 1988–9. Successor to Dalreoch Church, by *John McLeod*, built 1873 close to the junction of Cardross Road and Renton Road, but demolished in 1984. A neat oblong of fawn blockwork roofed by two tiled monopitches forming a clearstorey. In 2000 this was cleverly extended S as a glazed roof-light spine over an added hall; by *Gregor Design*. Between the two, a small apex belfry.

FREE HIGH CHURCH, Latta Street. By *Halley & Neil*, 1907–8.
Unremarkable gable-fronted Gothic in rough red sandstone
with ashlar dressings. All windows set in rectangular panels
slightly recessed from main wall plane. Only the corner belfry
tower, vaguely Arts and Crafts in flavour, the bellcast eaves of its
pyramid roof splayed through crenellated corners, rises above
the mundane.

HIGH CHURCH, High Street. Built as the Free High Church,
1863–4. A steepled kirk by *John Honeyman*, sited at the w end
of the town's eponymous main street, its high spire rising in
forgotten denominational rivalry with the Parish Church (now
Riverside Church, *see* below) to the E. Closed 1972. From 1981
rudely adapted to retail use. In spite of tawdry commercialism,
its townscape success is undiminished. Gable and steeple front
to High Street. The style is E.E. Gothic, of a 'similar character to
older parts of Lincoln Cathedral', said *The Builder*; the masonry
square-snecked rubble and ashlar, generally in poor condition.
Three tall lancets with clustered shaft mullions of black Carnock
stone dominate the façade gable. Below is a gabled entrance with
cusped-arched doorway flanked by blind pointed recesses. From
a square base to the r., buttresses emerge to clasp the corners of
the steeple. At belfry stage, marked by tall, louvred, pointed openings, they splay inwards, transforming to obelisk finials guarding lucarnes at the base of the spire. Five bays deep behind the
steeple, the nave roof falls in bellcast profile over the aisles.
Plain lateral elevations lit by tall lancets. Galleried interior.

LENNOX EVANGELICAL CHURCH, Risk Street. By *James Oliver*,
1973–4. Constructed in the ubiquitous purply-brown bricks used
throughout the redeveloped town centre. Raking, book-end
walls flank the street entrance, a steeper version of those carrying the church's monopitch roof behind. High clearstorey throws
w light on the table.

OLD PARISH CHURCH OF CARDROSS, Levengrove Park. Ivy-
drenched medieval relic among yews and holly. Low walls define
a small oblong chamber open in the w. Fragmentary suggestion
of a smaller chancel (?) on the E, though the opening between
the two appears to have been built up. – On the w side of this
dividing wall, a blind arcade of three pointed arches on bell
capitals and cluster shafts with a pink granite panel in the central
bay; a MURAL MONUMENT to glassworks industrialist Robert
Dixon †1862. – On the E side, a grey granite MURAL TABLET to
his son Robert Dixon †1912, above which is the family crest
depicting an arm brandishing a cutlass and the words FORTES
FORTUNA JUVAT.

RIVERSIDE PARISH CHURCH, High Street. Originally Dumbarton
Parish Church. By *John Brash*, 1810–11. Erected to replace the
old post-Reformation parish kirk, 'a quaint, begalleried, cruciform
structure'* which, built *c.* 1565, had been repeatedly repaired
and, by the early years of the C19, was decidedly unsafe. The new
building, incorporating materials salvaged from the old in order

* *Ordnance Gazetteer of Scotland*, ed. Francis H. Groome, ii (1882), 384.

to reduce the contract price, was ambitious. Capacious enough to accommodate some 1,400 worshippers, it was also confident enough in form to have a distinctly urban impact. It still dominates the slow westward curve of the town's High Street.

Marking the threshold from street to tree-shaded kirkyard, two
18 broad ashlar GATEPIERS, 1813, each penetrated by a gated lintelled opening and hanselled above a generous cornice by a squat urn, flank the entrance gateway. The principal w façade lies in axial alignment, a three-bay, two-storey wall of droved ashlar gabled with a severely plain pediment. Pilasters carry a simple entablature across the central entrance door, on the lintel of which is the date of construction, 1811. A stringcourse marks first-floor level. Whether calculated or the fortuitous consequence of economy, this restraint is fitting for it serves, so to say, to heighten the impact of the steeple on the High Street. Set axially above the apex of the wide pediment, it rises in two square stages, the first windowed between coupled Ionic pilasters under a dentilled cornice, the second plain save for the clock on each face. Illuminated clock dials, mounted in 1901, by *J. T. Joyce & Co.* of Whitchurch, Shropshire. Above this are four fluted urns positioned at the corners around a low octagonal belfry from which the ashlar spire tapers to a gilded weathercock.

N and s elevations are again plain, no more than a series of five superimposed lintelled windows. The rather boldly patterned glazing bar arrangements are later, of 1855. At the centre of the pedimented e gable a segmental arch encloses a tripartite window with ashlar mullions and lintel, a replacement for the two windows which originally lit the church at this end.

The church is entered from a tall wide vestibule. Doors open l. and r.; stairs rise symmetrically in the wings. At the upper landing an Ionic doorway flanked by glazed side panels opens under a segmental pediment to the gallery. This entrance and the adjacent garrison pews, originally reserved for soldiers serving at the castle, restored 1996. The interior is airy and without spatial complexity. Flat panelled plaster ceiling with four decorative circular ventilation grilles. Panelled U-plan gallery with dentilled cornice. Opposite the pulpit, where the balcony face projects slightly, is a cautionary clock set between the burgh arms and the Burning Bush, both in heraldic colour. Cast iron columns under the gallery; support below the rear gallery added in 1835. More extensive structural alterations, including foundation reinforcement, the replacement of gallery beams and a new roof, were effected in 1908. It seems likely that at this time the original, almost Baroque, timber backdrop set against the e wall (a central three-tier pulpit advancing between pedimented organ-pipe screens canted on each side) was superseded. – The present PULPIT, half-octagonal and still centred, projects from a three-bay timber wall panelled in regimented Perp style. – Organ pipes dismantled when the original *Willis* instrument was removed in 1993. – Very wide COMMUNION TABLE with open, late Dec tracery at ends and sides. – STAINED GLASS. Above the pulpit, a three-light window to James and Catherine Denny, designed in 1938 by the Dumbarton-born *C. E. Stewart* but not erected until 1946: a rose-tinted Christ, bathed in a circling aura of nacreous light, ascends over darker-robed disciples. – On the N, St Margaret with two children, by *R. Douglas McLundie* of the *Abbey Studio*, 1946. – On the S, four ground-floor windows. First, two memorial windows by *W. & J. J. Kier*, 1876: Christ blessing the children and 'Blessed are the peacemakers'. Then, in memory of Rev. Andrew Gray †1881, a richly coloured, painterly 'Blessed are they that mourn', by *Stephen Adam & Thomson*, 1886. Finally, a silvery-white Christ, crucified and ascendant against deep reds and purples, from the studio of *Morris & Co.*, post-1915; the symbols of nails, chalice and crown are repeated as border motifs.

Parallel and uncomfortably close to the S are the HALLS, by *Wright, Kirkwood & Partners*, 1975–7. Flat-roofed boxes of brown rustic brick lit by clearstorey windows. Where once glebe and graveyard stretched to the banks of the Leven, the site is now mercilessly crushed by industrial building towering between church and river. Thus compressed in plan, unable to keep a respectful distance, these C20 additions are inevitably graceless. Tombs, too, have suffered. The GRAVEYARD, which once accommodated hundreds of memorials, was greatly reduced in 1910 when land was sacrificed to shipbuilding and the present S wall built. Only a handful of graves were preserved; the oldest HEADSTONE retained, now in the E wall, records the death of Janet McIntyre †1721 in naïvely crushed lettering. There are two BURIAL VAULTS. In one, dated 1846, blind Gothic arcading carries inscriptions to the Napiers of Shandon, a local family renowned as pioneers in marine engineering and shipbuilding. The other, of the mid C19, dedicated to the Campbells of Barnhill, has Tudor-arched recesses, a bench seat and three lying SLABS, one commemorating Rev. James Oliphant †1818, moved here in 1972. Both vaults are oblong spaces, roofless walled enclosures entered through gated pointed-arched openings.

ST ANDREW, St Andrew's Brae, Bellsmyre. 1958–9. Utilitarian hall church. Low-pitched roofs over roughcast walls with a few panels of orange facing brick.

ST AUGUSTINE (Episcopal), High Street. By *R. Rowand Anderson*, 1871–3. From 1856, Dumbarton's Episcopal congregation worshipped in St Luke's, a small First Pointed chapel on Cardross Road. In 1873 they moved to the centre of town. The new church, designed to accommodate 550 worshippers, presents an ashlar gable to the street. At the centre of this S façade is a large, hooded, pointed window with simple Dec tracery. Below this, a pointed doorway, much moulded on the arch but not the jambs. To the r., a lean-to aisle. To the l., obtruding across the face of the W aisle, a bulky, blockhouse vestry built as the base of a projected tower; given an ill-fitting piend roof, it still merits the '"sticket" steeple' description given by Groome in 1882. The E elevation, exposed only to a narrow lane, is plain, dull indeed, with coupled clearstorey windows above the aisle roof and a single, small, ungainly obstruction buttressing the chancel arch.

What this disappointing exterior lacks, Anderson's INTERIOR, 'invested with an air of sublimity', more than makes up for. A pointed-arched arcade, carried on alternating round and octagonal pink sandstone piers with bell capitals and splayed bases, separates nave from aisles over the five bays to the chancel arch. The nave roof is not trussed but ribbed with closely spaced scissor spars, a procedure repeated in simpler terms over the aisles. Since 1996, when lath and strap work was removed, red sandstone walls of coursed rubble have been exposed and pointed below the aisle roofs. Timber flooring renewed in the 1990s. A moulded pointed opening with tall cluster shafts rising to floral capitals marks the entrance to the chancel where the nave-and-aisles width of the church is continued for three more bays with pointed arcades on cluster-shaft piers l. and r. Carving of the capitals completed 1899. Steps rise in three stages to chancel, sanctuary and altar. Stone strip floor patterned in square and diamond grids with decorative brass grilles and *Minton* tile infill in dull orange and red. To the r., the E aisle continues to reach a side door in the last bay. On the W, the aisle is closed to form a second vestry. The chancel roof is a boarded timber vault with arch-truss ribs carried on capitals set between the clearstorey windows. Clearstorey arcading returns for one blind bay on each side of the cusp-tracery window in the upper N wall. Below are two quatrefoil discs carved with the figures of the Archangels Gabriel and Michael. Between these, an intricately crocketed canopied niche set on the stepped centre of the Gothic REREDOS, installed, with the ALTAR, in 1893. Both were designed by *Anderson* and carved in red Corsehill sandstone by *W. Birnie Rhind* of Edinburgh. At the centre, between arcaded panelling, Christ in Glory is raised in a large quatrefoil frame flanked by statuettes of the four evangelists; a second quatrefoil depicting the Lamb fills the central panel of the table. The original altar was removed to St Mungo's, Alexandria (q.v.).

FURNISHINGS were mainly installed 1899–1923. – At the S end of the W aisle, an octagonal oak-lidded FONT carved on each face with religious symbols. – Beside the chancel arch, a cylindrical PULPIT of onyx with eight cusped lancet insets. – Brass eagle-headed LECTERN by *Jones & Willis*, Birmingham, 1899. – ROOD SCREEN in delicate ironwork arcuated with lacy cusping and spindly barley-sugar twist verticals. – Oak CHOIR STALLS. – Low oak COMMUNION RAIL; cusped arches with bowing angels carved on gateposts, by *R. M. McNaught* of *Denny & Blain*, 1923. – ORGAN console and pipes by *Spring & Brook*, Glasgow, 1880, incorporated in polished pitch pine casing. – In the E aisle beside the chancel, an altar WAR MEMORIAL in oak, by *McNaught*, 1923. – STAINED GLASS. In the four-light S window, SS. Columba, Patrick, Kentigern and Ninian over Augustine, Ambrose, Jerome and Gregory, with lamb and dove in two hexafoils above; by *Shrigley & Hunt*, 1903. – Below l., a small two-light window depicts Christ orange-cloaked, walking on water, and, in deep Prussian blue and red, speaking of the lost sheep; erected early C20. – Beside the font, a more youthful Christ with

1. Stirling, King Street, with the Athenaeum, by William Stirling I, 1816–17

2. Blairlogie

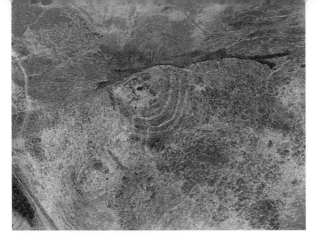

3. Kilmahog, Dunmore, Fort, iron age

4. Falkirk, Tamfourhill Road, Antonine Wall ditch, mid second century

5. Bearsden, Roman Road, Roman bath-house, second century

. Dunblane, Cathedral Church of St Blane and St Laurence, twelfth and thirteenth
enturies, restored in the ninteenth century

7. Dunblane, Cathedral Church of St Blane and St Laurence, west door, thirteenth century

8. Dunblane, Cathedral Church of St Blane and St Laurence, interior, thirteenth century

9. Stirling, Church of the Holy Rude, chancel, early sixteenth century

10. Stirling, Church of the Holy Rude, interior of chancel,
early sixteenth century

11. Cambuskenneth Abbey, bell-tower, *c.* 1300

12. Airth, former Airth Parish Church, twelfth century, recast and tower added in 1647, and with aisles of *c.*1480, 1593 and 1614

13. Kirkintilloch, former Kirkintilloch Parish Church (Auld Kirk Museum),1644 altered in late seventeenth and eighteenth centuries

14. Alloa, Old St Mungo's Church, tower, *c.* 1618–3

15. Stirling, St Ninian, tower, 1734

16. Baldernock Parish Church, 1795

17. Falkirk, Falkirk Old and St Modan Church, by James Gillespie Graham, 1810–11, with tower by William Adam, 1738, and porch-cum-session house by Wardrop & Anderson, 1892

18. Dumbarton, Riverside Parish Church, by John Brash, 1810–11, with gatepiers of 1813

19. Alloa, St mungo's Parish Church, by James Gillespie Graham, 1816–19

20. Stirling, former Erskine Marykirk Church, by Allan Johnstone, 1824–6

21. Renton, former Millburn Free Church, probably by John T. Rochead, 1843–5

22. Renton, Renton Trinity Parish Church, by David Barclay, 1891–2

23. Bearsden, New Kilpatrick Parish Church, stained
glass, by Alfred A. Webster, 1914

24. Bearsden, New Kilpatrick Parish Church, stained
glass, by Alfred A. Webster, 1914

25. Larbert and Stenhousemuir, Stenhouse and Carron Parish Church, stained glass, by Douglas Strachan, 1914

26. Larbert and Stenhousemuir, Stenhouse and Carron Parish Church, communion table, by John J. Burnet, with figures by William Vickers, 1921

27. Carriden Parish Church, by P. MacGregor Chalmers, 1907–9

28. Alloa, Alloa West Church, sanctuary and furnishings, by
Sydney Mitchell & Wilson, 1902–4

29. Falkirk, St Francis Xavier (R.C.) Church, by R. Fairlie & Partners, 1958–61

30. Dumbarton, St Peter (R.C.) Church, by Garner, Preston & Strebel, 1970–1

31. Bearsden, Scotus College, chapel, by James F. Stephen, 1997

32. Inchmahome Priory, graveslab of
Sir John Drummond, fourteenth
century

33. Muiravonside Parish Church,
headstone, 1761

34. Clachan of Campsie, former Campsie Parish Church,
Lennox mausoleum, 1715, heightened, 1819

35. Falkirk, Callendar House, Forbes mausoleum, by Archibald Elliot,
1815–16

36. Renton, Smollett Monument, 1774, and fountain, 1886

37. Killearn, Buchanan Monument, by James Craig, 1788–9

38. Stirling, Valley Cemetery, Star Pyramid, by William Barclay, 1863

39. Stirling, Valley Cemetery, Martyr's Monument, statuary, 1858–9, in structure by the Sun Foundry, 1867

40. Stirling, former Erskine Marykirk Church, Erskine Monument, by Peddie & Kinnear, 1859

41. Bridge of Allan, Fountain of Nineveh, 1853, heightened, 1895

42. Clydebank, Dumbarton Road, Nos. 421–481, crving, early twentieth century

43. Grangemouth, Zetland Park, War Memorial, by John J. Burnet, with sculpture by Alexander Proudfoot, 1922–3

44. Stirling, Back Walk, Town Wall and bastion, mid sixteenth century

45. Stirling Castle, Palace, 1537–c. 1550

46. Stirling Castle, Chapel Royal, 1594

47. Stirling Castle, Gatehouse, *c.* 1500–6, altered, 1810, Palace, 1537–*c.* 1500, and prince's Tower, *c.* 1500–6

48. Stirling Castle, Great Hall, *c.* 1500

49. Doune Castle, late fourteenth century

50. Dumbarton Castle, Portcullis Arch, probably fourtheenth century

51. Blackness Castle, mid fifteenth century, with curtain wall strengthened in, 1536–44

52. Castle Campbell, fifteenth and sixteenth centuries

53. Sauchie Tower, fifteenth century

54. Alloa, Alloa Tower, late fifteen century, altered, *c.* 1700-15

55. Old Sauchie, late sixteenth century

56. Edinample Castle, sixteenth century

57. Bo'ness, Kinneil House, tower, late fifteenth century, recast and pavilions added in late seventeenth century; 'palice' range to right, mid sixteenth century

58. Bo'ness, Kinneil House, 'Parable Room', mid sixteenth century

59. Strathleven, Strathleven House, early eighteenth century

60. Touch House, 1757-62, with sixteenth-century tower at right

61. Airthrey Castle, 1790-1 by Robert Adam, enlarged by David Thomson, 1889-91

62. Airth, Airth Castle, north-west front, by David Hamilton, 1807-9

63. Ross Priory, by James Gillespie, Graham, 1810-16

64. Garden House, east front, by William Stirling I, 1830

65. Meiklewood House, perhaps by R. & R. Dickson, *c.* 1832

66. Falkirk, Callendar House, south front, remodelling work carried on from c. 1500 to mid nineteenth century

67. Callendar House, Library, by David Hamilton, 1827–8

68. Lennox Castle, by David Hamilton, 1837–41

69. Overtoun House, by James Smith, 1859–62

70. Gribloch House, south front, by Basil Spence, 1937–9

71. Gribloch House, hall, by Basil Spence, 1937–9

72. Dunmore Park, The Pineapple, 1761

73. Westquarter, doocot, probably early eighteenth century

74. Doune lodge, Stables, by William Stirling I, 1807–9

75. Stirling, Old Bridge, *c.* 1500

76. Muiravonside, Avon Aqueduct, by Hugh Baird, 1818–22

77. Old Kilpatrick, Erskine Bridge, by Freeman, Fox & Partners, 1967–71

78. Airth, High Street, Market Cross, 1697, and View Villa, 1722

79. Stirling, Town House, by Sir William Bruce, 1703–5

80. Stirling, Cowane's Hospital, by John Mylne Jun., 1637–48

81. Stirling, Old Jail, by Thomas Brown Jun., 1845–7

82. Falkirk, Town Steeple, by David Hamilton, 1812–14

83. Stirling, Athenaeum, by William Stirling I, 1816–17

84. Dumbarton, Sheriff Court House, by James Gillespie Graham and Robert Scott, 1822–6, with wings added by William Spence, 1862–3

85. Alloa, Sheriff Court House, by Brown & Wardrop, 1862–5

86. Stirling, Municipal Buildings, by J. Gaff Gillespie, 1914–18

87. Clydebank, Municipal Buildings, by James Miller, 1900–2

88. Alloa, Museum and Library, by John Melvin & Son, 1874

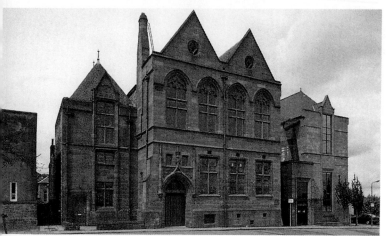

89. Falkirk, Falkirk library, by McArthy & Watson, 1900–2, with addition at right, by Falkirk District Council, 1991–2

90. Clydebank, Clydebank Library, by A. McInnes Gardner, 1912–13

91. Alexandria, Ewing Gilmour Institute, by Robert Thomson, 1881–4

92. Alexandria, Masonic Temple, by John A. Campbell, 1888–91

93. Alloa, Speirs Centre, by John Burnet, Son & Campbell, 1895–8

94. Alloa, Mar Street, No. 15 (former Liberal Club), by William Kerr, 1904

95. Falkirk, High Street, Nos. 138–140 (former Commercial Bank), 1829–31, probably by James Gillespie Graham, with ground floor altered in twentieth century

96. Alloa, Mill Street, former British Linen Bank, by Peddie & Washington Browne, 1906

97. Alloa, Bank Street, former gas showrooms, by William Kerr and John Gray, 1935–6

98. Dollar, Dollar Academy, Playfair Block, by W.H. Playfair, 1818–21

99. Alloa, St John's Primary School, by Kerr & McCulloch, 1907–8

100. University of Stirling, by Robert Matthew, Johnson-Marshall & Partners, 1966–72 (photo by John Dewar, 1970s)

101. Bannockburn, Bannockburn High School, by Central Regional Council, 1977–9

102. Balloch, Lomond Shores, Visitor Centre, by Page & Park, 1998–2002

103. Clydebank, Playdome Leisure, by the Ellis Williams Partnership, 1991–4

104. Stirling, Mar's Wark, 1570–2

105. Stirling, Argyll's Lodging, sixteenth and seventeenth centuries

106. Dumbarton, High Street, Glencairn's Greit House, 1623,
with ground floor arcade, by William A. Macartney, 1924–5

107. Stirling, Spittal Street, Darrow Lodging (No. 56),
seventeenth century

108. Dunblane, Cathedral Museum, Dean's House, 1624, heightened and forestair erected, *c.* 1765

109. Alloa, Kirkgate, No. 25, by Tobias Bachop, 1695

110. Bo'ness, South Street, No. 11, by Matthew Steele, 1907, and No. 13, 1750

111. Bo'ness, North Street, No. 74, 1786

112. Grangemouth, Bo'ness Road, Avondhu (No. 168), by James M. Maclaren, 1878

113. Alloa, Inglewood House, hall, by Sydney Mitchell & Wilson, 1895 (photo by Bedford Lemere, *c.* 1900)

114. Stirling, Friars Street, Nos. 29–31 (Friers Gait), by John Allan, 1902

115. Alloa, Gean House, living hall, by William Kerr, 1912

116. Callander, Stirling Road, veterans' houses, by Stewart & Paterson, 1919–20

117. Bo'ness, Corbiehall, Nos. 191–199, by Matthew Steele, 1935

118. Alva, Braehead, housing, by John Fraser & Sons, 1938

119. Dollar, Bridge Street, Mitchell Court, by Keir & Fraser, 1995–7

120. Clydebank, Great Western Road, late twentieth century

121. Bo'ness, North Street, Nos. 1–13, former warehouse, c. 1800

122. Tillicoultry, Clock Mill, 1824

123. Deanston, Deanston Spinning Mill, 1830–1

124. Falkirk, Grahamston Iron Works, gateway, 1886

125. Fishcross, Deven Colliery Beam Engine House, *c.* 1880

126. Alexandria, former Argyll Motor Works, by Halley & Neil, 1905–6

127. Alloa, Kilncraigs Factory, office block extension, by William Kerr and John Gray, 1936

128. Grangemouth, B.P. Oil Refinery and Petrochemical Works, late twentieth century

children; by *Stephen Adam*, 1897. – In the clearstorey, St Peter, the single realization of a plan to install the twelve apostles at high level in the chancel, 1901. – Also in the clearstorey, an ascended Christ in wine-purple robes. – In the traceried three-light N window, Christ in majesty amidst angels and apostles; by *Morris & Co.*, early C20.

ST MICHAEL (R.C.), Cardross Road, Dalreoch. A long church built in rust-red brick with a high boldly glazed belfry. By *Gillespie, Kidd & Coia*, 1952–4. There are similarities to their contemporary St Lawrence Church in Greenock but the escape from traditional forms is stronger here. The design takes full advantage of an elevated site. Raised on extensive underbuilding, the nave runs with the contours parallel to the road below. Steps climb to the W gable entrance from which a canopied concrete terrace wraps itself around the tall belfry to a glazed porch in the S wall. From a solid base the brick bell-tower is dramatically glazed to the S for almost its entire height. Only at the top does the glass grid change to a grid of brick, open like a doocot to the belfry proper. BELL cast by *Steven & Struthers*, 1953. Beyond the tower, nine diamond-framed windows mark out the long clearstorey. Brick boxes housing confessionals and the Lady Chapel project below. At the E end tall shadowed recesses throw light on the sanctuary. The roof is shallow-pitched; originally sheeted in corrugated asbestos, it was covered in copper in the 1960s and again in 2000.

Internal walls and flat ceiling are plaster, though the lower wall surfaces have been hypocritically clad in mock marble plastic laminate. Woodblock floor. At the W end are the main vestibule, a library room and a small chapel recess and office. From the vestibule a stair rises in the glazed belfry to reach the choir loft which crosses the W gable. Of the nine columned bays below the S clearstorey, two are glazed to a porch entry immediately E of the belfry, four project from the side aisle as confessionals and three open as the Lady Chapel at the E end. On the N, where small square windows are aligned below the clearstorey, two bays at the E end form the Sacred Heart Chapel. The chancel, raised five steps, is wide and open. Light falls on the sanctuary from windows recessed to the N and S. Drapes are hung on the E wall. Travertine paving in the chancel and side chapels.

All three ALTARS are similar in design; travertine in a white marble frame. – Octagonal, fawn marble FONT on a splayed base. – ORGAN by *Lewis & Co.*, installed in Dumbarton High Church in 1903, rebuilt in the choir gallery in 1981. – Bronze-painted plaster STATUE of St Michael in the S porch by *Benno Schotz*, 1963. – Hanging behind the belfry glazing, a crucified Christ with Mary and John; by *Jack Mortimer*. – STAINED GLASS. In the W window, St Michael again, framed by a vesica shape from which rainbow colours radiate, 1996; unexceptional and difficult to view in full. The five strongly coloured cross motif panels set in the Lady Chapel windows are much better.

ST PATRICK (R.C.), Strathleven Place. By *Dunn & Hansom* of Newcastle, 1901–3. A gabled, eight-bay, nave-and-aisles church

in rough-faced red Dumfries sandstone with ashlar dressings.
The w façade is solidly E.E. in character: three tall lancets
under a circle of three trefoils with a pointed-arched bipartite
window to each lean-to aisle. Below a gableted parapet, twin
entrance doors separated by a round-arched recess and flanked
by spear-steep blind arches. Consecration cross, dated 1901,
carved on the foundation stone on the l. jamb of N doorway;
above it, a consecration cross of 1950. Along the N and S elevations, coupled cusped lancets light the aisles and clearstoreys. Two
porches on S. In 1926–7, *Pugin & Pugin* added the square belfry
tower to the S, linking it to the church with a small Mortuary
Chapel (now designated as a Memorial Chapel). The junction
is seamlessly done. Materials are identical and the move to a more
Dec Gothic idiom seems entirely acceptable in such a show-
piece. The tower, buttressed on the angles, rises in three stages.
At the second stage, in niches set between quatrefoil-topped
cusped windows, the statues of three saints: St Patrick (w), St
Peter (S) and St Andrew (E); by *Boulton* of Cheltenham. Three-
light louvred belfry openings above conceal a carillon of twenty-
three bells, the first of its kind in Scotland, the tenor BELL cast
by *Gillett & Johnston*, Croydon, 1927. At the top, a crenellated
parapet with tall crocketed finials at the four corners. The parapet
has open tracery: quatrefoils to the E and N; the letters SANCTUS
to the W and S. At the E end of the church the roof ridge drops
twice; first for the chancel (the original sanctuary) and again for
the present sanctuary, added in 1935–6 when Dunn & Hansom's
E wall was removed by *Pugin & Pugin*. From the Sacristy,
extended in 1936, a glazed timber-framed Gothic corridor
connects to the PRESBYTERY, built in matching sandstone,
1906–8.

A timber screen, with leaded glass patterned in cusped ogee-
arched forms, separates the W vestibule from the nave. Above is
the choir loft reached by a stair in the SW porch. Gallery front
panelled with blind Dec tracery. Baptistery on N side of vestibule. Seven nave bays with red sandstone pointed-arched
arcading to aisles. Sandstone dressings to aisle and clearstorey
windows. Walls plastered above timber dado. Pitch pine boarding along cove cornice at wallhead. The roof is also boarded in
pitch pine, with gridded ribbing marking slope changes set by
scissor-trussed spars. Vestibule, centre and side aisles paved in
white marble. Red sandstone pointed chancel arch carried on
corbelled colonnettes at high level. In the chancel, a single
pointed arch l. and r., closed from the adjacent side chapel by
an oak screen carved in delicate Perp Gothic but open above
the springing point. Veined marble steps and paving, the latter
incorporating the symbols of the Four Evangelists. Roof as nave
but to a pointed vault section. In the SACRED HEART and LADY
CHAPELS, N and S, variegated patterned marble flooring and
lean-to boarded ceilings. A second high arch opens from the
chancel to the two-bay sanctuary. Red sandstone ashlar walls lit
by two lancets N and S and a pointed-arched window with a
traceried circle in the E. Boarded roof as in nave and chancel

but here twice sloped in 'mansard' section. Arch-braced truss on plain corbels. To the r. of the Lady Chapel, patterned marble floors lead to the SACRISTY and MEMORIAL CHAPEL. The latter, square in plan and walled in red sandstone ashlar above fluted dado panelling, has a coffered timber ceiling in dark oak. White marble floor inset with the symbols of the Crucifixion. In the SW corner, a door gives access to the belfry tower stair. Beyond the Sacristy, a *Minton* tile floor leads through the glazed connecting corridor to the Presbytery.

FURNISHINGS. The church is particularly well plenished. Several changes in arrangement have occurred. – Gabled, white marble BALDACCHINO of 1935–6 with six green marble columns surmounted by the sculpted figures of Aaron, l., and Melchizedek, r. Freestanding and bathed in light behind the chancel, it intensifies the depth and drama of the sanctuary. – Beyond is a white marble REREDOS, 1936: cusped arches with a domed canopied niche rising at the centre, all richly carved with crocketing and finials; coloured mosaics of Abraham's Sacrifice and the Feeding of the Five Thousand. – Here the HIGH ALTAR (now the Blessed Sacrament Altar) has a stepped marble mensa and a trefoil-gridded front of white Livorno marble reconstructed from the 1927 altar rail in 1998. – At the same time, the splayed ALTAR in the chancel was assembled, using white marble panels with cusped recesses taken from the E wall, the CREDENCE TABLE constructed from fragments of the dismantled altar rail, and the semi-octagonal PULPIT, 1927, moved to its position at the chancel arch. Marble reconstruction by *Tom MacMillan*. The pulpit, which is ornamented with small statues of Jesus and the four Evangelists, is white marble with rust marble panels and a dark green cornice. – Canopied oak CHOIR STALLS, six each side of chancel, 1927 (1936?) – Hanging in the chancel arch, a CALVARY of Continental provenance; the crucified Christ flanked below by Mary and John carried on octagonal colonnettes speared by the cross's transom; brought here *c.* 1908. – FONT, *c.* 1894, brought from the first St Patrick's Church built at Church Street in 1830; a deep stone bowl with fluted curved sides carried on clustered colonnettes on white marble base. – Richly elaborated Gothic ALTARS of white Livorno marble in the Sacred Heart and Lady Chapels; the former, brought from Italy, erected first. Each designed with a central canopied statue between carved panels recessed under cusped arches, 1927. In the Sacred Heart Chapel, Jesus between scenes set in Gethsemane and on the Emmaus road. In the Lady Chapel, Mary between her Annunciation and Coronation. – STATUARY. Flanking the Baptistery, St Anthony of Padua and St Joan of Arc, 1916; both made in Paris. – Marble figures of SS. Joseph and Patrick, 1935, stand guard at the chancel steps. – On the Sacristy side of the Lady Chapel is a white marble statue of Christ as the Infant of Prague with crown and orb. – Pietà in the Memorial Chapel by *W. Vickers & Co.*, Glasgow, 1928. – Placed centrally against the vestibule screen, an elongated, figural stone shaft with holy water cups corbelled on each side. A remarkably potent image of a

rainbow-winged St Michael the Archangel, whose aid is invoked
in the inscription on the socle. Sculpted, painted and lettered by
*Eric Gill*, 1920. Raised in memory of Father Michael Gordon
†1917 who fell in Flanders. The saint is shown triumphant over
evil, a snake painted in hoops of black, red and yellow which
may symbolize the colours of the German foe. – At the w end of
the s aisle, St Theresa of Lisieux carrying a crucifix and rose
garland. – ORGAN in the choir loft by *Andrew Watt & Son*,
Glasgow; the oak casing by *Pugin & Pugin*, 1927. – STAINED
GLASS. In the E window, a majestic red-cloaked Christ between
Pope Urban and Pope Pius X. – Two windows in the Memorial
Chapel: Christ raising Lazarus and Christ the King with Our
Lady of Mount Carmel. – Beside the door leading to the Sacristy
and Presbytery, a twin-light window with narrative panels depict-
ing apocryphal scenes from the life of SS. Anne and Joachim. –
In the Baptistery, '*Ecce Agnus Dei*'; Christ's baptism in the
Jordan.

Fortuitously hidden behind the church is the PARISH HALL
by *Alfred K. Gorra*, 1963. A few gratuitous Gothic arches in
brick do nothing to relieve its grim exterior.

30 ST PETER (R.C.), Howatshaws Road, Bellsmyre. 1970–1. Perhaps
*Garner, Preston & Strebel*'s finest achievement in Dumbarton and
a surprising discovery hidden on a hill of council housing. The
concept is familiar enough in C20 religious architecture; two
opposed slated monopitches rising steeply to create a high-level
clearstorey. Here the higher roof is continued at the E end to
form a belfry like a sharp elongated dormer. Walls are brick,
dark purply red in hue. Linked to the church around a paved
forecourt and garden is the Presbytery stepping downhill to the
s. Roofed in monopitches, it, too, is brick, the two-storey S
elevation articulated in a series of buttresses and mullions.

The interior is lofty and dark, immediately sensed as sacred.
The same brick prevails. The floor is dark too, glazed tiles varying from brown to maroon. Overhead, laminated pine beams
fall across a boarded ceiling to the N wall. The E wall, partially
hung with white drapes, steps back to allow side light to spill
across the sanctuary. The church space was originally intended
to continue under the lower monopitch (brick confessional
boxes project below the s eaves) with a choir secretly housed in
an attic gallery. Shuttered concrete walls and columns survive
below the clearstorey, *matières brutes* indeed, but the need for
ancillary accommodation has encroached on the worship space,
altered the confessional arrangement and left only a narrow side
aisle leading to a small chapel in the E.

The stone ALTAR, widely splayed from a central pedestal,
replaced the original wooden table in 1993. A splendid, perfectly
proportioned and positioned CROSS of laminated pine, elegantly
poised on a metal shoe, stands behind. – CHOIR STALLS and
PEWS plainly detailed in varnished pine. – Delicately worked in
brass sheet, the STATIONS OF THE CROSS, by *Berry* (?), may
be too abstract to be naïvely didactic but sparkle against the
dark brickwork of the N wall.

THE WEST KIRK, West Bridgend. Originally Bridgend United Presbyterian Church. By *John McLeod*, 1886–8. Restoration by *Richmond Architects*, 1993–9. The third church on the site. The original Relief Church of 1793–4, a whitewashed, piend-roofed, Georgian Gothic box, was superseded in 1859–60. This second building, West Bridgend Church, designed by *William Spence*, survives as hall accommodation, a plain gable-ended L-plan with Tudor-arched windows and a particularly attractive splayed-back steeple in the re-entrant. The present church abuts N facing the street. The E façade is a tall gabled front buttressed between nave and aisles with a ten-light wheel window of colonnaded spokes set at the centre. Below this, a gabled pointed-arched entrance with moulded ingoes and shafts. To l. and r., gabled staircase wings lit by triple lancets at the front and sides. On the roof ridge, a louvred roof ventilator with a leaded ogee dome, the bottle-rolled lead of the flared base in diamond pattern. Lateral elevations are plain with pilaster strips dividing the five bays. At the w end, a symmetrical, single-storey outcrop of piend roofs with a central gablet.

The church vestibule has a good mosaic floor and a ribbed plaster vault. Gothic glazed screen to inner vestibule. High five-bay interior, galleried on sides and rear. Cast iron cluster columns with shaft-rings and bell capitals continue through the balcony to leaf capitals under roof-beams. Plaster ceiling, panelled on slopes and soffits but decorated with a cusped-arch motif running along vertical faces at strut line. Similar motif repeats on gallery panelling. Pointed chancel arch with corner shafts rising to leaf capitals which align at abacus level with four-bay blind arcading l. and r. on the w wall. Above the organ pipes in the chancel is a ten-light telephone-dial w window with central cinquefoil. Raised central PULPIT on a canted bay plan of Gothic timber panelling. – STAINED GLASS in both gables and eight of ten two-light ground-floor windows. w and E wheel windows disappoint, the tracery filled with small decorative panes in green and yellow. – At the w end of the s wall, Christ appears to Mary in the Garden, white against an earthy warmth of plants and fruit trees. – Then, Christ in prayer in Gethsemane. – Next, Christ meets the woman at the well; by *G. Maile Studios*, London, 1965. – Last in line, SS Andrew and Paul, a memorial to the fallen of both World Wars, sadly blurred by fading lettering. – On the N wall is a window picturing Christ blessing little children, 1888, a memorial to the opening of the Sabbath School (*see* below). – Then, another Christ and two angel figures, female and mailed male; on the l., the designers' names, *J. T. Stewart* and *C. E. Stewart*, and on the r., *William Meikle & Sons*. – In the Reid memorial window, a crucified Christ with Mary and John, and to the r. Jesus appearing from the tomb; by *John Blyth*, 1980. – Lastly, a rose-robed Christ bearing the chalice, the design similar to SS Andrew and Paul, and on the r. a variegated ship launch scene, by *C. W. S. Design*, Lisburn, 1968.

Uphill, behind the 1860 church and the site once occupied by the first manse, is the old SABBATH SCHOOL, by *John*

*McLeod*, 1874, symmetrical Gothic now adapted without undue disfigurement to residential use.

CEMETERY AND PARKS

DUMBARTON CEMETERY, Stirling Road/Garshake Road. Opened 1854. Laid out by *Stewart Murray*, landscape gardener; a large area attractively landscaped with gently contoured paths and thickly planted with the usual accumulation of C19 and C20 gravemarkers. The main monuments are on the lower slopes not far from the gates. – Ringed Celtic CROSS precisely carved with scroll and figural ornament, the swelling base edged with chevron and interlace borders, *c.* 1920, commemorates Daniel Jackson †1931, his wife, sons and daughter; by *J. Gilfillan*. – Broken COLUMN on a rock base scrolled with inscription to Edwin Griffith †1907. – Dedicated to the masonic dead, a slender but strongly sculptural TOTEM in polychromatic marble, flanked by draped urns, 1900. – HEADSTONE to Daniel McAusland †1849, victim of cholera; inscribed white marble in a sandstone frame, guarded by putti. – In memory of the family of William Denny †1887, an immense white marble CROSS on a grey granite base, austerely impressive. – To Archibald Denny †1866, a cross-topped Gothic FINIAL by *James Young*. – Tall, plain OBELISK on a Classical stepped base raised by 'The Working Men of Dumbarton ... in the warmth of disinterested appreciation' to an older William Denny (1815–54) whose shipbuilding enterprise 'restored the drooping fortunes of the Ancient Town'. – Small temple MAUSOLEUM in banded sandstone, to more members of the Denny family; by *J. Gilfillan, c.* 1902. – A tall Gothic MONUMENT carrying an octagonal granite shaft, once banded, with a floral capital and gableted finial; to Peter Denny †1895, his wife and nine children. – James Denny †1864 and his wife are content with a simple OBELISK. – Another bossed Celtic CROSS carved with interlacing ornament and set on a swelling base, probably by *Gilfillan*, bears the name of Janet Macleod †1894, John Babtie †1916 and family. – Also perhaps the work of *Gilfillan*, on a stepped base, a grey granite Grecian MONUMENT, pedimented on four faces and domed above; a memorial to members of the town's second shipbuilding dynasty, John McMillan †1891 and his wife Jane †1893. – Similar but less grand, a domed granite MONUMENT with an aedicular front commemorates Robert McMillan †1912 and family; by *J. Gilfillan*. – To John Paterson †1855, a Graeco–Egyptian MONUMENT by *James Shanks* of Glasgow; draped urn perched on a battered base swept up to a gorge cornice. – Unusual in its triangular plan, a sandstone OBELISK to John McKechnie †1863, the shaft cut with masonic symbols. – Unusual for its material, another OBELISK carrying a draped urn, a rusting cast iron memorial to members of the Glen family, late C19. – Gothic SPIRE carried on small crocketed arched recesses on four pink granite colonnettes on a stepped base; late C19, to the Kirk family. – On the higher central ground of the graveyard, a massive pink granite SARCOPHAGUS to the

Whites of Overtoun. – In the same material, in an abstemious Gothic idiom, another SPIRE, rising from a tripartite base, honours the newspaper proprietor and editor Samuel Bennett †1876. – To Archibald Fraser Garvie †1901, a flat-topped grey granite OBELISK carrying a bronze wreath; decorative carving on the shaft flavoured with Art Nouveau. – Another Celtic CROSS, similar to those noted above, signed by *G. Buchanan*; to Allan Maclean †1891. – On a tall sandstone plinth, the bronze STATUE of John Proudfoot †1875, merchant in Liverpool, Rio Grande do Sul and Montevideo. – On the w boundary, a MEMORIAL WALL of five blind cusped pointed arches records the deaths of James Blair Risk of Meadowbank †1875 and his family. – Nearby, a Classical version of the same is dedicated to Alexander Campbell of Barnhill †1862; from an entablature-topped MEMORIAL WALL of five round-arched panels framed by coupled pilasters, a domed porch projects at the centre. – To shipowner's daughter Janet Rankin †1867, the cemetery's tallest SPIRE rising from a complex Gothic base with squat corner finials, gabled aedicules and colonnettes of pale green marble; by *Charles B. Grassby* of Glasgow. – In the shadow of the trees, a canopied CRUCIFIX watches over the graves of the Sisters of Notre Dame.

LEVEN EMBANKMENT. Dumbarton's sheltered riparian situation with easy access to the Clyde estuary gave it early importance both as a port and as a centre of shipbuilding and repair. It played a vital role as a base for the pacification of the Western Isles carried out by James IV in the last decade of the C15. Docks were constructed in 1505. In 1642 a new quay was built on the left bank of the Leven at the foot of the narrow lane known as Quay Pend. A decade later the town spurned an approach from Glasgow which could have boosted its status as a port. Its river commerce diminished. But by the C19, shipbuilding had boomed, especially after the deepening of the Leven in the 1850s. Docks, jetties and tidal basins appeared between the Parish Church and the Rock. The old pier became an esplanade in 1875. In the course of 1960s redevelopment this embankment area has been strengthened and landscaped as a pleasant walk-way with a series of tree-shaded car parking zones off Riverside Lane. Beyond the distillery, which blocks the way to the castle, shipyard land is being reclaimed.

LEVENGROVE PARK. A beautiful riverside park of mature trees, sweeping lawns and well-clipped hedges gifted to the burgh by shipping magnates John McMillan and Peter Denny, 1885. *John McLeod* appears to have been the architect responsible for the new sea-wall, lengthening the esplanade and designing the original conservatory, greenhouse, fern house and bandstand (all now demolished). At the entrance from Clyde Shore Road, a whimsically Tudor LODGE, 1884–5, with decorative plaster-work in half-timbered gables and a verandah porch framed by ogee-headed arches. Islanded in flower-beds, a truncated basin FOUNTAIN on four stub columns of pink granite. A small symmetrical PAVILION with a bellcast roof, its walls roughcast

above a red brick dado, has been boarded up. The town's WAR
MEMORIAL, erected 1920, sits at the S edge of the park beside
the Clyde. By *John Burnet, Son & Dick*. Blunted ashlar obelisk
enclosed by spear-headed iron railings and gates set on a stepped
base between quadrant walls; on a low stone pedestal projecting
from the N face, a bare-breasted bronze angel holds aloft a
wreath. Almost hidden by trees at the centre of the park are the
fragmentary remains of the Old Parish Church of Cardross (*see*
Churches, above).

### PUBLIC BUILDINGS

ARTIZAN BRIDGE. 1972–4. A long, elegantly understated, five-
span box-girder carriageway carried on inverted goal-post piers.
Designed to take the realigned A814 across the Leven, by *Babtie,
Shaw & Morton*, engineers, in consultation with architects *Garner,
Preston & Strebel*.

BRAEHEAD PRIMARY SCHOOL and MEADOWVIEW NURSERY,
Meadow Road. Built in red sandstone ashlar as Dumbarton
Academy to a competition-winning design by *John Rogerson* of
*McWhannell, Rogerson & Reid*, 1912–14. Coolly composed and
Classically erect, the symmetrical S front, nineteen bays wide
and two storeys tall, overlooks the Meadows. At the centre, an
open semicircular pediment interrupts the parapet to mark the
round-arched entrance below. Three triple-bay units recede and
advance l. and r., unified by a continuous eaves cornice toothed
with modillions. Hipped roofs reflect the rhythmic articulation
of the façade. Blockhouse toilet wings W and E. Domed ventilators rise from the ridge 'like Baroque tempiettos'. Large
segmentally-arched windows, placed asymmetrically on the N
elevation, light the assembly hall. To the W, off Townend Road,
the JANITOR'S HOUSE, dated 1914, makes play with pedimented
dormers passing through a sprocketed eaves. Extended in the
early 1930s.

BURGH HALL, Church Street. Plans to build a new Burgh
Academy with associated public halls and committee rooms were
originally prepared by *Thomas Gildard* in 1864. Although this
'chaste and elegant' Classical design was approved, the intervention of James White of Overtoun led to a vastly increased
budget and the appointment of architects *Melvin & Leiper* who
had 'little more than commenced business'. Building was completed 1865–6, though not without criticism. A writer to the
*Dumbarton Herald*, dissatisfied at the treatment of Gildard,
remarked upon some awkward planning, poor acoustics and a
staircase that had given way, asserting that the designers had
been prepared to 'sacrifice the *utile* to the *dulce*'.

The Hall, which presents a French Gothic façade in square-
snecked Kenmure sandstone to Church Street, certainly has
architectural aspiration. Symmetrical gabled block of two tall
storeys with large plate-traceried windows at first floor and five-
bay, pointed-arched arcading on the ground floor. At the centre,
a high belfry tower, its base open to the street, more *porte cochère*

than porch, with moulded arches, hooded and cusped, rising from broad piers. Also open, a second stage, aligned with the first floor behind, features a gabled Gothic aedicule set on a corbelled balcony parapet. Above this, the tall belfry with coupled lancets and, at the top, gabled telephone-dial windows framed by corbelled corner finials. Rising behind the conical stone peaks of these finials was a steep slated spire, the whole composition of the steeple intriguingly similar to that proposed by Sir George Gilbert Scott for the tower of Glasgow University. A fire in 1882 destroyed the spire, which was never rebuilt. The building was, nevertheless, restored by *William Leiper* who made provision for a School of Art in the attic, 1884. The six small dormer windows with cusped bargeboards belong to this conversion. By the time of the First World War a new burgh school had been built at Braehead and the building entered a period of changing administrative and commercial use. In 1976, a second fire destroyed the halls at the rear leaving the surviving fabric on Church Street in poor condition, especially the mullioned and transomed windows and half-octagonal stair towers on the E elevation. Extensive additions, including offices, library, a new hall and inner courtyard, were proposed by the local authority in 1976. All that was built, however, was the present BURGH HALL, a disciplined buttressed box in grey concrete blockwork, by *Dumbarton District Council*, 1984.

DALREOCH RAILWAY VIADUCT. Steel girder bridge, *c.* 1870, crossing the Leven E of Dalreoch Station in five spans. Tapering ashlar piers with rounded cutwaters to high-tide level. Vaulted occupation arches in W and E abutments. The five laminated timber arches of the original bridge, built 1847–8, were replaced with steel beams, shortly after the North British Railway took over the line.

DENNY CIVIC THEATRE, St Mary's Way. By *Alan Reiach, Eric Hall & Partners*, 1968–9. A bleak box in the town centre's ubiquitous blue-black brick. Brutalist escape stair in shuttered concrete. A new N entrance formed in a shallow convex bow continues to conceal any inner life.

DUMBARTON ACADEMY, Crosslet Road. 1935–7. The original Hartfield School buildings, readily identified by a symmetrical, immensely wide, two-storey façade, are the work of the unsung County Architect *Joseph Weekes*. Beneath a slated pyramid, the central entrance is in red brick edged with Art Deco detail. Lennox arms in the round arch of the first-floor window. On each side, twelve-bay classroom wings stretch out, skewed at mid-point to enfold the forecourt. The walls are roughcast above a red brick dado; the windows no longer original. At the ends, parapeted red brick pavilions with pilaster fins. Low boundary walls in brick and roughcast with Art Deco gates. Extensive later additions cannot match the coherence, nor the modishness, of this precious period piece.

DUMBARTON BRIDGE. In 1682, at the Convention of Burghs, a proposal was made to bridge the River Leven. It was not, however, until 1765 that the construction of a five-arched bridge was

completed by the local mason *John Brown*. Segmental arches,
with radial masonry fanning from the voussoirs, are carried on
piers with massive rounded cutwaters. In 1768 *John Smeaton*
reported on a sunken pier, advising Brown how to make good
the damage. In 1884 *W. R. Copland* added concrete footpaths
and balustrades, supporting this extra width on iron cantilever
brackets set between the cutwaters. Further reconstruction in
reinforced concrete by engineers *F. A. MacDonald & Partners*,
1933–4, added the concrete balustrade.

DUMBARTON CENTRAL STATION, Station Road. Built for
Dumbarton & Balloch Joint Railway by the Lanarkshire &
Dunbartonshire Railway. It replaced the earlier North British
Railway station of 1874, itself a successor to the original mid-
century station of the Caledonia & Dunbartonshire Joint
Railway. Construction in two stages, 1895–8; designed by a Mr
*Bonn* of engineers *Formans & McCall*. Renovation, 1992. High-
level tracks retained by pink sandstone walls running in parallel
along Station Road and Bankend Road. Crenellated parapets
and octagonal buttressing in red brick. Mock cross gunloops to
N. At the E end, arcuated Perp Gothic bays in stone and brick
define shops, ticket office and the under-bridge entrance to the
station above. All these now blocked. Access restricted to W
pedestrian tunnel from which long ramps rise to the two island
platforms; stair-flights at the E end of the platforms closed.
Waiting rooms, etc. in glazed brick; cream with orange dado.
Tudor-arched windows with leaded glass. Pitched roof over
offices extends W and E as continuous glazed roof-light on
arched lattice trusses carried by cast iron columns. Tapered lattice beams cantilever timber-boarded roofs over platforms.

DUMBARTON COTTAGE HOSPITAL, Townend Road. By *R.
Thornton Shiells & Thomson* of Edinburgh, 1888–90; some additions 1898 and 1904, the latter by *James M. Thomson*. Single-
storey, crowstep-gabled block in polychromatic sandstone. Over
a Gothic entrance is a square tower with mock machicolation
and pyramid roof.

DUMBARTON EAST STATION, Glasgow Road. 1896. Below the
railway bridge, behind two cast iron columns with egg-and-dart
capitals, moulded archways in triumphal arch arrangement
open to a diagonal flight of stairs. A central ironwork railing has
been retained from the original station but everything else has
gone. On the island platform, a small glazed shed; the impos-
turous, impecunious legacy of 1984 reconstruction.

DUMBARTON JOINT HOSPITAL, Cardross Road. By *J. M.
Crawford*, 1898–1901. Administration block in square-snecked
sandstone. Both the three-bay frontispiece and the gables are
pedimented. Domestic in scale and Georgian in disposition;
some aberrant detail around the entrance and vestigial scrolls
on the flanks vaguely redolent of ecclesiastical Baroque. Several
pavilion wards.

HEALTH CENTRE, High Street. Built in 1973 by *Western Regional
Hospital Board* on the site of the old Artizan settlement which
had grown up around the town's glassworks since the C18. A

collection of dull, flat-roofed CLASP-built pavilions unimproved by the green, profiled metal roof of the adjacent Out-Patients' Clinic. Tree-planted car parking but no response to the riverside site.

KNOXLAND PRIMARY SCHOOL, Leven Street. By *Dumbarton County Council*, 1973–4. Flat-roofed, single-storey classrooms in grey brick with cream-panelled fascias. Clearstorey-lit recreation hall embedded in plan.

MASONIC TEMPLE, Church Street. 1973–4. A building of severe elegance, though in the forbidding purple-dark facing brick favoured by *Garner, Preston & Strebel* in their extensive re-shaping of the town centre. Solid walls, glazed gaps and dark shadows in a composition of prismatic simplicity. Recessed windows w and s with battered brick plinths. Beside the canopied E entrance, a grey granite TABLET with Dumbarton's armorial elephant.

MEADOW SPORTS CENTRE, Meadow Road. Swimming pool and gymnasia, 1986–8. A vast industrial shed of a building with buttressed walls in brown and cream brickwork, the colour changed on arbitrarily drawn diagonals. The profiled metal of the roof, curved at the eaves, seems equally wilful in its raking edges. Glazed triangular-arched N entrance. A few diamond-shaped windows complete the obsession with decorative obliques.

Former MUNICIPAL BUILDINGS, College Street. By *James Thomson* of *John Baird & James Thomson*, Glasgow, 1899–1903. Baronial-Jacobean in square-snecked, Locharbriggs red sandstone. Both the s and E fronts, two storeys high, have an eaves line agitated by stepping gables, parapets and decoratively pedimented eaves dormers. All openings have roll-moulded jambs. Below a crowstepped gable at the w end of the s façade, the first-floor Council Chamber is lit by tall mullioned and transomed windows in a heavily corbelled, canted bay. The Chamber has two tall ogee-capped ridge ventilators. Central s entrance tower with four storey-height bartizans, a dated crowstepped gablet and flanking chimneys around a flat-topped French roof. E entrance tower similar in scale but with four tourelles and a leaded ogee roof. Entrance hall walls decoratively tiled. Panelled doors with Art Nouveau finger-plates. – STAINED GLASS. Coronation memorial staircase window shows King Edward, a view of the Castle and the heads of Bruce and Wallace; won in competition by *William Meikle & Sons* to a design by *J. T. Stewart*, 1903–4. – Windows by *Shrigley & Hunt* honour three of the town's provosts: the figures of Justice and Truth in a 'vigorous Renaissance' design for John McAusland †1901, installed 1907; Science and Engineering for Dr Peter Denny †1895; Faith and Fortitude 'well drawn . . . in a wealth of pure colour' for John Dixon †1822, installed 1909.

Erected in the grounds, 1902, a bronze STATUE of Peter Denny (1821–95) standing on a high Aberdeen granite plinth; figure by *William Hamo Thornycroft* of London, 1898. Bas relief panels on two faces of the plinth depict Denny's professions of shipbuilding and engineering. – Standing further E, a tall, red sandstone CROSS with a bossed head and plant scrolls carved on the shaft; a memorial to those who fell in the Boer War (1899–1902). *See* also Description, below, 'The College Bow'.

OLD PRISON, Glasgow Road. By *James Gillespie Graham* and *Robert Scott*, 1824–6, altered 1841, enlarged 1863 before being closed in 1883; the original two-storey cell-block was finally demolished in 1973. Fragments are incorporated into the landscaped verges along the S side of the A814: some low rubble walling, two twinned round-arched openings with iron grids (formerly windows to first-floor cells) and the entrance portal in its original position. The door, a studded timber yett, sits in a round-arched opening with imposts; above the cornice, the parapet carries the Dumbarton arms. Built into the wall nearby is the CROWN STONE ('GR' crowned between scrolls) which once adorned a chimneystack axially placed over the portal.

OUR LADY AND ST PATRICK'S HIGH SCHOOL, Hawthornhill Road. Characteristic horizontality by *Boissevain & Osmond*, 1967–8. A six-storey classroom block striped with continuous glazing and exposed aggregate spandrel bands. Detached assembly hall and grey brick ancillary buildings.

POLICE HEADQUARTERS, Stirling Road. By *Dumbarton County Council*, 1967. Low elongated offices with a ground floor unconvincingly faced in random rubble. At the gated entrance, a Baronial lodge by *James Thomson*, 1895 (*see* Description, below).

PUBLIC LIBRARY, Strathleven Place. 1908–10. Competition-winning design by the local architect *William Reid*. The narrow S front of Reid's design appears to be half a building, as if he anticipated a mirrored extension to the E. The Renaissance façade of white Dalreoch sandstone, only three bays wide, is in channelled ashlar. To the r., a round-arched entrance. At the middle of the façade, set slightly ahead of the door plane, a bay of recessing aedicule frames around a central window. Furthest forward, the two-storey corner, again aedicular, but with open pediments and a tall attic parapet returning W. The plan of this original building is long and deep with good-quality internal joinery and plasterwork. The old Reading Room has a nave and aisles arrangement with a segmental vault in panelled plaster under metal roof trusses, though this interior was altered and compromised when the Library was extended in a parallel strip plan on the E by Dumbarton Burgh, 1966–8. No attempt was made to reflect Reid's façade and the Strathleven Place elevation sadly continued as little more than bland roughcast wall. Mounted in 1969 in less than respectful isolation on the E wall is a bell-shaped stone TABLET, dated 1732 and 1790, a dormer fragment from the C18 MacKenzie House which stood on the N side of High Street opposite Quay Street until the extensive central redevelopments of the 1960s and 70s. The stone was originally part of the fabric of the Collegiate Church of St Mary (*see* Description, below); it bears the carving of a mitre flanked by the thistle and fleur-de-lis and the inscription TU DES CORONA DECUS.

ST MICHAEL'S PRIMARY SCHOOL, Cardross Road. By *West Dunbartonshire Council*, 1996–8. Bleakly symmetrical red brick front with a wide central gable. Steel roller shutters over every window add their own indictment.

St Patrick's Primary School, Crosslet Road. By *Dumbarton County Council*, 1971–2. A relaxed grouping of brown brick classrooms with cedar-boarded fascias and brown, concrete-tiled, monopitch roofs. Invitingly landscaped.

Scottish Maritime Museum (Denny Ship Model Experiment Tank), Castle Street. 1882–3; opened as a museum, 1988. A long, pitched-roof shed containing the 100m. hydraulic experimentation tank designed for Denny's Shipyard by *E. R. Mumford* and *J. McQuorn Rankine*. The street gable in polychromatic sandstone carries a carved bust and plaque commemorating William Froude (1811–79), 'THE GREATEST OF EXPERIMENTERS / AND / INVESTIGATORS IN HYDRODYNAMICS'. Besides the tank, which is still in use, workshops and timber-lined drawing office are preserved. Mounted in the grounds, the one-cylinder engine which *Robert Napier* designed in 1821 and installed in the wooden paddle-steamer *Leven*, built by James Lang at Dumbarton. Moved here from the Rock in 1969.

Sheriff Court House, Church Street. Originally a jail and court house, then Dumbarton County Buildings. Central w-facing block designed by *James Gillespie Graham* and *Robert Scott*, 1822, and built in fine ashlar, 1824–6, contemporary with the prison (q.v.). It replaced the Old Tolbooth, erected on the High Street 1640–1, and subsequently demolished in 1830. Cool Classicism: set on a channelled base, coupled Ionic pilasters mark out the three bays of a tall *piano nobile* carrying an eaves 84 entablature pedimented at the centre in front of a piended roof. Below the pediment, a tall window in a blind round arch; in the flanking bays, openings of similar height enhanced by architraves, cornices and elongated consoles. Below the central window, a pedimented porch with Tuscan columns, barely elevated from the tarmac and ill-served by a replacement architrave in steel. Forecourt and low enclosing wall with convex quadrants to axial entrance. Lower N and S wings in three-bay matching style with balustraded façade parapets, added by *William Spence*, 1862–3. At the rear, extensions N and S by *Duncan McNaughtan*, 1895–1900. Police offices, 1895–6. In the s wing, 1898–1900, a Council Chamber with a large Venetian window carried out in Gibbsian style, an echo of the *trompe l'oeil* windows painted on the E wall of Gillespie Graham's block. Lower building added between by *Halley & Neil*, 1906. The court room in the central block retains its original simple wooden furnishings. Columns with Corinthian capitals flank the panelled front of the judge's dais. Iron balustraded s gallery carried on two tall cast iron columns. Fine cornice with anthemion motif. In the Council Chamber (now serving as a court), arch-braced roof trusses with elaborate pendants, high corniced dado with fielded panels, and two glazed wall cases in which are mounted C18 flags. Open well stair. Some Art Nouveau leaded glass.

West Dunbartonshire Council Offices, Garshake Road. By *Lane, Bremner & Garnett*, 1962–5. Won in competition,

1960. A five-storey slab of offices regularly gridded with structural mullions forms the spine of the composition. To the NW, a
two-storey block, wide enough to contain inner courtyard
space, flanks the main approach which, passing under the spine,
reaches a granite-clad council chamber raised on pilotis to the SE.

DESCRIPTION

*1. Town Centre*

HIGH STREET retains its medieval line bending with the left bank
of the Leven. Both sides of the street are continuously developed. Beginning on the NE side, where C20 changes have been
more extensive, there is little now to recall the pattern of
narrow-fronted rig sites that characterized the old town. College
Street, which followed the line of the medieval Cross Vennel,
has gone. Across the street, however, close-packed properties
do still reflect something of the original tenure arrangements.
Always the more favoured feus, since the tofts here ran down to
the river's edge, the plots on the SW side of the street have few
wide frontages and are intermittently penetrated by vennels
running through to the Leven quay. Yet only one late medieval
building survives: Glencairn's Greit House (*see* below). The
architecture of Dumbarton's main street is comprehensively
C19 and C20 in provenance.

The Parish Church, now known as Riverside Church (*see*
Churches, above), is located at the SE end of High Street, where
a place of worship has stood since the C14. Ironically, the glebe
no longer stretches to the Leven banks. Cut off in the C19 by
McMillan's shipyard, from the 1930s its separation from the
river was cruelly reinforced with the construction of what was
then the largest whisky-making plant in Europe. Outrageously
tall boiling and rectifying columns and huge spirit receivers are
housed in bright red brick. Built by the Canadian giant Hiram
Walker & Sons, 1937–8, the grain DISTILLERY towers over the
church, dominates the town and can be seen for miles around.
Bottling and blending buildings were soon added and in the
second half of the C20 the complex continued to grow; the result
is an industrial colossus, red brick sculpture engineered on a
gigantic scale. Assertive and exciting in its own right, a man-made
rival to the Rock downstream, its impact on town and river is
implacable, even intimidating. Yet Riverside Church, drowned
in distillery shadow, somehow manages to keep its dignity. God is
not mocked; the steepled W front of the church looks out through
the kirkyard gates with axial concern, a more benign watchtower
on the quotidian life of High Street.

The SW side of the street begins in some style. No. 3, 1881–8,
is a fine five-bay palazzo built as offices for McMillan's Shipyard.
A symmetrical façade in ashlar with round-arched openings and
a pedimented aedicule entrance at street level, first-floor windows
with lugged architraves, and, above a heavy eaves cornice and
parapet, aedicule attic dormers. Quality continues at the BANK

OF SCOTLAND, 1897–8, a more or less symmetrical three-storey Tudor Gothic façade in pink sandstone, by *Peddie & Washington Browne*, for the British Linen Bank. Arched doorways, corbelled canted bays and mullioned and transomed windows, all exquisitely detailed. Across Riverside Lane at the ROYAL BANK, bolder, less fastidious ideas prevail; two shadowed walls of glazing set back below broad bands of cream tiling, by *Douglas Sanderson*, 1972. At Nos. 45–51, two three-storey tenements with shops below, mid C19. Architraved windows and a single stringcourse at the second-floor sills; simple street-wall sense. Then something special in black and white, the first of several Art Deco façades. First, No. 53, built for the Clydesdale Bank by *John Baird & James Thomson*, 1939. Five bays wide with three advanced and raised slightly at the centre. Fluted mock-Ionic pilasters with armorial crests in the capitals define this centre under a dentilled cornice. Also Art Deco, Nos. 55–63; two tall storeys, the windowed upper façade clad in cream tiling with chevron ornament in black, green, orange and cream edging the parapet, the same colours picked up in decorative motifs on the flanks. Built as tea-room, restaurant and shops; by *W. J. B. Wright*, 1938. Next, a high, narrow tenement with a half-timbered gable oversailing twin bays corbelled from first floor; late C19. At Quay Street, which leads to the Leven Embankment (*see* Parks, above), No. 79 retains some crude Deco detail: multiplication crosses banded horizontally and vertically on a deep corner parapet.

Across the lane, a more sophisticated period piece; still intact above an altered shopfront, a Burton trade-mark façade in white faience, 1937–8. Then, amazingly it seems, a C17 survivor. GLENCAIRN'S GREIT HOUSE, now used as local authority offices, was constructed in 1623 as the urban residence of the Earls of Glencairn. Built in a mixture of snecked and coursed rubble that was (and should be) harled, the façade is carried on an arcade of three round arches introduced by the Burgh Engineer, *William A. Macartney*, in 1924–5. A fourth, lower arch on the E is original. It opens to a vaulted passage, Quay Pend, that leads down to the river. Four regularly spaced lintelled windows light the floor above. Above these, four eaves dormers with varied decorative pediments. Art Deco again at Nos. 97–99, a buff-tiled, five-bay façade with finned mullions and a stepped parapet; by *Whyte & Nicol*, 1938. At Nos. 105–107, mid-C19 tenement modesty. Equally reserved, though with added cornices, seven tall first-floor windows at WINDSOR BUILDINGS, Nos. 121–125, *c.* 1870. Cut down from three to two storeys and mauled at street level, this once elegant tenement retains a high pend leading to the rear. Next to it is another wide-fronted, three-storey-and-attic tenement, Nos. 127–135, dated 1854. The five-bay façade is symmetrical with pilastered Venetian windows crushed at the centre of the first and second floors. After that there is little else to remark as the street wall drops in scale to Riverside Lane (formerly Brewery Lane). But then, with an abrupt eponymous surge, the tall tapering steeple of the High Church (*see* Churches, above) restores respectability, closing the curving vista w from High Street with almost as much urban percipience as the pedimented gable and spire of the Parish Church terminating the view E. A last three-storey tenement looks isolated and suburban scale weakens the corner of Bridge Street.

The NE side of High Street starts badly with a crudely horizontal brick office-block corner to Church Street. The gable of St Augustine's Church (*see* Churches, above) lifts the spirit a little, though not perhaps as high as might have been had its steeple not been clumsily aborted. Three-storey, ashlar tenements at Nos. 4–6 and 8–10 establish a street wall. Both are late C19, the former (dated 1888) with decorative carved panels below the second-floor sills and twin chimneys linked by a balustrade. The SAVINGS BANK, 1938, Art Deco Classicism by *Eric Sutherland*, is a subtly and elegantly proportioned ashlar façade marred by an added box fascia. Another good tenement at Nos. 16–20, *c.* 1885; two neat narrow dormers with round-arched windows front and sides are a bonus. No. 22, built for the Bank of Scotland, *c.* 1880, is a tall two-storey palazzo in granite and ashlar with dentilled cornices, a central doorpiece on raised pilasters, and a row of pilastered-arched windows at first floor. Next, Nos. 24–32, a long Art Deco wall: plain but rhythmically windowed shops and flats in granite and ashlar, built by Dumbarton Equitable Cooperative Society in 1938. Suddenly, the scale drops. Set back behind a row of silver birches is the main-street face of renewal effected by *Garner, Preston & Strebel* in 1966–9, part of their grand redevelopment plan won in competition in 1960. Below, in the shade of poured concrete canopies, shops; above, a floor of offices panelled in flint aggregate slabs (originally planned as gallery shopping).

At COLLEGE WAY this two-storey formula leads N into a pedestrianized TOWN SQUARE: more trees, a children's play area and the same grey uniformity raised on the N to three storeys. Despite the covered walkways and the leafy wash of foliage across the façades, a grim consistency of material and form make this a hard, uneasy place. Shops are vacant, maintenance is poor, town life is demeaned.

Urban activity holds to High Street. Urban architecture, too. At Nos. 84–92, the street's grandest tenement; four storeys of red sandstone alive with corniced windows, shallow canted bays and chimneystacks twinned by balustrades above the eaves. At Nos. 106–114, more shops and flats built by the Cooperative Society, 1938, in muted Art Deco. The ashlar façade of coupled windows is unimpaired but at street level only two of the grey granite shopfronts have managed to preserve their original decorative grilles. From here to Risk Street, mediocrity is rampant.

Between High Street and the dual carriageway sweep of the A814 everything is new. In the 1960s a radical programme of redevelopment razed the densely built-up core of the old town. In place of streets and lanes there is open space and much car parking; the urban structure has become amorphous, the lines of circu-

lation ambiguous. On the W, bounded by a realigned RISK
STREET, an enclave of medium-rise housing by *Garner, Preston
& Strebel*, 1965–70; four five-storey flatted blocks paired in
U-plan service courts, each open to the S but closed to the N by
a six-storey tower. The materials are those of 60s Brutalism,
blue engineering brick and off-the-shutter concrete. But the
geometries are strong, balconies accessing maisonette flats at
first and third floors arranged in a step-section profile. Nearby,
memories of COLLEGE STREET linger, more imagined than
visible perhaps. A civic agenda is evident in the creation of a
Town Square (*see* above). But the architecture is inadequate.
The Denny Theatre (*see* Public Buildings, above) turns a bare
brick back. The demolition of *John McLeod*'s North Church
does not help. The RIALTO CINEMA, 1914, survives in banal
isolation, reduced to bingo. Alone in this urban vacuum, the
Masonic Temple (*see* Public Buildings, above) has some robust
dignity. But it lies beyond the centre, sharing with the Burgh
Hall and Sheriff Court (*see* Public Buildings, above) a more
traditional relationship with CHURCH STREET which remains
as the link between the Glasgow Road roundabout and High
Street. Opposite the Sheriff Court is CHURCH COURT, *c.* 1980;
more flatted brick housing, lacking the polemical commitment
of the Risk Street flats but none the less pleasantly unassertive.

On the N edge of the town centre, a ramped underpass dips below
the dual carriageway. COLLEGE STREET reappears on the other
side. On the gushet with STATION ROAD, a four-storey Baronial
tenement, by *J. M. Crawford*, 1898, with broken-pedimented
eaves dormers and a canted bay on each street face. Above blind
coupled windows on the chamfered corner, a crowstepped gablet
with a single, suitably asymmetrical bartizan. More tenements,
*c.* 1900, run W down Station Road, Nos. 3–7 and 10–14, into
MEADOWBANK STREET, the corners marked by slated cones.
Across the street is the railway, elevated behind a battlemented
brick skyline as if on the parapet walk of some medieval town
wall.

In COLLEGE PARK, the former Municipal Buildings (*see*
Public Buildings, above) confront the traffic, here sprayed radially
from a town centre roundabout. Standing in the gardens of the
Municipal Buildings is the ancient arc of 'The College Bow',
relic of the COLLEGIATE CHURCH OF ST MARY founded
*c.* 1453–4 by Lady Isabella, Countess of Lennox and Duchess
of Albany, probably an adaptation or rebuilding of a chapel
dedicated to the Blessed Virgin Mary in the early C14. It was
partially destroyed in the late C16, became ruinous, was used as
a quarry in the C17 and was finally demolished in 1758. The surviving arch of chamfered voussoirs is carried on octagonal piers,
one of which incorporates new ashlar masonry. In 1850 the arch
was removed from its original site close to the present Central
Station and re-erected at the foot of Church Street, the last
fragments being cleared from the site when the railway arrived
in 1858. In 1907 it was again moved and rebuilt in the grounds
of the town's new administrative offices.

## 2. The West End

The A814 goes W over College Street underpass. Crossing the Artizan Bridge (*see* Public Buildings, above), it continues through Dalreoch en route to Helensburgh and the Gareloch. DENNYSTOWN, a gridded suburb of low flatted houses built for shipyard workers in the 1850s, has gone. In its place, three sixteen-storey point blocks, 1970. Past the West Kirk (*see* Churches, above), WEST BRIDGEND meets the Old Bridge (*see* Public Buildings, above). A long masonry wall, castellated with high merlons, conceals the grounds of Levenford House (*see* Mansions, below), the entrance to which is soon dramatically revealed. Powerfully poised on a massive outcrop of sandstone, LEVENFORD LODGE soars up in a splendid Baronial fusion of crowstepped gable, chimneystack with broached flues and a round cone-topped tower. Three straight flights of stairs climb to a round-arched bridge carrying Helenslee Road to the lodge gates. Below the bridge the drive that once led to Kirkton Quarry now goes nowhere. Opposite this theatrical conceit, tenements curve into a two-storey terrace along CLYDE SHORE ROAD. At No. 9, an ancient cobbled pend. On the l., past Veir Terrace, is Levengrove Park (*see* Cemetery and Parks, above). On the r., the leafy suburb of Kirktonhill, Dumbarton's West End. DIXON DRIVE has several solidly respectable late C19 villas by the local architect *John McLeod*. THE RECTORY and WESTCROFT, a high semi-detached block forming Nos. 2–4, have mullioned and transomed windows and neat truss-fronted dormers. A double-height five-light bow, good ridge ironwork and a magnificent conservatory distinguish No. 6, LYNFAIRN. Scale and quality are much the same along KIRKTON ROAD. On HELENSLEE ROAD, however, the great wealth accrued by Dumbarton's industrial barons makes itself evident. Pyramid-topped gatepiers are all that survive of *William Leiper*'s DUNMORE, a towered French Gothic mansion built as Kirktonhill House in 1866 for one of the directors of shipbuilders William Denny and Bros. But Levenford House, Garmoyle, Helenslee and Methlan Park, all of them built for the town's shipbuilding aristocracy, survive (*see* Mansions, below).

More modest middle-class houses line OXHILL ROAD which marks the W edge of Kirktonhill. Some black-and-white half-timbering appears; downmarket Arts and Crafts. Nos. 40–42, a three-storey semi-detached villa, is exceptional: two floors, with canted bays, in hard red brick, a half-timbered third storey jettied on timber brackets with a balcony between gables. No. 56 and No. 60 play a more orthodox game in similar idiom. To the w, the hilly fringes of town are covered with local authority housing; Brucehill, 1934–6, to the s of the A814, Castlehill, built a generation later, to the N. On CARDROSS ROAD (the A814), a relic of late C18 rural housing. Built for Easter Hole Farm by the architect-surveyor *Charles Ross*, BRUCE'S STABLES (also known as Braehead Cottages and 'Foule Hole') present a symmetrical screen-wall of three naïvely Gothick gables filled with blind ogees, lancets and gunloops and battlemented on the skews; behind each outer gable, a simple vernacular cottage.

## 3. The East End

GLASGOW ROAD runs E from the town-centre roundabout at the N end of Church Street. It is almost immediately suburban, passing between St James Retail Park on the N and a super-market to the S. A few late C19 cottage villas have survived this onslaught of commercialism. Star-and-scroll ironwork on the gables of Nos. 41–43. Further E, Nos. 67–69, late Georgian semi-detached; good dormers on a piended roof. Across the street, standing firm against Mammon, the Congregational Church (*see* Churches, above). Suddenly, at Newtown, urban intensity returns. On the l., Nos. 129–171, dated 1906, a long four-storey tenement range with ground-floor shops, corbelled chimneystacks and canted bays bursting through the overhang-ing eaves. At the E end, a curved windowed gushet capped by a slated cone looks over the railway bridge at Dumbarton East station (*see* Public Buildings, above).

Across the street, Nos. 96–106 are three-storey and plain, though with frontal chimneystacks stepping above the eaves; by *John Black*, 1882–4. Nos. 108–114, GRANGE PLACE, by *John G. Campbell*, 1905–6, have tripartite windows at all three levels. These are the tenements of KNOXLAND, a residential suburb built over a twenty-five-year period by Dumbarton Building Society on ground acquired from the local shipbuilder Peter Denny. Houses were intended for labourers, craftsmen and managers in the local yards. The plan is a simple grid with a central open space, KNOXLAND SQUARE, 1890.

Three parallel streets run S from Glasgow Road. WALLACE STREET has more tenements with stepped chimneys and round-arched close entries, Nos. 5–27, 1880s. Nos. 18–24 are similar in scale but with pulvinated architraves and keystoned cornices over the close entries, probably 1890s. Nos. 29–55 form a continuous range of cottage villas with tripartite windows below gabled eaves dormers; by *John G. Campbell*, 1904–5. Opposite is a line of ten similar but semi-detached houses, Nos. 26–64, probably also by *Campbell*. *Black*'s tenements recur along both sides of VICTORIA STREET, 1880s, and continue on the N side of Knoxland Square, Nos. 1–11, where they have brick turnpikes at the rear; probably mid 1890s. More of the same at Nos. 4–10 Bruce Street. On the S side of the Square, Nos. 2–24, a one-and-a-half-storey terrace with two-storey canted bays; by *George Budge*, 1897–9. A similar, though not identical, cottage-villa row at Nos. 26–52 Victoria Street. Nos. 9–37 BRUCE STREET and 10–28 BUCHANAN STREET, semi-detached like those in Wallace Street, must be by *Campbell, c.* 1905. More tenements by *John Black* line the N side of CASTLEGREEN STREET marking the S wall of the suburb. Nos. 1–11, 1880s (?), are without frontal stacks. At Nos. 15–27, 1890s (?), where rehabilitation has blocked a number of close entries, the stepped stacks return and there are more brick turnpikes at the rear facing Castlegreen Lane. Further E, ROCKVIEW TERRACE, a later stretch of red sandstone tenements with canted bays from street level, also built by Dumbarton Building Society, 1907–8, to the design of *John G. Campbell*; Nos. 33–37 rough-faced, 41–45 and 47–49 in hammered ashlar. Continuing the line of Victoria Street S of Castlegreen Street, Castle Road leads arrow-straight to the fortified Rock (*see* Dumbarton Castle, above).

Knoxland has lost several of the amenities originally provided to support the community: the church by *John McLeod*, 1884–5, demolished 1986; the school, also by *McLeod*, begun in 1885, doubled in size in 1889 and demolished 1974; and the bandstand in the Square with its pagoda roof fringed in filigree ironwork. A new school (*see* Public Buildings, above) has been built on Leven Street, its original site filled by a DISABILITY RESOURCE CENTRE, 1979–81, a low building in fawn brickwork saved from dreariness by a soldier course at lintel level, a corbelled eaves, and, inside, a bright, roof-lit hall. The only other addition worth a glance, notable more for its aggression than elegance, is a 1930s tenement at Nos. 12–14 Wallace Street which pushes forward two glassbrick-lit stair towers that seem almost Mayan in ambition.

BEECHWOOD TERRACE extends Glasgow Road further E in a long row of tenements with canted bays and T-plan frontal chimney stacks; Nos. 200–216, by *John G. Campbell*, 1908–13. Mirroring this model across the road is OVERTOUN TERRACE, a late tenement of twenty-one bays built in concrete blockwork as if in sandstone, 1930. It retains all its original stained-glass windows. SILVERTON AVENUE and OVERTOUN AVENUE are both delightfully tree-lined with terraces of red sandstone cottage villas, 1914–23, designed by *Campbell* (like the tenements and terraces of Knoxland) for Dumbarton Building Society. Thereafter, suburban mediocrity succeeded by the bleak walls of bonded warehouses. DUMBUCK HOUSE HOTEL none the less maintains a determined Classical symmetry – almost. Built *c.* 1824 as an estate mansion, it has been several times remodelled and extended. Flanking wings l. and r. are original but the parapeted piended porch and E wing are late 1980s additions. Tripartite windows appear at three levels; at first floor tall and corniced, in the attic shaped to form dormers with colonnette mullions.

### 4. The North

From the town-centre roundabout STRATHLEVEN PLACE leads NE between the Library (*see* Public Buildings, above) and the lanceted gable of St Patrick's Church (*see* Churches, above). On the r., a few early- and mid-Victorian mansions. BEN VIEW is grimly Gothic with quatrefoils cut in the bargeboards. DEVERON HOUSE, *c.* 1850, has Classical poise, symmetrical and piended, with a cornice carried across the façade from its central doorway. DRUMOYNE, formerly Strath Cottage, 1853, by *J. T. Rochead*,

Gothic again, but tepid Tudor. Tired and ill-treated, MANSFIELD HOUSE, 1837, has lost its self-respect.

Under the railway bridge BONHILL ROAD is tenemented. The scale is three-storey with full-height canted bays: Nos. 3–21 and 16–22, 1901–3, by *John G. Campbell*. But there is a black-and-white Tudor twist to this familiar theme. Crossing the gable of No. 3 is BANKEND, a one-and-a-half-storey house with a dormered, half-timbered upper floor. Similar tenements with similar villa-like adjuncts appear in WILLIAMSON AVENUE. And at the start of Meadow Road is AVALON, square-snecked below with stop-chamfered jambs, half-timbered above with gableted dormers; a charming little Tudor house looking w across Meadow Park. It seems likely that all of this is by *Campbell*. So, too, a tenement row in LATTA STREET (Nos. 2–9). Ranges at Nos. 23–29 and 36–40 Bonhill Road are flatter with fewer bays; dated 1889 and 1885, they are probably by a different designer. Earlier still are WESTONLEA HOUSE, *c.* 1845, and HARTFIELD HOUSE, 1853. Both are detached ashlar mansions of some Classical distinction, the former pedimented at the centre over a tripartite window and double-pilastered porch, the latter particularly elegant with canted bays l. and r. at ground floor.

Several late C20 attempts have been made to maintain the initial tenement scale of Bonhill Road. But none of this new housing has the necessary robust dignity. Beyond Roundriding Road, however, the mood changes as late C19 suburban villas line the road. The quality is modest but some details catch the eye. Intricately fretted canopies on console brackets shade the entrances to Nos. 74 and 76. Nos. 85 and 87 affect vaguely Romanesque windows at first floor. At No. 93, trefoil-headed windows. Nos. 103 and 105, last in line, have good ridge finials and tall round-arched staircase windows at the rear. On Townend Road, lowering the scale to single-storey, the LANGCRAIGS CENTRE, built for residential and day care by *Strathclyde Regional Council*, 1984–5, is a wide spread of low tiled roofs, one of which rises s over a clearstorey-lit central hall opening to a SE conservatory. More sheltered accommodation at WILLOX PARK HOME, off Colquhoun Street; by *Gillespie, Kidd & Coia*, 1959–60. Snaking single-storey rows with continuous glazing and some random Ronchamp-derived windows thrown in for modish measure; odd enough to win a Civic Trust Award in 1960.

Bonhill Road and Townend Road converge on a second round-about. Here local traffic encounters the A82 through-route linking Glasgow with Loch Lomond and Argyll. Bypassing the town, the tourists speed on to the NW. On the hill is Bellsmyre, a vast labyrinthine suburb of post-Second World War housing worth penetrating to discover St Peter's Church (R.C.) (*see* Churches, above). The A82 dual carriageway runs SE as STIRLING ROAD, passing between the inter-war housing of Silverton (naïve but optimistic Modernism now compromised by conservative re-hab) and later residential development uphill at Garshake. E of the Cemetery (*see* above), on the NE side of the road, are West

Dunbartonshire Council Offices and the Police Headquarters
(*see* Public Buildings, above). The latter has a gated approach
guarded by WEST OVERTOUN HOUSE, 1895, a small towered
and gabled lodge-house by *James Thomson*, confidently and
comprehensively Baronial. It once marked the start of a long
drive up-country to Overtoun House (q.v.). Not quite so distant,
but hidden in secluded grounds off Argyll Avenue, is CROSSLET
HOUSE, 1858, a rambling, bay-windowed mansion with consoled
eaves and an ashlar porch of Tuscan columns and pilasters added
(?) as a re-entrant entrance. The interior retains some consoled
cornices and dado panelling but fire regulations have ruined the
spatial impact of a galleried stairwell. The last houses on the
A82 are at Fourth Avenue, beyond which the road runs on
below the riven heights of Dumbuckhill Quarry to meet the
A814 at Milton (q.v.).

## MANSIONS

GARMOYLE, Helenslee Road. Pre-Lorimer Arts and Crafts Baronial
or 'old Scottish domestic', by *John Burnet, Son & Campbell*,
1890–2, the stylistic marriage reflected in red tiles and snecked
pink sandstone walls. Built for Lt.-Col. John M. Denny, from
1934 the house has served the needs of the Carmelite order.
The approach is from the N. Between three crowstepped gables,
asymmetrically arranged and randomly peppered with large and
small windows, red roof planes spill forward over the entrance.
From the l., the roof of the E service wing returns across one of
the gables 'to form a wide canted porch integrated with the
screen wall of the service court'. The welcoming attraction of
this shaded porch has been lost to later accretions added since
the house became a convent. To the S, three storeys look across
a tiered garden to the Clyde. SW drum corner with a conical
copper-clad roof. Stone dormers with boat-shaped pediments,
dated and monogrammed, break the eaves. To the r., a crowstepped gable with corbelled canted bay at second floor. More
sculpturally complex, the E elevation assimilates a mullioned
and transomed bay, another crowstepped gable and the curved
bow of the main staircase rising to a corbelled parapet that
encloses a bellcast copper cone. Uninspired residential extensions to the E, 1984. The interior is much altered. Behind the
wide round-arched entrance door, a mosaic floor in a plaster-
vaulted Hall.

HELENSLEE, Helenslee Road. Built 1855–6; remodelled and
enlarged 1866–7. In 1853 Peter Denny commissioned *J. T.
Rochead*, then engaged on the design of Levenford House (*see*
below) for James Denny, founding partner of the shipbuilding
dynasty. Surviving drawings show a two-storey T-plan mansion
symmetrical about the N–S stem of the T, with the entrance porch
located at the E end of the long cross axis. W, S and E elevations
are Italian Renaissance in spirit with round-arched windows set
in pilastered bays. Offices extend irregularly to the N. To what
extent these plans, dated 1854, were fully realized is difficult to

determine, for in 1866–7 *John Honeyman* radically reshaped the Denny residence. The orientation of the main entrance and the location of the staircase and N service quarters appear to have been respected but a tall tower, two of its bays four storeys high and two of them three, was added on the cross axis W of the stair. Beyond these higher additions, two more piend-roofed bays were built, reiterating the lower scale of the earlier house. It seems that Honeyman must also have extended the original building by two bays to the E, a decision which entailed the design of a new entrance porch. In the mid-1920s Keil School transferred to Helenslee from Southend in Kintyre and the house remained in educational use until 2000.

The entrance porch, at the centre of the E front, has broad-banded coupled Ionic columns with pilasters behind. Blind niches flank a doorway with entablature lintel and round-arched fanlight but the treatment of the three-bay E elevation is otherwise rather dull. Plain lintelled windows repeat along the six bays of the S front E of the tower, though a symmetrical 2-4-2 rhythm is achieved by canted bays at each end of the ground floor and a Regency-like balcony of light ironwork laid across the central four bays at first-floor level. Honeyman's tower culminates in a French roof, its balustraded parapet interrupted on three faces by a pedimented dormer. At second-floor level, another scrolled ironwork balcony links two corniced windows. At the same level, on the adjoining lower part of the tower, a pilastered tripartite window opens on to the roof of a two-storey canted bay. From this balcony an escape stair, no doubt neces-sitated by the building's conversion to educational use, corkscrews to the ground. At the W end, a two-bay extension repeats the treatment of the E portion of the building. A five-light bow window projects from the W gable. On the N, altered and extended service accommodation projects in confusion. Beyond this, as the ground rises, a congeries of temporary classroom sheds has accumulated chaotically.

INTERIOR. Far from immune to the rough rigours of school life, the house's original splendour has struggled to survive. A black and white mosaic floor with Greek fret margins, damaged and unrepaired, sets the sad tone at the threshold. In the inner porch, a decorative *Minton* tile floor is intact. Above is an excep-tionally fine plaster ceiling, circle in square, with the most delicate combination of Classical mouldings. This ceiling, on which Etruscan motifs are depicted, is polychromatic, a last example of the house's earlier refinement. The porch doorways, variations on the Palladian motif, establish a recurring pattern. Here they are lintelled between Corinthian columns held free from the walls with semicircular fanlights in the arch above. Further E down the central corridor, where, for example, they mark the staircase zone, they are without lintels. Columns may be coupled or single. In the main Hall there is a modillioned cornice and a second tiled floor, multi-coloured and patterned in a complex geometry of squares and diamonds. To the r., the main stair rises in three flights through an open well. Some

naïvely floral STAINED GLASS in three tall round-arched N
windows carries the motto FORTIS ET BENIGNUS and a heraldic
hand raised in blessing. This Denny family crest also appears
worked in the ironwork balusters of the staircase. The Library,
at the centre of the building on the S side of the corridor, is
divided into two zones by a wide lintelled opening framed by
coupled Corinthian columns and pilasters. Magnificent plaster
ceilings and cornices in each part of the room; an oval ring with
small pendants in the W, a circle in a square in the E. Two
round-arched fireplaces in ochre-flecked black marble. In the
room at the W end of the ground floor there is another ornamental plaster ceiling divided by ribs into hexagonal, square,
trapezoidal and arrow-shaped panels. A cornice-ringed rose
responds to the W bow. Slender column-mullions divide the
window's five lights, their wide-spreading scroll capitals redolent
of those Alexander 'Greek' Thomson would use a few years
later on the façade of Egyptian Halls in Glasgow. Marble fireplace similar to those in the Library.

On the lawn E of the house is a larger-than-life bronze
STATUE of Sir William Mackinnon (1823–93), whose bequest
founded Keil School in 1915. Dated 1899; by *Charles McBride*
of Edinburgh. It stands high on a tapering cylindrical base of
pale pink granite. Below the cornice is a series of bronze panels
depicting the family crest and galleons in full sail. Above the
stepped base, a bronze ring of thistles. Moved here from the
original school's site at Southend, Argyll.

The L-plan STABLES, designed by *Honeyman* in 1865, lie
some 0.4km. N. Gothic, with hooded pointed-arched lancets
and doors opening to a cobbled courtyard in the re-entrant.
The capitals of several jamb shafts remain uncarved. From the
attic, a canted bay pushes through the crowstepped S gable,
carried by corbelling on to the Composite capital of a single
pink granite column. At the SE corner of the E arm of the plan,
a round tower with a slated cone roof; it bears a clock by *James
Ritchie & Son*, Edinburgh. Gothic GATEPIERS with beheaded
lamp standards mark the entrance to the yard, but there are no
gates. Three-bay single-storey LODGE at the entrance to the
drive from Helenslee Road; *c.* 1865, also by *Honeyman* (?). Low
quadrant walls and corniced GATEPIERS with ball finials.

LEVENFORD HOUSE, Helenslee Road. Exuberant Baronial by
*J. T. Rochead*, 1852–3. Built for the shipbuilder James Denny
who hitherto had 'resided over and against the old churchyard'
in a noxious and far from salubrious part of town. Denny's new
house, on higher, healthier ground, was the first of several
mansions to be built on Kirktonhill by the industrial elite of
Victorian Dumbarton. Sated on the architectural meat provided
by R. W. Billings' recently published *Baronial and Ecclesiastical
Antiquities of Scotland* (a work to which Rochead had subscribed),
it soon became known as 'Castle Folly'. It does indeed possess
a high tower, square in plan with boldly rounded corners, visually
commanding if not actually defensive. Situated at the SE corner
of the house, it rises through four rubble storeys to a heavily

machicolated parapet walk from behind which emerges a gabled caphouse. Mock cannon and gunloops are spaced along the parapet wall. Tall windows lighting apartments at ground- and first-floor levels, including a segmental bow corbelled on the E, penetrate the thick walls. The other rooms of the house pack around the tower on the W and N with lower offices, coach-house and two-stall stable spreading around a small NW court-yard. A two-storey canted bay to the S corbels asymmetrically to one of several crowstepped gables. But it is difficult to deter-mine the exact extent of Rochead's work, for Levenford was later considerably enlarged to the W. In 1890 *John Burnet, Son & Campbell* added a new Dining Room, Library and Study, at the same time remodelling the entire interior. Thus altered, the house remained a home for several decades until in 1938 it was gifted to the local authority. Now used by West Dunbartonshire Library Services, it survives without undue impairment. For Levenford Lodge, *see* Description, above.

INTERIOR. The E entrance to the house, placed by Rochead at lower ground-floor level, is still in use. Under a mural panel carved with a galleon in full sail, a round-arched doorway with a fine cable moulding opens abruptly to a staircase that rises to the Hall above. In the stairwell, lit by a tall three-light window with stepping sills, an ornate timber chimneypiece carved with the heads of Walter Scott, John Knox, Robert Burns, George Buchanan and James Stewart, Earl of Moray. *Burnet*'s entrance, however, is through the W porch, a heavily half-timbered pitched-roof structure squeezed between his new Dining Room and Library. The porch has a mosaic floor and, on the N wall, a dado of glazed maroon tiles. Above, unglazed rust-coloured tiles inset with two carved stone tiles and a copper panel depict-ing a young girl holding a flower. The Hall has high dado panelling plastered above to a heavy egg-and-dart cornice. Round-arched panels above a number of doors are filled with decorative plaster strapwork. On the S wall, a massive stone chimneypiece: engaged columns carved in the capitals with Celtic ornament; mottled sage green tiling in the fireplace. Centred on the chimneypiece, a narrow ceiling void with semicircular ends (now glazed) opens to the upper hall. Two original brass and crystal light pendants: glass bell clasped by three curved and scrolled stems. In the Dining Room, a low dado, plaster walls and a dark timber ceiling, beamed, joisted and boarded. Stained oak chimneypiece with rounded corners; a Mannerist arcade above the mantel carries an entablature and chimney-breast above. Fawn-flecked black marble fireplace. Four painted glass panels in the N bay window are coloured copies of Slezer's 1693 views of Glasgow, Stirling Castle, Dumbarton Castle and the Castle of Edinburgh. The Library also has a boarded timber ceiling. Door-height bookstacks on all four walls. Another characteristically *Burnet* chimneypiece; here the recess above the mantel contains a framed mirror below a pedimented dentilled cornice. Below the mantel a moulded timber surround and thin pale pink marble frame; in the fireplace, mottled sage green tiles. Double doors open to the Drawing Room. Knobbly cake-icing cornice and ceiling rose. White marble chimneypiece carved with garlands on a deep mantel panel carried by angel-headed fluted consoles. Inset above the mantel is a mirrored panel behind thin twist colonnettes. A number of small marble and tile fireplaces remain in the bedrooms on the upper floor. Timber-boarded bathrooms retain their original fittings including niche showers and lidded water closets.

METHLAN PARK, Clyde Shore Road. A large if not particularly attractive mansion raised to distinction by a tall tower. By *John McLeod*, 1880–1, for the McMillan family. In 1935 the house became a home for soldiers, sailors and shipyard workers, later passing into the care of the Salvation Army. Abandoned since 1993.

The Italianate tower, set over an entrance placed, like that at nearby Helenslee (*see* above), against the centre of the E front, rises in four stages to a shallow-pitched pyramid roof. A porch of coupled Composite columns carrying an entablature and balustraded parapet with ball finials projects E. Ground- and first-floor stages of the tower repeat the quoins, strings and eaves cornice of the main house. In the upper stages, however, the architectural treatment is more ornate. Quoining continues. At second-floor level, two round-arched windows on each face; at the third floor, below a consoled eaves, a four-light pilastrade. This elaboration finds no echo in the exterior of the house itself, though the S front is articulated by a canted bay and five-light bow, both carried through two storeys. The interior, however, has decorative plasterwork and timber panelling. In the Drawing Room, a ribbed stencilled ceiling and Corinthian-columned screen. There are several chimneypieces; that in the Smoking Room decorated with tiles by *Moyr Smith* depicting scenes from the writings of Sir Walter Scott. STAINED GLASS in the three tall round-arched windows lighting the N staircase illustrates three scenes from McMillan clan history, including the separation of the eponymous Methlan from his brother Buchanan in 1214.

Single-storey L-plan LODGE, 1880–1, also by McLeod. Quadrant walls linked to GATEPIERS with bracketed cornice and decorative cap.

DUN, Dumbowie. 1km. NE. About 9m. in diameter within a wall 4m. thick. Excavated in 1895, the customary assemblage of stone and bone implements, whetstones and querns was discovered. There was also a collection of fake artefacts comparable to those from the nearby crannog at Dumbuck, a *cause célèbre* at the time.

FORT, Sheep Hill. 2km. SE, on an isolated rocky knoll overlooking the Clyde. Of two periods, the earlier being the small stone walled defence on the summit, later destroyed by fire. The later and larger fort has entrances to N and S. Excavation discovered pottery, moulds, jet bracelets and a blue glass bead broadly dating from CI BC to CI AD.

CAIRN, Dumbarton Muir. 1.7km. S of Wester Cameron Farm, The 'Lang Cairn' measures about 56m. in length and still stands almost 2m. high; two lateral chambers within the mound are still visible as is the façade of upright stones at the ESE end with panels of drystone walling between them. Twin portal stones at the centre of the façade formerly gave access to the principal chamber, but the precise arrangement is not clear. Some 5.5m. to the SW there is a round cairn 8m. in diameter.

# DUNBLANE S 7000

A cathedral city, though small, on the Allan Water 7 km. N of Stirling. Medieval belief asserts that St Blane (or Blaan, a rather shadowy figure at best) established a place of worship *c.* 600, on a dun or Pictish fort elevated above the l. bank of the river, but there can be no certainty of this. By the C9, however, Dunblane had become a monastic centre and it is possible that relics were brought here from Blane's missionary base at Kingarth on Bute following Norse raids on the island. In the C12 the bishopric was confirmed and a stone church built. After 1237 the cathedral began to take shape, the lower storeys of its S tower retained from the earlier building. By the following century the town had become a burgh and, at the start of the C15, the river was bridged. But it was the development of weaving in the late C18 which stimulated growth. By 1820 over 700 handloom weavers worked in the cottages of Bridgend W of the bridge, in Mill Row and High Street on the more populous E bank, and in the linear township of Ramoyle which curved NE from the cathedral between Laigh Hill and Holme Hill. Shortly after the arrival of the railway from Stirling in mid century the first villas were built. As the textile industry died, enthusiasm for the local mineral springs (favourably analysed in 1873) turned the town's attention to its visitors. Fostered by good road and rail links and by the restoration of the cathedral, tourism remains important.

## CATHEDRAL CHURCH OF ST BLANE AND
## ST LAURENCE

### CATHEDRAL AND CLOSE

As in medieval Aberdeen, Elgin and Glasgow, worship and trade produced a 'pattern of two towns' (McKean, 1996). The separation is not great here but the distinction of ecclesiastical from secular is still perceptible. Rising above town and river, Dunblane's Cathedral sits apart. Beyond The Cross, in an open rectangular plot defined by low-scale buildings on the S, E and N, a grassy

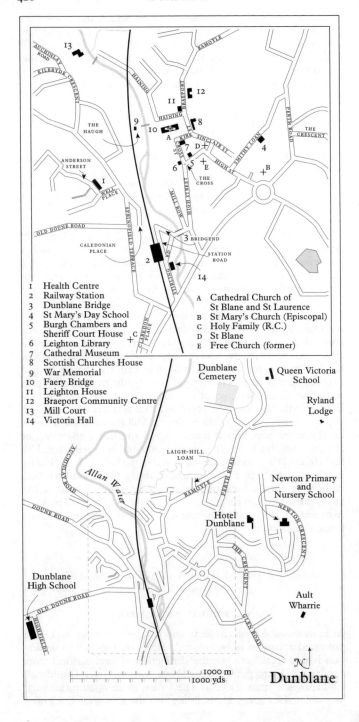

1   Health Centre
2   Railway Station
3   Dunblane Bridge
4   St Mary's Day School
5   Burgh Chambers and
    Sheriff Court House
6   Leighton Library
7   Cathedral Museum
8   Scottish Churches House
9   War Memorial
10  Faery Bridge
11  Leighton House
12  Braeport Community Centre
13  Mill Court
14  Victoria Hall

A   Cathedral Church of
    St Blane and St Laurence
B   St Mary's Church (Episcopal)
C   Holy Family (R.C.)
D   St Blane
E   Free Church (former)

Dunblane

graveyard garth gives the great church space and presence. It dominates the N end of the burgh, the horizontality of its elongated mass only partly balanced by the verticality of the tower part-way down its length. Ruskin found the unrestored cathedral 'the loveliest ruins in Scotland (and in its own way the loveliest in the world)'. He may have seen more, but not much more, of the old ecclesiastical enclave of the chanonry, long windswept from the W and lacking the enclosure it probably enjoyed in medieval times, with the bishop's palace flanked by manses for the dignitaries and canons, and a residence for the chaplains. Of all this, only fragmentary remains of the bishop's palace (*see* below) survive in identifiable state, though it may be that more than one of the manses has provided the nucleus of more recent buildings.

## The Medieval Cathedral*

The site is ancient, sacred perhaps from the C7. The existence of a religious settlement around the C8 and C9 is attested by two cross slabs, and it may later have developed into an episcopal centre. The first certain mention of a bishop, however, is in 1155, but it is likely it was by then already well established, under the protection of Malise, Earl of Strathearn. Dunblane is in the Menteith part of the diocese, and there may have been another episcopal centre in the Strathearn area, at Muthill. There was another important religious community within Strathearn at Inchaffray and, following the election of the Dominican friar Clement as bishop in 1233, there were thoughts of relocating the see to the Augustinian abbey there. At the time of Clement's arrival the church at Dunblane was said to be roofless and the finances of the diocese in disarray but, following a papal mandate of 1237, rebuilding of the cathedral commenced on the present site. By the later C13 the cathedral had an aisled nave incorporating an older S tower, and an aisleless choir with an adjoining N range providing sacristy and Chapter House. The cathedral was eventually served by a chapter of four dignitaries, the archdeacon and eleven prebendaries; there were also twelve choral chaplains by the time of the Reformation.

## The Cathedral since the Reformation

The first impact of the Reformation was felt in June 1559, when orders were given by the Earl of Argyll to purge the cathedral of 'Monuments of idolatrye'. By 1562 there was a reformed minister in place, and it was perhaps soon afterwards that the decision was taken to limit parochial worship to the chancel. In 1622 the nave was said to have lost its roof and Slezer's view of 1693 confirms this, excepting the tower and E bays of the S aisle, which we know was increasingly in use as a burial place. The existence of internal galleries in the chancel is indicated by a forestair against its E bay.

*The account of the cathedral (with the exception of the stained glass) has been written by Richard Fawcett.

To understand the present state of the cathedral it is necessary to take account of the restorations it underwent in the C19. The first major restoration, limited to the chancel and its adjacent N range, was carried out by *James Gillespie Graham* in 1816–19. Tracery inspired by English 'Perpendicular' forms was inserted in the windows of the S flank and on the N side of the presbytery, with an intersecting design containing cusped roundels in the E window. By that date the original tracery had evidently been lost, and Graham's designs were stock pattern-book types. Internal floor levels were also raised. In 1860–2 the roofs of the chancel and N range, which may until then have been still essentially medieval, were renewed to a flattened section, by *Thomas Brown Jun.* of *Brown and Wardrop*; the S chancel parapet was restored at the same time. Repairs to the tower and its spire were carried out in 1866–8 by *H.M. Office of Works*, at a time when the state was increasingly becoming involved in works at the Scottish cathedrals. The chancel was yet again deemed to be in a poor condition in 1873, and works were started, apparently with the advice of *G. Gilbert Scott* and of *Robert Matheson* of H.M. Office of Works. The original floor levels in the chancel were restored, efforts made to allow surviving medieval features to be seen to better advantage, and the windows above the chancel arch re-opened and glazed. In the course of this work two early cross slabs were found below the stair at the W end of the N chancel range.

The most far-reaching C19 campaign of restoration was that carried out in 1889–93 under the leadership of the Rev. Alexander Ritchie and to the designs of *R. Rowand Anderson*. By 1886 the capacity of the chancel was deemed to be insufficient and, after considering the possibilities of extending the chancel or of building a new church elsewhere, it was decided to bring the ruined nave back into use. Despite disagreements between architect and clients the work was carried through to completion at a cost of over £26,000, of which £19,000 was contributed by Mrs Wallace of Glassingal. The work was also carried out in the face of objections from John Ruskin, who poured scorn on Anderson's 'vulgar brutality', and the Society for the Protection of Ancient Buildings' consideration that the 'scheme must necessarily be of a destructive character'. However, driven by the spirit of the ecclesiological revival within the 'high church' wing of the Church of Scotland, and under the close vigilance of the Board of Manufactures, in whose ownership the cathedral had by then been vested, the end result attempted to pay close regard to the aims of the medieval builders. But it cannot have been easy to put it to Presbyterian uses once completed, with the communion table on the site of the high altar and a screen where the original chancel screen had been. Much of the restoration was based on analysis of surviving evidence, the main new elements for which there was no evidence being the insertion of tracery of C13 types in the chancel, the construction of a gable over the flank of the E bay of each of the nave aisles to give the impression of transeptal chapels, and the creation of triforium-like openings on the N side of the chancel into the upper floor of the N range. Nevertheless, there was much stone replacement with substitution of ashlar for rubble, and at least enough of the nave's clearstorey arcade was removed to allow the construction of an elegant little garden house at Glassingal! The re-medievalization of the chancel was completed when canopied stalls, a reredos-like screen behind the communion table, and a new organ case to the designs of *Robert S. Lorimer*, who had earlier worked with Anderson as his draughtsman, were provided in 1912–14.

Later works that must be briefly mentioned included the wainscoting and paving of the Chapter House and sacristy by *Reginald Fairlie* in 1934 and 1938, and the fitting out of the chamber in the SW nave buttress as the Clement Chapel by *Edith Burnet Hughes* in 1964.

## THE PLAN

The plan is composed of four principal elements dating from two main building operations: the first operation of the second quarter of the C12, the others of the second, third and fourth quarters of the C13.

At the E end is an unaisled rectangular chancel of six narrow bays. Running along the N side of all but the E bay of this chancel is a two-storeyed range which presumably housed the sacristy and Chapter House at the lower level, with a treasury and chapel above. This N range was originally entered either from a doorway between presbytery and canons' choir, or through a small vestibule opening off the Lady Chapel at the E end of the N nave aisle; also within this vestibule is a spiral stair to the first floor of the N range. There is a third doorway into the range, inserted in 1893 through the middle bay of the range's N wall. The nave has aisles along both flanks, and the eight bays into which it is divided are marked externally in most cases by buttresses; the two E bays, where there are chapels at the aisle ends, are narrower than the rest. Straddling the S aisle wall, and projecting irregularly into the third and fourth bays from the W, is the bell-tower, the only part of the earlier building to have been retained; it has a spacious spiral stair in its SW angle. The great processional entrance to the nave was at the centre of the W front. The principal lay entrance was, rather unusually, in the third bay from the E of the S aisle, where it was evidently originally covered by a porch in the re-entrant angle between the aisle and tower. Other doorways were provided in the second bay from the W of the S aisle and the third bay from the W of the N aisle. There is a spiral stair to the clearstorey and W front passages in the massive buttress at the W end of the N nave arcade. In the corresponding position on the S side is a small vaulted chamber; it has been suggested, but with no firm evidence, that this chamber may have been an anchorite's cell.

The basic plan of extended aisleless chancel and aisled nave was reflected in a number of other C13 cathedrals, the closest parallels being with Dunkeld (Perth and Kinross), where the chancel is C13 and the nave early C15. The closest parallel for

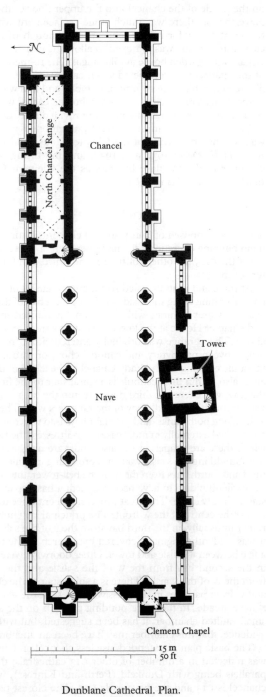

Dunblane Cathedral. Plan.

the elongated N range for Chapter House and sacristy is at Fortrose (Highland). But the most extraordinary feature of the plan is the incorporation of an earlier tower at a seemingly arbitrary point in the s nave aisle, and for this there are no close parallels. Asymmetrically placed bell-towers were certainly a common feature of major Scottish churches, though they were more usually placed at the NW corner of the nave, as at Glasgow Dunkeld (Perth and Kinross) and Brechin (Angus) Cathedrals (before the addition of the second tower) or at the abbeys of Lindores (Fife) or Cambuskenneth (q.v.). At Dunblane the situation was presumably complicated by the wish to retain an earlier freestanding tower, presumably for reasons of piety that can no longer be known, on a site that was both limited in size and possibly with unstable ground. A partly comparable approach was adopted at the Augustinian priory of Restenneth (Angus), where an early tower was retained to one side at the junction of the chancel and nave as rebuilt in the C13. As there, it is likely that at Dunblane the odd position of the tower would have been less evident internally when all liturgical furnishings were in place.

## The Medieval Building Sequence

The earliest part of the cathedral is clearly the four lower stages of the tower, which appears to have been initially a freestanding structure with an elevated entrance through its N face, and with belfry openings to all faces of its fourth stage. On stylistic grounds this tower should probably be placed in the second quarter of the C12, shortly before the first recorded reference to Bishop Laurence in 1155. Nothing is known of the church associated with this tower in the C12, though a number of chevron-decorated voussoirs displayed at the w end of the N nave aisle show that at least part of it was of similar date to the tower, and that it was work of some quality.

The continuous base course around the walls of the rest of the cathedral, although heavily restored in places, appears to be essentially authentic, suggesting that the whole of the cathedral apart from the tower was laid out in a single operation, no doubt after the settlement of the diocese's finances in 1237. The architectural evidence suggests that the order of construction after the base course had been laid out was first the N chancel range, then the nave and finally the chancel. This indicates either that an earlier chancel was retained in use for some years, or that a chancel as first built after 1237 was eventually deemed inadequate and rebuilt to the same plan but to a greater height.

The N chancel range, the administrative hub of the cathedral, was presumably built relatively quickly, with quadripartite vaulting over its lower storey, and simple groupings of lancets within containing arches. Construction of the nave was probably more protracted, and involved a number of changes of design. As first planned it was probably to have had lower arcades, and stone vaults over the aisles, but it seems that, after the outer aisle walls had been built, it was decided to heighten the arcades and abandon vaulting over the aisles. Later still, after the clear-

storey had been started, windows were introduced with a hybrid
form of plate and bar tracery in perference to the paired windows
of the earlier bays of the clearstorey or the grouped lancets of
the nave aisles. Bar tracery reached Scotland around the turn of
the third and fourth quarters of the C13, at Elgin (Moray) and
Glasgow Cathedrals and at Sweetheart Abbey (Dumfries and
Galloway), suggesting that completion of Dunblane's nave may
have been around the 1260s or 70s. Understanding of the date
of the chancel is hampered by the loss of the original window
tracery, but evidence suggests it post-dates the nave. From the
start its plan, as indicated by the buttressing laid out with the
base course, was for seven bays; narrower than those in the nave,
with presumably nothing more ambitious intended for the s
windows than grouped lancets. As eventually built, it was given
the very large windows usual for the later C13 (cf. Dunkeld), the
narrow spacing of the buttresses meaning that greater size had
to be gained by increasing their height. The relation of the chancel window mouldings to those of the nave arcades leaves little
doubt that these window openings are indeed of the later C13. It
seems equally clear that the chancel was raised to a greater height
than originally intended, evidenced by two openings above the
chancel arch, apparently first designed to be the E windows of the
nave, but now opening into the chancel.

   With the end of work on the chancel, the cathedral was substantially structurally complete, and there is evidence for only
minor subsequent medieval alterations, all of which can be
ascribed to one or other of the three bishops of the Chisholm
family who ruled the diocese between 1487 and 1569. It was
probably James (1487–1526) who heightened the tower by two
storeys, and whose arms are on the new parapet. Those arms
are also on the s chancel parapet which, with its pinnacles, must
have been reconstructed around the same time. Royal gifts of
drinksilver to masons in 1501 and 1502 show that work was in
progress in those years, and the provision of sumptuous new
chancel stalls by Bishop James (*see* below) was presumably the
culmination of a major campaign of repairs and remodelling.
One other likely Chisholm contribution was the reconstruction
of the chapel of St Blaise and the Holy Blood at the w end of
the N nave aisle, the position of which is indicated by two
enlarged windows. This was probably the work of its patron
Bishop William Chisholm I (1526–64).

### DESCRIPTION

Since the cathedral is not an unduly complex structure, it is best
to view first the exterior and then the interior in an essentially
chronological sequence. The order of discussion is therefore:
tower, N chancel range, nave, chancel.

6 *Exterior*

TOWER. The C12 tower, built of red (almost purple) sandstone rubble, rose through four storeys marked by stringcourses. The lowest storey is blind, and there are only simple arched or lintelled openings to the two intermediate storeys; the belfry stage has slightly larger arched openings, each subdivided by a shaft with a cushion cap carrying a pair of sub-arches. This tower, altogether unequal to the scale of the rebuilt C13 cathedral, and with its wallhead well below the roof apex of the adjacent nave, was heightened by two storeys of (mainly) buff-coloured ashlar, a crenellated parapet with angle rounds of red ashlar, and a low spire. The faces of each of the two added storeys have mean-spirited Y-traceried windows. Changes in the masonry suggest that these additions were not of a single operation, but the arms of Bishop James Chisholm on the parapet indicate a completion date of *c.* 1500. The slated splay-foot spire was extensively renewed in 1866–8.

NORTH CHANCEL RANGE. Like most of the rest of the C13 building, the N chancel range is of buff-coloured ashlar. It is divided into five bays by buttresses of relatively slight projection, with lateral intakes above the stringcourse at ground-floor window sill height, and with sharply weathered-back tops. The ground-floor windows, many of which are heavily renewed (that in the E wall is of 1873 and replaces a post-Reformation doorway), are groupings of three lancets within two-centred arches of either steeply pointed or depressed form, the hoodmoulds extending into a stringcourse that is cut by the buttresses. The upper storey has an asymmetrical grouping of three lancets to the E wall and small paired lancets to the first, second and fourth bays from the E. Since 1889–93 there has been a small doorway within a gabled salient in the central bay, and a determinedly Gothic boiler-house chimney further W.

NAVE. The N nave aisle wall is articulated by buttresses with two stages of intakes. In four of its eight bays are windows with group-ings of four lancets within slightly pointed containing arches. The four-light traceried window in the E bay of the aisle, together with the gable rising over that bay, is of 1889–93; in the two W bays of the aisle the three-light segmental-headed windows, with mullions reaching up to the arch, date from the early C16 remodelling of this area as a chapel of St Blaise and the Holy Blood. In the third bay from the W is a handsome doorway of three orders, two with detached shafts (now lost); evidence of a gabled salient around the doorway remains.

At clearstorey level, the bays are divided by slender gabled pilasters. The four E bays have pairs of wide lancets, but further W an early form of bar tracery is introduced (for all but the W half of the W bay), in which a quatrefoil is set between two light-heads. On this (presumably less visible) side of the building the spandrels between the windows are of rubble rather than ashlar.

The W front is the cathedral's finest external feature, rising over the Allan Water in sober, early Gothic elegance. Separating the blank aisle ends from the central part are tall buttresses of differing forms. The N buttress has a pyramidal cap while its S counterpart is gabled. The great processional doorway on the central axis of the front is deeply recessed, its lavishly moulded (but very weathered) arch having been carried on multiple shafts. Flanking the doorway are decorative blind arches, a similar arrangement to that at Paisley Abbey (Renfrewshire) and Inchmahome Priory (q.v.). Above this doorway, and rising up to the base of the gable, is a triplet of three elongated two-light windows, the central one wider than the others. At the head of these windows are two (heavily renewed) quatrefoils and a cinquefoil, treated in a way which represents an interesting cross between plate and bar tracery. Within the gable is a vesica with a dogtooth-decorated frame, a window that moved Ruskin to eulogize its creator and praise it as proof for the 'Nature of Gothic'.

The S flank of the nave is broadly comparable with that on the N, except that it is partly eclipsed by the tower in the third and fourth bays from the E. To the E of the tower is the carefully detailed principal lay entrance to the cathedral, which was designed to be covered by a vaulted porch, the wall rib and NE springing of which are still in place. A second, much smaller doorway opens through the second bay from the W, the string-course below the windows deflected around its head as a hood-moulding. Above this doorway is a small two-light window. In the clearstorey on this side of the nave the tracery starts from the second bay from the E, though frugally omitted behind the tower, where it would be invisible.

CHANCEL. The S flank of the chancel is divided into six bays by buttresses that rise sheer between intakes at stringcourse level and their rebuilt upper parts. The two windows to the E and W end bays are narrower than the others, and now have two broad lights rather than the four narrow lights of the others. The external reveals have broad chamfers terminating in quarter rolls, which closely relate to one of the nave arcade mouldings, and which show that the openings are probably of the later C13. The tracery, entirely of 1889–93, is of appropriate types, but based on no evidence. The parapet, and the upper parts of the buttresses with their distressingly starved pinnacles, are of the early C16; the arms of Bishop James Chisholm are displayed in the third bay from the E.

The E front is framed by angle buttresses; those projecting E are gabled, while those projecting laterally have partly restored pencil pinnacles. Below the centre of the window is a small gabled buttress. The window itself is attractively treated as a central four-light opening closely flanked by a lower lancet on each side. The tracery is, of course, of 1889–93.

*Interior*

TOWER. The C12 tower is entered from the S nave aisle by a doorway elevated *c.* 1m. above floor level. This round-arched opening was framed by nook-shafts (the shafts lost) with cushion caps, and it has a plain tympanum of coursed masonry above the lintel. The lowest storey is covered by an inserted pointed barrel vault with heavy chamfered parallel ribs. In the E wall is an arched altar recess; the lozenge decoration of the hood-moulding is similar to the decoration on a stringcourse at the smaller C12 tower of Muthill Parish Church, a reminder of their shared significance as diocesan centres. In the SW corner, a broad spiral stair, with the steps carried on the extrados of a helical vault, rises up to the original belfry stage. Within the later belfry stage is a late medieval bell frame.

NORTH CHANCEL RANGE. This range is entered from the chancel by an arched and shafted doorway with a trifoliate-headed inner arch. Its five bays are covered by quadripartite ribbed vaulting with foliate bosses. For reasons that are no longer clear, the prominent engaged responds that carry the vault are different on the two sides, those on the N being more slender and having both caps and full bases, while those on the S have chamfer stops rather than bases.

NAVE. The calm dignity of the nave interior is the cathedral's greatest beauty; one of the most satisfying architectural spaces to have come down to us from the Scottish Middle Ages. It is a perversely intriguing aspect of what we see that, although it was the part that was most fully restored in 1889–93, its C13 forms have been less interfered with than those in the choir, simply becaue it was so completely neglected for about three centuries.

The design is relatively simple, with a more or less regular rhythm of arcade arches on each side (albeit with the two E bays being narrower than the rest), over which runs a clearstorey with a delicately detailed inner arcade corresponding to the windows on the outer face of the wall; two arches in the clearstorey correspond to each of those of the main arcade. In many respects this design is a sophisticated advancement of ideas developed in northern England for two-storeyed elevations (cf. Hedon, Yorkshire). But behind the calm composure of the nave there is evidence of active thought processes, and of at least two changes of mind, and in fact this part of the building must be seen as representing an especially important stage in the development of the fully coordinated two-storey elevation.

A first pointer to the debate that lay behind the final design is the way in which the arcades are so very much taller than the outer walls of the aisles. Also significant is the fact that, while the N chancel range was stone-vaulted, and vaults were constructed over peripheral parts of the nave itself (the S porch, the vestibule at the base of the NW stair, and the small SW chapel), the aisles themselves were not vaulted. It is true that aisle vaults were not an altogether essential element in major churches, and certainly the slightly earlier nave aisles at Elgin Cathedral seem not to have had them at first. But at Dunblane, where vaults were placed over other spaces, it seems odd that they were omitted over the nave aisles.

In fact there is evidence that aisle vaults were originally intended, but dispensed with when it was decided to have much higher arcades. At the E end of the S aisle, around the E window head there are traces of what must be interpreted as a cut-back

8

wall rib and vault springings, together with the seating for the webbing of the vault itself. It should also be noted that, from the level of the vault springing upwards, the E arcade respond is augmented by a corbelled-out additional shaft on the side towards the central vessel, indicating that the arcade was to be built to a more substantial form than first intended. Whether the original intention had been to have an elevation of three storeys, as in the choir of Glasgow Cathedral, or of two storeys, as in the nave of Elgin Cathedral, we cannot know; but the end result of the modified design is a building of the highest elegance that is the more endearing for its slight inconsistencies.

As already noted externally, there was a further change of design with the introduction of tracery into the later windows of the clearstorey and W front. This tracery was also introduced into the inner clearstorey arcade, from the fifth bay from the E onwards.

The arcade piers have the moulded capitals and water-holding bases expected in the mid C13, but the piers themselves are a variant on the type possibly first employed earlier in the century at Holyrood Abbey, with engaged shafts on the leading faces and in the angles of a core of stepped profile. At Dunblane there are slight variations between the two sides of the nave, with the S piers (and also the chancel arch) having the angles of the stepped-profile core cut back in a broad chamfer. The arches are more richly moulded towards the central space than towards the aisles, the outermost element being the broad chamfer ending in quarter rolls that was soon afterwards to be taken up in the enlarged choir windows. At clearstorey level a mural passage runs around all four sides of the nave, stepping down to the sills of the W windows. As in the clearstorey, the W windows have an inner traceried arcade and, on this enlarged scale, the interplay between inner and outer planes is particularly attractive. To the E, the clearstorey passage steps up to cross the base of the two openings above the chancel arch; on the E side of the passage these openings were evidently intended to be glazed, while towards the nave they are framed by moulded arches. It is an attractive possibility that the great rood was set between the two openings, and it has been plausibly suggested that a series of angled slots in the masonry below them could have supported a rood loft.

The most clearly modern feature of the nave is the pointed and ribbed wagon ceiling designed by *R. Rowand Anderson* as part of the 1889–93 restoration. While it certainly enhances the sense of space, it cannot represent the original nave covering, since it blocks the lower part of the vesica in the W gable.

CHANCEL. Though richly furnished, the chancel does not possess the symmetrical composure of the nave. Much is the result of post-medieval changes, especially of works since 1889, and therefore only a partial reflection of the ideas of its original builders. Apart from the chancel arch, virtually the only original architectural features are the window arches and the doorway into the N range. The two triple 'triforium' openings, NE tomb recess, window tracery and timber-ribbed wagon ceiling are all of 1889–93. The ceiling, with its cusped profile and exposed collars that interconnect the purlins running along the points of the cusps, is a particularly handsome contribution to the sense of space. Of equal importance for the total impact are the fixtures and furnishings (*see* below). Above the chancel arch are two openings. Close inspection suggests they should have been glazed on their E side, and thus presumably originally designed to look out over the apex of a choir roof, but were enclosed by the height of the roof as built in the later C13. They were blocked after the Reformation but re-opened and glazed in 1873.

*Fixtures and Furnishings*

CHANCEL. – COMMUNION TABLE, 1893, by *R. Rowand Anderson*, oak, three-bay arcaded front with foliate cornice. – REREDOS SCREEN, by *Robert S. Lorimer*, carved by *W. and A. Clow*, 1912–14, as a memorial to Bishop Leighton. Oak, divided into seven bays with salient canopy projected on tierceron semi-vaulting and with elaborate cresting above a vine-carved cornice. Seven Corporal Acts of Mercy carved in the tympana within the vaulting. – Large mural AUMBRY, at end of S wall of chancel, rectangular with provision for a metal grille, possibly intended as a relic locker. – Floor-mounted CANDELABRA on each side of communion table, brass, of French Renaissance design, presumably 1893. – CHOIR STALLS by *Lorimer*, carved by *W. and A. Clow*, 1914. Two banks on each side, the upper bank with lavishly carved canopies inspired by those from St Nicholas, Aberdeen (now in the National Museum of Scotland, Edinburgh); ogee arches, with traceried cusping, rise against a pierced traceried field, with enriched cresting punctuated by pinnacles and tall finials. The backs of the upper stalls have ogee arches against traceried fields. Lavish poppyheads to the bench ends. Placed l. and r. at the E end of the chancel, within the presbytery area, are two groups of three and one group of four stalls without canopies. Traditionally associated with Bishop Michael Ochiltree (1429–46), though the similarities with the Chisholm stalls (*see* below) are so close that it is perhaps more likely they are part of the same set. – ORGAN CASE, by *Lorimer*, carved by *W. and A. Clow*, 1914; oak, five bays stepping upwards to centre, trac-eried spandrels and flanks; the case was sensitively enlarged and extended outwards when the organ was rebuilt by *Flentrop Orgelbouw* in 1989–90. – CHOIR SCREEN, 1893, by *Anderson*, elegant design in oak inspired by French Flamboyant Gothic/ early Renaissance prototypes; two pairs of openings above a linenfold-panelled dado, on each side of a wide central arch capped by an ogee super-arch rising up through the crested cornice; decorated with figures of Moses, David, Isaiah, Jeremiah, John the Baptist and St Paul.

CHAPTER HOUSE and SACRISTY: WAINSCOTING and CUP-BOARDS, 1934 and 1938 by *Reginald Fairlie*.

NAVE. – CHOIR STALLS. Against the w wall, on each side of the w doorway, two sets of medieval, three-canopied stalls, originally set against the chancel screen. (The timber arch that interconnected them above the central opening is now in the cathedral museum; it has the arms of Chisholm in both spandrels.) The arms of one of the three Chisholm bishops, thought to be James (1487–1526), are also on two of the misericords. The canopies are articulated by miniature pinnacles, each canopy having a rounded multi-cusped arch embraced by a heavily crocketed ogee outer arch, with a finial penetrating the cresting above the cornice; in the fields flanking the arches is high-relief carving of foliage and mythical beasts. – PULPIT, 1893, by *Anderson*; oak, octagonal with linenfold panels to stem, and canopy with Jacobean pediments; below canopies at the angles of the pulpit itself, statues of St Blane, David I, Bishop Clement, Gilbert earl of Strathearn, John Knox, Bishop Robert Leighton and Principal Carstairs; the panels of the pulpit have inlaid designs below cusped ogee arches carved in relief. – LECTERN, designed by *Anderson*, a monumental composition in cast brass, with double desk and widely projecting candle-holders; the stem has a deeply moulded base supported by eight lions, above which are four evangelist symbols within tabernacles and below a crown. – PEWS, by *Lorimer*; oak, rectangular-framed ends with low-relief foliage decoration along top rail; animal terminals to front pews in nave and SE chapel. – FONT, 1893, by *Anderson*; red sandstone, around circular bowl eight quatrefoils containing carved evangelist symbols and emblems of regeneration. – Sanctuary LAMP, above font, from church at Edessa, given by Greek Orthodox Metropolitan Panteleimon. – LIGHT PENDANTS, 1935, by *J. F. Matthew*, wrought iron with foliate ornament. – In the N nave aisle, great BELL, founded 1612 and re-cast 1660 and 1809 by *T. Mears and Son*; lesser bell founded 1687 and re-cast 1723 by *Robert Maxwell*. – SE nave chapel: in S wall, a mural AUMBRY and PISCINA (the latter converted into a second aumbry). – CROSS-SLABS. Two C8 or C9 cross slabs found 1873 below the N chancel range during restoration works, now displayed at the W end of the nave. Larger slab has a cross on main side, undecorated apart from volutes at its top and bottom corners, spirals to ring connecting arms, and serpent heads to framing moulding at base. Reverse has five tiers of decoration of various kinds, including a confronted pair of beasts at top, horseman at middle and recumbent man holding a staff at base. The chief decoration on the smaller slab, apart from faint traces of an incised cross shaft on the main face, is along one edge, and consists of interlace, key pattern and zoomorphic interlace.

CLEMENT CHAPEL: Statue of Christ in Majesty, 1964 by *Maxwell Allan*.

TOMBS AND MEMORIALS. – MEDIEVAL MEMORIALS. S side of chancel to E of stalls, Tournai marble ledger slab with inset for rectangular plate. On central axis of chancel, three Tournai marble ledger slabs, now bearing brass PLAQUES provided in 1897 by the fourteenth earl of Perth claiming they commemorate Euphemia, Margaret and Sybilla Drummond, said to have been poisoned 1501. In a largely modern TOMB recess on the s side of the Presbytery, eroded effigy of C13 bishop in mitre and mass vestments with feet resting on wyvern-like creature, traditionally identified with Bishop Clement (1233–58). The supine figure has lost its right hand and crozier head. – In s wall of SE nave chapel, within triangular-headed mural TOMB recess, eroded effigy of C13 bishop wearing mitre and mass vestments, evidently truncated to fit into recess. – In N nave aisle, C13 double effigy; male effigy in mail armour and coif carrying long heater-shaped shield; female effigy wearing loosely draped belted gown and mantle; traditionally identified with one of the earls of Strathearn and his countess. – Fragments of two GRAVESLABS with incised foliate-headed crosses mounted on N nave aisle wall. – POST-MEDIEVAL MEMORIALS. s nave aisle. John Wallace of Glassingal †1908, Jacobean tablet in brown and grey marble with strapwork decoration. – Between s aisle arcade piers, a standing stone MONUMENT to the children of Dunblane murdered in 1996: warm Clashash sandstone on a black Caithness flagstone base, the four faces of the upright shaft incised with poignant words in exquisite lettering carved by *Richard Kindersley*, 2000. – N nave aisle, from E to w. William Stirling of Keir †1793, opulent Jacobean marble aedicule capped by cartouche and obelisks, by *R. Rowand Anderson*, 1909. – John and Patrick Stirling of Kippendavie †1816, by *Peter Turnerelli*, 1819, a grieving matron placing a garland on an urn. – James Finlayson †1808, austere grey and white marble Neo-Classical aedicule with reeded shafts and entablature capped by urn. – Strathallan family, C17, restored 1893 by eighth viscount Strathallan, Tuscan pilasters flanking an arched recess housing an armorial tablet. – William Coldstream †1787, framed marble tablet with simple pediment and consoles.

STAINED GLASS. The cathedral is richly endowed with an important ensemble of stained glass. – w window by *Clayton & Bell*, 1906: The Tree of Jesse bearing the genealogy of Christ. – In the Clement Chapel, the eponymous blue-cloaked bishop by *Gordon Webster*, 1964. – Four-light windows in the nave, s side, w–E: first, the baptism of Christ by *Douglas Strachan*, 1926; then three bays by *Louis Davis* of London, 1917. In these, figural forms sway across blue Art Nouveau seas and skies, especially in the Nunc Dimittis windows in memory of Dr and Mrs J.W. Barty. – Past the s door, four pairs of superimposed saints; to David and Janet Wallace of Glassingal †1877 and 1902. – E end of N aisle, the Compassion of Christ depicts twelve scenes from the ministry of Jesus; by *Gordon Webster*, 1968. – Choir, E window, 1901, by *C.E. Kempe*: it shows scenes from the last days of Christ flanked in the side lights by Old Testament prophets. – Along the s side, a magnificent six-window panoply of allegory and colour by *Louis Davis*, 1915. The symbolic programme is complex, with allusion both biblical and to William Blake; the surging forms, passing from blues to reds and greens to yellow, intoxicating. – Staid by comparison, the small memorial windows in the Chapter House by *Douglas Strachan*, 1920s, and *Gordon Webster*, 1959–65.

– Gethsemane window in the passage between Chapter House and nave by *Strachan*, 1934.

A well populated GRAVEYARD, defined by a low wall, surrounds the cathedral. On the E, RICCARTON'S STILE, a medieval archway, rebuilt 1814 by *William Stirling I*, surviving as a relic from the demolition of buildings on the W side of Kirk Street, 1884. – Several badly weathered sandstone HEADSTONES, early C19. – Some flat, cast iron gravemarkers, C19. – To the SW, a number of weathered stones bearing early C18 dates and inscriptions. Lying SLAB, 1745, to John Rob and Elizabeth Lennox: winged angel head, star and crescent, skull and bones. – OBELISK with inscribed white marble insets; to William McCowan †1864, Commander-in-Chief of the 58th Massachusetts Infantry who fell IN DEFENCE OF THE UNION / AGAINST THE REBELLION. – Three-panel Gothic WALL TOMB to Stirling family, including the local architect William Stirling (1772–1838).

BISHOP'S PALACE, 50m. SSW of the cathedral. C13 vaulted fragments on the scarp above the Allan Water. On the W-facing slope below, a dome-headed COLUMN, 1842, records the lease of a riparian bleaching green.

CATHEDRAL HALL, at the SW side of the cathedral close. Crisp Scots Renaissance by *R. Rowand Anderson*, 1903. Harled walls with ashlar margins and strapwork over the windows. Large, pilaster-edged, mullioned and transomed window in the E gable. Almost cruciform in plan with double-gabled N and S 'transepts'; the ecclesiastical allusion still more marked in the interior where two-bay pointed-arched arcades flank the W end of the hall. Segmental-vaulted ceiling boarded between ribs. Deferential additions by *McEachern, MacDuff*, 1996–8, extend the accommodation W to terminate in a two-storey octagon with five pedimented eaves dormers.

## CHURCHES

Former FREE CHURCH, Nos. 124–126 High Street. Dated 1843. Rubble-built in three bays, each with tall twinned round-arched windows through two storeys, except over segmental arch entrance l. Outer bays gabled. Also used as a school until 1876; later as a meeting room. Subdivided 1946–7. Now disused.

HOLY FAMILY (R.C.), Claredon Place. By *Reginald Fairlie*, 1935. Unassuming Romanesque in slivered rubble with ashlar dressings. Gabled NE porch with quadrant wall approach. Stained trussed-roof interior. A semicircular chancel arch opens to a domed apsidal sanctuary. – Three STAINED GLASS windows by *Shona McInnes* memorialize the Dunblane massacre of 1996; seventeen doves, seventeen flowers and seventeen fallen leaves honour the victims in sinuous allegorical compositions.

ST BLANE, High Street. Originally Dunblane Free Church by *J., W.H. and J.M. Hay*, 1853–4. Aisleless nave with transept gables N and S. At the SE corner, a gabled porch and small belfry tower with broached spire. Bands of fish-scale slating. The pointed windows have fine, sharply cut, Dec tracery brought forward to the outer wall plane. Semi-octagonal apse pushed through the W gable at a later date. Inside, arch-braced trusses, rising from corbels, carry purlins and a diagonally boarded roof. At the junction with the transept roofs the framing timbers are laminated and decorated with stencilled disc motifs. Ribbed timber-tent ceiling over the chancel beyond the pointed chancel arch. E gallery. – Semi-octagonal box PULPIT panelled with blind Dec tracery ornament. – Slender pedestal FONT, also carved timber. – STAINED GLASS in the chancel depicts the four seasons in scenes full of incidental delights (sheep, cattle, birds, a mouse, a snail, and various flowers); by *Roland Mitton*, 1995. – More orthodox saintly figures in two S windows: one female, to Elisabeth Corsar †1904; the other, a purple-cloaked St Andrew, to her husband, the Rev. William Blair †1916.

ST MARY (Episcopal), Perth Road. Routine First Pointed by *John Henderson*, 1844; simple but rigorous, with 'a clear grasp of what the ecclesiologists were trying to achieve'*. Gable-ended nave of four buttressed bays with a lower, angle-buttressed chancel, extended E *c.* 1900. Apex bellcote rises from W gable; the triple lancet below formed 1887. S porch entrance arch with nook-shafts and floral capitals. Simple plastered interior with corbelled arch-braced trusses. The pointed chancel arch springs from all-but-detached shafts with bell capitals. Below the E lancets, a blind arcade of seven cusped arches. Encaustic tile floor to sanctuary. – Octagonal FONT carved with bishop's saltire and chevron edging; pointed-arched arcade around base. – Stone PULPIT with ribbed pedestal richly carved with floral spandrels and upper panels of coupled cusped arches. – Straight-backed oak CHOIR STALLS carved with dagger tracery and vines. – ORGAN installed in segmental-arched recess l. by *Wood*, Edinburgh, 1845, retains its original pipes; rebuilt by *Bishop & Son*, London, *c.* 1887, and *Binns, Fitton & Haley* of Leeds, 1937. – More floral relief in quatrefoils of stone ALTAR. – STAINED GLASS. W of the porch, an abstract design, to Robert Mitchell †1981. – Centenary window N, Mary and the Christ Child, 1946, by *James Hogan* of *James Powell & Sons*. – By the same artist, the War Memorial window S, 1949; St Nicholas holding a crozier and galley. – Opposite, in memory of John Alexander Stirling †1957, a red fisherman on a blue river under a variegated web of moon, sun and sky, 1992. – Sanctuary lancets, diamond and vesica patterns in deep blue and red spill below the bishop's saltire. – W gable, leaded whorls and leaf motifs. – Nearby N is the RECTORY, 1851.

CEMETERY

DUNBLANE CEMETERY, Perth Road. Opened 1914. A well-tended graveyard on a gentle slope, unremarkable were it not for the Garden of Remembrance honouring the memory of the sixteen young children and their teacher who died tragically in

* Allan Maclean, 'The Scottish Episcopal Church and the Ecclesiological Movement', *Architectural Heritage*, viii (1997), 48.

the massacre at Dunblane Primary School in March 1996. Gently landscaped below a grassy knoll ringed with silver birches. Water spills from a grey granite fountain into shallow pools with variegated pebble mosaic beds, the names of the children set in darker grey granite letters into the kerb of the larger pool. Rough rubble walls with tumbled-in stone slivers. Paths laid in flagstones and granite cobbles.

## PUBLIC BUILDINGS

BRAEPORT COMMUNITY CENTRE, Braeport. Former school, c. 1875. Symmetrical Gothic without pointed arches. Gabled centre, advancing wings and obliquely set porches in the re-entrants; the first topped by a bellcote, the rest with ball finials. Former Infants' School, c. 1905, adjacent.

BURGH CHAMBERS, The Cross. 1900–1. By *R. M. Christie*. Rough-faced crowstep-gabled façade with hooded windows and a central round-arched entrance flanked by broad fluted pilasters.

108 CATHEDRAL MUSEUM, Cross Street and Kirk Street. A short range of vernacular buildings restored and converted to exhibition and library use in 1958. Dominating the corner is the three-storey former Dean's House. Erected in 1624 for James Pearson of Kippenross, appointed Dean of Dunblane Cathedral by James VI, it acquired its forestair and two upper storeys c. 1765. Pearson family crest on the wall. Some barrel-vaulted chambers.

DUNBLANE BRIDGE. First constructed 1409, but rebuilt and widened as a round-arched masonry structure in 1849. In 1927, the present girder bridge with its reinforced concrete balustrading was superimposed.

DUNBLANE RAILWAY BRIDGE. By *Locke & Errington*, c. 1846–8. Segmental skew arches crossing Dighty Water.

DUNBLANE HEALTH CENTRE, Anderson Street. 1986. Blockwork walls with corner windows under a low piended roof.

DUNBLANE HIGH SCHOOL, Highfields. By *Perth & Kinross County Council*, 1974–5. Dispersed classroom blocks with a three-storey core clad in exposed aggregate storey-height panels.

FAERY BRIDGE. Narrow footbridge across the Allan Water, first built in timber, c. 1880. In 1911 a ferro-concrete bridge was erected; hence, perhaps, the corrupted name 'Faery'. Rebuilt as a slim-line, segmental-arched span, also in reinforced concrete, by *Leitch & Sharp*, 1974.

LEIGHTON HOUSE, Haining. Originally the Dunblane United Associate Church Hall. 1835 by *William Stirling I*. s gable lit by a round-arched window with five-light Perp tracery and shouldered with Gothic epaulettes. To the r., the random rubble s gable of a simple roughcast block. Converted by *Honeyman, Jack & Robertson* (*see* Scottish Churches House, below). *Stirling's* church, a replacement for the so-called 'Red Hoose' church of 1758, was demolished in the 1950s. The porch, however, remains as the entrance to a small gated garden.

LEIGHTON LIBRARY, Cross Street. Modest yet powerfully prismatic, this simple gable-ended box is the only surviving C17 library building in Scotland, the foundation of Robert Leighton (1611–84), Episcopalian Bishop of Dunblane. Built by *Edward Lightmaker,* 1687, with *James Robertson,* Master of Works. Over 1,200 of Leighton's books are accommodated. Erected on part of the site of the medieval Bishop's Palace, masonry remnants of which may have been incorporated in its walls, the Library was constructed 1685–7 under the direction of Viscount Strathallan: 'the fabrick of the house, its furniture and everything as it stands . . . was by his contrivance'*. It is a small harled building comprising a vaulted basement, which served as the librarian's dwelling until the middle of the C18, the Library above, accessed by the E forestair, and a garret, originally reached by ladder. Lighting the Library are three round-headed windows, two W and one S, installed in 1766 by the local wright *Mungo Buchan* as replacements for the earlier smaller openings. Half a century later an extensive programme of repairs, 1815–17, carried out by *William Stirling I* realigned the forestair alongside the E wall, repaired chimneystacks and skews (the survival of crow-stepping only on the N gable may date from this time), raised the Library ceiling, and, removing the last of the original oak wainscoting, replastered the interior. Repairs were again effected 1952–7 by *Ian G. Lindsay,* and in the 1980s by *Honeyman, Jack & Robertson,* when the 1766 windows were replaced with copies, the ceiling of 1817 restored and roofing, harling and flooring renewed. Books and bookcases were also refurbished and twelve 'turkie leather chairs', dating from 1688, survive.

Set into the E wall is a Venetian marble PLAQUE, 1687, its vesica shape reminiscent of the same motif at the head of the cathedral's W gable. The tablet, commissioned from England by Lord Strathallan, carries the Leighton arms, surmounted by a once-gilded mitre, and bore the carved words BIBLIOTHECA LIGHTONIANA; originally coloured, it was repainted in 1752 and again in 1811–12. It awaits a further restoration.

MILL COURT, Auchinlay Road. Built as Springbank Mill, 1853, and in operation until 1980. In 1986, after demolition of late Victorian additions, the original two- and three-storey rubble-built piended sheds were converted to flats. N turnpike stair retained.

NEWTON PRIMARY AND NURSERY SCHOOL, Newton Crescent. By *Stirling Council,* 1995–6. Low walls of brown facing brick with soldier courses at the sills and below a widely overhanging eaves. Rising above the tiled piended roofs of the classroom wings, a gabled assembly hall with corbelled skews and a squat apex belfry capped with a leaded pyramid.

QUEEN VICTORIA SCHOOL, 1.5km. NNE. Boarding school built 1906–10 for the sons of Scottish servicemen and as a memorial to those Scots who died in the Boer War. By *John A. Campbell,* whose competition-winning design, with spreading symmetrical layout and Scots Renaissance idiom, doubtless pleased the architect assessor, R. Rowand Anderson. The built scheme, four roughcast storeys high, is still symmetrical but much more

---

* Robert Douglas, 'An Account of the Foundation of the Leighton Library' (1692), *Bannatyne Miscellany,* iii (1858), 243.

compact and austere. Facing N, a wide central block ends l. and
r. in bartizan-lugged bays, which return into crowstepped gables
like tower-house book-ends. E and W wings, recessed slightly,
extend the spread of the N façade. These, too, end in crowstepped
gables to which round stair towers attach. A central freestone
frontispiece comprises round-arched entrance, a Mannerist
aedicule-frame, with segmental pediment for the window above,
and, between the two, an ashlar balustrade on console brackets
(a horizontal stress reiterated and lengthened at third-floor level
between the end bays). The frontispiece marks the axis of a thick
oblong plan which develops behind into top-lit halls flanked by
classrooms.

Houses for staff and other ancillary buildings also by *Campbell*
maintain the roughcast Baronial manner of the main block;
among them, the small, asymmetrically arranged ANDERSON
MEMORIAL HOSPITAL, completed 1911, at once picturesque
and austere with pyramid roofs and bellcast eaves. The long
three-storey classroom and boarding block in grey brick and
finned curtain walling dates from the 1960s. Contemporary, but
more stylish, is the low, flat-roofed LIBRARY, seven bays glazed
between brick buttresses under overhanging eaves. At the NORTH
and SOUTH GATES, curving random rubble walls rise to massive
round piers with hemispherical tops.

Also by *Campbell* with *A. D. Hislop*, the MEMORIAL
CHAPEL, 1908–10; Baronial Gothic with broadly buttressed
gables E, W and S, and, hunched over the crossing, a dumpy tower
from which rises a slated octagonal pyramid. Large round-
arched windows in the gables divided by a central mullion with
two-light cusped tracery l. and r. Hefty S porch: above its elliptical entrance arch, an empty canopied niche flanked by thin
finial strips crocketed above the parapet. Plastered interior with
unadorned piers carrying two-bay, round-arched arcades between
nave and aisles. W gallery. Four high, pointed arches define the
crossing. Corbelled arch-braced trusses over the nave with spars
continuing down over the aisles. – Plain ashlar box PULPIT. –
Filling the S transept, the ORGAN by *William Hill & Son and
Norman & Beard* sits in an oak screen elaborately fretted and
finialled around the pipes. – STAINED GLASS in the E window
by *Alexander L. Russell*, 1954; SS Columba, Ninian, Kentigern
and, appropriately, Blane.

RAILWAY VIADUCT over the Allan Water. By *Locke & Errington*,
c. 1846–8. Four segmental-arched spans (one over N bank footpath) in rough-faced coursed sandstone with ashlar voussoirs.
Rounded piers on low cutwaters. The vaults, built in tumbled-
in brick and obliquely cut, have been strengthened with iron rail
ties.

RAILWAY STATION. 1846–8. Red brick walls with window dressings and crowsteps in ochre sandstone. Waiting room timber-
framed and boarded, on red brick base.

SCOTTISH CHURCHES HOUSE, Kirk Street. An ecumenical
centre and retreat accommodated in a row of C18 and early C19
dwellings saved from demolition in the 1950s. Their subsequent

conversion and extension, including dining room and library, by *Honeyman, Jack & Robertson* in the 1960s and 1970s, created a consistent, two-storey streetscape. White roughcast, except the entrance block, *c.* 1800, a skew-gabled house in whin rubble with dressed surrounds, a fine eaves cornice and a delicate sunburst fanlight in the round-arched doorway.

Embedded into the hillside behind is a single-cell, barrelvaulted CHAPEL, C13 (?), discovered during work on the Kirk Street buildings. Constructed in random rubble, it has a lintelled W door and window, each with relieving arches over, the latter with an inner round arch. Inside, there are two aumbries in the E wall. A free-standing CROSS of laminated oak, simple pedestal TABLE and bench seating have been provided for modern worship.

ST MARY'S DAY SCHOOL, Smithy Loan. Built *c.* 1850. Gabled Gothic with asymmetrical bellcote over entrance.

SHERIFF COURT HOUSE, High Street. Built as a jail, 1842–4. A dull and presumably didactic exercise in grim-faced Tudor by local architect *William Stirling II*; extended 1869 by *Brown & Wardrop* (the court house itself) and again in 1886. S front, severe and symmetrical, in heavily pointed random rubble. Two-light windows with mullioned and transomed crosses, those to the upper floor considerably taller. Ashlar parapet, stepped at the centre, terminates in bartizan chimneys. Battlemented porch with hooded round-arched entry and convex flanks; dated 1844 in the parapet. Later irregular additions spread E. To the W is a small garden, formerly the site of the prison cells, dem. 1963. In the S gable of the Burgh Chambers a heavily framed stone TABLET bears the armorial achievement of John Chisholm of Cromlix.

VICTORIA HALL, Stirling Road. By *Simpson, McMichael & Davidson*, 1926. Rebuilt six-bay structure with shaped buttresses, lateral parapets and window dressings in red sandstone ashlar. Curvilinear gables N and S, the former swept up into an apex chimneystack. Ogee-capped ridge ventilator. A parapet tablet records the date, 1887, and architect, *J. Young*, of the original hall, burnt down in 1925.

WAR MEMORIAL, on the Haugh by the river. By *James Miller*. Erected 1922 opposite St Mary's Church but relocated 1959. Flat-topped obelisk with bronze panels.

## DESCRIPTION

Not surprisingly, Dunblane Bridge (*see* Public Buildings, above) is at the historic secular heart of the town. W of the river, BRIDGEND and CALEDONIAN PLACE, a curving lane of unremarkable but still vernacular housing now split by the railway, marks the start of the ancient route to Doune. STIRLING ROAD has more of the same; at No. 5, 1735, a rubble gable raised above an C18 scroll skewputt. Built in snecked rubble with droved dressings, INCHALLAN and INCHALLAN HOUSE, two gable-to-gable, mid-C19 dwellings, form a tidy row. DUNBLANE HOTEL, *c.* 1849 and later, is more demonstrative with shallow bay-window glazing pressed into wide corniced openings and two attic bay dormers under octagonal pyramids spiked by iron finials. On STATION ROAD (Nos. 1–3), another row, dated 1902: two-and-a-half storeys high with tall pedimented doorpieces convexly curved on the ingo. But it is the red-painted STIRLING ARMS HOTEL, immediately E of the bridge, that makes the most prepossessing impact. At first (probably early C19) three-bay, two storeys high to the eaves, it was raised, c. 1870: canted oriels at second floor and canted attic bay dormers above now flank a curvilinear chimneyed gable at the centre of which is a small window with filigree ironwork balcony.

MILL ROW dips to the river from the bridge. It is quiet now (the last mill was demolished in 1954), the name merely evocative. A few early C19 harled houses, notably ALLAN COTTAGE, ALLANSIDE HOUSE, begun c. 1797, and RIVERSIDE HOUSE, retain vernacular dignity. On a higher contour, HIGH STREET runs N to The Cross, ancient and narrow and alive with small-town activity. The old carriageway cuts an animated cleft through three-storey buildings; late Victorian redevelopment which seems only to have intensified the urban intimacy of the street. At first, l. and r., the scale is two-storey, though the much-modelled front of the former Post Office at Nos. 2–12, by *John McLean* of Stirling, 1886–92, repeatedly gabled and peppered with urn finials, has grandeur enough. At first floor, above the convex fascias of two fine shopfronts (jutting dramatically over the corner entry of No. 2), is the Masonic Hall. A few vernacular dwellings survive: Nos. 14–18, late C18, roughcast with painted margins, plain and archetypal; Nos. 22–24, 1726, ruined by some bull-faced stucco but retaining a single swept eaves dormer to the attic; No. 23, where a small pedimented eaves dormer sits between two tripartite windows; and No. 31, with, below a frontal chimney, a weathered stone inset dated 1736 (?), saved in the rebuilding of 1895. Then, a varied series of three-storey shops and flats, all symmetrical. Early C20 roughcast Scots at Nos. 30–34, five bays wide with three of its ashlar dormerheads carved with a rose, thistle and fleur-de-lis. Shallow canted bays and a central chimneystack at Nos. 44–48, c. 1900. Side-by-side canted bays at Nos. 39–43, 1902, castellated at second floor and topped, pediment-like, by a bargeboarded gable. Nos. 47–49 intrude; late C18, two-storey, rubble vernacular again with irregular chamfered dressings. A narrow pend leads to steps dropping to Mill Row and the river. At Nos. 50–56, late C19, architraves, cornices and, flanking another central chimney, pedimented eaves dormers at the third storey. Classical, too, but more orthodoxly ordered below a console-bracketed cornice, Nos. 58–64, 1884; the 'first modern building' in the street, says a descriptive wall panel. At Nos. 66–70, late C19, tripartite windows l. and r. at first and second floors. At Nos. 72–76, also late C19, pedimented bipartites. Finally, after some jumpy asymmetrical disquiet at No. 53, 1886, the street opens up to The Cross, gated l. and r. by two slated peaks rising fortuitously from similar, though not identical, late C19 octagonal corners.

On the W side of the roundabout, the L-plan front of No. 61, early C19, has a Doric columned porch. BANK HOUSE (No. 63), of *c.* 1835, harled with painted margins, is standard three-bay Georgian in style with a disappointing doorpiece; a lower wing, advancing a gable to the street, looks better, with cornice and consoles at the entrance to the BANK OF SCOTLAND. Facing s is the Sheriff Court House (*see* Public Buildings, above). Beyond this the rising curve of High Street turns back to reach the Perth Road. Set against deep pink harl, a curving forestair and canti-levered stone platt draw the eye to Nos. 91–95, a mid-C18 cottage exuding charm to the street and creatively recast at the rear. Next, St Blane's (*see* Churches, above) and the DUNBLANE INSTITUTE, 1908–9, by *James Davidson & Son*, church hall and library combined behind big-windowed gables with Art Nouveau glass. Across the street are Nos. 108–112, early C19, plain, altered, but still respectable in random rubble, and the former Free Church (*see* Churches, above), abject and abandoned. Sprawled over the hill s, ST BLANE'S HOUSE, *c.* 1835, complex in layout but dull, enlivened only by a pedimented Roman Doric porch and pale pink-washed harl. Rubble walls channel the street uphill. All but out of sight l., the long, two-storey, vernacular front of BALHALDIE HOUSE, C18 (perhaps late C17 in part) and early C19, looks SE across its hidden garden. Finally, at Four Ways roundabout, the Gothic composure of St Mary's (*see* Churches, above).

CROSS STREET (also known as Cathedral Square) leads N past the Leighton Library (*see* Public Buildings, above) to the Cathedral (*see* Cathedral and Close, above). The Cathedral Museum, part of which was once the Dean's House (*see* Public Buildings, above), marks the corner with KIRK STREET, an L-plan wall of white roughcast wrapped around the Cathedral Close on the s and E. Most buildings are probably C18 or C19, though housing replaced the cloister court from the middle of the C17. Apart from the Dean's House and the TAPPIT HEN, a C19 block of three storeys with a central nepus gable chimney and a good Edwardian shopfront, the scale is two-storey. The re-entrant junction with SINCLAIR STREET's late C18 and early C19 houses is attractively casual and its vernacular charm well maintained by Scottish Churches House (*see* Public Buildings, above).

BRAEPORT climbs N from this cathedral enclave. On the r., the town's first schools (*see* Public Buildings, above). Of the small houses edging the incline, AURORA, early C19, is plainest and best: wide, roughcast vernacular with small windows. The street narrows into RAMOYLE, bending NE; this is the old township, a tight lane of handloom weavers' cottages, late C18 and early C19, much altered, but barely gentrified. Most are one-and-a-half storeys high, variations on a simple three-bay village street theme. The roughcast RAMOYLE HOUSE, wider and longer than most, adds a small window beside its centre door. Unusually, CLIFF COTTAGE has high pilasters at the entrance. TILLYVERE, more villa than cottage, boasts obelisk corner finials above a square-snecked façade. In the eaves-dormered gable of BRAEHOLM, an inscribed tablet, dated 1888, marks the corner with LAIGH-HILL LOAN. Further E, BACKCROFT COTTAGE, roughcast and slated, with a new door and window, has been splendidly revived.

PERTH ROAD goes leafily N, suburban and relaxed, from Four Ways roundabout. Some ironwork bedroom balconies with a lacy spiral stair enliven the gabled front of CAIRNDOW, KINCAIRN and ROSEBANK, a three-house villa row in red sandstone by *R. Rowand Anderson*, 1905. ANCHORFIELD, at the junction with Smithy Loan, is a harled and painted survivor from the C18; there is a well in its cobbled basement. Immediately N, the battlemented Tudor Gothic of HOLMEHILL HOUSE LODGE, *c.* 1826 by *William Stirling I*, has little to guard now for the big house uphill W has gone. Beyond the Hydro (*see* Hotel and Mansions, below) is LEDCAMEROCH, 1884, a bulky asymmetrical mansion entered through an arched N doorway with twisted Corinthianesque columns, beside which rises a tall central tower topped by a truncated pyramid. Further N, hard to the roadside, WHITECROSS COTTAGES, probably early C18, are already rural.

Uphill, E of Four Ways, lies villa-land. The rising ground with prospects S and W is similar to the Upper Town of nearby Bridge of Allan, though layout and architecture are more casual and varied. On GLEN ROAD, for example, TOMDORAN, *c.* 1860, is free Jacobean, GLENACRES, *c.* 1865, peak-gabled Gothic with a rubble-built summerhouse incorporating two pointed entrances that may have come from restoration work at the cathedral, while SILVERBURN, built by *Alex Strang* in 1967, is a glass-walled pavilion of uncompromising elegance lying long and low 'beside the lake, beneath the trees'. Uphill, on the road to Sheriffmuir, the steadings of KIPPENROSS HOME FARM have been quietly and tidily converted to residential use by *Robert Halliday*, 1997–8. On THE CRESCENT, several houses sport scrolled bargeboards; NEWTON COTTAGE, dated 1870, is typical. NETHERBY, probably of *c.* 1880, is decidedly English: roughcast half-timbered façades and gables with a big red-tiled roof. ANNFIELD, more urban Scots in warm ochre sandstone, has a strongly consoled doorpiece flanked by double-height canted bays. Wide, single-storeyed and symmetrical, GLENLUSS, late C19, stretches between bow-windowed ends roofed in truncated cones; the full façade fringed with eaves fretted like a doyley. Then, incongruously bulky beside Ochlochy Cottage at the S end of The Crescent, a tall cylindrical DOOCOT, C18, built in half-harled rubble with a corbelled parapet encircling a central 'cupola', ball finial and weathervane.

## HOTEL AND MANSIONS

AULT WHARRIE, by *George Walton*, *c.* 1900, hidden in landscaped grounds above Leewood Road, is a widespread red brick house, agitated by gables, bays and balconies. Ill-arranged externally, its interiors are rich in Glasgow Style detail: wall panelling with flat coved cornices, tapered newels and chamfered balusters, leaded lights. In the entrance lobby, an elliptical plastered vault and a tessellated floor.

HOTEL DUNBLANE (former Dunblane Hydropathic), Perth Road. By *Peddie & Kinnear*, 1875–8; Dining Room added N, 1884. Reconstruction, 1936, by *T. Scott Sutherland*. A huge but architecturally dull pile flattered by its dramatic setting above grassy terraces. Constructed in stone from Dunmore, Polmaise and Plean quarries, the long four-storey-and-attic W façade has five-storey N and S wings and is centrally accented by a tall, pyramid-roofed, Italianate clock tower; apart from console-bracketed eaves and stringcourses at every sill level, 'there is externally little attempt at ornamentation' (*Stirling Observer*, 1878). Decorative ironwork verandahs between tower and wings, added before 1910. The original landscape design of 1875 is by *William Gorrie*.

RYLAND LODGE (formerly Kippendavie House), E of Perth Road. A low, harled and painted, two-storey house, hip-roofed with overhanging eaves. Built to an L-plan, *c.* 1840; later extended E. Without the whimsy of the contemporary *cottage orné*, it is yet delightfully intimate and unassuming. Chamfered corners and jambs. Two French-windowed canted bays open S to landscaped lawns. In the glazed porch, a stone TABLET with heraldic arms and the date 1617 brought from the mansion built by the Stirlings of Kippendavie shortly after the estate became the family seat at the end of the C16.

STONEHILL FARM, 2km. E. C18. Three-bay, two-storey; ashlar chimneystacks and an arched entrance. Single-storey wing.

KEIR HOUSE. *See* p. 542.
KILBRYDE CASTLE. *See* p. 546.
KIPPENROSS HOUSE. *See* p. 564.
OLD KIPPENROSS. *See* p. 565.

DUNGLASS CASTLE    WD 4070

0.8km. w of Bowling

Sited on a low rocky outcrop with strategic riparian significance that probably attracted settlement from the earliest times. Roman occupation has been suggested and the possibility of a defensible outpost in visual communication with the W end of the Antonine Wall at nearby Old Kilpatrick (q.v.) – feasible if not proved. The earliest surviving masonry evidence appears to be from the late C14: two ruinous walls on the S and W. In 1439 Dunglass is known to have passed into the hands of the Colquhoun family and towards the end of the C16 Sir Humphrey Colquhoun of Luss built a dwelling within the fortified walls of the earlier castle. This late medieval house forms the NW portion of the present structure. Some inner walling has been absorbed by later construction; more visible is the oblique N perimeter wall running to the corbelled NW corner turret. During the C18 the castle was quarried until, in 1812, Alexander Buchanan of Auchentorlie became owner and began partial restoration. By 1831–2 the earlier house had been repaired and remodelled with a square two-storey bay added on the w wall. Early photographs show that a first-floor timber balcony carried on posts was originally applied to this gabled bay. More radical enlargement, 1852–61, added two-storey extensions s and e, the former Baronial in character with a round sw turret, the latter more in the manner of Alexander 'Greek' Thomson (though the working of window dressings is similar in both wings). The single-storey block which acts as a circulation link between these two Victorian wings once supported a large timber conservatory. Some time after acquiring the house in 1893, *Talwin Morris* built a lean-to porch to connect the entrance door to the e wing with the archway in the c16 n wall. This link, which Morris decorated with a mural of cats, has been demolished. In 1899 the Macdonald family, one of whose daughters, Margaret, would marry the architect Charles Rennie Mackintosh, bought Dunglass. The following year, the year of the marriage, *Mackintosh* designed new interiors for the Drawing Room in the s wing and the Dining Room in the e wing. In the latter this entailed a remodelled ceiling and a new fireplace with corner seat and a long mantelpiece 'with square pigeon holes'. These no longer exist *in situ*.

For many years the castle buildings have decayed, neglected and inaccessible in an impregnable Oil Terminal. Recently, however, with changes in industrial priorities, rehabilitation has begun. By 2000, Edinburgh architects *Simpson & Brown* had stabilized the ruinous structure, re-roofed to protect the interior fabric.

Built up above the water's edge is an ivy-cloaked beehive DOOCOT of c16 or c17 date. Inside are five rows of pigeon nests. – In 1836 a tall obelisk MONUMENT honouring the steamship pioneer Henry Bell was erected on rising ground se of the castle.

DUNIPACE

Village, originally named Herbertshire, which had a population of *c.* 760 by 1841 and became part of the combined police burgh of Denny (q.v.) and Dunipace in 1876. Some plain buildings of the later c19 survive in STIRLING STREET and MILTON ROW to its w; the rest is mainly c20 local authority housing.

Former DUNIPACE PARISH CHURCH, 1.3km. e. Disused. Late Georgian Gothic, by *William Stirling I*, 1832–4. Tall broached ashlar box of three bays by two. Buttressed sides; at the corners, diagonal buttresses with foliage-finialled pinnacles. Hoodmoulded mullioned and transomed windows, of three lights at the sides, of two lights at the e gable, all with late Gothic tracery in their heads; at the top of the e gable, a round window with cusped loop tracery. Square w tower of three stages, the octagonal corner buttresses topped by foliage-finialled pinnacles; pierced battlement. At the bottom stage of the tower, hoodmoulded Tudor doors, the w a dummy. At each face of the second stage, a hoodmoulded mullioned and transomed two-light window, with cusped openings both above and below the transom; a quatrefoil in the head. At the top stage each face contains a hood-moulded belfry opening of three tall pointed lights. In the W gable, each side of the tower, a hoodmoulded lancet window. Low E vestry with diagonal buttresses and hoodmoulded openings.

DUNIPACE PARISH CHURCH, corner of Stirling Street and Barnego Road. Originally Dunipace Free Church. By *William Simpson*, 1888–90. Broad rubble-built box with buttressed corners. Y-traceried pointed windows in the sides. At the SE gable front, a hoodmoulded window of five lancet lights above a boldly projecting porch. In the NE inner angle of the porch and main gable, a battered tower. The intaken top (belfry) stage is finished with a battlement, cannon-spouts sticking out from its angle rounds. Inside the battlement, a slated octagonal spire.

A HALL and CHURCH OFFICER'S HOUSE were added to the E in 1901. The house fronting Stirling Street is sturdy Jacobean with bullnosed masonry and mullioned windows. Very shallow gabled porch, its sides battered.

DUNIPACE PRIMARY SCHOOL, off Thistle Avenue. By *Central Regional Council*, 1992. Long and low, with red brick walls and a red-tiled piended roof. Two-storey off-centre 'centrepiece', its gable topped by a birdcage bellcote. The inspiration seems to be Supermarket English Traditional.

# DUNMORE

Small mid-C19 estate village beside the River Forth.

SCHOOL (now MORAY COTTAGE). Dated 1875. Picturesque school and schoolhouse, with bracketed broad eaves, barge-boards and a flèche.

The former School stands on the S corner of the approach road from the A905. On the N, THE VILLA, a two-storey Jacobean house of *c.* 1850. The village itself forms a square, the E side open to the River Forth. On the central green, a square shelter, presumably of 1879, its bargeboarded gables supported by squat columns. This covers a PUMP signed by *W. E. Baily & Sons*. It is of Italian Gothic inspiration with a lion's head spout. On the pump's E side, the inscription explaining that 'THE SCHOOL AND VILLAGE OF DUNMORE TOGETHER WITH THIS WELL BUILT BY CATHERINE HERBERT COUNTESS OF DUNMORE WERE COMPLETED A.D. 1879'. On the other side of the pump, a verse:

HERE QUENCH YOUR THIRST, AND MARK IN ME
AN EMBLEM OF TRUE CHARITY;
WHO, WHILE MY BOUNTY I BESTOW,
AM NEITHER HEARD NOR SEEN TO FLOW,
REPAID BY FRESH SUPPLIES FROM HEAVEN
FOR EVERY CUP OF WATER GIVEN.

On the W side of the green, a cottage-range dated 1840, the windows with stone mullions. Broad gable over the two-storey

centrepiece. Single-storey lateral wings, the N extended later
but in the same style. On the green's s side, a two-storey four-
house main block of the mid C19. Jacobethan, with steeply
pitched gables and gablets and mullioned windows. It is flanked
by double cottages, each with a two-storey centrepiece, its first-
floor window surmounted by a consoled stone canopy. Single-
storey wings; porches at their ends. At the E end of this side of
the green, a late C19 single-storey and attic range. Bracketed
broad eaves to the roof; bargeboarded dormer windows.
Horseshoe-shaped door at the E house.

On the N side of the green, a single-storey broad-eaved range of
cottages of the later C19. Stone canopies over the mullioned
windows of the advanced ends; bargeboarded wooden porches.
To the E, a plainer and slightly later single-storey and attic triple
house using most of the same motifs but to less happy effect.

8080                  DUNMORE PARK                      F
                    o.8km. ESE of Dunmore

Castellated Tudor-Gothic mansion house designed by *William
Wilkins* and built in 1820–5 for the fifth Earl of Dunmore. It was
partly demolished and shorn of detail in 1972 and what remains is
a ruin looking distinctly sorry for itself set on the edge of parkland
whose design has been obscured by neglect and commercial
planting.

The main house was built round a courtyard, the w range containing the entrance hall, business room and service rooms.
Along the s range was a suite of dining room, library and drawing room. The family rooms (boudoir, bedroom, bathroom and
dressing rooms) occupied the ground floor of the E range, with
the kitchen and servants' offices in the N range and a second
courtyard to the N. The ashlar-faced main ranges are of two tall
storeys. Hoodmoulded rectangular windows containing stone-
mullioned Gothic lights (the taller ground-floor windows with
transoms). At the s end of the w (entrance) front, a two-storey
*porte cochère*, its outer corners clasped by slender battlemented
octagonal turret-buttresses. Four-centred arches at the carriage
openings and the windows above. Behind the *porte cochère*
project three faces of the octagonal entrance hall. The join of
this range's broader and taller s section (containing the entrance
hall and business room) to the lower service section to the N is
marked by an octagonal tower. Symmetrical s elevation of nine
bays, with turret-buttresses of the *porte cochère*'s type at the outer
corners. Full-height canted bay windows at the gabled second
and eighth bays. The centre bay is carried up as a three-storey
tower, its front marked off from the rest of the elevation by
turret-buttresses. At the house's E side the s end is very slightly
advanced under a gable; turret-buttresses at the corners. Projecting from this, a two-storey canted bay window. The loss of
the wallhead battlements is particularly unhappy. Most of the N
part of the building has been removed.

Contemporary STABLES SW of the mansion house. Austere castellated, a gabled tower at the centre of the front.

EAST LODGE on the B9214 on the S edge of the parkland, 1.4km. SSE of the mansion house. Early C19 castellated, a semi-octagonal bay projecting at the front. Hoodmoulded mullioned windows. Contemporary octagonal corniced GATEPIERS.

The drive leads to the back of THE PARSONAGE (its front facing the A905). Large but plain Elizabethan double house, by *David Bryce*, 1845–6. It was built to house the factor and chaplain.

W of The Parsonage (0.4km.) is a complex of brick WALLED GARDENS, the S garden of the mid C18, the N probably of 1822. The S garden is open to the S. Its N wall, the top enlivened by dummy windows, is of double construction and housed stores and hot-water pipes to serve greenhouses in front. At the centre of this side is THE PINEAPPLE, a fantastic ashlar-built architectural 72

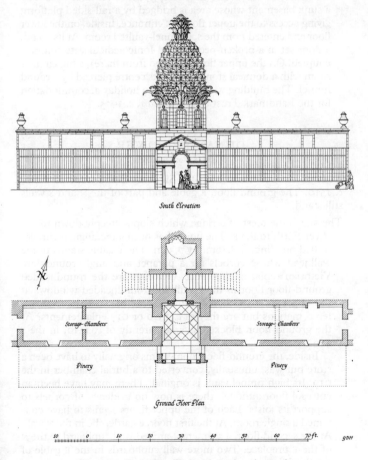

*South Elevation*

*Storage-Chambers*      *Storage-Chambers*

*Pinery*      *Pinery*

*Ground Floor Plan*

10   0   10   20   30   40   50   60   70 ft.

GDH

Dunmore Park, The Pineapple. S elevation and
ground-floor plan.

and structural show-off garden pavilion. To the S its lower storey is conventionally Palladian, fronted by an open-pedimented porch containing a Tuscan-columned Venetian doorway, its keystone carved with the date 1761. Above the centre opening has been inserted a panel bearing a heart charged with a cinquefoil (motifs from the Douglas-Hamilton coat of arms) and the motto 'FIDELIS IN ADVERSIS' ('Faithful in adversity'), probably erected to celebrate the marriage of Lady Susan Douglas-Hamilton to George, fifth Earl of Dunmore, in 1803. This lower floor serves as a pedestal for the octagonal Gothick upper storey, each slightly curved face pierced by an ogee-arched opening, its surround rising into a finial. At each corner, a thick column. This upper storey is crowned by the feature which gives the building its name, a realistically detailed 8.2m.-high stone pineapple, its leaves cantilevered out in a display of the engineer's and mason's skill. On the N side the ground rises steeply, the lower floor becoming a sunk basement whose area is bridged by a rail-sided platform giving access to the upper floor's N entrance. Inside, on the lower floor and entered from the S, a tunnel-vaulted room. At its N end, a door set in a broken-pedimented Ionic aedicule, its columns coupled. On the upper floor (entered from there), a tall circular room with a domical stone ceiling, its centre pierced by a round funnel. The building was converted to holiday accommodation for the Landmark Trust by *David Carr*, *c.* 1975.

## DUNMORE TOWER

0.6km. SW of Dunmore

Ruin of a tower-house built for Sir John Elphinstone of Airth, *c.* 1510. The ground floor, E gable and part of the N and S walls still stand.

The site is the crest of a ridge which slopes steeply down to the River Forth to the E. The house has been a rectangular rubble-walled building, *c.* 8.86m. by 7.31m. The E gable stands to the wallhead whose corbels for a parapet and angle rounds are Victorian replacements. Also Victorian are the roundheaded ground-floor door in the S wall and roundheaded windows at the upper floors. Other windows (some blocked) have chamfered margins but are they of *c.* 1510 or C17 enlargements? At the ground floor, blocked slits, apparently of *c.* 1510, in the S and E walls.

  Inside, the ground-floor room seems originally to have been a store but was, unusually, converted to a burial chamber in the C19. Its high tunnel vault is original. There may have been an entresol floor although there is now no evidence of corbels to support its joists. Each of the upper floors seems to have contained a single room. At the first floor, a garderobe in the N wall. At the second floor, a segmental-arched wall cupboard to the N of the E fireplace. Two more wall cupboards in the E gable of the third floor.

Ancillary buildings to the w of the tower were removed in the
C19 and replaced by a chapel and burial ground in 1850. The
chapel was demolished in the later C20. In the burial ground, a
Baroque granite MONUMENT of c. 1850 to Alexander Edward,
sixth Earl of Dunmore, †1845, a large coat of arms on the N face.

# DUNTOCHER                                   WD 4070

Now no more than a residential suburb of Clydebank. It is
difficult to imagine the Roman occupation, yet this is a location
towards the w end of the Antonine Wall which has yielded substantial archaeological finds. Among these, the remains of a fort,
underground passages and chambers thought to be part of a baths
building, and numerous artefacts from the same Roman period.
Almost as invisible is the evidence of a once-thriving textile industry.
From earliest times the wooded glen of the Duntocher Burn
provided power for a mill. By the 1780s the manufacture of coarse
woollens and cotton was under way, but it was the arrival of
William Dunn in 1808 that accelerated production. Dunn bought
and enlarged mills at Duntocher and Faifley, built new mills at
Milton and Hardgate and by 1835 had installed steam engines to
boost the output of spun and woven cotton. Within a decade of
his death in 1840 two of his mills had been destroyed by fire. By
1860 Duntocher's economy was in recession and in 1873 the mills
ceased production. A faint hint of the old village lingers along Old
Mill Road but the sense of prosperity is elusive. If not quite so
placeless as its neighbours Hardgate and Faifley, Duntocher has
all but disappeared under the rolling bleakly patterned carpet of
C20 council housing.

CLYDEBANK FAIFLEY PARISH CHURCH, Faifley Road. The
    original building, little more than a meeting hall with shallow-
    pitched roof, was completed in 1956–7. It now serves as ancillary
    accommodation for the more ambitious structure erected imme-
    diately E ten years later. A concrete-framed bell-tower stands in
    the wedge between the two. The church, by *Noad & Wallace*,
    1965–6, has a duodecagon plan, tall slot windows splayed from
    the wallplanes. Externally the roughcast group is untidy and
    unkempt but the interior of the church, designed for 'worship in
    the round', is much better. Pews fan out around a central pulpit.
    Above, laminated rib beams cross a boarded timber ceiling to
    meet under an apex roof-light.
Former DUNTOCHER FREE CHURCH, Dumbarton Road. Built
    1844–5. T-plan behind a s entrance gable castellated on the
    skews. Abandoned.
DUNTOCHER TRINITY PARISH CHURCH, Roman Road.
    Designed in 1949 by *William Reid* of Edinburgh but not built
    until 1951–2. Constructed in a reddish-brown facing brick
    inside and out, Trinity was the 'first blitzed church to be rebuilt in
    Scotland'. Cruciform plan and nave-and-aisles section are con-
    ventional enough but a shallow-pitched roof and steep parabolic

arches in the gables betray period preference. A square bell-tower abuts the w gable abruptly capped in height above three lozenge-shaped belfry openings. To the E, behind the crossing, halls and offices bed into the hillside. The brick interior imparts an unexpectedly austere gravitas. A decoratively textured brick wall divides vestibule from church. Four low parabolic arches open into low flat-roofed aisles on each side of the nave. Higher tapering parabolas at the transepts and chancel. Segmental plaster vault to the nave. Semicircular plastered apse. Wide, stone-panelled semi-octagonal PULPIT, fluted on the front face. In the vestibule, a pedimented white marble War Memorial TABLET saved from the bombed church.

DUNTOCHER WEST UNITED FREE CHURCH, Dumbarton Road. Originally Duntocher United Associate Church, 1822. Three-bay piended meeting house with a pilastered doorpiece. Tired but still respectable.

ST JOSEPH (R.C.), Douglas Muir Road, Faifley. Curving walls and roofs by *Nicholson & Jacobsen*, 1996–7; a replacement in grey blockwork and galvanized steel sheeting for *Gillespie, Kidd & Coia*'s church of 1963–4, destroyed by fire in 1993. Irregular plan with perimeter wall splays between glazing slots. Rounded wall ends become supports for coupled laminated beams rising in a slow arc from l. to clearstorey at r. Side-lit proscenium sanctuary with stepped bowed apron. Lean-to s vestibule opening to church through folding timber doors and glazed waffle grids. Cobbled forecourt and two-storey PRESBYTERY survive from 1960s.

ST MARY (R.C.), Chapel Road. Built in rust-red facing brick, 1952–4; by *Thomas S. Cordiner*. A nine-bay nave lit by pediment-arched lancets above low side aisles. Shallow-pitched roof sheeted in copper. In the w gable, the half columns of a stone portal with flat cornice slab carry the sculpted figure of the Virgin Mary, by *Jack Mortimer*. Behind her head is the Cross framed in a circular window. A link N, penetrated by segmental arches, leads to a tall bell-tower. High, well-lit interior, painted in pale blue and white. Segmental-arched aisle arcades l. and r. – Ahead, dominating the long space, a marble REREDOS rises from sanctuary floor to ceiling. The marble is light fawn in colour, so striated that it seems as if some organic parasite were clinging to the E wall. Framed in a vesica at its centre, Christ on gold. Diagonally above and below, the symbols of the Four Evangelists. – These and the ceiling BALDACCHINO with a dove were painted by local artist *James Brown*.

ANTONINE SPORTS CENTRE, Roman Road. Diagonal cedar boarding conceals what was a large industrial shed; adaptation by *Jenkins & Marr*, 1978. Small Hall added, using salvaged metal trusses, 1985–6. Brick health suite and sauna under wide-span, segmental roof by *Hutcheson, Fisher & Campbell*, 1998–9.

CARLEITH PRIMARY SCHOOL, Stark Avenue. By *Dumbarton County Council*, 1972–4. Two parallel classroom ranges with opposed clearstorey monopitches. E roof cut back flat over entrance area to assembly hall clearstorey.

DUNTOCHER BRIDGE, Roman Road. Two segmental arches with voussoir margins span the tumbling course of the Duntocher Burn. Groome reports the tradition that this is, or was, the work of the Romans. An inscribed tablet, inset in the W parapet in 1762 when Lord Blantyre restored the crossing, records the putative role of Quintus Lollius Urbicus, builder of the Antonine Wall in the C2. Added inscriptions report that the bridge was blitzed in 1941 and repaired in 1943. If the present structure is in any sense Roman, it can only be by virtue of some random masonry quarried for repair work from the nearby Antonine fort which was still, as Groome notes, 'distinctly traceable' in the C18.

EDINBARNET SCHOOL, Faifley Road. 1960–1. Three storey curtain-wall classroom blocks by *William T. Davie*.

GLENHEAD COMMUNITY EDUCATION CENTRE, Chapel Road. 1966–67. Well-ordered buff brick boxes. Rising above, a flat-roofed hall with an all-round clearstorey of close-spaced mullions.

GOLDENHILL PRIMARY SCHOOL, Stewart Drive. By *Gratton & McLean*, 1954–5. Symmetrical, eighteen-bay SE façade. At the centre, four parabolic arches form a ground-floor loggia entrance. First-floor classrooms fully glazed. Walls rendered in Dorset pea; bellcast piended roofs tiled.

ANTONINE WALL, Golden Hill. Only a section of the stone base of the Wall of *c.* 142 is visible. From the site of the fort on the summit of the hill the end of the Wall can be seen beside the Erskine Bridge as well as the manner in which the lie of the land is now against the Romans, underlining the interpretation of the Wall as a bureaucratic line rather than one of military defence.

COCHNO HOUSE. *See* p. 348.

## DUNTREATH CASTLE

S *5080*

3.2km. NW of Strathblane

Tower, mansion and gatehouse, primly placed in an immaculately tended landscape. Together yet apart, their relationship reveals little of earlier developments. The estate is ancient, originally part of the earldom of Lennox and, from *c.* 1434, in the possession of the Edmonstone family who built the tower towards the end of the C15. There is evidence of C14 work having adjoined the SE side of the tower but the precise layout of this earlier construction is unknown. Not until the late C16, when the tower's predecessor was perhaps recast as a chapel, does the castle's configuration become clear. By that time a courtyard arrangement had evolved with a NW gatehouse set between flanking walls, a SE kitchen range linked to the tower-chapel wing and a short SW range, the so-called 'Dumb Laird's Tower'. Of these, the gatehouse, erected by Sir James Edmonstone, sixth of Duntreath, at the turn of the C16 and C17, was the most notable, a three-storey structure described as 'one of the largest and most complete examples of its class in Scotland' (RCAHMS, *Inventory*, 1963). Abandoned a century or so later, the buildings fell into ruin and it was not until 1857 that restoration under *Charles Wilson* and *David Thomson* was begun. First, a new SW wing, with bartizaned gables and a turnpike stair tower in the W re-entrant, was built but soon the kitchen wing was demolished, the late C16 gatehouse reconstructed and a new outer gatehouse placed axially some distance NW of the courtyard. Further Baronial alteration and aggrandizement by *Sydney Mitchell & Wilson*, 1889–93, added a high SE range with a central drum-flanked entry to the courtyard opposite the restored gatehouse. This vast dwelling with its lavish interiors (illustrated by Hermann Muthesius in his exceptionally well-informed *Das englische Haus* of 1904–5) proved unsustainable in the C20 and in 1958 extensive demolition left only three separate elements.

The late C15 TOWER, built in random sandstone rubble with dressed margins and quoins, is oblong in plan and three storeys high with an attic and parapet walk restored above the wallhead corbel-course. An unusual rectangular stair tower containing a turnpike projects SW close to the S corner. It is twice intaken in its height, becoming semi-hexagonal at second-floor level and circular where it passes through the parapet; this round cap-house and its conical slated roof are not original. A thick cross-wall divides the ground floor into two vaulted chambers.

The Baronial MANSION, which formerly closed the SE side of the castle court, comprises the mid-Victorian range, built in square snecked rubble and identifiable from the stair tower in the E re-entrant and the carved panel dated 1863, and its rather grander late C19 encasing which, among its nationally symbolic embellishments, boasts a three-storey, round W tower with cone roof, a four-light mullioned and transomed NW window corbelled at first floor and a square bartizan at the N corner.

A little NW is the detached two-storey symmetrical GATE-HOUSE, *c.* 1857, with crowstepped gables facing NW and SE, and bartizans with ball finial tops at each corner. An ashlar barrel vault penetrates the structure, its arched doors sliding into recesses. Axially related but some distance SE of mansion and tower, tall GATEPIERS with swan's-head cresting mark the end of the now-disused SE drive: roll-banded square shafts with cornices and swan-topped coronets honouring the Edmonstone lairds. – EAST LODGE, early 1900s. NE, close to the A81, the U-plan Baronial STABLES in red sandstone rubble; late C19, as is the WEST LODGE. – PARK laid out *c.* 1857, the LOCH created in 1968.

STANDING STONES, 0.5km. SW of Duntreath Castle. An unusual linear setting of five standing stones. Excavations, 1972, produced a radiocarbon dating to the Neolithic period.

# DYKEHEAD

A hamlet on the B8034 halfway between Arnprior and Port of Menteith.

CARDROSS BRIDGE, 0.7km. SSE. Built 1774. Narrow, hump-backed bridge of three similar segmental arches, the central span 12.5m. Bold cutwater piers. Roughly dressed, dull red sandstone voussoirs; rubble superstructure. Inscribed panel on S side of E abutment records a royal contribution to the building costs from forfeited estates monies.

BRUCEHILL. Late C18. Two-bay farmhouse with round-arched first-floor windows, central oval panel and lower one-bay wings. Harled U-plan STEADING; central entrance archway under a bellcote.

DYKEHEAD COTTAGES. Late C18 or early C19. Two one-and-a-half-storey houses, gables at r. angles to each other, enclose a single-storey octagon. This, formerly a toll house and later a library, has a slated pyramid roof and gabled porch.

GARTUR, 2.4km. W. Probably late C18. Farmhouse and steading forming quadrangular court. Whitewashed rubble with pantiles to E range outbuildings.

MOATED HOMESTEAD, Ballangrew, 2.3km. ENE. C14–C15. Probably the site of a medieval hunting lodge which, before the agricultural improvements of the C18 and C19, must have been isolated in Flanders Moss. A trapezoidal area, 23m. by 21m., bounded by a broad water-filled ditch.

CARDROSS HOUSE. *See* p. 308.


## EDINAMPLE CASTLE          S *6020*
### 1.7km. SE of Lochearnhead

Picturesquely situated, harled Z-plan tower-house, dated 1584. Roofs modified and interior rearranged, *c.* 1790. Restoration began in the 1970s, first by *Peter Nicholson* who removed additions made in the early C20. Work continued throughout the 1980s and was completed in 1996-8 by *Raymond Muszynski* of *Ian Begg Architects*. The arrangement is classic: a tall, three-storey-and-attic, gabled oblong laid W–E with drum towers at the NW and SE corners. At the SW and NE corners at second-floor level, corbelled rounds with slated cone roofs. Quarter-round projections corbelled from first floor in the re-entrant angles between the NW tower and the N elevation and the SE tower and the E gable betray turnpike stairs. The main entrance, which faces W, is placed in the SE tower where the curve of its drum flattens briefly before abutting the s front. Doorway with roll-moulded frame. Above it, set between two superimposed windows, a weathered panel bearing the arms of Sir Duncan Campbell, builder of the castle. Most windows have rough rubble surrounds, some holed for shutter fixings. All are lintelled, those lighting the first floor Hall markedly taller. In the W gable at this level, a single round-arched window.

The castle looks N to Loch Earn. To the s the ground falls sharply into the valley of the Ample Water. A battered wall of large rubble boulders banks above a path that descends from the castle forecourt to the stream, its slow curve calculated to enjoy a view of a spectacular waterfall to the SW. Uphill S, at the entrance to the estate, is EDINAMPLE MAUSOLEUM, mid-C18, a gabled oblong with harled walls, rusticated quoins, a worn cavetto eaves course and a moulded stringcourse over its rubble base. In the w gable, a round-arched entrance under an uninscribed tablet set in a heavily moulded frame.

EDINAMPLE BRIDGE, 0.3km. s. Probably c18. Single-arch span over Ample Burn.

5070                    EDINBARNET HOUSE                    s
                         1.5km. NE of Duntocher

Baronial by *John J. Burnet* of *John Burnet & Son*. First built for Walter Mackenzie in a more exuberant turreted form than the present house, Edinbarnet was completed in 1882 and almost immediately destroyed by fire. Burnet at once prepared new designs, exhibiting these at the Royal Scottish Academy in 1895. How much of the fabric of the earlier mansion survived to be incorporated into these revisions is unclear (framed stone tablets dated 1882 are set in the w and s elevations), but around the parapet at the SE corner bay a carved inscription records that the rebuilding was carried out between 1889 and 1891. The house has been a nursing home since 1988.

The approach is from the w, where an open-gabled porch advances asymmetrically below a three-storey crowstepped gable of square-snecked ochre sandstone rubble. The porch is characteristically Burnet: bargeboarded with arch-braced timbers carried on red sandstone columns raised on plinths between which steps rise to the entrance doorway. Entangled in the thistle-heads and leaves carved in the column capitals are the letters W and M. In the apex of the gable behind, above a mullioned and transomed window, is a tablet carved with the antlered head of a deer. Recessed to the r. of this gable, a four-storey square tower forms the house's SW corner. Another stone tablet bears the monogram WM and the date 1882. Windows are placed randomly below a corbel course carrying a parapet battlemented at the corners. A stair turret with bellcast dunce's-hat roof spikes the NE corner. On the s face of the tower, a broad canted bay rises through two storeys to a balustraded balcony at second-floor level. To the r., the s wall continues on the same plane under an open eaves balustrade. A canted bay negotiates the two upper floors at the SE corner, the splayed faces of the parapet carved with the names of Walter Mackenzie and Elizabeth Campbell and the dates of the fire and rebuilding. From tripartite French windows at principal floor level at the centre of the E front, an external stone stair with ironwork railings and parapet walls capped by ball finials falls to a landing then divides in imperial plan to drop to the garden. To the r., a second broad canted bay two storeys high. Masking much of the N side of the house and extending E is a three-storey gabled bedroom wing added respectfully in the early 1990s. To the NW, a single-storey service wing. Inset in the w wall, a swan-neck pediment dated 1758; a fragment from an earlier house.

From the w entrance a stair rises to first-floor level where the main public rooms are located. Towards the e end of the Middle Hall is a round-arched stone chimneypiece cut with two simple trefoils and the initials WM. Plaster ceiling in the Library, panelled and ribbed. Lugged timber fireplace with green marble surround and a mirrored overmantel with dentilled cornice.

# FALKIRK          F *8080*

Conglomerate town formed from a C17 burgh of barony and the surrounding suburbs and villages which developed from the end of the C18. In 1769 Thomas Pennant described the burgh as 'a large ill-built town supported by the great fairs for black cattle from the Highlands' and, at that time, Falkirk was an unimportant urban centre which primarily served the drovers and cattle traders who met several times a year on the then moorland of Stenhousemuir to the N. Development of the areas to the N and E of the burgh began after the opening of the Carron Ironworks (*see* Carron and Carronshore) in 1760 and the Forth & Clyde Canal in 1773. The Falkirk Ironworks, begun in 1819, was a precursor of the industry which followed the opening of the Falkirk Grahamston station of the Edinburgh & Glasgow Railway in 1842, eleven large ironworks or foundries being established between 1856 and 1877, together with a brewery and distillery.

Suburban housing development to the s was a noticeable feature of the C20 which saw also the erection of a large aluminium rolling mill in 1944. Most of the traditional industrial ventures closed in the later C20, to be replaced belatedly by businesses connected with the high technology of the new global economy. Falkirk's most distinctive contribution to the cultural life of Scotland is as the centre for the manufacture of 'Irn-Bru', the fizzy non-alcoholic drink which has been taken round the globe by the Tartan Army of Scottish football supporters.

## TOWN CENTRE

Substantially the burgh of barony erected in 1600 under the feudal superiority of the Lords (later Earls of) Livingston whose seat was at Callendar House (*see* below). In 1647 the burgh was surrounded by a wall 'for keipeing furth of streingeris sua that nene may enter

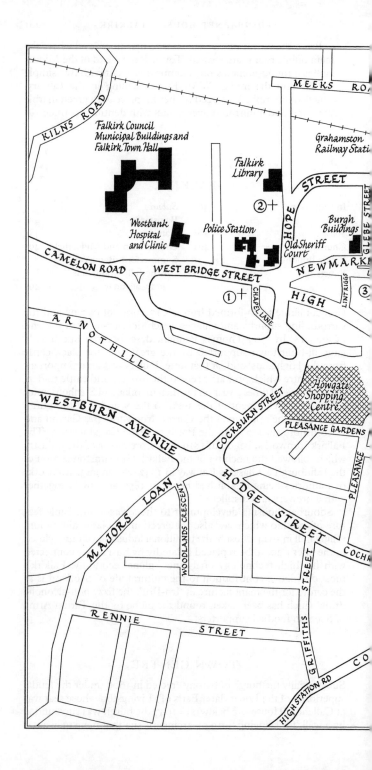

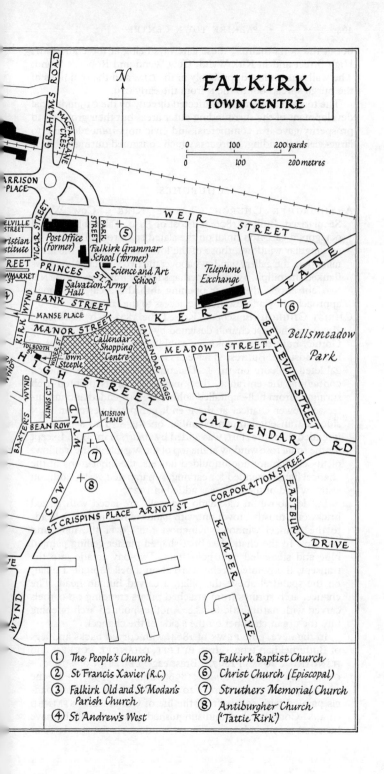

# FALKIRK
## TOWN CENTRE

N

| 0 | | 100 | | 200 yards |
| 0 | 100 | | 200 metres | |

GRAHAMS ROAD

MACFARLANE CRESCENT

HARRISON PLACE

MELVILLE STREET

Christian Institute

STREET

WEIR STREET

PARK STREET

Post Office (former)

Falkirk Grammar School (former)

Science and Art School

PRINCES ST

Salvation Army Hall

NEWMARKET ST

BANK STREET

MANSE PLACE

VICAR STREET

KIRK WYND

MANOR STREET

Tolbooth St

Town Steeple

WOOER ST

Callendar Shopping Centre

KERSE STREET

Telephone Exchange

BELLEVUE STREET

LANE

(+) (5)

(+) (6)

Bellsmeadow Park

MEADOW STREET

CALLENDAR RIGGS

HIGH STREET

BAXTER'S WYND

KINGS CT

BEAN ROW

COW WYND

MISSION LANE

(+) (7)

(+) (8)

CALLENDAR RD

CORPORATION STREET

EASTBURN DRIVE

WYND

ST CRISPINS PLACE

ARNOT ST

KEMPER AVE

T

F

| ① The People's Church | ⑤ Falkirk Baptist Church |
| ② St Francis Xavier (R.C.) | ⑥ Christ Church (Episcopal) |
| ③ Falkirk Old and St Modan's Parish Church | ⑦ Struthers Memorial Church |
| ④ St Andrew's West | ⑧ Antiburgher Church ('Tattie Kirk') |

bot at the ports thairof', these gateways being at the ends of the High Street and in Kirk Wynd, Cow Wynd and Robert's Wynd. The wall was removed, probably in the C18, and the buildings of the burgh spread out to the N from the early C19.

The town centre was little affected directly by the C19 industrial development of the surrounding outer areas but their growth and prosperity gave it a commercial and civic importance leading to large-scale rebuilding, a process which continued during the C20.

## CHURCHES

ANTIBURGHER CHURCH ('TATTIE KIRK'), Cow Wynd. Secularized. Built in 1806 at a cost of £850. Tall rubble-walled octagon, a cast iron finial on the slated spire roof. Two tiers of rectangular windows, those of the lower tier (lighting the area) taller than the gallery windows above; the two very tall S windows flanked the pulpit. SW door, perhaps for the minister. At the NE, two entrances, the lower opening into the area; the upper, approached by a forestair, gave access to the gallery.

CHRIST CHURCH (Episcopal), Kerse Lane. 1863–4, by *R. Rowand Anderson*, the first church designed by him to be built. Unfussy Gothic, built of buff-coloured rubble banded with courses of red sandstone. Buttressed nave, a Celtic cross on the W gable, a gableted bellcote on the E. Diagonally buttressed NW porch containing the entrance, the inner order of its pointed arch springing from bell-capitalled columns. Apse-ended and unbuttressed lower chancel at the E end; parapeted vestry on its N side, a transeptal organ chamber on the S. The S transept, intended from the start, was added by *Anderson* in 1902. Except for the small rose window at the top of the W gable all the windows of the church are hoodmoulded lancets, the label stops of the chancel lights intended for carving. A parapeted vestry addition at the W end of the nave was added in 1927.

Inside, above an oak dado the walls are faced with glazed brickwork, mostly brown but with bands of red; red brick heads to the chancel windows. Kingpost roofs over the nave and transept. In the chancel, a boat-shaped plaster ceiling painted blue and stencilled with gold stars. Two-bay arcade into the transept, the pointed arches carried on a bell-capitalled pillar; on the spandrel above the pillar, a carved human head. The chancel arch springs from attached pillars standing on corbels carved with naturalistic foliage. Another pointed arch opening into the organ chamber on the S side of the chancel.

In the nave, pine PEWS of 1864, with curved backs and legs of Butterfieldian type. – Iron PULPIT, CHANCEL SCREEN and HANGING CROSS of 1897. – Brass eagle LECTERN of *c.* 1900. – ORGAN by *Abbot & Smith*, 1896; rebuilt in 1987. – In the transept, a late C19 or early C20 wooden ALTAR, the front panels painted with scenes from the life of Our Lord. – STAINED GLASS. Complete but undistinguished. The sides of the nave have late C19 windows. – The W window on the N side (Our

Lord and little children) is by *James Ballantine & Son*, 1878, the
E window of this side (the Maries at the Tomb) by *Mayer &
Co.*, 1885. – In the W window of the nave, the S window of the
transept and the side windows of the chancel, mid-C20 glass,
the nave window incorporating late Victorian and Edwardian
fragments. – In the three lights of the chancel's apse, strongly
coloured late C19 work (Our Lord, Moses, and Elijah).

FALKIRK BAPTIST CHURCH, corner of Orchard Street and
Weir Street. By *G. Deas Page*, 1896–7. Gothic, built of bullnosed red sandstone ashlar with polished dressings. The breadth
of the front (E) gable of the nave is broken by crocketed pinnacled
buttresses. At the centrepiece, a four-light window with quatre-
foiled circlets in the head. Below this window, a battlemented
porch; the door surround of its gableted entrance is decorated
with rosettes. Gryphons stick out from the porch's E corners.
More gryphons at the corners of the nave gable. Yet more
gryphons at the corners of the W transepts which were added in
1904. Their gables contain large windows, each of three lights
under a cinquefoiled circlet. The roof's flèche is now missing.
To the W, a hall of 1904. It is joined to the church by a parapeted porch from whose corners lean out half-length male and
female figures.

Inside the church, the PULPIT and the Sicilian marble open
BAPTISTERY are of 1906. – STAINED GLASS. Three-light W
window (the Good Shepherd, with St John the Evangelist and
St Peter), by the *Blythswood Stained Glass Co.*, 1897. – In the N
transept, another window (Moses) of 1897 by the *Blythswood
Stained Glass Co.*, moved here from a side wall in 1906.

FALKIRK OLD AND ST MODAN, Manse Place, High Street and 17
Upper Newmarket Street. Large church, predominantly Georgian
Gothic but with a history of some complexity.

The building is a replacement for the medieval parish church
of Falkirk. That was cruciform with a crossing tower. The tower
was rebuilt to *William Adam*'s design in 1738. In 1810–11 the
medieval church was demolished and a new church built as a
straightforward rectangle abutting the N side of the crossing
tower whose lower part was reconstructed. At the same time a
mausoleum for the Earls of Zetland was built on the site of the
medieval sanctuary, i.e. as a SE wing to the new church. *James
Gillespie Graham* was the architect for all this work. In 1892
*Wardrop & Anderson* added a porch-cum-session house on the
site of the medieval S transept and an organ chamber on the N
side of the church. The organ chamber was rebuilt in 1970 and
halls added to the church's W end in 1996.

The church of 1810–11 is a broad rubble-walled box. A
battlemented parapet, the merlons with triangular tops, runs
along the N and S sides and round the corners which break
forward slightly like clasping buttresses. Crowstepped gables. N
side of four bays. At each of the two broad centre bays, a window
of four uncusped lights under simple loop tracery. The bottoms
of the windows are hidden by the shallowly projecting rectangular organ chamber of 1970. At each of the narrow corner

bays, a Y-traceried two-light window. Two-light windows of the same design at the corners of the gables. The centre window of the E gable is a clone of the centre windows of the N side, its counterpart at the W gable a variant of these. At the E gable, a battlemented porch. The W gable is overlaid by the flat-roofed link to the halls.

In the S side of the church, more two-light Y-traceried windows. At the centre of this front is the tower of 1738. It is square, ashlar-faced, with rusticated quoins (some of this work of 1810–11). At the W face, a raggle for the roof of the medieval nave. In the E face, a slit window and, both here and in the S face, blocked rectangular windows, all apparently C18. The W windows containing shouldered rectangular lights are of 1892. Above the tower's cornice, an octagonal belfry, a roundheaded opening in each face; slated roof with bellcast eaves. Attached to the S side of the tower is the two-storey porch-cum-session house added in 1892. It is Victorian Gothic, built of hammer-dressed masonry. Conventional battlement with straight-topped merlons. In the inner angles of the church and tower, low para-peted outshots, also of 1892, the rectangular window openings containing cusped round-arched lights.

The Zetland Mausoleum of 1810–11 at the SE is a sturdy buttressed and crowstep-gabled rectangle, ashlar-walled and with a stone slab roof. Hoodmoulded openings, the E windows with simple Georgian Gothic tracery. The tall dummy windows in the N and S gables have label stops (perhaps replacements) carved as human heads. Above the E door, the heraldic achieve-ment of the Earls of Zetland.

The Hall at the W end of the church is of 1996. Walls of polished ashlar contrasting with bullnosed rubble; steeply pitched stepped gable. Flat-roofed polished ashlar link to the church.

INTERIOR. Vestibule in the tower. Its N door into the church is set in a Neo-Classical surround designed by *J. G. Callander* and erected as a war memorial in 1923. Above it, a TABLET, perhaps early C19, inscribed in implausibly archaic lettering 'FVNDATVM/MALCOMO. III/REGE SCOTIA/A.M. †1057'.

The church itself is disappointingly bare. Large CEILING ROSE of simplified Gothic design, probably of 1811. – D-plan GALLERY on wooden Roman Doric columns. – At the centre of the N wall, a free Jacobean oak PULPIT of 1896. The canopy's gilded dove finial was re-used from the previous pulpit and may be of 1811 but perhaps of 1827 when a new canopy was made for that pulpit. – This is flanked by overly simple wooden SCREENS of 1992 masking the pipes of the ORGAN (by *Forster & Andrews*, 1892; rebuilt 1950). – STAINED GLASS. The two central N windows contain glass (Abel, Abraham, Moses and David; the Good Samaritan) by *Christopher Whall*, 1896. – In the large E and W gable windows, brightly coloured abstract designs by *Ballantine & Allan*, 1860–1, moved here from the N wall in 1896.

MONUMENTS. On the W wall of the vestibule, a large monu-ment to the Rev. John B. Patterson by *Alexander Ritchie*, 1838.

Neo-Classical frame containing a white marble tablet carved with the relief of a mourning lady and cherub beside an urn-topped sarcophagus whose side bears a portrait bust. – On the vestibule's E wall, a monument of 1889 to the Rev. William Begg by *J. & G. Mossman*. Gothic with a relief portrait bust.

In the passage E of the vestibule, two weathered stone EFFIGIES, one of a knight, the other of a woman. They may be mid-C15. – At the NE end of this passage are two medieval fragments. One is a roof BOSS carved with the coat of arms of Livingstone of Callendar. The second is a CROSSHEAD, perhaps originally from a headstone, each face of its boss carved with a rosette. – Also here is the large fragment of a GRAVESLAB bearing a coat of arms and Latin inscription. It probably commemorates Alexander, fifth Lord Livingstone, †c. 1550. – In the passage W of the vestibule, another and less worn pair of EFFIGIES, again of a knight and lady and perhaps of the later C16. – Also here, a GRAVESLAB bearing a coat of arms flanked by the initials RI, and a largely illegible Latin inscription apparently recording a death in 1600.

GRAVEYARD. At the SW entry from High Street, a simply moulded segmental-arched GATEWAY, one stone incised with the date 1659. Cast iron gates of the earlier C19. The graveyard was cleared of headstones in 1962 leaving only a few large monuments. Near the SW entry, a tall grey granite Celtic CROSS commemorating the men of Bute killed at the first Battle of Falkirk in 1298. It was erected by John, third Marquess of Bute, in 1877. – Just S of the E end of the church, the MONUMENT to Sir John Graham of Dundaff †1298 at the first Battle of Falkirk. It is enclosed in a cast iron cage of 1860. Axe-headed railings, crocketed finials at the corners and, on top, a lion rampant. On the N face of the cage, the heraldic achievement of Graham; on the E face, a panel, with thistles at the corners, bearing a rosette surrounded by the inscription 'VIRTVS VIVIT POST FVNERA' ('Virtue lives beyond the grave'). Inside this cage, a tall slab-ended table tomb, probably of 1772 but following the design of a tomb, possibly of the late C16, which existed here by 1697. Stacked under its lid are three slabs. The lowest is medieval and carved with an effigy, now badly weathered and difficult to see but apparently of someone (a man or a woman) dressed in a long robe; the identification with Sir John Graham is improbable. The middle slab, again badly weathered, is plain but has carried an inscription in raised letters. It is likely to date from the late C16 and formed the lid of the tomb until *c.* 1723 when the slab above was erected by *William Whyte*, wright in Falkirk, at the expense of the Duke of Montrose. Acanthus leaf frieze. The top is carved with an heraldic achievement and incised inscription copied from the slab below. This third slab was in turn displaced by a new lid (the present one) in 1772. This lid (restored, i.e. presumably recut, in 1860) is a replica of the slab of *c.* 1723. Marginal inscription apparently copied from the earlier lid:

HEIR LYES SIR JOHN THE GRAME BAITH WIGHT AND WISE ANE OF THE CHIEF RESKEWIT SCOTLAND THRISE AND BETTER KNIGHT NOT TO THE WORLD WAS LENT NOR WAS GVDE GRAME OF TRVTH AND HARDIMENT

Some of the wording is taken almost verbatim from Blind Harry's *Schir William Wallace*\* of which the first printed edition appeared in 1570. At the E end of the top, a further inscription: MENTE MANVQVE/POTENS ET/VALLÆ FIDVS/ACHATES/CONDITVR HIC/GRAMVS BELLO/INTERFECTVS/AB ANGLIS/XII JVLII/ ANNO 1298 ('Powerful in mind and hand, Graham, the faithful Achates of Wallace, is buried here, having been killed by the English on 22 July 1298'). On top of the tomb the replica of a sword thought to have been used by Graham at the Battle of Falkirk; it was cast by the *Falkirk Iron Works* in 1869.

SE of the Graham monument, a large MONUMENT erected in 1751‡ to Sir Robert Munro of Foulis and his brother, Dr Duncan Munro of Obsdale, both †1746 at the second Battle of Falkirk. Corniced pedestal surmounted by a sarcophagus decorated with carved drapery; grotesque heads at the ends and angels' heads at the sides of the sarcophagus. The pedestal's faces are panelled. At the S face, an heraldic achievement above drapery which is inscribed 'Job xix and 26 And though after my skin worms destroy this body. yet in my flesh shall I see god'. The N end of the pedestal is carved with martial trophies. The two long sides bear inscriptions, in Latin on the W, on the E its English translation:

HERE LYES INTERRED/The body of Sir ROBERT MUNRO of Foulis Knt & Bar/Colonel of a Regiment of foot./The life he had spent in the Parliament and Camp/With Honour He lost in the cause of Liberty and Religion/Near Falkirk/On the XVII of Jany MDCCXLVI aged LXII/As long as History Narrates the battle of FONTENOY/His Courage and Conduct on that day/In the Command of the HIGHLAND Regiment/ Will Be remembered./Sincere and active in the service of his FRIENDS/ Humane and forgiving to his Enemies/Generous and benevolent to all/His death was Universally regreted/Even by those who slew him./ With Sir ROBERT MUNRO was killed his brothr/Doctor DUNCAN MUNRO of Obsdale, aged LIX/Who unarmed would not forsake/His wounded Brother.

Just SE of the Munro monument, a late C19 MONUMENT to William Edmondstoune of Cambuswallace, also †1746 at the second Battle of Falkirk, and to members of the Dollar family. Neo-Jacobean red sandstone tombchest.

Near the E end of the churchyard's N wall, a MONUMENT to Patrick Murehead of Rashyhill and Margaret Buchanan, his wife, both †1723, an ambitious though provincial display of the mason's craft. It is a barley-sugar-columned aedicule, the frieze carved with reminders of death and, at the ends, angels' heads (symbols of the soul). Segmental pediment on which recline

---

\* 'I trow in warld was nocht a bettir knycht,
   Than was the gud Graym off trewth and hardement.'
‡ And restored in 1848 and 1972.

figures of angels. At the sides of the columns, feathered scrolls and bunches of grapes. Inscription panel in a foliaged surround, an angel's head at its top and skulls at the bottom. The aedicule stands on a ledge supported on piers with rounded corbels at their inner sides. A pair of recumbent effigies, their appearance surprisingly medieval, used to lie below the ledge. – To the w, a pedimented C18 MONUMENT, now with C19 inscriptions to members of the Wilson family. Below the pediment, attached columns from which spring roundheaded arches for the inscription panels (their lettering badly weathered). The spandrels of the arches are carved with reliefs of a skull, crossbones, hourglass, gravedigger's tools and a coffin.

ST ANDREW'S WEST, Upper Newmarket Street. Originally Falkirk Free Church. French Gothic, by *James Strang*, 1894–6, built of hammer-dressed and squared red sandstone. Broad and very tall nave, its E and W aisles hidden from the street by the NE porch and NW steeple. At the S end of the nave a shallow semi-octagonal apse pushes into the graveyard of Falkirk Old and St Modan's Church (*see* above). The apse windows are each of two cusped and pointed lights under a quatrefoil head. At the aisles, two tiers of lanceted windows, the lower single, the upper three-light. In the nave's front (N) gable a hoodmoulding-cum-stringcourse links the small cusped and pointed windows which light the vestibule; above, a five-light gallery window with cusped circlets in the head. The NE corner of the nave is gripped by a clasping buttress finished with an octagonal turret.

The steeple has a tower of four stages, its gableted angle buttresses stopped short of the top stage. Depressed arched entrance set in a pointed and hoodmoulded surround, the tympanum carved with the Free Church's emblem of the Burning Bush. At the second stage, a pair of cusped and pointed windows. A taller trio of nook-shafted pointed lights under a continuous hoodmoulding at the third stage. At the top of this stage, cut-out corners filled with foliage-capitalled nook-shafts; rosetted cornice. The belfry stage above is very tall and with its own sloping-topped angle buttresses. In each face, a pair of nook-shafted and hood-moulded openings containing fretted wooden louvres. Wall cornice, again carved with rosettes. This supports at each corner a spired octagonal turret with columned corners and niched faces. Within the turrets rises the steeple's octagonal stone spire decorated with two Gothic ornamented bands and stone lucarnes. Attached to the W side of the church, the contemporary hall, also Gothic but plainer.

Inside the church the nave is covered by a collar-braced roof, its ridge pierced by decorative ventilation openings. Nave arcades of stilted pointed arches carried on rather thin foliage-capitalled columns. D-plan gallery filling the aisles and across the N end. Pointed stone arch into the chancel. The CHANCEL FURNISHINGS (communion table, stalls, elders' chairs, lectern and pulpit) are all of 1930 in a Lorimerian manner. Behind them, the ORGAN by *Ingram & Co.*, 1913. – At the end of the E aisle, a (second) COMMUNION TABLE, carved with Celtic

motifs. It is by *P. Macgregor Chalmers*, 1915, and was formerly in
St Modan's Church. – STAINED GLASS. Chancel window
('Suffer the Children to Come Unto Me'), Glasgow style by the
*Blythswood Stained Glass Co.*, 1896. – At the E aisle, the S window
(David) is by *John Blyth*, 1994, a colourful example of simplified
realism. – The next window (St John), by *Douglas Hogg*, 1998, is
also colourful but much more freely drawn. – To the N, another
and more restrained window (St Margaret of Scotland) by *Blyth*,
1976. – In the W aisle, the S window (St Ninian) by *William Wilson*
and *D. Saunders*, 1954, is again colourful, the realism slightly
stylized. – Similar window (St Modan) of 1960, by *Wilson*, to the
N. – Further N, a window (Our Lord as the Light of the World)
of 1974.

In the vestibule, a marble wall MONUMENT to the Rev.
Lewis Irving, with a portrait bust in high relief. It is by *William
Brodie*, 1879.

ST FRANCIS XAVIER (R.C.), Hope Street. By *R. Fairlie &
Partners*, 1958–61. Dry-dashed nave and aisles almost hidden by
the screen front formed, at the end of the nave, by a panelled
29    ashlar-clad frame enclosing a huge chevron pattern of concrete
and glass, the base of each upright modelled with the emblem
of an Evangelist. Below, a low porch of hammer-dressed stonework. To the l., fronting the S aisle, a set-back ashlar slab bearing a gigantic relief figure of St Francis Xavier; semicircular
canopy over the inner angle. To the r., the N aisle is masked by
a lower projecting box housing the vestry.

Inside, the nave is divided into bays by the giant pointed
arches of the concrete framework. Plastered walls except at the
W (liturgical E) which is of brick, the sanctuary lit from side
windows hidden in diagonally walled recesses in the manner of
Coventry Cathedral. Flat-roofed nave aisles, the S occupied by
chapels, the N by confessionals. – STAINED GLASS. Modernistic
E window (scenes from the life of St Francis Xavier) by *Joseph
Vickers*, c. 1961. – In the clearstorey, laminated glass panels (the
Passion of Our Lord) by *Felix McCullough*, c. 1964.

STRUTHERS MEMORIAL CHURCH, Mission Lane. By *Alexander
Gauld*, 1897–8. Two-storey mission hall, the N front (now dry-
dashed) with a vestigial open pediment. Low pantile-roofed
tower at the NE corner.

THE PEOPLE'S CHURCH, West Bridge Street. Originally Relief
Church. Large Georgian box behind a Victorian front. The bulk
of the building is a rubble-walled rectangle by *Thomas Stirling*,
1799. In the side walls, two tiers of windows, the lower rectangular, the upper roundheaded, probably all of 1874 when the
pulpit was moved from the W side to the S end. In the W side, the
outlines of the original very large roundheaded central windows
and of a rectangular window to their l. are visible. In the S gable,
a pair of tall roundheaded windows under a small triangular
light, probably also of 1874.

The polished ashlar Italianate front was added in 1883 by
*James Boucher*. Broad aediculed centrepiece with Ionic pilasters
supporting the pediment. Within this frame, the huge round-

headed entrance, its arch springing from leafily capitalled pilasters, the keystone carved as a crowned and bearded human head. A rosetted guilloche band marks off the gallery level. Here, a window of three roundheaded lights with pilaster-mullions and projecting keystones. At each of the narrow end bays, a pedimented ground-floor window, its base lugged. The upper level of each end is framed by pilasters, their capitals again with leafy carving; between them, a round-arched pilastered and keystoned window.

Inside, a panel-fronted gallery carried on cast iron columns. This must date from the reconstruction of 1874.

Small GRAVEYARD on the w side of the church. The headstones were removed in the 1960s but mural monuments survive. On the w wall, a MONUMENT to the Rev. George Wade †1892, its alabaster plaque carved with a high-relief portrait by *Dow*.

## PUBLIC BUILDINGS

BURGH BUILDINGS, corner of Newmarket Street and Glebe Street. By *A. & W. Black*, 1876–9. Baronial, with crowstepped gables and gablets, and mullioned and transomed windows, all built of bullnosed masonry. In the three gablets of the s front, quatrefoil attic windows. Entrance with a depressed arch springing from columns with polished granite shafts and foliaged capitals; above the door, a pierced stone balcony. The SE corner of the building projects as a 'tower' under a Frenchy truncated spire with iron cresting. At the corners of the 'tower', Gothic turrets; at the front, a large canted oriel window, the base of its continuous corbelling supported on the outsize foliaged capital of an attached column. Spiked ball finials on the 'tower's' gables. High up in the E gable, a panel bearing the coat of arms of the burgh of Falkirk.

CHRISTIAN INSTITUTE, corner of Newmarket Street and Glebe Street. Italianate, by *G. Deas Page*, 1879–80. s gable front of polished ashlar, channelled at the ground floor, of three bays, the slightly advanced and pedimented very broad centre with channelled pilaster strips at the corners; frieze under the pediment carved with three human heads in high relief. At the centrepiece's ground floor, a shop. First-floor window of three lights, their stilted roundheaded arches springing from column-mullions, the heads of the windows decorated with bands carved with circles. Similar decoration at the heads of the first-floor windows of the outer bays. In these bays, segmental-arched openings. Long w elevation down Glebe Street, with segmental-arched windows at the ground floor and round-headed windows above.

FALKIRK COUNCIL MUNICIPAL BUILDINGS AND FALKIRK TOWN HALL, West Bridge Street. By *Baron Bercott & Associates*, 1962. Four-storey Municipal Buildings clad in alternating bands of glass and ribbed metal; penthouse on top. Projecting at the w end is the Town Hall, its frontage of mirrored glass.

FALKIRK GRAMMAR SCHOOL, corner of Park Street and Princes Street. Now the Park Street Office of the Falkirk Council Education Department. By *John Tait*, 1845–6. T-plan, mostly of a tall single storey but in places containing two floors in the same height. The long N jamb rubble-built and piend-roofed. At the piend-roofed main (S) block, an ashlar-faced corniced front of seven bays. Panelled parapet over the three-bay centrepiece whose architraved and corniced windows are linked by a consoled sill course. At the S end of the long jamb's E side, a pair of round-headed doors. The jamb was thickened to the W by *Alexander Black*, 1868.

89 FALKIRK LIBRARY, Hope Street. Urbane Gothic, by *McArthy & Watson*, 1900–2. Tall two storeys, faced with polished red sandstone ashlar. At the main block's four-bay E front, twin gablets; at their top, roundels containing cusped loop tracery. Basket-arched ground-floor windows, each of two mullioned and transomed lights and containing small leaded panes. The first-floor windows, their hoodmoulds linked by a stringcourse, also have leaded panes and are two-light with stone mullions and transoms but the lights have cusped heads and the windows are set in pointed overarches with blind Gothic tracery in their heads. At the S bay, the entrance, the head of its pointed arch filled by a wooden panel carved with the coat of arms of the burgh of Falkirk; above the door, a foliage-finialled ogee hoodmould, the label stops carved with figures holding books. At the ends of the hoodmould, diagonally set attached piers with crocketed pinnacles. Recessed at the S end, a one-bay section. Basket-arched lights in the windows, the upper rising into a gablet. N addition by *Falkirk District Council*, 1991–2. Glazed entrance and stair serving as a link from the original Library to the new rooms housed in a block which is again of two tall storeys and faced with red sandstone; tall windows and a gablet.

OLD SHERIFF COURT, corner of West Bridge Street and Hope Street. Now Falkirk Voluntary Centre. By *Brown & Wardrop*, 1865–8. Asymmetrical Scottish manorial, built of buff-coloured rubble. Relaxed display of crowstepped gables, semicircular pedimented dormerheads, strapwork and bits of carved heraldry. Over the ground floor, a stringcourse which forms hoodmoulds above the openings. Corbelled out in an inner angle of the stepped side to Hope Street is a fat round candlesnuffer-roofed turret displaying a quatrefoil dummy gunloop. At the West Bridge Street front, a round tower, again with a candlesnuffer roof. Corbelled out above the entrance, a square turret with another quatrefoil dummy gunloop and a Frenchy spired roof. At the W end of the elevation to West Bridge Street, the studded door and high-set small horizontal barred windows of the ground-floor cells.

POLICE STATION, West Bridge Street. Originally Stirling County Council District Offices. By *A. & W. Black*, 1904–5. Italianate, built of very badly weathered polished ashlar, channelled at the ground floor. Disconcertingly asymmetrical two-storey façade, of eight bays, the W three advanced with Corinthian pilastered corners supporting a pediment, its tympanum pierced by a foliage-framed round window in a Gibbsian surround. In the inner angle of the front, a Corinthian columned and balustraded portico. Rectangular ground-floor windows, their projecting keystones repeated at the baluster-aproned roundheaded first-floor windows set between attached Corinthian columns (pilasters at the window over the portico). Mutuled wallhead cornice and balustrade, topped by urns at the ends of the advanced section. Addition at the back by the Stirling County Architect, *A. J. Smith*, 1963.

Former POST OFFICE, corner of Vicar Street and Weir Street. By *J. Rutherford* of *H.M. Office of Works*, *c.* 1893. Small-scale but very smart collegiate Tudor Gothic, the two-storey façades faced with grey sandstone. At the main (W) front, a slightly advanced off-centre gable; a lion and unicorn holding shields at its ends, a crocketed finial at the apex. At the first floor of this gable, a shallow rectangular oriel, its parapet's blind arcading inter-rupted at the centre by the royal coat of arms surmounted by a crown set in a fleur-de-lis finialled pediment. The oriel's three-light window is flanked by diagonally set attached piers which rise through the oriel's parapet to foliaged finials. Below the oriel, mullioned and transomed ground-floor windows, each of two cusped ogee-arched lights; Tudor hoodmoulds above. In the outer bays, transomed windows, the N one at the ground floor of two ogee-arched lights; the window above has foliaged finials squashed under the wallhead cornice. In the S outer bays, a ground-floor window whose deep transom is carved with rosettes, and a Tudor-arched door with foliage decoration in the spandrels and a squat window serving as a fanlight above. At the building's NW corner, an octagonal turret is carried on continuous corbelling, the top course decorated with thistles. In the faces of the turret, cusped and transomed slit windows, their hoodmoulds linked by a stringcourse. On top of the turret, a crown spire formed by flying buttresses which join the foliage-finialled piers at the corners of the parapet to a central ogee-roofed octagonal cupola surmounted by a foliaged fat finial. Two-bay gable front to Weir Street, its windows with cusped ogee-arched lights.

SALVATION ARMY HALL, Bank Street. By *Oswald Archer*, 1909–10. Front of bullnosed red sandstone in a sort of free Jacobean manner with a battlement and crowstepped gablet.

SCIENCE AND ART SCHOOL, Park Street. Now in other use. Plain Renaissance, by *James Boucher*, 1878.

TELEPHONE EXCHANGE, Kerse Lane. Bland ashlar-fronted authoritarian modern-traditional building, by *H.M. Office of Works*, 1961.

TOWN STEEPLE, High Street. Falkirk's Neo-Classical assertion of civic status, erected in 1812–14* to house the Council chamber and municipal prison. The architect was *David Hamilton*.

Six-stage square tower built of polished Brightons ashlar, 82 channelled at the two bottom stages which are marked off from

---

* The top part rebuilt after being damaged by lightning in 1927.

each other by a cornice-like stringcourse. In each of the ground floor's w and s faces, a large opening, the w a window (originally of three lights), the s a door under a semicircular fanlight which rises into the stage above. At these openings the stringcourse is recessed as a transom, giving the masonry either side the appearance of broad pilasters. In the N face, a pair of small round-headed doors, one a dummy. Corniced second stage. At each of the w and s faces, a large window with a moulded architrave. The N face is pierced by a tier of three relatively small stair windows. The tall third stage is intaken, its cut-out corners occupied by fluted Greek Doric columns supporting a pediment at each face. Within these aedicules, round-arched windows with cavetto surrounds and balustered aprons. Much lower fourth stage, again intaken and with canted corners. At each elevation a round clockface framed by panelled pilasters. Above this stage's cornice, a stepped base to the tall belfry. This is an octagon with Ionic columns at the corners and a rectangular louvred opening in each side. Above, a very squat octagon, a segmental opening in each face, surmounted by the octagonal stone spire finished with a weathercock.

WESTBANK HOSPITAL AND CLINIC, West Bridge Street. By the Falkirk Burgh Architect, *A. J. M. Currell*, 1959. Three storeys of curtain walling under a shallow-pitched roof.

### STREETS

#### BANK STREET

For the corner building at the w end, *see* Kirk Wynd. Then, on the s, Nos. 3–7, plain mid-C19 Georgian survival with a bowed quadrant corner. It is followed by a development of flats and shops of the later C20. On the N, the red sandstone front of the Salvation Army Hall (*see* Public Buildings, above). Immediately to its E and set back from and below the street, VIOLET BANK of *c.* 1845. Single-storey L-plan; plain Tudor with a consoled block pediment over the main entrance. Further E, the former BANK STREET PICTURE HOUSE, a plain harl-fronted shed by *Neil C. Duff & Percival Cairns*, 1920. It incorporates the stone side walls and N gable of the former Bank Street Evangelical Union Church of 1844, its rectangular windows (now built up) still visible.

#### BAXTER'S WYND

On the w side, a car park. On the E, a couple of cottages (WHEATSHEAF INN and No. 23), probably of the early C19, both rubble-walled and with slated roofs. They are linked by a short two-bay pantile-roofed building of about the same date. s of these, on the corner of Bean Row, a two-storey harled building of *c.* 1840 with tall windows in its gable and s front.

## CALLENDAR RIGGS

Pedestrianization in the 1990s has provided the standard brick and concrete block paving and a row of trees in tubs down the middle. The two sides of the street display contrasting C20 architectural fashions. The E side is of the 1930s beginning with the Art Deco Nos. 1–9 by *J. G. Callander*, 1933, faced with pale cream-coloured sandstone. Plain red sandstone frontages at Nos. 11–13 of 1930 and Nos. 15–17. At Nos. 19–21, shopfronts in a busy Art Deco frame, again of cream-coloured stone. More Art Deco but unfussy at No. 25, by *Wilson & Tait*, 1935. Its corner to Meadow Street is bowed at the ground floor and concave above. N of Meadow Street, the multi-storey car park of the Callendar Square Shopping Centre. Concrete frame partly infilled with blockwork; piend-roofed towers at the corner of Kerse Lane.

On the W side, the CALLENDAR SQUARE SHOPPING CENTRE by *Clark, Tribble, Harris & Li* of New York, in association with *Hasler, Burke & Farthing* of Newcastle upon Tyne, 1992, occupies the triangle formed by Callendar Riggs, High Street and Manor Street. Tall three storeys, the fronts rendered and with stone trimmings. Shopfronts and windows of fairly traditional design. At the S corner, an ogee domed octagonal tower. On each of the elevations to High Street and Callendar Riggs, a pediment. At the N end of the Callendar Riggs front, ball-finialled pediments and a two-storey glass-sided bridge to the car park on the E side of the street.

## CHAPEL LANE

No. 3 is a two-storey early C19 house. Three-bay front of polished ashlar (eroded by stone cleaning), with panelled pilaster strips at the corners. Moulded architraves to the windows which are corniced at the ground floor; doorpiece with fluted Doric columns and a block pediment.

## COCKBURN STREET

Opened 1927. On the W side, a two-storey reinforced concrete block (Nos. 2–20) of *c.* 1930, with a bowed corner to West Bridge Street.

## COW WYND

At the N end, corner buildings with High Street (q.v.). Otherwise, mostly small-scale and rather altered C19 vernacular buildings, a few pantiled, and some C20 commercial blocks. At the S corner of Bean Row, the mid-C19 Nos. 19–21, with a block-consoled cornice over the door and a small battlemented tower. Set back on the E side, the Antiburgher Church ('Tattie Kirk'), for which *see* Churches, above.

## HIGH STREET

The main street of the burgh, winding along the ridge of a low hill. Pedestrianization, accompanied by its usual concomitants of new paving, benches, litter bins and tree-planting, took place in 1990.

At the w end, the s side begins with commercial blocks of the later C20. Nos. 1–33 by *Baron Bercott & Associates*, 1962, in brown brick and curtain walling. Glazed curtain wall at Nos. 35–37 by *Baron Bercott*, 1959. Vertical strips of aggregate cladding on Nos. 39–41, another glass curtain wall at No. 43 and aggregate cladding again at Nos. 45–51, all these part of the same development by *Ian Burke, Martin & Partners*, 1963.

The start of the N side is more rewarding. No. 2 on the corner with Upper Newmarket Street is by *Peddie & Kinnear*, 1879. Asymmetrical but austere Scots manorial, built of stugged buff-coloured stone. Jettied upper floors and crowstepped gables, one halted against a chimneystack. On the w elevation, a two-storey oriel window looking down West Bridge Street. The scale drops at Nos. 6–10, the former ROYAL HOTEL of *c.* 1760. Two storeys, now with a C20 mansard roof. Channelled masonry at the ground floor which has been rather altered but its Corinthian columned doorpiece survives. At the corners of the upper floor, rusticated pilaster strips; moulded architraves to the windows, which are joined by a sill course. Moulded wallhead cornice. The adjacent Nos. 12–16, by *Thomas Smith, Gibb & Pate*, 1978, attempts to be modern whilst evoking the traditional. Much taller and narrower mid-C19 three-storey building at No. 18. Polished ashlar three-bay front, the ground floor altered. At the upper floors, all the windows (the centre ones two-light) have moulded architraves and are joined by sill courses. Exceptionally tall first-floor windows. At the second floor the sill course is projected on squat consoles under the openings. Eaves course, again projected on consoles, the end ones large and elaborate. On the w corner of Lint Riggs, Nos. 20–24 High Street, perhaps late Georgian in origin but remodelled *c.* 1905 when it was given a domed octagonal turret corbelled out from the canted corner. After the Edwardian block on the opposite corner (*see* Lint Riggs) No. 32 High Street is a humble two-storey building, its rendered front late C19 in appearance, but set into the irregular E gable is a short row of corbels, perhaps to carry the ridge beam for a lean-to shelter at the entrance to Falkirk Old and St Modan's Parish Churchyard, for whose gateway *see* Churches, above. E of the grass bank on the s side of the churchyard, a narrow three-storey building of 1900 (Nos. 52–54) with two-light windows, corniced at the first floor. Then the early C19 Nos. 60–66, also of three storeys, followed by No. 68 of the later C19, which is of the same height as Nos. 60–66 but its ground-floor shop allowed room for only one floor above. This stugged ashlar upper floor is of three bays, the outer windows two-light. Weird detailing, the jambs and mullions of the first-floor windows all having consoles but they do not support the rather mean cornices which are skied above aprons. Much lower two-storey building (No. 70) next door. It is probably early C19 but much altered and the droved ashlar stonework now painted. Sticking out from the building line is the mid-C19 No. 72. C20 shopfront. At the upper floor, rusticated quoins and a three-light window. On the wall-head an open pediment which was given a Jacobean segmental-pedimented and scroll-sided topknot by *John P. Goodsir*, 1903; he added the balustrade at the same time. Then Nos. 74–78 by *Thomas M. Copland*, 1901. Squared-up Jacobean front of red sandstone ashlar. The following two buildings (No. 80 and Nos. 84–88) are much humbler, probably C18 in origin but badly altered. Then the block on the corner of Kirk Wynd (q.v.).

On the s side of High Street, just E of the churchyard, Nos. 59–63 by *James Monro & Son*, 1936, the full width of the front not completed until 1954, a bland ashlar façade above the long horizontal of the projecting shopfront. The two-storey and attic No. 65 is dated 1886. Enjoyable free Flemish. Segmental-arched first-floor windows. Slightly advanced centrepiece under a shell-topped gable surmounted by the statue of a unicorn holding a shield. No. 71 of 1908 is free Jacobean by *Thomas M. Copland*. At the first floor, recessed canted bay windows, their shaped gablets breaking the wallhead's balustrade whose uprights are supplied by balls. The twin-gabled No. 75 is by *A. & W. Black*, 1907, again with recessed first-floor bay windows but they project further and are mullioned and transomed; cornited windows at the second floor. Then No. 79, a large late C20 ashlar-fronted block, its perfunctory gablets a gesture to traditionalism. Also late C20 is the adjoining red sandstone gable containing an entrance to the Howgate Shopping Centre (*see* Howgate), followed by a pair of three-storey replica late Georgian rendered façades (Nos. 99–101). Both scale and quality rise at the four-storey polished ashlar front of WILSON'S BUILDINGS (Nos. 105–111) of 1848. At the first floor, blockily consoled cornices over the two huge tripartite windows; unusually, their outer lights are broad and the centre light narrow. The floors above are each of four bays. Over the second-floor windows, rosetted friezes and starkly simplified consoles under the cornices whose ends break forward. The overall parapet rises at the centre to form a panel carved with the building's name and date. Painted ashlar early C19 front at Nos. 113–117. Moulded architraves to the upper storeys' windows, those of the first floor cornited. Stugged red sandstone appears at Nos. 119–121 by *John P. Goodsir*, 1899–1900. Over the front's first-floor windows, steep triangular pediments; segmental pediment over the window at the E corner which is bowed back to the recessed building line beyond.

The N side, after the building on the E corner of Kirk Wynd (q.v.), resumes with a pair of three-storey buildings (Nos. 100–104) of *c.* 1800. Both are ashlar-fronted (the W now rendered, the E painted) with rusticated quoins and moulded window archi-traves. The following early C19 block (Nos. 106–112) is angled to allow space N of the Town Steeple (*see* Public Buildings, above). Tall three-storey and attic rendered façade crossed by sill

courses at the upper floors. Five bays, the first-floor windows
surmounted alternately by cornices and consoled pediments.
At the ground floor, an off-centre door set in an Ionic columned
and pedimented aedicule. The building line of this block is
continued E by Tolbooth Street (q.v.). High Street's main building line is resumed as a continuation of the S front of the Town
Steeple. Attached to its E side, a two-storey box (Nos. 118–120)
by *Saxone, Lilley & Skinner's Architects Department* (chief architect: *Ellis E. Somake*), 1964, the oversailing upper floor clad in
horizontal metal strips. The three-storey No. 122 of *c.* 1800 restores
urbanity. Rusticated quoins and moulded window architraves.

On High Street's S side, opposite Nos. 118–122, a three-
storey block (Nos. 123–127) of 1909. Squared-up free Jacobean
Renaissance, canted bay windows projecting from recesses at
the outer bays of the upper floors. Small pediment at the centre
of the wallhead. Over the entrance, a swan-neck pediment,
its tympanum carved with thistles and a cartouche. Then Nos.
129–131, mid-C19 Georgian survival, perhaps the remodelling of
an earlier building. Three-storey five-bay rendered front, with
rusticated quoins and sill courses. Consoled pediments over the
first-floor windows. At the second floor the window architraves
have square panelled blocks in the upper corners and moulded
brackets at the bottom. Moulded corbels under the wallhead
cornice which is topped by a low parapet. At the centre, a
depressed arch to the pend which gives access to King's Court
(q.v.). On the W corner of Cow Wynd, the LLOYDS TSB
SCOTLAND BANK (originally the Falkirk & Counties Savings
Bank), a pompous palazzo by *A. & W. Black*, 1895–6. Crowded
Renaissance detail; canted E corner.

On the N side of High Street, Nos. 128–130, a three-storey
building of *c.* 1840, with rusticated quoins at the W corner of the
seven-bay front. Architraves to the windows (some at the first
floor now enlarged to two lights) and a second-floor sill course.
Then an ashlar-fronted block (Nos. 132–136) of 1914. Broad two-
storey bay windows project from recesses at the upper floors
whose window architraves are all decorated with bead and reel
moulding. Central chimney on the wallhead. The adjoining former
95    COMMERCIAL BANK OF SCOTLAND (Nos. 138–140) is a
quietly powerful Classical block of 1829–31, probably by *James
Gillespie Graham*. It was set slightly back from the street line but
the space has been filled by a fussily detailed ground-floor addition
of *c.* 1930. The original design survives at the two upper floors.
These are of three bays, the recessed centre set between giant
Ionic columns *in antis*; pediment over the first-floor window.
Giant anta pilasters frame the end bays. Balustrades over the ends,
a parapet at the centre. The bank's restrained display of wealth
outclasses the ensuing pair of early C19 three-storey blocks. Both
are decently dressed, the first (Nos. 142–148) with cornices over
the first-floor windows, the centre window's consoled. At the
second (No. 150, the former RED LION INN), by *William
Stirling I*, 1828, a front of six bays, the first and fifth slightly
advanced, their first-floor windows with lugged architraves,

aprons and pediments. Cornices and aprons at the other first-floor windows. Then the Callendar Square Shopping Centre (*see* Callendar Riggs).

The final stretch of High Street's s side, E of Cow Wynd, starts with a three-storey Georgian survival building (Nos. 147–149) by *William Stirling III*, 1862. Cornices or pediments over the first-floor windows; canted corner to Cow Wynd. Then a pair of dead plain late Georgian buildings (Nos. 151–159) followed by a much lower three-storey piend-roofed building (No. 161) of the C18, rusticated quoins at its E corner. On the E side of Dundee Court, Nos. 165–169 by *William Graham & Co.*, 1960, a four-storey slab, its marble terrazzo panels looking more shoddy than cheerful. Then the 1930s No. 171 with Art Deco detail at the upper window. No. 179, probably of the 1920s, has a brick front dressed up with half-timbering and tile-hanging in an unconvincing evocation of southern England. At the mid-C19 No. 181, a pair of crowstepped gables. The adjoining No. 183 may be C18 but the surrounds to its first-floor windows are of the mid or later C19. Then unpretentious C18 or early C19 two-storey vernacular to the end of the street.

## HOPE STREET

The E side provides parking for the development at the W end of Newmarket Street.

On the W, at the corner of West Bridge Street, the Old Sheriff Court (*see* Public Buildings, above). To its N, a Jacobean double house of the later C19. Also Jacobean, but with an ecclesiastical flavour, is the adjoining clergy house by *James Strang*, 1901. This belongs to St Francis Xavier (R.C.) Church (*see* Churches, above). Then Falkirk Library (*see* Public Buildings, above). A little further N, BROCKVILLE HOUSE, a piend-roofed villa of *c.* 1840. Pilaster strips at the corners of the stugged ashlar front. Roman Doric columned and corniced doorpiece. At each end, a single-storey wing, its front containing an overarched window, the longer E wing with a door as well.

## HOWGATE CENTRE

Shopping centre and multi-storey car park by *Cockburn Associates*, 1986–90. Architecturally without distinction and, mercifully, mostly hidden behind High Street to whose shops it gives rear access.

## KERSE LANE

Unprepossessing street, now part of the main traffic route round the town centre. On the s, at the w end, the massive backside of the Callendar Square Shopping Centre's car park (*see* Callendar Riggs). On the N, at the corner of Princes Street, the ORCHARD HOTEL, an early C19 house with fluted pilaster strips at the corners and a fluted frieze under the wallhead's mutuled cornice.

Corniced doorpiece with fluted Roman Doric columns. Rosettes at the corners of the window architraves. Further E, the Telephone Exchange (*see* Public Buildings, above). On the S, at the corner of Bellevue Street, Christ Church (*see* Churches, above) and its RECTORY of *c*. 1870, also by *R. Rowand Anderson*, with a prominent display of bargeboarded gables.

### KINGS COURT

Well preserved but unexciting close bounded by low early C19 buildings.

### KIRK WYND

At the top, on the E side, the former COMMERCIAL BANK OF SCOTLAND (Nos. 1–9) between High Street and Manor Street, by *John Nisbet* of Glasgow in association with *Alexander Gauld* of Falkirk, 1904–6. Large four-storey and attic block faced with red sandstone ashlar. Squared-up free Jacobean; three-storey ogee-roofed turrets corbelled out from the canted corners. On the W side, at the corner of High Street, the former Railway Hotel (Nos. 2 Kirk Wynd and Nos. 96–98 High Street) of *c*. 1900. Scottish Baronial, again of red sandstone but hammer-dressed. Crowstepped gablets. Bowed corner under a witch's hat spire; corbelled out below the corner's second-floor window, a stone balcony, its front pierced by roundheaded arcading. Then No. 6 Kirk Wynd, a three-storey block of the earlier C19. Architraves at the upper floors' windows, those of the first floor corniced. On the corner of Manse Place another late Georgian building (Nos. 20–24) but covered in render.

On the E side at the N corner of Manor Street, a building (Nos. 11–17) dated 1913. Blocky Queen Anne, with a tall but thin octagonal turret topped by a cupola. Beyond, the large Art Deco No. 19 Kirk Wynd and No. 1 Bank Street, built as the Falkirk and District United Co-operative Society premises, by *J. G. Callander*, 1934–5.

### LINT RIGGS

Street effectively formed in 1903 when it was widened from *c*. 2.4m. to *c*. 12.2m., the layout and elevations for the buildings prepared under the direction of the Burgh Surveyor, *David Ronald*. The E side, built in 1903–6, is of polished yellow ashlar, the balustraded façade's detail eroded by stone cleaning. It is of three storeys. End sections, executed by *A. & W. Black*, treated in a free Jacobean manner with two-storey canted oriel windows rising from the shopfronts' cornice. Corbelled out from the splayed corners to High Street and Upper Newmarket Street are octagonal turrets, the N with a rounded dome surmounted by a cupola. The N turret's top stage bears panels carved with a shamrock, thistle and rose; above, an ogee-profiled dome. This side's Baroque main section is occupied by a Masonic Temple, designed by *Thomas*

*M. Copland* who departed from Ronald's elevation, the hall rising through the height of the two upper floors. End bays framed by Ionic pilasters, the three-bay centrepiece by Corinthian columns which carry an urn-finialled open segmental pediment, its tympanum carved with masonic symbols. Gibbsian surrounds to the windows, those of the ends and centre topped by pediments, the others by wavy cornices surmounted by cartouches bearing the dates 1876 and 1906 (for the foundation of the Lodge and the completion of the building).

The w side is also Edwardian and generally follows Ronald's elevations. s of the corner building with High Street (q.v.), the balustraded Nos. 2–6 by *James Strang*, 1903, with two-storey oriel windows sitting on the shopfronts' cornice. The next block (Nos. 8–16), by *Alexander Gauld*, 1904–6, originally an hotel, continues in the same manner but its walls are decorated with Baroque cartouches. Ogee-domed turret over the bowed corner to Upper Newmarket Street. Fluted chimneystacks (still intact on the N elevation) project slightly from the wall.

## MANOR STREET

For the w corner blocks, *see* Kirk Wynd. The rest is mainly small-scale and undistinguished C19 and C20. On the N, Nos. 8–34, a large late C19 block, plain except for the crowstepped central gablet and heraldic panels.

## NEWMARKET STREET

Buildings on the N side only. On the S, a garden in front of the retaining wall which divides Newmarket Street from Upper Newmarket Street. In this garden, two groups of statuary. The w is the SOUTH AFRICAN WAR MEMORIAL designed by *John A. Campbell* and executed by *W. Grant Stevenson*, 1905–6. Corniced pedestal of rock-faced granite, surmounted by a bronze group of a soldier of the Argyll and Sutherland Highlanders standing guard over the body of a wounded comrade. – To the E, the DUKE OF WELLINGTON STATUE by *Robert Forrest*, c. 1830. Weathered stone statue of the Duke standing beside his horse, erected in High Street in 1854, the pedestal executed by *James Gowans*, and moved to the present site in 1905.

The buildings begin at the w with a development by *Cockburn Associates*, 1976–7. Blocky architecture, faced with a mixture of polished ashlar and hammer-dressed masonry. On the corners of Glebe Street, the Burgh Buildings and the Christian Institute (*see* Public Buildings, above). E of the Christian Institute, Nos. 20–24 Newmarket Street, an idiosyncratic Italianate late C19 block. Polished ashlar façade. Late C20 shopfronts but the original entrance to the upper floors survives, with very heavy consoles supporting an anthemion-finialled segmental pediment carved with a rosette and rinceau decoration. The first floor's corniced outer windows are three-light with column-mullions and unorthodox Ionic pilasters at the jambs; guilloche carving on the friezes. Similar treatment at the two original central windows (the third is an insertion by *T. M. Copland & Blakey*, 1948) but they are single-light. Second-floor windows with heavy consoles under the cornices. More consoles under the eaves cornice. Much plainer three-storey block of *c.* 1900 at Nos. 26–30. The polished ashlar front is almost Georgian survival despite its asymmetry. Heavy consoles under the door's cornice. Two-light windows at the first floor, the r. corniced. The l. window is flanked by corbels which support an oriel window above. Another three-storey polished ashlar façade at Nos. 32–36. This is mid-C19 Georgian survival. Delicately consoled cornices over the outer first-floor windows but they and those above are two-light. At the centre bay of each of the upper floors, a window of three very widely spaced lights. Glass-fronted infill by *Millar, Crawford & Partners*, 1963, at Nos. 38–40. Another three-storey polished ashlar front at Nos. 42–46. It is Georgian survival of the later C19, the upper floors' windows with lugged architraves, but the outer windows are or were two-light (the mullions now missing from those of the second floor). Then the corner block (No. 48) with Vicar Street (q.v.).

### PLEASANCE GARDENS

On the N, a windowless wall of the Howgate Centre (q.v.). On the S is the early C19 two-storey piend-roofed MOUNT HOUSE. Three-bay ashlar front with rusticated quoins; corniced ground-floor windows and a Roman Doric columned portico.

### PRINCES STREET

Opened in 1933. For the W corner blocks, *see* Vicar Street. Then, on the S, Nos. 1–3, a 1930s two-storey stone frame containing shopfronts. At Nos. 5–13, by *T. M. Copland & Blakey*, 1935, a hint of Art Deco but there are oriel windows at the upper floor. On the N, the large ABC CINEMA by *C. J. McNair*, 1935. Plain except for the jazz-modern foyer at the W end. To its E, the former Falkirk Grammar School (*see* Public Buildings, above).

### TOLBOOTH STREET

Very short street, its S side occupied by the back of the Town Steeple (*see* Public Buildings, above). On the N, THE TOLBOOTH TAVERN, a two-storey building of *c.* 1800, with rusticated quoins. Moulded architraves to those first-floor windows which have not been altered. To its E, the gable of Nos. 2–4 Wooer Street (q.v.).

### UPPER NEWMARKET STREET

One-sided street looking down over a split-level double roadway to Newmarket Street. For the building on the W corner, *see* High Street. Then, two late C20 blocks. The red blockwork façade of the W, by *Willliam Hale*, 1990, is a not very happy pastiche of early C18 architecture. Concrete blockwork again at the second but Edwardian free style in inspiration. Simplified oriel windows at the upper floor, presumably attempting to relate to the block on the corner of Lint Riggs (q.v.), and an unnecessarily assertive w turret. E of Lint Riggs, the churchyard of Falkirk Old and St Modan's Church (*see* Churches, above). At the w end, one jamb of a round-arched window, the surviving fragment of the TOWN HALL (by *A. & W. Black*, 1879) demolished in 1968. At the E end, a pair of mid-C19 cast iron GATEPIERS with fluted Doric quarter-columns at the corners and acanthus leaf capitals. Then St Andrew's West Church (*see* Churches, above). At the E end of the street, Nos. 25–29, the former NATIONAL BANK OF SCOTLAND, by *David MacGibbon*, 1862–3. Determinedly Scottish with crowstepped gables, bartizans, corbelling and a jettied top floor, built of bullnosed rubble. On the N front, two large gablets, one with a thistle, the other a fleur-de-lis finial. The windows of the top floor break up through the eaves into steep pedimented dormerheads, one on the N front bearing a saltire, two on the E carved with floral designs. The elliptically arched dummy fan-lights over the two principal ground-floor windows display rose and thistle designs. On the battlemented porch, a statue of St Andrew (emblem of the National Bank).

VICAR STREET

The E side begins with a block (Nos. 1–3) by *Alan Jollie Associates*, 1985; canted corner to Bank Street. Then, the former PAROCHIAL BOARD OFFICES, a two-storey palazzo of *c.* 1870. Channelled masonry at the ground floor, its openings pilastered, a pediment over the principal entrance. This door is just off-centre to allow a secondary door to be squeezed between it and the window to the l. At the first floor, Corinthian pilasters at the corners and consoled cornices over the windows which are grouped 2/1/2 but with the middle window just r. of centre. On the s corner of Princes Street, a jazzy Art Deco bar (FINN MACCOOL'S) of the 1930s.

On the w side's corner with Manse Place, Nos. 2–18 Vicar Street of 1895. Free Jacobean Renaissance, an ogee-roofed dome over the canted SE corner. Shallowly projecting two-storey oriels. Over the first-floor windows, pediments (alternately broken) with rather mean carved decoration in their tympana. Much more lavishly carved heraldic panel at the s end of the E front. Then the former National Bank of Scotland on the corner of Upper Newmarket Street (q.v.).

On the s corner of Princes Street, Vicar Street's E side resumes with TUDOR HOUSE (Nos. 25–27) by *T. M. Copland & Blakey*, 1934. English Elizabethan with plenty of black-painted half-timbering decorating the white walls. It is followed by Nos. 29–31 (VICAR CHAMBERS) of *c.* 1900. Squared-up Jacobean with scroll-topped gablets; small cupola at the s end. More accom-plished is the red sandstone ashlar frontage of Nos. 39–43 designed by *George Washington Browne*, 1899, for the British Linen Bank. Characteristic Jacobean, with a steep pediment over the section containing the banking hall. This part is marked off

from the plain s wing by Roman Doric columns at the ground
floor and superimposed Ionic columns at the two upper floors.
Lozenge decoration on the banking-hall windows. At each of
the upper floors a six-light window with one light a dummy,
that at the first floor carved with the coat of arms of the bank,
that of the second floor with birds. For the former Post Office
on the corner of Weir Street, *see* Public Buildings, above.

The w side of Vicar Street between Newmarket Street and
Melville Street is filled by Nos. 24–38, a twelve-bay palazzo of
*c.* 1880. Ground-floor shops. The windows of the upper floors
are basket-arched, those of the first floor with consoled cornices,
the second-floor windows with lugged architraves. At each end,
a slightly advanced pavilion with a canted outer corner and pedimented stone dormers. Between Melville Street and Garrison
Place, three blocks of the 1880s. The first (No. 42) has consoled
cornices over the first-floor windows. The second (Nos. 46–50)
of 1887 is of three bays with a central wallhead chimney. First-
floor windows in moulded architraves with lugs at the bottom
corners; under their cornices are panelled friezes, fluted at the
ends. The outer windows were converted to oriels by *James Strang*,
1910. The third block (Nos. 52–58) also has a central chimney
but the wallhead is balustraded. Consoled segmental pediments
over the first-floor windows.

### WEST BRIDGE STREET

At the w end, set well back on the N side, Falkirk Council Municipal
Buildings and Falkirk Town Hall followed by Westbank Hospital
(*see* Public Buildings, above). On the s side, dead plain housing
(Nos. 1–11) of 1906. Then a late C19 terrace (Nos. 13–19),
probably by *A. & W. Black*, 1898. Front of bullnosed masonry,
with a procession of crowstepped gablets and shouldered-arched
doors; stringcourse jumping up to form hoodmoulds over the
segmental panels above ground-floor openings. After another
plain late C19 terrace (Nos. 23–39), a simple two-storey building
(No. 41) of the earlier C19 and The People's Church (*see*
Churches, above). Opposite, on the N, a motor car showroom
(No. 10) by *J. G. Callander*, 1933–4, the two-storey shopfront
enclosed in an Art Deco frame. Then the Police Station and Old
Sheriff Court (*see* Public Buildings, above). E of The People's
Church, Nos. 43–45, a rendered block, probably C18 but with a
shopfront by *Alexander Gauld*, 1907; pend arch at the E end. The
next building (Nos. 47–51) may also be C18 but its second
floor, the windows topped by bargeboarded dormerheads, is an
addition of *c.* 1900. For the corner building, *see* Cockburn Street.

### WOOER STREET

At the s end, on the w, the TOLBOOTH TEASHOP (Nos. 2–4), a
two-storey mid-C19 block. Tall ground floor. Consoled blocks
under the ends of the first-floor windows which are linked by a
sill course.

# SUBURBS

## BAINSFORD

Originally a separate village which developed from the late C18 both as a small industrial centre beside the Forth & Clyde Canal and to house workers at the Carron Ironworks. Large areas to the E and W were covered with housing in the mid and late C20.

### CHURCH AND PUBLIC BUILDINGS

BAINSFORD PARISH CHURCH, Hendry Street. Originally Bainsford Free Church. By *A. & W. Black*, 1879–80. Economical Gothic, its unarchaeological character surprising for the date. At the ends of the gable front, angle buttresses topped by pinnacles of late Georgian character with pierced clover-leaf finials.

BAINSFORD PRIMARY SCHOOL, North Street. By *Central Regional Council*, 1978. Two storeys, the ground floor harled, the upper floor oversailing as a tall attic broken up into small sections with wilfully bitty effect.

DAWSON PARK SCHOOL, Haugh Street. By *A. N. Malcolm*, 1935. Neo-Georgian with hints of modernity.

LANGLEES PRIMARY SCHOOL, David's Loan. By the Stirling County Architect, *A. J. Smith*, 1958–9. Curtain-walled but pitch-roofed.

NORTH END HALL, Mungalhead Road. Built as a Free Church mission hall, 1871, in the manner of thirty years before. Single-storey Georgian survival with a corniced doorpiece and bracketed eaves.

ST FRANCIS' R.C. PRIMARY SCHOOL, Merchiston Avenue. By the Stirling County Architect, *A. J. Smith*, 1958–9. Another version of Langlees Primary School (q.v.).

ST MUNGO'S R.C. HIGH SCHOOL, Merchiston Avenue. The modern-traditional core is by the Stirling County Architect, *A. J. Smith*, in association with *The Scottish Orlit Co. Ltd.*, 1949, and extended in the same manner by *Smith*, in association with *The Scottish Construction Co. Ltd.*, 1958–9. Large and sensible but unexciting flat-roofed additions by *Stirling County Council*, 1972, brown brick the dominant material.

### DESCRIPTION

MAIN STREET begins at the crossing of the Forth & Clyde Canal, the bridge rebuilt and a new lock provided in 1999–2001. On the street's NE corner with Bankside, No. 1, a two-storey house of the earlier C19, its broached ashlar walling now painted. The ensuing late C19 and C20 architecture is generally unappealing. But on the S corner of Smith Street is CHEYNES BAR, by *Alexander Gauld*, 1907, Edwardian free Baroque, the cornice over the ground floor becoming a swan-neck pediment above the entrance. The view down Smith Street is closed by Bainsford

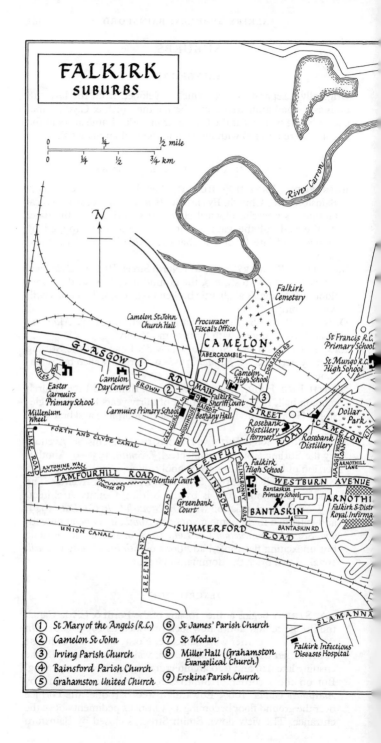

# FALKIRK
## SUBURBS

0    ¼    ½ mile
0    ¼    ½    ¾ km

N

*River Carron*

*Falkirk Cemetery*

*Camelon St John Church Hall*

*Procurator Fiscal's Office*

CAMELON

ABERCROMBIE ST

*St Francis R.C. Primary School*

*St Mungo R.C. High School*

GLASGOW RD

ST GILES

*Easter Carmuirs Primary School*

*Camelon Day Centre*

*Millenium Wheel*

BROWN

*Camelon High School*

DORRATOR RD

MAIN STREET

*Falkirk Sheriff Court*

*Bethany Hall*

CAMELON ROAD

*Dollar Park*

*Carmuirs Primary School*

BAIRD ST

CRAMBSTONE

MAISONHOUSE

*Rosebank Distillery (former)*

*Rosebank Distillery*

MAGGIE WOODS LOAN

ARNOTHILL LANE

FORTH AND CLYDE CANAL

LIME ROAD

ANTONINE WALL

TAMFOURHILL ROAD
*(course of)*

*Glenfuir Court*

GLENFUIR ROAD

WINDSOR ROAD

BLINKBONNY RD

*Falkirk High School*

*Bantaskin Primary School*

WESTBURN AVENUE

ARNOTHI

*Falkirk & Distr Royal Infirma*

*Greenbank Court*

BANTASKIN

SUMMERFORD

BANTASKIN RD

ROAD

UNION CANAL

GREENBANK

SLAMANNA

*Falkirk Infectious Diseases Hospital*

① St Mary of the Angels (R.C.)    ⑥ St James' Parish Church
② Camelon St John    ⑦ St Modan
③ Irving Parish Church    ⑧ Miller Hall (Grahamston Evangelical Church)
④ Bainsford Parish Church
⑤ Grahamston United Church    ⑨ Erskine Parish Church

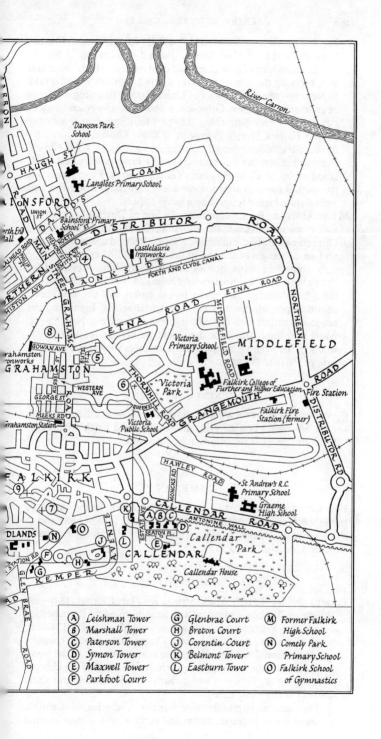

River Carron

Dawson Park School

HAUGH ST

LOAN

BAINSFORDS

Langlees Primary School

UNION ST

DAVIS

Bainsford Primary School

NORTH ST

SMITH ST

North End Hall

MAIN ROAD

CANALHEAD ROAD

PHILP ST

REDMILLS ST

GRAHAMS ROAD

NORTHERN AVE

WHISTON AVE

DISTRIBUTOR ROAD

BANKSIDE

Castlelaurie Ironworks

FORTH AND CLYDE CANAL

NORTHERN ROAD

ETNA ROAD

ETNA ROAD

MIDDLEFIELD ROAD

Victoria Primary School

MIDDLEFIELD

GOWAN AVE

Grahamston Ironworks

GRAHAMSTON

ETNA ROAD

THORNHILL ROAD

Victoria Park

Falkirk College of Further and Higher Education

DISTRIBUTOR ROAD

Fire Station

WESTERN AVE

CHESTER ST

GEORGE ST

MEEKS RD

Grahamston Station

QUEEN ST

Victoria Public School

GRANGEMOUTH

Falkirk Fire Station (former)

FALKIRK

HAWLEY ROAD

MONCKS ROAD

ST Andrew's R.C. Primary School

Graeme High School

ESTATE AVE

CALLENDAR ROAD

ANTONINE WALL

Callendar Park

SEATON PL.

GLEN BRAE ROAD

STATION RD

AVENUE

KEMPER

CALLENDAR

Callendar House

DLANDS

| | | | | |
|---|---|---|---|---|
| Ⓐ Leishman Tower | Ⓖ Glenbrae Court | Ⓜ Former Falkirk High School |
| Ⓑ Marshall Tower | Ⓗ Breton Court | |
| Ⓒ Paterson Tower | Ⓙ Corentin Court | Ⓝ Comely Park Primary School |
| Ⓓ Symon Tower | Ⓚ Belmont Tower | |
| Ⓔ Maxwell Tower | Ⓛ Eastburn Tower | Ⓞ Falkirk School of Gymnastics |
| Ⓕ Parkfoot Court | | |

Parish Church (*see* Church and Public Buildings, above). Further
N, on the E side of Main Street, the mid-C19 cottage at No. 61
is a rare reminder of how Bainsford used to look. Much larger and
of *c.* 1900 are the former CO-OPERATIVE SOCIETY PREMISES
at Nos. 75–79 on the corner of Union Street, flaunting a display
of crowstepped gables. Opposite, a dour Neo-Georgian block of
1930s two-storey flats (Nos. 42–72 Main Street), presumably
by the Falkirk Burgh Engineer, *William Gibson*, followed by
modern-traditional flatted housing of 1951 by *A. J. M. Currell*.
Further out, on the S corner of David's Loan, a large red sandstone ashlar block by *Alexander Gauld*, 1900–1. Plain Jacobean,
the canted corner carried up as a low octagonal tower finished
with a slated spire topped by a small cupola.

MUNGALHEAD ROAD continues the line of David's Loan to the
SW. Near its start, on the NW side, the North End Hall (*see*
Church and Public Buildings, above). Beyond are single-storey
and attic cottages of the end of the C19 and the beginning of the
C20, some (e.g. Nos. 40–86 Mungalhead Road) designed for
the Falkirk Building Society by *Thomas M. Copland*, 1899. Most
have been altered and given box-dormers but the mullioned
ground-floor windows of two segmental-arched lights and the
original dormers with carved bargeboards survive at Nos. 32–34.
More housing of the same date and type in the streets to the SE,
many of the original bargeboarded dormers surviving on the SW
side of PHILIP STREET.

### INDUSTRIAL BUILDING

CASTLELAURIE IRONWORKS, Bankside. Now in other use. Late
C19. M-roofed double pile, the walls of red brick with white
brick dressings. Tall round-arched windows.

## CAMELON

Former village, now part of the burgh of Falkirk. In the early C19
the inhabitants were employed in the manufacture of nails and at
the Rosebank Distillery. Redevelopment of the village began in
1866 and has continued since.

### CHURCHES

CAMELON ST JOHN, Main Street. By *David Rhind*, 1839–40.
Rubble-walled box dressed up with unarchaeological Romanesque
detail and a firescreen N front of roughly broached ashlar,
suggesting a nave and aisles behind. On top of the gable, a dumpily
spired octagonal bellcote. Projecting from the centre of the front,
a square two-storey parapeted porch. At the S end of the church,
outshots by *J. Jeffrey Waddell*, 1923–4, who added the short
chancel at the same time.

   The interior is mostly of the 1920s. Galleries with simple
panelled fronts in the transepts and at the N end. Kingpost truss

roof over the nave. Wagon roof at the chancel which is entered through a roundheaded arch. More roundheaded arches from the organ chamber into the chancel and E transept. – ORGAN of 1924, by *H. Hilsdon Ltd.* – PEWS of 1923. – In the chancel, a COMMUNION TABLE of 1923. – Simple wooden FONT, again of 1923, on the E of the chancel arch. – On the W of the arch, the 1920s PULPIT by *Helen Wilson*, the front carved with angels. – STAINED GLASS S window (Our Lord in Glory, flanked by the Virgin Mary and a Knight) by *Morris and Gertrude Alice Meredith Williams, c.* 1923. – On the W wall of the nave, a MONUMENT to the Rev. John Scott †1914, with a bronze portrait bust in relief.

IRVING PARISH CHURCH, Dorrator Road. Originally Camelon Free Church. By *G. Deas Page*, 1890. Plain Gothic, a bellcote on the gable front.

ST MARY OF THE ANGELS (R.C.), Glasgow Road. By *Gillespie, Kidd & Coia*, 1960. Flat-roofed L-plan grouping of church and clergy house, all faced with alternating bands of vertically and horizontally laid orange brickwork. Nave, with stepped buttresses along its E side, and a broad W aisle. The nave has a deep continuously glazed clearstorey on the W side; at its E side and the aisle narrower glazed bands under the wallheads. The two-storey clergy house projects W from the S end of the church.

Inside, the church's walls are again of exposed brickwork. Beamed wooden ceiling.

## CEMETERY AND CREMATORIUM
### Dorrator Road

The cemetery, well planted with trees and shrubbery, was laid out in the 1870s. By the entrance, a late C19 two-storey LODGE with bargeboarded gables and gablets. Large array of MONUMENTS and HEADSTONES. The earlier, at the S end, form a prosperous collection of Celtic crosses, obelisks, broken columns, and urns. A little W of the entrance, a large and elaborately carved Celtic cross to Jane Greig †1890, by *S. McGlashan & Son*. – A bit to its NE, the Celtic cross commemorating John Rennie †1904, signed by *W. Roberts & Son*. – Further N, a Celtic cross exceptional for its size and lavish decoration, including a coat of arms. It is a memorial of *c.* 1900 to the family of Hagart of Bantaskine executed by *S. McGlashan & Son*. – At the N end of the cemetery, CREMATORIUM by the Falkirk Burgh Architect, *A. J. M. Currell*, 1961.

## PUBLIC BUILDINGS

BETHANY HALL, Baird Street. Originally a United Free Church hall. By *James Strang*, 1903, a window of three lancet lights in the stepped front gable.

CAMELON DAY CENTRE, Glasgow Road. Originally an infectious diseases hospital. Main block by *A. & W. Black*, 1896. Large but plain villa, with a Tudorish door. The end bays were heightened with half-timbered gables by *A. & W. Black*, 1924. Single-storey wings were added by *David Ronald*, the Falkirk Burgh Surveyor, 1906–8. Also by Ronald, the contemporary lodge to the NW.

CAMELON HIGH SCHOOL, Abercrombie Street. The principal block, at the SW corner of the complex, is by *T. B. McFadzen*, 1874–6, but reconstructed and extended by *A. & W. Black*, 1906–7. It is a two-storey triple-pile, severely plain except for a Baroque bellcote over the centre of the S front of 1906–7. To the NE, a detached tall single-storey building, dated 1894. Simple cottage style, with mullioned windows and bracketed eaves. N and E of these earlier buildings are curtain-walled additions by *Alison & Hutchison & Partners*, 1959–60, and a further late C20 extension.

CAMELON ST JOHN'S CHURCH HALL, corner of Mansionhouse Road and Brown Street. Built in 1926–8. Straightforward dry-dashed rectangle with roundheaded windows and a gableted stone bellcote.

CARMUIRS PRIMARY SCHOOL, Carmuirs Street. By *James Strang*, 1900–2. Two-storey red sandstone block, the windows mullioned and transomed. Martial intimations are provided by small battlemented bartizans and gablets projected on 'machico-lation'.

EASTER CARMUIRS PRIMARY SCHOOL, St Giles Square. By the Stirling County Architect, *A. J. Smith*, 1959. Large assem-blage of flat-roofed dry-dashed boxes.

FALKIRK SHERIFF COURT, Main Street. By *Robert Matthew, Johnson-Marshall & Partners*, 1990. Hamfisted attempt to find a modern-traditional language for the late C20; the result is a mixture of Neo-Georgian, Art Deco and Postmodern. Two-storey red sandstone ashlar front, the oversailing upper floor supported on aggregate concrete columns. At the centre, a broad bow con-taining the entrance. Stringcourses, some serving as sill and lintel courses, are carried across the upper floor but abruptly interrupted by the window openings. These openings are too broad to look Georgian or Neo-Georgian but too vertical to suggest anything else.

PROCURATOR FISCAL'S OFFICE, Mansionhouse Road. By the *Property Services Agency*, 1992. Postmodern, with a heavy-handed open pedimented centrepiece.

## DESCRIPTION

MAIN STREET begins at the crossing of the FORTH & CLYDE CANAL (by *John Smeaton*, 1768–75). To the SW, canal locks with walls of stugged ashlar and brickwork (much refaced in 2000–1) and wooden lock gates. Beside these, on the S side of Main Street, the bonded stores of the former Rosebank Distillery (*see* Industrial Building, below) followed by a small public park. Set well back on the N, late C20 housing (DORRATOR COURT) by the Falkirk Burgh Architect, *I. A. Ferguson*, 1966. Near the S end of DORRATOR ROAD, Irving Parish Church (*see* Churches, above). At the N end, the Cemetery (*see* above). W of Dorrator Road Main Street acquires the character of the centre of a drab small town, with late C19 and early C20 shops under flats on its S side and late C20 housing on the N. To the N, in ABERCROMBIE STREET, the untidy complex of Camelon High School (*see* Public Buildings, above). Further W, on the S side of Main Street, Falkirk Sheriff Court (*see* Public Buildings, above) marks the end of the town centre. Behind it, in MANSIONHOUSE ROAD and BAIRD STREET, the Procurator Fiscal's Office, the Camelon St John's Church Hall and Bethany Hall (for these, *see* Public Buildings, above). The end of Main Street is marked by Camelon St John's Church (*see* Churches, above). In GLASGOW ROAD, set back on the S side, St Mary of the Angels (R.C.) Church and Camelon Day Centre (*see* Churches and Public Buildings, above).

## INDUSTRIAL BUILDING

ROSEBANK DISTILLERY, Main Street. The bonded stores of 1864 survive but have been converted to a bar (THE ROSEBANK). Two double-pile piend-roofed blocks forming an irregular L-plan, the outer corner of its NE heel bowed. Tall openings under semicircular dummy fanlights on the E side overlooking the Forth & Clyde Canal.

## GRAHAMSTON AND MIDDLEFIELD

Lying between the railway to the S and the Forth & Clyde Canal to the N, Grahamston was laid out in 1802 as 'the NEW TOWN of FALKIRK'. The feuing plan (prepared by 'an eminent architect'*) established a gridiron pattern with Grahams Road serving as the principal thoroughfare. Industry (principally iron works) was established along the canal although the area served also as a suburb of Falkirk. Middlefield to the E has been developed for housing since the 1930s.

## CHURCHES

GRAHAMSTON EVANGELICAL CHURCH. *See* Miller Hall, Public Buildings, below.

GRAHAMSTON UNITED CHURCH, Bute Street. Originally Grahamston Parish Church. Gothic of an early French type, by *T. B. McFadzen*, 1874–5. Nave with N and S aisles, each composed of three transeptal bays. At the W end of the N aisle, a low tower with a steep pyramid roof. At the end of the S aisle, a 33.5m. high steeple, its tower pierced by tall belfry openings; slated octagonal spire rising between spirelets on the corners of the tower. At the front (W) gable of the nave, a procession of five windows which light the vestibule. Above them, tall two-light windows with cinquefoiled heads; at the top of the gable, a roundel carved with the Church of Scotland's emblem of the

* According to an advertisement in the *Edinburgh Evening Courant*, 10 July 1802.

Burning Bush. In the gable of the nave, a huge rose window. Plain gothic HALL of 1897 to the N.

Inside the church, wagon roofs over the nave and each bay of the aisles. Panelled gallery along the sides and W end, the cast iron columns rising to foliage-capitalled columns supporting the roof. The E end is filled by the ORGAN (by *Rushworth & Dreaper*, 1903, and rebuilt by the same firm in 1966) and contemporary simple Gothic PULPIT. – STAINED GLASS. The E window's brightly coloured patterned glass, a small *Agnus Dei* in the centre, is by *David Small*, 1875. – At the S end of the E wall, a window (Our Lord, with King David and St Andrew by *Douglas Hamilton*, 1950, an example of stylized realism. – Next, an abstract window celebrating the Women's Guild, by *Roland Mitton*, 1988. – Also by *Mitton* is the adjacent Boys' Brigade window of 1989. – Two windows in the N aisle. The E (Madonna and Child), strongly coloured and realistic, is of 1950. – The W (Foundry men, the Family, Harvesters) is by *Mitton*, 1999.

ST JAMES' PARISH CHURCH, Thornhill Road. Originally St James' United Free Church. By *G. Deas Page*, 1898–1900. Accomplished late Gothic, the masonry of bullnosed red Locharbriggs sandstone. Broad buttressed box (the nave roof carried over the internal aisles); transepts and chancel at the W end. The E end of the nave projects beyond the aisles. In the NE inner angle, a *c.* 27.4m. high tower, a porch projecting from its E face. The tower is of three stages. At the two lower, simple cusped openings. The top stage is marked off by a cornice-like sill course under the hoodmoulded belfry openings. At the wall-head, a battlement with gryphons projecting from its crocketed corner pinnacles; inside the battlement, a thin octagonal slated spire. The E and W gables of the nave contain tall five-light windows. Three-light windows at the transepts. The windows of the nave aisles are also three-light but squat. On the S side, a link to the Hall, contemporary with the church and in the same manner.

## PARK

VICTORIA PARK, Thornhill Road. The park (little more than a playing field) was opened in 1895. At its entrance, a FOUNTAIN erected in 1912 to commemorate Sir John de Græme and his men killed at the Battle of Falkirk (1298); it is signed by *W. Roberts & Son*. Rusticated masonry of hammer-dressed granite ashlar, the domical top surmounted by a lion holding a shield.

## PUBLIC BUILDINGS

FALKIRK COLLEGE OF FURTHER AND HIGHER EDUCATION, Grangemouth Road and Middlefield Road. Large group of buildings on both sides of Middlefield Road, mostly flat-roofed and horizontal in emphasis. The W buildings are by the Stirling County Architect, *A. J. Smith*. Flat-roofed W block and pitched-roofed brick-walled hall of 1960–3. Low E extension of 1971–3.

The buildings E of Middlefield Road include a late C20 factory adapted in 1982. Nothing here to distract from the teaching.

Former FALKIRK FIRE STATION, Grangemouth Road. By the Stirling County Architect, *A. J. Smith*, 1955. Flat-roofed, the walls of brick and dry-dash. Red brick hose tower of 1958, also by *Smith*.

FALKIRK FIRE STATION, Distributor Road. By *Falkirk Council*, 2000. Postmodern, in pale-coloured blockwork and dark glass. Ribbed metal roofs, curved over the main block.

FALKIRK GRAHAMSTON RAILWAY STATION, Grahams Road. By the *British Railways Board's Architects' Department*, 1985. A small Postmodern building on each platform.

MILLER HALL, Gowan Avenue. Now Grahamston Evangelical Church. By *J. G. Callander*, 1912. Single-storey front (vestibule) block in a simplified Baroque manner. Taller utilitarian hall behind.

VICTORIA PRIMARY SCHOOL, Middlefield Road. By *Central Regional Council*, 1993. Large expanses of low-pitched red tiled roofs over brown brick walls; a birdcage bellcote on the two-storey central section.

VICTORIA PUBLIC SCHOOL, Queen Street. Now offices. Plain Italian Renaissance, by *A. & W. Black*, 1900. Two storeys, the first-floor windows roundheaded. Acroterion-finialled pediments at the centre of the N and W fronts. To the E, the contemporary single-storey INFANTS' DEPARTMENT, its N front again with an acroterion-finialled pediment.

DESCRIPTION

GRAHAMS ROAD begins N of the railway line. Below street level on the W side, Falkirk Grahamston Railway Station (*see* Public Buildings, above). On the E side, Nos. 1–9 Grahams Road by *James Strang*, 1903–4, a free Jacobean Renaissance block with large pedimented dormerheads. Ogee-domed octagonal cupola over the canted NW corner. Beyond, two late C20 shopping developments, Nos. 13–15, by *The Project Management Partnership*, 1997, with a pyramid-roofed tower, and TESCO by *The Parr Partnership*, 1994, with red tiled roofs. On Grahams Road's W side, two blocks, Nos. 12–16 by *A. & W. Black*, 1904, and No. 18, in a squared-up Edwardian free style, an ogee dome on the canted NE corner to Meeks Road. In MEEKS ROAD, on its N side, a pair of cottages (Nos. 6–8) of the later C19, both with round-arched doors and shouldered arches to the windows; wallhead parapet stepped up and corbelled out over the openings. N of Meeks Road, Nos. 26–38 Grahams Road, a two-storey and attic terrace of *c.* 1900, with shallow oriel windows at the first floor. Then the three-storey No. 40. Pompous late C19 classical, the polished ashlar stonework badly eroded. At the ground floor of the three-bay façade, a large Artisan Mannerist doorpiece with attached columns and a curvaceous broken pediment, flanked by a two-light window on the l. and one of three lights on the r., both with cornices and bracketed sills. The same asymmetrical use of two- and three-light windows at the upper floors, the top windows rising through the eaves into pedimented dormerheads. Then the two-storey GRAEME HOTEL (No. 42) of the earlier C19. Polished ashlar front of three bays. Moulded architraves at the windows; central entrance with cavetto-splayed jambs in a pilastered and corniced surround. No. 44 is contemporary with a doorpiece and architraves of the same design but the openings are more widely spaced and one of the ground-floor windows is of three lights. No. 48, on the corner of George Street, has been similar but its ground floor is now occupied by a late Victorian shopfront.

On the N corner of George Street, No. 50 Grahams Road, again of the earlier C19. Single-storey with an attic (now a C20 box dormer), the three-bay front rendered. Recessed Doric columns, their fluting and necking now lost, at the entrance. Panels decorated with ovals at the ends of the sills of the ground-floor windows which were probably originally hoodmoulded. After a gapsite, Nos. 58–60, a pair of semi-detached houses again of the earlier C19, of one storey over a fully exposed basement, its masonry with V-jointed rustication. Recessed entrances with Greek Doric columns; hoodmoulds over the ground-floor windows which are linked by a sill course. Opposite, on the E side of the road, the mid-C19 Nos. 41–43. Paired roundheaded and pilastered entrances (one now a window); windows with moulded architraves and bracketed sills. Bracketed eaves.

N of this, on both sides of the road, small-town commercial buildings of the late C19 and C20. In the side streets, terraced cottages, mostly of the later C19 and many with C20 box dormers. On the E side of Grahams Road, No. 53 is a relatively unaltered mid-C19 cottage. Broached ashlar front, with simply moulded architraves to the door and windows; canted dormers at the attic. Further N, the VICTORIA BAR (No. 75), again of the mid C19 but of two storeys and with a heavy pilastered and corniced doorpiece. Opposite, on the W side of the road, Nos. 92–98, originally a smartly detailed double house of the earlier C19. Ground floor now invaded by late C19 and C20 shopfronts but, at No. 94, a portico with fluted Doric columns which support an entablature with a fluted frieze and guttae. At the first-floor windows, moulded architraves and panelled sills, their ends decorated with rosettes and guttae. This stands on the S corner of Western Avenue whose vista is closed by Nos. 48–52 RUSSEL STREET, a two-storey double house of the mid C19. Georgian survival, with rusticated quoins, moulded architraves to the windows, and pilastered and corniced paired doors (one now a window); big and bad C20 box dormer. On Grahams Road's N corner with Western Avenue, the former ODDFELLOWS HALL of c. 1900. Large free Renaissance block, a two-storey bowed oriel window corbelled out at the canted SE corner. Pediment above the round-arched entrance whose keystone is carved as a bearded human head. Wallhead balustrade broken by a panel carved with a coat of arms and set in a scroll-sided segmental-pedimented frame.

N of this the W side of the road continues with plain two-storey and attic mid-C19 buildings containing flats above shops. Among them, the slightly earlier and classier Nos. 120–122 whose first-floor windows have moulded architraves and panelled sills, their ends decorated with ovals and guttae. Windows of the same type at the contemporary single-storey cottage of No. 91, its cornice brought slightly forward on tall consoles above the entrance. This stands on the S corner of Bute Street whose end is filled by Grahamston United Church (*see* Churches, above). Further N, on the W side of Grahams Road, Nos. 140–142, a mid-C19 two-storey and attic block. All the first-floor windows are dressed up with fluted pilasters, banded at the jambs; outer windows of three lights with Ionic pilastered mullions. Then GOWAN AVENUE. On its N side, the Miller Hall (*see* Public Buildings, above). At the W end, the gateway to Grahamston Iron Works (*see* Industrial Buildings, below). In Grahams Road, a little N of Gowan Avenue, the former GRAHAMSTON AND BAINSFORD CO-OPERATIVE SOCIETY premises of 1908. Two-storey front in a free Jacobean Renaissance manner. Shaped gables over the centre and ends, the central gablet topped by a pediment. At these bays are three-light windows with Ionic columned mullions, the end windows surmounted by open segmental pediments, the centre window by an inscription panel. At the N end of Grahams Road on the E side, No. 175, a large two-storey office block by *J. G. Callander*, 1936. It is a piend-roofed box with a jazz-modern front.

### INDUSTRIAL BUILDINGS

GASWORKS, Etna Road. By *William McCrae*, 1906. One large circular gasholder survives.

GRAHAMSTON IRON WORKS, Gowan Avenue. Almost all of the works founded in 1868 has been demolished. There remains the huge cast iron GATEWAY made by the works for the Edinburgh 124 International Exhibition of 1886. It is an elaborate High Victorian exhibition piece of the foundry's craft. Roundheaded arch in a pilastered and corniced frame; lavish floral decoration. In the spandrels, shields bearing the coat of arms of the City of Edinburgh; at the top of the arch, shields bearing the Royal Arms of Scotland. Above the ends of the cornice are urns; above the centre, scrolls and flags.

### SUMMERFORD, BANTASKIN, ARNOTHILL, WOODLANDS AND CALLENDAR

Large area on the S side of the town. Until the late C19 this was almost all rural. Since then it has been largely covered with housing, a few Victorian villas and a handful of churches and public buildings. The parkland of Callendar House provides an Arcadian contrast to the rest of Falkirk.

## CHURCHES

ERSKINE PARISH CHURCH, corner of Hodge Street and Cockburn Street. Originally Erskine United Free Church. By *A. & W. Black*, 1903–5. Large cruciform, built of hammer-dressed Eastfield sandstone rubble with broached ashlar dressings. Gothic of a generally thrifty character but with a few touches of Perp elaboration. Low N and S nave aisles. In the inner angles of the transepts, projections containing stairs to galleries. SW tower, its angle buttresses topped by crocketed pinnacles; pierced battlement. At the W gable, a five-light traceried window. Chunky spire-topped octagonal ventilator-cupola on the nave roof. Hall at the E end contemporary with the church.

Inside the church, pointed arcades from the nave to the narrow passage aisles. Big arches, again pointed, into the transepts and chancel. Galleries over the W vestibule and in the transepts. Stretched across the E wall of the chancel is the ORGAN by *Norman & Beard*, 1905, its rather bare Gothic case provided by *Whytock & Reid* in 1937. – In front, the oak COMMUNION TABLE, also of 1937 and by *Whytock & Reid* but its late Gothic manner much more delicate, with carved decoration of foliage and fruit, including wheat and vines. – Routine Gothic PULPIT of 1905, moved from the centre to the N side of the chancel *c.* 1965. – STAINED GLASS. In the chancel, a pair of Glasgow-style windows (the Resurrection; the Ascension) by *Stephen Adam*, 1905. – In the S side of the nave, two clearly drawn and brightly coloured clearstorey windows, the Penitent Woman Washing Our Lord's Feet by *Alexander Strachan*, 1937, and Our Lord as the Light of the World, in the same manner, of 1952. – In the N clearstorey, a window (Our Lord Washing the Disciples' Feet) of 1937. – Under the S transept's gallery, a modernistic light (St George) by *James Stewart*, *c.* 1975. – On the E wall of this transept, a large stone MEMORIAL TABLET to the Rev. James Aitchison, designed by *Alexander Black* and carved with a relief portrait by *Alexander Proudfoot*, 1937. – In the vestibule, the gilded wooden SCULPTURE of an eagle. It is of 1817 and served as the finial of the pulpit canopy in the congregation's former church (now demolished) in Silver Row.

ST MODAN, Cochrane Avenue. Now housing (ST MODAN'S COURT) and rather altered. By *P. Macgregor Chalmers*, 1914–15. Characteristically simple Romanesque, built of hammer-dressed buff sandstone. Nave with E and W (liturgical N and S) aisles, both low and with lean-to roofs at the S (liturgical W) end, the W aisle halted against a higher SW porch. At their N end the aisles broaden and rise higher under double-pitch roofs. In the garden outside, the FONT of 1915, a short round pier surmounted by a square bowl, its underside scalloped.

### PARK AND MONUMENT

DOLLAR PARK, Camelon Road. The park was opened in 1921. On its S edge, beside the road, a WAR MEMORIAL by *Leonard*

*C. Blakey*, 1925–6. Tall battered and corniced pedestal. On the front and back, bronze laurel swags from which hang shields bearing the coat of arms of the burgh of Falkirk. On the sides, swords and laurel wreaths. E and w Second World War Memorial extensions by the Falkirk Burgh Architect, *A.J.M. Currell*, 1953.

In the centre of the park is ARNOTDALE, an early C19 villa remodelled in the later C19. The late Georgian house consisted of three back-to-back blocks, increasing in width from s to N, all with panelled pilaster strips at the corners and corniced ground-floor windows. Refronting of the s block provided full-height open pedimented bay windows, each with a boldly consoled stone balcony at the first floor; in the centre, the entrance framed by fluted Doric columns. At the back of the house, two pavilions, each with a Venetian window to the front. Are they early C19 or do they belong to an earlier house, presumably of the late C18? – Behind, a two-storey DOOCOT, the rubble-built lower floor square. The upper stage is an ashlar octagon, a roundheaded dummy window in each face, one enclosing a stone sundial dated 1834, probably the date of construction. – W of this, a brick WALLED GARDEN, probably of the early C19.

MONUMENT TO THE SECOND BATTLE OF FALKIRK, Greenbank Road. By *A. & W. Black*, 1927. Pinnacled octagonal column, the ashlar masonry much patched with cement.

## PUBLIC BUILDINGS

BANTASKIN PRIMARY SCHOOL, Bantaskine Road. By the Stirling County Architect, *A.J. Smith*, 1958. Long, low and lightweight-looking; a small tower for vertical emphasis.

COMELY PARK PRIMARY SCHOOL, High Station Road. By *Falkirk Council*, 1995. Large but low, single-storey covered with shallow-pitched slated roofs. Entrance under a mansard-roofed canopy. Over the main block, a pyramid-roofed cupola containing a clock face.

FALKIRK AND DISTRICT ROYAL INFIRMARY, Majors Loan and Westburn Avenue. The earliest buildings, at the E end of the site, are by *William J. Gibson*, 1926–32. Unambitious harled Neo-Georgian, an open pedimented centrepiece at the main block's end to Woodlands Place. – To the N, ACCIDENT AND EMERGENCY and OUTPATIENTS, two storeys of curtain walling, by *Wilson & Wilson*, 1973. – W of this, the present MAIN ENTRANCE from Westburn Avenue, by *Wilson & Wilson*, 1992. Postmodern, the portico consisting of ball-topped piers supporting a glazed roof. On the w side of the entrance, the THEATRE BLOCK by *Keppie, Henderson & Partners*, 1963–6, the dark brown brick walls topped by a copper fascia. – W again, the WINDSOR and MATERNITY UNITS by *G. B. Horspool*, 1987. Walls again of dark brown brickwork but it is glazed and banded with red; metal-clad shallow bay windows.

Former FALKIRK HIGH SCHOOL, Rennie Street and Griffiths Street. Disused. Main block facing Rennie Street by *A. & W.*

*Black*, 1898. Simplified free Jacobean but not much fun. W extension by the Stirling County Architect, *A. J. Smith*, 1961–3. The freestanding block fronting Griffiths Street, again by *A. & W. Black*, was opened in 1910. Plain Neo-Georgian with channelled stonework at the ground floor and Gibbsian surrounds to the windows of the upper floor.

FALKIRK HIGH SCHOOL, Blinkbonny Road. By the Stirling County Architect, *A. J. Smith*, 1959–61. Three-storey concrete-framed box clad in a mixture of materials. Boxier and more expressive E addition by *Central Regional Council*, 1992, in best late C20 industrial estate style.

FALKIRK INFECTIOUS DISEASES HOSPITAL AND SANATORIUM, Slamannan Road. The ward blocks were replaced by houses in 2000–1. The single-storey administration block in a School Board Jacobean manner, by *A. & W. Black*, 1881, survives (converted to housing).

FALKIRK SCHOOL OF GYMNASTICS, corner of Cow Wynd and St Crispin's Place. Originally Volunteer Drill Hall. By *A. & W. Black*, 1898–9. Two-storey Neo-Georgian front block, faced with stugged red sandstone ashlar. Front of six bays, the centre two slightly advanced under a pediment, its tympanum carved with the coat of arms of the Argyll and Sutherland Highlanders. Cornices over the ground-floor windows and the door whose position in the l. bay of the centrepiece provides an asymmetrical touch. Behind, the hall itself, utilitarian and rather altered.

GRAEME HIGH SCHOOL, Callendar Road. Large but unexciting, by *The Parr Partnership*, 1999–2000. H-plan, the walls of reddish blockwork and panels of white harling; shallow-pitched and broad-eaved ribbed metal roofs with maltings-type ventilators. Front (S) block of three storeys, the top floor a band of continuous glazing. A pair of flat-roofed stair towers break up through the eaves to give vertical emphasis. Fully glazed rectangular bay window lighting a stair at the E gable.

MILLENNIUM WHEEL AND AQUEDUCT, off Lime Road. By *Robert Matthew, Johnson-Marshall & Partners*, in association with *British Waterways*, 1999–2000. Prominent display of engineering, the single most ambitious part of the reopening of the Forth & Clyde and Union Canals. This restored a link between the two canals whose former flight of interconnecting locks had been destroyed. A canal from the higher level Union Canal passes through a 0.145km.-long tunnel under the Antonine Wall. Just s of the Forth & Clyde Canal this emerges into the aqueduct carried on a single line of concave-sided piers whose circular heads contain the canal itself. At the N end of the aqueduct, the massive wheel composed of two spanner-shaped arms at the ends of the axle. The ends of each arm are pierced by round holes into which are slotted the ends of two water-filled 22m.-long 'gondolas' or caissons carried by the rotating wheel from the aqueduct down to a dry dock beside the Forth & Clyde Canal into which boats can then pass. – Beside the wheel, the contemporary glass-clad VISITOR CENTRE, in shape like a segment of an orange.

Falkirk, Millennium Wheel. Visualization.

ST ANDREW'S R.C. PRIMARY SCHOOL, Hawley Road. By the Stirling County Architect, *A. J. Smith*, 1973. Assembly of units covered with tiled monopitch roofs.

## VILLAS

ARNOTHILL. No. 3 is a sizeable Jacobean house of *c.* 1860, with a conical slate-roofed round tower. C20 additions for its present monastic use, including an oratory and tower on the S by *Reginald Fairlie*, 1937, and a two-storey octagonal chapter house by *R. Fairlie & Partners*, 1954. – Jacobean Renaissance No. 17 (ARNOTHILL HOUSE) of *c.* 1865. U-plan S front with two-storey bay windows projecting from the shaped gables of the advanced ends. Strapworked parapets; mullioned and transomed windows. Late C20 E addition trying hard to be tactful. – Late C19 bargeboarded villa at No. 19. Slim tower, its tall French pavilion roof topped by iron cresting.

ARNOTHILL LANE. HATHERLEY by *T. M. Copland*, 1904. Harled Arts and Crafts, with a broad-eaved roof and mullioned windows. At the centre, a pacific low tower, a broad crenelle in each face of its parapet.

CAMELON ROAD. For Arnotdale, *see* Dollar Park, above. DARROCH HOUSE is set well back from the road. Ashlar-faced mid-C19 classical. At the entrance front, an advanced and pedimented centrepiece; Ionic portico in its r. inner angle. Contemporary single-storey LODGE at the beginning of the drive. Pedimented gables, the E with a canted bay window, probably a late C19 addition.

KILNS ROAD. KILNS HOUSE is by *William Stirling III*, 1853. Large Jacobean bay-windowed villa.

MAGGIE WOODS LOAN. No. 7 (MAYFIELD HOUSE). Italianate of *c.* 1860. Tower with a flattish pyramidal roof.

## TOWER BLOCKS

EASTBURN DRIVE and SEATON PLACE. Seven fifteen-storey blocks (EASTBURN TOWER, BELMONT TOWER, LEISHMAN TOWER, MARSHALL TOWER, PATERSON TOWER, SYMON TOWER and MAXWELL TOWER) standing along the ridge on the N side of Callendar Park and enjoying the best views in Falkirk. All by *Crudens*, 1965, the layout plan by the Burgh Architect, *I. A. Ferguson*. More sensible than stylish, clad with rendered panels; cut-out corners provided balconies which were glazed in as part of a refurbishment in 2000.

FINISTERE AVENUE. BRETON COURT and CORENTIN COURT are by *George Wimpey & Co.*, 1967. Each is a fifteen-storey L-plan block, clad with concrete aggregate panels. Tiered balconies linked vertically by fins.

KEMPER AVENUE. GLENBRAE COURT and PARKFOOT COURT, by *George Wimpey & Co. Ltd.*, in association with the Falkirk Burgh Architect, *I. A. Ferguson*, 1965, and originally of the same design as Breton Court and Corentin Court in Finistere Avenue (*see* above). They were remodelled at the end of the C20 when pitched roofs were added and the two lowest storeys clad in pale brick and the floors above in white metal sheeting.

WINDSOR ROAD and GLENFUIR ROAD. GLENFUIR COURT and GREENBANK COURT are a pair of fifteen-storey blocks by *George Wimpey & Co. Ltd.*, 1969. Glenfuir Court was remodelled at the end of the C20 when the balconies were glazed in and gablets added.

## INDUSTRIAL BUILDING

ROSEBANK DISTILLERY, Camelon Road. Built in 1864 beside a lock of the Forth & Clyde Canal. V-shaped complex of two- and three-storey buildings, mostly of brick but the NW range's lower floors are of rubble and have blocked windows; they may incorporate part of earlier buildings (originally a brewery) on the site. Some roofs are piended. Tall circular brick chimney.

4 ANTONINE WALL of *c.* AD142 (*see* Introduction, p. 13–15). On the W side of TAMFOURHILL ROAD, an exceptionally well preserved stretch of the ditch which continues NW in less dramatic form on the N side of the road and reappears to the W of LIME ROAD.

## CALLENDAR HOUSE
### off Seaton Place

Strung-out mansion, its predominantly French Renaissance appearance the last of a succession of costume changes during the building's development from a medieval tower to a post-Restoration showhouse to a Victorian country house.

The lands of Callendar were granted to the Livingstons in 1345 and a 'castle' (*castrum*) was in existence by 1458. Doubtless originally accompanied by extensive other buildings, now lost, a late C14 or early C15 tower of this 'castle' is incorporated in the NW corner of the main block of the present house. It has been a stone-built near-rectangle (the N wall splayed), probably of two storeys and an attic, *c*. 7m. broad over *c*. 2.13m.-thick walls. Probably *c*. 1500 a 16.45m.-long wing was added against the S side of the tower and projecting to its E. Perhaps in the late C16 this wing was extended E by a slightly broader addition, *c*. 26.8m. long. Its first floor may have contained a new hall and great chamber, its second a long gallery.

Major remodelling and enlargement was carried out in the C17, probably in two stages. The first stage may have occurred soon after 1634 when James Livingston, first Lord Livingston of Almond (and later first Earl of Callendar), acquired the estate from his elder brother. In this the E wall of the original tower was removed, the tower extended E to a total length of *c*. 17.37m. and an octagonal stair tower was erected in the inner angle of the tower and S range. The second stage, probably built for Alexander Livingston, second Earl of Callendar, who inherited *c*. 1674, added a NE wing, *c*. 12.5m. square and projecting from the end of the S range, making the house a not very regular elongated U-plan with a shallow recessed centre to the N. A second octagonal stair tower, smaller than the first, was placed in the E inner angle of the U and both stair towers given tall spire roofs. Internally, this work provided a state apartment, the new state stair in the SE corner of the addition leading to an enfilade of rooms in the S range consisting of a dining room followed by drawing room, bedchamber, dressing room and closet.

James, fourth Earl of Callendar and fifth Earl of Linlithgow, took part in the Jacobite rising of 1715 and subsequently forfeited his honours and estates, Callendar being sold by the Government in 1720 to the York Buildings Company which then granted a lease of the house and lands to the attainted Earl's daughter, the Countess of Kilmarnock. It is likely that it was she who further extended the house to its present length by the addition at either end of two-storey L-plan wings, the E containing a kitchen, with stair towers in their inner angles.

In 1783 the estate was sold to the Scots-born but London-based entrepreneur William Forbes, who carried out extensive repairs and some remodelling of the mansion house in 1785–7. Further work, mainly new plasterwork in the principal rooms and the installation of marble chimneypieces but also including the making of a new library in the NW corner of the main block, was executed for Forbes's son and namesake to designs by *David Hamilton* in 1825–8. Two years after the completion of this work rival designs for additions to the house including a new N porch and entrance hall and new kitchen offices were procured from *David Hamilton* and *Patrick Wilson* but left unexecuted. However, in 1841–3 a new design by Wilson was used for the addition of a full-height protrusion containing a new entrance and stair hall, occupying most of the N front's recessed centre between the C17 octagonal stair towers, and, projecting from this, a *porte cochère*. Some internal alterations were carried out at the same time.

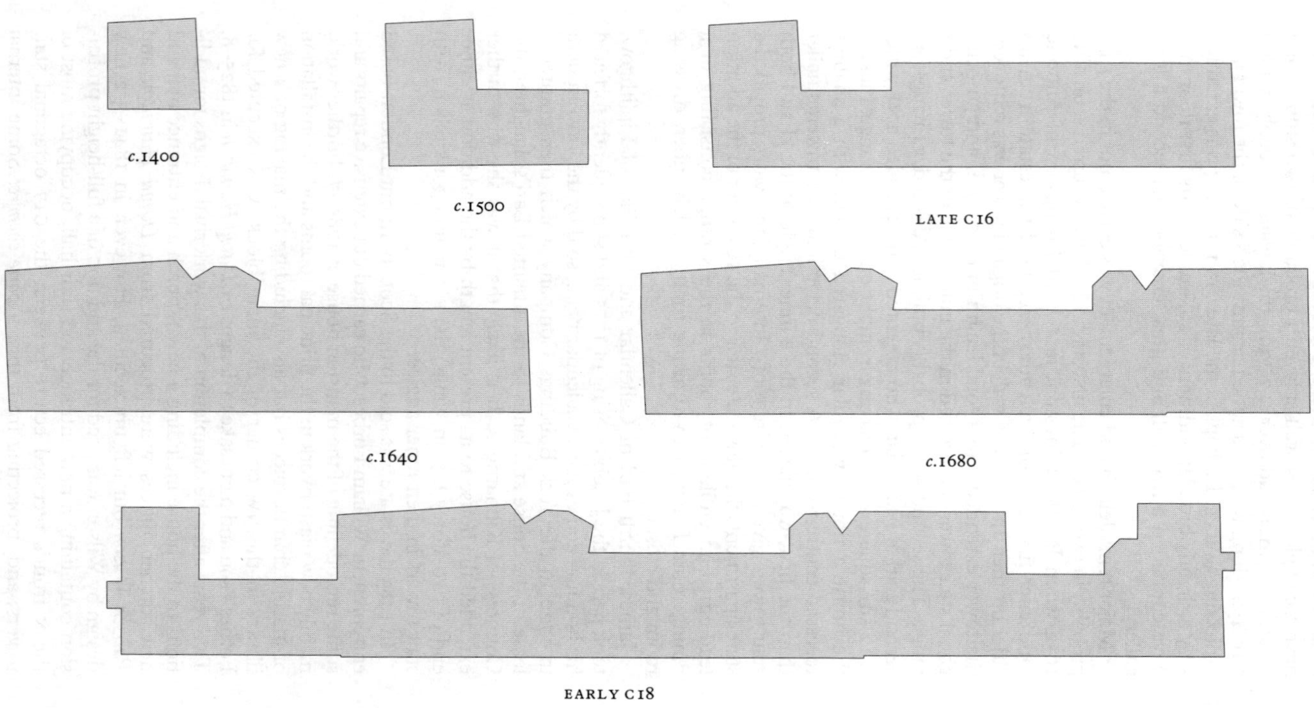

c.1400

c.1500

LATE C16

c.1640

c.1680

EARLY C18

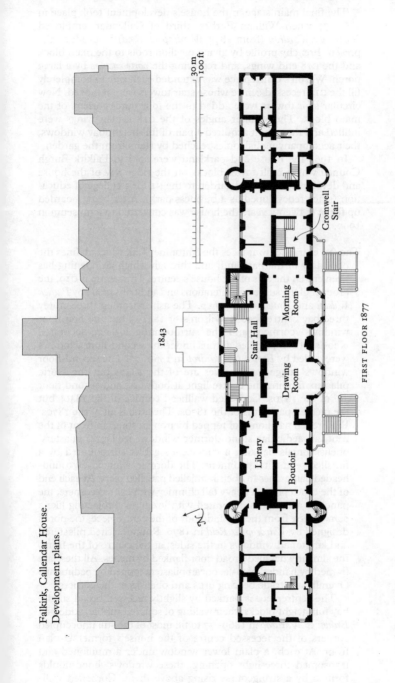

Falkirk, Callendar House.
Development plans.

1843

30 m
100 ft

Stair Hall

Library

Boudoir

Drawing Room

Morning Room

Cromwell Stair

FIRST FLOOR 1877

N

The final main stage in the house's development took place in 1869–77 when William Forbes, third of Callendar, employed *Brown & Wardrop* (from 1874 *Wardrop & Reid*) to produce the present Frenchy profile by giving pavilion roofs to the main block and the C18 end wings, and replacing the *porte cochère* by a large porch. Wilson's centrepiece was extended each side to completely fill the C17 recessed centre whose stair towers were removed. New circular stair towers were added to the four outer corners of the main block. The N inner angles of the C18 L-plan wings were infilled and the S front acquired a pair of full-height bay windows, their accompanying balconies reached by stairs from the garden.

In 1963 the house and parkland were sold to Falkirk Burgh Council which built tower blocks on the ridge NW of the house and developed the walled garden to the NE for a college of education (since redeveloped as a business park). After being boarded up for over twenty years the house was converted to a museum in 1997.

The (N) entrance front faces the Antonine Wall, which defines the boundary of the parkland, and through which an opening has been cut on the axis of the house's centre. This centre is C19, the product of the successive alterations and additions made by *Patrick Wilson* and *Brown & Wardrop*. The ashlar-fronted three-storey three-bay centrepiece is Wilson's of 1841–3 but the first-floor windows' cornices and the surmounting lozenge-decorated Neo-Jacobean panelled aprons under the second-floor windows were added by *Brown & Wardrop* in 1869–77. The second-floor windows' lugged architraves are of the 1840s but the Doric pilasters framing the centre light at both first and second floor are of the 1870s. Corbelled wallhead cornice of the 1840s but the pierced parapet is of the 1870s. The attic is all of the 1870s. Big French pavilion roof topped by iron cresting. In front of the roof, an aedicular stone dormer window, its Doric pilasters' obelisk finials flanking a curvaceous gablet surmounted by a finialled segmental pediment. The dormer is joined by round-headed half-arches to obelisk-finialled panelled piers. At each end of the centrepiece, a heavy tall chimney with canted corners, the panelled main faces decorated with lozenges. Projecting like a *porte cochère* from the ground floor of the centrepiece, the porch designed by *Wardrop & Reid* in 1876. Round-arched pilastered and keystoned windows in the sides; at the centre of the front, the similarly detailed broad door flanked by niches. All these are framed by banded Neo-Jacobean pilasters topped by pediments. Overall balustrade bearing urns and obelisks at the corners.

The centrepiece is flanked by slightly recessed broad single-bay full-height blocks, their walling of squared rubble, added by *Brown & Wardrop* in 1869–77 to fill most of the still unoccupied corners of the recessed centre of the house's former U-plan front. At each, a plain lower window under a mullioned and transomed three-light opening, these windows' hoodmoulds formed by a stringcourse rising above them. Corbelled wallhead cornice and pierced parapet like those of the centrepiece.

At the centre of each parapet, a dormer window, a smaller version of the one on the centrepiece but with consoled buttresses in place of the flanking half-arches and piers. At the outer corner of each block, a conical-roofed round turret carried on continuous corbelling.

E and W of the C19 centre are the harled outer bays of the N front of the house which had developed by the late C17, the inner ends of either block (the E broader than the W) additions of 1869–77 filling the last left-over spaces of the former recessed centre. The block W of the centrepiece is longer than the E and its front has a more pronounced splay. At both blocks are windows of late C17 type with roll-and-fillet mouldings, the windows of the W block narrower than those of the E. Between the two central first-floor windows of the E block, a plain ventilation hole for a C19 lavatory. Stringcourses across both blocks, added in the 1870s. Also of the 1870s are the wallheads' pierced parapets carried on continuous corbelling, each surmounted by a group of four tall chimneys, their tops joined by a single cope. At the outer corner of each block, a conical-roofed round tower of the 1870s, its top window framed in a Neo-Jacobean aedicule.

E and W of the main block's corner towers are two-storey three-bay harled links, their upper windows rising through the wallhead to steeply pedimented Neo-Jacobean dormerheads. These links are of 1869–77 when the inner angles of the L-plan C18 wings were infilled. The wings were originally of two storeys, the E with a basement, the W with dummy basement windows. Harled walls with chamfered surrounds to the openings; square first-floor windows. *Brown & Wardrop* added a jettied ashlar-clad and French pavilion-roofed attic over the N jamb of each wing, its front window rising through the eaves into a steeply pedimented dormerhead. A second and identical pavilion-roofed attic was added to the end of each S range behind.

The S (garden) elevation is a flat-fronted harled spread, sub- 66 stantially of the late C17 but overlaid and enlivened by the exposed stonework of the protruding Victorian towers and bay windows and the accompanying *château* roofs. At each end, the two-storey S range of an C18 end wing, the end two bays topped by the attic and pavilion roof added in the 1870s. The originally square upper windows of the wings' inner three bays were heightened by *Brown & Wardrop* to rise through the eaves into dormerheads like those over the corresponding windows of the N front. At the outer corners of the main block are conical-roofed round towers of the same design as those of the N front. The E of these is of 1869–77, the W earlier (probably part of *Patrick Wilson*'s additions of 1841–3) but remodelled by *Brown & Wardrop* to correspond to their three new towers. The main S range between the towers is of three storeys and an attic. Before the C19 alterations it was of fourteen bays, the windows all with moulded surrounds of late C17 character but not altogether regularly disposed and the W first-floor windows taller than those at the E; at the ground floor of the E end, a ventilation hole for a C19 lavatory. *Brown & Wardrop* gave the elevation French

Renaissance character by slightly heightening the two bays at each end under French pavilion roofs, their crested ridges transverse to the main roof; at each pavilion, a bargeboarded wooden dormer. More dormers of this type at the ends of the main roof. Roughly in the centre (in fact a little to the E) of the main block they added a pair of pavilion-roofed bay windows, their sides canted at the two lower floors above which they are corbelled out to the square; conical-roofed two-stage turrets at the outer corners. Three-light windows, transomed at the first floor, in the bays' faces, the centre openings at the second floor framed by attached columns whose panelled bases flank panelled aprons. At the front of each pavilion roof, a dormer window of the same design as those of the outer bays of the centre of the N front. On the outer sides of the bay windows, stone stairs from the garden to balustraded stone balconies under the adjoining first-floor windows. Another balcony across the two bays between the bay windows; between these, an uncarved late C19 panel in a bandaged frame. On the roof over this centrepiece, a large chimney of the 1870s, its faces panelled, the front with a lozenge ornament; from a little distance, where it stands against the central pavilion roof of the N front, it is clear that the 'centres' of the N and S elevations are out of alignment.

INTERIOR. The N porch is of 1876–7. Ionic pilastered and oak-grained walls; panelled ceiling, again grained. Floor of black and white marble. At the S end, steps up to the stair hall provided by *Patrick Wilson* in 1841–3. Oak stairs against the E and W ends rising to a cantilevered first-floor balcony along the S side. Oak panelling below the balcony and on the stair dado; panelled wooden ceiling. The style is unostentatious Jacobean, with touches of strapwork. Each side of the stair hall, a staircase of 1869–77 rising from the ground to the second floor, with turned balusters. Behind the stair hall, a ground-floor corridor whose S side is the N outer wall of the late C16 extension of the S range. It has a splayed plinth and windows with C17 roll-and-double-fillet mouldings. Behind the E half of this corridor, a large room (intended as the billiard room in the 1870s but later used as the dining room) which must have been the late C17 entrance hall. Its S bay window is of the 1870s, the other decoration of 1825–6. Egg-and-dart cornice; beamed ceiling with sparing Neo-Jacobean ornament. Heavy corniced doorpieces. In the N wall, besides the windows to the corridor, an off-centre roundheaded niche; another niche at the centre of the W end. E of this room is the late C17 stair hall (the CROMWELL STAIR), its oak panelling partly replicated in 1916. Scale-and-platt stair, with simple turned balusters and, along the walls, half-balusters and a vestigial handrail. Ceiling painted with a *trompe l'oeil* depiction of women looking down over a parapet and with cherubs holding garlands of flowers. It was probably of *c.* 1700 but repainted by *William Kay* in 1997. Two-panel late C17 doors. The W door at the top of the stair opens into the MORNING ROOM, the late C17 Great Dining Room, the first room of the state apartment. Its C19 character is the product of several alterations. Bay window of the 1870s on the S. At the E end of the room, a screen of Corinthian columns *in antis* erected by *Patrick Wilson* in 1841–3 but most of the plasterwork, the friezes of the walls and ceiling beams enriched with anthemion, urns and foliage, was executed by *John Bryson* as part of *David Hamilton*'s alterations of 1825–6. The walls are covered with stamped leather panels set in oak framework, probably introduced in the 1870s together with the oak chimneypiece, its fireplace jambs carved as caryatids, the Neo-Jacobean overmantel designed to contain a painting. Corniced doorpieces, apparently of the 1820s but the NW one must be of the 1840s when this doorway was made from the stair hall to the N. *En suite* to the W is the DRAWING ROOM, the drawing room of the late C17 state apartment but extended W in the 1780s or perhaps the 1820s to take in the former state bedchamber. Bay window of the 1870s but the Neo-Classical plasterwork and the corniced doorpieces with swagged friezes are of 1825–6. Desperately plain and rather small white marble C19 chimneypiece. The room to the W was made in the late C18 or early C19 out of the late C17 dressing room and closet. W of that, the C19 boudoir (now a book store) made from a C17 bedchamber and closet. This opens on the N into the LIBRARY, its main entrance off the stair hall, which was formed by Hamilton in 1827–8 by throwing together three rooms. The W end occupies the surviving part of the late C14 or early C15 tower, the thickness of the N wall revealed at the ingoes of the W window. Coffered tunnel-vaulted oak ceiling. Pilastered bookcases along the walls and the ingoes of the two W windows. Block pedimented doorcase at the E end. At the W end and N side, plain black marble chimneypieces.

At the SE corner of the house and filling most of the S range of the C18 wing is the KITCHEN. Two storeys in height, the hefty pilasters along the walls and coomb ceiling look early C18, as does the elliptical-arched E fireplace. In the N wall, a pair of keystoned segmental-arched recesses, probably of *c.* 1785. The E contains a cast iron bread oven, the W a hotplate decorated with Classical reliefs including a figure of Vesta; the oven and hotplate were supplied by the *Carron Company* in 1786. At the W end of the kitchen a room has been formed at the upper level, probably in the early C19, its mezzanine floor supported on columns. In this room's wall to the kitchen, a clock (a late C20 replacement) in an acanthus-leaf plaster border. Under the kitchen are vaulted cellars.

Some C16 and C17 rooms survive on the ground floor of the W part of the main block. Immediately W of the dining room is a pair of early C17 stores, now sharing a bay window of the 1870s. The W retains its tunnel vault. The next room to the W, in the addition of *c.* 1500, is also covered by a tunnel vault, its E end reinforced by an arch inserted in the later C16 or early C17. In the S wall, a blocked segmental-arched kitchen fireplace.

The surrounding PARKLAND is planted along late C18 lines. The N drive is cut through the Antonine Wall. Built into a mound on the drive's E side, an ICE HOUSE, probably of the later C18. Pedimented entrance from which the passage leads to a brick-lined domical chamber. – NW of the house are the STABLES. Front (E) courtyard of the mid C18. Piend-roofed ranges, the E façade of droved ashlar with rusticated quoins. Small and square first-floor windows but several have been heightened in the later C19 and now rise through the eaves to piended dormerheads. Keystoned elliptical-arched entrance. Coachhouse doors of the same type inside the court and, in the centre of the W side, a round-arched entrance to a pedestrian pend. Behind, a second court, developed from the early C19. On the N side, a two-storey ashlar-fronted range, perhaps of the 1820s. Elliptical-arched coachhouse doors at the ground floor; narrow lancet windows above. At the E end of the range, a battlemented rubble-built square tower of 1828, its top stage containing a doocot. – To the N, at the present entrance to the policies, a two-storey rendered LODGE of the earlier C19. At the E front, hood-moulds over the door and windows. Wallhead battlement with triangular-topped merlons. Late C19 NW extension in an unexciting Georgian survival manner.

o.8km. SW of the house, a BRIDGE of 1787 over a dried-up canal. Simple segmental arch faced with polished ashlar, the soffit of brick; curved abutments. The cast iron balustrades are now missing.

35          o.6km. SE of the house, MAUSOLEUM, by *Archibald Elliot*, 1815–16, in the form of a circular Greek temple. Podium of vermiculated ashlar masonry supporting the main drum surrounded by a Doric peristyle. Over the entrance, a Greek inscription taken from Lucian ('Mortals' possessions are mortal. . .').

FALLIN                              S

Colourless mining village on the flatlands E of Stirling; little more than a housing scheme laid alongside the A905.

RAILWAY BRIDGE. Six braced and bolted timber trestles on brick and concrete constructed in the late C19 to carry a single-line track across a small stream on the W edge of the village.

FINLARIG CASTLE                   S
                        o.75km. NNE of Killin

A ruined Z-plan tower set on a wooded mound on the N edge of the haughlands that stretch between the bend of the River Lochay and the W end of Loch Tay. It was erected in the early C17 by Sir Duncan Campbell, seventh Laird of Glenorchy, the same 'Black Duncan' who built Achallader, Barcaldine (Argyll and Bute), Edinample and Loch Dochart castles (qq.v.). The oblong core, lying E–W, is little more than a shell, barely surviving along the N wall but more preserved on the S and on the E where the gable stands to the fourth storey. Part of the vaulted basement remains towards the W gable and the plan of cellars and E kitchen, accessed from a S corridor, can be detected. A fragmentary mural stair at the NE corner appears to indicate a link to a NE wing, though there is no extant evidence of this wing. A SW wing does, however, exist, rising from a vaulted basement to an ivy-clad irregular wallhead at the third and fourth storey. Its construction incorporates huge rubble boulders. Windows are lintelled with rounded ingoes and shutter-fixing holes in the jambs, as they are in the main E gable. The entrance door, located in the re-entrant on the E wall of the SW wing, has partly intact roll-moulded jambs but no lintel, the masonry having fallen below its relieving arch. It leads to a staircase which originally returned to reach the first-floor Hall in the main block. Above the door is an armorial tablet with the date 1609.

Close to the N wall of the castle is a stone-lined tank. MacGibbon & Ross regard this as a provision for water storage but cannot forgo reference to the persistent tradition that this is a killing pit, the overflow being the hollow in which the unfortunate victim 'placed his neck for the convenience of the headsman'.

BREADALBANE MAUSOLEUM. Immediately to the E. Built 1829–30 by *William Atkinson*. A three-bay nave with a small chancel and porch constructed in brick but stuccoed to appear stone. The nave is buttressed with lancet windows. The structure has collapsed, its dereliction beyond the romantic affection of any latter-day Gothick sensibility. Nor is there evidence to permit any imaginative recollection of the Chapel of the Blessed Virgin which in 1523 Sir Colin Campbell, third Laird of Glenorchy, built here or hereabouts to house his remains. What do exist are two Celtic CROSSES, the gravemarkers of Sir Gavin Campbell, seventeenth Laird of Glenorchy and fourth Marquess of Breadalbane †1922, and his wife, Lady Alma Graham †1932.

## FINNICH MALISE                                        S 4080
### 0.7km. S of Croftamie

A three-bay, three-storey Classical mansion, *c.* 1815, uneasily sandwiched between two-bay, full-height wings added in 'sympathetic' style at different times during the C19. 1888 remodelling by *Percy G. Stone*. Good intentions are evident, but their aggregation unconvincing. The red sandstone dressings do not all come from the same quarry, the harling is inconsistent and the pitch of the piended roofs varied, low in the wings, steep (perhaps a C19 alteration) in the core. NE wing, 1937. The interior retains some Georgian panelling and chimneypieces. – On the S lawn, a timber SUMMER HOUSE, *c.* 1905, with a thatched pyramidal roof; ingeniously devised to rotate on a wheel mechanism to catch the sun. – In the WALLED GARDEN, *c.* 1815, a colonnaded seating area with half-cone roof, *c.* 1910, abuts the original N brick wall. Courtyard STEADING, *c.* 1830, 0.1km. SE. Five-bay N range with pedimented central bay over archway and pedimented door. W range has central pedimented pend-arch and open pedimented end bays. Horse-mill with slated cone roof at

the SW corner. – Harled GATE-LODGE, c. 1905, on the A809:
shallow-pitched roof with bracketed eaves. Six domed ashlar
GATEPIERS, rubble walls and robust Arts and Crafts timber
gates.

Two settlements in the upper Endrick valley. Clachan, the original
kirktoun, now little more than the church itself and a handful of
houses, developed just W of Gonachan Bridge. 1.5km. further W is
the modern village of Newtown of Fintry, founded to house the
workers in the cotton mill which Peter Spiers of Culcreuch established in the last decade of the C18.

FINTRY PARISH CHURCH, 1.2km. E. An ancient religious site
where a church has stood since the C13. The present church, built
1823, replaced a building of 1642, rising around its predecessor
until the latter, wholly enveloped, was demolished and removed
stone by stone. It is a skew-gabled rubble kirk, with a square W
tower crenellated between corner obelisk finials. Side walls lit
by three pointed-arched windows with splayed ingoes; E wall by
two four-centred-arched bipartite windows with cusped tracery,
formed in the early C20. Pointed windows light the staircase in
the tower. Above a stringcourse at ridge height, each face of the
tower is marked by a blank circular disc set within a diamond-
shaped panel. The same arrangements, compositionally and
decoratively, are repeated at Killearn Church (q.v.).

Plain plastered interior. W gallery carried on two slender cast
iron columns. Seating arrangements date from 1890; Dec timber
panelling rising to sill height on the E wall, early C20. – Between
the windows, a raised box PULPIT backed by a Gothic aedicule.
– Among the furnishings which clutter the chancel are an open-
frame COMMUNION TABLE, with cusped arches and a vine frieze,
and a bowl FONT resting on the gilded floral capital of a pedestal
column with four slender buttresses rising from its bell-shaped
base; both oak pieces came from Oban Parish Church in 1989.
– E wall l., two grey marble TABLETS: the plainer commemorates
Rev. William Grierson Smith †1870 and his wife Hannah †1891;
the other, shield-shaped, their two children †1848. – Three more
are placed on the S wall close to the gallery front: one, in memory
of Alexander Graham Speirs, is cut in an irregular leaf shape. –
Five windows have STAINED GLASS. Chancel l., Christ with
children, by *Gordon Webster* (?), c. 1955; r., the War Memorial
window, by *J. T. & C. E. Stewart*, c. 1928. – The others depict
Christ in Gesthsemane and in company with three disciples (N
wall); S, in warm browns and reds, the angel greeting the two
Marys at the empty tomb.

Mounted on the tower is the BELL, dated 1626, cast by *William
Maine* or *Mayne*.

A walled GRAVEYARD surrounds the church. It contains a
number of SLABS and HEADSTONES of the C17 and C18, difficult
to decipher. – In the SE corner, fronting a raised mound, a massive,

rough-faced granite CROSS to William Gibb †1903. – In the SW corner, before another elevated grassy plot, a tall Celtic CROSS with heavy simple interlacing and a monogrammed boss; in memory of Sir George Home Speirs, ninth Baronet of Blackadder †1887, and his wife Ann Oliphant †1907.

FINTRY BRIDGE, carrying the B822 over the Endrick Water. Built 1804. Three equal segmental arches separated by cutwaters. Coursed rubble with pilastered piers, a coping course and a horizontal stringcourse tangential to the projecting moulding marking each of the dressed voussoir curves. An earlier four-arch bridge, c. 1792, appears to have been short-lived.

FINTRY CASTLE, 2.5km. E. Late C15 or early C16. Little more than rubble footings of what may have been the hall-house of the Grahams of Fintry.

FINTRY LEISURE CENTRE. Formerly Stewart's School, dated 1839; by *William Stirling II*. Classrooms organized in a cruciform plan. The projecting gabled front is bargeboarded in a semi-circular arc over a clock and a bipartite window with sharply dentillated cornice. Decorative glazing-bar patterns.

LOW BRIDGE OF GONACHAN, 1.8km. E. Built 1750–1. A narrow, hump-backed, rubble bridge of two unequal segmental-arched spans, the dressed voussoirs of both arches recessed slightly under drip-moulds. The larger N span, 15.7m.; the smaller, S of an intervening cutwater pier, 5.5m. Decorative weathered date-stone on W keystone of principal arch.

MENZIES HALL, Main Street. Erected 1908, the gift of Walter Menzies of Culcreuch. Church-like buttressed hall with gabled E porch. The box ventilator on the ridge preserves its slated pyramid and weathervane.

## DESCRIPTION

Old Fintry is barely a hamlet. The CLACHAN INN, small, venerable but maltreated, claims a 1633 date above the plain cornice of its consoled doorway. Set back across the road are two manses: the Old Manse, DUNMORE COTTAGE, 1732, a low rubble house with ground-floor bipartite windows, early C19 (?), and single-storey wings l. and r., and the NEW MANSE, 1836, higher, with architraved windows and a pilastered doorpiece in a roughcast W front.

New Fintry is more attenuated, flatted millworkers' housing of c. 1795–1800 lining the S side of MAIN STREET. All of these are two-storey, rubble-built, but the details vary. Nos. 1–3 have small tripartite windows with stone mullions. No. 21 has an architraved entrance door with a simple pediment drip-mould. New windows have disfigured FINTRY INN. Typical rows survive at Nos. 43–51, Nos. 61–67, and Nos. 81–99, most of these with a characteristic small lobby window beside the street door. At a later cottage, No. 109, the doorway is canopied on carved consoles springing from timber pilasters. On the N side, building is more diverse. BURNBANK COTTAGE, mid-C19, is stark three-bay sandstone with a proper respect for the street. At the junction with the B822 is a four-bowl, cast iron FOUNTAIN, 1902, a Coronation concoction rising from lion base supports to a central lamp standard. N across Fintry Bridge (*see* above) is THE MILL, 1792–4, a three-storey (formerly four-storey) piended block of five regular window bays; now in domestic use, it is the SW remnant of two parallel ranges which extended NE. The mill-wheel has gone and the line of the lade is not wholly clear but THE MILL HOUSE, *c.* 1795, remains: plain standard Georgian with a glazed bow-fronted W wing added axially.

DUN, Craigton, 1.3km. NE. Traces of a squarish rubble enclosure, its maximum internal dimension some 14.5m. Some outer facing stones on the NW. Short stretches of NW and SE outer walls.

FORT, Dunmore, 1.1km W. Hilltop fortification defined by rubble remains of a 3.6m.-thick wall reinforcing natural rocky scarps. An area some 150m. by 45m. appears to have been enclosed. Entrance by a gully penetrating the middle of the N wall from a lower ridge surrounded by precipitous slopes except to the ESE, where traces of defensive walling survive.

MOTTE, 0.45km. W. Oval mound surrounded by a ditch. May have been the C13 residence of the Earls of Lennox.

MOTTE (SIR JOHN DE GRAHAM'S CASTLE), 6.6km. E. Near the NW end of Carron Valley Reservoir, a banked platform, 45m. square, with perimeter ditch.

STANDING STONES, Waterhead, 5km. SE. Known as the 'Machar Stones': one, more pillar than slab and 2.29m. in length, has fallen; the other stands 1.52m. high.

CULCREUCH CASTLE. *See* p. 354.

CULCREUCH CASTLE. *See* p. 354.

*8090*        FISHCROSS        C

Small village, the two principal streets (PITFAIRN ROAD and ALLOA ROAD) making an L-plan. Some C19 terraced cottages in Pitfairn Road. The inner angle of the L is filled with C20 housing.

FISHCROSS PRIMARY SCHOOL, Alloa Road. By *Thomas Frame & Son*, 1887. Built of hammer-dressed masonry, with mullioned and transomed windows. At the E elevation, a central gable buttressed by chimneys. U-plan S front, a window rising into a gable at the recessed centrepiece. To the S, contemporary SCHOOLHOUSE, asymmetrical, with bracketed broad eaves to the jerkin-headed roof. At the front, windows grouped 2/1 and an off-centre wallhead chimney.

MINERS' WELFARE INSTITUTE, Alloa Road. 1930, by *William Kerr* and *John Gray* of *John Melvin & Son* and characteristic of that firm's halls and institutes of the earlier C20, with harled walls and a red-tiled piended roof. Tall ball-finialled curvilinear open pediment at the E porch. To its N, a rectangular bay window, its sides and front glazed; another bay window of the same type at the N elevation.

125 DEVON COLLIERY BEAM ENGINE HOUSE, 0.7km. N. A solitary

survivor of the coal mine, now accompanied by flower beds.
The building is of *c.* 1880 when the mine was reopened after a
twenty-six-year closure. Tall two-storey piend-roofed rectangle,
the walls of stugged ashlar. Round-arched openings in the N, E
and W faces, the lower windows very tall. At the S face's upper
level, a broad opening from which projects the pumping engine
made by *Neilson & Co.* of Glasgow in 1865. The building was
restored by *Bob Heath* in 1993 when the interior acquired a
curvaceous gallery, elegant but not forgetful of industrial purpose.

SAUCHIE TOWER. *See* p. 651.

## GARDEN HOUSE                    S *5090*
### 1.6km. WSW of Arnprior

By *William Stirling I*, 1830. Piend-roofed mansion of two main   64
storeys and a sunk basement, harled with red sandstone dressings. Five bays wide under a strongly emphasized eaves cornice, the main E façade possesses an unspectacular but assured
classical composure. At the centre, reached by a perron, is a
surprisingly masculine Doric tetrastyle portico, its entablature
shading the broad segmental arch of a glazed entrance screen.
In the outer bays, slightly but significantly advanced, lugged
ground-floor windows with consoles carrying a pediment, a feature repeated on the N and S elevations. All other windows have
moulded architraves.

But there is more to Garden House than at first appears, for
behind this C19 block, which is only one room deep, lies the
original mansion, built by the Gartmore mason *David Tod*,
*c.* 1750. It is three bays wide and three storeys high, now in a T-plan
relationship with its later addition, but retaining its symmetrical
W façade. In the central bay of the C18 house is a geometrical
stair; its lowest flight is of stone. At the centre of the principal
floor of the C19 house is a vestibule with a coved and coffered
ceiling. A corridor permits communication between the two.
To the N is a single-storey extension, probably of *c.* 1840 and
designed by *William Stirling II*. – LODGE and GATEWAY on the
A811, by *William Stirling II*, 1838.

## GARGUNNOCK                      S *7090*

Hillside village on the S edge of Blairdrummond Moss.

Former FREE CHURCH, Station Road. *c.* 1844; reconstructed 1939.
   Low, hip-ended hall with two iron pepper-pot ridge ventilators.
   Now the Parish Church Hall.
PARISH CHURCH. Impressively poised uphill on the SE side of
   the village above the Gargunnock Burn. Erected 1774 to replace
   a C17 church. Crowstep-gabled, T-plan kirk built of rubble and
   originally harled. Dressed quoins, cavetto eaves course and margins
   rebated and holed for shutters. Windows are square-headed

except for two pointed lights flanking the pulpit on the S wall. On the E and W gables, cross and crescent finials taken from the earlier church. On the N aisle gable, a columned bellcote with ball finial and golden weathercock. Against all three, parapeted forestairs rise to galleries. Ground-level doors below W and E landings maintain the formal exigencies of the 'preaching house' plan but it is now the former only which serves as entrance. In 1833, these two doors and three windows below the galleries were formed. In 1891, *John Honeyman* made alterations which may have included new furnishings and the re-panelling of the gallery fronts. The treatment is classical, the panelling of the PULPIT, a square raised box at the centre of the S wall, enhanced by carved thistles, oak-leaves, acorns, and vines. – Behind it is the WAR MEMORIAL, 1919, by *Robert S. Lorimer*, fumed oak rising through the record of gilded names to three organically cusped arches under a cavetto canopy. – Roof renewed 1963; coomb ceiling tiled. – STAINED GLASS in the two pointed S windows probably by *William Wilson*: Christ the carpenter, 1956, and Christ the Sower, 1968.

Around the church, the walled hilltop GRAVEYARD has many tombs, though none appears older than early C18. Railed BURIAL ENCLOSURES of the Stirlings of Gargunnock and the Grahams of Meiklewood; both early C19, the latter with two armorial TABLETS in strong relief. – Walled ENCLOSURE, SE, entered under a lintel-stone bearing the name George Christison and an indecipherable date: to the r., a small TABLET marked 1727/MR/IW; to the l., a framed stone PANEL in memory of Rev. James Laurie †1843, with a long complimentary inscription. Inside, equally prolix, the TOMB of another minister, Rev. James Robertson †1832; ogee arch with column shafts and sill. – Among the graves, near the E door, a swollen baluster SUNDIAL, 1974. – At the roadside steps, a small piended rubble building; the old SESSION HOUSE, 1829. – GATEWAY to Manse garden lintelled with re-used C17 stone, perhaps from the former church.

GARGUNNOCK COMMUNITY CENTRE. The former village school, 1858, designed by a Stirling architect, *Robert Logan*. T-plan classrooms fronted by schoolhouse with dated porch.

### DESCRIPTION

Four roads meet at THE SQUARE in the centre of the village. A short row of one- and two-storey houses, probably late C18, lines the N side. TRELAWNEY COTTAGE, low on the corner, pushes out a square bay window; GLENFOYLE has moulded skewputts and applied shutters; McNAIR HOUSE, eaves dormers with shaped bargeboards. On the E, THE WHITE HOUSE, C18, once an inn, now a dwelling with a hip-roofed porch and single-storey wing. On the S, side by side, two three-bay, two-storey roughcast houses, ARRONLEA and EASTER HOUSE, again possibly late C18. A small sandstone FOUNTAIN, sitting in a hedged enclosure with radial slab paving, lies W: below its carved swag of fruit an inscription commemorates Jeanie Millar and records the provision of the village's water supply by her son, the Rev. Robert Stevenson, in 1909.

MAIN STREET climbs W, crossing the Gargunnock Burn by a rubble BRIDGE, *c.* 1775, of two segmental arches. S-facing gable-to-gable houses, mostly roughcast with painted margins, step up the hill. A cottage scale prevails. GARGUNNOCK INN is the exception; a dignified three storeys, plain with a moulded skew-putt surviving on the W gable. The same continuity of C18 townscape is missing across the street where later housing sits back above grassy banks. But some low older cottages remain; among them HAVEN COTTAGE, roughcast three-bay with a gabled porch on tree-trunk columns. At the top of the hill are MANSEFIELD and WOODSIDE, both lug-gabled C19 villas.

LECKIE ROAD has a single building of note: ARDLECKIE, 1995–6 by *Dakers Fleming*, a provocative venture in blindingly white Scotstyle. Three storeys high, it is entered from the S across a neat first-floor bridge. At the NW corner, generously glazed for views to the N, the obligatory round tower wearing a slated sun-hat roof problematically prominent across the carse.

STATION ROAD follows the Burn N. On the l., WATERSIDE, a respectable three-bay house, late C18, with a partially intact cavetto eaves, and then, reached by a narrow rubble bridge over the Burn, the Parish Church Hall (*see* above).

Uphill, SE of The Square, is the Parish Church (*see* above) and beyond the kirkyard, DUNNING HOUSE, *c.* 1750, the former manse. Gabled with rolled skews, it is duly austere, though inevitably compromised by later enlargement. Further E is VIEWFIELD, mid-C19, strongly symmetrical with hip-ended single-storey wings advancing l. and r., but far from dour.

MEIKLEWOOD HOUSE. *See* p. 607.
OLD LECKIE. *See* p. 628.
WATSON HOUSE. *See* p. 792.

## GARGUNNOCK HOUSE                    S 7090
0.85km. E of Gargunnock

The plain but imposing S front, three storeys high and seven bays wide, its central three bays advancing slightly below a pediment, is evidently C18. The walls are harled with stone dressings and the ground-floor entrance no more than a simple three-quarter-columned doorpiece. Three pediment urns flanked by balustraded parapets on an ogival-moulded eaves course provide the only other architectural ornament. In the harled tympanum of the pediment, a single small circular window. But this reserved economical classicism, carried out in 1794, is very much a façade; behind lies a complex aggregation of building begun two centuries earlier.

Gargunnock's oldest structure, a late C16, four-storey, L-plan tower-house, survives as the core of the plan, the main block aligned N–S with a NE wing at r. angles to this. A turnpike stair, in the re-entrant, has gone, demolished in 1794 when a geometric stair replaced it. Although the N and S gables of the main block

are now hidden by later building, the crowstepped gable of the
NE wing is largely unaltered, romantically accented by the sharply
conical roof of a round study corbelled on the SE corner at
second-floor level. Some time during the C17, the L-plan became
a Z-plan, a three-storey W wing being added against the S gable
of the main block. Its re-entrant turnpike stair remains, though
rebuilt, like the upper part of the W wall of the central block, in
the mid C18 when a second W wing of similar height was constructed against the N gable of the old tower-house. A third
turnpike, contained within the SE corner of this wing, afforded
easy circulation between the oldest and newest parts of the house.
In 1794, the SE wing was built, extending the S front, and the
opportunity seized to recast the whole S façade in its present
classical guise. At the same time, the Geometric stair mentioned
above was inserted between the two E wings. Minor single-storey
additions have been made on the NE and between the W wings.
The house has been flatted.

In the INTERIOR many door and window openings have been
blocked or altered as the house grew and room arrangements
changed. Barrel vaults, from which meat-hooks still hang, survive
over the ground floor in both wings of the old L-plan tower.
The original hall, at first-floor level in the N–S arm of the L,
remains a single apartment. Mid-C18 remodelling as a Dining
Room opened it up through the second floor; decorative plaster
ceiling with C-scroll motifs, rose-and-bracket cornice, some
timber panelling and a thin consoled mantelpiece of pine carved
with grapes and rinceau scrolls. Carved timber fireplaces of
Adamesque design in the S entrance hall and in the adjoining
apartment in the late C18 wing. In the Drawing Room above,
which also rises through two storeys, a marble fireplace elegantly
Neo-Classical in detail, and a delicately decorative plaster ceiling.

N of the house, the two-storey, hip-ended S front of the
STABLES, early C19, and NW, a high harled DOOCOT, early C19,
octagonal in plan with a castellated eaves and a centrepiece of
four columns supporting a castellated cornice and ball finial. –
Stone SUNDIAL with a copper dial bearing the arms of Sir
James Campbell of Ardkinglass and dated 1731. – Hip-roofed,
harled LODGE has a Gothic window with interlacing glazing
bars. Square GATEPIERS with obelisk finials. – To the W, the
WALLED GARDEN, trapezoidal in plan with a curved W wall.


6000                  GART HOUSE                      S
                   2km. SE of Callander

Originally The Gart. By *William Burn*, 1833–5. Built 'in the cottage
style'* as a modest gabled mansion beside the Teith, but a
mansion nonetheless, as Burn's surviving plans show. The original
two-storey-and-basement house, entered from the SE beside a
turnpike stair tower, was square in layout with a service wing

* *The Scottish Tourist*, ed. William H. Rhind (9th edn, 1845), 67.

extending NE and canted bays on the three other sides. Following a catastrophic fire, it was enlarged and recast in a muted Baronial idiom, 1903–4. Of this date, the parapeted porch box, the gabled NE wing with its dunce's-hatted E drum and, probably, the raising of the S corner into a square castle-like tower. Continuity in the use of pink conglomerate and ochre sandstone dressings, so typical for Callander, make the changes seamless. Many internal alterations have been made, notably a 90° relocation of Burn's well stair.

## GARTARTAN CASTLE *see* GARTMORE HOUSE

## GARTINCABER

S 6090

### 3.3km. E of Thornhill

A house composed of two gabled L-plan three-storey houses, the N arm of the earlier C18 dwelling clasped in the SW angle of its C19 enlargement. A magnificent avenue of lime trees runs W. Differing floor levels in the two arms of the older house may indicate a C17 origin but this is masked by uniform harling. The E arm, perhaps the oldest section, faces S on to a balustraded terrace overlooking a small walled garden. Entrance with moulded surround in the NE re-entrant. Here, at first floor, a single Venetian window and, above the eaves-height lintels of the second-floor windows, four pediments with relief carving and Latin inscriptions. Similar pediments, though plain, are repeated above the eaves of the three-bay N front of the 1820 block. This is a heightened version of its forerunner, particularly so in the tall *piano nobile*. Walls are harled but pediments, crowsteps, roll-moulded ingoes and other dressed details are in red sandstone. Demolition of a W tower, added 1843, has left the house with no proper point of contact between architecture and landscape. Restoration under way in 1997 may remedy this. In the interior of the older house, the first-floor study retains full-height timber panelling, C18 or earlier; in the sitting room, an Adam-style chimneypiece with urn and palmette frieze. Vestiges of a cornice with rinceau frieze survive in the principal public room of the C19 wing.

Rubble-built STABLES with semi-elliptical arches; *c.* 1825–30. – Gabled entrance LODGE, mid-C19, lavishly endowed with traceried bargeboards.

GARTINCABER TOWER, 0.8km. N. 1790. Two-stage octagonal folly with large pointed-arched windows to the upper storey. Cantilevered external stair. Ruinous.

## GARTMORE

S 5090

A planned village, early C18. A single straight street depends from the estate gates to Gartmore House (*see* below), rises to a small square then falls more sharply SW.

Former FREE CHURCH, The Square. By *William Gale*, 1847;
altered 1893. Five-bay buttressed nave serving as the Village Hall
from 1936. In 1978 (?) the roof was cut down leaving its gable
façade shorn of bellcote and finials. Three lancets and a central
pointed-arched door survive to confront the village with a low-
browed scowl.

GARTMORE PARISH CHURCH. Built as a gabled, oblong kirk
with bellcote and porch in 1790; by 1794 a chapel-of-ease; by 1834
the Parish Church. Much-pointed rubble walls with sandstone
dressings. Gothic wrought ironwork added to the ridge in 1872.
Recast and altered 1904 by *H. & D. Barclay*, when, although
the communion table was placed in the NE end, a central SE
doorway was re-opened. With the removal of galleries, the symmetrically arranged windows, hitherto of differing heights, were
carefully aligned: two pointed openings on the NW, four on the
SE. At the centre of the SE front a new belfry gable and hooded
lintelled window were formed with a small Gothic porch advancing
below. The church's BELL, 1800, was retained.

Plastered interior with flat boarded ceiling, boarded dado
and sanctuary panelling. – At the centre of the NE wall, a semi-
octagonal PULPIT with raised panels and carved putti; behind
it, a decorated panel of three cusped arches under a floral cornice.
– Carved timber FONT with four banded columns as pedestal. –
STAINED GLASS. Above the entrance, a declamatory full-frontal
Christ: 'I am the Way...'. – Flanking this, two mailed figures
bathed in a warm olive glow recall sons of the laird: l., by *Stephen
Adam*, commemorates Major John Sanders Cayzer †1908; r.,
by *Alfred Webster*, in memory of Arthur Bryant Cayzer †1909. –
In the three-lancet SW window Christ oversees scenes of fishing
and fishermen, a memorial to the laird himself, Sir Charles
William Cayzer, first Baronet of Gartmore, and his wife, Lady
Agnes Elizabeth; installed *c.* 1925. – To the l. of the sanctuary,
more marine imagery by *Gordon Webster*, 1963; to Sir August
Bernard Tellefson Cayzer. – Circular ceramic PLAQUE on the
NW wall 'in happy memory' of Sir August's son, Bernard
Cayzer †1891.

A walled GRAVEYARD separates street from church, while behind
lies a small cemetery garden, also walled, in which stands an
obelisk SUNDIAL, mid or late C17. Uniquely, all eight faces of
the collar or capital have bowl-shaped sinkings. – Set into the
NW wall are four inscribed TABLETS commemorating members
of the Cayzer family.

COBLELAND BRIDGE, 1.8km. NNE. 1752; repaired 1779. Rubble
crossing of the River Forth with heavy S abutments. Two
segmental arches, each with voussoirs recessed from wall plane.
Splayed cutwaters.

CUNNINGHAME GRAHAM MEMORIAL. 1937; moved here from
Ardoch, Dunbartonshire, 1978. A stand of random whin wall
commemorating the author, traveller, horseman and 'patriotic
Scot' Robert Bontine Cunninghame Graham (1852–1936), the
last Graham laird of Gartmore. Portrait head in circular bronze
relief by *Alexander Proudfoot* sits between two stone inserts

inscribed ARGENTINA and URUGUAY respectively. Above the head a verse of poetry by the eponymous Don Roberto.

## DESCRIPTION

A single street of side-by-side houses. The evident rigour of the plan implies some measure of architectural control; but there is none. Plot sizes may be more or less consistent but little else. An underlying three-bay order, perhaps; the predominance of white walls; here and there, the recurring theme of gabled timber porches accented with finials. Yet variety animates and energizes the street just as landscape invigorates its hilltop geometry. Only THE SQUARE, meanly defined and bleeding space, seems to break the continuity of enclosure.

## GARTMORE HOUSE    S 5090
### 0.8km. ENE of Gartmore

An overgrown house, overcome by vulgar hubris, which began conventionally as a restrained two-storey-and-basement Georgian mansion, pedimented at the centre of the NW front above Venetian windows. *William Adam* prepared a design, *c.* 1740–5, for Nicol Graham which appeared as Plate 83 in *Vitruvius Scoticus* but it is unclear whether he carried out the project. Though stylistically akin, the house built differed somewhat in plan and elevation from that published.

In 1779–80, *John Baxter Jun.* made major alterations: these probably included the symmetrical addition of SW and NE wings which, being of matching height, of considerable breadth and given semi-octagonal projections on the SE façade, annulled restraint and balance in the principal elevations. Worse followed in 1901–2 when, removing everything but the outside walls, *David Barclay* entirely reconstructed the house for Sir Charles Cayzer who had purchased the estate from Robert Bontine Cunningham Graham in 1900. Steeply pitched French roofs, punctuated by pedimented dormers, some with vaguely Art Nouveau ornament, now appear above the plain C18 parapets. Single-storey flat-roofed flanking wings spread out from the NW front, at the centre of which rises a three-storey frontispiece tower, elaborated in a manner both classical and Baronial. Above the door, the motto CAUTE SED IMPAVIDE ('cautiously but fearlessly'), only the latter half of which seems a fitting comment on such architectural inflation. Of the C18 only the simplicity of lintelled or round-arched window openings remained, their dressed stone margins set against roughcast walls. Nor was ambition yet satisfied, for in 1910, *Thoms & Wilkie* of Dundee proposed raising the outer wings from one to four storeys to accommodate additional bed-rooms. Their building rises no higher than the parapet of the original house. Part of this work includes extensions of similar height set into the S and E re-entrants between these wings and the main block. In the former, below the upper floor, a two-storey round-arched loggia, balconied at first floor, was created.

Inside, timber-panelled walls and low-relief plastered ceilings from the 1901–2 rebuilding. The long central ENTRANCE HALL is panelled to door height in dark-stained oak. Classical detail predominates; broken Baroque pediments over doorways framed by lugged architraves; Mannerist forms in the staircase balustrades and newel posts. Oak-panelled chimneypiece and overmantel with fireplace roll-and-hollow-moulded surround of green-veined marble. Jacobean ceiling. Art Nouveau STAINED GLASS in vestibule screen.

Terraced lawns fall gently SE, defined by long balustrading similar to that forming the parapets of the outer wings flanking the opposite side of the house. There is a WALLED GARDEN, mid-C18, built with masonry taken from nearby Gartartan Castle (*see* below), including an armorial panel dated 1686 over the S gate. – ESTATE GATES, axially aligned at NE end of the village main street. 1790. High, crudely crenellated wall with semi-circular archway. Harled with stone dressings. A classical conceit with quadrant flanks, unconvincingly disguised by cusped arches, quatrefoil openings and quatrefoil cluster shafts.

GARTARTAN CASTLE (Gartavartane Castle), 0.3km. NE of Gartmore House. Late C16 or early C17. Ruinous Z-plan tower-house. Of the two diagonally opposed round towers the E, standing over two storeys, has a corbelled staircase link at second floor. Vaulted basement. Some gun-loops and lintelled openings.

GARTARTAN LODGE, on A81. 1902, by *David Barclay*. A 'small baronial effort'[*] with a two-storey drum tower on the N side of the estate gateway.

MOATED HOMESTEAD, Peel of Gartfarran, 2.3km. SE. Possibly C13. 'One of the best-preserved homestead moats in Scotland'[‡]. Trapezoidal plan bounded by a low inner bank and flat-bottomed ditch, still easily discernible. W entrance over causeway.

<sub>5080</sub>                GARTNESS                          S

In a loop bend of the Endrick Water, the site of several ancient mills. At the Pot of Gartness, a stepping waterfall where tiered rock strata cross the river, there are vestiges of a meal mill with stones dated 1574 and 1684 and, on the N bank, a woollen mill and mill house. A short distance down-river on the r. bank was Gartness Castle, C16, once occupied by John Napier of Merchiston, the inventor of logarithms. Nothing remains. At Gartness Bridge, another woollen mill, C19, and a row of millworkers' cottages, now with varied dormers.

DALNAIR FARM, 1km. SW. Built as a manse, 1682. A three-bay, gabled T-plan house of three storeys, now much altered. Only

* Charles McKean, *Stirling and the Trossachs* (1985), 118.
‡ RCAHMS, *Stirlingshire*, i (1963), 178.

the painted rubble N front, from the centre of which a short full-height entrance wing projects, preserves something of its C17 character: the lintelled doorway, with in-and-out jambstones and voussoirs, sits to the r.; above it an empty recess with moulded frame, and above that, located centrally below the crowstepped gable, a second-floor window. Most other windows and eaves dormers have been altered, W and E gables have lost their crow-stepping and the S front has been rendered. A single-storey lean-to addition overlaps the W end of the N front, linking with C18 and C19 stone and brick outbuildings. Little survives inside. A turnpike stair fills the projecting N wing. The original kitchen fireplace, recessed into the E gable, has a wide segmental arch of damaged sandstone voussoirs.

DRUMQUHASSLE, 1.8km. W. 1839. A mildly Gothic red sand-stone house extended W *c.* 1930 when old and new were coated in roughcast. Sandstone outbuildings NE, much altered. – In the garden a SUNDIAL, dated 1710; red sandstone Roman Doric column supporting a table with copper plate and gnomon and inscribed with the name William Govane of Drumquhassle. – GATEPIERS with fir cone ornament also in garden.

DOOCOT, 0.25km. N of Drumquhassle. Dated 1711. Red sandstone square with monopitch slated roof. Ledges at 'first floor' S and on three walls at eaves-cornice height. Central S door with three arched openings for birds above the ledge. Crowstepped gables rise from scrolled skewputts to chimney-like upstands returning into the rear N wall, the corniced coping stone ornamented with five stone balls. Inside, brick gridding on three walls.

KILLEARN BRIDGE, 1.1km. NE. C19. Red sandstone crossing of the River Endrick in two high semicircular arches with central blunted cutwater.

# GARTOCHARN

A leafy roadside village.

GARTOCHARN CHURCH. Originally Kilmaronock United Free Church. Arts and Crafts Gothic by *H. E. Clifford*, 1911–12; decent but undistinguished. A step-gabled SE front in snecked red sand-stone; between buttresses a pointed arch embraces three narrow cusped lights over the hooded doorway. Single cusped lights repeat down the roughcast flanks. Gables hint at transepts.

Arch-braced trusses in stained oak define the six-bay interior. Shallow recesses at chancel and transepts. Raked floor. Charac-teristically Clifford are the shield motifs applied to the trusses and the castellated treatment of dado panelling. – In the vestibule, a white marble TABLET to the Rev. James Dunlop †1910: short fluted Composite pilasters support a pediment block with quatrefoil flower-heads on each side of a crown.

GARTOCHARN PRIMARY SCHOOL. By *Lane, Bremner & Garnett*, 1966–7. Neat monopitches and glazed classroom walls.

VILLAGE HALL, beside Gartocharn Church. By *Maclachlan Monaghan*, 1999–2000. A wide-based, slated, pyramid roof,

topped by an apex ventilator, masters the square plan. To the
SE, where the glazed vestibule is raised above steps and ramps
and set between walls of red sandstone ashlar, the building
appears to be single-storeyed. But the site falls to the NW allowing stretches of glazing at two levels: above, these open to cantilevered steel balconies; below, from the hall, to a paved area at
the rear.

Former VILLAGE SCHOOL, School Road. Dated 1876; extended
c. 1901. Red sandstone classrooms now offices. In the gabled
porch, a shouldered-arched doorway with roll-moulded jambs.

DESCRIPTION. A few dwellings date from the mid C19 or earlier.
The former T-plan MANSE, probably built c. 1840 and only later
acquired by the United Free Church, is white, three-bay and
two-storey, with a gabled porch and a lower piended wing to
the l. CLIFTON, dated 1851, is three-bay, too, but single-storey.
BRIDGEND COTTAGE, mid-C19, is similar but with gableted
dormers. Another three-bay cottage in whitewashed rubble,
CHIMES (originally known as Bridgend), has lost its austerity
in an attractive jumble of later piend-roofed additions. By contrast, several late Victorian villas are less rural, more suburban,
built in the red sandstone masonry so familiar in the Vale of
Leven. In 1937–9 an attempt was made to recapture the vernacular when the County Architect *Joseph Weekes* designed
CAMBUSMOON TERRACE on School Road, a white roughcast
range laid out to a U-plan with quarter-round corners and pends
in the re-entrants.

DUNCRYNE HOUSE, 0.7km. SE. Mid-C19 cottage transformed
in an Arts and Crafts enlargement by *John A. Campbell*, 1903.
Among the revitalizing ingredients are bargeboarded gables, half-
timbering, a canted oriel carried on brackets and a verandah
with carved wooden posts.

TULLOCHAN, 1km. W. Early C19. Standard three-bay, two-storey
farmhouse in painted rubble. Two timber dormers added in
respectful symmetry. A still earlier farmhouse with lower flanking wings is incorporated as the S range of the STEADING, which
has a quadrangular cattle-court and lean-to brick piggeries.

ASHFIELD HOUSE. *See* p. 185.
WESTERTON HOUSE. *See* p. 792.

ASHFIELD HOUSE. *See* p. 185.
WESTERTON HOUSE. *See* p. 792.

# GARTUR
1.4km. W. of Cambusbarron

Two-storey-and-basement ashlar mansion, early C19, perhaps by
*David Hamilton*. Dignified by austere detail: stringcoursing, eaves
cornice and a solid parapet fluted over the shallow projection of
end and centre bays. A wide flyover stair leads to a columned
entrance flanked by narrow windows. A fine semicircular fanlight depresses the door height. Above this, matching the width
of the stepped approach, is a bracketed ironwork balcony. The
house, one room deep, fronts a late C17, skew-gabled, harled
dwelling, now in ruins. – Hip-roofed, courtyard STABLES,

0.1km. E, in disrepair; symmetrical W front with central round-arched entry and blind round-arches in the wings. – LODGE with a four-columned Roman Doric portico at the entrance to the drive.

## GLENOCHIL
C *8090*

Small late C20 village composed of harled two-storey monopitch-roofed houses. It stands beside the former coal mine which opened in 1952 but closed soon after, the surface buildings subsequently converted to a prison.

H.M. PRISON AND DETENTION CENTRE. The earliest part of the complex includes the former Glenochil Mine's pithead baths, canteen and medical room, by the *National Coal Board Divisional Welfare Department*, 1957. These were converted to a detention centre in 1966. Young Offenders Institution built, 1973.

KING O'MUIRS, 0.4km. E. Early C19 two-storey piend-roofed farmhouse, a three-light first-floor window at the bowed centre of its three-bay front.

## GLORAT HOUSE
ED *6070*
### 1.5km. NW of Milton of Campsie

Unexciting Baronial house of 1869, enlivened by the conical-roofed tower, added in 1879, whose large cannon spouts and heraldic panel provide a welcome display of ostentation.

## GRANGEMOUTH
F *9080*

Surprisingly spacious and bosky town lying between the huge works of the chemical and oil-related industries which have been established here since 1914. The town owes its origin to the construction of the Forth and Clyde Canal, begun in 1768. Within ten years Sir Lawrence Dundas, owner of the Kerse estate, had laid out the village of Grangemouth beside the sea lock at the canal's E end. The village developed as a port during the C19 and became a burgh in 1872. Soon after this event what was effectively a new town was begun to the SE of the old village and separated from it by the railway line. This new town constitutes the commercial and civic centre of the present-day Grangemouth although housing has spread far to its S during the later C20. The original C18 village has been all but wiped out.

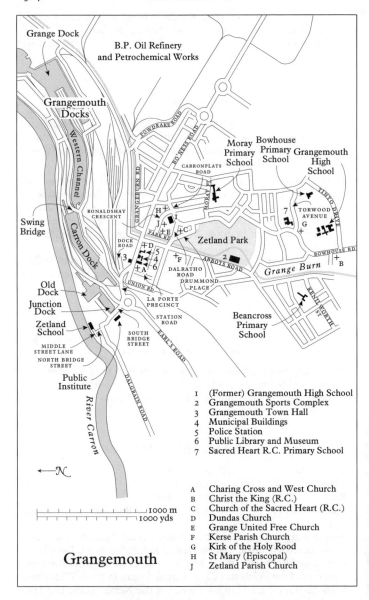

Grange Dock

B.P. Oil Refinery
and Petrochemical Works

Grangemouth
Docks

Western Channel

POWDRAKE ROAD

BO'NESS ROAD

GRANGEBURN RD

CARRONFLATS
ROAD

Moray
Primary
School

Bowhouse
Primary
School

Grangemouth
High
School

TINTO DRIVE

7    TORWOOD
AVENUE
G

RONALDSHAY
CRESCENT

Swing
Bridge

Carron Dock

H

I

J

E

C

PARK RD

Zetland Park

BOWHOUSE RD

DOCK
ROAD

D

5
4
6

A

3

F

ABBOTS ROAD

2

Grange Burn

B

DALRATHO
ROAD

Old
Dock

Junction
Dock

Zetland
School

UNION RD

DRUMMOND
PLACE

LA PORTE
PRECINCT

STATION
ROAD

SOUTH
BRIDGE
STREET

EARL'S ROAD

Beancross
Primary
School

KENILWORTH

KING ST

MIDDLE
STREET LANE

NORTH BRIDGE
STREET

Public
Institute

River Carron

DALGRAIN ROAD

←N

1000 m
1000 yds

Grangemouth

1   (Former) Grangemouth High School
2   Grangemouth Sports Complex
3   Grangemouth Town Hall
4   Municipal Buildings
5   Police Station
6   Public Library and Museum
7   Sacred Heart R.C. Primary School

A   Charing Cross and West Church
B   Christ the King (R.C.)
C   Church of the Sacred Heart (R.C.)
D   Dundas Church
E   Grange United Free Church
F   Kerse Parish Church
G   Kirk of the Holy Rood
H   St Mary (Episcopal)
J   Zetland Parish Church

## CHURCHES

CHARING CROSS AND WEST CHURCH, Bo'ness Road. Originally Zetland Free Church. By *J. McKissack & W. G. Rowan*,
1882–4. First Pointed, built of buff-coloured stugged masonry
with polished ashlar dressings. Fronting the street, the tall N
gable of the nave gripped by gableted corner buttresses with

octagonal turret finials. In the gable, three small hoodmoulded lancets which light the vestibule. Above, another three windows but much larger and linked and flanked by very narrow blind arches, all under continuous hoodmoulding. The central of these three windows is taller than the others and of two lights under a cinquefoiled head. The gable is flanked by transepts, each containing a broad doorway under a three-light window. Buttressed side elevations pierced by tall lancet windows.

Inside, narrow E and W aisles marked off by pointed arcades, their foliage-capitalled cast iron columns made by *M. Cockburn & Co.* of Falkirk. Over the nave, a polygonal wagon roof crossed by ribs. At the S end, a plain Gothic PULPIT with a huge ORGAN (by *Abbot & Smith*, 1902) behind. – STAINED GLASS of 1884. In the three-light S window, three roundels containing heads emblematic of Faith, Hope and Charity. – Floral designs in the screen between the vestibule and the nave.

CHRIST THE KING (R.C.), Bowhouse Road. By *Wilson & Wilson*, 1975. Church and a broader (W) hall under a single shallow double-pitch concrete-tiled roof, its S slope longer than the N; small triangular gablets.

Inside the church, zigzag windows in the N wall. The E wall behind the altar is of exposed grey brickwork.

CHURCH OF THE SACRED HEART (R.C.), Drummond Place and Dalratho Road. Early Christian, by *Archibald Macpherson*, 1925–7, the walls of stugged masonry, the roof now covered with concrete tiles. Small round-arched windows. At the W gable, a semi-octagonal portico, its minimally cusped arches springing from octagonal piers with simplified capitals. The roof of the portico is stepped to suggest a stair leading up to a canopied niche containing a statue of the Sacred Heart.

DUNDAS CHURCH, Bo'ness Road. Originally Dundas United Presbyterian Church. 1894, by *John Burnet, Son & Campbell*, and one of several churches designed by that firm between 1887 and 1900 which combine English village Arts and Crafts elements with Gothic and powerful Romanesque. Nave with a tower at its N end and a double-pitch roofed aisle on the W side. Projecting from the NW inner angle of the tower and aisle, a porch. SW hall range. The walls are of flush-pointed rubble: bracketed broad eaves. At the nave and aisle, lancet windows, mostly paired. At the half-timbered and bargeboarded W gable of the porch, a large rectangular bay window which contains the entrance. Along the N side of the hall range, a glazed corridor brought to a halt by the semi-octagonal projection of the vestry at the W end. The tower is powerful. Square but with chamfered corners. Round-arched windows. More roundheaded arches at the huge belfry openings, here with cushion-capitalled nook-shafts.

INTERIOR. From the vestibule at the E end of the porch, a door into the tower, intended to house a gallery of which only the rounded stone corbels on the E and W walls were erected. The S side of the tower opens through a large stone pointed arch into the nave. On the nave's W side, a three-bay arcade into the aisle, its roundheaded arches carried on moulded stone pillars without capitals. Wooden coomb roofs throughout, those of the nave and aisle with spindly braces and rafters supported on corbels. The three lights of the nave's s window are framed by jerky Gothic arcading, old-fashionedly fussy in the context. This end was reordered as a sanctuary in 1939 when sub-Lorimerian panelling was erected on the s wall. – The PULPIT of 1894 stands to the E side of the sanctuary. – Plain boxy pine PEWS of 1894. – Also of 1894 the ORGAN by *J. &A. Mirrlees* at the s end of the aisle. – STAINED GLASS. In the nave's s window, characteristic glass (the Agony in the Garden, Crucifixion, and Ascension) by *Douglas Strachan*, 1923. – Also by Strachan and of 1923 is a small window (St Cecilia) in the s end of the aisle. – At the aisle's N end, in the w wall, a strongly coloured window (Our Lord) by *William Wilson*, 1938.

GRANGE UNITED FREE CHURCH, corner of Park Road and Ronaldshay Crescent. Now housing (STRATHEARN COURT). Sizeable but plain lanceted Gothic, by *John B. Wilson*, 1902–3. The dominant impression is of redness, the colour of the hammer-dressed masonry, of the tiled ridge on the slated roof of the nave, and of the Rosemary tiles on the steep pyramid roof over the NW tower. Hall at the s end.

KERSE PARISH CHURCH, Abbots Road. By *John P. Goodsir*, 1897–9. Simple Gothic, with plain lancet windows along the sturdily buttressed sides. In the E gable of the nave and the N and s gables of the transepts at the w end, windows of three stepped openings; the centre openings are two-light, those of the nave and N transept with cusped loop tracery in their heads, that of the s transept with a quatrefoil. Octagonal flèche on the roof.

Hall to the w by *Wilson & Tait*, 1929–30. Loop tracery in the head of its E window. The Tudorish entrance is contained in the parapeted link to the N transept.

INTERIOR. Over the nave, an open roof combining hammer-beams and kingposts. Depressed arch into the chancel which is covered by a plaster ceiling; routine Gothic panelling on the chancel walls. – PEWS and PULPIT (to l. of the chancel arch) of 1898–9. In the chancel, an oak COMMUNION TABLE of 1921. – ORGAN by *J. J. Binns*, 1915, divided between the transepts, the cases of elaborate late Gothic character. – STAINED GLASS all by *William Wilson* and typically colourful. The four round lights in the chancel (Symbols of the Evangelists) are of 1951, the four-light E window (Our Lord as the Good Shepherd and the Risen Lord, flanked by Moses and St Columba) of 1954.

KIRK OF THE HOLY ROOD, Bowhouse Road. By *Wilson & Wilson*, 1961–3. Steep double-pitch slated roof above dry-dashed walls. Flat-roofed HALLS to the N. Inside the church, colourful semi-abstract STAINED GLASS in the E window.

ST MARY (Episcopal), corner of Ronaldshay Crescent and Carronflats Road. Simplest Early Christian, by *J. Maxton Craig*, 1937–8, the walls of crazy-paved rubble (buff-coloured weathering to grey), the roof slated. Five-bay nave and a lower two-bay chancel at the N (liturgical E) end. Round-arched windows, their surrounds chamfered; the side windows of the chancel and the entrance doorway are double-chamfered. In the chancel gable, a roundheaded window containing three round-arched lights.

The interior is plastered except for the ashlar roundheaded chancel arch. – Luridly painted HANGING ROOD of *c.* 1950, with figures of Our Lady and St John flanking the crucifix. – STAINED GLASS. Three-light E window (the Madonna and Child, with St Leonard and St Hedwig) of 1938. Stylized and effectively coloured with blues predominant. – W window (Grangemouth harbour and industry), again strongly coloured but much closer to abstraction, by *Gordon W. Stevens*, 1962.

ZETLAND PARISH CHURCH, Ronaldshay Crescent. Originally Grangemouth Parish Church. By *Wilson & Tait*, 1910–11. Scots late Gothic of a not unambitious sort, the main elevations to the street of stugged ashlar (the buff colour weathered to grey), the others of rubble. Buttressed nave and S aisle. At the W end, a N tower and S transept. At the E end, N and S transepts, a short low chancel, and a plain Gothic hall.

Cusped loop tracery in the heads of the nave windows. At the W gable, a pair of two-light windows separated by a buttress surmounted by a canopied empty image niche. The gable windows of the E end's transepts are each of three lights with an elaborate foiled dagger in the head. The battlemented NW tower has angle buttresses except at the NE corner where there is an octagonal stair turret, a small crocketed spire rising within its battlement. In the N face of the tower, the principal entrance with foliage-capitalled nook-shafts. Above, at each face, a belfry opening of two cusped arches. Inside, walls clad in grey ashlar; boarded roofs, a pointed tunnel vault over the nave, a wagon roof at the chancel. Gallery over the W bay of the nave. E of this, a three-bay arcade into the S aisle, the pointed arches carried on octagonal piers with corniced bulbous capitals. Tall pointed arches into the transepts and short chancel. In the E wall of the S transept, a blind arch. The aisle windows are framed by cusped arcading, the columns standing on the window sills. Decent but routine FURNISHINGS, the communion table placed in the chancel. – STAINED GLASS. In the four-light E window, strongly coloured gently modernistic glass (the Nativity, David, Our Lord in Glory) by *Joseph E. Nuttgens*, *c.* 1950. – In the S aisle, a three-light window with small-scale depictions of the Acts of Mercy, by *Gordon Webster*, 1966, the realism characteristically stylized. – ORGAN by *Henry Willis & Sons*, 1890. Originally in St George's Presbyterian Church, Brondesbury (London), it was rebuilt here by *N. P. Mander Ltd.*, 1983.

## PARK

ZETLAND PARK, Park Road. Extensive area laid out by *A. & W. Black* in 1882, extended 1920s and 1953. At the N entrance, two pairs of ashlar GATEPIERS with Doric friezes and large urn finials. These form part of the WAR MEMORIAL by *John J. Burnet* 43 of *John Burnet, Son & Dick*, 1922–3. Its powerful centrepiece is an ashlar cenotaph surmounted by the stylized sculpture (by *Alexander Proudfoot*) of the British lion killing the eagle of German militarism. – To the S, a cast iron FOUNTAIN of 1882 in the form of a lotus, the stem surrounded by kneeling fish-tailed angels. – Further S, a TENNIS AND BOWLS PAVILION by *J. C. Wallace*, the Burgh Engineer, 1926, built of red brick with a Rosemary tiled roof. At the N corners, octagonal turrets whose weathervanes depict a bowler and a tennis player.

## PUBLIC BUILDINGS

BEANCROSS PRIMARY SCHOOL, Kenilworth Street. By the Stirling County Architect, *A. J. Smith*, 1956–8. Curtain walls and shallow-pitched ribbed copper roofs.

BOWHOUSE PRIMARY SCHOOL, Tinto Drive. By the Stirling County Architect, *A. J. Smith*, 1966. Curtain walls and rendered brickwork under flat roofs.

Former GRANGEMOUTH HIGH SCHOOL, Carronflats Road. Now housing (BRYDEN COURT). By *Wilson & Tait*, 1908–9. Renaissance, the fifteen-bay façade faced with polished red sandstone ashlar. The channelling of the ground-floor masonry is carried up to frame the recessed walling of the slightly advanced and pedimented three-bay ends whose central windows are flanked by attached and paired Ionic columns. The centrepiece, also of three bays, is slightly advanced under a balustrade; at the centre of the balustrade, a plinth topped by a figure of Education. At each of the segmental-pedimented side elevations, an open-pedimented aedicule containing a round-arched entrance, one for boys, the other for girls, the keystone carved with the head of a child of the appropriate sex.

GRANGEMOUTH HIGH SCHOOL, Tinto Drive. By the Stirling County Architect, *A. J. Smith*, 1971. A curtain-walled mixture of glass, render and brick.

GRANGEMOUTH SPORTS COMPLEX, Abbots Road. By *Wilson & Wilson*, 1975. Like an industrial building but without panache.

GRANGEMOUTH TOWN HALL, Bo'ness Road. Classical, by *A. & W. Black*, 1884–5. Two tall storeys, the polished ashlar stonework of the front channelled at the ground floor. At the recessed centre, the entrance flanked by Ionic columns with shafts of polished granite and volutes joined by swags. The columns support a balustraded balcony under the console-corniced first-floor window. More consoled cornices over the windows at the first floor of the outer bays where each pair is framed by Ionic pilasters. Overall balustrade.

At the ashlar-faced W elevation of the front block, a console-corniced first-floor window flanked by niches. Both this and the plain E side are partly overlaid by additions by *Wilson & Wilson*, 1938.

MORAY PRIMARY SCHOOL, Moray Place. By the Stirling County Architect, *A. J. Smith*, 1955–8, in the lightweight-looking Festival of Britain manner, with a clock tower.

MUNICIPAL BUILDINGS, Bo'ness Road. Authoritarian stripped Neo-Georgian, by *Wilson & Tait*, 1936–7. Inside, STAINED GLASS stair window of 1937, displaying the burgh arms above a shipping scene.

POLICE STATION, Bo'ness Road. Modern-traditional, by the Stirling County Architect, *A. J. Smith*, 1959–61.

PUBLIC INSTITUTE, South Bridge Street. Disused. Built in 1876–7. Tall two-storey block, the walling of stugged ashlar. Five-bay front, its symmetry disturbed by having a round-arched and keystoned door at the r. bay as well as one at the centre. The centre itself is slightly advanced and carried up as a tower, the upper stages intaken, finished with an iron-crested French pavilion roof. NW extension of the 1920s, its stripped classicism hinting at Art Deco.

PUBLIC LIBRARY AND MUSEUM, Bo'ness Road. Renaissance, by *A. & W. Black*, 1888–9. Two tall storeys, the five-bay front's polished ashlar channelled at the ground floor. At each of the advanced ends, a door set between skinny Composite pilasters. Roundheaded first-floor windows with Ionic pilastered jambs and carved foliage in the spandrels. Corinthian pilasters between the three centre windows. The end bays are framed by Corinthian columned aedicules, their segmental pediments carved with large rosettes in foliaged frames. Set back at the w end, an addition by *Wilson & Tait*,* 1937–9, with a *moderne* door.

SACRED HEART R.C. PRIMARY SCHOOL, Torwood Avenue. By the Stirling County Architect, *A. J. Smith*, 1960–2. Flat-roofed classroom block; over the hall, a very shallowly pitched roof. N additions of 1968, also by *Smith*.

ZETLAND SCHOOL, Middle Street Lane. Now in other use and rather altered. By *A. N. Malcolm*, 1912–13. One tall storey, built of stugged masonry. Bracketed eaves broken by the windows which rise into piended dormerheads.

## DOCKS

The mouth of the River Carron is a natural haven off the Firth of Forth but its development as a man-made harbour followed the opening of the Forth & Clyde Canal in 1775. At the canal's E end was a basin joined by a cutting to the mouth of the Grange Burn which discharged into the Carron. Two years later, at the same time as he laid out the planned village of Grangemouth on either side of the canal basin, Sir Lawrence Dundas constructed a quay. At about the same time two basins for imported timber were formed opening off the s side of the canal.

The first major development of Grangemouth Harbour as more than an adjunct to the Forth & Clyde Canal came in 1838 –43 to designs by *J. B. Macneill*. In this scheme the Grange Burn was diverted to the E and the River Carron deepened. At the same time the E end of the existing timber basins was enlarged and joined by a short cutting to a new wet dock (now

* The firm's name changed to *Wilson & Wilson* during construction.

the OLD DOCK) constructed E of the village and with its own
entrance from the Carron E of the old canal entrance. In 1855–9
a second wet dock (the JUNCTION DOCK) was formed by
enlarging the cutting which joined the Old Dock to the timber
basins. Much more ambitious was the next development in
1877–83, executed for the Caledonian Railway Co. which had
recently acquired the Forth & Clyde Canal. This was designed
by *Blyth & Cunningham* who provided the CARRON DOCK, a
wet dock of 4ha. with a timber basin of 3.2ha. at its SW end joined
by a cutting or short canal to the SE corner of the Old Dock.
The entrance from the River Carron to the new dock was placed
at the very mouth of the river, 0.5km. E of the previous entrance.

The last major development of the docks and by far the most
extensive and expensive, costing *c.* £1,500,000, was carried out
by *John Wolfe Barry* in 1898–1906. This more than doubled the
size of the docks which were extended far beyond the mouth of
the River Carron, sheltered from the mouth of the Firth of
Forth by a massive scheme of land reclamation which created a
new promontory jutting into the firth. At the centre of the
extension is the GRANGE DOCK, linked by the new WESTERN
CHANNEL to the Carron Dock; at the new dock's E end, the
EASTERN CHANNEL leading to the Y-shaped entrance from the
Forth which is guarded by sea locks. A postscript to this work
was added in 1966 when the Eastern Channel was enlarged to
almost twice its original width and a new oil jetty constructed.

The size of the docks is impressive, their appearance utilitarian.
Ashlar facing at the Old Dock and Junction Dock, the rest
almost all of concrete. At the SE end of the Old Dock, a SWING
BRIDGE by *Crouch & Hogg*, 1936.


### DESCRIPTION

DALGRAIN ROAD, until bypassed to the S in the late C20, was the
W approach to Grangemouth. At its E end, North Bridge Street
leads NW to the former Zetland School (*see* Public Buildings,
above) in MIDDLE STREET LANE. SOUTH BRIDGE STREET
leads SE. On its SW side, overlooking Junction Dock (*see* Docks,
above), is THE QUEEN'S HOTEL. Front block of *c.* 1865 faced
with white-painted broached ashlar. Georgian survival but with
two-light windows and a bracketed cornice under the low parapet. The rendered rear wing is made up of various humble
buildings, probably late Georgian. Then the Public Institute
(*see* Public Buildings, above).

STATION ROAD leads towards the present town centre across the
line of the railway. On the road's NE side, at the corner of Dock
Road, a single-storey and basement classical building by *Wilson
& Tait*, 1912, its shopfront exuberantly Edwardian in character.
Then the town centre begins with ALEXANDRA HOUSE of
1913–14, also by *Wilson & Tait*, a long two-storey block with
ground-floor shops and an overall balustrade. Seven-bay centrepiece, its first-floor windows with lugged architraves and aprons.
At the centrepiece's end and centre bays are entrances set in

channelled masonry and, at the upper floor, aedicules, the outer ones with orderless panelled pilasters and segmental pediments, the central aedicule with Ionic pilasters and an open triangular pediment. The scale and early C20 classical manner continue at Nos. 2–10, again by *Wilson & Tait*, 1912–13. Five bays, the channelled rustication of the ground-floor masonry carried up at the upper floor of the slightly advanced ends. At the three centre bays, round-arched windows. At the first floor, the centre bay is marked off by pilasters, Ionic but with upside-down volutes, supporting an open pediment. On the SW side of Station Road, at the V-junction with Union Road and looking down Bo'ness Road, is the former COMMERCIAL BANK OF SCOTLAND of 1909–11. Tall single-storey block of three bays by three, faced with lightly tooled diagonally broached ashlar. At the E front, pedimented outer windows flank the boldly projecting centrepiece. This contains the entrance set in a Roman Doric pilastered aedicule, the spandrels of the round-arched doorway carved with reliefs of thistles, the keystone with a lion's head. The centrepiece rises above the eaves as a low square tower roofed with a steep copper dome surmounted by a ship weathervane. On each elevation of the ball-finialled upper stage, a clock face framed by a Roman Doric pilastered and pedimented aedicule. Pilastered side elevations, their centres topped by steep pediments. In the outer bays of the N side, panels instead of windows. The E panel is carved with the large coat of arms of the Commercial Bank.

On the S side of UNION ROAD, opposite the former Commercial Bank, Nos. 4–12 (CHARING CROSS), an Edwardian commercial Queen Anne block by *John P. Goodsir*, 1910, with shallow canted oriel windows, Dutch gablets rising behind their parapets. To the E, on the N corner of the La Porte Precinct, a pair of early C20 Georgian survival two-storey blocks (No. 2 Union Road by *Wilson & Tait*, 1910, and No. 2 Bo'ness Road) both with quadrant corners and buckle-quoined architraves to the first-floor windows.

LA PORTE PRECINCT, Grangemouth's commercial centre, is a redevelopment begun in 1967. Existing buildings were retained at its N end. On the W side, No. 12 of *c.* 1900, with pulvinated friezes over the first-floor windows and pediments (the outer segmental, the centre triangular) on top of the wallhead's mutuled cornice. To its S, the former BRITISH LINEN COMPANY BANK (Nos. 18–20) of 1905, by *Peddie & Washington Browne* in characteristic François I–Jacobean manner. Tall two-storey front of polished red sandstone ashlar. The first floor is of a symmetrical three bays with mullioned and transomed windows (four-light in the outer bays, two-light at the centre). Wallhead balustrade broken by obelisk-finialled shaped gablets above the outer bays. The ground floor is also of three bays but not quite symmetrical. Five-light mullioned and transomed window in the l. bay. In the r., a broader window-cum-entrance of five compartments. Its two l. compartments are occupied by a mullioned and transomed window. In the centre compartment, the roundheaded bank entrance placed between fluted pilasters. The r. two compartments are filled by the door to the agent's house under a two-light rectangular fanlight. The shopping centre to the N (by *Wheeler & Sproson*, 1967) is composed of flat-roofed two-storey blocks either side of the pedestrianized street.

BO'NESS ROAD starts at the W with a sense of civic importance. On the N side, the former EMPIRE ELECTRIC CINEMA of 1913. Utilitarian rendered auditorium, its bulk disguised by the lower vestibule block across its front. This is of red brick with buff-coloured sandstone dressings and is treated in a free C17 Scots manner. Tall ogee-roofed and Composite-pilastered corner pavilions. Stretched between them, a single-storey parapeted range. The central feature, inspired by monuments in Greyfriars Churchyard, Edinburgh, consists of a pilastered entrance under a square tablet flanked by scrolls and topped by an obelisk-finialled swan-neck pediment, flanked by more obelisks. W of the cinema, the Grangemouth Town Hall (*see* Public Buildings, above). Opposite, on the S side of Bo'ness Road, is Charing Cross and West Parish Church (*see* Churches, above) followed by the Public Library and Museum, the Municipal Chambers and the Police Station (*see* Public Buildings, above). To their E, Dundas Church (*see* Churches, above).

ABBOTS ROAD and PARK ROAD are the names of the W and E sides (mostly occupied by small villas of *c.* 1900) of a single broad street whose centre is occupied by an avenue flanking the Grange Burn, its line artificially straightened in 1838–43. In Park Road, on the S corner of Ronaldshay Crescent, the former Grange United Free Church and, just to its E, Zetland Park Church (*see* Churches, above). At the S end of the street, the entrance to Zetland Park (*see* Park, above). Abbots Road continues further to the S, Kerse Parish Church (*see* Churches, above) on its W side, the Grangemouth Sports Complex (*see* Public Buildings, above) on its E. Leading E from the end of Park Road is DALRATHO ROAD. On its N corner with Drummond Place, the Church of the Sacred Heart and, further E, at the beginning of CARRONFLATS ROAD, the former Grangemouth High School followed by St Mary's Church (*see* Churches and Public Buildings, above).

## VILLAS

BO'NESS ROAD. No. 59 is a late C19 single-storey and attic house. Three-bay front of stugged ashlar, the corniced doorpiece with skinny fluted Doric columns; it is flanked by hoodmoulded windows, their mullions now missing. Iron-crested parapet and rope-moulded club skewputts. Two canted dormer windows and a small roundheaded central dormer. – No. 140 is English picturesque of *c.* 1900. Harled and half-timbered, with a red Rosemary tiled roof. Part of the upper floor is jettied. – MAHRATTA VILLA (No. 173), another single-storey and attic house of the late C19. Mansard roof and over the advanced centre a ridiculous Frenchy truncated spire topped by iron cresting. – AVONDHU (No. 168) is by *James M. MacLaren*, 1878. Scottish manorial of a free Jacobean character. Projecting from the front, a large full-height bow window under a conical spire. Plenty of restrained relief decoration. Ball-finialled gatepiers carved with swags. – AVON HALL (No. 170) also by *James M. MacLaren*, 1878, but its bullnosed masonry is more aggressive. Balustraded round tower over the entrance. Full-height canted bay window with an octagonal slated spire. The gatepiers are decorated with oval panels and surmounted by obelisks standing on balls.

DALGRAIN ROAD. No. 51 is a small but extravagantly Baronial late C19 house built of bullnosed masonry. Canted bay window corbelled to the square at the upper floor. Crowstepped gables and a bartizan. Relief of a huge thistle.

## INDUSTRIAL BUILDINGS

AVECIA FACTORY, Earl's Road. Chemical works on both sides of the road, first begun for Scottish Dyers Ltd. in 1919. On the SE side of the road, two blocks of two-storey OFFICES, the windows segmental-headed. They were built in 1928 and the E block extended in 1949 by *Imperial Chemical Industries' Architects' Department*. On the NW side of the road, a long low range of late C20 OFFICES. Walls of red and brown brick with a ribbed metal fascia and shallow-pitched roof. Behind, three large industrial blocks (PROCIONS, MONASTRAL and PYRIMIDINES PLANTS) by *Peter R. Nuttall*, 1967–71. Straightforwardly inelegant, the walling of ribbed metal.

B.P. OIL REFINERY AND PETROCHEMICAL WORKS, Bo'ness Road. Huge complex developed since 1924 when Scottish Oils Ltd. opened the refinery. This now forms an L, one of its arms stretching NE from Bo'ness Road, the other bordering the Firth of Forth. Filling the inner angle of the L and spilling over to the SW side of Bo'ness Road is the petrochemical works opened by British Hydrocarbon Chemicals in 1951.

The structures for the most part provide an unashamed 128 display of industrial functionalism given excitement by discharges of flames and steam but the offices and laboratory buildings strung in a line along Bo'ness Road are genteel. At the W end, on the corner of Powdrake Road, the OIL REFINERY EXHIBITION CENTRE of 1961. Two storeys of brick trimmed with artificial stone. It is followed by ADMINISTRATION AND TECHNICAL BUILDINGS (by *Scottish Oils Ltd. Architectural Department*, 1935), their brick-built Neo-Georgian timidly aware of the Modern Movement. To the E, on both sides of Bo'ness Road, the ADMINISTRATION AND LABORATORY BUILDINGS of the petrochemical works. These are mostly by *Yates, Cook & Darbyshire*, 1948, brick-built with horizontal windows, their mullions of brick or artificial stone, and low towers. A couple have been extended later and two are linked by a self-confident aggregate-clad block by *Alison & Hutchison & Partners*, 1964–5, to form the CHEMICALS BUSINESS SUPPORT CENTRE. Disturbing the gentility is the POWER STATION, large and boxy, not bothering to attempt elegance.

FOUNDRY OFFICE, Grangeburn Road. Large two-storey block of *c.* 1900. Italian Renaissance, with pedimented ground-floor windows. Above the balustraded central porch, a three-light window whose consoled segmental pediment breaks through the wallhead's balustrade-cum-parapet.

6090                    GRIBLOCH HOUSE                    S
                        1.6km. SW of Kippen

By *Basil Spence* of *Rowand Anderson, Paul & Partners*, 1937–9. A remarkable mansion of compromised Modernism, built for the steel magnate John Colville who had met Spence through their mutual involvement in preparations for the Empire Exhibition of 1938. The client's demands for sun and view were not easily resolved on a site that looked N, so a bent, two-storeyed 'inverted F-shaped plan'* was evolved. From the living room and dining room, which are placed symmetrically in a shallow curve on each side of a thinly columned entrance porch, there are splendid prospects of the countryside to the N, while from the S side of the house sunlight floods into a galleried staircase hall that lies between two short splayed wings, the W containing the formal 'Regency' Drawing Room. Extending E, a service range completes the stem of the F. Consultation with the North American architect *Perry M. Duncan* persuaded Spence to abandon his first idea for a circular hall in favour of an ellipse, around the sunny S side of which a single-flight, cantilevered staircase rises gracefully through the airy double-height space. The hall, like the large NW bow of the living room, is generously glazed; the remaining windows vertical or square in proportion with narrow margins. Walls are white harl with a coped parapet concealing a low-pitched copper roof. Yet, however white and boxy, Gribloch's Modernism is tempered by a certain dull solidity, some lingering symmetries, and a soft-centred sense of the picturesque. In 1938 Spence wrote that 'the feeling we are striving for is something more of the Regency type, freshened up to fit with modern conditions'; *Moderne* rather than Modernist, he might have said.

While some interiors remain traditional, the aesthetic of the hall and living room is fresh and clean, tastefully refined for comfortable bourgeois consumption. The design of the Living Room, including fireplace, semicircular bookcase alcove and colour scheme (originally grey, lime-green, aubergine and turquoise), is by *John Hill* of *Green & Abbot Ltd.* Furniture by *Betty Joel.* In the Hall, shell-and-rope cornices, the theme repeated in the oval carpet; also by *Hill*, after Colville had rejected proposals from *Nikolaus Pevsner*. Wave-and-circle wrought iron banister by *Raymond Subes*. Chandelier in chrome and glass by *Joel*. – SWIMMING POOL between the S wings; sea-lion fountain by *Compton Pottery*, Guildford (matched by an ebony and ivory sea-lion servants' bell in the dining room). – GARDEN design

* Caroline A. MacGregor, 'Gribloch: The Evolution of the Architectural and Interior Design of a 1930s Scottish Country House', *Architectural Heritage*, v (1995), 73.

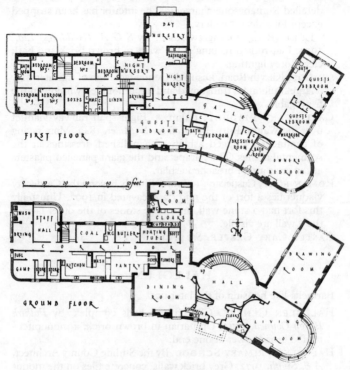

Gribloch House. Plans.

by the landscape architect *J. E. Grant White*; part walled and formal, part lawns merging into the surrounding heathland. – Sited 0.15km. E is the two-storey GARAGE BLOCK, designed by *Spence* to incorporate staff flats as well as vehicles: white again, more curves, a copper roof and a boldly symmetrical plan. – The LODGE, 1938, little more than a white bungalow, by *T. M. Copland & Blakey*, lies at the foot of the estate drive on the B822.

# HAGGS

Former mining village, a few late C19 cottages still surviving but the housing is mostly of the C20 and undistinguished except for four blocks in MARGARET AVENUE, by *Wilson & Wilson*, 1939. These are two-storey and flat-roofed, with cut-out corner windows.

HAGGS PARISH CHURCH, Kilsyth Road. Built in 1840, and very similar to David Rhind's Camelon St John's Church at Falkirk (q.v.). Red sandstone ashlar box, the side windows large and roundheaded. Firescreen S front suggesting a nave and aisles, the centre slightly advanced between pinnacled buttresses and topped by a spired octagonal bellcote. Projecting from the front, a parapeted two-storey porch, its door and windows of thinly detailed Romanesque character. The interior has been stripped except for a deep s gallery.

ST LUKE (R.C.), Garngrew Road. By *S. G. A. (Buildings) Ltd.*, 1974. Flat-roofed rectangle, the walls of brown brick and harl; clearstorey lighting.

SCHOOL, Kilsyth Road. Disused. Gentle Jacobean of the later C19, a large mullioned, transomed and hoodmoulded window in the front gable.

CASTLECARY VIADUCT, 1.1km. S. Eight-span railway viaduct over the Walton Burn, by *Grainger & Miller*, 1842. Main facing of channelled stugged ashlar, with polished dressings at the segmental arches. The parapet and the giant panelled pilasters at the ends are of broached ashlar.

ROMAN FORT, Castlecary, 1.2km. S. Shortly beyond the Castlecary viaduct lies a fort of the mid C2 excavated in 1902. Unusually this fort had a stone wall, and some stones of the outer face of the E wall are visible.

CASTLE CARY CASTLE. *See* p. 319.

8070    HALLGLEN    F

Barracks-like housing of the later C20.

HALLGLEN CENTRE. Church and halls complex, by *Falkirk Burgh Council*, 1974. Utilitarian in brown brick, a monopitch-roofed broad tower at one end.

HALLGLEN PRIMARY SCHOOL. By the Stirling County Architect, *A. J. Smith*, 1972. Grey brick walls, concrete tiles on the mono-pitch roof.

BRIDGE over the Union Canal, 0.3km. S. By *Hugh Baird*, 1821. Single large roundheaded arch of hammerdressed ashlar, the outer faces gently concave. The keystone on each face is carved with a human head, one smiling, the other weeping; above a rope-moulded frame enclosing an oval panel inscribed with the bridge's number (61) and the date 1821.

9090    HARVIESTOUN    C
1.8km. ENE of Tillicoultry

Harviestoun Castle, a mansion remodelled in castellated style in 1804, was demolished in 1965. Ancillary buildings survive. Beside the A91 are the early C19 E and W LODGES, both stodgy castellated. – Bordering the drive through the parkland, the late C18 STABLES. Ashlar-faced two-storey front range of thirteen bays, the two bays at each end slightly advanced and with round-arched carriage doors. Also slightly advanced is the pedimented three-bay centrepiece pierced by an elliptically arched pend. – To the E, HARVIESTOUN HOME FARM, an early C19 crowstep-gabled single-storey E-plan steading, now rather altered and partly heightened. At the centre, an octagonal steeple. Set diag-onally across each end, a two-storey house, its windows hood-moulded, its pyramidal roof topped by a chimneystack.

## HEAD OF MUIR

F *8080*

Housing, mostly of the late C20 but with a plain C19 development along the main street (DENNY ROAD).

HEAD OF MUIR PRIMARY SCHOOL, Haypark Road. By *Central Regional Council*, 1978. Single-storey, on a stepped plan, each unit with its own piended roof surmounted by a monopitch-roofed topknot.

## HIGH BONNYBRIDGE

F *8070*

Small C20 village.

HIGH BONNYBRIDGE BAPTIST CHURCH, Church Street. Originally St Helen's Church of Scotland. By *Wilson & Tait*, 1932. Early Christian with a Scottish flavour, built of hammer-dressed squared masonry; slated roofs. It comprises a nave and double-pitch-roofed S aisle; parapeted vestry at the W end of the aisle, a small chancel at this end of the nave. At the E end, a saddleback-roofed tower. Crowstepped gables at the tower and nave; straight skews at the aisle and chancel. Simple round-arched windows.

ST JOSEPH'S CHURCH (R.C.), Broomhill Road. By *J. Bell Morrison* of *Cowieson's Ltd.*, 1924–5, but altered and extended in 1936 by *Reginald Fairlie*. Church skied above a hall, all harled with brick dressings. A Gothic touch is provided by the pointed window in the front (E) gable; on the S side of this gable, a wooden belfry. – Piend-roofed CLERGY HOUSE to the NW, by *Fairlie*, 1936.

ROUGH CASTLE. *See* p. 647.

## INCHCAILLOCH

S *4080*

Island in Loch Lomond.

CHAPEL. Barely discernible traces of a small oblong chapel dating from the end of the C12 or early C13. Dedicated to St Kentigern. Abandoned 1621. The remains lie within a rectangular graveyard rewalled in drystone rubble, probably in the C19. Among the few tombstones is a TABLE TOMB carved with an armorial shield and inscribed to McGregor of that Ilk and dated 1693.

## INCHMAHOME

S *5000*

Island in the Lake of Menteith.

INCHMAHOME PRIORY lies close to the N shore. Augustinian foundation established by Walter Comyn, fourth Earl of Menteith, in 1238, on the site of an earlier island church. Long ruinous and roofless, but delightfully situated among trees by the water's edge; the surviving walls can still evoke a picture of the priory church and its conventual buildings ranged to the S. The W

gable is much cut down but preserves its magnificent processional doorway, a fine pointed opening defined by four orders
of moulded arches springing from the bell capitals of jambs
rippling with engaged shafts. Linked l. and r. are short arcades
of two blind lancets, a blind quatrefoil and trefoil in the
spandrels. Above this, a ruinous wallhead betrays signs that
the great W window may have had three lights. There is an
echo of the W end of Dunblane Cathedral (q.v.) in all this;
perhaps not surprising since it was the Bishop of Dunblane
who, on the authority of Pope Gregory IX, gave permission for
building.

The church, however, is altogether simpler in conception
than Dunblane: the NAVE no more than four bays long, the
choir and presbytery beyond of roughly equivalent extent. An
arcade of pointed arches, only the first two of which survive,
opened N into a lean-to aisle, now delineated by wall footings
only. Awkwardly located within the first bay, a square bell-tower
rises almost four storeys to a ragged wallhead. To the S, a solid
wall of rubble masonry separates the nave from the cloister garth.
Corbels and raking raggle lines indicate the roof construction
which must have covered the N cloister walk but, since nothing

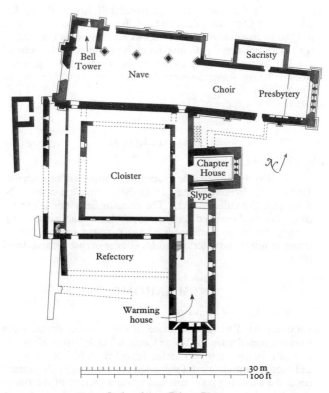

Inchmahome Priory. Plan.

remains of the upper walling, it is impossible to determine precisely how the nave may have been lit, though some form of clearstorey must have existed. The only penetrations of the S wall are two pointed, moulded doorways leading to the W and E cloister walks. Perplexingly, between these two openings, the wall does not run parallel with the N side of the nave, an anomaly of construction, or reconstruction, which results in the width of the choir being markedly less than that of the W front.

In the unaisled CHOIR, N and S walls revert to a parallel relationship. On each side they stand almost to the original eaves height, with several tall pointed-arched windows of varying widths. At the E end five high lancets are grouped within a framing arch on the inner face of the wall. These lancet lights, which have moulded jambs, rise from a sloping sill which returns down each side of the choir as a stringcourse linking the sills of the N and S windows. Below this course, at the E end of the S wall, are three SEDILIA with moulded arches on stub columns, the seat closest to the E end raised slightly above the level of its neighbouring recesses. Between this and the E wall are the PISCINA and a small aumbry. On the N, a door leads to the lean-to sacristy, of which only the lower walls remain. Opposite, a hooded pointed doorway presumably connected the church with a night stair from the canons' dormitory over the E cloister range, though neither stair nor dormitory survives.

The CLOISTER walk is discernible on all four sides. On the N and S, it seems likely that there were simple lean-to constructions, but on the W and E it is evident that the walks were incorporated into ranges of two-storeyed buildings. Set at r. angles and centred on the E range is the CHAPTER HOUSE, which owes its steep skew gables and fine state of preservation to a C17 adaptation as a mausoleum for the Earls of Menteith. It is a single barrel-vaulted chamber lit by three lancets in a segmental-arched recess in the E gable. A stone bench runs round three sides. Various lapidary fragments and gravestones. Among them, the DOUBLE EFFIGY of Walter Stewart, Earl of Menteith †c. 1295, and his countess, Mary; two well-weathered figures, elongated, elegant and immediately appealing. – A second EFFIGY, incomplete, of a knight carrying the Stewart arms on his shield. – GRAVESLAB of Sir John Drummond, C14; carved in low relief, 32 a mailed figure bearing spear, sword and shield with smaller images l. and r. of the head depicting St Michael killing the dragon and a bishop standing on a serpent. – Also displayed, a broken GRAVESLAB incised with the splendidly interlaced head of a cross and a sword hilt.

Immediately S of the Chapter House a narrow passage or SLYPE crosses W–E from the cloister walk. Beyond this, extending S, the ruins of the Warming House, from which a small day stair at the SE corner of the cloister rose to the dormitory above. At the S end of the Warming House, a double fireplace and beyond that a latrine block. With the exception of a stretch of walling at the SW corner of the cloister, which contains a doorway and the vestiges of a turnpike stair, little remains beyond footings to provide any reliable picture of the remaining domestic buildings. The refectory probably formed the s range with cellarage in the narrow w range under the prior's lodging.

*3080*          # INCHMURRIN          WD

The largest island in Loch Lomond.

Vestigial remains of the C14 CASTLE of the Earls of Lennox can be seen near the pier at the SW end of the island. Nothing of the adjacent medieval chapel of the eponymous St Mirin or Mirren survives.

*5000*          # INCHTALLA CASTLE          S
0.2km. SW of Inchmahome

In the Lake of Menteith, the island stronghold of the Earls of Menteith from the C14. The island is 'crowded with buildings'*, the much overgrown ruinous remnants of which, dating from the C17, indicate a quadrangular courtyard plan. To the N, a hall, aligned W–E, with a small staircase tower NW; to the S, a kitchen block and so-called High House, which may retain some pre-Reformation masonry. This last has a vaulted ground floor and, on the outer face of the S wall at first-floor level, a series of corbels and putlog holes betraying what MacGibbon & Ross judged to be 'a remarkable example of the provision made for the defence of castles by means of outside hoardings'‡. A few Gothic fragments suggest that Inchmahome Priory (q.v.) was quarried for stone.

*4020*          # INNISHEWAN          S

Placename in Glen Dochart.

GRAVEYARD. Rubble-walled graveyard of the Macnabs of Innishewan, *c.* 1758. Tombstones from 1766.

DOCHART HOUSE BRIDGE, 4.5km. WSW. Built *c.* 1800. Long rubble crossing of the Dochart on five segmental arches of irregular span. The largest arch springs from the N bank to a cutwater pier.

*3010*          # INVERARNAN          WD

A couple of inns N of Loch Lomond at the entrance to Glen Falloch.

DROVERS' INN. C18, perhaps earlier in part. A rugged, irregular, whin rubble structure of three storeys with wide eaves, gabled

---

*John A. Stewart, *Inchmahome and the Lake of Menteith* (1933), 54.

‡David MacGibbon and Thomas Ross, *The Castellated and Domestic Architecture of Scotland*, iv (1892), 287.

attic dormers and a gabled w porch. Alterations in the early c19 and the addition of an extra storey to the E wing, 1853, carried out in Breadalbane vernacular.

STAGGER INN. Early c19. Former U-plan court of offices. E façade has three gables with a four-centred arch at the centre, now a boarded doorway.

# INVERSNAID                                                  s *3000*

End-of-the-road hamlet on the E side of Loch Lomond, at the mouth of the tumbling Arklet Water. Originally important as a ferry point on the journey w from the Trossachs, it is now a valued stopover for walkers on the West Highland Way route N.

ST KENTIGERN. By *Thomas Leadbetter*, 1895. Arts and Crafts Norman in roughcast and red sandstone with 'something of the rustic cottage order' (*Building News*, 1895). Collared gables, small round-arched windows and a swept pagoda ventilator on the ridge exert persuasive charm. Closed in 1986, it was converted without impairment to an Outdoor Centre for the Boys' Brigade by *Wylie Shanks & Partners* in 1991–2. – Five memorial panels of STAINED GLASS have been retained in an illuminated internal screen. – Hanging in a canopied frame in the graveyard is the BELL, cast by *Felix van Aerschodt* of Louvain, Belgium, 1909.

BARRACKS. In 1718–19 the Hanoverian government, intent on quelling further Jacobite revolt, began to build a series of barracks across the Highlands. The choice of Inversnaid as one of them was doubtless also influenced by the local depredations of the outlaw Rob Roy Macgregor. The 'Surveyor and Chief Director' of the works was *James Smith*, replaced in January 1719 by *Andrews Jelfe* who was given the title 'Architect and Clerk of Works for this office in Great Britain'. In 1803 the Wordsworths found 'a very large stone building, a singular structure, with a high wall round it'. They thought it 'exactly like one of the spittals of the Alps, built for the reception of travellers'. By 1823 the buildings were ruinous. Of the three-storey barracks blocks on the N and s sides of the standard courtyard plan, only a few low stretches of masonry survive at Garrison Farm. On a slope which falls from the farm to the Snaid Burn is the GARRISON GRAVEYARD, a small fenced enclosure with several crude c18 headstones now much overgrown. A c19 gravestone commemorates those men who died at Inversnaid, 1721–96.

INVERSNAID HOTEL. From its beginnings as a two-storey, three-bay inn of *c.* 1820, the hotel has stepped N uphill with successive enlargement. The phases are easily identifiable. By 1900 a gabled three-storey wing had been added; by the First World War, two further bay-windowed, gabled bays; more recently a number of plainer bedroom wings, the latest, 1990, on the site of the old coach-houses.

INVERSNAID LODGE, 1km. SW. Built as a shooting lodge by the third Duke of Montrose, 1790.

LOCH ARKLET WATERWORKS, 2km. E. 1909–14; *J. R. Sutherland*, engineer. Battered concrete dam, faced in red sandstone; 320m. long and 10.67m. high, its castellated dam-walk wall continues in a curve by the roadside. Three-bay flatted HOUSE with corbelled upper floor; roughcast with dressings. Central stair tower with slated ogee roof. Adjacent cottage has crowstepped gables.

*3080*                      JAMESTOWN                      WD

Barely perceptible as a place on the road between Bonhill and Balloch. Created to house the labour force in Levenbank Works, it was never a town and now is hardly a village.

JAMESTOWN PARISH CHURCH, Main Street. By *Clarke & Bell*, 1868–9; the design modelled on that for the Parish Church in Blantyre, rebuilt 1863. Square-snecked red sandstone with dressed margins. In the gabled W front is a hooded pointed window traceried with a ten-dagger wheel. To the l., a belfry steeple clasped by corner buttresses that transform themselves first into engaged octagons and then break free as obelisk-topped finials around the spire. At the base of the steeple, a pointed entrance door with single shafts in the jambs. Staircase r. of gable. Four-bay nave with superimposed pointed windows. N and S transepts have a rose window with quatrefoil motifs; wheel window in E gable. Ogee-ribbed ceiling on thin columns with floreate capitals. Horseshoe gallery.

JAMESTOWN PRIMARY SCHOOL and NURSERY SCHOOL, Main Street. 1859–61. Single-storey classrooms in red sandstone with two-storey gabled projection at centre forming a T-plan. School-teacher's accommodation was provided on the upper floor. Two-storey wing to r., 1872, originally for a second teacher's dwelling. Keyhole-headed Gothic; windows grouped in twos, threes and fours, some with stone transoms.

*7090*                      KEIR HOUSE                      S
                      2.7km. SSW of Dunblane

Large estate mansion of cumulative grandeur but diminishing delight. Vast and complex in plan, the present rather dully pompous pile is the result of successive aggrandizement. Bulky and unbalanced, it nevertheless began in the C18 in coherent orthodoxy. A contemporary pencil drawing shows the principal E façade of a symmetrical, three-storey building eleven bays wide, at the centre of which three bays rise under a pediment. This was the seat of the Stirling family who, having forfeited the estate for their support of the 1715 rebellion, later regained their lands from the Commissioners. *David Hamilton* was first to infract the house's respectable, if unremarkable, Georgian order, adding the offices at the rear W and the SW wing of two high storeys aligned with the existing eaves, 1829–35. This wing contains a long N gallery and a magnificent drawing room, its symmetrical layout inflated into a wide segmental bow taking advantage of the views s across the carse. Hamilton also remodelled the interior of the old Dining Room at the s end of the C18 house, breaking out a tripartite pilastered window to capture the same prospect and raising the ceiling height (a move which co-ordinated the windows along the new s front but disastrously disrupted relationships with the fenestration of the E façade). In 1849, shortly after he had inherited the family estate, the collector and art historian *Sir William Stirling* (later *Stirling-Maxwell*) undertook yet more radical interventions. Collaborating with the little-known architect *Alfred Jenoure*, he relocated the main entrance to the N end of the house where he made the new driveway, gate, arcade and a two-storey *porte cochère*, crowned in a semicircular tympanum emblazoned with heraldic carving, 1851. Where the original pedimented entrance block had been, there now appears a five-light segmental bow, rising to an open third-floor loggia of balustraded round-arched openings under the glazing of a shallow-pitched conical roof (later slated and closed in). The similar but lower E bow was erected between the N end of the C18 house and the new entrance. In 1863 the *porte cochère* was raised to its present four storeys and acquired a steep French roof. Further expansion was yet to come. *R. Rowand Anderson* added the NW wing of kitchen offices and developed the garden, 1899–1905, and in 1911–12 *A. F. Balfour Paul* of *Rowand Anderson & Balfour Paul* built the apsidal chapel which, displacing the earlier arcading, extends E in a long finger parallel to the approach to the N entrance.

Extensive internal alteration and refurbishment accompanied these changes. Nothing, however, surpassed Hamilton's treatment of the Drawing Room with its axial opposition of fireplace and five-light bow flanked respectively by doors and niches and echoed above by a decorative circle-in-square plaster ceiling with coffered margins W and E, executed by *Leck & Johnston*. Notable, too, is the marble and mosaic interior of the CHAPEL sanctuary, 1926, by *Boris Anrep*, which depicts the risen Christ, the Dove and the Hand of God against a gold background.

Scattered across the estate is the evidence of sustained C19 development. The entry is distinguished: ESTATE GATES, 1820, by *David Hamilton*, re-erected near the roundabout that terminates the M9 just s of Dunblane, 1969. Flanking the drive, two tall round arches in channelled ashlar fronted by Greek Doric columns carrying an entablature combine to bear a blocking course and attic plinth on which sits a large sculpted hound. Adjacent is Hamilton's SOUTH LODGE, 1820, a pilastered ashlar drum symmetrically engaged in a lower piend-roofed oblong. Alas, the promise of this Neo-Classical conceit is not realized. Instead, a freer mid-Victorian eclecticism, the product of Sir William Stirling's building programme, 1849–62, predominates. The Doune road LODGE, dated 1861, is characteristic: rock-faced rubble with ashlar dressings, detailed in a chunky classical manner with blue tiles in the eaves frieze. It is linked to polygonal GATEPIERS, carrying hefty foliage-draped urns, which mark the way to the HOME FARM. Laid out by *David Bryce*, 1832–3 (proposals by *Hamilton* appear to have been rejected), but remodelled and enlarged with brashly idiosyncratic gusto by *Jenoure* and *Stirling*, 1856–61: a huge cattle court bounded by varied one-and-a-half-storey N, E and S ranges. There is a high sharply coped chimneystack on the N and, at the SE corner, a three-storey clock tower with two obliquely set clock faces lettered with cautionary mottoes, much roguish carving and a swept French roof, fish-scale-slated and crested with ironwork. – Several BRIDGES, GATEWAYS, and HOUSES for estate-workers, most in rock-faced rubble, date from the period of Sir William's patronage. – NW of Keir House is the WALLED GARDEN, *c.* 1820: the brick S wall, which has a pedimented centre between greenhouse ranges, by *David Hamilton*, 1833; the gated three-arched loggia and pavilions on the NW are mid-Victorian. Gothic, pyramid-roofed BATHING HOUSE *c.* 1893; William Adam-style STAIRCASE on the W terrace, 1899–1901; swan-topped baluster SUNDIAL, dated 1906: all by *R. Rowand Anderson*. Brick, egg-type ICE HOUSE, early C19.

ARNHALL CASTLE. 0.65km. WSW of Keir House. 1617. Ruinous L-plan tower-house reduced to two- and three-storey stands of red sandstone rubble. The re-entrant has gone completely but corbelled bases of rounds at N and S corners survive. Some gunloops.

# KENNET                                C

Small former mining village strung along the NE side of the road.

DESCRIPTION. At the SE end, a long terrace of single-storey cottages (Nos. 1–20 KENNET) of *c.* 1800 (No. 3 with the date 1804 painted on its door lintel). All have fronts of broached ashlar and, except for No. 1 which has a fourth bay, are of three bays. Most are now roofed with red pantiles (replacing dark blue salt-glazed pantiles) with slated easing courses; at No. 5 clay pantiles have given way to slates and at No. 8 to concrete tiles. A mid-C19 cottage in the lane behind. At the NW end of the terrace, the late C20 OLD ROAD GARAGE and LYNDON, followed by a mid-C19 *cottage orné* and a short terrace of four mid-C19 cottages, three with bracketed eaves to their roofs and piended dormers.

BRUCEFIELD. *See* p. 288.

# KERSIE MAINS                          F
0.5km. SW of South Alloa

White harled L-plan farmhouse but formerly a laird's house, its building history not immediately apparent. The house was originally a simple rectangle, perhaps of two storeys and an attic, probably built in the C16 for the Abercrombies who, by 1595, held the lands of Kersie in feu ferme from the Crown as successor to

Cambuskenneth Abbey. It was remodelled first in the mid or later
C17 and then again in 1842 by *James Smith* of Edinburgh.

The house's earlier development is best understood from inside
what is now cellarage but, before the banking up of the surrounding soil, was the ground floor. The main block and NW jamb
each contain an unvaulted room. The room under the main
block has had a large kitchen fireplace at its W end, now built up
but a fragment of the roll-moulded N jamb still visible. S of the
fireplace, a recess (formerly shelved), the small window in its
back wall still containing early glass but blocked externally.
Three irregularly spaced small windows (the E two built up) in
the S wall. In the E gable, a window which has been inserted,
perhaps in the late C17. Two original windows in the N wall, the
E built up. The W of these is a slit which now looks into the
jamb but must originally have been to the outside.

The room in the NW jamb has also been a kitchen. It probably
dates from extension and remodelling of the house to its present
shape and height in the mid or later C17. In this room's N gable,
a large fireplace (now built up), its roll-moulded lintel apparently re-used from the fireplace of the earlier kitchen in the
main block. In the W wall, a blocked door, perhaps an insertion,
and window. At the N end of the E wall, a stone sink with a
drain to the outside. Both rooms are entered from the foot of a
stair tower in the NE inner angle of the house. Rounded margins
at the stair tower's entrance.

In *Smith*'s remodelling of 1842 the existing ground floor was
abandoned for use, the ground banked up round it, a new
entrance made from the centre window of the S front into the
new ground (former first) floor, and a plain single-storey extension added to the jamb's N gable. The S front, except for Smith's
plain doorway, is however still that produced in the C17 remodelling. Regular five-bay elevation, the windows with roll-moulded
margins; it must have looked incongruously sophisticated when
viewed above the original ground floor with its small and
randomly disposed openings. At the SW corner, a diagonally set
square sundial. In the gables of the main block, more windows
with roll-moulded margins. Roll-moulded margins again at the
jamb's first-floor windows and the N window of its ground floor
but this floor's S window has been converted to a door, probably
in 1842, and then back to a window but with plain margins. C19
piend-roofed porch at the centre of the jamb's front.

Much altered interior but in the W rooms on the ground and
first floors of the main block are identical stone fireplaces, their
basket-arched openings surrounded by roll moulding crossed
just below the springing level by crude cornice-capitals; triangular panels in the spandrels, and a cornice-like mantelshelf.
Are these C17 or archaizing insertions of 1842? In the attic of
the jamb the adze-dressed roof timbers are exposed, their posi-
tioning numbers visible.

To the NE, a not very formal courtyard STEADING by *James
Smith*, 1840–2, the walls of whitewashed rubble, the piended
roofs covered by pantiles.

# KILBAGIE

Just a paper mill and laird's house.

KILBAGIE HOUSE. Rubble-built laird's house, the main block of
c. 1775. Three-bay S front, a single round attic window at its
centre; lugged architrave to the door. Bow-fronted early C19 W
addition.

KILBAGIE PAPER MILLS. Originally a distillery founded in the
later C18 but converted to a paper mill in 1874. Utilitarian
buildings of the later C19 and C20 but with a battlemented
Italianate brick water tower of 1874 to give presence. On the W
side of the complex, the early C19 KILBAGIE MILL HOUSE, a
chimneyed gablet over the two centre bays of its front.

# KILBRYDE CASTLE
### 3.7km. NW of Dunblane

A stolid flat-chested Baronial mansion wonderfully landscaped
above the deep wooded cleft of the Ardoch Burn.

Of the C17 L-plan tower-house, which MacGibbon & Ross were
able to illustrate, only the E gable, with its square Pinkie-style
bartizans l. and r., remains. Evidently, ill-judged mid-C19 interference provoked a partial collapse of the structure, a situation
recovered by the Perth architect *Andrew Heiton Jun.*, whose
recasting of the four-storey house in rough-faced, square-snecked
red sandstone with ochre sandstone dressings was completed in
1877. A conically roofed stair tower, corbelled to the round from
a ground-floor octagon, marked the N entrance. Crowstepped
gables, battlemented parapets and corner rounds appeared, but
the wall planes remained flat; even the S front, looking out on a
terraced lawn which suddenly drops in a steep plunge to the
stream below, lacks modelling. Perhaps deliberately so, for this
restraint intensifies the cumulative drama of landscape and
architecture. Only the eaves, penetrated by pedimented dormers
bearing the monograms J C and C S, and the attic behind, from
which the conic roofs of four narrow round-fronted dormers
push forward, are busy with sculptural incident. A weathervane
over the N tower and numerous hopper-heads bear the date
1877. Two rooms lined with pilastered panelling may be
restorations of C18 work.
   Linked to the N front by a battlemented wall is a two-storey
SERVANTS' WING with its own NW tower. c. 0.2km. W, the
STABLE BLOCK, c. 1770, has a symmetrical front in which two-
storey, three-bay units (each with a circular first-floor window)
combine on either side of a segmental-arched pend under a
pedimented central doocot.

KILBRYDE CHAPEL, 0.5km. S. Dated 1864. Crowstep-gabled
Gothic: three buttressed bays with a gabled porch centre S. Paired
pointed windows in shouldered lintelled openings, except in
the gables where this relationship is reversed. Raised as the

mausoleum of the Campbells of Aberuchill in a walled GRAVE-
YARD of more ancient date. – Several C18 graves, though most
are now illegible. Lying SLAB dated 173?, carved with skull and
crossed bones.

# KILLEARN                                          S 5080

An affluent village on the A875 2km. ENE of the confluence of the
Endrick Water and Blane Water. Lavishly, and all but contigu-
ously, endowed with four churches and an obelisk.

Former FREE CHURCH, Balfron Road. Built c. 1845, renovated
c. 1900. Plain gabled Gothic in heavily pointed red sandstone
rubble. Adapted as church hall, 1954, and enlarged 1971.

Former KILLEARN PARISH CHURCH, Balfron Road. 1825–6,
but superseded by the neighbouring church of 1882; it has become
the village hall. More finely judged than its twin at Fintry (q.v.)
though indecently assaulted by lower accretions of 1953. The
gabled hall with its axial tower is the same, but white-painted walls
intensify the simplicity and sharpen the restraint of the mouldings. The square N tower carries identical finials and circle-in-
diamond motifs but the quatrefoils and hooded trefoils are
more regularly placed. The tall pointed windows have splayed
ingoes too, but the slender five-part interlacing of the glazing
bars imparts a special elegance. VESTRY and SESSION HOUSE,
added 1874, are unfortunate, the flat-roofed extensions wrapped
around the base of the tower in 1953 simply uncivil. – Set between
whin rubble piers, the CORONATION GATES, 1953, compound
this insult with their anglicized EIIR monogram.

KILLEARN PARISH CHURCH. By *John Bryce*, 1880–2. A replacement for its early C19 neighbour to the N (*see* above), the church
was the gift of Archibald Orr Ewing of Ballikinrain in memory of
his daughter Ella who died, aged sixteen, in 1878. Respectable
E.E. in rough-faced, square-snecked, ochre sandstone. Reversing
the traditional liturgical orientation, the six-bay plan has N and S
transepts at the W end, the E end presenting a gabled entrance
front to Balfron Road. At the centre of this façade, below three
tall hooded lancets, is the main door, a pointed opening plain in
the splayed jambs but much moulded above. To its r. is a 30m.-
high steeple pinned by heavy angled buttresses which diminish
in successive stages before transforming themselves into four
obelisk-topped finials rising like miniature corner steeples below
the spire. Triple-lancet plate tracery in the transept gables. Ten-
light wheel window in W gable.

The E door leads into the vestibule from which a stone stair
rises r. within the steeple base. Wide nave with decorative arch-
braced trusses dropping to wooden corbels on short column
shafts carried in turn on floral corbelstones. Purlins support a
sparred and boarded roof. Plastered walls. The rear gallery projects on corbelled brackets through a two-bay pointed-arched
arcade. Similar arcades to the transepts which have bracketed
arch-braced scissor trusses. – In the S transept, three brass

PLAQUES and seven stone TABLETS commemorating members of the Orr Ewing family, including a white marble pointed-arched panel with sunburst and stars and a floral border, dedicated to the young Ella Orr Ewing. – On the N transept gable, four large brass PLATES on which are inscribed l. the Ten Commandments and r. the Creed and Lord's Prayer. – Oak panelling to sanctuary wall coved l. and r. below organ pipes and curtained between. – CHOIR STALLS with fleur-de-lis finialled ends and other chancel FURNISHINGS by *Alexander Lorne Campbell*, 1926. – To the l. of the chancel area is the stone FONT by *John Rhind*, 1882, a kneeling angel holding a shell as baptismal bowl; again in memory of Ella. – Four of the nave's double-lancet windows have STAINED GLASS. N, two abstract designs in brilliant blues and reds, by *Sadie McLellan*, in memory of Thomas Downie †1979; and Joseph and Mary with the Infant Jesus, by *William Meikle & Sons*, 1911. – On the S, to the Jamieson family, residents at Gartness Mill for two centuries, Jesus and Moses under Gothic aedicules; and, to Andrew Cathcart, SS Andrew and Peter with saltire and keys: both by *Meikle* (?). – Ten-light W window: a ring of angels from which radii of white lilies and red roses converge on a central portrait of the ill-fated Ella Orr Ewing; by *James Ballantine & Son*.

Linked SW is the gabled SESSION HOUSE, 1967. Two round-arched windows have STAINED GLASS by *Sadie McLellan*, 1969.

OLD CHURCH. 1734. Roofless skew-gabled shell built of coursed dull-red sandstone rubble with dressed margins and rusticated quoins. Set in a busy graveyard which still contains some C17 tombstones. Both gables have rolled skewputts and a central round-arched window. The W window encloses a narrower lintelled opening rising through its sill (probably an access door, for both gables have internal scarcements for galleries), while the E one, which is without margins, may be an insertion. The S wall is symmetrically arranged with four round-arched upper windows, the outer pair set above round-arched doorways, the inner over lintelled openings, now blocked. At the centre is a round-arched door surmounted by a roughly cut datestone. Ornamental window keystones, scrolled or masks, overlap the eaves course. Round-arched openings over blocked lintelled windows also at each end of the N elevation, but at the centre this wall is solid and recesses slightly, rising to a shallow pediment-like gable. This is evidently infill, a curtailment of the church's perimeter from its C18 T-plan form, no doubt done in the C19 when the shell was stabilized and adapted as a burial enclosure. TOMBS include grave-slabs, headstones and wall tablets; a white marble Romanesque AEDICULE commemorates Ella Orr Ewing †1878 (*see* Killearn Parish Church, above).

In the GRAVEYARD some barely legible C17 tombstones. Two mantled HEADSTONES, C18, bear the usual symbols of mortality, skull, crossbones and hour-glass: one, dated 1766, to John McKinlay and his wife Mary; the other, illegible and more primitive, carved with the naïve head and wings of an angel. – Tall Roman Doric cast iron COLUMN carrying an urn commemo-

rates William Paterson †1832. – Two HEADSTONES with incised
Neo-Classical ornament, by *J. & G. Mossman*, the larger erected
1881 in memory of the Jamiesons of Gartness Mill. – Ringed
Celtic CROSS, bossed and interlaced with serpents, to Andrew
Buchanan †1902, and his wife Jean †1906.

BUCHANAN MONUMENT, in a railed plot 0.1km. S of Killearn 37
Parish Church. Erected by public subscription 1788–9 to honour
George Buchanan (1506–82), linguist, historian, wit and scholar
of genuinely European stature: the architect, *James Craig* of
Edinburgh, gave his services free. Obelisk of local millstone grit,
over 31m. high. In 1850 the monument was restored and a white
marble tablet inscribed with a long Latin panegyric added to
the N face of the tall classical base. The plan to commemorate
Buchanan seems to have been a consequence of Enlightenment
pride. In 1781 the Glasgow polymath John Anderson delivered
a paper concerning 'the Propriety of Erecting an Obelisk In
Honour of Buchanan', in which he called for a monument 150ft.
high 'to be placed at the Head of Buchanan Street in Glasgow',
i.e. fronting St Enoch Church. In the event, despite its suitably
civic and urban appeal, this proposal was not realized. Nor was
a design prepared by *John Adam* of Glasgow adopted. Buchanan's
birthplace, Killearn, was ultimately preferred for the location
while Craig, who had built the obelisk monument to Linnaeus
in Edinburgh in 1779 to the designs of Robert Adam and may
well have competed in the submission of designs for that commission, became the architect.

LEISURE CENTRE (former School). Built 1874 in square-snecked
red sandstone. Gabled classrooms in cruciform plan. Open bellcote on decoratively bargeboarded SE gable.

THE OLD MANSE, behind the Buchanan Monument. Late C18
and 1825. Three-bay, two-storey-and-attic, harled house. Kitchen
wing, originally a separate cottage, has a door lintel dated 1815.
A block of red sandstone in the STABLES bears the date 1671.

WAR MEMORIAL, Balfron Road. Dedicated 1924. Ashlar sandstone column carved with wreathed crosses on three of its six
faces. Hexagonal socle on raised rubble base.

## DESCRIPTION

Opposite the Old Church (*see* above) is THE SQUARE, four white
cottages of differing ridge heights, a gable-to-gable late C18 row.
At its SE end, turning the corner to Crosshead Road, KNOWE
HEAD, dated 1804 over a thinly pilastered door. All restored
by the Killearn Welfare Trust, 1937–9. Established in 1932 to
'promote the welfare and amenities of Killearn Parish', the
Trust intermittently acquired and reconditioned some of the
village's older properties. Round the corner is THE BLACK
BULL, a standard three-bay inn, probably late C18, later elongated l. and r., and next to it the Buchanan Monument (*see* above).
Then come the three other church buildings (*see* above), rub-
bing shoulders with one another along the W side of BALFRON
ROAD, and beside them the HEALTH CENTRE, 1981, a neat

aggregation of tiled monopitches over dry-dashed walls. This is the village centre, signalled by the Monument and by a sharp bend in the A875. Opposite the churches is another row of low cottages, early C19. Most are painted but one, the TOLL HOUSE, c. 1840, is red sandstone with a gabled porch crossing the pavement. The same material has been used for the former Free Church MANSE, of the mid C19, a low parsonage with hooded windows, and GREENEND, late C19, a high house with a consoled doorway and stop-chamfered window jambs. NE, on the edge of the village, is KING'S MILE, 1955, its two-bay front of provincial Venetian windows and narrow pedimented dormers belying its date.

At the War Memorial (*see* above) the road turns sharply into MAIN STREET. A long gradual fall SE begins. There is good, though not unbroken, containment, first by building but latterly more by greenery. On the l. is THE OLD SCHOOL HOUSE (No. 5), c. 1830, a fine three-bay residence with a pilastered doorpiece and lugged window margins, well painted and well presented. BRUCE COTTAGE, early C19, is low vernacular with a sprocketed slated roof eaves-on to the street. Then the gabled eaves dormers of Nos. 15–17 and 19–21, the latter dated 1863, a short one-and-a-half storey row, and at No. 27, attic bay dormers and a decorative cast iron eaves railing. On the r. there is more cottage continuity; Nos. 12–24, an early C19 painted rubble row with two segmental arch pends. Also single-storey but in red sandstone, No. 28 has a datestone over the door inscribed JG/1875. At Ibert Road the street cranks S. TOWNFOOT is a long, low, white, early C19 cottage with small windows, restored by Killearn Welfare Trust, 1967. Then, on each side of the street, some respectful roughcast HOUSES by *Stirling County Council*, 1935. More adventurous, CAMELOT, c. 1964, pushes a half-round wall forward, glazed at first floor under a conic roof fringed with decorative leadwork. Uphill E behind banked lawns is CLEVEDEN, 1961–2, by *Thomas J. Beveridge*, a large harled house with a curvilinear gable. Cottages return to mark the street line briefly: Nos. 65–67, BLACKLANDS, 1786, with a single rolled skewputt preserved, another restoration by Killearn Welfare Trust, 1967, and No. 74, probably early C19, hidden behind a hedge. Kirkhouse Burn passes under the road, bridged E by an arcuated VIADUCT of rough-faced red sandstone of the mid C19. The trees thicken, hiding a succession of villas; among them, WHITE COURT, a white-gabled villa of 1933.

AUCHENIBERT, 0.9km. ESE. By *Charles Rennie Mackintosh*, 1905–7. Sited on rising ground like Windyhill, Kilmacolm, and The Hill House, Helensburgh, Auchenibert enjoys wide views, but there the similarity ends. There is nothing Scottish here, nor any intimations of C20 Modernism. This is Arts and Crafts architecture, Cotswold-style in Cotswold stone. Evidently the client, F.J. Shand, had his own agenda: Mackintosh wrote offering 'a home in the Tudor or any other phase of English architecture'. A rambling composition of gabled blocks, tall broad chimneystacks and small vertical lights gathered in horizontal groups evolved; all good enough, and in fine snecked masonry, but not the new Jerusalem. At length, the 'strain of apostasy'* snapped the bonds between architect and client. *A. D. Hislop* finished the job. Internal restoration in 1983 by *H. Karlin*.

DRUMTIAN FARM, 2km. N. Early C19, rubble-built barn and byres under one roof. Segmental-arched cart entries. Ventilation slits to hay-loft.

GLENGOYNE DISTILLERY, 3.6km. S. Built as Burnfoot Distillery, 1833; enlarged through C19. Various harled buildings.

KILLEARN HOUSE, 2.4km. SW. Roofless and dilapidated in 1997. Erected 1829–30 in a style suggestive of downmarket *William Burn*: gables with saddleback skews, plentiful hoodmouldings and octagonal chimneystack groupings. Under the stepped hoodmoulding over the SW door a monogrammed marriage stone, dated 1850, records the house's enlargement. Offices abut NW.

LITTLE CARBETH, Drumtian Road, 1.6km. N. By the *Boys, Jarvis Partnership*, 1977–8. White roughcast modern vernacular in U-plan arrangement.

CARBETH HOUSE. *See* p. 308.

# KILLIN                                   S *5030*

A long one-street village at the W end of Loch Tay strung out N from the spectacular Falls of Dochart to the mouth of Glen Lochay.

KILLIN AND ARDEONAIG PARISH CHURCH. Built in 1744 by *Thomas Clark*, mason in Dunkeld, who was also responsible for now-demolished churches at Ardeonaig and Strathfillan. The design was probably by the Edinburgh architect *John Douglas*, later engaged by the Campbells of Breadalbane at nearby Taymouth Castle (Perth & Kinross). At first an octagonal kirk with cupola-topped roof and gabled E, W and N 'aisles' of equal width, it was enlarged in 1831–2 by widening the E and W aisles on their N side, a change which left the S wall untouched but, by absorbing the N side of the octagon, entailed new gabled roofs E and W. Doubtless the pulpit remained at the centre of the S wall in what had effectively become a canted bay projection until, in 1890, fashionable apostasy from proper Presbyterian order further dishonoured the building's spatial integrity by orientating worship to the E. Minor later excrescences have also abused the church's external symmetry and, regrettably, remain unrectified. Walls are roughcast with painted dressings; windows round-arched with Y-tracery or lintelled, except the central S window which has a four-centred arch. A crude birdcage bellcote survives on the N gable. BELL, 1632, by *Robert Hog*.

Entry is now by the W door. A narrow vestibule briefly conceals the inner conflict between liturgical and architectural axes. But the absurdity of the layout is quickly apparent: a meaningless canted recess to the S and, off-centre l., two tall fluted cast iron

* Charles McKean, *Stirling and the Trossachs* (1985), 135.

columns introduced in 1831–2 to carry the original timbers of the C18 roof structure. The ceiling is flat save for this disconcerting octagon with its beams and cornices. In this N aisle, a laird's loft, with panelled front and pilasters at the sides, relates badly to the repositioned focus of worship in the E. The gallery is reached by a timber winding stair from St Fillan's Prayer Room partitioned off below. Chancel furnishings are ill co-ordinated. – Octagonal PULPIT with Dec tracery motifs, finialled arrises and scalloped base. – Seven-sided medieval stone FONT, holed for lid and drain, on octagonal sandstone pedestal. – Clumsily boxed in the NE corner, a two-manual ORGAN, *c.* 1925, by *Ingram & Co.*, Edinburgh, brought from Killin U.F. Church in 1932 and reputedly 'one of the finest small Pipe Organs in Scotland, with an especially bright top register'. – STAINED GLASS. E window, 1901; the resurrected Christ appears to the two Maries in the garden, his head haloed against a fiery sky. – Central S window by *R. Douglas McLundie*, 1948; a War Memorial. – Lilies of the Field in the small W window over the vestibule.

The old GRAVEYARD is situated NE behind the adjacent hotel. Nothing of the earlier church remains but SLABS and HEADSTONES, C18 and C19, cover the hilly site. Several have scrolled pediments and fluted pilasters; that to Donald McNicol, late Fisher at Kenmore, †1776, among the better preserved.

ST FILLAN (Episcopal). Erected as a private chapel by the seventh Earl of Breadalbane for his shooting-party guests, 1876; hence its local nickname, 'Grouse Chapel'. Extended E in the early C20. Cruciform, gabled, and clad in corrugated iron. Timber-framed and pine-lined interior with thin scissors trusses. – ALTAR painted by *George Watson*, Edinburgh.

BREADALBANE FOLKLORE CENTRE (St Fillan's Mill). Two-storey L-plan mill in heavily pointed rubble, built *c.* 1840. A broad eaves and pointed-arched windows with rubble voussoirs; the so-called Breadalbane Gothic house-style. Converted to an information centre with restored working millwheel and timber-railed riverside terracing, 1994, by *Stirling District Council*.

BRIDGE OF DOCHART. Long curving rubble structure leapfrogging the rock-strewn course of the River Dochart in four segmental arches of differing widths. Dated 1760 and 1831, the second phase of building resulted from flood damage to the principal span. The broad white-water Falls of Dochart lie to the SW side of the bridge.

BRIDGE OF LOCHAY. Probably C18. High semicircular arch in rubble.

CLAN MACNAB BURIAL PLACE, Innis Bhuidhe. C18. Island site approached from a gate in the NE parapet of the Dochart Bridge (*see* above). The path passes between two tall rubble piers with ball finials, then a rubble wall with three segmental archways before coming to an oblong rubble enclosure beautifully set among pines, rhododendrons and scented azaleas with the river on each side. To Dorothy Wordsworth in 1814 it was 'altogether uncommon and romantic – a remnant of ancient grandeur: extreme natural wildness – the sound of roaring water, and withal, the ordinary half-village, half-town bustle of an every-day place'. Inside the enclosure are fifteen graves, nine of these clan chiefs. A lying SLAB, late medieval, bears the weathered effigy of a kilted warrior (?). – Outside are three HEADSTONES; one, dated 1777, to Patrick McNab, 'Taylor in Aucharn'; a second, dated 1811, commemorating a Dun McNab with some ill-arranged cautionary verses.

FIRBUSH POINT FIELD CENTRE, 3.2km. ENE. Norwegian pine-log structure by *A. C. M. Forward*, 1966–8.

LOCHAY POWER STATION, 3.5km. NW. By *Robert Matthew, Johnson-Marshall & Partners*, 1957–9. Gabled block with a shallow-pitched, metal-deck roof and a low curved tail of office accommodation.

McLAREN HALL. By *A. &. L. Barr* of Stirling, 1935. Buttressed roughcast hall with piended roof. Toy fort front of square-snecked stone has a raised central storey with pyramid roof. Saltire patterned parapets.

STEWART MONUMENT, in front of the church. Gothic plinth in pink granite, shaft and cross-topped obelisk in grey. Commemorates Rev. James Stewart †1789, minister at Killin and first translator of the New Testament into Gaelic.

WAR MEMORIAL, Grey Street. 1922 (?). Kilted soldier on rubble base into which are set three panels cut with the names of the dead. A certain similarity with the Memorial at Crianlarich (q.v.) suggests it may be the work of *Beveridge* of Perth. Stone benches. In the cobbled paving the words LEST WE FORGET and the dates 1914 and 1919.

## DESCRIPTION

Despite its length and largely riparian route (little short of 2km. from Bridge of Dochart to Bridge of Lochay), MAIN STREET is something of a disappointment. There are no buildings of note, though here and there older houses sustain continuity. On the W, BIRCHBANK, GLENGARRY and ASHLEA, all C18, combine to create an attractively irregular wall of two-storey rubble dwellings. Across the street, CRAIGVIEW, CLEMATIS COTTAGE and ANTAGGART COTTAGE form a simpler, lower, gable-to-gable row. Further N, there is more of the same; roughcast cottages, again C18, again hard to the pavement, with rubble footings clearly seen at BARNACARRIE. Comparable in date and still vernacular in character, KILLIN HOTEL is grander, three storeys plus hipped attic dormers, raised in height by *Dick Peddie, McKay & Jamieson*, 1945–7, after a fire, 1941, but sadly dis-figured by a full-width rubble and glass porch. The ground floor of INVERTAY HOUSE, C18, has also been altered, but more successfully: standard three-bay symmetry with two three-light square bays added l. and r. Late C19 villas and hotels are plentiful. FERNBANK has a strangely Gothic porch with a large octagon glazed into its lean-to gable; at GREENBANK, eaves and bargeboards are cut with thick fleur-de-lis shapes. Such

intermittent incident is never urban, though it can be fun: at the
CAPERCAILLIE RESTAURANT, for example, where, under a
clearstorey peak, another cottage breaks out into a glazed pavilion
overlooking the river; by *Gray, Marshall & Associates*, 1986–7.
But main-street scale remains elusive. Only DREADNOUGHT
PLACE, *c.* 1900, a symmetrical, three-storey block of shops and
flats with canted end bays corbelled from first floor into gabled
dormers, comes close.

To the S across the Dochart on GREY STREET, there is the sense
of a separate bridgend village. At the gates of Kinnell Estate, a
row of three two-storey roughcast houses, probably late C18,
has become the CLACHAIG HOTEL. Uphill, also overlooking
the Falls, more single-storey rubble cottages, probably early C19;
some rehabilitated, some still with corrugated iron roofs.

AUCHMORE, 1.3km. E. A long estate road leads to the site of
Auchmore House. Little more than a cottage, the house was
altered and enlarged for the 1st Marquess of Breadalbane by
*Archibald Elliot* in 1806–07. Rebuilt as a large Baronial mansion
by *Peddie & Kinnear*, *c.*1870, it was demolished a century later.
The surviving Victorian whin rubble OFFICES and STABLES,
which originally incorporated servants' quarters, were adapted
for flats in the 1950s; two symmetrical blocks, gables and dormers
bargeboarded in Breadalbane style, face each other across a
gated courtyard. A tunnel, which took servants to the mansion
house, has been blocked. 0.2km. E is a ruined roofless GAS HOUSE
with portholed pediment and chimney.

KINNELL HOUSE, 0.5km. NE. White harled house begun *c.* 1580,
its five-bay, two-storey composition of C18 provenance later
cast in a more rural asymmetrical mould by mid-C19 additions
and extensions. Tall first-floor windows. The SE centre bay
projects slightly under a chimneyed gable given Breadalbane
Gothic bargeboads. Attic dormer r. and lower NE wing eaves
dormer similarly bargeboarded. Long lean-to GREENHOUSE
extends SW. – WALLED GARDEN to NW. SUNDIAL on rough
rubble base; gnomon and plate by *William Osmond*, Salisbury,
1822. – U-plan STEADING court with two-storey SW and NE
ranges and cottage row NW. – The W drive from Bridge of
Dochart passes through three sets of round rubble GATEPIERS,
C18; the first topped by urns, the second by ball finials, the third
by carved lions possibly oriental in origin. Close to the W gate,
the eponymously roughcast, two-storey-and-attic YELLOW
COTTAGE is the former estate office; late C18 (?) but later recast
in Breadalbane Gothic. – Hidden in riparian trees, a disused
RAILWAY VIADUCT, 1885–6: five skew arches with crenellated
parapet and bartizans.

MOIRLANICH LONGHOUSE, 1.7km. NW. Late C18 or early C19.
Township survivor now in the care of the National Trust for
Scotland. Rubble walls with thatched cruck roof under corrugated iron. Byre in W end; dwelling in E has a hanging lum
(flue) of wood and clay.

STONE CIRCLE, 0.6km. E. Six uprights up to 2m. high set in a flattened circle 9.5m. by 8.5m. Particularly massive stones on sw. Three cupmarks on the northernmost stone.

FINLARIG CASTLE. *See* p. 508.

# KILMAHOG S 6000

A few houses at the T-junction of the A821 with the A84.

ST BRIDE'S CHAPEL, 3km. NW. Rubble foundations of a small oblong chapel with clear step up to E sanctuary. – In the walled GRAVEYARD, rebuilt 1932, a FRAGMENT of an Early Christian cross and a few lying SLABS. – A single fine HEADSTONE with an angel face and wings compressed under its flattened ogee top; to James McKinlay, tacksman of Inverchagernie †1823, and his son Peter †1828.

KILMAHOG GRAVEYARD. Rubble-walled enclosure, probably late C18, entered through a gabled portal with semicircular archway. BELL carried in a small round-arched opening in the gable apex. – Foundations of the pre-Reformation ST CHUG'S CHAPEL are indiscernible. – Many moss-covered lying SLABS. – Plain but well preserved TABLE TOMB in rust sandstone to Flory McNab †1806. – Several pedimented or arch-topped HEADSTONES, late C18 and early C19, including a tall stone with pediment block erected by Francis, Earl of Moray, in memory of Robert Stewart, tenant in Glenfinglas, †1840. – Two piers with dentilled cornices flank the MACFARLAN MONUMENT, a sandstone wall with block pediment carrying an elegant urn commemorating William Macfarlan of Bencloich, Stirlingshire, and Luggiebank, Dumbartonshire (*sic*), †1851; sculpted by *Barclay* of Glasgow. – C19 MORT-HOUSE.

GARTCHONZIE BRIDGE, 1.3km. SSW. 1777. Rubble crossing of Eas Gobhain. Two segmental arches with central cutwater. Inscribed tablet records date and royal funding from Annexed Estates.

KILMAHOG BRIDGE. Dated 1777. Rubble structure crossing Garbh Uisge. Two wide segmental-arched spans with central cutwaters.

KILMAHOG WOOLLEN MILLS. C19 with two-storey additions, 1965 and 1969. Three low rubble gables to the road. At the rear, the lade and a 4.27m. wood and iron undershot wheel, still in use.

LOCH VENACHAR SLUICE HOUSE, 1.7km. SW. 1856–9, by the engineer *James Bateman*. Symmetrical wall of rock-faced masonry on eleven segmental sluice arches. Pavilions at centre and ends are pedimented.

DESCRIPTION. A few rubble cottages, early C19, survive. One, formerly the TOLL HOUSE, has a canted gable to the road with an added canted bay. Of the villas, THE HIRSEL, late C19, is distinguished by the steep bellcast pyramid roof of its square entrance tower. GREEN SHADOWS, by the river, fills a splendidly bargeboarded gable with a timber canted bay. Across the river at BRIDGEND COTTAGE there are gables and decorative barge-boards in abundance.

INVERTROSSACHS HOUSE, 5.8km. SW. Built as a shooting lodge, 1844, but later extended and recast in 1911. Some further rebuilding, 1968. Hipped and dormered W front attractively irregular with a small ogee-roofed entrance tower. A second similarly roofed tower at NE. Duller S and E fronts, symmetrically organized with projecting hip-roofed ends, open on to terraced gardens. On the W lawn, a concrete baluster SUNDIAL, the plate dated 1767. Some 0.3km. E, close to the approach drive, is a small symmetrical KENNEL-HOUSE with hipped gables.

LENY HOUSE, 0.3km. N. Small Scots Jacobean mansion by *David Bryce*, 1845–6, with the expected proto-Baronial crowstepping, double-height bay window and canted bay below corbelled gable, plus a conically capped, round entrance tower at the NW corner (a feature later familiar in Bryce houses). Lugged roll-moulded doorway under armorial panel. Harled C17 house with dressed margins and pedimented eaves dormers forms N façade. – V-plan C18 WALLED GARDEN to W. Obelisk SUNDIAL, *c.* 1630, much weathered.

FORT, Bochastle, 0.7km. SE. Remains of C1 Roman earthworks.

3 FORT, Dunmore, 1.1km SW. on the S flank of Bochastle Hill, an impressive situation overlooking the flood plain. Iron age. Four walls provide defence except on the E where the steep slope must have sufficed.

Church and castle.

KILMARONOCK CHURCH. The parish, dedicated to St Ronan, dates from the C14. The present church, pleasantly situated in a tree-shaded graveyard, replaced an earlier, possibly part medieval, building in 1813. It is austerely classical, a three-bay hall with pedimented W and E gables, built in red sandstone rubble, harl-pointed with ashlar dressings. A squat square belfry, lead-domed over a cornice, sits at the W end of the roof ridge; it bears the 1813 date, though it was repaired in 1849 and again in 1909 when the church roof was renewed and re-slated. W entrance door and radiating fanlight in a round-arched ashlar portal, plain but corniced. Above this, but below the pediment, a blank sandstone tablet. In the N and S walls, three multi-paned double-hung windows, with radiating glazing in the upper sash, sit in tall, broad, round-arched openings. A Venetian arched window in the E gable, 1898, by *James Thomson*. In the cramped vestibule, a timber screen names the incumbents from 1325. To the l., a stone stair climbs to a small W gallery which crosses the first window bay to be carried on thin cast iron columns. Pipe ORGAN in the gallery. Segmental plaster vault ceiling, introduced by *H. E. Clifford*, 1909. – Original pews. – In the sanctuary, refurbished in oak in 1898–9 by *James Thomson*, dado panelling, an octagonal PULPIT, and a COMMUNION TABLE with a cusped open front carved in the spandrels with wheatsheaves and vines. – There are several commemorative brass PLAQUES. Erected 1890, a mural TABLET in white marble on black to the Rev. William Berry Shaw Paterson. – In the gallery, a large but plain white marble TABLET in memory of Sir George Hector Leith Buchanan †1903, his wife Eliza Caroline Tod †1899 and their fourteen children who are all named; sculpted by *James Young*. – STAINED GLASS only in the E window; by the *Abbey Studio*.

The church sits in a GRAVEYARD first walled in 1695. The kirkyard has been several times enlarged, reaching the roadway in 1901 and spreading E in 1921. Plain square GATEPIERS with corniced copings mark the entrance from the road. A short stretch of coursed masonry with saddleback coping stones survives but much of the walling is ruinous. The oldest graves lie closest to the church; among them a few, generally indecipherable, lying SLABS, C18, and several early C19 HEADSTONES with well-lettered inscriptions. – A broken SLAB, incised with the lines of a cross, leans against the W gable; it may be late medieval in origin. – Among the familiar funerary designs is an unusual MONUMENT to the Rev. Andrew Whyte †1834: a short fluted obelisk and urn standing on the moss-quilted table of a squat square base cornered with fluted quarter-columns. – Built into the wall at the NW corner of the graveyard is a short flight of steps leading W across a lane to ruinous OUTBUILDINGS, early C19, forming a simple U-plan. Beyond that is the MANSE, 1803–4, a decently plain L-plan dwelling with rendered walls and ashlar dressings.

WAR MEMORIAL, 1.7km. SW. Designed by *D. Y. Cameron*; erected 1921. High boulder cairn carrying a tapered Peterhead granite shaft crowned with a small ringed cross. Inset in the base, a granite slab inscribed with the names of the war dead. Outer ring of spaced boulders.

KILMARONOCK CASTLE (Mains Castle). A C15 tower-house, probably built by the Dennistoun family but now hollow, holed and roofless. Its four high storeys, constructed in red sandstone rubble with dressed quoins and margins, rise from a steeply battered base or talus. Held in precarious stability by shrouds of parasitic vegetation, the masonry has collapsed in several places. The gables have gone and only a fragment of corbelled parapet moulding remains at the NE wallhead. Windows, most little more than slots, have chamfered jambs with deep splays penetrating walls more than 2m. thick. Traces of round-headed openings appear at third floor. At second-floor level, above a gap in the masonry on the E face, a larger round-arched opening is discernible. This appears to have been the entrance doorway leading, according to MacGibbon & Ross, directly into the Hall. A fireplace in the W wall is flanked by narrow windows with deep splayed reveals. Providing more generous light to this end of the Hall on the now heavily overgrown N and S walls are two larger windows evidently once divided by mullion and transom. The interior of the tower, originally vaulted at ground-, first- and second-floor levels, is void but it is clear that the upper walls contained many small chambers and recesses. A small staircase, barely evident in the SE corner of the tower, led down to two vaulted storeys below; a turnpike in the NE corner evidently rose to the upper levels.

KILMARONOCK HOUSE, beside the castle. Dated 1901. A modest mid-C19 house reworked as an Arts and Crafts villa with Baronial attitude. Crowstepped gables and a round entrance tower with a bellcast leaded dome, a roll-moulded entrance doorway and studded door all assert indigenous allegiance. More Anglophile, the cream roughcast wall, a gratuitous buttress, and the two-storey hall wall of leaded glass held in a mullioned and transomed grid, crude in execution yet vaguely redolent of Lutyens.

GARGOWAN LODGE, 0.6km. W on the N side of the A811, marks the entrance to the South Avenue leading to Buchanan Castle (q.v.). It is a mid-C19 dwelling with a narrow bargeboarded gable and hoodmoulded door at the centre of the SW front. WOODEND LODGE comprises two L-plan cottages, late C19; one in snecked sandstone, the other painted. Both have mullioned and transomed windows and Tudor hoodmoulds. Quadrant walls and Egyptian-style GATEPIERS were probably built in 1854, the work of *William Burn*, designer of the now-ruined castle which lies 2km. NE. A cast iron girder BRIDGE, probably a mid-C19 replacement for an earlier suspension bridge, takes the Avenue across Endrick Water.

# *7000*    KINBUCK    S

A village with an untidy one-sided street scarcely worthy of its pleasant site on the banks of the Allan Water. Near derelict spinning mill by the river.

KINBUCK BRIDGE, 0.4km. N. Dated 1752. A narrow carriageway carried on two segmental arches. Rubble structure with splayed cutwaters stepping back above and carried below on a flared concrete base. Heavily reinforced with plated steel ties. Blockwork-faced abutments to the S.

OLD GLASSINGAL HOUSE, 0.8km. SE. Mid C18. Three-bay, two-storey, gabled simplicity. Roman Doric pilastered doorpiece. Lower outbuildings form U-plan court on E. Of the Victorian mansion built 1863–4 by *Pilkington & Bell*, for Thomas S. Smith (1815–69), founder of the Smith Art Gallery and Museum, Stirling (q.v.), nothing remains. Demolished 1966; only GATE-PIERS and two quirkily detailed LODGES, evidently by the same architects, survive on the B8033.

WESTER CAMBUSHINNIE, 1.5km. N. Probably C18. Single-storey cottage, harled with margins. Attached bothy incorporates sculptured baluster, perhaps a sundial fragment.

CROMLIX HOUSE. *See* p. 353.

# KINCAID HOUSE *see* MILTON OF CAMPSIE

# KINCARDINE-IN-MENTEITH
## PARISH CHURCH *see* BLAIR DRUMMOND

## KINLOCHARD                                    S  *4000*

Hamlet at the w end of Loch Ard.

MILL OF CHON. One-and-a-half-storey painted rubble dwelling
with piended eaves dormers. Boulder footings at rear.

## KINNAIRD HOUSE                                F  *8080*
### 1.8km. N of Carron

Ponderous Scots Jacobean, by *James Thomson* of *John Baird & James
Thomson*, 1895. At the centre of the entrance front, a battlemented low tower and *porte cochère*, its corners topped by dome
finials.

## KINNEIL HOUSE *see* BO'NESS

## KIPPEN                                        S  *6090*

A village stretching along the N-facing slopes above Flanders Moss
with wonderful views N to the Menteith Hills and Ben Ledi.

Former FREE CHURCH, Main Street. By *F. McKinnon* of Stirling,
1878–9. E.E. gable front with square belfry tower to r.; built in
coursed and squared red sandstone rubble with ochre stone
dressings. In 1908 the spire was declared unsafe and demolished.
Since 1944 secularized and now brutalized beyond redemption.

Former PARISH CHURCH. Built, or rebuilt, 1691. In 1777–8 it
was repaired and enlarged by *William Thomas*, wright at Killearn,
and became a T-plan kirk with three galleries reached by internal
stairs. The crowstepped W gable of red sandstone rubble still
stands, carrying a fine four-columned bellcote with a swept and
moulded pyramid and weathervane. BELL dated 1618, its inscription recording that it was recast and enlarged in 1726. Short N and
S walls buttress the gable and return to form a small enclosure.
The four-centred-arched door in the S wall is a reconstruction
but preserves original jambstones at low level W. On the E face
of the gable were three step-arched memorial TABLETS, C19:
one is missing, the remaining two illegible, but adjacent panels,
1923, record the original inscriptions commemorating members
of the Galbraith family.

There are numerous lying SLABS and TABLE TOMBS, C18
and C19, in the walled GRAVEYARD. Among a variety of HEAD-
STONES, a simple red sandstone marker recurs: minimally
inscribed, these bear dates ranging from 1766 to 1829. – Celtic
CROSS incut with interlacing pattern and a bead and reel edging;
to local farmer John McNiven †1866.

PARISH CHURCH, Fore Road. Good parish church Gothic of
1823–7, by *William Stirling I* and *William Stirling II*. Reconstruction, alterations and refurbished interior, 1924–8. The formula is
familiar: a skew-gabled, three-bay nave fronted by a square, three-
stage N tower. Hooded pointed-arched windows are tall and broad
with Y-tracery. In the tower, a BELL cast by *J. & W. Young* of
Glasgow, 1873, its oak crosshead from the tower of the Old
College, Glasgow, 1696. Above the belfry are four clock faces,
installed by local watch- and clockmakers *Robert & John Dougall*,
1881, and above these a castellated parapet with four high finials
rising from diagonal buttresses. The church appears to have been
galleried on three sides with the pulpit located on the S gable. In
1878, *David Robertson* of Edinburgh recast the seating arrangements. Half a century later a major transformation occurred.
  Between 1924 and 1928, under the direction of *Reginald
Fairlie*, the chancel was added with a high segmental arch of pink
Biggar stone broken through the S gable. The roof was reconstructed with a seven-bay panelled and beamed ceiling, and a
new N gallery, accessed from the cantilevered stone stair in the
tower, was formed. In 1931, turning water to wine, *Eric S. Bell*
converted The Grove, a cottage lying immediately E of the
chancel area, into the present CHURCH HOUSE (*see* below), an
oblong hall of red sandstone with a crowstepped E gable from
which a canted buttressed bay with three pointed windows projects. How independently the two architects worked is unclear
but they must surely have collaborated on the design of the hall,
staircase and buttressed half-octagon entrance bay which unite
church and Church House at the angle of their L-plan relationship. Over the pointed-arched doorway an ogee hoodmoulding
terminates in a slender statue of the Virgin. Later still, 1938, *Bell*
built the PRAYER CHAPEL (*see* below). Tucked against the W
side of the tower, it is constructed of Locharbriggs stone inside
and out. A stone Christ with uplifted palms 'as on the threshold of
His ascension'* rises from the parapet; the work of *Hew Lorimer*.
  FURNISHINGS. Accompanying the external alterations a whole
new interior emerged; richly appointed thanks largely to *Fairlie*
and the sustained patronage and design involvement of *D. Y.
Cameron*, examples of whose art and craftsmanship are to be
found throughout the building. – Octagonal PULPIT, r. of the
chancel arch, by *Andrew Thom & Sons* of St Andrews, 1985, its
cornice carved with oak-leaves and acorns, lapis lazuli and onyx
ball finials on the newel posts of the stair. – Under the chancel's
timber vault, on the S wall, hangs a BANNER of silk rose damask
designed by *Cameron*. – Below it, four wooden FIGURES: the
Risen Christ and John the Baptist by *James A. Woodford*, London,
and two cherubs by *John Crawford* of Glasgow. – BRONZE,
'Youth with the Cup of Life in his Hand' by *Henry Wilson*,
London. – Timber PANELLING, given an attenuated Gothic
treatment where it is raised under the banner, by *Whytock &
Reid*. – MINISTER'S CHAIR, LECTERN, PRAYER DESK and

* R. W. A. Begg, *The Renovation of Kippen Parish Church, 1924–1961* (1962), 28.

COMMUNION TABLE by the same workshop, 1935; the last, carved with wheat and grapes, sits on Iona marble. – ELDERS' CHAIRS and STALLS by *Thom & Sons*, 1985. – Silver VASES and ALMS DISH by *Edward Spencer* of the London Artificers' Guild, *c.* 1935. – HANGING LAMPS of remembrance by *Fairlie*. – STAINED GLASS, 1924, by *Herbert Hendrie*: l., the figures of Faith and Hope robed in crimson and yellow; r., Charity in blue.

In the BAPTISTERY, to the l. of the chancel arch, a silver bowl, 1848; pedestal FONT by *William Wilson* on a base of Greek Ionian marble; arched timber CANOPY, 1931, by *Morris Maclaurin* carved with symbolic fruit, flowers and birds. – Bronze STATUE of Charity by *Alfred Gilbert*. – Hoptonwood stone TABLET, 1925, by *Herbert W. Palliser* records names of ministers from 1574 to 1920; a second stone, 1985, by *Allan & Sons Ltd.*, continues the roll. – ORGAN by *William Hill & Son and Norman & Beard* of Norwich, 1928. Cyclamen carved around the console and, above, 'Innocence' carrying a lily, the work of *James A. Woodford*. – Framed ALTAR FRONTAL, with Old Testament figures, from Assisi, early C16. – Ash PEWS from St Oswald's Parish Church, Edinburgh, installed 1964. – The CARVING of ceiling bosses, flying and kneeling angels, and the burning bush on the gallery front (this last designed by *Douglas Percy Bliss*, 1929) carried out by *Thomas Good*. – All six windows have STAINED GLASS. Those closest to the chancel, both by *Herbert Hendrie*, coruscate with light around the images, the glass like 'crushed jewels and mother of pearl': w, the sacrifice of Mary of Bethany, a memorial to Lady Jean Cameron †1933; E, the themes of Motherhood and Childhood, to Annie Henderson †1934. – Middle of the w wall, an almost Celtic intertwining incorporating holly, rose, snowdrop, daffodil etc. by *Gordon Webster*, 1971. – Opposite, two cusp-arched panels by *A. Ballantine & Gardiner*, 1895, show the Good Shepherd and what appears to be the dispensing of bread to some far from emaciated Victorian children. – Below the gallery, w and E, more warm-toned C19 inset panels by *James Ballantine & Son*. – Above w, scenes from a faithful life by *Gordon Webster*, 1963, and E, Sowing and Reaping by *Hendrie*, 1928.

PRAYER CHAPEL. Easel PAINTINGS by *Cameron* and *Sir Thomas Monnington*. – BRONZES of St Elizabeth of Hungary and the Virgin Mary which the sculptor, *Alfred Gilbert*, intended as trials for the Duke of Clarence's Memorial in the Chapel Royal, Windsor. A third bronze, a Head of Christ, by *Alfred Hardiman*. – HANGING LAMP by *Robert S. Lorimer*, a trial-cast for the Thistle Chapel, St Giles Cathedral, Edinburgh. – STAINED GLASS in both lancet windows: Christ at prayer. In the tower, a bipartite window, 1930, illustrating Christ's entry into Jerusalem and St John setting down his vision of the Holy City.

In the entrance hall between church and Church House, a Hoptonwood stone TABLET cut with a biblical text by *Hew Lorimer*. – ALMS BOX from Florence, C17. – Of four STAINED GLASS windows, those designed by *John K. Clark* are most idiosyncratic: one, 1985, in which the artist *Willie Rodger* also had a hand, commemorates James Carmichael of Shirgarton with images of his house, his trade, his dog and two geese; the other, 1986, displays the varied interests of a Glasgow lawyer, James Lyndsay Orr.

The CHURCH HOUSE interior is an intimate, even domestic, space still redolent of its cottage origins. Two arch-braced trusses, in part adze-wrought, carry a broad-boarded ceiling of pitch pine. Bolection-moulded wall panelling by *Scott Morton & Co.* brought from Moray Place, Edinburgh. Sandstone segmental-arched chimneypiece on S wall; keystone carved with angel head and wings. Fluted oak pilasters frame a fielded panel above the fire bearing the inscription BLESSED ARE THE PURE IN HEART / FOR THEY SHALL SEE / GOD. – Refectory TABLE by *Whytock & Reid*. CARVINGS of St Andrew and St John by *James A. Woodford*. – 'Entry into Jerusalem' BRONZE by *Alfred Hardiman* on a high stone base designed by *S. Rowland Pierce*. – In the E bay, four STAINED GLASS scenes from Christ's life by *Herbert Hendrie*.

BRIDGE, Boquhan Burn, 1.9km. NE. Late C18. Red sandstone structure of three segmental arches on rounded cutwaters, the central span higher and wider. Ashlar arch rings. Parapet-height piers on the bridge between centre and S arches. Ruinous E side.

GILLESPIE MEMORIAL HALL, Fore Road. Now a house. Four-bay E.E. hall by *David Robertson*, 1877–8. Saddleback skews. Gable to street with three hooded lancets with vesica over.

KIPPEN READING AND RECREATION ROOMS, Main Street. 1906; refurbished 1992. Gable front, shaped at the apex and lit by a large Venetian window, linked l. to square tower with plain corbelled parapet. Roughcast with red sandstone dressings.

WAR MEMORIAL, Main Street. By *A. N. Paterson*, *c.* 1920. Octagonal base of Northumberland stone with inset panels of grey-green Ellswater stone inscribed with the names of the fallen. From this rises an Ionic column with marked entasis, its capital enriched with Saltire carving and carrying an apex cross on back-to-back open pediments of an almost Gothic profile. Around the base is a low octagonal wall of red sandstone.

### DESCRIPTION

Beside the kirkyard is the village's oldest street, RENNIE'S LOAN, still much as it was in the C18. Little more than a lane, it is a secret inner space at once urban and domestic. A hanging anvil sign identifies the SMITHY, a roughcast two-storey dwelling now in the care of the National Trust for Scotland. Stepping downhill beside it, a similar house with a single-storey pantiled extension, and across the lane another, also pantiled but with slated eaves. An iron wheel, set decoratively in the cobbles, recalls the cartwright's craft. Ahead, framed in this intimate fragment of C18 townscape, is the BLACK BULL, dated 1729, a two-storey, three-bay house, gabled with scrolled skewputts, its roughcast walls irregularly edged by red sandstone margins and quoins. Once an inn on the Back Road from Stirling, it too has been restored by the National Trust for Scotland.

As at Buchlyvie (q.v.), MAIN STREET is generously wide, broad enough for market days. A few trees shade the verges. There is, however, no mercat cross, though the War Memorial (*see* above) might be mistaken for one. It stands by the kirkyard gates, where the street is widest, marking the village centre. N of the burial enclosure lies GLEBE HOUSE, another late C18 dwelling with the familiar text PAX INTRANTIBUS SALUS EXEUNTIBUS BENEDICTIO HABITANTIBUS over its central door and a bow window added by *R. F. Brebner*, 1907. Across the road, hard to the pavement, HILLSIDE HOUSE, three-bay, late C18, with red sandstone skews and a single-storey NE extension. Linked to this is KIRKHILL, also late C18 but with a gabled Gothic porch of 1844 facing the garden.

Downhill on STATION ROAD, garden walls conceal the former home of Sir D. Y. Cameron, DUN EAGLAIS, a harled two-storey dwelling in Lorimeresque style by *Charles E. Whitelaw*, 1902–3. Later alterations in a Scots Renaissance idiom, by *A. N. Paterson* and *Cameron* himself, added the SW drum and entrance loggia, 1911, a two-storey NW wing and drawing room, dated 1923–4, and a studio to the NE in the 1920s. Interior plasterwork and joinery combine classical detail with the intimacy of Arts and Crafts and the more abstracted naturalistic motifs of Art Nouveau.

Uphill, MAIN STREET begins in two-storey, gable-to-gable vernacular. On the N side, the CROSS KEYS HOTEL, part late C18; roughcast with painted margins, a three-bay house with two later bays added W. The former Free Church (*see* above), scarred by crass conversion, disrupts the scene but the mid-C19 CARSEVIEW and its neighbour, each with simple pediment block lintels over pavement doors, restore village scale. On the S, there is comparable unpretentious quality at the POST OFFICE, a five-bay block of two houses, probably late C18, separated by a pend and enhanced r. by the insertion of an early C20 glazed shopfront with a dentilled cornice. Thereafter continuity breaks down. Running SW from the Recreation Rooms (*see* above), a short terrace of three red-tiled gable-fronted houses, *c.* 1910 (?), attempts to re-establish the street wall. But detached houses now predominate. The TOLL HOUSE, a wide three-bay cottage with attic bays, claims a 1782 date. It marks the transition into FINTRY ROAD and the brief onset of bungaloid suburbia. Fortunately, rural values reassert themselves at CAULDHAME where a series of low, rose-bordered cottages lines the NW side of the road. LAUREL COTTAGE is best, its steep slated roof accented by three piended attic-bay dormers.

FORE ROAD has more good cottages. Among them are ROSE COTTAGE, skew-gabled, obliquely set to the road close to the junction with Main Street, and, further downhill on the village edge, LOMOND VIEW COTTAGE, long and low with two gabled porches. These, and the CROWN HOTEL, an adaptation of a couple of two-storey three-bay houses, are probably of early C19 date. So, too, is HELENSFIELD, opposite the Parish Church (*see* above), though it is grander, decidedly symmetrical with three wallhead gabled dormers and a decorative rectangular fanlight over its central doorway. Symmetrical, too, though nominally romantic, BEECH COTTAGE, late C19, pushes two slate-hung canted bays through a wide bellcast eaves to become eaves dormers, each splayed piended roof oddly horned with a curved ridge tile.

LARABEN DOOCOT, 2.8km. WNW. Late C18. Brick structure, square in plan; now roofless. Decorative stringcourses above door height and at the wallhead.

MAINS OF GLINN, 4.2km. SSW. Mid-C18. Five-bay, two-storey laird's house. Restored by *McGurn, Logan, Duncan & Opfer*, 1994–5. Harled with dressed surrounds and all the more ascetic for its moorland setting.

SIGNAL BOX, 1.6km. ENE. 1893; disused since 1959. High brick base with timber-framed glazing on three sides.

MOTTE, Keir Knowe of Drum, 1.7km. WNW. Raised oval promontory on 'the steep slope of an ancient shore-line'.* Excavations show this to have been a stockaded motte from the early Middle Ages. At the centre, nine post-holes were found indicating a timber structure *c.* 4.5m. square.

BOQUHAN HOUSE. *See* p. 275.
GRIBLOCH HOUSE. *See* p. 534.
WRIGHTPARK. *See* p. 793.


KIPPENROSS HOUSE                    S
                          1.5km. S of Dunblane

Classic two-storey-and-basement Georgian with asymmetrical later additions; built for the Pearson family as a successor to Old Kippenross (*see* below). The core of the house is of *c.* 1770, harled with rusticated quoins and moulded architraves to all windows. Five-bay SW façade, three bays advancing slightly under a pediment, unadorned though capped with urns, as are the flanking balustraded parapets. A flying stair rises to a central entrance door with Roman Doric columns and a pedimented entablature, both modern. In 1789 *James Playfair* proposed a variety of ideas for enlarging and ennobling this elegant but unremarkable conceit for the Stirling family. None was undertaken, but in 1810, or perhaps a few years later, *William Stirling I*, maintaining the original height, materials and detail, built a SE wing to form a simple L-plan arrangement, extending the façade by three bays. Later, *c.* 1832, the less grand NW wing was added, also L-shaped with service accommodation returned on the NE to create an inner courtyard. In 1881 *R. Rowand Anderson* recast the interior, replacing the central staircase with a beautiful well stair rising r. from the rear of the hall in a slow ascent through sumptuous space to an arcaded gallery above. Archways in both the lower and upper halls were enriched with decorative plaster-work. A double-height canted bay was also added to the rear elevation, lighting ground- and first-floor rooms NW of the stair.

* RCAHMS, *Stirlingshire*, i (1963), 176.

A more radical intervention, which left the house in its present form, occurred in 1967–9 when Anderson's successor firm, *Sir Rowand Anderson, Kininmonth & Paul,* cut back both wings to the width of the original house. A pedimented SW porch was removed and a new flying flight of steps built in reinforced concrete. Within, a room was added at centre rear on the first floor, and though this entailed the sacrifice of the Venetian window which originally lit Anderson's staircase, a single round-arched light, inserted by *Anderson* halfway up the principal flight, remains. Although some splendid decorative ceiling plasterwork was lost, some fine plaster ceilings survive. In the Morning Room, ground-floor r., above a consoled cornice, paired birds and baskets of flowers are incorporated into a symmetrical pattern of tendril-like scrolls. Beyond, in Stirling's wing, the Cupola Hall and Ballroom have a more Neo-Classical theme: Greek key, Vitruvian scroll and rinceau.

Close to the SE gable is a baluster-type SUNDIAL, dated 1830. – A short distance uphill, the U-plan STABLES COURT, 1822, opens S, its W and E ranges, with segmental-arched cart entries, terminating in slated pyramids. – To the W, the estate drive is carried across the Allan Water on the high rubble superstructure of KIPPENROSS BRIDGE, C18, borne by two segmental arches on a rounded cutwater.

OLD KIPPENROSS. An earlier house of 1646 was partially destroyed by fire in 1768. The present harled structure was erected on the older barrel-vaulted cellars which, opening to the garden, form an extra storey to the S. A symmetrical house of three in-line parts, the outer units under slated pyramids, the centre similarly roofed but a storey higher with a N gable. Axial and cubic, the feeling is nonetheless Gothick, imparted by quatrefoils at each end of the N entrance front and a central pointed window at high level S. In the N gable, two inset stones. One, a FRAGMENT with roll-moulded lower edge, bears the words SOLI DEO GLORIA. The other, a framed marriage TABLET with family arms, the initials AS and IM and the date 1617. – Over a gateway in the WALLED GARDEN, another inscribed marriage PANEL, dated 1703.

CAIRN 0.4km. N. Large mound 21m. in diameter and 2.3m. high; kerb-stones on S.

# KIRKINTILLOCH                      ED 6070

Town which began *c.* 1212 as a burgh of barony under the superiority of William Comyn who held a castle here. Burgh status was later lost, perhaps at the beginning of the C14, but regained in 1526. The town developed as an industrial centre, cotton spinning the principal activity, after the opening of the Forth & Clyde Canal in 1775. In the C19 the burgh's architecture and layout received unfavourable comment, the *Parliamentary Gazetteer* of 1851 noting: 'It is an irregularly built, strangely arranged, confused looking little town, conveying by its aspect the idea of such

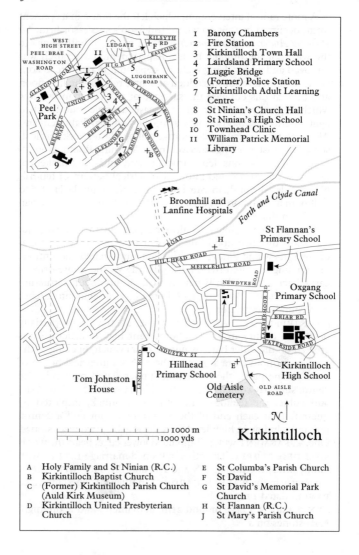

1  Barony Chambers
2  Fire Station
3  Kirkintilloch Town Hall
4  Lairdsland Primary School
5  Luggie Bridge
6  (Former) Police Station
7  Kirkintilloch Adult Learning Centre
8  St Ninian's Church Hall
9  St Ninian's High School
10 Townhead Clinic
11 William Patrick Memorial Library

Kirkintilloch

A  Holy Family and St Ninian (R.C.)
B  Kirkintilloch Baptist Church
C  (Former) Kirkintilloch Parish Church (Auld Kirk Museum)
D  Kirkintilloch United Presbyterian Church
E  St Columba's Parish Church
F  St David
G  St David's Memorial Park Church
H  St Flannan (R.C.)
J  St Mary's Parish Church

entire devotement to trade and manufacture as precludes nearly all attention to the graces of exterior appearance.'

Some rebuilding took place at the end of the C19. The C20 brought massive expansion of the town, large housing estates being developed to the E and much of the old centre redeveloped.

CHURCHES

HOLY FAMILY AND ST NINIAN (R.C.), Union Street. By *P. P. Pugin*, 1891–3. Late Gothic, built of bullnosed red sandstone ashlar. Nave with E and W (liturgical N and S) aisles; one-bay chancel. The S (liturgical W) front is approached by elaborate flights of steps. These, together with the flat-roofed baptistery and porch in front of the gable, were added in 1954. In the gable, a hoodmoulded pointed window of five small lights under a huge circlet filled with cinquefoils and cusped loop tracery. At the aisles, the windows are set in slightly recessed panels. In the rectangular openings, cusped pointed lights; the windows at the four centre bays are three-light, the others one-light. At the chancel's N gable, a short hoodmoulded and pointed window entirely filled with cusped loop tracery; foliaged stops at the ends of its sill.

Inside, a scissors roof over the nave; S gallery. Pointed arcades with octagonal stone pillars. At the N (liturgical E) end the arches are narrower and the pillars' shafts are of polished granite. – Elaborate Gothic REREDOS and ALTARPIECES of *c.* 1900 over the High Altar (by *Boulton & Son*, 1893) and the altars at the ends of the aisles, marble and alabaster lavishly used. – Late C19 STAINED GLASS in the N windows, that over the High Altar depicting the Holy Family surrounded by Angels and with Emblems of the Evangelists; in the window of the N aisle, King David and St Ninian, in that of the E, Angels.

KIRKINTILLOCH BAPTIST CHURCH, Townhead. Built as Kirkintilloch Original Secession Church, it is by *Malcolm Stark Jun.*, 1892–3. Cheap Gothic.

Former KIRKINTILLOCH PARISH CHURCH (AULD KIRK 13 MUSEUM), Cowgate. Crowstep-gabled cruciform church built in 1644 (the date on a panel above the window in the S gable). Later alterations and additions have transformed a not unambitious essay in Gothic survival into a much couthier example of a Scottish kirk, its 'historic' character emphasized since 1890 when the harling was stripped from the rubble walls.

As first built the church's W gable was surmounted by a bellcote and contained a pair of pointed windows above a rectangular door. Each of the other gables contained a large pointed window, its outer order chamfered, the inner with a cavetto moulding. The window's sill served as the lintel for a door with a chamfered surround. At the inner end of each of the side walls of the limbs was a tall rectangular transomed window, its surround again chamfered. On the S slope of the E gable, a large stone sundial.

Alterations seem to have been made from early in the building's history. The first, perhaps in the late C17, may have been the contraction of the W door, the inserted jamb again chamfered. Possibly also in the C17 a door or window was inserted in the W side of the S limb and the W limb's original S window was converted to a door; it was later again altered to form a window. In the earlier C18 a basket-arched door was inserted in the W side of the N limb.

More drastic alterations were carried out in the late C18. Between 1788 and 1798 galleries were erected. Access to these was by stone forestairs built against both sides of the N and S limbs and cutting across the C17 windows in the side walls of all the limbs; these windows were consequently built up. Doors were inserted at the head of the forestairs. Another forestair was built against the W gable, one of whose windows was converted to a door. Also part of this late C18 work was the rebuilding of the bellcote by *James Lang* in 1798. This is of birdcage type, with a segmental arched opening in each face. In 1839 *John Herbertson* dressed up the N door with battlemented piers, the front of each decorated with a pointed panel. Later C19 alterations, probably those made in 1890 by *John W. Small*, added dormer windows to the E and S limbs and a wooden cupola over the crossing. In the C20 a couple of cement-margined windows were inserted on the N side of the E limb and the S side of the W. The E door was widened for the present museum use *c.* 1980.

Inside, the W gallery of 1788 survives. So too does the E, a replacement of 1839 but apparently replicating its predecessor of 1792. Both have panelled pine fronts, with anta pilasters at the ends and flanking the central roundels; dentil cornices. – At the W side of the entrance to the S limb, the tall PULPIT made by *John Scott* in 1782. Panelled bowed front. The back has a pair of Gothick panels framed by fluted pilasters which carry two tiers of Doric entablature under a mutuled cornice; above, a large plaster shell. – In the E vestibule, a BELL signed by *Gerhard Koster*, 1663, and bearing the arms of the city of Glasgow. It was bought for Kirkintilloch Parish Church in 1769.

GRAVEYARD. Laid flat in gravel S of the church are the top slabs of several table stones and some headstones. One of the headstones is roundheaded and bears the date and initials 1742 and TAL together with the relief of a wright's tools including a setsquare and dividers.

KIRKINTILLOCH UNITED PRESBYTERIAN CHURCH, Kerr Street. Now The Park Centre. Built in 1854–5, adapting a design by *John Dick Peddie*. Simple Gothic. Buttressed gable front, the hoodmould of its entrance with large foliaged label stops. Above, a stepped arrangement of three lancets under continuous hoodmoulding, the label stops again foliaged. Quatrefoil opening at the top of the gable which is surmounted by a gableted bellcote.

ST COLUMBA'S PARISH CHURCH, corner of Waterside Road and Old Aisle Road. By *Robert B. Rankin*, 1968–9. L-plan group of church and hall, all clad in dark brown brick. Over the church, a steep tiled gablet-roof. Convex N gable with a tall window in the centre. Inside, boarded ceilings expressing the roof pitches. Simple wood and glass screen behind the sanctuary. – STAINED GLASS. In the N window, one light (the Angel of the Lord) by *Norman M. Macdougall*, 1921, formerly in the now demolished St Andrew's United Free (originally Free) Church.

ST DAVID, corner of Ledgate and Kilsyth Road. Secularized. By *John Herbertson*, 1836–7. Broad piend-roofed box, the N front and W side of broached ashlar, the other elevations of rubble. Tall pointed windows. At the N gable's slightly advanced centre, a Y-traceried window under an ogee-arched hoodmould whose large foliaged knot finial serves as a corbel under the bellcote. This is tall, with panelled pilasters and a small crocketed spire; the corner pinnacles are now missing. The N front is badly obscured by the desperately plain HALL added by *Honeyman & Keppie* in 1895–6.

ST DAVID'S MEMORIAL PARK CHURCH, Alexandra Street. Originally St David's United Free Church. Expensive but simple Gothic with a Scottish inflexion, by *J. Jeffrey Waddell*, 1924–6, following a design of *c.* 1921 by *P. Macgregor Chalmers*. It is built of stugged and squared khaki-coloured masonry with lightly tooled ashlar dressings; roofs covered with Lake District slates. Six-bay nave with N and S aisles, the N aisle diagonally buttressed. The aisles' W bays are narrow, with monopitch roofs; at the three E bays they are broader, with double-pitch roofs. Buttressed semi-octagonal chancel at the E end. NW steeple.

In the buttressed W gable of the nave, a pointed window with cusped loop tracery in the head; foliaged label stops to the hood-mould. In the sides of the nave, roundheaded and cusped clear-storey lights. At the narrow W bays of the aisles, pointed windows with cusped heads. At the aisles' E bays, depressed arched windows, each containing three cusped lights. The E gable window of the N aisle is also of three lights but taller and round-headed, with quatrefoil tracery; hoodmould with foliaged label stops. The chancel windows are pointed and hoodmoulded, the label stops again carved with foliage. In the heads, tracery of cusped loops and quatrefoils.

The steeple is tall. At the bottom of the square tower, N entrance in a pointed arch, its hoodmoulds' label stops carved with tightly curled foliage. In the W face, a very simple round-headed window. The tower's second and third stages, the third slightly intaken above a stringcourse, are marked only by narrow slit windows. Lofty fourth stage, again intaken above a string-course and with chamfered corners. In each main face, a pair of tall belfry openings. The outer label stops of their hoodmoulds are again carved with foliage, the inner with heads. Battlement with hefty stone spouts and corner pinnacles. Within it, an octagonal stone spire studded with projecting blocks of stone. At the SW corner of the tower, a sloping-topped buttress-like stair turret.

E of the church, a plain Gothic HALL by *William Baillie*, 1910–11, overlaid by harled additions by *Keppie, Henderson & Partners*, 1977 (restored after a fire in 1986). E extension by *John W. McDonald*, 1962–3. – In front of the hall, a Celtic cross WAR MEMORIAL designed by *P. Macgregor Chalmers* and executed by *A. Muir & Sons*, 1922.

INTERIOR. At the bottom of the tower, a vestibule, the beams of its wooden ceiling supported on rounded corbels. The walls of the church itself are faced with ashlar lightly tooled with diagonal broaching. Nave arcades with pointed arches carried on pillars with octagonal capitals. Boarded wagon roofs over the nave and aisles whose floors are laid with orangey red tiles. Tall chancel arch with narrow bands instead of capitals, the N band carved with corn and grapes, the s with foliage. Another wagon roof over the choir whose floor is raised by two steps and paved with green and white marble; oak-panelled walls. On the s side of the choir, the organ chamber (containing an ORGAN by *Charles Anneesens & Fils*, 1899; rebuilt by *Ingram & Co.*, 1926) with pointed arches to the N and W. Another pointed arch from the choir into the groin-vaulted sanctuary, its floor raised by a further three steps and again of green and white marble. Its walls' oak panelling is slightly more elaborate than that of the choir and with an elders' bench.

FURNISHINGS of 1926. In the choir, an elaborately carved Gothic oak COMMUNION TABLE. – CHOIR STALLS again of oak, bearing Celtic and late Gothic motifs. – On the s of the chancel arch, an oak PULPIT, the bands above and below the body carved with oak leaves and acorns, the upper band also containing the depiction of a bird. – N of the chancel arch, a brass eagle LECTERN. – Studiously simple oak PEWS in the nave and aisles.

STAINED GLASS. The chancel's E window (the Ascension) is of 1926. Realistic in strong dark colours, the heads of the Apostles apparently portraits. – In the N window of the choir, one light (Loyalty, Love and Purity). It was erected in Park (originally Kirkintilloch United Presbyterian) Church in 1967 and moved here in 1992. – At the N aisle, the E gable's window (the Good Shepherd) is by *William Glasby*, 1926. – Also by *Glasby* the con-temporary window (the Penitent Woman Anointing Our Lord's Feet) in the N wall. To its W and more effective are two windows of 1946 (the Beatitudes) and 1939 ('I have fought a good fight') by *Gordon Webster*. – In the s aisle, at the E end, another narra-tive window (Our Lord Commissioning the Apostles to Make Disciples of All Nations) by *Glasby*, 1928. – Much better is the stylized realism of the single light (King David) of 1926 in the W bay of this aisle.

ST FLANNAN (R.C.), Hillhead Road. By *William J. Gilmour*, 1969–70. Walls of brown brick pierced by tall narrow windows. Huge double-pitch concrete tiled roof. Porch at the glazed s gable. At the N, a chancel, its gable V-shaped with a central buttress and large side windows. Fin-like concrete vertical feature at the NE corner of the nave.

ST MARY'S PARISH CHURCH, Cowgate. By *George Bell II* of *Clarke & Bell*, 1912–14. Large but earthbound late Gothic, built of stugged and squared red sandstone with diagonally broached dressings. Broad nave with low and narrow E and s aisles and N transepts; rectangular chancel taller than the nave. At the s end of the aisles, semi-octagonal stair turrets. Angle-buttressed square tower at this end of the nave. It is of three stages. Squat bottom stage containing the entrance placed in a broad arched and hoodmoulded recess flanked by large but empty canopied image niches. The two upper stages are lofty. At the first of these, a tall pair of lancets in the s face. The top stage has rather more elaborate two-light belfry openings. Battlement with fussily detailed tall pinnacles.

The nave's clearstorey is articulated by heavy stepped

buttresses, their lower parts hidden inside the aisles. Three-light clearstorey windows with cusped loop tracery. At the aisles, simple lancets except at the W bay of each where there is a rectangular opening containing three cusped lights. The transept gables are divided by buttresses into two bays containing tall two-light windows with mouchettes in their heads. In the chancel's gable, a large five-light window with cusped loop tracery.

Inside, hammerbeam roofs over the nave and transepts. Round-headed arches from the nave into the aisles. Broad pointed arches to the transepts and S tower from which a gallery pushes forward. Another pointed arch, flanked by narrow arches containing organ pipes, into the short chancel whose sides are pierced by more pointed arches containing pipes of the ORGAN (by *Norman & Beard*, 1915). – On the chancel walls elaborate Gothic oak arcading. The COMMUNION TABLE of 1914 occupies the centre of the chancel. On the E side of the chancel arch, the contemporary stone PULPIT with a wooden Gothic canopy. On the W, a large combined stone LECTERN AND FONT supported on veined black marble columns.

STAINED GLASS. The five-light chancel window (Te Deum), strongly coloured and tightly drawn, is by the *Stephen Adam Studio*, 1926. – In the W transept, a pair of two-light narrative windows (Scenes from the Life of Our Lord) by *Atkinson Bros.*, 1914. – In E transept another pair of windows (Ezra, Nehemiah, Our Lord as the Carpenter, Christ the King) in a stylized realistic manner, by *Douglas Hamilton*, 1954. – In the aisles, highly accomplished small windows (the Six Days of Creation) designed by *Willie Rodger* and executed by *John K. Clark*, 1987. – At the S end of each aisle, another window by *Willie Rodger* and *John K. Clark*, (the Nativity of Our Lord; the Passion, Deposition from the Cross, and Resurrection of Our Lord), 1991–2.

CEMETERY AND PARK

OLD AISLE CEMETERY, Old Aisle Road. The name commemorates the pre-Reformation St Ninian's Chapel which stood here. At the NE entrance, a sturdy GATEWAY probably of the early C18. At the E face of the roundheaded arch V-jointed rustication as high as the springing; in-and-out voussoirs to the arch itself. On top of the archway, reached by a flight of steps on the N side, an ashlar-walled square room, its slabbed pyramidal roof topped by a birdcage bellcote. Square chimney at one corner.

Large array of Victorian and later monuments, several looking decidedly expensive. In the N row of the cemetery's NW section, a big MONUMENT to Beatrice Clugston, founder of Broomhill Hospital, designed by *W. F. Salmon*, 1891. Red sandstone Gothic frame containing a bronze relief by *Pittendrigh MacGillivray* depicting a nurse tending a woman and, above, a portrait bust of Miss Clugston and cherubs' heads.

PEEL PARK, Peel Brae and Union Street. Laid out in 1898 on the site of the medieval castle of Kirkintilloch, the rectangular mound on which it stood still partly visible; 30m. by 17m. with a broad ditch on the S and E sides. At the entrance from Peel Brae, a classical WAR MEMORIAL GATEWAY of 1925, designed by *John Shanks* and constructed of grey New Zealand marble donated and cut by the *Fletcher Construction Co.* Shallow pediment over the round-arched central entrance; rectangular pedestrian gateways. At the ends, screen walls bearing bronze panels (by *Charles Henshaw*) inscribed with the names of the dead. – A little W of this, an octagonal cast iron BANDSTAND made by the *Lion Foundry*, 1905. Artisan Mannerist Composite columns and leafy spandrels; small dome on the centre of the roof. – W again, a drinking FOUNTAIN, also of cast iron and by the *Lion Foundry*, 1905. High relief lions' heads on the pedestal which is topped by the classical statue of a lady holding a vase on her head. – Cutting across the NW corner of the park is a small section of the base of the ANTONINE WALL (*see* Introduction, p. 13–15).

PUBLIC BUILDINGS

AQUEDUCT, E of Barleybank. By *John Smeaton*, 1768–75, to carry the Forth & Clyde Canal over the Luggie Water. Ashlar, a single broad segmental arch, its lower part infilled in 1826 when an embankment was constructed for the Monkland & Kirkintilloch Railway (the line now removed). The walling above the arch is slightly recessed and gently concave. Plain corbels support the parapet topped by a cast iron railing.

BARONY CHAMBERS, corner of West High Street and Cowgate. Built as a combined townhouse and parish school in 1813; *Andrew Galloway* was the architect. Dead plain three-storey three-bay block, the front faced with rough ashlar. Projecting from its centre is a steeple which gives civic status to the building and the burgh. The tower's base is plain; in the W side, a door reached by a forestair. The upper stages are all intaken and corniced. At the main stage above the base, giant angle pilasters and a roundheaded window (the E and W dummies) in each face. The next stage is lower. Angle pilasters again but panelled; elliptical arched windows (the E and W again dummies). Then a cubical clock stage. Belfry with chamfered corners and rectangular openings. Octagonal stone spire.

BROOMHILL AND LANFINE HOSPITALS, off Kilsyth Road. Disused. Two originally separate but adjoining institutions which amalgamated in 1960 but closed in the 1990s. BROOMHILL HOSPITAL, founded in 1875 by Miss Beatrice Clugston as a hospital for incurables, occupies the former Broomhill House, a substantial early C19 villa extended at each end in the mid C19. The E wing and end tower, its slated spire topped by a cupola, were added in 1884 by *James Salmon & Son.* In 1895 the same architects further enlarged the original house by the addition of a W wing containing nurses' accommodation. A new nurses' home immediately W of the hospital was designed by *John Shanks* in 1923 and opened the next year. – LANFINE HOSPITAL to the E, built as a cottage home for incurable consumptives, is by

*James Salmon & Son*, 1904. Single-storey L-plan ward block
backed by a two-storey administration building, half-timbering
in its gable. Verandahed addition by *John Shanks*, 1909–10.

FIRE STATION, Glasgow Road. By *A. J. Smith*, 1955. Utilitarian,
with a brick hose tower.

HILLHEAD PRIMARY SCHOOL, Newdyke Road. By *James Taylor*,
1955–6. In the Festival of Britain manner, with a low brick tower.

KIRKINTILLOCH ADULT LEARNING CENTRE, Southbank
Road. By *Richard Murphy Architects*, 2001, the roof swept down
towards the Forth & Clyde Canal.

KIRKINTILLOCH HIGH SCHOOL, Briar Road. By *Keppie,
Henderson & Partners*, 1969–71. Woefully utilitarian.

KIRKINTILLOCH TOWN HALL. Free Baroque on a budget, by
*Walker & Ramsay*, 1904–6. Symmetrical front, its badly eroded
ashlar stonework largely covered by flaking cement render. Tall
and narrow windows at the upper floor lighting the hall behind.
Slightly advanced three-bay centrepiece, higher than the rest
and corniced. Projecting from this, a bowed porch, its small
upper windows set between alternating stumpy Doric columns
and piers which support a plain frieze under a mutule cornice of
extravagant projection. In front of each end bay, a balustraded
single-storey block, its inner corner rounded. Domed octagonal
cupola on the roof. Plain single-storey w addition of *c.* 1930.

LAIRDSLAND PRIMARY SCHOOL, Kerr Street and Queen Street.
Begun in 1874–5 by *W. & R. Ingram* as a tall single-storey U-
plan building fronting Kerr Street; advanced and gabled ends.
The main block was raised to two storeys in 1893 when *James
Mitchell* added the parallel rear block facing Queen Street. This
block's N elevation is quite plain except for a central gablet containing a round window.

LUGGIE BRIDGE, High Street and Eastside. Bridge over the
Luggie Water, built in 1672. Three segmental-headed ashlar
arches with triangular cutwaters. The bracketed iron footpaths,
with latticed railings and ornamental lamp standards, were
added by the *Kirkintilloch Foundry* in 1881.

OXGANG PRIMARY SCHOOL, Lammermoor Road. By *Dumbarton
County Council*, 1968. Flat-roofed, with brown brick walls and
white painted fascias.

Former POLICE STATION, corner of Townhead and Luggiebank
Road. By the Dumbarton County Architect, *Joseph Weekes*,
1934. Harled Scots domestic, with boat dormers and a large
gablet.

ST FLANNAN'S PRIMARY SCHOOL, Newdyke Road. By
*Dumbarton County Council*, 1958–9. In the Festival of Britain
manner, with a low brick tower. Extension by *R. J. Walker &
Smith*, 1964.

ST NINIAN'S CHURCH HALL, Union Street. Two-storey building developed in two stages. The earlier part, built as a school
and chapel in 1875, faces w. At this front, mullioned and transomed windows, all of three segmental-headed lights; two gablets
at the wallhead. In 1895 *W. Gowan* remodelled the four-bay s
elevation and extended it E by a further six bays, the windows

again mullioned and transomed but their lights minimally pointed.

ST NINIAN'S HIGH SCHOOL, Bellfield Road. Large but thrifty Neo-Georgian, by the Dumbarton Deputy County Architect, *B. P. Gibb*, 1929–31.

TOM JOHNSTON HOUSE, Lenzie Road. 1984–5, by *Strathkelvin District Council* as its own offices. Of two and three storeys, large and sensible but unexciting, with bands of dark brown brick and glass; ribbed metal roofs and a canopy over the entrance.

TOWNHEAD CLINIC, Townhead. By the Dumbarton County Architect, *Joseph Weekes*, 1932. Neo-Georgian, harled with red sandstone trimmings. Piend-roofed two-storey main block and single-storey pavilions, these with Venetian windows, the tops of their arched lights dummies.

WILLIAM PATRICK MEMORIAL LIBRARY, High Street. By *Strathkelvin District Council*, 1994. Restrained Postmodern, of two and three storeys, with blockwork walls and piended tiled roofs.

DESCRIPTION

GLASGOW ROAD is the approach from the W. A few late C19 villas lead up to the Fire Station (*see* Public Buildings, above). This is followed by the late C20 GEORGIAN HOUSE (No. 5), its determined attempts to live up to its name comically misguided. No. 1 is late Georgian, the entrance with Roman Doric columns *in antis*. Roundheaded attic window in the pedimented E gable. It stands on the corner of WASHINGTON ROAD whose E side is taken up by the extensive garden of CAMPHILL HOUSE, a large late C19 bay-windowed villa. Italianate touches; iron cresting on the roof. E of the entry to Washington Road, on the N side of Glasgow Road, a former TOLLHOUSE (No. 12) of the earlier C19. Bracketed stone canopy over the door which is flanked by dummy windows painted with the toll charges.

WEST HIGH STREET runs E off Glasgow Road. Its N side begins with WESTERMAINS FARM (No. 78), a rendered short terrace of vernacular cottages of the earlier C19, mostly crowstep-gabled and originally thatched. At the bottom of the garden of the E cottage, an octagonal GARDEN HOUSE, again of the earlier C19 and with pointed windows. E of Coal Road, Nos. 60–62 West High Street, by *John Shanks*, 1905, a Glasgow-style three-storey tenement with battlemented bay windows. It is followed by KELVIN COURT of *c*. 1990, whose narrow triangular oriel windows break forward from an otherwise bland front. Then, Nos. 18–24, a three-storey block of flats over shops by *Robert Wemyss*, 1906. Oriel windows topped by shaped gables at the ends; at the centre, a curvaceous chimneyed gablet decorated with a carved calf's head. Pend to the close behind in which is a two-storey house, its first-floor entrance reached by a forestair. No. 16 West High Street is of *c*. 1800; one gable is crowstepped. Plain mid-C19 buildings on the S side of West High Street, the E (Nos. 17–19) with a central gablet. At the E end, Peel Brae

leads up to Peel Park (*see* Cemetery and Park, above). On Peel
Brae's E side, at the corner of West High Street and Cowgate,
Barony Chambers (*see* Public Buildings, above).

HIGH STREET continues the line of West High Street. At its W
end, looking down Cowgate, is the William Patrick Memorial
Library (*see* Public Buildings, above). Beside it, BABYLON, the
former BLACK BULL CINEMA by *John Fraser* of Dunfermline,
1921. Pedimented centre at the front block containing the foyer;
large shed behind. Then a sharp drop in the ground to New
Lairdsland Road, a late C20 relief road which cuts across High
Street. E of this barrier, on High Street's N side, a *moderne* garage
of 1934. At the end of High Street, the Luggie Bridge (*see* Public
Buildings, above). Immediately across the bridge, on the S side
of EASTSIDE, a polished Peterhead granite obelisk erected in
1877 as a MONUMENT to Hazelton Robert Robson who had
drowned the year before trying to save a child when the Luggie
Water was in flood. Eastside's buildings are generally unambitious and undistinguished late C19 but at Nos. 23–29, on the E
corner of Ledgate, an early C19 two-storey block. Chimneyed
wallhead gablet and rope-moulded club skewputts. In Ledgate,
St David's Church (*see* Churches, above).

COWGATE is Kirkintilloch's principal street. At its N end, on the
W side, Barony Chambers (*see* Public Buildings, above) is
followed by the churchyard of the former Kirkintilloch Parish
Church (Auld Kirk Museum), for which *see* Churches, above.
Much of the rest of Cowgate was rebuilt in an inoffensive manner
in the later C20. At Nos. 48–52, on the N corner of Union Street,
a block by *John Fairweather*, 1900, with corniced first-floor
windows and an octagonal corner turret. In UNION STREET,
Kirkintilloch Town Hall and St Ninian's Church Hall (*see* Public
Buildings, above) and, set back on the edge of Peel Park, Holy
Family and St Ninian's R.C. Church (*see* Churches, above).
On the E side of Cowgate, S of Broadcroft, a DRINKING FOUN-
TAIN presented to the town by John Watson of Earnock in 1893.
It was made by *J. Whitehead & Son*. Grey granite battered
pedestal, the bowls projecting from shell-headed niches. Italianate
open superstructure. At each of its pedimented faces, a pair of
roundheaded arches, the supporting columns with shafts of pink
granite. After the fountain, some C19 buildings on the E side of
Cowgate followed by St Mary's Parish Church (*see* Churches,
above). In KERR STREET, Lairdsland Primary School and the
former Kirkintilloch United Presbyterian Church (*see* Churches
and Public Buildings, above). In ALEXANDRA STREET, some
cottages of the mid or late C19. Among them, No. 23 with a tall
semi-octagonal gableted dormer and No. 35 with fluted piers at
its cast iron porch. For St David's Memorial Park Church, *see*
Churches, above.

TOWNHEAD continues the line of Cowgate S of the Forth &
Clyde Canal. For the former Police Station on the corner of
Luggiebank Road, *see* Public Buildings, above. It is followed by
a short stretch of C19 buildings. Among them, the early C19
Nos. 23–27 with a pedimented wallhead gablet. More wallhead

gablets but of the later C19 at Nos. 37 and Nos. 39–43 (of 1876).
On the W side of Townhead, a three-storey red sandstone block
(Nos. 2–14) by *John Shanks*, 1896–1900. Georgian survival of a
sort, with consoled cornices over the first-floor windows. Then
late C20 buildings containing flats over shops, followed by
Kirkintilloch Baptist Church (*see* Churches, above) and a mix-
ture of C19 and C20 blocks. No. 91 was built for the Kirkintilloch
Co-operative Society in 1913. First-floor windows framed in open
pedimented Doric aedicules. At its s end, Townhead swerves
to the SW. On the SE side, the Townhead Clinic (*see* Public
Buildings, above). On the NW, MUIRHEAD HOUSE of *c.* 1840,
with an anta pilastered and corniced doorpiece. In INDUSTRY
STREET, Townhead's continuation to the SE, a grey granite
DRINKING FOUNTAIN presented to the town by James
Dalrymple of Woodhead in 1905. Stripped classical, topped by
a small dome.

THE STABLES, Glasgow Bridge, 2.2km. SW. Standing beside the
Forth & Clyde Canal, a piend-roofed stable block (now a
restaurant) of *c.* 1820. Two-storey seven-bay front of droved
ashlar, the centre advanced under a pediment containing a
round dummy window. Segmental-arched doors and windows;
above the centre door, a loft opening. Single-storey W wing,
perhaps a mid-C19 addition.

*6000*    LANRICK CASTLE    S
2km. W of Doune Lodge

In 1801 Ramsay of Ochtertyre thought the house 'more magnificent than convenient'. Over eighty years later Groome was
impressed by 'a handsome modern castellated edifice, with very
fine grounds'. Abandoned in the 1950s, it survived as an empty
shell, still sufficiently intact to keen the sadness of its fate, until in
February 2002 it was demolished.

For much of the C18 the estate remained in the hands of the
Haldane family. From 1791, however, when improvements were
first made, the old house was transformed by a sustained programme
of aggrandizement carried out at the behest of the new owners,
the MacGregors. Clan Gregor Castle, as Lanrick became known
for a time in the early part of the C19, was all that Groome admired.
What was the nature of the earliest architectural changes and who
carried them out is by no means clear but a rough sketch surviving
in the National Archives of Scotland suggests that the house may
have been castellated before 1800. By 1803 *James Gillespie Graham*
was at Lanrick in the employ of the owner, Sir John MacGregor
Murray. The architect's further involvement is recorded in 1822,
1826 and 1828 and it was certainly he who, over a period of thirty
years or so, gave the castle its final Gothicized symmetry.

At the centre of the s front, doubtless incorporating some of the
fabric of the C18 dwelling, is a harled, skew-gabled, three-bay
block rising to three storeys. It is flanked by lower two-bay
wings, also gabled. Both the centre and wings have lintelled

windows with dressed margins; at the wallhead are corbelled ashlar parapets, battlemented with wide plain merlons. Corbelled bartizans capped with slated cones accent the skews. On the slated slopes behind the parapets, small rounded dormers given conical roofs to match the bartizans were added later, probably by *Andrew Heiton Jun.*, *c.* 1875. Flanking the two-bay wings are lower two-storey additions, each cornered with three-storey cylindrical towers against which abut single-storey-and-basement bowed ends. These elements, too, are harled under closely crenellated ashlar parapets. Single tripartite windows, large below but smaller and hooded above, light the links to the towers. In the towers themselves and the curved terminations beyond, all the openings have pointed arches. Fronting the full width of the three-storey centre is an ashlar porch and *porte cochère* with castellated octagonal corner buttresses, traceried pointed-arch windows and four-centred archways opening to the covered entrance. More than anything else, this frontispiece declares the hand of Gillespie Graham.

The interior possessed a number of rooms in late Adam style. Entrance hall and staircase Gothicized *c.*1815.

U-plan, two-storey, Gothic STABLE BLOCK with a pyramid-roofed tower at the centre. Rubble-built Tudor COTTAGE linking to KENNELS with tree-trunk column verandah; *c.* 1825. Set into the river bank is a vaulted GROTTO with rustic Gothic arch; late C18. – L-plan N LODGE, *c.* 1845; crowstepped with porch in re-entrant. – Baronial S LODGE with arched gateway and long curving screen wall; *c.* 1875. – Estate WALL penetrated by a Tudor archway gate; by *Gillespie Graham*, 1828.

BRIDGE, 0.2km. E. Constructed *c.* 1875 to replace the original suspension bridge which *James Smith* of Deanston had designed in 1842. Single segmental span; wrought iron with cast iron parapet. Abutments have ashlar crenellations.

MACGREGOR MONUMENT, 0.4km. SW. Late C18 or early C19. A strange clan memorial. Hidden in the woods, it seems to surge up out of the earth like the spirelet of some subterranean steeple. The base is exceptionally tall rising from the forest floor in the form of an ashlar-faced tree trunk, the shaft romantically carved with the stumps of two cut branches and the scars of other lopped limbs. At the top of the trunk is a serrated parapet of triangles within which stands an attenuated three-column Roman Doric rotunda carrying an entablature on top of which is placed a single tall Roman Doric shaft. An urn once stood on the capital of this topmost column while another column was originally located at the centre of the rotunda.

## LARBERT AND STENHOUSEMUIR    F *8080*

Agglomeration of late C19 and C20 housing. At each end, a church (Larbert Old Church and Stenhouse and Carron Church) and some shops. Halfway along the 2km. Main Street the Dobbie Hall provides a weak civic centre.

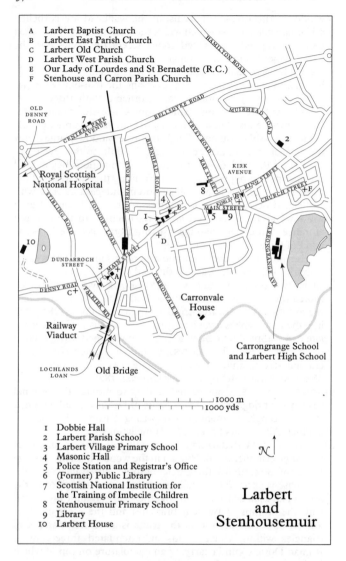

A Larbert Baptist Church
B Larbert East Parish Church
C Larbert Old Church
D Larbert West Parish Church
E Our Lady of Lourdes and St Bernadette (R.C.)
F Stenhouse and Carron Parish Church

1 Dobbie Hall
2 Larbert Parish School
3 Larbert Village Primary School
4 Masonic Hall
5 Police Station and Registrar's Office
6 (Former) Public Library
7 Scottish National Institution for
  the Training of Imbecile Children
8 Stenhousemuir Primary School
9 Library
10 Larbert House

Larbert
and
Stenhousemuir

Stenhousemuir developed from the late C18 as housing for workers at the Carron Ironworks (*see* Carron and Carronshore). Larbert remained a small village beside its parish church until the mid C19 when the railway was opened and an ironworks founded.

### CHURCHES

LARBERT BAPTIST CHURCH, Main Street. By *Ferrier Crawford*, 2000. Rendered walls, the tops of the gables glazed, and a broad-eaved double-pitched roof. Low round tower at the NE corner.

LARBERT EAST PARISH CHURCH, corner of Main Street and Kirk Avenue. Originally Larbert East United Free Church. By *James Strang*, 1900–2. Large but mechanical Geometric, the masonry of bullnosed buff sandstone. Slated bellcast roof. Battlemented SE tower. To the N, a villagey HALL by *Wilson & Tait*, 1923–4.

LARBERT OLD CHURCH, Denny Road. Georgian Gothic, Perp in flavour though not in detail, by *David Hamilton*, 1818–20. Big buttressed and parapeted box, built of yellowish ashlar, droved at the main walling, polished at the buttresses, all sadly eroded by sandblasting. The breadth is disguised at the front (W) gable by an angle-buttressed square tower, its battlement's corners pinnacled. In the belfry openings, intersecting tracery. Crocketed pinnacles on the angle buttresses at the W corners of the church; plainer pinnacles above the diagonal buttresses at the E corners. At the E end, a chancel flanked by an organ chamber and vestry, all added by *P. Macgregor Chalmers*, 1909–11, in the same style as the church.

Inside, the ceiling was replaced with an open wooden roof by *John McLaren*, 1887. Also of 1887 the D-plan GALLERY, its front decorated with blind Gothic arcading. – The stone CHANCEL ARCH is by *Chalmers*, 1909–11, the inner order with foliaged capitals and standing on foliaged corbels. – N of the arch, a routine Gothic oak pulpit made by the *Bennet Furnishing Co.* to McLaren's design in 1887. – Brass eagle LECTERN of *c.* 1900 S of the arch. – In the ashlar-faced chancel, a COMMUNION TABLE of 1911. Behind it, a canopied REREDOS with figures of Prudence and Fortitude, erected as a war memorial in 1923. – On the N side of the chancel, the ORGAN by *Wilkinson & Sons*, 1887, rebuilt in this position by *Ingram & Co.*, 1911.

STAINED GLASS. E window (the Transfiguration of Our Lord) by *R. B. Edmundson & Son*, 1859. Very brightly painted in the style of contemporary Munich glass. – In the N wall, a series of windows under the gallery. The E of these (Acts of Charity) is by *Gordon Webster*, 1962. – The next window (Our Lord's command to St Peter; Our Lord Administering the Chalice to a Saint) is of 1935. – Then a strongly coloured window (St Christopher; Our Lord as a Child) by *Gordon Webster*, 1930. – The W window of this wall (Feeding the Hungry; Visiting the Sick) is of 1912. – In the S wall, the E window (Angels) is by *Stephen Adam & Son*, *c.* 1900. – Next to it, a cool-coloured narrative window (the Presentation of Our Lord in the Temple) of 1912. – Then a colourful but not very good window of *c.* 1895. – At the W end of the wall, a Glasgow-style window (the Risen Lord appearing to the Disciples on the Road to Emmaus) by *Stephen Adam & Son*, *c.* 1900.

GRAVEYARD to the W of the church. Just inside the E entrance, the rubble-built BURIAL ENCLOSURE of the Elphinstones of Quarrel, the N, S and W walls probably rebuilt in the early C19. The E wall seems to be C17 and contains a blocked entrance, its lintel inscribed with the initials RSE and EDC (for Sir Robert Elphinstone of Quarrel and his wife Dame Euphame Carstairs) and the date 1663. Inside the enclosure, built into the W end of the N wall, are the parts of a broken stone bearing the Elphinstone coat of arms and a Latin inscription commemorating Michael Elphinstone †1645 at the Battle of Kilsyth. – Beside it, a stone commemorating, among others, Michael Elphinstone †1640; it bears at the top his initials and coat of arms and those of his wife Mary Bruce. – Just S of the Elphinstone Enclosure, a HEAD-STONE to James Muir †1761 'who lost his life (with another of the hands) at Hispaniola in Mounta-Christa river (going over the Barr for fresh water) out of the long boats belonging to the Prince Ferdinand'. The top of the stone is carved with a head and skull, the narrow sides with an anchor and a pierced heart and coffin; on the W face, the relief of a ship in full sail. – Near the E end of the graveyard's N wall, a TABLET whose inscription has been recut, probably in 1764. It reads:

> HERE.LYES.INTRRED [*sic*].WITHIN.HIS.URNE
> THE.CORPS.OF.HONEST.GOOD IOHN.BURNE
> WHO.WAS.THE.EIGHT.IOHN.OF.THAT.NAME
> THAT.LIVD.WITH.LOVE.AND.DIED.WITH.FAME
> IN.CHANGING.TYMES.SADDEST.DISASTER
> TREW.TO.HIS.KING.LORD.AND.MASTER
> KYND.TO.HIS.KEVERED.NEIGHBUR.FREND
> WHOS.GOOD.LYFE.HADE.ANE.HAPPIE END
> HIS.SOUL.TO.GOD.HE.DID.BEQUEATH
> HIS.DUST.TO.LYE.THISSTONE.BE(N)EAT(H)
> ANNO 1653 REPAIRED 1764

Just W of this tablet, an ENCLOSURE with early C19 spear-head railings containing monuments to the Robertsons of Carron Hall. At its N end, the ashlar MONUMENT to Duncan Robertson †1824, with Roman Doric pilasters and a swan-neck pediment over the central compartment. – To the W, a cast iron MONUMENT to George Smith †1833, the corniced pedestal supporting an obelisk, its urn finial now on the ground.

At the W end of the graveyard, a large BURIAL ENCLOSURE with ornate cast iron railings of the earlier C19. At its centre, the ashlar MONUMENT erected by the Carron Company to Joseph Stainton of Biggarshiels †1825, manager of the Carron Works for thirty-nine years. Corniced pedestal supporting an urn-topped fluted Doric column. The inscription records of Stainton that 'BY ECONOMY, DILIGENCE, AND SCIENTIFIC SKILL, HE RELIEVED THE COMPANY FROM EMBARRASSMENT, AND PLACED IT IN UNRIVALLED PROSPERITY'. – E of this monument is one to Thomas Dawson †1873, a Neo-Gothic sarcophagus, the top carved with a floriated cross. – Beside it, a lower sarcophagus monument to Anne Dawson †1888, the top again carved with a cross but it is of interlaced Celtic type; the monument is signed by *John Hutchison*. – In the SE corner of the enclosure, a large granite tomb-chest MONUMENT to William Dawson yr. †1867. Doric entablature with rosetted metopes. The top rises into scrolled ends. On the S face, a high-relief bronze portrait bust. – W of the Stainton monument, a tall grey granite Celtic CROSS on a base of pink granite. It commemorates Margaret Dawson †1867 and is signed by *A. Macdonald, Field & Co.* of Aberdeen. – At the w end of the enclosure, the MAUSOLEUM of William Dawson †1874. Pedimented Doric temple, the bronze door decorated with rosettes and a laurel wreath. Inside, a marble statue of the Angel of the Resurrection, signed by *John Hutchison*. – s of the enclosure, a HEADSTONE of 1815 to George Calder and Margaret Lyon, its E face bearing the low relief of a ship in full sail.

LARBERT WEST PARISH CHURCH, Main Street. Originally Larbert West United Free Church. By *J. P. Goodsir*, 1900–1. Big broad box with transeptal outshots; late Gothic detail. Hall of 1898 to the E.

Inside the church the focus is on the ORGAN by *Norman & Beard*, 1903.

OUR LADY OF LOURDES AND ST BERNADETTE (R.C.), Main Street. By *Reginald Fairlie*, 1934–5. Harled hall-church, the slated roof piended at the E end. To the s, a piend-roofed and rendered clergy house of 1936, also by *Fairlie*.

STENHOUSE AND CARRON PARISH CHURCH, Church Street. Originally McLaren Memorial Church. By *John J. Burnet*, 1897–1900, and one of the most satisfying of an impressive series of churches designed by Burnet that mix Romanesque, Gothic and Arts and Crafts influences. The church consists of a nave and w tower, s aisle and sw porch, and is joined by a contemporary SE hall range to the manse (also by Burnet) of 1905–7. The walls are all roughcast, with red sandstone dressings; roofs covered with red tiles. In the N wall of the nave, paired fattish lancet windows, the E pair with cusped heads. In the E gable, a window of three lancet lights. On top of the gable, a Celtic cross. The w tower is muscular. In its w face, a two-tier window, the lower part consisting of two cusped lights, the upper a large Romanesque opening, its nook-shafts' cushion capitals decorated with Neo-Celtic carving; panel between the two tiers carved with a tree and inscription. Above, belfry openings, each of two huge round-arched lights with cushion-capitalled nook-shafts. The tower is finished with a parapet which breaks out into angle rounds at the corners. Inside the parapet, a pyramidal tile-roofed and lucarned spire. At the sw corner of the tower, a low semi-octagonal stair turret. The upper part of each corner is treated as a column, its capital carved with foliage and a bird. Projecting from the inner angle of the tower and s aisle is the long sw porch, its s end with an open-sided and bargeboarded wooden superstructure. Inside the porch, the door to the church has a semi-octagonal head; above, a minimally pointed window. The s aisle is flat-roofed and parapeted. In its s wall, three-light windows, their openings all shouldered arches with cusped heads. Hall range extending s from the E end of the aisle, with windows like those of the aisle and a basket-arched w door. Boldly bellcast roof. At this range's s end, the two-storey manse. Bay window at the w gable. At the s front, the position of the recessed entrance is marked out by half-timbering at the upper floor.

INTERIOR. s nave arcade of depressed arches springing from

octagonal piers without capitals. Depressed arch from the nave to the W tower in which is placed a gallery, its front panelled with Gothic blind arcading. In the aisle and nave, open wooden roofs of some complexity, the braces of the nave roof supported on moulded corbels, except at the E end where the brace rises from attached round columns, their capitals carved with Neo-Celtic decoration. Here is a rood beam carrying a wooden arch containing a pedestal, perhaps intended for a statue. This marks off the chancel, raised two steps above the nave and covered by a tunnel-vaulted boarded ceiling. In the chancel's N wall, a two-light hoodmoulded window. On the S side of the chancel, a depressed arch into the organ chamber.

Above an ashlar dado the walls are stencilled in imitation of green-coloured ashlar, the 'pointing' picked out in gold, each 'stone' bearing a gold fleur-de-lis. The chancel's E end, its floor level raised in 1921, is marked off as a sanctuary by a scalloped brace springing from corbels carved with angel musicians. More carved angel musicians on the ingoes of the E window whose three lights are framed by attached columns; foliaged label stops to the window's hoodmoulding. Round the sanctuary walls, a band of stonework carved with foliage and mythical beasts and the words 'HOLY HOLY HOLY'.

The FURNISHINGS are of as high a quality as the architecture.
26    In the sanctuary, the COMMUNION TABLE of 1921, designed by *John J. Burnet* as the church's First World War Memorial. It is of oak, the panels on its front and sides decorated with a floriated and gilded ground to which are fixed oak shields bearing the names of the fallen. At the centre of the front, a broad canopied niche containing the figure of Our Lord flanked by worshipping angels. In image niches at the table's W corners, figures of St Andrew and St George. All these figures were modelled by *William Vickers*. – In the chancel, oak CHOIR STALLS of 1899, decorated with floral bosses and carved by *Porter* of *Wylie & Lochead Ltd.* – PULPIT of 1899 on the N side of the entrance to the chancel. On the principal face of the semi-octagonal and marble-topped stone front, a relief of the *Agnus Dei*. Two other faces bear consecration crosses. On the S face, the high relief of an angel musician and, at its E end, an empty image niche. The back of the pulpit is of oak. – On the S side of the chancel entrance, an oak READING DESK in the same manner as the choir stalls. – In front of this, a silvered bronze FONT by *Albert H. Hodge*, 1900. Circular bowl supported on a sensuously modelled octagonal stem with figures of naked dancing children at four of the faces. – Studiedly simple pine PEWS in the nave. – ORGAN by *J.J. Binns*, 1902. – The STAINED GLASS is all by *Douglas Strachan*. E window (the Revelation of Heaven to St
25    John the Divine) of 1914. Jewel-like strong colours, the stylized figures set in swirling motion. – In the chancel's N window, the E light (the Supper at Emmaus) is of 1922 but much less dramatic. – The W light (the Angel at the Tomb of Our Lord) of 1950 is painterly. – At the E end of the nave's N wall, a strongly coloured dramatic but stylized narrative window (the Crucifixion) of 1937.

PUBLIC BUILDINGS

CARRONGRANGE SCHOOL AND LARBERT HIGH SCHOOL,
Carrongrange Avenue. Large but unexciting complex. At the N
end, Carrongrange School and an extension to Larbert High
School, both of 1999–2000, by *The Parr Partnership*. Walls of pale
buff blockwork enlivened by white and blue render and cladding
of the same ribbed metal as is used on the shallow-pitched roofs
on which sit maltings-type ventilators. At the S end, the flat-
roofed Larbert High School, by *Central Regional Council*, 1977,
the walls faced with brown brick and ribbed metal.

DOBBIE HALL, corner of Main Street and Burnhead Road. Earthbound Baroque, by *A. & W. Black*, 1900–1. Round-arched
broad entrance, its architrave with Gibbsian rustication, set in
an Ionic pilastered and swan-neck pedimented aedicule; above,
a second aedicule but with columns which would be orthodox
Corinthian were the volutes not upside-down and a broken
segmental pediment.

LARBERT HIGH SCHOOL. *See* Carrongrange School and Larbert
High School, above.

LARBERT PARISH SCHOOL, Muirhead Road. Now in other use.
Built by *James Burns* and *Alexander Wright*, 1826, but the present
appearance dates from 1862 when *Alexander Black* heightened
the walls by *c.* 1.3m. Tall single-storey rectangle. Painted front
of six bays, the openings all roundheaded and with projecting
keystones. The two S windows are set closer than the others. In
the next bay, a shallowly projecting entrance under a round
window; above, a bellcote, the top of its gablet with concave
sides.

LARBERT VILLAGE PRIMARY SCHOOL, Main Street. Restrained
late Victorian Classical, by *A. & W. Black*, 1891. Two storeys,
the ashlar masonry channelled at the ground floor of the front.
This is of six bays, the two outer bays at each end slightly
advanced with Corinthian pilasters at the corners of their upper
floor. The jambs of the ground-floor windows are treated as
attached Roman Doric piers; consoled cornices over the first-
floor windows.

LIBRARY, Main Street. By the Stirling County Architect, *A. J.
Smith*, 1971. Single-storey, the projecting ends of the flat roof
supported on up-ended I-beams.

MASONIC HALL, Main Street. By *A. & W. Black*, 1902–3. Two-
storey façade, with a segmental-pedimented entrance, large
first-floor windows and an overall balustrade.

OLD BRIDGE, Lochlands Loan. Built over the River Carron in
1782, it is of rough ashlar with arch rings of polished ashlar.
Two segmental arches (the NE a floodwater arch), triangular
cutwaters projecting each side of the pier.

POLICE STATION AND REGISTRAR'S OFFICE, Main Street.
Originally the Police Station and Larbert Parish Council Offices.
Plain Jacobean, by *A. & W. Black*, 1900–1.

Former PUBLIC LIBRARY, Main Street. By *A. & W. Black*,
1902–4. Single-storey pedimented front with a Venetian window.

RAILWAY VIADUCT over Falkirk Road and the River Carron. Designed by *Locke & Errington* and built for the Scottish Central Railway, 1848. Fourteen-span viaduct. Battered piers of bullnosed ashlar support the segmental arches whose arch rings and V-ended voussoirs are of stugged ashlar, the spandrels of hammer-dressed ashlar.

ROYAL SCOTTISH NATIONAL HOSPITAL, Old Denny Road. A development on the parkland of Larbert House (*see* Mansions, below) which had been acquired as a second site by the Royal Scottish National Institution (originally the Scottish National Institution for the Training of Imbecile Children, q.v.), in 1925. At the centre, the ADMINISTRATION BLOCK by *William J. Gibson*, 1928–35. Harled free Jacobean of two storeys; over the central entrance, a battlemented and oriel-windowed tower. The contemporary ward buildings (also by *Gibson*) are villa-like, each with an advanced and gabled centre containing a Venetian window. Verandahs across the front ending in low towers. – Near the E end of the site, a flat-roofed HOSPITAL by *James Miller* of Glasgow, 1935. – Undistinguished but friendly late C20 additional buildings.

SCOTTISH NATIONAL INSTITUTION FOR THE TRAINING OF IMBECILE CHILDREN, Central Park Avenue. Disused. The site is now mostly covered by a redevelopment of the 1990s but two buildings survive of the school and home for children with severe learning difficulties which was begun in 1862 and closed in 1989. They are of 1862, designed by *F. T. Pilkington* in his characteristic rogue Ruskinian Gothic manner, built of bullnosed masonry. At the N block, pierced chimneys, their simplified detail providing a foretaste of Art Nouveau. The S block has a centre tower and is encrusted with carving.

STENHOUSEMUIR PRIMARY SCHOOL, Rae Street. By the Stirling County Architect, *A. J. Smith*, 1954–7, in the Festival of Britain manner.

## DESCRIPTION

STIRLING ROAD is the approach from the S. It by-passes the Old Bridge and goes under the Railway Viaduct (*see* Public Buildings, above) on its ascent to Larbert Old Church (*see* Churches, above) at the corner of Denny Road. In DENNY ROAD, W of the churchyard wall, the OLD MANSE, the key dates of its building history provided by the lintel of a first-floor N window inscribed 'BUILT FEB/1635 AN' (the initials those of Alexander Norie, minister of Larbert from 1619 to 1645) and by a window in the E gable inscribed '1957 RESTORED LRH'. Rubble-walled, with crowstepped gables and a steeply pitched roof, now pantiled but probably thatched originally; chamfered margins to the windows. Irregular fenestration at the N wall; at the S (entrance) side, windows of regular size but their arrangement missing symmetry. To the W, Kirkmalling (*see* Villas, below). On Denny Road's N corner with Stirling Road, the COMMERCIAL HOTEL, small-scale mid-C19 Georgian survival with a quadrant corner.

On the opposite corner at the beginning of Main Street, the harled RED LION HOTEL built in the later C19, with a trio of simple Jacobean gablets.

MAIN STREET starts with a bitty collection of buildings of the mid and late C19 and of the C20. On the w corner of Dundarroch Street, Nos. 24–34 Main Street by *D. Frew*, 1900–1. Bullnosed red sandstone masonry. Bowed corner rising into a low round tower, its slated roof a truncated cone topped by exuberant ironwork. This block's use of shallowly projecting canted oriel windows and chimneys corbelled out from below the wallhead is repeated at the contemporary Nos. 36–44 (also by *Frew*) whose bowed corner is finished with a battlement. A little further E, on the s side, Larbert Village Primary School (*see* Public Buildings, above). Beside it, a late C19 cottage (No. 92 Main Street) with mullioned windows and bracketed eaves followed by Larbert Baptist Church (*see* Churches, above).

On the N side of Main Street at its corner with Foundry Loan, STATION TERRACE (Nos. 185–203 Main Street), built *c.* 1900 and originally of three storeys and an attic but cut down and drastically remodelled in the later C20 when the surviving upper floor was dry-dashed and a mansard roof put on. The Edwardian ground floor's Ionic pilastered tall shopfronts remain. On the E side of FOUNDRY LOAN, the STATION HOTEL, its present appearance of *c.* 1900. White painted walls with black trim, half-timbering and bargeboards. Lugged architraves and cornices at some of the windows. One is a broad rectangular oriel. Over one corner, a slated octagonal spire. E of the hotel, the RAILWAY STATION, a brown glass box of the late C20.

On Main Street's s side immediately E of the railway, the villa-like CLYDESDALE BANK of *c.* 1865. Relaxed cottage style, with bracketed broad eaves and bargeboards; sparingly applied Jacobean detail. In 1905 *John Baird & James Thomson* extended it E by one broad bay in the same manner. This is followed by small villas and cottages of the later C19. Among them, on the s side, Nos. 1–8 BROOMAGEBANK, double houses of the 1930s, each block piend-roofed with a centre chimneystack. Projecting centrepieces with rounded corners and horizontal windows; *moderne* doorpieces. A little further E and also on the s side, Larbert West Parish Church (*see* Churches, above). Beyond, on the N side at its corner with Burnhead Road, the Dobbie Hall and former Public Library (*see* Public Buildings, above). In front of the Dobbie Hall, a WAR MEMORIAL by *George Washington Browne*, 1922, its stonework now painted. Cenotaph, with a band of Greek key ornament above the inscription panel and a pulvinated frieze. Further E, St Bernadette's (R.C.) Church on the N and the Masonic Hall on the s (*see* Churches and Public Buildings, above). After the Masonic Hall, Main Street jinks to the SE, marking the beginning of Stenhousemuir. On the s, at the corner with Park Terrace, the Police Station and Registrar's Office (*see* Public Buildings, above). On the N, the PLOUGH HOTEL of the later C19, faced with white-painted render, the details picked out in black. Over the ground- and first-floor windows are hoodmoulds, those of the ground floor joined by a stringcourse. Beyond, the s side of Main Street contains small-town commercial architecture of the late C19 and early C20. The N side of Main Street and the s side of King Street have here been removed to provide a triangular car park for the shopping precinct of 1965–80 on KING STREET's N side. Also late C20 on the s side of Main Street is the Library (*see* Public Buildings, above). Beyond, Main Street continues with buildings on both sides. At the E end of King Street, on its corner with Tryst Way, the two-storey former STENHOUSEMUIR EQUITABLE CO-OPERATIVE SOCIETY LTD. BUILDING of 1889. Plain except at the canted NE corner where, above the wallhead, there is placed a pedimented panel containing an empty roundel intended for a clock face; flanking the panel, octagonal turrets of free Jacobean character. A little to the E, on the corner of Main Street and KIRK AVENUE is Larbert East Church (*see* Churches, above). The line of Main Street now turns again to the SE and is continued W by CHURCH STREET. Church Street and the streets to its N are mostly occupied by late C19 cottages. At the E end of Church Street, C20 local authority housing. Among this, Stenhouse and Carron Parish Church (*see* Churches, above).

<h2 style="text-align:center">VILLAS</h2>

CARRONVALE ROAD. TORWOODHALL. Large and rambling harled villa of *c.* 1900. Bargeboards and bracketed eaves at the roof; on top, an octagonal gazebo. – AIRLIE HOUSE. By *Frank Sheen* of Ingatestone, 1908. English Arts and Crafts, with white harled walls and red tiled roofs. Two-storey bow window at the gabled s bay of the E front; some porthole windows. – WOODCROFT. By *Thomas L. Watson*, *c.* 1890. English domestic with half-timbering, bargeboards and a red tiled roof, '. . . pleasing enough but not in any way remarkable' said *The Builder*.[*] CARRONVALE HOUSE. *See* Mansions, below.

DENNY ROAD. KIRKMALLING. Sizeable Arts and Crafts by *A. & W. Black*, 1908. Hammer-dressed stone walls with half-timbering at the gables; bellcast roof with bracketed eaves, covered with Lake District slates. The entrance is placed in a cut-out corner, the walling above supported on a squat Tuscan column.

<h2 style="text-align:center">MANSIONS</h2>

CARRONVALE HOUSE, Carronvale Road. Georgian house of *c.* 1780 reconstructed and enlarged in 1897 by *John J. Burnet* for the Glasgow businessman George Sheriff. The house which Sheriff had inherited in 1896 was unpretentious. Piend-roofed two-storey three-bay harled main block, its gentility asserted by consoled cornices over the ground-floor windows and the anta pilastered and corniced central door; at each end, a tall single-storey one-bay wing of *c.* 1820, bay windows added in the mid C19. Now used by the Boys' Brigade.

In his reconstruction of 1897 Burnet retained the Georgian main block but gave it a broad-eaved roof covered with red Rosemary tiles and replaced the entrance door by one decorated with guttae under the top panel. He also raised each of the existing wings to two storeys, with squat two-light mullioned lights at their new upper floors. At each end of the house was placed a set-back two-storey addition, slightly taller than the main block, the ashlar-faced upper floor enlivened with squat Artisan Mannerist Ionic pilasters topped by low-relief urns. The symmetry is disturbed by a single-storey block in the NW inner angle, its parapet a continuation of that over the bay window to its S. At the S end, recessed from the two-storey addition, a further but lower two-storey service wing, a two-bay round-arched ground-floor loggia at its front; to its S, a balustraded screen wall. On the N side of the house a broad verandah with ashlar piers rising through its roof to finials carved with high-relief swags of flowers and fruit, covers the E end. At the back of the verandah is the bowed N wall of the billiard room, a tiled frieze surmounting its rendered finish. Plain E elevation overlooking the brick walled garden. S of the house, an unfortunate addition of *c.* 1970.

The INTERIOR is of 1897. The front door opens into a small internal porch, occupying the SW corner of the vestibule, constructed of wooden panelling with etched glass panes set behind mullion-like balusters, its inner side carved with foliage and gryphons; Roman Doric columns at the inner door into the VESTIBULE which was formed by throwing together the Georgian entrance hall and the room to its N. Floor of veined marble, the marble carried up as a surround to the N fireplace; overmantel with bulging Doric columns. In the W window, a painted glass view of Dumbarton Castle. At the N end of the E side, a free Jacobean wooden screen, its pierced panels carved with gryphons, beyond which is a corridor-like INNER HALL. Free Jacobean with a high dado and lugged architraves to the doors, those at the ends with segmental-arched heads. On the E side, at the N end, a screen, its octagonal piers partly fluted, opening on to the undemonstrative Jacobean stair. To the r. of this screen, a Venetian door, partly glazed and incorporating pieces of stained glass, opens on to a small courtyard. On the Inner Hall's W side, a door into the STUDY (the S room of the late C18 house), its 1897 fireplace surround composed of Delft tiles set in an architraved wooden frame. At the S end of the Inner Hall, the DINING ROOM in the early C19 S wing and Burnet's principal S addition. Trabeated wooden ceiling; bay window on the W side. At the N wall's fireplace, a wooden overmantel of three diamond panels framed by spindle balusters. NE sideboard recess marked off by a beam, its end supported on corbels decorated with carved cherubs. In the top panes of the windows, restrained Glasgow-style stained glass.

The DRAWING ROOM is entered from the N end of the

Inner Hall. Above a low dado the walls are divided by wooden stiles into panels topped by a shelf-like cornice. Above the cornice, a deep plaster frieze decorated with cartouches set in swags of fruit. Coved ceiling, its enrichment of geometrical Jacobean type, with pendants. Opulent chimneypiece in the s wall. Bulging Doric marble columns, their shafts highly patterned. Overmantel with squat Ionic columns, again bulbous, supporting a frieze under the room's cornice which rises here to form a segmental pediment. Above, the room's frieze bulges forward and upward, its decoration more elaborate and including cherubs, gryphons and human heads as well as swags of fruit and a central cartouche. The small fire opening is placed in a cast iron surround, its top panel bearing a relief of *putti* musicians. On the N side of the room, a pair of recesses created by Burnet's alterations. The w is deeper but flows into the room. The E, marked off by an elliptical arch, has a glazed china cupboard and French doors to the garden. E of the drawing room is the BILLIARD ROOM. Dado and simply enriched plaster ceiling with a huge oval centrepiece. Lugged surround to the fireplace, its mantelshelf supported on corbels. Bulging Doric columns at the overmantel. The room's N wall is a shallow bow containing three French windows on to the verandah.

On the first floor, a broad corridor above the Inner Hall, the coved ceiling crossed by beams which spring from corbels decorated with plaster *putti* in high relief. Simple plasterwork in the Bedrooms.

LARBERT HOUSE, off Stirling Road. Mansion house which has grown in piecemeal fashion. The original house, built *c.* 1800 for the Riddells of Ardnamurchan, constitutes the E part, its front elevation still fairly intact. This comprised a centre block of two tall storeys with a broad bow at each end of the front. Fluted bandcourse studded with circlets under the first floor whose centre window has been converted to a fire escape door; bold wallhead cornice. This block was joined by recessed single-storey links to end pavilions. In the front of each link, a three-light window, the N now a door. In the late C19 the s link was given an upper floor, its stonework much yellower than the original, the sill of its two-light window projected on corbels. The end pavilions are two-storey but only a little higher than the links. At the front of each, a shallow bow containing a three-light window. The wallhead cornices repeat that of the main block but the s pavilion has acquired a crowning Victorian balustrade and the rusticated quoins of its s corner have been removed, apparently when the house was recast in the 1820s.

The remodelling of 1822–5 for Sir Gilbert Stirling was carried out by *David Hamilton* who thickened the house to the w and moved the entrance to a new s front. This is of polished ashlar, its overall balustrade an addition of *c.* 1900. At the four outer bays, console-corniced ground-floor windows. Projecting from the very broad centre, a *porte cochère* with paired fluted Doric columns and a coffered ceiling, its balustrade again of *c.* 1900. Apparently also of the 1820s is the pavilion at the s end of the w elevation, its design very like that at the same end of the E front but faced with broached ashlar and without quoins.

At the end of the C19 the house was again remodelled for John (later Sir John) H. N. Graham, a Glasgow merchant. Hamilton's *porte cochère* was resited further out and a broad bow-cornered open-sided porch built behind it. Above the porch, a low tower, its mullioned and transomed first-floor window framed in an aedicule, its banded Ionic pilasters supporting a segmental pediment broken by a coat of arms. Other late Victorian and Edwardian additions and alterations at the W and N elevations including the W conservatory and stair window of simplified Romanesque character. The two-storey bay window at the N end of the W side was added by *D. Thomson & C. Menzies* in 1904.

## LATHALLAN HOUSE    F 9070
### 1.9km. E of Polmont

Poised on a hill, an Elizabethan villa-country house (originally Laurence Park), by *Thomas Hamilton*, 1826. Two storeys and an attic, the walls of ashlar. Entrance (N) front of five bays hinting at but carefully avoiding symmetry. Hoodmoulds over the windows of the three centre bays, two-light at the upper floor, single lights below, but a curvily gabled porch is placed in the l. of these bays. At the advanced and gabled ends, three-light ground floor windows and windows of two lights above but the r. end is broader than the l. and its windows, that of the ground floor without a hoodmould, placed in a shallow projection surmounted by a prominent chimneystack. A pair of canted bay windows at the W elevation, its S end advanced and gabled. Late C19 SE addition with a conical-roofed tower. Inside, at the Entrance Hall, a rather small black slate chimneypiece in an idiosyncratic stripped Tudor classical manner, its overmantel rising into a triangular centrepiece topped by an obelisk. In the main rooms, more conventionally Elizabethan chimneypieces; a ribbed ceiling in the Drawing Room.

## LAURIESTON    F 9080

Village laid out in 1756 along the road from Falkirk to Linlithgow by Francis, fifth Lord Napier of Merchiston, who named it New Merchiston. It acquired the present name after the superiority was acquired later in the C18 by Sir Lawrence Dundas. Late C19 and C20 redevelopment and expansion have given it its present untidy character.

LAURIESTON PARISH CHURCH, Polmont Road. By *A. & W. Black*, 1893. Very plain lancet Gothic. S additions (transepts, chancel and SE vestry) by *P. & C. Hamilton*, 1906. Bellcote on one side of the nave's S gable.

Simple INTERIOR. Tudor arch into the semi-octagonal chancel; two-bay arcades with pointed arches into the transepts.

– Plain late Victorian PULPIT. – In the s bay of the w transept,
an ORGAN by *Andrew Watt & Son*. – STAINED GLASS. In the N
window, colourful patterned glass of the later C19. – In the
chancel, centre window (Our Lord with workers in local industries) by *Margaret Chilton* and *Marjorie Kemp*, 1926. – The flanking lights (Saints) are of 1932, also by *Chilton* and *Kemp*. All are
clearly drawn with a characteristic hint of febrility.

DESCRIPTION. MARY STREET is the main street of the C18
village but the buildings are now a drab mixture of C19 and
C20. At its centre, the street broadens to the N to form MARY
SQUARE. On the square's E side, Nos. 96–98 Mary Street, free
Jacobean Renaissance of 1910, with an ogee-domed octagonal
corner turret. Further E, on the N side of POLMONT STREET,
No. 2, an early C19 house of two storeys and a basement.
Three-bay front of polished ashlar (damaged by stone cleaning)
with V-jointed rustication at the ground floor. Roman Doric
portico, its top forming a balcony for the centre window of the
first floor whose outer windows are architraved and aproned. E
of this, on the s side of the street, Laurieston Parish Church (*see*
above). E of the church, late C19 villas. These are generally
small but at the end of the village, set back on a hillside which
rises to the N, is the late Victorian FORT KNOWE, its walls
plentifully decorated with half-timbering; large monkey-puzzle
tree in the garden.

*7090*                **LECROPT**                                        S

Church, manse and school.

LECROPT CHURCH, poised above the M8 motorway. By *William
Stirling I*, 1824–6. Built to replace an earlier church, with late C13
origins, in the pinnacled Perp Gothic manner of *David Hamilton*,
whose involvement is probable. Of ashlar masonry, four-and-a-
half bays long, each bay buttressed between cusped pointed-
arched windows. Low castellated porches project W and E from
the second bay. A short gable-ended s chancel between pinnacled
octagonal buttresses; below it, where the ground falls away, the
burial vault of the Stirling family. Dominant against the N gable,
a square, angle-buttressed, belfry tower rises in three high stages
to a castellated parapet with crocketed finials at the corners.

The N entrance, originally reserved for the Stirling family,
leads through a small vestibule in the tower base to the Keir
Loft. Across the width of this raised loft, three plaster-vaulted
bays arcaded on cluster shaft columns with bell capitals. Over
the door from the tower a white marble pointed arch encloses a
niche with a marble bust of James Stirling of Keir (1766–1831)
who commissioned the building. Arranged symmetrically l. and
r. on this N wall, six similar memorial PANELS and circular
TABLETS each incorporating inset busts of members of the
Stirling family, 1877. A central stair of eight steps, introduced
1963–4, descends into the nave between the pine-panelled faces
of the gallery. The four structural bays of the church proper are

also plaster-vaulted but are divided into eight panels by four-centred transverse-arched ribs springing from moulded corbel-stones at the cornice. Deep friezes inscribed with texts run the full length of the nave: to the r., BLESSED . ARE THE . PURE IN . HEART . FOR THEY . SHALL . SEE . GOD and to the l., PROVE . ALL . THINGS . HOLD . FAST . THAT . WHICH . IS GOOD. The small chancel, which has a plaster groin vault, is raised three steps. – Of the original furnishings only the timber PULPIT survives: an octagonal box supported on eight Roman Doric columns and a central column pedestal, its panels, pilasters and frieze inlaid with delicate classical motifs in lighter wood. – To the r., an oak screen of restrained Baroque design behind which is the ORGAN, by *Blackett & Howden*, 1885, moved here from Keir House (q.v.), 1905. – STAINED GLASS in four of the two-light side windows. Two by *Stephen Adam*, 1907: S end E wall, Christ's baptism pictured in glowing colours with angels above and water lilies and poppies below; over the door to the W porch (converted to a vestry, 1905), Christ surrounded by children. – Immediately N of the E porch, a cool elongated Nativity by *A. Carrick Whalen*, 1972. – Opposite this, local scenes and an Indian tiger and elephant are combined by *Roland Mitton* in memory of the Rev. William Stewart and his wife, Wilma Davidson, who spent thirty years as missionaries before coming to Lecropt in 1967. – In the four-light S window, angels play on the instruments of praise, by *Alfred A. Webster*, 1911.

LECROPT MANSE, 0.45km. E of church. By *William Stirling I*, 1812. A two-storey three-bay harled house to which a bay window, attic dormers and rear wings have been added. Within a pilastered Roman Doric doorpiece a round-arched fanlight with interlacing glazing bars.

LECROPT SCHOOL, 0.45km. E of church. Low, two-storey, three-windowed schoolmaster's house erected at the same time as the church. By *William Stirling I*, 1826. Bracketed doorpiece with block pediment. In 1846, the schoolroom was removed from the E gable and reconstructed on the W.

# LENNOX CASTLE ED 6070
1.5km. W of Lennoxtown

On the edge of the ravine formed by the Glazert Water, a massive mansion-house by *David Hamilton*. It was built in 1837–41 for John Lennox Kincaid Lennox who, in 1833, had inherited the estate of Woodhead from his aunt, Margaret Lennox. She had attempted to prove, despite convincing evidence to the contrary, her right to the earldom of Lennox which had fallen to the Crown in 1459. In 1813 she backed the publication of *The Case of Margaret Lennox of Woodhead, in Relation to the Title, Honours and Dignity of the Ancient Earls of Levenax or Lennox* which opened with the assertion that 'The family is of high antiquity. It is of Saxon origin. . .'. The claim to the earldom may have inspired her nephew to give the name of Lennox Castle to the new house he built at Woodhead, the claim to the family's Saxon origin may have determined its generally Romanesque detail. But stylistically Lennox Castle cannot be pigeonholed. Its powerful and near-symmetrical massing owes not a little to Robert Smirke's 'New Square' style (Greek-revival stripped of ornament) and its battlemented outline derives from Robert Adam's Castle Style. Pretty it is not, but as a brutal assertion of status it cannot be denied success.

68   The house, of droved ashlar with polished dressings, is H-plan but with a tower protruding on the W side of the cross-bar and a *porte cochère* and porch projecting from the N front. The battlemented *porte cochère* pushes out almost to the edge of the ravine. At its corners, set-back buttresses topped by battlemented square finials panelled with Romanesque blind arcading. In each exposed face, a roundheaded carriage opening, the rosetted outer order of the arch carried on columns, their capitals carved with stylized foliage. On the corbelled battlement of the N front, a panel carved by *William Mossman* with an heraldic achievement. Inside, the *porte cochère* is covered with a sexpartite stone vault. Behind the *porte cochère*, a single-storey and basement porch, again battlemented and with a window of three roundheaded lights in each side, joins to the centrepiece of the front. This is a battlemented tower of four storeys above the unsunk basement which projects all round the building as a heavy splay-topped plinth pierced by severely plain rectangular windows originally hidden by screen walls (removed *c.* 1930). At each corner of the tower, a battlemented clasping pilaster-buttress, its corners cut out at the upper floors and filled with exaggeratedly tall and slender cushion-capitalled nook-shafts; Romanesque blind arcading at the top. At the front of the tower, roundheaded windows, those of the first floor with nook-shafts in their moulded ingoes and with hoodmoulds whose label stops are carved as human heads. Slightly set back from this centrepiece are flanking blocks, each with a large ground-floor window set in a nook-shafted and dentillated rectangular over-arch. But, although these blocks are of the same length, the W is further recessed than the E and a storey lower (two-storey and basement instead of three-storey and basement) and has, at its outer end, a square three-storey and basement projecting corner tower whose front wall is aligned with that of the E block. This asymmetry of the entrance front may be partly explained by the internal plan of the house but is also a response to the siting of the building. This necessitates an oblique NE approach which would have caused the W block to be hidden by the *porte cochère* had it not been given the extra length of its corner tower which also counteracts the foreshortening imposed by the approach.

The E (garden) front is almost symmetrical, the wallheads battlemented. Five-bay centre block of two storeys and a basement set back between broad three-storey and basement towers. The corners of the N tower are cut-out and nook-shafted like those of the centrepiece of the N front, the corners of the S tower

given set-back pilaster buttresses. The battlement of the N tower
is carried on heavy square corbels, that of the S on corbelled
roundheaded arcading. At each tower, a large ground-floor
window of three roundheaded lights in a nook-shafted and
dentillated rectangular over-arch (the lintel and tops of the shafts
now missing) and three hoodmoulded first-floor windows,
again roundheaded, their label stops carved with human heads,
but, at the second floor of the N tower, are five close-set roundheaded windows (two dummies), at the S three more widely
spaced windows in shaft-sided rectangular frames. At the centre
block as elsewhere, all the windows above the basement are
roundheaded. They are hoodmoulded with human-head label
stops at the ground floor, set in dentillated over-arches at the
first. At the wallhead, an uncrenellated parapet above a cornice
studded with heraldic devices.

The S elevation is again near-symmetrical, with a recessed
centre and end towers, but the corners of the E tower have set-
back pilaster-buttresses and its battlement's corbelling continues
that of the tower's E face; at the W tower, a battlement carried
on corbelling like that of the NE tower. At each tower, a large
roundheaded ground-floor window in a nook-shafted and dentillated rectangular over-arch; hoodmoulded first-floor window,
again roundheaded, with human-head label stops. At the second
floor of the E tower, roundheaded windows in shafted rectangular
over-arches; at the W tower, a trio of round-arched openings in
a dentillated rectangular over-arch. At the recessed centre
block, its cornice and parapet like that of the E front's centre,
the roundheaded ground-floor windows are grouped 2/1, the
isolated E window of two lights, its hoodmould's label stops
carved with human heads. At the first floor, again a 2/1 grouping (a fourth window is apparently a later insertion) but these
windows, also roundheaded, are all single lights and set in dentillated over-arches.

The W elevation of the house faces on to a service court, its N,
S and W sides enclosed by single-storey ranges enlivened by
plain Romanesque detail. This front of the house is E-plan, the
centre stroke provided by a battlemented tall stair tower with
pilaster-buttresses at its corners and the centre of the front;
square caphouse on the SE corner. Boldly projecting tower at
each end of the front, the broader S tower of three storeys and a
basement, the N tower a storey lower except at its N end.

The INTERIOR is now (2002) disused. The entrance from the
*porte cochère* to the porch opens into a hall containing a straight
stair from basement level to the principal floor. At the side
walls, three-light windows, their roundheaded arches springing
from foliage-capitalled bundle-shafted columns. Flattish vaulted
plaster ceiling with heavy ribs and Tudorish bosses, executed,
like all the plasterwork, by *John Leck*. At the head of the stair, a
vestibule, its ceiling a flattened fan vault. At the S, a depressed
arch springing from bundle-shafted responds into a lobby where
a second depressed arch opens on to a *c.* 27.4m.-long corridor
covered by a compartmented ceiling of Tudor character. The

central section of the corridor is marked off by more depressed arches. On the W side of this section, a trio of roundheaded arches, the larger central one opening on to the main stair to the first floor, its trabeated ceiling enriched with pendants. The principal rooms were on the E side of the corridor. Dining room at the NE corner of the house and drawing room at the SE, both with elaborate trabeated and compartmented ceilings ornamented with pendants.

Hidden in trees immediately NE of the mansion house is its predecessor, WOODHEAD CASTLE, whose late C16 tower-house nucleus was converted to a picturesque ruin in 1840–1. This tower was built by John Lennox of Balcorrach and Woodhead, probably soon after he inherited the estate in 1572. Rectangular main block, c. 12.6m. by 7.8m., the rubble walls built of large blocks of stone. It was of three storeys and an attic but is now badly ruined, especially at the W end, and overgrown. A round attic turret projected on continuous corbelling remains at the NE corner; it has been finished with a moulded eaves cornice (partly surviving). In the main block's half-fallen S wall, a good-sized first-floor window with chamfered margins, apparently of the late C16. At the S end of the E gable, a blocked door inserted in the C17 or C18 and the jambs of a C17 first-floor window. In the N side, a couple of ground-floor doors. Both have had unmoulded jambs and are presumably C18 insertions. To their W, a window, probably formed in the C18, its lower part checked for a shutter; a chamfered jamb has been inserted in its upper part. Three windows survive at the first floor of this side, all with chamfered jambs. The two E, quite big but of unequal sizes, are C17 enlargements or insertions, the small W window seems to be C16. Projecting S from the W gable, a formerly rectangular stair jamb lit by a quite large C17 W window. The jamb itself is C16 but its original turnpike stair, the inner wall of its S segment now exposed, was replaced by a larger turnpike, placed slightly to the N and intruding into the main block, in the C17.

The C16 entrance was in the SW inner angle and opened on to a tunnel-vaulted corridor (the E end surviving) along the S side of the main block. Off the corridor are two rooms. The W was the kitchen, covered by an ashlar tunnel vault (its S part now fallen) and with a fireplace (later narrowed) at its W end; locker at the E end of the N wall. The E room, also tunnel-vaulted, was a store. Deep recess at the SE corner; built-up locker in the W end of the N side. The first-floor hall used to be vaulted; fire-place at the E end. The second floor and attic, originally reached by a turnpike stair in a turret in the jamb's inner angle, have had wooden floors.

The Lennox Castle estate was sold to Glasgow City Council in 1927 and land to the E of the mansion house developed from 1931 as a HOSPITAL for those with learning difficulties. The architects were *Wylie, Wright & Wylie* (later, *Wylie, Shanks & Wylie*). Their buildings are of red brick with slated piended roofs, the architectural manner generally simple Neo-Georgian.

The main ward blocks are at the N of the site, a single-storey complex with, at its centre, a refectory of one storey and an attic, with piended dormers and a verandah. Some late C20 buildings on the edges of this group. Uphill to the s, larger 1930s buildings (workshops, etc.). – On the E drive, a couple of battlemented Tudorish BRIDGES, presumably of *c.* 1840.

# LENNOXTOWN     ED <i>6070</i>

Large village laid out at the end of the C18 which developed as a small industrial centre with a cloth and calico printfield and an alum works.

## CHURCHES

Former CAMPSIE PARISH CHURCH, off Main Street. Disused and roofless but theatrically sited on a low hill. Late Georgian Gothic, by *David Hamilton*, 1827–8. Big broad box faced with orangey-coloured broached Bishopbriggs sandstone ashlar; the N chancel, its gable pierced by three tall lancets, was added *c.* 1950. In the sides of the main block, tall hoodmoulded and pointed windows, each divided at gallery level by a panelled band of stonework; simple pointed lights below and taller cusped openings above. The S bay on each side is marked off by buttresses and contains a four-centred door with quatrefoil panels in the spandrels. Diagonally buttressed N corners; s corners clasped by buttressed and battlemented octagonal turrets. In the S gable, windows like those in the sides. They flank the angle-buttressed tower. Even in its present truncated state this is powerful. The lower four stages survive. At the bottom, the s door is a repeat of the doors of the main block; hoodmoulded and pointed window in each side. At the second stage, a tall hoodmoulded two-light window in each face. The three-light windows of the third stage are relatively squat, their label stops carved as foliaged knots. Above, a clock stage, the circular surrounds to the missing faces decorated with carved foliage. The tower's top stage, a very tall battlemented belfry, has been removed except for stubs of masonry.

GRAVEYARD. In the NW corner of the older (s) section, a large late C19 MONUMENT to members of the Macleod family. Its centrepiece, a tall Celtic cross commemorating the Rev. Norman Macleod †1862 and his wife †1879, is flanked by panels decorated with Celtic enrichment. – Built against the retaining wall at the back of this, a MONUMENT to the Very Rev. Donald Macleod †1916, its panels carved with reliefs of a galley and the Burning Bush (emblem of the Church of Scotland); interlaced work in the borders. – At the NE corner of this part of the graveyard, a very large but routine Celtic cross to Thomas Reid of Carlestoun †1896. It is signed by *J. & G. Mossman.*

CAMPSIE PARISH CHURCH, Main Street. By *Fleming Buildings Ltd.*, 1988. Pyramid-roofed square church, with a piend-roofed vestibule in front and a large hall at the back. Spirelet on top of the church roof. Dry-dashed walls and concrete-tiled roofs.

Inside, the church roof is supported by diagonal braces. – COMMUNION TABLE of 1988 carved with reliefs of the Four Seasons, each with a woman (pregnant in Spring, a widowed grandmother in Winter). – STAINED GLASS. Behind the communion table, a panel (a rainbow over three crosses on a hill) by *Bryan Hutchison*, 1988. – Another panel (scenes from the Bible and from the history of the Church in Campsie) at the s end of the vestibule. It was also executed by *Bryan Hutchison*, 1989, using designs by local children.

ST MACHAN (R.C.), Main Street. Large and lumpy 'Saxon' of 1846. Battlemented and buttressed nave, the angle buttresses topped by pinnacled turrets; tall and narrow round-arched windows. Gabled w bellcote; battlemented sw porch. At the E end, a lower one-bay chancel, a two-light window in its s side. In the chancel's gable, two single-light windows flanking a three-light central window (now blocked).

Inside, a wooden ceiling over the nave, its panels painted with angels and shields bearing Christian symbols. Roundheaded arch into the chancel whose wooden ribbed tunnel vault is stencilled with angels. – STAINED GLASS. The two brightly coloured pictorial E windows (St Andrew and St Patrick) are late C19, by *Mayer & Co.* – The chancel's similar s window (St Joseph and St Francis Xavier) is of *c.* 1900. – Pre-Reformation FONT BOWL, a hollowed-out octagonal stone block; one side is indented, perhaps to fit against a pillar. It came from the former Campsie Parish Church at Clachan of Campsie (q.v.).

### PUBLIC BUILDINGS

CAMPSIE MEMORIAL HALL, Main Street. Dated 1867. Quite plain except for a very shallow corniced porch containing the shouldered-arched entrance; above, a three-light mullioned and transomed window.

LENNOXTOWN PRIMARY SCHOOL, School Lane. The earlier part at the w is by *H. & D. Barclay*, 1894–6. Mullioned and transomed Venetian windows in the gable. Over the entrance, a tower whose belfry stage has, at each face, a pair of round-headed openings sharing a central Roman Doric column; ogee-profiled dome with an Art Nouveau-ish weathervane. Additions to the E, by *A. N. Malcolm*, 1926.

ST MACHAN'S SCHOOL, St Machan's Way. By the Stirling County Architect, *A. J. Smith*, 1963. Flat-roofed boxes of one and two storeys.

### DESCRIPTION

C20 housing is the norm but a few buildings are earlier. On the w corner of SERVICE STREET and CROSSHILL STREET, a block of 1895 (No. 2 Service Street and Nos. 1–3 Crosshill Street). Free Jacobean, built of hammer-dressed red sandstone. Stone

shell over the canted corner; some strapwork decoration. On
the w side of Crosshill, plain early C19 terraced housing (Nos.
11–27), Nos. 11–17 dated 1821 and with paired doors; paired
doors again but also corniced at Nos. 19–21 and Nos. 25–27.
Further up the street, MEADOWBANK (No. 102) of 1822 is a
two-storey three-bay villa with a pilastered and corniced doorpiece; piend-roofed single-storey wings. Off the E side of
Crosshill Road, ST MACHAN'S WAY leads to St Machan's
School (*see* Public Buildings, above).

Station Road leads s from Service Street. Off it to the E is
WINSTON CRESCENT developed for the Lennoxtown Housing
Association in 1940–1 to a design by *T. O. W. Gratton,* with
Dudok-inspired flat-roofed double houses, their walls harled
and with brick trimmings. Each is L-plan with a brick chimney-
stack serving as a hinge in the inner angle.

In MAIN STREET at the entrance to the path up to the former
Campsie Parish Church (*see* Churches, above), a First World
War MEMORIAL GATEWAY of 1923. It is castellated and
pinnacled in the manner of fifty years earlier; canopied image
niches contain tablets inscribed with the names of the dead. To
the E, in SCHOOL LANE, Lennoxtown Primary School (*see*
Public Buildings, above). In Main Street just E of School Lane,
St Machan's R.C. Church and Campsie Parish Church (*see*
Churches, above) face each other across a small square.

MAIDEN CASTLE, Garmore. 1km. NE. Originally a circular motte,
eroded on the E side, measuring about 17m. in diameter across
the summit. Possibly set within an oval bailey.

FORT, Meikle Reive. 1km. NE, occupying a promontory protruding from the Kilsyth Hills. Central enclosure measuring about
44m. by 36m. with entrances to E and W. Further ramparts and
ditches provide additional defence on the more vulnerable N
and NE flanks. Excavations in 1954–5 produced fragments of
pottery and a shale armlet of Iron Age date.


# LENZIE                                                                    ED 6070

A suburb of Glasgow although separated from that city by open
country. A station on the main railway line from Edinburgh to
Glasgow was opened here in 1842 and a village, originally and
misleadingly named Campsie Junction, begun. In the 1850s the
Edinburgh & Glasgow Railway Company offered five-year free
railway travel to those who built houses within a mile of the
station but it was not until the 1870s that Lenzie (its name changed
to that of the medieval parish in 1869) developed seriously with
leafy streets of prosperous villas. These have been followed by C20
housing estates.


## CHURCHES

LENZIE OLD PARISH CHURCH, corner of Kirkintilloch Road
and Garngaber Avenue. Built as a chapel of ease in 1874; the

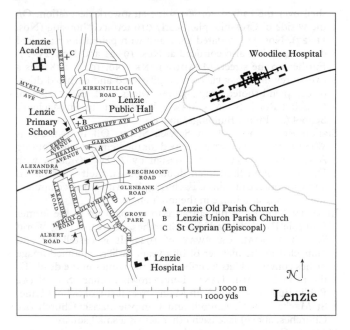

Lenzie Academy

Woodilee Hospital

MYRTLE AVE

BEECH RD

KIRKINTILLOCH ROAD

Lenzie Public Hall

Lenzie Primary School

MONCRIEFF AVE

FERN AVENUE

HEATH AVENUE

GARNGABER AVENUE

+C

+B

A

ALEXANDRA AVENUE

BEECHMONT ROAD

GLENBANK ROAD

VICTORIA ROAD

ALEXANDRA ROAD

GLENHEAD RD

HERIOT ROAD

ARCHIBALD ROAD

KIRKINTILLOCH ROAD

GROVE PARK

ALBERT ROAD

A   Lenzie Old Parish Church
B   Lenzie Union Parish Church
C   St Cyprian (Episcopal)

Lenzie Hospital

1000 m
1000 yds

N

Lenzie

architects were *Clarke & Bell*. Large but plain Gothic edifice. Nave and aisles, with minimally projecting transepts and a lower chancel, its gable topped by a chimney. At the W front, a transeptal stair projection on the N, a steeple on the S. In the main W gable, a quintet of lancets lighting the vestibule and a huge wheel window above. In the stair projection's N front, the head of the lower window is carved with the relief of a bird standing on a fruiting branch. The steeple's tower is of two tall stages. At the lower, clasping buttresses which are broached to semi-octagons, their alternate faces gableted. At the pointed and gableted entrance, nook-shafts, their large capitals carved with naturalistic foliage. The corners of the tower's second stage are clasped by pinnacled octagonal buttresses. In each face, a two-light window with cinquefoil tracery in the head. Octagonal spire, large lucarnes at its base.

LENZIE UNION PARISH CHURCH, corner of Kirkintilloch Road and Moncrieff Avenue. Originally Lenzie United Presbyterian Church. Plain E.E., by *Campbell Douglas & Sellars*, 1874–5. The breadth of the nave is disguised at the W front by cut-out corners filled with minimally projecting transepts containing the gallery stairs. A little elaboration at the entrance where there is stiff-leaf carving of the nook-shafts' capitals and of the frieze over the door. N transept added by *Honeyman, Keppie & Mackintosh*, 1906. Flat-roofed and harled E chancel built together with plain halls in 1923–5; by *Keppie & Henderson*.

Inside, a wagon roof over the broad nave; gallery at the W

end. Three-bay arcade into the N transept, the pointed arches carried on bell-capitalled columns. Rose window above the stone arch into the chancel which is covered by a panelled ceiling; on each side of the chancel, a pointed arch filled by part of the organ case. The ORGAN itself is by *Conacher & Co. Ltd.*, 1925; rebuilt by *J. W. Walker & Sons*, 1971, and enlarged by *R. C. Goldsmith* in 1981 and 1991. – Oak COMMUNION TABLE of *c.* 1925, in a routine Lorimerian manner. – On the S side of the chancel arch, PULPIT of 1925, also of oak but much more accomplished, with carved cherubs' heads and fruit in the manner of Grinling Gibbons.

STAINED GLASS. Three-light chancel window by *Charles Paine* of *J. & W. Guthrie & Andrew Wells Ltd.*, *c.* 1950. Christian symbols on a strongly coloured blue background. – In the S wall of the nave, Glasgow-style W window (Our Lord Blessing Little Children) of 1904. – The two windows to its W (the Maries at the Sepulchre; the Risen Lord on the Road to Emmaus) are by *Alexander Ballantine*, 1904, competent but uninspired. – Next, a restrained expressionist window (the Sower and the Reaper) of 1921. – The W window of this side (King David) is of 1939. – In the N wall of the nave, one window (small-scale Scenes from the Life of Our Lord) by *J. & W. Guthrie & Andrew Wells Ltd.*, 1923. – In the E wall of the transept, two windows. One ('Faith') is gently expressionist of 1938. The other ('Boys' Brigade Window') is of 1984. – In the large rose window over the chancel arch, late C19 glass, a dove depicted in the central roundel. – Abstract patterned glass, also of the late C19, in the rose at the top of the W window. – In the vestibule, two lights (the Madonna and Child; the Good Shepherd) of the mid C20.

ST CYPRIAN (Episcopal), Beech Road. By *Alexander Ross*, 1872–3, in the 'old Scotch Gothic' style, built of stugged and squared buff-coloured masonry. Tall nave and chancel with a steeply pitched roof and SW porch; steeple against the W bay of the chancel. In the W gable, a stepped arrangement of three narrow tall lancets joined by continuous hoodmoulding and also by a sill course which is carried round under the simple narrow lancets in the sides of the nave. Under the nave eaves, beakhead ornament. The W side of the gabled porch is pierced by trefoil lights; stiff-leaf capitals to the nook-shafts of its S entrance.

The steeple and its octagonal SW stair turret are crossed by stringcourses, two of them continuing the lines of the sill course and eaves course of the nave. At the first stage of the tower, lancet windows like those of the nave. Cinquefoil lights at the second stage. At the third, nook-shafted and hoodmoulded belfry openings. At the top of both tower and turret, a quatrefoil-panelled band from which stone gryphons lean out at the corners of the tower. Both the tower and the turret are finished with chevron-decorated stone spires, the turret's octagonal, the tower's pyramidal and lucarned.

Placed high up in the E bay of the chancel's S side are quatrefoil openings; a trio of pointed windows in the N side. In the E gable, a large plate-traceried rose window under a small quatrefoil light.

Vestry of *c.* 1926 on the N side of the choir. To its E, a hall of
1961.

Inside the church, open wooden roofs over nave and chancel.
Their collar braces, the heads pierced with quatrefoils, spring
from stone corbels which are carved with foliage in the nave and,
in the chancel, with angels, the W two with hands clasped in
prayer, the hands of the other pair covering their faces. Pointed
stone chancel arch enriched with dogtooth ornament; foliage-
carved capitals at the supporting columns. – FURNISHINGS. In
the arch, a wrought iron SCREEN of *c.* 1935. Simple Gothic, with
snakes curling round the uprights. The windows in the N wall of
the sanctuary are set well back in an arcaded surround, its
columns with polished granite shafts and stiff-leaf capitals. The
walling on the S side below the quatrefoil lights was intended to
be covered by a sedilia; it looks bare without. On the S side of
the choir, the stencilled false pipes of the former ORGAN (by
*Frederick Holt*, 1873; now replaced by an electronic instrument).
– REREDOS of 1949, a copy by *Phyllis Dodd* of Leonardo da
Vinci's Last Supper. – Brass eagle LECTERN of 1919. – Stone
PULPIT of *c.* 1920. – The nave's Gothic PEWS are of 1873.

STAINED GLASS. In the rose window of the chancel's gable,
glass (the Ascension) by *John Hardman & Co.*, 1873, a characteristic strongly coloured archaic design. – Also of 1873 and by
Hardman are the three small lights (the Nativity, Crucifixion
and Resurrection of Our Lord) in the N side of the sanctuary and
the three quatrefoils (angels bearing symbols of the Eucharist)
in the S side. – In the S wall of the nave, the E window (King
David) is of 1937. – Next, a narrative light (Our Lord Walking
on the Water) by *James Ballantine & Son*, 1873. – Then a window
(St Margaret of Scotland) of 1948, a competent example of
stylized realism. – More naturalistic the next light (the Guardian
Angel) of *c.* 1930. – In the N wall, the overbright E window (St
Matthew) is of 1993. – Next, a window (a Saint) of 1929. –
Then a window (Our Lord Blessing Children) by *James Ballantine
& Son*, 1875, followed by another light (St Luke) of 1993 and a
window (the Good Shepherd) of 1873, again by *James Ballantine
& Son*. – The three-light W window (the Resurrection, St Peter
and St John) is by *G. J. Baguley*, 1901.

At the entrance to the surrounding garden, a bargeboarded
wooden LYCHGATE of 1919.

## PUBLIC BUILDINGS

LENZIE ACADEMY, Myrtle Avenue. By *Thomson, McCrea &
Sanders*, 1958–60. Uneasy compromise between traditional and
Modern Movement. Two storeys of red brick and curtain walling
cladding a precast concrete frame. Beside the principal entrance,
a slender pitched-roofed tower, its belfry opening a fussily detailed
grille.

LENZIE HOSPITAL, Auchinloch Road. Originally Glasgow
Convalescent Home, built in 1870–1 to a design by *James
Thomson*. Like a large villa but plain except for a pyramidal-

roofed Italianate tower. Additions of 1891–4 including a smaller tower bearing the date 1892.

LENZIE PRIMARY SCHOOL, corner of Kirkintilloch Road and Fern Avenue. Carefully unified but built in two stages. The N range is by *J. C. Rankin*, 1886–7, the rest by *Thomas Baird*, 1909–10, all faced with stugged ashlar. The manner is thrifty Italianate. Tall two-storey N and S ranges, each with round-arched windows, their sills consoled, in its front gable to Kirkintilloch Road. Between them, a piend-roofed block of three storeys but lower. At the S range's twelve-bay S elevation to Fern Avenue, the four centre bays are slightly advanced under a broad gable; at this centrepiece the windows are again round-arched and with consoled sills.

LENZIE PUBLIC HALL, Kirkintilloch Road. By *Baldie & Tennant*, 1892. Symmetrical Scots Jacobean, built of stugged and squared buff-coloured stone. Two storeys, the front of three bays. At its ground floor, round-arched openings, their imposts linked by a stringcourse. Sill course under the tall mullioned and transomed first-floor windows, each surmounted by a crowstepped gablet.

WOODILEE HOSPITAL, off Garngaber Avenue. Originally the Barony Parochial Asylum, a pauper lunatic asylum serving the Barony parish of Glasgow. The first buildings, designed by *Salmon, Son & Ritchie*, were put up in 1871–5. The main range was 213m. long, with twin towers at the centre and a chapel linked to the rear. All but one of the blocks composing this range were demolished after a fire in 1990. Free Jacobean hinting at Italianate. At the centre, an Ionic portico; above, a clock tower with stumpy corner finials. In 1894–5 *W. Forrest Salmon* of *James Salmon & Son* extended the original main range at each end to a total length of *c*. 435m. These E and W additions largely survive. Each is of two storeys with a loggia occupying the ground floor, the openings formed by segmental arches carried on corniced piers. Segmental-headed windows at the low first floor. The ranges are enlivened by projecting saddle-back-roofed towers with shaped gables and oriel windows. N of these fragments of the main range, a detached villa-like two-storey block (Home for Imbecile Children) by *R. A. Bryden*, 1899–1900. Florid Jacobean, again with Italianate hints. Five-bay front, its centre advanced under a Dutch gable on whose ends stand urns. Projecting from this centre, a canted two-storey bay window, the curvaceous parapet embellished with strapwork and coroneted shields. – To the W, at the beginning of the drive from Garngaber Avenue, a Jacobean LODGE, dated 1874. Iron cresting on the roof of its bowed projection.

## DESCRIPTION

KIRKINTILLOCH ROAD and AUCHINLOCH ROAD, its continuation S of the railway, provide a long main thoroughfare off which are streets containing villas (*see* below). At the S end of Kirkintilloch Road are Lenzie Union and Lenzie Old Parish

Churches, together with Lenzie Primary School and Lenzie Public Hall (*see* Churches and Public Buildings, above). Here too, s of Heath Avenue, is the small commercial centre consisting of two blocks of flats above shops. One (Nos. 90–96 Kirkintilloch Road) was built by *George Bennett*, *c.* 1865. Piended roof with bracketed eaves; canted N corner to Heath Avenue. The other (Nos. 98–110 Kirkintilloch Road) is commercial free style of 1887, with canted bay windows and a pedimented central gablet. Broad-eaved cottage (No. 112) of the later C19 on the edge of the Railway Station's car park. s of the Railway Station (a late C20 replacement), at the E end of ALEXANDRA AVENUE, a single-storey building (No. 1) of *c.* 1900 provides a bit of much-needed enjoyment. Harled and half-timbered, with a gambrel roof and a small pyramidal-roofed tower topped by a Tuscan-columned and ogee-domed cupola.

## VILLAS

ALBERT ROAD. The harled No. 12 (GLENHEAD HOUSE) was built *c.* 1875 but owes its present appearance to a remodelling by *William B. Whitie*, *c.* 1910. Very Scottish, with crowstepped gables, a curly dormerhead, conical-roofed tower and martially corbelled balcony.

BEECH ROAD. NETHERHALL (No. 5) is a routine late C19 villa, but with Art Nouveau GATEPIERS of *c.* 1900. Battered pylons with lid-like cornices. On the fronts of the piers, panels carved with reliefs of stylized foliage.

BEECHMOUNT ROAD. No. 7 (COACH HOUSE) is a late Victorian two-storey pavilion, its first-floor front window of two round-arched lights sharing a central column. Long single-storey range of offices at the rear.

GARNGABER AVENUE. THE TOWER. Straightforward two-storey villa of the later C19 but with a battlemented round tower, crowsteps at some gables, and outsized strapwork decoration.

GLENBANK ROAD. Nos. 14–16 form a late C19 single-storey double house. Half-timbering in the broad gables of the end bays, each containing a column-mullioned window of five round-headed lights (the outer lights dummies). Long and low broad-eaved porch at each end.

GROVE PARK. U-plan development of detached cottage villas round a central garden, built *c.* 1900. Carefully picturesque but the hammer-dressed masonry dispels thoughts of frivolity.

HERIOT ROAD. WARWICK CROFT and No. 43 ALEXANDRA ROAD. Asymmetrical broad-eaved villa of *c.* 1880 using motifs culled from Alexander 'Greek' Thomson. At the s front, a broad gable over the E bay, a piended roof over the w whose first-floor window is of five lights with pier mullions, the responds marked only by capitals. At the recessed centrepiece, a three-light ground-floor window and one of two lights above. Classical porch at each end. At the w elevation, a rectangular window, its frieze decorated with circles. – Nos. 5–7, a late C19 pair of small detached villas built on reversed plans. The front of each has a steeply pitched and bargeboarded gable at one end from which projects a single-storey bay window; three-light mullioned window above. At the other end of the front, a large steeply pitched and bargeboarded dormer window.

MYRTLE AVENUE. Nos. 10–12 and Nos. 14–16 are a pair of two-storey villas (now flatted) of c. 1890, both with crazily patterned rustication at the quoins and the surrounds to the doors and windows. Each is of three bays, with ground-floor three-light windows flanking the advanced centre whose corners are canted at the ground floor and corbelled to rectangles above. At the upper floor each villa is individually treated, Nos. 10–12 with gableted dormerheads and a centre gable, all with carved bargeboards, Nos. 14–16 with piended roofs and bracketed broad eaves.

VICTORIA ROAD. No. 3 (BAILILISK) is late C19 Georgian survival but with wackily detailed Ægypto–Greek GATEPIERS of 'Greek' Thomson inspiration. – Two-storey double house dated 1881 at No. 25 Victoria Road (ARDEEN) and No. 16 Glenhead Road (DALVEEN). Generally Italianate but with 'Greek' Thomson touches, e.g. at the S entrance whose flanking pilasters are expressed only as capitals, and the stonework behind the entablature is recessed. Single-storey bow window on the S side; two-storey bow window to the W. – No. 27 (INVERSHIEL), again of the late C19 and strongly under Thomson's influence. It is of two storeys and an attic. At the ground floor of the ashlar-faced front, broad rectangular bay windows with pier mullions. The windows' entablature is carried across the centre where it is supported on columns to form a porch. Bracketed eaves to the piended roof whose platform is crowned with a broad-eaved attic. – Another late Victorian villa at No. 34 (SHERBROOKE) but heavy-handed Italianate, with roundheaded windows and a pyramidal roofed tower. – No. 39 (MACHRIE-MHOR) is accomplished piend-roofed and symmetrical Neo-Georgian of 1909. Harled walls with stone dressings and angle pilasters. At the garden entrance, mild steel GATES by *John Creed*, 1992, with extravagant water-lily uprights.

# LINLITHGOW BRIDGE F 9070

Tiny hamlet at the W end of the eponymous bridge over the River Avon, the buildings including THE BRIDGE INN, white harled vernacular of c. 1800.

AVON VIADUCT. By *Grainger & Miller* for the Edinburgh & Glasgow Railway, 1838–42. Twenty large segmental arches (each of 15.24m. span) and three smaller roundheaded arches (each of c. 6.1m. span) at the E end, built of stugged and channelled ashlar, now reinforced with metal straps.

GLENAVON HOUSE, 0.2km. N. Overblown villa of 1886, the style a mixture of Brycean cottage and Jacobean Renaissance, the bargeboarded roofs covered with Rosemary tiles. Ogee-roofed squat round tower at the SE corner.

MANUEL HOUSE, 1.8km. SW. Mid-C19 spikily gabled Jacobethan.

Conical-roofed round tower but too inconspicuously placed to make much impact. – Two-storey LODGE of *c.* 1900. Harled with half-timbering in the gables.

MANUEL PRIORY. *See* p. 606.

9070                              LOAN                              F

Hamlet of C19 and C20 cottages. One (FIRVIEW COTTAGE) of the earlier C19 has blockily pinnacled buttresses and a curly top to the doorpiece.

CANDIE HOUSE, 2.2km. SW. Unpretentious two-storey Georgian laird's house, built of harled rubble. The main block is probably of the later C18. Four bays, the openings grouped 2/2 (the l. first-floor window now blocked and harled over); corniced door-piece. Across the W end, a full-height piend-roofed wing of the earlier C19, its short N extension perhaps a little later.

4020                   LOCH DOCHART CASTLE                   S
                        1.5km. E of Crianlarich

Late C16 or early C17, built by Sir Duncan Campbell, 7th Laird of Glenorchy. Much reduced island ruin, engulfed by vegetation. Oblong plan with vestiges of circular SE tower and N and S stair turrets. Inglenook fireplace at centre of S wall.

5020                      LOCHEARNHEAD                      S

Waterside village at the W end of Loch Earn. Apart from nearby Edinample Castle (q.v.) it is without architectural sophistication. But it does retain some early C19 vernacular rubble cottages, espe-cially at Craggan, in Glen Ogle, and along the A85 on the N side of the loch. Several have corrugated iron roofs and have not been 'improved'. The railway viaducts on the dismantled line N through Glen Ogle to Killin are of considerable engineering interest.

Former PARISH CHURCH. Early C19. Gabled kirk built on a cruci-form plan. Cusped timber tracery. Converted to a dwelling by *David Hardwick*, 1992–5, but subsequently destroyed by fire. Under reconstruction in 2002.

ST ANGUS (Episcopal). By *G. T. Ewing* of Crieff, 1888. Miniature Arts and Crafts Gothic in grey rubble with red sandstone dress-ings. Cusped lancets grouped in square-headed frames above a splayed base. Eye-catching ridge bellcote with four gablets contains a BELL, *c.* 1880, cast by *John Murphy* of Dublin. Plain interior with simple arch-braced roof. Pointed chancel arch with timber inset. – Painted and gilded REREDOS, 1909, with twin-panel folding doors hinged each side, depicts SS Blane, Ninian, Angus and Columba. – In the five-light sanctuary window, STAINED GLASS in memory of clan chief Rear Admiral Sir Malcolm MacGregor †1879: Christ on the cross with Mary and John and two other saints.

BRIDGES, Glen Ogle. A series of rubble-built single semicircular arch crossings constructed to serve the military road built by *Major William Caulfield, c.* 1749. The present structures may be early C19.

EDINCHIP BRIDGE. Cast iron footbridge over railway by *B. &E. Blyth, c.* 1865. Arched and decoratively bracketed to sandstone rubble abutments.

GLEN OGLE TWEEDS. By *Andrew Jackson,* 1968–9. Well judged neo-vernacular grouping with roughcast walls and dormered slated roofs arranged in an artfully casual L-shaped plan stepping around a forecourt. Carefully detailed timber interior to shop.

RAILWAY VIADUCTS, Glen Ogle. 1869–70. Two structures of rock-faced coursed masonry; one of three segmental arches, the other of twelve. A third structure of 1901–5 with nine semi-circular arches curving to the line of the track is built in concrete with channelled rendering. Disused.

RAILWAY VIADUCT over Kendrum Burn, 1.9km. SW. By the engineers *Simpson & Wilson,* 1901–5. Five round arches to S with two to N, the girder span between now removed. Concrete structure channelled in the spandrels.

RESTAURANT. Built as a boathouse, 1980–1, by *Finlayson & Campbell.* From the low eaves of a steeply sloping roof, random rubble lateral walls extend as buttresses on each side of peaked, timber-boarded gables.

SCHOOL. C19. Classroom block roofed transversely with rough-cast triple gables NE and SW. Schoolhouse abuts SE.

WAR MEMORIAL. *c.* 1920. By *George Washington Browne.* Standing stone slab incut with an armpitted cross above and the names of the fallen below. Rubble base with short quadrant walls.

DESCRIPTION. A few single-storey rubble-built cottages survive in the village. AUCHTOO, possibly mid-C18 but rebuilt in part, has battered walls, traces of hanging lums and a corrugated iron roof replacing its original thatch. WESTER AUCHRAW is similar but retains a cruck roof structure. BRIAR COTTAGE: two in-line rubble dwellings, reputedly dating from the mid C17 and mid C18. Rehabilitation by *Findlay, McKinnel,* 1997–2000. Thatching restored and original cruck roofing members retained and exposed internally.

EDINAMPLE CASTLE. *See* p. 459.

# LOGIE OLD KIRK and LOGIE PARISH CHURCH
## *see* BLAIRLOGIE

# LUIB
S *4020*

Isolated buildings in Glen Dochart.

LUIB HOTEL. Originally a three-bay, single-storey dwelling with a gabled two-storey centre; probably late C18. Altered and extended 1829, 1842 and 1849 when it was remodelled in bargeboarded Breadalbane Estate Gothic style.

SUIE LODGE HOTEL, 0.6km. W. Two-storey, three-bay house, C18; gabled attics and arcuated glazing bars betray Breadalbane Gothic remodelling, C19.

9070                     MADDISTON                     F

Village, mostly made up of C20 housing but in MAIN STREET S of Maddiston Primary School (*see* below) some late C19 cottages and the mid-C19 MADDISTON INN. Perched on a hill at the S end, Cairneymount Church (*see* below).

CAIRNEYMOUNT CHURCH, High Road. By *James Strang*, 1903–4. Lumpily detailed Gothic box built of bullnosed masonry. On one side of the front gable, a gableted bellcote.

CENTRAL SCOTLAND FIRE BRIGADE HEADQUARTERS, Main Street. By *A. J. Smith*, c. 1960. Dry-dashed walls and a flat roof.

MADDISTON PRIMARY SCHOOL, Main Street. The main block facing the road was built in two stages. The N end, by *James Strang*, 1896–7, was built as an infants' school. Minimally pointed windows. At each of the N and W elevations, a slightly advanced and gabled bay containing a hoodmoulded window of three lights. In 1911 *Malcolm & Robertson* extended the building S by a further ten bays, making a symmetrical fifteen-bay frontage, but the windows of the addition are segmental-arched. Rear addition of c. 1930.

VELLORE. *See* p. 791.

9070                  MANUEL PRIORY                  F
<br>1.3km. SW of Linlithgow Bridge

Upstanding fragment in a field beside the River Avon.

The priory, a Cistercian nunnery, was founded by Malcolm IV c. 1160 and what survives is probably of the late C12. This remnant consists of about half of the W gable of the small convent church which, according to Cardonnel's drawings of c. 1739, was a straightforward rectangle. The gable is built of rough ashlar (now patched with later masonry), the N corner carried out as a sloping-topped buttress. In the centre of the gable was a roundheaded doorway; the moulded base of one nook-shaft remains. Above the level of the door, corbels to support the roof-beam of a lean-to porch or galilee. Over these were three pointed windows (the N window and the N jamb of the centre window surviving) jointed by a splayed sill course. Above the windows, a stringcourse which was carried down at the ends of the gable. In the top of the gable, a segment of a round window survives. A fragmentary stump of the church's N wall projects E from the gable.

# MEIKLEWOOD HOUSE

S *7090*

2.5km. NE of Gargunnock

A restless congeries of Tudor and Jacobean forms in snecked pink-grey sandstone, *c.* 1832; perhaps by *R. & R. Dickson*. The s front porch (almost a *porte cochère*) has a wide four-centred archway flanked by octagonal buttress shafts which become chimney-like finials above its balustraded parapet. Directly behind, similar buttresses rise three storeys to clasp a curvilinear gable. The plan is a double-L. The single-storey E wing ends in an octagonal larder with ogee roof and ventilator. Another, more elongated, bell roof caps the turnpike stair in the W range re-entrant. The interior has panelled Tudor ceilings with a plaster fan vault and pendant over the upper landing of the main staircase. The principal public rooms have deeply modelled plasterwork of a very high class of design and execution, the Drawing Room cornice being particularly handsome. Marble chimneypieces. – STABLES COURT, 1832, restored 1880, lies N. Symmetrical W front with semicircular carriage arch, over which are a pedimented round-arched window and bellcote. This raised centre contains a doocot with flight holes on the court-yard side and incorporates a stone dated 1696 bearing the initials MS. – Harled MOTOR-HOUSE, 1907, with half-timbered gables.

# MENSTRIE

C *8090*

Sizeable village, formerly a centre of woollen manufacture.

## CHURCHES

BLAIRLOGIE UNITED FREE CHURCH, Main Street. Built as a mission church in 1891, it is by *Thomas Frame & Son*. Plain lancet-windowed box. At the front (s) gable, a quatrefoil opening above the porch.

MENSTRIE PARISH CHURCH, Main Street. Plainest Gothic, by *James Collie*, 1880. To the E, HALL of 1898, also Gothic but more appealing. Front of hammer-dressed masonry, the hood-mould of its three-light window having label stops carved with foliage. Cupola-ventilator on the roof.

## PUBLIC BUILDINGS

DUMYAT CENTRE, Main Street East. By *Baxter, Clark & Paul*, 1987–8. Square two-storey main block, the brick walls enlivened by patterning; huge pyramid roof. Lower outshots, the NE covered by a downward projection of the main roof, the others with their own roofs. The effect is of one strong idea compromised by afterthoughts.

DESCRIPTION

MAIN STREET EAST is the entry from the E overlooked on the N
by Broom Hall (*see* below) and with C20 housing on the S. The
village centre is announced by the Dumyat Centre on the S (for
this, *see* Public Buildings, above). Then, on the N, the small
HOLLY TREE HOTEL, its front Art Deco but of the 1950s
rather than the 1930s. On the S, a long two-storey building of
the later C19, its triangular clock turret dated 1897 and probably
an addition. Beside this, Menstrie Parish Church (*see* Churches,
above). To its W, harled cottages, probably of the mid C19 but
altered. They face over the street to a green. At its SW corner,
the WAR MEMORIAL of *c.* 1920, an ashlar pillar with an arched
top. At the green's NW corner, a humpbacked segmental-arched
BRIDGE over the Menstrie Burn. It was built in 1656 and later
widened to the N, perhaps in the C19. On the S face, a weathered
armorial panel. Brook Street leads S from this end of Main Street
East. Off it, in CASTLE ROAD, Menstrie Castle (*see* below).
MAIN STREET WEST, W of the Menstrie Burn, starts on the
N with a small housing development (MIDTOWN) by the
Clackmannan County Architect, *W. H. Henry*, *c.* 1960. Built
into the S gable, a stone panel, probably late C17, carved with the
heraldic achievement of the Holburnes, owners of the Menstrie
estate from 1649 to 1719. On the S side of the street, the
BURNSIDE INN, a *cottage orné* of *c.* 1840, followed by MENSTRIE
HOUSE, old people's housing by *Central Regional Council*, 1982.
To its W and set well back from the street, the former Elmbank
Mill (*see* below) followed by 1930s housing by *Thomas Frame &
Son*. Opposite, houses of the mid C19, most originally single-
storey but several having acquired upper floors, the alteration
clearest at No. 18 whose upper floor has different stonework
and is much higher than the ground floor. At No. 50, a single-
storey cottage of 1871, energetically Gothic with shouldered
arches to the openings in the hammer-dressed red sandstone
front; it bears the monogram MD. The pair of cottages at Nos.
54–56 with bargeboarded gablets over the doors are dated 1872
and bear the monogram 'D & J' (for Drummond & Johnston,
the owners of the Elmbank Mill). The same monogram and
stugged buff-coloured stonework appear at Nos. 64–74 (OCHIL
PLACE) of 1873 but this terrace is two-storeyed and quite plain.
More decorative are Nos. 100–106, a pair of late C19 double
cottages built on reversed plans, each having a canted bay
window, iron-finialled canted dormers and a bargeboarded
porch, that of Nos. 104–106 still with tree-trunk supports. At the
end of the village, Blairlogie United Free Church (*see* Churches,
above).

MENSTRIE CASTLE
Castle Road

The surviving W and S ranges of a presumably quadrangular house
built for Sir William Alexander of Menstrie, first Earl of Stirling,

at the beginning of the C17, now standing among 1950s housing. After a long period of dereliction the exterior was restored and the interior converted to flats by *W. Schomberg Scott* in 1961.

Both ranges are built of rubble, formerly harled. Three-storey W range, the N gable crowstepped. The upper floors of the W front are of an almost regular six bays, the windows, all with chamfered margins, quite generously sized at the first floor but only a little taller than they are broad at the second where they are linked by a lintel course under the moulded eaves cornice. At the S bay, a bowed turret (originally containing a stair from the first to the second floor) is jettied out on continuous corbelling and covered with a sloping stone-slabbed roof. The top course of the corbelling is cavetto-moulded and carried across the four bays to the N as a stringcourse; projecting from it, a couple of decorative cannon spouts which flank the off-centre entrance to a pend running through the range to the courtyard. The pend entrance is placed in a rectangular ashlar surround of triumphal arch derivation, the architrave of its crowning entablature formed by the stringcourse carried across from the turret. Above, a pulvinated frieze under a shallowly projecting cornice. The round-arched entrance itself is surmounted by a rosetted hoodmould with pendant label stops. Under the hoodmould, a band carved with nailhead ornament. Inside this, a projecting rope-moulded order which springs from attached columns with tall weathered capitals but no bases. At the arch's inner order, a roll-and-hollow moulding. The lower parts of the outer corners of the frame have been removed. Were they perhaps pilastered? S of the entrance, a fairly small ground-floor window; at the N bay of the ground floor, a plain door with a window (renewed) beside it.

The S range, again of three storeys, projects to the E. Crow-stepped and chimneyed gables; at the W gable, a moulded cornice under the base of the chimney. The wallhead of this range is slightly lower than that of the W and the second-floor windows rise through the eaves to corniced dormerheads. These have catslide roofs, as they did before the work of 1961, but were they originally pedimented? At the SW corner of this range (i.e. the SW corner of the house), a round second-floor turret carried on continuous corbelling; decorative quatrefoil gunloops in the NW and SE segments of the turret. The E gable of the S range is quoined but also has tusking and contains evidence of a first-floor door, its level apparently lower than that of the first floor of the surviving range, and fireplaces at the two upper floors, so there seems to have been a slightly lower E continuation of the range, not necessarily contemporary with it.

The courtyard is reached through the pend under the W range, its passage covered by an ashlar segmental tunnel vault. On each side, an elliptical arched recess containing a low stone bench; W of the N recess, a plain rectangular cupboard.

Inside the courtyard, the W range's E elevation is similar to its W, the windows' spacing again almost regular. Towards the N end, a corniced first floor reached by a forestair. From this

forestair a cavetto cornice studded with cannon spouts is carried
s above the ground floor. At the ground floor the pend entrance
is treated simply with only a roll-and-hollow moulding. Low
plain door at the s end of the range. In the courtyard's sw inner
angle, a monopitch-roofed square stair tower, a replacement of
1961 for an earlier round tower.

Inside, at the N end of the ground floor, a room with pseudo-
C17 plasterwork motifs of 1961. To its s, a tunnel-vaulted store.

BROOM HALL, Long Row. Absurd Scots Jacobean villa placed
high to enjoy the s view. It was built in 1874 for James Johnstone,
owner of the Elmbank Mill; *Francis Mackison* was the architect.
Conical-roofed round turrets and a two-storey bay window
under a corbelled-out square tophamper at the main block;
round corner turret at the E wing. In the inner angle, a preposterously tall square tower containing the entrance. Angle rounds
at three corners of its corbelled parapet; at the fourth, a tall
round turret finishing in an ogee-roofed caphouse. – At the
entrance to the drive, crowstep-gabled LODGE and STABLES
contemporary with the house.

ELMBANK MILL, Main Street West. Now offices. Two-storey
woollen mill of 1864. Georgian survival five-bay front, its piended
roof hiding the M-roof behind. Pilastered and corniced door;
at the centre of the wallhead scrolls support an anthemion-
finialled circular surround for a clock. Plain fourteen-bay side
elevations.


5070                    MILNGAVIE                    ED

A small village was in existence here by the late C18, its name
taken from Gavin's (or Guy's) Mill (*see* Industrial Building, below).
By the mid C19 some industry (calico printing, cotton spinning,
corn mills, a bleach works and a distillery) was established, making
use of the water power provided by the Allander Burn running
down what was then the w edge of the settlement. The railway to
Glasgow was opened in 1863 and Milngavie became a burgh
twelve years later. In the late C19 considerable villa development
took place. Industry disappeared in the later C20 but the town
underwent major expansion of its housing, especially to the w for
its present primary function as a Glasgow dormitory.


CHURCHES

CAIRNS CHURCH, corner of Cairns Drive and Buchanan Street.
Originally Cairns United Free Church. Dec, by *John B. Wilson*,
1902–3. Dramatically positioned on a steeply sloping site, the
church is a broad buttressed box, built of hammer-dressed
masonry. On the roof, a square cupola-ventilator with an Art
Nouveau-ish finial. Interest is concentrated at the s end. This
consists of a buttressed semi-octagonal 'chancel' (in reality
the vestibule) with pointed entrances and traceried windows.
Transeptal stair projection on the w. On the E, a steeple. The

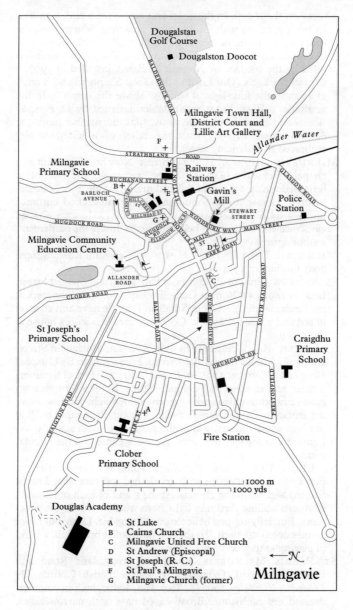

Dougalstan
Golf Course

■ Dougalston Doocot

_Allander Water_

Milngavie Town Hall,
District Court and
Lillie Art Gallery

F
+
STRATHBLANE        ROAD

Milngavie
Primary School

Railway
Station

BUCHANAN STREET

B +

BARLOCH
AVENUE

CAIRNS DRIVE

HILL ST

HILLHEAD ST

+ E

G +

Gavin's
Mill

STEWART
STREET

Police
Station

GLASGOW ROAD

MUGDOCK ROAD

MUGDOCK
RD

ELANGOWAN

DOUGLAS ST

WOODBURN WAY

MAIN STREET

Milngavie Community
Education Centre

MAIN
ST

D +
PARK ROAD

ALLANDER
ROAD

+ C

CLOBER ROAD

BALVIE ROAD

CRAIGDHU ROAD

St Joseph's
Primary School

SOUTH MAINS ROAD

Craigdhu
Primary
School

DRUMCARN DR

PRESTONFIELD

CRAIGTON ROAD

KIRK ST

+ A

Fire Station

Clober
Primary School

|————————————| 1000 m
|————————————| 1000 yds

Douglas Academy

A    St Luke
B    Cairns Church
C    Milngavie United Free Church
D    St Andrew (Episcopal)
E    St Joseph (R. C.)
F    St Paul's Milngavie
G    Milngavie Church (former)

← N

Milngavie

tower's two lower stages are plain. Above, an octagonal belfry of
polished ashlar, with diagonal buttresses at four corners and
pointed and cusped two-light openings. Octagonal spire covered
with red Rosemary tiles; Art Nouveau-ish finial.

INTERIOR. Nave with two-bay arcades, the depressed arches
carried on octagonal stone pillars. Another depressed arch to a

recess at the N end. In the aisles and across the S end, a gallery, its front panelled with Gothic blind arcading. Wagon roof, the space between the tie-beam and ceiling filled with arcading. – Exceptionally roomy Gothic PULPIT. – The recess behind is filled by the ORGAN by *Norman & Beard*, installed in 1907. – STAINED GLASS (Our Lord as the Good Shepherd and Saints) of 1907 in the four-light N window above the organ. – In the vestibule, a WAR MEMORIAL tablet designed by *D. Forrester Wilson* and executed by *James Gray*, 1921, the manner hinting at Art Nouveau. Bronze, with the relief of a kilted soldier embraced by a dancing angel.

MILNGAVIE CHURCH, Hillhead Street. Now housing. Built as a chapel of ease in 1840–1. 'Saxon' rectangle, the S front of broached ashlar, the rest of squared rubble. At the front, a battlemented narrow tower containing the round-arched entrance under a round-arched window. Above that, a lozenge-shaped clock face and rectangular belfry openings. Inside the battlement, a stone spire.

MILNGAVIE UNITED FREE CHURCH, Craigdhu Road. Simple boxy Gothic, of 1934–5.

ST ANDREW (Episcopal), corner of Park Road and Stewart Street. Built in 1892 as a Roman Catholic chapel for Irish labourers at the Craigmaddie Reservoir. Small and simple nave and chancel in red and white brickwork. Contemporary two-storey house at the N end.

ST JOSEPH (R.C.), corner of Station Road and Buchanan Street. Originally Milngavie and Baldernock Free Church. By *Campbell Douglas & Morrison*, 1895–6. Broad buttressed box of hammer-dressed and squared buff-coloured stone. In the S (liturgical W) gable, a hoodmoulded and Y-traceried three-light window above the entrance. On the gable's E side, a tower, its parapet bulging out into angle rounds; within the parapet, a small slated spire. Pointed windows in the sides. At the N gable, a large circular window.

ST LUKE, Kirk Street. By *King, Main & Ellison*, 1971–3. Economical but effective, with dry-dashed walls and slated roofs. Canted E gable to the church. At the E end of each of its sides, sawtooth walling directing light from windows on to the sanctuary. Butterfly-topped bellcote on the W gable. Large but lower piend-roofed W porch. To the S, a flat-roofed brick hall, a band of glazing at the top of the walls.

ST PAUL'S MILNGAVIE, corner of Strathblane Road and Baldernock Road. Originally Milngavie Parish Church. By *Leadbetter & Fairley*, 1903–6. Scots late Gothic, built in hammer-dressed red sandstone. Broad-eaved nave with narrow aisles. Diagonally buttressed two-bay transepts; battlemented semi-octagonal chancel at the N end. Purposefully blocky SE porch intended to form the base of a bell-tower; on top of the porch, the bell from the former Milngavie Church (q.v.). Hoodmoulded and loop-traceried W window of nine lights. In the aisles, rectangular windows, each containing two roundheaded lights. Elliptically arched clearstorey windows, their pointed lights with concave-sided heads. Loop tracery again in the two-light transept windows and cusped loops in the side windows of the chancel; a cusped circlet in the head of the N window. HALLS on the E built in 1961–4, their front to Baldernock Road added by *Beaver Construction Ltd.*, 1981–2.

INTERIOR. Walls of hammer-dressed and squared red sandstone rubble. Broad four-bay nave, the arcades to the aisles with depressed arches springing from octagonal piers, their main faces rounded, their tops without capitals. At the crossing, tall two-bay arcades to the transepts, their centre piers and responds all with capitals. Large arch into the shallow semi-octagonal chancel whose walls are panelled in pine with some linenfold decoration. Over the nave, an almost flat ceiling, its beams supported on hammers.

On the W side of the chancel arch, an oak PULPIT of 1906, the frieze carved with vines; emblems of the Evangelists at the corners. – ORGAN at the NW corner by *J.J. Binns*, 1914, its chamber opening into the chancel and transept. – STAINED GLASS. In the chancel, the centre (N) First World War memorial window (the Crucifixion) is of 1920 by *Douglas Strachan* in his restrained rather bitty manner. – Wishy-washy W window of the chancel (the Sermon on the Mount) by *William Meikle & Sons*, 1927. – The chancel's E window (Our Lord healing the Epileptic Boy) is of 1931. – In the W nave aisle, Women's Guild and Girls' Brigade windows of 1987 and 1993. – In the W clearstorey, a window (the Vine topped by the Victor's Crown) by the *Abbey Studio*, 1951. – Much more successful window (Our Lord calling the Apostles) of 1979 in the E clearstorey. – In the porch, a wall MONUMENT to the Rev. Robert Bell †1898, with a portrait bust in relief.

## PUBLIC BUILDINGS

CLOBER PRIMARY SCHOOL, Kirk Street. By *Dumbarton County Council*, 1963–4. One- and two-storey flat-roofed H-plan, of light brown brick and curtain walling.

CRAIGDHU PRIMARY SCHOOL, Prestonfield. By *Strathclyde Regional Council*, 1976. Assembly of single-storey monopitch-roofed blocks.

DOUGLAS ACADEMY, Craigton Road. By *Boissevain & Osmond*, 1964. Long, low and polite. Flat-roofed and curtain-walled.

FIRE STATION, Craigdhu Road. Built *c.* 1970. Brown brick walls, with a metal fascia over the glazed doors of the engine house. Oversailing dry-dashed upper floor at the adjoining offices.

MILNGAVIE COMMUNITY EDUCATION CENTRE, off Allander Road. By *Strathclyde Regional Council* (project architects: *W. F. Cameron* and *D. W. Hodge*), 1980. Two flat-roofed boxes faced with brown brick and with white fascias; linking foyer. The W block, placed at a lower level than the E, stands beside a pond towards which it pushes a cantilevered balcony.

MILNGAVIE PRIMARY SCHOOL, Hillcrest Street and Hillhead Street. Two-storey front (N) block by *Henry Higgins*, 1903–7, built of bullnosed buff-coloured masonry. Thrifty Jacobean, with mullioned windows and shaped gablets. Porch at each end, the E for girls, the W for boys. To the S, a second block built as Milngavie Public School in 1874–5; *Hugh H. Maclure* was the architect. Single-storey ashlar front. Pedimented centre-piece of four bays, its windows corniced. Piend-roofed W addition by *J. L. Cowan*, 1896, its three-light windows also corniced.

MILNGAVIE TOWN HALL, DISTRICT COURT AND LILLIE ART GALLERY, Station Road. By *Michael Bowley*, 1961–2. Understated and unexciting group, the exposed concrete frame infilled with red brick and glazing. Tall windows in the W side of the Town Hall which is covered by a shallow double-pitch roof. Flat-roofed District Court to the SE. Irregular sawtooth roof over the Lillie Art Gallery at the E end of the complex.

POLICE STATION, Main Street. Sizeable brick box, by *Taylor & Davie*, 1958.

RAILWAY STATION, Station Road. Built in 1863. Main building on the E platform, a broad-eaved long *cottage orné*. Over the platform an awning supported on cast iron columns with fluted bases and foliaged capitals.

ST JOSEPH'S PRIMARY SCHOOL, Craigdhu Road. At the front, a tall single-storey building of the 1930s, its centrepiece, marked by greater height, and wings all with piended roofs. Behind, a flat-roofed two-storey block, by *Frank Burnet, Bell & Partners*, 1964.

### DESCRIPTION

St Paul's Milngavie Church (*see* Churches, above) on the corner of STRATHBLANE ROAD and Baldernock Road stands as a sentry at the entrance to the town centre. STATION ROAD leads to the W. On its N side, Milngavie Town Hall, District Court and Lillie Art Gallery (*see* Public Buildings, above) is followed by St Joseph's R.C. Church on the W corner of BUCHANAN STREET which runs uphill to Cairns Church (for these *see* Churches, above). Set below Station Road's S side, the Railway Station (*see* Public Buildings, above). W of this Station Road is pedestrianized. On its N, a couple of prosperous late C19 villas. No. 41 has a two-storey bow window, a bargeboarded gable and gablet, and gentle 'Greek' Thomsonesque touches. At EDINA (No. 39) a pair of steeply pitched bargeboarded gablets and a pilastered and corniced doorpiece. Then the street becomes commercial. On the S, Nos. 30–44, a long two-storey block of *c.* 1900 containing flats above shops. First-floor oriel windows and a slated conical spire over the E corner. A stodgier version (Nos. 2–28), also of *c.* 1900, follows. On the N side, at the corner of Mugdock Road, the CROSS KEYS, an early C19 inn, its broached ashlar now painted.

DOUGLAS STREET continues the line of Station Road. Its buildings, an unexciting redevelopment of *c.* 1970, are by *Jack Holmes & Partners*. On the S side, the burgh's WAR MEMORIAL by *G. H. Paulin*, *c.* 1920, a bronze statue of a lady holding a lamp.

MAIN STREET goes off to the s. At its head, a pedestal bearing a large CLOCK of the earlier C20 formerly on the (demolished) Copland & Lye's department store in Sauchiehall Street, Glasgow, and erected here in 1981. On the w corner with Douglas Street, a big English-looking block (Nos. 4–8) of c. 1900. Two tall storeys, the ground floor with late C20 shopfronts. At the upper floor, a pair of very broad bargeboarded and half-timbered gables, each containing a large mullioned and transomed rectangular oriel window. A much lower and less self-confident near-contemporary version of this at Nos. 10–18, followed by the very plain red sandstone CO-OPERATIVE BUILDINGS of 1896. On the s corner of Stewart Street, THE TALBOT ARMS, dated 1885, a broken segmental pediment over the canted corner. On the e side of Main Street, the façade of the former BLACK BULL HOTEL, the main block built in 1827, with a heavy Roman Doric columned doorpiece. It was extended s in the later C19, the addition's N corner bowed under a crowstepped gablet. It is now incorporated in a shopping development by *The ADF Partnership*, of 2000. Then the late C20 Nos. 13–25. Harled neo-vernacular, the ground-floor shops set behind a piazza. An underpass under Woodburn Way leads to a car park. On the car park's e side, TESCO, late C20, a valiant attempt to disguise the commercial shed by draping it with 'mansard' roofs; glass-topped pyramid over the entrance. On the w side of the car park, Gavin's Mill (*see* Industrial Building, below) standing beside the Allander Water.

## VILLAS, ETC.

BALDERNOCK ROAD. – CARFAX (No. 14) is English Arts and Crafts of the early C20. Harled walls; display of red Rosemary tiled roofs of various pitches. Narrow windows at the entrance front, a bow window on the e. – DOUGALSTON DOOCOT, on Dougalston Golf Course. Early C19 two-storey hexagon. Rubble-built with polished ashlar dressings. Strip quoins; concave-moulded corbels under the eaves course. A stringcourse cuts across the ground floor's dummy windows at the level of the springing of their roundheaded arches; in the s face, a corniced door with a semicircular panel above. Horizontally proportioned windows at the first floor. The roof (a replacement of 1972) is a truncated spire topped by a cupola.

BARLOCH AVENUE. BARLOCH COTTAGE, a white-painted villa of the earlier C19. Main block of two storeys and three bays, with a pilastered and corniced doorpiece. Single-storey piend-roofed wings. Horizontal glazing in the windows.

## INDUSTRIAL BUILDING

GAVIN'S MILL, Main Street. Now a bar. Probably of earlier origin but of the mid C19 in its present form. Rubble-built two-storey double pile. Overshot wheel on the w side.

A number of substantial, mainly late C19, mansions enjoying the wooded waterside landscape at the E end of Loch Ard.

JEAN MCALPINE'S INN. Perhaps C18 in origin; restored early 1990s. Three low gabled vernacular buildings in random rubble. Roof structures have been carefully reconstructed using scarf-jointed couples and thatching of bracken, broom and rushes. W unit has a re-created 'hangin lum' formed from wattle and daub over framing.

MILTON MILL. C19. Plain rubble structure built to an L-plan on sloping ground. Quoinstone inscribed 16 WM 67. Segmental arch with console keystone.

DESCRIPTION. The road W twists along the narrowed tail of the loch affording the most picturesque views of water and forest. On the l. are CORRIENESSAN, 1887, by *John J. Burnet*, red sandstone and roughcast with half-timbered gables and roofs falling W over a glazed ground floor, and, shoreside, DUNDARROCH which, despite its white, parapeted and piended Georgian look, complete with Roman Doric porch, dates from a *c.* 1922 rebuilding. On the r., in rubble and ashlar: CREAG ARD, inverted V-shaped gables trimmed in ragged-edged bargeboarding; CRAIGENVEOCH, with a twin-gabled porch and gables galore above; DALDRISHAIG, which has a two-storey canted bay capped by a faceted hip-end with raking sides; and CUILVONA, dated 1887, with a steep pyramid roof over its octagonal SW corner.

DUKE MURDOCH'S CASTLE, Loch Ard, 2.9km. W. Early C15. Fragmentary remains on the tiny island of Dundochil; reputedly built by Murdoch, Duke of Albany.

DUCHRAY CASTLE. *See* p. 385.

Once a textile hamlet dependent on the tumbling waters of the Milton Burn but now no more than a suburban cluster of varied C20 housing on the N side of the A82 E of Dumbarton. By far the best of this housing is WHYTE'S CORNER, a flatted crescent in the roughcast Scots vernacular practised by the County Architect, *Joseph Weekes*. The design, which dates from 1933, won a Saltire Award in 1937.

MILTON HOUSE, 0.4km. N. Built *c.* 1792 as the mill manager's residence. Harled five-bay classical mansion pedimented over the central three bays but with no projection of the façade. From the gable skews low eaves parapets collide with the pediment. Pilastered doorpiece and short flying stair. Urns on the skews and on the GATEPIERS at the entrance to the drive.

MILTON MILL, 0.4km. N. Nothing remains of the water-powered textile mill of *c.* 1790 save two ruinous towers of five and three storeys. Both are battlemented. Both have superimposed Palladian Gothick windows, some blind, some with astragals.

BARNHILL HOUSE 1.6km. N. A largely Victorian accumulation of hipped roofs and bays. Some vestiges of the C16 dwelling of the Colquhouns of Milton may have been absorbed by C18 and C19 expansion.

OVERTOUN HOUSE. *See* p. 629.

## MILTON OF BUCHANAN S *4090*

A delightful village clinging to a bend and dip in the road between Drymen and Balmaha.

BUCHANAN PARISH CHURCH. By *John Adam*, 1761–4. Skew-gabled, roughcast kirk aligned E–W with a projecting N aisle forming a T-plan. At the apex of the N gable is a round-arched bellcote topped with ogee dome and cross, probably not original. Venetian window in the E gable; in the W, a single round-arched light over a door with segmental lintel. Four round-arched S windows. The church was repaired in 1828 and described as 'a plain edifice, very neatly finished' in the *New Statistical Account* of 1845. There was originally a laird's gallery for the Duke of Montrose and his family but in 1938 the interior was destroyed by fire; within a year, however, refurbishment by *Clarke & Bell & J. H. Craigie* was complete. Only the N wing was altered externally: in the gable, across which a narrow stone moulding maintains the impression of a pediment, a two-light window with ashlar surrounds and keystones was introduced and below this a single-storey porch, its ashlar ingoes splayed under a wide segmental arch, also heavily keystoned.

Internally, the C20 renewal, carried out in light oak save for pointed rubble walls above the panelling, is airy and spacious and consistently detailed in classical style. There is no gallery. Coomb ceiling with arch-bracing springing from timber corbels. The N wing forms a full-height aisle closed on the N by a timber panelled wall behind which is the vestibule and, above it, reached by a winding pitch pine stair, the vestry. At the W end, an oak doorpiece with broad fluted pilasters and a plain cornice. – In the E end are the choir stalls, lectern and PULPIT, an octagonal box with fielded oak panels, each bearing a carved religious symbol. – A copper ALMS PLATE with Art Nouveau pewter shield and heart-shaped inlays.

The church is approached axially from the N through the GRAVEYARD. Close to the N gateway is a fluted stone SUNDIAL shaft, 1922; it has a copper dial-plate but has lost its gnomon. – Most graves to the N are of recent date but S, behind the church, are some C18 and C19 TABLE TOMBS and HEADSTONES. A small W plot contains the graves of the sixth and seventh Dukes of Montrose and other members of the Graham family; a variety of Celtic crosses, C19 and C20.

BUCHANAN PRIMARY SCHOOL, early C20, extended at the rear in 1964, has a half-timbered gable projecting symmetrically from its main classroom block.

MEMORIAL HALL, built *c.* 1920 as a public hall and museum; an

uncomfortable L-plan block with round arches to the windows
and a corner doorway set between rubble 'bastions'.

DESCRIPTION. At the centre, located on the E bank of the Burn
of Mar since at least the mid C17, is BUCHANAN MILL, a plain
rubble block, late C18 or early C19, with a segmental-arched SE
doorway and a mill-wheel seemingly ineffectually ditched in
a pit against the SW gable. In fact, the water channel reached
the wheel by an underground channel. Across the road, the
OLD SCHOOLHOUSE, probably late C18, two dwellings in one
white piend-roofed cube with small timber sashes sliding vertically in the downstairs windows but horizontally above. For the
Buchanan Primary School and Memorial Hall *see* above. Uphill
E is MILTON FARM, a late C18 inn, painted rubble with a
piended roof, small stone-mullioned windows and a minimal
stone porch. Beside it, white too and piended, are WESTMOST
and EASTMOST COTTAGES, *c.* 1800, a two-house row of former
farm dwellings.

GARTINCABER, 0.6km. NNW. C19. Standard two-storey three-
bay house. Windows wider than usual with stone mullions.

AUCHMAR. *See* p. 186.


# MILTON OF CAMPSIE

Sizeable village, a few of the buildings C19 but mostly housing of
the later C20.

MILTON OF CAMPSIE PARISH CHURCH, Antermony Road.
Built in 1888. Broad lancet-windowed box, the walls of stugged
buff masonry. At the front (S) gable, a slightly advanced centrepiece containing a three-light window and crowned with a
gableted bellcote. Gabled porch in the SE inner angle. In the
gable, a large round window with a smaller one above. – Inside,
STAINED GLASS designed by *Willie Rodger* and executed by
*John K. Clark*, 1987–8.

CRAIGHEAD COMMUNITY EDUCATION CENTRE, Craighead
Road. Former school, by *David Sturrock*, 1902–3. Stugged buff
stonework, the detail eroded by cleaning. Single-storey, with
broad eaves and mullioned and transomed windows. In the
gablets, relief portrait busts of men.

CRAIGHEAD PRIMARY SCHOOL, Craighead Road. By the Stirling
County Architect, *A. J. Smith*, 1966–8. Dry-dashed walls and
felted monopitch roofs.

BALDORAN HOUSE, Campsie Road. Two-storey rendered villa,
of the mid C19 in its present form. Main block of three bays,
with a cast iron verandah across the front. At the S end, a further
bay which is advanced and pedimented, with a three-light window
at each floor. Balustraded porch in the inner angle.

BALDORROCH HOUSE, No. 2 Antermony Road. Two-storey
three-bay house of *c.* 1800, built of white-painted rubble. At the
main (S) front, looking away from Antermony Road, a pilastered
and pedimented doorpiece. Piend-roofed single-storey wing at
each end.

KINCAID HOUSE, off Birdston Road. Country house-villa designed by *David Hamilton, c.* 1812, in a light-hearted castellated manner. Two-storey piend-roofed main block of three bays by two with round towers at the corners, all faced with droved ashlar except at the slightly advanced centrepiece of the E (entrance) front whose ashlar stonework is polished. At this front's outer bays, rectangular three-light windows. The tall and hoodmoulded ground-floor windows have segmental-arched centre openings flanked by narrow roundheaded lights. The windows above have equal-sized rectangular lights and are set in moulded frames rising from a sill course which is carried round the block. Over the outer bays, a corbelled low battlement. The centrepiece is taller and finished with a corbelled parapet pierced by round-arched openings; at its corners, pinnacled miniature turrets. At the ground floor, a semicircular portico, its columns with bundled shafts and bell capitals; guttae under the cornice which supports a battlement, the merlons pierced by keyhole openings. Behind the portico, a side-lit entrance under a segmental-arched fanlight. First-floor window of three pointed lights set in a rectangular overarch. Visible behind the centrepiece is the battlemented tower over the main block's rear; in each of its E and W elevations, a large pointed window. At each corner tower, tall and narrow roundheaded ground-floor windows with hoodmoulds skied above them. Stone cupolas inside the towers' battlements.

The N and S elevations are each of two bays, their windows (some dummies) like those of the outer bays of the E front but of two lights instead of three. The S elevation's E bay is covered by a late C20 conservatory.

Protruding N from the back of the early C19 main block is a double-pile wing. The harled and crowstep-gabled S half may be late C17 but much altered. The piend-roofed N half is of the mid C18 but the droved ashlar front may be a refacing of *c.* 1812, the likely date for the segmental-arched ground-floor windows and the battlemented clasping buttress at the NW corner.

Inside, a screen of fluted Doric columns with vestigial capitals at the E end of the entrance hall. At its W end, the main staircase, a late C19 replacement. Some thinly enriched plaster ceilings in the principal rooms.

Early C19 piend-roofed LODGE at the entrance to the drive. Elliptical-arched windows; corner pilasters supporting the heavy wallhead cornice.

BIRDSTON FARM, 1.3km. S. Small two-storey laird's house of the mid or later C18, the roof's slates replaced by concrete pantiles in the later C20. S front (now dry-dashed) of five bays, the upper windows linked by a lintel course under the moulded eaves course, the surrounds to all the openings dressed up with false keystones. Scrolled skewputts with rosetted centres. The house forms the centrepiece of a U, the whitewashed SE and SW ranges built as farm offices in the early C19, their concrete pantiles again C20.

GLORAT HOUSE. *See* p. 523.
WOODBURN HOUSE. *See* p. 793.

Residential enclave in pleasant elevated countryside. A brief
village street of white roughcast dwellings surrounded by a clutch
of grander houses.

CRAIGALLION, 2.1km. WNW. Robust Baronial-Tudor mansion
built in bull-nosed rubble by *James Ritchie*, 1883–5 (dated 1884).
Rising above the gables and bays of the SW façade, a three-storey
entrance tower with corbelled parapet from which emerge a
timber caphouse and cone-topped turret. Many mullioned and
transomed windows. SE conservatories in disrepair. Timber
interiors in oak, walnut, sequoia and pitch pine.

CRAIGEND CASTLE, Mugdock Country Park, 1.7km. NW.
Completed by *Alexander Ramsay*, 1816–17, after work on the
enlargement of an earlier house, following plans prepared by
the amateur architect *James Smith* of Jordanhill, was abandoned.
Strongly influenced by Smith's planning and by the medievalist
designs of Robert Lugar at Tullichewan and Balloch (qq.v.),
Ramsay's castellated Gothic mansion, constructed in droved
ashlar, survives as a romantic roofless shell. The SE façade has a
three-bay centre of superimposed hoodmoulded windows, E
corner octagon tower and a three-storey square S tower with a
band of cusped pointed arches under its corbelled parapet. This
last motif repeats above the four-centred arches of the *porte
cochère* which projects between tower and centre. Only a few
windows preserve any tracery.

    STABLES. Probably by *Alexander Ramsay*, 1812. Converted to
Mugdock Country Park Visitor Centre by *The Pollock Hammond
Partnership*, 1987–96. Castellated Gothic like the castle itself
but built in squared whinstone with hefty ashlar dressings, roll-
moulded at the quoins and around hooded doors and windows.
Symmetrical S façade with centrepiece arched entry and end
pavilions, the linking battlements holed with trefoil-headed
pointed-arch openings. Behind, around an inner courtyard,
stables, byre, coachhouse and steading have been adapted to
leisure use with exhibition area, tea-room, ranger's offices etc.
Semicircular byre on W transformed into clearstorey-lit lecture
room. Waterpen, kennels and stores survive at NW. To the SE
is the WALLED GARDEN, restored 2000–2001 as Mugdock
Plantaria, with railings along its low SW wall and the Millennium
Bandstand sited axially at its centre.

DINEIDDWG HOUSE, 0.2km. S. By *Honeyman, Keppie &
Mackintosh*, 1905–06. Ambitious in scale if not in architectural
accomplishment. Turgidly respectable bulk in square-snecked
sandstone with mullioned-and-transomed widows and parapeted
gables. The former offices survive in separate residential use as
THE STABLES, their three-storey, crowstepped tower rising
above converted coachhouses etc. on the S side of the village
street. Apsidal conservatory entered through a round arch in
roughcast screen wall.

EASTERTOUN HOUSE, 1km. ESE. Respectable mid-Victorian

house enhanced by internal remodelling, new porch and three-storey hip-roofed W wing by *A. N. Paterson*, *c.* 1914. NW tower with swept cone roof. Garden layout, SUMMERHOUSE and DOOCOT also by *Paterson*.

MUGDOCK CASTLE, Mugdock Country Park, 0.9km. WNW. Picturesque ruin on high ground at the SW end of Mugdock Loch. Begun in the late C14, perhaps by Sir David de Graham, it was extended in the C15 and until the beginning of the C18 remained the fortress of the Montrose family. The square tower which survives may be one of several which punctuated the original enceinte. It is entered from a forestair on the courtyard side through a round-arched opening at first-floor level. The chamber at this level is vaulted on splayed ribs. Remains of a second tower lie some 0.2km. N connected by the C14 curtain and it is possible that this arrangement was mirrored on the E side of the castle court. A ruinous gateway SE of the intact tower retains door rebates and grooves for the portcullis. Part of the C15 enclosing wall, with inverted keyhole gunloops and a ruinous C16 range behind, extends NW. Traces of walling then continue N along a steep bank for *c.* 0.09km. Some distance N of the ruined tower are the remains, rectangular in plan, of what may have been a chapel. – The WALLED GARDEN was added *c.* 1820.

Half a century later in the 1870s, *James Sellars* of *Campbell Douglas & Sellars* began to transform the E block into a mansion house conceived in the 'Old Scotch' style. Much of the medieval work was taken down but the castle tower was retained with a library on the first floor connected to the dining room of the new house by a half-timbered bridge. In its turn, Sellars' house has been demolished.

# MUIRAVONSIDE                                                    F *9070*

Isolated church.

MUIRAVONSIDE PARISH CHURCH. Tall harled box of 1811. Pointed windows with wooden mullions and Y-tracery. Ball-finialled birdcage bellcote on the W gable. On the E gable, a circular stone carved with a Maltese cross, probably late medieval; it was erected here in 1947 when the E porch was added.

The interior was also recast in 1947 when the present E gallery was put up, the pews (probably dating from *Black & Learmonth*'s repairs of 1873) rearranged, and the pulpit (also probably of 1873) moved from the S wall to the E end. – STAINED GLASS. In the two centre windows of the S wall, colourful scenes (Acts of Mercy) of *c.* 1885.

GRAVEYARD. Immediately NE of the church, a mid-C18 HEADSTONE to James Nimmo of Wardlaw, mason, bearing a coat of arms supported by naked boys, one holding a square, the other compasses. It is an outlier of a remarkable collection of thick HEADSTONES of the mid and later C18 which stand to the S of the church. These are carved variously with angels' heads (representing the soul), reminders of death, coats of arms, naked

boys, and grapes. A few have pilasters or attached columns. Among them, just s of the e bay of the church, is a stone of
33  1761, its w face displaying figures standing on coffins and blowing looped trumpets. – s of the centre of the church, a stone whose w face is carved with a snake coiling round bones. – Just to its sw, three more stones with trumpeting figures standing on coffins. – s of the w end of the church, a stone crudely carved with a man wielding a pick. – To its n, a stone whose w face is carved in fairly high relief with a flying angel and emblems of death. It commemorates Patrick Calder †1718.

76 AVON AQUEDUCT, 1.6km. SE. By *Hugh Baird*, 1818–22, to carry the Union Canal over the River Avon. Built of hammer-dressed rough ashlar. Twenty segmental arches, the piers battered and tapering towards the top; plain parapets.

MUIRAVONSIDE COUNTRY PARK, 1.8km. SE. Muiravonside House, a small mansion which had grown from the C17 to the C19, has been demolished but dwarf walls mark its outline on a lawn in its garden, now part of the Country Park. e of the site of the house, a wall which screened the stable offices from the garden. At the wall's e end, a large crowstep-gabled lectern DOOCOT, probably of the earlier C19. Rubble-built, the front (s) wall harled. At the front, above a boldly projecting cornice-cum-ratcourse, a pair of steeply pedimented stone dormers, each containing two tiers of round-arched flight-holes; upstanding blocks on the ends of the cornice. On the n side of the wall, a mid-C19 court of STABLE OFFICES, a crowstep-gabled centre-piece at the e range. – 0.41km. n, partly built into the n bank of the Bowhouse Burn, remains of a mid-C19 circular LIMEKILN. Three tunnel-vaulted chambers survive, with bullnosed masonry at their round-arched entrances.

MYREHEAD, 1.1km. NE. Mid-C19 farmhouse and rubble-built steading, rather altered. At the NW corner of the steading, a bottle-shaped round WINDMILL tower.

ALMOND CASTLE. *See* p. 173.

MUIRHOUSES*                       F

C19 hamlet, the houses built for workers on the Carriden estate. Some C20 development, mostly tucked discreetly away.

DESCRIPTION. On the approach from the n up CARRIDEN BRAE, on the w side, GRANGE LODGE, a mid-C19 Jacobean cottage with hoodmoulds over the mullioned windows. It is followed by C20 bungalows. The e side of the road is open to the fields except for a LODGE of 1844 to Carriden House. Picturesque with bracketed broad eaves and a jerkin-head gable. At the top of the hill, an informal group of seven single-storey cottages (HOPE COTTAGES) dated 1854–74, all with snecked rubble masonry, bracketed broad eaves and jerkin-head

*Account based on that by Colin McWilliam, *The Buildings of Scotland: Lothian* (1978).

gables. Among them, on the corner of Acre Road, THE OLD
SCHOOLHOUSE built as a girls' school in 1866. Steep-pitched
gablet at the school; at the adjoining schoolhouse, a rustic porch
and a bay window of two storeys, the lower semi-octagonal,
the upper corbelled to the square. Latticed glazing in the
windows. To the W, set back from the S side of ACRE ROAD, is
GRANGEWELLS by *Matthew Steele*, 1911, an L-plan villa crisply
dressed in white harl with black-painted trimmings. Art
Nouveau touches. Battered chimneys. Half-domed bow window
at the S gable; two-storey canted bay window at the NW jamb.
Low service wing on the E side.

## NATIONAL WALLACE MONUMENT    S *8090*
### 2.3km. NE of Stirling

By *J. T. Rochead*, 1861–9. In 1851, Charles Roger, the leading
promoter of the movement to raise a monument in honour of
Scotland's C13 freedom fighter, William Wallace, declared that
'a colossal statue of the national hero ... would be peculiarly
suitable for the summit of the Abbey Craig'. Eight years later,
reviewing the full range of proposals made, William Stirling
of Keir disagreed: 'For a position which is a landmark to so
vast a range of country, a statue, however colossal, is manifestly
unsuited.' Such controversy was not new. Since 1818, when the
idea of a monument had first emerged, neither location nor design
had won consensus. At length, the counter claims of Glasgow and
Edinburgh rejected, the Abbey Craig, a high wooded crag rising
dramatically out of the flat carseland close to the site of Wallace's
victory at the Battle of Stirling Bridge in 1297, was chosen as the
site. In June 1856, 20,000 people gathered in Stirling's King's
Park to acclaim the intention to proceed. In the final event, a
national architectural competition was held and in 1859 the
design submitted by Rochead was declared the winner.

This is the ultimate totemic expression of Scots Baronialism:
an immense, rocket-shaped shrine of myth and memory wrapped
in a knobbly carapace of rock-faced stone. It is seen for miles
around, the craggy shaft over 60m. high, more elevated on its
hilltop site than Stirling Castle itself. Yet the pilgrim, climbing
through the trees, comes upon it suddenly. Out of the summit,
a mass of battered masonry, as much as 4.5m. thick at the base,
rears up into a high tower. Linked S is the KEEPER'S HOUSE
(now a small tea-room), bulkily gabled and crowstepped, its heavy
corbelled bartizans spiked with gargoyles. Between the two, opening off a terrace that looks W to the carse, a huge round arch,
circled by screw-twist and cable mouldings and surmounted by
armorial bearings and a thorn-wreathed thistle-head, marks the
entrance. Above l., set into the SW corner of the tower, a larger-
than-life bronze sculpture of Wallace by *D. W. Stevenson*, 1887.
Clasped against the NW corner, above the tower's battered base,
a narrow turnpike stair twists upwards, enclosed in an octagonal
ashlar cage repeatedly banded by raking cable mouldings and

National Wallace Monument. Engraving of proposal by
J. T. Rochead, c. 1861.

small coupled openings. High above, the tiered buttresses of a
crown spire arch over the wind-seared viewing platform at the
summit.

The great w ARCHWAY originally gave into a courtyard
between tower and Keeper's House but from 1874, when this
inner space was provided with a glazed roof, it has served as
Entrance Hall. The tower's ground-floor chamber l. (now a
shop) is a lofty, barrel-vaulted volume with splayed corners, the
first of four similar superimposed spaces. Walls and vault are of
large coursed rubble blocks. N, E and S segmental-arched windows
with steeply sloping sills. Along the w side of the tower a long
straight-flight staircase rises in a narrow slot to first floor and

the start of the spiralling ascent at the NW corner. Here is the HALL OF ARMS. Above this, the HALL OF HEROES. Both are lit by single segmental-arched windows in each wall. In the ROYAL CHAMBER at third-floor level the barrel vault is pointed, each side penetrated by two oblique shafts bringing light from above. Finally, the climb ends. A high-walled parapet defile passes around the tower through the eight ribs that form the great crown spire, each triple-tier flyer, crested with three crocketed pinnacles, arching against its opposite number over an upper platform set back behind the walkway below.

At each level sentiment and story combine. Not the least addicted to national glory is the STAINED GLASS installed by *James Ballantine & Son* in the tower's eleven windows, 1885. At ground floor, the Honours of Scotland flanked by unicorns bearing the lion rampant and the flag of St Andrew. – Hall of Arms: the arms of Great Britain, Scotland, Wallace and the Burgh of Stirling. – Hall of Heroes: Wallace, Bruce, an archer and a spearman. Here, too, are ranged fifteen white marble BUSTS of the country's principal cultural luminaries, all by *D. W. Stevenson*, 1886–9. Bronze HEAD of Thomas Carlyle by *Pittendrigh Macgillivray*, 1891.

## NEWTOWN OF FINTRY *see* FINTRY

## OLD BALLIKINRAIN *see* BALLIKINRAIN CASTLE

## OLD KILPATRICK WD *4070*

A residential village bypassed by the boulevard traffic on Great Western Road, only to be cast in the baneful shadow of Erskine Bridge.

OLD KILPATRICK BOWLING CHURCH. Originally Old Kilpatrick Parish Church. The parish church built in 1812 in 'later English style'. Droved ochre sandstone courses with polished ashlar dressings. Three tall windows N and S, pointed-arched openings divided by Y-tracery and crossed by a single stone transom. Diagonal buttresses at the corners of the church and inset W tower. Hooded four-centred-arched entrance doorway on the tower's S face. Above the skews, louvred Y-tracery belfry openings under hooded pointed arches. Above these, four clock faces in lozenge frames. BELLS, installed 1898, by *Gillett & Johnston*, Croydon. Crenellated parapet with obelisk finials. At the E end, a battlemented canted organ apse and session house, added 1897–8. Four lancet lights under a pointed arch. Re-roofed and interior renovated, 1928. After heavy war damage the church was restored in 1949.

The interior is distinctly lofty. Collar ceiling with the ties and struts of roof trusses exposed. U-plan gallery carried on eight remarkably slender cast iron columns and panelled in oak. – Chancel furnishings are by *P. Macgregor Chalmers*, 1897–8. – High hexagonal oak PULPIT on arched stone pillars on a marble base, 1898. – Wide stone cup FONT on pedestal, 1897. – Memorial WALL MONUMENTS on N wall: white marble tablet to Rev. John Reid †1867, by *Alexander Clubb* of Glasgow; brass on veined green marble to Col. George James Ferguson-Buchanan of Auchentorlie †1928 and his wife Grace Hamilton †1935. – On the S wall, brass on green marble to Hannah Ralston Cumming †1914, installed 1946; another of the same to Claud Hamilton Hamilton of Barns and Cochno †1900; and a white marble tablet with a relief portrait of Rev. Robert Henderson †1893. – Bronze RELIEF of Robert Filshie, beadle for sixty-five years. – Bronze War Memorial PLAQUES, the grander, to the fallen of World War I, by *Donaldson & Burns* of Edinburgh. – STAINED GLASS. In the apse, the Ascension, gifted 1916; in two windows N and S, the Four Evangelists: by *A. Ballantine & Gardiner*, 1898.

An extensive walled GRAVEYARD contains many interesting grave-markers. The church plinth and the street wall are incised with lair numbers. – Slab EFFIGY of an armed knight, C14 (?), stands near the W door of the church. – A few C17 and C18 SLABS; the oldest stone, bearing the initials TP and IP, is dated 1616. – Wide variety of C19 HEADSTONES. On the W wall, a cast iron TABLET in memory of John Clark, a calico printer at Little Mill, †1776, and his heirs; erected 1829. – In the SE corner, the STIRLING OF LAW MAUSOLEUM, dated 1658; a U-plan walled enclosure with ball finials on the corners and, above a framed panel and angels' wings, a small strapwork rise in the street wall flanked by scrolled coping. – Close to this, a mural TABLET to the McNair family with fluted pilasters carrying an entablature and dumpy ogee pediment carved with hourglass and inscription. – Skew-gabled rubble structure NW of the church is the HAMILTON OF BARNS MAUSOLEUM; applied panel dated 1875–87. – To the N, the ruinous Gothic MEMORIAL plot to the Nobles of Ardmore, of the mid C19. – Nearby, an unnamed MEMORIAL, mid-C19; an ashlar pyramid on a pedimented cubic base from which massive acroteria have fallen. – E of this, the BUCHANAN OF AUCHENTORLIE MAUSOLEUM, a three-bay classical box with pilaster strips, coupled at the ends, and a dentilled cornice; tomb restored 1887, though, as the inscription records, the family have been buried here 'since the year 1600'. – On the N wall of the kirkyard a gabled pointed-arched portal, 1878, opens to a second burial ground. Further enlargement, 1906.

Former RELIEF CHURCH. Built *c.* 1795. A three-bay box with small windows and a steeply piended roof. Stark and symmetrical, it would be stunning were its harled walls to be whitewashed, as they should be. Converted to residential use. Low rubble walls curve and rise to carry an iron arch at the axial entrance.

ST PATRICK (R.C.). By *Nicholson & Jacobsen*, 1979–80. An elegantly simple composition of two overlapping intersecting monopitch roofs. White roughcast walls, the S gables carried beyond the building as screens penetrated by round-arched openings leading to lateral paths. Entrance in the SE re-entrant below a plain cross mounted on the upper wall. Recessed in the E wall, two vertical windows with splayed jambs and sills light each side of the sanctuary. The walls of the church interior are roughcast under a wide pine-boarded ceiling falling to the E. Confessionals and offices to W. A grey granite boulder ALTAR recalls the mass rock of earlier days.

CHURCH HALLS, opposite Old Kilpatrick Bowling Church. 1897. Two roughcast skew-gabled buildings with a mutual wall. A square entrance block set into the NW re-entrant has lost its slated pyramid roof. The mood is ecclesiastical: arched windows and doors dressed in red sandstone and a buttressed, half-octagonal E end to the S hall. Over the entrance door, a sandstone tablet with the curtailed monogram RE(X) LE(X) DU(X) LU(X).

ERSKINE BRIDGE. By the engineers *Freeman, Fox and Partners*, 1967–71. High, wide and, in the estuarial landscape, decidedly handsome. A cable-stayed, box-girder structure, at once monumental and elegantly slender. The curving carriageways, slung in the sky across the Clyde, have a central span of 300m. and two anchor spans of 110m. Eight approach spans rise gradually from the N, four from the S. The tracks reach a height of 55m. above high-tide level.

GLENARBUCK HOUSE, 0.7km. N. Early C19. An elegant white-walled mansion well sited on the lower slopes of Kilpatrick Braes above the A82. A three-bay, two-storey house with a Roman Doric porch set between pedimented tripartite windows. Instead of gables, full-height windowed bows bulge W and E.

DESCRIPTION. Housing is strung along DUMBARTON ROAD. Here and there a few red sandstone tenements, *c.* 1905, survive. Best is a short range at No. 230; a symmetrical block with slated peaks on corbelled corner bays. The ETTRICK BAR is in fact a cut-down tenement reborn as a black-and-white gabled pub with a quaint corner dormer by *Iain M. Barclay*, 1975. Local authority housing built by the County Architect, *Joseph Weekes*, is much in evidence. In a variety of cottages and flats built between 1920 and 1946, HAWCRAIGS, mid 1930s, at the W end of the village is outstanding; roughcast cottage vernacular, intimate in scale, Scots in allusion, and cunningly planned in oblique arrangements that create a series of pleasant external spaces. There are few detached houses of quality. But a handful of 1870s villas on Lussett Road have acquired Conservation Area status. CRAIGVIEW is enhanced by a gabled timber porch that still preserves its stained glass flanks. More spectacular, the filigree ironwork porch at VIEWARD. The quirkily detailed LUSSETT HOUSE has bowed projections W and E, both with slated conical roofs, the latter sporting an iron finial dripping with florets.

# OLD KIPPENROSS *see* KIPPENROSS HOUSE

OLD LECKIE                    s
                    1.7km. w of Gargunnock

Late c16. Three-storey laird's house with four-storey s wing form-
    ing T-plan: 'a good example of the passage of the Scottish style
    from the castle to the mansion'*. Walls are harled, now without
    margins, and the gables, including the reflection of the s wing at
    the centre of the n wall, crowstepped. A witch-hatted staircase
    turret, corbelled from first floor in the se re-entrant, completes
    the traditional repertoire. Below the banded cone of the turret's
    corbel-courses, a segmental-arched recess in the e wall of the s
    wing marks the original entrance. Two blocked machicolations,
    a gun-loop and a spy-hole make this 'almost the only defensive
    feature of the house'‡. Access is now gained on the opposite
    side of the projecting wing where a plain doorway leads to a
    corridor hall and a narrow turnpike rising in the sw re-entrant
    to first and second floor. At first-floor level, in what was the
    original Hall, a wide stone chimneypiece survives, its deep plain
    lintel supported on short half-columns. A two-storey extension
    on the e gable, c18, and a small hip-roofed first-floor porch and
    staircase added later have wisely been removed in late c20 restora-
    tion. To the s, built in red sandstone rubble, are the courtyard
    OFFICES, early c19, entered from the e through a segmental-
    arched pend, and the OLD BRIDGE, a single semicircular arch
    over the Leckie Burn, with an inset parapet stone dated 1673
    and inscribed EX BENEVOLENTIA/OB SALUTEM ('Out of bene-
    volence, for safety's sake'). se of the house is an obelisk SUNDIAL,
    c17, without its obelisk.

OLD SAUCHIE                   s
                    2km. sse of Chartershall

   An elongated aggregation of estate buildings of varied date. The
55  oldest is the TOWER-HOUSE, late c16, situated at the se end of
    the range. It stands three storeys high, an L-plan shell built in
    random rubble with dressed surrounds. The walls, once harled,
    rise to a cavetto eaves course with gables crowstepped on the
    nw and se and on the sw jamb. At the middle of the se wall a
    segmental bulge corbelled from just below first-floor level to eaves
    height betrays the turnpike stair within. At second-floor level
    corner turrets are corbelled from the n and e angles on layered
    roll-moulded courses; though roofless, they preserve windows
    and pistol-holes below a cavetto eaves. Pistol-holes, peep-holes
    and gun-loops are plentiful, particularly around the ground-
    floor walls. Despite this evident concern for defence, the propor-
    tions of several of the lintelled windows lighting the first-floor
    hall are generous; in fact, only two of six such tall windows have
    not been subject to later widening. The doorway in the w re-

---

* David MacGibbon and Thomas Ross, *The Castellated and Domestic Architecture of
Scotland*, iv (1892), 84.
  ‡ RCAHMS, *Stirlingshire*, ii (1963), 373.

entrant has roll-and-hollow moulded jambs but is without its original lintel. It originally gave access to a scale-and-platt stair which led to the turnpike above.

A vestigial tusk of masonry at the W corner of the jamb hints at the possibility of a barmkin wall and suggests that the approach was first from the W or N. The present drive rounding the S corner is probably not original for it is precariously close to a dramatic and dangerous gorge on the E side of the tower. Moreover, to permit this access, the course of the Sauchie Burn, doubtless also an element in the natural defences of the tower, has at some time been culverted *en route* to its discharge at the foot of a concave cliff of rubble masonry falling into the precipitous valley below.

The short two-storey kitchen wing was added to the NW gable of the tower early in the C17. A century or so later this NW expansion continued a further 30m. in a range of two-storey rubble offices. These buildings, now restored, serve as offices.

DOOCOT, 0.4km. NE. A two-chamber rubble structure now ruinous but formerly with a penthouse roof. Two S entrances; both compartments lined with nesting-box grids. A fallen stone panel is dated 1700.

HOWIETOWN FISH FARM, 0.6km. E. Fish ponds formed to the specifications of Sir James Maitland, 1874–8. Three of the ponds lie in parallel and drain through brick-lined channels and a small circular pool into the principal transverse pond at the centre of which, islanded on brick arches, is a timber-framed-and-lined SUMMERHOUSE. In plan a hexagon set between two squares, it has a slated gabled roof rising higher in faceted planes over the centre. Floor hatch for feeding fish. A narrow gangway on coupled cast iron columns gives access from the bank. – Nearby are the now residential rubble buildings of HOWIETOWN MILL, C18.

MILNHOLM HATCHERY, 0.9km. SSE. Dated 1881. Unremarkably rectangular in plan but anomalous in section. Built two storeys high in buff brick with tooled stone dressings, its windows and battlemented parapet step down W–E following the slope of concrete floor slabs laid to permit water flow by gravity. A short FOOTBRIDGE with decorative cast iron balusters, *c.* 1880, crosses Auchenbowie Burn to reach the hatchery.

NORTH THIRD FILTERS, 2.5km. NW. 1931. Four-bay roughcast building on battered basement. Thermal windows below eaves and in the S gable. Broad NE tower with low pyramid roof.

## OVERTOUN HOUSE
WD *4070*

1.6km. N of Milton

Victorian hubris funded with 'new money' by James White, chemical manufacturer in Rutherglen, and designed with Baronial bravado by *James Smith*, 1859–62, in local stugged stone with polished dressings. White, who had purchased the estate because it lay near his wife's childhood home at Barnhill (Milton), intended the approach to be from Dumbarton. However, unable to buy the intervening Garshake Estate, he was obliged to travel the 'two miles from the beach at Milton' to reach his house. Much later, in 1895, having negotiated the purchase, his son, Lord Overtoun, bridged the Overtoun Burn, laid down the link w to Dumbarton and built West Overtoun Lodge (*see* Dumbarton). In 1939 Dumbarton Town Council acquired the mansion and from 1947 until 1970 it was used as a maternity hospital. Since then, although the estate has become a Country Park, the house has had an unsure future.

69    At the centre of the N façade is a colossal *porte cochère* of three round moulded arches springing from the foliate capitals of colonnettes inset in massive square piers with splayed plinths. Machicolated upperworks carry stepped parapets with bartizans at the corners. Ribbed quadripartite vault with thistle boss. Above the surprisingly simple round-arched entrance door is a tablet carved with a quotation from Psalm 150; similar texts appear on the link parapets that connect the porch to the main building. The N front, set on a lower-ground-floor plinth lit by a series of segmental-headed windows, is dramatically asymmetrical. To the l., a corbelled bartizan, cone-roofed with fish-scale slating, nudges against a high crowstepped gable pedimented at the apex. In the gable, a two-light mullioned and transomed window lights the main staircase. Further E, a pair of two-storey bays with tall pedimented eaves dormers and a domed bartizan on the NE corner. To the r., a still higher gable, crowstepped again, with a chimneystack at the apex and a framed panel dated 1868. Then a three-storey link; coupled windows below a broad two-light eaves dormer with a strapwork gable. Finally, a massive square tower with symmetrical hooded windows, lugged on the NW corner with yet another cone-capped bartizan. The height of this dominant feature, five storeys on the basement storey, was raised during construction at White's express behest. Behind its cannon-spiked battlements is a caphouse.

A double-height canted bay window, carried on the basement plinth, projects from the w face of the NW tower. To the r., the façade recesses to a crowstepped half-gable leaning against the tower. Then a second recess to a three-bay, three-storey wing with another canted bay, hooded windows and pedimented eaves dormers, all of this fronted by an added escape-stair cage of steelwork. On the SW corner, another bartizan.

On the E side of the house a high cylindrical tower, machicolated below a tall attic and slated cone, is gripped in a deep re-entrant. To the r., at the return from the N front, a crowstepped gable with two tall hooded windows under a first-floor window with a strapwork-filled pediment. To the l., more strapwork in the gables of two dormers and a tripartite window set in a parapeted square bay.

The s front, which looks out across terraced banks and lawn on soft rolling country, reverses the asymmetrical arrangement of the N. Rising l., a three-storey crowstepped gable fronted by a double-height canted bay. On the r., a two-storey crowstepped gable with a canted bay to the ground-floor storey only. Between these two gables, four windowed bays dropping in the middle from three to two storeys, the corner of the gable thus exposed accented once more with a bartizan. At ground-floor level a balustraded verandah, carried on massive corbel brackets, fills the space between the two outer gables. From this balcony a central staircase descends in two short flights to a grassed terrace. Two banks slope down to an expansive lawn bounded on the w, s and e by a low wall the balustrading of which repeats the open circular motif of the verandah. Bowed viewing areas articulate the sw and se corners of this wide sward. At the centre of the s wall is another short staircase.

LANDSCAPING by *Edward Kemp* of Birkenhead, *c.* 1863. Extensive offices with stabling for twelve horses, vineries, greenhouses and forcing houses, a castle folly built not far N of the main house, and the East Lodge have all been demolished. Square GATEPIERS with pyramidal caps and ball finials, probably by *James Smith*, *c.* 1863, survive at the entrance to the s drive. Immediately w of the house a spectacular BRIDGE, designed by *H. E. Milner* of Westminster, crosses the deep glen of Overtoun Burn. The scale is titanic, the masonry appropriately rough and rugged. A high round arch flanked by lower, smaller arches carries the carriageway across the narrow valley. Cutwater buttress piers corbel under the parapet to become semicircular refuges. Built in 1895, it marks the start of the long drive which Milner laid through the Garshake Estate to the Stirling Road.

# PLEAN

A village once dependent on coal-mining, now depressed by its demise.

PLEAN PARISH CHURCH. 1879. Gable-fronted church constructed in sandstone rubble with chamfered dressings and lit by segmentally-arched two-light mullioned and transomed windows. Applied to the E entrance gable is a squat parapeted porch. Small hefty bellcote corbelled from gable apex; mini-obelisks at the skews. s transept forms session house. Triple lancet in the chancel gable, the centre light filled with STAINED GLASS. Church sits in graveyard.

BRIDGE, West Westfield, 4.5km. E. Built *c.* 1750. Single span, 3.2m., carrying B9124 across Pow Burn.

EAST PLEAN PRIMARY SCHOOL. Asymmetrical accumulation; two storeys rising to three. The schoolhouse is dated 1874 but rough-faced, square-snecked sandstone and half-timbered classroom gables suggest that much of the building may be by *McLuckie & Walker*, *c.* 1905.

WILLIAM SIMPSON'S HOME. 1833–7, by *William Stirling I*. A low *cottage orné* in droved ashlar, symmetrical but picturesque. N entrance with good fanlight. Chamfered angles hook-stopped below eaves. Enlarged w by *Wardrop & Reid*, 1872. WALLED GARDEN to N.

CARNOCK TOWER (Bruce's Castle), 2.3km. E. Early C15. Rectangular tower-house on a rocky rise reduced to a tall stand of ruinous masonry.

PLEAN FARM, 1km. NNW. Probably late C18. Smart black-and-white piended dwelling built on a T-plan with a central piended projection S.

PLEAN HOUSE, 0.7km. SW. Sited in a country park created from Plean Estate, 1993, to commemorate the miners who worked in the local pits. Now roofless and ruinous, the mansion house, c. 1820, survives as an ironic testimony to past privilege. Its SE façade, built in finely droved ashlar, is five bays wide, the ends advancing slightly between full-height pilasters, the centre enhanced by a portico of coupled Greek Doric columns, reached by a flying stair. On the NW façade the three central bays have blind round-arches at ground floor over lintelled windows and doorway. Abandoned 1970. – The STABLES COURT is even more degraded; only a high portal of coupled Roman Doric pilasters flanking a segmental archway gives some sense of former grandeur. – WALLED GARDEN.

PLEAN TOWER, 1.5km. E. Mid-C15 TOWER-HOUSE built in roughly coursed rubble with dressed quoins and chamfered window margins. The home of the Somerville family, Barons of Plean for some 300 years. At the start of the C20 only the outer walls were intact, standing to a continuous corbel course at the wallhead where a parapet and caphouse must originally have existed. Re-inhabiting the building c. 1905, *David Menzies* added a tall, castellated top storey with oriel rounds at the NW, SW and SE corners. A round-arched W door was blocked, new windows and a door formed at ground-floor level S, and the main entrance at first floor, originally located at the E end of the S wall, and once probably reached by a forestair, altered to become a window. Far from scholarly, Menzies also left his cavalier mark by inscribing his name and armorial bearings in the stonework of lintels, arches, chimneypieces, etc. with indiscriminate liberality. A second restoration was undertaken in 1992 by *John P. Wright* working with the architect *John W. Brown*. A new ground-floor entrance doorway was formed at the E end of the S wall and a new internal stair made in the NE corner to connect with the still partially extant turnpike above. At the W end of the first-floor Hall, a segmentally lintelled fireplace, retaining its original N jamb, has been re-created using stone fragments from the Menzies period. Painted timber ceiling by *Brown*. Above are bedrooms and above these the early C20 top storey, under a new low-pitched leaded roof.

Adjoining the tower at its SW corner, the remains of a C16 HALL-HOUSE stretch S. These comprise three vaulted chambers in a line standing to first-floor height, the upper works having been demolished in the C17. Stabilized and castellated during the Edwardian 'restoration', they supported a raised garden until the house was rebuilt, 1992–5, to designs by *Bruce P. Wright* as a three-storey L-plan dwelling with crowstepped gables N, S and E. A round-arched E entrance doorway is set in the NE re-entrant angle below a corner turnpike stair corbelled from the first floor. At the SE corner a SUNDIAL, C17, has been built into the wall. The principal windows to the upper level apartments (three openings on the W, two on the E) are aligned vertically, those to the second floor being stone-gabled eaves dormers carved with initials and dates which include T.S. 1539 for Thomas Somerville, the first laird, and J.P.W. 1995 for the latest restorer. Corbelled from first floor on the W front behind a new fireplace, a broad projection rises above the eaves to a shouldered chimneystack.

Both tower and hall-house have been roughly harled in a warm ochre colour, and while the dressed stone used in the former matches the grey-green colour of the original and Edwardian margins, that in the latter, which seems to blush with a hint of pink, has been cut from material shipped from India. Tower and hall-house enclose a cobbled yard, pleasantly irregular in plan and level. Along the S side of this forecourt, again built on earlier foundations, is a harled COTTAGE, 1992, with more crowstepping and a slated cone at the SW corner. Downhill to the SW, landscaping has created a small pond where a mill once stood.

WEST PLEAN HOUSE, 2.5km. WNW. Early C19 and later. Aggregated in plan but given Gothic credibility by gables and hoodmouldings along the long SE front. Consistently domestic in scale; stone and harl painted to farm-like freshness.

BROCH, Tappoch, 2.1km. S. Well-preserved broch with an internal diameter of 10m. within a wall up to 7m. in thickness; entrance passage has bar holes and a lintelled roof. Clearance in 1864 and excavation in 1948–9 produced quernstones, spindle whorls and pottery of Iron Age type.

TORWOOD CASTLE. *See* p. 776.

# POLMONT

F *9070*

Large and sprawling village. Its first houses were built near Polmont Old Parish Church at the N end, but a 'Newtown' was laid out around Main Street *c.* 1800 and a further and separate development took place later in the C19 around the Railway Station to the S. Most of the housing is now C20.

## CHURCHES

POLMONT FREE CHURCH. *See* Brightons Parish Church.

POLMONT OLD PARISH CHURCH, Bo'ness Road. Simplified Lombardic Romanesque, by *John Tait*, 1844–5. The church is a buttressed broad box, the tooling of the stugged ashlar masonry eroded by cleaning. Gripping the corners of the front (E) gable are shallowly projecting towers, the top (belfry) stage of each intaken and surmounted by a pyramidal stone-slabbed roof. Over the gabled entrance of this front, a hoodmould whose label stops are carved with human heads. Above the entrance, a hoodmoulded window of three stepped lights.

Inside, two STAINED GLASS windows (the Annunciation; St Paul Preaching at Athens) by *James Ballantine & Son*, 1876.

In the graveyard, to the N, the roofless and ivy-clad remains of the FORMER PARISH CHURCH built in 1731–2; the mason was *Adam Howison*, the wright probably *Archibald Chessels* who provided the seating in 1733–4. Rubble-walled T, the gable of the N jamb formerly with a bellcote. In the S wall of the main block, large roundheaded windows, their sills lowered in 1798. Between them, a blocked rectangular door which gave access to the pulpit; above the door, a small rectangular recess (formerly filled by a sundial) with a moulded sill. In the E and W gables, rectangular doors and roundheaded gallery windows (the upper part of the E gable now demolished). Rectangular openings at the jamb and the N wall of the main block. The interior contained galleries at the E and W ends and in the jamb.

Between the two churches and to their W, a good number of quite deeply carved C18 HEADSTONES displaying the usual emblems of death and angels' heads (symbols of the soul). Among them, next to the centre of the S wall of the former Parish Church, a stone of 1755. Fluted Doric pilasters on the E face, human figures on the sides, and a crowned hammer (emblem of the smiths) and a horseshoe on the W face. – To its SW, aligned with the W gable of Polmont Old Parish Church, a stone (now with an inscription to William Williamson †1888) of 1752, its W face bearing a large coat of arms supported by naked boys. – Some way to the NW, nearly in line with the W gable of the former Parish Church, a stone of 1754. On its W face, an egg-and-dart bordered panel carved with a depiction of Adam and Eve in the Garden of Eden. Above the panel, the incised inscription: 'SOLOMON. IN.ALL.HIS.GLORIE.WAS NOT.ARAYED LIK ON OF THESE'. – Beside the S wall of the graveyard, at the W end of Polmont Old Parish Church, another stone, of 1786, depicting Adam and Eve, carved in exceptionally high relief. – Beside this, the MONUMENT to James Montgomery †1789, parish schoolmaster for over fifty years. Tall panelled pedestal surmounted by an urn.

## PUBLIC BUILDINGS

BRIDGE, Station Road. Built over the Union Canal *c.* 1822. Single segmental arch, the stonework of roughly dressed ashlar.

POLMONT PARISH CHURCH HALL, Main Street. By *James Strang*, 1898–9. Plain Gothic. Late C20 W addition by *John Deans*.

RAILWAY STATION, Station Road. Built *c.* 1842. Piend-roofed Georgian survival block standing on the steep side of the railway cutting so the N front is single-storey, the S facing the line of two storeys.

ST MARGARET'S PRIMARY SCHOOL, Salmon Inn Road. By *Central Regional Council*, 1977. Bitty collection of two-storey buildings, the upper floors with steeply pitched tall roofs broken by roof-lights and clearstorey windows.

SCHOOL, Main Street. Now in other use. By *T. B. McFadzen*, 1875, incorporating the fabric of the former parish school designed by

*John Miller* in 1852. Small-scale School Board Gothic with a bellcote.

## DESCRIPTION

BO'NESS ROAD is the entry from the N. At its start, the graveyard containing Polmont Old Parish Church and its predecessor (*see* Churches, above). Immediately S of the bridge over the M9 motorway, the entrance to a drive to the harled KINNEIL HOUSE, the former Polmont Parish Manse. This began *c.* 1735 as a two-storey three-bay block with a corniced Gibbsian surround to the door. Plain Jacobean gable-fronted W addition, probably part of the work carried out by *John Tait* in 1830. To the E, two low parallel ranges of office houses rebuilt in 1787, the S gable of the E range pierced by flightholes to a doocot inside. At the S end of Bo'ness Road, a T-junction with Main Street.

MAIN STREET'S E part is occupied by housing, some of it C19 and mostly rather altered and some C20 and undistinguished. But TURRET HOUSE on the S side is a Jacobean villa of *c.* 1840. Round corner turrets at the boldly advanced centre, its steep gable topped by a spiky finial. Battlemented outer bays with pinnacled diagonal buttresses at their ends. Hoodmoulds over the door and windows.

The W stretch of Main Street begins, on the corner of Bo'ness Road, with a mid-C19 lodge-like cottage. Bracketed broad eaves at the piended roof; Italianate doorpiece. Immediately to the W and set below road level, a brick-walled shopping development and public house (THE CLAREMONT), a small diagonally set cupola on top of its concrete-tiled pyramid roof, by *Thorburn, Twigg, Brown & Partners*, 1984–5. Housing to the W, partly late C19 but mostly C20, and Polmont Parish Church Hall and the former school (*see* Public Buildings, above).

STATION ROAD runs S from Main Street just W of the junction with Bo'ness Road. Near the top end, the Railway Station (*see* Public Buildings, above). Between this and the bridge over the Union Canal (*see* Public Buildings, above), a small late C19 group of respectable but unpretentious houses and a short commercial terrace (PRETORIA PLACE) of *c.* 1900.

PARKHILL HOUSE, off Buchanan Gardens. Small Palladian mansion house built *c.* 1790 for James Cheape of Sauchie. Main block of two storeys and a basement. Broached ashlar front of three bays. At the advanced and pedimented centre, the former main entrance with sidelights and an overall semicircular fanlight. The door was converted to a window in the late C19 when the flight of steps up to it was replaced by a stone balcony. At the outer bays, Venetian ground-floor windows with balustered aprons. At each end, a single-storey and basement link to a projecting pavilion, again of one storey above a basement. In the front of each pavilion, a tall roundheaded window set in an overarch. Beyond these pavilions and with their fronts set back are tall mid-C19 wings, perhaps part of *William Burn*'s alterations of 1835, which project to form two sides of a courtyard at the rear. In the pedimented front of each wing, a Venetian window.

To the NW, fronting Main Street, late C18 fluted GATEPIERS; rosettes on the friezes and pyramidal tops.

ANTONINE WALL, Polmont Woods, 0.7km. NE. A stretch of the ditch survives.

LATHALLAN HOUSE. *See* p. 589.

# POOL OF MUCKHART

Village of well maintained cottages, mostly of the early or mid C19 but some C20, several with roses or honeysuckle round their doors. The overall prettiness is much greater than the sum of the humble individual parts.

MUCKHART PARISH CHURCH. Built in 1838. Three-bay box, the rubble walls harled except at the S where most of the harling has been removed. Depressed arched windows. Corbelled out at the W gable, a birdcage bellcote with panelled piers. Ball-and-spike finial on the E end. Built into this gable, four stones, one inscribed 'ANNO', the others bearing the dates 1620, 1659 and 1715, referring to the building and repair of the previous church on the site; higher up, a couple of projecting rounded stones. The low session house-cum-porch at the W end is an addition of the earlier C20.

The interior is entered from the porch through the original depressed-arched external door. Over the E bay, a gallery, its cast iron columns with bundled shafts. – Boxy PEWS of 1838. – The PULPIT looks like a replacement of *c.* 1900, now missing its canopy.

GRAVEYARD. Against the church's E gable, a large MONUMENT of *c.* 1875 to the Christies of Cowden. It is free Romanesque but incorporates Celtic interlacing around the heraldic achievement over the central inscription panel. – SE of the church, a HEAD-STONE of 1748 to James Sharp. The panel on the front is flanked by weirdly capitalled attached columns; above, an angel's head (the soul), its wings looking very like a wig. NE of the church, the weathered SLAB of a table stone, dated 1732, commemorating AD and AW. It is carved, on the r. of its border, with the relief of a woman and, on the l., with a skeleton; crossbones at the bottom, a skull at the top.

MANSE to the SW, by *William Stirling I*, *c.* 1832. Two-storey house, a block-pedimented door at the centre of the three-bay front.

# PORT OF MENTEITH

T-junction hamlet at the NE edge of the Lake of Menteith.

PARISH CHURCH. Five-bay nave by *John Honeyman*, 1876–8, its simple Gothic qualities compromised by badly weathered local freestone. A replacement for an earlier church of 1771. Dourly dignified by a square SW belfry tower with broad clasping buttresses and a slated pyramid above the parapet. Hooded lancets except in the E gable where three circled cinquefoils are inscribed within a spheric triangle. From the NW porch stairs rise into the vestibule and then, in the tower, to a rear gallery which pushes forward over two cast iron columns. The plastered interior is bare rather than austere. Arch-braced trusses in stained ash have curved struts above the collars and arcuated cross-bracing under the spars. Chancel platform floored in oak. – Centrally placed in front of the E wall, on an octagonal stone base, is an oak PULPIT, finely carved with Late Dec blind tracery panels, probably of c. 1905. – White marble FONT with onyx pedestal. – In the gallery, a Victorian ORGAN, probably by *Joseph W. Brook*; pipes gathered in a Gothic screen with cusped ogee arch. – STAINED GLASS in geometrical tracery of the E window by *Stephen Adam*, 1879; to Sir James and Lady Campbell of Stracathro. – Lancets have red and yellow edging. – In the vestibule, two memorial wall TABLETS: one, a pink sandstone aedicule to John Elphinstone Erskine †1887; the other, a pedimented frame in grey sandstone to Matilda Graham †1839.

On the W side of the GRAVEYARD, built on a battered base close to the lochside, the GRAHAM MAUSOLEUM, by *William Stirling I*, c. 1817, a pedimented cell of dimpled dull red sandstone with a stone-slabbed roof and central ogee-arched E entrance set within a segmental-arched recess. Among the mainly C19 graves are a few older SLABS and TABLE TOMBS with some gravemarkers dating from the C17.

PRIMARY SCHOOL. C19 schoolhouse and classroom, though a school has existed here from the late C17. Roughcast, single-storey, pitched roof addition, continuing E as a monopitch with a glazed piended bay set into the SE re-entrant; by *Central Regional Council*, 1990–91.

TOLL HOUSE, on the A873 opposite the Arnprior road-end. Early C19. Painted rubble; piend-ended T-plan with a central gable from which a two-light canted bay projects.

LOCHEND, 1.8km. SE. Steeply roofed three-bay dower house of Cardross; dated 1715 above architraved door. Additions of 1871 and 1893.

MENTEITH HOUSE. The former manse, much aggrandized. S-facing with a fine prospect of the Lake, it was begun in the early C19 in the customarily severe three-bay idiom of the time. Enlargement at the rear, c.1865, created a double-pile L-plan arrangement. In 1958 it ceased to serve the church and by 1960 had been transformed in character by the addition of flat-roofed, single-storey accommodation on the S and W sides. The new S front, though wider than the manse behind, is built in random rubble like the original and respects its symmetry. At the centre is a recessed porch with Ionic fluted timber columns flanked by timber pilasters, also fluted. To l. and r. are large glazed openings with French doors opening to the forecourt. Beyond these, on each side, a Venetian window. Timber pilasters marking the W and E ends of this principal façade are linked across the full width of the front by strongly moulded superimposed timber cornices under a plain parapet coping. This heavily corniced wallhead returns on the short E and longer W fronts. A single Venetian window and two larger glazed areas with French doors repeat on the W elevation. It seems likely that the manse's three first-floor eaves dormers may have received their undulating roofs and timber mouldings as part of the 1959–60 changes. Oak dado panelling and one door casing in the Library brought from Buchanan Castle (q.v.).

To the E of the house is a long, single-storey rubble building which may be a remnant of an earlier farm engrossed by the manse. At the drive entrance, early C19 quatrefoil-plan stone GATE PIERS caged by Gothic cast iron.

ARNTAMIE. *See* p. 184.
BLAIRHOYLE. *See* p. 241.
REDNOCK CASTLE. *See* p. 640.
REDNOCK HOUSE. *See* p. 641.

*9080*    POWFOULIS MANOR    F

2.6km. SE of Airth

Carpenter's Gothic villa of *c.* 1820 with fairly tactful mid-C19 additions. The early C19 house is of two storeys above a tall basement which is masked at the W (entrance) front by a ramp, its parapet pierced by pointed openings. This front was originally of three bays, the walling of droved ashlar with polished dressings. At the outer corners, slender octagonal turrets, their faces enlivened by tall and narrow dummy windows, their finials crocketed spires. In the outer bays, two-light windows, the taller ground-floor openings transomed and hoodmoulded. The slightly taller centre is narrowly advanced between two-stage pilasters, the faces of their upper tier decorated with Gothick panels enclosing narrow dummy windows; gableted and crocket-spired finials, dumpier than those at the outer corners. At the ground floor, now enclosed by a big pedimented wooden porch of *c.* 1900, a four-centred arched entrance flanked by narrow pointed openings. First-floor window of three roundheaded lights. The ground- and first-floor windows are tied together by sill courses. Wallhead parapets, pierced by octagonal openings at the outer bays and lattice work over the centre. At each end, a one-bay mid-C19 addition, its front windows of three lights, hoodmoulded at the ground floor. Corbelled and Gothick-panelled corner turrets; parapets with blind arcading.

At the other elevations the basement is fully exposed. At the ends of the N and S additions, big wallhead chimneys; shallow rectangular bay window at the S. The E (garden) elevation is a much plainer version of the front. At the additions, hoodmoulded two-light windows to the principal floor with three-light windows above. The end corners of the early C19 house have turrets of the same design as those at the front and the centre bay is again advanced but without pilasters. The windows were probably all originally two-light with hoodmoulds at the principal floor but unequally sized canted bay windows have been added at the outer bays, c. 1900.

Inside, a plaster vaulted entrance hall, the arches springing from corbels modelled as smiling and weeping human faces. Behind, the stair, its lower flight geometric, the upper scale-and-platt. In the s addition, the ground-floor Drawing Room decorated c. 1900, with an elaborate frieze and beamed ceiling, its panels decorated with reliefs of thistles and acorns. Doric-columned marble chimneypiece. At the NE corner of the early C19 house, the Dining Room with a bowed end and black marble chimneypiece.

Uncomfortably close to the NE corner of the house is an undistinguished HOTEL BEDROOM BLOCK of the later C20. – Further E, crowstep-gabled STABLES AND COACHMAN'S HOUSE of c. 1860, a tall round conical-roofed doocot turret corbelled out at one corner. In the N gable, a reset early C17 dormer pediment inscribed 'D/MR/TO GOD', the initials those of Dame Margaret Rollox, wife of Sir James Bruce of Powfoulis. It presumably came from the present mansion house's predecessor. To the W, single-storey harled and piend-roofed LODGE of the earlier C19, its windows hoodmoulded; it has been extended to the rear.

## POWIS HOUSE    S *8090*
### 1.3km. SSW of Blairlogie

Built 1746–7. Solid and stolid, hip-roofed mansion-house, with broad chimneystacks swept up from the W and E gables on ogival haunches. Harled walls with quoins and window margins in header-and-stretcher bond. Three storeys high but only three bays wide; rather small lintelled windows, coupled in the centre bay of the N façade above a columned portico, semicircular in plan, which shelters the fanlit doorway. At the rear of the entrance hall a scale-and-platt staircase rises under a cupola. – NW lie the STABLES, late C18 or early C19, now converted to housing; a square court with a sharply domed octagonal doocot. – 0.18km. S, a stone SUNDIAL shaft, monogrammed and dated 1745.

## QUARTER HOUSE    F *8080*
### 1.8km. N of Dunipace

Piend-roofed and white harled late C18 two-storey laird's house. At the entrance (W) front, a corniced porch with coupled Tuscan columns. On each side, a three-light ground-floor window, its hoodmould probably an early C19 embellishment. At the first floor, five regularly spaced windows, the second and fourth dummies. The central section of the front rises a little above the wallhead to support a chimneyed open pediment pierced by a circular dummy window. Inside, the entrance hall opens through an elliptical arch to the geometric staircase.

## REDDING

9070                                                                              F

Village, the housing mostly C20.

REDDING AND WESTQUARTER CHURCH, Main Street. By *Wilson & Tait*, 1906–7. Dumpy late Gothic, with a slate-spired low tower.

## REDDINGMUIRHEAD

9070                                                                              F

Village of plain C19 and C20 houses, the Wallacestone Methodist Church, the Community Centre and the red brick frontage of the free Jacobean CO-OPERATIVE SOCIETY BUILDINGS (now THE RED HOUSE) of *c.* 1900 providing a centre in Shieldhill Road.

WALLACESTONE METHODIST CHURCH, Shieldhill Road. Built in 1873. Straightforward box, with panelled and pinnacled pilasters at the ends of the ashlar-faced front gable. Projecting from the centre of this front, a ball-finialled porch containing a roundheaded door. At the top of the gable, a circular window. Only the corbels survive of the crowning bellcote. Roundheaded windows in the side walls.

BRAES HIGH SCHOOL, Newlands Road. By *The Parr Partnership*, 1999–2000, using the same formula as at their contemporary schools in the area (e.g. at Bo'ness, Falkirk and Larbert). Walls of buff-coloured blockwork and cream render, shallow-pitch roofs covered with ribbed metal. Glazed stairs at the ends of the three-storey classroom block; parallel but lower hall block.

BRIDGE, Reddingmuirhead Road. Humpbacked bridge of *c.* 1822 over the Union Canal, built of roughly dressed ashlar. Single segmental arch.

H.M. YOUNG OFFENDERS' INSTITUTION POLMONT, Newlands Road. Assembly of C20 buildings, their style ranging from Neo-Georgian to Postmodern but none of much distinction.

REDDINGMUIRHEAD COMMUNITY CENTRE, Shieldhill Road. Originally a Board school. By *T. B. McFadzen*, 1875–6. Picturesque, with bracketed eaves, bargeboards and a pyramidal-roofed and spike-finialled bellcote. Exceptionally fat round GATEPIERS at the entrance in the boundary wall.

## REDNOCK CASTLE

5000                                                                              S
1.9km. ENE of Port of Menteith

C16. Little more than a cylindrical rubble stair tower rising approximately three storeys; circular in plan below, rounded square above. NE doorway. Stub walls N and ENE.

# REDNOCK HOUSE

S *6000*

1.75km ESE of Port of Menteith

By *Robert Brown* of Edinburgh; designed 1821 but not built until 1827. Two-storey-and-basement, three-bay E front of droved ashlar. Eaves cornice, central pediment and tall windows to the principal floor. Greek Doric portico of paired columns reached by steps flanked by cast iron eagles seated on squat columns. Above the porch, a tripartite window. Within, a square vestibule leads to a circular domed saloon ringed at first floor by a railed gallery with niches in the corners and top-lit through a central cupola. On the W, behind the C19 mansion, is a U-plan rubble block with shaped gables, early C18. At the junction of the two, Baronial screen walls of *c.* 1840 terminating in conically roofed stair towers project symmetrically N and S.

The STABLE BLOCK, recast by *Brown*, 1827 (earlier work by *James Ramsay*, 1797, though an 1811 date has been revealed on plasterwork) lies 0.2km. N. Four ranges enclose a court; the main S range has pediment gables at the centre and ends with three blind round-arched windows in the links. Segmental-arched openings in the end pavilions with a central round-arched entry; domed octagonal tower removed in the 1980s. – Overgrown WALLED GARDEN, constructed between 1816 and 1820, has a hollow N wall for heating. – Nearby, W, a ruinous egg-type ICE HOUSE, perhaps of 1827, the outer masonry of its dome exposed between two bouldered gables.

# RENTON

WD *3070*

'The Renton', as it is colloquially known, has seen better days. Founded in 1782 as a manufacturing village dependent on thriving bleachfields and printworks sited in the meandering loops of the Leven, it is now depressed and depressing.

## CHURCHES

Former MILLBURN FREE CHURCH, Main Street. Abandoned 21 Disruption kirk attributed to *George Meikle Kemp*, but more probably the work of *J. T. Rochead*, 1843–5. Traditional T-plan, gabled N, S and, at a slightly lower height, on the W. The suggestion of Kemp's authorship seems to derive from the steepled entrance tower which advances axially E, a tapering compacted composition of thin buttresses and finials, evocative in silhouette though not detail of his Scott Monument in Edinburgh. Here the Gothic is First Pointed; plain lancet windows on all faces, tripled in the gables. Angle buttresses twice intaken on all corners. Gables with dumpy obelisks on the skews and apex crosses. W gable results from the curtailment of the nave. The church is roofless, its gables ragged; vegetation sprouts from the steeple.

In the GRAVEYARD, which stretches W to the railway, many

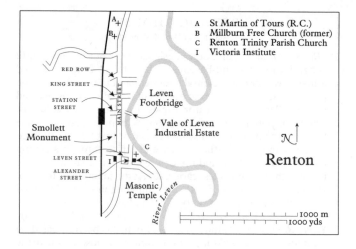

A  St Martin of Tours (R.C.)
B  Millburn Free Church (former)
C  Renton Trinity Parish Church
I  Victoria Institute

Renton

1000 m
1000 yds

Victorian headstones have fallen. – OBELISK to John Hathieson
†1874. – Tall tapered MONUMENT with buttressed sides, topped
by an open horseshoe arch from which sprouts a lotus leaf finial;
to William Murray †1872 and family.

22 RENTON TRINITY PARISH CHURCH, Alexander Street. By *David
Barclay* of *H. &D. Barclay*, Glasgow; 1891–2. Late Gothic in
square-snecked red sandstone with ashlar dressings and rough-
faced quoins. The w belfry tower, three stages high with a castellated parapet and small corner finials, looks down Leven Street.
(BELLS by *James Warner & Son Ltd.*, Glasgow.) At the base of
the tower, a four-centred-arched entrance with dual doorways
and blind tracery. Placed axially behind the tower is a wide
castellated gable falling to low diagonal buttressing topped by
tall crocketed finial shafts. Four-bay nave with traceried Perp
windows. N and S transepts and lower E chancel have similar
windows.

The interior has been recast, *c.* 1983, the original nave now
serving as a Hall. Worship is now orientated N–S across the
transepts. In the N transept, which is entered from the W, a
vestibule has been created from which a glazed screen opens to
pew seating re-arranged to face a new chancel raised in the S
transept. Boarded purlin roof on open trusses with round-arched
bracing carried down to stone corbels. Plaster ceiling over original
chancel.

Most FURNISHINGS date from 1911–12. – Heptagonal oak
PULPIT box, its traceried panels carved with a hint of Art
Nouveau. – Perp Gothic, three-bay oak COMMUNION TABLE.
– ORGAN by *Rushworth & Dreaper*; pipes crowded into the S
chancel. – Nearby, an octagonal bowl FONT on marble column
pedestal. – STAINED GLASS, gifted by John B. Aiken of Dalmoak,
installed 1912 in the four-light windows of the S, E and N gables;

by *Oscar Paterson*. In each case the design is divided by the window transom: Abraham, Moses, David and Elijah above Christ delivering the Beatitudes; Matthew, Mark, Luke and John above the Last Supper; SS Stephen, James, Peter and Paul above Christ's Baptism in Jordan. In the last scene, a portrait of the donor is incorporated. In the E windows of the N and S transepts, 1924, *Paterson* depicts the somewhat esoteric female figures of Lydia of Thyatra and Phoebe of Cenchrea; a memorial to Jane T. Aiken of Dalmoak †1922.

St Martin of Tours (R.C.), Main Street. By *Charles W. Gray*, 1970. Despite a stepped approach and paved forecourt the exterior is unprepossessing; roughcast walls, apsidal to the S, gabled to the N above a flat-roofed vestibule, faced in artificial stone. But the interior is spacious and full of light. A full-width glazed screen divides vestibule from church. Four-bay nave with wide portal frames, their tapered shafts marking narrow aisles W and E. Confessionals and apsidal Lady Chapel open to W below square clearstorey windows, three to each bay. On the E wall, a series of tall slot windows with clearstorey light above the apsidal Sacred Heart Chapel. Five steps rise to the sanctuary apse which is bathed in light from tall windows l. and r. – Pedestal ALTAR of pink granite, swept in a scotia profile, carries a black marble table. – Behind the altar, raised three more steps, is a tall four-poster BALDACCHINO canopied in timber above the monstrance. – STATIONS OF THE CROSS; incised wood panels by *Gabriel Loire* of Chartres. – STAINED GLASS fills the N gable: SS Martin and Patrick, their faces and figures strongly conceived in Byzantine style, fill a leaded-glass mosaic shading from turquoise blue to ultramarine.

## PUBLIC BUILDINGS

LEVEN FOOTBRIDGE, Station Street. Narrow walkway carried between lattice beams supported by concrete frame piers. Built to form a convenient link to Vale of Leven Industrial Estate, established on the E bank of the river in 1948.

MASONIC TEMPLE, Alexander Street. Tall, two-storey W front in red sandstone; *c.* 1885. Classically symmetrical and severe. Tripartite façade with tripartite windows l. and r. and at the centre above a lintelled doorway. Full-height engaged columns with plain abacus capitals flank this central zone. Strong but plain cornice with modillion blocks.

SMOLLETT MONUMENT, Main Street. 1774. An impressively tall 36 Tuscan column commemorating the novelist Tobias Smollett (1721–71), born locally at Dalquhurn. On the base is an inset panel bearing a long inscription in Latin; 'miserably bad – as Coleridge said, such as poor Smollett, who was an excellent scholar, would have been ashamed of'.

VICTORIA INSTITUTE, Main Street. 1887. Plain E façade in red sandstone ashlar; two storeys with a square bay l. and two- and three-light lintelled windows.

Renton, Smollett Monument. Drawing by Joseph Irving copied from *The Book of Dumbartonshire*, 1879.

## DESCRIPTION

MAIN STREET is almost all there is. Sandwiched between the A82 and the coiling course of the Leven, length and straightness are its only distinctions. Buildings are intermittent, generally bleak or tawdry. A few earlier houses, *c.* 1840–50, retain respectability without pretension. At Nos. 16–22 there is a plain pilastered doorpiece and a pend with a segmental voussoir arch. ARGYLE COTTAGE and LENNOX COTTAGE also have good doorways, one pilastered, the other columned. GLENLYON is a standard three-bay, two-storey, gabled dwelling with a stringcourse running full-width from the cornice of its Tuscan doorpiece. A wearied dignity clings to some stretches of red sandstone flatted terraces built in the late C19 when industry prospered. The best of these are in LEVEN STREET and ALEXANDER STREET where a first-floor window, uniquely corbelled and splayed on the corner of FORESTVILL, merits mention. On Main Street, there are several stretches of interwar local authority housing by *Joseph Weekes*, County Architect of Dunbartonshire. Though not without invention, much has lost its savour. Roughcast flats at Nos. 145–153, 1929, have neatly framed dormers in a mansarded third storey and recessed open balconies at the rear. Also by *Weekes*, 1934, long runs of three-storey flats at Nos. 216–222 and 224–230 (the former with second-floor corners chamfered with a window evidently copied from Forestvill on Alexander Street) have been pleasantly but unrecognizably rehabilitated in coloured render and facing brick as part of 1990s improvements. On RED ROW, however, some one- and two-storey roughcast housing from 1935 in Weekes's vernacular Scots style is relatively, if precariously, intact.

Of civic or commercial building there is little to remark. The

Victoria Institute (*see* Public Buildings, above) is no more than ordinary. The Cullaloe stone obelisk of the village WAR MEMORIAL, designed by *James Dempster*, 1922, seems humbled, humiliated even, by the hubris of its neighbour, the Smollett Monument (*see* Public Buildings, above). A dried-up FOUNTAIN 36 under a domed cast iron canopy, four arches ornamented by scrolls and cusps, mocks its memorial dedication to the opening of Renton Water Works in 1886. More by neglect than intent, the CENTRAL BAR, dated 1893, has kept a five-arched shopfront; below a pulvinated fascia stopped by fluted consoles the narrow spandrels retain some leaded glass. At what was once Renton Cross, boarded-up shops and flats at Nos. 155–157, 1891, contribute an all but exhausted energy to the corner of King Street; polychromatic Baronial with a corbelled corner bow and turret. Marooned on STATION STREET, yet another red sandstone relic; eight identical bays long and two storeys high under an overhanging eaves, retained, so a placard ironically claims, 'for the use of the people of Renton'.

KIPPEROCH FARMHOUSE, 1.8km. SW. Early C19 symmetrical three-bay dwelling with single-storey wings returning to form U-plan court at rear.

KIPPEROCH HOUSE, 1.5km. SW. Late C19. Two-storey, three-bay villa with some Baronial detailing. Monogram ABJS in bracketed parapet above doorpiece. Additional monograms, JE and AR, at first-floor level l. and r.

DALMOAK HOUSE. *See* p. 355.


# ROSS PRIORY WD 4080
2km. NW of Gartocharn

The name implies some ecclesiastical provenance but this is no more than C19 romantic affectation. Speculative suggestions that a fraternity of monks lived at Ross Abbey until the middle of the C17 when they were replaced by nuns from Inchcailloch are unconvincing. On the other hand, the site has been settled at least since medieval times and was the seat of the Buchanans of Ross, probably from the C14. Vestiges of this early structure may have been retained in the cellars of a house begun in 1695 and completed in the C18. This in turn was radically recast between 1810 and 1816. Commissioned by Hector MacDonald Buchanan, *James Gillespie Graham* removed the wings of the older classical mansion, embedding its substantial core in a new larger house clad in Gothick garb. It is this neo-medieval conceit that remains. In 1971 the estate was purchased by the University of Strathclyde, which has carried out extensive restoration of both house and landscape, first in 1971–3 and again in 1991. The Priory now serves as rural retreat and club for academics.

At the entrance to the estate is a single-storey Gothic LODGE, *c.* 1810, by *Graham*. It has pointed-arched windows with cusped astragals and a piend-roofed porch of four-centred arches carried on clustered shafts. Ahead, a long straight avenue, almost 1km.

in extent, approaches the Priory obliquely from the s. Gradually, through framing trees, it appears against the background of loch and mountain.

63    The E entrance front, built in ashlar, is still classical in its organization but decidedly Gothic in detail; nine bays wide, two storeys elevated on a basement. A perron stair with lancet balustrading rises to a three-bay porch at the centre of the façade. Porch of three pointed openings divided by buttress piers with crocketed finials linked by a quatrefoil parapet. In the shadows, under pointed arches, a fanlit doorway and flanking windows with Gothic astragals. Above the porch, four narrow lancets. To l. and r., at all three levels, paired windows flank tripartites. All are lancets, those to the upper levels cusped and, in the case of the ground-floor tripartite windows, hooded. Four octagonal buttresses with tall crocketed finials stand like pikestaffs, two clasping the central porch, one at each end of the façade. A second quatrefoil balustrade crosses the eaves above the porch while at the lower outer levels the eaves parapets are traceried with lozenge shapes. Diamond-set chimneystacks rise from low piended roofs.

On the N elevation, the finialled buttress at the NE corner is repeated on the W side of a shallow full-height bow lit with lancets. Then, a wider wall with Gothic tripartite windows at all three levels. At the NW corner, another pikestaff buttress. To the W, the C18 house becomes apparent: six bays, roughcast with red sandstone margins. At the S end of this plain, unequivocally rear elevation *Gillespie Graham* added yet another finialled buttress. But the length of the W elevation of the older house does not match that of the new on the E. A lower two-storey service block, built in red sandstone random rubble, fills the SW corner.

The interior maintains the medieval idiom. From the corners of the small square Vestibule, four ribbed plaster squinches fan out to a circular rosette of dagger tracery. The panelling of doors and ingo recesses is also ribbed with Gothic forms. In the Dining Room, a Gothic fireplace in black marble. The ceiling is without ornamentation and the cornice repeats a simple anthemion motif. In the CARNEGIE ROOM the fireplace is again Gothic, in white marble, the ceiling beamed but devoid of added decoration. In the BAR LOUNGE, formerly the Ante-Dining Room, another Gothic fireplace which has lost its original overmantel of finialled niches. The well stair rises under an oval cupola; cantilevered stone treads with slender iron balusters.

STABLES, dated 1794, lie at the lochside 0.25km. NNE. Formerly quadrangular, they have been much altered and now form a single-storey L-plan with a pyramid-roofed upper storey over the segmental-arched pend entry. Roughcast walls with red sandstone dressings. Adapted as residential accommodation during 1990s renovation. Adjacent, a lean-to pigsty and piend-roofed bothy; both derelict.

WALLED GARDEN, 0.2km. SW, probably late C18, re-created with four lawns, greenhouses, wooden pergola and Moongate

in SE wall by *Maurice Wilkins*, *c.* 1990. At its centre a SUNDIAL
on a swollen pedestal; gnomon plate dated 1988. Nearby, in a
natural garden of wooded walks, a pentagonal oak SUMMER-
HOUSE by the *University of Strathclyde Estates Department*, 2000.
– Hidden in trees, 0.5km. ESE of the main house, is the
BUCHANAN GRAVEYARD, a small walled enclosure planted
with coupled yews. WALL MONUMENT; in a cusped arch recess
between gableted buttresses, a white marble panel records the
deaths of Hector MacDonald Buchanan †1828, his wife Jean
Buchanan †1852 and their nine children.

# ROUGH CASTLE                     F *8080*
### 1.4km. NE of High Bonnybridge

ROMAN FORT. The best-preserved fort on the Antonine Wall.
The broad (6m. wide) ramparts of the fort enclosed the usual
group of buildings, which were revealed during excavations in
1903, 1935 and 1957–61: headquarters, commander's house,
granary and barrack-blocks, none now visible. An inscription
found in 1903 revealed that the correct name for the HQ was
*principia* not *praetorium* as had hitherto been believed. The sites
of the four gates of the fort are clear and beyond the ramparts
lie two ditches, with an additional third to the W. To the E of the
fort lay an annexe which had contained the bath-house. Three
ditches protected the E side but there was only one on the S.
Fort and annexe were attached to the rear of the Antonine Wall
rampart, being added to the Wall during its construction. Beyond
the upcast mound the 1903 excavations revealed an extra defence,
a series of pits, generally called *lilia*, after Caesar's description of
them in Gaul. Several are still visible. The reason for their appearance at this particular location is not clear.

The rampart, ditch and upcast mound run W from the fort.
Immediately to the W of the Rowan Tree Burn the *agger* (mound)
of the Military Way appears. Beside it lie the remains of a small
(? medieval) house and similar remains lie on both sides of the
rampart just to the E of the car park. 5m. beyond the cattle grid,
the prominent mound attached to the rampart is an 'expansion'.
Excavation has shown that a stone base 5m. square supported a
turf platform. Although the base was separate from, if attached
to, the rampart, the turves of the expansion and the rampart were
continuous higher up. This indicates that the 'expansion' was
part of the original building programme. The pair of this expansion lies in the grounds of Bonnyside House just to the W of the
area in the care of Historic Scotland. Between the cattle grid and
the W boundary of the Historic Scotland site are several quarry
pits, from which gravel was extracted to build the Military Way
which here lies under the modern track. The existence of a
quarry pit below the 'expansion' demonstrates an early date for
the Military Way.

# ROWARDENNAN                                    s

Youth Hostel and hotel on the E shore of Loch Lomond; between
the two, a pier from which, in summer, a small passenger ferry
crosses the loch to Inverbeg. Now an overnight stop on the West
Highland Way.

ROWARDENNAN HOTEL. An inn has existed here since the late
C17. The present white-painted five-bay two-storey rubble inn
with its gable hard to the road seems early C19. Abutting at
right angles W is a higher mid-C19 house incorporating additions
by *Wylie, Wright & Wylie*, 1931.

VISITOR CENTRE. 1999–2001, by *Richard Shorter* in association
with *Simpson & Brown*. A building of simple form imaginatively
conceived to use natural materials obtained locally. Under a
slated saddleback roof with gentle double curvature, the plan
centres on a circular foyer grasped by two trapezoidal shapes.
Oak frames, mud walls and composting toilets.

YOUTH HOSTEL. Mid-C19 shooting lodge, later enlarged. The
original gabled and dormered building, of brownish whin with
red sandstone margins, now forms the E wing. Corbelled from
an octagonal base, a low drum tower with dunce's cap roof sits
in its SW re-entrant. Extended first around the present entrance;
more extensive additions in grey whin spread W. Decorative
bargeboards holed by trefoils shelter windowed gables on the S
and W. In each case, spun barley-sugar posts drop from the
purlin ends in front of the first-floor windows to the sloping
roofs of wide, square or canted bays below.

# RUMFORD                                         F

Small village, its housing mainly C20.

Former ST ANTHONY'S (R.C.) CHURCH, South Craigs Road.
Simple Gothic, by *Canon William Grady*, 1891. Bellcast-roofed
nave, with continuous clearstorey lighting above the windowless
side aisles. W tower, its intaken top stage with canted corners
and a battlement, the crowning pyramid-roofed open wooden
bellcote an addition, probably dating from alterations of 1913.

ST ANTHONY'S (R.C.) CHURCH, Maddiston Road. By *Fleming
Buildings Ltd.*, 1985. Square pavilion, the walls dry-dashed, the
pyramid roof covered with concrete tiles. Big S porch. Small
detached brown brick bell-tower. Inside the church, a boarded
ceiling expressing the external shape of the roof. – Small but
powerfully modelled bronze STATIONS OF THE CROSS by
*Vincent Butler*, c. 1978. – STAINED GLASS roundels (scenes
from the life of Our Lord), of 1936, originally in the former
Roseburn Free Church, Edinburgh.

WALLACESTONE PRIMARY SCHOOL, Braemar Gardens.
Lightweight-looking, by the Stirling County Architect, *A. J.
Smith*, 1962–4.

THE HAINING, 1.1km. E. Big two-storey villa of 1825 (the date on the N end). Ashlar-faced E front of four bays, the second and fourth advanced. At the r. bay, a shallow portico with paired Roman Doric columns. Hoodmoulded ground-floor windows of three lights. Hoodmoulds also over the first-floor windows but they are single-light and joined by a sill course. Mutules under the broad eaves. At the N elevation, two tiers of pointed windows. Large but plain additions, perhaps of *c.* 1900, at the rear.

# ST NINIAN'S *see* STIRLING

## SAUCHIE

C *8090*

Large village contiguous to Alloa but still with its own identity. Mining was the chief industry here from the C16 to the C20, with distilling and woollen manufacture established in the C18 and C19. Most of the housing is of the mid and later C20.

SAUCHIE AND COALSNAUGHTON PARISH CHURCH, Alloa Road. Built as a chapel of ease in 1841–2. The design was based on that of Camelon St John's Church at Falkirk (q.v.). Straightforward rectangle with an E (liturgical W) tower, built of reddish sandstone, rubble at the sides of the church, the E gable and tower of rough ashlar. At the sides, round-arched windows, their wooden mullions introduced in 1889. The gable walls project beyond the sides as stepped lateral buttresses. At the E gable, the walling each side of the tower is divided by a slender buttress into two bays, the inner bay containing a narrow round-arched window and finished with a sloping parapet, the outer bay with a horizontal parapet. The square tower is of four stages, each of the upper stages slightly intaken except at the corners which form simplified pilasters at the second stage and clasping buttresses at the third and fourth. At the tower's E front, a round-arched entrance beneath a window of three tall round-arched lights, the centre rising above the two which are dummies; at the third stage, the surround for a circular clock face (missing) inside a lozenge. At each face of the top stage, a large roundheaded belfry opening. On top, a pierced parapet, stepped up at the centre of each face; pinnacled pedestals at the corners.

Behind, a crowstep-gabled HALL, by *J. S. Leishman*, 1900. S of the church, a HALL, by *L. Twigg*, 1956–7.

Inside the church, a deep E GALLERY of 1972. – Late C19 PEWS, probably dating from improvements of 1889. – COMMUNION TABLE of *c.* 1930. Sub-Lorimerian, with naturalistic carving. – STAINED GLASS. The two W windows (Faith, Hope and Charity; the Bible, Holy Spirit, and *Agnus Dei*) are late C19, with small panes including figurative roundels. – In the N and S sides, two late C19 windows containing emblems of the Evangelists.

SAUCHIE AND FISHCROSS UNITED FREE CHURCH, Church Grove. Modern Gothic, by *John Bruce*, 1931–2. Dry-dashed rectangle, with tiled roofs and broad pointed windows. The entrance is contained in the pyramid-roofed clock tower at the NW. Another pyramidal roof over the square ventilator at the church's E end. NE HALL.

ALLOA COLLIERY SCHOOL, Rosebank. Now housing (ROSE-BANK GARDENS). Built in 1819 but now rather altered. Long low block, the windows hoodmoulded; late C19 spired ventilator on the roof. At the E end, a battlemented tower, its windows again hoodmoulded.

CLACKMANNAN COLLEGE, Branshill Road. Originally Forebraes Junior Secondary School. Large spread of rendered buildings, by the Clackmannan County Architect, *W. H. Henry*, 1958.

CRAIGBANK PRIMARY SCHOOL, Newtonshaw. By *Central Regional Council*, 1976–7.

DEERPARK PRIMARY SCHOOL AND LOCHIES SCHOOL, Gartmorn Road. Flat-roofed boxes, by *Crudens Ltd.*, 1965. Big brick-faced HALL with large segmental-arched windows, a late C20 addition.

FAIRFIELD SCHOOL, Pompee Road. By *Thomas Frame & Son*, 1905. Free Jacobean Renaissance; single-storey, built of hammer-dressed purplish masonry with polished buff sandstone dressings. Strapwork decoration in the gables; mullioned and transomed windows.

SAUCHIE DISTRICT HALL, corner of Fairfield Road and Mar Place. By *William Kerr* of *John Melvin & Son*, 1911, the rear (N) wing added by the same architects in 1925. White harled walls and red tiled roofs. The piend-roofed main block is free Queen Anne. Shaped gable at the porch, large windows with wooden mullions and transoms, and a cupola-ventilator with a flattened ogee roof. At the rear wing, catslide dormerheads over the windows and a tall tile-hung ventilator. – In front, a stone WAR MEMORIAL designed by *William Kerr* of *John Melvin & Son* and executed by *R. McGee*, 1922. Octagonal shaft topped by scrolled corbels on which stand a pair of angels holding a crown in front of the cross finial.

SAUCHIE HOSPITAL, Parkhead Road. Originally a fever hospital. By *John Melvin & Son*, 1892–5. Single-storey detached blocks, the central building with an attic. Free Queen Anne, the walling of hammer-dressed rubble with rendering in the gables. To the N, a block of 1938, by *William Kerr* and *John Gray* of *John Melvin & Son*. Late C20 two-storey brick-walled block to the S.

SAUCHIE LEISURE CENTRE, Main Street. By *Clackmannan District Council*, 1995.

SAUCHIE SCHOOL, Mar Place. Now an annexe of Clackmannan College. By *Thomas Frame & Son*, 1887. Single-storey, built of hammer-dressed red sandstone, with mullioned and transomed windows.

## DESCRIPTION

Two entries from the s. The se is by HALLPARK. On its w side, Hallpark Mill (*see* Industrial Building, below). At the end of Hallpark, Burnbrae leads e into housing of the later C20. Among this, in ROSEBANK, the former Alloa Colliery School (*see* Public Buildings, above).

The sw approach is along PARKHEAD ROAD. On the e side, Sauchie Hospital (*see* Public Buildings, above). To the w, in CHURCH GROVE, Sauchie and Fishcross United Free Church (*see* Churches, above). N of this, on the N side of POMPEE ROAD, Fairfield School (*see* Public Buildings, above). On Pompee Road's s side, late C19 double cottages with big bargeboarded gablets bracketed out at their centres, a couple still with wrought iron finials.

FAIRFIELD ROAD lies at the e end of Pompee Road and the N end of Parkhead Road. At its se end, on the corner of Mar Place, Sauchie District Hall and, to the e, the former Sauchie School (for these, *see* Public Buildings, above). At the N end of Mar Place is MAIN STREET. On its NW side, the late C19 MANSFIELD ARMS, Georgian survival but the painted masonry is hammer-dressed and the wallhead has a scroll-sided chimney. NE of this, the Sauchie Leisure Centre (*see* Public Buildings, above). The rest of Main Street is almost all of the later C20, mostly housing, with five-storey flatted blocks on the se side, and a few shops. Near the end, on the NW side, a two-storey commercial block dated 1905. Lugs at the bottom of the first-floor windows' architraves; segmental-pedimented clock turret at the centre of the wallhead. Further out, on the w side of ALLOA ROAD, Sauchie and Coalsnaughton Parish Church (*see* Churches, above). Still further out, on a low hill to the w of the A908, the round rubble-built tower of a WINDMILL, perhaps of *c.* 1700, its battlement an early C19 embellishment possibly contemporary with the building's conversion to a doocot.

## INDUSTRIAL BUILDING

HALLPARK MILL, Hallpark. Long woollen mill. The oldest surviving part, at the s, is dated 1908. Rubble-built two-storey block with a tall ground floor. Six bays by nine, the parapet on the shorter e front rising to a shaped central gablet. Eight-bay double-gabled brick extension of *c.* 1930. Further N extension, again of two storeys but lower and with large windows, built in 1947.

## SAUCHIE TOWER
### 0.4km. NW of Fishcross

C *8090*

Shell of the tower-house of the Schaws of Sauchie, standing on a steep slope down to the River Devon*. It was probably built in the mid or later C15 by James Schaw who was Comptroller of the royal

---

* Restoration was begun by *Simpson & Brown* in 2000.

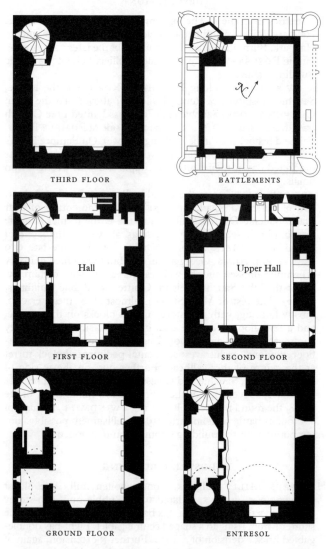

THIRD FLOOR

BATTLEMENTS

Hall

FIRST FLOOR

Upper Hall

SECOND FLOOR

GROUND FLOOR

ENTRESOL

Sauchie Tower. Plans.

household in the 1470s and appointed captain of Stirling Castle in
1489. The tower was superseded in the C17 by a new house, since
demolished, which stood a little to its w.

The building is an almost square five-storey rectangle, c. 11.3m.
by 10.1m., built of dark buff-coloured ashlar. The walling rises
unbroken by stringcourses or intakes to a parapet projected on
individual moulded corbels; at the corners of the parapet, con-

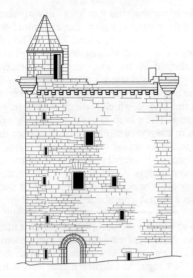

W ELEVATION

15 m
50 ft

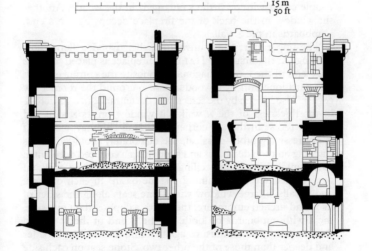

SECTION LOOKING NE          SECTION LOOKING SE

Sauchie Tower. Sections.

tinuous corbelling carrying rounds. Immediately S of the NE
round, machicolation for a wallhead garderobe. Set back within
the battlement of the NW round, remains of a polygonal slab-
roofed caphouse, almost identical to the caphouse on the refectory of Dunfermline Abbey (Fife). At the ground floor of the W
front and near its N end, the round-arched and heavily chamfered
entrance checked for an outward-opening door and a yett behind.

To its N, a tier of narrow stair windows, all with glazing grooves. Some way S of the entrance, a pair of small ground-floor windows (both hidden by the present ground level). The other ground-floor windows are in the E wall, again originally narrow slits; the N has been enlarged. At the floors above, the principal windows are generously sized; slit windows light the garderobes.

The entrance opens into an irregularly shaped cruciform lobby contained in the W wall, which is much thicker (c. 3m.) than the others (c. 1.5m.). The S limb of the cross was a guardroom, its N the approach to the NW turnpike stair which rises the full height of the tower and gives access to all the upper floors. To the E the lobby opens into the principal ground-floor room. At this room's S end, a bowed recess containing a well. Segmental-arched embrasures to the E windows. At the S end of the W side, the entrance into a mural chamber. This floor together with the entresol above are covered by an ashlar tunnel vault. On the side walls, corbels to support the wall-plate of the now missing wooden entresol floor. At the entresol, another large room. In each of the E and S walls, a good-sized window, the S with stone seats and a cupboard in its E ingo. At a slightly higher level than the entresol and opening off the stair is a long and narrow tunnel-vaulted room in the thickness of the W wall. This was the kitchen. A couple of slit windows (the S enlarged) in the W side. Another slit window in the back of the fireplace occupying the S end. Cupboards in the E wall.

The upper storeys are unvaulted, their wooden floors now missing. At the first-floor HALL the fireplace is placed towards the S end of the E wall, diagonally opposite the entrance which was partitioned off by a wooden screen around the room's NW corner. Also hidden by the screen was the entrance to a garderobe in the thickness of the N wall; slit window on its N side and a lamp recess in the SW corner. The Hall chimneypiece itself is impressively proto-classical, the elaborately moulded jambs standing on moulded bases and supporting a corniced deep lintel; overmantel rising to the ceiling. At the E end of the N wall, an ogee-arched recess containing a stone basin. In each of the E and S walls, a large window with stone seats along the sides of its round-arched embrasure, the E with a cupboard on one side, the S with cupboards on both. At the N end of the W wall, a third window, its embrasure again round-arched but broader and deeper than those of the other two. Stone seat on each side but the S seat is cut through to allow access into a wall chamber which has a small window to the outside and a larger window into the Hall. Along the E and W sides of the Hall, cornice-like continuous corbelling which has carried the wall-plate of the floor above.

The second floor is again occupied by one principal room (a GREAT CHAMBER or UPPER HALL) but here the main W wall is reduced to about half the thickness it shows below and, instead of W wall chambers, there is a recess roofed at a lower level than the rest of the room. At the N end of this recess, a W window with stone seats. At the recess's S end, the entrance to a window-

less gardrerobe in the s gable. Two more windows in the principal
room's N and E walls, both with stone seats, the N with a basin
in the sill, the E with a cupboard on one side. In the wall thickness of the house's NE corner, a dog-leg garderobe with a slit
window to the N and a lamp recess. At the SE corner, an L-plan
recess covered by segmental tunnel vaults set at r. angles to
each other. In each limb of the recess, a window, the s partly
blocked; stone seat along the w end. In the centre of the s end
of the Great Chamber, a broad fireplace, its corniced deep lintel
projected on moulded corbels and surmounted by a sloping
hood. Again there is cornice-like continuous corbelling along
the E and W sides of the room to support the wall-plate of the
floor above. This third floor seems again to have been occupied
by a single room. Fireplace at the W end of the s wall with a
small cupboard beside it. Recesses with splayed ingoes near the
E end of the s wall and the W end of the N. About two-thirds of
the way up the side walls, rows of very simply moulded corbels
which support an inward jettying of these walls which are also
thinned externally so as to allow sufficient breadth at the wall
walk for a person to squeeze past the NW caphouse and the E
chimneystack. Above, an attic entered from the caphouse, with
a window at each end.

## SAUCHIEBURN HOUSE      S 7080
### 1.8km. sw of Chartershall

By *Honeyman, Jack & Robertson*, 1973. A white gabled house with
a conically roofed entrance tower; somewhat overglazed for its
size and Scottish pretension, and emasculated by comparison
with its robustly red Baronial predecessor, which *Sydney Mitchell
& Wilson* had built for Sir James Maitland, 1890–1. – On the
lawn, an obelisk SUNDIAL with the inscribed date 1692. A second
SUNDIAL, its upper obelisk-shaped section detached from a
plinth carved with a mask on each face, is also late C17. Both
are believed to have come from Barnton House, Midlothian. –
MIDDLE LODGE lies 0.7km. SE, a small piend-roofed late
Victorian dwelling with a log-columned porch and lattice-glazed,
round-arched windows. – To the N, the STABLE COURT survives
from the C19; symmetrical s front with a central semicircular-
arched entry and crowstep-gabled wings, restored as a Riding
Centre for the Disabled by *McEachern, MacDuff*, 1994. –
WALLED GARDEN.

## SHERIFFMUIR      S 8000

Bleak battlefield country on the w flanks of the Ochil Hills, the inn
standing at the junction of moor roads from Dunblane, Bridge of
Allan and Greenloaning.

CAULDHAME, 1.1km. SSE. White-harled C18 drovers' inn, towered
and castellated in the C19.

MACRAE MEMORIAL, 1.2km. w. Bicentennial cairn, erected 1915. High pyramid of rubble boulders, square in plan with concave sides, set in a walled and fenced enclosure by the roadside. Gaelic and English inscriptions recall the Macraes who fell at the Battle of Sheriffmuir, 1715.

SHERIFFMUIR INN. Mid-C19 recasting of earlier house. Three-bay, two-storey, with gablets to upper windows.

SHIELDHILL                     F

Village begun in the late C19.

BLACKBRAES AND SHIELDHILL PARISH CHURCH, Main Street. Originally Shieldhill Free Church. Plain lanceted Gothic of 1887, a gableted bellcote on the front (N) gable. The architect was probably *G. Deas Page* who extended the building in 1894. C20 re-roofing with red concrete tiles which provide colour but not cheer.

SHIELDHILL PRIMARY SCHOOL, Main Street. Flat-roofed box, by the Stirling County Architect, *A.J. Smith*, 1961.

DESCRIPTION. On the N side of MAIN STREET, Blackbraes and Shieldhill Parish Church, and, on the S, towards the W end, Shieldhill Primary School (for these, *see* above). Further W, the former REDDING CO-OPERATIVE SOCIETY PREMISES (now a bar) of 1903. Inexpensive free Jacobean but with a large panel carved in relief with the Society's emblem of a handshake.

SLAMANNAN                     F

Former mining village which developed from the mid C19.

CHURCHES

CHURCH OF CHRIST, New Street. Originally Slamannan Methodist Church. Humble Gothic of 1874.

SLAMANNAN PARISH CHURCH, Main Street. Built and perhaps designed by *James Warden*, wright in Falkirk,\* 1810–11. More secular than ecclesiastical in appearance, it is a tall rubble-walled box. Rectangular windows and doors, the two centre windows of the S wall (flanking the pulpit) taller than the others. Birdcage bellcote on the W gable. In the centre of the S wall, a bronze SUNDIAL, probably early C19. Built into the wall below the sundial, a pedimented dormerhead with the damaged superscription '16[—] I AM TH[E] LIGH[T] O[F] TH[E] W[O]RLD', and also a stone, probably also C17 and originally a lintel, inscribed 'KEIP MY SABBATH AND (REVE)RENCE MY SANCTUARY LEVIT [xix 30]'; they may have come from the church's predecessor.

Inside, an Adamish plaster umbrella rose at the centre of the

\* But various designs were prepared by *Hume & Richardson* in 1809.

ceiling. Semi-octagonal gallery, its pine front panelled, supported on tapering Tuscan columns. – At the centre of the s wall, an oak PULPIT of 1810, with a stem pedestal and semi-octagonal body finished with a dentil cornice. Back with a roundheaded panel, its arch springing from acanthus-capitalled pilasters; pediment skied above. – The simple oak COMMUNION TABLE and ELDERS' PEWS were designed by *Alfred Greig* and executed by *Scott Morton & Co.*, 1935. – Victorian PEWS. – ORGAN, its two halves sitting on the s ends of the gallery, by *Ingram & Co.*, 1923, originally in the (demolished) Grahams Road United Free Church at Falkirk. – STAINED GLASS. In each of the windows flanking the pulpit, a small panel (the Ascension; Our Lord in the House at Bethany) of *c.* 1900.

GRAVEYARD. At the w entrance, stumpily pinnacled GATE-PIERS, probably of the earlier C19, and a piend-roofed SESSION HOUSE of *c.* 1850.

HEADSTONES. S of the church, a mid-C18 stone bearing the initials I G and A R (for James Gray and Agnes Rankin), the w face carved with two human heads, the E with an angel's head (the soul) and hourglasses. – Further S, a stone of 1740 to I M and M R, the top carved with an angel's head and a skull, crossbones and hourglass. – Beside it, a stone of 1745 commemorating Robert Kirkwood. On the w face, foliage-capitalled attached barley-sugar columns surmounted by naked boys flanking a coat of arms. On the E face, a leafily bordered inscription panel on whose top recline two angels and which is flanked by standing human figures and bunches of grapes. The intention is more sophisticated than the execution.

PUBLIC BUILDINGS

FIRE STATION, New Street. By the Stirling County Architect, *A. J. Smith*, 1961. Small flat-roofed brick-walled building.

PARISH CHURCH HALL, Main Street. Built in 1900–1. Crow-stepped front gable built of bullnosed masonry and containing hoodmoulded tall Jacobean windows.

SLAMANNAN PRIMARY SCHOOL, Bank Street. By *Alexander Watt*, 1876.* Single-storey, in a very plain Jacobean manner. Rear addition by the Stirling County Architect, *A. N. Malcolm*, 1932, and NW extension by Malcolm's successor, *A. J. Smith*, 1966–8.

DESCRIPTION

MAIN STREET leads in from the N. On the E side, a few altered mid-C19 vernacular cottages, followed by the motte (*see* below) and Slamannan Parish Church (*see* Churches, above). On the w, just s of the church, the Parish Church Hall (*see* Public Buildings, above). Across the Culloch Burn, NEW STREET goes off to the SE. On its E side, the Church of Christ and the Fire Station (*see* Churches and Public Buildings, above). On the w

* The date 1873 on the front was added in 1932.

side, reached from KIRKBURN, a crowstep-gabled cottage in
the Jacobean style of thirty years earlier than its date of 1877. S of
the junction with New Street, Main Street has plain buildings
of the mid and late C19 on the E side. On the W, THORNDENE
TERRACE by *G. R. M. Kennedy & Partners*, 1980. At Main Street's
S end, on the E corner with HIGH STREET, the ROYAL HOTEL,
Georgian survival of 1866. On the W corner, the ST LAURENCE
BAR of about the same date and also Georgian survival but
dignified by cornices over the ground-floor windows and a
pilastered and corniced entrance.

On the s side of High Street, on the axis of Main Street, a MONU-
MENT of 1902 to George Ralston Peddie Waddell. Octagonal
pillar, its capital carved with birds and beasts among thistle
foliage; *Joseph Hayes* was the sculptor. It supports a square clock
by *James Ritchie & Son*, topped by a stumpy stone pinnacle. At
the E end of High Street, on its corner with Station Road, WAR
MEMORIAL of 1921. Polished granite pillar of routine design,
with a stylized iron finial. Round the memorial are three plinths
bearing recumbent lions, all of red sandstone.

MOTTE, Main Street. Probably formed in the C12 or C13 and now
rather damaged. It is a truncated cone, *c.* 3.96m. high, with a
diameter of *c.* 27.43m. at the base and of *c.* 11.28m. at the summit.

GLEN ELRIG, 2.8km. NE. The mansion house has been demolished. At the end of the N drive, a LODGE of the earlier C19.
Single-storey L-plan, with scrolled skewputts and pointed
windows.

Small bitty village, the houses almost all C19. This was the S end
of a ferry across the River Forth established by John Francis
Erskine of Mar, *c.* 1790.

Former SCHOOL, 0.7km. S. Simple Jacobean, dated 1875, the
two-storey schoolhouse (now DUNDARROCH) intact, the tall
single-storey school rather altered.

KERSIE MAINS. *See* p. 544.

# STIRLING

## INTRODUCTION

A fortress town at the crossroads of Central Scotland. Few other places have a history more grounded in geography. Topography is decisive; indeed, it is visibly and literally crucial. Here, at the lowest point on its course where the Forth could be bridged, the craggy basalt of the Castle Rock bursts out of the flat alluvial carse. From its defensible heights nothing is hidden. Routes radiate in all directions: E by the Hillfoots to Fife; NE through Strathallan to Perth; NW by Doune and Callander to Strathyre and Breadalbane; W across Flanders Moss to Strathendrick, the Vale of Leven and Dumbarton; and S, branching SE through Falkirk to the Lothians and Edinburgh or SW to Lanarkshire, Glasgow and the Clyde. Such elevation at the convergence of so many strategic routes must always have attracted settlement. Some form of early hillfort stronghold seems likely, for several sites in the area testify to Iron Age occupation. But archaeological corroboration is elusive. Nor is there more than scant evidence of a Roman presence, still less from the millennium that followed their departure.

By the C12 a royal castle, probably still largely of timber construction, had been raised on the precipitous W flank of the Rock. From the crag, a small castletoun straggled down the sloping tail

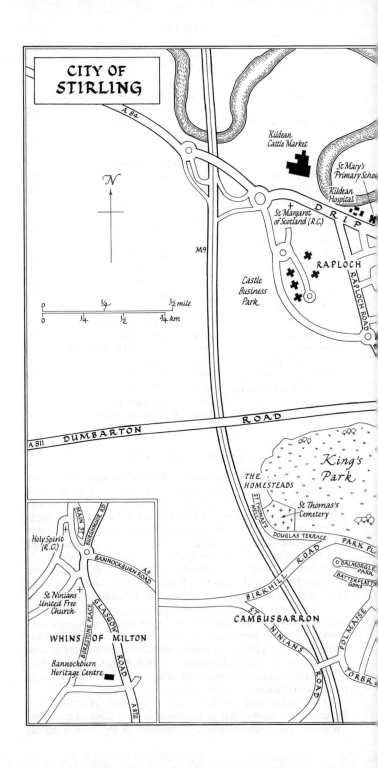

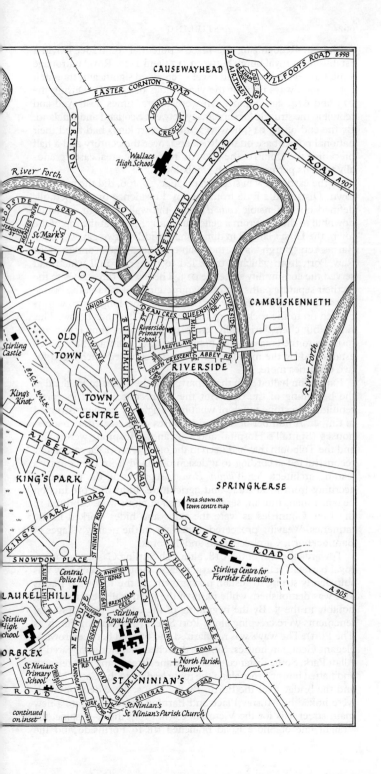

CAUSEWAYHEAD

EASTER CORNTON ROAD

HILLFOOTS ROAD B998

ALLOA ROAD A907

A9

CORNTON ROAD

LOTHIAN CRESCENT

AIRTHREY RD

LOGIE RD

GLENTANA

Wallace High School

River Forth

WOODSIDE ROAD

ROAD

CAUSEWAYHEAD ROAD

St Mark's

FERGUSON2 ST

NELLIES DALE

CAMBUSKENNETH

R O A D

UNION ST

DEAN CRES

QUEENSHAUGH DR.

RIVERSIDE DRIVE

Stirling Castle

OLD TOWN

BURGHMUIR

COWANE ST

ROAD

Riverside Primary School

MILLAR

ARGYLL AVE

ABBEY RD

River Forth

King's Knot

TOWN CENTRE

FORTH CRESCENT

RIVERSIDE

BACK WALK

ALBERT PL.

GOOSECROFT ROAD

KING'S PARK

SPRINGKERSE

KING'S PARK ROAD

ST NINIAN'S ROAD

COLQUHOUN ROAD

←Area shown on town centre map

KERSE ROAD

A 905

SNOWDON PLACE

Central Police H.Q.

ANNFIELD GDNS

VILANDS GATE

BRENTHAM CRES.

STREET

Stirling Centre for Further Education

LAUREL HILL

LAUREL HILL

NEWHOUSE

RANDOLPH RD

CLIFFORD RD

SPRINGFIELD ROAD

Stirling High School

ORBREX

RANDOLPH TERR.

BELLFIELD RD

Stirling Royal Infirmary

North Parish Church

St Ninian's Primary School

ST NINIAN'S

ST M UIR

SHIRRAS BRAE ROAD

ROAD

KIRK WYND

MAIN ST

St Ninian's †

† St Ninian's Parish Church

continued on inset ↓

to the SE. Recognizing the place's potential for trade, David I established a royal burgh between 1124 and 1127. Royal patronage – military, ecclesiastical and fiscal – remained significant, though it could not always prevent the vicissitudes of conflict. During the C13 and C14, castle and town were several times destroyed and rebuilt in the struggle for supremacy between Scotland and England. By the end of the C15, however, the Stewart kings had fixed their national power base on the Rock and, over the century and a half preceding the Union of the Crowns in 1603, the great castle gradually took its permanent form (*see* below).

As the castle grew in size and prestige, so, too, did the medieval town. Distanced a little from the royal residence by an open, ill-defined but defensible *cour d'entrée*, the walled burgh stretched downhill to the SE. From a generous market-place at the top of the town, the High Gait fell in diminishing width to two gateways: the Barras Yett (Burgh Gate), the main entry from the S, and the Dirt Raw Port, from which a track led to the grain mill which had served the community since the C13. There were three gates to the N, their separate paths out of town merging not far S of the bridge crossing of the Forth. SW of the castle, the long narrow tofts backed on to the rocky scarp that fell to the flatlands below. This simple but characteristically linear urban pattern, similar in many respects to the crag-and-tail plan evolving at Edinburgh, was well established by the middle of the C16. It remained unchanged for two centuries more.

Expansion halted with the departure of the Court to England at the beginning of the C17. But the town consolidated its form, rebuilding in stone much of what had originally been constructed in timber. A number of fine town houses were erected, two alms-houses (Spittall's Hospital and Cowane's Hospital) were built, and the Tolbooth that had risen in the old market-place completely reconstructed according to a design obtained from the country's leading architect, *Sir William Bruce*. Augmenting the prosperity accruing from local trade and agriculture, industrial production began. Linen, muslin, serge and worsted cloth were exported to the Low Countries as were the skins and hides worked in the tanneries. Weaving prospered, especially in the nearby villages of Bannockburn, Cambusbarron and Torbrex.

Towards the end of the C18, although Stirling Castle was now a royal barracks rather than a royal palace, the town's economy was sufficiently strong to sustain new growth. In the 1770s the Barras Yett was demolished, while parts of the town wall were removed, notably in the E. By the beginning of the C19, a few extramural tenements were creeping along Port Street (then known simply as The Port). The way S was regularized and banked between rows of elegant Georgian houses. Similar detached mansions appeared in Allan Park. Some distance N, on Cowane Street, ranges of terraces and flatted housing rose along the route leading to the Cattle Market and the bridge over the Forth. By the 1840s, these developments were linked by Murray Place and Barnton Street to create a new main street axis for the Victorian town. From this N–S spine, the straight line of Shore Road branched NE to Forthside and the steamboat quay from which twice-daily services connected with South Queensferry downriver on the Firth. Within a few years, however, the use of river transport had declined as communications were greatly improved by the railway, which reached Stirling in 1848. Benefiting from the ease with which goods and people could now be transported, the town continued to grow. Below the castle, s from Dumbarton Road, the salubrious suburb of King's Park spread rapidly through the middle years of the century. A residential ribbon stretched s as far as St Ninian's village which, with the weaving hamlet of Torbrex, had already been absorbed into the burgh in 1833. By the 1870s houses were being built in Laurelhill and Annfield. The same decade saw the beginnings of serious industrial development in Springkerse while the textile mills in Cambusbarron were employing over a thousand people. But in addition to the stimulus given to building by the need to house a growing population of industrial workers, tradesmen, merchants and professional men, the impact of Victorian travellers was also a significant factor in the town's economy. With the development of nearby Bridge of Allan as a spa and the building of the National Wallace Monument at Causewayhead, Stirling began to realize its attractive potential as a tourist centre. Not only was the castle wonderfully situated and rich in romantic historical association but the town was in effect the gateway to the sublime landscapes of the Trossachs and the North.

The provision of housing dominated the town's growth during the C20. In the years before the First World War low terraces and semi-detached houses were built E of the railway in the almost peninsular suburb of Riverside at The Shore where the old harbour and quay had been. In the 1920s public housing extended this quiet quarter. In the 1930s, Raploch took shape back o'hill on flat land N of the Castle Rock. A Parliamentary Act of 1936 brought Causewayhead, Cambuskenneth and Whins of Milton within the burgh boundaries, though further residential development of these areas was delayed by the Second World War. Extensive local authority building continued after the Second World War in Cornton, St Ninian's and Braehead. Speculative housing began in the inter-war period in Causewayhead and Livilands, but it was during the last three decades of the century that private developers became particularly active on several peripheral estates. Rehabilitation of the Old Town has also been an important preoccupation. Since the formation of the Thistle Property Trust in 1928, the retention of old fabric or the sympathetic intervention of new housing has been a commendable aspect of Stirling's approach to its late medieval urban heritage. Although the Trust was dissolved in 1952, conservation has continued to contribute to civic self-respect, extending not only to the streets of the Old Town but, at the level of national concern, to the castle itself.

Late C20 road developments, which in so many communities have disrupted townscape, have been relatively kind to Stirling. The M9 motorway, running well W of the town, makes little impact. This is less true of Burghmuir Road, a dual carriageway route which connects St Ninian's with the bridge over the Forth 3km. N.

It dips and curves in a series of long flowing curves and, if it exposes a good deal of backlands commerce through the centre of town, much of this the consequence of the massive Thistle Centre and Thistle Marches shopping mall projects of the 1970s and 1990s, it does at least cling close to the railway, already a strong barrier to urban continuity. Only Riverside and Springkerse lie E of the railway, the latter a visually chaotic concentration of industrial estates, most of which have sprung up in the last quarter of the century after the burgh extended its boundaries in this area. Much more coherent in architectural terms is the Castle Business Park, attractively landscaped close to the motorway on the W fringes of Raploch. Stirling was granted city status in 2002.

# INNER STIRLING

## STIRLING CASTLE[*]

Stirling Castle was one of the outstandingly important royal castles of medieval and early modern Scotland. Its buildings represent not only the most ambitious but also the most complete surviving complex of structures built for the occupation of the Stewart dynasty. Set on its high rock the castle presents an extraordinarily varied series of images, depending on the vantage point, the time of day and the quality of light. From the wallhead of Doune Castle to the NW, its narrow and strongly vertical silhouette gives it something of the appearance of a distant ship sailing along the Forth valley, while from Cambuskenneth Abbey to the E, its buildings crown the ridge above a more gentle build-up of hills and valleys. But despite inappropriate modern developments in the valley, perhaps the most dramatic views are still from the W, across Flanders Moss, from where the sheer rock face can be seen rising through the belt of trees along its base, with the Ochil Hills swelling beyond.

The reasons for building so important a castle here are not hard to see. Indeed, the combination of a naturally strong rock platform with a location at the geographical heart of the kingdom was a coincidence of circumstances which made the construction of a castle almost inevitable. This is especially the case since it is at the junction of a number of the most strategically important land and water routes.

The castle rock itself is a high quartz dolerite volcanic sill, on which the action of glaciers during the Ice Age created almost vertical cliffs on the W and N sides, with downward-stepping hills on the E, and a gentler SE slope along which the dependent burgh was to develop. From this site the castle overlooks a narrow section of the Forth valley, where it is restricted by the Ochil Hills to the NE and the Gargunnock and Touch Hills to the SW. Through this area, routes run both E–W across the Midland valley and N–S between the Highlands and Lowlands. The military advantages of the castle site were of even greater significance before the late C18,

---

[*] This account has been written by Richard Fawcett.

since much of the land w of the castle was covered by marshes, the Flanders and Blairdrummond Mosses, and it required detailed local knowledge to avoid the routes which passed below the castle. Whoever controlled the castle rock was thus well placed to monitor communications through the heart of the kingdom.

### BUILDING CHRONOLOGY

*The early history, up to the C12*

It is inherently possible that such a naturally dominant site was defended from prehistoric times, though no physical signs of this have survived, and archaeology has so far failed to find any evidence. The rock could have been a stronghold of one or both of the tribes known to the Romans as the Maeatae and Votadini (or of the successors of the latter, the Gododdin). Later legends associated Stirling with King Arthur, and even suggested it could have been Camelot. More plausibly, in the C7 and C8 the rock may have been Urbs Iudeu, where Penda of Mercia is said to have pursued Oswy of Bernicia in 654. According to Hector Boece, writing in 1527, Kenneth MacAlpin besieged the rock in 842 as part of his campaign to establish control over both the Pictish and Scottish parts of Scotland.

*The early C12 to the late C15*

The earliest certain reference to the castle is in the time of Alexander I who, between 1107 and 1115, endowed a chapel within it, suggesting the castle was well established by then. During the C12 and C13 Stirling became a favourite royal residence, and for a while it possibly functioned as the main centre for the administration of royal finances. David I (1124–53) founded an Arroasian (later Augustinian) abbey in a loop of the Forth at Cambuskenneth, which enjoyed a relationship with the castle similar to that of Holyrood Abbey with Edinburgh Castle or Kelso Abbey with Roxburgh Castle. He also established a hunting forest in the valley beyond, later enclosed to form Scotland's first royal park. Stirling was one of the castles surrendered by William the Lion under the humiliating terms of the Treaty of Falaise of 1174, by which William was forced to accept Henry II of England's overlordship of Scotland. This acknowledgement, despite being later revoked, was to lie at the root of Scotland's troubles with England from the end of the C13 through much of the rest of the Middle Ages.

Stirling was hotly fought over during the long 'Wars of Independence' which erupted in 1296. Edward I of England took it immediately on the outbreak of warfare, though in 1297 it was recaptured by the patriots William Wallace and Andrew Murray, after the battle of Stirling Bridge. Again re-taken by the English in 1298, it was once more in Scottish hands in 1299. During the successful English siege of 1304 the mysterious engine referred to ominously as the 'War Wolf' was devastatingly deployed. In the next phase of warfare, during the reigns of Robert I in Scotland and Edward II in England, possession of Stirling was the cause of the battle of Bannockburn in 1314: after the Scottish victory Robert destroyed it as part of his policy of ensuring that castles could not be held against him. But the site was again in English hands from 1336, during the minority of David II, and was re-fortified for the English Warden, Sir Thomas Rokeby. It was besieged by the Scots in 1337, when guns were used for perhaps only the third time on Scottish soil, but it was only finally re-taken in 1342.

Many of the castle's first buildings and defences were evidently of earth and timber, though in 1287 the Exchequer Rolls record works by *Richard the Mason,* and by the C14 there are increasing numbers of references to building in stone and lime. Traces of what may have been an early stone curtain wall were found through excavation in 1994 on part of the highest point of the castle rock, behind the Chapel. The earliest structure to survive above ground, however, may be the lower parts of the North Gate; this could be part of a larger building campaign recorded in 1381 in the time of Robert II, the first of the Stewart dynasty.

*The apogee of the castle as a royal palace: building for the Stewart kings from the late C15 to 1603*

Most of the Stewart kings were architecturally active within the castle, and it may have been James I who confirmed the tradition of making it part of the queen's jointure and, in consequence, frequently the royal nursery. However, the most outstanding period of the castle's architectural history was from the late C15 to the late C16, when it was rebuilt for the three monarchs who were Scotland's greatest patrons of palatial architecture: James IV, James V and James VI. The result of this activity was an architectural complex conceived and executed on a more expansive scale, and to a more sumptuous degree of finish, than at any other Scottish royal residence. Both individually and collectively these buildings are of paramount importance for our understanding of secular architecture in the later Middle Ages and earlier Renaissance. Several of the existing buildings, together with the siting of others, appear to stem from the wishes of James IV (1488–1513) to have a more fitting residence at Stirling, at the same time that he was building at Edinburgh Castle and the palaces of Linlithgow, Falkland and Holyrood. His works at Stirling Castle include what was probably his own residence (the King's Old Building) and the Great Hall, on opposite sides of the main enclosure, the Inner Close. They also include the great towered wall across the main approach, the Forework. If he had not been killed at Flodden in 1513, he would probably have built other structures around the Inner Close; he certainly magnificently endowed the Chapel Royal, which stood along its N side, even if he did not replace the building.

Further major works were carried out for James V (1513–42). The quadrangular Palace, on the S side of the Inner Close, was built to provide more suitable accommodation for himself and his French queens. James V's daughter, Mary Queen of Scots, who succeeded to the throne as a baby in 1542, was crowned in the Chapel the following year. During her absence in France as wife of the future François II it is likely her mother, Mary of Guise, continued work on the Palace and commissioned the major artillery defences commanding the approaches to the castle. These survive in part, embedded within the later Outer Defences. Following her return to Scotland, Mary Queen of Scots evidently did little building, but both before and after her abdication in 1567, the young James VI spent much of his infancy at Stirling. A report of 1583 suggests that many of the main buildings were in disrepair, with the Great Hall and Chapel Royal leaking, the towers of the Forework roofless and the W side of the Palace in a state of pending collapse. James VI's Chapel, on the N side of the Inner Close, was the last major royal building to be constructed within the castle, being raised in haste in 1594 for the baptism of Prince Henry.

## Building after the Union of the Crowns and the response to the Jacobite threat

James VI succeeded to the English throne as James I in 1603, and made only one homecoming to Scotland, in 1617, for which repairs and improvements were carried out. There was much redecoration and some structural changes for a brief visit by the art-loving Charles I at the time of his Scottish coronation (at Holyrood) in 1633. The most visible traces of this visit are the wall paintings in the Chapel and the earthworks of the gardens in the valley SW of the castle. Charles II visited Scotland in 1650–1, after the execution of his father, when he was accepted as king of Scotland, but in reprisal Stirling Castle was taken by English parliamentary forces after a siege by General Monk in 1651. Charles II's visit to Scotland was the last by a ruling monarch for nearly two centuries, and with the decline of royal interest there was little need for palaces north of the Border. Consequently, most of the buildings in Stirling Castle were progressively adapted to military or more mundane uses.

Many of the late C17 to late C18 additions and changes made to the castle were in response to the threat represented by the deposed Jacobite line in the persons of James VII and II, his son Prince James (the Old Pretender) and his grandson Prince Charles Edward (the Young Pretender).

The revolution which ousted James VII and II in 1689 was accompanied by a rising led by John Graham of Claverhouse, Viscount Dundee, and measures were taken to strengthen the castle, including the construction of new artillery batteries and the closing of all but the main entrance. The next alarm was the appearance of a French squadron in the Firth of Forth in 1708, sent in support of the Old Pretender's claims. This led to the immediate construction of massive outer works, incorporating parts of the mid-C16 artillery defences.

The next significant rising, in 1715, was led by the hereditary Governor of Stirling Castle, the sixth (or eleventh) Earl of Mar, an enlightened patron of architecture but an inadequate general. He had earlier made various changes to buildings within the castle, especially on the top floor of the Palace, where he had his own apartment. (While in exile in Paris after the failure of this rising, he drew comfort from working up abortive designs for remodelling the Palace for himself as Governor and for the restored Stewart dynasty.) The main impact of the last seriously threatening rising of 1745–6, led by the Young Pretender, was a mis-handled siege following the rebel army's withdrawal from Derby. This was mounted from the adjacent Gowan Hill, under the direction of the Comte Mirabelle de Gourdon, but the grand battery of the castle made short work of the emplacement. The Jacobite army then marched off, with the Duke of Cumberland in close pursuit, to final defeat at Culloden.

*Building history 1790–1997*

Building operations within the castle from the later C18 were all for military uses. Some of the new buildings, including the Main Guard House and the Fort Major's House, while utilitarian in spirit, were nevertheless handsomely detailed and carefully built. More damaging was the progressive adaptation of all the royal buildings, at times when accommodation was needed for an enlarged garrison, though such adaptation did at least ensure the continued existence of the buildings. In the late 1790s, when Britain was at war with France, the Great Hall was sub-divided by floors and walls to create barrack rooms; the work was possibly designed by *John Sanders*, architect to the Barrack Department of the War Office from 1794. The hammerbeam roof, perhaps beyond repair by then, was destroyed. Similar operations were carried out in the King's Old Building and to a lesser extent in the Palace and Chapel.

A more historically conscious (if highly inventive) approach was signalled by *R. W. Billings'* reconstruction of the N end of the King's Old Building after a fire in 1855. But it was only following the intervention of Edward VII in 1906 that greater regard was paid to the castle's historic qualities than to the immediate needs of the army. It was then decided that maintenance should be dealt with by the Office of Works rather than the War Office. As a result of modified attitudes, the kitchens below the Grand Battery were excavated in 1921, while in the 1930s the dining hall, school and stores were removed from the Chapel; the outbreak of war then halted further restoration. The next turning point was in 1964, when the castle ceased to be a military depot. While accepting the importance of the army's post-1707 role in maintaining the royal buildings and in adding significant new ones, since 1964 conservation works have been initiated in most of the buildings, including all of the principal structures around the Inner Close. This has involved the stabilization of historic fabric, the removal of unsympathetic insertions and some restoration of missing elements where this can be done authoritatively. Most ambitious has been the restoration of the Great Hall, started in 1964 and completed in 1999.

## PLAN

The summit of the castle rock is an irregular elongated oval aligned roughly from SE to NW. Its steepest sides are to the W and N, and the natural line of approach is from the SE. The platform of the summit steps down E in a series of terraces towards the Ballengeich Pass and Gowan Hill. The large surface area of the rock, and the great length of its perimeter, mean that fortifying it was never easy. Consequently, the full extent of the area eventually fortified was probably only achieved relatively late; archaeological investigations have hinted at the possibility of a walled enclosure at the highest point by the C13, but most of the perimeter walls appear to be C15 or later in their existing state.

The castle is subdivided into three main parts, with various subdivisions within them. Massive defences, combining works of the mid C16 and early C18, guard the entrance and occupy much of the lower terrace on the SE side.

The central part, roughly triangular in shape, is approached through the Forework of *c.* 1500. Within the Forework is the Outer Close, with kitchens and domestic offices on its E side. The main focus of the central part is the grouping of royal buildings around the Inner Close, approached by a road up from the NW corner of the Outer Close. Archaeological evidence suggests that the area of the Inner Close was earlier occupied by buildings laid out on a predominantly E–W axis, probably in response to the terracing of the underlying rock; the chief upstanding survivor of this earlier axis is a block at the S end of the King's Old Building, now known to have been a chapel. It was only from the late C15 that the present more regular quadrangular layout was planned, though the relatively steep slope of the platform at the top of the castle rock must always have made difficult the creation of a suitably dignified space without building up the levels at the lower end of the site. The present regular gradient of the Inner Close is probably largely a modern creation, and there was evidently a balustraded terrace at the top end in the early C18. The W and E sides of the Inner Close are defined by the King's Old Building and the Great Hall respectively, while the Chapel Royal occupies the N side and the Palace the S side. Behind the Chapel Royal is an area known as the Captain's Garden in the C18, though it was then subdivided by walls (now gone) running back from the Chapel and King's Old Building to the North Curtain Wall. W of the Palace is an area known as the Ladies' Hole, from which the ladies of the court could overlook the gardens below the castle.

To the N of the central part, beyond the North Curtain Wall, is the third part, the Nether Bailey; the two parts are connected by

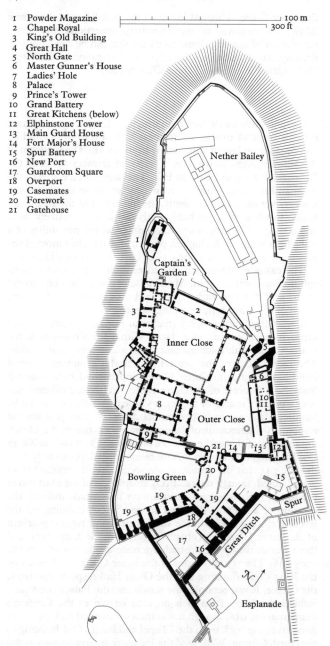

100 m
300 ft

Nether Bailey

Captain's
Garden

Inner Close

Outer Close

Bowling Green

Great Ditch

Spur

Esplanade

N

Stirling Castle. Plan.

the North Gate. Since the late C17 strengthening of the castle perimeter the Nether Bailey has been a cul-de-sac, though there used to be two postern gates through its walls. This area now contains little more than C19 magazines with their guard house and the remains of a firing range, but it may once have accommodated a number of the castle's ancillary activities.

## OUTER DEFENCES

The ESPLANADE, the open area at the head of the volcanic tail in front of the entrance to the castle, was levelled as a parade ground in 1809, after extra land was acquired from the burgh. On the Esplanade a number of MONUMENTS: NW, a memorial to members of the Argyll and Sutherland Highlanders who fell in the South African War in 1902, by *W. Hubert Paton*, 1905–7; on a red granite plinth, a bronze kilted soldier is shown advancing. Beside it, a pink granite cross commemorates the soldiers of the 75th Stirlingshire Regiment who fell in the Indian campaigns of 1857–8. NE, a statue of Robert the Bruce, designed by *George Cruikshank* and sculpted by *Andrew Currie*, 1876–7; on a high base, the tall mailed figure of the victorious king sheathes his sword.

The OUTER DEFENCES present a starkly forbidding first impression from the Esplanade, appropriate to their role as a massively constructed but low-set barrier designed to absorb the impact of artillery bombardment. The chief elements are a straight wall pierced by a single gateway, and a flanking gun battery at the N end. They date largely from 1708 to 1714, following the attempted invasion of 1708 by the Old Pretender, though it is now known that they incorporate important earlier work and also that there was a major change of plan during the work started in 1708.

The earlier work was possibly started after Mary of Guise became Regent for the absent Mary Queen of Scots in 1554, at a time of conflict between the Catholic pro-French party led by Mary of Guise, and those favouring closer links with Protestant England. Views before the changes of 1708–14, especially the plan and perspectives by John Slezer of *c.* 1680, show that it took the form of a great bastion-like spur with a pyramidal reinforcement at the prow, and with smaller spurs to each side. The E spur was an orillon demi-bastion, while that to the W, which flanked the entrance, was of larger and less regular form. In the siting and planning there are parallels with the destroyed outworks at Edinburgh Castle, for which an Italian deviser was paid in 1547–8. Excavations in 1977 confirmed that the French (E) Spur still stands much as first built, albeit with a wall across the recessed mouth of the flank to provide additional gun emplacements. Much of the E face of the Great Spur itself also survives within the later walls, with part of its curved prow in evidence N of the gate; in addition, other fragments, including part of a retaining wall of the ramped approach road, have been identified in existing masonry or through excavation. The link of Mary of Guise with this work is circumstantially supported by unidentified arms with the French fleur-de-lys on the prow of the E spur, and by the fact that it was referred to as 'the French Spurre' from at least the time of Slezer.

Following the alarm of 1708, *Theodore Dury*, the Military Engineer for Scotland, suggested strengthening the Outer Defences by constructing a large triangular enclosure with a gatehouse at its apex in front of the outworks of Mary of Guise; this would have occupied much of the upper area of the present Esplanade. About 67m. of the S wall of this enclosure was built and survives in modified state, with one end projecting from the S side of the Outer Defences as eventually completed. However, work was stopped when *Captain Obryan* from London expressed concern, offering instead a design for more ambitious bastioned outworks on the castle's most vulnerable NE and SE sides. In 1711 a further report was prepared by Dury's and Obryan's superior officer, *Talbot Edwards*, and work to the present design was resumed in April of that year by Dury, with some assistance from the architect *James Smith*, and with *Gilbert Smith* as mason.

The main feature of the final design is a wall extending across much of the line of approach, incorporating and extending S from the E face of Mary of Guise's Great Spur. It has a single arched gateway, known as the NEW PORT, within a rusticated rectangular frame of slight projection at the centre, as the only entrance to the castle. Running in front of this is a deep, flat-bottomed, partly rock-cut dry ditch, which, like the wall itself, was an extension of the earlier outworks; this ditch was defended by two vaulted caponiers, one of which survives (the other was probably lost when a rackets court was built in the ditch in the early C19). The New Port is reached across a retractable bridge which, in the C18 (and probably before), was in the form of drawbridges suspended from an archway built above a pier in the middle of the ditch. On top of the new section of wall is a covered way for footsoldiers behind a turfed glacis, with an ogee-domed sentry box corbelled out at the S end. Behind the retained E face of the C16 Great Spur two-storeyed casemates were formed with a series of walls at r. angles to the spur wall bridged by barrel vaults. A battery was provided along the covered way on top of these vaults, with embrasures for three cannon through the turfed glacis, and with another sentry box at its S end. The main change to the French Spur was the walling across of the recessed flank to provide two levels of embrasures for cannon directed along the ditch, those of the lower level being casemated and opening through rusticated arches. On the upper level, in addition to the two cannon embrasures directed along the ditch, are two embrasures facing out towards the main approach, and four others in the NE face directed towards the Forth valley and the bridge that crossed it.

Within the New Port an enclosure now known as the GUARD-ROOM SQUARE was formed to trap any who had penetrated so far. The two inner walls defining this enclosure are strengthened behind by casemates carrying a glacis-fronted covered way. The covered way facing the entrance was for footsoldiers, and has a third sentry box at its s end; that on the N wall has three cannon embrasures above the OVERPORT, the gateway through to the rest of the castle. Running in front of the inner walls is a second dry ditch, of dog-legged plan; it was originally defended by a caponier at each end, the E one surviving below the guard room of 1813. Also within the Guardroom Square is a small stable (E), probably late C18, now housing lavatories, and a straw store of 1813 (S), later converted into a garage and now a shop. An arched stone bridge crosses the inner ditch to the OVERPORT, the archway of which is flanked by rusticated Tuscan pillars with the crowned initials of Queen Anne on its keystone.

Beyond the Overport is the area known as the COUNTERGUARD. Behind a sunken area NE of the Overport are the four bays of originally two-storeyed casemates set against the retained section of the Great Spur; these could be used as barrack rooms in times of emergency. The casemates, and a modern extension, now house a restaurant. Beyond the casemates is the terrace of the Spur Battery. W of the Overport, an archway (below the road up to the covered ways overlooking the Guardroom Square) leads through to a garden used as a bowling green from at least the late C17. Along its SE side are six bays of vaulted single-storeyed casemates behind the W wall of the Guardroom Square, and beyond those are three casemated cannon emplacements designed to provide fire along the S flank of the Outer Defences, at the point where the castle rock becomes less steep and thus more vulnerable. (These replaced an earlier battery built by *Tobias Bachop* in 1689.) Along the SW side of the green a low wall with a wall-walk overlooks the the gardens in the valley below. Along the NW side of the green, below the walls of the Forework and Palace, is a terrace with at its W end the remains of a balustraded parapet, which is thought to have been constructed in 1628–9 in preparation for Charles I's homecoming in 1633. The Masters of Works' Accounts record payments to *Robert Norie* and *James Rynd* for their work on 'balesteris for the law torres'. This parapet stops against a short length of wall which is probably the N end of the mid-C16 outer wall of the spur W of the Great Spur. Built into it is a window gablet, thought to have come from the Palace, which has the crowned initials M R, for either Mary of Guise or Mary Queen of Scots.

Dominating the Counterguard is the FOREWORK, James IV's outer wall across the main line of approach, with the later Palace rising behind its W section. Constructed at least partly on the line of an earlier wall, the Forework provided a magnificent frontispiece, a foretaste of the residence of a monarch who regarded Europe – and not just Scotland – as his stage. Although now badly damaged, with the gatehouse reduced to less than half-height, the flanking round towers largely or completely gone, and only one of the terminal towers standing to full height, the Forework can still be seen to have been a glorious piece of work.

Indeed, it was perhaps more reminiscent of painted castles in French illuminated manuscripts than of a functional artillery fortification of *c.* 1500. At the centre was the soaring gatehouse with cylindrical corner towers (originally conically roofed), and with two half-round towers to each side; terminating the walls stretching from each side of the gatehouse were large rectangular towers, known as the Elphinstone Tower (NE) and the Prince's Tower (SW).

The Forework was evidently under construction before 1501, when work was recorded on the foretower (perhaps the gatehouse) in the Treasurer's Accounts, and there was work on the kitchen tower (possibly the Elphinstone Tower) in 1503. The portcullis was ready for installation in 1504, and the 'forewerk' as a whole was nearing completion by 1506. Among the principal masons were *John Yorkston* and *John Lockhart*.

The curtain wall, capped by a broadly crenellated parapet carried on a decorative double-corbelled cornice, was probably thick enough to withstand all but a determined bombardment, while the towers of the gatehouse were pierced by at least three tiers of dumbbell-type shot-holes, suggesting that a defensive role was still a factor in its design. But the overall design of the Forework reminds us that Renaissance kings – in common with growing numbers of their more educated subjects – had a keen sense of history and of the messages which architecture could be programmed to convey. In the soaring towers and fantastic roofscape of the Forework there may have been more than a passing reference to chivalry and to the Arthurian legend, in both of which James IV is known to have had an enthusiastic interest. The closest parallel to this frontispiece in the other works of James IV was the multi-towered Outer Great Bulwark added in front of the entrance at Linlithgow Palace, though that was planned on a much smaller scale.

47

The GATEHOUSE is the principal focus of the Forework. Comparison with early views, and especially Slezer's, shows that, in addition to having been truncated, it has lost two three-quarter towers to the rear. It may have been damaged in the siege of 1651, and C18 engravings show that its upper storeys were then ruinous. Its present droved ashlar upper courses, with their mean crenellations, are of 1810. Originally the gatehouse was a tall rectangular block with three-quarter towers at all four angles, and with a *chemin-de-ronde* running around the steeply-roofed caphouses which rose above the wallhead. There are vaulted prison chambers below the principal level of the main body of the gatehouse and of the front towers, which are entered through floor hatches in the diagonally-set passages between the towers and the pedestrian ways. Chambers from which the portcullises were operated are above the pedestrian ways.

The ultimate inspiration for the overall form of the gatehouse is likely to have been the tower keeps with round-towered angles and *chemins-de-ronde* of C14 France, as at the royal castle of Vincennes. The idea was taken up widely elsewhere in Europe for both gatehouses and donjons, from England (as at Nunney in Somerset) to Italy, though the relationship between parapet and caphouse suggests a French prototype directly inspired the Stirling gate. A striking feature here is its imposing triplet of gateways, with smaller pedestrian ways flanking the central carriageway; each of these has a round-headed arch within a rectangular labelled frame, with provision for both portcullises and timber doors. (One portcullis still remains in place in the w pedestrian passage.) Triple openings to afford prominence to an entrance façade had, of course, been common for several centuries in major churches throughout Europe. There are also a number of earlier gatehouses which have them, from the early C15 gate of St Osyth's Priory (Essex) to some of the city gates of Bruges, while parallels have also been suggested with the city gates of Classical and Renaissance Italy. They were also to be seen by the mid 1530s in the gateways of Whitehall Palace in London. Their appearance in such impressive form at Stirling c. 1500 is nevertheless precocious.

At the w end of the Forework, the PRINCE'S TOWER is of three storeys, with a fourth in the caphouse. Apart from altera-tions to the windows and the loss of the merlons of its crenel-lated parapet, it is externally complete. The Elphinstone Tower, which rises from a lower level, now has only its two lowest storeys and is capped by a late C17 embrasured parapet for artillery (for description of the interiors *see* below).

OUTER CLOSE

Within the Forework is the OUTER CLOSE. It is dominated to N and w by the soaring gable of the Great Hall and the most impressive of the Palace's façades, as a prelude to the royal splendours of the Inner Close (q.v.). Leading down the E side of the Hall is the road to the North Gate, around which are ancil-lary buildings, some of which were separately enclosed by the early C18 in an area known as the King's Office Houses. Imme-diately E of the Forework gatehouse is the FORT MAJOR'S HOUSE (earlier the Storekeeper's House), with a three-bay, two-storeyed early C19 ashlar front of pleasing proportions. Its later functions had previously been supplied by the N block of the King's Old Building. Next to it is the Main Guard House, a handsome late C18 two-storeyed structure with a three-bay loggia between salient pavilions, which replaced a simpler one-and-a-half-storeyed range projecting at r. angles behind the Forework. Beyond the Main Guard House, modern steps lead down into the two remaining floors of the ELPHINSTONE TOWER. On the lower floor are two vaulted cellars, on the upper floor a kitchen, a room with a fireplace and a latrine, and a small lobby off the spiral stair which connected the floors. It seems likely the tower was designed to provide a substantial self-contained lodging for some officer of the castle; the upper storeys were probably demolished at the time of the Revolution of 1689 in order to provide a platform for the three-gun battery, at which time the lower storeys would have been packed with earth.

Running SW from the Elphinstone Tower, against the curtain wall of c. 1500 which stretches back from it to the North Gate, are the restored GREAT KITCHENS; they are now largely hidden below a turf-covered bank, and it is uncertain what their original external appearance was. The Great Hall was first served by kitchens in the rebuilt superstructure of the North Gate (q.v.) and the range along the inner face of the curtain was built to supplement those. The Great Kitchens may have been linked with the Hall through the North Gate in a way that is no longer clear. They had their vaults removed in 1689, when the Grand Battery was formed above them, and were infilled to provide a firm gun platform. Seven large cannon embrasures were constructed in the new parapet wall above the curtain here, with smaller embrasures for hand-held guns at each end. The central section of the Kitchens was excavated and revaulted in 1921; three barrel-vaulted chambers, with a barrel-vaulted corridor running along part of their SW side, are now accessible. The N chamber was a bakehouse, with mouths for two ovens behind a twin-arched fireplace, and a servery hatch opening on to the corridor. The central chamber was probably for food preparation and had two hatches to the corridor. The kitchen itself was to the S, and had a twin-arched fireplace. The complete range was clearly originally longer, and may have extended SE to the Elphinstone Tower and NW to the North Gate. But rising above the chamber at the N end of the kitchens, and obscuring its relationship with the North Gate, is the MASTER GUNNER'S HOUSE. It dates back to the late C17 or earlier, but was much remodelled in the C18 and C19 when its SE face was given four symmetrically arranged windows: it was used as the Barrack Warden's Quarters by 1870. (For description of the North Gate *see* below.)

### INNER CLOSE

The INNER CLOSE, at the heart of the castle and on the crown of the rock, was the area around which the main buildings of the royal residence were grouped. Before the late C15, this area evidently had buildings across it on an E–W diagonal alignment. The chief survivor of this earlier alignment of buildings is the block at the S end of the King's Old Building (behind the early C18 stair to the upper floor of the Palace), which originally extended further E, and is now known to have been a chapel. On a parallel alignment to that block were the pre-1594 Chapel Royal and the North Curtain Wall. It was probably James IV who decided to create a more regular quadrangular space.

### KING'S OLD BUILDING

The KING'S OLD BUILDING has an elongated L-shape and possibly incorporates older structures on the earlier alignment at its s end. It extends along the w side of the Inner Close, at the highest point of the castle rock, rising directly above the rock edge, from where it commands superb views across to the hills around Loch Lomond. This was clearly one of the most prestigious sites within the castle, and internal evidence for planning and architectural details suggests it was James IV's own lodging. It was thus probably the building referred to in 1496 as the 'king's house', for which there is a contract with the royal master mason, *Walter Merlioun*, in the Treasurer's Accounts. The main rooms were elevated above a ground floor subdivided into a series of barrel-vaulted compartments, and were reached by a spiral stair in a square projection topped by an octagonal caphouse. Rooms which appear to have been the king's own hall and outer chamber extend to the N of the stair, with a small kitchen to the s; an inner chamber was probably in the lower range projecting at r. angles from the N end of the main block. Traces have been found of large rectangular windows in the main rooms, looking over the Inner Close, and fragments of green-glazed tiled floors within the window embrasures; on the evidence of surveys of 1719 and 1741 the rooms were covered by wagon ceilings of polygonal profile. A latrine draining over the cliff at the N end may have been connected to the main building by a timber structure, since it seems the main N gable was initially well to the s of the latrine, and there could have been a closet and wardrobe within that timber structure. (Striking analogies for the overall planning and forms of the King's Old Building are to be found in the s range at Castle Campbell, the principal lowland house of the earls of Argyll.) Timber galleries may also have run in front of the kitchen, where there is now a stone lean-to.

During the C17, C18 and C19, the building was greatly modified to provide accommodation for officers of the garrison by the insertion of extra floors and subdivisions, and the piercing of new windows; some of the lower floor vaults were removed or modified. The N end of the building was burned out in 1855, and that part was rebuilt and enlarged in baronial style by the architect *Robert William Billings*, whose publications were of particular importance for publicizing the qualities of Scottish medieval and Renaissance architecture. Particular emphasis was given to the 'Douglas Room', at the E end of the N wing, within which it was then thought that James II had murdered the Earl of Douglas in 1432; it is lined with cast iron linenfold panelling in timber framing. The whole building is now occupied by the Regimental Headquarters and Museum of the Argyll and Sutherland Highlanders.

As already said, the rectangular block at the s end of the King's Old Building, behind the stair to the upper floor of the Palace, is on an E–W alignment and probably predates other structures around the Close. Excavation below the NW corner of the Palace has shown that this block originally extended further E, while excavations within it in 1997 exposed a number of burials; this shows it was one of the chapels within the castle, and perhaps the 'ald kyrk' for work on which *John Yorkston* was paid in 1504–5. In this particularly prestigious situation it may have been the privy chapel serving the royal lodgings.

GREAT HALL

48 The restored GREAT HALL, the most ambitious and impressive building of its type in Scotland, is on the E side of the Inner Close, where it faces across to the King's Old Building. Though a tradition dating back to the late C16 suggested it was built for James III by his (largely apocryphal) favourite Thomas Cochrane, there can be little doubt that the present building was largely or entirely erected for James IV. It was evidently under construction around the same years as the Forework and the King's Old Building, references in the Treasurer's Accounts to plastering in 1503 indicating it was then nearing completion. Records refer to previous halls of various kinds within the castle, presumably serving both as the outer rooms of lodgings and as the principal public room of the castle; but nothing of this scale had been attempted before either in Stirling or in Scotland as a whole. It is a basically rectangular structure about 42 by 14.25m., elevated to the level of the Inner Close above a vaulted basement (which is fully exposed towards the Outer Close). Towards its S end, a symmetrical pair of projecting bay windows lights the E and W sides of the dais, with ribs applied to the soffits of their rear-arches giving the appearance of rib vaulting. The E bay was treated externally more richly than the W bay, with transoms in the form of intersecting arcs, and elaborate miniature tabernacle work on the piers. Otherwise, the main source of lighting is a series of paired rectangular upper windows above a stringcourse; they are set on the inner wall plane within segmentally arched openings to the exterior. Between some of the windows are image tabernacles.

The Hall is entered through a doorway towards the N end of its W wall, and there was presumably originally a timber bridge across a sunken area on this side. Internally there are five fireplaces, one for the dais at the S end, and the others arranged asymmetrically along the E and W walls. Four spiral stairways run between the main floor of the Hall and the other levels, two being within the screened-off service area immediately within the entrance. The NW stair runs the full height of the Hall, connecting basement, Hall, the loft over the screens, and the wallwalk behind the crenellated parapet. That at the NE corner connects only basement and Hall. An externally projecting stair near the middle of the E wall connects basement, Hall, a loft within an arched recess at upper window level (presumably for the use of privileged observers or musicians), and the wallhead. A fourth stair in the N jamb of the SE bay was possibly suppressed at an early stage, but had connected the dais and a mezzanine level below the bay; this stair is now restored, though the details of its caphouse are conjectural. The Hall is covered by a replica of the original hammerbeam roof based on survey drawings of 1719 and 1741; it has significant relationships with the contemporary roof over the smaller hall of Edinburgh Castle without being identical.

Externally, a restored pentice runs along the w side of the Hall, towards the Inner Close. Initially the ground level of the Inner Close here was a little lower, and beneath the pentice was a sunken area giving light to a series of windows and doorways opening into the w side of the Hall basement. When the ground level next to the Great Hall was raised, perhaps in the later c16, the sunken area was covered by a segmental barrel vault, across which the surface of the Close was extended. Probably around the same time, a lean-to service gallery was built along the N side of the Hall, connecting the Hall with the servery area between Hall and kitchens on the first floor of the North Gate.

The Hall was under construction at the time of James IV's marriage to Margaret Tudor in 1503. At this period there is evidence of renewed architectural interchanges with England after many decades during which Scottish patrons and masons had generally preferred to pursue their own course. It is therefore significant that the Hall's overall design is related to that of a number of English royal halls, such as that at Eltham Palace. This is seen particularly in the choice of a hammerbeam roof (as in the slightly later hall at Edinburgh Castle) and in the paired bays flanking the dais (a feature that was possibly also reflected in the hall at Falkland Palace). It is also worth noting that the plasterer at work in 1503 was said to be English. Nevertheless, despite the English inspiration for some elements, these ideas were firmly assimilated to their Scottish context.

The Hall was modified on several occasions. In 1594 it was fitted out for the baptismal celebrations for Prince Henry, when a new doorway at the centre of the w wall (now blocked) was probably cut. After the Union of the kingdoms in 1707, and the subsequent decline of royal interest in the castle, in 1709–10 there were proposals to subdivide it to form a smaller hall and a chapel with barrack-rooms above. It is doubtful how much was done, but by 1719 there was an inserted floor along at least part of its length. Also probably in the c18 the pentice along its w face was fully enclosed, and the wallhead parapet had its crenellations removed. The greatest changes came in the later 1790s, when it was subdivided to provide barracks for a greatly enlarged complement of soldiers, probably by *John Sanders*. The hammerbeam roof (which by then was probably in a precarious state) was replaced by a utilitarian structure and the parapet entirely removed. Two additional floors, five cross-walls and two flights of stairs were inserted, and the original windows were replaced by sash windows lighting the individual barrack-rooms. In the later c19 growing appreciation of the Hall's architectural merits led to calls for its restoration, but this only became possible after 1964; restoration was completed forty-five years later.

When James IV commissioned the King's Old Building as his lodging he was a bachelor, and it seems that after his marriage in 1503 existing lodgings (possibly on the site of the w quarter of the later Palace) were simply refurbished for his queen's use. James V successively married two French princesses (Madeleine, daughter of François I, in 1537; and Mary of Guise-Lorraine, daughter of the Duke of Guise, in 1538) and it was to house both himself and his queen that the Palace was built. The intention was clearly to meet this need in a manner as creditable to Scotland as possible, resulting in an enormously impressive building that is arguably one of the first of clearly Renaissance design to have been raised in the British Isles. Together with the work carried out for him at Falkland, Holyrood and Linlithgow, the Stirling Palace reveals James V as an architectural patron of major importance.

The Palace is a highly enriched quadrangular structure along the s side of the Inner Close, which extends back to the Forework and abuts the Prince's Tower, with imposing façades to N, E and S. The W side, which was perhaps never finished, partly collapsed in the early C17. It incorporates some earlier structures within its lower storey and at its SW corner and, though these were not allowed to impinge on the design, the need to align the four main façades of the Palace towards the areas they face did necessitate some irregularities of planning. Work was probably started after the Principal Master of Works, *Sir James Hamilton* of Finnart, was recorded as coming to the castle in 1537–8, presumably to oversee the work; dendrochronological analysis of timbers in the queen's lodging has given a felling date of 1538. The designer of the Palace was possibly one of several French masons known to have been in James V's employment, among whom were *Mogin Martin*, *Nicholas Roy* and *John Roytell*, though it is likely that Hamilton of Finnart was himself closely involved in the design process. The shell may have been nearing completion by the king's death in 1542, though it is doubtful if it was fully completed for several years, and there were payments for glazing the rooms of the queen's lodging as late as 1558.

The Palace is of outstanding interest as an example of Renaissance royal planning, magnificently reflecting contemporary ideas on royal authority and the increasingly sophisticated protocol of courtly life. It contains a symmetrical pair of royal lodgings, each composed of a hall (or outer hall), an outer or mid chamber (or inner hall), and a chamber, with a series of smaller closets within. The rooms are carefully graded in scale from the larger spaces of the outer halls, to which many would have access, through the progressively smaller spaces of the outer chambers and chambers, to the diminutive closets, into which only the king's or queen's closest intimates and servants would have been received. (By 1585 the main rooms were described as outer hall, own hall and chamber, but by 1613–14 the middle room was called the Chamber of Presence, and by 1628–9 the outer hall was called the Guard Hall.) These rooms are grouped around three sides of a rectangular central courtyard (known as the Lion's Den, possibly because a lion bought for the king in Flanders in 1537 was housed there), with a gallery connecting them on the W side. From a central doorway in that gallery a stair (now restored in timber) gave access to the courtyard. The King's Closets are in a lean-to range along the E side of the central courtyard, while the Queen's Closets evidently stretched back behind the Forework wall to the Gatehouse, but are now lost. Set behind the Forework wall, the queen's lodging had the added advantage of a raised terrace at wall-walk height. The King's Outer Chamber is connected to the dais end of the Great Hall by a bridge over the route from the Outer to the Inner Close. In its present form the bridge is of Gothick design, but there are indications of its original arch and windows at the SW angle of the hall, which indicate that the earlier bridge was on a slightly different alignment from the one now seen.

Though the principal rooms were level with the upper side of the Inner Close, with a ground-floor entrance at the NW corner, the steep slope of the land meant that a vaulted lower storey was required below much of the building, resulting in a particularly impressive façade towards the Outer Close. It is thus not clear how far the ground-floor entrance was a matter of choice, or a consequence of the castle's complex ground levels. A first-floor (*piano nobile*) position for the lodgings would certainly be more expected. The entrance was at the point closest to the King's Old Building, and it is possible that it was intended to link the two buildings in some way, as was certainly proposed in 1709–10. (The link could have been a timber gallery of a type known to have existed elsewhere in the castle, and it would be interesting to know where the timber and glass gallery for which payments were made in the Treasurer's Accounts for 1576–8 was built.) The top floor of the Palace was partly within the roof space, set back behind the crenellated parapet; it was lit by gableted dormers (now gone, but is the gablet with the crowned initials MR on the Counterguard terrace from here?) and by windows in two crowstepped gables surmounted by heraldic beasts at the ends of the E façade. A small winding stair connects the top floor with one of the King's Closets, though the original main means of access to that floor is unknown (the present stair, adjacent to the entrance porch, is *c.* 1700).

The N, E and S PALACE FAÇADES have alternating recessed and salient panels. In a somewhat Mannerist reversal of what might be expected, the large heavily barred rectangular windows are within the salient panels, below segmental tympana inscribed J5, while in the recessed sections are statues elevated on two-stage decorated balusters beneath multi-cusped arches. Above the arched recesses, and in front of the parapet, are smaller statues on balusters. Defining the base of the parapet is a deep cornice decorated with winged angel heads and spiralling ribbons, and there is a stringcourse with angel heads below the main windows. The sources of this tantalizingly hybrid design will probably never be fully understood. In the alternation of raised and recessed sections capped by a crenellated parapet, is it even possible to see some reflection of the keeps which still formed a cherished element of some royal palaces in England and France (the Tower of London and Fontainebleau for example)? And in the alternation of windows with niches for statues is there a Scottish response to a type of façade design to be found in contemporary prestigious buildings across Europe, from Rome to Heidelberg, Bruges and Paris? Whatever the underlying sources of inspiration, however, some elements of this architectural vocabulary have their closest counterparts in France. Multicusped arches above statuary recesses are found in many French buildings. Among these are the frontispiece of 1501–12 at the ducal palace at Nancy, where the polygonal stair tower of the rear courtyard wing (now destroyed) had two tiers of statues on balusters. (Nancy was one of the principal residences of the dukes of Lorraine, the senior representatives of Mary of Guise's own family.) Multi-cusped arches, together with elongated balusters to support statues, are also to be found on the façade of the main stair at Châteaudun, started in 1502 (a home of the family of Mary of Guise's first husband, the Duc de Longueville). Nevertheless, while such comparisons help to clarify the wider European background against which the Stirling Palace was produced, it remains an enigmatic and only partly comprehensible building.

The Palace façades are enriched by a virtuoso display of carving that cannot be described in detail here. Several hands were evidently responsible and the quality varies but, though most of those hands were probably native, the strongly emphasized realism and solid characterization suggest inspiration from the work of German artists, and some of the more classicizing figures are known to have been derived from the engravings of Hans Burgkmair. The statues include one of James V himself (NE corner) and depictions of a hermaphroditic devil (s face) and of St Michael (one of the patrons of the Chapel, s end of E face). It has been demonstrated, however, that there is a strong sun theme running through the predominating depictions of Classical gods and goddesses. At the higher level, the smaller statues along the s side, which overlook the Forework, depict soldiers, including a crossbowman. Some of the finest and best preserved carvings are the baluster-supporting corbels along the E and N façades: one, with a dragon biting a woman's breast, may symbolize Luxuria or Lust, suggesting that others also had allegorical significance. Among the most delightful carvings are the creatures acting as corbels and waterspouts, including what appear to be pigs, elephants and a range of mythical beasts.

Internally, the best features to survive *in situ* are the fireplaces in the main rooms, which have three-quarter round or square shafts carrying capitals with heavily carved anthropomorphic, zoomorphic or foliate decoration. Traces of a tiled floor have been found in one room, and at least some of the rooms had richly decorated ceilings. The best of these ceilings was evidently in the King's Outer Chamber, which had oak roundels (known as the Stirling Heads) set within a grid pattern of ribs (according to an engraving by Edward Blore of 1817). The heads were taken down in 1777, when they were threatening to fall, and only thirty-eight now wholly or partly survive, most of which are displayed within the Palace, while others are held by the National Museum of Scotland. A number of the heads (including a jester) are so carefully characterized that they could represent figures at the court, while others illustrate mythological or biblical subjects. These roundels were one of the clearest indicators of the Classicism of the Palace and, as with some details of the exterior, many parallels for their use in various contexts can be found in France, e.g. at the Ducal Palace of Nancy; within Scotland, the earliest roundels may have been those of stone along the courtyard façades at Falkland Palace, started the year before the Stirling Palace. Significantly, the wright *Robert Robertson* had worked at Falkland before coming to Stirling in 1541. Others who could have worked on the heads are the French craftsman *Andrew Mansioun* and the king's master wright *John Drummond*.

The incorporation of earlier work at the NW corner of the Palace, together with the precarious condition of the rock on the W side, evidently contributed to structural problems. By 1583 the outer part of the W range was in a state of collapse, and similar reports were made by the master mason *William Wallace* in 1625, though it was only in the 1670s that limited remedial works were carried out. By then the main function of the Palace was the use of the top floor as a residence for the Governor. Bolection-moulded fireplaces and doorcases on that floor probably date from works associated with the masons *Tobias* and *Thomas Bachop* between 1699 and 1703. Presumably at the instigation of the 6th Earl of Mar, new windows were cut through the parapet on the outer façades, and through heightened walls towards the Lion's Den. Mar probably also had the new enclosed stair to the upper floor constructed, together with the two-storeyed porch over the entrance to the Palace itself; these front the truncated diagonally-set block at the S end of the King's Old Building, now identified as a chapel. By the C19 the Palace was increasingly used by the garrison, and many changes and additions were made, some of which have since been reversed. These included a cook-house added against its W side, an octagonal latrine within the Lion's Den, an archway between the two royal bedchambers, inserted subdivisions, and the formation of a large officers' mess hall with a timber wagon ceiling at the W end of the upper floor of the S range.

CHAPEL ROYAL                                                  46

A chapel was the first recorded building at the castle, in the early C12, and for much of the Middle Ages there were two chapels within its walls. The main chapel, dedicated to St Mary and St Michael, was probably always towards the N side of what eventually became the Inner Close. Archaeological excavations have traced two earlier buildings below the present structure, one of far smaller scale and simple rectangular plan, and the other a much larger building flanked by lateral spaces, presumably in the form of aisles, and with a central S projection assumed to have been a porch. Both James III and James IV spent considerable sums on the chapel structure and its furnishings (the choir stalls were specified as the model for those of Glasgow Cathedral in 1506). By 1501 James IV had magnificently endowed a collegiate foundation as a basis for its becoming the Chapel Royal of Scotland. Since the alignment of the chapel which existed *c.* 1500 meant that it would have partly blocked the entrance to James IV's new Great Hall, it is likely that he hoped to rebuild it further back, but that he was prevented by his death at Flodden in 1513. A report of 1583 makes clear that the chapel was still regarded as inconveniently placed and also in bad repair.

The present Chapel Royal was built in 1594 for the baptism of Prince Henry, the son of James VI and Queen Anne of Denmark, and was reputed to have cost £100,000 Scots. In rebuilding, it was decided to set it out on a more appropriate axis for the Inner Close as regularized by James IV, leaving the façade of the Great Hall fully exposed. The documentation for the building is lost, but it was perhaps a work of the royal Master of Works, *William Schaw*. It is a large rectangular structure measuring 34.3 by 11.4m., connected by a bridging section to the King's Old Building at its W end (where there was perhaps a royal gallery), and eventually also to the Great Hall at its E end. There may have been a vestry off its N side. The main façade, of ashlar, is on the S side, towards the Inner Close.

The central doorway is emphasized by a frontispiece designed as a Classical triumphal arch, with paired columns flanking an arched doorway. Flanking this are three pairs of round-headed windows within round containing arches, a type ultimately inspired by those of Florentine quattrocento palazzi. Within the containing arches are faint traces of applied cartouches, the 'siferis' (cyphers) of which were repainted in 1628–9. Surveys of 1719 and 1741 show the chapel was covered by a polygonal wagon ceiling, and the accounts of 1628–9 record it as painted in predominantly 'blew gray' colours, with floral trails and 'antikis' on the ribs. The main historic feature is now a heavily restored painted entablature with decoration extending upwards into the two gable walls; this was executed as part of a wider scheme of decoration in 1628–9 by the artist *Valentine Jenkin* in advance of Charles I's visit of 1633. There is a *trompe l'oeil* window in the W gable, and within the frieze of the painted entablature cartouches with the honours of Scotland (sword, sceptre and crown) and the royal cypher of Charles I, interspersed with festoons. These paintings were rediscovered in the 1930s and subsequently restored. A surviving but badly damaged pulpit, possibly that for which the minister John Duncanson was paid £20 in 1574–6, may have been used in this Chapel.

Like the other buildings around the Inner Close the Chapel was adapted to various uses after 1707. By the time of a survey of 1911 it contained the soldiers' dining hall and school-room at ground-floor level with store-rooms on an inserted floor. These were removed in the 1930s, but proposals to restore the whole building for use as the Chapel Royal of Scotland were interrupted by the outbreak of war; reinstatement of the ceiling (in modern materials) was eventually completed in 1996.

In the Captain's Garden behind the Chapel Royal and the King's Old Building is an early C18 stone-vaulted POWDER MAGAZINE, on the site of one built in 1681. Later converted into the Quarter Master's Store and Office, when new windows were cut through the walls, it is now a meeting room. Also in the garden, the shaft of a C17 SUNDIAL, with the remains of four tiers of panels framing sunk dials of a variety of geometrical forms.

Leaving the Inner Close, one may return to the Outer Close and down through the North Gate to reach the Nether Bailey.

## NORTH GATE AND NETHER BAILEY

The NORTH GATE interconnects the main part of the castle and the Nether Bailey, though before the latter assumed its final form it is possible that the gate was an external entrance, supplementing the main gateway on the side facing the burgh. The North Gate is traditionally known as the Mint, though there is no certain evidence that coins were ever minted here. It may incorporate the earliest upstanding masonry within the castle, the outer section probably forming part of the work carried out for Robert II in 1381. That outer section has a dog-legged barrel-vaulted passage opening through a pointed arch equipped with a chase for a portcullis towards the Nether Bailey. There was a postern gate in the W flank of the passage, bridged over when the superstructure was rebuilt. The form of the original super-structure of this gatehouse is unknown, since it has been rebuilt several times. The main changes were perhaps in 1511–12, when the Treasurer's Accounts record payments to the mason *John Lockhart* for work on the great tower in the N part of the castle. To provide adequate space for kitchens to serve the Great Hall, the gatehouse was extended S and W, giving space for a rectangular first-floor room vaulted in two compartments carried on two central segmental arches, and with a large fireplace (now reinstated) in each compartment. W of the gate, a triangular link building containing a servery was formed in the space between kitchen and Great Hall, partly by bridging over the space between the North Gate and the adjacent curtain wall; hatches open from the kitchen into this servery. Only part of the S wall of this link building survives. Possibly as an extension to this operation, the lean-to gallery was built at the N end of the Great Hall, though clear evidence of how all these elements were connected has been lost. The gate was further heightened in at least two stages on the evidence of a change of masonry and of the way the NE half-gable is simply butted up against the chimneystack. The second floor was entered from the adjacent wall-walk, and by 1719 was used as the Gunner's Store; above that was an attic.

The NETHER BAILEY, beyond the North Gate and to the N of the central part of the castle, is a large irregular enclosure following the contours of the rock. It is contained by a curtain wall of various dates. On its E side is a postern doorway walled up in 1689 with the C19 (?) inscription 'OLD SALLYPORT' on its lintel; Slezer shows a spur of wall affording protection to this postern. There was a second postern through the W wall of the Nether Bailey, which was possibly the main means of access to the gardens in the C16; payment in 1530 to *John Bog* for his work 'to mak ane passage doun... to the park' could refer to this, since the N boundary wall of the garden evidently joined the castle wall at this point.

Three POWDER MAGAZINES, with a single-storeyed L-shaped guard house to the SE (the latter subsequently converted to a guard house and prison) were built *c.* 1810, and occupy much of the level ground within the Nether Bailey. The magazines are covered by parabolic vaults, and had baffled vents in the side walls; they are surrounded by a high wall. At their NW end a fourth magazine was constructed in a separate enclosure not long after 1860 for the Volunteer Corps recently raised. In 1908 the three main magazines (but not the fourth, which was left unchanged) were converted into transit stores, and the porches at the SE end of each removed before they were connected by link buildings; windows were pierced through the side walls and the baffled vents blocked.

### 'KING'S KNOT' AND ROYAL GARDENS

There were certainly gardens in the valley to the SW from the time of James IV, and probably from much earlier. They were overlooked by some of the most prestigious buildings within the castle, and the main route down to them seems to have been from the W side of the Nether Bailey; any other route was perhaps lost when the Esplanade was formed in 1809. The gardens underwent major restoration before Charles I's visit of 1633: the English gardener *William Watts* was at work from 1625 (the present earthworks probably date from then), while the Masters of Works' Accounts record activity in 1628–9 on the king's orchard and garden. The most prominent feature is a three-tiered octagonal stepped mound within a square pattern of paths. N of this is a lower earthwork parterre with a cross-pattern of paths leading to a central square of paths enclosing a circle. These earthworks presumably formed the basis for part of a formal garden layout in which the main lines would have been emphasized by low borders of trimmed hedges, with specimen shrubs to emphasize certain points. On the lower platforms of the parterre there may have been more complex patterns of hedges. Somewhat confusingly, however, the most prominent earthworks appear on neither Vorsterman's view of the castle of 1673–4 nor on maps of 1725 and 1740, and the latter maps show additional parterres to the N, of which little is now visible. While there seems little doubt that the main earthworks date from the 1620s, this discrepancy suggests there has been more substantial restoration than might otherwise be suspected.

## TOWN WALL

Substantial stretches of the battered defensive wall built in random
whin rubble in 1547 still reinforce the wooded rock face on the
SW side of the castle ridge. An ascent can be made below the walls
following BACK WALK from Dumbarton Road to the Castle
Esplanade. First conceived by W. Edmonston of Cambuswallace
in 1723 and relandscaped by *Stirling District Council* in 1993,
the walk gives increasingly panoramic views across the Carse.
Behind Allan's School (*see* Public Buildings, below) the climb
passes under a single surviving gunpowder BASTION. This is a 44
powerfully sculptural beehive fortification of domed masonry
embedded in the hillside. The structure has been adapted as a
doocot, though a few primitive gunloops can still be seen. Along
the wall there is evidence of forestair accesses to the gardens in
the tofts behind. At Academy Road a mural TABLET, dated 1530,
recalls Robert Spittal, tailor to James IV (*see* Old High School in
Public Buildings, below). Higher still, a path returns to climb up
to Cowane's Hospital (*see* Public Buildings, below) and the Church
of the Holy Rude (*see* below). At length the Walk reaches the
summit where, at the NW corner of the Valley Cemetery (*see*
Cemeteries, below), a flight of steps rises to the Esplanade.

## CHURCH OF THE HOLY RUDE*

The late medieval churches of the greater burghs collectively
represent what is arguably Scotland's greatest contribution to the
art of their period, and Holy Rude at Stirling is one of the most
ambitious of them. The fact that most burghs were single parishes,
and that at this stage of their existence few had tolbooths likely to
provide a rival focus of civic loyalty, gave a particular significance
to the mother church in the community's life. The burgh churches
thus came to be regarded as the most important architectural
expression of corporate pride, and a number were rebuilt on a scale
that surpassed that of the lesser cathedrals. In order to achieve
this, several burghs – including Stirling – had to overcome the
problem that the fabric of the chancel was the responsibility of the
body to which the church was appropriated (Dunfermline Abbey
in the case of Stirling). In such cases it is a striking demonstration
of the significance of the churches for burgh life that the onus of
rebuilding the chancel might be taken on with that of the nave.

The services and rituals performed within the churches gave
spiritual meaning to the pride expressed in the buildings themselves. In several cases this was emphasized when their clergy were
established as a collegiate body, which ensured a perpetual round
of religious observation based on that of the cathedrals and religious houses.

The lavish expenditure on the burgh churches is particularly
remarkable when it is remembered that the later Middle Ages was

* This account has been written by Richard Fawcett.

a period of economic recession; though this in itself partly explains why several of the burgh churches were never fully completed, and Stirling is one of those. But despite its unfinished state, Holy Rude is highly impressive. In particular, the eastward expansion of the building during the final phase of building called for lofty sub-structures to support the new work, and the E apse consequently towers over the NW end of St John Street, offering one of the most memorable views of any church in Scotland.

## BUILDING CHRONOLOGY

The first church in the Stirling area was possibly at St Ninian's (q.v.), earlier known as Eccles, where there was perhaps a foundation as early as the Ninianic mission in the C5. The earliest certain reference to a church in Stirling itself was *c.* 1150, when David confirmed an earlier grant of two churches within the vill (one possibly being that in the castle) to Dunfermline Abbey. Nothing remains of any building of the C12, the present church being the result of total reconstruction in two main phases in the C15 and early C16.

### The medieval campaigns

The spur to rebuilding was evidently a fire, on the evidence of a grant towards repairs recorded in the Exchequer Rolls for 1414, and since the nave was the first part rebuilt it was presumably that which was most damaged. But heraldic evidence suggests its reconstruction was a protracted process, and it is possible new impetus was given by damage resulting from the Douglas riots of 1455, since there was a further royal grant in 1456. The arms of Adam Cosour and Katherine Fotheringham in the W bay of the S nave aisle vault indicate a date between the 1440s and 1480s for the completion of vaulting there, though, since Adam is known to have founded altars in the S aisle in the 1470s, a date towards the end of that period is more likely. Cosour also added St Mary's Aisle off the W end of the S aisle in 1484. St Andrew's Aisle, off the E end of the N aisle, also appears to have been completed about the same time for the Forestar family.

The start of rebuilding the chancel is marked by an agreement of 1507 with Abbot James Beaton of Dunfermline, by which the burgh agreed to carry out the work in exchange for certain concessions. Timber was being provided in 1523, presumably for the roof, though in 1529 the mason *John Couttis* was said to be still at work. The arms of Bruce of Stenhouse and Airth on one of the buttresses support the idea that building was in progress around the 1520s. Completion of the W tower, along with unfulfilled proposals to heighten the nave, probably also date from this campaign. But it is likely work had been halted by 1546 when a college was founded, with the vicar as its head; a collegiate foundation had probably been the ultimate goal at the time the chancel was started. Indications of unfulfilled intentions to add a third storey over the chancel as well as the nave, to build transepts and a central tower, and to construct a spire over the W tower, suggest that shortage of funds prevented completion of a scheme that was simply too ambitious for the burgh's resources.

## Post-Reformation work

The church's post-Reformation history was almost as complex as its medieval history. In *c.* 1656 the building was split into two separate churches by a dividing wall on the W side of where the transepts would have been; by this time the first of a random accretion of galleries was being installed. A survey of 1803 showed that the West Church, in the nave, had E, N and W galleries, with the pulpit against the second arcade pier from the E on the S; at that stage three projecting chantry aisles and the S nave porch still survived. In the East Church, which included both the chancel and the crossing area, the pulpit stood against the first pier from the W of the N arcade. Stirling was no exception to the general rule that invasively draconian restorations in the earlier part of the C19 were followed by more scholarly reconstructions from the later part of the century, as greater understanding of medieval architecture developed. As the first stage in this process, the East Church was restored and re-ordered by *James Millar* in 1803, and the West Church by *James Gillespie Graham* in 1818. In the East Church Millar relocated the pulpit within an elegantly curved exedra beneath the crossing. In the nave, Graham demolished all projections apart from St Andrew's Aisle, and placed plaster vaults over the central space. Further restoration of the East Church was carried out by *James Collie* in 1869, when a new entrance front was created in the S wall of the still incomplete S transept. In 1911–14 the West Church was thoughtfully restored by *Thomas Ross*. The two churches were eventually reunited as a single building in 1936–40 by *James Miller* (of Glasgow), who also rebuilt a porch over the S nave doorway and extended the transepts to a length closer to what had probably been initially intended, but stopped short of adding a crossing tower.

### SITE, PLAN AND STRUCTURE

Holy Rude is set out on a correctly orientated axis across an irregularly sloping site, a combination of circumstances that caused its later builders major problems. Although the small terrace on which its central part stands was probably sufficient for its presumably far smaller C12 first building, it was inadequate for the church in its final extended form. Consequently the ground to the W and NW stands higher than the interior, while the chancel is elevated well above ground level, soaring obliquely above St John Street where it turns to become Castle Wynd.

The NAVE, which is almost unseen from the street because of the angle at which the church is set, rises to a lower height than the E arm, though there is evidence of a secondary intention to

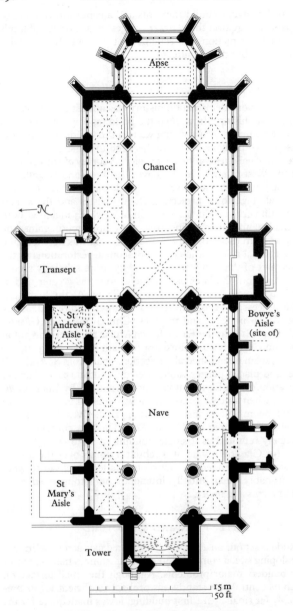

Stirling, Church of the Holy Rude. Plan.

increase its height. It is of five bays with an aisle along each side, and has a W TOWER of telescoped form with a stair turret at its NW corner. Openings through the E face of the tower point to an intention to heighten the nave at a later stage of building operations. Against the second bay from the W on the S is a porch

covering the main lay entrance, a modern replacement of an
earlier structure. There was a smaller corresponding N doorway
(now blocked) without a porch. The main processional entrance
(now also blocked) was through the W tower. At least three chapel
aisles were added against the nave flanks in the course of building to serve as chantries and burial places for the families of
their founders. These have gone except for that built for the
Forestar family and dedicated to St Andrew in the E bay on the
N side, in the re-entrant angle with the transept. The lost chapels
were Bowye's Aisle and a chapel for the Cosour family. Bowye's
Aisle was off the E bay of the S nave aisle, corresponding to St
Andrew's Aisle on the N; by the 1630s it had been taken over
by the earl of Stirling. The Cosour family chapel, dedicated to
St Mary, was off the W bay of the N aisle.

W of the chancel are mid-C20 TRANSEPTS of unequal length;
they are of pink sandstone to differentiate them from the medieval
work. Transepts, with a second tower above them, had evidently
been part of the intention when the chancel was being rebuilt in
the early C16. (The only other Scottish church known to have
been planned for twin axial towers is Kelso Abbey, of the C12.)

The CHANCEL is of three aisled bays, terminating in a five-
sided E apse slightly wider than the main body of the chancel;
the clergy had a small entrance in the W bay of the choir N aisle
(now blocked). Although it is taller than the nave, there are
indications of an unfulfilled intention to give the chancel even
greater height, because of the way the present clearstorey seems
to have been first intended as a gallery, suggesting a true clearstorey may also have been planned.

Several aspects of the design exemplify the openness to continental influences of Scottish patrons and masons at this time,
as might be expected in one of the major trading burghs. These
aspects include the telescoped form of the W tower, the polygonal
E apse, the lateral gables of the nave chapels and the cylindrical
nave arcade piers. Some of these may have been inspired by
Netherlandish prototypes.


EXTERIOR

The APSE of the post-1507 E limb rises through both levels of the
chancel, and has widely projecting buttresses with multiple offsets. There are tabernacles at the level below the windows on
both the buttresses and E apse face; the buttresses are capped
by disproportionately meagre pinnacles. A crenellated parapet
runs round the wallhead, behind which is a stone-flagged roof
with a crowstepped E gable. The E face of the apse, wider than
its other faces, has a six-light window with the simplified rectilinear tracery which had a limited fashion around the time of
James IV's English marriage. The round-headed main lights,
with undivided panel lights above them, are grouped within a
pair of sub-arches between which is a pair of curved daggers.
The other windows of the apse and chancel are variants on
standard late medieval types. The three-light windows in the

angled faces of the apse have light heads linked by intersecting arcs, above which are inward-deflected daggers. The N and S apse flanks have a related type of tracery, in which the intersecting arcs are omitted, and there is a pointed quatrefoil at the window head above the daggers. All these windows have arched transoms at mid-height.

9    The CHANCEL is considerably taller than the nave, as is particularly evident in the great height of the chancel aisles. Dividing the aisles into bays are pinnacled and tabernacled buttresses similar to those around the apse; the tabernacle corbels have decayed heraldic decoration, two shields on the S apparently having the arms of Bruce of Stenhouse and Airth, and of Bully. The N aisle has three different windows (all restored): that in the E bay is a four-light variant on those of the apse flanks, while the four-light middle window has a circlet with three spiralling daggers. The three-light window in the W bay is related to those of the angled faces of the apse. In the W bay is a blocked priests' doorway. In the S aisle the windows of the E and W bays are like that of the E bay on the N, the central window is like its N counterpart.

The rather squat clearstorey is an enigma. Before 1869 the windows opened into the roof space over the aisles and were unglazed, meaning that they were a gallery-like feature rather than a row of clearstorey windows. This could indicate an intention to have a third stage – a true clearstorey – above. The impact of the E arm would thus have been even more impressive than now, particularly if there had been a central tower behind it. Perhaps it was nervousness at building quite so loftily above such steeply falling ground, as well as shortage of funds, which led to abandoning the idea.

The TRANSEPTS of 1936–40 are of pink sandstone. Faced with the difficult task of bridging between the differing heights of nave and chancel, *James Miller* continued the wallhead level of the nave, but took many details from the apse and chancel, including the squat buttress pinnacles and the crowstepped gables set behind the parapet. The roof runs unbroken between N and S gables, with the slightly lower nave roof abutting it to the W, and the W gable of the chancel rising above it to the E; no architectural reference is made to the tower apparently planned for the E crossing in the early C16. The N transept, which houses the organ, is larger than the S, but has only a two-light window to the N and a minor doorway on the E (now blocked by a heating flue). Greater play was made with the S transept front, which has a major doorway with multiple continuous mouldings below a four-light window.

The NAVE aisles are divided into bays by substantial buttresses. Most are set below the parapets, except for those at the W angles which rise through the wallhead and are capped by pinnacles, that at the SW angle being diagonally set and that at the NW angle being a C19 creation. The rest have a wide top weathering, and a smaller off-set at mid-height, though those flanking the porch have an additional off-set. The half-gable at the W end of the N aisle was rebuilt with straight skews, whereas that to the S is crowstepped. The restored windows of the aisle flanks are of three-light cusped intersecting form, though three are C19 insertions where chantry aisles have been removed and a doorway suppressed. The windows at the aisle W ends are two-light versions of the same type. The porch, like the transepts, dates from 1936–40. On the N side are the remains of a small blocked doorway, corresponding to the S porch.

The walls of the central vessel above the aisles are unarticulated by buttresses; on the S there is a simple sequence of five round-headed clearstorey windows, but on the N there never were windows, and the roof there now covers much of the wall. Stirling is not unique in asymmetry of clearstorey fenestration, other examples being the chancel of Perth, St John, and possibly the (now rebuilt) nave of Edinburgh, St Giles. It seems likely that during the post-1507 operations it was intended to raise the central vessel of the nave, possibly by adding a new clearstorey and converting the existing clearstorey into a gallery. Thus both nave and chancel would have had three-storeyed elevations. The evidence for this is on the E face of the heightened W tower, where there are pairs of openings at two levels above the present roof, with a roof moulding between the upper pair. The lower openings, which give access to the two sides of the wall-walk behind the parapet, are evidently secondary cuttings through the tower wall. The upper openings appear to be contemporary with the heightening of the tower and were apparently intended to give access to a higher wall-walk that was never built. Even at this increased height the nave would not have been as high as a three-storeyed chancel (*see* above), but the discrepancy would have been less obvious if there had been a central tower. It was clearly intended that the collegiate choir should be more prominent than the parochial nave.

ST ANDREW'S AISLE projects in the re-entrant angle between the N aisle and transept. There is a simple three-light intersecting N window, and a rectangular window subdivided by a mullion in the W wall; the latter largely rebuilt in 1911–14. This chapel has the same base course as the nave, so cannot postdate it significantly. The gable above its N face rises almost to the top of the N aisle parapet. BOWYE'S AISLE, corresponding on the S side, has left very little trace apart from discrepancies of masonry coursing.

ST MARY'S AISLE, at the W end of the N side, has gone, apart from the lower courses which revet the external ground levels. However, it can be seen that the roof was higher than that of St Andrew's Aisle: the vault wall rib rises to near the top of the aisle parapet, while its roof crease rises through much of the central vessel parapet. (In this almost random accretion of laterally gabled chapels there is perhaps an echo of the manner in which chapels were added around the town churches of the Netherlands, though the most extreme example of this in Scotland was St Giles, Edinburgh.) The chapel was entered from the nave through a wide archway with foliate capitals, the upper part of which now frames the window in this bay. The similarity of the jamb mouldings of this arch to the SE nave arcade pier, and of the chapel base course to that below the rest of the nave, shows that (as with St Andrew's Aisle) it belongs essentially with the main nave building campaign. In what was the interior E wall of the chapel, S of the site of its altar, are an ogee-headed credence recess and the mutilated remains of a piscina bowl.

The W TOWER is one of Holy Rude's finest features. Its three-dimensional geometry is highly satisfying, and in the intake at two-thirds height it is possible it was partly influenced by the telescoped tower of Dundee, St Mary, which must itself have been largely inspired by Netherlandish prototypes. On the evidence of masonry changes, the first part of the W tower to be built rose little higher than the nave roof apex. It is rectangular rather than square in plan, being longer on its N–S than its E–W axis. A spiral stair rises at its NW corner, now entered through an external doorway, rather than by the original internal doorway. The W processional doorway was blocked in the early C19, when the two-light W window was extended downwards. Only the bases and lowest courses of the door jambs are now evident. It was so wide that it was probably subdivided with a central trumeau. The upper stages of the tower are the result of a later heightening, possibly as part of the post-1507 works. One further storey was added to the same plan as the lowest storey, with a single lancet W and S; the roof moulding and openings on the E face of this stage have already been mentioned. (Pockmarks on the N and W faces of this stage may be a result of defensive fire from the castle during the siege of 1651.) The two upper storeys above this first additional stage are much more complex. They are made square in plan by intakes to N and S, and by corbelling out to E and W. There is a parapeted wall-walk to N and S above the two lower storeys, carried by corbelling which is continued round the E and W sides to support the salient faces of the tower there. The NW stair turret becomes more prominent at the upper levels because of the way it continues the line of the tower's lower W and N faces, and it is topped by an octagonal spirelet with pinnacles at the four angles. The main body of the tower is capped by a crenellated parapet. A spire was probably intended as the culmination of the tower, behind the parapet, on the evidence of internal squinches.

## INTERIOR

The vista down the central vessel is particularly fine. There is none of the smoothly handled articulation of space seen at what was probably Scotland's first apsed and aisled church, Queen Mary of Gueldres' Trinity College Chapel in Edinburgh, founded c. 1460 and therefore roughly contemporary with the nave of Stirling. But that was probably not the effect emulated here, and one senses such smooth – and possibly Burgundian-inspired – sophistication might have been regarded as effete by the burgesses. What is memorable here is the way the eye is drawn

along the relatively low space of the nave, with its robust sense
of architectural mass, and through the dark square of the crossi-
ing before moving on to the less elongated but more vertically
attenuated proportions of the chancel, culminating in the closed
space of the apse.

The TOWER opens off the nave through a tall arch with its
apex at the level of the nave wallhead. It is covered by a sexpartite vault with a bell-hole and an extra intersection to accommodate the angled face of the stair turret. Scottish masons
evidently developed a fascination for older vault types in the C15,
and sexpartite vaults are also found in towers at Dunfermline
Abbey and Linlithgow, St Michael.

The five-bay aisled NAVE has arcades in which the supports
of all but the E bays are large cylindrical piers of the type found
in several of Scotland's major churches of the later C14 and
early C15. These include Aberdeen Cathedral nave, pre-1380;
Dunkeld Cathedral nave, post-1406; St Andrews Cathedral S
transept, post-1409; St Andrews, Holy Trinity Church, post-
1410. The revived use of such piers, like the design of the tower,
probably owes its ultimate inspiration to Netherlandish prototypes and reminds us of the strong continental links enjoyed by
the trading burghs. The E arcade pier on each side is of more
complex type: that on the N has filleted rolls to the cardinal
directions separated by salient quadrant hollows; that on the S
has filleted rolls flanked by smaller rolls in the cardinal directions,
with further filleted rolls in the hollows of the diagonal faces. The
reason for such enrichment is uncertain though, in view of the
more elaborate sections of arcade in the area of the high altar
found at Edinburgh, St Giles, and Perth, St John, these piers
may have been intended to emphasize the site of the nave altar
in front of the chancel screen. The capitals of the cylindrical piers
have continuous rings of mouldings, some with one or two bands
of foliage in the hollows. The more elaborate E piers have caps
with diagonally continuous mouldings to each face, which only
minimally respect the individual shafts of the piers; this type of
cap is seen elsewhere perhaps as early as the 1430s (cf. Torphichen
Preceptory transepts, Lothian). The arcade arches each have
pairs of chamfers with a hoodmould. The nave aisles are covered
by quadripartite rib vaults with ridge ribs, which rise from corbels
along the outer walls.

The nave clearstorey walls are separated from the arcades by
a stringcourse set a little above the arch apices; short shafts topped
by caps (foliate on the S) rise from that string to the wall-posts
of the roof. As we saw externally, only the S side of the clearstorey level has windows, the N wall being blank. Along the
walls are faint traces of the plaster vault inserted in 1818 and
removed in 1911–14. The ROOF, although extensively restored,
is one of the few of medieval date to survive in Scotland; like
that over the chancel of Perth, St John, its appearance is of
rugged sturdiness rather than high finesse. It is of double-raftered
tie-beam construction, with two couples to each bay, those above
the piers having wall-posts and arched braces. Above the ties

are kingposts and angled struts, with braces from the kingposts to the ridge-piece, and from the inner struts to the upper of the two purlins.

ST ANDREW'S AISLE, at the E end of the N aisle, is entered through an archway in which both responds and arch have paired chamfers. It is covered by a tierceron vault, with arms assumed to be those of Forestar on the central boss. There is a small ogee-headed credence recess in the E wall, S of the altar site. The archway that led into St Mary's Aisle (now demolished) from the W bay of the N aisle has a window set within it. In the bay E of this the blocked doorway is flanked by a restored holy water stoup.

The CROSSING is largely C19 and C20, other than the multi-shafted NE pier and parts of the SE pier. The W crossing piers, inserted 1936–40, copied the E piers, but incorporated the medieval semicylindrical responds at the E end of the nave arcade. The crossing itself has a modern ribbed vault. In the S TRANSEPT steps lead down to the S doorway.

10    The three-bay CHANCEL has bundled-shaft piers of eight filleted shafts. The heavily moulded caps have three or four tiers of diagonally continuous mouldings, above compressed bell and necking mouldings that follow the profile of the pier shafting; the S arcade caps and E respond have foliage sprigs on the bell. The aisles have rib vaulting with ridge ribs. Along the N aisle walls the vaulting springs from corbels; in the S aisle, there are short barley-sugar shafts below the corbels. The E walls of the aisles are blank, presumably to accommodate altar retables, and in the S aisle there is a small ogee-headed credence recess S of the altar site. In the N aisle, between the second and third windows from the E, is an arched recess, usually said to be an Easter Sepulchre (*see* Furnishings). E of the blocked priests' doorway in the W bay is a damaged holy water stoup. The stair at the NE angle of the N aisle leads down to vestries created below the chancel in 1936–40.

The CHANCEL CLEARSTOREY is separated from the arcade by a string a little above the arch apices; wall-shafts rise from the arcade capitals on the N and from corbels on the S, passing through the string to support the roof wall-posts. The windows are round-headed, each containing two round-headed lights. These were originally openings into the roof space above the aisles, and towards the interior they are of a type related to those of the gallery openings of the three-storeyed elevation of the nave of Linlithgow, St Michael, supporting the possibility that Stirling was intended to have a third storey in both nave and chancel.

The APSE is slightly wider than the chancel. The sill of its E window is a little higher than those of the angled faces, which are in turn slightly higher than those of the flanks, presumably in order to accommodate the high altar. In the side walls, faint traces of the organ screen that occupied the lower level of the apse before 1936–40. The apse vault is one of Holy Rude's less satisfactory features. The N–S span is first reduced by two orders of segmental wall-arches to N and S. The space is then bridged by a pointed and ribbed barrel vault, whose E segment is humoured awkwardly into the angled faces of the apse. The touching faith of many late medieval masons in the idea that a barrel vault could be adapted to all situations is nowhere more evident – but perhaps nowhere less justified.

## FIXTURES, FURNISHINGS AND MEMORIALS

FONT. In St Andrew's Aisle, a stone carved with tracery designs, found in vicinity of Cambuskenneth Abbey, and hollowed out to form basin. – PULPIT. 1911–14 by *Thomas Ross* for West Church, but incorporating C17 work; circular with Corinthian pilasters and carved panels. – EASTER SEPULCHRE (?). In N chancel aisle, a deep recess within a three-centred arch with continuous mouldings, but in a position so far away from the high altar perhaps more likely to have been a tomb recess. – PISCINAE, CREDENCE RECESSES and HOLY WATER STOUP. *See* above. – CONSECRATION CROSSES. Ten inscribed at various points around interior of both nave and chancel. – CHOIR STALLS. Designed by *W. A. P. Jack*, made by *Whytock & Reid*, 1965, with ogee-arched canopies and raised and fielded panels with traceried holes, and separated by pinnacles to desk fronts. – ORGAN by *Rushworth & Draper*, 1940. – ROYAL ARMS. C17, over entrance to St Andrew's Aisle; originally on E gallery of West Church; re-tinctured 1959.

MEMORIALS. Four in floor of St Andrew's Aisle: Alexander Durham, Purse Bearer to Mary Queen of Scots and James VI †(?)1584, a slab with two shields; Alexander Foster of Garden †1598, a slab with a marginal inscription and two shields; Agnes Leishman, wife of Duncan Forestar †1633, a slab with two shields; an undated stone with traces of six shields. – N choir aisle: W bay, Janet Roger (†1786, erected 1791), a Classical aedicule surmounted by maiden weeping over urn. – S nave aisle: W end, David Doig (†1800), black Classical aedicule surmounted by books, pen and urn. – N nave aisle: W end, the Rev. James Somerville (†1817, erected 1819), black Classical surmounted by urn. – TOWER: memorials to five benefactors of Stirling set within Gothic wall arcade blocking W doorway.

## STAINED GLASS

E ARM. – Apse: central, memorial to John Cowane †1633, founder of Cowane's Hospital (Last Supper, Sermon on Mount, Acts of Mercy), by *James Ballantine*; SE, to John King, 1870 (scenes from ministry of St Paul); NE, given following visit by Glasgow Society of Sons of the Rock in 1868 (Christ teaching in Temple, Paul instructing Timothy, miracle at Cana, parable of Good Samaritan), by *James Ballantine*. – S choir aisle: E bay, to William Galbraith and Christian Littlejohn, 1880 (scenes from life of Christ), by *Adam & Small*; second from E, to Alexander Munnoch †1879 (illustrations of hospitality), by *Cottier and Co.*; third from E, Munich glass (dated 1883) to John Thomson †1854 and Henry

Ainslie †1877 (Old and New Covenants). – N choir aisle: E bay, to James Reid †1879 (Agony in Garden, Christ's First Appearance to Disciples), by *James Ballantine & Son*; second from E, to James Monteath †1867 (parables of Talents, Good Samaritan); third from E, to George Galbraith †1847 (Christ healing centurion's servant). – Window above chancel arch: a vesica-shaped window installed *c.* 1869 when pulpit of East Church was still sited within the arch (an angel). – S transept: to John Risk (Benedicite), by *Douglas Strachan*, 1945. – NAVE. – S nave aisle: second from E, the Guildry window (incorporating a merchant's mark, evangelists' symbols, arms of cities and countries with which Stirling had trading links), by *Crear McCartney*, 1993; third from E, to John Dick †1865 (erected 1869) (Christ's Words of Comfort); W, to Patrick Connal †1887 (illustrating man's mortality), by *W. & J. J. Kier*. – N nave aisle: third bay from E, to Charles Randolph †1878 (wedding at Cana), by *W. & J. J. Kier*; W, to Emily Jessie Campbell (Connal) †1877 (on theme of the good wife), by *W. & J. J. Kier*. – Tower: to Michael †1812 and Patrick Connal †1854 (Sermon on Mount).

## CHURCHES

ALLAN PARK SOUTH, Dumbarton Road. Originally Allan Park United Presbyterian Church. Gabled Gothic by *Peddie & Kinnear*, 1865–76. The church sits across the contours, elevated an extra storey as the land falls SW. In the NE entrance gable, a rose window, ten quatrefoil lights around a cogwheel centre; below, a pointed-arched doorway with moulded reveals and engaged shafts. Facing NW and SE, two conjoined gables, each with a hooded, two-light, pointed window with cinquefoil plate tracery. In the SW gable, the rose is repeated above five two-light windows with quatrefoils, the additional lower storey lit by three sets of coupled windows with shouldered lintels. Abutting r., a square spireless S tower, abruptly parapeted, the skyline barely redeemed by the sharply pyramidal copper roof of a curtailed corner stair turret. The tall belfry stage of the steeple, which originally soared to a deeply corbelled parapet and pyramidal roof, was demolished in 1954–5 in an extensive reconstruction which also included the strengthening of the SE gable and repairs to the roof. Plastered interior. Two cast iron columns rise through the U-plan gallery to support the valley of the cross-gabled roof. In 1963, *Gordon & Dey* created a more spacious chancel with panelled organ pipe housings raised on each side of a large cross centrally hung in front of an 'argent-curtained reredos' masking the rose window in the N gable. – Oak COMMUNION TABLE with the Apostles' symbols carved on the rim. – ORGAN by *Forster & Andrews*, 1898, rebuilt 1904. – STAINED GLASS. War Memorial window, SE lancet l. of chancel: St Michael slaying a dragon above a scene depicting Stirling Bridge; by *Gordon Webster*, 1948. Opposite, the Virgin and Child against a rainbow-crossed background of farming activity; by *Isobel Goudie*, 1937.

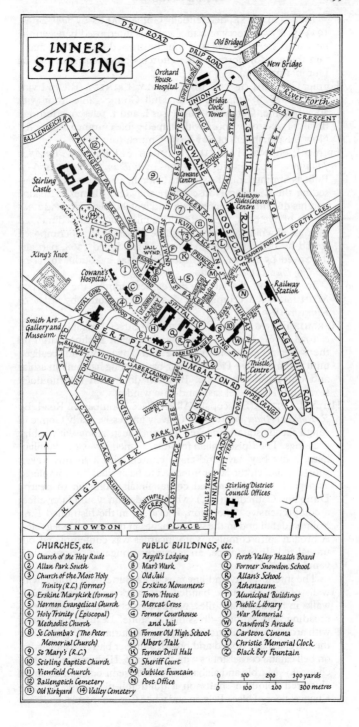

INNER STIRLING

DRIP ROAD
Old Bridge
New Bridge
River Forth
DEAN CRESCENT
Orchard House Hospital
UNION ST
Bridge Clock Tower
BURGHMUIR ROAD
BALLENGEICH RD
BALLENGEICH PASS
Stirling Castle
King's Knot
Cowane's Hospital
Smith Art Gallery and Museum
Rainbow Slides Leisure Centre
Cowane Centre
FORTH CRES.
Railway Station
ALBERT PLACE
DUMBARTON RD
Thistle Centre
VICTORIA SQUARE
UPPER CRAIGS
KING'S
SNOWDON PLACE
Stirling District Council Offices

## CHURCHES, etc.
1. Church of the Holy Rude
2. Allan Park South
3. Church of the Most Holy Trinity (R.C.) (former)
4. Erskine Marykirk (former)
5. Hermon Evangelical Church
6. Holy Trinity (Episcopal)
7. Methodist Church
8. St Columba's (The Peter Memorial Church)
9. St Mary's (R.C.)
10. Stirling Baptist Church
11. Viewfield Church
12. Ballengeich Cemetery
13. Old Kirkyard
14. Valley Cemetery

## PUBLIC BUILDINGS, etc.
(A) Argyll's Lodging
(B) Mar's Wark
(C) Old Jail
(D) Erskine Monument
(E) Town House
(F) Mercat Cross
(G) Former Courthouse and Jail
(H) Former Old High School
(J) Albert Hall
(K) Former Drill Hall
(L) Sheriff Court
(M) Jubilee Fountain
(N) Post Office
(P) Forth Valley Health Board
(Q) Former Snowdon School
(R) Allan's School
(S) Athenaeum
(T) Municipal Buildings
(U) Public Library
(V) War Memorial
(W) Crawford's Arcade
(X) Carlton Cinema
(Y) Christie Memorial Clock
(Z) Black Boy Fountain

0        100        200        300 yards
0     100      200      300 metres

Linked to the SE, deferentially Gothic HALLS by *John Bruce*, 1933–5. A two-storey entrance gable is interposed between the beheaded steeple tower and four buttressed bays which maintain the window forms of the church's basement storey along Dumbarton Road.

Former CHURCH OF THE MOST HOLY TRINITY (R.C.), Irvine Place. 1836–8; enlarged 1860. Dull Gothic gable front with apex bellcote. Octagonal buttresses l. and r. telescope into tall finials. Two-storey house with shaped gable entrance attached l. Now the parish hall of St Mary's Church (q.v.).

20 Former ERSKINE MARYKIRK CHURCH, St John Street. By *Allan Johnstone*, 1824–6; with alterations by *William Simpson*, 1876–7. Built as Stirling United Associate Church, a Seceders' kirk superseding the Meeting House where the Rev. Ebenezer Erskine and his dissenting congregation had worshipped since 1742. NE façade of five bays, the centre three pilastered and pedimented in coursed whinstone with freestone dressings to superimposed round-headed windows and doors. Abandoned 1968, partially destroyed by fire in 1980, but adapted as a Youth Hostel by *Stirling District Council*, 1992.

40 In front, on the site of the earlier church, the ERSKINE MONUMENT, a Tempietto with a fish-scale dome, by *Peddie & Kinnear*, 1859.

HERMON EVANGELICAL CHURCH, Bow Street. Probably designed *c.* 1938 by *Sir Frank C. Mears* working with Stirling Burgh on the wider redevelopment of the Old Town, but not realized until the mid 1950s. Piended, four-bay meeting hall built in ashlar and bull-faced sandstone. Boarded door with roll-moulded surround. High-level sash-and-case windows.

HOLY TRINITY (Episcopal), Albert Place, Dumbarton Road. By *R. Rowand Anderson*, 1875–8. Gravely impressive Early Gothic in rough-faced, square-snecked Bannockburn stone with ashlar dressings. The Episcopalian formula, aligned NW–SE, is familiar: here, a five-bay nave-and-aisles church with a slightly lower, shorter chancel, the latter intended to be apsidal but completed as a gable with buttressed corner finials. Allusion to nearby Dunblane Cathedral (q.v.), where Anderson would later effect a comprehensive restoration, is evident in the restrained First Pointed detail and in the vesica shapes in the NW and SE gables. A broach spire complete with lucarnes was contemplated but unrealized. In its place, an elegantly elongated, copper-clad, ventilator *flèche*.

The interior, lofty and linear, is more Butterfield Gothic with walls of polychromatic banded brickwork and aisle and nave walks in red and black tiles. Nave piers, chamfered round-arch arcading and window dressings in stone. Lean-to aisle roofs with arch-braced half-trusses supporting purlins and spars. Over the nave, a dark, ribbed and boarded timber barrel vault carried on bell capital corbelstones with fluted tails. High pointed arch to chancel. – Marble and alabaster PULPIT, semi-octagon on squat clustered coloured shafts on a quatrefoil-plan base, 1878. – Chancel floor of black Belgian and white Carrara marble, by *Robert*

*S. Lorimer*, 1921–2. – Wrought iron SCREEN also by Lorimer, 1922. – Choir STALLS in Pensacola red pine. – ALTAR and carved and painted REREDOS, a splendidly complex Nativity, by *C. E. Kempe*, 1878. – On the N side of the chancel the Memorial Chapel, formerly the sacristy, created by Lorimer, 1920–1: marble altar and floor, panelled walls, oak roof with carved bosses. – On the S, painted organ pipes fill the pointed arch at the end of the aisle. *Conacher* ORGAN, 1878, rebuilt by *Binns, Fitton & Haley*, 1935; reconstruction by *David Loosely*, 1979–81. – At the rear of the nave, the FONT. – Mounted on the E wall at the end of the S aisle, a white marble MURAL TABLET with Latin inscription commemorating Bishop George Gleig †1811, by *David Ness*, Edinburgh; brought from *John Henderson*'s Christ Church on Barnton Street, which had been built for the Episcopalians in 1845. – STAINED GLASS. Memorial window to Colonel Priestly by *James Ballantine & Son*; first erected in the Barnton Street church, 1868, and transferred, 1878. – Lady Clerk memorial picturing St Michael and angels by *Burlison & Grylls*, London, 1896. – But the best windows are more recent. Outstanding are the figures of saints in the aisle lancets by *Margaret Chilton*, 1947–55; SS Elizabeth of Hungary, Mary Magdalene, Andrew, Francis of Assisi and Columba. – In the Memorial Chapel, SS George, Michael and Victor of Marseilles by *J. C. Bewsey* of London, 1921.

METHODIST CHURCH, Queen Street. Built *c.* 1850. Shaped ashlar gable front lugged with small square bartizans. Hooded round-arched windows. Obelisk apex finial.

ST COLUMBA (The Peter Memorial Church), Park Terrace. By *J. J. Stevenson*, 1899–1902. A big, admirably Gothic brew of *fin-de-siècle* medievalism, creatively infused with flavours of Baronial, Tudor and Art Nouveau. Fine masonry; the contrast between rough-faced square-snecked walling and keenly cut ashlar dressings and detail especially effective. The N tower dominates. Diagonally buttressed, with pairs of traceried pointed belfry openings at the uppermost stage but without its projected crown spire. NE pointed doorway with blind tracery above the lintel. To the l., the crowstepped gable of the nave with a segmental-arched door below two tall two-light pointed windows. Facing NW, along Park Terrace, three broad bays with pointed-windows below and coupled lintelled openings above, the latter separated by narrow crocketed finials which rise through a crenellated ashlar parapet. This continues around an advancing crowstep-gabled caphouse with superimposed mullioned and transomed windows that connects the church to the buttressed bays of the Hall beyond, their relationship not unlike that of transept and chancel. All windows, other than those in this link, have Stevenson's distinctive tracery with its sinuous Art Nouveau interpretation of Gothic.

A magnificent roof dominates the interior. Queenposts and ceiling ties are exposed; sloping soffits and boxed margins boarded with superimposed panel patterning. Five trussed bays relate to five pointed-arched SE windows while on the NW an arcade of three high pointed arches defines aisle and side gallery (the latter closed in to create the Anderson Hall, 1988). Stone well stair in the tower leads to the rear gallery, its form subtly splayed at the ends, panelled in a four-square pattern centred on a raised pyramidal base. High, narrow, pointed chancel arch, its profile continued as a panelled plaster vault. – The ORGAN, by *J.J. Binns* of Leeds, 1903, fills the space like a giant reredos. – Oak FURNISHINGS, installed *c.* 1958 when the chancel apron was created, are severe and plain save for decorative insets in gold and blue symbolizing the dove in the lectern and font and sheaves, cross and vines in the communion table. – STAINED GLASS, in the middle lights of the four SE windows, by *John Blyth*, 1988: the Good Samaritan, a saintly figure 'sure and steadfast' on a sea-girt rock, the Good Shepherd, and St Columba. – Above the chancel arch, two small cusped windows in a warm sap green with yellow Art Nouveau rose motifs, 1902 (?).

ST MARY (R.C.), Upper Bridge Street. 1904–5; by *Pugin & Pugin*, the gabled nave-and-aisles arrangement, built in thick and thin courses of rough-faced red Dumfriesshire sandstone with crisp ashlar dressings and tracery, instantly recognizable. Approached through a hillside garden (the ironwork gates disappointingly pusillanimous), the SE gable is impressive. Three tall pointed windows, set between buttresses and inventively traceried with circles, daggers and mouchettes, intensify the verticality: above is a canopied niche with a statue of the Virgin; below, two pointed doorway recesses separated by a traceried circular window. To the l., the splayed projection of a stair rising to the choir and organ gallery. To the r., a buttressed octagon; the baptistery. Behind this entrance façade the nine-bay nave stretches back between lower lean-to aisles to a splayed apse, the window tracery more curvilinear around the sanctuary.

Lofty nave-and-aisles interior, renovated and restored 1987–8. Pointed-arched arcading carried on round stone piers. From corbels, carved as angels with musical instruments, thin shafts thicken into octagonal columns in the clearstorey. Pointed, barrel-vault roof, the plaster surface gridded by timber ribs. Walls stencilled with rose and leaf pattern in cream and orange (restoration, 1988). 'Lean-to' arches over the aisles. Pinewood floor with tiled passages; strongly patterned tiling in the chancel. – In the sanctuary, a Gothic REREDOS, carved from beerstone, its attenuated step-profile culminating in a canopied niche set just below the clearstorey stringcourse. – Stone block ALTAR, 1988. – Set to the l. are timber settles, three-seater Gothic SEDILIA, high-backed and canopied. – Sanctuary CHAIR by *Tim Stead*, 1982. – Both side chapels have elaborately detailed Gothic altars in marble. – In the baptistery, a variegated marble FONT; brass-domed white bowl on pink pier. – Almost all windows have STAINED GLASS honouring saints and benefactors; richest in colour are those in the five baptistery windows where Christ's baptism is flanked by SS Augustine and Matthew, Ambrose and Mark, Luke and Gregory, John and Jerome; by *Gunning* (?), Dublin.

STIRLING BAPTIST CHURCH, Murray Place. Originally the South Free Church, 1851–3, by *J., W.H. & J.M. Hay* of Liverpool. Closed 1971. Radically converted for the Baptist Church with outstanding success by *Inglis & Carr*, 1987–9. Gabled pointed portals open from the street to stair flights rising symmetrically to a central entrance. Below, a doorway to the undercroft; above, a gable façade with a five-light Late Dec window. An octagonal stair turret r. buttresses a steeple tower with louvred belfry lancets, four steeply pyramidal finials and a high, lucarne-fringed spire.

After 1987 the exterior was restored and the interior cleverly recast, reducing the volume of the church by the insertion of a new floor at lower gallery level. Below this raised worship area, the ground floor accommodates foyer, lounge, classrooms and lecture theatre, while in the basement, which can be entered from the street, there is space for crèche, multi-purpose hall, kitchen, etc. A lift housed in the tower connects all levels. A Sports Hall was added to the rear.

VIEWFIELD CHURCH, Viewfield Place and Irvine Place. Built as Viewfield United Presbyterian Church by *F. & W. Mackison*, 1858–60. Gable and steeple dominate the rising corner. In the former, a four-light pointed window with Dec tracery. Plain tower with a diagonal corner buttress, triple lancets to the belfry, and a spire shorn of its lucarnes. The church, lit by coupled pointed windows, is five buttressed bays deep. Raked interior. – The original gallery, over the SE vestibule, extended to a U-plan in 1876. – Furnishings, 1946–7. – ORGAN by *Lewis & Co.*, Brixton, installed 1949; the Gothic screen carries a decorative frieze of grapes and pomegranates.

## CEMETERIES*

BALLENGEICH CEMETERY, Ballengeich Road. C19. Hillside graveyard with no sepulchral monuments of architectural note but a splendid view from the summit.

OLD KIRKYARD, surrounding the Church of the Holy Rude on the W and NW. There are many early SLABS and COPED STONES, several dating from the C16 and most from the C17. The symbols of mortality – skulls, bones, hour-glasses and angels – are frequently visible but inscriptions, if still legible, can be read only with difficulty. Located centrally, the oldest SLAB bears the date 1579, its mason's tools and armorial carving suggesting a link with the quarrier Peter Gibb. – Lying S of this, another shield-bearing SLAB, to Andrew Baird †1692. – Several COPED STONES with pie-crust margins, probably C17, lie close to the W side of the church tower. – A few small C17 HEADSTONES survive. A mutilated pair bearing a date from the 1670s appear to be the oldest. – Much larger, the HEADSTONE probably carved

---

*Research on the gravestones of Stirling's cemeteries carried out by John G. Harrison in 1997 is gratefully acknowledged.

by the mason *John Service c.* 1636 for his father, also John Service, also a mason. It is situated on the N boundary. On its W face, surrounded by a serpent, are figures that appear from 'speech balloons' to be speaking, the imagery drawn from Francis Quarles' *Emblems Divine and Moral* published in London in 1635. The E face, which is decorated with strapwork, is also carved with an illustration from Quarles, The Farewell. This 'appears to be the earliest known use of motifs from an Emblem Book on a gravestone'. – Fifteen HEADSTONES shouldered with 'mirrored S' scrolls are unique to Stirling. They carry dates between 1696 and 1736. On one, dated 1696 but incised with a later inscription of 1779, a maltman's shovel and three sheaves of corn indicate the family trade. On another, to Robert Fergusson †1695, the dividers and set-square of a wright and a horned face with ribbon streamers trailing from the mouth. On another the scrolls become birds' heads, probably pelicans symbolizing the self-sacrifice of Christ. Best of the group, dated 1728, the grave of James Stevenson, located not far N of the centre of the kirkyard; swags, hour-glass, skull, crossed bones and the familiar injunction MEMENTO MORI. – S of the centre, marking the grave of the Cambuskenneth gardener John Simson †1724, a HEADSTONE with initials and a serpent coiled around a pruning hook on one face and spade, shears and rake on the other. – Nearby, on the S boundary, is a large MURAL MONUMENT to John Sconce, John McCulloch †1689, a former provost of Stirling, and others. Coupled columns carry a corniced pediment above a body surrounded by skulls, putti and strapwork.

Many C19 stones are interspersed with these older markers, the graves merging imperceptibly with the Valley Cemetery to the NW (*see* below). All the familiar forms of funerary sculpture are in evidence. A high HEADSTONE with scrolled top and draped ovoid shield; to John Wingate †1829 and his wife Janet †1832. – Dated 1858, a tall panelled pillar MONUMENT, square in plan, with a wide cornice carrying an elegantly flared urn on a stepped base; to the merchant John Murray †1863 and his family. – Another of the same with inset panels of white marble; to Rev. Robert Shirra †1804. – Leitch family commemorated in a thick urn-bearing COLUMN raised on a corniced plinth; one of several similar tombs. – Beside the church, in the SE corner of the graveyard, the most elaborate sandstone COLUMN, to Rev. Archibald Bennie †1846 and many others of his family. It sits on an octagonal plinth carved with *putti* and open Bibles, inscriptions and inverted torches alternating on the chamfered faces of the tall shaft; sculpted by *James Ritchie* of Edinburgh. – On the N edge of the Old Kirkyard, a high Celtic CROSS in pink granite, ringed and much ornamented with interlacing on the face and sides, to Professor Henry Drummond †1888 and his wife and sons.

VALLEY CEMETERY, below the Castle Esplanade. Laid out in 1857–8 by *Peddie & Kinnear* largely at the instigation of William Drummond (1793–1868), 'seedsman and evangelist', whose grave is here but whose greater monument lies, like Wren's, all around. Most spectacular, and most immediate in its impact on entering the graveyard from Castle Wynd, is the STAR PYRAMID, 38 by the sculptor *William Barclay*, 1863; not, in fact, a tomb but a tribute in stone to the cause of Scots Presbyterianism so assiduously promoted by the Drummonds' tractarian publishing business. Constructed in hammered ashlar blocks, the pyramid sits on a massive three-step base built on a rocky knoll. At the base of each face are open Bibles sculpted in white marble. Pious inscriptions, texts and biblical references abound. A flight of steps with low parapet walls carrying ball finials incised with lines of latitude and longitude falls to the S. – Nearby, beyond a small rock-rimmed pool, is Drummond's grey granite SARCOPHAGUS grave, ascetically plain save for a Greek fret rim. – A number of sandstone STATUES on high plinths, by *Alexander Handyside Ritchie*, 1858–9, are sited at different points among the tombs. They honour those Protestant divines admired by Drummond: Ebenezer Erskine, James Renwick, James Guthrie, Andrew Melville, John Knox and Alexander Henderson. The last three are grouped together on a grassy bank shaded by a birch tree; below them, a grotto-like white marble fountain with a shell basin. – No less sentimental the MARTYR'S MONUMENT erected by 39 Drummond to Margaret Wilson, 'Virgin Martyr of the Ocean Wave', said to have died in the Solway in the 1680s refusing to disown her allegiance to the Scottish Covenant. On an octagonal base, two young girls sit under the protection of a draped angel. In 1867 the group was encased, glazed in a domed cast iron structure manufactured by *George Smith & Co.*'s *Sun Foundry* of Glasgow. Only in the dome has the glass survived. Close by is the Ladies' Rock viewpoint, a rocky eminence to which, it is said, the women of the castle would come to enjoy the prospect of the landscape below.

There are many gravemarkers from the C19 and C20. Among the usual headstones, crosses, columns, obelisks and aedicule tombs are these. To the Wordie family, a Celtic CROSS with interlacing ornament on the face and base, by *J. & G. Mossman*, Glasgow, 1902. – Octagonal shaft CROSS with flared extremities, wrapped asymmetrically in a sculpted floral wreath; to James Guthrie †1900 and his wife and sons. – Raised on a stepped base with a bold scotia moulding, a grey granite block MONUMENT with corner columns carrying entablature, urns and dome; on pink granite panels, the names of W. Crawford †1894, his wife Margaret McKenzie †1882 and their family. – Rough-cut OBELISK with inset copper portrait panel of the local veterinary surgeon Thomas Logan Houston †1924. – Commemorating Agnes Bunten Muir †1894, a STATUE of a seated woman with hands clasped on her lap. – To the Rev. Dr Alexander Beith, †1891, 'courageous leader in the Disruption of the Church of Scotland in 1843', and his wife Julia †1866, the cemetery's tallest OBELISK, in pink granite.

## PUBLIC BUILDINGS

ALBERT HALL, Dumbarton Road. Pompous urban palazzo in
rough-faced snecked rubble and ashlar by *William Simpson*, 1881–3.
The streetside façade is disturbingly not quite symmetrical with
advancing pedimented end bays flanking a *piano nobile* of six
round-arched windows beneath a balustraded parapet with
swagged swollen urns. Central round-arched doorway covered
by a balustraded balcony on coupled consoles. On the SE front,
a similar pedimented portal to the main entrance, approached
across a paved forecourt, landscaped by *Ian White Associates*,
1994. Above it, a five-bay 'pressed in' portico, pilastered and
pedimented.

ALLAN'S SCHOOL, St John Street. A replacement for the original
school of 1836. Queen Anne style by *Ronald Walker*, 1888–91;
refurbished 1991. Tall, three-storey classroom block with mullioned and transomed windows. Four bays wide; the outer bays
steeply pedimented, the inner capped by swept dormerheads.

1, 83 ATHENAEUM, King Street and Spittal Street. Designed as the
town's Merchants' House by *William Stirling I* of Dunblane and
built in good ashlar by *Allan Johnstone*, 1816–17; it served as
burgh offices from 1875. The building responds magnificently to
a gushet site poised between uptown history and downtown
commerce. A tall tower, five chamfered stages below a circular
columned belfry and spire, commands the axis of King Street,
advancing between convex three-storey shoulders that curve
back into streets beginning the climb to the Old Town. Embar-
rassingly chunky domed porch, added 1859, supports a statue
of local hero Sir William Wallace, by *A. Handyside Ritchie*.

BLACK BOY FOUNTAIN, King's Park Road. 1849. Black-painted
cast iron by *Neilson & Co.* of Glasgow. A fine two-bowl pedestal
fountain supporting the figure of a young boy. Octagonal stone
base and pond.

BRIDGE CLOCK TOWER, Union Street. By *Ronald Walker* of
*McLuckie & Walker*, 1910. Domed ashlar tower on a diagonally
buttressed plinth. Four gabled clock faces. Gifted by Provost
David Bayne.

CARLTON ALLANPARK CINEMA, Allan Park and King's Park
Road. By *Samuel Runcie*, Glasgow, 1936–8. A wide rounded corner
opening in a gaping maw, with a later glazed upper lip canopy and
a stepped parapet fronting the high auditorium shed behind. Brick
pilastered wall to Allan Park. Feisty opposition to the project raised
by residents in nearby King's Park can well be understood.

CENTRAL POLICE HEADQUARTERS, St Ninian's Road. Parallel
to the road, a long three-storey office block by *Stirling County
Council*, 1970–1. First and second floors repetitively clad in
storey-height precast concrete panels; over thirty identical splay-
framed windowed bays of white exposed aggregate planes interrupted asymmetrically by a brown brick stair tower marking the
entrance.

CHRISTIE MEMORIAL CLOCK, King's Park Road. By *A. M.
Lupton* of Stirling, 1905–6. Thick fluted shaft with a densely

floral capital from which cherub heads peep out. On top is a boxed clock, its four aedicular faces crowned by segmental pediments broken by elaborate cartouches.

Former COURT HOUSE AND JAIL, St John Street and Jail Wynd. By *Richard Crichton*, 1806–11. Additions made on the s side of the Tolbooth (q.v.) to provide prison cells and a double-height Court Room. Ground-floor rooms and those in the sw corner of the first and second floors are vaulted. The Court Room, lit by three round-arched windowed recesses on the w and e, has a coffered plaster ceiling vault. Tenement height, suitably solid, symmetrical and spartan, the Jailhouse faces St John Street; ashlar Neo-Classicism at once ascetic and assertive. Four-window front with five arched ground-floor openings. On the w gable, a Gibbsian door with bearded head keystone.

A radical conversion by *Richard Murphy Architects*, 2001, adapted the Court Room as a 200-seat theatre auditorium, altering its axis from n–s to w–e and adding a cantilevered extension with bleacher seating which will project into the courtyard on the e side of the existing building. An entrance pend passing from Jail Wynd through one of the vaulted ground-floor rooms will give access to this inner space. Artists' accommodation, a recording studio and bar will be accommodated in the Jailhouse building with a secondary performance space added in the attic. While existing street elevations remain intact, the proposals carry the promise of an intervention in which the new and the old will cohere, Scarpa-like, in uncompromising excitement and honesty.

COWANE CENTRE, Cowane Street. High gabled classrooms rear up behind a playground forecourt elevated above the w side of the street. These are the 1884 extensions to the mid-c19 Territorial School, an oddly rusticated, single-storey block of eleven segmental-headed windows, three of which step up at the centre under a gablet. Adapted as a community centre, 1974.

COWANE'S HOSPITAL, St John's Street. A finely conceived, late medieval almshouse constructed between 1637 and 1648. Funded from a legacy left by the prosperous Stirling merchant John Cowane (†1633), the building was built 'for sustenying therintill the nomber of tuelf decayed gildbroder, burgessis and induellars' of the burgh. *John Mylne Jun.*, master-mason to the Crown, provided the design. Built in freestone quarried at Elphinstone and Plean, the structure took shape under the direction of the local mason *James Rynd*. In 1852 some reconstruction work was carried out by *Francis Mackison*.

The hospital, two storeys high to the entrance front on the 80 ne and three on the sw where it falls to Back Walk below, is laid out to an E-shaped plan. The main block lies nw–se between steep crowstepped gables with apex chimneys. Short end wings, lower in height, project ne to similar gables. Advancing at the centre is a four-storey, three-stage stair tower with a leaded ogival roof. The lowest stage, which is two-storeyed, is asymmetrical with the simple entrance door and window above placed to the r. Moulded stringcourses mark out the upper stages:

below, an aedicule-framed niche with a statue of the donor; above, similar but narrower belfry aedicules. Above the entrance are two inscribed TABLETS. The larger, dated 1639, reads: THIS HOSPITALL / WAS ERECTED AND / LARGLY PROVYDED BY JOHN COWANE / DEAN OF GILD / FOR / THE ENTERTAIN-MENT / OF DECAYED GILD / BREITHER. On the lower, the familiar biblical text from Matthew 25 enjoining charity. The statue of John Cowane dressed in ruff, doublet and breeches is by *Mylne* and is based on a preliminary study by *John Service*, a local mason and contemporary of Cowane (*see* Old Kirkyard, above). To l. and r. of the tower is a single window; above each an eaves dormer; all four openings blocked during C19 altera-tions. Similar windows with adjacent door openings occur on the inward-facing SE and NW walls of the wings. The doorway to the SE wing has been altered to become a window, the neigh-bouring window a door. Biblical texts are carved on the lintels of both original doorways. High in the gables of both wings are oval panels with a moulded surround each bearing the initials J C and the date 1639 in relief.

A tall three-light window with moulded mullions, frieze and a cornice carrying strapwork ornament fills the centre of the SE gable of the main block. Symmetrically below are two corniced doors bearing more strapwork incorporating Cowane's mono-gram J C. These doorways open on to a flagged terrace over-looking the Bowling Green (*see* below). The NW gable is less grand, with only a few small lintelled windows. There are three mural TABLETS, two with textual inscriptions. On the SW front, dramatically visible on the Castle Rock skyline, three high shoul-dered chimneystacks alternate with three tall two-light windows which break through the eaves to gables.

The three chimneys no longer function, the fireplaces that warmed the ground-floor 'Hospital Hall' having disappeared, possibly in the first quarter of the C18 when the partitions sub-dividing the first-floor 'Over Hospital' were removed to create a second hall space. From this time the term 'Guildhall' was regularly applied to this upper hall, though the Patrons allowed the building to be used 'for a great variety of purposes besides the ordinary meeting place of the Gildry'. If the fireplaces were retained in this conversion they did not survive the changes of 1852 when Mackison removed the floor dividing the two halls, thus creating a single lofty chamber. The three splendid SW windows, together with the window in the SE gable introduced in these Victorian changes, light this main apartment of the hospital. Entered from a small lobby in the tower, it is five bays long with a gallery at the NW end and an open timber roof. Pointed-arched trusses and intermediate rafter trusses carry purlins, spars and boarding, the principal trusses springing from elaborately carved corbelstones set into plastered walls. The gallery, which has a panelled front bearing the reversed '4' mark of the Guildry of Stirling, is reached by a stair in the adjacent wing. A smaller domed balcony recessed at the centre of the NE wall, its panelled projection carried on coupled consoles identical to the roof truss corbels, is accessible from the tower. Three niches are also indented at balcony level in the NE wall. The Hall walls are panelled to door height. In the SE gable, a fireplace which may be original in part. Above it, colourful STAINED GLASS by *James Ballantine* depicts the building's patron, John Cowane.

The terrace that extends along the SE gable of the hospital looks across an open balustrade with widely spaced balusters, dating from the late 1660s, on to the BOWLING GREEN, laid out in 1712, probably on the site of an earlier garden. In the nearby Dutch Garden is a pedestal SUNDIAL. The incised inscription on the brass dial bears the date 1727 and records that the maker was *Andrew Dickie* of Stirling. The octagonal base may, however, be a surviving part of the sundial bought from *John Buchanan* in 1673.

CRAWFORD'S ARCADE, linking King Street and Murray Place. By *John McLean*, 1879–82; restored in the early 1980s by *Honeyman, Jack & Robertson*. Built as a private investment for the local councillor William Crawford. Behind narrow, four-storey street façades at each end (*see* Description, below) ramped shopping alleys lead at r. angles to an inner court. The alleys, two glazed storeys high, are lit from a clearstorey and a continuous pitched roof-light carried on arch trusses. The five-bay court is a storey higher, the upper floors glazed between pilasters with entablatures at each floor level decorated with cartouches and anthemion ornament. Covering the court is a hipped roof-light on timber and steel tie trusses.

Former DRILL HALL, Princes Street. Dated 1892. Built for the Argyll & Sutherland Highlanders. Symmetrical gatehouse Baronial at the head of the brae. Early Renaissance detail. Moulded doorpiece centred in a crowstepped gable sandwiched by cone-roofed drums; an echo of the castle forework?

FORTH VALLEY HEALTH BOARD, 33 Spittal Street. Classical gravitas. Built as the Commercial Bank, 1825–7, to a design by *James Gillespie Graham*; a six-bay ashlar block with projecting tetrastyle portico in Greek Doric. Altered by *Peddie & Kinnear*, 1873–4, it became the Royal Infirmary, acquiring parapeted wings in repeated enlargements, 1878, 1883 and 1913.

JUBILEE FOUNTAIN, Viewfield Place. Dated 1887. Three-branched light sprouting from the capital of a pink granite shaft. The column sits on a four-basin plinth enlivened by colonnettes and lion-heads. Stepped octagonal base in grey granite.

MERCAT CROSS, Broad Street. Restored 1891. Octagonal shaft on a stepped circular base with typical royal burgh crown of armorial shields and unicorn (known locally as 'The Puggy'). The unicorn alone survives from the original C16 cross which was removed in 1792.

MUNICIPAL BUILDINGS, 8–10 Corn Exchange Road. Won in 86 competition by *J. Gaff Gillespie* of *Salmon, Son & Gillespie* in 1908 but not built until 1914–18. Ambitious in conception (the project began in 1894 with the creation of a new road from Spittal Street downhill to Dumbarton Road), only the central block and SW wing of a grandly symmetrical proposal were realized. The architecture is distinguished in composition and character, the scale impressively civic, especially where the land falls s at Back Walk. The main seven-bay block, two storeys and attic high, is dominated by a central gable from which a corbelled canted bay pushes forward at first floor under a swept ogee roof. At the gable apex, a sculptured finial statue of Mary, Queen of Scots. The oriel has two column mullions: at the top of one are carved the initials J.G.G. and a pair of compasses, for the architect; at the top of the other, W.G. and a mallet, for the builder, *William Gourlay*. To l. and r., canopied niches house the tall figures of a warrior and cleric. Below the niches, carved unicorns and, over the door below, the inscription SPAIR NOTHT. CONSIDER WEIL. SPEIK FURTH, an adaptation of lines carved on Mar's Wark (*see* Mansions, below). The doorway is round-arched, its keystone carved on the soffit with the initials A.W.Y. for the sculptor, *A. W. Young*, the imposts bearing inscriptions recording the laying of the foundation stone, 1914, and the opening, 1918. On each side of the door are three round-arched windows above which are two-light, mullioned and transomed windows in heavily moulded lintelled frames. A stepped parapet partially conceals attic gablets. The taller sw wing advances l. on a channelled storey-height plinth lit by three large round-arched windows, its symmetrical street façade rounded on the flanks under conical roofs. Set between these Holyrood-like drums, ahead of the glazed wall of first- and second-floor offices, is a four-columned screen *in antis*. Only the cornice is continuous, the remainder of the entablature recessing between each column. The entrance to this wing, at the base of the E tower, is framed by columns carrying a curved entablature over which carved angels support the burgh shield. High on the convex face of this tower is another shield and an inscription to the tailor Robert Spittal 1530, Town Council patron of Spittal's Hospital (*see* Description: Old Town). On the s tower, a corresponding honour is accorded John Cowane 1633, patron of Cowane's Hospital (*see* above). Round the corner on Back Walk, the sw front climbs to seven storeys below a steeply pedimented clock tower.

The entrance hall and staircase of the central block are inlaid with a variety of marbles, pilaster capitals bearing emblematic figures representing the Scottish infantry regiments. Columned upper hall. Tripartite STAINED-GLASS window over stair depicts Alexander II presenting the town's royal charter in 1226; designed by *Gillespie*, 1915, and executed by *William Meikle & Sons*, 1916.

In 1937 proposals to complete the project were prepared by *Gillespie, Kidd & Coia*, the successor practice to Salmon, Son & Gillespie. After the Second World War a bay was added to the r. of the porch following the original design. Following the demolition of the Corn Exchange Hotel, further extensions by the Burgh Architect, *Walter H. Gillespie*, 1965–8, provided three storeys of offices turning the corner into Spittal Street (*see* Description: Old Town, below).

NEW BRIDGE. Built 1831–2 to a design prepared by the engineer *Robert Stevenson*, 1822. Built in rough-faced whinstone (smooth to the carriageway). Five segmental arches with radial masonry from its voussoirs. Round-ended cutwaters.

OLD BRIDGE, Bridgehaugh Road. Late C15 or early C16; SW arch 75 rebuilt 1748; repaired 1927. Perhaps the most strategically important river crossing in all Scotland, yet strangely quiet and detached from the town. A bridge, probably of timber construction, existed at least as early as the mid C13. Built in coursed square rubble, the present structure is 82m. long with a cobbled carriageway of 4.56m. There are four semicircular arches with chamfered double-ring voussoirs between cutwater piers set on oval rubble foundations. Over the central cutwaters the bridge parapets form refuge recesses which, until the C18, rose to crowstepped gables. From here, parapets with weathered coping stones step down to what were the SW and NE gates, originally arched but, since mid-C18 rebuilding, marked by square pillars with tall pyramidal finials. Abutments, renewed in random rubble, stretch back on each bank, those N of the river attractively curved in plan.

Former OLD HIGH SCHOOL, Academy Road and Spittal Street. By *J., W. H. & J. M. Hay*, 1854–6; extended 1887–90 by *J. M. MacLaren* and further enlarged by *McLuckie & Walker*, 1905–7. Closed in 1962. Converted and extended to become Stirling Highland Hotel, 1990–1, by *Coleman, Ballantine*.

Dated 1854, the wide, almost symmetrical Gothic Revival front on Academy Road, built on a site once occupied by a monastic school, is constructed in dark whin with Bannockburn sandstone dressings. End bay gables with mullioned and transomed windows. Vaulted pend under central tower; above the pointed entry, a two-storey window (surmounted by sculpted children by *Alexander Handyside Ritchie*), belfry, clock, parapet gables, bartizans and slated pyramid roof. Rising above the gable to Spittal Street, an octagonal belfry with cusped ogee arches and a stone pyramid roof. At the junction with Back Walk, the PRIMARY HIGH SCHOOL, added by *McLuckie & Walker*, 1905–7, maintains mullioned and transomed windows. On the wall, a stone TABLET, dated 1530, commemorates Robert Spittal, TAYLOR TO KING JAMES THE FOURTH / DONOR OF THE HOSPITAL IN THIS BURGH / FOR RELIEF OF DECAYED TRADESMEN, with the scissors of his own trade carved below the inscription.

The main extension to the school, 1887–90, is by *J. M. MacLaren* (completed by *Robert Watson*), who won the commission in competition. Three storeys stretch down Spittal Street to a five-storey observatory tower, the gift of Sir Henry Campbell-Bannerman. Above a high ground-floor storey of hammered ashlar, the walls are of snecked whin with fine sandstone dressings. Eight bays of mullioned and transomed windows light the first-floor classrooms; at the second floor, three push up as tall dormers, their semicircular pediments carved with thistle, rose and lily. Framing the high cusped portal at the base of the tower, more carving: Zodiac panels in the splayed reveals and, above, the Tree of Science and the Tree of Life with the inscription HIGH SCHOOL and the date 1888. The late C16 arched doorway with

diamond-faceted pilasters and strapwork capitals seems originally to have come from the house of Adam Spittal of Blairlogie.
The tower is windowed to Spittal Street but beyond the rounded
corner it is tower-house solid: a cliff of snecked masonry soaring
to an ashlar parapet and copper-domed observatory. A round
stair drum bulging s converts to an octagon below the parapet,
over which is a recessed caphouse with ogival roof. The allusions
are Scottish, though overall the building is much more eclectic.
Practising in the milieu of Arts and Crafts London, MacLaren
mixes his sources, Scots and English, Gothic and Renaissance,
with Free Style Edwardian ease. Yet this tower, however 'remotely
Baronial'*, was to prove seminal. Gaunt gable and turreted
tower, traditional forms traditionally transformed, were noted by
Charles Rennie Mackintosh, to be recycled once more, first in
the skyline of his *Glasgow Herald* building in Glasgow, 1893,
then in the E end of the Glasgow School of Art, 1897.

The conversion to a hotel has created a closed inner courtyard. NW and NE ranges by the *Hays*: the former a symmetrical
eleven-bay wall with a towered centrepiece and arcaded outer
bays (now glazed); the latter a three-bay arcade of buttressed
arches (also glazed) under tall bipartite windows breaking the
eaves with finialled dormerheads. *MacLaren*'s more complex
SW range, towered to the r., maintains the Victorian collegiate
atmosphere. *Coleman, Ballantine* have adapted these buildings
to hotel use with considerable care. Less convincing, their three-
storey bedroom block in dry-dash sienna-coloured render striped
with ashlar stringcourses closing the quadrangle on the SE side.

81  OLD JAIL, St John Street. By *Thomas Brown Jun.*, 1845–7. Built
to supersede the Tolbooth prison (*see* former Court House and
Jail, above), then deemed the worst in Britain. Ingeniously and
excitingly restored as an interpretation centre and offices by
*Stirling District Council*, 1994–6. Darkly castellar in lugubrious
whinstone rubble with crenellated ashlar parapets. Symmetrical
arrow-head plan, the cells layered in three storeys over a basement in each wing. Pinned between the cells at the centre of the
S front, a drum tower with octagonal off-centre turret. The
basement cells have been restored, as has the circular LAUNDRY
which, located in the drum, has a central stone column with a
corbelled capital supporting a ceiling of radial stone slabs. From
this exhibition area, at the lowest level, visitors are conveyed in
a glass-walled lift to viewing galleries on the roof. Above ground
floor, the three-storey cantilevered gallery interior accommodates
three floors of offices created from cells. The superimposed
circular chambers in the drum, each with cast iron columns at the
centre (including what was once the domed guardhouse), are
now meeting rooms. In the former DEBTORS' ROOM, top floor
centre, the conversion has introduced a helical steel stair rising
under a glazed cupola to a viewing platform on the roof. Crenellated boundary WALLS and GATEPIERS command the entrance
from St John Street.

---

* Fiona Sinclair, *Scotstyle* (1984), 55.

ORCHARD HOUSE HOSPITAL AND HEALTH CENTRE, Union Street. A disparate group of dull low buildings including vestiges of the former Poorhouse, Hospital and Lunatic Asylum by *John Dick Peddie*, 1855–6, now adapted as a Geriatric Unit, and *McLuckie & Walker*'s Union Street Hospital of 1904–5. Health Centre in brown brick by *Alex Strang & Partners*, 1982.

POST OFFICE, 84–86 Murray Place. By *W. W. Robertson* of *H.M. Office of Works*, 1894–5. Symmetrical ashlar palazzo, two tall storeys high and four lights wide (round-arched at ground floor, lintelled above). In the outer bays, pilastered entrances under pedimented aedicules. Above a dentilled and consoled eaves cornice, these end bays rise into blind aedicule dormers with shell pediments and flanking urns.

PUBLIC LIBRARY, Corn Exchange Road. Competition-winning design, 1901, by *Harry Ramsay Taylor* of *Lessels & Taylor*. Built 1903–4. An impressive testimony to the generosity of Carnegie funding. A street wall full of Scots Renaissance ornament 'with liberal touches of Elizabethan'*, especially in the great mullioned and transomed windows which light the Reading Room NW and SW. On the skyline, pyramid, ogee and cone; the last rising from a tall tower, circular drum over octagonal oriel, that marks the corner with Back Walk.

RAILWAY STATION, Goosecroft Road. 1913–16, by *James Miller* with the Caledonian Railway Co.'s Superintending Engineer, *W. A. Paterson*. Proposals to upgrade *A. &A. Heiton*'s small station of 1855 were first made at the end of the C19‡ but it was more than a decade before extensive reconstruction was finally undertaken. Streetside, the new station retained the rather sober crowstepped gable idiom of its mid-C19 forerunner, but behind is a new world of light and line. Glazed roofs stretch N and S along the platforms rising in piended pavilions linked by a covered footbridge. Curves are everywhere: in the semicircular concourse, bowed bookstalls and bending stairflights; in the steel lattice trusses that arch and branch from the flat-topped capitals of cast iron columns. Miller's glasshouse magic was not new; ten years earlier at Wemyss Bay, much influenced by the railway company's chief engineer, Donald Matheson, he had linked platform and pier with an elegance that cannot quite be matched at Stirling.

RAINBOW SLIDES LEISURE CENTRE, Goosecroft Road. 1971–3. Rectangular swimming-pool hall clad in grooved exposed aggregate concrete panels sandwiched between a dark brick plinth and copper fascia. Lower entrance block with random rubble facing. Cast concrete mural by *Charles Anderson*, 1973.

SHERIFF COURT, Viewfield Place. Designed as County Buildings and Court by *Thomas Brown Jun.*, 1864; executed by *Brown & Wardrop*, 1874–6. Symmetrical with flanking crowstepped gables, a high *piano nobile* of mullioned and transomed windows and a steep hipped roof with decorative ironwork at the ridge. At the

* Charles McKean, *Stirling and the Trossachs* (1985), 35.
‡ In 1900 *T. M. Barr* produced plans in Elizabethan style. Two years later *Peddie & Washington Browne* exhibited a Queen Anne version at the Royal Scottish Academy.

second floor, three dormers, capped by attenuated finial-like gablets, rise between wallhead parapets. Gothic porch, Renaissance strapwork, Baronial stair turrets. Hammerbeam roof in Court Room. Linked N, symmetrical 1912 extension, a single crowstepped gable compressed between chimneystacks and pedimented entrances.

SMITH ART GALLERY AND MUSEUM, 40 Dumbarton Road. By *John Lessels*, 1871–4. Elegantly calm and classical temple to the arts; 'unequalled out of London' said the *Stirling Journal and Advertiser* (1874) with exaggerated pride. Tetrastyle Doric portico with entablature and pediment; the tympanum adorned with the arms of Stirling and those of the founder, the painter and collector Thomas Stewart Smith. Placed symmetrically behind, a wider, piend-roofed block, its parapet picking up the line of architrave and frieze. Behind this, a deep plan of parallel galleries, the SE elevation of which, nine bays long, is framed by pedimented gables with Venetian windows. Inscriptions, including the name of the architect, in the tympana. Inside, the long roof-light over the main gallery is crossed by lattice beams decoratively pierced (unexpectedly) with trefoils. On the forecourt, two cast iron lamp standards by *McDowall, Steven & Co.* of Glasgow, their fluted shafts and classical ornament colourfully painted.

Former SNOWDON SCHOOL, 31 Spittal Street. Collegiate Gothic by *J., W.H. & J.M. Hay*, 1855. Two gables with cusped lancets; the l. a later addition, the r. with a corbelled corner belfry, square then octagonal with trefoil-headed openings under a bellcast polygonal roof.

STIRLING COUNCIL OFFICES, Viewforth, St Ninian's Road. An extensive campus, testimony to the expansion of local authority bureaucracy through the C20. Two large C19 mansion-houses have been assimilated to administrative need. At the N end of the site, closest to the town centre, is VIEWFORTH, 1855, a rugged Baronial concoction, spiked with square and round bartizan turrets, by the Liverpool architects *J., W.H. and J.M. Hay*. In 1932 the County Council occupied the house after alterations had been carried out by *James Miller* of Glasgow. Within a few years more space was required and Miller added a long two-storey wing, 1934–7, stretching E at the rear of the house. Built in white-pointed russet-brown brick laid in Flemish bond, these offices are entered from the S through a three-bay centrepiece of ashlar fluted pilasters. Placed l. and r. of the bronze entrance doors are statues of Wallace and Bruce by *A. Handyside Ritchie*, 1856, relocated from the old house. An axial approach leads through the entrance hall to the Council Chamber which projects N. At the S end of the site, *William Leiper*'s LANGGARTH (formerly Viewfield), dated 1897, is also in administrative use. A sprawling composition in C17 Scots style with circular tower, corbelled turret and crowstepped gables. The influence of Lorimer is clear; even more so in Leiper's harled LODGE, dated 1899, a delightful piece of white vernacular sculpture, roofed with pyramid and cone. Landscaped across the gentle slope between

PUBLIC BUILDINGS 715

these two Victorian residences stretches NEW VIEWFORTH, by the Stirling County Architect *A. J. Smith*, a vast development of five-storey offices constructed between 1968 and 1971. Cruciform in plan, the design is relentlessly regular in elevation, every lozenge-shaped window framed by precast concrete panels (themselves cruciform in shape) with an acid-washed finish of Creetown granite aggregate.

STIRLING ROYAL INFIRMARY, Livilands Gate. Begun 1925–8 by the Glasgow architect *James Miller*, whose home was in nearby Randolphfield. This earliest phase of building is now buried at the centre of an agglomeration of later *ad hoc* growth added intermittently throughout the C20. Miller's neo-Georgian work retains dignity with difficulty. Its symmetrical hip-roofed central block, nine bays wide with two-bay outer wings advancing slightly, is a regular aggregation of two-storey-high reddish-brown brick panels with superimposed brick-arched windows separated by broad pilaster strips. At the centre is a columned porch with quasi Tower of the Winds capitals. All this is ordered and relatively untouched. But flanking flat-roofed ward blocks, arranged in paired relationship to the NE and SW, have suffered badly from later encroachment and alteration. Less impaired is the 1933 out-patients' department (now Ward 9) which Miller added at the SW end of the circulation axis of his plan. A single-storey roughcast building with a dormered mansard attic, its SW front is eleven bays wide. Workshops and stores of 1941 (?). Chest diseases unit, 1955. Nurses' training school, 1961. Out-patients' department, 1964. Two-storey-and-basement maternity unit clad in white precast concrete panels by *Keppie, Henderson & Partners*, 1967–9. Extensive additions carried out to the NW in dark brown brickwork are dominated by the Queen Elizabeth Wing, 1996–8, by the *Common Services Agency*, a wide-fronted, four-storey block articulated by square bay projections.

THISTLE CENTRE. Phase 1, E of Port Street and Murray Place, by *Walter Underwood & Partners*, 1973–6; Phase 2, crossing Goosecroft Road to Burghmuir Road, by *Comprehensive Design*, 1995–7. An extensive development of covered shopping malls linking the town's commercial centre with lower car parking decks and a bus station to the E. In Phase 1 the malls are lit by continuous segmental roof-lighting carried on lightweight bow trusses triangulated with a complex network of steel ties. In Phase 2, known as The Marches, the malls are higher, brighter and whiter with canted beams supporting lean-to patent glazing. On the SE edge is a large restaurant space lit by a wide band of glazing giving views across roadway, railway and industrial backlands to the Ochil Hills.

TOWN HOUSE, Broad Street and Jail Wynd. A three-storey-and- 79 attic tolbooth with a NW tower, built 1703–5 to replace its C15 predecessor, by then dilapidated and dangerous. The work was carried out by master mason *Harie Livingstone* and *John Christie*, wright, to a design commissioned by the magistrates and Council from *Sir William Bruce*. Livingstone dealt directly with Bruce, travelling to Kinross to obtain 'ane draught or sceme of the

work'*. Three storeys high and originally only three bays wide
to Broad Street, the new Town House appears to have incorporated surviving masonry from the C15 building, especially behind
facing stone in the lower stages of the tower and on the S side
away from the street façade. In 1785 the building was extended
a further three bays E by *Gideon Gray*. The enlargement is barely
betrayed by a slightly broader gap between windows at the centre
of the elevation but otherwise the heights, spacing and detail of
the windows remain the same. All have lugged moulded architraves and pulvinated friezes, those at first- and second-floor
level linked by stringcourses at the sills. Three windowed bays
with plain offset margins face Jail Wynd. Sockets for iron grilles
cut around the upper halves of all these windows indicate the
probability that the lower sections were originally shuttered. A
doorway, detailed in similar fashion to that of the windows,
opens from Broad Street adjacent to the tower. A second, similar
entrance on the W wall, S of the tower, is now a window.

At the corner, the six-storey tower rises to a moulded eaves
cornice and iron-railed parapet within which sits a timber belfry
under a steeply swept leaded roof with ogival cap and gilded
weathercock. Clock in a moulded stone frame and 'ane new moon
glob sufficientlie guilded [*sic*]' by *Duncan Ker*, 1704, the former
replaced by a new mechanism made by *Andrew Dickie*, 1728.
From Broad Street a round-headed archway with a grotesque
keystone opens to a straight stair which penetrates the tower
over a vaulted ground-floor cell; at first floor, a vestibule leads l.
to the council chamber. Over the street arch is a niche set in a
rectangular frame carved with egg-and-dart and above that a
window similar to and aligned with those lighting the tolbooth
at second-floor level. In the upper part of the tower, demarcated
by a stringcourse which coincides with the eaves cornice of the
tolbooth, two small superimposed windows.

Quadripartite plaster vault over the tower stair, the central
bell-hole filled by a painted panel carrying the burgh seal and
the motto STIRLINI OPPIDVM. A round-arched doorway with
roll-and-hollow surround leads to the vestibule. From here a
door with a lugged architrave opens to the first of two large rooms
separated by the original early C18 gable wall. Panelled walls with
dado and moulded cornice. On the E wall, a stone fireplace with
fluted Ionic pilasters and painted landscape overmantel, early
C18. In the second room, dado panelling, decorative plaster
cornice, scrolled plaster brackets and chimneypiece, late C18. A
BELL, dated 1656, hangs in the fifth storey of the tower. In the
belfry, a recast BELL of 1864 and a chime of sixteen BELLS, two
dated 1729.

In 2001 a major programme of repair and restoration was in
train, directed by architects *Simpson & Brown*. The project,
initiated in 1999, also entailed the integrated rehabilitation of
the former Court House and Jail buildings (q.v.) which abut the
Tolbooth tower on the S.

* *Extracts from the Records of the Royal Burgh of Stirling, 1667–1752* (Scottish Burgh
Records Society, 1889), 97.

UNIVERSITY OF STIRLING (*see* p. 789).
WAR MEMORIAL, Corn Exchange Road. By *George R. Davidson*
of Stirling, 1922. Shaped stone pillar carrying bronze lions and
standard. Balustraded Scots Renaissance terrace.

## MANSIONS

ARGYLL'S LODGING, Castle Wynd\*. This delightful building, 105
the finest surviving example of a C17 noble town house in
Scotland, has a more complex building history than its first
appearance of architectural homogeneity might suggest. Four
main phases of work have been identified, in the course of
which a modest mid-C16 house was progressively expanded to
provide a fine urban residence by a succession of three later aristocratic owners, all of whom had estates in the area. These later
owners were Adam Erskine (a kinsman of the Earl of Mar), the
first Earl of Stirling, and the ninth Earl of Argyll (from whom
the house takes its name). The two latest building phases, *c.* 1630
and *c.* 1670, correspond to periods when a greater royal presence in Scotland was anticipated, and the house may have been
intended to accommodate its owners in appropriate style when
they attended the royal court hoped for at the nearby castle.

### The mid-C16 hall house and the SW street range

The earliest identifiable part of the building is at its NE corner,
where there is what appears to have been a compact two-storeyed
house. The ground floor of this house survives largely intact,
though this is only readily discernible internally; it has a barrel-
vaulted kitchen at the E end, and two vaulted chambers connected by a vaulted corridor to its W. Little of its upper floor is
identifiable, but it is assumed it would have contained a hall
and chamber, reached either by an external forestair or by an
internal stair in a narrow compartment at its W end. The ownership of this building is not known with certainty, though there
are records of the conveyance in 1559 of a tenement by John
Traill, a burgess of St Andrews, to a servant of Adam Erskine;
since the latter appears to have been the owner of the Lodging
in its next phase of existence, it was possibly the house on this site
that was being conveyed. Around this time there may already
have been a building on the site of the later SW range, running
along the line of the street; possibly an earlier residence of the
earls of Argyll, who evidently had property in this area.

### The urban tower house of c. 1600

The hall-house was enlarged by the addition of a jamb off the E
end of its S face, and heightened by two extra storeys *c.* 1600.
Most of the jamb was destroyed in the course of later extensions,

---

\* This account has been written by Richard Fawcett.

but there is still a spiral stair corbelled out at what was the re-entrant angle of the two parts, which connects the higher floors from first-floor level upwards. These enlargements resulted in a tall L-shaped house comparable with many rural tower-houses found throughout Scotland. But such tower-house-like structures were once also common as residences in the burghs, with examples still to be seen in the manse at Anstruther Easter, the lodging of the Earl of Kellie in Pittenweem (both Fife and of c. 1590), or in the splendid town residence of the earls of Cassillis in Maybole (Ayrshire, early C17). On analogy with such houses elsewhere, it seems likely the rooms on the first floor would have been a hall and chamber, with access to them by a spacious stair within the jamb, and with chambers on the upper floors of both the main block and jamb reached by the surviving spiral stair. At some stage an office wing was added w of the house, with a larger kitchen at its far end; this wing forms the ground floor of the N quarter of the house in its final form.

At this stage the house was possibly owned by Adam Erskine, Commendator of the secularized abbey of Cambuskenneth from 1562 to 1608. In 1604, he resigned 'a new and great house or manor' in Stirling to his kinsman, Sir James Erskine of Craig, which may have been this house.

## The house of c. 1630

In 1629 the house and adjoining land were acquired by Sir William Alexander, later first Earl of Stirling, one of the leading courtiers and men of letters of his generation, and Secretary for Scotland from 1626. His wife was a member of a cadet branch of the previous owner's family. Parts of the building are dated by inscription to 1632 and 1633, suggesting a burst of activity in anticipation of Charles I's long-awaited homecoming in 1633 for his Scottish coronation. In the course of that visit Alexander, already a viscount, was elevated to an earldom.

Stirling's main contribution was an imposing three-storeyed range extending s from the main body of the earlier tower-house, and subsuming the original s jamb of that house. At the s end of the new range a shorter range was built at r. angles to balance the main block of the c. 1600 building. Stirling's house was in the highest fashion of its day, presumably reflecting his ability to call on the services of the royal masters of works and master masons. It was perhaps built with the involvement of his second son, *Sir Anthony Alexander*, who was appointed joint royal Master of Works in 1629, but the possible authorship of the design is discussed more fully below.

## The house of c. 1670: Argyll's Lodging

Lord Stirling died in debt in 1640, leaving his Stirling house to his fifth son, but the burgh foreclosed on mortgages on the property, after which there were proposals to turn it into an almshouse. The house was eventually disponed to the ninth Earl of Argyll in 1668. Significantly, the families of the earls of Argyll and Stirling were closely connected. It had been the seventh Earl of Argyll who took the future Earl of Stirling on the tour of Europe, and who had probably later introduced him at court. Additionally, the Alexander family's seat at Menstrie (E of Stirling) may once have formed part of the lands of the earls of Argyll, who had their main Lowland seat at nearby Castle Campbell (q.v.).

Argyll further remodelled the Lodging, possibly in expectation of visits by the king to Scotland and Stirling, around the time that work started on the rebuilding of the palace at Holyrood in 1671. Argyll's most clearly identifiable work is on the s side of the courtyard, where the architectural evidence suggests he may have connected up the Earl of Stirling's house with an existing range to the sw. He may also have partly remodelled the N quarter, and added a new external frame to the courtyard entrance; he certainly did much redecoration within the house. Comparison with the contemporary work at Holyrood, however, suggests that, with the exception of the new gateway, Argyll's work was not in such high fashion as Stirling's had been.

Inventories were drawn up in 1680 and 1682 as part of the jointure arrangements after the house was settled on Argyll's second wife, which help understanding of how the house then functioned; unfortunately, we do not have comparable evidence to explain how the rooms of the house had been used before then.

## The later history of the house

The house was sold by the fourth Duke of Argyll in 1764 and passed through various hands before being acquired by the crown in about 1800. It was then used as a hospital in connection with the military use of the castle. During this use, c. 1862, much of the sw range was demolished, apart from its N end; the outer wall of the ground floor of the rest of that range was retained as the enclosure wall towards the street. After Stirling Castle ceased to be a military depot in 1964, the house was used for about thirty years as a Youth Hostel. In 1996–7 major works of conservation were carried out, and the main rooms are now presented as they might have been furnished in 1680.

## PLAN

The house is laid out around three sides of a courtyard, with the principal quarter of c. 1630 on the E, facing a screen wall which cuts off the courtyard from the road. In this plan the inspiration of French *hôtel* layout is evident. Such inspiration was not entirely new, and is to be seen on a smaller scale and less regularly arranged in the c. 1600 nucleus of Culross Palace, Fife (Sir George Bruce's house, where the screen wall is now gone) and at Acheson House off the Canongate in Edinburgh (started in 1633 for the Earl of Stirling's fellow Scottish Secretary, Sir Archibald Acheson); but Argyll's Lodging is by far the grandest surviving C17 expression of the idea. A fourth range extended down

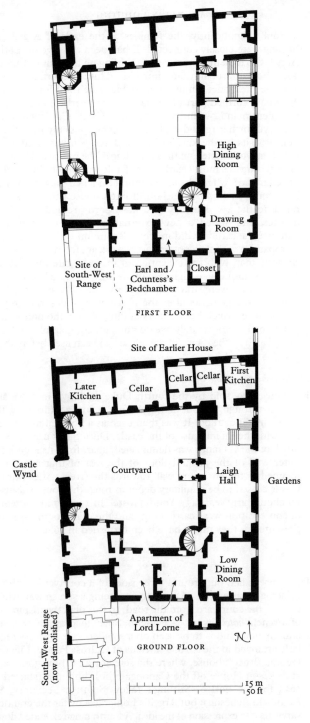

High
Dining
Room

Drawing
Room

Site of
South-West
Range

Earl and
Countess's
Bedchamber

Closet

FIRST FLOOR

Site of Earlier House

Later
Kitchen

Cellar

Cellar

Cellar

First
Kitchen

Castle
Wynd

Courtyard

Laigh
Hall

Gardens

Low
Dining
Room

Apartment of
Lord Lorne

N

South-West Range
(now demolished)

GROUND FLOOR

15 m
50 ft

Stirling, Argyll's Lodging. Plans.

along the street front from the SW corner of the house, though much of this was demolished *c.* 1862. There are circular or polygonal turrets for spiral stairs at all four internal corners of the courtyard, though that at the NE corner, surviving from the house of *c.* 1600, is behind the face of the E quarter because of the way the inner wall of that quarter overlapped the remains of the *c.* 1600 jamb.

Despite the complex architectural history of the house, the first impression of regularity is striking. The main deviation from this is the impingement of the N end of the SW range into the area of the courtyard. This anomaly supports the possibility that the SW range was a *c.* 1670 remodelling of an earlier structure. When it was connected to the *c.* 1630 Lodging, a narrow closet block was added in the re-entrant angle towards the courtyard.

The house is entered at the centre of the E quarter through a porch, which opens on to the Laigh Hall. The principal stair at the N end of the Hall leads up to the main rooms on the first floor. The ground floor of the N quarter is occupied by kitchens and domestic offices, while at the junction of the E and S quarters on the ground floor is the Low Dining Room. Individual rooms, or groups of rooms forming apartments, fill the rest of the ground floor of S and SW ranges. It is uncertain how the sequence of rooms functioned *c.* 1630, but by *c.* 1670 the principal accommodation was on the first floor of the E quarter and the E part of the S quarter. It starts with the High Dining Room at the head of the stair, beyond which was the apartment of the earl and countess, consisting of a drawing room, closet, bedchamber and stool closet. (It was presumably the relatively limited space in their town house which meant that the earl and countess shared an apartment, since by this date they might have been expected to have separate apartments in their main houses.) Much of the rest of the upper floors of the house was evidently subdivided into a series of two-roomed apartments, each of which could be reached either from the main body of the house through other apartments or, with greater privacy, by way of the spiral stairways at the corners of the courtyard and on the garden side of the SW wing. There were no corridors apart from a short section in the domestic offices of the N quarter. The W ends of the upper floors of the N and S quarters are now physically separated from the rest of the house, and are only accessible by the spiral stairs. The use of the second floor in the E quarter possibly changed between the 1630s and 1670s. It may eventually have been used as a gallery, and is certainly now a single open space; but the existence of mural stool closets at each end suggests it was originally subdivided into two apartments.

The evidence of C18 maps shows there were extensive terraced gardens, laid out with formal parterres, E of the house.

## EXTERIOR

The chief elements of the STREET FRONT are a pair of gable walls, each with a crowstepped gable capped by a chimney, between which runs the screen wall containing the arched gateway to the main courtyard. Extending S from this is the wall towards the street of that part of the SW RANGE which survived the demolition of *c.* 1862. To the N is a boundary wall pierced by a modern gateway (1995). The N gable wall has a slightly irregular arrangement of three small windows with pediments of double-ogee shape, and with two blocked windows to the attic. The S gable has a balanced arrangement of triangular-pedimented windows (with the boar's-head badge of Argyll within each pediment), two to each of the three floors, and with a pair of smaller windows to the attic. However, the S gable does not in fact represent the end wall of a range, and it is possible it was only given the appearance of a gable when the SW range of which it formed the N part was embodied within the house *c.* 1670. Apart from the irregularity of the SW range's relationship to the courtyard, the form of the doorway opening off the street into the destroyed part of the range is further evidence for this part being earlier than *c.* 1670. This doorway, which may be a composite piece, has a continuous foliage trail around jambs and lintel of a type usually datable to the earlier decades of the C17: cf. a fireplace in Clackmannan Tower, or the doorway into the courtyard range at Roslin Castle, Midlothian, dated 1622. The pediment above the doorway, with the Argyll crest, was inserted as part of the *c.* 1670 remodelling.

The internal and external faces of the GATEWAY appear to be of different dates. Externally it is framed by Tuscan pilasters, and both arch and pilasters have heavy chamfered rustication, a design based on an engraving of Alessandro Francini (presumably the English translation of 1669 rather than the original publication of 1631). It has been pointed out[*] that, since Francini's designs were a source for Robert Mylne's monument to John Mylne (†1667) in Greyfriars churchyard, Edinburgh, *Mylne* could be a candidate for the authorship of the *c.* 1670 work on the Lodging. References to the designs of Francini are also found in Mylne's work at Thirlestane (Borders),[‡] which further supports this possibility. Internally the arch is flanked by rather spindly fluted Corinthian pilasters that appear to be of *c.* 1630.

*The courtyard*

The French-inspired *hôtel* plan of the house, with three residential quarters around the sides of a COURTYARD and a screen wall towards the street on the fourth, is here most clearly evident. Three main phases of building are discernible. At the NE corner, the main block of the tower house phase of *c.* 1600 (with the earlier hall house at its base) is identifiable from its higher roof line, its general absence of windows, and from the way its stair is set back behind the face of the E quarter. The lower storey of the rest of the N quarter incorporates the domestic range which was added on to that house, but which is no longer identifiable

---

[*] By Dr Aonghus MacKechnie.
[‡] John Dunbar, pers. comm.

externally following remodelling *c*. 1670. The main E quarter, with a shorter range returning at its S end, is of *c*. 1630. The original extent of the shorter S range is identifiable by a run of buckle-decorated quoining, and by changes from strapwork gablets to triangular pediments above the main windows. In their present form the remodelled N end of the SW range that projects into the courtyard, the closet block behind it, and the infill section that connects that range with the *c*. 1630 work, are all of *c*. 1670.

The E quarter, i.e. the main block of Lord Stirling's Lodging of *c*. 1630, is of four bays and three storeys, the windows of the top storey rising through the wallhead as dormers flanked by fluted Tuscan pilasters. In the re-entrant angle of the E and S quarters is a stair turret. This corresponds to the stair retained from the *c*. 1600 house at the N end of the E range, which is set back within the body of the range; but the later SE stair is treated more boldly, being extruded from the angle rather than concealed.

The MAIN ENTRANCE is centrally placed in the E range. It is covered by an open-sided porch, dated 1632 in the gablet, and with engaged fluted Tuscan angle pilasters on socles at the angles. The way this porch partly obscures the surround of the doorway, which also has fluted Tuscan pilasters, suggests it was brought from elsewhere in the building to this position, presumably having been displaced *c*. 1670. On the wall above the doorway are Lord Stirling's arms in a square cartouche. These include a Red Indian and a mermaid as supporters, and a beaver as crest, in reference to his attempted colonization of Nova Scotia; the badge of the baronets of Nova Scotia is placed on a shield in pretence. The windows, doorways and armorial cartouche have complex strapwork decoration.

Although no firm conclusion on the identity of the designer of the work of *c*. 1630 seems possible, this is perhaps an appropriate place to consider some possibilities. Close analogies for the combination of strapwork decoration and pilastered dormers are to be seen at Winton House (Lothian), remodelled by William Wallace 1620–7; related details, together with buckle-decorated quoins, are also at George Heriot's Hospital in Edinburgh, another work started by Wallace before his death in 1631. Since Wallace was for about two years Master Mason to the Crown at the time that Lord Stirling's son *Sir Anthony Alexander* was joint Master of Works to the Crown, it could be possible that *Wallace* and Alexander cooperated in providing a design soon after Stirling acquired the property in 1629. Wallace died before building was completed (the only dates on the work are 1632 and 1633) and it could be that, after a design had been supplied, supervision of construction passed to a successor. Among possible candidates as successor are *William Ayton*, who took over from Wallace in building Heriot's Hospital, or *John Mylne Jun.*, who became Royal Master Mason in 1636. Ayton is known to have been consulted about the building of Cowane's Hospital (q.v.), a short distance from Argyll's Lodging. Mylne, however, was very much more closely involved in that project and this could further support his candidature. But these are not the only individuals to whom authorship might be attributable. Parallels have been seen* in the work of *Sir James Murray* of Kilbaberton, Principal Royal Master of Works between 1607 and his death in 1634, part of that time conjointly with *Sir Anthony Alexander*.

The clearest difference between the work carried out for Stirling and Argyll within the courtyard is the abandonment of strapwork gablets on the later part in favour of simpler triangular pediments: those to the first-floor windows of the w parts of the N and s quarters have concave sides with ball finials and contain the boar's-head badge of Argyll, while those to the second-floor dormers are of steep triangular form. The date of this phase is indicated by the doorway at the base of the sw polygonal stair turret, which has a segmental pediment dated 1674. There is also evidence of a change in the method of glazing (though all windows now have sashes). The windows of *c*. 1630 were designed for glazing set directly into the masonry of the upper part of the opening, with internal shutters; those of *c*. 1670 were evidently designed for casements. However, all is not as straightforward as might appear. The pediments and gablets of the upper floors of the heightened N range are identical with those in the s range, yet contain the initials of Lord and Lady Stirling; equally confusing, the pediment of the doorway at the base of the nw stair turret is identical to that at the base of the sw turret (dated 1674), yet has the defaced date 1633. On balance, and taking account of the close connections between the families, it seems possible that all of these pediments were in fact the work of Argyll, but that he was recording his own work in the infill section and remodelled end of the roadside range on the s side of the courtyard, and that of his predecessor in embellishing the windows and adding the stair turret on the n side.

## The outer façades

Less care was taken to create an appearance of unified architectural composition on the GARDEN FRONT of the house, and the distinction between the four-storeyed *c*. 1600 tower-house and Stirling's three-storeyed E quarter is consequently clearer than in the courtyard. On this side even the s wall of the SE jamb of the tower-house has been retained, with a gable added above to bridge the junction between the work of *c*. 1600 and that of *c*. 1630. Most window openings of the earlier phases of work on this side are distinguished by their plainness, generally with only simple rounding of the arrises. Stirling's work has strapwork gablets to the garden doorway, the window above it and to the dormer windows of the top storey. The other windows of the ground and first floors of Stirling's work have segmental pediments with elaborate fruit festoons and winged cherub heads. Some of these show striking similarities with *William Wallace*'s

---

* By Dr Aonghus MacKechnie.

top-floor windows in the rebuilt N quarter at Linlithgow Palace of 1618–20, and further support the idea that he was responsible for the design. At the S end of the garden front blocked doorways at first- and second-floor level suggest there were timber galleries, overlooking the gardens.

As on the garden front, the tower-house is distinguishable at the E end of the N FRONT by its greater height and more irregular pattern of windows. On this side it has a projecting oriel bay corbelled out above ground-floor level. However, changes to adapt the internal floor levels of the tower-house to those of the later work further W are apparent from the three rather than four storeys of its W part.

The S SIDE presents the most irregular face of the house, with no attempt to form a unified façade. To the E is the gable end of the E quarter, next to which is a lower offshoot housing closets. W of that offshoot is the rest of the c. 1630 S quarter and the link section between that and the SW range; following the demolition of all but the N end of the SW range, the consequently salient corner of the link section was finished with a circular buttress. Part of the site of the SW range is now occupied by a modern single-storey lavatory block.

### INTERIOR

The names of the rooms used throughout the description of the interior are based on those of the 1680 and 1682 inventories, though not all of them can be identified with certainty. The main doorway opens into the LAIGH HALL. Changes in the plaster cornice suggest there was once a screen separating the entrance and stair area at the N end from the rest of the space. There was certainly a timber partition here from at least the mid C19 until relatively recently, though no differentiation is specified between the two parts in the inventory. The principal surviving feature of c. 1630 is the fireplace, in the centre of the S wall, with crescents (one of the charges of the arms of Lord Stirling) on the blocks at the ends of the lintel, and with mouldings at the angles of the chimneybreast. In the E wall is the garden doorway, and N of that is the GREAT STAIR, of c. 1670 in its present form, which leads only to the principal rooms on the first floor. This is of timber scale-and-platt type, winding around three sides of a square space, with heavy turned balusters and square newels capped by (mainly 1996) ball finials. In the W wall of the hall, between two windows, is a buffet recess (with doors of 1996). W of the fireplace, doorways open on to the SE spiral stair and into the Low Dining Room (see below), the doorway into the latter having geometrically patterned painting to the flanks and soffit of the embrasure. At the N end of the Hall doors in the timber partition below the stair open into a small timber-lined closet (used as the pharmacy of the military hospital) and into the domestic corridor in the N quarter.

The three vaulted rooms at the E end of the N quarter formed the ground floor of the original hall house, but were called bakehouse, ale cellar and pantry by 1680. The BAKEHOUSE had clearly been the kitchen of the first house. It has a semicircular arch opening into the fireplace, which occupied about one third of the room, with a bread oven and salt box within the fireplace itself, a blocked slop outlet to the N and a blocked window to the S. The (later) KITCHEN, at the far W end of the domestic range added to the *c.* 1600 tower-house, was double the size of its predecessor. It has a slop basin in the N wall and a bread oven at the back of the fireplace, though only the mouth of the oven survives.

The LOW DINING ROOM, at the S end of the Laigh Hall, has for its (now truncated) fireplace a smaller version of that in the Laigh Hall, and there is a buffet recess in the W wall. Beyond the Low Dining Room part of the S range was occupied by the APARTMENT OF LORD LORNE, the future first Duke of Argyll, consisting of an 'Utter Roume', and his own 'Roume' (bed-chamber); beyond was a 'Roume Wtin'. The bedchamber has a stool closet in its N wall. The first two rooms of this sequence are now subdivided by modern partitions. On the W side of the outer room, the side towards the bedchamber, is a section of chamfered plinth course showing that this was an external wall *c.* 1630, and this plinth corresponds with the section of buckle-decorated quoining on the courtyard side of the S quarter. It is an interesting pointer to attitudes in the planning of such houses that, although the relatively modest mid-C16 house had a corridor connecting the rooms of the domestic offices, there were no corridors in the principal rooms of the house in its far more ambitious *c.* 1630 or *c.* 1670 states, and access to the rooms was either through other rooms or from the exterior.

The chief goal of those ascending the great stair is the HIGH DINING ROOM (referred to in 1682 as the High Hall). It is entered through a handsome doorway with a lugged architrave and pulvinated frieze, capped by a pediment with the painted coroneted initials of the ninth Earl of Argyll. (Opposite the doorway, concealed behind a panel, is part of the originally external cor-belling of the stair in the re-entrant angle of the tower-house.) The High Dining Room is a fine space with three bays of windows along each side and *trompe-l'oeil* Corinthian pilasters painted around the walls, extending up to a painted modillion course around the edge of the ceiling. (This decoration is a rela-tively late reflection of a fashion seen as early as 1626 in Provost Skene's House in Aberdeen, and perhaps confirms the suspicion that, apart from the remodelled entrance gateway, Argyll's work was not in such advanced taste for its time as Stirling's work had been for *c.* 1630.) The painted pilasters along the timber partition at the entrance end of the room are largely untouched, but the rest is a modern restoration (1996) above lining paper protecting the few surviving fragments. The contract for this painting of 1675, with *David McBeath* of Edinburgh, specifies that the foliage trails of the frieze were to be based on those of the existing fireplace; it also seems clear that the pilasters were based on those of the inner side of the courtyard gateway. The richly carved fireplace of *c.* 1630 on the s wall is supported by terms, one female and one male; traces of rich colouring have been found on the carving below later stone-coloured paint.

The DRAWING ROOM, beyond the High Dining Room, was the first room of Lord and Lady Argyll's apartment, and has another fine fireplace of *c.* 1630. Its lintel is supported by figures with human heads, console-like bodies and lion's paws, which may have been intended as sphinxes; the central block of the lintel has the carved crescent of Stirling's arms, and on the lintel to each side are raised ovals with the arms of Lord and Lady Stirling. s of the fireplace a blocked doorway perhaps led to a timber gallery overlooking the gardens. The CLOSET opens off the sw corner of the Drawing Room and has a restored (1996) fireplace and three windows. The EARL AND COUNTESS'S BEDCHAMBER can be entered both from the Drawing Room and from the se spiral stair, so that the outer rooms could be bypassed if required. Like most of the other bedchambers, this has a stool closet, lit by a discreet slit window. There is the ghost of a window rear-arch in the w wall which, like the plinth course on the floor below, shows that this wall was once external. Since the fireplace is below the blocked window, this was clearly not its original position.

Some of the other rooms on the first and second floors deserve brief mention. w of the Earl's bedchamber is a chamber with early c18 wainscoting, perhaps dating from *c.* 1706, when work was being carried out for the second Duke. Within the N quarter several interesting rooms lie within what was the *c.* 1600 tower-house. On the first floor is what was probably the hall of that house: this has an oriel on the N side at what was presumably the dais end, and opposite it corbelling supports the lower flight of the spiral stair in the re-entrant angle of the tower-house. The bedchamber E of the tower-house hall has a latrine closet, N of the flue which rises from the first kitchen below. The third-floor chamber at this corner has a large fireplace truncated both by a rise in floor levels and by a lateral contraction of the opening; the raising of the floor level resulted from the wish to create more spacious rooms on the second floor of the *c.* 1630 house. The first-floor chamber w of the hall of the *c.* 1600 tower-house must have been another room of importance, having a fireplace with a lugged bolection-moulded surround and a pulvinated frieze to the cornice. The inventory of 1680 appears to indicate that it was the chamber of Lady Sophia Lindsay, who was both the ninth Earl of Argyll's step-daughter and the future wife of his third son. (It was dressed as her page that the Earl escaped from prison when awaiting execution in 1681.)

MAR'S WARK, Castle Wynd. Built 1570–2, at a convenient but respectful distance from the castle, it was commissioned by John, first Earl of Mar. It was a palace fit, if not quite for a king (the young James VI), then for his regent, a post Mar obtained in 1571 only a year before his death. There is an urban grandeur about the ashlar façade on Castle Wynd: two octagonal towers flanking a heavily moulded round-arched gateway, 'like a port 104

entering to a city'. Fragmentary banded column shafts flank the
central opening and similar vestiges can be traced on the arrises
of the towers. A pediment moulding, now much reduced, surmounts the archway. Doorways are located at the foot of each
tower and on the outer walls beyond, the latter with small companion windows – surely shops opening on to the market-place.
A strongly horizontal stringcourse marks the first-floor level,
dropping only to the sills of windows lighting the landings of the
stairs which originally rose in the towers. Above these two openings are highly ornate framed panels bearing armorials for Mar
and his wife. Between them, above the entrance arch, is a central
window opening, above which the royal arms are gloriously displayed. Carved corbelstones, evidently intended to carry statues,
project from the upper walls. At the top of the towers where false
cannon gargoyles protrude, it seems likely that slated cones
would have capped a third storey. The interior is little more
than a large roofless rectangle. Vestigial cellars in the s and tusking stones at the N end of the building seem to indicate that
wings extended W forming a U-plan courtyard. If such existed
their foundations must now be buried under the Old Kirkyard
of the Church of the Holy Rude which rises abruptly behind.
Some of the barrel vaulting over nine of the ground-floor
chambers survives.

In 1715 soldiers were billeted in Mar's Wark. Repairs were
carried out in that year and again in 1733 but in 1745 the building was badly damaged. Within a generation it was without a
roof and deteriorating fast. By the end of the C18 masonry was
being quarried for other building projects. Yet, however hollow,
its magnificent Renaissance façade continued to provide a rich
scenographic backdrop to the play of quotidian events in the
square below, its considerable bulk shielding the open space of
Broad Street from the direct onslaught of the W winds blowing
across the valley under the castle walls. That it was this sheltering effect rather than any worthy architectural consideration
that seems to have saved the structure from total destruction in
the C18 and C19 may be an indictment of the priorities sometimes shown by the stewards of Scottish culture. But it stands
still, a testament to courtly aspiration and the cosmopolitan
culture of an earlier age.

### DESCRIPTION

*1. Old Town*

Early settlement must have prospered under the protection of the
castle. Set a little apart, the dependent community spilled down
the ridge that falls SE from the fortified crag. By the C13 a church
(later to be known as the Church of the Holy Rude) had been
built. Thatched timber dwellings were probably ranged around
three sides of the market, evidently a relatively large space
bounded by tofts lining what is today the N side of Broad Street,

the s side of St John Street and the E side of Bow Street. Several
times warfare or fire frustrated growth, houses had to be rebuilt
and the community remained small; even by the late 1300s perhaps
no more than a few hundred people lived in the 'Top of the Town'.
Yet by the beginning of the C15, the burgh had increased in area,
spreading SE in a linear development along the High Gait from
the s side of the market past the monastery of the Grey Friars and
on downhill to the Barras Yett (Burgh Gate). Since a burn flowed
in this same direction, it has been suggested that this High Gait
must have been broad enough to ensure a dry thoroughfare beside
the stream with houses built gable-to-gable down the s side of
Spittal Street and, later, along the N side of today's Baker Street.
Narrow lanes, St Mary's Wynd and Friars Wynd, descended to
the N.

The coming of the royal Court and with it a succession of major
building projects embellishing the castle fabric did much to foster
the prosperity and growth of the town. In 1547 defensive walls
were built along the SW scarp of the Rock and continued in the E
on lower ground; 'for resisting of oure auld innimeis of Ingland'
said the Burgh Council minutes. Protective measures taken on the
N were 'less formal in character', probably a combination of timber
palisading, earth ramparts and ditches. On the streets, stone began
to replace timber as the principal building material. The nobility
erected substantial town-houses. By 1600 the population exceeded
2,000. The lines of Broad Street and St John Street had been
finally defined by a block of short-toft plots which, perhaps from
as early as 1470, had filled much of the 'good market-place'*
around the old Tolbooth. In the lower town, similar infill on the
High Gait created the narrow track of Baker's Wynd (later Baker
Street), while a few properties began to appear along the NE side
of Spittal Street. Gradually the gaps were built up, creating the
elongated plan of parallel streets that survives today. Cross links
were formed: Jail Wynd, Bank Street and a series of tight vennel
connections between Spittal Street and Baker's Wynd. Development
on the narrow medieval feus grew more and more intense, so
much so that in 1706 St Mary's Wynd had to be widened because
of the constricting encroachment of forestairs.

During the C18 the centre of commercial activity moved downhill away from the old market-place. By 1820 The Athenaeum 1
had been built at the gushet junction of Baker's Wynd and Spittal
Street. It faced E looking down Quality Street (today's King Street)
to what would soon become the heart of Victorian Stirling (*see*
Town Centre). New water and sewage systems were laid down in
the 1840s and 1850s. But, as the new town grew, the tightly packed
houses of medieval Stirling fell into decay and disrepair. Proposals
for improvements in several of the old streets were finally approved
in 1913 but it was not until the years after World War I that progress
was made. Rehabilitation and conservation began with the emergence of the Thistle Property Trust, founded in 1928 'to retain the
features which made Stirling famous'. By the 1930s *Frank C. Mears*,

* John Ray, 'Itinerary' (*c.* 1662), in *Early Travellers in Scotland*, ed. P. Hume Brown
(1891), 236.

working closely with the burgh's own architects, had determined design guidelines which would direct the realization of renewal over the next twenty years.

Despite the architectural promise of The Athenaeum (*see* Public Buildings, above), the climb to the Top of the Town makes a blighted beginning as SPITTAL STREET starts badly between banal bursts of repetitively mullioned Modernism. On the l. are the 1960s extensions to the MUNICIPAL OFFICES (*see* Public Buildings, above), a two-storey curtain of spiritless geometry; twenty-six bays in green slate and ochre sandstone; 1967–8. On the r., some bleak grey mosaic; the offices of the INLAND REVENUE, 1962–3, flimsily finned in aluminium. But things improve uphill. First l. comes Allan's School, next the Gothic Revival gable of the old Snowdon School, then the classical portico of Forth Valley Health Board; still more impressive, the observatory tower of the Old High School (for all these *see* Public Buildings, above). Across the street, humbler events. At No. 32, a red tenement with flat-roof 'drying green', the dipping parapet edged in the coping with faint touches of Glasgow Style Art Nouveau; 1903, by *McLuckie & Walker*. Then, Nos. 40–50, a short, two-storey row in Dorset pea render, the last house dated 1892. Gabled to the corner of Bank Street, an older harled dwelling, now THE COTTAGE TEA SHOP, perhaps C17. It looks on to a small landscaped garden which in the early C20 replaced a densely built-up block of housing stepping down to Baker Street (*see* below).

SPITTAL'S HOSPITAL at No. 54 Spittal Street survives as a good example of C17 urban building. Harled under a steep slated roof, its two storeys increase to three at the crowstepped E gable. A half-round stair tower, with an entrance to the w, projects from the street wall; part of an extensive restoration carried out by *Sir Frank Mears & Partners* in 1959. Inset to the r. is a tablet which records that the hospital was founded by Robert Spittal, tailor to James IV, 'for the support of the puir' in 1530. It seems probable that this was transferred from the original Nether Hospital building when it was demolished in 1751. Next door at No. 56 is the DARROW LODGING (also known as Glengarry Lodge), similar in character and date, but three storeys high with swept eaves dormers. Another turnpike stair, with a w door and small pointed-arched windows with intersecting glazing at the landings (a legacy of the building's adaptation to Episcopal worship), pushes on to the pavement. Restored by *Mears* in 1959.

ST JOHN STREET continues the climb. To the l. is a brief cul-de-sac enclave of one-, two- and three-storey housing by the Burgh Architect, *Walter H. Gillespie*. Completed in 1962, the dwellings are varied in finish but consistent in their slightly heavy-handed Scots detail; roll-moulded doorways, eaves dormers, crowstepped gables, and a series of inset stones carved with the symbols of the town's seven incorporated trades. A high wall marks the boundary with the former Erskine Marykirk Church (now a Youth Hostel; *see* Churches, above) and another, penetrated by

107

a castellated gateway, that of the Old Jail (*see* Public Buildings, above). Both buildings sit back, contributing strongly to the skyline of the Castle Rock seen from the S. At No. 33 the street redefines itself with a five-bay, three-storey town-house of late C18 date, rubble-built, symmetrical and starkly plain but for a pedimented Tuscan doorpiece. Similar, but severer still, the two-bay Nos. 35–37. Then, at Nos. 39–41, comes BRUCE OF AUCHENBOWIE'S HOUSE, perhaps *c.* 1520, though much altered since. A round stair tower, set off-centre, has a swept roof, small landing windows and a roll-moulded W door recessed under a squinch corbel. A separate doorway gives entry to the vaulted basement. Across the street from No. 2 to No. 8, some respectable, if too strenuously varied, 1950s residential renewal of two and three storeys. At No. 36 is the BOYS' CLUB, a two-and-a-half storey reconstruction of a C17 building in respectable Scotstyle by *Eric S. Bell*, 1929. Built in random rubble with crow-step gables, a lugged eaves dormer with pointed-arched pediment and a thistle apex, and a doorway with roll-moulded surrounds and St Andrew's Cross. Several carved imperatives on lintels; among them PLAY THE GAME and KEEP SMILING and, on the gable of the Hall which returns along Jail Wynd, QUARREL-ING IS TABOO. Returning on the NW to face the Church of the Holy Rude (*see* Churches, above) is a short stretch of rubble-built housing with four gabled eaves dormers, one a medieval frag-ment, another dated 1937.

BAKER STREET parallels the slow ascent of Spittal Street. It, too, makes an indifferent beginning. On the l., filling the street-to-street plot behind the spire of The Athenaeum, is the grey bulk of the INLAND REVENUE building, its two-storey NE face a dull, mosaic-clad structural frame of glazed shops and offices. Older shops and flats follow; Nos. 11 and 13, late C18 or early C19, each three-bay and three-storey, one rubble, the other cement rendered. At No. 11a, a low narrow pend leads into SMA' VENNEL, a cobbled lane link to Spittal Street. Nos. 21–25, a high red sandstone tenement, 1899, reflects the façade of No. 32 Spittal Street (*see* above). Nos. 27–29 is early C18, though much altered, five bays wide and four storeys high with an armorial plaque centred at second floor. Short three-storey ranges, early to mid C19, step up the hill. A crowstepped gable façade at Nos. 49–53, 1891, incorporates a datestone from its 1715 pre-decessor. Ending the street wall in unexpected style, No. 55 is a Tudor tower-house in polychromatic brick standing tall on the corner with Bank Street. Brick-arched windows at first floor, a broad bay corbelled at second, and a jettied top storey of black-and-white half-timbering under bargeboarded gables; scarcely contextual, despite being badged with the burgh arms, but con-ceived with bravura by *John Allan*, 1890.

Nothing comparable disturbs tenemental continuity on the opposite side of Baker Street. THE HOGSHEAD pub, three storeys in three different finishes, perhaps by *McLuckie & Walker, c.* 1905, marks the chamfered junction with Friars Street with a slated peak set on a low octagonal corner. But the climb is otherwise calm and consistent, a series of three-storey, ashlar tenements, of the early and mid C19, packed in two- and three-bay steps. There is a good pilastered shopfront at Nos. 28–30, plain but potentially elegant. Here a narrow alley, DALGLEISH COURT, terminates axially in a small classical town-house of *c.* 1810, built in coursed whin with rusticated quoins and a Roman Doric doorpiece at the head of a short flying stair. Some high flatted housing, 2000–1, continues the street wall to Morris Terrace. Then Nos. 52–68, a range of housing designed by *Frank C. Mears* working in association with the Burgh Architect in 1938 but not built until the mid 1950s. Subtly articulated in plan profile and storey height, varied in material (polished ashlar, square-snecked and rough-faced stonework, random rubble and roughcast are all employed) and designed in the idiom of vernacular form and detail, these dwellings have a respectable earnestness that escapes pastiche. At No. 68 a tall crowstepped gable stands at the corner of a vennel leading to SAUCHIE HOUSE, a three-bay ashlar mansion of 1830 with coupled pilaster quoins, a modillioned cornice and balustraded parapet. Once the National Bank, it is now a nursery. More *Mears* housing at Nos. 70–78. Under a curvilinear gable, the close entry to No. 72 is surmounted by a tablet dated 1956 and inscribed with the letters RBS for the Royal Burgh of Stirling. Finally, on the corner, the Hermon Evangelical Church (*see* Churches, above).

In BOW STREET, more residential renewal in Scots vernacular; Nos. 1–3, dated 1960, a perhaps too couthy grouping by *Walter H. Gillespie.* Across the street, sturdier urban stuff. No. 18, known as DARNLEY'S HOUSE, though more properly the Erskine of Gogar House, dates from the late C16 or early C17. A four-storey tenement residence with three pedimented eaves dormers (two triangular, one semicircular), its façade constructed in squared rubble and ashlar. A C19 carved tablet centred at second-floor level suggests that here was the nursery of James VI and his son Prince Henry but this has been doubted. At ground floor four narrow lintelled openings front two parallel segmental-arched stone vaults. There is a pend to the r., entered under a semicircular arch closed above impost level with inset masonry dated to record the renovations of 1957–8. It leads through to MOIR OF LECKIE'S HOUSE (No. 16), an L-plan town-house, probably of the mid C17. In the E elevation are two superimposed Venetian windows introduced in the early C18. Rehabilitated 1957–8. No. 20 is an early C19 tenement, plain but solid.

Bow Street leads into ST MARY'S WYND, the ancient way N to Stirling Bridge. Some dull C20 tenements make a poor introduction. JOHN COWANE'S HOUSE, dating from 1603, survives as a rubble ruin three storeys high with a projecting square stair tower and a corbelled NE corner. Salvaged dormerheads dated 1633 and 1697 are in the garden of Knockhill House in nearby King's Stables Lane. THE SETTLE INN, dated 1733, claims to be 'Stirling's Oldest Ale House'; a crowstep-gabled dwelling with a steep bellcast roof and stuccoed walls. The ground floor has been mauled but four windows at first floor preserve something of their original vernacular dignity. The tall attic bay dormer is Victorian. Upper Bridge Street (*see* Description: Town Centre, below) continues downhill.

Retracing our steps uphill *en route* to the castle, BROAD STREET, as the name implies, is generous in width. This was the market-place of the medieval town. There is time and space to pause and catch breath before continuing the climb. Signposted by the Mercat Cross (*see* Public Buildings, above), halfway up the incline on the SE side, is the towered mass of the Tolbooth (*see* Public Buildings, above). Dominating the scene, it is neither too tall nor too ornate, but erect with civic rectitude. It stands a little separated from its neighbours. Downhill, No. 21, by *Sir Frank Mears & Partners*, *c.* 1955, a four- and three-storey roughcast tenement with five bays of pedimented eaves dormers. Uphill, at No. 39, an early C19 three-bay three-storey flatted structure in droved ashlar with round-arched openings at ground floor and a roughcast turnpike stair added to the SE gable as part of reconstruction carried out 1972–3 by the Burgh Architect, *Walter H. Gillespie*. No. 41, another three-storey tenement designed by *Frank C. Mears* in 1937, incorporates an ogival tablet with armorial carving brought from the demolished Lawrie's turnpike on Baker Street.

Housing on the NE side of the street varies in date but not in scale; sound urban parataxis, reminiscent of Edinburgh's Canongate, though considerably lower in height and decidedly provincial. At the lower end of the slope, more by *Mears*. A salvaged tablet inset in the harled wall of Nos. 4–8 is dated 1715. No. 10 has another with the inscription NISI DOMINUS FRUSTRA and a stone sundial with Roman numerals. The fabric of PROVOST STEVENSON'S LODGING at Nos. 12–14 is C17, though the harled five-bay front is C19 and the whole rebuilt in 1963. A C17 fireplace with stone bolection moulding survives at the attic floor. No. 16 (JAMES NORRIE'S LODGING), is also C17, but was largely rebuilt by Stirling's Burgh Architect, *Walter H. Gillespie*, 1958–9. Its crowstep-gabled ashlar façade is tall and narrow, three storeys of three bays over a ground floor framed by a roll-moulded cornice carried at the ends on diapered columns. Every window is pedimented, the tympana carved with Latin mottoes, initials and the date 1671. No. 18 is confusingly applied to two properties; the lower section, harled but dignified by twinned crowstep gables, was the GRAHAM OF PANHOLES LODGING. Though its off-centre street doorway is modern, the house may be early C17. A plaque at the rear records 'Restored 1959'. Nos. 20–22 is an early C19 tenement. Three round-arched openings (window–door–window) define a shop, to the r. of which is a segmental-arched pend. No. 24 is older; a five-bay C18 tenement built in random rubble. Older still, perhaps late C17, the last tenement in the stepping range (No. 26), again five-bay but harled, with a low segmental-arched pend giving access to the turnpike stair at the rear. Tall GATEPIERS, which seem to have added tops with cornices and ball finials, guard the gap to MAR PLACE HOUSE. Here the street makes a cultural leap to end in Neo-Classical decorum. The early C19 mansion-house front is symmetrical, a raised entrance door with pilastered jambs, dentilled cornice and a fluted frieze placed between tripartite windows similarly pilastered and corniced. Now a restaurant; applied lettering overburdens the building's otherwise unimpaired architectural integrity. Nonetheless, the street ends well.

Between the two impressive Renaissance mansions of MAR'S WARK (q.v.) and ARGYLL'S LODGING (q.v.), CASTLE WYND climbs slowly N, the prospect of the castle still notional rather than visual. Set back on the l. is VALLEY LODGE, a three-bay C18 house, tall, skew-gabled and white. A Regency porch, its swept roof carried on slender fluted pillars, conceals a corniced doorway with a double-vesica fanlight. At the rear are two Venetian windows. Further up the hill, located between the entrance to the Valley Cemetery (*see* Cemeteries, above) and steps leading up on to the Castle Esplanade, is THE PORTCULLIS HOTEL. Built as the town's Grammar School by the local mason *Gideon Gray* in 1788, its classical character is nevertheless essentially residential. A pediment with a blind oculus and apex chimney sits over the two central bays of a four-bay, three-storey façade. Classically robust but without the charm of Valley Lodge. Less visible on the opposite side of the cobbled street, MAR'S LODGE, *c.* 1817, seems single-storeyed, a symmetrical cottage villa in dark whin ashlar with a pedimented centre and Ionic porch. But seen from below from the E, it falls to a lower storey with bold full-height bows advancing l. and r.

The cobbled channel of MAR PLACE bends up to the open summit before the castle. To the r. is the VISITOR CENTRE, an C18 vernacular structure comprising two three-bay buildings, transformed by *Johnston & Groves-Raines*, 1971–2. It too deceives; what appears to be little more than a single-storey dwelling drops four storeys to Upper Castlehill. White roughcast walls sculpt the approach to a bowed porch on the SW. On the NE wall the windows are blind save for three ampoule-shaped oriels at the top. Inside, a small steeply stepped auditorium cleverly exploits the change in level.

Winds blow across the wide expanse of THE ESPLANADE; ahead is Stirling Castle (*see* above).

## 2. Town Centre

The heart of modern Stirling lies along the N–S armature of Port Street, Murray Place and Barnton Street. Wood's map of 1820 makes clear the beginnings of a shift in the town's centre of gravity from the old market area of Broad Street downhill to Quality Street (today's King Street). With the removal of town gates and the destruction of some stretches of the medieval walls towards the end of the C18, the built-up edges at the tail of the town had started to spread. Port Street, Melville Terrace and Allan Park were under construction to the s (*see* King's Park, below). Houses lined the Airth road (The Craigs) as far E as the lade serving the burgh mill. In 1816, the Athenaeum steeple rose up at the head of Quality Street marking the gushet site entry into the Old Town and in 1839 the Corn Exchange was built nearby. On the N side of the medieval burgh, both Friar's Wynd and St Mary's Wynd extended down-hill, the latter continuing as Upper Bridge Street and Lower Bridge Street intermittently lined with houses all the way to the Forth. From St Mary's Wynd, the terraces and town houses of Irvine Place and Queen Street stepped down to the E. By 1820 it was already clear that a new road linked to these various developments on the NE side of the Castle Rock would be necessary, but it took more than two decades before Murray Place and Barnton Street were laid down. By the second half of the century, however, civic build-ings, banks, shops, churches and flatted housing were raising the urban scale and dignity of central Stirling along this new route N from Port Street; it had become the main artery of the Victorian town.

In the second half of the century, keeping pace with this expan-sion, improvements in municipal amenities such as sanitation, water supply, street and pavement surfacing, and lighting were under-taken. More streets appeared E of the new commercial spine, though expansion here was always restricted by the railway and the river beyond. Cowane Street, partially built up as early as 1820, acquired its tenements. Later, more intensive tenemental development took place around Bruce Street. Rather grander flatted housing rising three storeys above street-level shops lined each side of Murray Place and Barnton Street, and in 1880 covered shopping became possible when the Crawford Arcade connected Murray Place with King Street. Finally, in the 1890s, Corn Exchange Road broke through the town wall on the SW side, curving in a steep bend down the hillside to Dumbarton Road. This intervention not only conveniently connected the Old and New Towns with the Albert Hall, the Smith Art Gallery, and the new villas in King's Park, but within twenty years or so was itself a street of considerable civic presence. By the end of the First World War, new Municipal Buildings, a splendid Library and a lavishly carved Bank had com-bined with the spired tower of the Athenaeum to define an urban space rich in architectural quality.

Later C20 developments have not altered Stirling's municipal focus. Nor has the pattern of commercial activity been radically changed. Despite the extensive and prolonged construction of vast areas of retail accommodation, covered car parking and roads associated with the Thistle Centre, this seems to have augmented rather than destroyed existing patterns of shopping. The new malls are entered through the largely C19 street walls on the E side of Port Street and Murray Place. Regrettably, a stretch of low-scale shopping at the junction with Station Road exposes the worst of latter-day indifference to the lessons of the past.

The tour begins outside the Thistle Centre at the intersection of Port Street, King Street and Murray Place. Here the climb W up through the Old Town (*see* above) to the castle (*see* above) can commence. Here the historic N–S route through Scotland passes through the heart of the modern burgh. Here Stirling's streets are at their busiest, its architecture at its most urban.

PORT STREET, as the name implies, originally gave entry to the town from the S. Today, though only brass studs record the site of the old Barras Yett (Burgh Gate) at the intersection with Dumbarton Road, there is still a sense that where Port Street ends suburban Stirling begins. It is a distinctly urban channel, for the most part four storeys high. Pedestrianized from King Street, the W side begins calmly and consistently; mid-C19 ashlar ranges with windows architraved and occasionally corniced. Then, abruptly, at the junction with Dumbarton Road, there is more classical elaboration. On the N, identified as WOLF'S CRAIG on a carved corbelled tablet just around the corner, Nos. 38–40 by the local architect *Ebenezer Simpson*, 1900–1. Between two pediment-gabled street elevations, busy with corniced windows and much Gibbsian banding, a splayed bay bordered by partly fluted pilasters climbs to an urn-carrying entablature. Above this is an octagonal third-floor corner capped by a slated peak roof. Across the road, another of the town's prominent turn-of-the-century architects, the idiosyncratic *John Allan*, abjures historicism; built as a grocer's emporium, No. 42, 1897–8, is extraordinary in every way. Five storeys of Welsh red Ruabon brickwork sweep round the corner below a strange lead-covered 'cup-and-saucer' dome. At the end of each street front, a tier of shallow bow-windows with puzzling, quirkily symbolic, carved stone panels in the spandrels. Allan's original shopfronts, with fluted pilasters and inverted egg-and-dart capitals, survive. Grey granite tablets are inset on the Dumbarton Road elevation: on one, the architect has signed his name, with the date 1897; on the other, below a sculptured wolf, the words 'Here in auld days / The wolf roam'd / in a hole of the rock / in ambush lay'. At Nos. 46–50, 1901–2, orthodoxy returns; three storeys and an attic mansard with a frontal chimneystack flanked by dormers. Then more red brick from *John Allan*, Nos. 52–56, 1901, this time Knightsbridge Queen Anne and 'surprisingly gracious'*; a symmetrical elevation with two broad canted bays at first- and second-floor level, four-light windows above each and a balustraded eaves cornice with a deep floral frieze. Red again at Nos. 58–72, a wide-fronted sandstone tenement, 1900–1, with 'pressed-in' bays l. and r. and coupled at the centre under a steep gable. Between the shops, two narrow close entries with fluted pilasters and dentilled pediments seem stretched to Glasgow Style attenuation. Nos. 74–78, 1934, drops to two storeys, a different, more Deco, modishness in its balcony railings. Domestic, too, a delightful late C18 town-house in painted ashlar at No. 80. Pedimented from a modillioned cornice, with urns at apex and skews, its C18 four-bay front necessitates an off-centre entrance, the door simply but elegantly enhanced by a decorative frieze and dentilled cornice. This is the last building on the W side of the street, an intimation of the Georgian scale to come in Allan Park and Melville Terrace (*see* Description: King's Park, below).

The E side of the street keeps comparable scale. A white

---

* Charles McKean, *Stirling and the Trossachs* (1985), 43.

faience façade of Deco classicism looks up King Street. Built as
a BURTON'S store in 1928, its pilastered symmetry is insulted
by a crassly commercial shopfront. Beside it, the first of two
entrances to the Thistle Centre (*see* Public Buildings, above),
each signposted with a triangulated grid of steel struts and ties
projected above shop level. Nos. 7–11 is a red tenement, 1905–6,
four storeys high with superimposed canted bays at each end,
tripartite windows at the centre and a series of fluted shafts and
chimneystacks rising from a corbelled second-floor sill course.
Further s, some rare dignity at Nos. 23–27; a plain, three-bay
front of *c.* 1840, precisely symmetrical and precisely detailed.
Another tenement at Nos. 45–49, late c19; end bays between
pilaster strips, a frontal chimneystack and dormers in the mansard
roof. At Nos. 55–57, twinned bays side by side, splayed back
under a gabled attic. This narrow sculptural façade was 'rebuilt
1887', perhaps by *John Allan*. A full four storeys by *Ebenezer
Simpson*, 1914, turn into Upper Craigs, the corner chamfered,
pilastered and pedimented. On the s side, which is lower and
more delicate in detail, the corner curves. Nos. 65–67, with
gableted attic dormers at the eaves, is the first of three early c19
ranges. Nos. 75–81 is the last, simplest and best; six plain bays
in coursed rubble. A pend leads to a small cobbled courtyard,
an intimate anachronistic space surrounded by more rubble-
built, early c19 housing. Finally, at Nos. 83–91, a neat mid-c19
tenement, with tripartite windows at each end above the shops.

UPPER CRAIGS, running e off Port Street opposite Dumbarton
Road, is a street of modest tenements varying in height. No. 42,
dated 1906, follows a familiar four-storey model with canted
bays on the flanks and a central chimney gable. Nos. 44–48 is
similar but flat-faced. Nos. 62–66, still four storeys, is flat-roofed
with a partly railed parapet. Across the street, some lower, early
c19 housing, built in rudely coursed whin blocks, rounds the
corner into Cameronian Street. Further e, at Nos. 57–59, a
three-storey office and showroom layered with continuous glazing and red brick spandrels sweeps round a wider corner into
Goosecroft Road. Designed by *John Begg*, 1935, its streamlined
horizontality mirrors the flow of passing traffic. Were it not for a
steeply pitched roof this would be the very stuff of European
Expressionism. CRAIGS HOUSE, on the other hand, a little
isolated to the s, is poised calmly above the rush. A three-bay,
two-storey-and-basement mansion of *c.* 1815, it may be the work
of the local architect *Alexander Bowie*. Balustraded parapet and
Roman Doric porch with curved ends. Converted to a Masonic
Temple by *John Bruce* in 1933. Adapted as a bank in 1994–5 by
the *Davis, Duncan Partnership* and extended symmetrically with
short wings w and e. Columned door screen with a transom
and wide segmental fanlight, echoed in the sunburst spray carving of blind segmental arches over tripartite windows lighting
the ground floor.

At KING STREET, history connects with commerce. Uphill is the 1
Old Town; downhill, shopping. Once the burgh's High Gait, by
the beginning of the c19 it was known as Quality Street. Renamed

for George IV in 1821, its urban classicism is more or less consistent, its axial rise towards the steeple of the Athenaeum (*see* Public Buildings, above) almost regal. The material is generally ochre sandstone ashlar, the scale four-storey, the continuity of the street walls uninterrupted. A rounded corner to Port Street has pedimented first-floor windows and a cornice course at third-floor level. This simple mid-C19 formula continues up the s side of the street at Nos. 3–7, five bays wide with a simple arched close entry between shops, and at Nos. 11–15, where two first-floor windows are pedimented on consoles. The former ROYAL BANK at Nos. 21–25, by *Peddie & Kinnear*, dated 1863, has a consoled eaves cornice, finely moulded architraves and a Vitruvian scroll course below the second-floor sill line. Recessed symmetrical street entrance in grey and black granite with Greek Doric columns flanking the central bronze doors. Nos. 27–31 has a French roof with attic dormers. At Nos. 42–45 heavy first-floor cornices sit on pulvinated architraves over lugged surrounds. Above its street-level shops the symmetrical tenement front of Nos. 53–59 has canted bays l. and r. framed through three floors by pilaster strips. Finally, in an elaborately articulated curve, the former CLYDESDALE BANK, 1899–1900, by *James Thomson* of *John Baird & James Thomson*, breaks the mould; three tall storeys in red sandstone, still classical, but ornately detailed. Arched windows round the rusticated corner below a balustraded balcony jutting out on console brackets. Aedicule-framed windows rise through the upper floors to carved pediments, a canted bay carries a swept gablet with flared urns, a bow window with Ionic mullions swells out below an oval opening surmounted by a lion finial: rich urban sculpture exuberant to the verge of Baroque. Round the corner, the Library and Municipal Buildings (*see* Public Buildings, above) face each other at the head of CORN EXCHANGE ROAD, their steep-roofed façades erect with civic pride.

Back downhill, beginning the N side of KING STREET, the BANK OF SCOTLAND; an opulent palazzo with a splayed entrance bay porched and chimneyed to make the most of its corner site. Tall first-floor windows; balustrades below, heavy pediments above. Fronting the steep roofs of the attic storey, a series of pedimented oval dormers. Designed by the Liverpool architects *J., W. H., & J. M. Hay*, 1862–3, as the Drummond Tract Depot. The heads of Luther, Calvin, Zwingli, Wycliffe, Knox, Guthrie, Whitefield and Chalmers, originally carved over the ground-floor windows, have been removed. Much quieter at No. 4, a former CLYDESDALE BANK of the early C19, though altered later. Three-bay Roman Doric colonnaded shop front with a dentilled transom but no proper entablature. Then THE GOLDEN LION, begun in 1786, perhaps by *Gideon Gray*. Its plain C18 dignity, in Aberdeen bond masonry, is enhanced by a wide pediment rising at the eaves and a symmetrically set unfluted Greek Doric doorpiece, but its initial mansion-house symmetry unbalanced by two later E bays. Restored 1994. Two shopfronts at Nos. 6–8, attractively designed with fluted mullions and an arcuated leaded glass screen above door height, are early

C20 intrusions. Next, a four-storey red sandstone tenement, by *McLuckie & Walker* for the Co-operative Society, 1897–9. Above the shops, at each end of its symmetrical front, pressed-in canted bays (becoming bows at second- and third-floor levels) flanked by full-height pilaster strips. Behind a balustraded eaves parapet, two slated cones. Then Nos. 22–24, another palazzo, formerly the BANK OF SCOTLAND, *c.* 1840; a five-bay façade with pedimented first-floor windows and a modillioned cornice with a triglyph moulded frieze. Two square-column Corinthian porches placed symmetrically l. and r. suggest the hand or influence of *David Hamilton.* Nos. 26–28, *c.* 1830, is plain three-bay ashlar with architraved windows and a cornice stringcourse at the third-floor sill. Then, the former Temperance Hotel, a narrow generously glazed façade with canted bays l. and r., its three bays defined by tall pilaster strips crested with *antefixa* above the eaves; by *John McLean,* 1881–2. At street level, a flimsy glazed porch over the entrance to Crawford's Arcade (*see* Murray Place, below, and Public Buildings, above). Yet more glass at Nos. 36–38, a four-bay, cast iron, warehouse-frame front capped at attic level by an undulating parapet of four ovoid dormers. Dating from the early 1860s and remodelled *c.* 1903, it has a blandly Art Deco shopfront of 1930s provenance. Thereafter, some flat-fronted painted ashlar, perhaps late C18, until at Nos. 42–48, a three-window convex curve by *William Burn,* 1833, the street wall curves to the r. Also by *Burn,* another BANK OF SCOTLAND, 1833. Here, unlike the Hays' bank at the foot of the street, the mood is more austerely classical: superimposed tripartite windows and a muscular Roman Doric porch to King Street; to the w, two heavily balustraded first-floor balconies, each carried on four console brackets.

Burn's bank, built on the site of the old Saracen's Head Inn, turns the corner into FRIARS STREET, now a pedestrianized link falling N to Murray Place (*see* below). Nos. 17–19, built *c.* 1900, still to the late-medieval plot width, is gabled with broad canted bays constructed in timber at first- and second-floor levels and a boarded shop fascia curved to a bold *cyma reversa* profile between coupled consoles. Equally narrow, but wholly unique, FRIERS 114 GAIT, at Nos. 29–31, climbs four tall storeys to a scrolled Baroque gable. Glazed walls, reversing the plan profile of a canted bay, open on to three superimposed railed balconies indented between red brick flanks. This inventive façade of 1902, inset with a number of enigmatically carved tablets, is recognizably that of *John Allan.* Above its shopfront are two of Allan's home-spun precatory appeals: HONOR . PRINCI . PLE and DO . YER . DUTY. No. 33 is a more than respectable three-storey tenement, 1862–3, with ornate consoles under decoratively crested cornices to its four first-floor windows.

MURRAY PLACE extends the slightly curved spine of the Victorian town and continues N from Port Street. First feued in 1842, its commercial importance intensified when the railway arrived a few years later. It is still a busy shopping street, though less grand than it once was. From the s end at King Street, four-storey tenements of the mid C19 maintain an urban scale. In the six-bay front of BRITISH HOME STORES three first-floor windows have become a six-light glazed opening with cast iron column mullions. Nos. 16–24, also six bays wide, remains unimpaired. Nos. 13–17, flat-fronted 1930s, is stolidly symmetrical, with a stepping parapet and Deco balconies at first and second floors. At Nos. 25–29 and 31–35, the familiar canted bays stacked between pilaster strips; late C19. Nos. 26–30 is grander with a six-window first-floor pilastrade running between two-bay flanks, tripartite windows at second floor and a French roof with pedimented attic dormers. Dated 1863, a rugged tenement with hefty roll-moulded window openings ends the street wall on the E; its gable end, sculpted with a boldly corbelled chimneystack, returns to the stepped threshold of the Thistle Centre (see Public Buildings, above) as the street cranks NW. From here to Station Road, the NE side succumbs to mediocrity, only redeemed by the high symmetrical assurance of Nos. 60–66, c. 1900, five ashlar storeys full of classical invention.

On the SW, a four-bay front, pilastered and corniced at first- and second-floor levels, negotiates the change of direction in a gentle curve. Then come a vigorously modelled red sandstone gable eroding badly, a plain four-storey ashlar façade with corniced tripartite windows and, at Nos. 55–61, more 1930s minimalism, a framed structure fully glazed at the upper levels. Crawford's Arcade (see King Street and Public Buildings, above) reappears at Nos. 63–67, formerly the Douglas Hotel: two-storey canted bays l. and r. with tripartites above, a large round-arched window centred at first-floor level and, below a good modillioned cornice, rehabilitated shops flanking the entrance to the Arcade that recesses, reversing the splays of the bays above. Next the raised gable-front and spire of the South Baptist Church (see Churches, above) and, at the junction with Friars Street, Nos. 77–79, the former Commercial Bank by *David Rhind*, 1872, a three-storey corner in Italian Renaissance style with arched first-floor windows corniced on consoles. Across the street at Nos. 80–82 is the ROYAL BANK OF SCOTLAND, another Italianate finance-house exquisitely detailed in ochre sandstone; built as the Edinburgh and Glasgow Bank by *John Dick Peddie* in 1854–5, its palazzo façade of arched windows is surmounted by a decorative entablature and strongly modillioned cornice. The Post Office (see Public Buildings, above) comes next, half a century later, its façade similarly composed and no less decoratively enriched.

BARNTON STREET takes the Main Street axis N. From Friars Street (see above) a three-storey ashlar wall, the former Royal Hotel, 1840, continues for seven windowed bays. It is plain above but, below a modillioned cornice, possesses a good run of early C20 shopfronts (the close entry at No. 3 records their remodelling for the Co-operative Society in 1905–6). At No. 9, a two-bay front in channelled red sandstone with giant Ionic pilasters clasping double-height canted bays; early C20 but still strongly classical. Darkening suddenly, the street becomes a tenemented canyon with a city-like severity. Four-storey cliffs rise on each side. On the r., dramatizing the gushet junction with Maxwell Place, is a narrow bay-windowed façade capped by an octagonal roof peak spiked with a weathervane wolf. A rounded shop projects at street level, its flat roof edged with a decorative cast iron parapet. This piece of tower-like townscape is the start of a long stretch of shops and flats, *c.* 1880. Nos. 2–24, plain in elevational treatment but peppered at the skyline with hip-roofed dormers. Nos. 26–30, even plainer. At Nos. 32–44, a patera frieze above the shops, incised ornament on lintels and eaves, and a series of pedimented timber dormers breaking through a mansard roof. Nos. 46–48, similar but simpler, with round-arched doorways coupled under a roll-moulded, three-centred archway. On the opposite side, the slow curve of the street wall, Nos. 11–49, dated 1904–8, is equally consistent in its repetitive order, though much more rhythmically modelled. Then, at VIEWFIELD PLACE, there is breathing space. The streetscape widens, in deference, it seems, to the effusive façade of the Sheriff Court (*see* Public Buildings, above). But the scale drops on one side to reveal the gable and steeple of Viewfield Church (*see* Churches, above) on the rising ground behind. Across the road, a more elegant, more classical terrace, Nos. 1–10, 1835–40, accented by pairs of Roman Doric pilastered doorpieces. But while Main Street scale is lost, three streets running w uphill to the Old Town retain their urban coherence.

PRINCES STREET is a steep incline ending in the double-bastion front of the old Drill Hall (*see* Public Buildings, above). Mid-C19 terrace houses step up the hill l. and r. Some have Roman Doric doorpieces, others arched openings with consoled cornices. At Nos. 15–17, trailing vines are carved above the doorways. No. 18, a three-storey tenement dated 1916, powerfully massed at the centre with two chimneystacks, interrupts the dominant eaves line.

IRVINE PLACE is older; though less intact it has evident pretension, with a number of detached early C19 town-houses. No. 2, *c.* 1835, has a Greek Doric doorway with partly fluted columns and a quasi-triglyph frieze. Nos. 4–8 have Roman Doric doorways. So, too, does Nos. 9–11, a two-storey-and-basement double house with a curving forestair rising to a shared entrance landing. A pediment appears at Nos. 13–15, a larger four-bay house of three storeys built in whin rubble with lintelled windows at ground floor set in segmental-arched recesses. Here the doorway is placed asymmetrically at the head of a widely splayed stair. No. 12 is different, a muscular mid-Victorian mansion vigorously splayed to a vaguely triangular plan with a pyramid-roofed tower swallowed up between canted bays. Across the street is the Dutch gable of ST MARY'S PARISH HALL, 1838, which, as Trinity Chapel, housed the town's Roman Catholic congregation until the building of the Pugins' St Mary's Church on Upper Bridge Street (*see* Churches, above).

QUEEN STREET is severe; parallel, two-storey, terrace houses built in whin rubble or ashlar stepping gable-to-gable with the slope. Setting the classical tone at the gushet with Viewfield Place is Nos. 2–4, the former Royal Hotel, an abstemious early C19 building of three storeys and three façades of three bays. Apart from this, the rest of the street, almost all of it designed by *Allan Johnstone*, 1824–6, is unified in conception yet diverse in detail. Paired units are distinguished by differing doorways. Nos. 7–9, 11–13 and 38–40 have cornices on pulvinated architraves. There are simple round-arched entries at Nos. 6–8, 10–12, 26–28 and at No. 36 which has a voussoir arch and a fine fanlight. Nos. 42–44 is pedimented. As in Irvine Place, the shaped gable of a small church, the Methodist Church (*see* Churches, above), breaks the continuity of the street face on the S. Uphill, on the corner with Upper Bridge Street (*see* below), is the BOY SCOUTS' HALL, a rubble-built malt barn from the C19, with a roughcast second floor, gabled to Queen Street, added much later.

UPPER BRIDGE STREET connects with St Mary's Wynd (*see* Old Town, above), continuing the medieval route descending from the castle to the crossing of the Forth. Under a piended roof, a good three-bay late Georgian town-house with a Roman Doric doorpiece sits back at No. 11, *c.* 1824. Retiring, too, behind the red Gothic of St Mary's Church (*see* Churches, above), the PRESBYTERY at No. 15, late C18, has a pedimented façade with tripartite windows l. and r. of a pilastered entrance and a false, pediment-gabled wing to the N. Downhill, across the street, a long wall of two- and three-bay early C19 houses, Nos. 26–54, stepping with the slope. No. 30 and No. 48 both have tripartite windows l. and r. of a central doorway; No. 42 has a Gibbsian doorpiece; at No. 50 the door is corniced over a reeded frieze. Further N, isolated but self-assured, Nos. 53–57 LOWER BRIDGE STREET, a three-storey, three-close tenement; rough-faced, square-snecked sandstone, dated 1881 under a central barge-boarded gablet.

UNION STREET runs N towards the river where a roundabout resolves the nodal intersection of routes at the S end of the New Bridge (*see* Public Buildings, above). On the W side, Orchard House Hospital and Health Centre (*see* Public Buildings, above); on the E, some two-storey terrace housing built in stages, 1879–93. BRUCE STREET, a quiet tenemented enclave, links Union Street with Douglas Street. Three-storey walls built in the 1890s and barely relieved by some stop-chamfering and a few semicircular pediment mouldings over the close entries: power-fully urban and uncompromising. Slated peaks mark the street corners. On WALLACE STREET, more of the same at Nos. 8–10, dated 1891–2, and at Nos. 21–27. SPITTALMYRE at No. 19 is, however, unique; built in rough-faced, square-snecked sand-stone, it has four-light windows and a central gable chimney dated 1906. There are more tenements on COWANE STREET: dull three-storey houses from the second half of the C19 and an equally plain two-storey range, pre-1850. A single four-storey unit stands out; dated 1871, its flat-fronted façade is liberally stop-chamfered and crowned with a heavy dog-tooth eaves. A parapet, stepped at the centre to an ironwork balustrade with trefoil ornament, conceals a flat roof.

Cowane Street and Wallace Street lead back in an arrowhead junction to Viewfield Place (*see* above) and Stirling's Main Street spine. Below the backs, the bleak avenue of Goosecroft Road passes the far from colourful Rainbow Slides Leisure Centre (*see* Public Buildings, above) to reach the Railway Station (*see* Public Buildings, above), where Station Road diverts uphill to Murray Place (*see* above) back into the centre of town.

## 3. King's Park

Spacious residential suburb lying below the castle, s w of the town centre. Once a royal deer park and later burgh land, the area was gradually acquired by Spittal's Hospital from the early decades of the c18. Spittal's Trustees envisaged development and a feuing plan, indicating a row of houses along what is today Port Street, was drawn up by *William Chrystie* as early as 1741. Some time after 1745 improvements were made to the old road running s w to Cambusbarron but it was not until the last quarter of the c18 that building began. Stretches of the town walls on the E side of the medieval burgh were demolished in the 1770s and from 1785 feus were offered and subtle level changes contrived on opposite sides of St Ninian's Road, the main route s. Shortly after the turn of the century, the first mansions were being built on Melville Terrace and Pitt Terrace. By this time, too, the Dumbarton Road turnpike had been laid down, running w out of town towards the King's Knot. At its E end, it was linked in an L-plan bend to the Cambusbarron road (now King's Park Road) by Allan Park, a quiet residential enclave developed between 1810 and 1826.

A proposal to construct a Stirling branch to the Forth & Clyde Canal with basins and wharves in Southfield, which lay between St Ninian's Road and King's Park Road, came to nothing. It did, however, delay the implementation of the Southfield feuing plan prepared by *William Legate* in 1834. This introduced Snowdon Place to connect the two older roads, an ornamental circular garden with radiating residential streets placed at the centre of the new road. By the 1850s, the plan was at length being realized. Park Terrace and Park Avenue, both generously planted with elms, were elevated in parallel along the rising curve of King's Park Road, repeating the arrangement already successfully introduced at St Ninian's Road. But Legate's ideas were only partially achieved. Drummond Place and Gladstone Place were built on the N side of Snowdon Place but the passage s into Laurelhill had to await later less elegantly urban development.

Contemporary expansion also took place in the Spittal's Park area lying between King's Park Road and Dumbarton Road, where feuing had already begun in 1837. Here the plan prepared in 1856 by *Francis Mackison* is similarly orientated on an open space, Victoria Square, located at the centre of a simple rectilineal street grid. On the s w, the curving line of Queen's Road and Victoria Place marks the suburb's boundary with the open space of King's Park. It was here, facing the park, that the first villas appeared. While building continued around the Square through the 1860s and 70s, closer to the town centre the feuing of Glebe Avenue and Glebe Crescent, by *James Ronald*, did not begin until 1879. Almost a century later King's Park became a Conservation Area.

MELVILLE TERRACE (originally Melville Place), raised above the level of through traffic on St Ninian's Road, maintains a sheltered air of detached elevation. A street of plain but dignified classical mansions sharing a common Georgian model while differing subtly in detail, almost all were built in the period 1810–30 (Nos. 1–9 are recorded on John Wood's map of 1820). Nos. 1–2 is a four-bay double house in whin ashlar with a modillioned eaves and sunburst fanlights over its pilastered arched doorways. No. 3, HERMES HOUSE, is three-bay with a Roman Doric door-piece with frieze and fanlight. The next four dwellings repeat this detached, three-bay pattern. The TERRACES HOTEL, harled and whitewashed, has an added canted bay. Segmental-arched tripartite windows flank the Ionic doorway at No. 5, a painted ashlar house made grander still by single-storey wings ornamented with urns. There is another Ionic pilastered door at No. 6, this time with a dentilled cornice. At No. 7, a half-columned Roman Doric doorpiece. Nos. 8–9 is a double house, the entrance to No. 9 given asymmetric attraction by a quirkily glazed porch. No. 10, *c.* 1850, is the exception; three-bay still, but with full-height canted bays l. and r. and an Ionic porch crested with decorative ironwork. More semi-detached mansions follow. Nos. 11–12 and 13–14, both in whin ashlar, both with arched doorways; the latter, *c.* 1821, extending screen walls to pedimented wings. Nos. 13–14 has been attributed to *Allan Johnstone* and it seems likely his hand is at work in others in the series. At Nos. 15–16, *c.* 1825, more pilastered doors and quoins. At Nos. 17–18, *c.* 1825, columned Ionic doorpieces. Then two detached mansions, also of post-1820 date. No. 19 asserts a commanding presence; three-bay ashlar, piend-roofed, with a wide Roman Doric door and broad pilaster quoins. Scarcely less impressive, No. 20, ROSS HOUSE, is gabled, ashlar again with architraved windows and another Ionic doorpiece. Both are linked to single-storey-and-loft garden houses with segmental archways.

Across St Ninian's Road, the short length of PITT TERRACE (originally The Terrace) retains few traces of its early development. No. 3, 1797, is almost intact; a severe three-bay gabled mansion in whin ashlar with tripartite windows at ground floor flanking a round-arched doorway. No. 5, too, has an arched door which, together with a conical-roofed, two-storey bowed projection to the l., is all that survives of the original dwelling of *c.* 1800. Later C19 additions, Nos. 6 and 7, abut gracelessly to the s. Then come three similar, though not identical, double houses in ashlar sandstone, *c.* 1855. Each is crisply symmetrical, distinguished by differing twinned doorways; Greek Doric columns, Roman Doric pilasters and pedimented consoles.

s of Melville Terrace, the w side of ST NINIAN'S ROAD opens up to some undistinguished government offices and the repetitive white façade of the Police Headquarters (*see* Public Buildings, above). Across the road are the District Council Offices, an extensive campus linking the mansions of Viewforth and Langgarth (*see* Public Buildings, above). To the S, residential scale prevails. WOODLANDS HOUSE, *c.* 1840, is a symmetrical mansion with added ground-floor bays, coupled windows at first floor and a dentilled eaves cornice. THRUSHVILLE, dated 1865, has a tall façade of elongated window shapes rising under finialled gables. Mullioned and transomed windows feature in EARLSGATE HOUSE, *c.* 1870, a large semi-detached villa altered and adapted like its two neighbours to commercial use.

ALLAN PARK, *c.* 1815–35, is tranquil and as classically reserved if not quite so architecturally consistent as Melville Terrace. From Dumbarton Road it begins in WELLINGTON PLACE, a two-storey-and-basement ashlar range with railed stepped entries bridging the areas behind the pavement; a unified façade designed by *Alexander Bowie* and *Thomas Traquair* before 1820. At its centre is No. 5, two parapeted bays wide with segmental arches over window and door at ground floor. Symmetrically l. and r. are four-window units, Nos. 1–3 and 7–9, with pedimented gables across their full width and shallow segmental-arched recesses framing the two inner entrance bays. No. 11 is a small three-bay mansion, like those in Melville Terrace; columned Roman Doric doorpiece with fanlight. Similar doorways mark the entrances at Nos. 13–15, a four-bay detached dwelling, and at No. 17 and No. 19, both again detached. On the opposite side of the street, Nos. 2–6, by *Bowie*, *c.* 1825, correspond but do not exactly match with Wellington Place; here the arrangement of window bays in the three-dwelling range is 3–3–3 rather than 4–2–4. Earlier, probably *c.* 1818, *Traquair* had designed Nos. 8–10, a semi-detached block with cavetto splays at the doorways but no fanlights. Decorative fanlights reappear over the arched doors to Nos. 12–14, built by *Allan Johnstone*. Above the pilastered doorway of THE HERITAGE HOTEL, No. 16, is a Regency ironwork balcony. The ALLAN PARK HOTEL at No. 20, by *Alexander Bowie*, 1818–20, is in the same three-bay mould enhanced by its flying stair, Roman Doric door and flanking single-storey wings. No. 22, still three-bay, is much plainer; harled and whitewashed with concave splays at its architraved entrance. No. 24, now painted ashlar, has a Greek Doric porch and a later two-storey canted bay r. Both these houses, situated W and S of the elbow bend in the street, benefit greatly from their axial aspect.

DUMBARTON ROAD is straight and broad. It is, at least on its N side, a distinctly civic avenue. Lined up below Back Walk (*see* Town Wall, above) and the rocky backdrop of the castle crag is a succession of large object buildings, a little stiff with parade-ground dignity. First, past the battered rubble beginnings of the old town wall, the gabled bulk of Allan Park South Church (*see* Churches, above). Then a green gap where the sweep of Corn Exchange Road, breaching the town walls in the last decade of the C19, curves down from the Old Town. In the gardens, several monuments. Terraced on the hillside, the town's War Memorial (*see* Public Buildings, above). Bronze STATUE of Robert Burns by *Albert H. Hodge* of London, 1914, the handsome figure of the poet standing on a grey granite plinth bearing illustrative bronze panels. Uphill, a second bronze STATUE; Sir Henry Campbell-Bannerman in the robes of the Order of the Bath, sculpted by *Paul R. Montford* of London, 1911–13, on a pink granite base. Much less dignified is *Benno Schotz*'s STATUE of Rob Roy, 1973; mounted on a rocky cairn, brandishing a sword, yet somehow peculiarly short-legged in proportion, the kilted outlaw evokes neither respect nor fear. Across a landscaped paved forecourt is the Albert Hall (*see* Public Buildings, above) and, beyond this municipal grandeur, Holy Trinity Church (*see* Churches, above). A few mid-Victorian villas attempt to establish a more suburban character. Notably idiosyncratic at the junction with Clarendon Road, No. 26A, perhaps by *John Allan*, is dormer-laden, crested with decorative ironwork and peculiarly endowed by carved portrait-head bosses. Decorative bargeboarding enlivens No. 30. Nos. 32–34, a rather gauche semi-detached villa in rough-faced rubble, is indeed by *Allan*, built for himself in 1878. But the public face of the street reasserts itself, albeit briefly and unconvincingly, with the temple front of the Smith Art Gallery and Museum (*see* Public Buildings, above) already a little incongruously peripheral. Finally, No. 42, a mid-Victorian semi-detached dwelling with two three-storey Italianate towers and coupled pilastered doorpieces, by *John Allan*. Conceived with decidedly Thomsonesque detail, it turns the corner to ROYAL GARDENS, also by *Allan*, a one-sided street of late Victorian houses looking W across the King's Knot to the wide carse beyond.

On its S side DUMBARTON ROAD sustains residential formality. At first, however, as it emerges from the town centre, it is aggressively and impressively urban. Facing N, stretched along the street, are the former premises of the DRUMMOND TRACT DEPOT, 1887–8; good commercial classicism for a once thriving religious publishing house. The street wall, three storeys under a dentilled eaves with a mansard attic above, extends to twenty-three bays, symmetrically composed in two identical glazed ranges, each with pyramid-peak-roofed, pilastered margins, and separated by a single central bay of superimposed canted windows under a Palladian motif at third-floor level. Lowering the scale, No. 35 has a pleasant rusticated doorway with a delicate fanlight. Then, identical chimneyed gables flank the entrance to Allan Park (*see* above). At WELLINGTON HOUSE, a robust pedimented portal with columned doorpiece.

Beyond Glebe Avenue, ALBERT PLACE begins, reserved, residential and redolent of the town's early suburban expansion. Ranked along the S side of the road is a row of classical cottages, built between 1837 and 1850, the ashlar sandstone of each three-bay façade carried to a high parapet concealing upper-floor accommodation lit from the side and rear. Details vary. No. 1 has pilaster quoins. No. 3, set between lower side wings, has a Greek Doric entrance and consoled pediments to the windows, the latter treatment repeated at No. 7. Several dwellings have windows with architraves and cornices; at No. 8 the architraves are lugged, the cornices tweaked with *antefixae*. There are segmental arches over the windows and doors of Nos. 13 and 14. Interrupting this cool sequence at Clarendon Place and Victoria Place are two pairs of asymmetrical matching mid-Victorian villas, Nos. 10 and 11 and Nos. 18 and 19, agitated by gables, dormers and porches with decoratively fretted bargeboarding. No. 15, too, is two-storeyed but remains classical; pilasters and cornices framing the ground-floor windows, doorway, and, at quoins and eaves, the full façade of the house. No. 21 reverts to the cottage formula, last in the line. Thereafter, four ashlar-fronted double houses (Nos. 22–27) of the mid C19, each with coupled pilastered doorpieces.

In the area s of Dumbarton Road (formerly Spittal's Park) the broad residential streets around Victoria Square are prosperously suburban. Substantial stone villas, detached and semi-detached, symmetrical and asymmetrical, many raised imposingly on a sunken basement storey, share a common scale and character. Built over a fifty-year period from the late 1850s, all are respectably, though by no means academically, classical, varied in detail by a Victorian taste for eclectic experiment. Good stonework from local quarries at Denevon and Thorny Dyke – ashlar, channelled, rough-faced and snecked – prevails. Bay windows, columned porches, pilastered doorways, consoled openings are everywhere evident. Houses in ABERCROMBY PLACE are typical and among the earliest to be built. In CLARENDON PLACE, too, there is quality, Nos. 5–15 designed by *Francis Mackison* and his nephew *William Mackison*, 1860–3. But here variations begin. No. 17, BEECHCROFT, also by the *Mackisons*, is Italianate dramatized by a four-storey entrance tower with an elaborately consoled doorway under a balustraded balcony. No. 12, on the other hand, has a Neo-Jacobean pilastered porch. On VICTORIA SQUARE itself, Nos. 1–3 is also Neo-Jacobean, while Nos. 13–15, with mullioned and transomed canted bay windows, a tall chimney and some half-timbering on the gables, might almost be classified as Neo-Tudor. Pointed arches, gables and trefoil ironwork give No. 2 QUEEN'S ROAD a mid-Victorian Gothic quality, drawn perhaps from Blackie's *Village and Cottage Architecture* published in 1868. Still more exotic, the Egyptianesque dwarf doorway columns and chimney pots at Nos. 2–4 BALMORAL PLACE, a late Victorian double villa, probably by *John Allan*. Allan may also be the designer of the quirkily piended villa at No. 7 GLEBE CRESCENT. In this street and its continuation N, where none of the houses was constructed before 1880, there are several inventive details. Nos. 3–5 is fronted by a colonnade of short square columns carried on fluted socles. Nos. 12–14 is outstanding; ornamental iron balcony, gables and gablets decoratively braced in carved timber, spired bellcast roofs with fish-scale slates and diapered crenellated chimney pots. Heavily carved stone friezes surmount the doors of Nos. 16–17 and 18–19 GLEBE AVENUE, while small, first-floor bays at Nos. 20a–21 jut out in timber on Art Nouveau brackets. Among the trees on PARK AVENUE, Nos. 7, 7a and 8, dated 1859, is another large Italianate villa with tall tower, canted bays, pedimented entrance and a detached billiard room lit by shouldered tripartite windows filled with stained glass. Next door, on the corner, No. 8 is inventively bayed and dormered, by *John Allan*, 1895. Hidden at No. 14 Windsor Place is THE INCLOSURE, built by *Robert Watson*, a pink-harled house which has survived from the early C18; two storeys, three bays, the centre projecting slightly with a raised attic and off-centre circular window.

On the SE side of King's Park Road, in Southfield, more C19 residential development. On PARK TERRACE, which, like Park Avenue across the road, is raised above the level of the through route to Cambusbarron, only a few properties had been constructed by 1840: Nos. 29–30, semi-detached with arched entries and rusticated quoins, No. 32, PARK LODGE HOTEL, ennobled by a balconied Greek Doric doorpiece and balustraded eaves, and No. 33, a simple three-bay dwelling with another Greek Doric entry. Nothing else was built until the mid 1850s. The parade begins past St Columba's Church (*see* Churches, above). Nos. 1–2 is transitional Baronial, symmetrical crowstepped gables and cable moulding framing windows and doors. No. 3 affects Neo-Jacobean. Nos. 8–9, semi-detached with Ionic columned doorpieces, persists with Georgian. Thereafter, a succession of good ashlar villas differentiated by their classical detail. Further s comes greater eclectic elaboration. At Nos. 27–28, Neo-Jacobean returns with decorative consoles, strapwork and crenellated parapets, and at No. 34, THE WHINS, a staged aggregation of Renaissance elements combined with Victorian bravura; columned porch with swagged capitals, tripartite windows, rusticated quoins and a French roof with ironwork cresting. More repetitively regular semi-detached mansions face one another across the broad avenue of DRUMMOND PLACE. On GLADSTONE PLACE, where building did not begin until the 1870s, there is much of the same but variety too. A five-storey Italianate tower at No. 2 marks the corner with Park Terrace; at its base, a cranked staircase rises to an Ionic doorway. Nos. 6–12 are plain but elevated to some dignity on a grassy banking. Across the street, the Baronial Nos. 5–7 with canted bays corbelled to square below advancing gables. At No. 17 a French roof dramatizes another corner junction.

SNOWDON PLACE runs from St Ninian's Road to King's Park Road, much of its straight length lined with leafy verges. Nos. 3–5, *c*. 1820, is semi-detached Georgian (cf. Melville Terrace, above), a gabled whin ashlar house with fanlit arched doorways. But it is an exception for the street is otherwise entirely Victorian. No. 7 is Italianate, a Roman Doric porch at the base of a three-storey tower. Set back in its own grounds, No. 9 is immense; a towered assemblage of canted and rectangular bays under a steep French roof. Across the road, Nos. 2–4 is no less cubic and bulky, similarly roofed, and characterized by bold stop-chamfering on all openings. Then, ranged around the landscaped circle of SOUTHFIELD CRESCENT, come three imposing villas with good decorative doorpieces approached up a flying stair balustraded in cast iron. SOUTHFIELD, busy with gables, reconnects with Snowdon Place. Across the street, No. 15, CARLTON, is symmetrical and much more reserved, with canted bays flanking an Ionic porch with banded columns. It sets a calmer pattern which prevails behind the trees as far as King's Park. Only the French attic to Nos. 21–23, lit by Venetian dormers, interrupts the douce semi-detached respectability.

## OUTER STIRLING

### CHURCHES

HOLY SPIRIT (R.C.), McGrigor Road. By *Boyd Barratt*, 1963–4. Elongated steep-roofed block, gable-ended with small peaked transepts. N entrance gable glazed under triangular arch with Alpha and Omega mosaic in gold and blue over door.

NORTH PARISH CHURCH, Springfield Road, Braehead. By *Gordon & Dey*, 1970–1, succeeding the original North Church of 1842 in Murray Place. Three-gabled space with aluminium-sheeted roof slopes swept up to a silvery finial spire. Y-plan with the tall gables defined internally by laminated timber arch-frames. The triangle-based pyramidal roof structure above the gables was originally lit by patent glazing but in 1992 *Andrew Rodger Associates* removed the roof-lighting, added the spire and opened up larger timber-gridded windows in each of the gables. – Symmetrical interior with axially placed semi-octagonal PULPIT and blocky COMMUNION TABLE, 1936, the latter carved with a distinctly Art Deco flavour; both brought from Murray Place. – Three STAINED-GLASS panels in each gable window, by *John Blyth*, 1981. Biblical imagery honouring the Trinity: God the Father (blue background), Christ the Son (green) and the Holy Spirit (red).

Linked in cumbersome relationship to the E are bulky rough-cast HALLS, originally flat-roofed but pitched with hip ends in the mid 1980s.

ST MARGARET OF SCOTLAND (R.C.), Drip Road, Raploch. By *Central Regional Council*, 1993–4. An eye-catching slated pyramid roof rising to an apex roof-light with walls of polychromatic brickwork, buff and dark brown, lit by clearstorey windows running below a wide-eaved boarded fascia. Gridded glazed panels flanked by darker brick mark the cross axes. Roofing the interior, laminated timber portal frames rise on the diagonal. Boarded ceilings on laminated purlin beams. Maintaining the same materials and details, hip-roofed HALL and HOUSE to W and S create a U-plan courtyard.

ST MARK, Drip Road, Raploch. By *Harry Taylor*, 1964–6. Utilitarian, pitched-roof hall, glazed in vertical stripes below the eaves. Belfry wall slices through the NW gable ridge. – STAINED GLASS by *A. Carrick Whalen*: the Lion of St Mark, 1966; St Martha, 1969.

ST NINIAN, Kirk Wynd. The medieval parish of St Ninian remained separate from that of Stirling Burgh and today, around the church, the sense of kirktoun village still survives. By the end of the C17 the kirk was in disrepair, though it was not until 1721–2 that plans were drawn up by three competing 'architects'. By 1725, the successful designer, *Robert Henderson*, mason in Alloa, had completed extensive alterations and additions and in 1734 he, with *Charles Bachop* of Stirling, rebuilt the ruinous STEEPLE, an improvement recommended by the presbytery fifty years before. Despite the destruction of the church in 1746, resulting from the explosion of Jacobite gunpowder stored there, this tower still stands. Rubble-built with rusticated quoins and stringcourses, it rises *c.* 18m. to a fine eaves cornice above which is an ashlar dome carrying a small stone drum, also domed, and a weathervane. Urns on three corners. A new clock mechanism, added by *James Ronald*, 1901, replaced the original of 1735 which would 'not keep time with any other clock in the neighbourhood'. – A detached fragment of the repaired church, part of the square-ended chancel, probably C16, now encloses the graves of the Murrays of Touchadam. Blocked tripartite window and round-arched doorway; inside, an aumbry and an unusual PISCINA with two arched recesses, perhaps for ciborium and chalice. – Two tall slender GATEPIERS, constructed of alternately plain and fixed blocks and bearing ball finials, by *Henderson* and *Bachop*, 1734, mark the entry to the crowded GRAVEYARD. – WHEEL-CROSS, probably C11.

ST NINIAN'S PARISH CHURCH, Kirk Wynd. The church, completed *c.* 1750–1, stands a short distance E of its medieval predecessor. Successive enlargements have done little to enhance it, although the rubble-built N wall with five sets of superimposed lintelled windows under relieving arches retains the rough simplicity of the original gabled rectangle. Vestry on the S wall by *McLuckie & Walker*, 1886. Alterations by *Simpson, McMichael & Davidson*, 1937–40, produced a T-plan arrangement, a scrolled gable (unbalanced by a single-storey excrescence to the r.) advancing from the centre of the S wall. In the rubble gable, three windows at low level; thistle, acanthus and rose carved in the lintels. Two tall S windows l. and r., their rusticated margins matching the gable quoins, light the church; sculpted panels in the outer windows mask the galleries. In 1962, an ungainly trio of session house, vestibule and chapel appeared on the W gable. In 1965–6, the E gable received its chancel-like vestibule. Gable-fronted, T-plan CHURCH HALL, 1843–5, with wide bracketed eaves. At the apex, an arched bellcote with scrolled base. Gabled porches in the re-entrants.

Among tombs in the surrounding GRAVEYARD are several small gravemarkers bearing dates from the C17 onwards. In the enclosing wall N, three MURAL TABLETS make an almost symmetrical group; framed centre panel to Robert Belsches †1796 and his relict, Elizabeth Buchanan. – In the N wall of the church, two white marble TABLETS commemorate the Steuarts of Steuart Hall.

ST NINIAN'S UNITED FREE CHURCH, Borestone Place. 1934. Simple hall with blockwork vestibule fronting the E gable.

## CEMETERY

ST THOMAS CEMETERY, Douglas Terrace. Laid out 1948–9. C20 gravemarkers, many of polished granite with gilded inscriptions. Worth discovering, an elegantly simple sandstone HEADSTONE to David Russell †1999; tall, with a smooth vertical edge to the l. but ragged on the r., carved with two doves and beautifully incised with the words WITH WARM / BREAST / AND WITH AH! / BRIGHT / WINGS.

## PUBLIC BUILDINGS

BANNOCKBURN HERITAGE CENTRE, Glasgow Road. By *Wheeler & Sproson*, 1966–7. A smart Modernist composition in white roughcast; flat-roofed rectilinear austerity relieved by mono-pitch skyline accents and lower curving walls in the foreground. Auditorium and Information Centre dedicated to recalling the victory of the Scots over the English in 1314. – Orientated to the putative battlefield, the BANNOCKBURN MONUMENT, 1962, lies 350m. WNW: a *plein air* rotunda defined by a timber ring-beam circling above two unequal arcs of ribbed concrete-block walling. In the centre, a tall, two-part iron flagstaff, erected 1870, and rubble CAIRN with inset bronze panel. – Nearby, an immense bronze STATUE of Robert the Bruce raised on a polished grey granite plinth; by *C. d'O. Pilkington Jackson*, 1963–4.

KILDEAN CATTLE MARKET, Drip Road, Raploch. By *Alex Strang & Partners*, 1966–7. A rippling waveband of undulating concrete carried over cattle halls on arched ribs. To the S front, single-storey shops and two-storey offices in grey brick and exposed aggregate cladding panels.

KILDEAN HOSPITAL, Drip Road, Raploch. By *Ebenezer Simpson*, 1903–4. Two storeys in rough-faced square-snecked stone with a central pediment, carved with the armorial devices of several local burghs, raised above the eaves line. Below the pediment cornice, carved proud on a pulvinated frieze, are the words THE STIRLING COMBINATION HOSPITAL. Detached single-storey wings W and E with multi-piended roofs.

NATIONAL WALLACE MONUMENT. *See* p. 623.

RIVERSIDE PRIMARY SCHOOL, Alexandra Place, Riverside. An agglutinative assemblage of red brick boxes begun by the County Architect, *A. N. Malcolm*, 1926–7. Swimming pool added 1931–2.

ST MARY'S PRIMARY SCHOOL, Drip Road, Raploch. By the County Architect, *A. N. Malcolm*, 1938–9. Wide implacable symmetry: two-storey N front of white-pointed red brick class-rooms with a bulky assembly hall at the centre. Glazed corridors run W and E to outer stair towers beyond which single-storey wings splay forward to semicircular termination.

ST NINIAN'S PRIMARY SCHOOL, Torbrex Road. Symmetrical gable-fronted Board School of 1878. Extended W, 1892, with matching details. To the W, flat-roofed classroom block by the County Architect, *A. N. Malcolm*, 1931–3.

STIRLING CENTRE FOR FURTHER EDUCATION, Kerse Road. Low, sleek and smooth; by *Reiach & Hall*, 1997–8. Two long rectangular blocks of classrooms, laboratories and offices slide in parallel against a central services core. Aluminium glazing grids with *brise-soleils*. At the E end a free-form common-room bulge hints at Thirties Modernism.

STIRLING HIGH SCHOOL, Ogilvie Road, Torbrex. By *Stirling County Council*, 1960–2. Four-storey, flat-roofed classroom block and ancillary buildings. Gridded glazing, rust-coloured profiled cladding, red brick and a dash of random rubble. Much enlarged by *Central Regional Council*, 1976–7.

UNIVERSITY OF STIRLING. *See* p. 789.

WALLACE HIGH SCHOOL, Marlborough Drive, Causewayhead. By *Stirling County Council*, 1970–1. A cumulative composition of flat-roofed boxes in grey-brown brick. Four-storey, curtain-wall classroom block with yellow spandrel panels.

## DESCRIPTION

### 1. Causewayhead

A hamlet N of the Forth developed around the T-junction linking Stirling with Bridge of Allan to the W and the Hillfoots and Alloa to the E. The name indicates the head of the Lang Calsey which originally traversed the marshy ground to the N of the town's Old Bridge (*see* Inner Stirling: Public Buildings, above). Absorbed by Stirling Burgh in 1939, the suburb has continued to spread SW. Up on the Abbey Craig, dominating the flat landscape of the carse for miles around, the barbed Baronial shaft of the National Wallace Monument (q.v.) surges out of the trees, as if intent on release from its scenic launching pad.

The best sites, above Airthrey Road looking W across the carse, are on GRAHAM AVENUE. FRIARSCROFT, *c.* 1900, a symmetrical front of broad square bays linked by a balustraded balcony, has a cylindrical porch on the N gable capped by an ogee dome and finial. ST CLAIR is a gabled confectionery of chocolate tiling, cream harl and orange-red stone and brick. Nos. 30–32, all white, revert to wide bays, but shallower under gable triangles. At No. 22 LOGIE ROAD, early C19 ashlar sobriety: a three-bay, piended mansion with a consoled doorway. Uphill, sunk below HILLFOOTS ROAD, Nos. 12–18 are skew-gabled, white vernacular. Higher still is ABBEY CRAIG PARK HOUSE by *John Allan*, 1879 and 1919, rock-faced masonry like the Wallace Monument (q.v.) on the summit, but gabled and bowed with an Italianate Thomsonesque tower, the Baronial bacillus confined to huge thistle-heads sprouting from the gatepiers.

On Alloa Road, LOGIE KIRK HALL, the former Logie Parish Mission Hall by *McLuckie & Walker*, 1888, presents a narrow pedimented front between piended flanks.

Hidden in suburban villa-land N of Wallace High School (*see* Public Buildings, above) is a wholly unexpected gem. *Patricia*

*Coelho*'s extension and alteration to 56 LOTHIAN CRESCENT, 1994, raises an otherwise unremarkable semi-detached dwelling to the level of inventive architecture.

## 2. The Homesteads

Tucked below a low scarp on the S side of King's Park, this tiny cluster of unremarkable houses, designed by *James Chalmers* of Glasgow, 1909–10, is still remarkable as an experiment in socialist community living. Turn-of-the-century enthusiasm for co-operative ownership, the planning ideals of the Garden City movement and smallholding cultivation combined to foster the idea of The Homesteads settlement. In 1908 Ebenezer Howard gave a lecture in Stirling at the invitation of the Glasgow & West of Scotland Garden City Association. Stimulated by this and the committed promotion of one of the Association's activists, Robert MacLaurin, who soon became their chairman, a local group was established and a suitable site for development sought.

At first, the group's political affiliation frustrated progress. Proposals to build at Raploch Road were defeated on appeal but in 1909 the 'amateur agriculturalists', as the *Stirling Sentinel* called them, obtained Crown land on the fringes of town near the village of Cambusbarron. Chalmers, who had just won a prize for cottage designs in a competition sponsored by the Garden City Association, was commissioned to prepare plans and by 1910 a handful of detached and semi-detached dwellings and a small farm had been built. The houses are architecturally modest, harled walls and red pantiled roofs; indeed, as the *Stirling Journal* reported, 'they fall short of expectations ... there is certainly nothing unusually attractive or pretty in the appearance of the houses ... The picturesqueness which was claimed before their erection is lacking ...'. Yet they are distinguished by some well-fashioned Glasgow Style furnishings and fittings designed and produced by The Scottish Guild of Handicraft Ltd. which, again under the creative influence of MacLaurin, had set up workshops in Stirling in 1906. Among the artists who contributed fireplaces, chairs, tiles, ironmongery, etc. were *Hugh Allan, Janet Aitken, P. W. Davidson, Eliza Kerr, Jessie King* and *H. T. Wyse*.

Hopes for sustained agricultural production were never realized but The Homesteads survived as a co-partnership housing association until 1975.

## 3. Laurelhill and Torbrex

Residential suburb spreading S of King's Park but separated from Cambusbarron (q.v.) by the M9 motorway. All but engulfed in this expansion of private and local authority housing, the former weaving village of Torbrex survives as a single narrow street. A succession of feuing plans (1867, 1881, 1902, 1924, etc.) documents the development of speculative housing in the area lying between Torbrex and Polmaise Road. Although some semi-detached dwellings were built in the 1880s, everything else is C20. Nothing is remarkable.

The finest mid-Victorian houses are on PARK PLACE where the scale and quality established in earlier developments W and E of King's Park Road are maintained. In particular, the vogue for tall Italianate towers, intermittently appearing in Spittal's Park and Southfield, is here even more evident. GLENELM, NO. I, has its tower with an open pediment carried on consoles over the doorway at its base. There are pyramid-roofed towers, too, at No. 15, where spear-headed finials pierce the skyline, at No. 23 (ROCKDALE LODGE), c. 1855, which has a tripartite doorpiece with a basket arch fanlight, and at Nos. 31–35 (THE SHEILING), 1860, where the balustraded top stage of the four-storey square tower is chamfered at the corners. This splay-angled treatment recurs on the mini-tower of THE GAZEBO, formerly the lodge house of The Sheiling. Nos. 11–13 and 19–21, on the other hand, are two-storey double houses with little more than rusticated quoins to relieve their severity. Different again are No. 8 (ASHFIELD HOUSE), dated 1863, gable-fronted with decorative bargeboarding, and Nos. 39–41, sharp, triangular-arched Gothic with hooded windows and canted bays corbelled at first floor below frontal gables. This latter 'Rogue Gothic' character reappears further S on BIRKHILL ROAD on the high-gabled façade of No. 4 (THORRINGTON). Its more massive neighbour, No. 2 (CLIFFSIDE), dated 1866, is cast in muted Jacobean. To the r., Douglas Terrace leads to St Thomas's Cemetery (*see* above) then dips down to a last residential cul de sac circling the pond at ST THOMAS'S WELL. Here an early C19 FARMHOUSE, the standard three-bay, gabled model with a fanlit doorpiece and cavetto eaves course, has been sucked back into the built-up edge of town. Beyond lie The Homesteads (q.v.).

POLMAISE ROAD leads S of King's Park. In DALMORGLEN PARK (the name and a pointing hand carved in a tablet inset in the rubble wall leading into the street) are a few early C20 villas of some quality. But immediately S better is to come. Three grand, late C19 villas sit in detached splendour. Elevated on a landscaped knoll to the E, SPRINGWOOD HOUSE, c. 1870, now flatted, is vigorously built in rock-faced red sandstone, Baronial but without Brycean invention. Steep crowstepped gables packed around a 'dummy tower-house nucleus'*. No less large and certainly more spectacular is *John Allan*'s BATTERFLATTS, 1893–5. This is hard-edged towered Tudor. Under gabled and piended red-tiled roofs, the black-and-white upper storey and attic are half-timbered and roughcast but it is red Ruabon bricks below, elaborated with much decorative cast detailing around canted bays, mullioned and transomed windows, balustrading and porch, that seem to make the building as much engineered as crafted. Out of sight in bushy seclusion a little to the S, ENDRICK LODGE (formerly Deroran) is genuinely Arts and Crafts in provenance

---

* Historic Scotland, Descriptive List of Buildings of Special Architectural or Historic Interest.

and no less so in its materials – rubble, harling, half-timbering and tiles. A widespreading L-plan mansion by *William Leiper*, 1899–1900, it has a castellated circular entrance tower in the N re-entrant and an engaged, peak-roofed, octagonal stair tower. The former lodge, now No. 16, is *Leiper* in lighter mood; cream-harled walls, red-tiled roof with overhanging eaves spars and a charming porch inset at the roadside corner behind a single swollen timber column carved, like the eaves beam it carries, with naïve Ionic allusion. Convex balustraded walls curve in to wrought iron gates set between octagonal GATEPIERS carrying ball finials.

Polmaise Road continues S before swinging E past the bridge to Cambusbarron to become TORBREX ROAD. Confusingly named, TORBREX is a narrow vehicular route N, more lane than road, once the village street. Some early C19 cottages remain, though several have been radically altered. TORBREX INN is older; a stone tablet in the wall carries the date 1721, but dry-dash render, mock stonework and an added porch compromise its vernacular integrity. The long low roughcast walls and slated roofs of No. 14 are much more convincing. Here, too, there is a mural tablet: 17 AR AS 56. Denying its original innate austerity, ROSE COTTAGE has assumed the pretension of shallow bay windows. But KERMODE COTTAGES are less changed; roughcast walls with rudely cut door dressings. To the N, a hedge-bordered footpath passes Stirling High School (*see* Public Buildings, above) to connect with St Ninian's Road and the route back into town.

## 4. Raploch

A bleak suburb of inter-war local authority housing lying below the NW face of the Castle Rock. Emerging W of this environmental desert, the glossy putative prosperity of the Castle Business Park makes a bittersweet neighbour.

DRIP ROAD runs W out of town, long and straight, as if to escape to open country as fast as possible. Neither side has much to offer. To the N, unprepossessing council housing. To the S, the same only worse; street after street of grey abandoned houses, their windows and doors built up with concrete blockwork. St Mark's Church (*see* Churches, above) offers little to delight the eye. But there are some redeeming elements. Nos. 66–74 is a carefully composed block of continuous Scotstyle housing by *Eric S. Bell*, 1936. Symmetrical, with a seven-bay central section raised to three storeys, it is linked by screen walls to flanking wings which establish a long street-to-street façade. Arched roll-moulded close entries, ogee domes on the corners, and scrolled gables with crudely shaped thistle and fleur-de-lys finials are repeated around the block in MENZIES DRIVE, FERGUSON STREET and WOODSIDE ROAD. The tarnished dignity of this short streetscape is the exception. Mediocrity and neglect triumph.

Further W, between the road and the bend of the River Forth, Kildean Hospital (*see* Public Buildings, above) presents a respectable façade. Across the street, St Mary's Primary School (*see* Public Buildings, above) is seriously symmetrical, its long brick front barely lightened by porthole-window flirtation with Thirties modishness. Next, last in line, latest in time, St Margaret of Scotland (R.C.) Church (*see* Churches, above) proclaims its status with a slated pyramid. Beyond, on the edge of town to the N, is Kildean Cattle Market (*see* Public Buildings, above).

Over the course of the last decade of the C20 the CASTLE BUSI-NESS PARK has been developed on flat open land between Raploch and Junction 10 on the M9 motorway. Conceived as a prestige business village, the site has acquired six upmarket IT office buildings and a restaurant and conference centre. While design control has remained in the hands of the *Hurd, Rolland Partnership*, with landscaping by *Ian White Associates*, the archi-tectural character has changed over time. SCOTIA HOUSE, ARGYLL COURT and ERSKINE COURT, 1994–6, represent the initial approach. Each unit is cruciform in plan with four two-storey wings, gable-ended or hip-roofed, meeting in a three-storey, pyramid-roofed, central tower. Walls are clad in random-coursed reconstituted ashlar to first-floor sill height, above which run bands of continuous glazing. Staircase towers sit in the re-entrant or are appended to roughcast gables. Roofs are slated. Midway through the 1990s a somewhat different idiom appeared. Materials remained the same but the elevational form of three further speculative office units became more overtly expressive of the buildings' frame construction. At LOMOND COURT, 1996–7, the name has some eponymous legitimacy for here four two-storey office ranges are arranged around an inner court-yard. BERMUDA HOUSE and KATRINE COURT, 1998–9, on the other hand, revert to the cruciform plan. All three have slated roofs with a distinctly shallower pitch than their prede-cessors and share wide eaves overhangs carried on slender brackets springing from first-floor sills.

Located at the entrance to the Business Park strategically close to the M9 motorway, THE RIVER HOUSE provides conference facilities, restaurant and bar. It, too, is by *Hurd, Rolland*, 1995–6, with interior refurbishment by *Nicoll Russell Studios* in 2000. Four octagonal timber-framed structures with slated peaked roofs are linked together by lead flats. Lead-lined canopies pro-ject under the eaves. Around two of the octagons, balconies are bracketed out over the edge of a shallow lochan landscaped with pebble and rock shores between timber groynes. Water and wood combine well; it is easy to see why the project was originally known as 'The Crannogs'.

## 5. Riverside

A quiet residential enclave folded in a loop of the Forth. A few houses had appeared by *c.* 1830 but, all but islanded by the rail-way, it was only fully developed from the last decades of the C19. Some of the burgh's earliest four-in-a-block local authority hous-ing survives from the 1920s.

From the centre of town, SEAFORTH PLACE crosses N over road and railway. The scale is immediately domestic; terraces, generally two-storey, a few villas and some later local authority housing. The earliest houses, *c.* 1825, are in FORTH PLACE. Nos. 1–27, most in whin ashlar, have pilastered Roman Doric doorways with architraved first-floor windows at Nos. 17–19 and 25–27. Running alongside Shore Road, FORTH CRESCENT, too, is modest. First, a terrace, Nos. 1–13, the doors merely consoled, though canted bays appear and chimneystacks accent the entrances. Next, some small sleepy villas, one dated 1888. No. 30 is best; a detached early C19 three-bay dwelling in black whin with a central arched doorway, pilastered below the fanlight. Then a plain two-storey range, Nos. 31–40. With yet another terrace, ABBEY ROAD continues the centuries-old route to the river where a modern footbridge supersedes the ancient ferry crossing to Cambuskenneth (q.v.): Nos. 29–37, in rough-faced square-snecked rubble, the last house bearing the date 1911. Similar two-storey street walls define Nos. 29–37 MEADOW PLACE and Nos. 1–27 MILLAR PLACE, *c.* 1905–6. Both sides of RONALD PLACE are also terraced: two-storey ranges dated 1894 and 1905, three-storey, 1879. Some pleasant late C19 houses in rough-faced masonry look NW across DEAN CRESCENT to the river. On the embankment, STIRLING ROWING CLUB, dated 1906, a symmetrical, white roughcast box, two storeys to the river, with castellated octagonal corner turrets and a slated pyramid over the pedimented entrance from Queenshaugh Drive.

### 6. St Ninian's

Originally a kirktoun settlement, also known as St Ringan's, straggling in 'one long narrow street along the great south road from Stirling'*. Gradually, from the late C18 through the C19, village and town grew together, absorbing the hamlets of Newhouse and Bellfield along the line of St Ninian's Road. A few of the 'curious and old-fashioned' dwellings noted by Groome survive in rehabilitated form close to the church. The area is now a residential suburb with a linear development of mixed, predominantly mid to late C19 house types, on the old road S and a later, more salubrious, quarter of villas and bungalows bounded on the E by the dual carriageway of Burghmuir Road.

KIRK WYND alone retains something of the old village character. At one end, the tall gatepiers and clock-tower steeple of the C18 kirk (*see* Churches, above). Beyond the graveyard, a solitary C18 dwelling marks the entrance to Shirra's Brae Road: DROGAN COTTAGE, now isolated from the village nucleus by the barrier of Burghmuir Road. Roughcast and crowstepped, it has kept its red tile roof. At the other end of the Wynd, turning the corner into Main Street, some pleasant vernacular housing, a much restored courtyard group of fragmentary antiquity; single- and two-storey, crowstep-gabled dwellings, dating from the C17 and C18. No. 31 has a seven-bay front incorporating a 1629 datestone, while at the rear a forestair climbs to an upper doorway dated

* *Ordnance Gazetteer of Scotland*, ed. Francis H. Groome, vi (1885), 317.

1603. A swept loft opening on one of the lower houses is dated 1674. But all is largely reconstruction of 1975–6; slates replacing pantiles, mock stone dressings, dry-dash render rather than harling. The former MANSE at Nos. 3–5 Kirk Wynd, part of the same restoration programme, is no less architecturally modest, though here, too, are problematic datestones, 1677 and 173(1). MAIN STREET itself (the name scarcely appropriate) is now little more than a brief cul de sac of tired, two-storey, gable-to-gable shops with flats above. Nos. 1–7, c. 1820, retains some rolled skewputts. Nos. 9–11 is a roughcast intruder, dated 1905, but respectful enough to engross crowstepped gable, pedimented dormers and a gated pend in its design. More crowstepping at Nos. 13–17 and Nos. 19–21, both early C19 but deteriorating rapidly.

RANDOLPH TERRACE runs N back towards King's Park and the Town Centre. On the E side, the plain, two-storey terraces of THE GLEBE, of the mid C19, still linked in scale to the vestigial village. Across the street, however, a later, denser life-style: three-storey tenements at No. 20, RANDOLPH BUILDINGS, dated 1911, and Nos. 24–26, CALEDONIAN PLACE, 1903. On the wall of the former, a stone tablet with the date 1724, some initials and a selection of carved tradesmen's tools, a salvaged example of those 'rude sculpturings' which Groome had observed on the cottages of St Ninian's village in 1885. A succession of respectable late C19 semi-detached villas with full-height canted bays or bows asserts suburban scale. Then the earlier elegance of several detached cottage villas, mid-C19 dwellings similar to those in Albert Place (see King's Park). ALLERTON at No. 75 NEWHOUSE is typically restrained with architraved windows on each side of a pilastered doorpiece.

BEECHWOOD sits back on the W side of the road behind a thick stand of tall trees. A five-bay, two-storey-and-basement mansion of mid-C18 date, with skew gables and flanking parapeted wings. The canted porch with its basket arch entrance may be part of the alteration work effected by *Charles Wilson*, c. 1855. Brightly roughcast and painted in shades of cream, it is now flatted; rehabilitation by *Stirling District Council*, 1992–3. Tucked away to the S of Beechwood Park off Berkeley Street is WILLIAMFIELD HOUSE, a plain, crowstep-gabled dwelling with a C17 origin, a piend-roofed wing from the C18 and a two-storey canted bay added in the C19. A 1682 datestone set in a stuccoed wall bears the initials WW for William Wordie of Torbrex and IM for his wife Jean Mill.

NEWHOUSE continues N. At No. 25, MONA PLACE, a flat-fronted tenement constructed in rough-faced square-snecked stone. It is dated 1897 and bears a strange N point incised in a tablet below the frontal chimneystack; perhaps by *John Allan*. More cottage villas follow, linked by flanking walls, all with added dormers. Their corniced doorways differ: No. 19 has an entablature with triglyphs, a flower spray is carved on the frieze of No. 21, while No. 23, though plain, is the only one framed by pilasters. Then, a gently curving tenement range, very plain with only stop-chamfered openings and frontal chimneystacks to relieve the street wall of square-snecked masonry; Nos. 7–17, its constituent closes variously dated 1880, 1888 and 1890. No. 1 is another three-bay cottage villa, *c.* 1850, attractively abstemious in detail. Across the street, No. 2, dated 1904, is softly Scots, roughcast with a jettied upper storey, a lugged stone doorway and a lead-finialled round at the NE corner.

E of Newhouse and St Ninian's Road, shielding the spreading campus of Stirling Royal Infirmary (*see* Inner Stirling: Public Buildings, above), is a network of quieter residential streets lined with villas and bungalows, mostly early C20, many of which gain interest from decorative doorways, dormers and verandahs. Imposing late-Victorian semi-detached mansions line CLIFFORD ROAD, those on the S side notable for their ornamental bargeboards. At the foot of Annfield Gardens, ANNFIELD HOUSE, built in 1785, altered and extended in the C19 and saved from the brink of dereliction in 1997, is now a well scrubbed if somewhat gawky nursing home. But three houses are outstanding. Commissioned by the owner of Hayford Mills at Cambusbarron, BRENTHAM PARK HOUSE, 1871, in Brentham Crescent, is in aberrant Baronial style; cone-roofed corner turrets, shaped gablets and an octagonal entrance tower balustraded at the eaves below a dormered French roof. Off Livilands Gate, down a driveway entered between obelisk-topped gatepiers, is WESTERLANDS, a Scots Renaissance mansion by *McLuckie & Walker*, 1899, built in good square-snecked rough-faced masonry. On the SE elevation, a large sundial tablet carved with the inscription UT . ME . LUX . SOLIS . REGIT ./ SIC . VOS . LUX . COELESTIS . REGA. At Nos. 23–25 RANDOLPH ROAD, an asymmetrical, Arts and Crafts Tudor villa by *James E. Ronald*, *c.* 1910, commands the corner with Bellfield Road. Several half-timbered gables front a complex tent of red-tiled roofs. The roughcast upper floor, here balconied, there jettied on hefty wooden brackets, sits on a ground-floor base of red sandstone ashlar, the stone decoratively carved around windows and round-arched porches.

## 7. Springkerse

A wide expanse of flat country lying S of the river on the E side of town, entirely given over to late C20 industrial estates, business parks and mass retail outlets. A few shining car showrooms sparkle in a morass of architectural mediocrity.

E along KERSE ROAD the Stirling Centre for Further Education (*see* Public Buildings above) catches the eye almost immediately. Nothing else merits the detour, except perhaps the GRANARY BUILDING, *c.* 1885, now isolated beyond a car body workshop on the S side of Kerse Road. Three storeys high, faced in polychromatic brick, a memory of Victorian industrial enterprise. Below a large oculus, segmental brick arches define bays on the gables. On the W and E sides, windows and doors with brick soldier arches and, carried on timber outriggers and struts above the first-floor windows, two gableted brick projections which

housed the hoisting apparatus for lifting goods to the upper floors
and loft. Abandoned and anachronistic but still architecture.

### 8. Whins of Milton

A suburban ribbon trailing SE from Stirling along the A872.

On both sides of GLASGOW ROAD a few rubble cottages recall an
earlier C19 hamlet. Best are Nos. 92–96, two-storey, roughcast
with painted margins; and Nos. 98, 112–116, and 153–157, all
single-storey, but varied in finish. In BORESTONE PLACE, two
white roughcast villas, *c.* 1905, have a vernacular charm; at THE
GABLES, an asymmetrical chimneyed gable; at HILLCREST,
an inventive amalgam of quirkily quaint Scots allusion.

STRATHBLANE

Valley of the Blane Water on the flank of the Campsie Fells.
Settlement focuses on the villages of Strathblane and Blanefield,
once separate but now continuous commuter country.

ST KESSOG (R.C.), Campsie Dene Road. 1893. Village Gothic in
rough-faced, square-snecked sandstone, greatly enhanced by its
setting above grassed terraces. Five-bay hall church with lancet
lights. Priest's house linked w. s gable with five-ring circular
window and lean-to porch. All windows have simple memorial
STAINED GLASS by the *Abbey Studio*: lancets with scrapbook
angles, St Kessog in the porch.

STRATHBLANE PARISH CHURCH, Strathblane Road. By *John
Brash*, 1802–3; a four-bay, gabled box in coursed rubble, lit by
lancets and a pointed-arched w window with intersecting tracery.
Gabled bays N and S, each with apex vesica, lancet light and
pointed entrance, lead into a w vestibule with tight winding
stairs rising to the gallery from the NW and SW corners. *Charles
Wilson* re-roofed the church in 1844–5 and effected further
repairs in 1862. In 1870 the building was buttressed, the roof
pitch increased, a w bellcote added, and a three-light Gothic
window with plate tracery introduced in the E gable; probably
the work of *David Thomson*. Today, only the s entrance is in use,
the NW stair has been removed, and the w bay recast at ground-
and first-floor level, 1958–9. Arch-braced trusses (coupled at the
middle two bays) spring from corbelstones; stencil patterning
between rafters and purlins. Painted traceried panelling to gallery.
Framed below the E window, under a brass panel recording
the refurbishment by the Edmonstone family, 1870, the Ten
Commandments are lettered in gold on a dark blue background.
– To l., a squat, square, stone pedestal FONT with white marble
bowl. – Hexagonal box PULPIT in grained timber, carved with
Gothic tracery. – ORGAN at r. by *Ingram & Co.*, *c.* 1908; thin
Gothic tracery screen to pipes above cavetto cornice. – All win-
dows have STAINED GLASS of Victorian Gothic design. In the
E, Christ's Ascension, colourful but sentimental, flanked by
lancets filled with texts and the symbols of the four Evangelists;

by *W. & J. J. Kier* of Glasgow, 1870. – On the N wall, closest
to the E gable, the parable of the talents commemorates the
patronage of Sir Archibald Edmonstone; by *Kier*, 1874 (?). –
Next, the Good Shepherd, also by *Kier*, 1874. – Then comes a
sombre Christ walking through steel-blue waves; by *William Butler*
of *W. B. Simpson & Sons*, London, 1888. – Opposite this on the S
wall, set against yellow flames in a blue ellipse, Christ the Light
of the World; unattributed, *c.* 1903. – Then, the Resurrection,
by *David Gauld* for *J. & W. Guthrie*, *c.* 1896. – Finally, a rather
stiffly grouped Christ, Nathaniel and Philip; by *Kier*, 1871.
Beneath each window a brass panel gives memorial details.

The GRAVEYARD, terraced downhill N and W, contains many
grave-markers. There are numerous lying SLABS, several C17;
one stone said to be dated 1482. C18 and early C19 HEADSTONES,
several mantled or scrolled. – HAMILTON MONUMENT, *c.* 1840;
tall Neo-Classical block of weathered ashlar with pilaster strips
bearing inverted torches. – Set within a railed circular enclosure
close to the NE corner of the church is the EDMONSTONE
MAUSOLEUM, *c.* 1802: steeply roofed gabled Gothic with the
family arms in the W gable apex, VIRTUS AUGET HONOREM,
above a moulded pointed arch, high and sharp, with intersecting
tracery over a lintelled doorway set between clustered shafts. –
Later tombs include a wall aedicule MEMORIAL with open
pediment and flanking cornices: to Professor Archibald Barr
†1934 and family. – MURAL PANEL, inscribed on a boldly plain
sandstone block, to Sir Harald Edgar Yarrow †1962 and his
wife Eleanor Etheldreda Aitken †1934.

Former UNITED FREE CHURCH. The original Free Church,
1867, was recast and extended by *John Honeyman*, 1893, but
destroyed by fire, 1905. Rebuilt 1906–7. Five-bay Dec Gothic
with SE porch. Converted to residential use by *Hughson Crawford*,
1963–4.

MOSS BRIDGE. Built *c.* 1730.

VILLAGE CLUB, Glasgow Road By *Davis & Emanuel* of London;
dated 1911. Restoration by *C. T. M. Design Ltd.*, 2001. More
Anglified Arts and Crafts; roughcast with half-timbered gables
and a porch carried on gnarled tree-trunk columns. Red-tiled
roofs gabled and hipped. Tapering chimneystacks.

VILLAGE HALL, Glasgow Road. By *David W. Glass*, 1926. Gabled
roughcast box with symmetrically splay-fronted porch.

WAR MEMORIAL, Glasgow Road. By *Robert S. Lorimer*, 1921.
Cross-topped column on high plinth.

DESCRIPTION. Some village survivors. On Dumbrock Road, THE
COTTAGE, probably C18, crowstepped painted rubble. On
Glasgow Road, NETHERTON HOUSE and WOODBANK are
tarnished three-bay, two-storey; NETHERTON COTTAGE is
single-storey, painted rubble with hipped attic dormers. At
WOOD PLACE, WEST ROW and NEW CITY ROW, an L-plan
group of two-storey flatted housing with open stair access; built
for workers in the now-demolished calico printworks. All these
early C19. More characteristic are the villas and bungalows of
the C20, the best of them scattered in leafy seclusion off OLD

MUGDOCK ROAD. Among them, a low, wide and white ranch, No. 40 by *Wilson, Hamilton & Wilson*, 1957; DEIL'S CRAIG DAM, also 1957, by *Jack Holmes*, a flat-roofed waterside pavilion, white-walled and timbered; and, comfortably Scots, roughcast with stone-dressed gables and eaves dormers, MOORHOUSE, *c.* 1938.

BALLAGAN HOUSE, 1km. E. 1896. Broad-fronted and square-bayed, with a three-storey Italianate SW entrance tower. 1694 datestone built into gable of mid-C18 block at rear.

BALLEWAN, 2.2km. NW. Dated 1702. A small laird's house now absorbed in later building.

LEDDRIEGREEN HOUSE, 0.5km. NNE. Built *c.* 1760–70. Standard three-bay, two-storey laird's house linked l. and r. to lower, pedimented pavilion wings with Venetian windows and blind oculi. Five-light square bays, *c.* 1913, flank central rusticated doorpiece.

LEVERN TOWERS, 1.2km. NW. By *John Lawrence*, 1938. A robustly pretentious two-storey-and-attic house built on a butterfly plan with updated Baronial bravura. Walls are in dulled cream roughcast with generous dressings of ochre sandstone. Flanking the central entrance, two cone-roofed circular towers act as hinges to skew-gabled wings l. and r. There is an idiosyncratic disregard for stylistic convention, the buildings's supervening symmetry as ill-at-ease with Baronial allusion as any such Scots aspiration is with its Anglophile Arts and Crafts detailing. For all that, this last lends a delicacy to what might otherwise have been oppressively monumental. This is especially so in the semi-detached LODGE where formality is mitigated by angle buttressing, wide eaves and a steep hip-dormered roof.

CARBETH GUTHRIE. *See* p. 307.
DUNTREATH CASTLE. *See* p. 457.

# STRATHLEVEN                                    WD

Since 1946, an industrial estate bounded on the E by the Dumbarton–Bonhill road and on the W by the looping course of the River Leven between Cordale Point and Dalquhurn Point. Marking the entrance is a short stand of ashlar wall fronted by a tetrastyle Ionic portico. Above the pediment, the traces of Roman letters announcing 'Vale of Leven Industrial Estate' are still visible. Industrial estate layout by *Keppie & Henderson*.

Noteworthy among the collection of industrial buildings, Allied Distillers' OFFICES AND BOTTLING HALL, 1999–2000, by architects *Jenkins & Marr* working with *Charles Scott & Partners*. A four-storey façade of curtain walling, horizontally stressed with *brise-soleil* sunshading and swept in a gentle curve to a sharp ship-like prow.

### STRATHLEVEN HOUSE
At the heart of Vale of Leven Industrial Estate

One of Scotland's earliest and most important classical country houses, precociously refined in a provincial Palladian manner that David Walker has described as 'in a special class even within the definition of outstanding'. Known as Levenside until 1836, it was built by William Cochrane of Levenside and Kilmaronock, perhaps as early as 1690, more likely in the first years of the C18. Cochrane's arms and those of his wife Grizel, daughter of the Marquess of Montrose, whom he had married in 1687, appear in the pediments of the N and S façades, their initials and the date 1708 in the tympanum over the S entrance door. Through marriage Cochrane was related to the architect *Sir William Bruce* and it is conceivable that Bruce might have been consulted. A much more plausible designer is *James Smith* whose houses at Whitehill (now Newhailes), near Edinburgh, 1686, and Raith, Kirkcaldy, 1693, exhibit notable similarities, all three houses having single-pile tripartite plans and steeply pitched piended roofs. A drawing by Smith held in the RIBA Library may be a preliminary study for Strathleven, though the façade is shown with a segmental pediment rather than the more orthodox built version.

Compromised by the industrial transmutation of the estate, by the 1970s Strathleven was in serious disrepair, suffering from dry rot and vandalism. Original panelling and plasterwork were removed to storage. Threats of demolition were resisted and in 1986 the Scottish Historic Buildings Trust purchased the house with rehabilitation in mind. Funding negotiations dragged on. In 1992 a fire resulted in the removal of the T-plan Roman Doric porch which had been added to the principal S façade *c.* 1860; it has been re-erected at Broadwoodside, Gifford, East Lothian. A year later, however, a full-scale restoration programme, aimed at transforming the mansion house into a business centre, was begun under the direction of *Nicholas Groves-Raines*. This painstaking work of recovery, which has entailed stabilization of the structure, the replacement of the roofs, reharling and the reinstatement of the plaster and panelling that had been removed, was finally completed in 2000.

Like Newhailes and Raith, Strathleven is a seven-bay house of 59 two storeys set on a raised basement. The central three bays of the S entrance façade advance slightly and are pedimented, the frieze and cornice of the entablature rising above the eaves cornice of the outer bays. In the tympanum are two blind oculi with the family arms between. The piended roof is bellcast at the eaves, the leaded hips flashed to the slate courses. Dormers inset on the W and E slopes were introduced *c.* 1850. On the platform above the steep piends, rising from each of the two crosswalls of the plan, are two sets of panelled ashlar chimneystacks with heavily moulded coping cornices. Walls are harled with raised sandstone quoins, plain window margins and stringcourses at floor and sill levels. At basement level, channelled ashlar with voussoirs over the windows. The S entrance door, re-exposed since the removal of the Victorian porch, has architrave mouldings and a segmental pediment with the date 1708 in the tympanum. Apart from this door, the N elevation is identical. Narrow links with *oeil-de-boeuf* windows connect the main block of the house to W and E wings which advance but remain in parallel plane. Harled with sandstone quoins and margins, these are much lower though two-storeyed with four simple windowed bays to the s and five to the n. Steep piended roofs with platforms and panelled chimneystacks match those of the main house.

Original interiors have been reinstated in the main Entrance Hall, the Oak Room in the w wing and the Pine Room at first-floor level in the e wing. A hanging stone stair with moulded nosings dog-legs from r. to l. rising in the Hall to a galleried upper floor. Both stair and gallery have a decorative timber balustrade carved with pierced foliage and roses. The Cochrane arms are centred over a lugged doorpiece opening to the basement stair. The panelling in the Oak Room has a rose and bracket cornice, a rich frieze of fruit, flowers and flute-playing angels, and incorporates fluted Corinthian pilasters flanking the chimneypiece and w doorway. Overmantel and doors have beaded architraves with egg-and-dart ornament and foliage-framed panels above. All is carefully composed and wonderfully carved with classical detail that recalls Wren's City churches, several of which Smith had almost certainly seen. This woodwork has some similarities to the work of *William Morgan* at Smith's Hamilton Palace and Bruce's Kinross House, though not perhaps of quite such a high quality, and it has been suggested that *James Maclellan*, Morgan's assistant at Hamilton, may have been responsible for the Strathleven commission. This attribution does not apply to the panelled Pine Room where Ionic pilasters flank the chimneypiece in an altogether simpler scheme.

STABLES, 0.05km. E. Dated 1727. Roofless two-storey offices in pink sandstone rubble showing traces of harling. The U-plan court opens to the w. Windows and cart entries blocked.

DOOCOT, a little to the N between the house and stables. A high, two-storey, square-plan box built in pink sandstone with evidence of cream harling. Parts of an eaves cornice and an ashlar s pediment gable survive. Below this at first floor is a disintegrating ashlar niche with architrave mouldings, imposts and keystone. On the N face a lintelled first-floor window frames a round-arched recess. All doors are blocked. The now inaccessible upper chamber, which is carried on a stone vault, has a stone nesting grid.

STRATHYRE                  s

A linear valley village concatenated along the e side of the A84.

BUCHANAN MONUMENT. Erected 1883. Thick Gothic finial of sandstone with inset columns of grey and pink granite and four small fountain bowls, now cemented over. Three granite panels carry quotations and commemorative inscription to Dugald Buchanan (1716–68): HE WAS A TRUE POET / AN ELOQUENT MAN, AND / MIGHTY IN THE SCRIPTURES.

STRATHYRE BRIDGE. C18. Narrow carriageway carried on two segmental rubble arches with faceted cutwater piers over River Balvag. E abutments.

DESCRIPTION. Gabled eaves dormers are the local predilection; they recur repeatedly. The long white roughcast wall of THE INN, of the mid C19, has ten of them. There are some exceptions to this roadside rule. Among them, BEN SHEANN HOTEL, late C19, with two wide canted bays, a full two storeys under steeply peaked roofs, linked by a first-floor balcony carried on cast iron columns. Another is CORRIEGOWRIE, of the mid C19, with a pilastered doorpiece and two smart cone-roofed attic dormers. Only a few houses sit back from the road: DUNELLAN, mid-C19, tidy three-bay basic in square-snecked sandstone, and DOCHFOUR, probably early C20, a broad, hip-roofed, semi-detached house in pink sandstone with symmetrical bows under a full-width balcony with decorative cast iron balustrade. IMMERVOULIN is a single-storey-and-attic farmhouse with outbuildings forming a U-plan court; *c.* 1830.

ARDCHULLARIE MORE. *See* p. 183.

## STRONACHLACHAR S 4010

Some houses and a roughcast pavilion pier with a red-tiled piended roof and a cast iron arcade, all tidily landscaped on the W shore of Loch Katrine.

GLENGYLE HOUSE, 3.6km. NW. Isolated, three-bay roughcast house, much altered in a series of changes difficult to discern and date. Part of the fabric may date from the first years of the C18 but the house was burnt in 1715 and 1745. Crenellated porch, mid-C19, incorporates two datestones, one 1764 (altered to read 1704), the other 1728. Later remodelling, *c.* 1930, raised the upper storey and added crowstepped wallhead dormers. Rob Roy MacGregor was born at Glengyle, 1671.

MACGREGOR OF GLENGYLE BURIAL PLACE, on a raised promontory 0.7m. SE of Glengyle. C18. Rubble enclosure with segmental entrance arch; 'a square enclosure like a pinfold, with a stone ball at every corner . . . a dismal spot, containing four or five graves overgrown with long grass, nettles, and brambles [and] a marble monument to the memory of one of the lairds'*.

## STRONVAR HOUSE *see* BALQUHIDDER

## THORNHILL S 6000

Ridge-line village NE of Flanders Moss. Thornhill proper, planned and feued at the end of the C17, stretches from crossroads to church. To the E is Norrieston, once a C15 fermtoun.

Former NORRIESTON FREE CHURCH. Built in 1844. Rudimentary double-pile farm-shed rubble kirk. Now serves as church hall.

NORRIESTON PARISH CHURCH. Gabled nave and steeple in

* *Journals of Dorothy Wordsworth*, ed. E. de Selincourt, i (1941), 269.

workmanlike E.E. by *William Simpson* of Stirling, 1878–9. Hooded lancets, tripled in the s front over central, pointed-arched entrance door. Attached angle-buttressed SE steeple breaks free at belfry stage below a broached ashlar spire. Circular window with quatrefoil tracery in N gable. Arch-braced pitch pine trusses spring from moulded corbelstones; pine roof boarding, alternately light and dark, parallel to purlins. Rear gallery over vestibule accessed by steeple stair. – Central PULPIT corral with half-octagon projection reached by stairs l. and r. Framed pitch pine front with herringbone infill, a motif repeated in later FONT, 1968, and LECTERN, 1980. – Brass barley-sugar LIGHT STANDARDS on pews, choir rail and pulpit, carry false tilley lamps. – Brass PLAQUE, l. of pulpit, finely engraved in Trajan script; to Rev. James Gordon Mitchell, minister here 1879–1927. – Adjacent to W vestry, a framed PANEL with painted inscription to Rev. James Hughes †1800; retained from earlier Chapel of Ease. – Attractive abstract STAINED GLASS margins and banding.

GRAVEYARD, W of the church. A number of C17 stones have gone or are illegible. Several C18 table tombs, lying slabs and headstones. – SARCOPHAGUS with urns carved in elliptical insets on sides and ends. – Cusp-headed HEADSTONE, dated 1767, to Rob family; masonic symbols, unicorn, winged angel head, crossbones and hourglass. – Another, dated 1736, carries similar symbols of mortality but is severely weathered. – Tall HEADSTONE to Robert Downie †1886 depicts the Charity of Saint Martin in recessed relief. – Among those recorded on the gravestone of the McLarens of Middleton is the architect James M. MacLaren (†1890).

BLAIRHOYLE MASONIC HALL. By *S. Henbest Capper*, 1893. Crossroads-conscious, a square tower rises above the slated bellcast roof of 'the smallest purpose-built lodge in Scotland' to accent the village's hilltop skyline. Roughcast walls with red sandstone sills and stringcourses but the Arts and Crafts affinities are more Germanic than Scots. The tower, broadened slightly at the topmost level on a moulded corbel course and lit below a sprocketed open eaves by all-round glazing, is capped by a red-tiled pyramid with a masonic weathervane at the apex. On its s face is a high entrance doorway with a red sandstone surround surmounted by a cornice and decorative dated tablet. A suspended ceiling conceals the scissors roof timbers over the hall.

LION AND UNICORN HOTEL, Main Street. 1635 (?), but much altered. Named for the twin tablets that flank a small armorial boss above its first-floor windows, it was formerly the Commercial Hotel and before that probably a drovers' inn. In the small ground-floor dining room is a high stone chimneypiece with a salt recess r. and a small aumbry l.

NETHERTON BRIDGE, 1.3km. S. 1827. Segmental-arched span over Goodie Water with semicircular land arch each side. Inscription records the patronage of Henry Home Drummond of Blair.

WAR MEMORIAL. Erected 1920. On a swollen boulder-cairn base, a hefty obelisk of rough-faced sandstone culminates in a blocky Swiss cross.

DESCRIPTION

MAIN STREET is long, straight and severely Scottish; a hard-edged urban canal running E from the crossroads, tightly confined by gable-to-gable cottages. Most houses, late C18 or early C19, are single-storey, many with added attic bay dormers. No. 61, stripped to struck-pointed rubble, is among the oldest; extant deeds record 1749. In scale, it is typical. But roughcast or painted render finishes are more frequent, as at No. 28 which has a corniced doorpiece with panelled pilasters, or Nos. 10–18, 56–62 and 67–75 where a common eaves line persists. Occasionally, the street wall steps up. At No. 8 a canted timber bay window projects at first floor. The CROWN HOTEL, too, is two-storey, door-in-the-middle, with tiny consoles under the sills. Larger consoles appear at ALBION HOUSE (No. 70) scrolled under the fretted bargeboards of its entrance canopy. At SLATEHAA (No. 83) more fretwork and a scallop-corbelled corner. Here the street line kinks N before reaching the Lion and Unicorn Hotel (*see* above). Further E is the church (*see* above) and the former manse, BLAIRHILL, a three-bay house, dated 1848, with lying-pane glazing and a pilastered doorpiece and moulded window architraves in red sandstone. Opposite, the rough window margins of NORRIESTON HOUSE and HEATHERLEE betray an older, more vernacular provenance, *c.* 1740. Beyond is PIPER'S COTTAGE, probably late C18, now without the piper once carved on its gable, and, on the corner of the Doune road, BURNHEAD, probably of the mid C19, with a gabled porch on Roman Doric columns.

THE HILL, running W from the crossroads, has several C18 dwellings. HILLVIEW (No. 3), mid-C18, has a central door with lugged architraves and cornice. LOW TOWN and DOIG STREET, which lie parallel downhill to the S, retain some C18 weavers' cottages. No. 2 Low Town, 1701 (?), was once the village school.

BRAENDAM HOUSE, 3km. NW. Three-bay, three-storey, hip-roofed mansion, 1742–4; revised *c.* 1790. Roman Doric columned porch flanked by thermal windows. At first floor, three tripartite windows. – Single-storey ashlar LODGE, *c.* 1830, with piended roof and segmental-arched porch. – SW is a disused MILL, probably late C18, with W and E segmental-arched entries opposed at lower level.

COLDOCH HOUSE, 4km. ESE. By *K. Darling*, 1964. Two-storey mock-vernacular with crowsteps and entrance gable. Fragments from late C18 predecessor set in roughcast.

COLDOCH BROCH, 3.4km. ESE. Hidden in a wood above a S-facing slope. Overgrown rubble remains with masonry courses intermittently intact to less than 1m. height. Internal dia. *c.* 8.85m. Entrance gap E. Some evidence of mural chambers.

GARTINCABER. *See* p. 517.

# TIGH MOR TROSSACHS                              S
## 2.5km. w of Brig O' Turk

Formerly the Trossachs Hotel; the original three-bay, three-storey
E section, with a central coupled round-arched window at first
floor and symmetrical angle towers, was built 1848–9 by Lord
Willoughby d'Eresby with architectural advice from *G. P. Kennedy*,
then at work on Trossachs Church (*see* Brig O' Turk). Additions
were made in 1853, 1877 and 1891 turning it into a Highland
Camelot, an austere but magical pile of round towers and crowstepped gables in grey-green random rubble with a roofscape of
dormers and chimneys gathered below three high candlesnuffer
cones, decoratively slated and subtly bellcast at the eaves. Now
converted to holiday apartments with added NW and E wings
and separate courtyard block built W, 1992–3, by *John White*;
suitably muted if dully deferential.

# TILLICOULTRY                                    C

A burgh of barony was founded here in 1634 but by the end of the
C18 consisted only of two villages (Eastertown and Westertown).
These developed into the present town after 1830 as a centre for
the woollen industry, which was succeeded by paper manufacture
in the C20.

## CHURCHES

HILLFOOTS EVANGELICAL CHURCH, Bank Street. Rectangular-
windowed rubble box of 1853, a broad W porch with Tudor
Gothic windows relieving the plainness. The W gable's bargeboards and half-timbering look like embellishments of *c.* 1900.

TILLICOULTRY BAPTIST CHURCH, High Street. Gothic box of
1896, built of purplish stone, hammer-dressed at the front gable
and its porch.

TILLICOULTRY E.U. CONGREGATIONAL CHURCH, High
Street. Broad Gothic box, by *Robert Keir*, 1875–6. In the diagonally buttressed stugged ashlar front gable, a door flanked by
two lancet windows each side, all linked by a moulded string-
course-cum-hoodmould; above, a large rose window and a
trefoil opening in the apex of the gable.

TILLICOULTRY PARISH CHURCH, Dollar Road. Unarchaeological lumpy Perp, by *William Stirling I*, 1827–9. The church
is a short droved ashlar rectangle covered with a piended platform
roof. At the centres of the three-bay E and W sides, buttressed
flush transepts, their roofs lower than the main roof; at the
outer corners, diagonal buttresses topped, like all the buttresses,
by sturdy octagonal pinnacles with large foliaged finials. At the
N and S ends, slightly advanced centrepieces between octagonal
buttresses. Corbelled out from the gable of the N (entrance)
front's centrepiece, a heavy octagonal bellcote; within its battlement, a foliage-finialled stone spire. The Tudor-arched N door

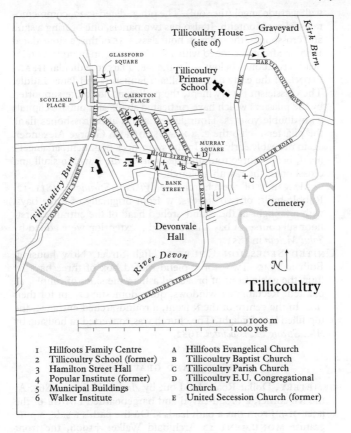

GLASSFORD
SQUARE

SCOTLAND
PLACE

CAIRNTON
PLACE

Tillicoultry House
(site of)

Graveyard

Tillicoultry
Primary
School

MURRAY
SQUARE

HIGH STREET

BANK
STREET

Devonvale
Hall

River Devon

ALEXANDRA STREET

Tillicoultry

|    | 1000 m |
|----|--------|
|    | 1000 yds |

| 1 | Hillfoots Family Centre | A | Hillfoots Evangelical Church |
| 2 | Tillicoultry School (former) | B | Tillicoultry Baptist Church |
| 3 | Hamilton Street Hall | C | Tillicoultry Parish Church |
| 4 | Popular Institute (former) | D | Tillicoultry E.U. Congregational |
| 5 | Municipal Buildings | | Church |
| 6 | Walker Institute | E | United Secession Church (former) |

is placed in a diagonally buttressed and battlemented surround.

The church interior is open-roofed but presumably had a plaster ceiling originally. In 1921–2 *P. Macgregor Chalmers* replaced the 1820s horseshoe gallery with the present deep gallery at the N end. Also by *Chalmers*, 1921–2, are the COMMUNION TABLE and PULPIT. – The brass eagle LECTERN was introduced in 1929. – STAINED GLASS. Colourful but relatively restrained three-light W window (the Crucifixion; Jacob and Joseph; David and Solomon) by *Douglas Strachan*, 1924.

Plain Gothic HALL of 1889–90 at the back. Harled HALL, by *George Bain*, 1929–30, to the SE. At its E end, a single-storey rubble-walled fragment of the manse offices built by *Watson Kirkham* and *Alexander Westwood* in 1813.

GRAVEYARD E of the church. Aligned with the N front of the church, the MONUMENT erected in 1859 by Robert Walker to the memory of his father, George. On the front, the high relief figure of a barefoot lady clasping a book to her bosom. – To the NE, near the churchyard wall, a couple of early C18 HEADSTONES. One (largely buried) has two roundheaded panels, each carved with a crude angel (the soul). The other, dated 1727, commemorates Mary Monteith. It also has two panels, one bearing a skull and crossbones, the other an hourglass. – SE of this, a stone dated 1687, the front decorated with a skull wearing an hourglass on his head; crossbones below. – To the NE, a larger aedicular HEADSTONE of the early C19 to William Jamieson and Janet Liddle. The classicism is very inept, the pediment not quite supported by the pilasters which have rusticated shafts and outsize capitals with double volutes. Hourglasses, skulls and crossbones flank the pilasters. – To the E, a HEADSTONE to George Alexander, again probably early C19. In the swan-neck pediment, an angel's head; below, three roundheaded panels, the l. with a skull and crossbones, the r. with a plough.

MANSE S of the church, by *William Stirling I*, 1811–12. Rubble-built, of two storeys. W front originally of three bays, with a fanlight in the round-arched head of the entrance; first-floor sill course. A bay window and N extension were added by *John Melvin* in 1851.

UNITED SECESSION CHURCH, High Street. Now housing. Built in 1840. Two-storey piend-roofed box of three bays by four, the gable front of broached ashlar, the sides of rubble, all painted. Rectangular windows, quite domestic except for their size. In the centre of the N front, a round-arched entrance, the top filled by a fanlight. The church was converted to housing by *Alex Strang & Associates*, 1982.

### CEMETERY AND GRAVEYARD

CEMETERY, Dollar Road. Laid out by *Archibald Sutter*, 1861. At the NE corner, a broad-eaved and bargeboarded LODGE of the later C19. From this a path leads S. On the path's L side, a pink granite MONUMENT to Archibald Walker †1906, the front bearing the relief of a Celtic cross together with other Celtic motifs and a portrait bust of Walker. – Just to its SE, an elaborately decorated granite Celtic cross to James Fullarton Caldwell Conn †1917; at its head, panels carved with reliefs depicting the Ascension. – An almost identical cross of *c.* 1920 to members of the Brown family stands beside the N path across the cemetery's W section. – N of this path, the FIRST WORLD WAR MEMORIAL, by *Henry Hutcheon Ltd.* of the *Aberdeen Granite Works*, 1921, a tall rock-faced granite pedestal bearing the rather small figure of a mourning lady ('Memory'). – To its N, the SECOND WORLD WAR MEMORIAL of *c.* 1950, a semicircle of small headstones, each incised with a cross and the name of one of the fallen.

GRAVEYARD, Fir Park. Small unfenced graveyard, formerly the site of a pre-Reformation church or chapel. At the W end, an aedicular HEADSTONE (now on the ground), with bulbous baluster-pilasters and a simplified swan-neck pediment carved with an angel's head (the soul). The aedicule frames reliefs of a skull, crossbones and hourglass, and a mason's set square, mallet and chisel. To its E, near the N boundary of the graveyard, a weathered HOGBACK STONE, its sloping sides carved with scalloped decoration. It may be C12. – S of this a rather similar COPED STONE, probably late medieval, its ridge much broader and now bearing the initials HD, IP. On the N side, an incised sword and what was probably a cross; two more badly worn crosses, set base to base, are carved on the S side. – Just S of this, a slab carved with the date 1522 and the initials IM, ID at the top and a large incised spade at the bottom. – To the SE, a HEADSTONE, now lying flat, with the initials IM, ED and MD and the date 1722, together with emblems of death and a weaver's shuttle and stretcher. – Immediately E of the first of the hogback stones, a broken slab commemorating Robert Meiklejohn, skinner and burgess of Edinburgh, †1651, bearing a shield incised with a glove. – Immediately E of this, a HEADSTONE whose top rises into a pair of roundheaded quasi-pediments, each displaying the head of a mournful angel. Below, three panels, the centre bearing initials and the date 1723. In the l. panel, reliefs of a skull, crossbones and hourglass; in the r., a plough. On the back (W) side, the incised inscription:

.I.AM.LAID.IN.THIS.COLD
.BED.AND.CVRTINE
OVER.MEY.IS.SPREAD

– At the graveyard's E end, a slab, probably of the C18, which displays a skull, crossbones and hourglass and a large shovel, probably as the emblem of a maltster.

## PUBLIC BUILDINGS

DEVONVALE HALL, Moss Road. Neo-Georgian going on Art Deco, by *Arthur Bracewell*, 1938–40.

HAMILTON STREET HALL, Hamilton Street. Dated 1864. Single-storey rectangle built of stugged masonry. At the gables, widely spaced crowsteps and, on the W, a pinnacled ball finial. Finial of the same type on the W porch whose front window is roundheaded.

HILLFOOTS FAMILY CENTRE, High Street. By *Central Regional Council*, 1988. Octagonal front block, its pitched and slated roof topped by an octagonal cupola whose glazed sides provide clear-storey lighting to the hall within. Behind, a long single-storey range.

MUNICIPAL BUILDINGS. *See* Description, below.

POPULAR INSTITUTE, Ochil Street. Only the E gable and tower remain. The main block was built in 1858–60. Its surviving gable, built of stugged and squared pinkish sandstone, is diagonally buttressed and crowstepped but has lost its corner turrets; Tudor-arched windows. The weirdly Baronial tower was added by *John Melvin & Son*, 1878–9, also of pinkish sandstone but the masonry is stugged ashlar. Diagonally buttressed bottom stage. Pointed doors, the W with nook-shafts and ballflower and fleuron ornament on the arch; foliaged ball label stops to the hoodmould. Above, the E corners are chamfered and contain slender nook-shafts, their lower part of barley-sugar type; at the

E front, a stone balcony on heavy corbels below the mullioned and transomed window. This stage is finished with a corbelled battlement; round turrets at the corners and boldly projecting drainage spouts. Inside the battlement, a tall octagonal belfry, its broader N, S, E and W sides each having a mullioned and transomed two-light opening under a clock face; at each of the other faces, a tall pointed panel. Gryphons project from the corners of the belfry's cornice which supports a quatrefoil-pierced parapet. The finishing touch was a cast iron crown spire, sadly now lost.

TILLICOULTRY PRIMARY SCHOOL, Fir Park. By the Clackmannan County Council Architect, *W. H. Henry*, 1966. Four-storey flat-roofed main block and lower wings, the walls rendered with dry-dash.

TILLICOULTRY SCHOOL, Institution Place. Now offices. Utilitarian, by *William Kerr* and *John Gray* of *John Melvin & Son*, 1938.

Former WALKER INSTITUTE, Stirling Street. The main block is a house of *c.* 1860. Two-storey broad-eaved T-plan, the corners of the tail's S gable canted at the ground floor and corbelled to r. angles above. At the gable, heavily hoodmoulded entrance; first-floor window of two roundheaded lights. On top of the gable, a round-arched 'bellcote' feature, perhaps a late C19 addition. This became the Walker Institute in 1914. Single-storey N wing, a porch on its W side, added by *William Kerr* and *John Gray* of *John Melvin & Son*, 1919.

### DESCRIPTION

The A91 enters the town from the W, crossing the Tillicoultry Burn by a BRIDGE by *Buchanan & Bennett*, 1891, its structure of iron, the parapets of ashlar. Immediately NE of the bridge, a grey and pink granite FOUNTAIN of 1900, with squat Roman Doric columns at the corners and a cupola on top. In LOWER MILL STREET to the S, the former Paton's Mill (*see* Industrial Buildings, below). UPPER MILL STREET N of the bridge starts, on the E side, with housing by *A. G. Bracewell*, 1961, followed by plain housing of the mid and later C19. More mid-C19 housing in the side streets of CAIRNTON PLACE and GLASSFORD SQUARE to the E and SCOTLAND PLACE to the W. Among them, a couple of single-storey pantile-roofed cottages (No. 5 Glassford Square and ·No. 3 Scotland Place). Similar cottage (CLOCK MILL COTTAGE) at the top of Upper Mill Street itself. This looks across the burn to the Clock Mill (*see* Industrial Buildings, below). Above the mill the road crosses the burn on a plain C19 rubble-built BRIDGE and climbs uphill to a two-storey house (No. 85 Upper Mill Street) of *c.* 1840 with a pilastered doorpiece; single-storey and attic E wing.

HIGH STREET begins at the SE corner of Upper Mill Street with the ROYAL ARMS of *c.* 1840, its doorpiece heavily pilastered and corniced, followed by a white-painted two-storey terrace, also of *c.* 1840; a couple more heavy pilastered and corniced

doorpieces at Nos. 8 and 10. Beyond this and extending to
Union Street, three-storey housing by *A. G. Bracewell*, 1968–70,
traditional and very boring. On the s side of High Street, another
two-storey terrace of the earlier C19. Set back at its end, the
Hillfoots Family Centre (*see* Public Buildings, above). After the
Family Centre, two late C19 buildings. No. 25 is Georgian
survival of a sort. The larger free Jacobean block of Nos. 27–35
attempts to establish the scale of a small-town commercial centre
but is let down by redevelopment set back from the street immediately to its E. Further E the urban quality is re-established by
a mid-C19 terrace (Nos. 55–69) containing flats above shops.
Then plain late C19 as far as Institution Place in which stands
the former Tillicoultry School (*see* Public Buildings, above).
Across Institution Place, the former United Secession Church
(*see* Churches, above).

On High Street's N side, at the corner with Stirling Street,
CURRAN COURT by *P. C. Edney*, 1996–8, a curious revival of
the dourer sort of late Victorian architecture but with a clock
on the canted corner to hint at civic importance. In front of
the corner, the grey granite BAKING COMPANY'S JUBILEE
FOUNTAIN, dated 1896 but not unveiled until the next year.
Attached columns at the corners and incised anthemion ornament; lion's head spouts. In STIRLING STREET, after its late
C20 SE end, terraced cottages of the mid or later C19 on the SW
side; on the NE side, similar cottages but also some villas. Set
behind a front garden, the two-storey No. 11 of *c.* 1840, with
hoodmoulded ground-floor openings and a cavetto-splayed doorpiece. Also set back is No. 15, again of *c.* 1840 but piend-roofed
and with a pilastered and block-pedimented doorpiece. Contemporary No. 17 but it is quite plain and fronts directly on to the
street. At the top end of Stirling Street, the former Walker
Institute (*see* Public Buildings, above).

In High Street E of Stirling Street, No. 92, a two-storey mid-
Victorian Jacobean villa. Further E, a mid-C19 terrace (No. 102)
of flats above shops, with a bowed quadrant corner to Ochil
Street. In OCHIL STREET, Victorian vernacular housing of one
and two storeys. At its N end, the remains of the Popular
Institute (*see* Public Buildings, above).

On the s side of High Street E of Institution Place, the MUNICIPAL
BUILDINGS, a substantial harled house of *c.* 1830. The front
faces the garden to the s. Piend-roofed main block of two
storeys and three bays, with rusticated quoins. Architraved windows, those of the ground floor with block pediments; a late
C19 bay window has been added at the E end. Set back from the
front at each end, a lower wing projecting to the N. The E wing,
taller than the W, has rusticated quoins (as has the NW corner of
the main block) and, at its N gable, a Doric portico and three-
light ground-floor window. To the E, on the corner of Bank
Street, the CLYDESDALE BANK of *c.* 1870, like an oversized villa,
the architecture Georgian survival but with an Italian flavour.
On the E side of BANK STREET, set back from High Street's
building line, the Hillfoots Evangelical Church (*see* Churches,

above). To the E, High Street continues with an undistinguished shopping and housing development of the later C20. Hardly more distinguished the late C19 buildings on the N side of High Street between Ochil Street and Hamilton Street. In HAMILTON STREET, single-storey Victorian vernacular cottages, Nos. 18–20 on the W side with pantiled roofs. On the E side, HAMILTON STREET HALL (see Public Buildings, above).

ARTHUR BETT COURT on the S side of High Street is of 1994. Four-storey Postmodern with pyramid-roofed lower towers cantilevered out above the W corners. At the centre of the W front, a shaped gable; three-storey oriel window at the E bay of the N elevation. To the E, a plain two-storey mid-C19 block followed by Tillicoultry Baptist Church (see Churches, above). On the N side of High Street between Hamilton Street and Hill Street, C19 vernacular. E of Hill Street, No. 150 High Street, a mid-C19 single-storey and attic house with hoodmoulded ground-floor windows and a pilastered and corniced doorpiece. Next door, the gable of another mid-C19 house (No. 152), its door-piece's pilasters panelled; an oriel window was added to the front gable c. 1900. Then, Tillicoultry E.U. Congregational Church (see Churches, above).

MURRAY SQUARE on the S side of High Street serves as a bus station. At the square's E end, a half-timbered pyramid-roofed CLOCK TOWER of 1931 supported on spindly legs.

MOSS ROAD leads out to the S. On its NE corner, a prosperous villa (No. 2) of c. 1860. Heavy-handed Georgian survival, with big blocky consoles supporting the cornice over the door. The outer windows, corniced at the ground floor, are of two lights set in slightly advanced rectangular bays. To the S, late C19 and C20 houses. Nos. 36–46 and 52–62 are by *Arthur Bracewell*, designed in 1935 and 1937 to house workers at the Devonvale Mills; rendered walls and red-tiled roofs, with Art Deco touches. On the E side of the street, the Devonvale Hall (see Public Buildings, above). At the S end, the Devonvale Mills (see Industrial Buildings, below). On the W side of the road, a SECOND WORLD WAR MEMORIAL by *C. d'O. Pilkington Jackson*, 1948, a stone sculpture of a kneeling angel holding a sword. At its S end Moss Road becomes ALEXANDRA STREET which leads over the River Devon to the hamlet (now effectively a suburb of Tillicoultry) of DEVONSIDE. On the S side of the river, W of Alexandra Street, the Devonpark Mills (see Industrial Buildings, below).

DOLLAR ROAD continues the line of High Street to the E. On its N side, sizeable but unexciting late Victorian villas well-screened by planting. At their end, a single-storey piend-roofed LODGE of c. 1840 to the (demolished) Tillicoultry House. At the three-bay droved ashlar W front, an advanced and pedimented centre-piece: stone canopies over the door and windows. Opposite, on the S side of the road, Tillicoultry Parish Church (see Churches, above). To the E, Dollar Road becomes bungaloid. On the S side, the Cemetery (q.v., above).

HARVIESTOUN GROVE, going uphill to the N from the E end of Dollar Road, contains late C20 housing but at the top are the early C19 TILLICOULTRY HOUSE STABLES. Piend-roofed U, the ashlar-faced W front of nine bays. Broad three-bay U-plan centrepiece, its outer bays containing segmental-arched doors under blind panels. At the centre bay, a rectangular pend entrance contained in a giant segmental-headed overarch, a small oculus at the top. Above is a cupola-topped drum placed within a square of Roman Doric columns to which it is joined by outward projections of its parapet. To the N but reached from Fir Park, a small graveyard (*see* Cemetery and Graveyard, above).

At the E end of the town, also leading N off Dollar Road, is BARDS WAY. On its W side, the former TILLICOULTRY MAINS STEADING (now HARVIESTOUN COUNTRY INN), a broad-eaved U-plan of the later C19. Segmental-arched doors and windows. Corner pavilions, their piended roofs tweaked up into gablets over the canted corners.

## INDUSTRIAL BUILDINGS

CLOCK MILL, Upper Mill Street. Now offices. Rubble-walled three-storey and attic woollen mill built for J.&G. Walker in 1824. Ball-finialled three-bay S gable containing a clock face. Nine-bay side elevations. Attached to the N end, a slightly later, lower and narrower piend-roofed house (BRIDGEND HOUSE) of two bays by two.

DEVONPARK MILLS, Alexandra Street. Late C19 woollen mill. At the SE, a triple-pile range. To the NW, more ranges, one with its centre rising as a double-pitch-roofed nave between lean-to aisles.

DEVONVALE MILLS, Moss Road. On the E side of Moss Road, the Victorian woollen mill complex of J.&R. Archibald. At the NW of this group, a two-storey piend-roofed office block of the later C19, with a slightly advanced and pedimented centrepiece. To the S, the three-storey mill building (now a shopping complex) of c. 1870. Triple-pile, with corrugated iron piended roofs, built of white painted stugged ashlar; two-light windows. At the W end, a slender square tower of painted brick, now topped by a corrugated iron pyramidal roof. To the S of the complex, the canteen (now restaurant) by *A. G. Bracewell*, 1954.

PATON'S MILL, Lower Mill Street. Now housing. Two ranges survive of the woollen mill complex begun by J.&D. Paton in 1825. The W range facing the street is a late C19 faintly Italianate three-storey office block. The rubble-built S range, a mill block, is of c. 1836. Three storeys and an attic, the frontage of thirty-four bays; over-enthusiastic display of roof-lights added on its conversion to housing in the late C20.

HARVIESTOUN. *See* p. 536.

# TORBREX *see* STIRLING

# TORRANCE

Sizeable loose-knit village, formerly housing miners at the Balmore coal pit, the buildings C19 and C20.

TORRANCE PARISH CHURCH, School Road. By *Young & Gault*, 1998–9. Unexciting, with rendered walls and concrete-tiled pitched roofs.

ELECTRICITY SUBSTATION, Campsie Road. Flat-roofed builders' *moderne* of the 1930s. Rendered walls enlivened by horizontal brick bands; metal windows.

TORRANCE COMMUNITY CENTRE, School Road. Built as a Board school in 1876; *W. & R. Ingram* were the architects. Tall single-storey school and two-storey schoolhouse. Some gables are bargeboarded, others jerkin-headed; mullioned windows.

TORRANCE PRIMARY SCHOOL, West Road. By *Strathclyde Regional Council*, 1976–8. Linked pair of single-storey polygons, their flat roofs topped by glass cupolas.

# TORWOOD CASTLE
## 2.8km. S of Plean

Hybrid of a hall-house and tower-house occupying the S side of a courtyard whose other buildings are now fragmentary. The lands and office of Forester of Torwood were held by the Forestars of Garden from the mid C15 until the earlier C17 and Alexander Forestar's 'hous of Torwood' is mentioned in 1573. The date 1566 on a broken stone (now in Falkirk Museum) which was found built into a dyke *c.* 0.18km. from the house may well be that of its construction. Restoration of the roofless building, including rebuilding of the wallheads, was begun by *Gordon Millar*, 1960, and is still in progress (2000).

The house is L-plan, composed of a long two-storey and attic S range (*c.* 25m. by 9m.), with a small rectangular SW projection, and a four-storey and attic NW jamb (*c.* 6m. square); in the inner angle of the S range and the jamb, a rectangular stair tower. The walling is of rubble and the gables have been crowstepped. A stringcourse above the ground floor is carried round the exposed faces of the jamb and stair tower but halted abruptly against the N front of the S range and, even more disconcertingly, at the join of the jamb and this range's W gable although the jamb's splayed basecourse is carried across the gable. At the ground floor of the jamb and stair tower, oval gunloops of characteristic mid-C16 type. The jamb's E face contains the principal entrance to the house, the door surround with a roll-and-hollow moulding. Above the door the stringcourse rises to frame the aedicular surround for a missing armorial panel; the pilasters of the surround have almost weathered away but the obelisk finials on the ends of the cornice survive, as does the crowning semicircular pediment, its tympanum carved as a shell. Good-sized windows with moulded margins at the upper floors of the jamb; smaller windows, again with moulded margins, at the stair tower. Corbelled out at the

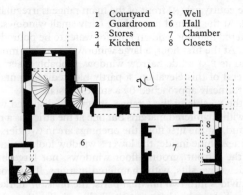

| | | | |
|---|---|---|---|
| 1 | Courtyard | 5 | Well |
| 2 | Guardroom | 6 | Hall |
| 3 | Stores | 7 | Chamber |
| 4 | Kitchen | 8 | Closets |

FIRST FLOOR

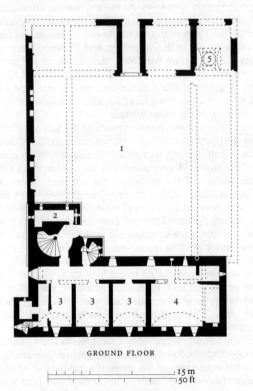

GROUND FLOOR

├──────────────┤ 15 m
├──────────────┤ 50 ft

Torwood Castle. Plans.

stair tower's SE corner, a round turret, its lowest part contained
in the roof space of the S range suggesting its position was an
afterthought. Was it originally intended to be at the NE corner
but switched to the SE to give a more martial emphasis to the
house as seen from the low ground to the S?

The courtyard (N) front of the main range is irregularly composed. At the ground floor, three fairly small windows, all with
chamfered margins, and an inlet for water to be poured into the
house. At the first floor, a large window, its margin moulded. A
little to its E, a crude narrow window, probably inserted. Near
the E end of this elevation, a partly blocked segmental-arched
door, formerly approached by a stone forestair.

At the E gable of the S range, irregularly disposed windows,
most with chamfered margins but one at the attic has a moulded
surround. At the first floor the openings are in two tiers disclosing a mezzanine inside; the lower S window looks an insertion.

At the S front, ground-floor windows, not large but more
than defensive slits, with chamfered margins. This front's first
floor divides into two unequal parts, the division marked by an
intermediate gable between the hall and chamber. Moulded
margins to all the windows. At the E (chamber) third, one large
window and, to its E, a smaller high-set horizontal opening. The
larger W (hall) part of this elevation is symmetrical, of four bays,
with tall windows in the outer bays and, between them, a pair of
smaller almost square windows, their lintels at the same level.
At the W end of this front, a small diamond-shaped opening.

The W gable of the S range and its SW projection contain
windows with chamfered margins. Gunloop below the ground-
floor window of the main W gable.

INTERIOR. The ground-floor entrance to the jamb is checked for
a door and yett. A bolthole extends through the N door jamb
into the E gunloop of a narrow guardroom which occupies the N
end of the jamb. More gunloops in the guardroom's other two
outside walls. Off the W side of the entrance lobby, a broad
turnpike stair (renewed in concrete) which rises to the first floor
where it is covered by a tunnel vault. Along the N side of the S
range, a tunnel-vaulted ground-floor corridor. Off its N side, the
entrance to the quite comfortable turnpike in the stair tower. S
of the corridor are four tunnel-vaulted rooms. The W three were
stores, each with a window and aumbry in the S wall. Opening
off the W store (subdivided in the later C20) is a small room in
the SW projection and, to its S, contained in the wall thickness,
a tight turnpike service stair (now partly missing) which rose
to the attic. The E ground-floor room was the kitchen, its
segmental-arched E fireplace largely rebuilt in the later C20; in
its S side, an aumbry, probably a salt box. In the S wall, a pair of
unequal-sized windows; at their embrasures are stones cut to
serve both as the tops of the splayed jambs and as springers for
the segmental-arched heads. The same detail recurs at the N
windows of the corridor. Below the E of the two kitchen windows, a slop drain.

The two N stairs open on to the W end of the first-floor hall,
the principal stair through a segmental-arched doorway, that of
the stair tower through a rectangular opening. The service stair
at the SW opens into a small room in the projection, its E wall
now missing. In the S side of the hall, a symmetrical disposition
of two large end windows and, between them, a pair of windows

which are truncated, probably so that a large buffet could be placed beneath them. Towards the E end of the N wall, a large fireplace, its square pilaster jambs C16, its arched top C20. The hall's original height is disclosed by rounded corbels which supported the missing attic floor.

At the NE corner of the hall, a moulded doorway to the chamber. This room was subdivided in the later C20, a passage and stair inserted on its N side. In the W wall, a fireplace whose attached column jambs are C16, its hood C20. The flue of the kitchen chimney projects into the E end of the chamber. Each side of it was a C16 arrangement of two rooms, one above the other, the lower a closet, the upper open to the chamber to which its window gave clearstorey lighting. The W line of these rooms is now marked by a C20 elliptical arch at the lower level and a wall pierced by three round-arched openings at the upper.

The attic floor of the S range, reached from both the turnpike in the stair tower and the SW service stair, seems to have contained two rooms above the hall, each with an end fireplace and an L-plan garderobe in the S wall. There was a third room above the chamber and another on the second floor of the NW jamb. The turnpike in the stair tower has continued upwards to give access to the third floor of the jamb. From this level another turnpike contained in the turret at the stair tower's SW corner gave access to a missing caphouse on top of the stair tower.

The courtyard's other ranges were probably of the earlier C17, perhaps replacing wooden outbuildings. Of the W range much of the rubble-built W wall, butted against the NW jamb of the house, survives, as does the raggle of its monopitch roof cutting across the first-floor window of the jamb and its stringcourse. The building has been of two-storey height on its W side but a low single storey on the E. On the inside of the W wall, ground-floor fireplaces and lockers. Of the N and E ranges there remain little more than foundations. At the NE corner of the courtyard, a WELL, perhaps of the C15 or C16, its square shaft surmounted by a circular opening whose surround is carried on vaulting.

## TOUCH HOUSE
### 2.5km. w of Cambusbarron

S 7090

Elegant in composition and execution, its S façade 'perhaps the most distinguished example of Georgian architecture in the county [of Stirlingshire]'*, Touch remains elusive in attribution. Stylistic arguments have been advanced for *William Adam* and for *John Adam*, while an C18 drawing showing plans and elevations as built bears the note '1747 Took House by *James Steinson*'. A tenuous link between John Adam and the Seton family who commissioned the mansion has been pointed to by Macaulay‡ while, since William Adam died in 1748, contemporary contact between the mysterious

*RCAHMS, *Stirlingshire*, ii (1963), 376.
‡James Macaulay, *The Classical Country House in Scotland, 1660–1800* (1987), 140.

*Steinson* and the Adam family, *père et fils*, is also possible. Building accounts make no mention of the building's designer though they do record the name of the mason-contractor, *Gideon Gray* of Stirling, and confirm the period of construction as 1757–62.

60 In fact, the house is an amalgam of C16, C17 and C18 work. By the late C17 the house consisted of two parallel ranges, each with a tower at one end, separated by a narrow courtyard. Of this building the principal remnant is the C16 SE TOWER, a narrow rectangular structure built in whin rubble with dressed quoins and margins. Aligned N–S against the E gable of the later C18 mansion, it rises through four storeys to a corbelled crenellated parapet behind which is an attic storey with crowstepped gables. A re-entrant angle which existed at the NE corner has been filled by a rubble chimneystack added in the C19. A tier of single lintelled windows, the lowest of which is not original, lights the tower's apartments from the S, the N end of its plan being taken up by a turnpike stair. A second C16 tower, also rectangular but aligned W–E, has been invisibly incorporated into the W end of the C17 NORTH RANGE, a three-storey building with crowstepped gables, which established an L-plan relationship with the SE tower and now lies along the rear of the Georgian house. This is a plain harled affair, pleasantly vernacular in character, crested with pedimented eaves dormers by *Robert S. Lorimer*, 1927–8, and dramatized by sloping ground falling to the N.

But it is the MANSION HOUSE, replacing the earlier S range, that gives Touch its architectural distinction. Built in Longannet ashlar, rusticated on the ground floor, the three-storey, seven-bay S façade is a design of real classical sophistication. The three central bays, bordered by quoined edges like the outer margins of the elevation, advance under a pediment carved with scrolls and the full armorial bearings of the Seton family. Urns sit on ashlar supports at the apex and sides of the pediment. The roof is hip-ended, its slated planes falling to a sprocketed eaves. Below a corniced eaves moulding a continuous ashlar course is coincident with the lintel margins of the second-floor windows, a treatment seen also at Blair Drummond House (q.v.). Windows lighting the first floor, the *piano nobile*, are taller, have moulded architraves and carry pediments, alternately triangular and segmental. Those to the ground floor, smaller again, have boldly rusticated voussoirs. Only at the central entrance, which has narrow side lights set in Gibbsian rustication, is there a sense that something is not quite right; the bracketed pediment over the door seems compressed, its flanking cornice mouldings an unnecessary elaboration.

The S door opens into a large hall from which, axially placed on the N, climbs a beautiful elliptical staircase with cantilevered stone treads and a scrolled iron balustrade. This is of *c.* 1810, probably designed by *James Gillespie Graham* and a replacement for an C18 stair occupying the former courtyard. The stair coils slowly through the full height of the house, lit from above by a twenty-four-light elliptical cupola ringed by a Vitruvian scroll

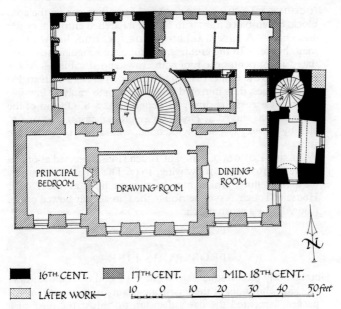

16TH CENT.  17TH CENT.  MID. 18TH CENT.
LATER WORK—

10 0 10 20 30 40 50 feet

N

Touch House. First-floor plan.

frieze. At first-floor level there are three magnificent rooms, their
C18 decoration probably supplemented by *Lorimer* in 1927–8.
The Dining Room, in the E, is fully panelled in pine: there is a
low dado and a generous cornice, its frieze carved with acorns
and oak-leaves. Moulded ribs divide the plaster ceiling into
compartments filled with thin, mainly Rococo, motifs; the work
of *Thomas Clayton*. In the W wall, a severely classical chimneypiece in grey and white marble. Full-height pine panelling also
lines the central Drawing Room, beneath a finely carved frieze
and cornice and a *Clayton* ceiling which, though not compartmented, is more freely decorated with vines and tendril-like
Rococo ornament. There is a large marble chimneypiece with
rinceau relief below a consoled cornice mantel. The W room, a
Bedroom, is less well appointed; its ceiling is simpler and the
walls are unpanelled, though the doors retain the moulded
architraves of the neighbouring rooms. On the E side of the
staircase, corridors communicate with the apartments of the N
range and NE tower. Bedrooms take up the second floor of
the house proper. The walls of two of these are partly panelled
and there is a delightful plaster ceiling, similar in decorative
spirit to that in the Drawing Room, in the W bedroom. In the
Library on the second floor of the N range the ceiling is coved
above a dentillated cornice and has plaster busts set into each
corner.

Service buildings link E to L-plan STABLES COURT, early C19.
Hip-roofed and built in droved ashlar and rubble, the S front
has a central pediment with a SUNDIAL in the tympanum

(I COUNT THE SUNNY HOURS) and a weathervane on the apex block. Seven-bay E front with segmental-arched entries at centre and ends. – A large WALLED GARDEN, *c.* 1810, lies W of the main house. – In the grounds, a ruinous rectangular DOOCOT, dated 1736; penthouse roof with crowstepped gables. – At the entrance to the estate, rusticated ashlar GATEPIERS with angled coping stones, their mirrored slopes seeming to imply an invisible pediment across the drive; by *Lorimer*, 1927–8. On top of the piers, falcons carved by *Phyllis Bone*. – Roughcast GATELODGE, also by *Lorimer* (?), steeply piended, with a bell roof over the stair.

SETON LODGE, 0.4km. N of Touch House. Erected as offices between 1797 and 1810; W wing, 1947. The original two-storey harled dwelling, which may have been built as the Dower House of Touch, is symmetrical to the S, its slightly bowed centre fronted by a Tuscan porch.

4000

# TROSSACHS PIER                                                S

Outrageously picturesque narrows at the E end of Loch Katrine. Ruskin, who thought the lacustrine beauty of the scene unsurpassed, lamented the C19's decision to 'thrust the nose of a steamer into it, plank its blaeberries over with a platform, and drive the populace past it as fast as they can scuffle' (1885). Today, a spur of the A821 reaches the embarkation point for leisure cruises on the S.S. *Sir Walter Scott*, built at Denny Brothers, Dumbarton, 1899, and still plying the waters during the tourist season. From here the road opens into a sylvan bowl. To the r., the CAPTAIN'S REST, a rubble-built Victorian tearoom, refurbished 1955, with a high piended roof extended over an enclosed verandah. Ahead, a red-tiled, gable-ended SHOP pushes W into the loch. A perjink KIOSK, octagonal with a copper roof and leaping deer weathervane, provides tourist information. To the l., clinging to the tree-drenched rocky shore, the long access finger leading to the PIER, timber-framed with a red-tiled saddleback roof, might have been transported from the wallhead walk of some fortified medieval German town. Indeed, the whole scene has a romantic Germanic look about it, were it not for an unimaginative handling of car-parking and an inexplicable C20 deference to tarmac.

A bronze PLAQUE set in the rubble wall of the CENTENARY WELL, 1955, recalls the Act of Parliament that led to the construction of Loch Katrine Waterworks, a massive engineering feat undertaken by the Corporation of Glasgow, 1855–9, which continues to supply the city with fresh water.

8090

# TULLIBODY                                                     C

Large village, its small C19 nucleus near the site of a former tannery, the rest overspill development from the 1950s.

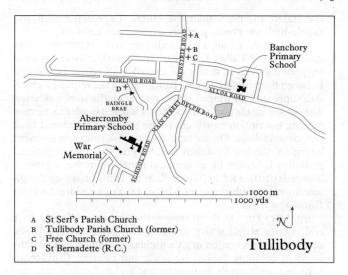

A  St Serf's Parish Church
B  Tullibody Parish Church (former)
C  Free Church (former)
D  St Bernadette (R.C.)

**Tullibody**

## CHURCHES

Former TULLIBODY PARISH CHURCH, Menstrie Road. Roofless rectangular church of a parish which was in existence by *c.* 1170, reconstructed in 1539 but unroofed in 1560 by French soldiers who used the timbers to construct a bridge over the River Devon; forty years later the parish was united to Alloa. A new roof was put on the old church *c.* 1760 when the building became the mausoleum of the Abercrombies of Tullibody and, after another re-roofing in 1824, the interior was fitted up in 1833 as a chapel of ease. A new church (St Serf's Parish Church, q.v.) was built in 1904 and the pre-Reformation church again unroofed twelve years later.

The building is a straightforward rectangle, *c.* 19.2m. by 6.7m., the W, N and S walls built mostly of cubical ashlar, their masonry and the dimensions suggesting a C12 date; the E gable is of rubble and clearly later. At each gable the masonry is intaken at the level of the main wallhead, perhaps the result of one of the C18 or C19 re-roofings. The gables' crowsteps are probably replacements or embellishments of the early C19. On the W gable, a birdcage bellcote, probably of 1833, its roof supported on stumpy Roman Doric pillars. In this gable, lancet windows, clearly insertions of the later C19, perhaps dating from repairs carried out in 1873. Small rectangular window, now built up, set high towards the E end of the N wall. Windowless E gable. In the S wall, rectangular windows and doors, all with roll-moulded margins and dating from a reconstruction of 1539, the date carved together with a weathered crozier on the lintel of the E of the two doors. The window E of this door, probably provided to light a short sanctuary, is of two lights and more

elaborately moulded than the others. Crowstep-gabled and
rubble-built SW porch, perhaps an early C19 addition.

Inside, on the E wall, a large aedicular MONUMENT to George
Abercromby of Tullibody †1699. The Corinthian columns stand
on pedestals whose fronts are carved with reliefs of torches.
Between the pedestals, a long panel bearing the relief of a graveslab supported on winged skulls; resting on the slab, a skeleton
with angels' heads (souls) at its ends. Floriated border to the now
missing inscription panel; above the border, a weathered head
and carved foliage. On the main frieze, crossbones and a winged
hourglass, flanked by angels' heads. The aedicule's segmental
pediment is broken by an armorial panel. – On the W gable, a
bronze MONUMENT to Alistair Ramsay Tullis †1949 aged eighteen months, with the relief portrait bust of a toddler by *Percy
Portsmouth*, 1950.*

GRAVEYARD. On the N wall of the church itself, near its E
end, a large MONUMENT to George Haig, dated 1715. It is a
country mason's version of a Corinthian columned aedicule, the
attached columns flanked by skulls and rosettes. Curvaceous
pediment with scrolls on its sides and an urn finial; tympanum
carved with a trumpet-wielding angel, together with a skull and
crossbones.

Surrounding the church, a wealth of C18 HEADSTONES and
three (just SW, just NW and S of the E end of the church) of the
1690s. The late C17 and many of the C18 stones have incised
carving. Others (the earliest apparently of 1709) are carved in
relief. Some of the stones bear angels' heads but the dominant
motifs are skulls and crossbones, together with emblems of the
trades of the deceased, the most common the plough and harrow
of the farmer, but others include the shears and iron of the tailor,
the horseshoe, tools and crowned anvil of the blacksmith, the
shuttle of the weaver, and the setsquare and dividers of the wright.
The largest of these stones (NE of the church) is set on its side.
The W face, commemorating the family of John Colley, is
divided into three panels, two bearing inscriptions, the round-
arched centre panel a skull, crossbones, hourglass, and plough
and harrow. On the other side, in higher and cruder relief, a
skull, crossbones, hourglass and plough, and the date 1729,
together with the initials E S and E P, all these now set sideways,
suggesting that the slab may originally have stood upright and
was later taken over by Colley and placed on its side. But if so,
it would have been quite exceptionally tall for an upright headstone and the carving of the two sides, although apparently by
different hands, does not look very different in date. – Stylistically
more ambitious than the generality of the C18 headstones,
although remarkably inept in execution, are a couple of early
C18 stones immediately N of the church, placed a little W of its
centre, both having curvaceous pediments which are almost but
not quite supported by Ionic pilasters framing crossbones and
hourglasses; stone skulls on the ends of the pediments.

*In 1928 the RCAHMS noted a stoup at the W end of the S wall and an aumbry at
the S end of the E gable. Neither of these is now (2001) clearly visible.

FREE CHURCH, Menstrie Road. Now church hall. Built in 1844. Sizeable but plain Gothic rectangle, with a gableted 'bellcote'.

ST BERNADETTE (R.C.), Baingle Brae. By *Peter Whiston*, 1961–3. Two broad dry-dashed boxes (nave and chancel), the W's monopitch roof sloping down to the W, the roof of the slightly narrower and lower chancel sloped down to the E to allow a clearstorey at the end of the nave. The chancel's E wall is fully glazed. – STAINED GLASS. In the E window, a light (St Bernadette and Our Lady) of *c.* 1965.

ST SERF'S PARISH CHURCH, Menstrie Road. Small rubble-walled Early Christian church, by *P. Macgregor Chalmers*, 1904. Nave with a low N aisle and E apse; gabled SW porch and NE vestry. In the S wall of the nave, plain round-arched windows. Simple moulding at the door of the porch. Another round-arched window but bigger and with nookshafts in the W gable of the nave. At the W end of the aisle, a round-arched window like those of the nave's S side. In the aisle's N side the windows are small rectangles. At the apse, more round-arched windows but with blind heads.

Inside, exposed rubble walls and open wooden nave and aisle roofs, that of the nave of braced collar type. The N arcade's roundheaded arches spring from squat columns with block capitals. Chancel arch again roundheaded, its nookshafts with scalloped capitals. Over the semicircular apse, a half-dome plaster ceiling. – Furnishings all of 1904. Simple plain PEWS. – Round stone FONT. – STAINED GLASS. In the apse, two pictorial lights (Our Lord holding bread; Our Lord holding a chalice), probably of 1904, by *Stephen Adam & Son*. – The W window of the nave (the Adoration of the Magi; the Agony in the Garden; Our Lord in Glory) is signed by *Stephen Adam & Son* and probably of 1904.

S of the church, a C20 wrought iron stand decorated with flowers, fruit and corn. It holds a BELL of 1838 which used to hang in the bellcote of the former Tullibody Parish Church.

## PUBLIC BUILDINGS

ABERCROMBY PRIMARY SCHOOL, School Road. By the Clackmannan County Architect, *W. H. Henry*, 1951. Prominent hall, with a low clock tower at one end. Flat-roofed classroom block.

BANCHORY PRIMARY SCHOOL, Alloa Road. By *W. H. Henry*, 1958–9. Pitched-roof hall and flat-roofed classroom blocks of one and two storeys.

BRIDGES, 1.3km. W. Two adjacent bridges over the River Devon. The OLD BRIDGE is a combination of causeway and bridges across the river and its flood plain. The bridge of Tullibody is first mentioned in 1560 when it was said to have been cut by Kirkcaldy of Grange in an attempt to prevent French troops crossing the Devon on their way to Stirling. In 1616 the Privy Council authorized the levying of a toll for repair of the bridge which was of four arches ('bowis'). Further levies or tolls for repair were authorized by the Privy Council in 1675 and by Parliament in 1681 after a report of 'some of the arches and bowes being fallen down'.

The causeway begins some way E of the river, the raised pathway bounded by rubble retaining walls rising to form a plain parapet. Over the river itself, two obtusely pointed arches with thickly ribbed soffits. Between the arches, at each face, a broad triangular sloping-topped cutwater. Heavy buttresses at the abutments. All this looks C16. To the W, a stretch of causeway, perhaps a late C17 substitute for one of the arches which existed in 1616. There follows an arch over a side-channel of the river, its head almost semicircular, its soffit with thick ribs like those of the arches to the E. Is it C16 or late C17? To the W, a causeway pierced by two small roundheaded arches, the E hoodmoulded; they may date from the earlier C19.

The late C19 BRIDGE immediately to the N is by *A. J. Main & Co. Ltd*. At the ends, battlemented stone piers with large crosslet dummy arrowslits; latticed iron span.

### DESCRIPTION

MENSTRIE ROAD is the N entry. On its l., the ecclesiastical trio of St Serf's Parish Church, followed by the roofless former Tullibody Parish Church and the old Tullibody Free Church (*see* Churches, above). Then the MANSE (originally Free Church Manse) by *John Melvin*, 1847–8, with block pediments over the ground-floor windows and an anta-pilastered doorpiece. The adjoining No. 14, also mid-C19, is more lighthearted, a single-storey harled Jacobean villa. T-junction with STIRLING ROAD which leads out of the village to the W. On its S side, St Bernadette's Church (*see* Churches, above). The E continuation of Stirling Road is ALLOA ROAD, its S side formerly dominated by a huge tannery. Further out, on the N, Banchory Primary School (*see* Public Buildings, above).

MAIN STREET runs s from the junction of Stirling and Alloa Roads. It is a thoroughfare which serves housing and a small shopping centre of the later C20, the buildings unexciting but pleasantly placed among trees and well-kept gardens. In DELPH ROAD to the E, a handful of C19 cottages, one with a pantiled roof. In SCHOOL ROAD, the s continuation of Main Street, Abercromby Primary School (*see* Public Buildings, above).

*3080*

# TULLICHEWAN CASTLE    WD

### w of Alexandria

'The first asymmetrical Gothic house in Scotland'*, Tullichewan was built on the lower slopes on the W side of the Vale of Leven not far s of Loch Lomond. It was a large house with all the appurtenances of country living including extensive gardens

---

* John G. Dunbar, *The Historic Architecture of Scotland* (1966), 127.

provided with greenhouses, vineries, a fernery and a melon house. John Stirling of Cordale purchased the estate in 1792 but building seems to have been delayed until he obtained charters of confirmation for the estate lands in 1808. In that year *Robert Lugar*'s design, picturesquely replete with castellated towers, was exhibited at the Royal Academy when it was said to be 'now building'. Thereafter construction of the battlemented mansion with its equally romantic offices and lodges went ahead, the layout of the estate grounds fashioned by *Alexander Nasmyth*. Nearly a century and a half later, in 1954, the Castle was blown up. Roadways and housing schemes have subsequently obliterated all traces of Lugar's medievalizing conceit. – Dilapidated STABLES remain, isolated above the dual carriageway of the A82, a symmetrical Gothic fort in coursed rough-faced masonry crowned with a battlemented octagonal tempietto of open lancet arches. – The SOUTH LODGE and GATEPIERS also survive on Alexandria's Main Street (*see* Alexandria).

# TWECHAR

ED 6070

Village built from *c.* 1880, originally to house miners.

## CHURCHES

ST JOHN OF THE CROSS (R.C.), St John's Way. By *Alexander McAnally*, 1968–9. Tall circular red brick building with a cross-finialled triangular 'spire' on the centre of the roof. Full-height bow-fronted S porch. Rectangular openings to both church and porch.

TWECHAR PARISH CHURCH, Main Street. By *James Davidson*, 1900–2. Simple Gothic, built of hammer-dressed Closeburn red sandstone. Nave, N aisle, transepts and W chancel; NE tower. In the S side, lancet windows. Y-traceried two-light windows at the transepts and N aisle. Stepped arrangement of three lancet lights in the chancel's gable. At the E gable, two tiers of windows. The lower are four-centred, their hoodmould's label stops carved with foliage. The three upper windows are pointed and stepped under a continuous hoodmoulding, its label stops carved with the heads of two men, one apparently a depiction of John Knox. At the NW, the former MANSE (converted to a hall in the 1960s) also by *Davidson*, 1902, with a battlemented bay window.

## PUBLIC BUILDINGS

TWECHAR INSTITUTE, Main Street. Opened in 1901. Tall single storey, built of stugged masonry. Lugged architraves and consoled sills to the windows. Broad elliptical-arched entrance, the surround with Gibbsian rustication. At the N end of the front, a projecting broad gable masked by an unhappy late C20 addition. In this gable, a round-arched window flanked by two rectangular lights placed too far apart to form a Venetian window.

TWECHAR PRIMARY SCHOOL, Main Street. The piend-roofed front (E) range by *A. McG. Mitchell*, 1888, is dressed up with Jacobean pilasters, their Mannerism very Artisan. The other ranges were added in 1927, forming a quadrangle. In 1937 the N and S ranges were heightened from one to two storeys and the W range extended N.

## DESCRIPTION

At the N end of MAIN STREET, the Twechar Institute (*see* Public Buildings, above) and fairly plain late C19 housing. At the S end, St John's R.C. Church hidden away to the W, and Twechar Parish Church and Twechar Primary School fronting the road (*see* Churches and Public Buildings, above). Immediately N of the school, the single-storey and attic SCHOOLHOUSE of 1888, its front door framed by pilasters just like those of the school. In MACDONALD CRESCENT to the SW, neatly traditional rendered housing by the Dumbarton County Architect, *Joseph Weekes*, 1939, with prominent gables and some catslide dormers. More utilitarian housing of 1955 to the W.

EASTERTON, 0.9km. SW. Former school and schoolhouse of *c.* 1830. Single-storey harled asymmetrical Jacobean marred by late C20 solar panels and the enlargement of one window. In the schoolroom's projecting S gable, a hoodmoulded elliptical-arched window of four pointed lights. Segmental-arched door at the schoolroom's gabled porch.

GARTSHORE EAST LODGE, 0.9km. SW. Gartshore House (demolished, 1963) was by *James Thomson* of *John Baird & James Thomson*, *c.* 1890. The contemporary lodge survives. Baronial, built of hammer-dressed stone; ball finials on the crowstepped gables.

ROMAN FORT, Bar Hill, 1km. NE. A long access track follows the line of the Antonine Wall to Bar Hill. On the small rocky crag sat an Iron Age fort, probably abandoned by the Roman period, its defences surviving as a series of slight terraces. On a clear day both sides of the country are visible from here. The ditch swung round the N side of the Iron Age fort, but was not fully completed. The Roman fort lies to the W, unusually, detached from the rampart. The low mounds of the E, N and W ramparts are visible: the S is followed by the modern site boundary. Inside are visible the stone foundations of the headquarters building and bath-house. The artefacts discovered during excavations in 1905 and 1974–9 are in the Hunterian Museum of the University of Glasgow. The ditch can be followed W down the hill to Twechar. W of Twechar the Wall is only rarely visible.

TYNDRUM                    S

A village at the head of Strathfillan where roads and railway lines branch N to Fort William and W to Oban.

TOURIST INFORMATION CENTRE. 1998. Smartly simple gabled structure in creamy roughcast. Against the glazed NE wall, a flat-roofed, steel-columned verandah provides a sheltered entrance.

UPPER TYNDRUM STATION. 1894. Hillside halt with an island platform. Standard West Highland Line station by *James Miller*: brick dado, timber framing and shingle cladding under a bell-cast piended roof. Unmanned, tidy, but with all windows boarded up.

DESCRIPTION. Everything serves the traveller; tourists passing through by bus or car, walkers on the West Highland Way. The dominant building is the BEN DORAN HOTEL, 1990–1, three roughcast storeys and a piend-roofed storey with wide triangular dormers and glazed attics. The ROYAL HOTEL, late C19 but enlarged in the early 1990s, is not dissimilar. Both are liveried in cream, green and brown, both have wide conservatory vesti-bules and both are fronted by immense *porte cochère* canopies of trussed timber. Of Highland village life there is only the faintest suggestion, a row of white roughcast COTTAGES with corru-gated iron roofs lined up across the burn at the NW end of the settlement.

# UNIVERSITY OF STIRLING    S *8090*
### 3km. N of Stirling

A beautifully landscaped rural campus gathered on the slopes of Airthrey Loch, part of the early C19 parkland demesne of Airthrey Castle (q.v.): a 'beautiful varied park with a large artificial lake' (*The Gardeners' Magazine*, 1842).

The University was established in 1966, Scotland's first new uni-versity since the foundation of Edinburgh University in 1583. Between 1966 and 1972 *Robert Matthew, Johnson-Marshall & Partners* transformed the 340-acre Airthrey Estate into an out-of-town campus unique in Scotland. The essential disposition of the development plan has remained unchanged.

Placed centrally, immediately S of the Loch, are the LIBRARY and MACROBERT ARTS CENTRE of 1969–72, the academic and social core of the student community. Elevations have a pro-nounced horizontality, a formal approach consistently favoured by the architects, though here relieved by the volumetric demands of the auditorium plan and section. Theatre and Library, lying on opposite sides of a N–S circulation spine which cleverly exploits the interactive possibilities of level changes, combine with a restaurant, bar and shops to make this the hub of campus activity. A covered pedestrian route S bridges Queen's Court to connect with teaching and research accommodation in the COTTRELL BUILDING, 1969–70. This is laid out in a ladder-plan arrangement with parallel spines linked by rib rungs form-ing a series of inner courtyards with integral lecture rooms ingeniously located where the spines make oblique changes of direction. Three and four storeys high, the elevations are again striped, dark alternating with light; continuous glazing with

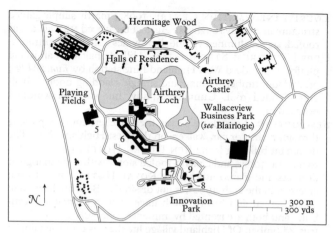

University of Stirling. Plan of campus.

1  Macrobert Arts Centre
2  Library
3  Pathfoot Buildings
4  Principal's House
5  National Swimming
   Academy Building
6  Cottrell Building
7  Scion House
8  Bio Reliance Building
9  E.R.D.C. Building

concrete mullions running between bands of precast concrete finished with Torrin marble exposed aggregate.

N of the Arts Centre an open BRIDGE, 1970, of starkly simple U-section of reinforced concrete carried on splay-legged frames, provides a cardinally straight line across Airthrey Loch to the HALLS OF RESIDENCE, erected 1969–72 on the s-facing slopes below Hermitage Wood. Eight blocks of housing, four halls of residence and four flatted units climb up the hillside in stepped U-plan formation. Built in structural concrete blockwork with exposed aggregate facing, generally four or five storeys high, and banded with horizontal glazing, they seem like an 'Alpine sanatorium, gleaming from the first flush of the Modern Movement' (McKean, 1973).

Between the Loch and the A9, which skirts the campus on the w, are the University playing fields and the NATIONAL SWIMMING ACADEMY BUILDING. By *Faulkner Browns Architects*, 2000–01. A sparkling silver shed. Spanning the breadth of the 50m. pool hall, an aluminium standing seam roof, boldly curved back to a tilted E wall, falls gently W. At the eaves a long clearstorey separates this higher form from a long low linear block of flat-roofed offices and changing rooms clad in acrylic render and stained hardwood lining. To the NW, overlooking the entrance to the estate, is the PATHFOOT BUILDING, 1966–7, three flat-roofed single-storey terraces, each comprising two parallel, corridor-plan blocks linked by courtyards. Walls are glazed below deep precast concrete fascias finished with exposed aggregate. The gridded plan arrangement incorporates a variety of room types (a necessary aspect of its being the first building on the campus) and has readily accommodated change and extension.

High in the NE corner of the estate below Hermitage Wood, on a site that served first as the stable yard of Airthrey Castle (q.v.), is the elegant, flat-roofed PRINCIPAL'S HOUSE, 1966–7, by *Morris & Steedman*. Rubble walls have been retained to create a court-yard, the overlapping white walls of the house placed against the inner face of the yard's obtuse SW angle in an arrowhead plan that points the view through a glazed corner living-room.

The E corner of the University campus is occupied by an Innovation Park, fostering scientific and light industrial enterprise. Several buildings attain a measure of architectural quality:

BIO RELIANCE BUILDING, Phase 2 by *Oberlanders Architects*, 1998–99. Red brick with box projections in mirrored glass under a segmental roof.

E.R.D.C. BUILDING, by *Davis, Duncan, Harrold*, 1999–2000. Sophisticated two-storey steel frame offices on a gently bent plan, the long elevations suavely gridded with glass, glass bricks and tiling.

SCION HOUSE, by the *Davis, Duncan Partnership*. Phase one, 1993: two-storey L-plan block built in ochre brick with dark brown striping. Glazed galleried hall in the re-entrant. Behind this a glazed corridor links to Phase 2, 1995–6, connecting diagonally to the glazed entrance apex of its triangular plan. From above this second hall the roof falls across wide two-storey bays with exposed steel columns set between.

# VELLORE
F *9070*

o.8km. E of Maddiston

Lighthearted castellated small mansion house of *c.* 1800, with an earlier back wing and additions of 1905–12 by *James Strang*.

The N front is all of *c.* 1800. Rubble-walled two-storey main block of three bays by two, the wallhead's battlement ending in round corner turrets. Hoodmoulded windows. Battlemented porch, the ogee-arched entrance flanked by columns of bundled shafts. Slightly recessed low single-storey links, their parapets scalloped. In the front of each, a hoodmoulded pointed window flanked by pointed dummies. The end pavilions are battlemented and conical-roofed round towers of two low storeys. At their ground floors, huge crosslet 'gunloops'; pointed windows to the first floors.

C18 three-storey back wing, its top windows' segmental-pedimented dormerheads dating from the early C20 alterations which also added a two-storey extension to the wing and single-storey pavilions (recreation room and smoking room) at the SW and SE corners of the front block.

# WALLACE MONUMENT *see* NATIONAL WALLACE MONUMENT

## WATSON HOUSE                                                     s
1.4km. w of Gargunnock

*6090*

Originally New Leckie. By *David Hamilton*, 1829–35. An asymmetrical Jacobean jumble of shaped gables, chimney ranges and
hooded windows, described as 'English Baronial style'*. The s
front has a central *porte cochère manquée* to the l. of which is a
tall stair window in Perp Gothic. Vestibule has a panelled ceiling and almost imperceptibly Gothic glazed screen leading to an
inner hall. Timber tracery balustrade to stair. Lower E wing,
dated 1830. NE service court entered N under four-centred arch
supporting heavy birdcage belfry. EAST LODGE, 1843, roughcast
with dressed quoins and skews, much enlarged s.

*4080*

## WESTERTON HOUSE                                                 WD
0.9km. SE of Ashfield House (q.v.)

Early C19, with additions, 1909–10. A two-storey classical house
of five bays to which a broader sixth bay has been added l. The
s front has an urn-capped pedimented centrepiece over a broad
first-floor window set between blind oculi. Tripartite door with
blind semicircular fanlight. Paired pilasters flank the outer bays.
Part of the two-storey service wing may originally have served
as a family chapel, for the N elevation has a pointed-arched
window, blind cruciform arrow-slits and three blind quatrefoils.

*9070*

## WESTQUARTER                                                     F

Garden suburb, originally for miners, in the grounds of the
demolished Westquarter House. It was laid out in 1936 by *John
A. W. Grant* who also designed the housing. The winding streets
respect and exploit the well-wooded sloping site. Two-storey
semi-detached houses and flatted blocks, with rendered walls, red
Rosemary tiled roofs, and front gables the principal architectural
features. A few intruders of the later C20 have crept in.

CHURCH HALL, Elm Drive. By *Wilson & Wilson*, 1939. Tall and
narrow pebble-dashed rectangle. Curvaceously shaped front
gable of Lorimerian Cape Dutch inspiration. Projecting from it,
a crowstepped two-storey porch.

WESTQUARTER PRIMARY SCHOOL, Westquarter Avenue.
Symmetrical free Neo-Georgian, by *John A. W. Grant*, 1939.
Two tall storeys, with white-painted rendered walls and red-tiled
roofs. Recessed centre block topped by a small ogee-domed
copper-clad cupola. Long lateral wings; projecting from each, a
single-storey bow window.

73 DOOCOT, Dovecot Road. Rubble-built lectern doocot, probably
of the early C18. On the tall s wall, a scalloped parapet, one of
its ball finials surviving, which returns at the crowstepped gables

---

* *Ordnance Gazetteer of Scotland*, ed. Francis H. Groome, iv (1883), 479.

to terminate in panel-fronted corniced piers topped by stumpy pinnacles. One moulded ratcourse. Above the N door, a panel, apparently re-used, bearing the quartered arms and initials of Sir Henry Livingstone of Westquarter and Dame Helenore Livingstone, his wife, and the date 1647.

## WHINS OF MILTON *see* STIRLING

## WOODBURN HOUSE ED *6080*
2.8km. E of Milton of Campsie

Rubble-built two-storey laird's house built for the Buchanans of Auchenreoch *c.* 1800. Front of three bays, the centre advanced under a chimneyed pediment. Corniced three-light ground-floor windows in the outer bays. A boldly projecting porch was added *c.* 1825. It is Gothick, with hefty octagonal buttresses at the corners and blind arcading at the front; hoodmoulded windows in the sides.

## WOODHEAD CASTLE *see* LENNOX CASTLE

## WRIGHTPARK S *6090*
2.25km. SSW of Kippen

A seriously Georgian house of 1750–1, severe rather than elegant. Five bays wide and three storeys high. The principal E front, which is in ashlar, has a ground floor with channelled joints, above which are plain pilasters (their capitals unwrought) supporting a heavy entablature with pulvinated frieze and, over the central three bays, a pediment and urns. Architrave and frieze return briefly from the façade, the cornice continuing as an eaves course above the harled N, S and W walls. The fanlit entrance door, at the centre of the E front, sits within a round arch; lintelled windows on each side similarly recessed. Architrave mouldings surround the tall *piano nobile* windows and the smaller openings above.

# GLOSSARY

Numbers and letters refer to the illustrations (by John Sambrook)
on pp. 806–13.

ABACUS: flat slab forming the top of a capital (3a).

ACANTHUS: classical formalized leaf ornament (3b).

ACCUMULATOR TOWER: see Hydraulic power.

ACHIEVEMENT: a complete display of armorial bearings (i.e. coat of arms, crest, supporters and motto).

ACROTERION: plinth for a statue or ornament on the apex or ends of a pediment; more usually, both the plinth and what stands on it (4a).

ADDORSED: descriptive of two figures placed back to back.

AEDICULE (*lit.* little building): architectural surround, consisting usually of two columns or pilasters supporting a pediment.

AFFRONTED: descriptive of two figures placed face to face.

AGGREGATE: see Concrete, Harling.

AISLE: subsidiary space alongside the body of a building, separated from it by columns, piers or posts. Also (Scots) projecting wing of a church, often for special use, e.g. by a guild or by a landed family whose burial place it may contain.

AMBULATORY (*lit.* walkway): aisle around the sanctuary (q.v.).

ANGLE ROLL: roll moulding in the angle between two planes (1a).

ANSE DE PANIER: see Arch.

ANTAE: simplified pilasters (4a), usually applied to the ends of the enclosing walls of a portico (q.v.) *in antis*.

ANTEFIXAE: ornaments projecting at regular intervals above a Greek cornice, originally to conceal the ends of roof tiles (4a).

ANTHEMION: classical ornament like a honeysuckle flower (4b).

APRON: panel below a window or wall monument or tablet.

APSE: semicircular or polygonal end of an apartment, especially of a chancel or chapel. In classical architecture sometimes called an *exedra*.

ARABESQUE: non-figurative surface decoration consisting of flowing lines, foliage scrolls etc., based on geometrical patterns. Cf. Grotesque.

ARCADE: series of arches supported by piers or columns. *Blind arcade* or *arcading*: the same applied to the wall surface. *Wall arcade*: in medieval churches, a blind arcade forming a dado below windows. Also a covered shopping street.

ARCH: Shapes see 5c. *Basket arch* or *anse de panier* (basket handle): three-centred and depressed, or with a flat centre. *Nodding*: ogee arch curving forward from the wall face. *Parabolic*: shaped like a chain suspended from two level points, but inverted.
Special purposes. *Chancel*: dividing chancel from nave or crossing. *Crossing*: spanning piers at a crossing (q.v.). *Relieving* or *discharging*: incorporated in a wall to relieve superimposed weight (5c). *Skew*: spanning responds not diametrically opposed. *Strainer*: inserted in an opening to resist inward pressure. *Transverse*: spanning a main axis (e.g. of a vaulted space). *See also* Jack arch, Overarch, Triumphal arch.

ARCHITRAVE: formalized lintel, the lowest member of the classical entablature (3a). Also the moulded frame of a door or window (often borrowing the profile of a classical architrave). For *lugged* and *shouldered* architraves see 4b.

ARCUATED: dependent structurally on the arch principle. Cf. Trabeated.

ARK: chest or cupboard housing the tables of Jewish law in a synagogue.

ARRIS: sharp edge where two surfaces meet at an angle (3a).

ASHLAR: masonry of large blocks wrought to even faces and square edges (6d). *Broached ashlar* (Scots): scored with parallel lines made by a narrow-pointed chisel (broach). *Droved ashlar*: similar but with lines made by a broad chisel.

ASTRAGAL: classical moulding of semicircular section (3f). Also (Scots) glazing-bar between window panes.

ASTYLAR: with no columns or similar vertical features.

ATLANTES: *see* Caryatids.

ATRIUM (plural: atria): inner court of a Roman or C20 house; in a multi-storey building, a toplit covered court rising through all storeys. Also an open court in front of a church.

ATTACHED COLUMN: *see* Engaged column.

ATTIC: small top storey within a roof. Also the storey above the main entablature of a classical façade.

AUMBRY: recess or cupboard, especially one in a church, to hold sacred vessels used for the Mass.

BAILEY: *see* Motte-and-bailey.

BALANCE BEAM: *see* Canals.

BALDACCHINO: freestanding canopy, originally fabric, over an altar. Cf. Ciborium.

BALLFLOWER: globular flower of three petals enclosing a ball (1a). Typical of the Decorated style.

BALUSTER: pillar or pedestal of bellied form. *Balusters*: vertical supports of this or any other form, for a handrail or coping, the whole being called a *balustrade* (6c). *Blind balustrade*: the same applied to the wall surface.

BARBICAN: outwork defending the entrance to a castle.

BARGEBOARDS (corruption of 'vergeboards'): boards, often carved or fretted, fixed beneath the eaves of a gable to cover and protect the rafters.

BARMKIN (Scots): wall enclosing courtyard attached to a tower house.

BARONY: *see* Burgh.

BAROQUE: style originating in Rome

c.1600 and current in England c.1680–1720, characterized by dramatic massing and silhouette and the use of the giant order.

BARROW: burial mound.

BARTIZAN: corbelled turret, square or round, frequently at an angle (8a).

BASCULE: hinged part of a lifting (or bascule) bridge.

BASE: moulded foot of a column or pilaster. For *Attic* base *see* 3b. For *Elided* base *see* Elided.

BASEMENT: lowest, subordinate storey; hence the lowest part of a classical elevation, below the piano nobile (q.v.).

BASILICA: a Roman public hall; hence an aisled building with a clerestory.

BASTION: one of a series of defensive semicircular or polygonal projections from the main wall of a fortress or city.

BATTER: intentional inward inclination of a wall face.

BATTLEMENT: defensive parapet, composed of *merlons* (solid) and *crenelles* (embrasures) through which archers could shoot (8a); sometimes called *crenellation*. Also used decoratively.

BAY: division of an elevation or interior space as defined by regular vertical features such as arches, columns, windows etc.

BAY LEAF: classical ornament of overlapping bay leaves (3f).

BAY WINDOW: window of one or more storeys projecting from the face of a building. *Canted*: with a straight front and angled sides. *Bow window*: curved. *Oriel*: rests on corbels or brackets and starts above ground level; also the bay window at the dais end of a medieval great hall.

BEAD-AND-REEL: *see* Enrichments.

BEAKHEAD: Norman ornament with a row of beaked bird or beast heads usually biting into a roll moulding (1a).

BEE-BOLL: wall recess to contain a beehive.

BELFRY: chamber or stage in a tower where bells are hung. Also belltower in a general sense.

BELL CAPITAL: *see* 1b.

BELLCAST: *see* Roof.

BELLCOTE: bell-turret set on a roof or gable. *Birdcage bellcote*: framed structure, usually of stone.

BERM: level area separating a ditch from a bank on a hillfort or barrow.

BILLET: Norman ornament of small half-cylindrical or rectangular blocks (1a).

BIVALLATE: of a hillfort: defended by two concentric banks and ditches.

BLIND: *see* Arcade, Baluster, Portico.

BLOCK CAPITAL: *see* 1a.

BLOCKED: columns etc. interrupted by regular projecting blocks (*blocking*), as on a Gibbs surround (4b).

BLOCKING COURSE: course of stones, or equivalent, on top of a cornice and crowning the wall.

BÖD: *see* Bü.

BOLECTION MOULDING: covering the joint between two different planes (6b).

BOND: the pattern of long sides (*stretchers*) and short ends (*headers*) produced on the face of a wall by laying bricks in a particular way (6e).

BOSS: knob or projection, e.g. at the intersection of ribs in a vault (2c).

BOW WINDOW: *see* Bay window.

BOX FRAME: timber-framed construction in which vertical and horizontal wall members support the roof. Also concrete construction where the loads are taken on cross walls; also called *cross-wall construction*.

BRACE: subsidiary member of a structural frame, curved or straight. *Bracing* is often arranged decoratively, e.g. quatrefoil, herringbone. *See also* Roofs.

BRATTISHING: ornamental crest, usually formed of leaves, Tudor flowers or miniature battlements.

BRESSUMER (*lit.* breast-beam): big horizontal beam supporting the wall above, especially in a jettied building.

BRETASCHE (*lit.* battlement): defensive wooden gallery on a wall.

BRICK: *see* Bond, Cogging, Engineering, Gauged, Tumbling.

BRIDGE: *Bowstring*: with arches rising above the roadway which is suspended from them. *Clapper*: one long stone forms the roadway. *Roving*: *see* Canal. *Suspension*: roadway suspended from cables or chains slung between towers or pylons. *Stay-suspension* or *stay-cantilever*: supported by diagonal stays from towers or pylons. *See also* Bascule.

BRISES-SOLEIL: projecting fins or canopies which deflect direct sunlight from windows.

BROACH: *see* Spire and 1c.

BROCH (Scots): circular tower-like structure, open in the middle, the double wall of dry-stone masonry linked by slabs forming internal galleries at varying levels; found in W and N Scotland and mostly dating from between 100 B.C. and A.D. 100.

BÜ or BÖD (Scots, esp. Shetland; *lit.* booth): combined house and store.

BUCRANIUM: ox skull used decoratively in classical friezes.

BULLSEYE WINDOW: small oval window, set horizontally (cf. Oculus). Also called *oeil de boeuf*.

BURGH: formally constituted town with trading privileges. *Royal Burghs*: monopolized foreign trade till the C17 and paid duty to the Crown. *Burghs of Barony*: founded by secular or ecclesiastical barons to whom they paid duty on their local trade. *Police Burghs*: instituted after 1850 for the administration of new centres of population and abolished in 1975. They controlled planning, building etc.

BUT-AND-BEN (Scots, *lit.* outer and inner rooms): two-room cottage.

BUTTRESS: vertical member projecting from a wall to stabilize it or to resist the lateral thrust of an arch, roof or vault (1c, 2c). A *flying buttress* transmits the thrust to a heavy abutment by means of an arch or half-arch (1c).


CABLE or ROPE MOULDING: originally Norman, like twisted strands of a rope.

CAMES: *see* Quarries.

CAMPANILE: freestanding belltower.

CANALS: *Flash lock*: removable weir or similar device through which boats pass on a flush of water. Predecessor of the *pound lock*: chamber with gates at each end allowing boats to float from one level to another. *Tidal gates*: single pair of lock gates allowing vessels to pass when the tide makes a level. *Balance beam*: beam projecting horizontally for opening and closing lock gates. *Roving bridge*: carrying a towing path from one bank to the other.

CANDLE-SNUFFER ROOF: conical roof of a turret (8a).

CANNON SPOUT: *see* 8a.

CANTILEVER: horizontal projection (e.g. step, canopy) supported by a downward force behind the fulcrum.

CAPHOUSE (Scots): small chamber at the head of a turnpike stair, opening onto the parapet walk (8a). Also a chamber rising from within the parapet walk.

CAPITAL: head or crowning feature of a column or pilaster; for classical types *see* 3a; for medieval types *see* 1b.

CAPONIER: a vaulted gallery for flanking fire along a ditch.

CARREL: compartment designed for individual work or study, e.g. in a library.

CARTOUCHE: classical tablet with ornate frame (4b).

CARYATIDS: female figures supporting an entablature; their male counterparts are *Atlantes* (*lit.* Atlas figures).

CASEMATE: vaulted chamber, with embrasures for defence, within a castle wall or projecting from it.

CASEMENT: side-hinged window. Also a concave Gothic moulding framing a window.

CASTELLATED: with battlements (q.v.).

CAST IRON: iron containing at least 2.2 per cent of carbon, strong in compression but brittle in tension; cast in a mould to required shape, e.g. for columns or repetitive ornaments. *Wrought iron* is a purer form of iron, with no more than 0.3 per cent of carbon, ductile and strong in tension, forged and rolled into e.g. bars, joists, boiler plates; *mild steel* is its modern equivalent, similar but stronger.

CATSLIDE: *see* 7.

CAVETTO: concave classical moulding of quarter-round section (3f).

CELURE or CEILURE: enriched area of roof above rood or altar.

CEMENT: *see* Concrete.

CENOTAPH (*lit.* empty tomb): funerary monument which is not a burying place.

CENTRING: wooden support for the building of an arch or vault, removed after completion.

CHAMBERED TOMB: Neolithic burial mound with a stone-built chamber and entrance passage covered by an earthen barrow or stone cairn.

CHAMFER (*lit.* corner-break): surface formed by cutting off a square edge or corner. For types of chamfers and *chamfer stops see* 6a. *See also* Double chamfer.

CHANCEL: E end of the church containing the sanctuary; often used to include the choir.

CHANTRY CHAPEL: often attached to or within a church, endowed for the celebration of Masses principally for the soul of the founder.

CHECK (Scots): rebate.

CHEMIN-DE-RONDE: a protected walkway or passage around a feature; frequently used to refer to a wall-walk around the caphouse at the head of a tower.

CHERRY-CAULKING or CHERRY-COCKING (Scots): decorative masonry technique using lines of tiny stones (*pins* or *pinning*) in the mortar joints.

CHEVET (*lit.* head): French term for chancel with ambulatory and radiating chapels.

CHEVRON: V-shape used in series or double series (later) on a Norman moulding (1a). Also (especially when on a single plane) called *zigzag*.

CHOIR: the part of a church E of the nave, intended for the stalls of choir monks, choristers and clergy.

CIBORIUM: a fixed canopy over an altar, usually vaulted and supported on four columns; cf. Baldacchino.

CINQUEFOIL: *see* Foil.

CIST: stone-lined or slab-built grave.

CLACHAN (Scots): a hamlet or small village; also, a village inn.

CLADDING: external covering or skin applied to a structure, especially a framed one.

CLEARSTOREY: uppermost storey of the nave of a church, pierced by windows. Also high-level windows in secular buildings.

CLOSE (Scots): courtyard or passage giving access to a number of buildings.

CLOSER: a brick cut to complete a bond (6e).

CLUSTER BLOCK: *see* Multi-storey.

COADE STONE: ceramic artificial stone made in Lambeth 1769–c.1840 by Eleanor Coade (†1821) and her associates.

COB: walling material of clay mixed with straw.

COFFERING: arrangement of sunken panels (coffers), square or polygonal, decorating a ceiling, vault or arch.

COGGING: a decorative course of bricks laid diagonally (6e). Cf. Dentilation.

COLLAR: see Roofs and 7.

COLLEGIATE CHURCH: endowed for the support of a college of priests, especially for the saying of masses for the soul(s) of the founder(s).

COLONNADE: range of columns supporting an entablature. Cf. Arcade.

COLONNETTE: small column or shaft.

COLOSSAL ORDER: see Giant order.

COLUMBARIUM: shelved, niched structure to house multiple burials.

COLUMN: a classical, upright structural member of round section with a shaft, a capital and usually a base (3a, 4a).

COLUMN FIGURE: carved figure attached to a medieval column or shaft, usually flanking a doorway.

COMMENDATOR: receives the revenues of an abbey *in commendam* ('in trust') when the position of abbot is vacant.

COMMUNION TABLE: table used in Protestant churches for the celebration of Holy Communion.

COMPOSITE: see Orders.

COMPOUND PIER: grouped shafts (q.v.), or a solid core surrounded by shafts.

CONCRETE: composition of *cement* (calcined lime and clay), *aggregate* (small stones or rock chippings), sand and water. It can be poured into *formwork* or *shuttering* (temporary frame of timber or metal) on site (*in-situ* concrete), or *pre-cast* as components before construction. *Reinforced*: incorporating steel rods to take the tensile force. *Prestressed*: with tensioned steel rods. Finishes include the impression of boards left by formwork (*board-marked* or *shuttered*), and texturing with steel brushes (*brushed*) or hammers (*hammer-dressed*). See also Shell.

CONDUCTOR (Scots): down-pipe for rainwater; *see also* Rhone.

CONSOLE: bracket of curved outline (4b).

COPING: protective course of masonry or brickwork capping a wall (6d).

COOMB or COMB CEILING (Scots): with sloping sides corresponding to the roof pitch up to a flat centre.

CORBEL: projecting block supporting something above. *Corbel course*: continuous course of projecting stones or bricks fulfilling the same function. *Corbel table*: series of corbels to carry a parapet or a wall-plate or wall-post (7). *Corbelling*: brick or masonry courses built out beyond one another to support a chimney-stack, window etc. For *continuous* and *chequer-set* corbelling see 8a.

CORINTHIAN: see Orders and 3d.

CORNICE: flat-topped ledge with moulded underside, projecting along the top of a building or feature, especially as the highest member of the classical entablature (3a). Also the decorative moulding in the angle between wall and ceiling.

CORPS-DE-LOGIS: the main building(s) as distinct from the wings or pavilions.

COTTAGE ORNÉ: an artfully rustic small house associated with the Picturesque movement.

COUNTERSCARP BANK: low bank on the downhill or outer side of a hillfort ditch.

COUR D'HONNEUR: formal entrance court before a house in the French manner, usually with flanking wings and a screen wall or gates.

COURSE: continuous layer of stones etc. in a wall (6e).

COVE: a broad concave moulding, e.g. to mask the eaves of a roof. *Coved ceiling*: with a pronounced cove joining the walls to a flat central panel smaller than the whole area of the ceiling.

CRADLE ROOF: see Wagon roof.

CREDENCE: shelved niche or table, usually beside a piscina (q.v.), for the sacramental elements and vessels.

CRENELLATION: parapet with crenelles (*see* Battlement).

CRINKLE-CRANKLE WALL: garden wall undulating in a series of serpentine curves.

CROCKETS: leafy hooks. *Crocketing* decorates the edges of Gothic features, such as pinnacles, canopies etc. *Crocket capital: see* 1b.

CROSSING: central space at the junction of the nave, chancel and transepts. *Crossing tower:* above a crossing.

CROSS-WINDOW: with one mullion and one transom (qq.v.).

CROWN-POST: *see* Roofs and 7.

CROWSTEPS: squared stones set like steps, especially on a crowstepped gable (7, 8a).

CRUCKS (*lit.* crooked): pairs of inclined timbers (*blades*), usually curved, set at bay-lengths; they support the roof timbers and, in timber buildings, also support the walls. *Base:* blades rise from ground level to a tie-or collar-beam which supports the roof timbers. *Full:* blades rise from ground level to the apex of the roof, serving as the main members of a roof truss. *Jointed:* blades formed from more than one timber; the lower member may act as a wall-post; it is usually elbowed at wall-plate level and jointed just above. *Middle:* blades rise from halfway up the walls to a tie-or collar-beam. *Raised:* blades rise from halfway up the walls to the apex. *Upper:* blades supported on a tie-beam and rising to the apex.

CRYPT: underground or half-underground area, usually below the E end of a church. *Ring crypt:* corridor crypt surrounding the apse of an early medieval church, often associated with chambers for relics. Cf. Undercroft.

CUPOLA (*lit.* dome): especially a small dome on a circular or polygonal base crowning a larger dome, roof or turret. Also (Scots) small dome or skylight as an internal feature, especially over a stairwell.

CURSUS: a long avenue defined by two parallel earthen banks with ditches outside.

CURTAIN WALL: a connecting wall between the towers of a castle. Also a non-load-bearing external wall applied to a C20 framed structure.

CUSP: *see* Tracery and 2b.

CYCLOPEAN MASONRY: large irregular polygonal stones, smooth and finely jointed.

CYMA RECTA and CYMA REVERSA: classical mouldings with double curves (3f). Cf. Ogee.

DADO: the finishing (often with panelling) of the lower part of a wall in a classical interior; in origin a formalized continuous pedestal. *Dado rail:* the moulding along the top of the dado.

DAGGER: *see* Tracery and 2b.

DEC (DECORATED): English Gothic architecture *c.* 1290 to *c.* 1350. The name is derived from the type of window tracery (q.v.) used during the period.

DEMI- or HALF-COLUMNS: engaged columns (q.v.) half of whose circumference projects from the wall.

DENTIL: small square block used in series in classical cornices (3c). *Dentilation* is produced by the projection of alternating headers along cornices or string-courses.

DIAPER: repetitive surface decoration of lozenges or squares flat or in relief. Achieved in brickwork with bricks of two colours.

DIOCLETIAN or THERMAL WINDOW: semicircular with two mullions, as used in the Baths of Diocletian, Rome (4b).

DISTYLE: having two columns (4a).

DOGTOOTH: E.E. ornament, consisting of a series of small pyramids formed by four stylized canine teeth meeting at a point (1a).

DOOCOT (Scots): dovecot. When freestanding, usually *Lectern* (rectangular with single-pitch roof) or *Beehive* (circular, diminishing towards the top).

DORIC: *see* Orders and 3a, 3b.

DORMER: window projecting from the slope of a roof (7). *Dormer head:* gable above a dormer, often formed as a pediment (8a).

DOUBLE CHAMFER: a chamfer applied to each of two recessed arches (1a).

DOUBLE PILE: *see* Pile.

DRAGON BEAM: *see* Jetty.

DRESSINGS: the stone or brickwork worked to a finished face about an angle, opening or other feature.

DRIPSTONE: moulded stone projecting from a wall to protect the lower parts from water. Cf. Hoodmould, Weathering.

DRUM: circular or polygonal stage supporting a dome or cupola. Also one of the stones forming the shaft of a column (3a).

DRY-STONE: stone construction without mortar.

DUN (Scots): small stone-walled fort.

DUTCH or FLEMISH GABLE: see 7.

EASTER SEPULCHRE: tomb-chest, usually within or against the N wall of a chancel, used in Holy Week ceremonies for reservation (entombment) of the sacrament after the mass of Maundy Thursday.

EAVES: overhanging edge of a roof; hence *eaves cornice* in this position.

ECHINUS: ovolo moulding (q.v.) below the abacus of a Greek Doric capital (3a).

EDGE RAIL: see Railways.

EDGE-ROLL: moulding of semi-circular section or more at the edge of an opening.

E.E. (EARLY ENGLISH): English Gothic architecture *c.* 1190–1250.

EGG-AND-DART: see Enrichments and 3f.

ELEVATION: any face of a building or side of a room. In a drawing, the same or any part of it, represented in two dimensions.

ELIDED: used to describe a compound feature, e.g. an entablature, with some parts omitted. Also, parts of, e.g., a base or capital, combined to form a larger one.

EMBATTLED: with battlements.

EMBRASURE: splayed opening in a wall or battlement (q.v.).

ENCAUSTIC TILES: earthenware tiles fired with a pattern and glaze.

EN DELIT: stone laid against the bed.

ENFILADE: reception rooms in a formal series, usually with all doorways on axis.

ENGAGED or ATTACHED COLUMN: one that partly merges into a wall or pier.

ENGINEERING BRICKS: dense bricks, originally used mostly for railway viaducts etc.

ENRICHMENTS: the carved decoration of certain classical mouldings, e.g. the ovolo with *egg-and-dart*, the cyma reversa with *waterleaf*, the astragal with *bead-and-reel* (3f).

ENTABLATURE: in classical architecture, collective name for the three horizontal members (architrave, frieze and cornice) carried by a wall or a column (3a).

ENTASIS: very slight convex deviation from a straight line, used to prevent an optical illusion of concavity.

ENTRESOL: mezzanine floor subdividing what is constructionally a single storey, e.g. a vault.

EPITAPH: inscription on a tomb or monument.

EXEDRA: see Apse.

EXTRADOS: outer curved face of an arch or vault.

EYECATCHER: decorative building terminating a vista.

FASCIA: plain horizontal band, e.g. in an architrave (3c, 3d) or on a shopfront.

FENESTRATION: the arrangement of windows in a façade.

FERETORY: site of the chief shrine of a church, behind the high altar.

FESTOON: ornamental garland, suspended from both ends. Cf. Swag.

FEU (Scots): land granted, e.g. by sale, by the *feudal superior* to the *vassal* or *feuar*, on conditions that usually include the annual payment of a fixed sum of *feu duty*. Any subsequent proprietor of the land becomes the feuar and is subject to the same obligations.

FIBREGLASS (or glass-reinforced polyester (GRP)): synthetic resin reinforced with glass fibre. GRC: glass-reinforced concrete.

FIELD: see Panelling and 6b.

FILLET: a narrow flat band running down a medieval shaft or along a roll moulding (1a). It separates larger curved mouldings in classical cornices, fluting or bases (3c).

FLAMBOYANT: the latest phase of French Gothic architecture, with flowing tracery.

FLASH LOCK: see Canals.

FLATTED: divided into apartments. Also with a colloquial (Scots) meaning: 'He stays on the first flat' means that he lives on the first floor.

FLÈCHE or SPIRELET (*lit.* arrow): slender spire on the centre of a roof.

FLEURON: medieval carved flower or leaf, often rectilinear (1a).

FLUSHWORK: knapped flint used with dressed stone to form patterns.

FLUTING: series of concave grooves (flutes), their common edges sharp (arris) or blunt (fillet) (3).

FOIL (*lit.* leaf): lobe formed by the cusping of a circular or other shape in tracery (2b). *Trefoil* (three), *quatrefoil* (four), *cinquefoil* (five) and *multifoil* express the number of lobes in a shape.

FOLIATE: decorated with leaves.

FORE-BUILDING: structure protecting an entrance.

FORESTAIR: external stair, usually unenclosed.

FORMWORK: *see* Concrete.

FRAMED BUILDING: where the structure is carried by a framework - e.g. of steel, reinforced concrete, timber - instead of by load-bearing walls.

FREESTONE: stone that is cut, or can be cut, in all directions.

FRESCO: *al fresco*: painting on wet plaster. *Fresco secco*: painting on dry plaster.

FRIEZE: the middle member of the classical entablature, sometimes ornamented (3a). *Pulvinated frieze* (*lit.* cushioned): of bold convex profile (3c). Also a horizontal band of ornament.

FRONTISPIECE: in C16 and C17 buildings the central feature of doorway and windows above linked in one composition.

GABLE: peaked external wall at end of double-pitch roof. For types *see* 7. Also (Scots): whole end wall of whatever shape. *Pedimental gable*: treated like a pediment.

GADROONING: classical ribbed ornament like inverted fluting that flows into a lobed edge.

GAIT or GATE (Scots): street, usually with a prefix indicating use, direction or destination.

GALILEE: chapel or vestibule usually at the W end of a church enclosing the main portal(s).

GALLERY: a long room or passage; an upper storey above the aisle of a church, looking through arches to the nave; a balcony or mezzanine overlooking the main interior space of a building; or an external walkway.

GALLETING: small stones set in a mortar course.

GAMBREL ROOF: *see* 7.

GARDEROBE: medieval privy.

GARGOYLE: projecting water spout, often carved into human or animal shape. For cannon spout *see* 8.

GAUGED or RUBBED BRICKWORK: soft brick sawn roughly, then rubbed to a precise (gauged) surface. Mostly used for door or window openings (5c).

GAZEBO (jocular Latin, 'I shall gaze'): ornamental lookout tower or raised summer house.

GEOMETRIC: English Gothic architecture *c.* 1250–1310. *See also* Tracery. For another meaning, *see* Stairs.

GIANT or COLOSSAL ORDER: classical order (q.v.) whose height is that of two or more storeys of the building to which it is applied.

GIBBS SURROUND: C18 treatment of an opening (4b), seen particularly in the work of James Gibbs (1682–1754).

GIRDER: a large beam. *Box*: of hollow-box section. *Bowed*: with its top rising in a curve. *Plate*: of I-section, made from iron or steel plates. *Lattice*: with braced framework.

GLACIS: artificial slope extending out and downwards from the parapet of a fort.

GLAZING-BARS: wooden or sometimes metal bars separating and supporting window panes.

GLAZING GROOVE: groove in a window surround into which the glass is fitted.

GNOMON: vane or indicator casting a shadow onto a sundial.

GRAFFITI: *see* Sgraffito.

GRANGE: farm owned and run by a religious order.

GRC: *see* Fibreglass.

GRISAILLE: monochrome painting on walls or glass.

GROIN: sharp edge at the meeting of two cells of a cross-vault; *see* Vault and 2b.

GROTESQUE (*lit.* grotto-esque): wall decoration adopted from Roman examples in the Renaissance. Its foliage scrolls incorporate figurative elements. Cf. Arabesque.

GROTTO: artificial cavern.

GRP: *see* Fibreglass.

GUILLOCHE: classical ornament of interlaced bands (4b).

GUNLOOP: opening for a firearm (8a).

GUSHET (Scots): a triangular or wedge-shaped piece of land or the corner building on such a site.

GUTTAE: stylized drops (3b).

HALF-TIMBERING: archaic term for timber-framing (q.v.). Sometimes used for non-structural decorative timberwork.

HALL CHURCH: medieval church with nave and aisles of approximately equal height. Also (Scots C20) building for use as both hall and church, the double function usually intended to be temporary until a separate church is built.

HAMMERBEAM: see Roofs and 7.

HARLING (Scots, *lit.* hurling): wet dash, i.e. a form of roughcasting in which the mixture of aggregate and binding material (e.g. lime) is dashed onto a wall.

HEADER: see Bond and 6e.

HEADSTOP: stop (q.v.) carved with a head (5b).

HELM ROOF: see 1C.

HENGE: ritual earthwork with a surrounding ditch and outer bank.

HERM (*lit.* the god Hermes): male head or bust on a pedestal.

HERRINGBONE WORK: see 6e (for brick bond). Cf. Pitched masonry.

HEXASTYLE: see Portico.

HILLFORT: Iron Age earthwork enclosed by a ditch and bank system.

HIPPED ROOF: see 7.

HOODMOULD: projecting moulding above an arch or lintel to throw off water (2b, 5b). When horizontal often called a *label*. For label stop see Stop.

HORIZONTAL GLAZING: with panes of horizontal proportions.

HORSEMILL: circular or polygonal farm building with a central shaft turned by a horse to drive agricultural machinery.

HUNGRY-JOINTED: see Pointing.

HUSK GARLAND: festoon of stylized nutshells (4b).

HYDRAULIC POWER: use of water under high pressure to work machinery. *Accumulator tower*: houses a hydraulic accumulator which accommodates fluctuations in the flow through hydraulic mains.

HYPOCAUST (*lit.* underburning): Roman underfloor heating system.

IMPOST: horizontal moulding at the springing of an arch (5c).

IMPOST BLOCK: block between abacus and capital (1b).

IN ANTIS: see Antae, Portico and 4a.

INDENT: shape chiselled out of a stone to receive a brass. Also, in restoration, new stone inserted as a patch.

INDUSTRIALIZED or SYSTEM BUILDING: system of manufactured units assembled on site.

INGLENOOK (*lit.* fire-corner): recess for a hearth with provision for seating.

INGO (Scots): the reveal of a door or window opening where the stone is at right angles to the wall.

INTERCOLUMNATION: interval between columns.

INTERLACE: decoration in relief simulating woven or entwined stems or bands.

INTRADOS: see Soffit.

IONIC: see Orders and 3c.

JACK ARCH: shallow segmental vault springing from beams, used for fireproof floors, bridge decks etc.

JAMB (*lit.* leg): one of the vertical sides of an opening. Also (Scots) wing or extension adjoining one side of a rectangular plan making it into an L-, T- or Z-plan.

JERKIN HEAD ROOF (Scots): see 7.

JETTY: the projection of an upper storey beyond the storey below. In a stone building this is achieved by corbelling. In a timber-framed building it is made by the beams and joists of the lower storey oversailing the wall; on their outer ends is placed the sill of the walling for the storey above.

JOGGLE: the joining of two stones to prevent them slipping by a notch in one and a projection in the other.

KEEL MOULDING: moulding used from the late C12, in section like the keel of a ship (1a).

KEEP: principal tower of a castle.

KENTISH CUSP: see Tracery.

KEY PATTERN: see 4b.

KEYSTONE: central stone in an arch or vault (4b, 5c).

KINGPOST: see Roofs and 7.

KNEELER: horizontal projecting stone at the base of each side of a gable to support the inclined coping stones (7).

LABEL: see Hoodmould and 5b.

LABEL STOP: see Stop and 5b.

LACED BRICKWORK: vertical strips of brickwork, often in a contrasting colour, linking openings on different floors.

LACING COURSE: horizontal reinforcement in timber or brick to walls of flint, cobble etc.

LADE (Scots): channel formed to bring water to a mill; mill-race.

LADY CHAPEL: dedicated to the Virgin Mary (Our Lady).

LAIGH or LAICH (Scots): low.

LAIR (Scots): a burial space reserved in a graveyard

LAIRD (Scots): landowner.

LANCET: slender single-light, pointed-arched window (2a).

LANTERN: circular or polygonal windowed turret crowning a roof or a dome. Also the windowed stage of a crossing tower lighting the church interior.

LANTERN CROSS: churchyard cross with lantern-shaped top.

LAVATORIUM: in a religious house, a washing place adjacent to the refectory.

LEAN-TO: see Roofs.

LESENE (lit. a mean thing): pilaster without base or capital. Also called pilaster strip.

LIERNE: see Vault and 2c.

LIGHT: compartment of a window defined by the mullions.

LINENFOLD: Tudor panelling carved with simulations of folded linen.

LINTEL: horizontal beam or stone bridging an opening.

LOFT: gallery in a church. Organ loft: in which the organ, or sometimes only the console (keyboard), is placed. Laird's loft, Trades loft etc. (Scots): reserved for an individual or special group. See also Rood (loft).

LOGGIA: gallery, usually arcaded or colonnaded along one side; sometimes freestanding.

LONG-AND-SHORT WORK: quoins consisting of stones placed with the long side alternately upright and horizontal, especially in Saxon building.

LOUVRE: roof opening, often protected by a raised timber structure, to allow the smoke from a central hearth to escape. Louvres: overlapping boards to allow ventilation but keep the rain out.

LOWSIDE WINDOW: set lower than the others in a chancel side wall, usually towards its w end.

L-PLAN: see Tower house and 8b.

LUCARNE (lit. dormer): small gabled opening in a roof or spire.

LUCKENBOOTH (Scots): lock-up booth or shop.

LUGGED ARCHITRAVE: see 4b.

LUNETTE: semicircular window or blind panel.

LYCHGATE (lit. corpse-gate): roofed gateway entrance to a churchyard for the reception of a coffin.

LYNCHET: long terraced strip of soil on the downward side of prehistoric and medieval fields, accumulated because of continual ploughing along the contours.

MACHICOLATIONS (lit. mashing devices): series of openings between the corbels that support a projecting parapet through which missiles can be dropped (8a). Used decoratively in post-medieval buildings.

MAINS (Scots): home farm on an estate.

MANOMETER or STANDPIPE TOWER: containing a column of water to regulate pressure in water mains.

MANSARD: see 7.

MANSE: house of a minister of religion, especially in Scotland.

MARGINS (Scots): dressed stones at the edges of an opening. 'Back-set margins' (RCAHMS) are actually set forward from a rubble wall to act as a stop for harling (q.v.). Also called rybats.

MARRIAGE LINTEL (Scots): door or window lintel carved with the initials of the owner and his wife and the date of building work, only coincidentally of their marriage.

MATHEMATICAL TILES: facing tiles with the appearance of brick, most often applied to timber-framed walls.

MAUSOLEUM: monumental building or chamber usually intended for the burial of members of one family.

MEGALITHIC: the use of large stones, singly or together.

MEGALITHIC TOMB: massive stonebuilt Neolithic burial chamber covered by an earth or stone mound.

MERCAT (Scots): market. The Mercat Cross of a Scottish burgh was the focus of market activity and local ceremonial. Most examples are post-Reformation with heraldic or other finials (not crosses).

MERLON: *see* Battlement.

MESOLITHIC: Middle Stone Age, in Britain *c.* 5000 to *c.* 3500 B.C.

METOPES: spaces between the triglyphs in a Doric frieze (3b).

MEZZANINE: low storey between two higher ones or within the height of a high one, not extending over its whole area.

MILD STEEL: *see* Cast iron.

MISERICORD (*lit.* mercy): shelf on a carved bracket placed on the underside of a hinged choir stall seat to support an occupant when standing.

MIXER-COURTS: forecourts to groups of houses shared by vehicles and pedestrians.

MODILLIONS: small consoles (q.v.) along the underside of a Corinthian or Composite cornice (3d). Often used along an eaves cornice.

MODULE: a predetermined standard size for co-ordinating the dimensions of components of a building.

MORT-SAFE (Scots): device to secure corpse(s): either an iron frame over a grave or a building where bodies were kept during decomposition.

MOTTE-AND-BAILEY: CII and CI2 type of castle consisting of an earthen mound (motte) topped by a wooden tower within or adjoining a bailey, an enclosure defended by a ditch and palisade, and also, sometimes, by an inner bank.

MOUCHETTE: *see* Tracery and 2b.

MOULDING: shaped ornamental strip of continuous section; *see* Cavetto, Cyma, Ovolo, Roll.

MULLION: vertical member between window lights (2b).

MULTI-STOREY: five or more storeys. Multi-storey flats may form a *cluster block*, with individual blocks of flats grouped round a service core; a *point block*, with flats fanning out from a service core; or a *slab block*, with flats approached by corridors or galleries from service cores at intervals or towers at the ends (plan also used for offices, hotels etc.). *Tower block* is a generic term for a high multi-storey building.

MULTIVALLATE: of a hillfort: defended by three or more concentric banks and ditches.

MUNTIN: *see* Panelling and 6b.

MUTULE: square block under the corona of a Doric cornice.

NAILHEAD: E.E. ornament consisting of small pyramids regularly repeated (1a).

NARTHEX: enclosed vestibule or covered porch at the main entrance to a church.

NAVE: the body of a church w of the crossing or chancel, often flanked by aisles (q.v.).

NEOLITHIC: New Stone Age in Britain, *c.* 3500 B.C. until the Bronze Age.

NEPUS (Scots): a small gable rising directly from the wallhead at the front or rear of a building, often with a window or chimney.

NEWEL: central or corner post of a staircase (6c). For Newel stair *see* Stairs.

NIGHT STAIR: stair by which religious entered the transept of their church from their dormitory to celebrate night offices.

NOGGING: *see* Timber-framing.

NOOK-SHAFT: shaft set in the angle of a wall or opening (1a).

NORMAN: *see* Romanesque.

NOSING: projection of the tread of a step (6c). *Bottle nosing*: half round in section.

NUTMEG: medieval ornament with a chain of tiny triangles placed obliquely.

OCULUS: circular opening.

OEIL DE BOEUF: *see* Bullseye window.

OGEE: double curve, bending first one way and then the other, as in an *ogee* or *ogival arch* (5c). Cf. Cyma recta and Cyma reversa.

OPUS SECTILE: decorative mosaic-like facing.

OPUS SIGNINUM: composition flooring of Roman origin.

ORATORY: a private chapel in a church or a house. Also a church of the Oratorian Order.

ORDER: one of a series of recessed arches and jambs forming a splayed medieval opening, e.g. a doorway or arcade arch (1a).

ORDERS: the formalized versions of

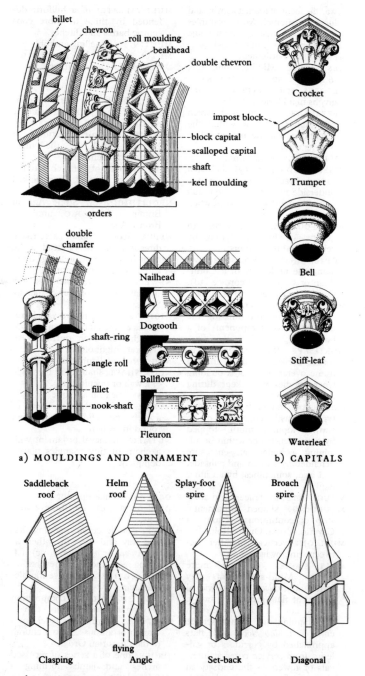

a) MOULDINGS AND ORNAMENT

b) CAPITALS

c) BUTTRESSES, ROOFS AND SPIRES

FIGURE 1: MEDIEVAL

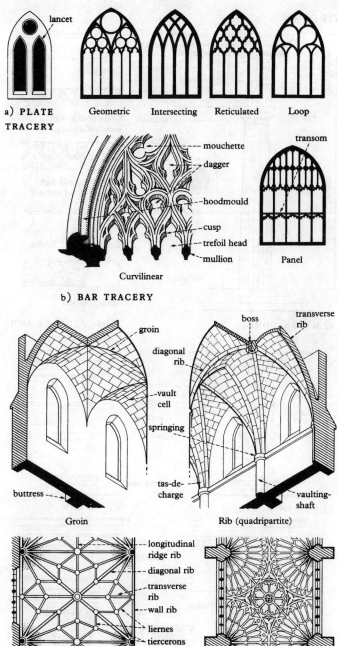

a) PLATE TRACERY — lancet, Geometric, Intersecting, Reticulated, Loop

b) BAR TRACERY — mouchette, dagger, hoodmould, cusp, trefoil head, mullion, Curvilinear; transom, Panel

c) VAULTS — Groin: groin, diagonal rib, vault cell, springing, buttress; Rib (quadripartite): boss, transverse rib, tas-de-charge, vaulting-shaft; Lierne: longitudinal ridge rib, diagonal rib, transverse rib, wall rib, liernes, tiercerons; Fan

FIGURE 2: MEDIEVAL

## ORDERS

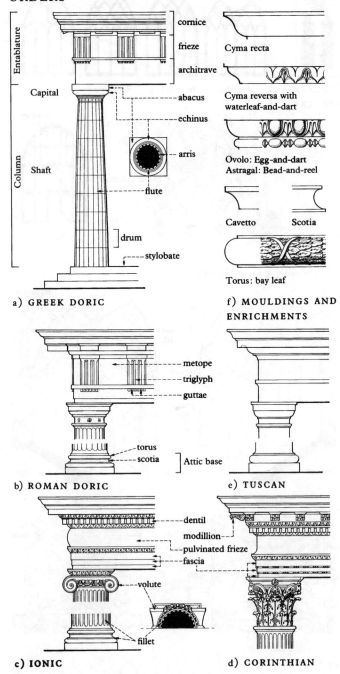

Entablature
— cornice
— frieze
— architrave

Capital
—— abacus
—— echinus
—— arris

Column
Shaft
—— flute

drum
—— stylobate

a) GREEK DORIC

Cyma recta

Cyma reversa with
waterleaf-and-dart

Ovolo: Egg-and-dart
Astragal: Bead-and-reel

Cavetto     Scotia

Torus: bay leaf

f) MOULDINGS AND
ENRICHMENTS

—— metope
—— triglyph
—— guttae

—— torus
—— scotia  } Attic base

b) ROMAN DORIC

e) TUSCAN

—— dentil
—— modillion
—— pulvinated frieze
—— fascia

—— volute

—— fillet

c) IONIC

d) CORINTHIAN

FIGURE 3: CLASSICAL

a) PORTICO

Anthemion & Palmette

Guilloche

Key pattern

Rinceau

Husk garland

Vitruvian scroll

Console

Diocletian window

Acanthus

Broken pediment

Segmental pediment

Venetian window

Lugged architrave

Shouldered architrave

Open pediment

Swan-neck pediment

Gibbs surround

b) ORNAMENTS AND FEATURES

FIGURE 4: CLASSICAL

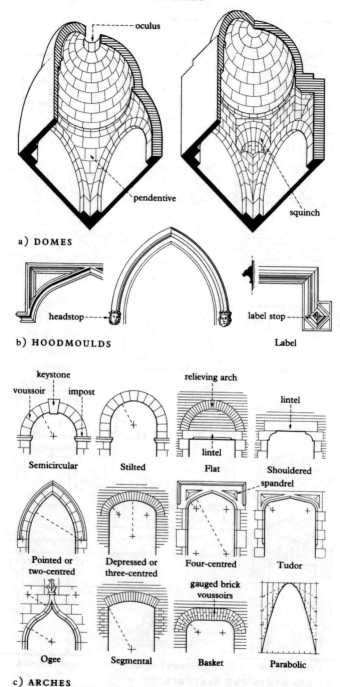

a) DOMES

b) HOODMOULDS

Label

c) ARCHES

FIGURE 5: CONSTRUCTION

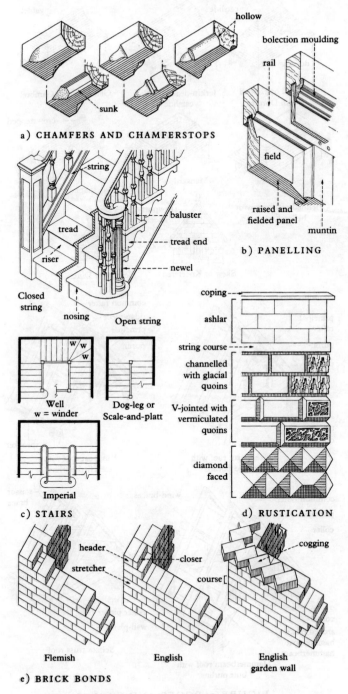

hollow

**a) CHAMFERS AND CHAMFERSTOPS**

sunk

bolection moulding

rail

field

raised and fielded panel

muntin

**b) PANELLING**

string

baluster

tread

tread end

riser

newel

Closed string

nosing

Open string

w / w / w

Well
w = winder

Dog-leg or Scale-and-platt

Imperial

**c) STAIRS**

coping

ashlar

string course

channelled with glacial quoins

V-jointed with vermiculated quoins

diamond faced

**d) RUSTICATION**

header

closer

stretcher

course

cogging

Flemish

English

English garden wall

**e) BRICK BONDS**

**FIGURE 6: CONSTRUCTION**

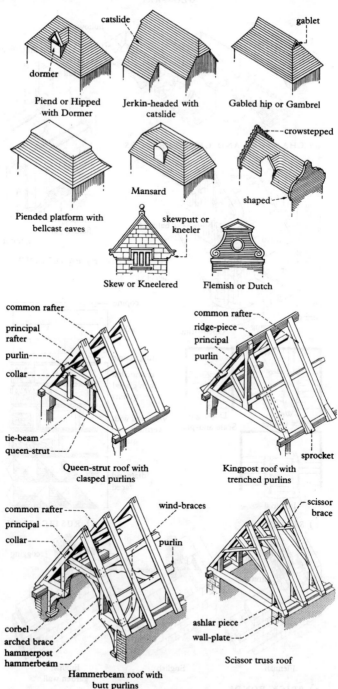

FIGURE 7: ROOFS AND GABLES

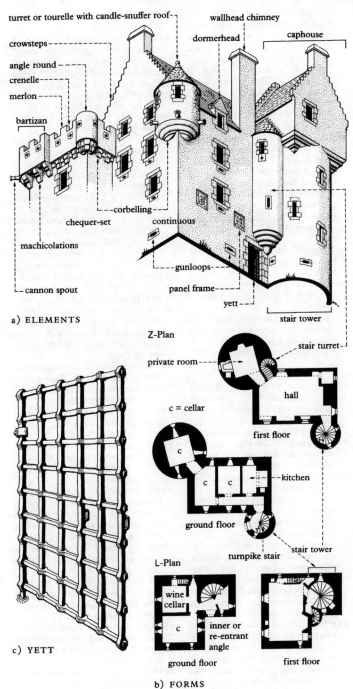

turret or tourelle with candle-snuffer roof

wallhead chimney

crowsteps

dormerhead

caphouse

angle round

crenelle

merlon

bartizan

corbelling

chequer-set

continuous

machiolations

gunloops

panel frame

cannon spout

yett

stair tower

a) ELEMENTS

Z-Plan

stair turret

private room

hall

c = cellar

first floor

kitchen

c    c    c

ground floor

wine cellar

c

inner or
re-entrant
angle

turnpike stair

stair tower

L-Plan

ground floor

first floor

c) YETT

b) FORMS

FIGURE 8: THE TOWER HOUSE

the post-and-lintel system in classical architecture. The main orders are *Doric*, *Ionic* and *Corinthian*. They are Greek in origin but occur in Roman versions. *Tuscan* is a simple version of Roman Doric. Though each order has its own conventions (3), there are many minor variations. The *Composite* capital combines Ionic volutes with Corinthian foliage. *Superimposed orders*: orders on successive levels, usually in the upward sequence of Tuscan, Doric, Ionic, Corinthian, Composite.

ORIEL: *see* Bay window.

ORILLON: the ear-like extension of the face of a bastion (or demi-bastion) to provide protection for a flanker (an inset gun emplacement).

OVERARCH: framing a wall which has an opening, e.g. a window or door.

OVERDOOR: painting or relief above an internal door. Also called a *sopraporta*.

OVERTHROW: decorative fixed arch between two gatepiers or above a wrought-iron gate.

OVOLO: wide convex moulding (3f).

PALIMPSEST: of a brass: where a metal plate has been reused by engraving on the back; of a wall painting: where one overlaps and partly obscures an earlier one.

PALLADIAN: following the examples and principles of Andrea Palladio (1508–80).

PALMETTE: classical ornament like a palm shoot (4b).

PANEL FRAME: moulded stone frame round an armorial panel, often placed over the entrance to a tower house (8a).

PANELLING: wooden lining to interior walls, made up of vertical members (*muntins*) and horizontals (*rails*) framing panels: also called *wainscot*. *Raised-and-fielded*: with the central area of the panel (*field*) raised up (6b).

PANTILE: roof tile of S section.

PARAPET: wall for protection at any sudden drop, e.g. at the wallhead of a castle where it protects the *parapet walk* or wall-walk. Also used to conceal a roof.

PARCLOSE: *see* Screen.

PARGETING (*lit*. plastering): exterior plaster decoration, either in relief or incised.

PARLOUR: in a religious house, a room where the religious could talk to visitors; in a medieval house, the semi-private living room below the solar (q.v.).

PARTERRE: level space in a garden laid out with low, formal beds.

PATERA (*lit*. plate): round or oval ornament in shallow relief.

PAVILION: ornamental building for occasional use; or projecting subdivision of a larger building, often at an angle or terminating a wing.

PEBBLEDASHING: *see* Rendering.

PEDESTAL: a tall block carrying a classical order, statue, vase etc.

PEDIMENT: a formalized gable derived from that of a classical temple; also used over doors, windows etc. For variations *see* 4b.

PEEL (*lit*. palisade): stone tower, e.g. near the Scottish-English border.

PEND (Scots): open-ended ground-level passage through a building.

PENDENTIVE: spandrel between adjacent arches, supporting a drum, dome or vault and consequently formed as part of a hemisphere (5a).

PENTHOUSE: subsidiary structure with a lean-to roof. Also a separately roofed structure on top of a C20 multi-storey block.

PEPPERPOT TURRET: bartizan with conical or pyramidal roof.

PERIPTERAL: *see* Peristyle.

PERISTYLE: a colonnade all round the exterior of a classical building, as in a temple which is then said to be *peripteral*.

PERP (PERPENDICULAR): English Gothic architecture *c.* 1335–50 to *c.* 1530. The name is derived from the upright tracery panels then used (*see* Tracery and 2a).

PERRON: external stair to a doorway, usually of double-curved plan.

PEW: loosely, seating for the laity outside the chancel; strictly, an enclosed seat. *Box pew*: with equal high sides and a door.

PIANO NOBILE: principal floor of a classical building above a ground floor or basement and with a lesser storey overhead.

PIAZZA: formal urban open space surrounded by buildings.

PIEND AND PIENDED PLATFORM ROOF: *see* 7.

PIER: large masonry or brick support, often for an arch. *See also* Compound pier.

PILASTER: flat representation of a classical column in shallow relief. *Pilastrade*: series of pilasters, equivalent to a colonnade.

PILE: row of rooms. *Double pile*: two rows thick.

PILLAR: freestanding upright member of any section, not conforming to one of the orders (q.v.).

PILLAR PISCINA: *see* Piscina.

PILOTIS: C20 French term for pillars or stilts that support a building above an open ground floor.

PINS OR PINNINGS (Scots): *see* Cherry-caulking.

PISCINA: basin for washing Mass vessels, provided with a drain; set in or against wall to S of an altar or freestanding (*pillar piscina*).

PITCHED MASONRY: laid on the diagonal, often alternately with opposing courses (*pitched and counterpitched* or herringbone).

PIT PRISON: sunk chamber with access from above through a hatch.

PLATE RAIL: *see* Railways.

PLATEWAY: *see* Railways.

PLATT (Scots): platform, doorstep or landing. *Scale-and-platt stair*: *see* Stairs and 6c.

PLEASANCE (Scots): close or walled garden.

PLINTH: projecting courses at the foot of a wall or column, generally chamfered or moulded at the top.

PODIUM: a continuous raised platform supporting a building; or a large block of two or three storeys beneath a multi-storey block of smaller area.

POINT BLOCK: *see* Multi-storey.

POINTING: exposed mortar jointing of masonry or brickwork. Types include *flush*, *recessed* and *tuck* (with a narrow channel filled with finer, whiter mortar). *Bag-rubbed*: flush at the edges and gently recessed in the middle. *Ribbon*: joints formed with a trowel so that they stand out. *Hungry-jointed*: either with no pointing or deeply recessed to show the outline of each stone.

POPPYHEAD: carved ornament of leaves and flowers as a finial for a bench end or stall.

PORTAL FRAME: C20 frame comprising two uprights rigidly connected to a beam or pair of rafters.

PORTCULLIS: gate constructed to rise and fall in vertical gooves at the entry to a castle.

PORTE COCHÈRE: porch large enough to admit wheeled vehicles.

PORTICO: a porch with the roof and frequently a pediment supported by a row of columns (4a). A portico *in antis* has columns on the same plane as the front of the building. A *prostyle* porch has columns standing free. Porticoes are described by the number of front columns, e.g. tetrastyle (four), hexastyle (six). The space within the temple is the *naos*, that within the portico the *pronaos*. *Blind portico*: the front features of a portico applied to a wall.

PORTICUS (plural: *porticūs*): subsidiary cell opening from the main body of a pre-Conquest church.

POST: upright support in a structure.

POSTERN: small gateway at the back of a building or to the side of a larger entrance door or gate.

POTENCE (Scots): rotating ladder for access to doocot nesting boxes.

POUND LOCK: *see* Canals.

PREDELLA: in an altarpiece, the horizontal strip below the main representation, often used for subsidiary representations.

PRESBYTERY: the part of a church lying E of the choir where the main altar is placed. Also a priest's residence.

PRESS (Scots): cupboard.

PRINCIPAL: *see* Roofs and 7.

PRONAOS: *see* Portico and 4a.

PROSTYLE: *see* Portico and 4a.

PULPIT: raised and enclosed platform for the preaching of sermons. *Three-decker*: with reading desk below and clerk's desk below that. *Two-decker*: as above, minus the clerk's desk.

PULPITUM: stone screen in a major church dividing choir from nave.

PULVINATED: *see* Frieze and 3c.

PURLIN: *see* Roofs and 7.

PUTHOLES or PUTLOG HOLES: in wall to receive putlogs, the horizontal timbers which support scaffolding boards; not always filled after construction is complete.

PUTTO (plural: putti): small naked boy.

QUARRIES: square (or diamond) panes of glass supported by lead

strips (*cames*); square floor-slabs
or tiles.

QUATREFOIL: *see* Foil.

QUEEN-STRUT: *see* Roofs and 7.

QUILLONS: the arms forming the
cross-guard of a sword.

QUIRK: sharp groove to one side of a
convex medieval moulding.

QUOINS: dressed stones at the
angles of a building (6d).

RADBURN SYSTEM: pedestrian and
vehicle segregation in residential
developments, based on that used
at Radburn, New Jersey, U.S.A.,
by Wright and Stein, 1928–30.

RADIATING CHAPELS: projecting
radially from an ambulatory or an
apse (*see* Chevet).

RAFTER: *see* Roofs and 7.

RAGGLE: groove cut in masonry,
especially to receive the edge of a
roof-covering.

RAIL: *see* Panelling and 6b.

RAILWAYS: *Edge rail*: on which
flanged wheels can run. *Plate rail*:
L-section rail for plain unflanged
wheels. *Plateway*: early railway
using plate rails.

RAISED AND FIELDED: *see* Panelling and 6b.

RAKE: slope or pitch.

RAMPART: defensive outer wall of
stone or earth. *Rampart walk*: path
along the inner face.

RATCOURSE: projecting stringcourse on a doocot to deter rats
from climbing to the flight holes.

REBATE: rectangular section cut out
of a masonry edge to receive a
shutter, door, window etc.

REBUS: a heraldic pun, e.g. a fiery
cock for Cockburn.

REEDING: series of convex mouldings, the reverse of fluting (q.v.).
Cf. Gadrooning.

RENDERING: the covering of
outside walls with a uniform
surface or skin for protection from
the weather. *Lime-washing*: thin
layer of lime plaster. *Pebbledashing*: where aggregate is thrown
at the wet plastered wall for a
textured effect. *Roughcast*: plaster
mixed with a coarse aggregate
such as gravel. *Stucco*: fine lime
plaster worked to a smooth surface. *Cement rendering*: a cheaper
substitute for stucco, usually with
a grainy texture.

REPOUSSÉ: relief designs in metal-
work, formed by beating it from
the back.

REREDORTER (*lit.* behind the
dormitory): latrines in a medieval
religious house.

REREDOS: painted and/or sculptured screen behind and above an
altar. Cf. Retable.

RESPOND: half-pier or half-column
bonded into a wall and carrying
one end of an arch. It usually terminates an arcade.

RETABLE: painted or carved panel
standing on or at the back of an
altar, usually attached to it.

RETROCHOIR: in a major church,
the area between the high altar
and E chapel.

REVEAL: the plane of a jamb,
between the wall and the frame of
a door or window.

RHONE (Scots): gutter along the
eaves for rainwater: *see also* Conductor.

RIB-VAULT: *see* Vault and 2c.

RIG (Scots): a strip of ploughed land
raised in the middle and sloped
to a furrow on each side; early
cultivation method (runrig) usually
surrounded by untilled grazing
land.

RINCEAU: classical ornament of
leafy scrolls (4b).

RISER: vertical face of a step (6c).

ROCK-FACED: masonry cleft to
produce a rugged appearance.

ROCOCO: style current between
*c.* 1720 and *c.* 1760, characterized
by a serpentine line and playful,
scrolled decoration.

ROLL MOULDING: medieval moulding of part-circular section (1a).

ROMANESQUE: style current in the
CII and C12. In England often
called Norman. *See also* Saxo-
Norman.

ROOD: crucifix flanked by representations of the Virgin and St
John, usually over the entry into
the chancel, painted on the wall,
on a beam (*rood beam*) or on top
of a *rood screen* or pulpitum (q.v.)
which often had a walkway (*rood
loft*) along the top, reached by a
*rood stair* in the side wall. *Hanging
rood*: cross or crucifix suspended
from roof.

ROOFS: For the main external
shapes (hipped, gambrel etc.) *see*
7. *Helm* and *Saddleback*: *see* 1c.
*Lean-to*: single sloping roof built
against a vertical wall; also applied

to the part of the building beneath.

*Bellcast*: sloping roof slightly swept out over the eaves.

Construction. *See 7*.

*Single-framed* roof: with no main trusses. The rafters may be fixed to the wall-plate or ridge, or longitudinal timbers may be absent altogether.

*Double-framed* roof: with longitudinal members, such as purlins, and usually divided into bays by principals and principal rafters.

Other types are named after their main structural components, e.g. *hammerbeam, crown-post* (*see* Elements below and 7).

Elements. *See 7*.

*Ashlar piece*: a short vertical timber connecting an inner wall-plate or timber pad to a rafter.

*Braces*: subsidiary timbers set diagonally to strengthen the frame. *Arched braces*: curved pair forming an arch, connecting wall or post below with a tie- or collar-beam above. *Passing braces*: long straight braces passing across other members of the truss. *Scissor braces*: pair crossing diagonally between pairs of rafters or principals. *Wind-braces*: short, usually curved braces connecting side purlins with principals; sometimes decorated with cusping.

*Collar* or *collar-beam*: horizontal transverse timber connecting a pair of rafter or cruck blades (q.v.), set between apex and the wall-plate.

*Crown-post*: a vertical timber set centrally on a tie-beam and supporting a collar purlin braced to it longitudinally. In an open truss lateral braces may rise to the collar-beam; in a closed truss they may descend to the tie-beam.

*Hammerbeams*: horizontal brackets projecting at wall-plate level like an interrupted tie-beam; the inner ends carry *hammerposts*, vertical timbers which support a purlin and are braced to a collar-beam above.

*Kingpost*: vertical timber set centrally on a tie-or collar-beam, rising to the apex of the roof to support a ridge piece (cf. Strut).

*Plate*: longitudinal timber set square to the ground. *Wall-plate*: along the top of a wall to receive the ends of rafters; cf. Purlin.

*Principals*: pair of inclined lateral timbers of a truss. Usually they support side purlins and mark the main bay divisions.

*Purlin*: horizontal longitudinal timber. *Collar purlin* or *crown plate*: central timber which carries collar-beams and is supported by crown-posts. *Side purlins*: pairs of timbers placed some way up the slope of the roof, which carry common rafters. *Butt* or *tenoned purlins* are tenoned into either side of the principals. *Through purlins* pass through or past the principal; they include *clasped purlins*, which rest on queenposts or are carried in the angle between principals and collar, and *trenched purlins* trenched into the backs of principals.

*Queen-strut*: paired vertical, or near-vertical, timbers placed symmetrically on a tie-beam to support side purlins.

*Rafters*: inclined lateral timbers supporting the roof covering. *Common rafters*: regularly spaced uniform rafters placed along the length of a roof or between principals. *Principal rafters*: rafters which also act as principals.

*Ridge, ridge piece*: horizontal longitudinal timber at the apex supporting the ends of the rafters.

*Sprocket*: short timber placed on the back and at the foot of a rafter to form projecting eaves.

*Strut*: vertical or oblique timber between two members of a truss, not directly supporting longitudinal timbers.

*Tie-beam*: main horizontal transverse timber which carries the feet of the principals at wall level.

*Truss*: rigid framework of timbers at bay intervals, carrying the longitudinal roof timbers which support the common rafters. *Closed truss*: with the spaces between the timbers filled, to form an internal partition.

*See also* Cruck, Wagon roof.

ROPE MOULDING: *see* Cable moulding.

ROSE WINDOW: circular window with tracery radiating from the centre. Cf. Wheel window.

ROTUNDA: building or room circular in plan.

ROUGHCAST: *see* Rendering.

ROUND (Scots): bartizan, usually roofless.

ROVING BRIDGE: *see* Canals.

RUBBED BRICKWORK: *see* Gauged brickwork.

RUBBLE: masonry whose stones are wholly or partly in a rough state. *Coursed*: coursed stones with rough faces. *Random*: uncoursed stones in a random pattern. *Snecked*: with courses broken by smaller stones (snecks).

RUSTICATION: *see* 6d. Exaggerated treatment of masonry to give an effect of strength. The joints are usually recessed by V-section chamfering or square-section channelling (*channelled rustication*). *Banded rustication* has only the horizontal joints emphasized. The faces may be flat, but can be *diamond-faced*, like shallow pyramids, *vermiculated*, with a stylized texture like worm-casts, and *glacial* (frostwork), like icicles or stalactites.

RYBATS (Scots): *see* Margins.

SACRAMENT HOUSE: safe cupboard in a side wall of the chancel of a church and not directly associated with an altar, for reservation of the sacrament.

SACRISTY: room in a church for sacred vessels and vestments.

SADDLEBACK ROOF: *see* 1C.

SALTIRE CROSS: with diagonal limbs.

SANCTUARY: part of church at E end containing high altar. Cf. Presbytery.

SANGHA: residence of Buddhist monks or nuns.

SARCOPHAGUS: coffin of stone or other durable material.

SARKING (Scots): boards laid on the rafters to support the roof covering.

SAXO-NORMAN: transitional Romanesque style combining Anglo-Saxon and Norman features, current *c.* 1060–1100.

SCAGLIOLA: composition imitating marble.

SCALE-AND-PLATT (*lit.* stair and landing): *see* Stair and 6c.

SCALLOPED CAPITAL: *see* 1a.

SCARCEMENT: extra thickness of the lower part of a wall, e.g. to carry a floor.

SCARP: artificial cutting away of the ground to form a steep slope.

SCOTIA: a hollow classical moulding, especially between tori (q.v.) on a column base (3b, 3f).

SCREEN: in a medieval church, usually at the entry to the chancel; *see* Rood (screen) and Pulpitum. A *parclose screen* separates a chapel from the rest of the church.

SCREENS or SCREENS PASSAGE: screened-off entrance passage between great hall and service rooms or between the hall of a tower house and the stair.

SCRIBE (Scots): to cut and mark timber against an irregular stone or plaster surface.

SCUNTION (Scots): reveal.

SECTION: two-dimensional representation of a building, moulding etc., revealed by cutting across it.

SEDILIA (singular: sedile): seats for clergy (usually for a priest, deacon and sub-deacon) on the S side of the chancel.

SEPTUM: dwarf wall between the nave and choir.

SESSION HOUSE (Scots): a room or separate building for meetings of the minister and elders who form a kirk session. Also a shelter by the church or churchyard entrance for an elder collecting for poor relief, built at expense of kirk session.

SET-OFF: *see* Weathering.

SGRAFFITO: decoration scratched, often in plaster, to reveal a pattern in another colour beneath. *Graffiti*: scratched drawing or writing.

SHAFT: vertical member of round or polygonal section (1a, 3a). *Shaft-ring*: at the junction of shafts set *en délit* (q.v.) or attached to a pier or wall (1a).

SHEILA-NA-GIG: female fertility figure, usually with legs apart.

SHELL: thin, self-supporting roofing membrane of timber or concrete.

SHEUGH (Scots): a trench or open drain; a street gutter.

SHOULDERED ARCH: *see* 5a.

SHOULDERED ARCHITRAVE: *see* 4b.

SHUTTERING: *see* Concrete.

SILL: horizontal member at the bottom of a window-or door-frame; or at the base of a timber-framed wall into which posts and studs are tenoned.

SKEW (Scots): sloping or shaped stones finishing a gable upstanding from the roof. *Skewputt*: bracket at the bottom end of a skew. *See* 7.

SLAB BLOCK: *see* Multi-storey.

SLATE-HANGING: covering of overlapping slates on a wall. *Tile-hanging* is similar.

SLYPE: covered way or passage leading E from the cloisters between transept and chapter house.

SNECKED: *see* Rubble.

SOFFIT (*lit.* ceiling): underside of an arch (also called *intrados*), lintel etc. *Soffit roll*: medieval roll moulding on a soffit.

SOLAR: private upper chamber in a medieval house, accessible from the high end of the great hall.

SOLDIER ARCH: flat arch, using a soldier course (q.v.) in the head of the opening.

SOLDIER COURSE: a course of bricks laid vertically in rows.

SOPRAPORTA: *see* Overdoor.

SOUNDING-BOARD: *see* Tester.

SOUTERRAIN: underground stone-lined passage and chamber.

SPANDRELS: roughly triangular spaces between an arch and its containing rectangle, or between adjacent arches (5c). Also non-structural panels under the windows in a curtain-walled building.

SPERE: a fixed structure screening the lower end of the great hall from the screens passage. *Spere-truss*: roof truss incorporated in the spere.

SPIRE: tall pyramidal or conical feature crowning a tower or turret. *Broach*: starting from a square base, then carried into an octagonal section by means of triangular faces; *splayed-foot*: a variation of the broach form, found principally in the south-east of England, in which the four cardinal faces are splayed out near their base, to cover the corners, while oblique (or intermediate) faces taper away to a point (1c). *Needle spire*: thin spire rising from the centre of a tower roof, well inside the parapet: when of timber and lead often called a *spike*.

SPIRELET: *see* Flèche.

SPLAY: of an opening when it is wider on one face of a wall than the other.

SPRING OR SPRINGING: level at which an arch or vault rises from its supports. *Springers*: the first stones of an arch or vaulting-rib above the spring (2c).

SQUINCH: arch or series of arches thrown across an interior angle of a square or rectangular structure to support a circular or polygonal superstructure, especially a dome or spire (5a).

SQUINT: an aperture in a wall or through a pier, usually to allow a view of an altar.

STAIRS: *see* 6c. *Dog-leg stair* or (Scots) *Scale-and-platt stair*: parallel flights rising alternately in opposite directions, without an open well. *Flying stair*: cantilevered from the walls of a stairwell, without newels; sometimes called a *geometric* stair when the inner edge describes a curve. *Turnpike* or *newel stair*: ascending round a central supporting newel (8b); also called a *spiral stair* or *vice* when in a circular shaft, a *winder* when in a rectangular compartment. (Winder also applies to the steps on the turn.) *Well stair*: with flights round a square open well framed by newel posts. *See also* Perron.

STAIR TOWER: full-height projection from a main block (especially of a tower house) containing the principal stair from the ground floor (8a).

STAIR TURRET: turret corbelled out from above ground level and containing a stair from one of the upper floors of a building, especially a tower house (8a).

STALL: fixed seat in the choir or chancel for the clergy or choir (cf. Pew). Usually with arm rests, and often framed together.

STANCHION: upright structural member, of iron, steel or reinforced concrete.

STANDPIPE TOWER: *see* Manometer.

STEADING (Scots): farm building or buildings; generally used for the principal group of buildings on a farm.

STEAM ENGINES: *Atmospheric*: worked by the vacuum created when low-pressure steam is condensed in the cylinder, as developed by Thomas Newcomen. *Beam engine*: with a large pivoted beam moved in an oscillating fashion by the piston. It may drive a flywheel or be *non-rotative*. *Watt* and *Cornish*: single-cylinder; *compound*: two cylinders; *triple expansion*: three cylinders.

STEEPLE: tower together with a spire, lantern or belfry.

STIFFLEAF: type of E.E. foliage decoration. *Stiffleaf capital*: *see* 1b.

STOP: plain or decorated terminal to mouldings or chamfers, or at the end of hoodmoulds and labels (*label stop*), or stringcourses (5b, 6a); *see also* Headstop.

STOUP: vessel for holy water, usually near a door.

STRAINER: *see* Arch.

STRAPWORK: decoration like interlaced leather straps, late C16 and C17 in origin.

STRETCHER: *see* Bond and 6e.

STRING: *see* 6c. Sloping member holding the ends of the treads and risers of a staircase. *Closed string*: a broad string covering the ends of the treads and risers. *Open string*: cut into the shape of the treads and risers.

STRINGCOURSE: horizontal course or moulding projecting from the surface of a wall (6d).

STUCCO: decorative plasterwork. *See also* Rendering.

STUDS: subsidiary vertical timbers of a timber-framed wall or partition.

STUGGED (Scots): of masonry hacked or picked as a key for rendering; used as a surface finish in the C19.

STUPA: Buddhist shrine, circular in plan.

STYLOBATE: top of the solid platform on which a colonnade stands (3a).

SUSPENSION BRIDGE: *see* Bridge.

SWAG: like a festoon (q.v.), but representing cloth.

SYSTEM BUILDING: *see* Industrialized building.

TABERNACLE: safe cupboard above an altar to contain the reserved sacrament or a relic; or architectural frame for an image or statue.

TABLE STONE or TABLE TOMB: memorial slab raised on freestanding legs.

TAS-DE-CHARGE: the lower courses of a vault or arch which are laid horizontally (2c).

TENEMENT: holding of land, but also applied to a purpose-built flatted block.

TERM: pedestal or pilaster tapering downward, usually with the upper part of a human figure growing out of it.

TERRACOTTA: moulded and fired clay ornament or cladding.

TERREPLEIN: in a fort the level surface of a rampart behind a parapet for mounting guns.

TESSELLATED PAVEMENT: mosaic flooring, particularly Roman, made of *tesserae*, i.e. cubes of glass, stone or brick.

TESTER: flat canopy over a tomb or pulpit, where it is also called a *sounding-board*.

TESTER TOMB: tomb-chest with effigies beneath a tester, either freestanding (tester with four or more columns), or attached to a wall (*half-tester*) with columns on one side only.

TETRASTYLE: *see* Portico.

THERMAL WINDOW: *see* Diocletian window.

THREE-DECKER PULPIT: *see* Pulpit.

TIDAL GATES: *see* Canals.

TIE-BEAM: *see* Roofs and 7.

TIERCERON: *see* Vault and 2c.

TIFTING (Scots): mortar bed for verge slates laid over gable skew.

TILE-HANGING: *see* Slate-hanging.

TIMBER-FRAMING: method of construction where the structural frame is built of interlocking timbers. The spaces are filled with non-structural material, e.g. *infill* of wattle and daub, lath and plaster, brickwork (known as *nogging*) etc., and may be covered by plaster, weatherboarding (q.v.) or tiles.

TOLBOOTH (Scots; *lit.* tax booth): burgh council building containing council chamber and prison.

TOMB-CHEST: chest-shaped tomb, usually of stone. Cf. Table tomb, Tester tomb.

TORUS (plural: tori): large convex moulding, usually used on a column base (3b, 3f).

TOUCH: soft black marble quarried near Tournai.

TOURELLE: turret corbelled out from the wall (8a).

TOWER BLOCK: *see* Multi-storey.

TOWER HOUSE (Scots): for elements and forms *see* 8a, 8b. Compact fortified house with the main hall raised above the ground and at least one more storey above it. A medieval Scots type continuing well into the C17 in its modified forms: *L-plan* with a jamb at one corner; *Z-plan* with a jamb at each diagonally opposite corner.

TRABEATED: dependent structurally on the use of the post and lintel. Cf. Arcuated.

TRACERY: openwork pattern of masonry or timber in the upper part of an opening. *Blind* tracery is tracery applied to a solid wall.
*Plate tracery*, introduced *c.* 1200, is the earliest form, in which shapes are cut through solid masonry (2a).
*Bar tracery* was introduced into England *c.* 1250. The pattern is formed by intersecting moulded ribwork continued from the mullions. It was especially elaborate during the Decorated period (q.v.). Tracery shapes can include circles, *daggers* (elongated ogee-ended lozenges), *mouchettes* (like daggers but with curved sides) and upright rectangular *panels*. They often have *cusps*, projecting points defining lobes or *foils* (q.v.) within the main shape: *Kentish* or *split-cusps* are forked.
Types of bar tracery (*see* 2b) include *geometric(al)*: *c.* 1250–1310, chiefly circles, often foiled; *Y-tracery*: *c.* 1300, with mullions branching into a Y-shape; *intersecting*: *c.* 1300, formed by interlocking mullions; *reticulated*: early C14, net-like pattern of ogee-ended lozenges; *curvilinear*: C14, with uninterrupted flowing curves; *loop*: *c.* 1500–45, with large uncusped loop-like forms; *panel*: Perp, with straight-sided panels, often cusped at the top and bottom.

TRANSE (Scots): passage.

TRANSEPT: transverse portion of a cruciform church.

TRANSITIONAL: generally used for the phase between Romanesque and Early English (*c.* 1175–*c.* 1200).

TRANSOM: horizontal member separating window lights (2b).

TREAD: horizontal part of a step. The *tread end* may be carved on a staircase (6c).

TREFOIL: *see* Foil.

TRIFORIUM: middle storey of a church treated as an arcaded wall passage or blind arcade, its height corresponding to that of the aisle roof.

TRIGLYPHS (*lit.* three-grooved tablets): stylized beam-ends in the Doric frieze, with metopes between (3b).

TRIUMPHAL ARCH: influential type of Imperial Roman monument.

TROPHY: sculptured or painted group of arms or armour.

TRUMEAU: central stone mullion supporting the tympanum of a wide doorway. *Trumeau figure*: carved figure attached to it (cf. Column figure).

TRUMPET CAPITAL: *see* 1b.

TRUSS: braced framework, spanning between supports. *See also* Roofs.

TUMBLING or TUMBLING-IN: courses of brickwork laid at right angles to a slope, e.g. of a gable, forming triangles by tapering into horizontal courses.

TURNPIKE: *see* Stairs.

TUSCAN: *see* Orders and 3e.

TUSKING STONES (Scots): projecting end stones for bonding with an adjoining wall.

TWO-DECKER PULPIT: *see* Pulpit.

TYMPANUM: the surface between a lintel and the arch above it or within a pediment (4a).

UNDERCROFT: usually describes the vaulted room(s) beneath the main room(s) of a medieval house. Cf. Crypt.

UNIVALLATE: of a hillfort: defended by a single bank and ditch.

VAULT: arched stone roof (sometimes imitated in timber or plaster). For types *see* 2c.
*Tunnel* or *barrel vault*: continuous semicircular or pointed arch, often of rubble masonry.
*Groin vault*: tunnel vaults intersecting at right angles. *Groins* are the curved lines of the intersections.
*Rib vault*: masonry framework of intersecting arches (ribs) supporting *vault cells*, used in Gothic architecture. *Wall rib* or *wall arch*: between wall and vault cell. *Transverse rib*: spans between two walls to divide a vault into bays. *Quadripartite* rib vault: each bay has two pairs of diagonal ribs dividing the vault into four triangular cells. *Sexpartite* rib vault: most often used over paired bays, has an extra pair of ribs springing from between the bays. More elaborate vaults may include *ridge-ribs* along the crown of a vault or bisecting

the bays; *tiercerons*: extra decorative ribs springing from the
corners of a bay; and *liernes*: short
decorative ribs in the crown of a
vault, not linked to any springing
point. A *stellar* or *star* vault has
liernes in star formation.
*Fan vault*: form of barrel vault
used in the Perp period, made up
of halved concave masonry cones
decorated with blind tracery.

VAULTING-SHAFT: shaft leading
up to the spring or springing (q.v.)
of a vault (2c).

VENETIAN or SERLIAN WINDOW:
derived from Serlio (4b). The
motif is used for other openings.

VERMICULATION: *see* Rustication
and 6d.

VESICA: oval with pointed ends.

VICE: *see* Stair.

VILLA: originally a Roman country
house or farm. The term was
revived in England in the C18
under the influence of Palladio
and used especially for smaller,
compact country houses. In the
later C19 it was debased to
describe any suburban house.

VITRIFIED: bricks or tiles fired to a
darkened glassy surface. *Vitrified
fort*: built of timber-laced masonry, the timber having later
been set on fire with consequent
vitrification of the stonework.

VITRUVIAN SCROLL: classical running ornament of curly waves
(4b).

VOLUTES: spiral scrolls. They occur on Ionic capitals (3c). *Angle*
volute: pair of volutes, turned outwards to meet at the corner of a
capital.

VOUSSOIRS: wedge-shaped stones
forming an arch (5c).

WAGON ROOF: with the appearance
of the inside of a wagon tilt; often
ceiled. Also called *cradle roof*.

WAINSCOT: *see* Panelling.

WALLED GARDEN: in C18 and C19
Scotland, combined vegetable
and flower garden, sometimes
well away from the house.

WALLHEAD: straight top of a wall.
*Wallhead chimney*: chimney rising
from a wallhead (8a). *Wallhead
gable*: gable rising from a wallhead.

WALL MONUMENT: attached to the
wall and often standing on the

floor. *Wall tablets* are smaller with
the inscription as the major element.

WALL-PLATE: *see* Roofs and 7.

WALL-WALK: *see* Parapet.

WARMING ROOM: room in a religious house where a fire burned
for comfort.

WATERHOLDING BASE: early Gothic
base with upper and lower mouldings separated by a deep hollow.

WATERLEAF: *see* Enrichments and
3f.

WATERLEAF CAPITAL: Late Romanesque and Transitional type of
capital (1b).

WATER WHEELS: described by the
way water is fed on to the wheel.
*Breastshot*: mid-height, falling and
passing beneath. *Overshot*: over
the top. *Pitchback*: on the top
but falling backwards. *Undershot*:
turned by the momentum of the
water passing beneath. In a *water
turbine*, water is fed under pressure
through a vaned wheel within a
casing.

WEALDEN HOUSE: type of medieval
timber-framed house with a central open hall flanked by bays of
two storeys, roofed in line; the
end bays are jettied to the front,
but the eaves are continuous.

WEATHERBOARDING: wall cladding
of overlapping horizontal boards.

WEATHERING: or SET-OFF: inclined, projecting surface to keep
water away from the wall below.

WEEPERS: figures in niches along
the sides of some medieval tombs.
Also called *mourners*.

WHEEL HOUSE: Late Iron Age circular stone dwelling; inside, partition walls radiating from the
central hearth like wheel spokes.

WHEEL WINDOW: circular, with
radiating shafts like spokes. Cf.
Rose window.

WROUGHT IRON: *see* Cast iron.

WYND (Scots): subsidiary street or
lane, often running into a main
street or gait (q.v.).

YETT (Scots, *lit.* gate): hinged openwork gate at a main doorway,
made of iron bars alternately penetrating and penetrated (8c).

Z-PLAN: *see* Tower house and 8b.

# INDEX OF ARTISTS

Robson, Adam (glass-stainer,
  b. 1928) 363
Rochead, John Thomas (1814–78)
  42, 88, 418, 420, 422–3, 623, 641,
  Pl. 21
Rodger (Andrew) Associates 749
Rodger, Willie (artist, b. 1930) 35,
  561, 571, 618
Rogerson, John (1862–1930) 406
Rogerson (Robert) & Philip Spence
  217
Romer, Captain John Lambertus
  (1680–?1754) 390, 392, 394
Ronald, David 82, 480–1, 490
Ronald, James 744, 750
Ronald, James E. (1873–1924) 89,
  759
Ross, Alexander (1834–1925) 27,
  281, 599
Ross, Charles (1722–1806) 416
Ross, Launcelot H. (1885–1956) 192
Ross, Thomas (1839–1930) 351, 689,
  697
  see also MacGibbon & Ross
Roxby, Park & Baird 337
Roy, Nicholas (mason) 680
Roytell, John (mason) 680
Runcie, Samuel 706
Rushworth & Dreaper (organ
  builders) 189, 213, 353, 363, 384,
  492, 642, 697
Russell, Alexander L. (glass-stainer)
  444
Russell, Thomas (builder) 114
Rutherford, J. 473
Ruthven, J. 227
Rynd, James (mason) 673, 707
St Enoch Glass Co. (glass-stainers)
  272
St Enoch Glass Studios
  (glass-stainers) 310, 363
Salmon (James) & Son (James
  Salmon, 1805–88; William Forrest
  Salmon, q.v.) 572, 573, 601
Salmon, Son & Gillespie (William
  Forrest Salmon, q.v.; James
  Salmon Jun., 1873–1924;
  John Gaff Gillespie, q.v.) 709
Salmon, Son & Ritchie (James
  Salmon, 1805–88; William Forrest
  Salmon, q.v.; James Ritchie, q.v.)
  78, 601
Salmon, William Forrest (1843–1911)
  571, 601
Salviati, Antonio (mosaicist,
  1816–90) 31, 137
Samuel, Drew, 186
Sanders, John (1768–1826) 668, 679

Sanderson, Douglas 413
Saracen Foundry (founders) 125,
  282, 309
  see also Macfarlane (Walter) & Co.
Sauer, Wilhelm (organ builders:
  Paul Walcker) 210
Saunders, D. (glass-stainer) 470
Saxone, Lilley & Skinner's
  Architects Department 478
Schaw, William (d. 1602) 684
Schotz, Benno (sculptor, 1891–1984)
  41, 227, 399, 746
Scott Bennett Associates 330
Scott (Charles) & Partners 762
Scott, Sir George Gilbert (1811–78)
  428
Scott (J.N.) & A. Lorne Campbell
  (John Nichol Scott, b. 1863;
  Alexander Lorne Campbell, q.v.)
  27, 250
Scott, John (wright) 568
Scott Morton & Co. (decorators
  and cabinet makers) 562, 657
Scott, Robert (d. 1839) 73, 276,
  410, 411, Pl. 84
Scott, Stephen & Gale (Robert Scott,
  q.v.; John Stephen; William Gale,
  q.v.) 276
Scott, W.M. (engineer) 231
Scott, Walter Schomberg (1910–98)
  609
Scott, William 245
Scottish (The) Construction Co.
  Ltd. 485
Scottish Co-operative Welfare
  Society's Architects' Department
  161
Scottish Oils Ltd. Architectural
  Department 533
Scottish (The) Orlit Co. Ltd. 485
Sellars, James (1843–88) 59, 621
Service, John (mason) 704, 708
S.G.A. (Buildings) Ltd. 226, 536
Shanks, James (sculptor) 404
Shanks, John (b. 1866) 42, 572, 573,
  574, 576
Shaw, Christian (glass-stainer) 138
Shearer, James Grant (1881–1962)
  288–9
Shearer (James) & Annand (James
  Grant Shearer, q.v.; George
  Annand) 105
Shearer, Robert & Mark 361
Sheen, Frank 586
Shiells, R. Thornton (1833–1902) 27
Shiells (R. Thornton) & Thomson
  (R. Thornton Shiells, q.v.; James
  M. Thomson) 246, 408

# INDEX OF PLACES

Principal references are in **bold** type; demolished buildings are shown in *italic*.